THE WRITER'S HANDBOOK

The Writer's Handbook

Edited by

SYLVIA K. BURACK
Editor, The Writer

Publishers   THE WRITER, INC.   Boston

CONTENTS

BACKGROUND FOR WRITERS

HOW TO WRITE—TECHNIQUES

GENERAL FICTION

JAN   1994

Background for Writers

1

WHAT MAKES A WRITER TICK?

BY WARREN KIEFER

EVERY WRITER DREADS THE BORE who says, "You're just the person I always wanted to meet, because I've got this incredible, surefire idea for a runaway bestseller and a fantastic film. You write it and we split the money."

My most common defense is to pretend I'm deaf and immediately focus my attention elsewhere. Writers are still vulnerable, however, to the other kind of literary groupie whose question is, "Where do you get your ideas?" He or she may be less obsessed than the one who thinks he has a story to tell, but just as ignorant of what makes a writer tick.

And what *does* make a writer tick? Lots of answers have been suggested by writers themselves, and all of them are probably true. Ego is a powerful goad. Writers tend to be uncommon egotists even when they hide behind pseudonyms or ghostwrite other people's books. But there's nothing wrong with ego if it keeps them working. A lack of confidence, in fact, is tough on talent.

The desire to see one's name in print has usually been enough to drive more than one recalcitrant talent to work hard enough and long enough to overcome early rejection and finally to succeed.

But incentives provide only a partial answer to the key question. If there were a recipe for creating an original, pleasurable, readable, salable manuscript and getting the finished product sold and published, it might read something like this: one part *idea,* two parts *talent,* and three parts *motivation* seasoned with *patience.* Trim excess fat from idea, simmer in talent, mix in motivation, and bring to a boil. If patience runs thin, add fresh discipline until it stands by itself.

A reading public is essential, of course, and luckily it is still out there. It may be fickle, biased, or poorly prepared, but then again, it probably always was. Dickens complained when his editors asked him to write down to his readers, while Proust held the public in such contempt he wrote only for himself. Most working writers cannot afford such luxury, but must reach out to their markets, regularly. Today's reading public may be more inclined to rent a video or spend eight dollars going to a ninety-minute film than twenty dollars on a book that lasts a lifetime, but that is of no concern to the writer. Without him video and film wouldn't be there either.

So one starts with the idea. I can't speak for an entire profession, but if I hadn't been brimful of story ideas clamoring to get out, I never would have become a writer. I've never had a problem coming up with themes, characters, and/or plots. The real problem is selection.

Assuming you have a good idea, you can first ask yourself a few simple questions to make sure it is good enough.

Is it truly original, or has it been used before? If it has been used before (and most good ideas have), will your treatment of it be sufficiently fresh or outstanding to give it a chance anyway in a highly competitive market?

Is it of compelling interest to others outside your immediate family and circle of admirers?

Are the characters you envision strong enough to sustain the idea (as well as the writer and the reader) throughout the hundreds of pages necessary to express it?

If the answer is "no" or even a reluctant "maybe" to any of the above, the idea should be shelved without a second thought.

Over the years I've stocked files with notes on storylines that include enough dramatic incidents, dynamic relationships, and intriguing situations to fill a hundred books. I've overpopulated these files with real or imaginary characters whose idiosyncrasies include inventories of everything from the color of their socks to the quality of their minds.

Most of this material I'll never look at again, but the process of writing it down and filing it feeds that data bank of the mind I call the creative subconscious. What I retrieve later may be insignificant, or it may become the driving idea behind a new book. The filing itself is a refining process, and even if the material never sees print, it filters into my daily work, coloring and affecting what I write and perhaps defining my literary style.

Talent is obviously vital and not something one acquires like a suntan but has from birth, like 20/20 vision, hand-eye coordination, or good muscle tone. Yet talent can't succeed without motivation. A writer must want to write more than anything else. Mark Twain described this compulsion as a curse worse than madness, as debilitating as a disease, while Balzac said it was an itch he had to scratch with his pen every day.

Motivation is no substitute for talent, however, any more than money can take the place of motivation. A person anxious to get rich can choose from a hundred professions more remunerative than writing. There are always a few writers—like Stephen King or Danielle Steel—who reach the top income bracket, but according to the Authors Guild, $7,000.00 is the average annual income for professional writers, placing them well below the poverty level.

Assuming one has the talent, the motivation, and the stamina to write, one still needs the time. But that, too, is relative. Full-time employment usually takes only forty hours of a 168-hour week. Allowing for a job, sleep, food, and exercise, anyone with a little self-discipline can always wring another forty writing hours from an ordinary week.

But even with the time to write, when does one decide the idea is important enough to form the basis of a novel, and how does one extrude a publishable work from the bare bones of the idea? In my case, this happens only when I feel the need to explore something in greater depth than I can through my normal habits of thought or random conversation with friends. The make-believe space afforded by the novel allows me to ask questions, probe character, plumb emotions, and circle closer to a clearer understanding of the human condition.

For example, I have always found the question of identity absorbing. Who are we, each of us, really? How many roles do we play in life and how do we perceive others in the roles they play? Race, gender, age, profession, height, weight, education, and cultural background all figure in the identity equation. Alter any one to the least degree and you have a different person. This has been a recurring theme in my work.

I dealt with it first in *The Lingala Code,* a suspense novel about war and violence in Africa. The man telling the story is a U.S. ambassador, married and with children, who had once been an Air Force fighter pilot and CIA agent. Flashing back to his days in the Congo with the CIA, he tells how he investigated the murder of his best friend, nearly got himself killed, and wound up with a red-headed French girl he eventually married. The reader assumes he is white until the very end of the book when I reveal that he is black. This changes nothing basic

5

about the character, but it sharply alters the reader's perception about race and identity, which was my precise intention. The book won the Edgar Allan Poe Award as the year's best mystery novel and brought in hundreds of letters from readers both black and white, who said they'd had to rethink the story in view of their own unconscious prejudices and assumptions.

In *The Stanton Succession,* I returned to the question of identity and people's perception of others, but in an entirely different way. One of the main characters, a corporation vice-president of immense charm and demonstrated ability, is exposed on page 12 as an ex-convict who had once served time in prison for fraud, forgery, and embezzlement. The shock of learning this gives the company president a fatal heart attack, and infighting begins for the successor of his job.

The Stanton Succession is told from the point of view of the company's Wall Street attorney, a man of some rectitude and conscience who nevertheless lets himself be drawn deeper and deeper into a web of corporate criminal intrigue as he balances questions of law and morality against the rampant greed, fear, and ambition around him. His deep misgivings about abandoning old shibboleths in favor of a new morality of convenience reflect my own concern for a society that sometimes seems to be telling us that anything goes as long as you can get away with it.

Unlike my lawyer character, I tend to have ambiguous feelings about the law. And I had some hard questions I hoped to explore in depth while writing the book. I was taught to respect and fear the law, but I also mistrust it, particularly when I see educated, respectable people who know better ignore its moral intent and violate its social constraints in order to further their personal ambition or fill their pockets. In writing *The Stanton Succession,* I found myself asking whether the fault was in the law or in us.

Perhaps there are no clear answers to such questions, but writing a novel does offer a unique way to examine them. Besides entertaining readers, good fiction should also bring both author and reader a little closer to otherwise elusive truths about ourselves and how we relate to the world around us.

For the novelist who likes to enjoy himself at other people's expense, writing a book is a wonderful way to get even. But getting even can also involve a serious shift in one's perception of others, as I once found out to my dismay. I made the main villain in one of my early books a sinister, nasty charmer of the kind who'd sell crack to his kids if there was a buck in it. I modeled him on a former boss in such a way that anyone who knew the real-life man could not fail to see him in my fictional portrait. It was revenge on my part, pure and simple, from the gray in his hair to the flaws in his character. I made the hero of the story his opposite—a younger, handsome, decent sort of fellow with all the right instincts.

A few days after the book was favorably reviewed by *The New York Times,* I received a call from my old boss.

"Congratulations, big shot."

"Ah . . . well . . . thanks."

"When can we do lunch?"

"Well, I dunno . . . let me look at my agenda and . . ."

"Quit stalling. I read your book." He was never one to suffer indecision if he could steamroll his way over you.

I showed up at the restaurant ten minutes early. I told myself I should have talked to a libel lawyer beforehand, and when I saw his grim expression as he walked in, I was sure of it. He sat down heavily and laid an enormous package on the nearby chair. "You did one hell of a job on me," he said flatly. "I give you that."

"Well, look, you know, don't take it . . . I mean . . ."

"Don't take it personally? How am I supposed to take it? The minute I got past the first page I saw what you'd done."

"No harm was meant. . . ." I lied.

"I loved it."

"You. . . ?"

". . . loved it! I recognized myself as the main character immediately. You made me younger and better looking than I really am, but that's O.K.—poetic license, right? Otherwise you got me down to a T. I didn't realize you knew me that well. I liked the heavy, too. He was a well-drawn character." He winked. "I can guess who you had in mind there, but I'll never tell."

I was stunned that he could ever have imagined himself as the hero, and I had no idea whom he thought I'd used as the model for my villain. I simply stared in disbelief as he wrestled his package closer and opened it. Inside were twenty copies of my book with a list of all the people he wanted them inscribed to.

2

TALKING ABOUT WRITING

BY URSULA K. LE GUIN

PEOPLE COME UP TO YOU if you're a writer, and they say, I want to be a writer. How do I become a writer?

I have a two-stage answer to that. The first-stage answer is this: You learn to type (or to word-process). The only alternative is to have an inherited income and hire a full-time stenographer. If this seems unlikely, don't worry. Keyboards are easy to learn.

Well, the person who asked, How do I become a writer, is a bit cross now, and mumbles, but that isn't what I meant. (And I say, I know it wasn't.) I want to write short stories, what are the rules for writing short stories? I want to write a novel, what are the rules for writing novels?

Now I say Ah! and get really enthusiastic. You can find all the rules of writing in the book called *Elements of Style,* by Strunk and White, and a good dictionary—I recommend the *Shorter Oxford*; Webster's is too wishy-washy. There are only a very few rules of writing not covered in those two volumes, and I can summarize them thus: Your story may begin in longhand on the backs of old shopping lists, but when it goes to an editor, it should be typed, double-spaced, on one side of the paper only, with generous margins—especially the left-hand one—and not too many really grotty corrections per page.

Your name and its name and the page number should be on the top of every single page; and when you mail it to the editor it should have enclosed with it a stamped, self-addressed envelope. And those are the Basic Rules of Writing.

I'm not being funny. Those are the basic requirements for a readable, therefore publishable, manuscript. And, beyond grammar and spelling, they are the only rules of writing I know.

All right, that is stage one of my answer. If the person listens to all that without hitting me, and still says All right all right, but how *do* you become a writer, then I can deliver stage two. How do you become a writer? Answer: You write.

It's amazing how much resentment and evasion this answer can arouse. Even among writers, believe me.

The most frequent evasive tactic is for the would-be writer to say, But before I have anything to say, I must get *experience.*

Well, yes; if you want to be a journalist. But I don't know anything about journalism, I'm talking about fiction. And of course fiction is made out of experience, your whole life from infancy on, everything you've thought and done and seen and read and dreamed. But experience isn't something you go and *get*—it's a gift, and the only prerequisite for receiving it is that you be open to it. A closed soul can have the most immense adventures, go through a civil war or a trip to the moon, and have nothing to show for all that "experience"; whereas the open soul can do wonders with nothing. I invite you to meditate on a pair of sisters. Emily and Charlotte. Their life experience was an isolated vicarage in a small, dreary English village, a couple of bad years at a girls' school, another year or two in Brussels, and a lot of housework. Out of that seething mass of raw, vital, brutal, gutsy Experience they made two of the greatest novels ever written: *Jane Eyre* and *Wuthering Heights.*

Now of course they were writing from experience; writing about what they knew, which is what people always tell you to do; but what was their experience? What was it they knew? Very little about "life." They knew their own souls, they knew their own minds and hearts; and it was not a knowledge lightly or easily gained. From the time they were seven or eight years old, they wrote, and thought, and learned the landscape of their own being, and how to describe it. They wrote with the imagination, which is the tool of the farmer, the plow you plow your own soul with. They wrote from inside, from as deep inside as they could get by using all their strength and courage and intelligence. And that is where books come from. The novelist writes from inside.

I'm rather sensitive on this point, because I often write science fiction, or fantasy, or about imaginary countries—stuff that, by definition, involves times, places, events that I could not possibly experience in my own life. So when I was young and would submit one of these things about space voyages to Orion or dragons or something, I was told, at extremely regular intervals, "You should try to write about things you know." And I would say, But I do; I know about Orion, and dragons, and imaginary countries. Who do you think knows about my own imaginary countries, if I don't?

But they didn't listen, because they don't understand. They think an artist is like a roll of photographic film: You expose it and develop it and there is a reproduction of Reality in two dimensions. But that's all wrong, and if any artist tells you "I am a camera," or "I am a mirror," distrust them instantly; they're fooling you. Artists are people who are not at all interested in the facts—only in the truth. You get the facts from outside. The truth you get from inside.

O.K., how do you go about getting at that truth? You want to tell the truth. You want to be a writer. So what do you do?

You write.

Why do people ask that question? Does anybody ever come up to a musician and say, Tell me, tell me—how should I become a tuba player? No! it's too obvious. If you want to be a tuba player you get a tuba, and some tuba music. And you ask the neighbors to move away or put cotton in their ears. And probably you get a tuba teacher, because there are quite a lot of objective rules and techniques both to written music and to tuba performance. And then you sit down and you play the tuba, every day, every week, every month, year after year, until you are good at playing the tuba; until you can—if you desire—play the truth on the tuba.

It is exactly the same with writing. You sit down, and you do it, and you do it, and you do it, until you have learned how to do it.

Of course, there are differences. Writing makes no noise, except groans, and it can be done anywhere, and it is done alone.

It is the experience or premonition of that loneliness, perhaps, that drives a lot of young writers into this search for rules.

Writing cannot be shared, nor can it be taught as a technique, except on the most superficial level. All a writer's real learning is done alone, thinking, reading other people's books, or writing—practicing. A really good writing class or workshop can give us some shadow of what musicians have all the time—the excitement of a group working together, so that each member outdoes himself—but what comes out of that is not a collaboration, like a symphony performance, but a lot of totally separate, isolated works, expressions of individual souls. And therefore there are no rules, except those each individual makes up.

I know. There are lots of rules. You find them in the books about The Craft of Fiction and The Art of the Short Story and so on. I know some of them. One of them says: Never begin a story with dialogue! People won't read it; here is somebody talking and readers don't know who, and so they don't care, so—Never begin a story with dialogue.

Well, there is a story I know, it begins like this:

"*Eh bien, mon prince!* so Genoa and Lucca are now no more than private estates of the Bonaparte family!"

It's not only a dialogue opening, the first four words are in *French,* and it's not even a French novel. What a horrible way to begin a book! The title of the book is *War and Peace.*

There's another Rule I know: Introduce all the main characters early in the book. That sounds perfectly sensible, mostly I suppose it is sensible, but it's not a rule, or if it is somebody forgot to tell it to Charles Dickens. He didn't get Sam Weller into the *Pickwick Papers* for ten chapters—that's five months, since the book was coming out as a serial in installments.

Now you can say, all right, so Tolstoy can break the rules, so Dickens can break the rules, but they're geniuses; rules are made for geniuses to break, but for ordinary, talented, not-yet-professional writers to follow, as guidelines.

And I would accept this, but very grudgingly. Put it this way: If you feel you need rules and want rules, and you find a rule that appeals to you, or that works for you, then follow it. Use it. But if it doesn't appeal to you or work for you, then ignore it; in fact, if you want to and are able to, kick it in the teeth, break it, fold staple mutilate and destroy it.

See, the thing is, as a writer you are free. You are about the freest person that ever was. Your freedom is what you have bought with your solitude, your loneliness. You are in the country where *you* make up the rules, the laws. It is a country nobody has ever explored before. It is up to you to make the maps, to build the cities. Nobody else in the world can do it, or ever could do it, or ever will be able to do it again.

Absolute freedom is absolute responsibility. The writer's job, as I see it, is to tell the truth. The writer's truth—nobody else's. It is not an easy job. You know how hard it is to say to somebody, just somebody you know, how you *really* feel, what you *really* think—with complete honesty? You have to trust them, and you have to *know yourself,* before you can say anything anywhere near the truth. And it's hard. It takes a lot out of you.

You multiply that by thousands; you replace the listener, the live flesh-and-blood friend you trust, with a faceless unknown audience of people who may possibly not even exist; and you try to write the truth to them, you try to draw them a map of your inmost mind and feelings, hiding nothing and trying to keep all the distances straight and the altitudes right and the emotions honest. . . . And you never succeed. The map is never complete, or even accurate. You read it over and it may be beautiful, but you realize that you have fudged here, and smeared there, and left this out, and put in some stuff that isn't really there at all, and so on—and there is nothing to do then but say O.K.; that's done; now I come back and start a new map, and try to do it better, more truthfully. And all of this, every time, you do alone—absolutely alone. The only questions that really matter are the ones you ask yourself.

3

EDITORIAL CRITICISM: HOW TO TAKE IT—AND USE IT

BY DIANE LEFER

WHEN I FIRST STARTED WRITING FICTION, I knew most writers didn't make a lot of money, but—in my naïveté—I did believe getting published was a matter of course. I was shocked when my first stories came back. As my stack of form rejection slips grew, along with well-meaning remarks such as "near miss," my desperate longing changed its focus. Of course I still wanted publication, but what I wanted even more was criticism—or so I thought. When criticism finally came, I was not prepared to take it.

Part of the problem had to do with my expectations. After so much frustrating isolation, I dreamed an important editor would suddenly recognize my genius and ask, "Where have you been hiding all these years?" The other fantasy was that an editor would mark up my manuscript and provide simple step-by-step instructions on how to turn a flawed but promising story into a masterpiece. In fact, however, most comments I received were too general, and the specific criticism often confused me as editors contradicted each other. With no opportunity to ask questions or to explain my work when it seemed clearly misunderstood, I simply filed editorial letters away. In time, though, I stumbled over a few ideas that have helped me make constructive use of editors' comments.

Yes, all criticism is subjective. An editor may be wrong. But now I always test my work against a simple question: *What if* he or she has a valid point—or is even 100% right?

When I'm frustrated because I can't talk to the editor, I've learned to have an imaginary conversation. Suppose an editor doesn't understand a character's behavior or can't figure out the ending? I have to admit my first reaction can be, "It's obvious!" But when I come down off my high horse and write out a thorough explanation as if in response and then reread the story, all too often I realize that the points I came up with so easily and cogently in my explanation are completely missing from the story itself. I may need a new illustrative scene, or a line or two taken from my written response and strategically placed in the story may do the trick.

Editors can be very astute at zeroing in on weak spots. I've found that even when I disagree with suggested solutions, they often point out the areas of the story that need more work. For example, it's very tempting to call an editor hopelessly sheltered and naïve when *he* says a situation is unbelievable and *I* know I took it from real life. But what aspects of the true experience or context did I change or omit? How did my modification affect verisimilitude? If an editor says a character's grim family background is unbelievable, the problem may be that the character in the story seems too unaffected and unscathed for the shocking background to ring true.

What if an editor complains that the family I've praised in glowing terms actually acts like a nest of vipers? It's possible this particular editor suspects "dysfunction" in every family, but it's also possible I've been missing the implications of my story situation. I don't sit right down and start revising. Instead, I daydream. I'll give up my feeling of ownership of the material and let the characters and their situation "free float" as I try out different scenarios, some of which conform to the editor's vision. Sometimes the new pictures in my mind will seem flat and false. But sometimes, new ideas will suddenly surface and gel and I know I'm on the right track.

When it's obvious that an editor has entirely missed the point of a story, it is indeed possible he or she didn't read it carefully enough. But—remembering the fault may be mine—I read the manuscript and try to figure out what might have made my presentation misleading. In my own work, it sometimes turns out to be a matter of metaphors being taken literally. When the context is at all ambiguous, I find that changing metaphors to similes may help.

(Incidentally, editors have a knack for getting smarter every day. When I first read an editor's letter, I often find comments off-base or irrelevant. If I go back and look at the criticism a day later, more objectively, it sometimes makes an awful lot of sense!)

When an editor complains that a character is undeveloped or one-dimensional, use your logical analytical mind first. Is the character a

14

stereotype in which all traits line up to form a clichéd image or type? If the answer is yes, ask yourself how your character can surprise you. Has your character ever done or thought anything uncharacteristic? Switch into imaginative mode. Picture your character in a variety of vivid and detailed scenes. Maybe you'll come up with something new you can use. A clear view of a character in context—interacting with others or moving through a specific, detailed environment—can sometimes do more to bring the character to life than piling on more physical description, psychological exposition, and memories of childhood.

How do you know when to revise, when to stick to your guns, and when to look for another opinion?

Many writers I know won't revise a story unless an editor specifically says, "I'll consider publishing it if you make the changes." Otherwise, why bother changing a story to suit the taste of someone who's not going to publish it anyway? But I'm not interested in pleasing one editor; I'm trying to make my stories as good as they can be. If a comment raises a serious question, I'll consider it.

That doesn't necessarily mean rewriting. If, on rereading, the story continues to hold up for me, I'll keep sending it out unchanged. One of my stories that several editors found "unfocused" and "not really a story" ended up published in *The Literary Review* and nominated for a Pushcart Prize. I sold another story on the 91st try! The editors who accepted it have no idea what other people said about it; they love it just as is.

At this point, I don't consider *any* editor's reaction or criticism an ultimate judgment, unless it makes sense to me. For example, an editor recently returned a story of mine. Though she was not interested in seeing it again, she mentioned that one weakness was that the main character, Jody, was a nurse in a New York City hospital but that the job seemed to have had no effect on her. The editor didn't believe that anyone could work in that intense and stressful environment without being marked by it. She was right. I'd made Jody a nurse just as a device through which she could realistically meet some of the other characters. First I considered taking the easy way out—changing Jody's job. But when I began to imagine how her experiences on the job would affect her outlook and her other relationships, Jody began to take shape for me in a different way. I'm a lot happier with the story now. I won't send it back to the editor (*don't,* unless you've been

15

specifically asked to), but I remain grateful that she took the time to share her opinion.

Of course, if an editor does ask to see a story again after revision, publication is a distinct possibility—and so most writers are likely to get right to work on revising, but don't rush it! Unless the editor specifies a deadline (which may happen, for example, if a story is being considered for a special theme or holiday issue), take your time. Fiction editors are impressed by well-thought-out, effective rewrites, not by speed. When you are ready to send the manuscript back, be sure to mark your envelope "Requested Revision." But before you make any changes, it's important to consider *why* the editor is suggesting the revisions.

Some requested changes may have more to do with the magazine's audience and image than with the effectiveness of the story, as, for example, if a major magazine asks you to come up with an upbeat ending or to change the ages of the main characters. In these cases, you must use your own judgment and decide if tailoring the story to meet those specific market guidelines will ruin it. You may want to give it a try and see. If the result is a travesty, don't blame the editor. Just stick by your original version and submit it elsewhere. Keep the editor in mind for more appropriate material.

Similarly, editors often suggest cutting a story because of space limitations. You may legitimately feel it's impossible to do justice to your subject in 2500 words. On the other hand, if an editor writes, "This story goes on too long for what it has to say. Do you really need all the flashbacks?" the comments are directed at the material itself. Do take another look at the manuscript and consider whether the background really adds to the reader's understanding. If you feel that all the scenes *do* contribute to the overall effect, you might still respond to the editor's concern by seeing if you can cut without sacrificing anything essential. Do you make the same point over and over? Is your prose repetitive? Does the dialogue merely echo what has already been said in the narrative or vice versa? Do you go into unnecessary detail in your transitions? When the editor of *The Virginia Quarterly Review* accepted my story, "Little Virgins," he said he would be happy to publish it as written but hoped I'd "take a look at the story again with the possibility of cutting it down somewhat." I could have told myself, *It's been accepted! Why bother?* Instead I went through the manuscript again carefully, word by word and line by line, pruning excess. I'm glad I was nudged into doing so: The story as it appeared was tighter and better than the story I submitted.

Should you talk to the editor?

No matter how much imagination you have, one-way written criticism is rarely as helpful as an exchange of ideas. Never phone an editor to demand an explanation, but if you're invited to call and talk about a story, by all means take advantage of the chance. If you're sensitive about criticism, it makes sense to wait a couple of days, to give yourself time to cool down, reread the letter and your manuscript and think about it objectively. Be prepared with questions. Pin down the source of the editor's reservations. If the editor has suggested a solution you don't like, emphasize the aspects of the advice you found most valuable, and brainstorm about ways to solve the problem. Even if you think you have no questions, it's worthwhile to talk in order to confirm that you understand the editor's points correctly. Sometimes new ideas or areas of misunderstanding will emerge unexpectedly from the conversation. Besides, a personal chat may give you an idea of the editor's taste and interests—a good way to help you judge if you have other stories that might be especially appealing. It's also a chance to get some firsthand knowledge that editors are human—and on your side.

Knowing how to "take it" doesn't mean that criticism doesn't sting. It doesn't mean you must always follow advice blindly or trust other people's opinions over your own instincts. It does mean paying attention with an open mind, being receptive and guarded at the same time, both confident and flexible.

Criticism that helps improve a story is a true gift and, like anything of great value, doesn't come along every day, but any editorial response can lift a writer's spirits. Imagine yourself for a moment in the editor's place, faced with hundreds or even thousands of manuscripts and a magazine that can publish only a handful a year. When you think of all the demands on an editor's limited time, even the rejection letter that seems harsh takes on a friendlier glow. The editor who devotes time and effort to criticizing your story believes in the value of you and your work.

4

IS THERE A SECRET TO GETTING PUBLISHED?

BY KATHERINE PATERSON

ONCE UPON A TIME THERE WAS A WOMAN who wanted to write. No, delete that first sentence. Once upon a time there was a Maryland housewife with first two, then three, then four children under the age of six who was constantly composing in her head and furiously writing down the bits whenever she had a moment, who wanted desperately to publish. She became a celebrated, award-winning commercially successful writer of books for children and lived happily ever after. The end.

What a minute! That's no story.

What do you mean "that's no story"? You have "once upon a time" and "happily ever after." What more could anyone want?

A middle! A story must have a beginning, a middle, and an end.

But that's the boring bit. Delete "boring," insert "depressing." Besides, it's a story the audience will know all too well. The slogging away at manuscripts she has no hope will ever see the light of day— the wistful attendance at writers' conferences—the seven dismal years of self-addressed envelopes jammed into the mailbox—the coffee-stained manuscripts that have to be painfully retyped before they can be submitted to yet another seemingly heartless editor—the drawers of printed rejection slips—the wondering if it is worth the headache, not to mention the postage. She doesn't think about the time—her time evidently has no value.

Through the years, she tries everything—stories, poems, articles, fillers—but nothing sells except one story and one poem. The tiny magazines that buy them immediately fold.

She is, obviously, not meant to be a published writer. She doubts that she has any talent at all. In all other ways, she is a fortunate

18

woman—she has a good husband and four happy, healthy children. Isn't that enough? Why can't she be content?

But if she'd been content in the middle, the happily ever after wouldn't have happened.

What you've just read is an internal debate between my creative side and my business side. The business side is, frankly, a bit surprised that anyone would ask me to speak about "writing for the market." Years ago she made noble efforts to steer me toward writing something that might be marketable, but it became sadly evident that I was simply incapable of that kind of writing. The creative side wants me to tell the middle of the story, hoping it might help other weary writers, though she's not quite sure how. . . .

So, I pulled myself together and called my editor to tell her that I'd been asked to speak on writing for the market. "What are you planning to say?" she asked nervously. "Well, that's what I'm trying to figure out," I said. "What do *you* think I should say?"

"Well," she said, "I'm right now reading through the slush pile, and I wish everything weren't so market driven. I think people should write what they need to write."

"Can I quote you on that?" I asked.

"No, wait a minute. I have to phrase this very carefully. Writers have to know what's being published today and what's selling. It's not enough to go to libraries. Writers have to go to bookstores to find out what's being published and what's selling. But, having said that, I believe they should write what they need to write."

"Do you think new writers have a chance today?"

"It's harder," she admitted, "though it's always been hard. But today there are fewer editors willing to read slush-pile submissions. Though I can't understand it. How are they going to find good first novels if they don't read slush-pile submissions?"

No wonder my story turns out well. Does anyone in the world have such a terrific editor?

But back to the middle of the story. The question I suppose I need to address is how I got from there to here—how the frustrated, practically unpublished housewife became, if not exactly a household name, at least a respected and well-paid writer.

Let me say first of all that no one has been more surprised by my success than I have. But everyone seems a bit surprised. When people

19

first meet me, I watch the way they think I ought to. Here's this woman, not nearly so clever as I, they're thinking, and she's supposed to be this well-known writer. Then often, surprise moves to questioning—or to be more specific, to what is sometimes known as the "trick" question. Which is, what is your trick? There must be some trick, some secret that you know that I don't. So, be generous, tell me your secret, so I can be rich and famous like you.

It doesn't do to say that there is no trick. The person will just think you're being selfish. And advice, even good advice, comes without a guarantee. It reminds me of the Mother's Day card I got from one of my sons this year: "Mom," it says, "all the advice you gave me growing up is still as clear in my mind as the day you gave it—And to this day, I always look both ways before accepting candy from strangers. . . ." Hm-m.

But, anyhow, for what it's worth, here it is: The middle of the story—the trick—the secret—the advice. It boils down to what my editor suggested: I did read what was being written in the field of children's books, but when I sat down to write, I wrote what I *needed* to write, I wrote what I *wanted* to write, what, as it turned out, I *could* write.

There is a wonderful story about the writer Conrad Aiken who during his lifetime received awards and critical respect, but very little in the way of actual money. During the 1920s and 1930s, he was a struggling writer with a house full of children to support. He was publishing, but only in toney little literary magazines too high class to insult contributors by paying them for their work. But what Aiken needed most of the time was cold, hard cash.

He decided to change his ways. Forget literature. Write something that would put groceries on the table. He went about his assignment scientifically. Taking most of the almost non-existent family budget, he bought copies of all the magazines that paid real money to writers for their stories. There were a lot more of them in those days than there are, alas, now: *The Saturday Evening Post, Liberty, Collier's*. He studied and analyzed all the stories in these publications until he figured out the key. Then he deliberately wrote a *Saturday Evening Post* story, one he was sure the editors would not be able to resist.

Well, of course, the *Post* rejected his "perfect" story, as did all the other high-paying magazines. (His "Silent Snow, Secret Snow" was eventually published in some obscure place, but it has been repeatedly anthologized in the years since Aiken's death as an example of a great literary short story.)

The moral of this cautionary tale is, you can study the market to a fare-thee-well, but in the end, you write what you can.

When children ask me where I get my ideas, I turn the question back on them. Ideas are everywhere—a dime a dozen. But before I write a book, I look at the idea, or rather, the complex of ideas I am proposing to turn into a story, and I ask two questions: Is it worth all the trees? And, the second question, which gets more relevant for me with every passing year—is it exciting enough, important enough for me to live with it for the year, two years, maybe three years of my ever-shortening life that it will take me to write it?

You may wonder why I ever write a book—so do I. And yet I do, because, like you, somehow I must. It's what I do. But I only write books that I truly need to write—that matter deeply to me.

I began to write my first novel back in those grim days when nothing I wrote was getting published. A lady in the church where my husband was pastor felt sorry for me, home with all those little children. She took me on as a kind of good work. "How about attending a writing class through the county adult education program?" she asked. She knew I was trying to write, but without success. It sounded great— Mom's night out. I started in a general writing course. Then the next year I took a course on Writing for Children. I was writing something— a story or a poem—every week, and publishing nothing, when it occurred to me that if I could write a story a week, I might be able to write a chapter a week. And at the end of the year I would have a book.

I wanted to write a story set in Japan, because I had lived there for four years, back when I was a competent single woman, and I was a little bit homesick for Japan. If I wrote a story set in Japan in the past, I would have an excuse to read Japanese history, something I loved doing. I don't think I ever knew that if I did that I would be committing historical fiction. I wasn't thinking about genre, I was thinking about story. I'm sure I didn't know that a book for children set in 12th-century Japan would be for all practical purposes totally unmarketable.

But a novel has to have more than fascinating setting and well-paced plot. It has to have an emotional core. It has to be written out of passion. And the heart of this novel set in 12th-century Japan came

21

from an unexpected source. It came to me from my then five-year-old daughter.

Lin was born in Hong Kong in the fall of 1962. When she was about three weeks old, she was found on a city sidewalk by a policeman and taken to an orphanage out in the New Territories, where she lived for more than two years before she came to be our daughter. Her initial adjustment was horrendous, and again when we moved from New Jersey to Maryland in 1966, a lot of it came unglued and had to be redone. But by 1968 when she was five, life had settled down pretty well for her. Still, there were times when for no reason we could discern, the bright, happy little daughter she had become would disappear. And in her place would be a silent waif. It was as though the child we knew had simply pulled down a curtain that we could not reach through, often for several days at a time. And it scared me to death. Where had she gone? What was going on behind that blank stare? And how on earth could I reach her? I had tried everything—cajoling, begging, holding her. Nothing worked. One evening I was in the kitchen making supper and she came in. Without a word she climbed up on a high kitchen stool and sat there, her tiny body present, but the rest of her completely closed away. I tried to chat with her in a normal tone of voice. There was no answer, no indication that she even heard. The harder I tried, the more tense I became.

Finally, I did what any good mother would do under the circumstances, I lost my temper and screamed. "Lin," I yelled, "how can I help you if you won't tell me what's the matter?"

She jerked to life, her eyes wide open. "Why did that woman give me away?" she demanded.

And then it all began to pour out. Why had she been given away? We'd never told her that she was a foundling. It seemed too harsh— just that her mother had not been able to keep her and wanted her to have a home. I repeated this, adding that I was sure her mother hadn't wanted to give her away, and wouldn't have if there had been any possibility that she could take care of her. Was her mother alive? Was she all right? I couldn't answer her questions, but she let me try to comfort and assure her. She never again, even in adolescence, pulled down the curtain in just that way.

She is a mother herself now—a wonderful, loving, funny mother, giving our baby grandchild all the care that she herself never had but

22

that somehow she knows how to give. She is a wonder, and I cannot tell you how I admire her.

But what she gave me that day was not only herself, but the emotional heart of the story I wanted to write. What must it be like, I wondered, to have a parent somewhere that you do not know?

I look at this book—*The Sign of the Chrysanthemum* is its title—and it's no marvel to me now that I had difficulty finding a publisher. It is set in the midst of the civil wars of 12th-century Japan. The central character is a thieving bastard who is searching for the father he never knew. The girl he cares about ends up in a brothel; I didn't put her there because I wanted to scandalize my readers, but because a beautiful thirteen-year-old girl in 12th-century Japan who had no one to protect her would, most likely, end up in a brothel, and the penniless teenage boy who loved her would be powerless to save her.

Now at some point I must have realized that I hadn't seen a lot of books for young readers along this line, but when I wrote *The Sign of the Chrysanthemum* I wasn't, to be honest, worrying about readers. I was writing a story I needed and wanted to write, as honestly and as well as I knew how.

For those of you who have been wondering about the difference between novels for young readers and adult novels, the adult bestseller at about the same time my book was published—a bestseller that was breaking every sales record since *Gone With The Wind*—was the sentimental tale of an overachieving seagull *Jonathan Livingston Seagull*, by Richard Bach. Then how on earth did my book ever see the light of day?

It almost didn't. It made the rounds of various publishers for more than two years. And then a miracle happened. It was taken out of the seventh or eighth publisher's slush pile by a young woman just out of college who read it and loved it. She took it to the senior editor, who had just come back from a visit to Japan and who was and is a woman of vision in the field of children's books. She has always dared to publish books that she feels will open up unknown worlds for children. She had no illusions that the book would sell well, but she wanted young readers to have a chance to read the book, and she wanted the writer to have the chance to write more books.

Though *The Sign of the Chrysanthemum* has never sold well in hardback, it sells remarkably well in paperback. This is particularly satisfying to me, because children and young people buy paperbacks, and it means that the book is reaching the people I am writing for.

Well, that's pretty much the middle of the story. It is harder to place a first novel now. The corporate giants who control most of the New York publishing houses do not have the vision of my first editors. Fewer chances are being taken.

There was a depressing article a few years ago in *Harper's Magazine* entitled, "Reading May Be Harmful to Your Kids." It included the twenty best-selling paperback children's books of 1990. Nine of the top ten had the words "Teenage Mutant Ninja Turtles" in the title. There were only two genuine books on the whole list. One of these, number fifteen, was E. B. White's *Charlotte's Web,* published in 1952, and the other, number twenty, was Maurice Sendak's *Where the Wild Things Are,* published in 1963.

So those of us who haven't the patent on Ninja Turtles might just as well devote our energies to writing something we really care about. And which, not incidentally, may be the only thing we really can write.

It is well to remember that by the time you write a book for the market and that manuscript has gone through the long process of selling itself to an editor and being published, the market may have long before gone somewhere else and left your book far behind. But a beautifully written book, a well-crafted story, a work of honest human feeling and deep passion, like the stories of Conrad Aiken, E. B. White, and Maurice Sendak, will never go out of style. And I still believe there will be a few horribly underpaid, sensitive, unjaded young people ploughing through the slush pile who will find your manuscript and take it to one of the rare remarkable editors left in the business, who will dare against all trends to put it between covers.

It will take a miracle, of course. But who am I to deny the existence of miracles?

5

No, No, A Thousand Times No

By Nick Lyons

BY THE TIME I HAD DECIDED to write stories and poems, I was in my middle 20's.

I lived alone in a dirty-green room on West 10th Street in Greenwich Village. The room—once a walk-in closet or a john—was exactly four and a half strides long. The bed wedged sideways into two snug alcoves at the far end; there was a sink whose porcelain had been gnawed away in a dozen places by rust; there was a hot plate, a tiny desk, one chair. On one of the dirty walls a previous tenant had hung a Christ with a crown of thorns, ripped from a magazine and put carelessly into a Woolworth frame. The half window over the bed opened onto the alley-way to a posh restaurant and, on warm spring nights, I could hear the constant clanking and clinking sounds of dishes, smell a dozen amiable mixed scents and hear occasional high laughter. I wrote, often for a dozen hours or more a day, not for fame or glory—or even money—but to fill some great hunger in my heart.

Still, every morning after I had lingered in the dark hallway for a glimpse of Diane, the young ballet dancer next door, I checked the mailbox. Since I wrote at a ferocious rate and sent my miserable words out into the world like so many arrows, randomly shot, the mailbox was host to a steady stream of rejections. At first, all of the rejections were printed notices to the effect that (a) the magazine received a huge number of submissions; (b) someone had in fact read what I had scraped off my brain; (c) what I had done was not—for some good but unnamed reason—for them. *The New Yorker* returned my poems and stories so fast that in the mad blur of those intense days in the mid-1950's I often thought I had submitted the work the day before—or even that morning.

Though I might not be writing for fame or money, these curt slaps hurt. They always do.

Rejection and acceptance, encouragement and tougher forms of counsel are, of course, central to the publishing process. The nature of what one accepts, the blindness—or vision—with which one rejects: all reveal the editor as surely as *le style c'est l'homme* (or *la femme*).

Less is found in what are ungraciously called "slush piles" today because fewer editors fish in such waters, and many book and magazine publishers even flatly refuse to accept unsolicited manuscripts because the odds are so poor, the dross so thick. Some have fired all of their "first readers" and make short shrift of what comes in unsought, without the protection of a known friend or a respected literary agent. There just isn't time, they say, and point to the thousands of manuscripts that arrive like this—perhaps one in 20,000 worth print.

There are ways of insulating yourself from rejection, perhaps—risking little, wanting (and needing) nothing—but such protection reminds me of Swift's jibe at stoicism: that it supplies our wants by lopping off our desires, cuts off our feet when we need shoes.

Mostly, those who create are painfully vulnerable, whatever success they've had.

Try as we will, I suspect we need to be accepted on some terms (though some feed on rejection, which confirms some deep-seated sense of fate). Mostly, of course, the work counts—perceived or not. But how can we remember that? We crave that word or two that will fan our hopes, that will help us hold what we do against the best we know, of whatever time, that will keep us free from those temporarily in the saddle. For editors change. And what barely got a look from one is praised and bought by another. I have seen it happen dozens of times with magazines, newspapers, book publishers. What, then, truly matters, beyond some simple encouragement to keep from going batty, other than the work itself?

Some of us grow, with luck, a bit wiser in the particular risks we take, and that, I am sure, is prudent (I would not dream of submitting anything to *The New Yorker* ever again, for more reasons than my perfect certainty of rejection); occasionally, when some of us migrate to the other side of the submission, we at least remember how it was.

My own thickening skin, on both sides of the mailbox, has seen several changes in the past decade; I still write what I like, mostly from the heart, always essays now, and the several hundred acceptances and some sure sense that, somewhere, I can find a home for anything I write make turndowns less painful, though never painless; and having started a small publishing house of my own, I can now say yea or nay alone, restricted only by the fact that we're a small publisher and publish only books on outdoor leisure sport—no fiction or poetry. I prefer to accept, but I must daily find the strengths to reject.

I reject for any of a thousand reasons: the work is poorly done, it is on a subject that does not interest me, it is too expensive to produce, it would take more time than I have to give it the proper shape according to my lights—or for an even less tangible reason: I don't know why but I just don't want to do it. It may be good or great; it may be something someone else will surely publish. I did not hang out a shingle and say, "I will surely give you good and proper reason if I don't decide to invest my time and money in your book."

Am I obligated to do so?

I don't think so. Quietly, as I try to keep a small publishing house afloat, I have to say that I do not offer myself to the world as a free reader of manuscripts, nor do I claim to be an infallible reader of them. I have a fragile little business to run, and if I don't put my best energies into *that,* the rest of the questions will be academic and I will surely lose—for myself, my partner, my staff, the authors we publish—the whole show. No, I do not owe that close reading and the thoughtful rejection letter even to others who write, as I once did, to fill a terrible hunger in their hearts; I only owe my little business the best books I can find.

But I will say this: After the metamorphosis from supplicant author to tyrant publisher capable of administering the sternest punishment by rejection, I cannot help looking, myself, at every scrap of paper that comes my way, from whatever source. I look a little or a lot, and I try to find some frank helpful thing to say—if only a few words or a pointing in another direction or the encouragement to work longer, harder—about every manuscript that heads back to its origins. I do not do so out of any obligation other than the selfish one. I keep thinking that something of value, of specific value to my publishing firm, will be there.

Just last week I was playing the grim reaper with a stack of proposals—some of merely a few careless pages, some careful and complete manuscripts—and had been sad for the blood I knew I would draw. Fourteen, fifteen manuscripts came and fell. The last was a complete book on a subject on which I am fairly expert. I had never heard of the author, and I follow the literature of the field closely; in fact, he had died a few years earlier, and the book was submitted by his widow. The title was a cliché. I'd make short shrift of this one.

But I didn't.

It drew me in, and I smiled and traveled with the man and found— from the first paragraph on to the end—a person of intelligence and wit, a happy capacity for simple joys, a shrewd eye for the natural world (I later found out that he was a renowned ornithologist), and I grabbed it.

At 60 I have less hunger than I had in my middle 20's—but enough; I look less for improbable acceptances, from faces in a hallway, lotteries, literary long shots; I do what work I find to do and then try to find a proper home for it, and generally do. That green room, those endless white slips, didn't crucify me—and perhaps, just perhaps, they helped me find that good man's book and some slight stays myself against the discrete horrors of rejection—and even of acceptance.

6

WAITING FOR INSPIRATION

BY PEGGY RYNK

MANY WRITERS, ESPECIALLY BEGINNERS, OFTEN HAVE the notion that to write well they must be inspired.

That notion is wrong.

The belief persists that simply sitting down and writing without feeling inspired is not real writing, but hack work.

That notion is also wrong.

The truth is that most of what we read on the printed page, whether in books, newspapers, magazines, or whatever, was written by someone who just sat down and wrote it. That's the way the work gets done.

Do we have to feel inspired to pass an exam, get a degree, parent our children, do brain surgery, or fix a leaky faucet? Of course not. Neither must we feel inspired in order to write and write well. A good part of writing well depends on practice. If you wait to practice until you feel inspired, you will write very little.

One writer I know pens stories with well-rounded characters, plot lines that move the reader happily along and that are a pleasure to read. But in the years I've known her, she's finished few of them. Why? She says she runs out of inspiration before she reaches the final page. Her unfinished, unpolished manuscripts gather dust, not checks. At the rate she's going, she'll never see her byline anywhere.

What makes this "inspiration" nonsense even worse is that some writers have decided that inspiration is something mysterious that can't be harnessed. They think of it as some irresistible, magnetic force that draws them to the typewriter or keyboard where they then have no choice but to get it down on paper. And what happens when this force is missing? Why, of course, they can't do anything!

You're welcome to wait for inspiration if you prefer to, but you must recognize that waiting is an excuse not to write, not a reason. Why not write something while you're waiting and see how it turns out?

Nobody says you have to send it anywhere, or even keep it. You can toss it later if it turns out limp, lifeless, and dull.

But maybe when you read the work over later, it will contain something good, something unexpected, something you hadn't even realized you were thinking when you wrote it. Maybe it'll be worth polishing and submitting. Maybe an editor will buy it.

It's true that sometimes when you write, you feel as if you're being guided by some influence outside yourself. The words seem to flow onto the page almost by themselves, and they give you a warm glow of satisfaction. The next day when you read over what you've done, your writing may live up to your hopes and be a truly fine piece of work. This can be a heady experience—something like falling in love. It's great when it happens, but don't count on it to be an everyday occurrence.

More often, the writing you produce on demand is just as good, just as salable, and certainly more abundant because your creative energies are always flowing on one level or another, whether you're conscious of feeling those energies or not.

"But if I don't *feel* anything," you might ask, "what am I supposed to write about? What if my mind is a blank?"

These are good questions, and they have good answers. One is to read widely, copiously, so that your mind is constantly packed with facts, thoughts, questions, characters, suppositions, and what-ifs. Writing comes from what you know, what you think, and what you imagine, and these come from your store of information.

Another answer is to keep an idea file. When something occurs to you—a subject for an article, a plot twist for a novel or short story, an interesting character trait, an appealing phrase, even a question you'd like an answer to—jot it down. Keep these ideas and snippets on index cards, bits of scrap paper, scribbled in a notebook—whatever suits you. Then on days when you can't think of anything to write about, you will have something to work on. All you have to do is sit down and write. You're in business again.

A writing teacher I know gets his students off and writing with an exercise that piques the imagination. He'll ask the class for possible story titles—ordinary or odd, sane or lunatic—then writes them on the board. Out of those listed, he selects five. Each student then picks one and writes a story using it as a starting point. The story can move in any direction; it can be funny, serious, poignant, sassy. But by the next week each student must have written a story.

Come up with your own list of titles, right off the top of your head. Don't dig for them. Then use the list as a springboard to write a story, an article, a poem, an essay, or anything else. The results may surprise you.

If one title turns out to be a dead end, try another. Soon one will click. In the meantime, you'll gain practice and discipline, both of which are necessities for writers.

Each day set yourself a realistic goal—to write five pages, for example—and don't quit until you've reached it. If one page is more reasonable for you because of other responsibilities, that's fine, too. Don't set your goal as minutes or hours spent working; it's too easy to waste that time looking up one last fact, changing your margins, or when desperate, searching for a new pen.

If you meet this goal every day, five days a week, at the end of a month you'll have completed a substantial amount of work, an accomplishment you can see and touch, review and polish, not because you waited for inspiration, but because you didn't.

The more experience you have at practicing your craft, the easier the words and ideas will flow—much like learning to type, to play tennis, or to drive a car. Before long, you'll be able to produce high quality writing almost anywhere, almost anytime, and under almost any circumstance.

7

BRING YOUR IMAGINATION
BACK TO LIFE

BY CYNTHIA K. JONES

YOU ROLL A CLEAN SHEET OF PAPER into your typewriter, then sit staring at it, your mind a total blank. Frustration begins to build as minutes tick by and not one fresh idea comes to mind. The minutes stretch into an hour, and still nothing. In other words, your imagination is dead. To bring it back to life—almost instantly—take a stroll through a graveyard.

Yes, a graveyard. It needn't be large, but it should be old. Wander among the headstones, and don't just read what's written on them; study them, and ask plenty of questions, for every headstone is a story, somebody's story that could become your story with just a little probing.

In an old church cemetery rests Jonathan David West, who died at age 18 months. His headstone reads "John-John, gone so soon." And although he died over 40 years ago his grave is neat, cared for, and boasts fresh flowers. The work of the mother? The father? The still grieving sister who took care of him after their mother's death in childbirth? Or could it be the doing of a remorseful person who felt responsible for the baby's death?

In that same cemetery, there is another grave—small, crude, neglected, at least in appearance. But on several Sundays you notice a woman—old, unkempt, obviously poor—who comes to visit it. She always takes a creased and faded photograph out of the pocket in her frayed sweater and holds it to her heart as she stands silent over the grave. What is *her* story? But more important, what do you *imagine* is her story?

Why is James Johnson buried beside his first wife while his second wife and widow is buried alone 30 feet away? Did his children so hate her that they refused to allow her to be laid to rest beside their father?

32

Or did the widow come to so hate her husband—who continually praised his first wife—that she insisted on not being buried with him— and *her*?

Why did sisters Lucy, Jane and Mary never marry although they lived into their eighties? Too good for the rural boys of that small town? Or would no one have them in spite of their money?

And can you imagine the life of "Red," whose 1884 headstone declares that he was "legally hanged"? And was Anna Lee Smithson really a traitor at the age of 17, as her headstone claims? Or is her coffin empty, and her "death" was only a ploy designed to smoke out the real traitor? If so, what happened to Anna?

Even a seemingly ordinary headstone can set the imagination flying. Mary Ann Jones died in Virginia in 1926, just two weeks shy of her sixteenth birthday. Her headstone is large and very elaborate, suggesting that she was from a wealthy family. Think back over the years. Can you see Mary Ann, her mother, and grandmother, as they excitedly plan her "coming-out" party—an expected event for girls of wealthy families during that period. Can you imagine Mary Ann as she lies awake at night dreaming of her party—only two weeks away now! Do you feel her girlish excitement as she dreams of a certain young man, hoping he will ask to court her? For a novelist, Mary Ann doesn't have to die, and the party doesn't have to be canceled. In fact, Mary Ann could and should have a future far beyond anything she could have dreamed of.

Bring the dead back to life. Three-year-old Jennie died in 1893. Imagine her on her deathbed, feverish and weak, her small hand clasped in her 20-year-old mother's already work-roughened one, pleading in a small tired voice, "Mama, help me." The mother knows there's nothing she can do for her daughter. Can you see her valiant, reassuring smile? Can you feel the constriction in her throat as she answers, "Drink some water, dear, then get some sleep. You'll feel better soon. Mama loves you." We know the child dies, but how did her death affect her mother and the rest of the family? If you're a writer, you know they didn't just carry on as before.

Gravestone names can stir the imagination in many ways. Abraham McBain died at the age of 71, a bachelor. With a name like that he might have had a Jewish mother and an Irish Catholic father. Would neither group accept him and allow him to marry their daughters? Did he spend his life embittered, self-pitying, resigned, or well-adjusted? What kind of life did his parents have together?

In Montana in 1823 Kitty Morgan died, along with her two-year-old twins. What might have happened to them? Were they killed fighting Indians, disease, starvation, or by bandits? What were they doing that far West so early in our nation's history? Were they on their way back East, or firmly settled?

Captain David Wilson, a veteran of the Revolutionary War, is buried in a small fenced-in section of a tiny graveyard in South Georgia, along with his three wives and five infant daughters. What might their story be? Anything you want it to be, and if you're imagining, you can imagine anything.

Family graveyards can be especially interesting, particularly to those writing multi-generational novels. What would your imagination conjure up if you found a family graveyard neatly divided in half, the immediate family on one side and the daughters- and sons-in-law on the other? You might not want to be a part of such a family, but you might want to write about them.

Don't just read the engravings on the headstones, read *into* them. Tom Johnson's headstone claims he was a veteran of the Spanish American War, which ended when he was fourteen years old. What about the headstone that says, "He was ninety years old, and it was time for him to go"? A family glad to be rid of a burden or a compassionate family relieved to see a loved one released from pain and suffering?

Is there a poem or scripture engraved on the headstone or just the bare facts? Compare, "Nancy Smith, beloved wife of David," to "Nancy Smith, wife of David Smith, born 1932, died 1967."

Question the dead, pry open their secrets, don't take anything you see at face value, and your imagination will come to life.

8

THE FROG IN STEPHEN'S POCKET

BY VICKI GROVE

I GOT SOME GREAT NEWS TODAY. My editor called and told me my sixth book for young people has been accepted for publication. I intended to savor this victory as I jogged tonight, to smile a lot and to punch the air joyfully from time to time. But instead, I found myself thinking about this boy named Stephen who sat next to me in Miss Adcock's fifth grade.

Miss Adcock assigned Stephen and me seats next to each other in the back row because we were both new kids and both of our last names started with the same letter. I was shy, and he stuttered. We were sort of invisible back there. I guess you could say Stephen and I became friends those first weeks of September—if we really were friends—by default.

At first no one knew Stephen stuttered, because he never talked. About a week into school, Miss Adcock wrote his name on the board, but she spelled it wrong—Steven. Stephen waved his hand frantically in the air and jumped to his feet. "I-i-it's . . . puh-puh-p! Then i-it's aytch!"

Every kid in that class exploded with laughter. And though I've been privileged to meet hundreds of incredibly caring and sensitive teachers in my lifetime, I'm sorry to say Miss Adcock wasn't one of them. She laughed, too.

After that, Stephen didn't talk again. But one day I noticed something amazing. The left pocket of his shirt was moving! He saw me staring, propped his math book up on his desk to hide us from Miss Adcock, and leaned toward me, smiling. He carefully unbuttoned his pocket and opened it outward just enough for me to notice a tiny brown frog he had living in there, in a neat little bed of grass and clover.

My family moved again the first week of October. The last week I

35

was in Miss Adcock's class, she decided to force Stephen to talk, so she called on him to read from our history book.

He stood up, his neck bright red. He opened the book, looking straight down at the page. Several kids covered their mouths with their hands, poised to giggle.

"Th-the C-C-Consti-tu-tu . . ."

The explosion of laughter came, and Stephen slammed shut the book and stumbled toward the front of the room, toward escape through the classroom door over which, ironically, there hung a framed copy of the Constitution, which tried in its own way to assure some kind of respect for people's differences. But Stephen didn't make it out the door. He caught his foot on a desk in the front row and fell. Miss Adcock took him to the nurse's office, and he went home with a compound fracture of his left arm.

I moved a week later and never saw him again.

The book my publishers accepted today is called *Crystal Garden*. I began outlining it about three years ago, after speaking to sixth-graders in a school near where I live. A group of kids gathered around me, asking questions, all talking at once.

Allysa had dark-brown hair pulled back with a purple band. She worked her way toward me and said clearly, calmly, "My dad died when the fireworks factory blew up last year."

I felt stomach-punched. This wasn't the usual "I have a cat named Pearly" type of information I get from young people when I visit schools.

"Oh, I'm so, so sorry," I whispered, touching her wrist.

"They couldn't call us," she said in that same sturdy, controlled voice. "They couldn't call us!" she repeated, as the others pushed her on.

The bell rang, and the group dispersed in all directions. I went to find the reading teacher, and described the girl. "Allysa," she said. "Yes, her father was killed."

"But she says, she keeps repeating, that they couldn't call her. Why?"

"I heard they couldn't reach the family after the accident. They're very poor, and their phone had been disconnected. That's probably what she meant."

From another teacher I learned a tiny, but significant, bit more. Allysa's father lingered in the hospital for a few hours, but he died before Allysa could see him again, one last time.

Crystal Garden is Allysa's story, a story of frustration and rage directed against the fact that, yes, there are classes in America based on income, and yes, if you're in the wrong class, life can be pretty unbearably unfair at times. It's Stephen's story, too, because classes can also be based on physical differences. It's also the story behind a finger painting I saw hanging in the hallway of an inner-city school in Kansas City last spring, done by a second-grader named Keisha. It was a lovely scene of two girls swinging, with wide happy smiles, under a big also-smiling sun, and it was called "My Happiest Day." The text on a piece of tablet paper taped underneath it read, "This is my happiest day, when me and Lavonda were at the playground. That night her mom's boyfriend hit her with a gun and she bleeded to deth, and don't nobody care but me, and I can't do nothing about it."

I would never pretend to have the gut-level honesty or the literary grace of that young writer, yet I'm an adult who writes books for young readers. So it was up to me to write *Crystal Garden,* and though I tried and tried to get it right and spent a whole year on it, I got it wrong.

I sent my manuscript off to my publisher, and it came back loaded with yellow stick-on notes. The criticism was made by several editors about many major things, including the horrifying information that readers there had found my narrator, my Stephen/Allysa/Keisha character, "unsympathetic" and "whiny."

I put the manuscript aside for a week or two, till the pain subsided, and I could think more clearly. Then I began laboriously and tediously working on a total rewrite. It took me most of another year.

I sent it off again, and it came back to me, again with several major criticisms. The main problem was still characterization, and without that, what is there? I really wasn't any closer to having the book published this time around than I had been last time. My editor gently, kindly suggested I might want to put it aside for a while, which I'm sure, in editorese, must mean, "Give it up, stupid!"

Now this, I believe, is where you begin to separate out a few things within your own heart and soul. I had to ask myself why I was hacking away at this hopeless project, to the degree that I couldn't see it with any objectivity. I was wasting my time and the valuable time of some very gifted, very busy editors. Besides, I have to earn money with my writing!

Right about then I ran a writing workshop in that same Kansas City school, and saw the elegant picture of Lavonda and Keisha under the smiling sun. "Don't nobody care but me, and I can't do nothing about it." I stood right there and whispered, "Oh, Keisha, I care. I do!"

Then I went home, took scissors to *Crystal Garden,* cut it into pieces I thought might be salvageable, and began from scratch.

And this time around, it was accepted.

Lots of revising and editorial work are still ahead. And then the acid test will come. When it's published, will it move young readers, will it increase their awareness, their compassion, enhance their lives? Or will it be unread, or worse, read and quickly forgotten?

It's been said many times that writers must never give up on their manuscripts, that if you have faith your work will eventually find a home. I believe this is true, but I quibble with the word "faith." It's plain hard work—perhaps even harder than many unpublished authors believe—that gives a story an eventual home. And in my own experience, this more often means listening than anything else.

Listening to the voices around you, listening to your own heart, and, yes, listening to criticism, especially if you're fortunate enough to have good editors give you some along the way.

Keisha, I care. I wish you and Lavonda could still be swinging in the sun, and if I fail you by not doing anything about it, it won't be because I didn't try. It'll just be because I tried and tried and ultimately wasn't up to it.

Allysa, they couldn't call you, and I think that's how you'll remember your dad's death forever, and it's important that people know how that feels. Don't worry—I got your point, and I'll try to spread the word.

Stephen, I want more than anything for people to know who you really were, a boy with a frog in his pocket. How neat that was, what a nice little portable nest you made! I want to show you to readers as I saw you. But as you know better than anyone else I've ever met, if I stutter and stumble, they won't listen.

9

Imagining What You Don't Know

By Paula Fox

I HAVE BEEN UNABLE TO PUT out of my mind, though I have tried, a sentence I glimpsed in the last paragraph of an interview with a novelist that appeared in a national magazine a few years ago. The novelist, when asked about her plans, replied, "Now that I have succeeded as a writer, I'm looking for new forms of stimulation."

Such fatuousness is not exceptional, perhaps not even surprising during these days when one of the more intrusive catchwords has become *lifestyle,* with its implication that how one lives is entirely by choice, by will, and when the director of a national self-help organization announces from his platform that "We must applaud everything equally and give up the useless habit of evaluation."

Life is not a style, any more than death is a style, although if we give up the "useless habit of evaluation," we may not be able to tell the difference. And as for succeeding as a writer, a claim that in the days of my own youth no writer would have been caught dead making, and wouldn't, I venture to say, have secretly thought, here is what Cesare Pavese says about such self-congratulation in his diary, *This Business of Living:*

> Complacency is a deficiency whose penalty is a special perennial adolescence of the spirit. It is doubt which alone can make us probe and glimpse the depth of consciousness.

I have written and published six adult novels and twenty books for young people. Save for an occasional sentence, a paragraph here and there, I haven't been content with my work. "Eased" is closer to describing the sense of deliverance I feel when the last galley is corrected, when I am, for a time, free of the enveloping tension of work.

During those quiet days, a kind of truce prevails in me. I am relatively untroubled, either by doubt or certainty, volatile states in any case. In fact, for a little while, I rest almost in a torpor, its surface only faintly ruffled by mild, vague thoughts. I can hardly recall, in this state, the days of the years when work was like digging a trench in hard ground. I forget the times of confusion, of tedium, of a failure of nerve, of pulling myself together once more to go to my workroom, wishing the telephone would ring, resenting it when it does, wishing for any distraction, yet dreading all distraction. I forget, too, the moments when writing seems nearly effortless (there are few of those!), and a voice seems to speak through me. And I forget the deep pleasure of an absorption so complete that time itself weighs nothing.

Before the book is actually published, any judgment of mine on the possible failure or success of the book I have written bears on how effectively reviewers will encourage or discourage readers from buying it and reading it; the significance of that kind of success or failure is that it will—or will not—result in buying me time so I can begin once again.

The calm is soon over. A few reviews trickle in. A painful prospect opens up. My book will not be understood by anyone. It will not be read by anyone. Or if it is read and written about somewhere, it will be by that same happy and successful novelist whose words I quoted at the start of this article. And she will say about my book: It has not succeeded! Let the writer seek a new form of stimulation!

Hard and unremitting labor is what writing is. It is in that labor that I feel the weight and force of my own life. That is its great and nettlesome reward.

It is not easy to convince people who take writing courses just how much labor is required of a writer.

After all, their mouths are full of words. They need only transfer those words to paper. Writing can't be really difficult, like learning to play the oboe, for example, or studying astrophysics.

Pavese, in his diary, also writes:

They say that to create while actually writing is to reach out beyond whatever plan we have made, searching, listening to the deep truth within. But often the profoundest truth we have is the plan we have created by slow, ruthless, weary effort and surrender.

Most students of writing need little convincing about the deep truth they have within them, but they are not always partial to "slow, ruthless, weary effort." Few of us are. Yet there comes a time when you know that ruthless effort is what you must exert. There is no other way. And on that way you will discover such limitations in yourself as to make you gasp. But you work on. If you have done that for a long time, something will happen. You will succeed in becoming dogged. You will become resolute about one thing: to go to your desk day after day and try. You will give up the hope that you can come to a conclusion about yourself as a writer. You will give up conclusions.

The English critic, John Middleton Murry, wrote:

A writer does not really come to conclusions about life, he discovers a quality in it. His emotions, reinforcing one another, gradually form in him a habit of emotion; certain kinds of objects and incidents impress him with a peculiar weight and significance. This emotional bias or predilection is what I have ventured to call the writer's mode of experience; it is by virtue of this mysterious accumulation of past emotions that the writer, in his maturity, is able to accomplish the miracle of giving to the particular the weight and force of the universal.

People who see themselves as having succeeded so thoroughly at writing there is nothing left for them except to search out fresh fields of endeavor are not, in my view, in the right profession. Conclusions about life are just what such authors like best. They wish to believe there are answers to everything, and everything is defined by them as that for which they have answers.

I think that the character, the temperament, of their products, exhibit a kind of perverted social-workerism. And their fiction trivializes even as it sentimentalizes our lives no less than did the older, didactic literature of the past, toward which these new didactic writers often express such lofty contempt.

These are not tellers of tales, imaginers. They are answerers, like those voices on the telephone, which, for a fee, can provide a caller with a prayer, a joke, sexual stimulation, weather reports, or a list of antidotes in case one has swallowed poison.

In *The Tragic Sense of Life*, Miguel de Unamuno tells of Solon weeping over the death of his son. When asked why he is weeping, since it will avail him nothing, "That," replied Solon, "is why I was weeping."

Complacency is a deadweight on the spirit. It smothers imagination. But one rarely hears talk about imagination, especially in the class-

41

room. This is partly due, I think, to an insidious kind of censorship. Censors have always been around, wanting to ban books because they contain some sexual or social or political content that frightens or repels them.

But the new censors tell us that, as writers, our only valid subject is ourselves, or those identical to ourselves, as though we were clumps of clones distributed about the earth. Men are to write only about men, women about women, black people about black people, and so on.

What a foretaste of the intolerable boredom that lies ahead! What is to be done with Tolstoy's reflective hunting dog, with Gogol's Nose, with Turgenev's singers of the Brezhin meadow, with Sancho Panza's imaginary kingdom, with all the men and women and children and ghosts and gods and animals that have been imagined and made living for us in all the stories that witness and record our pleasures and our sufferings, the mystery of our lives?

Narrowing, ever narrowing, the new censors, their tiny banners inscribed with ominous declarations: *I can't identify with that! I can't relate to this!* seem to want to ban humanity itself, in all its disarray and difference!

"Maybe we're here," the poet, Rainer Maria Rilke, said, "only to say: house, bridge, well, gate, jug, olive-tree, window—at most, pillar, tower—but to say them, remember, oh! to say them in a way that the things themselves never dreamed of so intensely."

As I write Rilke's words, I think of the great silence into which we hold up our small bundle of words; it is like the blue light of our small planet glimmering in the darkness that is all around.

℥ 10

Keeping a Writer's Journal

By Marjorie Pellegrino, Lynne Weinberg-Hill, and Tama White

For many writers, the journal is more than a diary recording life's events. It is an essential tool resulting in deeper thinking. Writing about things outside yourself from an introspective point of view allows you to reach into your core to discover untapped resources. The journal is a place to find your voice, to experiment and play, to be alone with yourself.

Here are some suggestions—not rules—on how to keep a journal, what to write in it, and how the raw material you produce can be transformed into nonfiction, fiction, and poetry.

Use a notebook that doesn't restrict your writing. A loose-leaf offers more freedom than a small, dated diary. You can insert pages from your computer, magazine articles, letters, excerpts from books, even notes made on the backs of envelopes.

Date your entries, but don't worry about writing every day. Read aloud what you have written to discover the emotion beneath the words, but keep your journal private. If you decide to share what you have written, make a copy.

Here are some ideas to stimulate and enrich your journal writing.

- Dig deep. Sit in silence a few moments before you begin, and record what you really care about.
- Tell the truth, even if you have to write in code.
- Write quickly, so you don't know what's coming next.
- Turn off the censor in your head.
- Learn to be observant. Write down six things you notice each day.
- Write from different points of view to broaden your sympathies.
- Collect quotations that inspire you, and jot down a few notes on why they do.

43

- Set goals, and keep track of your progress.
- Record your dreams. Ask what the symbols remind you of, and describe what you think the dream is telling you.
- Use your journal as a non-judgmental friend to listen to your angry or confused thoughts.
- Make a list of the things you love. Note how often you make time for them.
- When words won't come, draw something—anything.
- Dedicate an entry to your muse or to a person you admire.
- Don't worry about being nice, fair, or objective. Be selfish and biased; give your side of the story from the heart.
- Write even what frightens you, *especially* what frightens you. It is the thought denied that is dangerous.
- Don't worry about being consistent. You are large; you contain multitudes.

Nonfiction

Well-crafted nonfiction excites and informs. The reader is drawn into the piece by an edge, an undercurrent, and kept involved by the flow of ideas. For nonfiction writing that sparkles, journal writing offers the essential ingredients, capturing the emotion of an idea, theme, or event. It locks in details that would otherwise vanish over time.

Two of my strongest nonfiction pieces, "September Sunday" and "Reunion," grew directly from journal entries. During a three-month period when my brother faced a life-threatening illness, I wrote in my journal every day to keep myself centered. Those pages resulted in a published poem, an article, an inspirational piece, and a nonfiction book proposal. Organizing, filling out, and editing came later, but the part that moved the reader found its voice in my journal.

While sometimes I pull an essay from my journal, other times I have a work-in-progress and use the journal process to edit, organize, or find a focus. I might ask myself, "Why am I writing this article? What is it about? What are the most important things the reader should know?" Through this exploratory writing, the thread of a meandering piece becomes clearer, and I'm more aware of excess baggage that needs to be lightened, or an essential point that needs to be moved to the forefront.

I also use my journal to focus nonfiction ideas that I will then develop into queries. A remark by a neighborhood child about my family's bike helmets resulted in several journal pages. I then decided to write a piece on bike safety, feeling that if as a parent I was concerned about how children could learn to be safe bike riders, other parents would probably be concerned as well.

Creating fiction

Fiction grows from the writer's imagination, but the seeds of the story can often be found in the writer's life. A scene, an event, a character, a remark overheard, can start those seeds growing.

Long before I became a fiction writer, I began keeping a journal. I recorded events of the day, feelings, settings, scenes, even dialogue. I didn't write in my journal every day, sometimes not even every week.

As I began taking my writing seriously, I used my journal as a compost heap, throwing in everything I wanted to recycle. Now when I'm writing a story and need fresh details from a long-ago scene, I can locate that memory in my journal.

For instance, when I went to court for a traffic violation, I described the courtroom in my journal, noting the high ceiling, wood paneling, flags, and signs on tables. In my first published story, "Walkers and Other Tribes," I used those details in a pivotal scene. Epi, an older Hispanic woman, has chosen to go to court alone and plead "not guilty" for having her dog off-leash in the park. Details enhanced the tension:

In the courtroom, Epi takes a seat on a low pew. The room is huge under a 30-foot-high ceiling, outlined by wood paneling. The judge faces into the room, behind a large bench, an American flag to his right and an Arizona flag on his left. Two large tables separate him from the wooden pews. The first table has a sign reading *plaintiff*. The second table says *defendant*.

Along with everything else I put into my journal, I record my dreams. While I was writing my second published story, "Roadrunner," I recorded this dream:

I was captured by Palestinian terrorists. Other captives and I were being driven in a mini-van. . . . Then I realized none of the terrorists were in the car. I suggested we not drive to the destined spot, but flee instead. Everyone agreed. I felt a moment of relief. When the driver turned the van in another direction, the terrorists shot him.

In my story, the character receives an unsettling call late in the evening. I framed the dream passage with, "I had a hard time falling asleep and then dreamed an odd dream," and ended with, "I found a microphone hidden on the front seat and wondered at my naivete. To think I could do combat with terrorists."

Not only does your journal help you understand what is currently going on in your life, it offers perspective on the past. As you dig through your journals, you rediscover old friends, buried feelings, past events, and forgotten details. With distance and insight, your life, as recorded in your journal, can yield many fiction possibilities.

Inventing poetry

Half of my journal entries are records of dream or waking reverie and are full of images and symbols coming directly from the unconscious. Capturing these images in a journal is the first step in the writing of poetry.

I use this type of journal entry in several ways. Most often I take an index card and lay it vertically on the left side of my journal pages, cutting off the first two to four words of each line. Reading down the page gives me such phrases as "standing at the top of my head." (You can use these in one poem, or you may choose just one as a jumping-off point or poem title.) That's how I came up with the titles "This Dream, A Road in the Mirror" and "This Elevator Could Be Considered." The middle of lines can be isolated using two cards, one on either side, and, of course, the ends of lines are equally useful.

A related method involves photocopying a page from my journal and tearing it into small pieces, each containing a few words that can be used together, as in the index card method. In that way, I created the title of my first published poem, "Grandmother, Do You Think Like Roses?"

"What I did today" journal entries can be used in similar ways or can serve as take-off points for longer, narrative poems, and even for a series of related poems revolving around a group of characters (suitably disguised, of course). A loose-leaf notebook is again useful, allowing you to remove pages and set them side by side, so that new lines can be constructed by reading across from one page to the next.

Journal writing is what keeps me going during dry spells. Even when I am producing little finished work, the time spent on my journal entries is not a total loss, as I have produced dozens and dozens of pages of raw material to work from when inspiration strikes anew.

11

SURVIVAL TACTICS FOR MAGAZINE WRITERS

BY EILEEN HERBERT JORDAN

I DON'T KNOW IF ANYONE HAS properly acknowledged magazine writers as survivors, but if no one has, it's a shame. Over the years, we have not only survived, but prevailed in the face of obstacles too numerous to mention.

There has always been, of course, the inevitable loss of the editors who have nurtured us, losses due to time, to altered lifestyles, to the changing winds that blow through publishing empires. Indeed, not only have editors disappeared, so have magazines we thought would last forever. To complicate matters, magazines that have *not* disappeared have been so reinvented and redesigned that we no longer even recognize them when we see them on the newsstand. The writer, nervously observing this, cannot help but notice that, when the art directors and the graphic artists have done their jobs, the finished product may look absolutely splendid—*but it contains less text.* In addition, new magazines have proliferated, and a quick word count of any one would show less text as well.

The greatest casualty in the reduction of text in popular magazines has been short fiction. This is true whether you are considering *Mademoiselle,* which discovered, among many others, Truman Capote, or *Redbook,* which prided itself once on publishing five or six stories in an issue, not to mention novellas. Since text is what we writers produce, it takes no prescience to see that it is survival time again.

And I have some survival tactics—perhaps not permanent, but at least temporary. They are by no means limited to fiction writers, either; anyone can play. We begin with the premise that writers write to be published. For one thing, they need the money. For another, they need the jolt to the ego one gets upon seeing one's name and material in print. Without the latter, any piece of writing is only a solo sung in an empty concert hall.

The best athletes usually acquire proficiency in more sports than one—why not us? Just as the gymnast may become a dancer, so the supple skills and the control you learn and use in writing fiction can serve you well in other fields. What I have in mind is the personal essay. A personal essay is a rather brief commentary on life as you see it. But it is more: It strikes a chord for many people—of nostalgia, of humor, of outrage, of whatever emotion you bring to it. It stands alone.

As an editor of *Woman's Day* Magazine, I bought many of these. Now as a free-lance writer, I have published several in the last couple of years, after a long career of writing fiction. It occurs to me that, since I have been on both sides of the desk, it might be helpful to share what I have learned. The good news first: The market is lively. In some magazines such essays are published in every issue; in others just occasionally. Look around and you will soon get a good idea of the opportunities available.

First, however, I have a secret to tell you about writing today, one which I hope you will keep to yourself and not repeat to everyone. It is the sensible way to proceed right now: *Write fiction as if it were fact and fact as if it were fiction.* I won't explore every interpretation of this, but you have only to watch a few television movies, all of which seem to consist of newspaper stories turned into melodrama, complete with hysteria, or to study *The New York Times* bestseller list and note the number of lawyers, those standard bearers of truth, who are writing fiction, to see what I mean. Bearing this in mind, consider the following:

1. *Keep it short.* No longer than a thousand words. Too much concentration on length can inhibit your creative processes; instead, focus on adjusting the rhythm of your writing, and set a goal for making your point rather than rambling on. An editor, especially with a beginning writer, is not going to plow through four thousand words to find the golden nugget. Stay in bounds.

2. *Give it form.* Like a short story, an essay requires a beginning, a middle and an end. It is not a character sketch; it is not a vignette.

3. *Tell the truth.* The truth as you see it, that is. The personal essay

48

expresses your opinion about one or more of life's foibles. The opinions don't have to be popular, but they do have to be honest. Don't write what you think the editor or the reader wants to hear. For instance, I dislike most television talk shows, and I published an article in *Modern Maturity* saying so—and why. I imagine there are plenty of people out there who like these shows, and that's perfectly O.K., but they couldn't write my piece! You would not believe them if they did.

4. *Get your facts straight.* If you use any figures, statistics, historical or geographical information in your essay, *make sure that they are accurate.* You may not be an investigative reporter, but you should pay as much attention to the precision of the facts you present as if you were. Editors will learn to distrust you if your work is not accurate, not to mention the fact that you will plunge yourself into a deep sea of bad habits.

5. *Say something.* Say something that is larger than its subject matter. The best short stories leave an afterglow with the reader, a point of view; the best essays should, too. For instance, my talk show piece was, in reality, a protest against the Peeping-Tom syndrome that is so widespread today. Another essay I did for *Woman's Day,* which dealt with the difficulty of coping in an electronic world, was really a plea to remember that people were here before machines.

6. *Don't lose your charm.* Because you are writing what is essentially a factual piece, don't think you must be sober and dull and abandon any style you ever had. Style is vital. If it is natural for you to be colloquial, be colloquial. If you work well with dialogue, find a way to use it. And don't be afraid to be funny. There's nothing wrong with laughing at some of the facts of life that otherwise could get us down; irreverence, in some cases, can mean survival, too. And readers love it.

7. *Remember the season.* Many subjects know no time of year, but some do. If you are thinking summer vacations, valentine messages you remember, Christmas wishes, etc., write about them at least six months before their season. It's a good idea to make a few notes on the subject as you think of them, then put them into essay form later.

8. *Consider your audience.* This is the first piece of advice every writer receives from every magazine editor I have ever known, in-

cluding myself, yet it cannot be repeated too often. And somehow, when people begin to write their personal opinions on a subject, they suddenly seem to think the whole world wants to listen. Not true. If you are commenting on life with young children, your ideal market is not *Lear's*. If you're doing a senior citizen peeve, forget *Mademoiselle* and *Glamour*. *Vogue* wouldn't have much room for coping with an old car, and *Woman's Day* probably less for how to handle servants. There are exceptions to every rule, including this, but use common sense.

9. *You can ask, but don't expect an answer.* Personal essays are almost always speculative ventures, just as short stories are. The exceptions may be for a very famous name (and if you have one you don't need me) or for a topic so unique that an editor would hardly duplicate it. If an editor tells you she already has something in her inventory on widgets, then widgets are not for her, so go elsewhere. On the whole, though, she will probably say, let's see how you have handled the subject. You bring so much of yourself to personal essays that querying beforehand is almost always a waste of time.

10. *Don't give up.* For one thing, you get better all the time, as you learn the steps and the proper moves. For another, since you are dealing in the business of opinion, you may have to do some networking before you connect with the editor who is looking for your point of view. Hang in there.

I hope this has been helpful. I hope this a lot, because I know the special rewards that lay ahead for you if you persevere. In a long publishing career, I have never received so many letters as I have from readers who have responded to my essays. It seems as if you strike a nerve when you publish one, and readers respond. Whether they agree or disagree doesn't matter; a dialogue is opened up. It is almost like making friends, and what could be better than that? I couldn't wish you more!

12

PURSUING YOUR DREAM

BY MARGARET CHITTENDEN

WHEN I WAS A VERY SMALL CHILD, I believed, sincerely and absolutely, that a lot of little people lived inside the radio. I believed that when you turned the switch to off, they knew to shut up.

Now I'm grown up, and I still believe in all those little people, though now they live inside my head. I know they are there because they talk to me.

Lots of people hear voices. Some of them are called mad and are shut up in rooms where they stare at the walls all day. Some of them are called writers, and mostly they do the same thing.

So here I am, a writer, staring at the walls of my office, trying to come up with something wise to say about pursuing the dream of becoming a writer. The room is silent. The voices aren't talking. The brain is dead. I've obviously burned out. I've said everything that is in me to say. This, by the way, is the same ritual of despair I go through when trying to start a new novel.

But always, quite suddenly, one of the little people in my head wakes up and starts talking to me, and my fingers start rattling the computer keys. In this case, the voice said, "Define the dream."

What exactly is the dream? What is *your* dream? If it's to be a writer, then you've got it made. Anyone can sit down with a typewriter, a pencil and paper, or a word processor, and write away, all day, every day.

If your dream is to be a *good* writer, then we've added a level of difficulty. And if your dream is to be a good *published* writer, we've added a steep hill to climb.

I'm going to tell you three very short stories.

The first, which I've always hoped was apocryphal, deals with a famous writer who was asked to speak at a writing seminar. He stood up in front of the microphone and said, "How many of you want to be

51

writers?" All the hands went up. And the famous writer said, "Then go home and write," and sat down again.

The second story I *know* is apocryphal because I made it up. It concerns a young man who graduated from M.I.T. and decided he didn't want to be an engineer after all; he wanted to be a violinist. He hadn't ever played an instrument, but he thought it looked pretty simple. So he went to a music store and bought a violin and came home and tuned the strings and put rosin on the bow and tucked the violin under his chin and played the "Intermezzo" from *Cavalleria Rusticana*.

The third story is about the Greek geometrician and mechanician, Archimedes, who once lowered his body into a filled bathtub, spilled a lot of water out onto the floor, and then jumped out and ran naked through the streets of Athens yelling "Eureka"—"I have found it." He had discovered the law of hydrostatics, which states that a body surrounded by a fluid is buoyed up by a force equal to the weight of the fluid it displaces.

It seems to me that the first two stories say the same thing, that if you want to do something badly enough, all you have to do is to go home and do it. I don't believe this for a minute.

The third story tells the truth. Archimedes was not visited by divine inspiration. He had devoted his entire life to research and experiment in plane and solid geometry, arithmetic and mechanics. In short, Archimedes had studied his subject. So when the water spilled over, he could go with the flow, so to speak.

We've all heard that we should study the type of writing we want to do. This is very good advice. But why not go a step beyond that? I spend a lot of very pleasurable time studying Sue Grafton and Sara Paretsky's mysteries for pace and suspense techniques; Joyce Carol Oates for atmosphere and anticipation and interesting story structure, as well as characterization in depth; John le Carré for good clean writing and a broad sweep to the story; Anne Tyler for storytelling techniques as well as terrific writing and characterization and style; Anne Perry for her command of historical detail. I study science fiction to stretch my imagination, newspapers for immediacy, and my favorite romance authors for sensual atmosphere, tight plotting, and the tensions that can occur between a man and a woman.

I study these various types of writing, not to copy those writers' techniques, but to develop and improve my own and to stimulate my imagination and creativity. The problem is, you see, that if we read only one type of writing, we may fall into the trap of writing in a way that we *think* is the proper way to write in that particular genre, rather than writing in a way that is natural to us and to our own style.

What we are after is a way to create writing that has what, for want of a better word, I call sparkle. I've read a lot of beginners' manuscripts in workshops and contests. Some were terrific. Some weren't. A lot weren't. They reminded me of my cake baking. I'm a good cook if I stick to dinners, soups, and pies. When I try to make a cake, it's disaster time. I don't know why this is. I use all the proper ingredients and utensils, but my cakes still turn out like flabby pancakes. So it is with some of the manuscripts I've read. The ingredients are all there, but the whole is not equal to the sum of the parts. There's no sparkle.

What exactly is sparkle? I don't know. It's rather like the judge's definition of pornography—I don't know how to define it, but I certainly know it when I see it. I'm willing to bet you do, too.

While pursuing the dream, it's a good idea to cultivate insomnia. I decided to learn how to write during the middle of a sleepless night, and I've had some of my most creative ideas while staring wide-eyed at the shadowed ceiling of my bedroom. Scott Fitzgerald talked about the real dark night of the soul, where it is always three o'clock in the morning. I've had many a real dark night of the soul. And I've learned that at such times I'm incapable of dishonesty. I can see with crystal clarity everything that is wrong with the novel I've been working on for four months. I'm reminded here of one of my favorite quotes, from H. G. Wells. "If you are in difficulties with a book, try the element of surprise: attack it at an hour when it isn't expecting it." Try three o'clock in the morning, run your latest manuscript through your mind and see if it tests positive for sparkle.

My old friend Archimedes would tell you that the shortest distance between two points is a straight line. But in the active pursuit of our particular dream, that's not always true. During the first two years of my writing career, I took a very circuitous approach. I wrote humor articles for my local newspaper's Sunday magazine, I wrote short stories for Sunday school papers, trade magazines, school publications. I suspected, rightly I'm sure, that I wasn't ready to write a novel. Nobody can really pick up a violin for the first time and play the

53

"Intermezzo" from *Cavalleria Rusticana*. It makes sense to practice scales and finger exercises and try to master "Twinkle, Twinkle, Little Star" before plunging headfirst into more difficult works.

Persistence pays. Put the emphasis on the pursuit rather than on the dream. Active pursuit. We have to look upon the road to publication as a journey. We have to resolve to have the patience and the stamina to stay with it, to persist in the face of rejection.

In my opinion, the only way to handle rejection is to meet it head on and leap over it. We should never interpret rejection as meaning we're no good; we should look upon it as a challenge. (I'm going to show *them*!)

Literary history is full of stories about great books that were rejected umpteen times and finally sold. My own first children's book was turned down by 25 publishers before finding a home. John Creasey, a prolific English writer who created several popular mystery series— altogether under 28 pseudonyms he published 600 books—collected 743 rejections before selling a single book.

It is very easy to get discouraged when you are a writer. Rejection slips do not drop upon us as the gentle rain from heaven, they come at us sideways from publishers' offices, arrows shooting straight to our hearts. Belief in yourself as a writer isn't always easy to sustain.

So I would offer this final thought for you to ponder. If the pursuit of the dream seems endless, if you receive more rejection than encouragement, if the road to publication seems impossibly long, bear in mind two very important words that were given to us by the ancient Romans. *Nil Desperandum,* which very loosely translated means, hang in there. Define the dream; pursue it actively, professionally, studying, learning, writing, rewriting, looking at your work with three-o'clock-in-the-morning honesty, trying at all times to make your work sparkle. Don't give up. Don't *ever* give up!

13

CORRESPONDENCE COURSES— ANYWHERE, ANYTIME

BY JOAN E. JUSKIE-NELLIS

I'VE BEEN TAKING CLASSES IN WRITING nonfiction and poetry part time for the past year and a half. One course in poetry taught by a widely published poet provided detailed critiques of my poetry. (I live in a small city that doesn't even have a college!) Too good to be true? No, it was by correspondence study!

Over 10,000 correspondence classes are offered by universities around the country, according to *The Independent Study Catalog,** a bible for people who wish to take correspondence classes. This catalog defines correspondence study as "individual instruction by mail" (also sometimes referred to as "independent study" or "home study"). Courses are listed by subject (look for writing classes under English or Journalism) and course title, and there are numerous possibilities for those who wish to learn to write, or improve their talent. Writing classes range from the introductory level to the more advanced critique-based workshops through the mail. You can find writing classes in fiction, poetry, and nonfiction (including some special genre areas like writing for children and journal writing), as well as in such supportive areas as grammar, editing, and expository writing.

Classes are offered noncredit, for undergraduate credit, and sometimes even for graduate credit. Tuition costs vary among institutions and programs: They range from about $70 for a short noncredit workshop to about $350 for a credit class at one of the more expensive institutions (some private schools may be even higher). Most programs allow you to sign up any time of the year, but an occasional one will

The Independent Study Catalog, published by Peterson's Guides, for the National University Continuing Education Association. May be ordered directly from Peterson's, P.O. Box 2123, Princeton, NJ 08543-2123, (1-800-EDU-DATA), for $16.95, plus $4.75 for shipping and handling.

go by the academic year and allow you to sign up only during registration time. Most give you a year to complete the course, but some run for shorter periods. I'd recommend the same process I went through when I decided to enroll in correspondence classes:

(1) Get a copy of *The Independent Study Catalog (I.S.C.)*.

(2) Find out which institutions offer courses in subjects in which you are interested.

(3) Send for their catalogs (addresses are in *I.S.C.*). Some institutions have a separate course description sheet or a syllabus for specific classes. Ask for one when you request the catalog.

(4) Evaluate which course seems right for your current needs. Introductory or advanced? (You may want to write to the instructor if the catalog doesn't specify.) Some advanced courses, like good writing programs, may require you to submit a writing sample to be admitted to the class. How many submissions does the class require? I found one with eleven submissions a lot more valuable than one with only five. Also find out if they have a page limit per submission. In one, all my prose submissions were limited to three typed pages; it's hard to develop an article within that limitation. Make sure you're getting *writing* rather than *literature*.

(5) After you get your first assignment back, reevaluate the course. Is this the type of feedback you are looking for? Having the right instructor is a very important part of the process. If the teacher has a writing slant very different from yours, you may have trouble accomplishing your objectives. In this case, consider changing courses before you continue. Check the catalog for the institution's policy for dropping a course. Most allow you to drop out within the first month or so, and will refund the charge (minus a slight processing fee). I made the mistake once, when I was very disappointed with the quality of critique, to continue throughout the entire course. It made me less motivated to put everything into it, and consequently I learned less. I should have dropped the class after the first lesson.

When I first began to take correspondence classes, I sent for about twenty catalogs from different schools (and there are still a lot more out there to investigate). Here are some of the highlights of my research into writing classes. Because details of course cost and availability continually change, it is essential to write for the most recent catalogs.

- Indiana State University offers *Intro to Photojournalism,* a subject not often available through correspondence.
- Indiana University offers the usual creative writing classes in poetry, fiction, prose, and drama, some requiring twelve submissions.
- Oklahoma State University offers fiction writing (three credits) for $139.95, and poetry writing (three credits) for $148.00. (These prices may have increased since I did my research, but I found them among the lowest for credit classes.)
- Texas Tech University had some interesting noncredit classes for only $44.00: *Creative Autobiography; Write and Publish Stories, Books & Articles;* and *Express Yourself in Poetry.*
- University of California, Berkeley, offers the largest selection of writing classes I've found. In addition to all the usual ones, they have a number of unique classes: *Editorial Workshop* "develops your skill in copyediting reports, newsletters, journals, books, and other nonfiction." *Individual Projects in Writing* is very individualized: "Design your own writing projects and determine form, content, and purpose." They also have a *screenwriting* course and genre writing in *romance, mysteries,* and other popular categories. A professional manuscript reading service is available for advanced writers. *Perfecting Your Poem: A Guide to Revision* caught my eye, along with *Poetry of the Self: The Writers Within,* described not as a poetry writing class, but a way to "explore your own ideas and experiences." The instructor has a background in Gestalt and Jungian psychology.
- The renowned University of Iowa offers correspondence courses in creative writing, often critiqued by participants in the Iowa Writer's Workshop.
- University of Minnesota has a *Journal and Memoir Writing* course, as well as the interesting-sounding *Topics in Creative Writing: Journaling into Fiction.* Their courses sometimes use cassette tapes.
- University of Wisconsin offers an outstanding variety of courses (almost as many as UC Berkeley), high-quality instruction, and affordability. Look for classes in both English and Journalism Departments. *Attack on Grammar* is a fun review class!
- Western Washington University offers *Journal Writing I* and *II,* open to beginning and experienced writers. Ask for a catalog and syllabus.

Writing works especially well in correspondence study because some of the most important skills required for correspondence study are also required for writers. First, strong reading skills are needed—and since most writers are also avid readers, they have an advantage here. Second, you must be able to work alone, make your own deadlines, set your work habits and follow them closely, and turn out material regularly. Again, this is part of a writer's life. I found that having to churn out new material for correspondence-course assignments increased my productivity. Finally, correspondence courses can increase your motivation to submit for publication. Having your manuscript come back with an "A" creates a strong incentive to make corrections and submit it to a magazine. You can learn to write by writing—it's a fun way to improve your skills.

§ 14

Don't You Know You're Beautiful?

By Arn Shein

ONE OF MY ALL-TIME FAVORITE movies is *The Inn of the Sixth Happiness,* a 1958 film starring Ingrid Bergman and Curt Jurgens. In one memorable scene, Jurgens asks why she never married and Bergman tells him she's not pretty.

"Don't you know you're beautiful?" he asks.

Long pause . . . reflective look . . . tilted head . . . shy smile.

"Once in her life," says Miss Bergman, "every woman should have that said to her. I thank you for being the one who said it to me."

Nearly 16 years later, poor health forced me to end a long and happy career as sports editor and columnist of a New York daily newspaper. Recognizing my need for a psychological lift, my wife talked me into joining a creative writing class. Smart woman! The old juices flowed once again and, with the help of an understanding teacher, I soon began pounding out one personal experience article after another.

It has long been my contention that if *you* don't think every word you put to paper is a gem, neither will the reader. And since I have never in my life written anything that I didn't think deserved a Pulitzer, I began sending my articles to upper-echelon magazines.

Over the next four years, I discovered that the editors of those publications didn't necessarily agree with my assessment. During that period, I amassed an impressive array of rejection letters—94 in all. My confidence was shaken, but each time an article came back in my self-addressed, stamped envelope (SASE), I stubbornly pulled out the red pencil, worked diligently to improve the copy, and sent it back out to another top-rated magazine.

The SASEs continued to find their way back to my mailbox. Most of the rejections were cold, impersonal form letters, without even a salutation. I was a no-name. Occasionally, a few editors would include a personal note with their rejections. And sometimes those notes included the suggestion that I must learn the difference between writing for a newspaper and a national magazine.

As you might imagine, with 94 submissions and 94 rejections, it's easy to have periods of self-doubt and depression. Mine became so bad at that stage that I went for many months without sending a single line of copy out into the world.

Then I began writing my autobiography. Perhaps that was my escape hatch, a way of continuing to write without having to face constant rejection. After completing the first 150 pages, I sat down to read what I had written. True to form, I came to the immodest conclusion that this was Pulitzer Prize stuff.

Then I had an inspiration. Putting my autobiography aside, I pulled out my old rejected articles to see if I could smooth out the rough edges. One of those, "Ida's Friend, God," was an inspirational piece about my late mother. It had already been turned down by at least a dozen of the finest magazines on the market. But that, I told myself, was when it had all those rough edges.

In my 60th year, I decided to give one of the country's leading women's magazines first crack at this resurrected piece. About a month later, I opened my mailbox, only to be greeted by the sight of that large, ugly manila envelope. This time, however, the rejection letter was a bit different. It was a far cry from a form letter.

"Dear Mr. Shein," it began.

Hey! It's got my name on it!

"Dear Mr. Shein: Thank you for sending us your very moving essay. Ida sounds like a truly unusual and terrific lady. That's why I'm especially sorry to have to say that we don't see a spot for the story in our magazine. Thanks, though, for giving me the chance to read and enjoy your piece."

Encouraged by those words, I smoothed out still another rough edge or two and shipped my article to *Reader's Digest*. It wasn't long before, on opening my mailbox, I was confronted by that big envelope—and a rejection letter.

Once again, however, the letter was different:

"Dear Arn:"

Dear Arn?

"Dear Arn: This won't quite work for *The Digest,* but it seems like a natural for *Guideposts*. I'd send it right off if I were you."

It was signed by a senior editor.

It was my 96th consecutive rejection letter. But there was something startlingly different about numbers 95 and 96. I raced out, made a copy of the *Reader's Digest* letter and sent if off to *Guideposts* with my own cover letter, the customary SASE, and my article, "Ida's Friend, God." On the 28th day after mailing the article, I opened my mailbox. There *was* a letter, a *thick* letter . . . from *Guideposts.* I pulled the contents out of the envelope and began reading the letter from the senior staff editor.

"Dear Mr. Shein: *The Digest* editor gave you good advice. Your story is beautiful, and we'd like to buy 'Ida's Friend, God.' Here's our offer in the usual legal language. *Guideposts* will pay you . . ."

But I kept looking at those first few incredible words: ". . . beautiful . . . we'd like to buy . . . will pay . . ."

I opened a file drawer, pulled out a copy of my article and stared at it. I didn't read it; I just stared at it. There was a long pause, a reflective look, a tilted head and a shy smile.

"Don't you know you're beautiful?"

Once in his life, every free-lance writer should have that said to him. I thank you, *Guideposts,* for being the one who said it to me.

§15

BEFORE YOU BEGIN TO WRITE

BY GINNY THOMPSON

THERE'S MUCH MORE TO LEARNING to write well than arranging words into sentences, and sentences into paragraphs, crafting your article or story into a fluid whole. In fact, learning to write well involves learning to do several other things well, which, in and of themselves, are not actually writing at all.

The basis of good writing is prewriting—everything you do before you start your first draft. During prewriting, you are observing, probing, and shaping raw writing material for content, for that needed angle or focus. Following this prewriting checklist will save you time and frustration.

Idea development

Provocative ideas and provocative writing come straight from the things people say. Train yourself really to listen to people's concerns and problems; that's where you will find excellent article material.

One afternoon, my neighbor talked to me about her friendship with a woman who was involved in a bad relationship with a man: "How do I tell Marcia what I really think of him and still keep our friendship intact?" she asked. Here was the *seed of an idea* that set my mind working.

Two days later, believing I was "onto" an article, I began developing the idea for an article that was to become, "When You Hate Your Best Friend's Man."* Generally, I'll start out with a What question. (Remember the 5Ws: *Who?, Where?, What?, When?* and *Why?*) *What* are the ways a man could drive a wedge between women friends?

Because a *what* question looks at the likely scenarios that fit the dilemma, it is a fine starting place for most types of writing, piquing

---

*Published as "When A Friend Falls for Mr. Wrong," in *Complete Woman,* with Kim Wiley as co-author.

your interest and curiosity, and prompting you to get your research off to a flying start. To find out what *actually* happens when you hate your best friend's man, I asked real people.

Here are some tips I've learned through trial and error, as I questioned people like you and me.

1) Imagine every outcome, motivation, or resolution to a problem or conflict. As I began to develop the idea, the thought of the friendship ending over a man seemed absurd. But I included that possibility on my question list and later learned it does happen.

2) Be flexible. Although you'll obviously know in advance the questions *you* want answered, it's best to allow the person you're interviewing to zero in on the questions that pertain most to her experience; you'll get deeper into what happens universally in the problem situation you're writing about and find a sharper focus.

3) Don't be afraid to eavesdrop or just talk: Everyday people will provide more clues that relate to your angle or theme.

After questioning "real people" for my article, I turned to some experts—psychologists and authors dealing with female/female friendships. What I learned from the discussions with "real people" gave me valid, not hypothetical cases for the experts to comment on.

A word on experts: Always start your interview with questions based on the article or story premise; for instance, ask the expert if she has observed the specific phenomenon you're researching. But be sure to bring in case histories; the responses you'll get will have even more authenticity when applied to real life.

A writer spends her lifetime observing. You're already curious. The ideas—if you're open to them—will come. And the questions that come tumbling forth will likely turn *your* observation into print. Simply continue listening and probing; if you pay attention, you'll get what you need for your article.

4) Reading. If you're writing nonfiction, you'll want to research what's been published on your subject to avoid duplication and to develop a different slant. As a general rule of thumb query magazines that haven't covered the topic in two years; but if your slant is unique, query on!

Make your public or college library your first stop. If your library subscribes to such magazine indexes as InfoTrac or Magazine Index, both of which cover hundreds of magazines, you'll be able to see quickly what's been written on your subject. To supplement your search, check out print sources such as *The Readers' Guide to Periodical Literature, Business Periodicals, Humanities Index,* and *Psychological Abstracts.* Buy on the newsstand sample copies of the magazines not covered by computer or print sources, or send for sample issues. (There is usually a modest charge.)

Once your preliminary research is complete, your mind will select what is relevant to your subject from everything you've read in the normal course of a day. As you relax, you may not realize it, but you're selectively scanning the pages of newspapers, magazines, and books for helpful hints for your current project—and inevitably you will come up with some gems: that missing link to your theme, just the right person to interview for your article, or the penetrating quote for your epigraph.

Trust your instincts when a bit of information makes you say, "Take this into consideration."

5) Notetaking. Of course, all along your prewriting journey you'll be taking notes. I constantly jot down sentences, paragraphs, and even possible titles and subtitles. The detailed notes you take of the source of a fact or a quote are essential later on for checking—an important factor in nonfiction writing.

I make a checklist of what I plan to have my current piece cover, a kind of informal outline. I keep a variety of spiral notebooks, scratch pads, legal pads, removable self-stick notes, and my favorite pens in my purse, in my car, and in every room in the house. If you've ever had a sudden inspiration for an article or story while driving and found yourself without so much as the back of a gas receipt to write on, you know the value of always having at hand these writer aids.

I put my notes in my first draft file, until I discover later what my article is *really* going to be about. I then mark the key quotes and anecdotes for articles, or dialogue and narrative for fiction.

Avid notetaking gives you confidence and prepares you for the next prewriting step: clarifying.

6) Clarifying. When you began to do research for a piece of writing, you could think about it in broad terms to determine what material

was available, but now, you have to sharpen your focus and tighten up. Of course, the angle you choose for your article or the conflict you select for your story may be the original one. But in the course of the prewriting process, you will be likely to discover a new, possibly narrower, focus. For example, you may decide that instead of writing about "Why Men Marry the Women They Do," you'll tackle, "Why Men Marry Up (or Down)." Whether you nailed down your point of view at the outset or have a new slant, you'll need to whittle away the tangential bits of information and detail—anything that won't drive your theme home for your reader.

7) Sleeping. Mulling over your basic material takes place while you're awake or asleep, in your conscious or unconscious mind. Some of your best insights may come to you when you aren't consciously thinking about the subject. So be sure to keep a pad and pencil on your night table, and when a compelling idea makes you sit up in bed, you can get it down on paper and not lose what may be your best approach or sentence or even word or title.

Prewriting your idea will give you more time to write, so don't feel guilty if you miss a day of actual writing: When you're listening, observing, talking, reading, taking notes, clarifying your initial ideas, you're still writing.

⚌ 16

FINDING THE EXACTLY RIGHT WORD

BY JOHN POWELL RILEY

HAVE YOU HEARD THIS MALICIOUS, libelous, and unfounded gossip? Noah Webster's wife, according to rumor, found him in bed with another woman and said, "Noah! I'm surprised."

The great lexicographer is said to have replied, with his characteristic precision in the choice of words: "No, dear. It is I who am *surprised.* You are *amazed.*"

Although one meaning of "surprised" is synonymous with "amazed," this illustrates an attempt to find the *"mot juste,"* and it strikes a responsive chord in me. My fascination with words began when I was four years old. I was riding with my father in his brand-new Model T Ford roadster on a bumpy dirt road. Dad smiled and said, "Johnny, this is an *abominable* road."

I picked up *abominable* right away. It delighted me. I kept repeating, "This is an abominable road." The meaning was clear from the context of the situation. It became my favorite word for everything unpleasant, and I still like it. Ever since that moment, words have done to me what colors do to a painter, and I'm convinced that vocabulary building can start at a very early age.

Recently, it occurred to me that it could be enlightening to read the dictionary from cover to cover as one reads a novel, so I did that, and was fascinated. I chose my old *Webster's Collegiate,* seventh edition. The last Z (zymurgy) falls on page 1041, and since I averaged ten pages a day (about 680 words), the 70,000-word project provided me with about fifteen weeks of pleasure. With a red ink pen I marked certain words with symbols that classified them in various ways useful to me.

I had often perused the dictionary for an hour or so at a time but never before thought of reading every definition systematically. Probably the seemingly endless task put me off, but doing it a bit each day was easy, exciting, and certainly more fun than work. I learned some things that might otherwise have forever escaped my attention. Do you know for example that *subtle* and *subtile* have different meanings?

There are words that are best suited to speech and others ideal for written expression. Some one would never use at all but should know because others may use them. One oddity I would never use is *pneumonoultramicroscopicsilicovolcanoconiosis,* unless unfortunate enough to catch the illness. It's the longest word in the English language. . . .

Other types of words are mainly useful as thinking tools. After all, most of us think in words, except for painters, musicians, sculptors, architects, mathematicians, and some politicians and bureaucrats, who don't think at all. I firmly believe that the more articulate one becomes, the more precise his thought processes will be. Why don't we make semantics a required subject in school at all levels, starting with kindergarten?

Would you believe that the dictionary is one of the most interesting books you could read? It's true, despite the lack of plot and many changes of subject.

I estimate that there are three to five thousand words from which to select when you want just the right one, the *mot juste,* to describe an individual. For example, careerist, careworn, carnal, case hardened, Cassandra, catty, caustic, cavalier, censorious, chameleon, changeable, charisma, charitable, charlatan, charm, chary, chaste, chatterbox.

English is the most expressive, most unambiguous, most concise, most beautiful language in the world. The French are vain and sensitive where their language is concerned, but English offers far more words than French. Quite a few words of French origin are the same in both languages but seem to have been poorly accepted by English-speaking people; for example, *camion, carrefour, ambiance, corniche,* and others. Not many of us use them. Then we have words like *dégagé, démodé,* and *déclassé* that we can pronounce but can't write properly on an American or English typewriter or some word processors, because the diacritical marks are not on the keyboard.

Among the remainder are words that sound pleasing to the ear. I have in mind the image makers like billow, enchanted, resonant, misty, phantom, or whispering.

Finally one finds in this treasure chest the sparkling gems and golden nuggets—words that have no synonyms. If you don't know the right word, you have to use a phrase or even a sentence to express the thought. It's so gratifying to know the exact word—words like ad hominem, aestivate, attrited, chirr, metonymy, comity, polysemous, deontology, doctrinaire, eclectic, elliptic. . . .

There's another category that delights the ear—the onomatopoeic words like boom, bang, clang, ding-dong, babble, zip, and burp.

Obviously the artful choice of words depends on your ability to gauge your listeners or readers and select words appropriate to their backgrounds. Certain words would sound pompous to some people but would be a good choice for others. Some words are more appropriate in conversation, keeping in mind the listener's age, sex, education, and social background. Other words are suitable for letters, dissertations, essays, or technical papers for special interest groups.

Some people resent unusual words and think you are being ostentatious if you use them—talking over their heads. These are the folks who never bother to look up words. They don't want to hear any that are not within the limiting confines of Basic English.

The English vocabulary has continued to grow, with over 460,000 entries now in *Webster's International Unabridged Dictionary*. Unfortunately, the average American knows only a little more than one per cent of these words. I understand that the average person uses only about 600 different words in a day. Shakespeare, by the way, used 34,000 words and that was before Samuel Johnson wrote the first comprehensive dictionary.

It should be the goal of everyone to increase his vocabulary by 5,000 words or more. To accomplish this, I suggest the following: 1) look up every word you don't understand, 2) read the dictionary cover to cover, 3) browse in the dictionary frequently, and 4) listen to tape-recorded word definitions in your car while you drive. The tape approach is particularly effective. By listening to the tapes repeatedly you will eventually absorb words by something akin to osmosis.

I read my dictionary, cover to cover, because I love words. I may seldom use most of them, except as thinking tools. One must use rare words and hot spices with some restraint. We must not err on the side of sesquipedalianism. Some writing doesn't depend on an extensive vocabulary. The King James version of the Bible is often cited for its simplicity, impressive dignity, and power, using fewer than 8,000 words.

Although that's small compared to Shakespeare's 34,000 words, it's still about 60 per cent greater than the average person's vocabulary.

I believe you can write good fiction of certain types with limited vocabulary. This style can have strong emotional impact that might be diminished by uncommon words, but there are other forms of writing, or styles, that are enhanced by them—characterization, erudite dialogue, scene setting, essays, any form that seeks to express subtle shades of meaning, thought-provoking logic, or new ways of thinking. A rich vocabulary stimulates and refines thought and is essential if you put those thoughts on paper.

Words are a writer's stock in trade. Use them or lose them. Why don't you start reading your dictionary today, cover to cover? It's a book that's hard to put down. Getting started is easier if you keep in mind that old Chinese proverb, "A journey of ten thousand miles starts with but a single step."

How To Write—Techniques
GENERAL FICTION

17

REMEMBRANCE OF
TENSE PAST

BY LYNNE SHARON SCHWARTZ

I BECAME AWARE, SOME YEARS AGO, of the spreading use of the present tense in fiction the way one becomes aware of an epidemic of flu. But while influenza does its worst to old people, the present tense for the most part strikes at young writers. Having grown up on fiction written mostly in the past tense, I at once felt the present tense as a deviation. I was aware of the writer's presence, not as narrative voice, which I would have applauded, few things being so appealing as the sound of a human voice, but as technician.

It was the jolt to the ear that bothered me, not the break with convention, good writing being by its nature a break with convention. But when breaking with convention, it's wise to know exactly why, and what you gain and lose, and whether you're simply substituting another convention with new and more disguised disadvantages.

I began asking my students why they wrote in the present tense. They chorused a short-answer reply: It gave a greater feeling of immediacy. When pressed to define what they meant by "immediacy," they said: that it's happening now, as you read.

What does that mean, that the action is happening as we read? John goes to the window, he parts the curtains and looks out; he sees a neighbor starting his car; his wife enters the room and says she is going to the store, and so on. Barely worth a yawn. However, it is happening as we read, or so we agree to believe. The tacit contract between reader and writer always asks for a considerable suspension of disbelief: To begin with, the reader agrees to assume that what appears on the page has objective truth and merits his time and attention. The present tense asks for even more. Besides everything else, readers are asked to believe the story is happening as they read.

And yet if a reader is presented with a series of incomplete actions, "happenings-as-he-reads," reflection and evaluation may be suspended as well, and indefinitely. In the guise of immediacy, the action is thrust so close that the reader is overwhelmed, or supposed to be over-whelmed, and must rely on the most superficial and quickest of re-sponses, which are not always the best and truest. His participation in the work becomes less an imaginative, reflective act than a passive, reflexive one, like a leg jerking when a doctor taps the knee.

"Immediate" means without mediation, without any barriers be-tween the action on the page and the reader. If the present tense pro-duces immediacy, then the past tense presumably acts as an intermediary. That is, no matter how intense an event or episode may have been, by virtue of being past, it is less crucial and cannot have as forceful an impact. This is a curious value judgment that raises questions of what fiction really is.

A belief in living in the moment is more salutary for real life than for fiction. Because life is chaotic, constantly recreating and rearrang-ing itself, we need to be unconstrained by the past, available and spon-taneous enough to seize what comes our way. Fiction, on the contrary, presents made-up people whose stories are told precisely because they have more than ephemeral import. Fiction is an artifice, giving coher-ence and boundaries to arbitrary swatches of life.

To understand a character, we need to see the trajectory of his or her experience, and we see it through the shape of the fiction. The present tense can be a way of evading scrutiny of that trajectory, evad-ing the obligation to apply sensibility and thought to one's material. After reading some present-tense fiction, we often have no more sense of what the characters' lives have been about, or mean, than we have of the lives of strangers glimpsed on the street. The implication is that all we can ever understand is what can be understood from a glimpse.

It has been noted before that today's preference for the present tense derives partly from television, with its reliance on immediacy, action, and visual impact. Fiction, though, is rooted not in visible action but in character and destiny. Its major events are often spiritual or emotional journeys impossible to illustrate by physical gestures, which is why many great books do not make great movies.

Television could not survive without action, but in fiction, the pres-ent tense has the dubious facility of suggesting action when nothing visibly significant is taking place, witness the example of John's looking out the window and seeing his neighbor's car, then hearing his wife say she's going to the store. While the action described has no interest, the real action may be taking place inside the character—if, for instance, John, a suspicious person, is shaken by the coincidence (?) of his wife and the neighbor going out at the same moment. The writer has offered the visible, however boring, and left us to infer the rest, like a host who serves his guests tunafish and lets them smell the hidden caviar.

The critical issue becomes, what exactly is being made immediate. One way of testing this is by transforming a present-tense passage into the past tense and seeing the results. The following (with the tense changed for illustration) is from "Three Thousand Dollars," by David Lipsky, in the November 11, 1985 issue of *The New Yorker*. The young man narrating is a college student:

I got a job working at a B. Dalton bookstore. The manager had to fill out some forms, and when he asked me how long I would be working—for the whole year or just for the summer—I said, "just for the summer," without thinking, and by the time I realized, he had already written it down and it didn't seem worth the trouble of making him go back and change it. Still, I went through the rest of the day with the feeling that I'd done something wrong. . . .

I was sent to the main floor, to the middle register, where old women came in pairs and shuffled through the Romance section. I ate lunch in a little park a block from the store, where a man-made waterfall kept tumbling down, and secretaries drank diet sodas. There was a cool breeze because of the water.

Admittedly, these sentences sounded more alive in the present tense. They sounded as though something, however amorphous, was being conveyed; in that sense, the writer made a wise choice of tense. Specifically, the novelty of "immediacy" of the present tense masked the poverty of diction and sensibility. Any emotion that might be generated by the passage is left for the reader to supply. With the tense changed, in this case one has to wonder what is left.

It seems to me that stories written in the present tense tend to sound more like each other, that is, to speak in the same voice, than stories in the past tense. I suspect this has to do with syntax and sentence structure. The present tense (with notable exceptions) has a colloquial tone and doesn't easily lend itself to complex structures, which can make it sound inflated and self-conscious.

An example of an exception might be the best proof: The following, from Russell Banks's story, "Firewood," in *Success Stories*, shows that the present tense need not always be used in the service of a reductive world-view. The character described, Nelson Painter, is an alcoholic who has spent the morning, as well as his whole life, becoming progressively more drunk:

It's [the snow's] deeper than he expected, eight or ten inches already, and drifting, a heavy, wet snow driven by a hard northeast wind and sticking to every surface that faces it, trees, houses, barns, chimneys, and now Nelson Painter, working his way down his driveway from the huge open door of the barn, a man turning quickly white, so that by the time he reaches the woodpile he's completely white, even his face, though he's pulled his head down into his coat as far as he can and can barely see through the waves of wind-driven snow before him.

And at the close, trying to return to the barn:

It seems so far away, that dark opening in the white world, miles and years away from him, that he wonders if he will even get there, if he will spend years, an entire lifetime, out here in the snow slogging his way toward the silent, dark, ice-cold barn where he can set his three pieces of firewood down, lay one piece of wood on the floor snugly against the other, the start of a new row.

How often do we find the present tense so well exploited to render, verbally and rhythmically, the feel of a character's being in the world? What Banks has done, and most present-tense writers are loath to do, is absorb his character's experience and let it permeate his own voice.

But when syntax and sentence structure are limited, the opportunities for diversity in voice are reduced, so that stories in the present tense will naturally resemble each other to some degree. And possibly that's what beginning writers want. Given the pressures of the marketplace and the difficulty of getting published, talented young people may feel they have a greater chance of success if they sound like their contemporaries who win acclaim at embryonic stages of their careers. Inevitably, their voices will tend to merge, the way voices on a telephone are less distinct and more alike than when they are heard in person. Reading fiction written in the present tense, one has the sense of hearing a telephone voice—in the worst of cases, a computer voice with all the hallmarks of a real voice except the breath and inflections of life.

76

This is a sharp contrast to the situation of say, fifty years ago, when writers prided themselves on distinctiveness of voice, not uniformity. For just as a speaker's voice shows her degree of attachment to the words, and a monotone empty of affect can deaden a listener, so the writer's voice shows whether her connection to the story is authentic and live, or dead and inconsequential.

The widespread use of the present tense suggests that, in addition to following trends, writers are resisting, perhaps are even afraid of, the sound of their own voices. They may feel comfortable being physically exposed, as the promotion of some recent books indicates, yet they seem bashful about their fantasies, the contents of their minds.

Rather than saying, the character I have invented did such and such, which means an accomplished act, a writer may say, my character does such and such, a tentative act always in the making, for which a writer does not need to take full responsibility. Can it be that the writers wish to separate themselves from what they're writing, mumble or murmur or mask their voices, as we do when we are uncomfortable about our words and prefer not to be held accountable? Very likely, since nothing is more revealing than the naked imagination and the naked sound of the intimate voice. And yet nothing can make fiction more authentic, more truly immediate.

There is also nothing that shows so thoroughly a writer's involvement in his work, and total comprehension of it. After all, if a writer does not appear to be fully invested in the fates of his characters, clearly no reader can be. Real immediacy, it would appear, has little to do with whether a story claims to be happening in the past or the present, and everything to do with the truthfulness of the emotion informing the work.

But how does a writer reach this truthfulness and comprehension? Joyce Carol Oates once said the prime trait a writer must possess is patience. Another well-known writer said perseverance. I would add nerve. Nerve is different from courage, which writers need simply in order to set pen to paper. There's a dashing, swift quality to nerve, to the word itself, a sense of peeking or lurching into something dangerous but thrilling, an almost cavalier quality. Nervy people are not so much brave as a little outrageous. A writer's nerve consists in serving as his or her own specimen and looking at the very aspects of human nature we all prefer to overlook. Looking in order to comprehend, and comprehending, to bring to light. The awareness of the range of human experience appropriate to each story must radiate from the words like an aura. It is this aura of knowledge and acceptance that gives great works their magic and lucidity. The integrity of the work comes to reflect the integrity of the writer.

Once this intimate comprehension of the work is gained, this close-to-the-bone feeling, the present tense might work as well as the past, or even in conjunction with it. A good example is Graham Swift's novel, *Waterland,* where present and past tenses beautifully interweave to display the simultaneity of past, present, and future in human destiny. The stories of Alice Munro, too, are firmly grounded in history; they move fluidly back and forth in time, and the tenses switch accordingly. J. M. Coetzee's superb novel, *Waiting for the Barbarians,* is written almost entirely in the present tense, and almost all of it takes place in the marrow of the spirit.

Finally, we can take heart from immortal writers like Dickens and George Eliot, among others, who used the present and past tenses in alternation to reaffirm the continuity of human experience, linking not only past and future, but action and effect, characters and readers, the world of the story and the world outside.

18

PLOTTING

BY ROBERT BARNARD

ONE THING THAT IS ALWAYS TRUE about my plots is that they come like Yeats' peace on the Lake Isle of Innisfree, "dropping slow." I have never been able to sit down and work a plot out in detail, have never begun a book knowing exactly what is going to happen. Agatha Christie, I believe, could do that, and it made the actual writing of her books a fast and comparatively straightforward process. My plots come to me, little by little, over a long period, and that period includes the time when I am writing the early chapters. This makes the plot-ideas notebook that I presume every writer has particularly important in my case.

It sits on the mantlepiece, and it mostly gets written in when I am listening to music in the evening. Many of the things that get noted down are simply phrases—funny twistings of clichés, for example, or odd things I have heard people say. But the first ideas for books will almost always be there, as well as subsequent changes, accretions, minor characters, twists that may mislead readers, and so on. Often I go back and read through the book, say if I am looking for an idea for a short story, and I don't remember the ideas that got there years ago, sometimes don't even understand what the scrawl was actually getting at, the idea that was behind my shorthand noting down of it.

I've gotten into a routine of writing a book between October and spring, with the interruption of Christmas to catch my breath in mid-book. This leaves late spring and summer for rewriting, revising, and writing the odd short story or magazine piece. At some stage during this "fallow" period, I will also decide which book for which I have some ideas will actually get written next. This doesn't always work out quite as I expected, and sometimes an idea will "take hold" of me and demand to be written *now,* as I remember my book called *The Skeleton in the Grass* did. I then take a new notebook and collect all the ideas I have had relevant to the new novel. That inevitably means that more ideas start coming, centering on the new project. All these I put at the beginning of the notebook.

Of course, the new ideas do not all concern the new plot: Some are, again, what we might call "little funnies," others are details of character, descriptions of houses, towns, and so on. But all have a tangential relationship to plot—plot is character in action; locales mirror the atmosphere that the plot needs, and sometimes prove an essential component in the actual murder (like the ruined castle on a steep declivity in my mystery novel, *Fête Fatale*). I am always very conscious that I have to write a book of two hundred pages or so, and have to have enough material, enough *story*, to fill those pages interestingly. My historical crime novel, *To Die Like a Gentleman*, written under the pseudonym Bernard Bastable, took me twelve years to write; it didn't take that long because it was long, but because it was short. The material didn't quite warrant two hundred pages, and, since I thought that what I had written was very good, I didn't want to spoil it with padding or by introducing subplots that detracted from the main interest. In the end, I had to take a deep breath and make a conscious decision to write a book rather shorter than usual.

I hope this suggests that to me, unlike E. M. Forster, the novel does and should tell a story, and I in no way regret this. How could I, whose main love is the Victorian novel, which so gloriously does tell a story? I laugh about a review that said that one of my books "has about as much tension as a wet noodle" (and, in passing, the convolutions of a wet noodle is not a bad image of a whodunit, which should be nicely tangled), but if I thought it was true, I would regard it as a serious charge: There must be tension, and there must be enough interest in what is happening to keep the reader reading. Otherwise, any piece of fiction that aspires to be popular literature has failed.

Often during the summer months I write the first chapter of what is to be the next book. First chapters to me are vital. If you don't believe me, read the first chapter of *Dombey and Son,* which simply compels one to read on, and compare it with the first chapter of *Martin Chuzzlewit,* which is a heavily laboured bore, and must have put countless people off a brilliant novel. The main thing is to seize the readers' interest, but also to give them the *feel* of the book, right from the start. One of the reasons I have mostly resisted having a series detective is that he dictates the feel, the tone, the atmosphere—call it what you will—of any book he or she is in. Agatha Christie regretted using Poirot in a book called *The Hollow,* and I think this was because it was a more serious book than usual, with greater depth of characterization, and Poirot simply did not fit in.

As well as setting the feel of the book, that first chapter in my case usually includes one or more of the central characters, and usually centers on the victim. I like to know the corpse before he becomes a corpse—having the character of the corpse gradually revealed after his death does not, for me, have the same immediacy. My bodies usually come around page sixty, or even later, and tend to be pretty unpleasant characters. This is for my own sake: When I have killed off characters I liked (as in *Fête Fatale,* and *A Corpse in A Gilded Cage*), it upsets me, and I feel rotten about it. And of course the nature of the victim's unpleasantness will be a major factor in setting the tone of the book: Is his or her unpleasantness dangerous, vicious, rather comic, or what?

Just before getting down to write, I start dividing the second half of the notebook into chapters and noting what each chapter will include. This I do about two or three chapters ahead: When I start the book I have, say, the first three chapters mapped out, and chapters get planned bit by bit as I write. All I've said has implied the cardinal element in my plotting: I get ideas as I write. Holding a pen is the most powerful stimulant to ideas (I'm sure tapping away at a word processor wouldn't have at all the same effect). So though I start the book with ideas, and have the main characters pretty firmly in mind—probably the victim, probably the murderer, too—I still have lots of room to maneuver, lots of minor characters to invent, lot of minor clues to think up. Charlotte Brontë started one of her juvenile pieces of fiction with the chilling words: "There is, reader, a sort of pleasure in sitting down to write, wholly unprovided with a subject." Oh no, there isn't, Charlotte, not for the reader, one is tempted to retort. On the other hand, a novel begun with a broad idea, a general notion of the most important characters, a sense of its tone, does have a sort of vitality and energy that a novel begun with everything already mentally in place will often lack.

Let me end by offering hostages to fortune in the shape of the two books I am planning. At this writing, I am not quite sure which of the two will be written first. One is a Robert Barnard novel called (very provisionally) *The Masters of the House.* The first chapter, already written, has a woman dying in childbirth and her husband going quietly mad with grief, or guilt, or something. The children of the house start a process of concealing their father's condition and taking over their own fates. I know who is going to get killed, I think I know who did it, and what is going to happen at the end of the book. More than that I don't know.

The other book is a Bernard Bastable called, definitely, *Dead, Mr. Mozart.* It is set, musicians may be puzzled to hear, in England in 1820. I have some main characters: Mozart, the manager of an opera company, a wealthy patron and his singer-mistress, King George IV, his mistress, and so on. I know roughly what is going to happen in the early chapters, but I am not at all sure who is going to get killed and know nothing about who killed him/her or why: This probably means this will not be the one that gets started first.

Let me say in conclusion that the above is not meant as any sort of prescription, merely as a description: This is what I do. I have no idea whether my practice sets a good example or a bad one for others. But I do in general believe that you have to allow yourself a bit of leeway, room to invent and expand while the book is being written. Whatever scheme for plotting a work of fiction is adopted, it has to be one that enables the work to stay fresh during the months or years that the actual writing takes. One must start a book with the ability to free-wheel, even though every chapter one writes necessarily limits that freedom.

19

THE FOUR DEADLY SINS
OF DESCRIPTION

BY BARNABY CONRAD

"WHY DON'T YOU JUST GET RID of 'em?" said the famous author to me. "Tear 'em up, get 'em out of there!"

He was talking about the first 72 pages of a novel I'd worked a whole year on, pages I'd written and rewritten lovingly. I was stunned. Where had I gone wrong?

I was twenty-four and visiting my parents in Santa Barbara, California, when I read in the newspaper that Sinclair Lewis was in the city. I'd always wanted to meet American's first Nobel prize winner, author of such works as *Babbitt, Main Street, Arrowsmith,* and *Elmer Gantry,* so I screwed up my courage and wrote him a note saying I was a would-be novelist and would like to say hello. To my surprise, he invited me to tea the following day.

Just seeing him was an event in itself. At the end of our visit, he asked to see some of my novel. I went home and brought back the first 75 pages of my hopes and dreams. I was quite proud of that beginning, lush descriptions of the Azores that my hero was visiting, so it was a terrible shock to me when, the next day, the Great Author told me to throw away the first 72 of those glorious pages.

"But—but," I protested, "I had to set the scene and mood, didn't I?"

"For 72 pages?" he retorted. "When I want to read about the Azores, I'll get *National Geographic,* not a novel."

And then he added this valuable advice for any writer: "People read fiction for emotion, not information. If they get some facts in with the emotions, that's O.K., but emotions come first. Pure description never made a novel great. Your narrative came to a dead stop when your ship stopped at those picturesque islands. But," he went on, "there was some fine stuff on those last three pages—conflict, emotion, characterization—let me see some more."

The upshot was that he liked the next pages and he hired me as his secretary-companion. I went off to Williamstown, Massachusetts, with him for six amazing and rewarding months.

There, I learned the first of The Four Deadly Sins of Description from a master of storytelling:

Don't let your description, no matter how beautifully written, bring your narrative to a halt.

This must always be kept in mind by the writer of fiction: Do not overdescribe anything, whether it be the Grand Tetons or the sunset or zebras on the beach at Waikiki; your narrative thrust will suffer for it, and you will put your reader's attention span in jeopardy.

Remember Elmore Leonard's golden rule: "I try to leave out the parts readers skip."

And readers tend to skip inert material.

What exactly is inert material?

A. B. Guthrie, that highly successful author of many books, including the classic *The Big Sky,* warned:

Anything off the story line constitutes what can be called inert material.

Exposition, explanation, description independent of your running narrative is inert. There it lies, an obstacle to the run of your story, a dam in the current.

And it is so easy to forget or ignore the simple fact that description of an object or process must be integrated with the story's movement.

This does not mean that if you are writing a story about a doctor, a lawyer, or a whaler, you cannot impart a lot of information about his profession. But you should do it subtly, weaving the information in and around the actions and conflicts of the protagonists and the thrust of the narrative. Painlessly, by osmosis, we learn about the law from Scott Turow, about submarines from Tom Clancy, and about Japan from Michael Crichton.

Keep your descriptions energetic but subservient to the central problem of the protagonists. Describe, if you must, the beautiful sunset behind the purple hills while the cows drink their reflections, but why not see it through the hero's or the heroine's eyes? He or she looks at the scene and compares its beauty to her present ugly predicament, or relates it to a more tranquil past, or whatever might give us an insight into her feelings or character, or whatever might give a push to the narrative.

Which brings us to our Second Deadly Sin:

Don't spend too much time describing non-essential surroundings.

I received a short story manuscript at a Santa Barbara Writer's Conference that contained a paragraph that illustrates this sin perfectly:

Connie looked out of the window of the train carrying her across the country to her marriage in San Francisco. The train stopped at the little town of Big River, Iowa (population 251, the sign said) and she saw the rows of drab houses, each unvarying in their sameness, almost all with a yellow dog sleeping on the porch. Originally, Big River had been a thriving mining town but now it was lifeless, finished. She saw a man on crutches selling newspapers on the station platform. The town had been founded in 1892 by Matthew Crump (1850–1899) and its greatest claim to fame had been that Teddy Roosevelt had visited it for a day in 1912. "Bully!" he had said about it. Now the train chuffed twice and Connie waved goodbye to the little town of Big River, never to see it again.

Z-z-z-z!

It would be a waste of space to include it in a long novel, much less a short story. The only reason for including this description of the town would be if Connie somehow related it to her past or her future, viz:

Though she'd never seen it before, Connie knew this little town well—it was all little towns and she hated them; she came from one exactly like Big River only it was called something else and it was in West Virginia. Now, thank God, she was going to a city, a big glamorous city where her beauty and singing talent could be appreciated. She could hardly wait until the train pulled out of this hideous town.

Or, the opposite reaction:

Connie immediately loved this little town, the tranquility promised by its tree-lined dirt streets, the little white church, the sleepy dogs. Maybe once they were married she could persuade Ed to leave crowded San Francisco and move to a little town exactly like Big River, a great place to raise the three children she planned to have.

In either of the above examples, there is a valid reason for the extended description of the town because we learn something about our protagonist, her hopes, her dreams, *her character.* Therefore we can

85

say that generally what validates and vindicates physical descriptions is our characters' reactions to their surroundings. And note the use of emotion to give emphasis to the description, *hate* in the first example, *love* in the second.

Novelist David Lodge has asserted:

> Description in a good novel is never just description. The danger of most set-piece descriptions is that a succession of well-formed declarative sentences, combined with the suspension of narrative, will send the reader to sleep.

Take Lodge's dictum to heart, type it on a strip of tape, and paste it on your computer or typewriter:

Description in a good novel is never just description.

Which brings us to our Third Deadly Sin:

Don't squander the reader's attention by focusing on an inconsequential action.

This is a more common fault among beginning writers than you might think. Here's a blatant example from a recent student manuscript:

> He got up slowly from the chair and went to the door. He hesitated. The metal handle felt cold to his freckled, moist, tan hand. He turned it slowly to the left and pushed the brown, panelled, oaken door which banged open. Then, one step at a time, his old shoes creaking, he walked out into the blazing noon day sun, and went down the stone steps. He started up his 1959 Ford pickup, drove to town, and shot his brother.

Obviously the focus here has been placed on the wrong actions!

One could enlarge this caveat by also warning writers not to focus unduly upon an inconsequential character whose presence is merely functional. Telling us, for example, that the "waiter had a rodential face and came from Yugoslavia with his widowed mother," or that "the waitress had hair the color of a saxophone, chewed gum, and was studying to be a court stenographer" might distract us from what was going on between lovers at the table, our protagonists.

Which brings us to the Fourth Deadly Sin of describing anything:

Don't generalize—Be specific.

> The sky was sort of bluish, the birds were flitting here and there, the mountains were hazy in the distance and the green fields smelled pretty good.

86

Z-z-z-z! We would know immediately that we were dealing with an amateur or, at best, a lazy writer. Why? Because this description is given in *generalities* that create a fuzzy, unfocused picture. We can improve things by taking a more specific look at the same landscape:

The sky was like the sky in a child's painting, the same deep blue from top to bottom. The jagged mountains in the distance looked like a dinosaur's back and a V of geese honked overhead. From the viridian fields came the scent of new-mown timothy grass.

If you feel you must write about static scenery or weather, try to do it with inventiveness and pizazz, like Virginia Woolf's description of heat in *The Waves,* which a lesser writer might have dismissed simply as being caused by "a blazing sun":

The sun beat on the crowded pinnacles of southern hills and glared into deep, stony river beds where the water was shrunk beneath the high slung bridge. . . . It beat on the orchard wall, and every pit and grain of the brick was silver pointed, purple, fiery as if soft to touch, as if touched it must melt into hot-baked grains of dust.

No one has summed up the deadly sin of generalization better than the great Russian writer Anton Chekhov. Here in a letter he urges a writer friend to avoid generalizations and the commonplace, especially when describing setting:

In my opinion a true description of Nature should be very brief and have the character of relevance. Commonplace description such as "the setting sun bathing in the waves of the darkening sea, poured its purple gold, etc." one ought to abandon. In descriptions of Nature, one ought to seize upon the little particulars, grouping them in such a way that, in reading when you shut your eyes, you get the picture. You will get the full effect of a moonlit night if you write that on the milldam, a little glowing star point flashed from the neck of a broken bottle, and the round black shadow of a god or a wolf emerged and ran, etc."

Obviously, the message is: *Be specific in your detail.*

Recently, I read a story in which the author opened with his heroine on a bus "reading intently." That's all.

Reading *what* intently? The author didn't say.

What an opportunity missed! Think of how much more about the heroine's character we would have known instantly had her reading matter been identified as *Anna Karenina* or *Playboy* or *Living with Cancer* or *Learning Law at Home* or *Field & Stream* or *How to Write Romance Novels* or *Gray's Anatomy* or—well you can see that each one of these choices reflects a very different person.

If it's a pretty young woman reading about cancer, we are interested. If it's a little girl reading *Field & Stream,* we are interested. If it's an old woman reading *Playboy,* we are interested. And certainly we know more about our protagonist than if we are told only that she is "reading intently."

So, then, remember when you sit down to write it is:

Not a *drink* but a *martini*; not a *dog* but a *poodle;* not a *flower* but a *rose;* not a *sleigh* but a *Rosebud;* not a *hat* but a *borsolino;* not a *cat* but an *Abyssinian;* not a *gun* but a *.44 Colt on a frontier frame;* not a *painting* but Manet's "*Olympia.*"

Let's counteract the Deadly Sins with the Golden Rule, Chekhov's Golden Rule, which all good writers follow in their descriptions:

Be specific!

§ 20

WHERE DOES YOUR FICTION "LIVE"?

BY SHELBY HEARON

ON MY EARLY MORNING WALKS, I pass a rural cemetery with a sign offering: PLOTS FOR SALE. My Oxford dictionary defines *plot* as "a small portion of any surface differing in character and aspect from the rest." And this seems to me to be a fine way to think about where fiction begins: with that plot, that parcel of ground, that place that you make yours and no one else's.

I always begin a novel with place. I might choose somewhere I have lingered or left, somewhere I took a fresh turn or turned my back, but when I step on the actual streets of my past, it is as if my story comes unbidden through the soles of my feet.

Sometimes you cannot go back to an actual place you have lived. Times change; houses and neighborhoods are not what they were. In these cases, I find a stand-in locale that has the deep emotional tug that the original had for me. For instance, in a novel called *A Small Town,* I moved a number of scenes from my childhood in Kentucky across the Mississippi River to Missouri, to a tiny town that once had coal-burning furnaces and felt then as my now-prosperous, bustling hometown had felt so many years before. Similarly, in a novel I'm researching now, I've picked a small town in the Blue Ridge Mountains of western South Carolina in which to set an important year when I was five and my daddy was mapping gold mines in north Georgia. I switched location because where we once lived in a rustic cabin has become a busy artists' colony and is no longer the site of my pine-scented memories. (I'm using small towns as examples, because so many of my novels are set there, but the same techniques would apply in choosing one neighborhood over another in any large city.)

Once I've selected my retrospective spot, I'm ready to get to know it from the ground up as it is today. I like to think of a place as having three faces: its history, its view of itself, and its significance to the people who live there. For the first, how it sees its past, I go to the local library's historical archives for clippings, photos, letters, first-hand accounts of earlier times; I investigate the geology and geography. Then, to get a picture of how the community sees itself now, I subscribe to the local newspaper, so I can follow the town through its civic seasons, learn its concerns, hear how it speaks of itself.

When I was working on my novel, *Hug Dancing,* which is set in Waco, Texas (a town that reminds me sharply of the smaller, more insular Austin of my child-rearing years), a lot of my plot grew out of a close reading of the paper. For example, when I saw that the front page of the sports section had a daily fishing column, giving the latest on lures and bait, river and lake conditions, I knew I must have a fisherman as a character. And when I read that the high schools were offering Japanese as a second language, I got a glimpse of what it meant for a little conservative city that had once supplied the whole confederacy with cotton to find itself on the burgeoning science corridor between Austin and Dallas.

But helpful though libraries and newspapers are, the only way you really get what a community is for its people, its voice, habits, ways of giving approval and disapproval, sanctions and prohibitions, is to walk the ground of the town yourself. I like to start my present-day acquaintance with a place by eating and eavesdropping. Meals tell a lot. For instance, in South Carolina on my last trip I had pork chops for breakfast, lunch, and dinner. Then, later that month, checking out the east Texas location where the other part of my fictional family lives, I was served a luscious morning meal of wild Russian hog sausage and batter-fried bacon. Knowing that hickory, pecan, and walnut trees go with such pork economies, I hunted out the rich aromas of green nut husks that will serve to tie my two locations together.

Eating leads to overhearing, of course; food and conversation go together. I always write down every interchange I hear, wanting to get the exact language of how, in this place, women and men talk together, parents and children, old-timers and outsiders. When I was working in Missouri on *A Small Town,* in my back booth at a Mom and Pop cafe, I kept hearing about "when we got the b'ar pit," and the "level of water in the b'ar pit." After a bit, curious, since the bare marshy river bottoms did not seem to me to be bear country. I asked the owner to explain. It seems the word was *borrow.* A borrow pit was a depression, filled up after the topsoil had been sold (borrowed), just as, years before, lumber companies had "borrowed" the region's stand of trees. From these conversations I gained a sense both of the area's language and of its way of dealing with loss.

Being on location in the place you have chosen, you can also see, with your own special vision, the sudden object or juxtaposition or absence you did not expect or did not recall. For example, in setting a novel called *Five Hundred Scorpions* in the small Mexican village of Tepoztlán, I was choosing a place that reminded me of how I'd felt the first time I went into a foreign-speaking country: a stranger in a strange land. I'd read seven books on the much-studied mountain village, and even had a map of the town when I arrived. But when I actually found myself on its steep tropical streets, I was struck at once by the fact that there was *no wood* anywhere. The rich homes had tile floors and metal doors and chrome chairs; the poor homes had dirt floors and hide chairs and rush doors. The local industry was charcoal—all the trees were burned before they reached lumber potential. At once I knew that my main character, who had left his wife and law practice behind in Virginia to come to Mexico, had left behind more than he counted on: handcrafted furniture, old oak doors, burnished hardwood floors. And this became a symbol of all that he missed that he had not expected to. Again—as happens every time I arrive on the streets of a chosen place—my story changed in response to what I saw.

Once you've picked a real place from your past or a stand-in place that conjures up the sounds, smells, and sights that remind you of old times and fuel your story, once you have been there and seen and heard what's there today, the final step is to make sure your setting is singular and significant for the reader. For you, it is special because you were there; for the reader, meeting it for the first time, it must be made memorable. In choosing Missouri for the setting of my childhood scenes, I selected a town that had fallen into the Mississippi River in 1811 in the worst earthquake of the western hemisphere—so that the reader would have a sense of shaky ground, of being in a spot that might at any moment disappear. Again, for my Carolina town, I have picked a community that before the Civil War was the site of the grandest artesian spa in the country, so that the reader will enter an area that feels itself to have been wiped out by history, will get to know people who feel their past has been taken away. And, in my Mexican village, I didn't select the locale I had actually visited before, but instead chose a place that had been studied by male social scientists from the Twenties through the Sixties, and I thought readers would enjoy the idea of two female social scientists studying the place in the present.

Having made your place particular for the reader, you are ready, by repetition, accrual, exaggeration, to do what I call "turn up the volume," so that the reader can hear what you have to say. Working on *Hug Dancing,* for example, I noticed that every day the newspaper had some big item about the weather. Reading up on record highs and lows, heaviest ice storms, floods, tornadoes, all the major acts of nature in Texas, I found that Waco was always right in the middle, getting hit with the worst of whatever was blowing in, most notably the tornado of '53, which leveled the entire downtown. So, after experiencing the gusty winds and sudden storms myself, I made sure that some of the most important parts of my plot hinged on the weather: a mother's drowning in a flash flood, a father's crash in an ice storm, lovers taking cover from hail, my fisherman stuck at home in a heavy duster. And also, weather became a central metaphor for the book: my characters' feelings reflecting those of the child-raising time in my life when everything seemed out of control.

Texas naturalist Roy Bedichek once said of the cabin where he worked: "The sights, sounds, odors and especially the feel of this place stimulate in me memories so warm and intimate that taking up residency here seems a homecoming." That is the feeling I set out to recapture when I select a location for a story: that feeling about place which is where fiction begins.

21

DIALOGUE THAT SPEAKS TO YOUR READER

BY JAMES MCKINLEY

IN WRITING DIALOGUE, THE EARS HAVE IT. Or, more properly, the ears you've been lent have it, those writerly ears that eavesdrop at every opportunity, that pick up the imaginary conversations of your fevered brain, those ears that you put on your characters so that *they* can hear one another and respond. Well, that's how I write dialogue anyway, with the critically important addition that what the ears have and hear needs hard editing, forceful shaping, to create one of fiction's miracles: artificial speech that seems as real as tapes from an anthropologist's field trip. To read the dialogue of Anne Tyler or John Updike, of Flannery O'Connor or Ernest Hemingway, to mention but four great writers of dialogue of the past sixty years, is to listen with your internal ears to hewn, forceful utterance that seems real but isn't. Take this brief passage from Updike's *Rabbit At Rest,* in which our worn protagonist, Harry Angstrom, talks about their son with his wife, Janice, who speaks first:

"Because he's grown up in the shadow of a dominating father."
"I'm *not* dominating. I'm a pushover, if you ask me."
"You are to him. Psychologically dominating. You're certainly a lot taller. And were a wonderful athlete."
"Were is right. A wonderful athlete whose doctors say he has to ride a golf cart and not do anything more violent than brisk walking."

And so they go on, as Updike practices exposition and foreshadowing of coming action in a passage that has little to do with how real parents would discuss a father-son conflict but everything with how to manipulate dialogue so it sounds real and furthers the story's action. How would it really have been to the tape recorder? Probably something like this:

"You scare him, that's all, he's just scared of you, who wouldn't be the way you bull around all the time, just scared, is all."

"Bull _____! *He's* a wimp, I got me a wimp for a son, why, when I was playing ball we wouldna let him. . . ."

"Like to see you play now with that gut you lug around. . ."

See? This, too, may sound real, but it's not going anywhere except a short way in the direction of characterization. It's just talk, not artful dialogue.

So, then, how do you get the feeling of reality and this artful shaping? I can only tell you some of what I've learned in years of putting words in characters' mouths and readers' ears.

Foremost, remember that dialogue is a main means by which your characters feel and behave, the way they express the node or action center of their scene. Playwrights live and die on dialogue, and the good ones today like David Mamet and Terrence McNally and Wendy Wasserstein know what all good dialogists know, that language is thought and feeling in action. So, the dialogue must be centered on an *action,* a thought or feeling or deed, that drives the scene forward. To write that dialogue well, you must first know what the scene's about, both in itself and as part of the work's whole scheme, so that you can think and feel for and through the characters. Then you're ready to write the words.

But—and this is second—you can't very well write these words, these emotions framed in language, unless you've had the feelings, either directly or through an imaginative projection. Want to write a jealous character speaking? Call on your jealousy, and if you don't have any, read *Othello.* Want to write catty, spiteful talk? Call on your envious self, or eavesdrop at an office party, in the faculty lunchroom, or any bar on a weekend night. And so on.

Naturally, once you've discovered the center of your scene—what the characters need to say in their situation, in that situation designed to carry the story's action forward—then you can apply the technical tricks of dialogue. Most writers know or discover them, but here are a few that I remind myself of every time I begin to construct the artifice that is fictional talk:

• Whenever possible, create distinctive speech patterns for each character, what I call "verbal gestures." This is especially true when the characters are about the same age, race, education, income level, and sensibility. F. Scott Fitzgerald made Jay Gatsby say "old sport" to Nick Carraway, both to distinguish Gatsby's doomed social-climbing temperament and to make sure the reader knew who was talking. In one gesture, Fitzgerald revealed character and solved a technical problem, which is never a bad idea.

• Following this, avoid speech tags whenever possible. They clutter the dialogue passage so much that the writer doesn't have space to concentrate on the motivation for the speech and its effect. Lazy writers often use tags instead of creating tense motivation for their characters. Parodying this tendency, Damon Runyon wrote his classic, "'Shut up,' he explained." The hoary "show me, don't tell me" rule applies forcefully here.

• Alter, at appropriate times, the usual pattern of dialogue passages, which is speech/surface reaction/speech to speech/deep reaction/speech. Here's an example of the first, more common pattern:

"Darling, I don't care less for you, just less *about* you."
Jane felt her eyes sting, but instantly steeled herself.
"Are you at sea about prepositions?" she asked in her nastiest schoolmarm's voice.

Here's the same passage in a different pattern:

"Darling, I don't care less for you, just less *about* you."
Jane's eyes stung suddenly, and an absurd question about prepositions came to her. But that wouldn't do, wasn't nearly hurtful enough. Besides, he looked paler now, as if the effort to be nasty and cute at the same time had exhausted his slender emotional resources.
"I see, oh, indeed I do."

The second, I think, moves the scene, and hence the story, faster. But suppose you don't care to use some kind of speech/deep reaction model (by "deep reaction" I mean a reaction by a character that goes deeper than the physical—stinging eyes—to an emotional or psychological level that enriches the gestural or spoken reaction). So, if you don't want that model, perhaps you're better off, if you can handle it, with the staccato stichomythia of writers like Hemingway and Joan Didion. Keeping the above example, this method yields something like:

"I don't care less for you, just *about* you."
"Cute. Been practicing prepositions?"

"Please, I'm trying to say something. Don't you understand?"

"Don't you understand grammar isn't feelings? You can't diagram our situation, you don't have enough verbs."

Here, clearly, we again try for the emotional center of the exchange, making words the servants of feelings, making the scene move the characters and their situations toward the plotted end.

• Give your characters speeches that include references establishing time, place, prejudices, past or future exposition. I don't mean lard the dialogue with extraneous talk, but do feel free to let readers know where, when, why, how things are. Here's a section from my story "Ozark Episode," that sets the action in our time of paramilitary paranoia mixed with confused Christian fundamentalism. A black youngster named Simon encounters an armed white man from a religious cult in the backwoods of the Ozark Mountains. The man demands to know if the boy's a Christian.

"You sure? Praise God?"

"Yessir I'm a Christian. No sinner." Simon took another small step toward his shoes. His daddy'd skin him if he lost them shoes.

"Praise God, then. Praise God. Boy?"

"Yessir. Praise God! Praise God!"

"You hate Sin, boy?"

Simon moved another foot backwards.

"Yessir. My daddy, he say hate the sin, love the sinner."

The man seemed not to hear. He was looking downstream, past where the dog was muzzling, near where the bullets hit.

"Boy, I don't believe you're a saved Christian," he said, still looking away. "Not saved. You're tribe of Ham, ain't you. Curse of Canaan and Cush. Slave folk. The Book says you ain't saved. Not black ones. Black is the Devil's color, you know that?" The man unslung his rifle. . . .

Well, here I hope is dialogue that captures part of our fractious times, identifies them, says something about prejudice and madness, *and* propels the tale.

In summary, your dialogue must be crisp, edited, artificial speech that seems real and whose only purpose is to move your characters and their story. To do this successfully, you must understand the emotional centers of your scenes, and then you must call upon your eavesdropping talents, your reading, your imagination, your journals to create characters that speak for themselves through you. Fortunately, all writers know that their characters will speak for themselves eventually. But it's the preparation and skill of the author that make the fictional people come alive and speak in distinctive, vivid, directed ways that carry readers to a story's intended and affecting end.

§ 22

TEASE TO PLEASE

BY J. MADISON DAVIS

FIRST-TIME NOVELISTS NATURALLY make a number of mistakes, but one that I've noticed also cropping up in many published novels by authors who should know better is giving up too much information too soon. In our age of switch-it-on entertainment and instant gratification, almost everyone with a desire to write knows that a novel must blast out of the gate and start racing down the track. A body drops out of a closet, a wife discovers the "other woman's" phone number in her husband's pocket, or the vampire emerges from his lair: Openings like these are bound to engage readers' interest, at least momentarily.

Yet, having aroused the readers' curiosity, many aspiring writers almost immediately slow down the forward motion by saying too much, too soon. Instead of letting details of character, personal history, and situation reveal themselves through the evolution of the action, all is plopped down with the same relentless summarizing of a *Masterplot*. Where can a novel go after its secrets are revealed? It drags on, reiterating what has already been said, giving no surprises and few pleasures.

Let's look at an example. I was once asked to read a manuscript about a naval pilot named Bob. It began marvelously. Bob is circling his aircraft carrier in a rough sea. He is low on fuel from his many attempts to land and the crew is about to raise a steel net that is used in desperate situations to snag the jets. This is dangerous, usually causes some damage to the expensive jet, and much paperwork for the pilot, if he manages to avoid injury. All the ingredients for a crackerjack opening are present: a man in danger, a situation that's intriguing because it's unusual, and the clock ticking to possible doom. From a purely mechanical point of view, most readers would learn about things they haven't known before, such as the steel net and the fact that many attempts are commonly necessary to land on a carrier. What's more, it was obvious the writer knew what it felt like to set an F-15 down on what from the air looks like a postage stamp. The cool fear was coming through loud and clear.

Sadly, however, the writer utterly dissipated the energy of his compelling opening by having Bob's entire life flash before his eyes as he made his last attempt to land without the net. Not just fragments of his life, but his entire life. Bob is a military brat. His father was a medal-winner. Bob wants to be in Vietnam but has been assigned to the Mediterranean. His girl friend has left him. His best friend is up on misconduct charges. He once had a dog named Rickenbacker, a mutt that was run over by a truck. Details like these poured out for half a dozen pages. When the pilot finally trimmed his air speed, the reader's excitement had already parachuted into the ocean.

So? What's wrong? Aren't you supposed to know your character well? Don't you want to give your reader a sense of a fully rounded character? First of all, most of this biographical material violated the old rule of "show, don't tell," but the problem arose less from that than from a well-intentioned misjudgment. The writer worried that if we did not know Bob well, we would be indifferent to Bob's problem. What he failed to understand was that the situation was sufficiently compelling that readers would sympathize with anyone caught in such a place. The details might make it more poignant—Bob speaks to his dead father or looks at a picture of his children—but we don't need at that moment to know how the father died or what the children's names are. When Bob lands safely, the reader still has things to learn. Who is this daring pilot? Why does he speak to his dad? Who are the children in the photo? Delicately dropped, these hints of more to learn tease the reader. Made too plain, they kill the promise of future rewards and decrease the urge to read on.

In another example, a student of mine began her novel with a nightmarish and very well-written scene in which a young girl shoots her father as he batters her mother. In chapter two, we leap ahead a decade or more, and Alice is a young woman who has suffered under the shadow of her act for all those years. So what's the problem? The novel begins fast. It piques our interest. It doesn't bog down with the background of the mother and father's relationship. There is little telling and much showing. The problem arises only when the second and third chapters flash forward. Once again, the teasing that pleases has been taken away. The possibility of discovery, which is so much of the pleasure of reading, has been denied.

When Alice is reintroduced, she has psychological problems. She behaves somewhat irrationally and Mike, the man who comes into her life, is going to have to cure her of the trauma. So far, so good. However, what is left for the reader to discover? Mike must ferret out the secret of her emotional scars, but the reader knows all about it. Every time Mike mistakes one reaction for another, he seems stupid. Why doesn't he know what we already know? Didn't he read the first chapter? Such a reaction might seem irrational—the novel doesn't exist in Mike's world—but we are likely to want to strangle him for not seeing the obvious. In movies, Roger Ebert calls this kind of situation an "idiot plot." There is much ado about nothing other than a lack of knowledge, as when one character is mistaken for another simply because everyone assumed the man in the Cadillac was the bank president and not his tailor. The frustration is a major turn-off.

Consider, on the other hand, if the writer teases a bit. Alice is afraid of going outdoors. Why? Someone lets slip that she killed her father. What happened? We discover bits and pieces along with Mike. We suspect this and that, and, most importantly, we keep turning pages to confirm our suspicions or to be surprised. Now we're hooked. Think how much energy would be lost from *Jane Eyre* if readers knew from the beginning that Rochester has a mad wife in the attic. How interesting would most mysteries be if we knew from the first chapter how and why the murder was committed?

Revealing too much at the outset derives from a number of causes. Novelist Philip Rosenberg once said that writing a novel is like walking to California from New York. You start out full of enthusiasm, the whole journey clear in your mind and all day you tramp, tramp, tramp until you are nearly exhausted, only to discover that you've barely entered New Jersey. As you begin writing a novel, it is all in your head from the Appalachians to the Plains to the Rockies, and quite naturally, you want to capture it all before it flutters away like money in a comic strip. Lacking confidence that you will get to all of these places you've mapped out, you lay it all out in the first twenty pages. It is hard to keep all the details of a three-hundred-page manuscript in your head, and you are nervous that you'll either forget some of it or leave something important out. Once you've worked your way through a few novels, you will have the self-confidence that you can handle it, but in your first attempts, you may be in a mad hurry to get it all down. Unfortunately, then, there is no discovery left to be made by the reader, no realization, and no illumination. The fun is gone. The walk becomes a packaged tour. If this is Wednesday, we must be in Cleveland.

Certainly good writers know their characters backwards and forwards, up and down. They know that Lord Dumont has an appendix scar and that his father was a cold-hearted antiquarian. They know that he has a weakness for older women and they know why. They must know the things he would do and the things he would not. The place, however, to get all these disparate aspects of character and history together is in the notes and outline of your novel, not in the first twenty-five pages. Let many of these aspects be implied, rather than explicit. Employ the power of suggestion. Remember Hemingway's dictum about a good story: like an iceberg, most of it is hidden. We can feel its great size and power when we see the part above the water. Somehow, the invisible part is even more impressive *because* we feel it instead of see it.

"Hold on!" you say. "Isn't it important to be clear?" Absolutely. It is more than important. It is essential. If you are not clear, your reader will put your book down faster than he would a tarantula. Teasing is not about being deliberately unclear. It is not about being clever by withholding information that would make the events understandable. If a passage is written to withhold that a character is angry when he says, "I love you," then you will be deliberately misleading and confusing your reader. Bad! If you explain every detail of the character's history and reasons for this combination, you will leave no chance for the reader to discover it. Also bad! If you create curiosity about this strange combination of anger and endearment, you will make your reader curious to know the reason. Now that's writing!

As in all writing, the choices are difficult and subtle, but their effects are profound. Every successful writer is aware of the pitfalls of revealing either too much or too little, mostly because every successful writer has made these mistakes. Are they fatal mistakes? Not if you edit them out. A mistake in a manuscript is a mistake that can be corrected. A mistake that's mailed to an editor, on the other hand, can lead to rejection. The largest difference between published novelists and unpublished novelists is that the former are fearless about rooting out their own miscalculations. Both of the aspiring novelists I mentioned earlier were able to put their egos aside and revise their openings. The chapter in which the child Alice killed her father has been tossed out of the book. This is one crucial reason this student author is soon to be published.

It is important to remind yourself that as a writer you are in the entertainment business. There are many different forms that the entertainment takes, from a deep intellectual to a blatantly commercial form, from deconstructive literary texts to "who-shot-Johns," but they are all intended for entertainment. Considered in this way, perhaps writing is little different from stripping. Both rely upon basic human compulsions and emotions, and both must be carefully composed so as to sustain the interest. And both rely upon teasing. In an age in which anyone can see anything he likes at any time, why is the hokey "art" of stripping—in both its male and female varieties—still economically viable? Like a good novel, the process of the strip is more interesting than the result.

The fan dancer reveals a wicked smile, an ankle, then a shoulder. Each revelation promises more, as the viewer assumes that each exposed part is attached to other more interesting parts, soon to be revealed. Each time an item of clothing is stripped away, another smaller one is beneath it. The relentless process of teasing moves on, gaining in intensity as the dance moves through time. Finally, when the tension has become unbearable, just before the teasing becomes tiresome, the unabridged truth is revealed. Only in this way is there any show at all. Otherwise, a striptease is just somebody getting naked. As in a novel, timing is everything, and too many aspiring novelists simply undress.

§ 23

POINT OF VIEW IN THE SHORT-SHORT STORY

BY MARIAN BATES

FOR BOTH CREATIVE AND COMMERCIAL REASONS, my favorite fiction form is the short-short, a preference that resulted from a process of trial and error. Some years ago, in less complicated times, I wrote a short story about the problems of a young girl emerging from childhood. Her shyness and resulting inability to make friends easily is compounded by an over-protective mother as well as by the unattractive braces on her teeth. (I used the braces as a symbol of childhood as well as the device by which the story is resolved.) When the braces are removed, the girl sees a new image of herself in the mirror and acquires self-confidence and a sense of self-esteem for the first time. This makes it possible for her to convince her mother that her childhood is over, and the time has come to let go.

When I finished the story and read it through, I was unhappy with it. While the beginning and end worked well, the middle seemed over-long and dragged out. There was a solution, I thought: I had never tried the short-short form before, but how hard could it be to pick up a pencil and cut my story to size, from 3,500 words to a thousand? Impossible, was the answer. That was how I discovered how unique the short-short story form is.

First and foremost, every word must count. In structure, a short-short must have a beginning, middle, and end, as in other fiction, but there the similarity stops. There is no room for intricate plot complications, lengthy descriptions, or numerous scene changes. For the same reason, it is crucial that the short-short author select the right viewpoint character—the one through whom the story can be told with the greatest economy. In my original story, I had chosen the girl as the pivotal character, but in rethinking it as a short-short, I decided that the mother should play that role, and provide the most significant emotional turning point in the story: the mother's bittersweet acceptance of the fact that her only daughter's childhood is over.

I was still not ready to begin writing. Now that I had my viewpoint character, I had to decide on the point of view, that is, the method of narration I would use. Most fiction writers prefer to write in the third person, which allows the most flexibility. With third person you can (if you wish) know everything about everybody, because you have personally created all the characters. That makes it easy—sometimes fatally, flatfootedly so—to lay out the lines of the plot and reveal each character's innermost thoughts and emotions. Using this omniscient point of view, it is even possible to switch viewpoint to a second character—or a third, a fourth—bearing in mind that you must do it deftly to avoid reader confusion. Or you can settle for less than omniscience, but still use the third-person point of view within whatever limits, wide or narrow, you want to set for yourself.

Writing in the first person (my preference) allows no such leeway. You must stay within the persona of the "I" of the story, which can be limiting. It can also be hard, because in using all those "I said"s and "I thought"s, you can be seduced into substituting your own persona for the character's, jarring to readers—unless the character really *is* you in disguise.

However, there is one outstanding advantage in the first-person approach: There is no faster, surer way to draw the reader directly into the heart and mind of the pivotal character. And in the case of my mother/daughter story, first person was a perfect fit, since I identified with the mother, being one myself (no daughters, though!).

I began the story in its new short-short form this way:

When Jennifer came beaming out of the orthodontist's office into the waiting room, I looked up from the magazine I was reading.

"Well, Mother, what do you think? Don't I look fabulous?"

It was Jennifer, and it wasn't Jennifer at all. The braces were gone. She was smiling, lips wide apart framing straight, perfect teeth. That much was brand-new, heart-stopping, beautiful. What I couldn't comprehend was the familiar, unfamiliar rest of her. Her shoulders, normally hunched forward so that the long butterscotch hair fell across her face, were flung back assuredly, accentuating small, lovely breasts, a slim waist, and narrow but discernible hips.

I knew I should have been as ecstatic as my daughter obviously was, sharing this longed-for moment with her, but all I felt was dismay. More than her braces had been left behind in the examining room, I thought, with a physical stab. It was as though her childhood had been left in the dentist's office too.

In the body of the story, the daughter is asked out on her first date. The boy's car develops clutch trouble; he calls from a gas station to say the car is being fixed and that he and the daughter will be late getting back. The mother's first impulse (which she struggles to resist) is to jump into her car and bring her daughter home.

At this point in the story, the problem was to show the mother working her way through the painful process of "letting go," taking care to make her change of heart believable to the reader. What I needed was additional insight into her character, insight she herself, as the viewpoint character, has to achieve. The question was how to accomplish it in very little space. After several false starts, I decided to use a memory from her childhood to confirm and strengthen the story's resolution:

> . . . but my own mother had managed what I was struggling to achieve. . . .
> The years rolled back. I had been younger than Jennifer was now—a new town, a new school, and on the day I had to report for the first time, I begged my mother to come with me.
> She had looked at me thoughtfully. "I will, Laura, if you insist, but I don't really want to. I think you can do this by yourself. Will you please try?"
> Years later I had asked my mother about that day. She had smiled.
> "The minute the door closed behind you, I wanted to run after you, take your hand, walk with you. . . . It seems now I held my breath for the entire day until I looked out and saw you skipping home, a new friend on either side. I was so proud—of you, of course—but more of myself."

From this point on, the story wrote itself. When the daughter returns at last, "glowing like a roomful of Christmas trees," she tells the mother that there has never been a day as special as this in anybody's life anywhere in the entire world, and that the mother, by not interfering, is the one who made it perfect.

I used the braces again as a metaphor to bring the story full circle. When the mother is in bed at last, after what has seemed the longest evening of her life, it ends this way:

> Drifting into sleep, I said a final, wistful good-bye to Jennifer's beautiful braces.

In another short-short story of mine, "Where Tomorrow Waits," the "I" of the story is Susan, a young woman too proud to admit she misses her small-town boyfriend when he, in a similarly mulish mood, visits her in the big city. Again, a symbolic object—Susan's grand-mother's candy dish and the associations it brings with it—provides a compressed but effective way of breaking the emotional logjam needed for the story's resolution.

A few words about another technique—writing from the male character's point of view, if you're a woman. (Male writers don't seem to need any encouragement to do the reverse; from the beginnings of the English novel—witness Samuel Richardson's *Pamela* and *Clarissa*—men have used a female persona whenever it seemed right to do so.) Indeed, there is no reason not to adopt whatever voice, male or female, young or old, is best suited to tell your story. If as the writer you—and by extension the reader—can identify with a male hero, step into his shoes, think and feel as he does in that dimension of his life you have chosen to explore, you'll have no problem.

Remember, too, that we are not talking about *War and Peace* here (though even if we were, the principle would be the same), but about light romantic fiction. And in that form, a male protagonist works particularly well; traditionally, the heroine has filled the central role, so a certain spice is added when the tables are turned.

My first story using the male character's point of view, "The Wonder of Jenny," was about a man who falls in love with a warm, generous caring girl, only to discover later that the very traits that drew him to her are a source of trouble in their relationship. Jenny's instinct for helping people thwarts Ben's efforts to be the focus of her attention, the center of her world. As he puts it:

There was a Good Samaritan streak in Jenny's nature a mile wide, and if I didn't learn to live with it we were both going to be miserable. Maybe she wasn't the girl for me after all. . . .

In creating Ben I had to walk a careful line. I wanted to portray him as a likable, sympathetic character, because I *knew* him and cared about what happened to him; at the same time, I had to show his unappealing self-centered side, or there would have been no conflict and therefore no story. The turning point comes when he finally realizes that unless he can learn to share at least some of Jenny's thoughtfulness for others, he will lose her. But he has to come to that realization *his* (masculine) way to make his conversion believable.

Endings

Does your short-short have a happy ending? Of course! Hadn't I known from the beginning that Ben and Jenny belonged together?

But before character, before point of view, before anything, comes plot. True, an imagined character sometimes becomes so real to a writer that he or she creates his or her own story. But most of the time, it's a situation that brings the characters to life. The idea for "Wedding Bell Blues" (another of my stories with a male protagonist) came from a snatch of conversation I overheard in a checkout line after a week of sitting at my typewriter fruitlessly searching for a short-short theme. The women behind me were discussing a wedding they'd been to. The gist of it went something like this:

> **First woman:** "I couldn't believe it when Doug showed up at Kate's wedding, could you?"
> **Second woman:** "I couldn't believe she invited him! Did you know he had bought her a ring just before she told him she was going to marry Brian?"

That was all, but it was enough to get me thinking. Looked at one way, it was a sad little snippet, but most young men, as we all know, are resilient creatures when it comes to romance. Just suppose, I thought to myself, "Doug" were to meet an ex-girlfriend of the groom at "Kate's" wedding—where else more likely?—and. . . . My imagination was off and running. Two days and three drafts later I had my story. Here the problem was to avoid a possible sad-sack connotation of two losers in love getting together on the rebound; using the first person for the engaging hero seemed the quickest way to head it off.

Today, few magazines actually have a special "short-short" fiction category. But as the demands on pages once allocated for fiction grow, a writer's ability to use this demanding but space-saving story form can be a marketing advantage.

One final word of advice: Often, other things being equal, a story with a seasonal or holiday theme may be just what an editor is looking for, if you can write it in time for the appropriate issue. But keep in mind the monthly magazines' long production lead time, at least three to six months.

24

ACHIEVING A SENSE OF REALITY IN YOUR NOVEL

BY LAVYRLE SPENCER

"HOW DO YOU MAKE THINGS SEEM SO REAL?" When an author is asked this question it is a compliment. If he is told, further, "I felt as if I were there. I could hear and smell and feel the places as if I had stepped onto the page," he has truly given the reader something special.

When I'm asked how I make things seem real I answer, "By appealing to the five senses." What writers don't always realize is that reality is achieved by appealing to the reader's five senses. It is simple enough to appeal to the visual sense, but how often do we include a smell, a sound (other than in dialogue), something tactile, or a taste?

I've been writing since 1976, yet I still keep on my office wall a list of five words: SEE, HEAR, FEEL, TASTE, SMELL. As I work on a scene, I refer to this list and consciously *plan* to put into it something with scent. It need not be a good smell; indeed, some offensive smells are wonderfully effective in creating reality. Consider the smell of spoiled fruit, as a character opens a refrigerator door; of rancid fat, as a man skins a bear; of gasoline on a woman's gloves after she fills her tank at a self-service station.

It is not enough to mention the scent at the outset of the scene; to get the most mileage out of it, you must refer to it again and again as you move your characters around. Let us suppose a man and woman are having an argument; he storms into the kitchen, shouting at her from the doorway, "I've had all I can stand of your mother living with us. The old lady better be out by the time I get back, or I'm packing my bags!" In setting up such a scene, I could easily have the woman baking a pumpkin pie (sweet, homey scent reminiscent of loving times like Thanksgiving), but the scene takes on a much more effective tang if accompanied by the acrid smell of pickling spices and vinegar from

108

the relish she is making. If the dialogue goes on for half a page, at one point I might remind the reader of the smell by a line such as this: *"I'm warning you, Nora, it's either her or me!" he said, looking as sour as the smell in the room.*

It is effective to turn that same sour smell into something sweet by *intentionally* having it accompany a tender scene. In such a situation, the addition of humor would most commonly be used.

Don't forget, as you go on writing a scene such as the one above, to show Nora continuing her canning as the argument goes on. As she's shouting a line of dialogue, she can burn her hand, then thrust it under cold running water. This, of course, heightens the sense of feel, again, not a pleasant feeling, but *real,* nonetheless. She can be pouring brine over the pickles and spill some, then have to wipe it up (wet). She can dry her hands on her apron (coarse cotton). She can feel sweat trickling down her forehead (heat, tickle). She can brandish a slotted spoon at him (hard, wooden handle) while shouting.

As the arguing grows louder, what other sounds might be heard? Does a dog saunter in and drink from the tin pie plate on the floor? (Slurp, slurp, slurp . . .) Does an old car chug by on the street outside? Are children's voices heard as they play in the yard next door? As the water boils in a canner on the stove, do the glass jars clink together?

How hot is it? Have you told the reader it's 95 degrees? If so, does your heroine have a glass of iced tea or iced coffee on the counter beside her pickling jars? When the argument ends, unsettled, with the man stomping out angrily, does she pick up the glass and take a swig of iced coffee, find it bitter, and make a face?

As you can see, it is possible to evoke all five senses in a scene such as the one sketched above, but to make this happen, the scene must be carefully planned. Most scenes will not lend themselves to using all five senses (taste is the most difficult to work in), but by using props, you can easily evoke four senses, and surely three in most scenes.

In dialogue, too, writers must work to create a sense of believability. Forgetting to use contractions, for example, will produce stilted dialogue. Contemporary Americans simply *don't* say *do not* very often, nor do they say *will not* when they can say *won't,* or *have not* in place of *haven't.* When in doubt about the reality of your dialogue, read it aloud, pretending you're an actor, speaking with the inflections that would be used on a movie screen or stage. If it sounds forced or unnatural, change it. Don't forget, people speak unfinished thoughts, so let some of your characters' sentences trail off. People ask questions of one another, so remember to make your characters do so, especially when they are getting to know one another. People sigh, chuckle, scratch their heads, puff out their cheeks, study their fingernails during a conversation. Make your characters do these kinds of things, too. People continue conversations as they go about their work. Use tag lines to create motion in a scene. Consider the following two:

"You never liked my mother!" Nora shouted. She slammed the kettle down.
"You never liked my mother!" Nora slammed the kettle down.

The second example increases tension, moves the scene along faster, and eliminates excess words, showing rather than telling the reader that Nora was shouting.

This is the perfect time to mention the rule by which I gauge all of my writing:

A moment of tension requires an economy of words.

I learned it from my tenth-grade English teacher many years after high school graduation. I'd written my second book but couldn't get several scenes to work. Something was wrong with the rhythm, and I couldn't figure out what, so I gave her the manuscript and asked for her comments and suggestions. Once she told me the rule and I applied it to the novel manuscript, everything became clear. In a tense scene, use shorter sentences, shorter words within those sentences, and fewer tag lines. Be brusque. When you do this, tension becomes inherent.

By contrast, in languid scenes in which a sense of tranquility prevails, use longer sentences, longer words, longer paragraphs, and more tag lines. Doing so automatically relaxes tension.

Realism is also established when you plan your novel before the first paragraph is written. Only through research can you paint accurate pictures of believable people performing their daily work amid the sights, sounds, smells, touches, and tastes that are indigenous to their surroundings. In researching my most recent novel, *Forgiving*, I learned much from books about old hand-printing presses, but only from a man who'd used them could I learn that a typesetter's efficiency (in 1889) was judged by listening to the *snick-snick-snick* of the metal type hitting his composing stick. Only from him could I learn that ink left out in the air on a brayer turns sticky and ruins the tool. Only from him could I learn that printers' ink and turpentine are the scents that pervade the air of an old-time newspaper office. Only by printing some sheets on his venerable old Washington Hand Press could I feel the thump of it against my hip, and realize a hip is used as much as a hand during this operation. Oh, you see what I've been doing again— now, let me see. . . .

snick, snick, snick (hear)
turpentine and printer's ink (smell)
thump on the hip (feel)
press, brayer, ink, office, composing stick (see)

Uh-oh! No taste. (Short sentences, short words, increased tension.)

Well, as I said earlier, taste is the toughest one to include, but four out of five isn't so bad.

Appealing to the senses and creating (or relaxing) tension with sentence structure will help you write stories that readers won't be able to put down because they're so real.

25

ABOUT FICTION WRITING: QUESTIONS AND ANSWERS

BY SIDNEY SHELDON

Q. At what age did you think about becoming a writer?

A. I began writing when I was very young. My first poem was published by a children's magazine when I was ten years old. I have always enjoyed working with language and ideas.

Q. What triggers a new novel: Character? Plot? Theme? Setting? How does each element relate to the others?

A. For me, a character comes to mind first, then the setting. In order for the story to be intriguing, the characters must be interesting. I let the characters dictate the plot through their personalities and interactions with others.

Q. After your characters, setting, and plot have taken shape in your mind, how do you know where to begin your novel?

A. I like to start a novel with a dramatic flashpoint, where a character is in trouble or about to be in trouble.

Q. Novels are often criticized in reviews for being too sentimental, or in "bad taste." Are these, in your opinion, flaws? How can these qualities be judged?

A. A novel can be judged in as many ways as there are readers. I do not consider sentimentality necessarily a flaw, and I find it difficult to judge for anyone else what I may consider "bad taste."

Q. What are the major risks in the writing life?

A. The major risk in a novelist's life is trying to make a living. The average novelist makes about $3,500 a year, and has to have an outside job to survive. It's not enough to want to be a writer; if you want to succeed, you *have* to be a writer.

Q. *Is it possible to write more easily when the characters seem to do all the talking, developing the story while the writer acts almost as transcriber?*

A. It's not only *possible*—it's the most exciting way to write a story. Each of the characters has his or her own voice and pattern of conduct.

Q. *Is it advisable for writers to read novels by other authors while working on their own?*

A. I don't read other novels while I'm working on my own books. I'm too immersed in the world of my own characters. When I'm not working on a novel, I read a great deal.

Q. *In the process of writing a novel, at what point are you more creator than critic? When does the critic take over?*

A. While writing the first draft of a novel, it's very important to let the creator take over and to keep the critic away. Once the first draft is finished, the critic should go to work. Being a critic of your work initially as you go along is much too inhibiting.

Q. *What "pre-writing" techniques do you use? Do you rehearse dialogue aloud? Keep journals? Scribble on bits of paper and tuck them into your pocket?*

A. Throughout my life I have jotted down ideas as they come to me for future consideration. The only "pre-writing" I do involves research for the book. Once I begin writing the novel, the characters direct the story.

Q. *What do you consider the most important portion of a story— opening, middle, or climax? Which is the most difficult to write?*

A. Every portion of a story is important. The opening introduces

113

the characters, the middle develops the circumstances, and the climax resolves the conflicts and/or mystery. A successful ending of a story is the most difficult part to write.

Q. *What practical ways have you found to solve problems in character and plot development?*

A. Before I begin writing a novel, I spend a great deal of time researching the characters and setting. By doing this, I experience fewer problems and less interruption once I begin writing.

Q. *A bestselling novelist has recently been quoted as saying that to satisfy her readers, she has to put erotic scenes in her books. She claims that her readers want to read erotic scenes because that's the only way to have safe sex these days! Could you comment on this?*

A. I don't believe it's necessary to put in erotic scenes to please readers. If you're trying to please the reader, you're in a lot of trouble to begin with. A writer should please himself or herself. If it's a good story and it's told well, the readers will be pleased. Putting in sex scenes arbitrarily is not the way to do it.

Q. *How do you react to advice and criticism from your editor?*

A. Since I do up to a dozen complete rewrites before my publisher even sees a manuscript, by then, it's pretty much ready for publication. The suggestions made are usually minor, and if they are helpful, I'm happy to adopt them.

Q. *What do you regard as an agent's role?*

A. A literary agent should not only represent the writer in the best light possible to as many publishers as possible, but he or she should be able to evaluate a manuscript objectively and, at the same time, be encouraging and supportive of the writer's projects and progress.

Q. *When a character completely absorbs you, do you find yourself* *almost chameleon-like, taking on a character's personality as you write, or shifting from one to another?*

A. The characters in my novels are very real to me while I'm writing their story, but life goes on, and I meet new characters every few years. I've had a few murderers in my books, so if I took on their personality, I'd be in real trouble!

26

BREAKING THE RULES

BY JOHN LUTZ

YOU'VE PROBABLY HEARD OR READ IT: The rule is there are no rules, and that's the only reliable rule for writing good fiction.

However, over the years and from countless creative writing classes, panels, and seminars, there has evolved what is known as the conventional wisdom. Beginning writers pay close attention to the various pearls of advice dropped by those established in the fields of writing or teaching fiction. Many of the pearls are false.

Writing is a uniquely individualistic endeavor, not for the most part mystical, and to a large degree teachable and learnable. But since it is, more than most activities, individual and personal, there are dangers in embracing what seems to be the soundest advice.

When aspiring writers attend seminars or read instructional books or articles, they should select very carefully what methods might work for their particular way of writing, then experiment with them before adopting them. Professional writers understand the difficulties involved in learning to write, and almost all of them are empathetic and really do want to share what they know to help others hone their craft or make that first sale. But advice given with wholehearted sincerity by established pros can sometimes harm more than it helps, in the way of strong medicine wrongly prescribed. I'm not saying it's always, or even usually, wise to reject the conventional wisdom, but I *am* saying you should always question it. Be extremely selective before incorporating it into your personal and distinctive method of writing.

The first piece of advice offered, even crammed down throats, in creative writing classes is to WRITE ABOUT WHAT YOU KNOW.

Wrong. Don't write about things of which you are entirely ignorant, but don't hesitate to build on scant knowledge and explore unknown territory. The fact is that no one "knows" enough about enough subjects to write expertly on the many elements that make up most stories

116

or novels. Probably you'll exhaust your expertise long before you learn how to write effectively. The trick is to learn to research in a way that complements your writing and to select which facts to use to capture the essence of the subject. Not so much the hard facts, but the nuances, the mood and character. In some instances, the reader will sense and share your pleasure of discovery when you've explored and chosen what's useful and representative and incorporated it in your fiction.

It's possible to know *too* much about a subject. For instance, I learned recently that many Revolutionary War battles weren't fought mainly at a distance with muskets and bayonets, but fought at close quarters with knives, hatchets and weapons known as spontoons. A spontoon is a sort of combination spearhead and axe head fitted to a staff about six feet long. Revolutionary War officers carried them rather than firearms because George Washington didn't want his field commanders concentrating on loading the inaccurate and time-consuming powder weapons of the era rather than paying attention to strategy and the ebb and flow of battle. However, the spontoon hardly fits the average reader's concept of Revolutionary War skirmishes, so were I writing fiction set in that period, I'd deliberately leave out that morsel of fact and probably arm my officers with muskets. Let's leave spontoons to the historians.

ALL GOOD FICTION IS ROOTED IN REALITY.

This is true only up to a point. Reader concept of reality is as important as the reality itself. We write fiction, not travelogues or instructional manuals. Your streets are not made to seem real because you've made sure the traffic is flowing in the right direction, or the street signs are spelled correctly, or the addresses match genuine house numbers, etc. Fictional streets are made real when your character bruises a heel stepping on a sharp stone, or stumbles over a raised section of concrete, or is made uncomfortable on sunbaked concrete by heat radiating through thin soles; when on a certain level the reader *feels* what the character feels.

It's a mistake to rely heavily on trying to create plausibility by impressing readers with a deluge of details and facts. You might educate them right out of suspension of disbelief. Of course, essential, widely known facts should be portrayed accurately so a glaring inaccuracy (a

117

mountain in Florida, a subway system in Milwaukee) won't puncture the illusion you're trying to create, but they have little to do with the actual creation of the illusion.

Using reality is fine unless carried to the extreme of emphasizing irrelevant or esoteric details rather than writing to engage the reader emotionally. That's what fiction's really about: engaging the reader's emotions. If you do everything else wrong but manage that, you've succeeded. Fiction isn't about facts, and sometimes facts need to be ignored, twisted, or embellished. Like Mark Twain's prematurely reported death, the importance of truth in fiction is greatly exaggerated.

CREATE AN OUTLINE BEFORE YOU BEGIN TO WRITE.

Here's another piece of conventional wisdom that can be a mistake. Most writers need some kind of map to lend their story sure-footedness and direction, but a rigid outline can lead to rigid, mechanical writing. It can be constricting as well as defining. I think it's best to keep the work fluid as long as possible, not close doors in the mind even before you sit down and begin writing. My own method is to work from a loose and free-flowing synopsis that provides general direction but at the same time leaves room for improvisation; maybe a clever new plot twist, expansion of the role of a previously minor character who's evolved surprisingly well, exploration of a subplot that's taken on life and interest, or a romance that's created more heat than anticipated. We cannot, and should not, know *everything* before we write the first word. If nothing else, that would take some of the fun out of writing.

KNOW THE ENDING OF A STORY BEFORE YOU WRITE THE BEGINNING.

Now, while I find this one to be generally true, and certainly true in my case, I know a few writers who begin without the slightest idea of the tail of their tale. Possibly this has to do with the way story concept takes root in their minds. Some writers seem to start with an interesting slant, startling incident or powerful theme, then charge ahead and somehow find not only direction, but a powerful and meaningful ending. Or they begin with some sense of direction, maybe even an outline, but project the ending only in simple or vague terms. That's fine if it works for them.

Each writer possesses a unique creative process, often not thoroughly understood even by the writer.

This rule is definitely one you should experiment with. Begin at least one story without any ideas as to how you'll end it. See what happens, the better to know thyself.

REVISE, REVISE, REVISE.

Again, this is true of me. But I've observed that there are writers who write "long" and writers who write "short" and then add (not pad) as well as cut and tighten. I fall into the "short" category unfortunately, and the more I embellish and revise the better the result. A well-known science fiction writer often told me he didn't revise at all, which I doubted until I went to his home and watched him sit at his typewriter and in a burst of creativity reel out one excellent page after another. Go figure. The point is, had he been following the conventional and usually correct advice to revise his work extensively, he'd probably still be unsold.

BASE YOUR CHARACTERS ON PEOPLE YOU KNOW.

This one can get you into serious trouble. While it will be easier to remember your characters' eye and hair color and little eccentricities, you should also take into account that your fictional characters must fit the requirements of your novel or story.

If you populate your fictional world with non-fiction people, it could cause you problems in character delineation and motivation. Your real Aunt Millie (the one you know so well) might indeed have done something your fictional Aunt Tillie does, though in the case of Aunt Tillie it might be totally out of character in the eyes of your readers, who've never met Millie.

The "real" person might in a number of ways get in the way of his or her fictional counterpart, might even behave in some fashion during the course of your writing that alters your perception of him or her. And the fact that someone does something in real life doesn't mean such behavior has been qualified to occur in fiction. Real people don't always behave logically, but fictional people almost always do. I've heard even professional writers complain, when an editor objected to a character behaving implausibly, that no revision was necessary because the real person on whom the fictional person was modeled actually behaved that way, so it *must* be in character. This often prompts the editor, who has heard this before, to sharpen a blue pencil.

CHOOSE A SUCCESSFUL WRITER WHOSE WORK YOU ENJOY AND ADMIRE, AND COPY HIS OR HER STYLE.

I've heard this dubious piece of advice a lot lately, and I'm sure it works for some. But then some people like eggplant. It seems to me that this game is supposed to be about originality. Publishers won't pay real money for imitation books or stories. Following this advice is rather like a singer or actress building her career on imitating Madonna. Lots of performers can do that, but there's still only one Madonna, and she tends to get the bookings.

Maybe you can imitate someone else's work long enough and exhaustively enough so that somehow your own style finally emerges. On the other hand, maybe your own style will be suppressed.

If I were you, I'd think hard about this one.

STUDY MAGAZINES SO YOU KNOW WHAT KIND OF FICTION THEY PUBLISH.

Well, if you were to read issue after issue of a magazine and then write a story almost exactly like most of the stories that had appeared in it, your story would probably be rejected for not being fresh. No editor wants to buy a story that reads too much like every other story. So much familiarity breeds rejection. Study the magazines again and in each story you'd probably find some unique angle or strength, something arresting, that made it different from all the others. That is why it was published.

A better approach might be to read a magazine to learn what it *doesn't* publish. Try to determine editorial taboos, then avoid them, and write the story *you* want to write. It will automatically fall within the parameters of what the editor's looking for, and at the same time be fresh.

As an example, one of the leading mystery magazines seldom publishes stories that feature diseases, denigration of the old, or subject matter that might even remotely risk legal action. Nor will you find in its pages graphic violence or sex (though a certain measure of subtle eroticism is acceptable), or stories involving spouse murder. These taboos, shaped by taste as well as marketing considerations, are for

120

the most part reasonable and easy enough to avoid, and they leave a wide range of subjects for good fiction.

These are only a few of the maxims launched the beginner's way when he or she seeks advice. Also heard are: "Set aside a certain amount of time each day to write." "Show your work to a friend whose judgment you trust before you submit it for publication." "Read some poorly written but strongly plotted 'formula' fiction so you can clearly see how it's constructed." And so on. There are many such standard pieces of advice floating around writers' conferences and creative writing classes. All of them are wrong at least some of the time.

While writers do have much in common, the odds on finding two who are alike are longer than with snowflakes. There are writers who require silence and writers who work with the radio blaring. Some who demand solitude and some who forge successful careers working in the company and din of a growing family. Some can't work without cigars or cigarettes in their mouths, or cups of coffee at hand, or cats in their laps. Some write in longhand, some type, some use word processors. Probably somewhere there is one who uses mud and a sharp stick.

Despite the established rules of creativity and marketability, writing remains an intensely personal and unique exercise, as mysterious as the labyrinth of the human mind. That might very well be why we write.

Before you wrap yourself too tightly in the security of the rules, ask yourself if a measure of daring might not be more valuable than any of them.

§ 27

HOLD THAT EDGE OF EXCITEMENT

BY PHYLLIS A. WHITNEY

THERE ARE A GOOD MANY EXCITING MOMENTS IN a writer's life. These happenings are all the more gratifying because of the rejections and discouragement that have gone before. I will never forget my first encouragement from an editor, or the first acceptance and appearance of my words in print. Of course I felt ecstatic when I held my first book in my hands.

However, I'm sure that the true "high" for any writer of fiction lies elsewhere. Fortunately, it is something that can come again and again, and we learn to treasure and encourage it. I mean that magical moment when the first glimmer of an idea for a story stirs in our minds. There can be a sense of marvelous "shimmer" around the flashing of those early indications of a story (or novel) to come. We always feel that *this* will be the best thing we've ever written.

While this miracle can occur for me in an instant—perhaps when I'm not even searching—it is something I may carry about with me for days or weeks, while the shining nucleus in my mind gathers more of its special sparkle, developing as if by magic. Perhaps creativity in any field is one of life's most satisfying experiences. That it doesn't last must be accepted and dealt with, so that it can be transferred to something that exists in the real world.

At first, the experience can be so invigorating that I need to hold back and not run around telling everyone what a remarkable book I am going to write. After seventy-three books, I can still be eager and even naive, though I know by this time that too much talking is a sure way to dampen the glow—and possibly even kill my own interest in what is happening.

Getting the idea down on paper in some form is much safer than bragging about it. Even a few words can capture it sufficiently so it won't get away for good. I do know, by now, that this glimmer is only that, and it won't be ready to become a full story or novel for quite a while. So, impatient though I may be, I have learned to wait.

When I was twelve years old, I discovered that I enjoyed making up stories. I could tell exciting stories to neighborhood children, making them up as I went along and delivering them with a dramatic flair that made up for their shortcomings. But I wanted something more permanent that could be read over again—by others, and by me.

My young brain teemed with stories, and I began to set them down on paper. I started out gloriously with story after story, but only now and then did I finish one. Whatever I wrote was never as wonderful as the dream. I was in too much of a hurry, and when I found I had created only the beginning of a story and must then find out where I was going, I lost interest. The magic disappeared and I gave up repeatedly.

There are two kinds of writers. I envy the writer who *can* run with the initial idea and develop it into a story or novel. (I have a private theory that these writers may need even more revision than I want or expect to do.) But my mind doesn't work that way; I can't find my story by writing it immediately, so I will deal here with my sort of writer. *We* need to find out where we're going before we attempt to write. I have developed a few methods that I use to hold onto that early shimmer and help it to grow. Or to be reborn. Somehow, in the course of three hundred pages or more, I must keep the initial excitement going so my interest will stay high until I finish the project.

How long that first edge of excitement will last differs with each book. I spend time with my notebook, developing my characters, collecting odds and ends of plot, discovering my direction, simply jotting down whatever comes to me—until the moment I *must* write. This always arrives before my planning is complete, and I know better than to deny the urge. At least I may get the opening for my story down. So I reward myself by writing several pages. My actors come onstage and begin to live. This is good for future planning, and I don't mind when the desire to write dies and I must go back to work on my characters and plotting.

When I read over what I've written, exhilaration runs high again, and I want to share this remarkable piece of writing with a reader. I never seem to learn, but perhaps it doesn't matter, since one part of my brain is being realistic and doesn't expect too much too soon. Of course, what I want is warm applause, approval—the same response to the "shimmer" that *I* have been feeling, even though I know that I am the worst possible judge of my own work when I am too close to the creative phase to see its faults.

Usually, my chosen reader, knowing the game, provides encouragement, with a hint of gentle suggestion that brings me down to earth. Sooner or later, I take another look at the first chapter and see if I can do a better version with a little more thought. For the beginner, there may be a danger in asking for criticism too soon. Our excitement over that first shining vision can be damaged all too easily. It's a lot safer to get the work done before we call on that necessary reader/critic.

Though I no longer expect that high point of excitement to last, I know it will return to engage and delight me—and keep me going. The writing of several hundred pages cannot be achieved on a single wave of exhilaration. Still, I can manage to lose myself in individual scenes that I feel are good. Along the way, wonderful new ideas attach themselves, and I take unexpected turns that lift me to the heights again. Fiction writers are allowed to be emotional people. If we write coldly and automatically, it will show.

It isn't wise to wait for these spurts of inspiration to come from out of the blue. I ask myself deliberate questions: What unexpected action can a character take at this point? What surprise event can I supply that will be logical and lift the story? I dream, see pictures in my mind, invent—and encourage lightning to strike repeatedly.

Let's consider three types of excitement that are involved in fiction writing. First and most important is the author's feeling about the story he or she is going to write. That's what I've been talking about. The second is the excitement the characters themselves feel as they play their roles in the story. If you examine what will excite each character and move him or her to action, you'll raise the excitement level.

The third type concerns the reader. If your interest and the interest of the characters remain high, the reader will live your story and take satisfaction from the experience. As writers, our purpose is to make the reader feel emotion along with the characters. But how does a writer retain that high interest level, often so difficult to achieve, when it's necessary to work on the same novel for months, or even years? Boredom for what we're writing and loss of perspective remain a real threat.

124

To avoid this and keep a certain freshness about the work, I make it a rule not to go back very far over what I've written. When I start work each day, I read only the last finished pages before moving ahead. This gives me a needed impetus to continue. Though I am dying to know what I've done and whether it's any good, I never allow myself to look back for more than a few pages—not for a while, anyway.

Eventually the time comes when I begin to feel sure that what I've written is a mess. I lose interest and courage. Since I expect this to happen, I now go back and read all those earlier pages that I'd stayed away from—read them up to the point where my writing stalled. They always seem much better than I expected, and I'm caught up again in the excitement of the story and can move ahead. I find that I even know my characters better after that rereading. This can be repeated a number of times in the course of writing a novel.

Often I receive letters from young writers—or even older ones who are still beginners—who are experiencing "writer's block." "Writer's block" is not a label I believe in. These pauses and stoppages are never incurable. We learn to set aside the "real" world with its worries and sorrows that can pull us away from our fictional scenes. The healing that results from our writing can be remarkable. We learn to turn the blows life gives us into stories, thus helping not only ourselves, but perhaps our readers as well. Nothing that happens to a writer ever needs to be wasted. We adapt and change and *use,* whether a happening is good or bad. For me the only writer's block occurs when excitement over my creation dies and my interest is suddenly gone. That could be fatal if I accepted the condition!

The problem came home to me repeatedly in the writing of my Charleston, South Carolina, novel, *Woman Without A Past.* I found myself breaking one of my own major rules: *to give my main character a strong, life-or-death drive*—a struggle she must engage in and deal with in order to save herself. In the course of writing this novel, I often failed to achieve this and my excitement for the story died along the way.

In the early stages of the novel, my heroine took action only when she was forced to by the characters around her. *They* all had plenty of drive and purpose, much of it tremendously important to them. My heroine's one goal was to solve the mystery of her birth. But that wasn't strong enough in itself and she drifted along without much drive behind her actions. I worried about her, but couldn't seem to correct the flaw. When I asked myself what she was striving for, fighting for, I came up with nothing strong enough. I ploughed through dull (to me) transition scenes, hoping I could fix them later. (Transition scenes are always hard for me to make interesting, so that was nothing new.)

During this struggle (on my part, if not on my heroine's) I called in every device I knew to keep myself interested in a character who wasn't fighting for her life, or for much of anything else. I examined my other characters—interesting enough—to discover how they would challenge my heroine and force her to act. This worked pretty well. My own interest quickened, and my excitement level rose—at times.

When the action sagged, I worked on emotion. It is all too easy in the middle deserts of a novel to lose contact with the main character's feeling. Each writer must find a way to recover lost emotion. Some play music that moves or stirs them; others take long walks that seem to free the creative mind. Or you may have a trusted friend—not necessarily another writer—with whom to discuss the problem. There are times when talking helps.

My own method is to read. Certain fiction speaks to me. I read, not to imitate or to get ideas, but to find a mood. My attention will wander from the page as something touches some emotion in me. Then I can write, because I have transferred that feeling to my main character. I rewrite the wooden love scene, and this time it works. Once you evoke your memories, they are endlessly useful and can be adapted to the needs of the scene you are working on. My heroine, I find, has a good deal to worry about.

I have also discovered that a good way to cure my loss of interest is to feed something new into my mind. Long ago, when I was teaching writing at New York University, I adopted a slogan: *Interest follows action*. When students would look at me blankly, with not a story idea stirring, I'd tell them to go out and *do* something new. Study something they knew nothing about—have fresh experiences. These need not be earthshaking, but just something to open the possibility of exploring a new field. They were always surprised that their own interest came to life when they took this sort of action, and very quickly they found themselves filled with fresh story ideas. First, you *do* something, and then you get interested. It never fails. While writing *The Singing Stones*, I went up in a hot air balloon. I had no idea how I could get that into a story—but it churned away at the back of my mind and gave me a lovely climax scene.

So when I was baffled by my problems with *Woman Without A Past,* I investigated a new subject, for me: what is known in the psychic field as "channeling," when a voice (from another dimension?) speaks through a living person. Or through a story character! My interest came to life, and I was able to develop several scenes that tied in with the plot. I even investigated cats for this novel, reading several books about them so I could understand and write about the cat in my story. Research about practically anything that will fit in can give you more material than you can handle. You, your characters, and your readers will profit from what you learn.

Nevertheless, when I finished the book, I had no great confidence in what I'd written. I knew there were some good dramatic scenes, and my Charleston setting offered wonderful material. Yet, my heroine's drifting continued to worry me, and I waited anxiously for editorial response. To my surprise, my agent and my daughter thought the story strong, exciting, satisfying. No one seemed to notice that my main character was more done-to than doing. By all the rules I know, it wasn't supposed to work—but it did. Why?

It took me some time to find the answer, and it's a useful one. I discovered the explanation in a book by Dwight Swain: *Creating Characters.* One of the goals he lists for a character is "relief from. . . ." Now I knew why my heroine had succeeded in spite of the author! I had written about a sympathetic young woman who is much put-upon (that's important) and who deserves to win out in the end. The goal of *relief-from-adversity* is legitimate and can be very satisfying to the reader.

A great deal of anxiety can be involved, in spite of having the main character take only minor action on her own. Often she is afraid, and this helped with my own interest as I became aware of her desperate, threatened state. She certainly needed relief from a number of unpleasant actions by other characters.

Anxiety can be a good tool to think about and use. However, I don't recommend that this rather negative goal be the sole direction of your main character. In my next novel, I shall make sure that my main character has a strong drive against tough opposition, though I'll certainly use the element of "relief-from" as well.

All such methods and devices are part of a writer's tool kit. We use them to keep our characters in a state of excitement that will convey itself to the reader and will grow from our own effort to hold that first shimmer of an idea alive—that edge of magical excitement that is the best reward of all to the fiction writer.

28

WHERE DO YOUR STORIES COME FROM?

BY RICK HILLIS

WHEN YOU TAKE YOUR FIRST EXPLORATORY STEPS onto a blank page, you're probably farther ahead if you're treading on something a tad more concrete than an idea. I'm talking about nuts and bolts: scene, character, tone of voice. As many short stories sprout from an interesting character you want to follow around for a bit, a curious image, a musical line of description, or even a mysterious title you keep scribbling onto cocktail napkins, as from any idea you might have.

Pre-formulated thoughts and politically correct opinions are not good short story fodder. Issues such as homelessness, child abuse, racial or sexual discrimination seem at first to be exactly the sort of topic a short story writer should take on. These ideas matter. You think they will make the kind of art that moves people to action!

But trying to cram big issues into seventeen pages is a lot like trying to shoehorn a whale into a wetsuit. In order to get your point across you have to manipulate the story's components so they add up right. Characters spout dialogue that sounds suspiciously like ventriloquism. They creak robotically, predictably, through moments more didactic than delicate and poetic. No mystery. No surprise. No discovery. The "epiphany" at the end clanks down like a hobnail boot.

Why? How come the story failed? Can't be the idea. There's nothing wrong with a noble idea.

In the real world, maybe not. But in the world of fiction, trying to dramatize conventional wisdom makes for a story that's too broad, too easy, too uncomplicated. None of the messy gray area that is the heart of most stories.

But now that a writer has this ball and chain of an idea and has invested time in a story, has something, no matter how lifeless, on the page, he or she will revise and rework and polish in a vain attempt to breathe life onto the page, changing everything *except* the idea. During the course of writing a story, things change. You make discoveries. Patterns emerge that weren't in your original game plan. In the end, the story may be about something totally different from what you intended, maybe something wholly different from what you believe at the moment.

In order for the story to become itself, characters, images, whole passages of prose you have sweated over often have to be sacrificed for the good of the story. Don't worry—these are spare parts to be used in another story. But knowing this doesn't help. Parting is always tough, especially parting with an idea. The idea *is* the story, right? That, in a nutshell, is the trap. An idea makes you want to create literature *before* you've built a story.

The best "idea" you can have for a story is to think in scenes. Stories are composed largely of scenes. The camera in close-up, paying close attention to detail, and the action unfolding dramatically at about the same pace as the time it is taking you to read it. Many stories are one long scene.

"Limbo River," the title story in my collection, is a good example of how a writer may build a story from image to image, discovering through these images and the scenes they spark, the story's central theme.

"Limbo River" came out of an image I had of a boy swirling around in a ride at a cheap fair. It was a cage. He was upside down, could see the stars between his running shoes. I'd just been at such a fair, and the experience triggered a memory of riding upside down on a similar ride when I was a kid.

On a napkin, I jotted down the image of the boy's "screaming at the stars between his shoes." I didn't know what the image suggested or why the boy was screaming, but it felt right to me, enough so that I not only thought about it, I wrote a mini scene to go with it, getting down as much detail as I could remember from the fair (broken bolts and nuts, cigarette butts, popcorn, change flying out of pockets on a ride, the sense of night). Here's the tail end of it:

It was a mesh cage that spun and orbited around a greasy hub like a planet around a star. There were broken bolts and nuts in the popcorn and cigarette butts scattered around the base, but we didn't care. "We're here for a good time, not a long time," Marcel laughed. And as he said this our cage jerked, lifted us into the night sky, and we spun upside down, and Marcel's change flew out of his pockets, whizzed past our ears like shrapnel. My heart tore free of my chest and I felt it in my mouth. We dove toward the ground, but at the last minute were scooped up, swirling through the blackness, me and Marcel, screaming at the stars between our shoes.

This could be the ending to any number of stories dealing with any number of ideas. But the important thing to me was that it seemed to *be* an ending, part of a climactic scene. Everything suggested a past history: It was night; there seemed to be a complicated bond built over time between the characters; the broken-down ride through the darkness seemed like the end of a journey; and the "stars between our shoes" suggested the arrival of some sort of personal philosophy. Something had changed in the boy to get to the point where he felt whatever he felt on that ride. Now all I had to do was find the rest of the pieces to fit the puzzle.

About the same time as I wrote the fair ride scene, another image came to mind, something I'd seen. Because of drought, a stream was drying up, and down river from a dam, huge fish were captive in isolated pools. You couldn't catch them because it was illegal to fish within a hundred yards of the dam.

Somehow I thought this image fit with the fair ride image. There seemed to be a connection between the freedom of the ride and the flowing river, and the same way that the ride's cage was a prison image, so were the shrinking, isolated pools in the river.

I could say it was intuition that made me link these images, and that intuition is a large part of writing fiction. And it is. But the truth is the images were linked because I wanted them to be. They were good material, and I wanted to use them in a story, so I made them fit.

Images that reinforce and build upon what's come before, like everything in short fiction, can accomplish several things at once. They can serve as events, flashbacks, humor, description. They are often the phrases that close out or open scenes, loaded with implication and beauty and tension. They are the joints of the skeleton of a story. And often, both for the writer and the reader, they hold the seed of what will become the story's idea. Throughout "Limbo River," I consciously remained on track, by reinforcing the basic ideas of the first images with more images that worked similarly:

"The Trip took so long, we felt like bugs trapped in a jar"; "Ralph was

131

swimming back and forth across the dark blue cage, slamming the windows, the wire mesh"; "The pen was located out where the blue vein of river wound through scrub prairie land"; " I went and nosed my car into a creek"; "By then the (drowning) victims were misshapen balloons hung up in the debris after spending all winter locked in their frozen bodies under the ice. . . ."

All but one of the stories in my collection *Limbo River* came about in this way. The one exception is "Blue," which, ironically, is one of my better stories. From the beginning, "Blue" was an idea. And I thought the idea was a winner. It had to be; it was all I had. Here it is: A woman gets hired on a pipeline construction crew. It's her one chance to have a solid, good-paying job. Her redneck coworkers are threatened. Sparks fly. O. K. It doesn't sound that great, but reduce any idea to a phrase or two, and it's going to sound idiotic. I think I liked this idea because it was the only one I'd ever had for a story— that, and I'd done pipeline work, so I had imagery stockpiled, ready to use when the story took shape.

But, it wouldn't take shape. In the first version of the story I tried to save my idea (the woman encountering the rednecks) so I could spring it on the reader in a climactic shootout. No matter how hard I revised, scenes seemed toenailed together, characters moved as if I were jiggling marionette strings. I was killing time until about page fourteen—*voila!* I could finally make this cardboard woman appear in the welding shop. And then, boy-oh-boy, the welders are not thrilled. Change had visited the men's traditional workplace, but dammit, it was time things changed!

Horrible, and I knew it was horrible, but I didn't know why.

One of the terrible things about an idea-driven story is that once the idea has hold of you, it won't let go. The more trouble you have doing the idea justice, the more precious and important it seems. It takes over. It haunts you.

About three or four years after I first started taking runs at "Blue" (I was calling it "The Wobble" then), it finally dawned on me that everybody knows that if a woman joins a pipeline, sparks will fly and things will be tough. That's no climax scene, no epiphany . . . it's a *beginning*.

So I wrote:

Lubnickie slams the truck door and leaps up the ramp to the shop. Nothing

132

new about that, but this morning Murdoch grabs his arm as soon as he steps inside, gives him a shake, gets his goddamn attention.

"You seen them yet?"

"Don't even think like that," says Lubnickie.

But when his eyes get used to the dark and he sees them, it's true. Three of them, two in their early twenties with faces like they got off at the wrong bus stop, the other one older, maybe thirty or so, and hard looking. She's got on men's jeans and dirty running shoes with the toes worn through on top. Her hair is reddish, tied from her face with a green scarf. One of the younger ones has on dress shoes with pointed heels and keeps lifting her feet one at a time like a flamingo . . .

By beginning with what I thought would be the climactic scene, exposing the idea on the first page, I stumbled on the prime short story axiom:

Start as close to the main action as you can. If your story is about a guy being stood up at the prom, don't begin in kindergarten.

Great. On the other hand, what happens next? Now that I'd opened with Norma encountering Ed in the welding shop, I'd written the sum of what I knew about the story by the end of the first page. I had no idea what was going to come next until out of nowhere:

Norma, the older of the women, fixes her eyes on a spot on the wall where no one is leaning. She is nervous, more frightened than she would ever admit, especially to herself. But seeing these cocky men with their pressed jeans and polished boots makes her think, *screw everybody.* Screw the younger ones with the muscle cars and designer jeans that cost more than the parka she's worn through at the elbows. Screw the older guys with their grade-eight educations, color TVs, second cars, houses with nice lawns, big weddings for their daughters, holidays in the summer. She knows who they are, because she's seen their wives in the mall, spending money their husbands made. . . .

So Norma had some real anger in her. Maybe even a chip on her shoulder. I hadn't realized that about her until I wrote it. Not only that, *I was in her mind, telling the story through her experience* as well as Ed's!

Which leads to a couple more axioms—or close to it: *Stories are not about issues or events* (sexism on the job, for example); they are about how these events affect *people.* Also when writing about a gathering of people, an outsider forced to be on the inside will provide an interesting point of view. For example, Norma can observe details Lubnickie would overlook. Everything is old hat to him.

By dispatching the rigid idea on the first page, I let myself be surprised and discover the natural structure of the story. Juxtaposing parallel moments between characters, each from their own points of view, came out of the blue. But once I had it, I knew the characters would drive the narrative. A day later the story was finished.

By setting out to dramatize an idea, it's unlikely you'll get beyond it. Three of a writer's chief tools—intuition, risk, and playfulness—will be left in the toolbox, and you won't enjoy one of a writer's great highs: discovery. Unless, in the end, you manage to say more than you intended (or even knew you knew), writing is just painting by numbers. It's not the idea you begin with that matters. It's the one you come away with.

29

THE ESSENCE OF STORYTELLING: DRAMATIZE, DRAMATIZE

BY ELIZABETH FORSYTHE HAILEY

DRAMATIZE, DRAMATIZE" IS THE ADVICE Henry James gave to writers of fiction.

His advice was reinforced in my own case by marriage to a novel-hating playwright who is not only my first audience but also my first editor. I knew when I started my first novel I would have to find a form that would engage and hold his attention—which is why I chose in *A Woman of Independent Means* to show the life of a woman from childhood to old age through the letters she writes, leaving the audience to imagine what her correspondents say to her in reply.

One of the keys to dramatizing is enlisting the imagination of your audience, forcing them to do some of the work and in effect making them accomplices in the conspiracy that is fiction.

Drama is the essence of storytelling. Wanting to know what happens next is what keeps a viewer in his seat or a reader turning the pages of a novel. But telling a story—like starting a fire—requires friction, two different elements striking against each other. Like natural combustion, the dramatic conflict that ignites a work of fiction requires antagonists.

In *A Woman of Independent Means* the main antagonist—the arch villain, if you will—is time. My heroine Bess, a character based on my own grandmother, was a woman with an extraordinary appetite for life. She wanted to see and do it all, and a single lifetime was not nearly long enough. She asked that her epitaph read "to be continued."

This central conflict was heightened when I adapted the novel into a one-person stage play. Thanks to a tour-de-force display of acting by stage and film star Barbara Rush, the audience was able to witness a lifetime in the space of two hours. Without benefit of makeup or costume changes, relying only on the most subtle adjustments in speech and movement, she was able to transform herself from a young girl of eighteen into a frail old woman facing death. The message of the book—to show how quickly even a long, full life passes—was translated into heightened dramatic terms on the stage.

The experience of adapting my first novel into my first stage play continues to serve me well when I return to the novel form.

I had no problem finding points of conflict and dramatizing them in my novel *Joanna's Husband and David's Wife.* It's the chronicle of a marriage over twenty-five years from a dual perspective—the point of view of both husband and wife.

Joanna starts a diary the day she meets David, determined to have a complete record of her relationship with the man she plans to marry. On their twenty-fourth anniversary, she returns to her parents, leaving the diary to her daughter, who has fallen in love for the first time. The diary is her way of showing her daughter what marriage is like (my characters have learned the secret of dramatizing: show, don't tell). But David discovers the journal first and decides to add his side of the story before their daughter reads it.

The device of the diary—and David's later discovery of it—allowed me to make use of two techniques that reinforce dramatic conflict: passage of time and point of view. The narrative spine of the novel is from Joanna's point of view—her diary entries. But David, looking back at an event, often remembers it differently—and there are times when he has no memory at all of what Joanna is describing. Using two points of view and locating them at different moments in time not only allows the characters to express hidden conflicts (those hidden from each other as well as those hidden from the reader), but encourages them to keep secrets. Sometimes what is unsaid between them can be more explosive than what is said.

However, in transforming *Joanna's Husband and David's Wife* into a two-character stage play, I had to write some of the novel's unwritten scenes, exploring the conflicts anew and allowing the characters to confront each other in the same time frame.

With my novel *Home Free,* my heroine took shape in my head a full year before I could come up with a story for her. I wanted to write about a middle-aged woman from a conventional, middle-class background who finds herself alone (I wasn't sure in the beginning whether

her husband would die or desert her for another woman) and is forced to redefine her ideas about home and family.

I had some vague idea that she would sell the house she had shared with her husband and, instead of finding another permanent residence, would become a housesitter for friends who traveled a lot or divided their lives among houses in different places. My idea was to make her a member (at least through marriage) of the moviemaking community—work that keeps people on the move. I saw her becoming involved in the lives of the different families for whom she served as a housesitter.

But even though I made a lot of notes on possible characters and situations, I knew in my heart of hearts I did not have the makings of a novel: The elements of conflict were missing. At best what I had was a book of interrelated short stories with my main character serving as a connecting device. But that was not what I wanted to write. My heroine, Kate Hart, was real and full to me, and I wanted to write a novel in which her actions would be focal.

Then three years ago at Thanksgiving I read a magazine piece on a homeless family in Los Angeles. The faces in the accompanying photographs seared my consciousness. There was a husband, a wife, a son, a daughter, even a dog—the all-American family—but they were living in their car. The article describing their ever more desperate plight changed all my comfortable assumptions about why and how people found themselves living on the street. Suddenly I saw my heroine opening the front door of the house where she now lived alone to a fictional family very much like the one whose faces now confronted me in the magazine. And I knew I had found the missing half of my novel. My heroine, who had a home but no family, was going to get involved with a family who had no home.

The story fell into place very quickly. I saw it in scenes, like a film, and used a device screenwriters often employ when constructing a movie script. I took a pack of index cards and, allotting one card for each scene, made notes of what I imagined happening between characters. The test of whether a scene deserved to be written was the strength of the potential conflict at the core of it.

I have a tendency in my first draft to spend too much time establishing characters and setting before zeroing in on the central conflict. But using the index card system forces a novelist to think in terms of scenes rather than endless chunks of prose.

When I first started plotting *Home Free,* I planned to show my two main characters in their separate settings before bringing them together. I wrote on my first index card: "Christmas Eve. Kate and her husband fight. He leaves." And on my second card: "Christmas Eve. Homeless man panhandles outside supermarket to buy presents for his family." Staring at my third index card, wondering how they would meet, I realized I had started the book too soon. The point of the novel was to make their two very separate worlds collide, and the sooner that happened, the more compelling and original my novel would be. So I put aside my first two index cards and started over. Notes for my new opening read: "Kate sees homeless man's car stall in front of her house as her husband walks out the door." Those two abandoned index cards saved me hundreds of unnecessary words.

Index cards are a terrific way to construct anything—novel, screenplay, magazine article, possibly even a poem (though I've never tried it)—much less cumbersome and rigid than a prose outline. You can shift scenes around or delete them with ease, and whenever a random idea occurs to you—a line of description, a scrap of dialogue—you can jot it down where you think it might fit.

The novel is such an open-ended form (running anywhere from several hundred pages to several thousand), it does not encourage disciplined dramatic construction. In contrast, the length of a play or film (with some well-known exceptions) is pretty much decided by the patience of the audience, and usually takes place within a two- or three-hour time frame. Also, economics can dictate the number of characters and settings.

But the novel is wide open—choices of scenes, characters, points of view limited only by the imagination of the novelist. The intoxicating possibilities of so much freedom can easily overpower a latent sense of dramatic economy. The task of the novelist is to practice from within the discipline imposed on the playwright from without.

It is not a coincidence that a lot of best-selling authors—Sidney Sheldon is a notable example—began by writing for the screen. They developed the craft of storytelling by learning how to construct scenes—scenes that would advance the action by entangling the characters in conflict.

138

In plotting your novel, try to see it as a film or play. Watch the story unfold before your eyes. Listen as your characters talk and argue.

My friend, the late Tommy Thompson, was a distinguished journalist and author of such nonfiction bestsellers as *Blood and Money* and *Serpentine* when he embarked on his first novel. Several chapters into it, he found himself for the first time in his life paralyzed by a massive case of writer's block. He had churned out hundreds of thousands of words under unrelenting deadline pressure as a journalist, but he was not prepared for the terror that comes from facing a blank page when the story is taking place only inside your own head.

Fortunately, he had a very wise editor who said to him, "Just because you're writing fiction doesn't mean you've stopped being a reporter. What you have to do is what you always do when you cover a story. Look at what's going on, listen to what people are saying, and report it—report all of it. The only difference is that the story you're reporting now is taking place in your imagination. But the process is the same."

I can imagine no better advice for a writer of fiction, whether novelist, playwright, or screenwriter. First see the scene, then report it. From that point on, you're home free.

Home free. Good title.

§ 30

REVISING YOUR FICTION MANUSCRIPT

BY JOHN DUFRESNE

REVISION IS NOT A MATTER OF CHOICE, yet many beginning fiction writers either resist, resent, or misunderstand its importance. When we read an impressive ten-page story, we may not be aware of the numerous discarded pages that preceded the finished product. If you were taught that writing is product and not process, that it's the articulation of thought and not thought itself, then revision may seem like punishment for not getting it right the first time. But writing is not supposed to be easy or extemporaneous. The writer has the duty and the opportunity to rework a story to try to find the best word, phrase, or scene, or do it over again until it is right.

If you are like Dorothy Parker, your revision begins with the first sentence of the first draft. She claimed that in writing seven words she revised five. The writing process itself is repetitive, erratic, messy. Planning, drafting, and revising seldom proceed in a linear fashion and, perhaps, should not be thought of as distinct tasks. All three go on in the first draft, as well as in the second and the tenth. But if we think of revision as a "seeing again," then we might say it starts when you have a beginning, middle, and end to your story. Now you can read it. Now you can see what you've said and sense what still needs to be said.

Revising means casting a critical eye on your work, and doing so makes the revision different from your first draft. You reorganize material; examine words, phrases, and paragraphs; consider character and plot; look at beginnings, endings, transitions, and composition. You add, delete, reshape. You examine your choices. There are a thousand steps in the process. It is in the revision stage that your imagination becomes deeply engaged with your material, when you come to know your characters and begin to perceive their motivations and values. Revision is not the end of the creative process, but a new beginning; it's a chance not simply to clean up and edit, but to open up and discover.

When you've completed a draft of your story, it's a good idea to set the manuscript aside and return to it later. Each time you read it over, you'll see something new. Read it aloud and note the places where the rhythms are smooth or hard, the prose graceful or awkward, a character's diction consistent and revealing, or jarring and unconvincing. Note the connections and tangents. Listen to your story. What is it trying to tell you? Try to visualize your characters, and before you go on to the next draft, imagine what they're doing or what they think they're doing and how they feel about it.

As the creator of a piece of fiction, you see what no one else sees. That's your job. Just as you notice every significant detail about your character's appearance—the thin scar on his left index finger, say—so you notice the confusing shift in tense, the awkward transition, the intrusive or extraneous adverb. You see what you wrote, not what you thought you wrote.

You look at your current draft and you ask yourself the right questions: Have I shown and not told? Is every scene necessary? Have I chosen the point of view that is likely to add interest and afford the reader clear access to the central conflict? Is the plot a causal sequence of events or a simple chronology? Has my central character changed? If so, how? Is the purpose of the change clear? Does each character have a distinctive voice? Have I made it difficult enough for my central character to get what she wants? Is the setting evocative? the theme fresh? Are the details vivid, precise, and revealing?

Answer the questions honestly. Make all necessary changes, and see if they necessitate additional ones. The substitution of a single word may sharpen the vision of an entire story. A character's precisely described gesture may be as effective as a page of exposition. Ask yourself more questions: What is my story about? Was that my intention? What emotional experience do I want the reader to have? Have I made that happen? Is the story as clear as it can be? If a scene drags, cut it; if dialogue rambles, tighten it. Make every word count.

All these rewrites and changes can't be done at once. Some writers may revise as they go along. Each of us has a different approach and process and needs to learn what works best. But for every writer, the first draft is an act of discovery; then the real labor begins. Be ruthless. The story should improve with each revision. Make a list of your "obsessions." Challenge your characters to take responsibility for their actions. Read each draft closely, because you must find the solution to the problems in the story itself. You begin to write better than you thought you could. You fix the problem, a new one appears, you persevere, and write on. If you never revise, you never learn to write. You see that the made-up characters you have created have become vivid and intriguing people who live interesting, but often heartbreaking, lives. You begin to resent the time spent away from them.

I write many drafts longhand, because it slows me down, gives me time to think. I change sentences, words, phrases as I write, often recopying the entire annotated draft from the first line to the point at which the corrections get so messy and confusing that I have to stop and make a fresh copy. In this way, I get to feel the rhythm of the prose, hear the tone of the narrative voice.

When I'm finally satisfied that the elements of plot are in place and I think I know what my characters want, I type this draft into the computer. I print it out, then put the copy away for a few days. When I read it again, I immediately begin to tear it apart. What I couldn't see in the heat of writing usually becomes clear now. I see that a story that I thought was good can be made even stronger. I make the changes, wait, reread, and start over.

There are some common stylistic problems that you will want to address in each stage of revision or at some point before the manuscript is finished. The following checklist may help you do that. By "challenge," I mean take out the offending word or phrase, read the piece again and only if the word or words in question are essential should you put them back in.

1. *Challenge every adverb.* Mark Twain said, "The adverb is the enemy of the verb." Often, what we need are not two words, one qualifying, thus weakening, the other, but one stronger word. Not "He walked unsteadily" but "He staggered." Adverbs modifying verbs of attribution are particularly intrusive and offensive. "'I see the problem,' she said confidently." *Show* us her confidence; don't tell us.

2. *Challenge every adjective.* Like adverbs, most adjectives are unnecessary. Often the adjectival concept is in the noun. A night *is* dark, an ache painful, a needle sharp. Color is often redundant, as in *blue* sky, *green* grass, and so on. Other adjectives are too conventional to

be either vivid or significant, like a *tender* heart or a *sly* fox. An adjective should never be simply a decoration; it must always be essential.

3. *Challenge every verb with an auxiliary.* Replace passive voice verbs with active ones that are immediate, clear, and vigorous. "I kissed her" is better than "She was kissed by me"—and shorter. Also, replace progressive forms of verbs with the simple tenses: "I brewed coffee" indicates a more definite time than "I was brewing coffee." (On the other hand, be sure to use the past perfect tense if denoting an action completed before a time in the past: "My mother had already called the plumber by the time I arrived.")

4. *Challenge the first paragraph.* Sometimes the first paragraph helps get the story going, but often it merely introduces the reader to the story we are about to tell. Action may actually begin in the second paragraph.

5. *Challenge the last paragraph.* If the last paragraph unnecessarily summarizes or explains the meaning of the story, cut it out.

6. *Challenge every line that you love.* Delete every word that is there only for effect, every phrase you think is clever, every sentence for which there is no purpose or point. Your concern must be with the characters and not with your own wit or style. Check your list of "obsessions" and correct them. Watch for your "pet" words—"just," "very," and "that" are common offenders—and delete them if they're not essential. Or perhaps your first-person narrators do too much telling and not enough showing, or you tend to shift tenses needlessly.

7. *Challenge every exclamation point.* Like adverbs, they are intrusive.

8. *Be alert for every cliché* or hackneyed word or phrase, every overused or unnecessary modifier. If you've heard it often, don't use it.

9. *Cut every nonessential dialogue tag.* In a conversation between two people you may need only a single tag:

"Doris, I'm home," Lefty said.
"In the kitchen, dear. Did you remember the milk?"
"Got it right here."

The new paragraphs clearly indicate who is speaking. When you're attributing dialogue, use "said" or "asked." Anything else focuses attention away from the dialogue.

10. *Eliminate those colloquial introductory words* in dialogue, like "yes," "no," "well," "oh," etc. What follows usually tells enough.

11. *Eliminate everything you're not sure of.* If you doubt whether a sentence, word, or behavior belongs, it doesn't.

12. *Read the draft aloud and listen* for awkward and repetitious words, inadvertent rhyme, faulty rhythm.

13. *Proofread* for clarity, consistency, grammar, punctuation, economy. And then proofread again.

Revision is not just a time to edit. It's a time to invent and surprise, to add texture and nuance. In writing fiction, you must be honest and rigorous. You cannot judge your characters or want to say something so much that you manipulate them, twist the plot, or ignore what *their* reactions and responses would be. You owe it to your characters to do justice to *their* lives. Revision continues until you feel that you have done all you can to make the story as compelling and honest as possible. Ask yourself if you care enough about these characters to put in the time, energy, and thought it takes to work a story into its best possible shape. If you quit, if you don't revise, then you don't care enough.

31

MOVEMENT WITH MEANING

BY LYNNE GESSNER

WHEN I FIRST BEGAN TO WRITE, I read all the books and magazine articles I could find about writing. They often stressed the need for action between characters, whether these people battled one another, climbed a hill, shot a gun, diapered a baby, or merely talked. I took the advice seriously, and my action scenes were acceptable. It was in the quieter ones, when my characters talked or listened, that I ran into trouble. In the mistaken belief that I was doing "tight writing," I thought a few terse words of "action" would suffice.

I filled my scenes with phrases like "he nodded," "she shrugged," "he stood up," "sat down," or "crossed his legs." That was action, wasn't it? I even had my characters *looking,* or *yawning,* or *smiling,* or *sighing.* All were part of my repertoire of "movements" shoved in between chunks of dialogue; I had mistaken movement for action. These manuscripts, cluttered as they were with these meaningless intrusions, limped back home.

Time and a few seminars in fiction writing helped me overcome this bad habit. I learned that these bland statements were nothing more than uneventful motion. But movement, combined with *emotion, attitude, posture,* or *expression,* became action that had meaning, action that characterized, action that created vivid pictures and brought dialogue alive.

Let me show you by example:

"Before she left," Hannah said, "Betsy told me there had been nothing between her and Luke—nothing at all." She looked at Helen and Carrie across the table. "Just gossip, that's all it was—just gossip."

What does "She looked at Helen and Carrie across the table" do? Nothing. It's natural for people to look at those to whom they speak; therefore, unless we tell *how* Hannah looks at Helen and Carrie (*defiantly, worriedly,* or *with amusement*), the sentence is superfluous.

Now I'll give meaning to this example:

She leaned forward, her eyes daring Helen and Carrie to defy her.

The leaning forward and defiant eyes convey intensity of feeling and also allow us to "hear" that she says the last sentence with emphasis and perhaps a touch of anger.

If I wanted to convey a different mood I might write:

She leaned back, glancing with amusement at Helen and Carrie.

In either case, that bit of narration is no longer intrusive, meaningless motion; it has become a necessary action.

Here's another example—a longer scene that includes the bits of useless narration often scattered throughout fiction manuscripts. Sergeant Hawkins and Lieutenant Carruthers are two police investigators who are discussing a murder case in the sergeant's office:

Hawkins looked at Carruthers. "There are several facts that don't connect, Lieutenant. This blue shoe—who does it belong to? And the key—just a lousy key. Does it fit a door, a padlock, or somebody's damned trunk?" Carruthers shrugged and Hawkins put the two items in his drawer.

Carruthers stood. "Maybe we'll have more information from the coroner." He walked to the door. "His report should be on my desk by now. Don't worry, Hawkins, I'm sure we'll have a wrap-up soon." He left the room.

This scene lacks drama. Note the bland verbs, *looked, shrugged, put, stood, walked,* and *left.* Not one portrays meaning, attitude, posture or expression. There is nothing here to indicate the emotion of either man.

See how the scene immediately comes alive when the bland verbs are changed to vivid movements:

Hawkins leaned forward, jabbing his fingers at the items on the desk. "There are several facts that don't connect, Lieutenant. This blue shoe—who does it belong to? And the key—just a lousy key. Does it fit a door, a padlock, or somebody's damned trunk?" He shoved them into his drawer and slammed it shut.

Carruthers smiled as he rose and patted Hawkins on the shoulder. "Maybe we'll have more information from the coroner. His report should be on my desk by now. Don't worry, Hawkins, I'm sure we'll have a wrap-up soon." He strolled out of the room.

146

Now the emotion of the scene is clear. Each action has posture, attitude, and expression. We see the irritation in Hawkins and the attempt by Carruthers to defuse that irritation. The words and movements complement one another.

Significant movement is needed to establish the mood of a scene. In the example below, two small boys are standing outside the gate of an old house.

"Come on, Johnny, let's go in," Billy said.
Johnny looked at him. "I hear it's haunted. Folks say they've seen ghosts."
"Aw, there ain't any ghosts. That's just scare talk." Billy walked up to the porch.
Johnny followed. Just as he reached the front door, he heard a scream. Immediately he turned and ran.

Here, again, are colorless verbs: *said, looked, walked, followed, reached, heard,* and *turned.* The dialogue leads us to believe Billy is daring Johnny to enter a haunted house. But the narration that supports the dialogue lacks posture.

Now, let the movement convey attitude, posture, expression or meaning, and you liven that scene.

"Come on, Johnny, let's go in," Billy dared him. Johnny paled, even as his voice trembled. "I hear it's haunted. Folks say they've seen ghosts."
"Aw, there ain't any ghosts. That's just scare talk." Billy strutted up the sidewalk, his glance a challenge to Johnny still hunched by the gate.
Johnny glanced over his shoulder, then finally inched his way closer. When at last he stood trembling by the front door, trying to look brave, he heard a scream. With a screech of terror he bolted down the steps and raced beyond the gate.

Now the mood of fear has been set. The small scene has life. It is clearly in focus.

In all three examples, the dialogue never changed, just the movement, and it was the improved movement that helped the reader understand the scene.

As a writing exercise, try adding meaningful movement to the same three scenes without changing the dialogue. For example, in the first scene, show that Hannah is sad. Next, indicate humor between Hawkins and Carruthers. Then lend a sense of adventure, rather than one of fear, to the scene between Billy and Johnny. Note how the dialogue comes alive when the reader can "hear" the tone in a character's voice.

For demonstration purposes, I used more movement in the policemen's scene than I ordinarily would: Though vivid and meaningful action can enhance a story, it can also interfere, if not used judiciously.

For instance, if you want a character to give your readers a specific block of information, such as pointing out what steps have been taken toward a solution, or what specific plan is being implemented, make sure that this information is not buried in a morass of action. Too much looking, or sighing, or shrugging, and even too much *meaningful movement* can interfere with the facts. To set the mood, confine meaningful movement to the beginning and end of the dialogue. If the mood changes as the story progresses, then it's vital that you use different movements that show the reader the altered posture, emotion, or attitude.

Some stories are written almost exclusively in the objective viewpoint; the author almost never goes into the protagonist's thoughts. In such cases, it is even more imperative that all action conveys distinct meaning, that posture portrays emotion and thought.

It sometimes takes more words to give meaning and drama to action, and in short stories especially, every word must count. So when your character does make a movement, be sure that action is vital to the scene. Remember, your writing will have more impact with one meaningful phrase than with a half-dozen movements that merely clutter.

32

TOO GOOD TO BE TRUE: THE FLAWLESS CHARACTER

BY MARY TANNEN

MY MOTHER ONCE BOUGHT a new table that came with a card printed on buff-colored heavy stock explaining that the table had been "distressed" with artful gouges and well-placed worm holes to give it a patina of age. We (her four children) thought this was hilariously funny and said that if we had only known she wanted distressed furniture we would have been happy to oblige and that clearly we had misinterpreted her screams of anguish every time we left a soda bottle on the coffee table or ran a toy car up the leg of the Duncan Phyfe chair.

The very phrase "character flaw" makes me think of that distressed table, as if characters were naturally shiny new and perfect and needed only the addition of a flaw or two, artfully placed, to make them more realistic. To me, a personality, whether actual or fictional, is not solid but liquid, not liquid but airborne, as changeable as light. What looks like a flaw might turn out to be a virtue. Virtue might, under certain circumstances, prove to be a fault.

When my daughter was reading *Billy Budd* and having a hard time with it, she came storming into my room to protest, and seeing the book I was working on in galleys, took it into her room to read. She brought it back the next day and announced that it was "better than *Billy Budd.*"

"Better than *Billy Budd!*" I could see it emblazoned across the book jacket. Actually, my novel isn't better than *Billy Budd,* but the style was a lot more congenial to my daughter. She was appalled by Melville's heavy symbolism, by the way Billy Budd was the representation of an idea, not an actual man.

Billy Budd had no flaws, physical or moral (except for his stutter). He was illiterate, of noble but unknown birth, untainted by the corrupting influence of either family or literature. He was a myth, "Apollo

149

with his portmanteau"! Melville never intended to create a realistic character. Billy Budd was Adam before the fall.

Sometimes when reading over a draft of a fiction piece I am working on, I realize that one of my major characters is suspiciously lacking in flaws. She is usually a person like me, but she is lacking in defects as well as in color and definition. When this happens in a piece of fiction I'm writing, it is a sign that I am identifying too closely with her. Just as I try to show my good and hide my bad, I am protecting this fictional person.

Recently I discovered a trick that helped me correct this. I was working with a character, Yolanda, a woman my age who ran a bookstore. Yolanda was nice. She was good. A nice good woman, and very bland. I couldn't get a grip on her or who she was. I went to my local swimming pool to do a few laps and take my mind off my troubles, when I saw a woman I'd seen many times before but don't know very well—a tall skinny woman with short elfin hair and wide-awake eyes. I decided to steal this woman's body and give it to Yolanda.

It worked miracles because now Yolanda was no longer me. She was this woman I didn't know very well. She began to exhibit all kinds of personality traits. She was allergic to almost everything and purchased her meals at the New Age Take-Out Kitchen. This explained why she was so thin. She spent lonely nights watching the families in the apartments across the street. The strange thing was that although Yolanda had many more weaknesses than she did before I discovered she wasn't me, I liked her better.

Another way to break the spell of the flawless character is to elicit the opinion of another character in the novel or story, one who dislikes, resents, or holds a grudge against the paragon of virtue. In *Second Sight,* I had a perfectly lovable older woman, Lavinia, who refused to believe that her philandering husband, Nestor, had left her for good. Instead of selling the house and investing the proceeds in order to live off the income, she managed on very little so that she could keep the house intact for Nestor's return.

Nestor (who had flaws to spare) had another version of the story. Lavinia's loyalty enraged him. He saw it as a plot to make him feel guilty and remain tied to her. Indeed, at the end when Nestor asked Lavinia to take him back, Lavinia realized she no longer wanted to return to her old life with Nestor. She wondered if perhaps instead of being noble and true all those years, she hadn't actually been taking out a genteel and subtle revenge.

A character without flaws has nowhere to go. He can't change or grow. In Philip Roth's *The Counterlife,* the novelist Zuckerman, who used himself as a character in his books, was writing about his younger brother Henry. Because Zuckerman had given all the faults to himself-as-character, he had doomed his brother-as-character to a life of virtue. Henry had always been the good son, the good husband, father, dentist. Writing about Henry at thirty-nine, Zuckerman imagined him as the suffocating prisoner of his perfect but shallow life. The only way Henry could break the pattern was to escape altogether, leave his family and practice in New Jersey and begin anew in Israel. Zuckerman went to visit Henry in his kibbutz on the West Bank and found that his younger brother had simply exchanged one slavish system for another. He was still the good brother. He could change the scene, but he couldn't change himself because he was a character without flaws.

I realize I have been using the term "flaw" as if it could mean anything from nail-biting to one of the Seven Deadly Sins. I think of a flaw as a personality trait I wouldn't confess to, except on a dark and stormy night to a stranger passing through. And then there are the flaws we hide from ourselves, or lack the insight to see, but which help determine the course of our lives.

When I'm writing, the flaws that interest me are not the ones I assign ("Q kicks small dogs"), but those that emerge in the course of the story. Take Yolanda, who tries to be good, to be virtuous, to do no harm to others: I was amazed to discover, somewhere near the end of the first draft, that she had used someone, a man, a friend, to get over a wound suffered long ago, and in using him had hurt him. Yolanda didn't see how she could hurt this friend whom she considered much more powerful and attractive than she. The more I work on that novel, the more I see that Yolanda's major flaw is her modesty. She lets people down because she cannot conceive that she means as much to them as they do to her.

In *Second Sight,* the opposite was true: A character's flaw proved to be her saving grace. Delia, the widowed mother of a twelve-year-old son, lacked all marketable skills. She lived on welfare and whatever she could make telling fortunes over the phone. Everyone, but especially Delia's career-minded sister Cass, faulted her for not taking her life in hand and finding a way out of the dead-end life of poverty she and her son had fallen into.

But Delia operated on another level from her more rational friends and relatives. She was watching for signs and portents, for signals that the time was right. She refused to force the unfolding of her life.

Delia did manage finally to bring about a change for herself and her son, to the amazement of the others, who began to see a glimmer of wisdom in her otherworldliness. Cass, however, could never accept that Delia's passivity had enabled her to recognize and receive love when it came her way. Cass would continue to take charge of her life, as Delia said, captaining it as if it were a ship, but never allowing for the influence of wind or tide or current.

People, fictional and real, are not perfect, like fresh-from-the-factory tables. They come with their faults built in, mingled and confused with their virtues. Whenever I find I am dealing with a character without flaws, and I am not intending a twentieth-century rewrite of *Billy Budd,* I take it as a sign that I have not done my work. I have not imagined my character fully, have not considered her through the eyes of the other characters. Finally, I have not cut the umbilical cord. I am protecting her, shielding her, and, at the same time, imprisoning her in her own virtue. It is time to let her go so she can fail and change and grow.

33

CIRCUMSTANTIAL EVIDENCE: SOURCE OF FICTION PLOTS

BY LEILA DAVIS

CREATING A CHARACTER BASED ON circumstantial evidence presents a writer with a different approach—and challenge. Law enforcement officers are often faced with that situation, a classic example being the "contents of a dead man's pockets." Identification may be missing, leaving as clues only what "John Doe" carried and wore. For example:

1) In John Doe's pockets they may find: a key chain with gold-tone golf cart medallion and seven assorted keys, nail clippers, black comb, two large rubber bands, partial book of matches from Tony's, one white shirt button, golf tee, receipt for three rolls of film, partial pack of mint Tic Tacs, two ticket stubs from a hockey game, a ⅜-inch brass nut, three nickels, six pennies, one quarter. A crumpled grocery list with these items: grapefruit, bread, coffee, chicken, light bulbs, Coors, cheese, carrots, tuna, hamburger, meat sauce, VCR tapes. No wallet was found.

The police have already taken the body to forensics; fingerprints and dental charts may eventually identify the man. Let's assume his body was found on the shores of Lake Michigan. Given the size of the Great Lakes, a boat could capsize and/or sink without ever being noticed or reported.

One writer might invent the following story: The victim, Mark, a cautious man, always stashed his wallet in the cabin so he wouldn't lose it if he fell overboard. He needed the ⅜-inch brass nut to repair the boat railing. Brass fittings are expensive, used mainly where equipment is subjected to a high degree of corrosion, such as a cabin cruiser. Mark also enjoys golf, but neither golf nor his boat gives him enough exercise to control the weight he's gained from frequent meals at Tony's Ristorante. The shirt button, strained to the limit, popped into his lasagna, and ended up in his pocket.

He'd left the three rolls of film on July 7 to be developed, pictures taken during a holiday get-together with other boating/golfing enthusiasts. Mark bought the groceries for the weekend he had custody of his son, who tapes movies off Dad's cable TV. The pair spent one evening at an exhibition hockey game.

Quite another story could be developed by a novelist: Randy, with the same items in his pocket, is found in an alley, victim of a mugger. Randy plays golf with the same foursome every week during the golfing season. The author imagines the button came off when Randy forgot to undo the left sleeve before pulling off his shirt in his rush to make starting time. He and one of his golf buddies are also rabid hockey fans, vocal in expressing their opinions. After a game, they often stop at Tony's to hash over the highlights of the day's game.

Smoking is not allowed in Randy's office, so he sucks a Tic Tac when he can't have a cigarette. The brass nut is to repair his leaking kitchen sink, too long neglected by the apartment manager. Randy pulled the large rubber bands off the bundle of magazines and letters delivered that day.

In addition to the key to his apartment and two car keys, he has a key to his basement storage locker, another to the apartment of one of his golf partners, as well as one to his parents' home, and one to his office. But, inexplicably, his key to the executive washroom is missing. Against company policy, Randy was having duplicates made. When his boss hears that Randy was killed, he's more upset about the missing executive washroom key than about Randy's death.

And here's a third possibility for developing a story from the same "evidence": Joe has never really liked golf, but his wife, Vanessa, loves it; he's more her caddy than her partner. The key chain was a stocking stuffer at Christmas, and now he carries on it a key to the apartment of his mistress, Melanie, who shares his love of hockey, a game Vanessa considers "common" and "vulgar." Melanie also shares Joe's interest in restoring antique cars. She picked up the brass nut for him at the hardware store where she works, and where they met. She and Joe occasionally meet at Tony's Lounge, a bar with a dim interior and high-backed booths.

The film is still at the drugstore where he'd left it because Joe's handwriting is so illegible that the envelope with the developed pictures is filed under Joshua, not J. Fisher. Vanessa has been nagging him for losing the pictures of their Miami vacation, but it was the crumpled grocery list she found in Joe's pocket that signed his death warrant. On it are chicken, hamburger, meat sauce. An ardent animal rights' activist and a vegetarian, Vanessa would never have asked Joe to buy these items. Enraged by his infidelity, she hired a hit-man to shoot Joe and make it look like a robbery.

2) Women usually carry handbags, and a woman carrying a Gucci handbag with gold-plated fittings is very different from one who carries a denim patchwork bag. Alison carried a red leather shoulder bag, gold-tone trim, one outside pocket, with one inside zipper pocket. Suppose a purse-snatcher removes Alison's wallet before disposing of the handbag in a trash can?

The person who discovers it opens the purse and finds these items in the zipper pocket: a twice-folded $20 dollar bill inside an address book, two community theater season tickets, a Hilton sewing kit, three Band-Aids, four safety pins, a pair of silver hoop pierced earrings. Loose in the purse are a black ball-point pen, a short Garfield pencil with worn-down eraser, three keys on a key ring, a small memo pad, a checkbook with scenic mountain "designer" checks, a receipt for dry cleaning—one suit, two sweaters—a packet of Kleenex tissues. Also in the purse is a floral cosmetic kit containing Clinique cosmetics—pink lipstick, mauve eyeshadow, brown/black mascara—a medium beige compact, comb, mirror, emery board, and an open pack of Tums. In the outside pocket are sunglasses and a Hallmark pocket calendar noting birthdays, anniversaries, teacher conference dates and orthodontist appointments for her daughter.

A writer may conclude that Alison is an upper-middle income mother. Her cosmetics are in a separate bag, not rattling around the bottom of her purse, demonstrating organization and the importance she places on her makeup. She can afford to keep $20 stashed away for emergencies, and supports the local theater. She has her sweaters dry cleaned, not hand-washed at home. At least one child has braces, seldom covered in full by dental insurance. The fact that she's willing to pay for her daughter's orthodontia and to arrange conferences with her teacher indicates a caring mother, but the Tums show she sometimes suffers from indigestion. Her scenic checks are another little luxury. Imprinted with her name and address, they may get her hand-bag back.

The Band-Aids, safety pins, sewing kit, tissues, and extra earrings indicate she's prepared for emergencies. With an address book in her purse, she has instant access to necessary information when she's away from home.

An alternative view casts Alison as a second-grade teacher keeping track of parent conferences and *her* orthodontist appointments. As an adult, she's opted to have the dental work her parents couldn't afford when she was a child. Her allergies led her to choose Clinique cosmetics, and the earrings were left at her home by an absent-minded guest. Alison plans to return them when she sees the woman at the next meeting of the community theater play selection committee. On the way to school, she dropped her husband's clothes at the cleaners; Alison is allergic to wool.

The red leather handbag was a birthday present from her mother, who lectures Alison about becoming dowdy. Mom also ordered the checks, a reminder of the annual family ski vacations in Vermont. Her mother's final gift was the address book listing all their relatives, including some Alison would like to forget.

A pupil gave Alison his Garfield pencil for her birthday. The memo pad is a necessity for a woman who writes notes to herself about everything. With her sensitive eyes, Alison wears sunglasses outdoors year-round.

3) Lacking a John Doe with pockets for you to explore, or a lost handbag, try to analyze character traits of fellow diners. Imagine a thirty-something couple seated across from you at a moderately priced restaurant at six on a weekday evening. The man is wearing a conservative suit but a flashy tie. His companion's raspberry suit is accented with a large pearl and rhinestone brooch. Both wear wedding rings.

He starts with a cocktail, but she shakes her head and drinks ice water. They share an appetizer of crab-stuffed mushrooms, then go on to soup, caesar salad, hers with peppercorn dressing, his with Roquefort. When the entrees arrive, he has a thick filet mignon that covers a platter, with large baked potato and sour cream on the side. She ordered chicken Kiev on a bed of rice. Later, the waitress brings two glasses of champagne, and offers congratulations. After clinking their glasses in a toast, the woman takes a few sips, then sets it aside. His dessert is "Chocolate Sin Pie," hers fresh strawberries and yogurt. Before leaving, she places three $20 bills on the table, under the check. What could the occasion be?

They could be celebrating an anniversary, or the birth of their first child. The early hour suggests they plan to go elsewhere after dinner, or perhaps their babysitter has an early curfew on a school night. The woman may have chosen not to drink much because she's on a medication that precludes alcohol, or she's more conscious of her health. In their haste to leave home, she forgot to give her husband the cash she'd picked up at the bank that day. Budget-conscious, they keep their credit cards locked in a desk at home unless they're traveling, also forgotten on this occasion.

But the writer reveals this couple is not married to each other. They're business rivals in the firm both work for. She lost her bet that she could outdo his sales figures for the month. Fearful that her husband—a tight man with a dollar—may find out how much the dinner cost, she paid cash, inwardly seething because her co-worker chose the most expensive items on the menu. The waitress offered congratulations after the man boasted they were celebrating a major triumph at work.

Whatever your basic information, try viewing it from at least three angles. "Circumstantial evidence" too often depends on personal interpretation. That's why it's seldom accepted in a courtroom. You see the teenager next door, with his deafening boombox and reckless driving, as a menace to society. To his girlfriend, he's a second Tom Cruise. His father glows with pride when he thinks of his son as a future partner in the family tire dealership. And you're *all* right.

34

HOW SHORT IS SHORT?

BY T. ALAN BROUGHTON

THE SHORT-SHORT STORY has gained respectability. We can say this with assurance now because it is not only being published, it is being anthologized. Increasingly, I am confronted with a bewildered writer or reader who wants some indication of "proper" length. How short is short, how long is long? When does a short story become a poem in disguise? When is it a novella? When does a story bloat on verbosity, or when does it shrink to mere anecdote? Frankly, I don't think length in itself has much to do with excellence. If it's good, if it works, so be it. For a writer, the task is simply to make the finest piece of writing that he or she can—and that's the long and short of it.

My usual advice to writers is, "in your first drafts of a story, write too much." I don't think a writer knows what the story is, who the characters are, where they are going, what needs to be revealed and what concealed until those first few drafts have been written. Begin wherever you can, but as soon as possible give yourself up to the story and try to find out where it really wants to go. I don't think you can find this out without risk of false starts, ramblings, foolish repetitions, stumbling around in the half-light of your dim perceptions and intentions. It takes a certain kind of indulgence in the beginning to get anything written. What follows, of course, is an openness to what that mass of material suggests and a willingness to be merciless in lopping off what does not help or in developing more if necessary. Economy may be the final result, but it's a "wasteful" process. Look at all the chips and stone dust that litter the floor in a sculptor's studio.

No writer *wants* to waste words. Brevity in a story is the art of including appropriate silence, of making each phrase, each sentence resonate with implications so that the story is much more than its length suggests—like one of those small dots of paper that, when dropped into water, opens out into the richly patterned illusion of a flower. But I've read just as many long short stories that do that as well as any short short. And vice versa.

Perhaps the trend nowadays in all things is toward the snack—eat less and eat more often, they say. In politics—sound bites, visual clips of a candidate's smile and honorable rhetoric—these are supposed to stand for substance. Children grow up in a world conditioned by the quick lies of commercials. Maybe editors are right in believing that we are all channel hoppers—read a few sentences in a story, get a cup of coffee, read a few more, pick up the latest issue of *USA Today*, read a paragraph further down the page, call someone on our cellular phones. Publishers see us as hyperactive kids on a sugar high, and we're expected to have fractured attention spans—at least when they give us credit for having any intelligence.

Pick up a copy of a nineteenth-century novel and compare its paragraphing to a novel or short story written today. You'll come to the conclusion that the paragraph in our time has shrunk to an average of three or four short sentences. Can you imagine how lost young readers are when they have to sink into a two- or three-page paragraph in a story by Henry James? Still, there's great art being made with brevity. No harm, as long as we don't forget to read the longer stories.

For instance, read aloud these sentences.

Out through the front of the tent he watched the glow of the fire, when the night wind blew on it. It was a quiet night. The swamp was perfectly quiet. Nick stretched under the blanket comfortably. A mosquito hummed close to his ear. Nick sat up and lit a match. The mosquito was on the canvas, over his head. Nick moved the match quickly up to it. The mosquito made a satisfactory hiss in the flame. The match went out. Nick lay down again under the blanket. He turned on his side and shut his eyes. He was sleepy. He felt sleep coming. He curled up under the blanket and went to sleep.

That's Hemingway, "Big Two-Hearted River, Part I." The story runs to about six printed pages.

Before he quitted London, however, he made a pilgrimage to May Bartram's grave, took his way to it through the endless avenues of the grim suburban metropolis, sought it out in the wilderness of tombs, and though he had come but for the renewal of the act of farewell, found himself, when he had at last stood by it, beguiled into long intensities. He stood for an hour, powerless to turn away and yet powerless to penetrate the darkness of death; fixing with his eyes her inscribed name and date, beating his forehead against the fact of the secret they kept, drawing his breath, while he waited, as if some sense

159

would in pity of him rise from the stones. He kneeled on the stones, however, in vain; they kept what they concealed; and if the face of the tomb did become a face for him it was because her two names became a pair of eyes that didn't know him. He gave them a last long look but no palest light broke.

That's Henry James in "The Beast in the Jungle." The story is about thirty-three printed pages long.

Fifteen sentences in Hemingway's paragraph, four in James's, and James's is about one third longer. I love them both.

If you keep your story very short, beware of the dangers. Don't put your reader in the position of beginning it in a state of admiration that ends in frustration because you did not live up to the story's implications. Risk using enough words to satisfy your reader's expectations. Too often stories I read present me with a situation, the sketch of a character or relationship, and never go beyond repetition of the same opening effects, admirable as they may be. Many authors have mastered the art of a good beginning, and part of a good beginning is not just the grabber, but a start that implies some intense consequences, or at least ones you can't wait to discover. A story that feels too short is one that richly suggests a potentiality that is not subsequently acted out. It is an anecdote, and although anecdotes are entertaining, they tend to contain caricatures rather than characters.

I'm even willing to follow a character for whom I have little sympathy and whom the author seems to regard at some distance also, but I want to be persuaded that my attention is worthwhile. I am willing to learn something about persons who might seem strange or unacceptable to me, because often in the process I find some unacknowledged aspect of myself is revealed. But this can be attained only if I am let fully enough into the thoughts and actions of characters to give me understanding. Then, even if they have been initially beyond my sympathy, when they make choices among the forces around them that are often beyond their control, I will be affected by their plight. This depiction of character ultimately reveals the author's vision to me, and I'm old-fashioned enough to believe that is essential to why I keep returning to certain authors.

But if the author has a vision, the smallest gestures will reveal it to readers. I'll gladly take mere hints of character when they are the kind that give me a glimpse into the larger workings of some human destiny. These are big words, but I don't mean epic actions. I am very fond of a story by the Welsh author Leslie Norris entitled "Blackberries." It's very brief. A boy goes to the barber shop for his first shearing, his mother buys him a new, expensive cap, he picks blackberries with his father, and when they use his cap for carrying the berries, it is ruined with berry stains. At home, his mother lashes into his father who responds angrily, the argument extends into the wider tensions in their relationship, and the boy has his first vision of how his parents' lives are unlike his, how he is utterly alone in his own grief. He is stepping out of his childhood, although nothing more has been ruined than his new cap. But I guarantee you will come close to weeping, will feel that center of loss Gerard Manley Hopkins identified so well in his poem "Spring and Fall" when he wrote, "Now no matter, child, the name: / Sorrow's springs are the same."

If you take on characters, dilemma, situation that has substance, you have to present all with enormous economy in a short story; that is the defining necessity of the form. But don't let "short" be a shibboleth. Try to live up to the material. Make your story as long or as short as it has to be to arrive at the truths of the human condition you need to reveal.

35

DIALOGUE: THE MEANING
BEYOND THE WORDS

BY TIM SANDLIN

THE FIRST NIGHT OF MY FICTIONAL FICTION CLASS, I walk to the front of the room, open the roll form conveniently provided by Central Wyoming College, and begin.

"George Singleton."

"Yo."

"Irene Bukowski."

"Present."

One by one, I call their names and they respond.

"Here."

"You got me."

"Yes."

"It is I."

One girl doesn't say anything, just raises her hand a half-inch off the desk.

"Accounted for."

"Sorry, I'm late."

And with each response, I learn something about the characters. The "Yo" guy will write comic pieces that start with the hero waking up hung over. The girl who won't speak will write a poem featuring death. The "It is I" girl won't take criticism, "You got me" is sneaky, and "Sorry, I'm late" will drop out after we read his first story.

Your snap judgments based on one or two words of dialogue may not match mine, but the point is that each member of the class gave a different response. And they stayed in character.

In real life, half the class would say "Here" and the other half raise their right hand about chin high, but this is fiction, and fiction is not real life. Don't forget that. If you write so realistically you can't stand the thought of that much diversification in a group, skip calling the roll

162

and go right to the scene where each student says a few words on "Why I'm taking this creative writing class."

Won't be any repeat answers there.

In fiction with energy, no two characters put any one thought the same. There are four primary ways to build a character—description, dialogue, and action, plus thought in your viewpoint people. To pass up the smallest opportunity to differentiate and build on your fictional people is a waste. Worse, it's stagnant. Even a story about stagnation can't be stagnant.

Several years ago in a show called "Charlie's Angels," three women with teeth and hair brought bad guys to bay with perkiness and spunk. But without dialogue. As far as the lines went, the women were interchangeable. Mostly, they took turns saying, "Come on, Charlie."

In putting words on paper, no one has enough teeth or hair to get away with this sloppiness. P. G. Wodehouse believed every sentence in a book must have entertainment value. That may or may not be true with every style of book, but it sure is true of dialogue. If the reader doesn't learn something new every time he ventures between the quotation marks, the writer has botched his or her job.

So what are these gems the reader is supposed to learn between the squiggly floating marks? Oversimplified, dialogue must do four things—show character, advance plot, give information, and set the voice, tone, and scene.

Show character. There are people in the English-speaking world of a certain cultural and educational background who actually say, "It is I." Imagine that. The secret is to nail down a character as quickly as possible. If you have her say "It is I," then follow up with a tight bun on her head and dark purple nail polish, you've pretty much done the job. Give her some matching action and send her down the road.

The idea is to supply one or two details that are so distinct, the reader can fill in all the others. A character who says, "I'm going to snatch you kids baldheaded," won't wear the same clothes or drive the same car as a character who says, "I have difficulty interfacing with children."

Even non-dialogue is dialogue. The girl who wouldn't answer but held up her hand a half-inch revealed character by not speaking. From there, you can have her go with the grain by keeping her in sweaters

163

four sizes too large and afraid to ride on an elevator unless it's empty, or you can blast against the grain—and be almost as trite—by turning her into a sex-crazed tigress when she lets down her hair.

Not speaking often says more than speaking, especially in tense climactic showdowns. It's a lot easier to write a scene where a man punches out his boss than a scene in which his anger is beyond words, and he walks away. That makes sense. By definition, "beyond words" is harder to put into words than a punch in the nose.

Here's a trick for keeping your characters in character. When I wrote a book about two 13-year-olds and their awkward struggles to overcome strange upbringings, I found my old junior high yearbook from 1963. Whenever one of my kids said something precocious, wise, or cornball, I looked at a photo of my 13-year-old classmates, and said, "Could this have come from Ronnie Craig's mouth, or Ann Humphrey's, or Annette Gilliam's?" The answer was usually "No," and the line got thrown out.

Advance action. This one should be self-explanatory. Story is how characters react to conflict, and much of the conflict between people in our modern world is caused by words. Communication—the thing that is supposed to resolve problems—actually causes more than it resolves.

We advance action by arguing, seducing, planning, slighting, gossiping, giving ultimatums—I could go find a thesaurus and stretch this into twelve column inches, but you get the idea.

Here's another place where fiction differs from real life. Most of those heart-to-hearts you have with your mother/husband/wife go in circles and dead-end. The same thoughts are constantly reported in slightly different ways, and when all this communicating is done, nothing has changed.

You don't have time for this jive in fiction. Each conversation must end with some condition different from what it was at the beginning. The relationship between the speakers has been slightly altered, or someone has grown wiser, or the speakers—at the very least, the readers—have information they didn't know before. Your viewpoint character is in more trouble or thinks he is moving closer to the solution to the conflict. Or maybe all she's done is order lunch. Ordering lunch reveals more about a character than his or her resumé.

164

A sidetrack on dialect. Anyone who tries it is braver than I am. Mark Twain pulled it off. John Kennedy Toole pulled it off. People think Eudora Welty pulls it off, but if you read her work carefully, you'll see she does it more with sentence rhythm and word choice than by dropping g's off walkin' and talkin'.

Check this out from her "My Life at the P.O.":

> I says, "Papa-Daddy, you know I wouldn't any more want you to cut off your beard than the man in the moon. It was the farthest thing from my mind. Stella-Rondo sat there and made that up while she was eating breast of chicken."

Not a misspelled word in the quote, yet after I read this story to my class, they all swore it was written in Deep Mississippi dialect.

Give information. This is the easiest one to mess up. The worst example I can think of in conveying information through dialogue happens on the soap operas.

> MAMA: "I saw Mildred Kinnicknick at the grocery store yesterday."
> DAUGHTER: "Is that the same Mildred Kinnicknick whose father was tried for murder, then he got off by claiming insanity because he'd eaten too many Twinkies and whose mother used to be married to Doc Watson, then she divorced him and married his brother Spud, only now she's back with Doc but carrying the baby of his older brother Bubba?"
> MAMA: "Yes."

Uh-uh. Dialogue doesn't work that way. To get information across, you have to be sneaky. This is part of the Show-Don't-Tell lesson you've heard 200 times. Don't say, "I see you wear glasses." Do say, "Your glasses are always dirty." This gets across that the character does wear glasses, and it also says something about his personality that they're always dirty and it says something about the speaker's personality that she notices the dirt and is brazen enough to comment on it.

This is especially true when you use dialogue to foreshadow. In mysteries by unskilled writers, there's always a line where someone says, "I notice you have a gun in your closet," or "We're spraying the rose bushes with Fetadetamiacin today, so don't stick any petals in your mouth or you'll die." Right then, I know that 200 pages from now, the gun or the Fetadetamiacin will pop up and kill somebody.

165

Foreshadowing, especially in mysteries, has to be done so when readers come to the place where the gun is used, they're totally surprised, but then they think about it and say, "Gee, that makes sense."

Anticipated surprises—they're what make endings fun. And the sneakiest way to foreshadow without getting caught is in dialogue.

Set the voice, tone and scene. Choosing the tone may be the most important decision you make when starting a story. I was once assistant editor at a literary magazine, and I read something like 200 stories in a weekend. Every one of those stories was competent—not a total loser in the batch—but what made an exceptional story rise above the others were the voice and tone.

The Holy Trinity of fiction is plot, character, and voice—Father, Son, and Holy Ghost. And, like the Holy Ghost, voice is the hardest to understand. Voice is that attitude of the writer to the story. It's the attitude of the writer toward his or her readers.

Sometimes I have my students write a two-page story, then rewrite it Erma Bombeck-style, then Edgar Allan Poe-style, then Louis L'Amour. The growth of these stories is amazing. And the easiest place to establish these styles is in the dialogue. People in Valley Girl High School speak differently from people in 1880s Bitter Creek or Transylvania. People about to be murdered on the moors speak differently from people chasing down the blue light special at K Mart. Doesn't take a Guggenheim grant to figure out that one.

Not everything to do with dialogue happens between the quote marks. The reader has to know who is talking and in what tone of voice. For this we use dialogue tags.

Dialogue tags seem to come in styles, like hats. What worked in 1932 looks slightly ridiculous now. There are no absolute rules in writing dialogue tags or anything else. If it works, you got away with it. But there are certain ways to playing it that work more often than not.

The easiest tag is none. Compare—Laurie crossed her arms on her chest. "Why do you say that?" to— "Why do you say that?" Laurie asked defensively.

If you can set the tone of the speech with a bit of action, you're better off than "Blah-blah," he said, adverb. If it isn't crystal clear who is speaking, use *he said* or *she said*. Once every couple of pages, sneak in a *he asked*. Don't, under penalty of personal castigation, use *he stated, she observed, the boy piped, George groaned,* or any other word for *said.* If you want George to groan, have him do it first.

George groaned. "I can't get up this morning."
Not—"I can't get up this morning," George groaned.

Trust me on this. You can't groan and talk at the same time.

And, if at all possible, avoid adverbs in dialogue tags. In the 1950s, riding the wave of the Hemingway revolution, adverbs were words to be avoided like the plague. I look at them as tools, and no tool should be banned forever.

However, use them with care. Hand grenades don't kill—people who throw hand grenades do kill. Pretend the adverb, when used in a dialogue tag, is a hand grenade. Don't play with it.

A word about typographical tricks. Say your character is really hacked off.

"GET OUT OF MY HOUSE." "Get out of my house!"
"Get out of my house."

Every editor in America is going to hate two of those three sentences, but I can't tell you which two, because it depends on the editor. Personally, I'd rather snort barbwire than use an exclamation point, and I can't even think of a metaphor disgusting enough to compare to dialogue in ALL CAPS, so I'm stuck with italics. Some editors can't stand italics. It's a pet peeve deal. If possible, work it into the action.

George smashed a glass on the linoleum floor.
"Get out of my house."

If that isn't strong enough for you, try one of the other three. I highly recommend against any combinations. *"GET OUT OF MY HOUSE!"*

And the worst, absolutely bottom-of-the-barrel method of expressing quoted frenzy is multiple punctuation.

"Get out of my house!!?!"
This was once Batman-style, but no more. I just looked in one of my son's *Ghost Rider* comic books, and do you think Mephisto himself screams questions!? Heck, no @#%&!

Of course, as soon as I say that, someone will mail in an example of James Joyce and the double exclamation point. Which brings us back to rule number one: There are no rules.

36

FACTS INTO FICTION

BY JOAN KING

FACTUAL INCIDENTS TURNED into fiction can make riveting reading. Yet a story is more than a series of facts. A story is people, conflict, motion, and emotion. Facts become important when the character needs them, when the reader needs them to understand the character, plot, and setting. It can be a daunting task to draw from your research the facts you'll need to create believable characters and scenes.

Stories plotted around famous battles, or figures of great historical significance, or perhaps an important scientific discovery, must yield to the facts. But facts must not overpower the story. It is the writer's job to select the best details to create the scene quickly.

When your research produces storage boxes full of index cards and photocopies gathered from long hours in the library, you may have the impulse to put it all down on your typewriter or word processor before it can slip away.

That is an impulse you should resist. Instead, shove the boxes into a closet, and sketch out the story. Keep in mind that the *story* is the main event and must remain the main event to the end. From what you know at this point—without reference to notes—ask yourself, what is the essence of this life, this story? Where are the conflicts, strengths, weaknesses, goals, motivators? Is the story clear? Are the characters three-dimensional and consistent?

Research gives you insights and authority and strengthens your story; it also keeps you from making embarrassing mistakes that will turn off editors and discourage readers. For instance, if you have a character listening to music by Beethoven at a time before Beethoven lived or composed the piece, readers will lose confidence in the story's authenticity, and even if the rest of the story is perfectly crafted, it will not be credible.

How much research is needed? Enough to get it right. If your main character is a detective, you must learn the latest advances in the field. If a character dies in an unusual way, you must get the medical facts straight. But just because you know all about substance-induced heart attacks, don't expect your reader to tolerate any more explanation than necessary to understand how and why. To avoid overloading the story with facts, stop researching when you have what you need. Some authors write the whole book first, then go back and plug in the holes. This would not work for every situation, but if all you need is authentic detail, this approach may work for you.

Research formed the basis of my biographical novels of artists. I learned everything I could about my subjects, their families, friends, their art, their social milieu, the places they lived, their politics, interests, and ambitions. I especially studied their letters for the language and attitudes of the time. I continued my research until I knew my subjects better than I knew myself, until I could carry on imaginary conversations with my characters.

My first drafts often contain too much research, making it necessary for me to go over them meticulously to delete extraneous material.

In my book about colonial artist Sarah Peale, the young Sarah had finagled her way into her uncle Charles's studio to watch heroic General Andrew Jackson pose for his portrait. The first-draft paragraph bulged with gratuitous facts:

Sarah stood still, hardly breathing, as she watched Charles ease the General toward the model's chair and greet the other men warmly. Colonel Johnson, Representatives Holmes of Massachusetts and Poindexter of Mississippi were there. Richard Johnson was in a buoyant mood, his face rosy as he arranged chairs for Representatives Holmes and Poindexter near the model's chair.

Story first, I kept in mind, as I tightened the manuscript, cutting out unnecessary facts, but retaining everything that was necessary for readers to understand the character, background, and storyline. With the dross removed, the reader has an easier time of it:

Sarah stood still, hardly breathing as she watched Charles ease the General and his party toward the model's chair. When they were settled, Sarah brought in the tea, struggling to hold the tray steady when Jackson smiled at her.

Only a small percentage of research can be used directly. But intensive background knowledge allows the writer to step surefootedly into the chosen historical or cultural setting.

Research for my biographical novels gave me the material I needed to analyze my characters and find out what motivated them.

Sometimes research turns up conflicting facts, making further study necessary and calling for the writer's best judgments. For instance, while researching for *Charles M. Russell: Cowboy and Artist,* I interviewed people who had known the western artist. One woman who had been his neighbor and friend told me, with authority and conviction, that Russell *never* drank alcohol. I accepted the fact as true *at the time she knew him,* but doubted if that had always been so. A man who had guided Russell into the mountains on hunting trips told quite a different story. "Russell never drew a sober breath," he said with conviction equal to the woman's. The real truth lay in between, and it meant more intensive investigation before I could judge what the truth was.

Some reports of incidents appear distorted or exaggerated. That was particularly true of Russell, who lived boldly and colorfully in a free-spirited frontier world, among the legendary westerners—vigilantes, outlaws, mountain men—while he became something of a myth himself.

To put the questionable stories in perspective, I visited the places Russell lived, painted, and worked in as a cowboy. In a roundup town, Utica, Montana, I ran across an unlikely item—the typewritten account of an old-timer's story:

Charles Russell shipped himself into Utica C.O.D. one time. After fall roundup, Charley had gone back with the cattle train to Chicago. . . . He spent all his money seeing the bright lights. He wanted to get back to Utica for the spring roundup and finally persuaded the railroad company to ship him out C.O.D. like a piece of freight.

It sounded like a tall tale, but not really out of character. This same story appeared in various other sources. Was it a tall tale that took on respectability by repetition? Possibly, but it was consistent with the reckless streak that typified Russell and his friends in those days. Then in Utica's frontier history museum I saw a slat from a wooden shipping box addressed to Utica, C.O.D. with Russell's name on it. It probably meant nothing, I told myself, but the C.O.D. caper could have happened as described. After much examination, I came to believe it did and included the scene, making it serve several purposes in my story:

Over and over Charley told about his friends in the Red Onion and Silver Dollar saloons who would be sure to pay the fee. He kept arguing because having to stay in Chicago, broke, stiffened his resolve. Finally, one of the agents said he would do it just to shut him up and teach him a lesson.

The crate made it to Utica with a shaken, cramped, hungry and miserable Charley. Frank Bright and his hired boy bent to heave the heavy crate into the post office's end of the general store.

"Take it easy. Your cargo's bruised and sore already."

Frank jumped and peered through the slats.

An hour later, standing with his high-heeled boot on the brass rail, Charley said, "I'm writin' down what I owe ya'all. I ain't going to forget my true friends." He grabbed a pencil and pad. "How much, Jim?"

"A few dollars, but I've been looking at that painting you left drying in the back room. I wish you'd paint me the part with the Snowy mountains and the horses."

Research can prove so stimulating, it opens the mind to plot possibilities you never before imagined. The more knowledge you bring to your fiction writing, the richer your story will be.

But all research is not equal. Studying issues, whether historical or contemporary, is fraught with pitfalls. Readers of fiction do not want lectures, lessons in art appreciation, or political or social analysis.

In *Impressionist,* my novel about Mary Cassatt, Mary and her mother went to Paris where Mary continued studying art. I included this account of their visit to the Louvre to show Mary's enthusiasm for study of the masters:

Mary took her mother's arm and led her along the corridor to find the Watteaus and Gérômes. But as they walked, Mary could not avoid stopping before a hauntingly beautiful portrait, *Girl in a Red Hat.* "Oh, look, a Vermeer. He understood how to let the light draw. I should like to copy that perfect mouth."

When I rewrote the scene, omitting the art appreciation "lecture," the reader perceived Mary's interest more subtly:

Mary led the way toward the Watteaus her mother wanted to see. Along the way, Mary tried not to pause at every turn. When they left the museum, she was amazed to walk outside into the fading sunset. "My goodness, the time! We'll be late."

Readers want to be swept into another, more exciting, or more significant life. If they happen to absorb some facts effortlessly and accurately without yawning, it's a plus, but it's not your purpose. Save issues and lessons for essays, articles, or nonfiction books, or use them sparingly.

But, what if an issue is part of a character? What if your heroine is a passionate suffragette? All the more reason to tread lightly. Readers soon tire of a character who sounds self-righteous. Nothing can sink a story faster than pontification.

Research can be an obstacle when a writer's enthusiasm for the subject takes over and allows facts to pour unchecked onto the pages, stopping the action of the story. Research enhances a story when the writer absorbs and reflects on the facts and selects only the most significant ones to weave into the story.

§ 37

BRIDGING TIME WITH MEMORIES

BY MARGARET WILLEY

[My younger sister, Cassie] told me a story about once trying to ask our mother a question about me, but not being able to remember my name. *That big girl,* Cassie had said to Mother, *that one who comes here sometimes.* And my mother couldn't figure it out because it didn't occur to her that Cassie would have forgotten her own sister's name.*

THIS BIT OF MEMORY—FROM MY SHORT STORY about a woman whose young sister brings her an unexpected Christmas gift—is part of a series of selected emotional events, past and present, which, when strung together, bring the older sister/narrator to an epiphany about her troubled life. Ordering time this way—emotionally rather than chronologically—is much like sorting through a bowl of multi-colored beads and stringing only one color. In "Cassie's Gift," the episodic beads that need to be strung together for the reader (and for Sally, the narrator) are the winter-blue beads of old and new partings—Sally's separation from her child, from her ex-husband, from Cassie, from her parents, from the landscape of her own childhood, and thus from the spirit of Christmas. With the forgotten-name incident, Sally's sister, Cassie, has found a most important bead for Sally—a memory that both explains and intensifies Sally's other losses.

I often string together memories this way when crafting a story, in order to establish an emotional truth about a character quickly. In only a few pages, "Cassie's Gift" spans three generations of emotional setbacks. Setting a story during the Christmas season speeds the process—Christmas is, in life and art, a reliable cornucopia of memories, including buried disappointments. Birthdays also have the potential for evoking memories, as do family reunions. But there are other, more ordinary occasions that a writer can use to make past and present

---

*From "Cassie's Gift" (*Good Housekeeping*)

overlap, circumstances that make memories connect with whatever is unfolding in the present.

One such circumstance—something I use often in my fiction—is an unplanned-for time of solitude. In my own life, finding myself alone unexpectedly will bring back memories, good and bad. In "Cassie's Gift," the absence of Sally's ex-husband and daughter at Christmas forces Sally to examine earlier Christmases. In my young adult novel, *The Melinda Zone* (Bantam), Melinda has been sent by her divorced parents to live with a cousin for the summer, a cousin who is too preoccupied to spend much time with her. The resulting solitude gives Melinda the time and freedom to look back, to reinterpret her two childhoods—as her mother's child and her father's—and to come to a better understanding of who she is as an individual, apart from either parent.

In these examples, I give my characters a spell of unplanned-for aloneness to ensure that memories will surface. Hence, the goal is the same for both writer and character: bead-stringing, reaching into the bowl for the particular memory beads that have brought one to a particular crisis. But for the character-in-solitude, the first bead to be strung will always be the question, *why am I here alone?*

Sometimes, conversely, it is an equally unexpected, unplanned confrontation that evokes memories. In a story I am working on now, the death of a character's mother leads to an unwanted reunion with a former childhood friend. Jean, the narrator, home for the funeral, is confronted by both her former friend and the friend's teen-age daughter. Past and present come together, memories swirl, and Jean must sort through the events of her life for one basic emotional truth: She had never forgiven her once-best friend for getting pregnant (at fifteen), for making them both grow up too suddenly.

Of course, neither situation guarantees that one story will proceed naturally and have the feel of real—not forced—memories. What is important, after all, is that the writer select the memories that *belong* in the story without making a reader feel manipulated. I try to avoid heavy-handed flashbacks in which the character actually finds him- or herself in a scene from the past, unless he or she is dealing with an understandably repressed memory, something either intensely revealing or intensely disturbing. Instead, I generally use "capsules" of narrated memories in which the character is firmly in the present, but

174

reviewing or *replaying* something from the past, examining it for information necessary to the story.

Creating a conversation that evokes memories is one of my most crucial, stylistic tools, perhaps because I believe that people can and do say things to each other in a few words that redefine years, decades, sometimes even lifetimes; such conversations are rare, but unmistakable. There are also conversations that go nowhere, that take the reader nowhere, that codify a character's separateness. Both types of conversations can send characters back to their origins. For instance, after Cassie tells Sally about the time she forgot her name, Sally remembers in a rush the many ways in her life that she has cut herself off from loved ones, thus making herself someone who could easily be forgotten. "It hurts me," she admits, both to herself and to Cassie, "that you forgot my name." Being able to share the sadness of that memory with Cassie redefines Sally and Cassie as sisters.

In *The Melinda Zone,* when Melinda asks her aunt, her mother's sister, why her mother even married her father, her aunt replies, "She was in love with him, honey." Melinda feels as though she has been waiting her whole life for this revelation. Finally, someone has given her this longed-for bead. She rearranges all her memories around it.

I often use the telephone to pull a character out of chronological time, sometimes even opening a story with a telephone conversation. We may speak in codes on the phone, but when a conversation has upset us, a load of painful memories can be stirred up, naturally surfacing at the moment of disconnection. In "Cassie's Gift," Sally first begins to remember her childhood after a brief phone call with her mother, during which her mother invites her home for Christmas. Sally quickly says no and then, after hanging up, must explain both to herself and to the reader why she didn't want to go. "I had never missed the sparse holidays of my childhood," she tells us, "both parents working night and day at their evergreen nursery, my brother Paul and I left alone." Sally is thus spun abruptly and naturally out of the present, into the past, and from the brief telephone exchange and the subsequent musings about her childhood, the reader has quickly learned a great deal about her, her past and her present situation.

There are also types of encounters that I use in my stories that create a juxtaposition of past and present for me personally—like seeing a place where I used to live, finding a photograph of an old lover, meeting

175

the children of someone from my past. If I make the same sorts of things happen to my characters, I can create a natural shift from present to past and back again. In my in-progress story about the childhood friend who became pregnant at fifteen, the narrator walks by the site of her old high school—a park now—and an unwanted memory erupts: helping this once-best friend into an empty lavatory in that long-gone school. "What was wrong with my friend," Jean wonders all over again, "my friend who was never sick?" Then, abruptly, the narrator is an adult again, walking back to her aging father's house, shaken but ready for more recollections.

And what happens when a character comes upon an old bicycle in the garage, a baseball mitt in the basement, a favorite doll in the back of a closet? These symbols of lost innocence wait in real closets and basements, but they are also found in the writer's top drawer. They are waiting to be brought to the light, to be reconnected to some present-day drama after a period of being forgotten.

In "Cassie's Gift," Cassie shows Sally her Christmas present for Sally's absent daughter—a doll that had once been Sally's. Now, thanks to Cassie, it will be passed along to Lydia, Sally's six-year-old daughter. Thus, a doll from Sally's past will help her begin the task of forgiving her parents for their long-ago emotional absence. She reconnects with the world, beginning with Cassie, her stranger/sister. It happens quickly, in only a few pages, culminating with a present-day Christmas and the hope of starting over. Memories have been isolated, events have been brought to the surface and connected in a new way, chronological time has given way to emotional time. Doing this subtly is a painstaking task—painful, too, sometimes—but the writer has to do it, to sort and string the beads, carefully and purposefully.

38

THE MISSING PIECE SYNDROME

BY RICHARD MARTIN STERN

NO PROFESSIONAL WRITER I know will challenge the need for discipline. It is the *sine qua non* of the trade, craft, business, call it what you will, of setting thoughts and ideas down on paper and selling them. A writer's place is at his desk facing his typewriter or word processor, *not* finding reasons why today he cannot write. And yet . . .

I speak here only of and for writers of fiction. Writers who deal with facts have, or should have, the facts in front of them before they sit down to write. The fortunate ones can wrestle with those facts, arrange and rearrange them, in effect play with their material as with the pieces of a jigsaw puzzle until the picture finally becomes whole and clear and ready to be presented as effectively as the writer can manage.

Fiction writers are in a somewhat different situation. We deal not with facts but with dreams and smoke and mirrors, and these *on occasion* refuse to fit together in a way that will make the illusion you are attempting to create, the illusion of reality, even inevitability in your tale, come off.

It is always possible that somewhere along the way your hand has slipped, and the picture you have presented of this character or that has thrown your entire story out of whack. Reading and rereading and frequently rereading again can usually turn up the cause of this aberration. You can then stifle the guilty character's propensity for taking center stage and shove him or her back into his proper niche in the story.

Or you may have made the mistake (all too easy to make) of putting certain scenes in the wrong sequence, thereby destroying the effect of building suspense, and what you intended to be a crashing climax fizzles like a wet match because you have told too much too soon.

It is also possible that in the delicately tangled web of your narrative you have overlooked a complete contradiction and, say, had Character

177

A behaving on the basis of knowledge he could *not yet have had*. It does happen. You might even have already killed off a character you now bring on stage to catch your reader's attention with his brilliant performance.

These, of course, are only a few of the possible flaws in your tale that have brought you to the discouraging but unavoidable conclusion that the story as written will not wash. To return to the jigsaw analogy, what I am talking about is the *missing* piece syndrome, the missing twist of plot, the character emphasis, the single, cohesive fact or feeling or force that can bring the entire story into sharp focus. In short, you do not yet have the handle, and this is when discipline, that *sine qua non* of writing, as I said, simply does no good at all.

This is one of the most discouraging of times for a writer. You *know* something is wrong, badly, basically, damnably wrong, but you don't know what it is. Reading and rereading what you've written turns up nothing but emptiness. You sit and stare at the machine and the blank page or screen. You go over and over the entire story as it first appeared in your mind—that shining, whole, flawless concept—and you realize that it does not even vaguely resemble what you have put down on paper, but you don't know why.

All of the characters are there, and the situations, the conflicts, the interplay of emotions and even the drama, carefully contrived. But the whole picture is askew, out of focus, whopperjawed, simply *not right*.

If you plow on, you tell yourself, it will all come out the way it should. If at first you don't succeed . . . But there also comes to mind the conclusion W.C. Fields put to that dictum: "Give up; stop making a fool of yourself." And sometimes W. C. Fields was right; a small voice tells you so, and *sometimes* you had better listen to that small voice, because if you do not, you are headed for nothing but disaster.

In every successful story there is something—and I will not even try to put a name to it because it is too nebulous, no more than a feeling—that binds the story into a whole, brings it alive, draws the reader into it page after page and in the end lets him put the tale down, satisfied.

Without that feeling, that binder, that whatever it may be called, there is nothing. And until you have found that essential force and have it firmly in mind, you will do well to throw discipline out of the window and wait for something within you, perhaps your unconscious, to come up with what is needed.

Only then, after balancing conscience against reality, is apparent sloth not only justified, it is mandatory.

I have recently begun the third complete revision of a new 135,000-word novel, and it has struck me with stunning force that I do not yet have the handle; in short, I do not know yet what the hell I am doing. I will now do nothing until the answer appears out of nowhere, as it will, bright and clear and good, tying everything together, bringing the story off the paper and into reality, making the entire tale *alive*.

Then, and only then, will I be able to proceed with confidence.

39

WHEN IS A STORY A SHORT STORY?

BY SUSAN R. HARPER

"THIS IS ON ITS WAY TO BEING a powerful short story," I once wrote on a manuscript—in fact, I've written something like that on any number of them, over the years. "But it isn't a short story yet," is how the second sentence goes, followed by sentences that offer thoughts on how it might become one.

The author of the piece I'm recalling right now asked to have his story read in class; he wanted it judged by a jury of his peers. I had to think about that for a minute; I never deliberately leave students open to embarrassment. But there's nothing inherently embarrassing about an early draft that falls short or isn't working—at least, there shouldn't be. Not in a workshop, anyway. That's what workshops are for. Besides, perhaps I'd been wrong: judged the story too harshly, missed its point. I've been crashingly wrong about stories at times.

I read the story out loud to the class, as I almost always do. That way the authors remain anonymous, and the criticism is directed toward the work, not the writers. I was careful to present the story as well as I could, as if I myself had written it. Then I asked for comments, first on what was working well (we usually begin with that), and then on what seemed not to work.

There was a lot to like in the story, everyone agreed: The characterizations were strong, the point of view consistent and convincing, the setting well evoked. . . . But? The comments suddenly became vague: "I didn't care for the ending."—a useless observation except that it did point to a problem area and got the group talking about it. "I wasn't ready for it to end."—a *bit* more helpful. "I don't know," said one young man. "Are we sure it *had* an ending? I felt more as if it had just quit. Like a plane that's supposed to come in for a landing, but instead just drops out of the sky."

"But did you have any idea *where* it would land?" asked another student.

"No," the first admitted.

"I didn't either. There wasn't any sense of a destination, or any suspense about whether or not the character would get there—wherever 'there' is."

"Right," someone else said. "It isn't that you don't care. The main character's too real for that; you can't be indifferent to him. But you don't know where he's headed, or what really matters to him. So when things happen to him, you don't know how you're supposed to feel about them."

Tell me a story

What's interesting to me about those comments is the way they spontaneously and almost innocently reveal what readers expect from a short story. There wasn't anything hifalutin' about the remarks—nothing technical or showoffy. People were just groping around for how they felt about that story.

Their feelings, I think, go all the way back to childhood, and beyond, to the beginnings of the human race. As we learned in high school biology, each of us repeats, in our individual lives, the whole history of our species. A lovely and intriguing thought! It assigns each generation more to absorb; it makes the "front ends" of our lives seem (in the abstract, at least) like speeded-up movies; and it offers one explanation, at least, for why things seem more frantic and more complicated with each succeeding generation.

When we sit around a long table in a seminar in San Francisco and listen to a story, we are doing something almost as old as humankind: gathering around a fire. And we are doing something we probably did when we were children. As soon as we became truly verbal, one of our requests was "Tell me a story."

What did we mean by that? I think that in a funny way I had a chance to find out as a kid. My parents came from a long line of raconteurs, and my father in particular was and is a very good storyteller. He has led an adventurous life, so he's continually adding to his repertoire, but the old stories are the ones we've heard the most and know the best. Even now, when we get together for a holiday or a reunion, we ask for these old stories by name. "Tell us 'Punk's Hack,'" we say. "No, how about 'Ham and Eggs and Gravy Legs'?" They are stories we've heard from childhood.

But I was a child of the forties and fifties, the era of the "shaggy-dog story"—a long, rambling narrative, the point of which was that it had no point. This type of story was, for some perverse reason, hilarious to my dad. So once in a while, if we asked for a story, we got a shaggy-dog story, told by him with great amusement and greeted by us with something close to mutiny. "That wasn't a *story*," we'd protest. I'm sure my father thought we were a pretty humorless bunch. But I can still remember my real disappointment, the sense of having been cheated. I wanted something with a *point,* something that started at A and went to B (or G, or Z). It was this desire, in fact, that the shaggy things exploited and mocked. So we weren't wrong in feeling that we were somehow being laughed at.

Were our desires different from most people's? Look at what the class members were implicitly looking for in the story I read aloud. They wanted an ending, certainly: an ending they were prepared for. "A destination," one of them called it—implying a journey: a shape of the whole story, as if it were a trajectory. "Suspense," one of them mentioned. Another talked about getting a sense of "what really matters," so that "when things happen to [the character], you . . . know how to feel about them."

The slice-of-life question

The key question in a short story workshop is: "What was the author's intention?" That is what we as readers must divine, if we are to do justice to the writer's work. In the last analysis, the writer may not do what we want, but has he achieved what *he* wanted?

That was the question at which our discussion arrived, and we were up in the air about answering it. "Since I couldn't tell where the author was going with this story," said the woman, "I never knew whether he or she got there."

Then a new voice joined the discussion. "I had the feeling that we were being shown something—like, say, a snapshot," he said, "and being asked to draw our own conclusions." And how had he felt about that? Was that a valid thing for a story to do?

"I guess anything is valid," he said (a true child of the seventies). "But how I felt was, well—it was as if I'd been given a test and had never found out if I'd passed. I always want to know the *author's* conclusions. Otherwise, why read an author's stuff, right?"

At that point, we turned to the author, who could hardly wait to speak. "That was the whole *idea,*" he said. "The story did just what I wanted it to do. It presented a slice of life. Period. The rest is up to the reader. It's *supposed* to make you feel frustrated; it's *supposed* to bring you face to face with life, and with the inevitability of making decisions and drawing conclusions and being alone in your judgments."

"O.K.," I said. "The author has done what he set out to do. His story affected us as he hoped it would. In that sense, he's entirely satisfied.

"The basic question now is: Has he written a short story? Does this piece have the hallmarks of what we call by that name? Or is it something else?"

"What else could it be?" someone asked.

If it's Tuesday, this must be fiction

One of the assumptions people fall into sometimes is that if a piece of writing is "creative" (as opposed to purely factual and expository) and if it's prose, it must be a short story. "What else could it be?"

The answer is that it could be a prose poem, or a novella, or a "short short story," or a vignette, or a character sketch. Each of these has particular attributes that distinguish it from the others. So-called slice-of-life stories usually turn out to be vignettes—brief incidents or scenes, or short descriptive sketches; moments, places in time, rather than trajectories—and I felt that the piece we were considering was probably a vignette. Because they're static, vignettes can't stand alone. And in that sense, they don't fulfill our expectations of the short story.

The short story, in fact, like the sonnet, can inspire (and fulfill) the most extravagant expectations. And even in its simplest, purest form, it is as rigorous, as rigidly circumscribed by "rules," and as demanding as the sonnet, though it doesn't have a prescribed number of lines or words or syllables, or a rhyme scheme with a name. But it has been interpreted—by writers, readers, and critics alike—with wide latitude. It flows between broad banks, retaining its fluidity and grace. Yet, like any chemical compound, including water, it has a specific structure that can be diagrammed, and a specific set of elements that go to make it up. These aren't arbitrary, and they aren't optional; they are what make a short story a short story rather than a vignette or a prose poem or a shaggy-dog story.

Like the child in the old television advertisement who is playing in the snow while waiting for his mother to make soup for lunch, we have certain definite expectations. "Is it soup yet?" the child calls in to his mother as she stands at the stove, stirring something in a pot. The child is expecting a hot liquid to be set before him in a cup or bowl. But if, when he sits down, his mother serves him tea—a hot liquid in a cup or bowl—he will protest, "This isn't soup!" We will expect the same response if she offers him oatmeal or chili. Soup is soup.

Call me a short story

We don't just decide that a piece of prose is a short story because we want it to be or wish it could be or don't know what else it is. We *know* whether a piece of prose is a short story by what is in it.

I'm thinking now of the injured man lying in the street, who cried out to a nearby hippie, "Call me an ambulance." Nodding, the hippie responded, "Like, man, you're an ambulance." I realize that the fact that this is one of my favorite awful old jokes shows the extent to which I am my father's daughter. But it's still true that if we dub something a short story without even thinking about it, we're as bad as the hippie. We're discouraging the author from understanding his or her work, and from confronting the standards by which it is measured. The short story is called a demanding form for good reason. And we don't write one by accident. Look at what Edgar Allan Poe wrote when he offered—more than 150 years ago—the critical definition of the short story that still stands today:

In the whole composition there should be no word written, of which the tendency, direct or indirect, is not to the one pre-established design. And by such means, with such care and skill, a picture is at length painted which leaves in the mind of him who contemplates it with a kindred art, a sense of the fullest satisfaction.

Pre-established design? At length? This is not the description of a casual process, but of a painstaking and specific (and perhaps lengthy) one. A rewarding one, too, for at its best it leads to that "sense of the fullest satisfaction" for reader and writer alike.

SPECIALIZED FICTION

⚭ 40

SCIENCE IN SCIENCE FICTION: MAKING IT WORK

BY JOAN SLONCZEWSKI

"WHERE DO YOU GET THOSE *IDEAS*?" That is the number one question I get as a writer of science fiction. The next question is, how do you make science ideas into a story? Most important, how do you extrapolate from known science to make it convincing and intriguing?

First it's important to realize that there are various kinds of science fiction today, in which science functions differently. Michael Crichton builds a thriller around technical details, even tables of data; character and "art" are less emphasized. Ursula Le Guin writes anthropological science fiction, emphasizing the social sciences and subtleties of character. A recent trend is the "future historical" novel such as Maureen McHugh's *China Mountain Zhang,* in which scientific extrapolation provides details of a vivid future setting for everyday people. My own work explores the interactions between science and society, and the human beings caught between them—even when, as in *A Door into Ocean,* we are not sure at first who is "human."

As a writer, you need to decide what role (if any) science extrapolation can play in your work. In fact, much of what is labeled "science fiction" today could as easily be labeled fantasy; and if your own style is distinctive enough, that may be the route for you. On the other hand, to take science seriously requires special attention. I can suggest some approaches that work for me.

Where to find ideas

The freshest ideas come straight from experience in an actual scientific laboratory. In my own lab and those of my colleagues, I regularly experience natural phenomena stranger than the strangest of science fiction: a superconducting magnet that suspends paper clips in the room next door; a dish of bacteria that generate thousands of mutations overnight; a flask of chemicals that "magically" turns color every few seconds. As a research scientist, and a teacher needing to range widely, I have an advantage. But any writer can telephone a research lab and even request a visit; most scientists love to talk about their work. INTERNET bulletin boards are another good source of expertise.

Next to the lab itself, the best source of ideas is research journals such as *Science* and *Nature*. These sources provide primary research reports of the latest discoveries, those of interest to a wide range of scientists. While the reading is a challenge even for a veteran scientist, most of the exciting finds reported here will never reach the popular science magazines. For example, I came across a report in *Science* of a bacterium that actually eats uranium. This fit right into the plot of my science fiction novel *Daughter of Elysium,* which required an organism to eat something no other creature would touch!

For readable reviews of emerging fields, use periodicals aimed at the scientifically literate readership such as *Scientific American* and Sigma Xi's *American Scientist.* Be wary of newspapers and the less sophisticated popular science magazines, whose accounts are likely to be superficial and contain errors.

Once you have a good idea, it's worth checking it out with experts, just as you might check out any other aspect of setting. Thus you can avoid obvious bloopers, as well as ideas considered total clichés by experts who would otherwise be sympathetic to your work. For example, physicists told me that an anti-gravity device would be written off as a cliché, but the use of a white hole as an energy source might be taken seriously.

In the end, you can take heart from the fact that "mistakes" may not be fatal, as far as popular success is concerned. Frank Herbert's bestseller *Dune* showed settlers on a desert planet distilling water from the air. This would work in an Earth desert only because Earth's atmosphere carries water from the oceans. Even if your science is "right" when the book is written, some aspects are bound to get outdated soon. *A Door into Ocean* depicted women who generate children by fusion of ova. Even before the proofs reached me, research had shown this to be impossible because paternal chromosomes carry essential modifications.

Credibility and consistency

What makes an idea "credible," then, is hard to define. Getting the facts exactly "right" and up-to-date is helpful; yet if none of your assumptions or extrapolations could be challenged, your work would not be science fiction.

Interestingly, the more common complaint I hear from inexperienced writers is that the "real science" they have carefully researched is declared false or unbelievable by readers or editors. What do we do when truth is stranger than fiction?

One way to make your ideas credible is to tie each invention to some easily verifiable event or fact on Earth. This can be done more or less subtly as a sort of in-text footnote. When Crichton shows his dinosaurs chomping through steel bars, "like hyenas," he offers a fact that I could verify. We can be sure that some hyena enthusiast out there will complain loudly if he gets it wrong! Similarly, when I created an alien organism with infrared vision in *The Wall around Eden*, I noted that known animals such as rattlesnakes possess infrared sensor organs. The focusing lens of the alien "eyes" was of sodium chloride, an infrared-focusing substance that living creatures commonly contain in their bodies.

Another source of credibility is consistency: Make sure that your facts and extrapolations, however reasonable on their own, make sense together in the story. If your imagined planet has twice the mass of earth, what is its gravity? The composition of its atmosphere? How close is it to its sun, and how long does it take to complete a year? Do the native animals on such a planet have thick, ponderous limbs, or delicate long ones? If voracious monsters descend upon your space visitors, what fauna do they normally prey upon?

The biological questions are frequently overlooked. In *Door into Ocean*, I created an entire ecosystem complete with microbial plants to photosynthesize, small phosphorescent grazers, both aerial and marine predators of a range of sizes, and scavengers, "legfish" that crawl up upon floating vegetation.

It may seem exhausting and frustrating to get all the parts to work together, but this extra craft is what distinguishes stories like *Dune* from more forgettable attempts. In my own work, I have come to rely upon a layered approach, in which I start at the beginning, write in a chapter or two until inconsistencies build up, then start all over from the beginning and try to get a couple of chapters farther. Inevitably the first chapter gets rewritten twenty times; but the reward is that my last one virtually writes itself.

A writer who develops a particularly complex worldview, or "universe," may choose to write several books within the same universe, exploring different aspects of its setting or theme. Just as Doris Lessing wrote a series of novels about Martha Quest in Africa, Ursula Le Guin wrote several books, including *Left Hand of Darkness,* within one imagined universe, where humanity's far-flung colonial worlds are linked by the "ansible" communication device. One must however take care to come up with enough fresh material to justify each new story in its own right.

Explaining your ideas

The biggest mistake is to lecture your readers, however intriguing an idea may be. The writer must blend science ideas seamlessly with all other aspects of experience that form the story. As always, "show, not tell" is the rule.

Try to let science ideas lead into character development, and vice versa. An example of this process occurred as I wrote *A Door into Ocean,* in which a population of women called Sharers inhabit a planet covered entirely by ocean. One day a researcher in my laboratory excitedly showed me a flask of purple protein he had just isolated from photosynthetic bacteria. When light shined upon the protein, it bleached clear, as it absorbed the light energy. This demonstration gave me the idea that my aquatic women characters would carry purple bacteria as symbionts in their skin, providing extra oxygen underwater. When their oxygen ran low, the Sharers' skin would bleach white dramatically. This ability to "bleach white" later developed a spiritual significance as well; the Sharers can enter a special kind of trance, called "whitetrance," which enables them to endure extreme physical stress while upholding their religious beliefs.

Another example from *A Door into Ocean* works in the opposite direction, of character development leading to science: The Sharers use Gandhian pacifist resistance to repel an armed invasion of their planet. I sought a metaphor from science to help describe the unexpected success of their resistance, which from the invaders' limited perspective seemed doomed to fail. The metaphor had to fit into the

190

perspective of the Sharers, who have advanced biological technology. I hit upon the idea of "electron tunneling," a phenomenon in which electrons can penetrate a seemingly impenetrable energy barrier. Electron tunneling occurs in the hemoglobin molecule as it collects oxygen in the blood, so the Sharers would know about it.

Some explanation is always necessary; the trick is, how much. It helps to weave necessary explication into dialogue, a sentence at a time, at a point where events demand it. For example, in *Daughter of Elysium,* a visiting scientist (new to the planet) discovers that his discarded culture dishes have come alive and are trying to gobble up his two-year-old son. A student comes to the rescue and explains that the "intelligent" culture-dish material (composed of billions of microscopic robots) has malfunctioned; it is designed to enclose tissue cultures, not children.

This example, by the way, also illustrates the time-honored gimmick for explaining any new setting: the naive "visitor," who needs everything explained. It works, if you don't make the lecture too obvious and do keep the plot moving. Michael Crichton's *Jurassic Park* essentially consists of a long lecture on cloning dinosaurs, kept moving by a fast-paced, and blood-thirsty, series of events.

One approach to the problem of explanation is to include all that the story seems to need in the first draft, even though you know it's too much for the reader to take. In later drafts, cut it drastically. Omit terms known only to experts, or redefine in simple language. (*Oogenesis* is "making eggs.") A typical science course introduces more new words than a first year of language. So try to use scientific terminology as you would use words from a foreign language—sparingly, for effect.

An occasional phrase of jargon may be worth keeping if it takes on a life of its own in the story. In *Daughter of Elysium,* I did keep one phrase of fetal development about the "primordial germ cells" which undergo a lengthy migration to reach the developing gonads before the fetus is born. The phrase set up a distinctive metaphor for the life journey of my central characters. But countless similar phrases were cut or redefined before my final draft.

How science and technology can advance plot

Complex technical information is best fed to the reader a little at a time and in such a way that it feels "inevitable" where it comes up.

This task is a challenge, but if done skillfully the development of ideas can advance your plot, heightening dramatic tension, much more so than if you had revealed all the implications at the start.

Daughter of Elysium depicts research connecting fetal development and aging, a field of daunting complexity. My opening chapter shows how the fetal heart tube forms and begins to pulse; later chapters depict more subtle processes of cells and tissues, and much later, the critical molecular events that determine whether the embryo will live or die—or live without aging. In between, various subplots incidental to research take up the scientist's time, much as they would in real life. Often the subplots make an ironic contrast to his work; for instance, when he faces his dying relatives back home, who will never benefit from his research on aging.

Another role for science in your plot can be to show how various characters react to change, and are themselves changed (or not). In *A Door into Ocean,* the invaders of the ocean world respond to the Sharers' life science in diverse ways. Some simply try to destroy it, and none of the bizarre setbacks they face changes their outlook. Others become intrigued by the new science, with its implications for their own medicine and agriculture. A few even take up the symbiotic purple microbes into their own skin.

The points I've made about finding ideas and using them have served me well in my own novels, and have worked for other writers too. At the same time, it is important not to get lost in the science. Remember that what makes a science fiction novel "work" in the long run is what makes any good novel work: connection, consistency, and characters that make us care.

🌮 41

WHEN YOUR SLEUTH WEARS A BADGE

BY MARGARET MARON

WHEN I BEGAN MY FIRST MYSTERY novel about Sigrid Harald, a self-conscious, awkward young woman who would be competent in her professional life but inept in dealing with her emotions, I simply intended to create a continuing character who could sustain my interest over a series of books and who had plenty of room for personal growth. My main worry was that I might not find enough plausible ways to involve her in one murder after another if she were a complete amateur; so, à la Willie Sutton when asked why he robbed banks ("Because that's where the money is!"), I naïvely made her a homicide detective because that's where the bodies were!

In short, Lieutenant Sigrid Harald of the New York Police Department was to be a traditional sleuth who just happened to wear a badge. New York's routine violence could provide more than enough background cases; I planned to concoct classic puzzles to occupy the foreground.

In the U.S., where each aspect of the mystery genre must fit into a neatly labeled category, using a police character automatically—and often mistakenly—tags that book a "police procedural." For me, the term "procedural" conjures up a novel fascinated with hardware, official hierarchies, and all the mechanical details of a technical investigation. More hardboiled in tone than traditional murder mysteries, the police procedural tends to emphasize the gritty *noir* side of city life. The victim is usually a random choice, devoid of personality, and merely serves as an excuse for readers to watch members of a homicide squad interact with each other as they investigate the crime. Of relatively little importance in these American procedurals are the killer's character and motivation.

Although true procedurals can be interesting to read, I didn't want to write them. Much closer to my own taste was what the British call "the police whodunit"—classically plotted puzzle mysteries with strong emphasis on character development, mood and setting. Ngaio Marsh, P.D. James, and Colin Dexter in England, Tony Hillerman and Susan Dunlap in America are good examples of this aspect of the genre.

In a *procedural*, the main emphasis is on *how* and *who*, not *why*, and we know that the killer will be unmasked as soon as enough witnesses have been interviewed and enough man-hours have been logged. The reader is merely a spectator.

In the police *whodunit*, the best writers "play fair," thus letting the reader become a participant who, if all the red herrings are eliminated, may actually solve the crime one step ahead of the police sleuth. Investigative processes are kept subordinate to the lives of the main characters.

When I began, I probably knew more about New Scotland Yard than about the New York City Police Department; and *One Coffee With*, my first Sigrid Harald novel, reflects my disinterest in technicalities: Details are focused and specific in the college scenes (a place familiar to me), vague and generalized in the scenes set in her office. *Death of a Butterfly* was much the same, but I had begun doing some research, and by the third book, the results were increasingly creeping onto my pages even though I still regarded actual police work as the least interesting part of Sigrid's life.

When I described the boredom of a routine stakeout or let an officer gripe about how long it takes the FBI to run a fingerprint, it was merely to add verisimilitude to the background. For me, the important thing was to show how Sigrid Harald was changing and growing as a person. Everything else was window dressing. Yet, as a professional, I tried to make my window dressing as accurate as possible.

I visited the bookstore at John Jay College of Criminal Justice and came home with used textbooks on gunshot wounds, arson investigations, and methods of police patrol. (My current forensics bible is *Practical Homicide Investigation: Tactics, Procedures, and Forensic Techniques.**) I borrowed books from the public library and browsed in the true crime section of used bookstores. Eventually, I even en-

---

**Practical Homicide Investigation* is part of a series edited by Vernon J. Geberth and published by CRC Press, 2000 Corporate Blvd. N.W., Boca Raton, FL 33431.

rolled in various criminalistics courses at my local community college. These teach the practical nuts and bolts of technical investigation and are usually geared toward police officers who want to move up in the ranks. Just listening to their slang, their turns of phrases, and their "war stories" provided reams of colorful details.

Through the years, I've found it relatively easy to get my facts straight when dealing with the investigation of the murder itself. Most medico/legal professionals will talk to you about postmortem cooling, lethal doses, blood-splatter patterns, etc., once you've explained clearly and concisely why you want to know. To find local experts, I usually start with the secretary of a specific department in a nearby college or teaching hospital. I describe the information I need and ask to be connected with a user-friendly professor or doctor. If the first one I get sounds harried, I apologize and ask if I can call later or if he could recommend someone else. Then when I call that "someone else," I can say, "Dr. X suggested that you might explain to me. . ."

If no one local can answer my questions, I've discovered that almost anyone in the country will answer a courteous letter, especially if I make it seem irresistibly easy. I decide beforehand what facts I absolutely must have and keep my questions as specific as possible. Triple-spacing between questions encourages the expert to answer directly on my letter so that all she has to do is jot down the facts and slip the sheet of paper into the self-addressed, stamped envelope which, of course, I have enclosed.

By contrast, getting the housekeeping details of precinct stations has been my biggest headache. Who reports to whom, what forms are used in which situations, who hands out the paychecks, to whom do the officers or detectives call in sick? These are the day-to-day background details that make a novel ring true and are much too easy to get wrong.

Networking outward from those early criminalistics classes, I met and talked with real-life police detectives and civil service clerks from many different commands. Over the years, they've given me updated organizational flow charts and guided me through their bureaucracy's constantly changing red tape.

Whenever I visit a detective's office, I take note of the sights and smells along a corridor, the stacks of papers piled on overflowing file cabinets, the mix of plainclothes and uniforms. "Who makes the coffee?" I ask. "How often do you use the pistol range in the basement? How do you requisition ballpoint pens and legal pads?"

In *Past Imperfect,* my seventh book about Sigrid Harald and the people in her life, Sigrid's personal complications were still very much in the foreground, yet the mystery itself—the murder of a colleague— required so many scenes that could take place only inside her station house that I kept getting hung up on minutiae I really didn't want to know—or use.

Less procedure and more whodunit, I reminded myself grimly. As I slogged through the final pages of in-house politics and bureaucratic trivia, I promised Sigrid, "Just get us to the end of this book, and you'll never have to see the inside of a police station again except to pick up your paycheck."

"I've already requested automatic deposit," she told me.

42

TIME, TRUTH, AND THE READER

BY JANE AIKEN HODGE

TRUTH AND TIME are twin problems for the historical novelist. Are you going to stick religiously to the historical facts of your background, and how are you going to make sure that your characters' fictional time, the events of their lives, mesh with the historical frame in which you have set them? I think there is some room for compromise in both cases, less over truth than over time. And you can save yourself a great deal of trouble by thinking hard about both problems in the early stages of planning your historical novel.

Of course, the basic facts of history are sacred. If you make the Confederate instead of the Union Army win the Battle of Gettysburg, you will lose your reader's confidence, and that is fatal. Nor can you alter dates. I think it is useful, in this context, to imagine yourself always being read by an expert in the field. Please them, and you will convince everyone, including yourself. There is no mistaking the absolute ring of truth in a solidly researched novel.

When it comes to using real people, probably as background to your story, there has to be a bit more latitude, but again you want to avoid making them do or say anything totally out of character. The best thing is to get to know them well before you start. And the more famous they are, the more careful you will need to be. If you introduce, say, the Duke of Wellington, or Abraham Lincoln, you will need to mind how you go. If Abraham Lincoln were to light a cigarette and say, "That's OK," then, I, the reader, would lose confidence in you as author and stop reading your book. Georgette Heyer, a past mistress of historical accuracy, used to weave quotations from, for instance, the Duke of Wellington's letters into her text, and they give a splendid ring of truth. Or you can use bits of actual recorded conversation, which will both give conviction and help you to tune your ear to the way your character talked, so as to get it right yourself.

I had a little trouble with someone called Lord William Bentinck in my novel *Escapade*. I decided to take a pair of heroines to Sicily in 1811, because they needed to get out of England, and with Napoleon in control of the rest of Europe, that was the only place they could go. So I looked into Sicily and found a most interesting situation. The Queen, Maria Carolina, was at daggersdrawn with this Lord William, who was sent out to take over as British Minister that summer. So I sent my heroines out on the same boat on which he sailed, and began by cheerfully providing him with a wife and children through whom they could all make friends.

Luckily for me, I went back to the library at this point and discovered a whole lot more information about Lord William. He was a most interesting, difficult character, with an evangelical wife and no children. I had outrun my research and had to go back, unravel the whole chapter, and knit it up again. It came out much better, as difficult bits often do, because I now knew enough about Lord William to make sense of him. I had met the queen before in a previous book, *Shadow of a Lady,* so I knew something about her; she was a passionately indiscreet letter writer, which helped. In fact, I got very fond of her, and there was a dangerous moment when she showed signs of taking over the book. I longed to drag it out to tell the sad end of her story, when Lord William won and drove her into exile, but this would have meant trouble with time. I would have had to keep my heroines in suspended animation for a couple of years, and it was not that kind of story. I sadly consigned the Queen's later adventures to a postscript, for anyone who had gotten fond of her, too.

The problems of truth and time are often linked like that. It is hard to tell, when planning the book originally, just how long things are going to take to happen. I often find that events move faster than I expect, so that the fictional climax turns up before I have come to the historical moment for which it was planned. That is trouble. In my book, *Windover,* I had meant to end with the infamous treason trials of May, 1794, but things speeded up, and the book was ready to end in the autumn of 1793. I went back to my source books and was luckier than I deserved. I found that a similar set of panic arrests and trials happened in Scotland in autumn, 1793. Word of them, reaching London, served to precipitate my crisis. Happy discoveries of that kind are some of the extra pleasures of the historical novel, but should not be counted on. The more you know in advance about the period on which you are working, the happier you will be, and the better your results.

There is a truth of language and detail, the small print of history, as well as of fact, and, in my view, it is equally important. It is the small details that give the feel of the period. The main reason I write historical novels, aside from the pure pleasure of it, is that I pine for a world with a moral structure, as against the moral and aesthetic chaos we suffer today. I write (and read) historical novels to recreate a world of rules and standards of behavior. My heroines conduct their lives by rules quite different from those (if any) that obtain today, and it is vital to keep the reader conscious of this. You need at the same time to keep readers aware that this is a different world, with different rules, and keep them gripped by the story.

Here, too, it seems to me to be a question of intelligent compromise. I have never set a book earlier than the time of the American Revolution because I feel that the language from then on is near enough to modern English so that such compromise is possible. There is no need for *pish* or *tush,* for *zounds* or *gadzooks.* One can remind the reader, perhaps with an Austen usage here and there, or a glancing reference to a *pelisse,* a *fichu* or a *fan,* that these are people who do not speak or think quite as we do today. Too much of it, and you risk losing the reader. I am very cautious with dialect and cockney, since I find, for instance, Walter Scott's Scotch novels unreadable, and have the same blank about anything heavily Irish. No use writing what one would not read oneself.

It is a kind of balancing act. You must keep your reader aware that your heroine is living by different standards, but be careful not to make her seem alien, or, worse still, priggish. You could call this the Fanny Price problem. Many modern readers of *Mansfield Park* identify with the naughty Crawfords instead of with good little Fanny. Jane Austen was writing with a different set of rules, and it is amusing to remember that contemporary critics tended to fault her books for not having a high enough moral tone. But then, she was daughter and sister of clergymen; religion was part of the air she breathed. It is part of the miracle she was that *Mansfield Park* is the only one of her books in which this does prove a possible barrier between her work and our more free-thinking age. I am surprised that no modern publisher has reissued her rogue book, *Lady Susan,* the story of a splendidly spirited and amoral adventuress, told largely in her own letters.

In my last two books, my heroines have been in revolt against the excesses of strait-laced puritanism, but I look on this as dangerous ground, to be gone over as lightly as possible. Religion is an explosive subject, to be handled with care. I have rather the same reservations about costume. It always comes as a shock to me when I get the jacket design for a new book, and there is my beloved heroine in poke bonnet and clinging muslin. This is not the way I think of her. Of course, that's what was worn then, but it was contemporary dress to them; they were not aware of it (unless they were fashion mad) and nor do I want my reader to be. We should think of them just as young women. It is one of the few points on which I differ from Georgette Heyer. I am bored by those long, detailed descriptions of every color and every frill, laboriously gleaned from *La Belle Assemblée* or *The Mirror of Fashion.* This seems to me an ostentation of research that risks alienating the reader.

Which is the one thing one must never do. In these days of fast everything, it is amazing to turn to a novel by Walter Scott and see the leisurely winding chapters with which he sets his scene. No time for that today. They had time in the nineteenth century. We do not. Or think we do not. You have to catch your readers quickly and never let them go. It is amusing to see how many novels open with a dramatic scene, culled from almost anywhere in the story, then fill in the background at leisure, bouncing around in time, maybe using several narrators to do so. I prefer to begin at the beginning, and keep the story simple, but then, what is the beginning? This is never so obvious as it might seem and it is vitally important. Get it right, and you are well away. A beloved Doubleday editor made me cut several first chapters of *Here Comes a Candle,* in which I had carefully built up to what is now the dramatic opening scene. It was painful at the time, but looking at it now, I see how right she was. And the work on the early chapters was not wasted. I had found my way into my characters and their situation. One should never underestimate the value of a good editor. More precious than rubies, they are.

Here Comes a Candle illustrated another interesting problem of the historical novel. My hero had an autistic daughter, but of course the word had not been invented, nor the condition recognized. This is true of all kinds of medical terms and conditions; the whole of post-Freudian psychological jargon is out of the question, and what a blessing that is. The subconscious did not exist, nor the Oedipus complex, nor a lot of other things one can manage very nicely without. I have an anorexic heroine in my new book. I hope readers will recognize the condition, but they will most certainly not find the word.

Plants are something else that must be handled with care. Your hero or heroine looks out at the garden, and what does he/she see? I thought of decorating my Sicilian gardens with bougainvillaea and cautiously looked it up in my favorite book of reference, the 1911 edition of the *Encyclopaedia Britannica*. And what a fascinating story I found. It was introduced from South America by Captain de Bougainville, who tried to colonize the Falklands for France, survived the French Revolution, was decorated by Napoleon, and died at 82 in the year of my book, 1811. Fascinating story; maybe I'll use it some day, but no bougainvillaea in the Sicilian gardens. It seems unlikely that it would have been anything like established by 1811.

I have not dealt at all with the kind of historical novel that uses real people for its central figures, because this is a game with totally different rules, and a very dangerous one at that, particularly when the characters are from the recent past. Splendid to recreate Alexander the Great for us, but to write books, for instance, vilifying Charles de Gaulle, and altering history to do so seems to me to be breaking a basic rule of the game.

Another of the games one plays with one's readers is trying to get enough basic information about time and place across without boring them into stopping reading. Dialogue is a great help here, as Alice so famously pointed out. Characters can discuss the events of the day, at the same time establishing themselves in the reader's mind and filling in their historical context. Much better that they should tell each other things than that you should prose on about them direct. After all, the writing of fiction is a kind of conversation, only the other party keeps silent. It is not much use going on with your story if your audience has crept away, one by one, from around the campfire. First you must catch them, then you must hold them. I think there is a great need, these days, for good old-fashioned storytelling. The straight novel has gone so far upmarket as to be almost invisible; the thriller has gone savage, and the mystery has gone glum. If you want to tell a plain romantic tale you must put it in disguise. Fantasy builds worlds of its own with its own rules; the historical novel recreates the rules of the past. It means that for both of them that delightful old-fashioned thing, the happy ending, is still a practical possibility.

43

IMAGINATION AND THE PAST

BY ROSALIND LAKER

NOTHING RINGS LESS TRUE in a historical story than the excessive use of outdated phrases and exclamations. All too often these cause amusement where none was intended. Atmosphere from the past can be conjured up in many other ways, and speech should be normal, provided care is taken to avoid words not in use at the time, such as "sadist" before the Marquis de Sade became notorious, or other more modern idioms. Readers have to be transported effortlessly from everyday life into another era, the present fading naturally into the past as the pages are turned. Colors, aromas, sights and sounds of the time have to be woven unobtrusively into the fabric of the plot, enabling the characters to move easily through their own world, taking the readers with them.

For this to be achieved, preparation is all-important. Although I always visit the place and the country in which I am setting a story, not all writers are able to do this, but there are no boundaries to imagination or to research. Before I write the first line of a new book, I will have studied the background to it, which means I will know how and where people lived, what they ate and drank, and whether historical events of the time will reach out to help or hinder my characters in the fulfillment of their plans and ambitions. People have not changed in their emotions throughout the centuries, but each generation has been governed by the customs and traditions of the period into which they were born. It is through taking account of these aspects that backgrounds can be firmly established and reality achieved.

Whether a writer has chosen to set a story in 18th-century St. Petersburg or 19th-century Paris, the chance to view such places is always there, either in great art galleries or in the art books that are to be found in every library. Here are pictures of landscapes and interiors and gardens as well as towns and villages painted by artists during their lifetimes. Not only do these evoke a period in accurate detail, even to the clothes worn and the tasks and pastimes, but they also convey the sounds that would have been commonplace at that time. One only has to look and listen imaginatively. Bells would be chiming in the church steeples, the wheels of a cart would rattle, and the clop of hooves be muffled by the thick mud of the lane. There would be a hiss of air from the turning sails of a windmill, and surely the sway of corn indicates a breeze rustling the stalks. There would be a stench in an ancient street, but the undaunted peddlers would be crying their wares while the carriers of sedan chairs shout for a way through the teeming, noisy crowd. The past is always within reach. A moment that stands out in my memory was when I was leaving Delft after researching the life of the 17th-century Dutch artist, Jan Vermeer, who had lived there. I looked back and literally caught my breath as I saw that the town's skyline had not changed since Vermeer had painted it in his famous landscape three centuries before.

It was for my novel, *The Golden Tulip,* that a study of Dutch paintings showed me that every household in 17th-century Holland had one or more box-like foot-warmers filled with hot coals. This in itself gave the information that those spotless chequered floors were cold in winter and that there were plenty of draughts. No wonder so many of the women's indoor jackets were fur-trimmed! The lovely flower paintings showed which blossoms had grown in abundance while the still lifes, with groupings of feathered game, fruit, bread, vegetables and decanters of wine, revealed what would be served at mealtimes.

To me the clothes of a past century help to summon up atmosphere in sensuous velvet, gleaming cloth of gold and tumbling satins. In *Gone With the Wind,* Rhett comments on the give-away rustle of his gift of a red silk petticoat that Mammy is wearing. What a seductive sound it must have been generally when a beautiful woman swept into a room, every frill aflutter like the wings of a bird. Actresses sometimes speak of the effect it has on them to wear the sumptuous though restrictive garments of another age, for immediately the clothes control their walking and their actions, a fact to remember when female characters are clad in attire of the past. Men's clothes have always given them freedom of movement through the necessity of allowing them to draw a sword quickly or to use their fists. Until the early 19th century, men were the peacocks, their clothes giving color to any scene, and I like to make use of this richness.

In my novel *Circle of Pearls,* I drew the contrast between the grim and sober regime of Cromwell with the colorful extravagance that followed the restoration of Charles II, a period afflicted by the Great Plague and the Great Fire of London. All these events affected the lives of everyone in the country, the repercussions rippling out. Inevitably these changed the course of my heroine's life and that of the man who loved her. A tumultuous background had formed from which there was no escape.

My book, *The Venetian Mask* was researched several years before I put anything down on paper. Venice had always fascinated me, and I knew that one day I would set an 18th-century story there, but before I was ready to visit the Serene City of the Sea, I studied everything I could about it. It is this kind of research that inspires twists and turns to a plot, for when I discovered that the eldest son of noble Venetian families did not automatically inherit, the father choosing the son he considered to be most suited, there sprang to my mind the jealousy and rivalry that must have torn those siblings apart. Added to this, only the heir was permitted by law to marry, so that the wealth and power of the head of the family would not be diminished. It left Venice full of restless young noblemen, which added to the strife and led to vendettas and duels, all grist for the mill of my plot.

When eventually I stepped ashore in Venice, my imagination had gone before me, and I saw at last all I had visualized of the city. The green water of the canals lapped against steps that had been ancient in the 18th century, the prows of the black gondolas cut through the early morning mists, the iron-studded doorways hinted at old dark secrets within, and the Doge's marble palace shone shell-pink in the sunsets. Such sights offered a surfeit of atmosphere, and it would have been easy to lose the force and suspense of the plot in such an excess of beauty and mystery, but the background must never swamp the action, nor must the aura of a place interfere with the progress of the story. In any case, lumps of description make tedious reading in what would otherwise be a fast-moving situation. It was far better for those wet steps to dampen a hem or allow a foot to be swamped. I described a gondola ride in a mist to aid a character's concealment. One of those sinister doors opened onto the development of the plot, and the vista of the glorious palace made an impression on the heroine for a special reason.

It has to be the same when handling great national events and disasters. Although at first it may appear that the characters are only flotsam on the tide, their resilience or their weaknesses will settle their own fates for better or worse. In *This Shining Land,* it was the heroine's courage that made her refuse to break under Nazi rule and brought her through. As for the villain in *The Golden Tulip,* it was his own greed for political status that caused him to be in the wrong place when the Dutch opened their dikes to let in the sea as a defense against attack.

I find old maps invaluable in research. In my imagination, I follow old paths and streets and lanes. Many history books publish maps of cities in past centuries, which enable writers to set locations accurately, but then it is my own golden rule that the past should be portrayed as it was. Nothing has changed in Venice for hundreds of years, but as my plot wandered through its squares and narrow ways, I used a map of the city to locate exactly the places featured in my story, from the historic orphanage renowned for its girls' choirs, where my heroine grows up, to the fictional site of her mask-making shop in a street where I found ruined premises that looked old as time. My camera also captured views and places for later reference.

As a footnote to my Venetian research I made a return visit to see the annual Carnival, which has always been a part of Venice and a feature in *The Venetian Mask.* These days the Carnival takes place in the last two weeks before Lent, and I arrived in deep snow in February during the Gulf War to learn that the Carnival had been canceled for fear of terrorism. Instead of hosting thousands of visitors in costume, Venice was virtually deserted, not a tourist to be seen.

So I thought myself alone in St. Mark's Square one snowy afternoon when there came a sudden development. Under one of the colonnaded arcades, previously deserted, there appeared an 18th-century gentleman in rose silk, white wig, a black eye-mask and a high-sided black tricorn hat sauntering along with an elegant, beribboned cane. Then from all directions others came in 18th-century costume, all masked, and they criss-crossed the square, the men bowing and the women curtseying when they met. These were the Venetians themselves, determined to maintain the spirit of Carnival and their ancient city in the face of difficult times.

To me, it was as if the pages of history had opened to present me with a scene from my own manuscript. Research can bring unexpected rewards in the most unusual ways.

§44

EXPLORING YOUR SCIENCE FICTION WORLD

BY SUE PACE

IN MY NOVEL, *The Last Oasis,* two teenage protagonists, Phoenix and Madonna, escape from the Mall (the last remaining semi-civilized city) and make a desperate run for freedom, heading for the hydroponics labs in Idaho. Four hundred miles, a couple of rivers, a half dozen unsavory characters, a proud tribe trying to save their home from environmental disaster, a nuclear waste dump, and a mountain range later, they make it.

That's an adventure story. The characters want something (in this case, a better life), and the whole world is dead set against their getting it.

When I began writing this young-adult adventure novel, I didn't think of it as science fiction; it's set in the twenty-first century. I had spent several weeks "on tour" in the future. I was familiar with the landscape, so familiar, in fact, that I sometimes forgot I was only a visitor poking through an imaginary country. And as an aspiring writer of science fiction, you must be that familiar with the world in which *your* story takes place.

Look at it this way: If you were going to trek through Europe or Africa or Asia for the next year, you wouldn't just throw a few odds and ends into your overnight case and take off, would you? Of course not! You would prepare. You would research. You would talk to others, possibly experts. You would decide where to go, what to see, and the best way to get there. You would worry about money exchange rates and where the bathrooms were.

That is what I did in plotting and pacing *The Last Oasis.* And I did much of it *before* deciding whom to take on the trip with me. Let me be your guide as you prepare to investigate.

Make a map

Take a large piece of blank paper and a pencil with an eraser and make a rough map indicating north, south, east, and west. Then lightly trace where you are at the beginning of your trip and draw a big X in the farthermost corner to show where you hope to be at the end of your journey—*and* your novel. Now put everything you can think of in between those two marks. Water hazards. Cities of Mutants. Nuclear waste dumps. Hostile populations. Ice-covered mountains. Whatever.

This may seem silly, but it works. Later on, when you and your protagonist(s) get stuck, you stare at the map and think, "Aha! She could go upriver on a fertilizer barge!" Or you could think, "Oh, no! He can't go that far west, or he'll never make it back to the ship before nightfall."

The map forces you, the author, to visualize the world you are creating. Is everything going to happen inside a space capsule? Then you should know *everything* about that capsule, even the wiring. Is everything going to happen in a time warp circling the planet Z-17 several million light years from here? Then you need to make a map so you don't catch yourself coming when you should be going.

Since my novel is set a few score years in the future, I pored over current geography maps and extrapolated rising water levels. I assumed melting polar ice caps and the return of dust bowls in what used to be the great grain belts. I spent hours in the library going through encyclopedias and articles in science magazines. But it paid off. My editors found the simple map I enclosed with *The Last Oasis* so helpful that they printed it in the front of the book.

See the sights

When I go on a trip, I make a list of the places I positively must visit. The Grand Canyon. The Louvre. The Taj Mahal. In *The Last Oasis,* I didn't want to miss New Hanford, the Snake-Shoshone Tribe, the balloon ride over the mountains, or the kayak ride through Hell's Canyon. As it turned out, I couldn't fit everything in and had to drop the Hell's Canyon run, but my two protagonists did come within spitting distance of it.

Decide what you absolutely must have in your science fiction world, and mark those spots on your map in ink. You will find that these very real, very physical places now begin to form a kind of time line for your adventure story. If you start in Portland, Oregon—as my characters did—and end up in Idaho, you have to slog through about four hundred miles. And, depending on the weather and the mode of transportation, that can fill up one day or five.

This will also get you to thinking about time. Not simply twenty-four-hours-in-a-day time, but also what-season-of-the-year-is-best-for-traveling time. A river that is fordable in March may not be in April, and you can't simply say, "Ah well, this is science fiction, and I'll just skip the spring thaw. In fact, I'll skip spring altogether." If there isn't a spring, then how does the food chain work? And what will your protagonist(s) have for dinner? You can see how these seemingly small details can add up.

Special people

Sometimes we visit relatives on a trip, or we look up old college friends. Or we attempt to meet people we wouldn't ordinarily be able to see—royalty or religious leaders or rock stars. In your science fiction novel, you need to know who has the wealth and who has the power. You need to know, with real titles and names, who runs the show.

This will get you thinking about monarchs and presidents and revolutionaries, about religion, prison, tariffs, and taxes. You will also be forced to think about slaves and servants and siblings. Names are helpful. Titles and gender are essential.

Write down the type of government your newly created world has. Then write down the type that came *before*. It is amazing what you will learn from just this simple act.

How long will you be gone?

If you spend twelve hours in Calcutta your trip will be significantly different from one that allows you two months there. And a story that spans two generations is far different from one in which everything happens in twenty-four hours. If you are writing for young adults, cram as much as possible into the smallest amount of time allowable. You can let the reader know far more about your characters by *showing* how they react in a tight spot than by telling how they spend their time mulling over the lunch menu. Unless, of course, the menu features fresh monkey brains and leg of man, and even those gimmicks will hold the serious reader only so long. Your young-adult science fiction readers want more than gimmicks; they want action. This means your characters will have to tour your world at breakneck speed. There won't be time for side trips or for hanging around at the beach waiting for the tide to change or for sleeping, either. There should be, however, a lot of dialogue about life-and-death issues, and there will also be a number of disagreeable people. (What can you expect with all that sleep deprivation?) This also means that a chapter usually ends before a scene does.

At the end of chapter four in *The Last Oasis,* Phoenix looks at Madonna and whispers, "I have an idea. Come with me." Chapter five is the answer to the question now in the reader's mind: What was Phoenix's idea? Again, at the very end of chapter twenty-eight, Phoenix and Madonna leap aboard a balloon heading east. They descend, feet dangling, smack dab into the middle of chapter twenty-nine. That's what creates enough suspense to keep the reader turning those pages.

The dry run

When I go on a trip, I try to take what I need. No more. No less. That means I have to look carefully at my itinerary; my points of interest, and the people I want to meet; my mode of transportation and my time frame. Then the questions begin. Can some be combined? Can some be eliminated? Those are the questions *you* must ask yourself.

How do people get around in your invented world? Do they walk everywhere, or do they sometimes take the bus? And what do they use for fuel? For food? For entertainment? For money? What if it rains? What if it doesn't? Remember, it is not enough to ask those questions. You must also attempt to answer them. This is the way a world is built, one question and one answer at a time. No shortcuts. No saying, "It really doesn't matter," because it does. If you are sloppy about your work, you will jar readers out of the fictional life you have created. They may put your book down and go for a walk, watch the Super Bowl, or have a dish of ice cream—and not come back!

The rules of the road

What kind of people will put up with the world you've created? Is there a kind of "good will among thieves" mentality, or is this a "me-first" universe? I like to write about regular people put in horrible, dire circumstances. I write about kids faced with the collapse of the world. You'd be amazed at how resourceful and just plain scrappy your babysitter could be if she had to. You'd be delighted at the depth of courage and inventiveness in the teenager who mows your lawn.

So, I go through the newspapers and weekly magazines and cut out human-interest stories from India, Liberia, Palestine, Los Angeles. As I read these stories, I ponder the miracles people can accomplish in the harshest of environments. "India debates rising traffic in human kidneys." "Armed children operate Liberian rebel roadblocks." "No school for an 11-year-old soldier." Those headlines are taped to the wall above my word processor, not to confirm what a terrible place the world has become, but to remind me of the conflicts young people face and of the effort many have to make just living each day, and to help me remember the teenage heroes.

Now you know the territory. You've poked around this new world long enough to be familiar with it. You can order dinner without checking your book of foreign phrases; you know where to spend the night, whom to avoid, and I hope, whom to invite.

Who's going?

The Last Oasis is a story about a boy and a girl. The boy, Phoenix, is a dreamer and an observer of life. He feels sorry for people and tries to figure out how things got so bad in the first place. He is a peacemaker. His sidekick, Madonna, is quick, tough, and streetwise. She is the one who acts. She doesn't back down in a fight, and she knows how to get along in a me-first world.

Phoenix is more like me. Madonna is more like my brother. I decided that if I were going on a dangerous trip, I'd better have someone like my brother along or I'd starve, and he'd better have someone like me to keep him out of jail. When I thought of the qualities my brother and I bring to the world, I tried to figure out if they were gender-related. I decided they weren't. My brother and I will never ever meld into one super-hero, and neither will Phoenix and Madonna. They are distinct characters but equally important for their trip to *The Last Oasis*.

List the qualities that are necessary for survival in *your* world. Does this list bring one person to mind, or will you need to take two or three friends along on the trek with you?

Who tells the story?

Using third-person point of view, I chose Phoenix to tell the story of *The Last Oasis,* because he's the thinker. It's within the scope of his personality to observe and reflect on the country, the people, the growing pains of this future world. That doesn't mean Madonna doesn't think; she's just too busy to take the time to write anything down. And nobody else of importance lived through it all. So in a sense, it's Phoenix's viewpoint by default.

I didn't set out to write a science fiction story; I tried to write a solid young-adult adventure story that happened to be set four-score-and-ten years into the future. But I didn't just race into the time warp. I spent two or three months touring the place first. It's amazing what a writer can discover with just a compass and a map.

❧ 45

DETECTIVE NOVEL WRITING: THE HOWS AND THE WHYS

BY STEPHEN GREENLEAF

PERHAPS THE BEST WAY TO ILLUSTRATE *how* I write is to discuss *why* I write detective novels. First, some factors that did not dictate that choice: I didn't begin in the mystery genre because it was so popular that the odds of publication were high. I began *Grave Error,* my first John Marshall Tanner novel, in 1977. The publishers and agents who saw and rejected the book were unanimous in their assurance that the hard-boiled detective was an anachronism, a relic of the 40s and 50s. I was advised to cast my lot with science fiction and fantasy, because that's where the fictive action was.

I don't write mysteries because I like poisons and drawing rooms and English butlers. I'm a bit of an Anglophobe, actually, as well as a realist, so the classic cozy was not my model. Rather, my inspiration came from Dashiell Hammett and Raymond Chandler and, above all, Ross Macdonald, writers who wrested the form out of the hands of the English masters and gave it an American voice and place and conscience. My inspirations were books which were driven not by plot or character or forensic verisimilitude, but by those that towered above the rest because of the strength and suitability of their style. Apocalyptic prose, I call it—words fit for the edges of experience, which is where these books take place.

Before writing *Grave Error,* I thought about what I liked about Macdonald's books, then tried to incorporate as many of those traits as I could. The result was undeniably derivative, but an instructive first step. Ten novels later, I have tried to make the Tanner books more my own than Macdonald's, but I hope I haven't strayed too far.

214

Images of the hero

Macdonald's Lew Archer novels suggested the essential building blocks. I wanted my books to have a hero. He would be the man I aspired to be, a man others would admire, but not a man so outsized that no reader could regard him as real. He would be more generic than remarkable, not of massive physical or mental makeup, just a guy in an office with a metal desk and an understuffed couch, two flights above the street. Although he would covet women and be expert in his work, he would not be entangled in a romantic relationship or ensnared in a police or other bureaucracy; he would, in other words, be less encumbered than most of us.

He would speak in the first person, because it is the most intimate relationship in narrative fiction and because the pact between the detective and his audience—the implicit pledge that the narrative will contain no fibs or non-disclosures and that only the reader is privy to it all—is the most hallowed tenet of the genre. Most important, my detective would define himself not through snippets of personal preference or paeans of self-aggrandizement, but by what he had to say about his world. The books are not about John Marshall Tanner; they are about the universe he inhabits: San Francisco, California, from boardroom to bordello, near the end of the twentieth century.

Motive for the crime

My stories have some common characteristics. The criminal catalyst usually has its genesis in the trauma of the past, which manifests itself in ways that reveal more about the psychological underpinnings of crime than about the methods and mechanics of the criminal. In other words, my novels focus less on *who* done it than on *why* it was done, and the presentation owes less to the novels of puzzle and deduction than to the novels of the picaresque. The underlying issues are more moral than maniacal, more political than criminal, more real than artificial, and more pathetic than pathological. Rather than beset by drug lords or Irish terrorists or Cosa Nostra kingpins, Tanner enters the lives of ordinary people who have been beset by circumstances that have produced extraordinary behavior.

I want the readers to believe that the events in the novel could be happening in the house across the street, or at least the bungalow down the block. And I would like them to believe they might have known,

215

once upon a time and only briefly, someone just like the guilty party. But one must not be seduced by experience: Just because it happened doesn't mean it's good for your plot. Reality can be improved upon; if you're a novelist, it's your job to try to do so.

The plot

A word about plot. I'd like to say that I sit down on day one of my journey toward a new novel and chart a brilliant scenario, beginning with a fiendish crime, proceeding through the accumulation of evidence as inexorably as a juggernaut, and ending with an inevitable yet unexpected revelation of the who and why of the crime. I'd like to, but I can't.

I don't know where I'm going when I begin. I know who's going to walk in the door and hire Mr. Tanner, I know what Tanner will be hired to do, and I know some themes I want the book to touch along the way—homelessness and libel law in *Book Case,* for example. Or racism in my novel *Southern Cross.* And that's about it.

The reasons for proceeding so haphazardly stem from my inability to engage the guts of a book until I'm actually writing it, until some people have come on stage and introduced themselves to me. Many efforts I've made to chart a clear and clever course before I start to write have inevitably ended in failure.

But I keep some essentials in mind. I make the investigation proceed logically, to have Tanner engage in a *purposeful* hike. I put enough people in the book to provide plenty of suspects to trot out when the time comes. As an aid, I make a diagram, putting the victim in a box in the center of the page, then drawing arrows to all the people who might reasonably have some connection to that person: parents, friends, lovers, etc. Then I imagine what kinds of connections these suspects might have had among themselves. Next, I litter the place with motive, means, and opportunity, and begin to write the first draft in longhand.

This method does not carry a recommendation. Its advantage is a certain flexibility of flow and a freedom from the sense that I am engaged in the equivalent of painting by numbers. But it is not without risks. I'm on Chapter 28 in the book I'm writing now, and the denouement has yet to reveal itself. I'm beginning to sweat, to draw some new

216

boxes, lines and arrows, and to consider shopworn devices such as incest, long-lost twins, and even a *deus ex machina*.

How you say it. . .

In my mind, more crucial to my books than theme and character is the nature and quality of its prose. It's not easy to say how a strong style is achieved. (It's also not for me to say whether or not I've achieved it.) Above all, it's a function of having read enough to distinguish good writing from bad. The essence of good prose can be absorbed by osmosis as well as analysis, I think, but the template must be first class, which means that reading can't be confined to one genre. A good short course for mystery writers would be to read *Paris Trout* (Pete Dexter), *The Zebra-Striped Hearse* (Ross Macdonald), and *The Elements of Style* (Strunk and White) within the same week.

The next step in producing good prose requires a desire to write well and a willingness to expend the effort necessary to make the book what you want it to be. Writing is rewriting, it's often been said, and the axiom holds for me. Because I don't outline beforehand, my first draft tends to be the literary equivalent of the blunt instrument. As I read through it, I sense that every adjective can be improved or, better yet, omitted; every exchange or dialogue can be shortened; every chapter can end several paragraphs before it does; and most of the philosophical musings of my narrator can be discarded as either puerile or irrelevant. This is not a fun time.

I go through the manuscript again. And then again, shortening, sharpening, shifting, slashing. I've rewritten some chapters ten times, and let others survive unscathed. I've discarded big chunks and small, put the last chapter first and vice versa, and changed the names of all the characters the day before mailing the manuscript to my editor. I try to make the novel accurate, so it says what I want it to say, and original, so it contains both scenes and people that have never appeared in a book before.

Accuracy is easier. It's mostly a matter of researching the facts and focusing the issue: What is the character trying to say and why is he trying to say it? What function is the scene performing, and is the bit about cults (or cars or cauliflower) really necessary? Tough choices, often, but essential. An editor will know when you haven't made them.

Originality is more elusive, since it comes mostly from effort. It is

217

my experience that each idea can be more precise, each action can be condensed and particularized, and each speech can be distilled, whether on the first reading or the fifth. What makes it easier is knowing what your story is about, whose story is it, what does it tell readers and why do they need to know it, and what does it add to what others have written about the subject.

What also makes it easier is "occupying" your characters the way an actor does a role, to the extent that you know what they would say and do in a particular situation, and, as important, what they definitely would *not* say or do, even with a gun to their head.

A novel should have a beginning, a middle, and an end, of course, and so should each chapter and so should each incident. The structure of a given scene will not necessarily be identical to any other, but there should *be* a structure, at least you should try to give it one. Use as few words as possible, start the story as close to the end as you can, and make sure each scene serves the plot and only the plot and contains an internal dynamic of its own.

Character is action, Fitzgerald said, but character and action flow from words. Different people speak differently, mostly because of where they're from and what they do. They dress differently, too, which is a clue to what they aspire to be. They eat different things as well, although in my view that's usually irrelevant.

Different emotions are evoked through words of different resonance, words that have essence and density, "bulbous," for instance, as opposed to words that are empty—"big." Words that are oddly matched, such as "the scar caressed his cheek," or that appear in unusual places, "he fell to the floor breathing blood," can be vivid and provocative. To evoke a given place, use words appropriate to its aura: "a pulsing brook" or "a languid stream." To be conscious of the rhythms in your writing, read it aloud for a better sense of its cadence. A teacher at a writers' workshop told me that whenever his rhythms went awry, he listened to a string quartet by Haydn. Others might prefer Madonna. Whatever works.

In the end, it comes down to language. It's the most important tool we have, it's what links us to Shakespeare and Jane Austen and to Danielle Steel and Stephen King as well. Language is, after all, what made us want to be writers in the first place. Let it sing and dance and strut its stuff, and leave them begging you for more.

46

SETTING IS MORE THAN PLACE

BY WILLIAM G. TAPPLY

AN INTERVIEWER RECENTLY ASKED ME WHY I choose to set my mystery novels in New England instead of, say, Nebraska. I was tempted to answer with the old vaudeville punchline: "Everybody's got to be somewhere." Every story has to have a setting.

Instead I told the interviewer the simple truth: My choice of New England was easy—New England is where I've lived my entire life. It's what I know best. I couldn't write about Nebraska.

I define setting broadly. It's more than place. Setting comprises all the conditions under which things happen—region, geography, neighborhood, buildings, interiors, climate, weather, time of day, season of year.

I feel fortunate. My New England provides me with a rich variety of settings from which to select. I can send my narrator/lawyer/sleuth Brady Coyne from the inner city of Boston to the wilderness of the Maine woods, from the sand dunes of Cape Cod to the farmland of the Connecticut Valley, from exclusive addresses on Beacon Hill to working class neighborhoods in Medford. New England has whatever my stories might call for.

New England also gives me the full cycle of the seasons and all the weather and climate that accompany them. It gives me Locke-Ober and pizza joints, museums and theaters, factories and office buildings, mansions and apartments, skyscrapers and fishing lodges, condominiums and farmhouses.

I don't know about Nebraska. I suspect that if I lived there and knew it as intimately as I know New England I'd find a similar wealth of possibilities. I have, in fact, sent Brady to parts of North Carolina and Montana that I'm familiar with. What's important is knowing my settings well enough to invoke the details that will bring them to life and be useful in my stories.

Settings must strike our readers as realistic. A realistic setting persuades readers to suspend their disbelief and accept the premise that our stories really happened. The easiest and best way to do this is to write knowledgeably about real places, places where our readers live or have visited, or, at least, places they have read about or seen pictures of. Readers, I have learned, love to find in a novel a place they know. They enjoy comparing their impressions of Durgin Park or the New England Aquarium with Brady Coyne's. They like to hear what strikes Brady as noteworthy about Newbury Street, the Combat Zone, the Deerfield River, or the Boston Harbor.

You must get actual places precisely right or you risk losing your readers' trust. No matter how much you might dislike it, you cannot avoid research. You *must* hang out in the places you intend to write about. Observe the people, listen to the sounds, sniff the smells, note the colors and textures of the place. I have spent hours loitering in Boston's Chinatown and prowling the corridors in the East Cambridge courthouse. I've wandered around the Mt. Auburn Hospital and the Peabody Museum, looking for the telling detail that makes the place unique and that will allow me to make it ring true for every reader who has been there.

Research need not be unpleasant, in fact. I make it a point to eat in every restaurant I write about, no matter how familiar it already is to me, at least twice—once just before writing the scene to fix it in my mind, and once again afterward to make sure I've rendered it accurately.

A realistic setting doesn't really have to exist, however, and the fiction writer shouldn't feel limited to using actual places if doing so will alter the story he wants to tell. A fictional setting can still be true. My rule of thumb is this: If the setting you need exists, use it; if it doesn't exist, make it up but make it true. I built Gert's on the North Shore and Marie's in Kenmore Square—where no such restaurants stand— because my stories demand there be restaurants like them there. Readers are continually asking me how to find Gert's and Marie's, which I take to mean that I have rendered them realistically.

I made up a hardscrabble farm in Lanesboro and a horse farm in Harvard—fictitious but realistic places in actual Massachusetts communities. In my first Brady Coyne novel, I moved a rocky hunk of Rhode Island coastline to Massachusetts, committed a murder there, and named it Charity's Point because that storyline required it. I've had readers tell me they believe they have been there. In *The Vulgar Boatman,* I invented the town of Windsor Harbor. Had I tried to set that tale in a real community north of Boston, too many readers would have known that no events such as the ones I invented actually happened there. They would have been unable to suspend their disbelief.

Gert's and Marie's, the farms in Lanesboro and Harvard, Charity's Point, and Windsor Harbor were like the characters that populated the books. Although they were not *real,* they were all *true*—places like them exist, and they *could* be where I put them.

Setting can—and should—serve as more than a backdrop for the action of the story. The conditions under which the action occurs should do double or triple duty for you. Setting can create mood and tone for your fiction. The places where they live and work can reveal the personalities and motivations of your fictional characters. Places, weather, climate, season of year, and time of day can cause things to happen in a story as surely as characters can.

Shakespeare and Conan Doyle understood how setting can establish mood and foreshadow events. The "dark and stormy night" had its purpose, as did the spooky mansion on the remote moor or the thick fog of a London evening. Contemporary writers can use thunderstorms and abandoned warehouses and the barrooms and alleys of city slums in the same way. Robert Louis Stevenson once said, "Some places speak distinctly. Certain dank gardens cry aloud for murder; certain old houses demand to be haunted; certain coasts are set apart for shipwrecks." Find such places. Use them.

But be wary. Such obvious settings can too easily become literary clichés. Misuse them, or overuse them, and they lose their punch. Clever writers understand the power of going against stereotypes. Seek subtlety and irony. Murder can be committed on a sunny May morning in a suburban backyard, too, and when it does, the horror of it is intensified by the contrast.

Carefully selected details of setting can delineate the characters who populate the place. Match the pictures or calendars that hang on every office wall with some trait of the man who works there. Is the policeman's desk littered with half-empty styrofoam coffee cups? What kind of tablecloths does your restaurant use? What music is piped into the elevator of the office building? Does a week's worth of newspapers litter the front porch of that Brookline mansion? Does a specimen jar containing a smoker's lung sit on the desk of the forensic pathologist? Does the lawyer keep a bag of golf clubs in the corner of his office? Does a stack of old *Field & Stream* magazines sit on the table in the dentist's waiting room? Such well-chosen particulars can reveal as much about a character as his dress, manner of speech, or physical appearance.

Think of your settings as characters in your stories. Settings need not be passive. They can act and interact with your characters. Rainstorms cause automobile accidents. Snowstorms cover footprints and stall traffic. Laboratories contain chemicals that spill and release toxic fumes. The bitter cold of a Boston winter kills homeless people. Water released from a dam raises the water level in a river and drowns wading fishermen.

Your choice of setting may, at first, be arbitrary and general—the city where you work, the village where you live. But as you begin writing, you will need to search out particular places where the events of your story will unfold. Visit them often enough to absorb them. If you're lucky, you'll find that your real settings will begin to work for you. You'll see a person whose face you'll want to use. You'll overhear a snatch of conversation that fits a storytelling need. You'll note a detail you didn't expect that suggests a new direction for your plot. On one backgrounding mission to a rural farmyard, I came upon a "honey wagon" pumping out a large septic tank. This suggested to me an unusually grisly way for a villain to dispose of a dead body; this murder method found its way into my story.

The secret of a successfully rendered setting lies *not* in piling exhaustive detail upon repetitive particulars. There's no need to lug your typewriter around a room describing the designs of the furniture, the colors of the rugs and drapes, the brands of the whiskey on the sidebar. Extended descriptive passages, no matter how poetic and clever, only serve to stall the momentum of your story and bore your reader.

Setting is important. It serves many purposes. But don't get carried away. It *is* only a setting, the conditions in which your characters can play out their conflicts. The key to creating effective settings lies in finding the *exactly right* detail that will suggest all of the others. Be spare and suggestive. Look for a water stain on the ceiling or a cigarette burn on the sofa. You may need nothing else to create the picture you want in your reader's imagination. As Elmore Leonard says, "I try to leave out the parts that people skip."

§47

THE ELEMENTS OF FANTASTIC FICTION

BY JANE M. LINDSKOLD

FANTASTIC FICTION EXISTS BY VIRTUE of an attractive paradox: Readers seek these stories for the elements of speculation and fantasy within, yet, simultaneously, the stories must be so believable as to present a viable alternative to the reality that we all know. Succeeding at the challenge of making the unreal real is one of the most enjoyable things about writing in this genre.

The term "fantastic fiction" can be used to define fiction from three categories: **science fiction, fantasy,** and **alternate history.** Science fiction is normally concerned with extrapolating from technological developments and imagining what impact these might have on the future. Fantasy usually involves some shift in what might be considered standard metaphysical values. That is, in fantasy magic works and magical creatures exist, not by virtue of genetic engineering or other scientific marvels, but because they are a natural part of the fantasy environment. Alternate history involves reinterpretation of the standard course of historical events so that the writer can investigate "What might have happened if. . ."

Although all of these sub-groups alter reality, the techniques for writing each type of book differ enough to warrant independent investigation.

Science fiction has been frequently called the literature of ideas. Often story ideas are inspired by new developments in the sciences. Even if a story is not going to be about those developments, the writer should be aware of what current technology is and where those developments are likely to lead. Technology has changed since the days when Robert Heinlein could write about space engineers who use slide rules and three-ton ballistic computers, as he did in the 1939 short story "Misfit." Ironically, in 1939 our slender credit card calculators, with their four basic functions, memory, and assorted other tricks, would have been dismissed as space-opera trappings, rather than good, solid science, because the revolutions in microcircuitry that we take for granted today had not been anticipated.

A science fiction writer doesn't need to be a technological wizard to write believable stories. An awareness of the current state of technology and where it is likely to go can be enough. A good general survey like Ed Regis' book *Great Mambo Chicken and the Transhuman Condition: Science Slightly Over the Edge* provides an amusing way for a non-scientist to become acquainted with what is going on in the sciences. Another useful tool is a magazine like *Science News,* which gives brief capsule summaries of new developments in a wide variety of scientific fields.

Certain scientific trends are particularly influential right now, including the projected Mars exploration project. Science fiction writers have never lost their fascination for "outer space," but lately the majority of space exploration stories have dealt with what happens once we are already "out there." The plans for actual exploration of Mars, rather than the orbital photography conducted by unmanned probes, have reawakened interest in fiction dealing with the nitty-gritty problems of planetary exploration and colonization.

Another intriguing area is those sciences that deal with "inner" rather than "outer" space, such as nanotechnology and virtual reality. Nanotechnology ("nano" indicates a billionth of a meter) is based on the theories of K. Eric Drexler, who postulated not only machines so tiny that they might even be used to manipulate atoms (a notion he shared with physicist Richard Feynman), but also that these increasingly complicated machines could be replicated organically, in a fashion similar to DNA's within cells. Drexler envisioned his nanomachines performing functions as widely varied as transforming cheap raw materials into prime beef and replacing human labor. In his most visionary materials, Drexler imagined nanomachines within the human body repairing and even refining existing structures. Needless to say, this is fascinating material for stories—whether positive extrapolations about worlds without hunger and disease or cautionary tales about what unforeseen dangers may result from manipulation of the atom.

Virtual reality computer technology (or simply VR) has become quite trendy, serving as a background element in stories that otherwise have nothing to do with computer technology. VR attempts to involve all of the senses within a computer-created reality. Most virtual reality devices in use today involve some sort of complicated interfacing equipment—gloves and goggles or even full bodysuits. Much of the fiction that uses VR bypasses these awkward devices in favor of purely hypothetical "jacks" that allow the user to plug into the computer, creating a direct electronic connection between the brain and the computer. Through these interfaces, the computer jockeys of the future enter a "matrix" or "cyberspace" created by the interplay of computers and the human mind. Here, rather than in physical reality, the people of the VR future work, socialize, educate their children, and even make love.

One of the most striking science fiction trends in recent years is **cyberpunk**—a sub-genre mostly credited to William Gibson and similar writers. In cyberpunk fiction, "inner space" rather than "outer space" is the main focus. Virtual reality and designer drugs become the means of investigating the mind, while body alternation, most visible through artificial "cyber"-augmented limbs and senses, permits a reshaping of the definition of what it is to be human. Yet, for all of its fascination with technology, cyberpunk's view of the future is dark. Corporations control most resources and the only escape for most people is through drugs or illegal activities. Although many critics claim that cyberpunk fiction is no longer as provocative and vital as when it first appeared, it has helped bring into the main focus elements that may become as standard as the robots and spaceships of earlier generations.

Fantasy also depends on alterations to the world as we know it, but rather than being based on scientific extrapolation, fantasy introduces elements that do not exist in our world. Perhaps the most common alteration is the introduction of magic—and for many editors and writers this is the one major difference between science fiction and fantasy. For instance, Anne McCaffrey's *Pern* books feature fire-breathing dragons large and small whose non-magical powers can be explained by science. Therefore, the *Pern* books are science fiction. If Pernese dragons breathed fire because of a "magical" ability to alter rock into fire, the books would be fantasy.

Although fantasy introduces magic, this is not an excuse to have everything and anything work "like magic." The best fantasy books have rules and limitations for how magic functions. In Jack Chalker's *Dancing Gods* books, these are included in the "Books of Rules"; in Robert Asprin's *Myth Adventure* books, they are limited by their ability to perceive and manipulate "lines of force." In fact, there are as many different magical systems as there are good works of fantasy. What is essential is that there are rules and that the rules be followed consistently. If magic exists without limits, then there are no reasonable challenges, and without challenges there cannot be a story.

Imagine the hypothetical kingdom of Diamond Mist. Magic is as common in Diamond Mist as musical talent is on our Earth; that is, not everyone has it, but almost everyone can manage a small spell or two and there are truly powerful magical talents who have "perfect pitch" for magic. Now take our heroine, Floriella. Floriella doesn't have "perfect pitch," but she does have quite a good "voice" that with training could be formidable. Floriella walks down a dark tunnel, torch in hand, her sturdy tunic soiled and torn from the exertion of searching for the lost prince who has been stolen by the dragon, Grimclaw, who has an appetite for virgins.

What's wrong with this picture?

Well, if magic is so common in Diamond Mist, why is Floriella walking around with a torch? Why doesn't she just summon a light? Why is her clothing dirty and torn? Can't she summon clean clothes or at least magically make some that would be immune to wear and tear? Why is she physically searching for the prince? How does a carnivore the size of a dragon affect the ecology of an area? What might a demand for a steady diet of virgins do to the age of sexual activity for the local population?

Clearly, Diamond Mist is in need of some refinement, yet, at first glance the scenario postulated above is not much different from what most people imagine when they consider writing a fantasy. However, the "side effects" of magic must be carefully considered. In this, writing fantasy is not very different from writing science fiction. As seen in the above example, magic in Diamond Mist will affect not only the abstract concept of "power," but much more concrete matters like economics, ecology, and social custom.

Alternate history is usually classified as a sub-section of science fiction, but it is just as viable an approach for fantasy. Essentially, alternate history takes some established historical event and changes some significant element. The story usually proceeds from there to investigate "what if. . ." the Spanish Armada had succeeded or Fidel Castro had gone on to become a Major League baseball player, or any other of a host of options. The key to writing strong alternate history is to know history well enough to anticipate all of the changes that an alteration will cause.

For example, take an alternate history that begins with the concept that Richard the Lionhearted died before he became king. Not only does this mean that Richard's Crusade would never have taken place—an obvious alternative to history—but it may also mean that there would have been no Magna Carta, since if the English nobility had not been angered first by Richard's absentee rulership and then by John's abusive rulership, they might not have risen up in protest.

However, there are more subtle differences than these. The Crusades reopened contact between Europe and the Holy Land. This meant that the Crusaders brought home knowledge that had been lost after the fall of the Roman Empire and ideas that had not yet evolved in Europe. This information included texts of the Greek philosophers, medical and astronomical theory, and even the concept of the zero. An alternate history that removes Richard the Lionhearted must deal with *all* of the consequences, not just the obvious ones. One could even argue that without King Richard and his Crusades, the European Renaissance might not have occurred.

Alternate history can be used as a fantasy device by introducing magic as an element in historical events. For example, the Spanish Armada might succeed because a powerful sorcerer overcomes the storm that historically destroyed it. Even more provocatively, the Armada might fail because Queen Elizabeth is a powerful sorceress who summons up the storm that sinks the Spanish fleet. In this magically altered history, the writings of poets like Edmund Spenser, who equated Elizabeth with Glorianna, the Fairy Queen of his epic, may become history rather than literary art. In this version of Elizabethan England, Sir Walter Raleigh might meet with the Red Cross Knight and go off to battle Acrasia for the heart of Elizabeth's lover, Leicester.

Fantasy has expanded alternate history to include reinterpretations of legends or myths. These are particularly attractive areas for fantasy writers because often magic is already an element. The writer, then, has the pleasure of explaining how that magic works and why events turned out as they did. Some legends exist only in bare bones structure—a fragment of an epic or a few lines of lyric. Here the writer extrapolates in the manner of a science fiction approach to alternate history, but feels free to include the magic that belongs to the original work. A fine example of this type of alternate history is Poul Anderson's novel, *Hrolf Kraki's Saga,* which mixes history, magic, and a fragment of recorded epic into a powerful novel.

Fantastic fiction in whatever form a writer chooses frees the imagination in a way that realistic fiction often cannot, inviting unique visions not only of what is, but also of what can be. The key to making the unreal real remains the same for all three: attention to detail and delight in reaching out for possibility.

48

IT'S NO MYSTERY

BY CAROLYN G. HART

WHAT CAN MAKE *YOUR* MYSTERY an editor's choice? The answer is no mystery—or it shouldn't be.

Superb books grab the editor in the very first paragraphs, the very first lines.

Superb books are as individual and as idiosyncratic as crusty Aunt Edith or affable Cousin Charles.

So these, in my view, are the two essential elements for a successful mystery novel:

Action.

Voice.

Action is creating the story as the reader watches.

Voice is the unmistakable reflection of the author's personality.

If your novel successfully combines action and voice, editors will vie to publish you.

I've always loved beginning novels with action, and in my Death on Demand mystery series, I use a technique I adore: the vignette.

A vignette is a small, swift cameo of a scene, featuring a character who is important to the novel in an act that relates to the theme of the novel.

Here are the opening sentences of the vignettes in the fourth book in the series, *Honeymoon with Murder:*

Vignette One: Jesse Penrick didn't miss much on his solitary nocturnal rambles. Lights at an odd hour. A visitor never before seen. An unfamiliar car.

Vignette Two: Lucinda Burrows darted through the crowd, her brown alligator heels clicking excitedly against the concrete. She'd done just as instructed, and the whole operation had gone without a hitch.

Vignette Three: The perfect crime. Who said it couldn't be done?

Vignette Four: Ingrid Jones had no idea she was being observed, she and the whole expanse of Nightingale Court.

What is accomplished? The reader is immediately plunged into the action. The reader knows things are happening, and the reader is made a part of the action.

Perhaps the single most enervating and deadly mistake a beginning writer makes is in trying to tell the reader what is happening.

Never *tell* a reader anything.

Let the reader become a part of the scene.

Look at it this way: People who read are smart or they wouldn't read. They've been going to films all their lives. When the movie opens with a chase scene, big guys with guns chasing Michael Douglas down an alley, the viewers don't know what's going on, but they are quite willing to find out *as the story unfolds.*

Let your story unfold.

For example, in *The Christie Caper,* my protagonist Annie Laurance, owner of the Death on Demand mystery bookstore, is planning a celebration of the centennial of the birth of Agatha Christie. What could be more boring than beginning a book with that information? For example, Annie might be talking on the telephone with her mother-in-law, Laurel, and she could tell Laurel, "I'm going to have a convention here on the island to celebrate the centennial, etc., etc."

That is telling the reader. Instead here is the beginning of the opening chapter:

Annie counted the magnums of champagne. Four. Five. Six. Surely that would be enough. She whirled on her heel and dashed out of the storeroom.

I don't *tell* the reader anything. The reader is there as Annie frantically readies the bookstore for an evening cocktail party for the convention attendees.

Action. Use it. Enjoy it. Live that scene, and your reader will live it, too.

There is always a way to provide information through action. When I received the editorial letter on *Deadly Valentine,* my editor suggested that readers needed to know more about the people who would be the focus at the Valentine Ball *before* the Ball began.

I created a scene before the party, when Annie and her mother-in-law, Laurel, walk down to the pier and look at the houses around Scarlet King lagoon, where Annie and Max live in their new house. If they'd walked down to the pier and Annie had simply described the houses and their occupants, it would have been what writing teachers call "tea party conversation," that is, the contrived exchange of information in a scene that doesn't move the story. Instead, there is action because of a subtle struggling between Laurel and Annie, Laurel intent upon gaining information, Annie reluctant to part with it. What makes it credible is that Annie is certain Laurel has some ulterior motive in asking for this information, and, as the reader discovers later, indeed Laurel did. This moves the story along and, at the same time, it satisfies the author's objective of introducing to the reader some of the people who will be at the Valentine Ball. Often, the author has several objectives in a scene in addition to the objectives of the characters. The characters' objectives in this scene are twofold: Annie wants to find out what her madcap mother-in-law is up to, and Laurel is quite determined to learn all about the neighbors.

Action can be mental. In *Design for Murder*, I used a vignette to give readers a clear picture of Corinne Prichard Webster's character:

... Her eyes narrowed, and she no longer looked at her reflection so she didn't see the transformation. At one instant, the mirrored face was soft and beguiling, almost as beautiful with its classic bones, silver-blonde hair, and Mediterranean blue eyes as on her wedding day at nineteen almost forty years before. Then, as Corinne Prichard Webster thought about her niece, Gail, throwing herself at a totally unsuitable man, the face hardened and looked all of its fifty-nine years, the eyes cold and hard, the mouth, thin, determined, and cruel.

In *A Little Class on Murder*, Annie is teaching a course at a college in Chastain on the Three Great Ladies of the Mystery: Agatha Christie, Dorothy L. Sayers, and Mary Roberts Rinehart. This is Annie's first teaching venture, and she's very self-conscious and certainly doesn't want anyone in the class whom she knows. I decided (unknown to Annie, of course) to enroll in the class Annie's ditzy mother-in-law, Laurel, her most opinionated customer, Henny, and the curmudgeon of Chastain, Miss Dora.

The day arrives for Annie's first class:

She was skimming her lecture notes when she stiffened, her senses assaulted.
Scent.
Sound.
Sight.

231

The scent came first. The unmistakable fragrance of lilac, clear and sharp and sweet.

Annie's hands tightened in a death grip on the sides of the lectern. Surely it couldn't—

It could.

Laurel swept through the doorway, beaming, of course. . . .

In short order, Miss Dora and Henny also arrive.

. . . The back of her (Annie's) neck prickled. That thump behind her!

It took every vestige of her will to turn her head to face the door to the hallway.

Thump. Thump. Thump.

Quick, purposeful, decisive thumps.

The ebony cane with its black rubber tip poked around the corner, followed by its mistress.

The tiny old lady (Miss Dora) stood motionless in the doorway. . . .

And then . . .

Oh God.

The sight framed in the doorway was almost too much for her to accept. Laurel was bad enough. Miss Dora would cast a pall on the Addams family tea party.

But this—

It wasn't as though she didn't recognize the costume: a large gray flannel skirt with a droopy hem, a full blouse with a lacy panel down the front, a shapeless rust-colored cardigan, lisle stockings, extremely sensible brown shoes, and hair bobbing in springy sausage-curl rolls.

"Henny," she moaned.

And poor Annie is facing her first class.

The reader saw it happen.

Action is yours for the asking. Pretend you're training a camera on your characters. Watch the scene unfold *with* your readers.

And with action, you will discover voice.

How you see the world, how you create scenes, will be a product of your personality, your experiences, and your willingness to dare.

Voice is perhaps the easiest element to recognize in successful fiction and, for uncertain writers, the most difficult to attain.

What is voice? It is the quality of writing that makes a passage instantly identifiable. If you handed me five unidentified pages written by Nancy Pickard, Sara Paretsky, Dorothy Cannell, and Joan Hess, I would have no difficulty at all in knowing who wrote what. Because each author's voice is so distinctive, so unmistakable.

This is perhaps the most elusive concept in writing. Maybe a few don'ts will make it clearer.

If you look at the bestseller lists, then write a book and send it to an agent or editor, saying this is just like Robert B. Parker or Mary Higgins Clark, that book won't sell.

Don't try to be another Parker or Clark. Don't imitate. Study, observe, absorb, but when you write, write it your way. You must write a book that absolutely no one in the world could have written except you. Each human being is unique. The passions and prejudices, the obsessions and revulsions that drive each person are different. Take advantage of this. Listen to your heart. Then you will have a voice.

You must write a book that matters enormously to you, not a Native American mystery because Tony Hillerman is hot, or a cat mystery because Lillian Jackson Braun is hot, or a serial killer because Thomas Harris is hot.

This isn't to say you can't set a book in New Mexico. Walter Satterthwaite and Judith Van Gieson are using that locale, but their books are succeeding because they are unmistakably their own, not Hillerman spinoffs.

If I look deeply into the books I have written, I realize that paramount to me is the exercise of power in relationships. This is my obsession, the element that fuels my books. I want everyone to be accountable for the way they treat others, so that is my focus.

And the way I write?

I love language. The sound of words matters to me. Is my fiction distinctive enough for readers to mark the words as mine? I can't answer that. That is for readers to say. But I know there are passages in what I have written that reflect the essence of my soul.

That is the price a writer pays to achieve voice. The writer must be willing to reveal what matters most of all to him.

If I were to select a passage that perhaps says the most about me, it would be from my novel, *Dead Man's Island*. This is the first novel in a new series featuring a retired newspaperwoman, Henrietta O'Dwyer Collins, as the protagonist. She's known as Henri O, a nickname given to her by her late husband, Richard, because he said she provided more surprises in a single day than O. Henry ever put in a short story.

Dead Man's Island is the story of a woman who responds to a call for help from a voice out of her past. She travels to a private island where murder and a hurricane threaten the survival of the stranded guests.

Toward the close of *Dead Man's Island,* Henri O awaits the return of the storm:

As I stood, fatigue washed over me. It would be so easy to drop down beside Valerie and close my eyes, let the warmth of the sunlight touch me with fingers of life and let my mind drift, taking memories and thoughts as they came.

But anger flickered beneath the exhaustion.

I suppose I've always been angry. That's what drives most writers, the hot steady consuming flame of anger against injustice and dishonesty and exploitation, against sham and artifice and greed, against arrogance and brutality and deceitfulness, against betrayal and indifference and cruelty.

I would not give up.

This passage is what Henri O is all about.

Should you as a reader care, this passage also tells you everything you'd ever need to know about me, the author. So when you write a book that offers your heart and mind and soul to readers, it will have voice.

Your voice.

§49

WHEN YOU WRITE
A HISTORICAL NOVEL

BY MAX BYRD

HOMER STARTED IT. Most of us are likely to credit Gore Vidal—or, if our memories are long enough, Sir Walter Scott—with establishing the "historical novel" as a popular literary form. But in truth, made-up stories about real events and people are just about as old as literature itself.

When my editor suggested a few years ago that I take a break from writing thrillers and try my hand at a historical novel, I sat down beside a pyramid of books and read as widely as I could in the genre. And the first thing I concluded was that Homer's *Iliad* three thousand years ago had established four major conventions of historical fiction that were still as up-to-date as *Burr* and *Scarlett*.

1) *Historical fiction gives a history of the tribe.* However much it may focus on individuals (Hector, Achilles), the real story always concerns the fate of nations.

2) *It tells about famous characters that everybody already knows,* or recounts famous events from the point of view of unknown participants ("His name is Rhett Butler, and he's from Charleston").

3) *It begins "in medias res,"* in the middle of the story, and makes no attempt to include the whole history of events from beginning to end, as a formal historian would. Long as it is, the *Iliad* covers only the climactic last year of the Trojan War, pretty much as Gore Vidal's *Lincoln* covers only Abraham Lincoln's five years as president.

4) *Its scale is long and deep,* ranging from the top of Mt. Olympus to the gloomy, dismal gates of the Underworld. There is no such thing as a *short* historical novel.

The little that Homer omitted as a convention in the *Iliad,* he took care of in the *Odyssey*, where the first "flashbacks" in western literature seem to occur: Telemachus sails away from home to learn the whereabouts of his famous father, and the old omniscient bore Nestor tells him in great detail (to the smell of endlessly roasting oxen) exactly what Odysseus did in the war and where he had wandered afterward. Few historical novelists since have been able to do away with the explanatory flashback (or diary or memoir or speech) that fills in the blanks.

What Homer hadn't established permanently as a convention of historical fiction I boiled down to three major questions of craft.

1) *What point of view should you choose?*

This is complicated by a factor that didn't bother Homer: If you are writing about a famous person (Freud, Napoleon, Catherine the Great), do you dare go inside that character's head? Can you really imagine yourself in Abraham Lincoln's consciousness? This was an urgent question for me, because I had agreed to write a novel about Thomas Jefferson, a man whose ideas and writings are known in such detail by millions of people (and who is a personal hero to so many of them) that it would seem arrogant, not to say foolhardy, to write in the first person, from Jefferson's point of view. Who could presume to speak for Jefferson?

I decided to avoid that implausibility and to write my historical novel in the third person, but then, of course, discovered that I had a further decision to make: Would it be the "third-person omniscient," such as the most Homeric of historical novelists Tolstoy uses in *War and Peace*? Or could it be instead "third-person limited," the story of Jefferson's life told from a single point of view, on the model of James Boswell observing Samuel Johnson, or Nick Carroway observing Gatsby? And given its advantages of immediacy and control, couldn't I let my *observer* at least narrate in the first person? Boswell certainly speaks in his own voice, pure first person, in those charming short stories collected in Lillian de La Torre's *Samuel Johnson, Detective*.

But those were short stories. Most historical novels are written in the third person and from many different points of view—a minimum probably of three, as in Gore Vidal's *Empire,* and as many as a dozen in Thomas Flanagan's epic *The Year of the French*. And this reflects that first important Homeric principle: If a novel tells the story of the tribe and the tribe is to be completely represented, you have to include the obscure and the downtrodden, as well as the heroes and princes. You need to have Thersites alongside Achilles, Sally Hemings beside the Master of Monticello.

And a further complication becomes apparent: When you write from several points of view in a historical novel, one of them should speak to readers in a modern voice. Doing so will make a story, though set in a very distant past—ancient Rome, for example, or the Middle Ages—seem less remote, more accessible to twentieth-century readers.

Most modern historical novels follow points of view revolving around either a central event or a central character. Michael Shaara's Pulitzer Prize-winning novel *The Killer Angels* simply tells us the story of the Battle of Gettysburg from the points of view (in repeated sequence) of Robert E. Lee, James Longstreet, and half a dozen other generals and soldiers. He uses the simple device of titling each chapter according to the point of view: "Longstreet," "Lee," etc. And most beginning historical novelists would probably do well to imitate his technique.

2) *How do you deal with what the distinguished novelist Oakley Hall calls "research rapture"?*

Any historical novelist understands what he means: the irresistible pull to learn *everything* there is to know about your subject, to read every diary, letter, and newspaper; to visit every geographical site, and *then* to cram it all in, every irrelevant notecard and fact, until your living fiction turns into a ponderous academic history.

One solution to the problem is obvious, if like Homer or Margaret Mitchell you have chosen the third-person omniscient. When it's tempting to indulge in grand exposition, to tell the facts without reference to your story, you just do it, as Mitchell did:

Hope was rolling high in every Southern heart as the summer of 1863 came in. Despite privation and hardships, despite food speculators and kindred scourges, despite death and sickness and suffering, which had now left their mark on nearly every family, the South was again saying, "One more victory and the war is over," saying it with even more happy assurance than in the summer before. The Yankees were proving a hard nut to crack but they were cracking at last.

Or there is a technique I call "cameos and conversation." Ciji Ware's

237

wonderful novel *Island of the Swan* is set in late eighteenth-century Edinburgh and recounts the story of the life of Jane Maxwell. It is clear that the author has read and seen everything possible about the period and the setting, and also (to the reader's delight) that she sometimes cannot resist bringing on stage, just for a moment, some of that research:

> Framed by the door's graceful moulding stood a well-proportioned young man of about twenty-seven or eight. The new arrival stared at his hostess with dark eyes that glowed with peculiar intensity as he surveyed the room. His luminous gaze paused momentarily on her lemon-colored bodice trimmed with white lace stitched around the scooped neckline, and lingered a second too long for delicacy. Jane sensed an almost animal-like magneticism about the man she immediately surmised was Robert Burns.

A writer in the grip of research rapture may also indulge in "brand-name brio" (the technique works best for novels set in late nineteenth- or early twentieth-century America). You might hand your hero a curious cigar-shaped metal cylinder with a pointed tip (the year is 1895) and have someone murmur, "This is the newest thing in our store, just invented. Doesn't need ink. It's called a ball-point pen."

To do this sort of thing well, however, the writer will need a journalist's eye for interesting concrete details and an editor's ruthless willingness to throw out most of them. Thus, in researching Thomas Jefferson's life, I found that I had incidentally learned quite a lot about ladies' fashions in eighteenth-century Paris, where Jefferson lived for five years just before the French Revolution. But since nothing is really more tedious and forgettable than dress lengths and wig lengths (actually, wig lengths are good), I ended up using two irrelevant details that I thought would nonetheless please a reader:

a) In grand French homes of the period, the stone floors were cleaned by young men called *frotteurs,* who poured soapy water across a room, strapped two huge scrub brushes to their feet, and glided back and forth like ice skaters. I open my story on such a scene.

b) For a variety of reasons having to do with the Catholic Church and the facts of life, divorce for a Frenchwoman in this period was obtainable mainly by something called "trial by impotence." If a woman wished to divorce an uncooperative husband, she might make the unnerving, not to say unmanning accusation that he could no longer perform his conjugal duty, and the husband who challenged the divorce could thereupon be required to demonstrate his prowess before witnesses in public trial. (I'm not going to say how I used *this!*)

One further dimension of research rapture to consider is a variety of documents as well as voices. Thus, Oakley Hall's *Warlock* punctuates its powerful narrative of the old West with numerous journals, letters, and newspaper clippings. These can be actual historical documents, copied right out of one's notes (Margaret Mitchell has Scarlett listen to a genuine 1866 poem about worthless Confederate money), or they can be made up by the writer in the style of the time; or even a mixture of both. And because a major goal of the historical novel is to bring a distant world to life dramatically, these authentic voices become a kind of guarantee to the reader that your fictional creation is undeniably real.

And for my final question of craft—

3) *How does the plot of a historical novel differ from other plots?*

My first answer is, of course, it doesn't. Whether you're writing a detective novel, a comic novel, a historical novel, or a warm, sensitive contemporary novel about gun-running vampires in suburbia, the elements of plot are always the same: suspense (not surprise), a dominating image that works like a refrain ("Tara"), reversals, obstacles, active characters driven by obsessions.

But it is well to remember that historical plots will normally have one of two relationships to "standard" history. If a writer chooses a story that describes famous events or characters, the plot must be bounded and limited by the historical facts. Lincoln dies, Troy falls; unless it is historical *fantasy,* the South loses the Civil War. Yet, paradoxically, this constraint of the well-known and the unalterable can actually strengthen the element of suspense in a plot. The fact that the reader already knows the end of your story somehow intensifies the drama of waiting for that familiar moment to arrive. A reader begins *Lincoln* completely aware of how it *must* conclude, but this only sets the heart beating faster as the carriage begins to roll toward Ford's Theater. Or—a double paradox—a historical novel may gain suspense because it *cannot* change history. Frederick Forsyth's *The Day of the Jackal* describes a hired assassin's attempt to murder Charles De-Gaulle—something we *know* did not happen—and yet the suspense is, if anything, greater than if it had.

A novel about famous people or events will probably work best with a subplot about obscure characters, historical or not, whose lives can give your imagination elbow room. A writer, no matter how dramatic his material, needs a little freedom from facts. In writing about Jefferson, I had to stick to the chronological truth about my hero, but I could give my primary observer, Jefferson's real secretary William Short, a private life of his own. Even less is recorded about the slaves Sally and James Hemings, the sister and brother who accompanied Jefferson to Paris, my main setting, so that through them and Short, I could strike out into almost any part of Jefferson's world.

On the other hand, a historical novel can exist in very loose relationship to historical facts, if the writer simply sets a story in a historical era and plays out a conventional plot against its canvas. These are the "period pieces" that nineteenth-century readers loved, adventure stories set between the lines of standard history: *Ivanhoe, The Three Musketeers, Scaramouche.* (The success of John Jakes's American Chronicle suggests that a vast audience still exists.)

Which kind of conventional plot works best?

For years I subscribed to the view that there were in fact only thirty-six different plots (from the title of Georges Polti's excellent book, *The Thirty-Six Dramatic Situations*). In writing novels for a decade, I boiled the number down to seven; and now, as I compact my natural laziness into ever denser bundles, I would agree with the idea I have sometimes heard expressed, that there are really just two basic plots in literature. And either one of them works perfectly in a historical novel.

1) A stranger comes to town—which is exactly how *Lincoln* begins, with the new President arriving at the Washington train station in 1861; and how Rhett Butler enters *Gone With the Wind;* and how the Connecticut Yankee finds himself suddenly in Camelot.

2) Somebody goes on a journey—as Odysseus does, and Huck Finn and Ivanhoe, and even Thomas Jefferson.

But these basic plots always have to be connected to the first and most important of Homer's conventions: What happens to individuals must reflect, explain, or symbolize the history of the tribe. The *Iliad* tells Greeks why Troy is no more. *Lincoln* tells Americans why the nation was reborn, in bloody union. I chose to write about Thomas Jefferson because, in his words and imagination, he could almost be said to have invented America and the idea of a democratic republic. Lesser lives, like that of Huck Finn, also have to be woven into the big world—in Huck's case, the world of ante-bellum slavery—and not permitted to exist unconnected to the life around them. That is why increasingly I have come to think of historical fiction as a healthy form for the inward-looking, self-absorbed modern imagination to take.

⚜50

HORROR FICTION: TIME FOR SOME NEW-FANGLED FANGS

BY GRAHAM MASTERTON

ABOUT SIX OR SEVEN YEARS AGO, horror started to become a very popular genre for new, young authors just starting out on a writing career.

This was partly because of the huge and obvious success of Stephen King, and partly because a new young generation of writers was coming of age, a generation brought up on horror comics, TV's *Twilight Zone,* and even books by me. They had a comprehensive reading background and a natural interest in horror.

But it was also because the horror market was rapidly expanding. Publishers were demanding more and more horror titles, and quite simply it was easier for a new writer to get his or her work published in the horror genre than almost any other.

So long as the fiction market in general and the horror genre in particular were expanding, this was fine, and in those six or seven years, many excellent new authors found their way into print. Only a couple of years ago, almost every major publisher had a horror list, and in almost every case that I know of, that list was administered by a young, enthusiastic, and dedicated editor. It was New Author Heaven.

But when recession struck the publishing industry, those horror lists were among the first casualties. Within a dramatically short space of time, opportunities for new horror writers have been considerably reduced, and it is now much harder for a new horror writer to get started in the genre, harder . . . but by no means impossible. More demanding, yes . . . but *because* it's more demanding, much more rewarding, too.

In fact, I can let you into a secret: If you have real faith in your writing skill and a deep and genuine interest in the development of yourself as a horror writer and horror fiction in general, it may even be a *better* time than ever before. But, you must be prepared to accept the challenge of a much tougher market, and be prepared to commit yourself to a considerable amount of preparation, writing, rewriting, and polishing. More than anything else, though, you must be prepared to stretch your imagination to the utmost. To succeed in horror fiction today, you must not only write skillfully, but you must come up with some *very* new ideas.

If you can invent a totally novel and unexpected terror, and present it with style and quality, then you have the chance not only of breaking into the horror market, but breaking into it at a time when it is much less flooded with other horror books . . . giving *your* book a better chance of standing out.

If there was ever a chance of your becoming the next Stephen King, it's now.

You see, one of the effects of a quickly expanding market was that publishers tended to bring out far too much category horror, much of it deficient in invention and quality of writing. Even some of the very best horror writers seemed to run short of new ideas and began to regurgitate themes that had lost much of their surprise, their shock value . . . and thus all of their *terror,* too.

Quite apart from the problems of recession, horror fiction began to show signs of creative exhaustion, the same kind of tiredness that, thirty years ago, affected the western. In particular, many leading writers seemed to forget that readers buy horror to be scared half to death and started to indulge in political and philosophical waffle along with the horror. There's nobody like a well-established horror writer for indulging in political and philosophical waffle.

An infallible sign of literary arthritis in *any* genre is when the books start getting thicker and thicker and thicker . . . as if length and verbosity can somehow make up for a fundamentally thin idea.

Publishers frequently send me new horror manuscripts to read, for the purpose of giving endorsements. In the past two years, I have seen nothing but the old, old stories. Vampires, werewolves. More vampires, more werewolves. Mutant babies. Children with unusual psychic powers. Children with *usual* psychic powers. *Exorcist III* asks, "Dare you climb these steps again?" and the answer is yes, we dare, but who cares? We know what's up there and it doesn't frighten us any more.

Even the recent books by the market leader, Stephen King (*The*

Dark Half and *Misery*) have, quite simply, lost their power to scare. Whereas, after rereading some of *'Salem's Lot* the other day, I still believe that it's frightening.

Clive Barker has become (by his own admission) more of a "fantasist" than a horror writer and the splatter-punk brigade (John Skipp and Craig Spector) are straining harder to think of new ways of being disgusting, to the point where the suspension of disbelief becomes stretched beyond breaking-point. A novel that you can't believe in is no longer frightening, by definition.

So what is a new horror writer supposed to do? He or she is faced with the very difficult task of creating a story that goes beyond the bounds of acceptable taste, as well as with the seemingly impossible task of creating a totally new terror—totally new, but believable, too.

How can this be done? Well, in my opinion, by rethinking the entire framework of modern horror fiction, by rejecting the patterns and devices and themes developed over the past two decades by Stephen King and John Farris and Rick McCammon (*They Thirst,* et al.) and, yes, by me, too. The way I see it, the future of modern horror fiction lies in far greater believability, and in the development of stories that are far less gimmicky and outré—stories that come closer to the quirks of real human psychology.

Stories, too, that are well-written, soundly constructed, and obey the fundamental principles of good novel-craft. That is: that they have engaging and three-dimensional characters, an interesting and credible setting, a strong forward movement, a heart-clutching beginning, a sound middle, and a huge mind-expanding climax. Easy, *ja?*

We have all tried to stretch the boundaries of the supernatural as far as we can. One of the most implausible stories that I recently attempted was *Walkers,* a novel in which the inmates of an asylum for the dangerously insane had escaped from captivity by disappearing into the walls. They traveled *inside* the bricks and out through the ground, and made good their getaway.

Of course, the basic notion of *Walkers* was utterly wacky. We all know Newton's Law that two objects cannot occupy the same space at the same time, which is one of the reasons that we have traffic accidents and bump into other shoppers in the supermarket. But I worked hard to develop a locale and an atmosphere that would make the reader want to believe that such a thing *could* happen. And that's the difference: *want* to believe.

It's comparatively easy to create a horror scenario in which the reader *doesn't* want to believe that such hideous events can take place. But it requires much more skill and much more thought to create a horror scenario in which readers are actually working *with* you, rather than against you, a horror scenario in which they actively help you to frighten them.

Enlisting the reader's support requires acute observation, writing discipline, and a strong empathy with other people's feelings. It requires not only believability, but a certain degree of *likability*. Your characters have to be not only real people, but *enjoyable* real people, people your readers wish they could spend some time with, whether they get involved in the Horror Beyond The Grave or not.

It also requires a fast, strongly constructed plot; a plot that trots; a plot that never allows your reader to get ahead of it. Sometimes, if your characters are really strong, you can get away with a certain amount of predictability. But you shouldn't take the risk. A horror novel should be a novel of sudden shocks and surprises, right to the end. It's better to make an unexpected change in your story line (unexpected even for *you*, the author) than allow your reader to guess what's going to happen next. The worst response a horror writer can hear is "I *knew* that would happen."

So let's take a look at all the demands that I've made. First, you need a startling new premise: an idea that's fundamentally frightening, but which nobody has ever thought of before. Here's a paragraph from *Walkers* that might give you a taste:

A little farther away, a *face* had emerged from the floor, too. A man's face, with a heavy forehead and a strong jaw, and a fixed triumphant grin. It looked as if it had been smothered in dry cement. There were powdery wrinkles and cracks around its mouth. Its eye sockets were totally black—*black,* like night, no whites at all, as if the inside of its head were empty. But it was alive, there was no question about that. It had risen straight out of the concrete floor, in the way that a swimmer emerges from the dust-covered surface of a lake.

It was alive and it was grinning at him and it was gleefully trying to drag him under the surface of the concrete, too.

No vampires, no werewolves. Something different. But something that can appear at any moment and threaten your hero or heroine with total fear.

It can be very fruitful to delve into occult archives to learn what demons and devils and odd monsters frightened people in the past. Many of the olden-day demons were created out of very strong and primitive fears—fears to which people can still be remarkably sensitive, even today. I used legendary Red Indian demons in *The Manitou* and *Charnel House*; Mexican demons in *The Pariah*; and stories about the real Scottish witch Isabel Gowdie in the third and last of my Night Warriors triology *Night Plague*. I altered many of the mythical details of their malevolent powers in order to suit my stories, and in some cases I changed their names. But they were all characterized by their elemental threat to human stability and human security; and this elemental threat was worth analyzing and translating into modern terms.

Demons and ghouls were created by the earliest storytellers as a way of giving shape and meaning to their most deeply seated anxieties and superstitions. Because they were the imaginary embodiment of such very basic terrors as fear of the dark, fear of inanimate objects changing into vicious creatures, fear of one's own reflection in a mirror, fear of children, they have a lasting potency that you can adapt and exploit, even today. Alternatively, you can use a modern artifact as a demon: a car *(Christine)* or a motorcycle, or a building, or a subway train. But I must warn you: Demonic possession of inanimate objects recently reached a nadir with a British horror-flick entitled *I Bought A Vampire Motorcycle,* and you will probably find it hard to have any similar ideas taken seriously after that.

Personally, I believe that a strong social theme has always been essential to a good horror novel (though beware waffle). In *The Burning,* a novel of fiery reincarnation, I attempted to deal with the issues of materialism, prejudice, and personal responsibility. So my characters had to deal with their own conscience and their own part in a larger society, as well as with horrific and supernatural terrors.

In his interview for horror-anthologist Stanley Wiater's collection of interviews, *Dark Dreamers,* David Morrell (author of *Rambo*) very correctly said that "when you're talking about a breakthrough book, it's not so much the field you're working in, it's the 'canvas.' I hate to use that overworked word, but it's one we all understand. The scope and breadth of a book."

246

He added (and I really can't put it better): "Most horror novels tend to be inbred: They rely on the ideas and concepts of others who have gone before them. Of course, a horror writer must be aware of the history of the genre. But to sell a lot of copies, a horror writer also has to find a large idea and head toward uncharted territory, announcing, in effect, that this book is *different* from other horror fiction."

The challenge to new horror writers is enormous. But it's a challenge that you *must* address if you're going to make your mark. When I wrote *The Manitou* in 1974, the horror market was Dennis Wheatley and me. Jim Herbert hadn't yet written *The Rats*; and Stephen King was unheard of. But now, many years later, a whole new generation of writers has emerged who were brought up on King and Straub and McCammon and me . . . and instead of being a field of four or five horror writers, as it was then, it's literally a field of thousands.

The next Stephen King will have to be a writer so innovative and striking that his (or her) talent spans many fields of thought and social relevance and be twenty times better than Stephen King—much more stunning than *'Salem's Lot* ever was. I really can't wait for this to emerge. That new writer could be you.

I discussed the necessity for characters who are both likable and real. The problem with many horror manuscripts that I've read recently is that the hero or heroines have been weak or corrupt or plain obnoxious or (even worse) unbelievable. I can understand why horror writers bring such characters into their stories. They have difficulty in dealing with the extremity of the threat their characters have to face. They don't attempt to imagine *how it actually feels* to witness a loved one having her head cut off in front of them, or *how it actually feels* to see a roaring demon emerging from their root-cellar.

Just because their fictitious threats are wild and imaginary doesn't mean that their characters should be wild and imaginary. In fact, totally the opposite. The more real the characters' response, the more frightening the threat turns out to be.

I can understand that, nervous of failure, many writers try to distance themselves from the raw emotions that any horrific or supernatural crisis would evoke. Have you ever witnessed a serious traffic accident? Have you tried to describe how you really felt about it? You should recognize that a horror novel will work well only if the characters react in a credible, true-to-life manner. So many horror movies

247

flop because teenage girls keep screaming whenever a monster appears. Watch the newsreels. Watch the way people really behave when they're desperately frightened. They don't scream. The way they really act is far more disturbing than the way so many writers make their characters act.

The characters in a horror novel should be as detailed and believable as the characters in any other novel. I've read so many horror novels in which the protagonists have no parents, no wives, no children, no job, even. They seem to be rootless, floating dummies, just waiting to have something Horrible inflicted on them. Just remember: their *raison d'être* isn't to be victims in your novel; they have their own *raison d'être*. And if you have a struggle making them believe in your horrific threat, and in making them respond to it, then so much the better. You will end up with a far more convincing story.

Make sure that even your minor characters are real. Bob Tuggey, a McDonald's grillman who witnesses the first ghastly immolation in *The Burning,* was described in three dimensions, even though his part in the novel was comparatively small:

. . .balding and overweight and by far the oldest employee at McDonald's Rosecrans Street. When his left eye looked west, his right eye looked nor-nor-west. . . . He had drifted through one menial government clerkship after another, black coffee, brown offices. He had started to drink, a bottle of Ricard a day, often more. Days of milk-white clouds and aniseed.

Make sure that your locations are real. Choose somewhere you know, or visit somewhere specially. I set *Walkers* in Milwaukee, which is an energetic city of varied weather and distinctive character, but which also suited the blue-coller personality of the hero. In contrast, I set *The Burning* in La Jolla, which was a perfect setting for the fashionable upwardly mobile restaurant owner who was the protagonist of *that* novel. Each setting in its own way was fascinating to discover and describe, and added to the depth of the novel.

Out of a strong combination of believability and daring imagination, I believe the next generation of horror fiction will eventually be born. The challenge is enormous; the creative task is very great. However, I am looking forward with considerable relish to the day when the advance manuscript arrives through the mail that will tell me somebody has given horror fiction the sharp new teeth it needs.

248

51

HAVING SOMETHING TO SAY

BY PATRICIA D. CORNWELL

I REMEMBER TAKING LITERATURE AND CREATIVE WRITING CLASSES AT Davidson College in North Carolina and being struck by a frustrating dilemma. It seemed that the best stories were told by the worst writers and the best writers had nothing to say. I have decided by now that this is a common problem, if not THE problem.

The sad reality is, talent does count. You cannot muscle your way to the top simply by doing enough research and spending twelve hours a day in your office. An example is my tennis ability. My pipe dream when I was a child was to play at Forest Hills. I practiced six hours a day, watched matches on TV, and kept *The Inner Game of Tennis* on the table by my bed. The highest I was ever ranked, I think, was fourteenth in North Carolina. The only way I was ever going to make it to Forest Hills was to sit in the stands.

Though you can improve your writing skills, just as you can improve your tennis skills, you cannot learn the inner poetry and descriptive brilliance that extraordinarily gifted writers seem to conjure up without trying. But instead of dwelling on the unsurprising revelation that few of us are geniuses, I'd rather assume that most of us fall into the category of the *good writer who has nothing to say.*

Your voice

I decided to write crime novels not because I liked to read them but because I had been a crime reporter for *The Charlotte Observer*. Beyond that, I cannot fully explain my fascination with violence, but I suspect it has to do with my fear of it.

In my college days, I think I imitated whomever I was reading at the time. This is fine when you are in your formative stages as a writer. But in order for you to write successfully, you must discover your voice and your story. Your voice is what you sound like when you no longer are consciously trying to imitate someone else. Perhaps your voice is dry and quite funny, like Sue Grafton's. Or it may be melancholy and richly poetic, like Pat Conroy's. When you really tap into your own voice, you are discovering a layer of yourself that is not necessarily apparent in the personality other people see when they meet you. For example, my writing is dark, filled with nightscapes and fear. Isolation and a sense of loss whisper throughout my prose like something perpetually stirring in the wind. It is not uncommon for people to meet me and find it incongruous that I write the sort of books I do.

Finding your voice requires endless writing, and you may discover your voice at the same time you discover your story.

Your story

What draws you in? When you read the newspaper in the morning, what do you look at first? Sports, comics, crime stories, or politics? My eye has always caught crime stories first, and that's been true for as long as I can remember. Ask yourself other questions, as well. Or maybe you already know your story. Maybe you're a lawyer like Scott Turow or know as much about horse racing as Dick Francis. Maybe you fought in Vietnam or work in law enforcement. Maybe your life has been a series of tragic romances—or no romances—and that's the song you want to sing.

Whatever your story is, if you write enough, certain themes will reappear. Watch for them. Don't be afraid to face them. Writing is an intensely psychological experience, or it should be, and the words don't have to be born of wounds, but they might be. My story is violence. I finally figured that out after years of failed manuscripts. My story is people who carry on in a world that is hard and cold and sharp around the edges. My story is not Southern or "clever" or derivative. It is an eyewitness account, the framework starkly wrought from what I see, the flesh and soul nurtured by my own experience and personality. I've done and continue to do a lot of research. Could I redesign my life, I would have been a chief medical examiner with a law degree who somehow found time to write novels featuring a chief medical examiner with a law degree. Then I would have discovered that my true gift was writing and could have lived off my intellectual investments for the rest of my literary life. But had I been a forensic pathologist with a law degree, I would have been far too busy and burned out to feel creative after hours. The truth is, I am a former journalist who majored in English in college. I hated chemistry and math, did not want to touch a computer, and was indifferent toward biology. By the time I was twenty-five I'd never been to a funeral because I was afraid of death.

I began work on my first murder mystery in the fall of 1984. A physician I knew recommended that I interview a medical examiner since forensic medicine is so important in modern criminal investigation. I was fortunate enough to get an appointment at the Office of the Chief Medical Examiner in Richmond, Virginia. I spent three hours talking with Dr. Marcella Fierro, the deputy chief. I was utterly fascinated, and I was horrified by how ignorant I was. I thought, "How can you write crime novels when you don't even understand what these people are talking about?"

I began to discover that subjects I had fled from in college not only fascinated me now, but I had an aptitude for them. Without realizing it, I had just embarked upon a grim and peculiar journey that, oddly, would lead me to my voice and story.

Authentic credibility

If you are interested in a particular field or intend to address a particular subject, you must learn something about it. Being a master at stringing words together or describing sunsets is not enough. If your story lacks credibility and authenticity, no one will care how exquisite your metaphors are.

For example, if your knowledge of journalism is limited to what you read in the paper or see in movies, don't decide to create a protagonist who is a journalist. Or if you do, start educating yourself. Get someone to introduce you to a journalist. Ask him if you can ride with him on his beat one day. Or see if you can do any sort of volunteer work in the newsroom on your day off from your regular profession.

For me, it is essential to experience directly what I'm writing about (within reason). I want to know what it looks like, feels like, smells like, sounds like. Writers are pests. We drive everybody crazy with our cries for help when we're getting started, and I've decided that you might just get what you want if you abandon any notion of entitlement. Don't think some harried reporter is going to be thrilled about having you ride shotgun while he rushes around on his beat. A lot of cops or other experts would get tired of you, too. Forget a medical examiner warming up to the idea of your hanging around the morgue. If you're determined to master a subject, apply the same rules that work in good business: You give me something, I give you something.

What would you like to master? Is there something you can do to help? Let's say you want to create a protagonist who is a gardener, yet you live in a fourteenth-story apartment in Manhattan. Find a greenhouse and go to work or volunteer. Expose yourself, somehow, to whatever it is you wish to understand. But never forget—if you want, you also must give. The irony is that when you're P. D. James, everybody wants you doing research at their facility when you no longer need it. When you're just getting started, you have to pay your dues because nobody cares.

I wanted to understand police work better, so I signed on as a volunteer police officer in Richmond City. I dressed in uniform. I took dog bite reports, directed traffic, and worked parades. I gave the city hundreds of hours of my time, but I got something extremely valuable in return. I know how to drive an unmarked car, get free coffee at 7-Elevens, talk on the radio and light flares. I've been to numerous homicide scenes and I know homicide detectives because I've ridden with them on their four to midnight shifts more times than I can count.

I know how Pete Marino, the homicide detective in my series, thinks. To learn how Dr. Scarpetta thinks, I went to work for the medical examiners. At first I assisted in technical writing. Eventually, I became their computer analyst. Though I work only as a consultant for them now, I was down there constantly for more than six years. I would place myself on the extreme end of the spectrum. Not everyone could or would throw himself into research to this extent. Most writers have other professions. Moderation for all things, but if you have a passion for westerns, at least go ride a horse.

Seeking advice

In the early days, I used to have friends read chapters as I wrote them. I wrote letters to P. D. James. I did everything most fledgling writers do, and now I know why. I thought I wanted advice. What I really wanted was assurance. What I got was a lot of confusion.

If it works better for you to discuss constantly a current project with someone, then do it. I can't. If meeting with groups of aspiring writers and commiserating and sharing ideas works for you, do it. I can't. In the first place, I feel that my ideas are private. I'm not going to tell you about this great plot I've devised. That places a burden on you to keep my secret, and the more I talk about my great plot, the more I relieve the tension necessary to drive me into my office. I have about concluded that the more someone talks about a book, the less he's working on it.

Writing is solitary. You can't write unless you are willing to spend a lot of time alone. I'm not saying you should never meet with groups or go to conventions. Much depends on your personality type. Some writers like crowds and derive much from panel discussions. Others, like me, choose to confide in a friend, but in the main, figure it out on their own. I believe trial and error is the best teacher, and that you can learn most about what makes a novel or story work by reading the best authors.

§ 52

CREATING SERIES CHARACTERS

BY ANNE PERRY

THE BEST SERIES CHARACTERS are those that readers come to know and like, that they enjoy meeting again and again. Some—Miss Marple, Poirot, or Columbo, for example—do not noticeably progress or have any personal life outside the plot of the current story. Others, whom I personally admire more, grow, have changing relationships, and inhabit a world of places and events that also develop. Dorothy Sayers's Lord Peter Wimsey is an excellent example of the latter type, with his World War I experiences as an officer in France, his family, his courtship and marriage of Harriet Vane. One wishes to read the next book not only for its mystery, but to know what happens next in *his* life.

I have never created a series character intentionally. I began with Charlotte and Pitt when they met in *The Cater Street Hangman,* and I rather lurched from one book to another for at least the first half dozen of my novels, always hoping the next one would be accepted but never sure in advance. After that, when I might have been confident enough to plan, it was far too late. The personalities and their histories and relationships were thoroughly established.

My second series character, Monk, was something of an accident, but I now realize, as I am beginning the fourth Monk novel, *The Gardener in White,* that by the greatest good luck, I have endowed him with many of the characteristics that make keeping him in a series relatively easy. I say "relatively," because there are still many pitfalls.

However, on thinking about it, I have come up with a list of qualities I would have given him, had I planned it, and why. (I will use the masculine simply to avoid saying "he" or "she" each time.)

When creating the past for a series character, leave plenty of spaces for events you may wish to put in later. I mean not only spaces in time, but also emotional spaces, unresolved ideas, brief mentions of experiences that may have been important. Be careful about too many unexplained hints; they can be very irritating to the reader. It is better simply to leave a space in your own mind with a possible way to account for it: service in a war, a period of living in a different country or a difficult social environment, a very unusual job, or anything else that allows for a variety of references in future stories.

With Monk, I have in my mind his entire past, which is unknown country to him because of his amnesia *(Face of a Stranger),* and slowly he is discovering past love affairs, people to whom he owes immense debts of gratitude, cases in which he failed and the consequences were very painful to him *(Defend and Betray).* Charlotte is very well known, but Pitt's youth is still largely unexplored, and I have plans for it in a future novel. But there are also all the subsidiary characters like Great Aunt Vespasia, who since she is eighty, must have a past with interesting adventures.

Relationships over time are very complex, and people are changed by closeness to one another. There are periods of intimacy and of distance, mutual injuries, misunderstandings, debts, dependencies, and all these will change and leave their mark on the characters. The people from the past can greatly contribute to your hero's personality, and later on you can introduce them if you wish, or insert such powerful experiences as a failure and the character's resultant sense of guilt; the death of someone close; a bitter injustice; or anything relevant to the story you are currently telling.

When inventing your hero's past, think hard about his family and other relationships—mentors, loves, professional rivals or friends, adversaries, etc. Do not draw him in such detail at the outset that you leave no room for layers of personality, conflicts, even contradictions to be revealed later on. People change from day to day, let alone from year to year, but we are all the sum of everything we have been. Our past, whether we remember it consciously or not, leaves its mark on us one way or another.

Show how your hero has been affected by the people he has known: those he loved, hated, feared, admired, or whatever. If you don't say too much to begin with, you will leave yourself room to bring in other people in later books. Suggest their existence with a sketch or a single reference or memory, then you may use them as key figures in a later story. This will not only provide a character for the plot, but will also affect your hero far more profoundly than a stranger might.

255

Let your hero be moved by the events of each story, and consequently be slightly changed, whether wiser, gentler, more compassionate; or if you prefer, more foolish, more arrogant, more cynical, whatever you feel would work for you. But remember, if *you* do not like your hero, your readers may not either, in which case they are unlikely to want to follow him through a series of novels.

I am not suggesting he become a saint, but simply that his adventures engage his emotions and that he will grow because of that. He may well have failings he never conquers, battles he wins, but wars he loses. Be careful of weaknesses like alcoholism or drug dependency, or a permanently bad marriage, or the inability to sustain a relationship. Such things can become very boring to readers after a while. Also, self-pity is tedious in real people, and not really any better in fictional ones. A short-lived problem can be interesting, but after two or three novels, it loses its appeal. Readers will begin to feel the hero should have dealt with his shortcomings or come to terms with them. I know that is not always the case in life, but if we wish our readers to continue to read and enjoy our stories, we have to make them enjoyable. I don't suggest a Pollyanna ending, but if a problem cannot be solved, be quiet about it. No one *has* to read our novels; we must write so readers will be eager to, and that means that the cardinal sin is to be boring.

Think how you yourself have grown, changed your feelings, your views; allow your hero or heroine to do the same. If you write a series over a ten- or twenty-year period, you will not be the same as when you started; neither should your characters be. Your readers should be able to trace the course of your characters as they mature from one novel to another—the development of their relationships; their skills; their inner spiritual life (if relevant).

For example, Charlotte's marriage to Pitt, a man of lower social status and income, changed her a great deal. She became more practical, learned to be less outspoken and to modify many of her previous judgments. That may be a reflection of my own friendships with a wide variety of people!

Monk has faced *much* more violent change in his discovery of his own past, his acts, and the character they portrayed. He was obliged to see himself as others had, without any knowledge of his motives at the time; his consequent assessment of himself shook him to the core. The examples are legion, and you can create them for yourself.

Beware of having a specific ending in mind when you start building a character, or you may find you reach the end before you mean to and have nowhere further to go.

In creating your series characters, try to create friends for yourself and others, people your readers will like so much they will not want you to let them die or disappear.

53

FREE-FORM PLOTTING THE MYSTERY NOVEL

BY MARCIA MULLER

PLOTTING THE MODERN MYSTERY NOVEL is a complex task that bears as little resemblance to so-called formula writing as Miss Jane Marple does to Lew Archer. One of the questions most often asked by aspiring mystery writers (frequently in tones of frustration, after being out-foxed by one of their favorite authors) is, "How on earth do you complicate your plots and still get them to hang together?"

Unhappily for those who seek instant solutions, there is no one sure-fire method of plotting. The techniques vary from writer to writer along a continuum that stretches from detailed, extensive outlining to what I call winging it (writing with no planning whatsoever). Writers adopt the type of plotting that best suits their working styles and personalities. Some hit on the appropriate type immediately, others gradually make their way toward it through experimentation—plus hard work and practice. There are no major shortcuts, but there are *little* shortcuts. Tiny ones, actually. What I'm about to tell you about plotting is only my highly individualized technique; all, some, or none of my suggestions may help.

I've learned my craft the hard way. In the past fifteen years I've made every attempt to "reinvent the wheel," especially where plotting is concerned. I began by making detailed character sketches, outlines, and time charts, a method distilled down to a lengthy storyline synopsis. I've tried winging it, with unsatisfying results. What I've finally settled into is a technique that I call "free-form plotting"; as the term implies, its key ingredient is flexibility.

Before we go on, however, let's discuss the concept of plot. If someone were to ask you what a novel's plot is, you'd probably say "the story." But if you examine a given *plot,* you'll see it's somewhat different from the *story.* The story is linear; it is the events that happen, both on and off scene. The plot is the *structure* you impose on those events. You select which to include, in what order, and how to tell each one. You shape your plot from the raw material—the story.

Here's an example of a crime story, simplified for our purposes:

1. Killer meets victim; they interact.
2. Killer murders victim.
3. Murder is discovered; detective enters case.
4. Detective investigates.
5. Detective solves murder; killer is apprehended.

Taking the raw material of this particular story, you could plot in a number of ways. You could tell it in a linear fashion, from step one to step five (although that's not likely to be surprising or dramatic). You could start with the discovery of the murder, continue through to the killer's apprehension, explaining in flashback or dialogue what went on in steps one and two. You could start with the actual murder, masking the identity of the killer. The steps may be ordered any whichway depending on what kind of book you want to write. It is up to you to decide how this simple story is told; the question we are addressing here is how you make and follow through on your decision.

What I like about free-form plotting is that it allows me to defer the decision, feeling my way as I write. It saves me from becoming locked into an inflexible plot outline that may, in the end, not suit my purposes. I can start a novel with a minimal idea of where I'm going, develop some ideas and characters, experiment with them, keep what fits, discard what doesn't. An example of this is how I plotted my Sharon McCone novel, *There's Something in a Sunday.*

When I started I had in mind a beginning situation, a few characters, a background, a theme, and a hazy idea of the ending. The situation has Sharon McCone being hired to follow a man who came to San Francisco every Saturday night and stayed through the early morning hours on Monday. The characters were the man, Frank Wilkonson; Sharon's client; a woman the man was looking for; and a married couple who were friends of the woman's. The background was dual: neighborhood activism and the plight of San Francisco's homeless people. The theme was the relationships between men and women, and how they go awry. And the ending—well, I won't reveal everything.

259

When I start a mystery novel, I like to set the situation in the first one or two chapters. In this case, it was Sharon following Wilkonson, observing his eccentric Sunday activities, and wondering if the client had told her the entire truth about his interest in Wilkonson. Because she observed Wilkonson's movements closely for nearly twenty-four hours, she feels that she knows him—and so did I, although he had not as yet uttered a single word of dialogue. In these two chapters, I had developed his character in some depth, and had begun to consider him a real person. As he developed, I began to think differently about Wilkonson and what I intended to do with him later on.

I employed the rule of flexibility very early. When I read my first two chapters, I found something was wrong: Taken together, they moved too slowly. So I broke them up, inserting a flashback chapter between them, in which I introduced the client, Rudy Goldring, and showed how Sharon had come to spend her Sunday tailing Wilkonson. By the time I finished the scene, both Goldring and the derelict who served as "doorman" at his office building had come alive for me, and I began to see new ways they could be used in the plot.

My next step was to introduce the supporting characters: the people at All Souls Legal Cooperative, where Sharon works. Again, something was wrong with the scene I'd planned. I was tired of writing about the co-op in the same old way. If I had to write the scene with Sharon sitting in her boss's office discussing the case one more time. . . . My solution was to introduce a new attorney and an assistant for Sharon, to give more prominence to an old character, the secretary, and to create personal problems for the boss, whose previous life had been placid. Now I had a situation that I was eager to write about, and a fast-developing personal subplot that (because the life of Sharon and the people at All Souls is an ongoing story from novel to novel) didn't necessarily have to be wrapped up at the end.

Of course, what happened in the scene at All Souls required going back and making minor adjustments in the first three chapters; the new attorney, for instance, was now the person who had handed Sharon the Goldring assignment, rather than her boss. This is a time-consuming necessity of free-form plotting but, as we'll see later, it has its advantages.

At this point I was ready to establish my other characters. And, while a lot had happened and a number of questions about Wilkonson and Goldring had been raised, I needed something more dramatic—the murder.

At the scene of the crime I was able to introduce another of the main characters, an unnamed woman who appeared suddenly and then vanished. In the next few chapters, as Sharon followed up on the case for reasons of personal satisfaction, I brought in the other characters who would figure prominently: the married couple, Wilkonson's wife, and his employer.

Most of these characters had turned out differently from what I'd first envisioned. A character "taking over" the story is a phenomenon that writers often discuss. No one knows exactly why or how this happens, but I suspect it has to do with the writer's being relaxed and "into" the story. As you sit at the keyboard, new ideas start to flow. Characters take on fuller identities as you allow them to speak and act and interact with one another. When this happens to me, I simply go along with whatever is developing; often I write pages and pages of dialogue or action, then pare them down or toss them out entirely. It's easier to cut or eliminate your prose than to go back and add material later. By setting down these free-flowing scenes on paper, you will avail yourself of the opportunity to create something that may vastly improve your novel. And (impossible in real life) you can always rip up the pages or hit the delete key.

One example of this phenomenon is the development of the married couple that I've mentioned—Vicky and Gerry Cushman. Originally, I'd seen them in a strictly functional sense, as friends of the woman who appears at the murder scene and then vanishes—the pivotal character in the plot. But, as Vicky began to take shape, what emerged was not the coolly efficient neighborhood activist I'd planned, but a woman with severe emotional problems. And in response to this development, her husband Gerry emerged as a selfish man who exacerbated her problems. I had created an unexpected conflict that wove nicely into the theme of the novel—and I was able to use it to further complicate my plot.

At this point—the end of your primary development stage—you can take full advantage of free-form plotting. You have your characters in all their individuality and richness; you have a situation that is ripe for additional complication; you have an idea of where you're going. Now

261

is the time to find out exactly where that is—and how you're going to get there.

The way I accomplish this is to read what I have on paper. Then I play the game of "what if." The game is a question-and-answer process: "What if such-and-such happened? How would that work?"

In *Sunday,* I reached this point just as Frank Wilkonson disappeared. He had gone to an abandoned windmill in Golden Gate Park; Sharon was following him, but lost him in the darkness and fog; Wilkonson never returned to his car. This was an unplanned development; the setting of the windmill had occurred to me while driving by it one day, and it seemed a perfect place for an eerie, late-night scene. The scene wrote easily, but at its conclusion I had to admit I had no idea why Wilkonson had gone there or where he'd gone afterwards. Time for "what if. . . ."

Why did he? I asked myself. The obvious answer was that he planned to meet someone there. Sometimes the obvious choice is the best. But who? I could think of one character who would have reason to be there, but no reason to meet Wilkonson. But what if he was asked to contact Frank? By whom? I knew who that might be. But then, why hadn't Sharon seen Frank meet the other person? What if Wilkonson had. . .?

By the end of this question-and-answer session I found myself in possession of a new plot twist: an eventual second murder and a killer who hadn't even been on my list of primary suspects. Because of my accidental choice of a setting and the manner in which I wrote the scene, my plot had taken on greater complication—and greater mystery.

A few chapters later I was faced with another situation calling for "what if." Sharon had finally located the woman from the murder scene. The woman had ties to all the major characters, but they were as yet nebulous. In a few cases, they were nebulous even to *me.* So I considered the connections among all six of these people. What if the client was an old friend of the woman? What if they had once been lovers? No, friends was better. But what if she had had a lover? What if it was Frank? Or Gerry? Or Frank's boss? Or. . .? Because the characters were well established at this time, I was able to come up with a logical answer.

As I've said, free-form plotting requires constant readjustments of scenes and details to make them consistent with one another. This is laborious at times, often necessitating extensive rewriting. But I'm convinced that it is also extremely beneficial. As you rewrite, you are forced to pay great attention to detail, to polish your prose, to reexamine your logic.

Logic is crucial to a mystery novel. If it is flawed, the whole plot—no matter how original your premise, fascinating your characters, or vivid your settings—simply falls apart. I advise frequent rewriting and rereading. Check every detail; make sure every place is described properly, especially if the action depends on the lay of the land. As I was preparing the final draft of an earlier McCone novel, *Eye of the Storm*, I found that I'd handled a description of a boathouse in two different ways. In the early chapters, it had been a building on pilings over the water; later on, it had a concrete foundation and boat wells. Since near the end something happened in one of those wells, the initial description made no sense whatsoever!

This may sound like an incredible error, but, believe me, things like this happen to professionals, too. When I discovered it, I had read the manuscript numerous times. A friend and frequent collaborator had read it twice. Neither of us had caught the discrepancy. So check your copy. Recheck. Publishing houses have copyeditors to catch the little things, but the big things are your responsibility.

There you have the basics of free-form plotting. Develop a general situation, background, theme, characters, and ending. Set the situation. Allow your characters to act and interact with one another. When the primary development stage is complete, complicate by playing "what if." Write some more. Be flexible; play "what if" again and again. Rewrite, reread. Check, recheck. And as you write, take advantage of the surprising things that develop—they will often point the way to a truly baffling plot!

263

§ 54

WRITING "TRUE" CRIME: GETTING FORENSIC FACTS RIGHT

BY STEVEN SCARBOROUGH

THE STORY READS LIKE THIS: Mitch Sharp, the skillful detective, solves the "Casino Slasher Case" by tracing cloth fibers and a drop of saliva found at the murder scene to the stealthy criminal.

What's wrong with the facts in this scenario? This simply can't be done. The evidence is scientifically dubious. When is a case plausible, and when does it stretch reality? A writer can know only by examining the type of forensic evidence necessary for the events of the story and then by doing the appropriate research.

Fingerprints

Fingerprints are the most conclusive form of forensic evidence; they are the only type of evidence that does not require corroborative proof. Though the probability of finding that elusive fingerprint or that single strand of hair is low, it can be woven into your story if you include the proper background. Fingerprint processing of a toenail and an eyeball of a murder victim in the *Red Dragon* is not only technically correct, but it also lends a gritty credence to Thomas Harris's novel.

Fingerprints command the most attention in court, and they should get equal billing in your crime story. In a city of about 300,000, fingerprints lead to the identification, arrest, or conviction of nearly one person every day.

While fingerprints are readily retrieved from glass, shiny metal, and paper, they are difficult to recover from fabric, textured objects, or finished furniture. Surface to surface, the methods of recovery differ, so the writer should know the proper processes for recovering incriminating fingerprints. It will make a story both interesting and accurate.

In *Presumed Innocent*, Scott Turow gives us an impressive account of the questioning of a fingerprint witness in court. His only lapse is in describing blue fingerprints developed on glass with ninhydrin powder. Ninhydrin, a liquid chemical brushed on paper, produces a purplish fingerprint. The common graphite powder method is used on slick surfaces such as glass.

A dramatic punch to your story might be to recover prints from one of your victims, and it can be done. Iodine fumes are blown over the body with a small glass tube and a silver plate is pressed against the skin to lift the print. However, at this time prints can be recovered only within two hours from a live person and within about twelve hours from a deceased one.

Is your antagonist trying to incriminate someone else? Maybe he has considered forging a fingerprint? Forget it; his attempts are sure to be futile. It is nearly impossible to recreate an accurate die of someone's fingerprint. A cast can be made, provided he has a willing or dead hand to cast. Yet, even then the resulting print will be reversed or backward if transferred to an object.

A fingerprint expert cannot testify to how long a fingerprint will last on an object. General rules suggest that a fingerprint will last days, not weeks, outside in the weather; weeks but not months in a residence; and a month would not be long for a fingerprint left on a mirror, especially if encased in a drawer or a safe. Fingerprints have been chemically recovered years later on the pages of a book.

When tracing someone from latent fingerprints, the investigator must have the suspect's name and fingerprint record on file to make a positive match. Lawrence Block captures the essence of fingerprints in *The Burglar Who Painted Like Mondrian*:

. . . you can't really run a check on a single print unless you've already got a suspect. You need a whole set of prints, which we wouldn't have, even if whoever it was left prints, which they probably didn't. And they'd have to have been fingerprinted anyway for a check to reveal them.

Historically, fingerprints have been filed using a ten-print classification system; without recovering latent fingerprints of all ten fingers, a person could not be identified. In the 1980s, the AFIS (Automated Fingerprint Identification System) computer was introduced, enabling jurisdictions with access to the computer to link a single latent fingerprint to a suspect previously fingerprinted. Writers should remember that AFIS computers cost over a million dollars, and your quaint Vermont village will not have one. The well-connected fictional investigator should know someone at a large agency or the FBI for a record check.

Body Fluids

Fingerprints may be the most positive form of identification, but what if your perpetrator does not leave any? In the absence of fingerprints, body fluids are a common type of evidence found at a crime scene. If an intact sample of adequate size is recovered, body fluids can be analyzed to obtain a DNA genetic profile that can be compared with the suspect's or examined for blood type.

Blood, semen, and saliva are all excellent media for determining a DNA match. DNA (deoxyribonucleic acid) is the blueprint of a person's genetic makeup and is absolutely unique for each individual.

Contrary to common belief, hair will not reveal a person's DNA pattern. Have your victim yank out a clump of hair with the skin cells to make a DNA match.

The equipment necessary to analyze DNA is highly specialized and costly. Again, if your story is set in a quaint village, it may not be feasible to run a DNA check. It also may take months to get results from one of the few laboratories that do DNA analysis. This need not be a negative; think of the desperation, the agony, of waiting for results while your killer still stalks.

Body fluids can be analyzed by the local crime lab to help your detective. An important factor associated with body fluids, including blood types, is secretor status. A secretor puts out, i.e., secretes, his ABO blood type into peripheral body fluids such as semen, perspiration, etc. It is possible for your fictional serial rapist to avoid any link to his body fluids by being one of the 15 per cent that are non-secretors.

What does blood type tell the investigator? Normally a blood type places a person in a broad portion of the general population. A community might have 45 per cent of its members with O blood, 40 per cent with A blood, and so on. Therefore, if standard ABO typing is done, the results are of little value because of the large population with that blood type.

Additional blood grouping techniques, specifically enzyme and protein analyses, enable the forensic chemist to assign a suspect to a narrower population. Your fictional crime lab should not give your detective a match on blood from the crime scene. They can limit only the number of people in your town that have that type of enzyme blood group.

The special equipment needed for thorough blood analysis is costly, and it is probable that numerous crimes go unsolved because sufficient testing is either too expensive or neglected.

Other evidence

Hair can be of forensic value. Strands found at the scene of the crime can be compared to a suspect's for similarities in color, shape, and texture, but it is difficult to determine race or even sex. An author can write that some of the suspects were eliminated because analysis concluded that their hair was not similar or consistent with the hair found at the crime scene.

Footwear prints, recovered by photography, fall into the class category. Except for the exceptional case, shoeprints can only be said to be made by the same type of shoe. Footwear, or any class type evidence (hair, fiber, ABO blood type) by itself would normally not be enough to convict your suspect in a court of law.

Handwriting cases rarely get into court. A handwriting expert renders an opinion after examining several varying factors such as letter height ratio and slant. If the writing is similar, then degrees of match probability are reported.

Criminals usually disguise their writing. It is unlikely that a kidnapper's ransom note, written in block letters will lead to the identity of your brutish villain. Words in blood dribbled on a wall may provide a strong clue and add color to your story, but they will not enable a handwriting examiner to point to your murderer.

Striations on a bullet are unique, much like the ridges of a fingerprint. Therefore, a bullet can be traced to a gun using the scratches or lands and grooves imprinted on it by the barrel of a gun. Unfortunately, if the barrel is damaged or changed, or if the bullet is mangled, the examination will be inconclusive. Careful scrutiny is necessary before including a firearms match in your murder mystery.

Thomas Harris was very skillful in weaving his forensic research throughout his novel. FBI Agent Will Graham explores the gamut of forensic evidence from fingerprints to blood typing to bite marks. *The Red Dragon* could be used as a forensic model for crime writers.

The increasing sophistication of today's readers is a two-edged sword: Readers are no longer satisfied with, "He was the only one tall enough who had a motive." A writer trying to add more realism to a story need not shy away from scientific evidence, but he must check his forensic facts for accuracy. Credibility is the key to a successful crime novel. Just as a character's action may lead the reader to say, "He wouldn't do that," an erroneous forensic fact can turn off the reader. Do your research well, and you will be rewarded by readers clamoring to pick up your latest authentic crime story.

55

CHARACTER: THE KEY ELEMENT IN MYSTERY NOVELS

BY JAMES COLBERT

BY DEFINITION, TO BE A MYSTERY a novel must have a murder at the beginning that is solved by the end. And by convention there must be a solution, whether or not there is an apprehension. This is the contract assumed by the reader when he or she picks up a book classified as a mystery. Yet despite this murder-solution requisite, mysteries offer the writer greater freedom, a basic structure around which to work plot, setting, and most important, character.

Without doubt, character is the most important element of a mystery. A clever plot helps, certainly, as does a strong sense of place, but those elements are secondary, best used to show how the central character thinks and responds to events and environment. One writer may have a native Floridian solving murders while another may send a New York City detective to Florida. While Florida, of course, remains the same, the interesting thing for the reader is to see how the character responds, how he or she integrates the sense of the place into an overall experience. The same is true of the plot. No matter how interesting, unless uncovered by a central character readers find engaging, events take on a flat, two-dimensional quality. "Just the facts, ma'am. Just the facts" has its place, all right, but that place is in a newspaper, not a mystery.

So how does a writer go about portraying an engaging character? The answer to that is as multi-faceted and as complex as the character must be, and it is accomplished one small step at a time. Think of a police artist putting together a composite sketch of a suspect. Thin sheets of transparent plastic, each with slightly different lines are laid one over another, composing different parts of the face until a whole picture emerges. While the medium is different, the technique is not dissimilar to the one a writer uses. First sheet: How tall is the character, and how much does he weigh? How is he built? Second sheet: What color hair does he have? What are his distinguishing characteristics? Third sheet: What is the setting, and what is the character thinking? Small elements are put together, one over another, until a whole picture emerges.

Where the police artist leaves off with the physical portrait, however, the writer is just beginning because the reader wants to know, well, what's this guy really *like?* Is he threatening or non-threatening? Well-read or illiterate? Optimistic or pessimistic? What kind of car does he drive? What does he eat? The nuances, eccentricities, habits, way of thinking and quirks are what separate a description of a character from one who starts to *live*; and all those things are revealed as the character responds to his surroundings and reacts to events—in a very good mystery, dynamic events make the character *grow.*

Growth and change are intrinsic, inevitable elements of the human condition. The growing and the changing, however, usually occur very slowly, day by day, not very noticeably. Within the usually limited time frame of a novel, this change is often very difficult to portray, but the mystery has the advantage of a dynamic structure. A murder occurs at the beginning and is solved by the end. Events, feelings, new understandings are speeded up, compressed into a very short time. As a result, it is credible that the characters change fairly quickly in response. Really successful mysteries allow the reader not just to know a character but to grow with him, to learn his lessons as he did, without actually having to endure the violent crime. Observe Burke in Andrew Vachss's novel, *Blossom,* or listen to the first-person narrator in Scott Turow's *Presumed Innocent.* Notice how they change during the course of the book. Observe what they learn and how the new understandings affect them. And watch how, with the characters firmly in hand, the authors thrust them into the events that form the respective plots.

Plots are usually very simple ideas extended. Even the most complex plot can be described briefly. (Excellent examples of this can be found in your Sunday paper, in the film listings, where even very involved movies are summarized in a line or two.) But unlike the step-by-step development of characters, plots appear complex at the outset and become more and more simple. Elements are stripped away rather than added. What appears confusing, even chaotic, at the start makes

270

sense later on when other motives and actions are revealed: In retrospect, all the twists and turns make sense. The reader is left with a clear sense of order, a good sense of character, and, one hopes, a strong sense of place.

Evoking a place is stage setting in its most basic form. Remember, it is crucial to have the stage set for the central character—and not the other way round. Overlong descriptions of a place and a recitation of facts about it are best left to travel guides, which is not to say that setting is *un*important. But it *is* secondary. When successfully used, setting becomes the character and helps to reveal his or her foibles and way of life. In John D. MacDonald's Travis Magee novels, Travis Magee's houseboat, for example, is very much a part of Travis Magee, accommodating, even making possible, a way of life that is so much a part of him that when he travels, he seems to embody one *place* confronting another. Readers envy Travis the beachbum freedom of his life, and we understand how it feels to leave the beach and go, say, to New York City or to Mexico—or, for that matter, just to go to work. The setting is integral to Travis Magee and enriches the whole series; but while it may be difficult to imagine him anywhere else, the fact is, readers can. (MacDonald even tells us how to go about it whenever Travis considers his options.) For the writer, however, the single most important facet of technique, as important in its own way as making character primary, is to make use of what you know.

If presented well, there is no human experience that is uninteresting. Very good books have been written about what might, from all appearances, be very mundane lives. Yet mystery writers too often feel the need to write not what they know but what they perceive they *should* be writing about. As a result, the characters they create do not ring true, or in particular, they are tough when they should not be, or have no real sense of what violence is really like. But despite the hard-boiled school of detective fiction, it is *not* necessary for a central character in a mystery to be either tough or violent—the book can, in fact, be just as interesting when a character conveys some squeamishness or distaste for violence. Not all detectives have to be built like linebackers and display a penchant for brutal confrontation.

The simple fact is, what you know is what will ring true. Andrew Vachss writes about violence and violent people because he knows his subject; but Tony Hillerman eschews that and writes about Navajo

271

Indians, which is what *he* knows. Scott Turow, the lawyer, writes about legal proceedings. All three have written very good books. But since Dashiell Hammett's *Continental Op*, far too many mystery writers have felt it mandatory to make their investigators tough, even when the writer has no notion of what real toughness is all about. The result is facade rather than substance—and the reader will sense it. In fiction, certainly, there is a need for imagination, but the imagination must spring from knowledge, not speculation. The most credible, most substantive books are those in which the author's grasp of his or her subject shows through. Allow your character to know what you know and do not attempt to impose on him what you feel he *should* know. Your character will appear shallow if you do, shallow, and most damning of all, contrived. With respect to that, it is important, too, that you consider your story first, *then* the genre it happens to fall into.

With my first novel, *Profit and Sheen,* I wasn't even aware that I had written a mystery until the first review came out. What makes me appear rather dense in one way worked to my advantage in another: I told my story as well as I knew how and was completely unencumbered by any feeling of restriction. The point is, tell your story as well as you know how and see how it comes out. *Then* worry about genre. If you start out with the expressed intent of writing a mystery, well and good; if you follow the rules. But if what you have in mind is a story with only some elements of a mystery, tell your story first and do not try to change it to conform to some vague idea of what a mystery should be. Your publisher will classify your book for you; genre classification is a subjective thing, nothing more than a handle, really, an easy and convenient way of breaking down different works into groups more for marketing purposes than for readers.

There are, of course, other aspects of writing a mystery to consider, but these are more difficult to pin down. Most notable among them, however, are point of view and voice. Selecting the right point of view is extremely important, because it determines what the reader will and will not learn. Voice is, really, the application of point of view to a consistent rhythm, a *voice* the reader hears. More often than not, point of view is intrinsic to the writing itself (the writer will begin "I . . ." or "He . . ."), but voice requires a certain conscious effort on the writer's part, an attempt to convey the story consistently through or around the central character—even when that central character's vision is rather limited or, to the writer, unattractive. The success of the voice is directly related to how true the writer remains to his character and how willing the writer is to remain "transparent."

If you work within the given structure, writing a mystery is not so different from writing any other kind of novel. Good mysteries do, in fact, have all the elements common to all good fiction: engaging characters, strong sense of place, compelling plot, believable voice. Allow the structure to work for you, write as honestly as you know how, and everything else will fall into place.

56

PLOT AND CHARACTER IN SUSPENSE FICTION

BY JOAN AIKEN

WHICH CAME FIRST, the chicken or the egg? Does plot arise from character, or character from plot? The question is in many ways an artificial one; most writers have felt, at one time or another, the heady excitement of knowing that a whole story, or at least its basic elements—plot, character, and development all tangled together—is struggling to emerge from the dark.

But if this does not happen?

"What is character," says Henry James in *The Art of Fiction* (1884), "but the determination of incident? What is incident but the illustration of character?" And the Old Master goes on to add (several pages later), "The story and the novel, the idea and the form, are the needle and the thread, and I never heard of a guild of tailors who recommended the use of the thread without the needle, or the needle without the thread."

Perfectly true, and you have to have both before you can begin. But, suppose you have only half of the combination?

Characters are generally the problem. *Plots* come a dime a dozen, they are easy to pick up. We read them every day in the papers. A mother, even after several years, remains positive that the death of her teenage son, classified as suicide, was not so; but whenever she pushes her inquiries about it, other unexplained deaths take place. The pet poodle of a notorious Chicago mobster is stolen. The CIA sets up a spurious marine engineering firm in an effort to salvage a sunken Soviet submarine. A middle-aged woman demands a daily love poem from her browbeaten husband. A descendant of one of the twenty-one victims of the Boston Molasses Disaster is still seeking compensation. A convention of magicians plans to meet in an Indian town, but the citizens raise strong objections. . . .

Any of these incidents, all culled from the daily press, might trigger a story, might produce that wonderful effervescent sensation, familiar to every writer (it really is like the working of yeast in one's mind), when different elements begin to ferment together and create something new. The best plots, of course, instantly create their own characters. That wife, that domineering wife, compelling her husband to produce a new love lyric every evening: we know at once what she would be like. And the cowardly put-upon husband, submitting to this tyranny, trudging off to the library for new rhymes and new verse forms, until the climactic moment when he rebels, and supplies you with the start of your story. Or the grieving, brooding mother, worrying on and on about her son's death, gradually acquiring little bits of information. It would be very easy to tell her story.

But if you have the plot without the characters?

There's nothing so frustrating for the reader as a potentially interesting, intricate story, full of turns and twists, in which the characters are so flat, machine-made, and lifeless that they form a total barrier to following the course of the narrative, because it is impossible to remember who is who. Is Miranda the actress or the secretary? Was it Wilmost whose car was stolen, or Harris? Is Casavecchia the gangster or the millionaire? Why *does* Kate hate Henry?

In murder mysteries and procedural detective novels, character portrayal is not so important. The reader won't expect great depth among the victims and suspects, while the detective probably has a number of well-established peculiarities, built up over a series of books: He is Spanish, wears elegant grey silk suits, and carries his exclamation point upside down; or he is very fat and drinks a pint of beer on every page; or he is a rabbi; or she is female, karate-trained, and has a huge wardrobe, which is just as well, since the vicissitudes of her job frequently reduce her clothes to tatters. We know all these and love them as old friends.

The problem of character arises most particularly—and can be a real handicap—in suspense novels.

Suspense novels are deservedly popular, but very hard to define. They are not murder mysteries. They are not just straight novels, because something nasty and frightening is bound to happen. That is the promise to the reader. They are not spy stories, and they are certainly not procedurals. One of the very best suspense novels ever written, *A Dram of Poison,* by Charlotte Armstrong, had no murder in it at all, not even any death (except a natural one in the first chapter, setting off the whole course of events), but it possesses more riveting tension than any other story I can recall.

In a suspense novel, the element of character matters very much indeed. The hero-heroine is pitted, not against organized crime or international terrorism, but against a personal enemy, a personal problem; the conflict is on an individual, adversarial level. And so, if either hero or hero's enemy is not a flesh-and-blood, fully rounded, recognizable entity, the tension slackens, the credulity drops.

In *A Dram of Poison,* all the mischief is caused in the first place by the arrival of the hero's sister, one of those terrible, self-satisfied, know-it-all characters (plainly Charlotte Armstrong wrote the story in the white heat of having recently encountered one of them) who can always interpret other people's motives and give them some disagreeable psychological twist. By her confident assertions, she soon has the heroine paralyzed with self-distrust and the hero downright suicidal. Then, in between the breathless excitement of trying to find what he did with that wretched little bottle of poison he had meant to swallow, the reader has the fearful pleasure of knowing that, in the end, odious Sister Ethel is bound to receive her comeuppance.

Charlotte Armstrong was particularly skilled at villains; the frightful parasitical pair of sisters who, in *Mask of Evil,* (originally published as *The Albatross*) come and prey on the two central characters are particularly memorable, with their sweet saintly selfishness. The sense of being *invaded,* taken over, in their own home, by repulsive aliens, was particularly well conveyed in that story.

The suspense novel is often a closed-world plot. The hero/heroine must battle it out against the adversary in a situation that, for some reason, allows for no appeal to outside help. There must be valid reasons for this. If not a snowstorm, with all phone lines down, then the villain has bruited it around that the hero is hysterical, unbalanced, alcoholic, a drug abuser, or just traumatized by recent grief so no call for help will be heeded or believed.

Ursula Curtiss had a particular gift for these enclosed-world situations, and she had a masterly touch with villains as well. It is an interesting exercise to compare some of her stories with others, for she was a very fertile creator of creepy domestic-suspense plots. Many of her ideas were brilliant, but some of them succeeded far better than others. Why? Because of the characters with which they were animated. *Voice Out of Darkness,* which has a fine snowy Connecticut setting and an excellent basic idea—harking back to the long-ago question of whether the heroine did or did not push her very unpleasant adoptive sister under the ice when they were both eleven—yet somehow fails to come off because it is peopled with rather stock characters: two handsome young men, two pretty girls, and some recognizable small-town citizens, the drunk writer, the gossipy lady. Her novel, *The Stairway,* however, is pure gold from the first page to the last. Why? Because of its villainness, the repulsive Cora. Judged dispassionately, the plot is simple and only just credible. Madeline, the heroine, is married to Stephen, an intolerable man whom she is about to divorce, a monster of tyranny who terrifies her small son. But Stephen falls downstairs and breaks his neck. Cora, the humble cousin, the poor relation, by pretending to believe that Madeline pushed him, gradually assumes more and more dominance over the household and seems all set to stay for the rest of her life. Madeline, in a bind because *she* believes that *Cora* pushed Stephen, feels that she can't betray her and is helpless. All this, given a moment's cool thought, seems hard to swallow. Why had Madeline married the horrendous Stephen in the first place? Why should she submit to Cora for a single moment? But Cora is made so *real,* with her greediness, her anxious, reproachful air, her dreadful clothes, her fondness for eating candy out of a paper bag and rustling the sheets of the newspaper, that all she does and says is instantly, completely credible.

Playwright Edward Albee once observed that the test he had for the solidity of his characters was to imagine them in some situation other than the play he had in mind and see if they would continue to behave in a real manner. The character of Cora would be credible and recognizable whether we saw her in a hospital ward, a supermarket, or a graveyard.

The Stairway was an early Curtiss novel, but one of her later ones, *The Poisoned Orchard,* contains the same terrifying claustrophobic, inturned quality, again because of its hateful and convincing villainness, the heroine's cousin Fen, and her accomplice, the cleaning lady, Mrs. List. This sinister pair have Sarah the heroine hog-tied, especially clowning, ugly, self-assured Fen, who continually manages to force her much nicer, much better-looking cousin into the unenviable role of straight man refusing to laugh at Fen's jokes. The relationship between the two is beautifully and most credibly realized, so that the reader is prepared to swallow the fact that Fen and her evil ally seem to be omniscient and omnipresent, able to anticipate Sarah's efforts to combat their plots almost before she can make a move. And what is it all about? We hardly know. A wicked deed, way back in Fen's past, that is catching up with her. And anyway, what can they *do* to Sarah? It hardly matters. The point is that they are menacing, and that she is more and more at their mercy. Fen is a wholly convincing monster, the more so because she is quick-witted and amusing, as well as being unprincipled. *Fear* is the essential ingredient of a suspense novel, and fear can be achieved only if the reader thoroughly sympathizes with the main character and thoroughly believes in the villain.

If the villain is less convincing, then the main character must be made more so.

Dick Francis, the English writer of deservedly best-selling mysteries with horse-racing backgrounds, wrote an interesting early novel, *Nerve*, in which all the jockeys on the turf were being persecuted by a well-known TV personality who secretly spread malicious gossip about them, prevented their getting to races on time, and had their horses doped. Why does he do this? Because he, son of a famous racehorse owner is terrified of horses, and therefore psychotically jealous of all who succeed in the horsey world.

What a preposterous theme it sounds, set down in cold blood. And the villainous TV star, Maurice Kemp-Lore, somewhat sketchily depicted, only just makes his murderous obsession credible to the reader. What does give the book immediate life, great energy and plausibility, so that it moves at a rattling pace and carries the reader along, completely hooked by the story, is the treatment of the hero. As always in Dick Francis novels, the hero tells the story in the first person; in common with other Francis heroes he is an odd man out, who has fallen into the racing world by a series of accidents. Descended from a family of professional musicians, he is the only non-musical one; despised by his kin, he has had to justify himself in some other direction. The contrast between the hero's elegant relations conducting Beethoven at the London Festival Hall, while he gallops through the mud at Ascot, is bizarre enough to be convincing, so that we are passion-

278

ately on the hero's side as he struggles to combat what he begins to recognize as a sinister plot against his whole *raison d'être*. The villain remains shadowy, but the hero, in this case, carries enough weight to sustain the story.

Given a satisfactory plot, it should not be too hard to equip it with characters. But what if the boot is on the other foot?

Some writers are compulsive character collectors. Wherever they go, they watch, listen, record, jot down notes and descriptions: the fat woman in the black-striped dress at the rail station with two elegant little pig-tailed girls, also in black-and-white-striped outfits, hanging on her arms. The lanky, unshaven six-foot male in the subway, with a shock of red hair and gold rings in his ears. The professional portrait painter, met at a party, who has produced a portrait every two months for the last twenty years, and has a photographic eye for a face. The woman who, though courteous and well-mannered, is an obsessive corrector, so that she can never hear a sentence spoken without chipping in to put the speaker right—politely, but *oh,* so firmly. . .

Character collecting is an excellent habit, because sooner or later some of these characters will start to move.

You have a whole cast of characters, but no plot. So: Make extensive notes about them—their preferences, dislikes, habits, childhood history. Like Edward Albee, set them in different environments, confront them with crises. What would the woman in the black-striped dress do if she were in charge of forty school children on a sinking cruise liner? Make them encounter each other. Suppose the portrait painter were sitting in a subway train, drawing lightning sketches, and the man with red hair and gold earrings, unaccountably angry at being drawn, grabs the sketchbook and gets out at the next stop? A character may suddenly get up and walk away, pulling a skein of plot behind him. Suppose they then meet by chance, somewhere else?

Imagine Jane Austen saying to herself, "Now, let's tell a story about a sensible practical sister and a self-indulgent, overemotional sister. What sort of men shall they fall in love with?"

Suppose in writing *Sense and Sensibility,* she turned her story the other way round. Suppose sensible Elinor had fallen in love with handsome, romantic Willoughby, and susceptible Marianne had been bowled over by reliable, prosaic Edward? But, no it won't work. Marianne could never have fallen for Edward, not in a thousand years. Jane

Austen, even at a young age (she was twenty-two), had her characters and plot inextricably twined together, one growing out of the other; there is no separating them. But it is fun to probe and investigate and reconsider; fun, after all, is what writing is all about. Jane Austen took huge pleasure in writing *Sense and Sensibility*. The fact is evident; she knew these characters entirely before she put pen to paper.

What is the best way of displaying your characters?

There are, of course, hundreds, but the worst way is to describe them flatly.

My recent novel, *Blackground,* has the theme of two characters who marry in romantic haste, and then, on a winter honeymoon in Venice where they are, as it were, suspended together in a vacuum, they discover that they had in fact met long ago and aren't at all the people each thinks the other to be. To make this as much of a shock as I intended, both for them and, hopefully, for the reader, I had to be familiar with their life stories right back to childhood. In order not to a) begin too early or b) bore the reader with too much flashback, I make Character A tell his story to Character B on the honeymoon, while hers is disclosed to the reader in snatches throughout the narrative.

Michael Gilbert, a writer of several different kinds of mysteries, whose characters are always remarkably individual and three-dimensional, adopts a very swift and vivid method of displaying his quite large cast of characters in his suspense novel *The Night of the Twelfth* (about sadistic murders in a boys' school). Sometimes a whole chapter is divided into blocks of conversation, often only about half a page— between A and B, between B and C, between C and A, between A and D—these fast-moving dialogues equally convey character and advance the action.

Sometimes you know your character *too* well; you could write volumes about his quirks and complications. But how do you get all this across to the reader without being pompous, or overexplicit?

How about portraying this person as seen through the eyes of another narrator, quite a simple soul (like Nelly Dean, the housekeeper in *Wuthering Heights,* who tells much of the story), or even a child? *What Maisie Knew,* by Henry James, can be an example to us all.

"Try to be one of those people on whom nothing is lost," said Henry James.

Perfect advice for a writer!

57

HOW TO WRITE THE POLICE PROCEDURAL NOVEL

BY O'NEIL DE NOUX

A PROMINENT CITIZEN IS MURDERED. The police are called in and find that clues are few, if any. So who's going to solve this baffling case? The gifted amateur; the college professor who moonlights as a P.I. on weekends; the spinster convenience-store clerk who is secretly a master sleuth? Unlikely. The case will be solved by hard-working homicide detectives.

Like its first cousin, the mystery novel, the police procedural novel features a well-structured, fast-paced chronicle of crimes and punishments. Unlike the mystery, the police procedural stresses the step-by-step procedures always followed by professional detectives in solving these cases: processing the crime scene to collect physical evidence; canvassing the neighborhood for witnesses or suspects; postmortem examination of the body to determine the cause and manner of death; identifying the victim; tracing the background of the victim; investigating associates of the victim, and those who reside or work near the scene of the crime; examining the method of operation of the perpetrator; and the continuing follow-up investigation.

These steps, although mandatory, can be described briefly or in detail by a writer, depending on the dramatic effect of the story. Don't let the specialization scare you away from writing police procedurals. There are seven basic guidelines that one should follow to write the successful police procedural novel.

Plot well

The *plot is the backbone* of the police procedural. A well-plotted scenario will allow the writer to create memorable characters, unforgettable scenes, uniquely described settings, so long as the writer does not forget to follow normal police procedures. Deviation from the norm removes credibility from your story. Strive for believability.

Although the hero or heroine travels step by step along a predetermined road, a good writer will fill that road with pot holes. The hero must then hurdle these obstacles. There are always complications, one damn thing after another, sequences of rising dangers relieved by moments of release, followed by increased danger. Remember the goal in fiction is to elicit an emotional response from the reader.

So where do you get your plots? Try the daily newspaper or the evening news. Murder has become an American pastime. Recently, I wrote a story based on a newspaper article about a rapist who served his time, and when released went straight out and kidnapped his original victim and raped her again. This story was filled with emotion and anger and irony.

Keep the novel action-oriented

Action is the flesh and blood of your story. Watch your pacing. Ask yourself if each scene moves the story forward. If it doesn't, toss it out. Do not go off on tangents or take vacations in the middle of working a case. Blend dialogue and descriptions with action, and you'll have no problem.

Although real police investigations include long, sometimes grueling days of unending canvasses, surveillances and dead-end leads, you should be selective. Short scenes with crisp dialogue can streamline the most mundane parts of an investigation. Leave out the boring parts.

Yet your story doesn't have to be all police work. Cops have private lives, too. A great deal of the action in Charles Willeford's Hoke Moseley series (*Miami Heat, Sideswipe,* and *New Hope for the Dead*) takes place at Hoke's home, with his family and friends.

In my novels, I include a strong ancillary plot revolving around my main character's relationship with the twin sister of a victim from his first murder case. That action, consequently, takes place away from the office.

Create well-rounded characters

As in all fiction, *character is the heart* of the police procedural. Although the hero/heroine of the police procedural is usually a police officer or someone closely associated with the criminal justice system, they are real people existing in a familiar world. What happens to them is extraordinary. Their reactions are usually courageous or clever.

In *The Silence of the Lambs*, Thomas Harris' heroine is FBI trainee Clarice Starling. Although only a trainee, Clarice exhibits extraordinary maturity and rare courage in her dogged pursuit of her villain. The hero of my novels is Dino La Stanza, a New Orleans homicide detective, a man with a perfect solution record who pursues his perpetrators with the tenacity of a hungry leopard. These characters are professional lawmen working within an admittedly imperfect legal system.

Joseph Wambaugh, perhaps the dean of police proceduralists, has focused on revealing, through his sometimes poignant characters, the pressures under which police officers live twenty-four hours a day. In *The Black Marble, The Glitter Dome,* and *The Secret of Harry Bright,* Wambaugh documents the ravages police work can inflict on the best of officers.

There is room to maneuver with your characters. They can ponder. They can do things against the grain. They can make profound statements and explore the secrets of the human heart. This is where you can insert your theme—your statement of the human condition. Unlike mainstream fiction, whose characters are sometimes obsessed with the discovery of their interior lives, police procedural characters have a crime to solve.

Your characters must think *with* action as opposed to pondering without action. You, the writer, must remain devoted to the sequence of the story.

Create a distinctive setting

The *setting is the skeleton* your story is built around. It is more than just the description of a place or time period; it is the feeling of that place and time.

Give the reader a distinct, vivid setting stressing sensory details: the acrid smell of gunpowder, the salty taste of blood, the tacky feeling of rubber grips on a .357 magnum when the hero's hand is sweating, the sexy sound of nylon when a woman crosses her legs, the way a culprit, when he is lying, will look away from the detective.

Your setting must be so realistic that the readers will be convinced the elements of your story could really happen. Charles Willeford, in his Hoke Moseley stories, paints a vivid picture of south Florida with snapshot descriptions mixed with plenty of action. Willeford once explained that capturing south Florida's fascinating society was a primary aim of his series.

In my series, set in New Orleans, I have attempted to make the setting equal in importance to character and plot. Reviewers have consistently commented on the richness of the setting and the interplay between my characters and the city, and their effects on one another.

Tony Hillerman places the hero of his Navajo police series, Lieutenant Joe Leaphorn, in a vividly rendered social and cultural environment, using the panorama of the west as a backdrop. James Lee Burke, a winner of the Edgar Allan Poe Award from the Mystery Writers of America, is a master of setting. His Detective Dave Robicheaux adventures, beginning with *The Neon Rain* (also *Heaven's Prisoners, Black Cherry Blues, A Morning for Flamingos,* and *A Stained White Radiance*) is an excellent example of a writer not only giving a visual description of a setting, but the feel, taste, and smell of the place through strong sensory details.

Use language accurately

Ever walk into a police station? If you do, be prepared to cover your ears. Policemen talk in harsh street language salted with profanity and jargon, particularly among each other. Criminals are worse. Neither uses flowery passages, and rarely speaks in complete sentences.

Through dialogue, you have an excellent opportunity to create emotion, from scintillating nails-on-the-blackboard passages uttered by creepy serial killers, to the soft whispers spoken to an overworked detective by a sympathetic lover.

Real cops, from Bangor to San Diego, from Seattle to Miami, verbalize their frustrations through black humor. Rope off a crime scene, fill it with policemen seasoned by years of sarcasm, and someone is bound to make derogatory or ludicrous remarks about the condition of the body of the murder victim. Describing a shot between the eyes as a perfect bulls-eye or viewing brain matter splattered on a wall and asking if anyone wants pizza later is nothing more than a release, an escape-valve reaction to the horrors of murder.

Be realistic

Make sure of your facts. Revolvers do not have safeties, nor can a silencer be used on one. Police do not have "Ballistics Labs," or ballistics examiners. They have firearms examiners. Ballistics is the study of objects in flight. Policemen are concerned with matching projectiles to weapons.

Do not depend on television or movies for accurate portrayals of police procedures. How many times have you seen chalk lines around bodies, or cops shooting suspects and then walking away for a couple of beers? Investigators never alter crime scenes with chalk. If an officer shoots someone, he is quickly spirited away by investigators who secure his weapon for analysis, who interview him in isolation, who secure his formal statement. In many departments an officer must endure a Superintendent's Hearing before he goes home. The officer must then face a Grand Jury investigating the death and the inevitable civil lawsuit automatically filed by overeager attorneys, no matter how justified the shooting.

Detectives take notes. How many times have you seen a movie or read a book and actually observed a detective taking notes? I was a detective for nine years. I never shot anyone, but I certainly killed a lot of pens. A pen is the detective's most useful tool and mightiest weapon. Every killer on death row began his long trek through the criminal justice system with a homicide detective taking notes at a crime scene.

Real detectives use *inductive* reasoning, conclusions from observations of facts, to arrive at a solution that fits all of the evidence. Amateurs, including many fictional detectives, use *deductive* reasoning, arriving at a specific conclusion from a general assumption. In other words, inductive reasoning involves relying on facts and only facts until only one conclusion is possible.

Have a definite resolution

Don't cheat the reader out of an ending to your story. Police cases end, usually with an arrest and trial, sometimes with a shootout. This

285

is a natural climactic event. Even cases that are suspended or closed without a solution have a climactic moment, when the investigators come face to face with the nightmare of someone getting away with murder. There have been successful stories written about The Zebra Killer and The Green River Killer, as well as about the ultimate unsolved murders by Jack The Ripper.

In your resolution, remember that something must be affirmed. Good triumphs over evil, or at least goes the distance.

So how does one learn the steps taken by lawmen in their pursuit of criminals or the procedures used by lawmen in the nineties? What is DNA or genetic fingerprinting, for instance? How does one learn that this scientific breakthrough, which may be more important than fingerprints, gives investigators the ability to isolate, identify and catalogue an individual's genetic fingerprint from a drop of blood, a tiny amount of semen, or a piece of skin found beneath a victim's fingernail? How does one learn that no two individuals have the same DNA fingerprint pattern, unless they are identical twins?

As a veteran homicide detective, I find that these procedures come second nature to me. But there are sources out there. The best is direct information from police officers or former police officers, who rarely shun the opportunity to share their war stories. Other sources can be found in your public library: *The Crime Writers' Handbook of Technical Information,* edited by John Kennedy Melling and *The Writer's Complete Crime Reference Book* by Martin Roth are two good examples.

Remember you are still writing a genre novel. The police procedural, like the mystery, science-fiction, or romance novel, will not have the prime space in bookstores, nor will it usually get the featured spot in your local paper's book section. But the sales will come. There is a large audience concerned about crime.

Mickey Spillane once said of crime fiction, "Those big shot writers can never dig the fact that there are more salted peanuts consumed than caviar."

§58

CHARACTERIZATION AND STORY

BY L. R. WRIGHT

THE BULLETIN BOARD IN MY OFFICE is studded with pieces of paper bearing aphorisms. Most are typed on index cards, the authors' names noted at the bottom. But some are scrawled on paper torn from whatever lay handy, written in ink now faded, and of these, a few lack attribution. One of these unintentionally orphaned maxims reads as follows: "It's the way we are that makes things happen to us."

The relationship between character and story is so close as to render the two indistinguishable: Each story must seem inevitable, given its characters. Writers are often asked where their stories come from, and my answer is, from our characters. The better defined we make our characters—the better we know them—the stronger the stories they tell.

But where do these people come from?

They emerge, gradually, from a conglomeration of memory, observation, and imagination. Some emerge easily, and some only with great difficulty.

Each of my novels, except one, evolved from a visual image of somebody doing something. *Among Friends,* for example, began as an image of a woman in an alley, at night, staring at something lying on the ground. When I started to write it, I knew absolutely nothing about this character, except that she was female. I began work on the novel by describing the picture that had lodged itself in my head. The character then began to come to life. (More accurately, by describing the scene in the alley, I began creating that character.) She developed into a woman in her late fifties who lives alone and works as a secretary-receptionist for a small news magazine. Because of the kind of person she is—reserved, proud, solitary—she doesn't ask for help when the underpinnings of her life give way. And because she is also frightened, and possesses an extravagant imagination, she conjures up a terrifying hallucination upon which to focus her fraying powers of concentration.

Although the following lines were written as the first paragraphs of the first draft of the book (there were at least three rewrites), in the completed novel they don't appear until page 132, at the beginning of Emily's crisis:

A few minutes later Emily stood immobile in a dark downtown lane, her concentration fixed on something lying on the ground. The blank surface of the lane looked wet and slick, and it shone dully in the light from the streetlamp at the end of the lane. Huddled against a brick wall, away from the light, an old man lay on his stomach with his knees pulled up; like a baby asleep in its crib. His right cheek was cuddled into the pavement, and his left hand clutched an empty wine bottle. His grey hair stood up in spikes and his eyes were tightly closed. A white shirt collar poked up from the old grey coat in which he was wrapped. He wore hiking boots and a pair of dark pants.

Emily turned slowly, holding her purse in both hands. She sighed, a soft, barely perceptible sound, and walked back toward the street. . . .

Any other night, she was sure, if her eye had been caught by something moving and glinting in a late night downtown lane, she would not have entered it but walked on. She couldn't understand what had possessed her to go in there. She remembered a feeling of detachment, and a sensation that she was invisible, or at least invincible.

Emily was a character who came easily.

Karl Alberg, though—that's another story. Alberg is the Royal Canadian Mounted Police staff sergeant in my three mystery novels, and perhaps it's because he was so difficult to "get" that I am especially fond of him.

Initially, I didn't know that my fourth novel, *The Suspect,* was going to be a mystery, even though it opens with the murder of one octogenarian by another. I had expected that once I'd written the crime (the visual image with which the book opens) and created the criminal, I would become immersed in a long flashback that would reveal the reasons for the murder, and this flashback, I thought, would constitute the book. But I became so caught up in the deed and its effects upon George, the elderly murderer, that momentum swept me along until the next thing that had to happen was a police investigation.

So I needed a policeman.

It was easy enough to decide upon his physical characteristics, his age, his marital status; but as hard as I tried, I simply could not make the man real.

Finally, somewhat desperate, I took him out of the book. I wrote about him in all manner of situations: in the middle of a funeral; grocery shopping; in conversations with people I know—fictional and real. All this was a painful, laborious attempt to breathe life into him. Nothing worked. He remained stiff, awkward, utterly unbelievable, until . . . One morning I armed him with pruning implements and dispatched him into his overgrown backyard to cut back the greenery. Then, who knows why, he suddenly became authentic.

It is because of the kinds of people George and Alberg are that *The Suspect* develops as it does. George feels no guilt about trying to evade punishment for his crime, because he knows that his suffering for earlier "crimes" far outweighs anything the law can do to him. Alberg grows, reluctantly, to admire George even as he suspects him; but he can't stand the thought of anybody—including George—getting away with murder.

A Chill Rain in January is the only one of my novels that didn't begin for me with a visual image and some sense of a central character, however vague and fuzzy.

I became curious about people who lack a conscience, who are incapable of distinguishing between right and wrong; sociopaths. For them, I thought, life must be complicated and hazardous—rather like trying to walk when lacking a sense of balance. They are also very dangerous people, because they are impervious to guilt. Psychiatrists differ about what causes this condition. Some think it is learned behavior, and others believe it is the result of a physiological abnormality, a chemical imbalance in the brain. I opted for the latter. My sociopath would be born that way.

For a while I struggled with a male character, because the books say that sociopaths are almost always male. But I soon decided that it would be more interesting if the character were female. A great deal of anger attends this condition, and a female sociopath would have to place stronger controls on her anger than would a male.

The process of creating her was different from anything I'd experienced before, since I had no picture in my head to get me going. I began by recalling events in my childhood that I associated with the emergence of my own sense of morality, and I described them, in the first person, as if I were another person, a child incapable of understanding "morality." Some of this work survived to become a part of the novel. Here's how it developed:

One day when I was very young, I scissored away some of the fur on my cat's back. In my memory, the cat (whose name was Myrtle) screeched and howled, tore herself from my grasp, ran out the door, and was never seen again. (My mother assures me that Myrtle, although she avoided me for a few days, didn't run away.) I remember a feeling of absolute amazement as it dawned on me that I had done something that caused another creature anguish, and that it was something I had had no right to do. I used this incident to create an imaginary one:

. . . The cat screamed and bashed around among the burning leaves and finally rolled out of the flames: it looked as if it had smoke coming out of it. It got to its feet and fled drunkenly across the park. . . .

Zoe's mother looked as if she felt dizzy or something. She kept staring at Zoe and saying her name, over and over again, as though she couldn't believe Zoe was really standing there, as if Zoe had just suddenly appeared, out of nowhere. . . .

"What did you do?" said Zoe's mother.

"I put Myrtle in the fire."

"But why? How could you do such a terrible thing?" She was staring at Zoe and hanging on to her purse with both hands. The purse had a couple of new scratches on it—places where the leather had been made less brown. Zoe thought Myrtle had probably done that, with her stupid claws.

"I don't know. She made me angry."

Her mother turned around so that her back was to Zoe, and then she turned the rest of the way around, so that she was looking straight at her again. "Didn't you hear it screech? Don't you know how much it must hurt?"

"But—it wasn't me," said Zoe.

"But you just said—you just said, I heard you, 'I put Myrtle in the fire.' You just told me that."

"Yes," said Zoe. "I mean, it wasn't me that hurt."

Again, it is what Zoe *is* that generates the story. When she feels threatened, the only "right" thing to do is the thing most likely to reestablish order in her world. The cost to others is irrelevant to her.

Situations of crisis, danger, dread, or distress are not hard to imagine; we've all survived a few. And it's amazing what's stored in our memories just waiting to be used—not the events themselves, but the ways in which we experienced them.

When I was about eight years old, I was attacked by a guard dog chained up behind a warehouse. He and I were friends, I thought. But on that day I approached him while he was eating, and that turned out to be a big mistake. Thirty years later I wrote a novel called *The Favorite,* in which a little girl gets beaten up by one of her schoolmates. While writing that scene, I used "sense memories" from the day the dog attacked me:

. . . she stood feeling small on the playground, blood running slowly from her nose, a bruise on the side of her head, ragged with dust, hair full of it, tangled and wild. . . .

Sarah aimed herself toward the sidewalk and started to move her feet, one after the other. She knew her body must be broken into hundreds of pieces. It wasn't falling apart because of her skin. She was grateful to her skin. It would have been awful if her whole body had fallen apart right there on the public sidewalk.

She struggled up the street and past the neighbors' houses and if she saw anybody she knew, she didn't remember it later. . . .

She walked up to her front door and hoped Muriel would know what to do about something like this. She knew her father would know what to do, but he was at work, and so was her mother. She put her hand out to take hold of the doorknob and saw that her hand was shaking, her whole body was shaking, she thought her skin wouldn't be able to hold in all the broken pieces if it kept on being shaken around like that and she opened the door and started to scream.

If you allow yourself time to develop characters who are concrete and substantive, you can, by making use of your own personal memories as well as your imagination, put these characters into any imaginary situation, into confrontations with any other fictional people, and discover, as you write, how they must react.

It is these stage-managed collisions—character with character, character with life events—that produce for me the best and often the most unexpected results in storytelling; the thing that everyone calls plot.

NONFICTION: ARTICLES AND BOOKS

59

LETTER TO A YOUNG ARTICLE WRITER

BY DONALD M. MURRAY

YOUR PIECES ARE FILLED with interesting, specific information; they have a clear focus; they are well written; but they are not likely to be published without revision.

What they lack is what professionals call an edge. The idea does not contain the tension that attracts and holds a reader. Note the first paragraph of my letter. It contains a surprise, an apparent contradiction, a conflict, something unexpected that engages the reader in a conversation. "What does he mean? The articles are written well, with focused information, and they are *not* publishable?" the reader asks, and the writer responds.

Your articles are pleasant and predictable. They do not have an urgency, a significance, an unexpectedness, a tension that will draw in a reader who is not already fascinated by your subject.

Editors find it difficult to describe what is missing in such good writing—and so do I. The problem is not with what is on the paper but what is not. Editors are looking for what they have not seen and cannot command. If editors know what they want, they can order it from professionals on their staff or from familiar free lancers like me. Doris Lessing said, "You have to remember that nobody ever wants a new writer. You have to create your own demand."

The demand is created when a writer expresses an individual, authoritative point of view toward our familiar world in a voice that is appropriate to the topic and the writer's attitude toward it. The voice communicates authority and concern.

Your ideas do not have an essential tension. Some of my daybook lines that have led to writing include:

"I cheered when we dropped the atomic bomb." [I was in the paratroops and scheduled to jump into Tokyo.]

"I'm lucky I had a sickly childhood." [It forced me to exercise my imagination.]

"I'm glad I have an old wife." [We have a shared history.]

"It was good there was no Little League when I was a kid." [We played sandlot ball and were not over-organized by competitive parents.]

My habit is to seek the tensions within my life and the lives of those around me. I inventory what sparks a strong emotional reaction: irony, anger, despair, humor, pain, pleasure, contentment, fear.

I read the mental and daybook or journal notes I make as I lead my life, asking such questions as:

- What surprises me?
- Where's the tension?
- What should be and what is?
- Where's the conflict?
- Where will these ideas, issues, people collide?
- What's the problem?
- What's different from what I expected?
- What are the implications—for me, for my readers?
- What are the connections?
- What contradicts?

Margaret Atwood says, "Good writing takes place at intersections, at what you might call knots, at places where the society is snarled or knotted up." Mary Lee Settle says, "I start my work by asking a question and then try . . . to answer it."

As I question myself, I hear fragments of language. These are rarely sentences, although they may be. Usually they are just phrases, words in collision, or words that connect in unexpected ways. Recently I wrote a column about my grandson learning to walk. The line came from his father, who said Joshua had "to learn to fall to learn to walk." That was an idea; it contained a truth expressed in a line that had a surprising tension.

I record such lines and scratch when they itch. A lead—the opening sentences or paragraphs—can hold an article in place so I can explore it in a draft written days or weeks later. For example, the other day I was doing errands with my wife when I had the following experience, and I immediately wrote (in my head), "have to get glasses tightened." When I got home, I turned the line into a lead:

We are driving to Dover, New Hampshire, to shop when Minnie Mae says, "I have to get my sunglasses tightened."

I pull up to Whitehouse Opticians and Minnie Mae asks, "Why are we stopping here?"

"To get your sunglasses tightened."

"They are home on my desk."

[She's just talking. I hear a problem to be solved.]

I have an idea, but that's not enough. In John Jerome's wonderful book on nonfiction writing, *The Writing Trade: A Year in the Life* (Viking, 1992), which should be on your desk, he quotes a colleague as saying that a 600-word essay needs about an idea and a half. That articulated an important truth about all articles for me.

My grandson's learning to fall so he could learn to walk was a good idea, but it was not enough. In writing the article I connected his need to learn to fall with writers, artists, scientists, and entrepreneurs, who need to experience instructive failure to succeed. Then I had an essay.

The anecdote demonstrating the difficulty I (who always want to solve a problem) have communicating with my female companion who is just commenting on life, is an interesting and amusing idea. It articulates a tension most male and female readers have experienced. But it is not yet publishable. I will write it when I come up with the essential extra half of an idea or, more likely, when I start drafting the piece and discover the extra half during the writing.

Your articles stop short of that significant half of an idea, that moment of discovery of a significant extra meaning that you and your reader share in the writing and reading of the essay.

To find that extra meaning I have to write with velocity so that I am thinking on paper, saying what I do not expect to say. Of course you will consider and reconsider, write and rewrite this discovery draft, but for me, it is essential to discover what I have to say by saying it. If I know just what I am going to say when I first start to write an article, the draft is flat, uninteresting. When I discover meaning during the writing, as I have in writing this letter to you, I may have something to share with readers that editors will want to publish.

Good luck. Draw strength from the fact that you can gather specific, revealing information; that you can focus it; that you can write a clear running sentence and a paragraph that develops and communicates a thought or feeling, and then go on to find the edge, the tension, that will make editors accept your articles and invite you to write more.

297

§ 60

PROFILE WRITING

BY SYLVIA WHITMAN

NEXT TIME YOU UNLOAD YOUR CART at the supermarket, check out what enquiring minds are reading. Headlines tease with the triumphs of Madonna and the travails of Princess Di. In a word: gossip. Even magazines that carry more cachet—that would never think of putting on the cover some mother who just gave birth to a space alien (unless he were the spitting image of Michael Jackson)—feature similar faces: Maria Shriver, Bill Clinton, Barbara Walters. As editors will testify, people fascinate people.

Fortunately for writers, that attraction has created a tremendous demand for profiles, from cameos of hot business owners, to biographies of offbeat scientists. If you socialize with the glitterati, you may need only to string together sentences to entrance a publisher. But connections won't make or break you in this field. Free lancers will find markets for the lowdown on any interesting person, celebrated or not.

Choosing the person

Fame sells. What superstars think isn't even feature fluff nowadays; it's news. The lucky few who make a living writing celebrity profiles earn their fat paychecks, however: Cozying up to stars requires patience and chutzpah.

Many of the rich and famous hire publicists to fend off writers. Busy actors usually don't chat on spec. While an assignment from a national magazine may open the door for you, "names" often demand quid pro quo—their photo on the cover, a plug for their latest project. Some celebrities require questions to be submitted in advance. If the latest heartthrob does grant you an interview, you may find your conversation has all the intimacy of a royal audience.

Dead celebrities offer a good alternative for writers outside of the

New York-L.A.-D.C. loop of cultural elitism. First of all, they're never too busy or too prickly. Secondly, they can't recant their quotes during the limbo between an article's acceptance and publication. On the other hand, the grave does lessen a star's newsworthiness, so a writer must try to give the profile a timely peg. That means working long enough ahead to allow for a magazine's lead time. A year before the 75th anniversary of the Girl Scouts, I started circulating a query about Girl Scouts founder Juliette Gordon Low. Think birthdays and decade milestones. I once sold to an airline magazine a retrospective that claimed, "Forty years after his death, W. C. Fields still reigns as the Dark Prince of American humor."

Beginners do well to follow the environmentalist motto: Think globally, act locally. Find someone close to home whose story deserves an audience. Local and regional publications love to introduce readers to their neighbors. Start with a topic. Who spearheads historic preservation in your town? Who shelters AIDS babies? Who runs an eco-store? When a city magazine asked me to write about child abuse, I contacted a Parents' Anonymous group and profiled an incest victim who had started to bully her own kids but was seeking help to break the cycle.

Hunt for people with extraordinary talents. By browsing widely, you may discover that the guy next door is better known outside the community than locally. After *The Wall Street Journal* described investment banker Anthony Gray as the Orlando money manager with a "Midas touch," a weekly in town enlisted me to interview him for a cover story. Few residents of Central Florida had ever heard of him.

Far more often, I pitch articles about local folks to national magazines. I mine my daily newspaper for likely candidates—someone with an unusual hobby, a recent award, or a bright idea—then pan through their backgrounds for an angle. While living in New Orleans, for example, I read a feature about a judge who assigns book reports to young offenders. Surely children's book writers would appreciate that. Indeed, the kids' lit trade magazine *Horn Book* bought my profile. Talking to the judge in chambers, I learned not only about her taste in literature, but also about the frustrations of administering juvenile justice. The wheels started clicking: law. I sold a revised version of the article to *Student Lawyer*.

The beauty of profiles lies in the many different ways you can slant them. Is your subject female? Try women's magazines. Does she work?

Hit professional journals. Where did he grow up? Query his hometown paper. Where did she go to college? Pitch an alumni magazine. Did he serve in the armed forces? Interest a military publication.

Recently, I learned about hotelier and philanthropist Henri Landwirth, who has opened an all-expense-paid resort near Disney World exclusively for terminally ill children and their families. First, I queried general-interest magazines with this story, but *Parade* had already run a profile on him, and others turned me down. Since Landwirth was nearing retirement age, I tried senior-citizen publications but again met rejection. Landwirth, a Holocaust survivor, said something that stuck in my mind: "I can relate to children who have no control over their lives. As a child, I had no control over mine." Wouldn't Jewish readers empathize with his motivation? Sure enough, a Jewish quarterly bought the manuscript.

Setting up the interview

It's not whom you know but how well you get to know them that counts. Usually, you get only one shot—one interview. You need to milk that conversation for all it's worth.

I try to schedule the meeting well in advance, at the subject's convenience. I also press for an open-ended time slot so I can have as much time as necessary. It takes a while for people to let down their defenses.

I prefer to tag along with someone on the job—or at least to meet on the interviewee's personal turf, whether home or office. "Midas" investor Tony Gray let me spend a morning in his office—a wonderful boon, since he had a speaker telephone, so I eavesdropped on traders angling for a piece of the stock action in the $1.5 billion pension fund Gray manages.

Look around. Knickknacks and photos often prompt questions. And observing someone in action supplies details that round out a profile. By taking our county appraiser to lunch, I could tell the readers of *Orlando* magazine that at age 79, he still climbs the stairs to his second-floor office and still considers a ham sandwich a grand meal.

Take photographs whenever possible—with the subject's permission, of course. Not only will the offer of a "package" tempt editors, but I find that pictures free me from objective physical descriptions—brown eyes, short hair, etc. When writing the piece, I can then focus on subjective details. I wanted to convey my impression of Kids Village founder Henri Landwirth as a businessman whose heart led him out of the executive suite: "A slim man at ease in a tie, he speaks softly with a European accent. Yet the children understand him . . ."

Lacking visual cues, I ask more probing questions during phone interviews, which sometimes stretch for hours. To protect her privacy, the incest victim I reached by phone didn't reveal her name. But I pried for enough information about her daily routine for readers to believe she was a normal, stressed-out parent:

Like most working mothers, Chris lives by the clock. Every weekday she wakes up at 5:30 a.m., dresses, mobilizes her three daughters, makes breakfast, drops the kids at school, works a full day as an interior designer, and picks up the kids at day care. Barring kickball games and teacher conferences, she usually arrives home around 5:30 p.m.—except on Tuesdays, when her 6-year-old takes ballet, and Wednesdays, when her 5-year-old dances, and Thursdays, when she buys groceries. . . .

On Mondays, Chris and her girls grab supper, maybe a bowl of cereal if they're rushed, and head to a church in Leon County. There . . . Chris and eight to 10 other [parents] discuss how and why they're not going to hurt their kids.

To prepare for interviews, I review all the information I have about my subject, but I make sure to verify what others have written. I jot notes and questions—but never in stone: Since I'm hoping for heartfelt comments, I aim to keep the conversation spontaneous.

For accuracy and later verification, most writers tape their interviews, provided the speaker agrees. Unless I'm worried about getting sued or planning to use extended or technical quotes, I don't use a tape recorder. Machines unnerve some subjects. Taking notes forces me to listen closely, and sometimes while I'm scribbling away, trying to catch up, my interviewee fills the pause with a golden afterthought.

Lastly, I solicit comments from friends, colleagues, a spouse. How to track them down? Ask the subject. Pals talk more freely when you have a referral, and unless you're writing about a controversial figure, fans serve just as well as critics. They often confirm your judgments but spare you from going out on a limb. When I wrote an article about Manlin Chee, winner of an American Bar Association award for public service, I let a legal-aid coordinator in Greensboro, North Carolina, describe her: "If you see Manlin, you would say she's a hippie. . . .

301

But what you see is not what you get. . . . She's just the person you want behind you, whatever your case."

Putting it on paper

I enjoy writing profiles because of their cohesiveness. I never have to drop bread crumbs to find my way back to the focus: Who is this person?

Chronology forms the outline for chunks of the article—where he came from, what she's doing now, what he hopes to accomplish in the future (or, in the case of a dead person, what she left as a legacy). Of course, I scramble the order of these blocks to pique a reader's curiosity. In the profile about the founder of the Girl Scouts, I started not with her privileged childhood in Savannah, but with her doldrums in the wake of a miserable marriage:

Although Juliette Gordon Low had just succeeded in recovering a fair share of her late husband's estate from his mistress, middle age looked as bleak as tundra. "I am just an idle woman of the world, with no real work or duties," she wrote from England to her mother around 1906.

From there, I fast-forwarded six years, to the mustering of the Girl Scouts who gave her life purpose. Then I rewound to her family history—dwelling on the resourceful women who influenced "Daisy" Low and the evolution of her daffy charm.

I always plant a statement or two in the lead about my subject's claim to attention, if not fame. At the same time, I try to establish a theme. In a profile of textile artist Lisa Williamson, I opened with her talking about a pair of sculptures in her yard, since yin and yang inform so much of her work. Writing the rags-to-riches story of Hector Hernandez for a teen magazine, I emphasized that as the son of migrant farm workers, he grew up a workhorse, not a clotheshorse:

. . . "My family shopped at the Salvation Army—long before that was trendy." Now as a designer for the prestigious Robert Comstock label, Hernandez helps to dress the most fashionable men in America.

Think of how you introduce a new acquaintance to an old friend: This is X—who works at X. She's the X who started X. Yeah, yeah, the one who X'd. Cool, huh?

No article ever writes itself, but you and your subject share the work

302

in a profile. You take turns at the mike. The writer arranges, condenses, describes, explains; the subject speaks in a loud, clear voice. Since tone reveals character, I insert a lot of direct quotes. Readers discovered Manlin Chee's modesty the way I did, by her humorous account of law school: "I went through my first year in a fog. . . . All I knew was Perry Mason." Yet I avoid transcribing monologues. Most people ramble. If the subject supplies the gems, then the writer must play jeweler, crafting a proper setting for every quote.

There's more to people than what they say, so a profile should include some of the writer's impressions. Does the subject flit from topic to topic like a hummingbird or lumber like a bear? You are the reader's intermediary: What strikes you? I noticed that high-rolling investor Tony Gray "does not dress the part of a tycoon—no silk, no monograms, just a watch and a wedding ring." Even if I'm casting someone as a hero or a villain, I often add asides that illustrate human contradictions. "Hippie" Manlin Chee told me that she sat through *Easy Rider* covering her eyes and ears because of the film's violence and profanity. Real people have many dimensions.

I usually save one of the better quotes for the last paragraph. When designer Hector Hernandez summed up his fashion philosophy, I tagged it for a conclusion: "Style is something personal; it's what you wear at home when no one's looking; it's who you are without airs." Then my editor tacked on another sentence about his rise up the ladder of success. Which brings me to a general lesson: Never make promises about the published form of a profile. No matter what a subject or a writer says, editors always get the last word.

§61

BREAKING INTO
MAGAZINE ARTICLE WRITING

BY CHARLOTTE ANNE SMITH

WHEN MEETING A WRITER, many people comment that they've always wanted to write. The question is, do they really want to write or do they want to have written? There is a vast difference, and the response to this question, in my opinion, is one of the primary ways to weed out the people who truly want to be writers from those who think being a writer would be glamorous.

There are some other questions that can help clarify these two desires, and you need to ask them of yourself before you embark on this often frustrating, extremely rewarding profession. And, yes, it is a profession, but resign yourself to being asked what you *really* do for a living.

Do you have a passion for the written word? Are you the despair of your family because wherever you are, there is always a pile of books, magazines, and paper? Do you think being a writer would be just the best life ever? Are you one of those people that just *have* to write? If you are, don't give up. That is a pretty good test to determine if you should be a writer.

Now that you have passed that test, let's talk about magazine writing. Nonfiction is easier to break into than fiction—not easy, just *easier*—because there are so many more markets for articles than for short stories. But there is still a lot of competition. In order to sell, you have to be aware of certain basic facts of magazine publishing.

First, be professional. How can you be professional if you've never sold anything? If you've written the right article for a particular magazine and present it in a professional manner, the editor doesn't usually need to know and may not even care if it is your first effort.

Whether you approach an editor by query or in a cover letter accompanying your article, state what is unique about it, compared to others on the same subject. It can be firsthand knowledge, access to documentation or interviews others have not had, specialized training in that field, or just a different viewpoint—i.e., a woman writing about football, a farmer about Wall Street.

For example, I have farmed, raised cattle, operated a bird-dog training kennel, performed in rodeos, trained horses, raised four children, taught Sunday school, played a musical instrument, sung in public, done standup comedy, refinished and reupholstered furniture, built two houses, fished, camped and hiked, and been a professional writer for 24 years. There are publications related to all of these things, and I have sold articles dealing with all of them. My experiences made my articles believable.

You can also use the experiences and expertise of others. My brother was a police officer for years; I have a friend who is a world-renowned livestock auctioneer specializing in thoroughbred horses; others are famous musicians, writers, artists, or just interesting people doing interesting or unusual things. I live in an area whose industries include oil and gas production, coal mining, and agriculture, and I have sold articles on all of these subjects. Some were technical, and I relied on my sources to fill in what I didn't know. The editor didn't care who the expert was, just as long as my article was accurate and the whole thing was readable.

How you present your manuscript is important. Don't submit one full of misspellings and typos. In this day and age, you are going to need equipment that will enable you to turn out a professional-looking manuscript. If you use a typewriter and your finished manuscript is covered with correction fluid, make a clean copy before you submit it.

Just because a market listing says, "replies in two weeks," don't get all upset if you don't hear from the editor by then. (If, on the other hand, the response time goes on much longer than originally indicated, you should contact the editor; things do get lost or forgotten.) If the listing says "don't call," then don't call, and if it says, "query; don't submit the complete manuscript," then follow those instructions. And *don't* send your manuscript by fax unless you know the editor wants to receive submissions that way.

One of the most common complaints editors have about free lancers—and it is a justifiable one—is that they're unfamiliar with the market. Don't send a poem to a publication that never publishes poetry, or an article on cooking wild game to a vegetarian magazine. Write for a sample copy of your target market, buy one on the newsstand, if available, or read several back issues in the library. Carefully reading the magazine you're aiming for will give you a feel for its subject matter, tone, and style. You can get specific information on word length, photo requirements, and method of submission by assiduously studying the market lists in this book.

Don't think that your words are so precious they can't be deleted or changed. Often a rewrite to change length or focus or to include additional information will make the difference between a rejection and a sale. The editor is the buyer; work with him or her. However, it is permissible to object to a suggested change that will destroy the meaning of the article, or will affect your credibility, since credibility is the one commodity a nonfiction writer must maintain to survive.

Ideas for articles are everywhere. If you can't recognize a potential article idea, you're in the wrong business. Everything you see, hear, feel, smell, taste, and touch is a possible article with a potential market. It is your job to make the match. Whatever your interest—a sport, craft, food, profession, hobby, lifestyle, religion—there is a publication (sometimes several) out there devoted to it. Find those magazines, study them, and then develop your article ideas. Markets are everywhere; look for them. Never pass a newsstand without checking it for publications with which you aren't familiar. While waiting for a train in Victoria Station in London, I picked up several magazines on horses and agriculture in England. Soon after I got home I sold an article to a British publication, *Sporting Horse*.

Almost every field has a publication that wants profiles. Consider your family and friends. What professions are they involved in? What are their recreational interests? Have they had a traumatic experience? Won an award or contest? Lived to be 100? The answers to these questions should generate many article ideas.

Train yourself to remember. You never know when what you see, hear, or read will be just right for an article. A fact learned long ago may give you the authenticity needed to make a sale today; an anecdote stored in your memory may be just the thing to put your personal stamp on an article.

Be realistic about what you expect to accomplish. Realize there will be months when you may not make any sales, and many publications still send checks with only two figures on the left of the decimal point. There is also a limit to how much work you can turn out in a given time, and this has to be taken into consideration when you are estimating your potential income. Don't quit your day job the day you decide to become a writer, or even on the day you make your first sale.

Often you won't be paid until weeks or months after you submit your work. Even publications that pay on acceptance may not actually accept the article until several weeks after it is received.

Aim as high as you can. If there are two publications into which your article would fit, always query or submit first to the one that pays more. If one pays on acceptance and the other on publication, but the amount is about the same, go with the pay-on-acceptance publication.

Don't work free. A publication doesn't expect its printer, advertising staff, typesetters or anyone else to work free, so why should the writer? Without the writer they don't have a publication.

I will make two exceptions to that rule. If you find a new publication that may be a steady market and can work out an agreement for payment in the future, go ahead, but have a firm understanding. This will give you credits to show editors, and they don't have to know you weren't paid.

The other exception is a publication dealing with something you are trying to promote—a religion, political viewpoint, or social issue, for instance.

Decide if you want to specialize. If you have expertise in a given field, you may want to write exclusively for that area. However, you may qualify in more than one area and that can make your work more interesting for you and your readers.

Don't expect to get rich, but keep in mind that there are good things in life besides money. I don't know of any other profession as enjoyable, that gives you the freedom to do what you want to do when you want to, that opens up the opportunity to meet so many interesting people— or that would have allowed me to be hugged by Roy Rogers.

62

Biography: Telling the Untold Story

By Steve Weinberg

In the preface to her book about the life of Frank Lloyd Wright, experienced biographer Meryle Secrest discusses difficulties she encountered. Paraphrasing Somerset Maugham, Secrest says that "there are three rules for writing biography, but, unfortunately, no one knows what they are."

I disagree, vehemently. There are guidelines that can help produce first-rate biography. After many years of trial and error, I think I know what they are.

Profiling a subject in a newspaper feature, magazine or book is more than gathering information and stringing it together. It is a big responsibility—thousands or maybe millions of readers will judge the subject primarily on the basis of what the author writes.

My principles of writing biography can, at the very least, serve as a starting point for discussion, even though writers and editors may disagree with them:

First, a life should be told chronologically. Actions of the main subject often make little sense if viewed in isolation. But those same actions become clear when viewed as the outgrowth of a previous action. In other words, a biographer owes it to readers to follow a life as it was lived—chronologically.

The most sensible place to depart from chronology, if at all, is in the opening chapter, when the biographer is trying to establish themes that will provide the reader with a framework for better understanding. The introductory chapter to my biography of Armand Hammer is set in a Los Angeles courtroom during 1976, when he was nearly seventy-eight years old. After that chapter, the book is almost entirely chronological.

Second, good biographers go the extra mile to check out everything, never settling for secondary data when additional effort might uncover primary data. Gaps or incomplete information can tempt biographers to rely on newspaper clippings, hearsay, and autobiographical writings without subjecting them to rigorous examination. A good biographer will tell readers that secret, specifying possible overemphasis and unreliable evidence: Newspaper clippings are often factually incorrect; hearsay might be motivated by spite or fraught with ignorance; and autobiographies are frequently more significant for what they omit than what they include.

Third, a good biography should provide the context of the times to help explain the life. William Abrahams, a biographer of George Orwell, says "One cannot leave the world out. Orwell was a product of his time. There is a direct relationship there that cannot be overlooked. He was deeply conscious of the world in which he lived. The Spanish Civil War was the centerpiece of his life."

Writing about the context of the life can be overdone. Anthony Edmonds notes that responsible biographers "walk a middle ground, placing their subjects within a historical context and emphasizing individuality. For example, it is legitimate in a George Washington biography to describe Indian tactics, but only to the extent Washington knew them and dealt with them."

Fourth, a biographer must refrain from using hindsight to intrude into the chronology. Biographers are sometimes inclined to comment about a decision by the subject as it is being made, but a biographer should not leap backward in time into his subject's life to poke him in the ribs on the basis of hindsight.

Fifth, a biographer should have sympathy or empathy for the protagonist, or should at least recognize the consequences of antipathy. The warning of Bernard Crick is apt for biographers from the investigative journalism tradition, who are trained to dig up the dirt: "Sympathy must be present in a biographer; otherwise one would grow sour living for so long with someone one disliked."

Being sympathetic is not the same as being in love. Nobody would expect biographers of Adolf Hitler or Joseph Stalin to love their subjects. But biographers of such monsters must try to see the world through their subjects' eyes.

In the end, interpretation of one's actions is tricky. Historian Allan Nevins has commented that "nearly all human acts and traits have a significance that varies with the sympathy or antipathy of the observer.

Is Jones a shifty, wavering, uncertain man? Or does he simply see both sides of an issue, so that his apparent vacillations are simply proof of open-mindedness and tolerance?"

Sixth, psychological analysis of the subject by the biographer, while allowable, should be practiced sparingly. We rarely know for sure what our spouses, parents or children are thinking, so how can biographers pretend to know the thoughts of a subject they have rarely or never met?

Mark Twain said it forcefully in his autobiographical writings a century ago: "What a wee little part of a person's life are his acts and words! His real life is led in his head, and is known to none but himself. All day long, and every day, the mill of his brain is grinding, and his thoughts, not those other things, are his history. His acts and words are merely the visible, thin crust of his world, with its scattered snow summits and its vacant wastes of water—and they are so trifling a part of his bulk, a mere skin enveloping it. . . . Biographies are but the clothes and buttons of the man—the biography of the man himself cannot be written."

One reviewer of my Armand Hammer biography called it "relentlessly non-judgmental." I do not think that was meant as praise, but I took it as such anyway.

Seventh, when looking into the minds of their subjects, biographers must concede and then explain the complexity of the human animal. This is true whether or not the biographer subscribes to Twain's belief, which, if subscribed to literally, could bring despair to the biographical enterprise.

Part of the complexity biographers must recognize is that their subjects, as well as their "supporting casts," are not static. In the best biographies, the people who surround the main subject evolve as he or she evolves; they change over time, and thus affect the actions of the main subject. A biographer must try to understand all the characters in the play, not just the one with the leading role.

If a biographer does light on a theme while attempting to make sense of a life, it must not become reductionist, must not be used to explain every thought, every action of the subject. Human beings simply are not simple. Joan Peyser, the biographer of Leonard Bernstein, said, "I wrote recently that I was clearly unable to decide whether Bernstein was an angel or a monster. . . . It is not a question of either one or the other. He could be both, and within minutes."

A biographer must be allowed some latitude in this regard. Biographies are, after all, not life—they are an arrangement and interpretation of a life. Without a theme imposed by a biographer, a book can become chaos, a self-contradictory narration that reflects the incoherence of life. Once a plan is chosen, the biographer should be faithful to it while also including as much relevant contradictory evidence as possible.

Eighth, a biographer must be honest with readers about filling in gaps. Every life leaves gaps in its public record, what biographer Victoria Glendinning calls "lies and silences." Gaps can lead a biographer to overemphasize periods for which there is ample documentation, and underplay important periods for which the documentation is sparse.

Ninth, biographers must make hard decisions about the appropriate length of the book. Sometimes setting out a smorgasbord of verifiable facts, enough reasoned (and maybe even alternative) hypotheses, can help make up for unreliable or uncooperative human sources.

Being selective when dealing with masses of material in order to keep a biography at a readable, publishable length is its own skilled form of interpretation. The task is harder than ever in an age of presidential libraries with millions of documents, videotapes and audiotapes, commercial computer databases that allow a biographer to search thousands of publications in a matter of seconds, and other resources that can lead to information overload.

Tenth, good biographers must take style as seriously as substance. Many investigative biographers writing on contemporary subjects discover fascinating new material, if only by serendipity based on sheer time spent. But precious few of those biographers have the talent to tell the tale compellingly. Interesting lives can too easily be rendered pedestrian by pedestrian prose. The best biographers not only arrange the facts logically, but also provide readers with the feel for the facts.

Some of the writing techniques used to create that "feel" are borrowed from fiction. Biographies and novels are concerned with birth, death, love, hate and moral dilemmas galore. The techniques used in each genre might include scene-by-scene construction based on immersion in a geographic setting, physical description of the key individuals, dialogue, imagery, symbolism, irony, contrast, and shifting points of view among various characters.

The dark side of the contemporary biography boom has been the large number of second-rate biographies. Nothing should be allowed to take the place of verifiable—and verified—information. Too many biographers today dig the dirt, then forget to look for the diamonds that might also be in the pile. They fall into a trap described by Jacques Barzun: "It is the principle Lincoln used to confound Grant's enemies—if drinking whisky wins victories, let all the generals be given a pint of Scotch. But Grant was not a drunkard who happened to win battles. He was a military genius who happened to drink. Similarly, all victims of biography are not idlers and profligates who were great artists on the side. They were artists whose characters were marred by adventitious elements precisely like certain other people that we all know."

63

THE MARKET FOR OP-ED ARTICLES

BY GENIE DICKERSON

THERE'S A LOT OF CONFUSION ABOUT OP-ED articles, the free-lance essays that newspapers publish opposite their editorial pages. Papers buy two kinds of op-ed pieces: personal experience and opinion or analysis. Most op-ed rejections result from the writer's confusion and blending of the two types.

Let's take the personal experience piece first. This offers writers the best and easiest way to get published by a newspaper. All that's required is 1) simple, clear, tight writing, and 2) an experience in some segment of public affairs.

Included in this type might be first-person narratives by a foreign defector, for example, or by personal victims of some horror. The whistleblower, the disaffected union worker, the member of an ethnic minority who has been discriminated against—all these may have special stories they want to tell. Any topical firsthand experience will work.

I've had op-ed articles published on my problems with neighborhood squirrels and on a conversation I overheard while having breakfast at a restaurant. Virtually everyone has at least one personal story that would interest newspaper readers.

Analysis or opinion op-eds

The analysis type of op-ed article usually sheds light on a public concern, or expresses a new point of view or opinion, but it does not involve personal experience. Here the writer uses the third person and turns out an impersonal commentary. The tone of an analysis should be firm and somewhat formal; its vocabulary is more likely to use polysyllabic words from the Latin, and the style is more sophisticated and knowledgeable. Facts and statistics must be verifiable. For instance, just because a person is sick and tired of the government's

313

budget deficit doesn't necessarily mean he should get paid to have his opinion set into print. The reader deserves more.

In dollars, how big was the deficit last year? Who is to blame? When did the problem begin? Do the United Kingdom, Germany, and Japan also run budget deficits? What evidence is there for these statements? The writer must present the facts in a logical essay and tie them together with an answer to one more question: What's the solution?

Experience is helpful but not necessary. I've sold opinion pieces on income tax, freedom of the press, and public funding for the arts, without having any special knowledge. Research at the library can fill in. Telephone inquiries to such sources as government bureaus and senators' offices are another good option.

With analytical op-eds, it's especially important to stick to one subject. Tossing in gratuitous comments on secondary issues may alienate readers needlessly. Avoid blanket criticisms of large groups like conservatives, liberals, ethnic groups, teenagers, college students, etc. Try to lead readers to look at an issue from a new angle without insulting any person or class. Balance should permeate the piece.

Writers of analytical op-eds should omit unnecessary personal facts: age, religion, race, political party preference, lifestyle choices, etc. If the writer seems to have an ax to grind, he'll lose the reader. The greatest pitfall in op-ed writing is mixing the personal, emotional narrative type with the impersonal, intellectual analytical type.

The first sentence is the most important part of any op-ed. It should be clever and concise, telling just enough about what is to come to hook the reader. The next most important sentence is the last one of the article, which should summarize the main point.

Humor is another valuable element in an op-ed. If the article can raise a smile or a laugh, so much the better. Although op-eds aim basically to provoke thought and discussion, the writer should offer readers some frosting on the cake. Although this sort of writing cannot be used in hard news reporting, it sells op-ed articles. But don't go too far. Fluff, purple prose, and padding will only bring rejections.

Titles and headlines

Newspaper headlines run longer than most magazine titles and often contain a verb. Also, individual newspapers use their own capitalization styles. Follow the style of the paper to which you submit. The paper may change your heading, but at least you have suggested a workable one and have shown your knowledge of the newspaper's style.

Follow normal manuscript form—typed, double-spaced—and include an SASE. Payment rates for op-ed pieces range from nothing to several hundred dollars, with larger-circulation papers paying the higher rates. Op-eds longer than the usual 700 to 800 words also command the higher-range fees, but few papers buy long pieces.

The best op-ed markets are hometown papers. Some newspapers refuse to buy from out-of-area writers, but most op-ed editors of metropolitan papers welcome the freshness brought by writers outside their region. Address the manuscript to "Op-Ed Editor" or to the editor by name. A few op-ed editors prefer queries, but many topics would be cold before the query was answered. Check the query policy of your targeted paper.

Whether or not to send a cover letter with the manuscript depends on what you've got to say in it and who the editor is. If you have relevant expertise, then a cover letter (or a bio line at the end of the manuscript) is in order. Rarely do op-ed editors welcome footnotes or a bibliography. If you have tearsheets on the same subject as the submitted manuscript, include them as support for your knowledge of the subject. Generally, however, the editor would rather just get to your manuscript without spending time reading extras.

If you prefer to test the waters before jumping into op-ed writing, try a short letter to the editor, similar in content to pieces published on the op-ed page. A success or two will build your self-confidence.

64

YOU DON'T HAVE TO GO TO SPAIN TO WRITE TRAVEL ARTICLES

BY BARBARA CLAIRE KASSELMANN

NO, I'VE NEVER BEEN TO SPAIN. OR PARIS, OR TAHITI OR TIERRA DEL FUEGO, for that matter. But I have been to Dayton, Woods Hole, Ludowici and Pittsburgh. And I do write travel articles and sell them.

I can assure you, you don't really have to travel to exotic locales and stay in fabulously expensive resort hotels to be a travel writer. If you can make the corner ice cream store come alive with your lively writing style, you can write and sell travel articles. I can show you how, by regaining that old childhood sense of wonder and carrying a notebook everywhere you go, you can turn any place, even the county fair or the local shopping mall, into a trip. And of course, a trip means a travel article. I have learned to make the most of where I can afford to go. And I have come rather to like that. With the travel writer's approach, I see the colors and hear the songs much more vividly, which leads not only to writing more travel articles, but it also makes life richer and more fun.

To be a successful travel writer, the first thing you have to do is to think like a travel writer. See every beach, every historical marker, every museum or restaurant as a possible destination or stop along the way for the curious tourist. Then experience that place and take notes on it. (No serious writer of any type should ever be caught without a notebook and a pen.)

Is the beach lonely or lively? Who swims or sunbathes here? Does it have palm trees or rocky cliffs, crashing waves or dramatic sunsets? Would you come here for peaceful meditation, great fried clams or to watch the beautiful people? If it's a historical site, make a note of what happened where and when. If you have time, visit the museum and eat at one of the restaurants.

Once you've found and explored that undiscovered little clam shack or archaeological wonder, check out the surrounding area. Are there other restaurants around? Budget motels or grand old hotels? Unusual gift stores or antique shops? And how about access? Is it near a major highway, public transportation or an airport? Travelers want to know how to get there, where they can stay, and if there's anything more to do when they get there than read one brass plaque. When you get ready to write your article, you'll want to combine a number of places and activities into a varied, interesting package for your reader.

Two very important lessons I learned the hard way are that my memory might not always be quite as clear as I thought it would be, and that I might not be able to go back again next week to get additional information. Hence, I carry not only my trusty notebook, but a big old canvas bag as well for items that might be pertinent to any article I may want to write: schedules of upcoming exhibits, festivals, or other special events, brochures, menus, local maps, business cards from hotels, restaurants, gift shops, bargain outlets, museums, theaters, and historical sites. If an establishment doesn't seem too busy, I say I am a travel writer and ask to speak to the manager to get some basic information. This personal contact makes it easy for me to call back later for more information.

When I get home, I immediately file all my literature by region, state, city and/or specific topic. The more deeply I get involved in travel writing, the more refined and explicit my files must become.

I also expand my files by reading, clipping, mailing, and calling information centers, convention and visitors' bureaus. I am an inveterate reader of the travel section of Sunday newspapers, as well as travel and airline magazines. Newspapers in particular are filled with 1-800 numbers, coupons, or addresses from which you can obtain travel packets of brochures, rates and information. I send for those from a place I might want to visit and write about within the next year or two. I also clip articles that might be related in some way to an area I am interested in exploring. All this literature helps me tremendously in making my travel and writing plans.

My budget limitations help curtail my files. I know there is no point in my accumulating massive files on Tahiti or Bora Bora this year. I stick mostly with literature about hidden treasures of New England (my home) and nearby Canada, which is also a possibility. I also consider the areas of the country I can visit because friends or relatives live there; my old hometown, and an occasional dream place like New Orleans or Montreal.

In general, I firmly believe that to write authentic, interesting travel articles, a writer must, in most cases, actually visit a place and experience it. I could write a good encyclopedia entry about Morocco or Melbourne without ever going there, but I probably couldn't write a great travel article that would make people want to hop the next plane and go there. So I write about Newburyport, which is a favorite old haunt of mine, 45 miles up the road from Boston, or Vidalia, just a lazy half-day's drive through the tall Georgia pines from my daughter's house.

It is possible, however, to write good travel articles without ever leaving the farm. It takes extra effort at traveling through research material, corresponding with possible sources and surveying markets. Target publications that prefer third person, informational pieces rather than personal accounts. Use your imagination and creativity to add spice, but be careful never to embroider the facts.

To be an effective travel writer, it's critical to maintain a childhood sense of wonder about the places you visit. Allow this funky little town, these rolling fields of graceful pecan trees or that musty old museum to sink into your senses.

Take a table at a little café or enjoy a picnic on the river bank, and absorb the world around you. Listen to the sounds of the street life, smell the aromas from the barbecuing ribs, feel the cool fog on your arms. Order a regional specialty dish—Maryland crab cakes, Cincinnati chili, Gulf shrimp. Relax, enjoy, and record. As you sit there soaking up the scene, take notes on the sights, the sounds, and the tastes. Make a list of shops you see up and down the street you will want to visit before you leave.

I always like to talk to the people in a region to get the flavor of their accents, their interests, and the styles that make that part of the country or the world special. If you make these people come alive in your writing, it will pique the prospective traveler's interest in the destination about which you will be writing. From the residents you can often pick up fascinating bits of local lore or find out about the best places to visit or dine, those little secrets and haunts not found in the tour books.

How important are photos? For me, they have been very important, but they are not essential. I took my first travel photo in the Smoky Mountains when I was five years old, and I have been clicking away ever since. While I do not have extensive photographic equipment, I do have a good quality camera and an eye for what will make a good picture. Along with my notebook, my camera is a permanent part of my gear. I never know when or where I will see that perfect hideaway to suggest to travelers. When I am proposing an article to a travel editor, I include a few color slides or mention their availability, which is definitely a plus.

If you are not a photographer, however, don't force it. Check with the information officer at local tourist sites and convention and visitors' bureaus to see what photos they have available, so you can mention specific photo possibilities when you query an editor. It is advisable to establish contact with good photographers; you can get their names from local newspapers, photographers' organizations, or the yellow pages.

When visiting an area, learn to look for the unusual. Why should readers want to visit this museum of art when they have a fine museum in their own city? Why should they travel 1,000 miles for an Italian dinner when they can get great ravioli right around the corner? Anticipate the questions your readers are going to be asking; it's your job to answer them. Show what things set a particular area apart from similar places to prove that it's worth the time and money to visit. Make a site come alive on the pages, and make it a special place worthy of a vacation, big or small.

To be a published travel writer, you have to learn about more than just the places you plan to write about. As with any article writing, you must study your markets and your readers. Read travel pages in the newspapers to which you'd like to submit, and study travel magazines, as well as the many general, regional, and women's magazines that use travel articles. *The Writer* Magazine is an important guide for free-lance writers seeking publication, with practical, precise information on where to send your manuscripts, who is buying, and how much they pay.

Select three or four publications that seem appropriate for your work. If you have an impressive line-up of clips from major magazines or newspapers, you can afford to start with the bigger markets, but if you are just getting started, small regional publications or the Sunday travel sections of small city papers are good places to start. Pay may not be high at first, but you will be compiling clips so you can gradually move up the ladder to bigger and better.

Get a feel for the style and editorial requirements of the publication to which you plan to submit your article. Are the articles 300 or 3,000 words long? Are they written in first, second, or third person? Do they feature local one-day trips, weekend getaways or exotic world tours? Are they aimed at wealthy world travelers, singles looking for an exciting weekend or families on a budget? Don't waste your time or the editor's by proposing an article on budget getaways to a decidedly upscale magazine, or suggesting a New York City weekend to a magazine for recreational vehicle owners.

Develop a query letter as soon as possible after visiting a place, while the sensations and sights are still fresh in your mind. As with all queries, make it vivid, but to the point. Make the travel editor want to go where you've just gone, and he or she will be hooked on your idea.

If you have kept all those brochures and menus and interview notes, you have the battle well under control when you actually begin to write the article. I like to peruse my literature, take a look at the slides I took of the region, and get back into the mode of the vacation place I am preparing to write about. This is much easier to do if I have visited a place within the past few weeks, rather than five years ago.

I organize my notes and write down every topic and angle I plan to cover. Then I number the topics in the general order I plan to use, highlighting points that might make a good lead and an effective conclusion. For most "on-the-move" travel articles, chronological order seems to work best. However, if you have stayed in one locale for a week, you might want to group and compare dinners, sports activities, beach days or evenings on the town. If you are a strict outliner, which I am not, use that approach; it will save you a great deal of grief.

Throughout the article, include specifics on places to stay, where to dine, how to get there. Give locations for historic sites or other points of interest. Some publications prefer a box or sidebar at the end of the article, with a wrap-up of hotels, event schedules and addresses or telephone numbers for travel and visitors' bureaus. Consider these points when surveying publications to which you plan to submit.

Many readers of travel articles do just what I do: clip them and use them in travel plans. Accuracy is vital: Make sure you've listed the correct addresses and phone numbers for hotels, restaurants, and other places mentioned in your article. Check and double-check your spelling, and the dates for any event that you include. If you're not positive about any piece of information, make a quick phone call to verify or update it.

If you're very lucky, you might sell your first travel article. However, it's more likely you will have to be determined, hard-working, persistent, and a reasonably good writer to crack the travel writing market eventually. If you have good skills and are willing to accept editorial criticism, it will only be a matter of time before you get a letter saying, "Yes, we would like to see your proposed article about visiting the sand dunes of western Michigan."

Of course, as soon as you get your first positive response from an editor, you'll stay up all night writing the dunes article. Then you'll start exploring and considering other towns or lakes you know and love, to get ready to write your next travel piece. Once you're on a roll, keep the momentum going, keep your writing alive, fresh, vivid, real, and full of sensations and specifics. Develop and hone your own style, and make the most of it.

These are the rules I follow, and they have paid off for me. I love traveling; I love travel writing. If you do, too, it will show in your writing, and before you know it, you, too, will be collecting checks for doing what you love to do.

As I continue to write and teach, I still keep one eye on my mailbox. I don't want to miss that letter saying, "We have continued to read and follow your travel articles, and we want to send you to a fantastic beach in Tahiti for a month so you will write an article for us." You say the plane leaves in an hour?

65

Nine Leads to Article Sales

By Lottie Robins

Twenty years ago, the instructor of a nonfiction course I was taking walked into the first class, fidgeted with some papers for a few minutes, then suddenly approached a young man in the front row. Pointing a finger at him, the instructor said, "Hey, you!" The young man looked up, startled.

"Did you hear me?" the teacher asked.

"Of course," came the quick reply.

"Good," said the teacher, walking back to his desk. "That's how to begin an article. You grab the reader's attention and say as few words as possible to make him listen, during which time you introduce your theme."

That teacher's dramatic illustration has stayed with me ever since.

Factual approach

Who, what, where, when, and why are usually the rules for the first sentence in a news article. For example, in a feature article entitled, "Home Schooling," published in *The Woman's Newspaper of Princeton,* my opening read:

Our son Jesse is a bright, normal boy of ten who reads five books a week, loves to browse through the encyclopedia, adores science fiction, and hates to take showers. He likes to swim and go to museums, adores his two-year-old sister, and hates to clean his room.

Today Jesse is attending a small private school. But from second grade through fourth, he was a home schooler, and although I do not have a degree in education, I was his only teacher.

Instead of straight facts, I bring an active character into the story, give his name, paint a word picture, give an important fact about the

322

narrator (my daughter, in this case), and state where Jesse is today in his education.

The fictional approach

To avoid sounding like a textbook, try the anecdotal lead, which is excellent for a subject without too much fictional or dramatic material. If you are planning to become a serious nonfiction writer, learn some fiction techniques and start collecting anecdotes.

In "I Can Hear the Water Running" *(The Woman's Newspaper)*, I used a story that had been told to me. My article began:

A number of years ago, a friend in her early 40's told me she had been deaf since the age of six and had just had surgery that restored her hearing. The biggest thrill, she told me, was when she awoke from the anesthetic and the nurse turned on the tap in the adjoining bathroom and she could hear the water running. It was like a symphony.

If I had begun with the history of hearing aids, or the statistics of how many hard-of-hearing people there are, I would probably have lost my audience immediately.

Begin with a character

To write an article for which you don't have statistics or for which they aren't really essential, plunge right in with a character who has a problem related to your theme. Here's my opening for "Start Your Own Singles Club" (published in *Pennysaver*):

Josephine is 51, recently divorced, and feels out of place with her married friends, even though they include her for a social evening in their home.

As I also wanted to draw in the male reader, two paragraphs later I introduce George, age 60, just widowed.

The Act I setting

After meeting two women who ran a personal service for senior citizens and deciding to write about them, I tried a half dozen openings before I came up with one I felt was just right. The reason I chose the following "stage setting" for "Help for the Elderly Housebound" *(Lady's Circle)* was that it best served my purpose to describe the service:

The telephone rings: "My elderly mother needs a series of X-rays that will take several days. I work and cannot take her. Can you escort her?"

I then listed two more telephone calls, using the same style, and continued:

Picking up the telephone and saying yes, they will be glad to help, is Personal Service of the Lehigh Valley, in Guthsville, PA.

The shocker

Sometimes, for a very dramatic emotional article, it is best to begin with a shocking statement, such as the one I used for "A Boutique to Save Babies" *(Life and Health):*

Scott died when he was five and a half. He was born on December 29, 1969, a delightful blonde boy with fuzzy hair and big blue eyes. He came from the hospital healthy, hungry, and spry.
Scott had Tay-Sachs disease.

Sometimes, when you wish to shock your reader into action, using the "you" technique is advisable. This method is excellent when your article is an exposé with a warning. In an editorial in *Seniorgram,* the author does just that: "Senior citizens, beware of the smooth-talking sales persons who tell you they're going to send you medical equipment that Medicare will pay for."

Ask a question

By opening with a question, you are getting your reader to think, and to participate in the answer. The question can come in the first sentence, or follow a few introductory remarks.

In "Seniors Go Back to School" *(Pennysaver),* I plunged in with:

Do you recall dropping your children off at a college dorm and wishing you, too, were going to experience the fun of college life?

Quotations

A popular type of opening is a quote from an authority, giving the person's title, background, and area of expertise. For my article, "Adult Condominiums—Why They Are for You" *(The Woman's Newspaper),* I open with the following quote, with permission of the realtor:

"New Jersey has more adult condominium developments than any other state in the metropolitan area," says Arlene Mulry, sales representative at Weichert Realtors.

Dialogue for human interest

Dialogue is one of the most important attention-grabbers a writer can use. For an article that needs drama, this type of opening will keep your editor reading beyond the first sentence. When I queried *The Saturday Evening Post* about an article on cults, the editor cautioned me that the story had to be dramatic as well as traumatic. In order to introduce both our son and us, I opened with:

"Mom, you've got to accept it. I have to give up everything I love for Reverend Moon and his Divine Principle," said Arthur, our twenty-two-year-old son, over the telephone. "My art, my drums, my apartment, my girl friend."

Make a statement

Lastly, if you cannot come up with any of the above catchy openings, then begin with a statement . . . but make sure it's an eye-opener, and keep your sentences as short as possible, each one having directly to do with your subject. Here's the opening for "Is the Law Abusing Women?," by Michael G. Dowd (*Woman's Day*):

My job is to defend women charged with killing the men who have abused them. I meet my clients in jail.

Here the opening not only gives the author authenticity, but in one short statement invites the reader to come into the jail with him.

With all these openings to choose from, pull out all your rejected manuscripts, and to grab your readers' and editors' attention, do what my instructor did years ago: Say "Hey, you! Are you listening? Because I've got something to say that you won't want to miss."

DO'S AND DON'TS

• When using first person, set the scene, the time, and the subject matter in the first sentence.
• If you are writing on a topic that requires authority, such as medicine, the law, social issues, literature, or even sports, be sure to identify

325

yourself in the first paragraph, and if possible, in the title, i.e. Tom Jones, M.D.

• If you are writing about a holiday, mention it not only in the title, but in the first paragraph.

• When writing about an ethnic group, be sure your reader knows, in the very first sentence, which group you are writing about.

• Make your lead catchy but not more dramatic than your article.

• Don't use long descriptive passages.

• Do use short sentences and small paragraphs.

🎇66

REVIEWING BOOKS

BY EDWARD HOWER

HAVE YOU EVER THOUGHT IT WOULD BE FUN to get paid for reading the latest books, and then for saying what you think of them? Then maybe you should think about reviewing books.

Getting started

You don't have to be an established book reviewer for your work to be published. A lot of hometown newspapers—including the local shopper's weekly—are glad to have reviews of books by local authors or about the area. Regional and special-interest magazines also run reviews, so if you're an expert on a particular part of the country or on some specialized subject, you should query those publications. If you have a book in mind that you'd like to review, say why you think the publication's readers might like to read about it—and why you are especially qualified to review it. An editor who is interested will respond by phone or letter to discuss it.

Early in your career, you may have to obtain your own copy of the book you select to review; you can do so by writing to the publisher's publicity department, saying that you want to review the book for whatever publication you have in mind. If you can get a note from the publication's editor indicating that he or she is interested in seeing your review, include this with your letter to the publisher. After you've published some reviews and editors get to know your work, they may send you bound galleys of forthcoming books—pre-publication paperback editions—in response to your letters to the publicity director.

Don't be surprised if you're paid nothing or almost nothing for your reviews, at first. Count it as a learning experience. I was paid only $5 apiece for my first several reviews in a local weekly, but later I used clips of these reviews to show to the editors at *The New York Times, The Boston Globe, The Chicago Tribune, Newsday,* and the other newspapers I write for today. Now I do about two reviews a month at $100 to $400 each. I also get free hardcover editions, which I can keep after reviewing them.

Once you've reviewed a few books, include photocopies of your published reviews with your next query letters to editors. Don't be afraid to mail out multiple queries, and to send follow-up letters if you don't hear from the editors after a few weeks.

Your letter should include a description of the kind of books you especially like; my specialty is contemporary fiction and books about the Third World. Other reviewers specialize in women's issues, American history, nature, sports, boats, or science. If your interest is too narrow, you may not get many responses to your queries, so it's a good idea to indicate that you'll be glad to review a wider range of books.

Each August and January, *Publishers Weekly* lists books, by publisher and date, that will be published in the coming season. Look through these issues in the library for titles that match your special interests. With your letters to editors include a short list of the books you'd be interested in reviewing for them.

Learning the trade

How do you learn to write reviews? First, as you read, take notes on the plot and content, and jot down comments you may want to make later. It's amazing how much more closely you read a book when you have pencil in hand. You can also learn a lot about reviewing by reading published reviews in newspapers and magazines. Many national and regional publications have book review sections or columns, often somewhere near the back.

It would be worth your while to spend time in the library looking through recent volumes of *Book Review Digest* and *Contemporary Literary Criticism,* valuable references that publish extracts from reviews of earlier books by most major authors. They're also useful for getting capsule plot summaries of books that you might not have time to read—good background for your own reviews.

You'll soon discover that a good review includes these elements:
• a lively opening: one or two brief paragraphs that mention the name of the author and the title and often some brief information about the author, as well as any past works, prizes, etc.

- a summary of the plot (if it's a novel) or of the main purpose and subject of a work of nonfiction
- the reviewer's opinion of the book's strengths and weaknesses
- a wrap-up sentence or paragraph that gives the reader a final impression of the book

The opening

Composing a good lead paragraph is the most challenging part of review writing. The purpose is to catch your readers' attention, making them eager to read what you have to say.

To get started, take notes. Ask yourself some questions:
- What's the main theme that runs through the book?
- What's special about the book, compared to others like it?
- What impact did the book have on me?

You're likely to find your lead in your answers.

The name of the author and the book title are often included in the first paragraph, but sometimes you can start with the book's most important idea, as if the review were an article on the book's subject.

Here's how I began the review of a satirical novel about college life that was published in *The New York Times:*

College campuses have been in turmoil for some time now. No, the students haven't been acting up. It's the professors who have been leaving trails of blood along the hallways of academe, bludgeoning one another over questions about what's called "political correctness."

Then, a couple of sentences later, I named the author (Ishmael Reed) and title *(Japanese by Spring).*

In the first paragraph, I called it a "funny, explosive new novel." Generally, I think it's a good idea to indicate very briefly at the beginning what you think of a book. An adjective or two will do, and you can expand on it later.

In reviewing nonfiction books, you can open with a short background to the topic the book covers, especially if the subject is likely to be unfamiliar to some readers. For instance, a review of mine in the *San Francisco Chronicle* started like this:

The recent news from South Africa has been both exhilarating and alarming. The nation seems on the verge of freedom, yet its people are rioting among themselves.

The next sentence gives the book's title, author, and some relevant information about him:

No recent book can better clarify South Africa's dilemma than *The Mirror at Midnight,* by Adam Hochschild, a former editor and co-founder of *Mother Jones* magazine.

The summary

People read reviews primarily to find out whether they want to read a book. You need to give them a taste of what's between the covers. When reviewing fiction, tell your reader something about the main characters but summarize only *some* of the plot. Nothing's more infuriating for both an author and would-be reader than to have a reviewer give away what happens in the end! I usually summarize the first third to half of the plot of a novel, omitting the subplots, and stop where a conflict is about to be resolved, a character is about to make a decision, or a major action scene is about to begin.

Reviews of nonfiction books, on the other hand, should provide an overview of all the important information. Include significant dates, people, places, and ideas, and a statement of how the author arrived at his or her conclusions.

Choosing good quotations from the book can make it come alive for your readers. Look for especially witty, moving, or powerful quotes, and describe the context in which they were made. But limit the quotations to no more than a sentence or two, unless an editor has given you the go-ahead to write a long review. Don't forget to give page references after each quotation, so that your editor can check them.

The opinion

Some reviewers don't mind trashing a book, and some seem positively to enjoy it. Not I. If I can't find at least something to like in a book's first twenty or thirty pages, I sent it right back, so another reviewer can try it. There are a lot of good books that deserve attention, so why waste my time on those I think unworthy? I do write mixed reviews, though; few books are without flaws, and it's my job to be honest with my readers about what I find in the books I'm reviewing.

When forming your opinion of a book, you might start by asking yourself these questions:

- What did this author set out to do?
- How well did he or she succeed?
- Did the book move me in some way?
- What did I like about the book?
- What did I dislike?

It's also helpful to divide your evaluation into two categories:
- Content: what the author said.
- Style: how he or she said it.

When considering the content of a work of fiction, ask yourself:
- Were the characters interesting and convincing?
- Did the plot hold my attention to the end?

As for style, decide what to say about the author's language.
- Was it simple, stilted, poetic?
- Impersonal, formal, moving?
- Hackneyed or original?

Try to come up with some fresh descriptive words. My rule: Any hackneyed adjectives that appear in a blurb are out of bounds for my review.

In reviewing nonfiction books, content is more important than style, though you do need to say whether or not the writing is clear and readable. Consider:
- How thoroughly and thoughtfully did the author cover the material?
- What is the author's major focus? Why?
- Were the conclusions justified by the material that the author presented?

You may disagree with the book's conclusions, but you must make every effort to be objective, not to argue with the author and say how *you* would have written it.

The wrap-up

Make your ending short, finding some strong words that sum up your opinion of the book. If possible, echo a statement you made in your opening paragraph.

At the end of my review of Ishmael Reed's *Japanese by Spring*, I echoed my opening statement, using different language and adding a twist:

331

. . .this clever, outrageous novel is just the sort of weapon we need in the war against academic pedantry.

The last paragraph of my review of Adam Hochschild's book echoed its opening, and, taking it one step further, added what I thought was the work's most important accomplishment:

The Mirror at Midnight is an ambitious and thoughtful book. It's strength lies not only in explaining what has been happening in South Africa, but in letting us empathize with its people.

Remember, your goal is not just to finish writing about a book, but to put a memorable ending on the review itself, making it a first-rate piece of journalism that you'll be proud of long after the book has been forgotten.

67

HOW TO WRITE AND SELL A SPORTS ARTICLE

BY TOL BROOME

WHAT WOULD YOU SAY ABOUT A MARKET THAT IS HUNGRY for quality writing and for which most free lancers can write? A market that includes books, newspapers, newspaper weeklies, annuals, programs and promotional material, as well as more than 600 regularly published magazines?

You may be surprised to learn that the market to which I am referring is the sports market. The arena of sportswriting has broadened considerably in recent years and now includes opportunities for publication not only in the big three sports—baseball, basketball and football—but also on a host of other topics: hockey, running, boating, skiing, sports medicine, and sports-card collecting, to name just a few.

Here is a step-by-step approach that I have used to publish several dozen sports articles in a variety of publications over the past six years:

The game plan

There are two key rules of thumb to follow to generate ideas. First, be a fan. You will come up with a healthy number of ideas from attending or participating in sporting events, watching sports on television, and reading about athletic events.

A couple of years ago while I was watching a 49ers game on television, the commentators began to discuss Roger Craig's amazing year in 1985. That made me wonder how that sensational season stacked up against superlative performances by other running backs. A good bit of research answered my question and resulted in the publication of an article, "Running For Glory: The Greatest Seasons Ever For Running Backs," in *Sports Collectors Digest*.

The second "rule" is to keep current and be aware of sports anniversaries. For example, in 1991 on the 50th anniversary of Joe DiMaggio's

333

56-game hitting streak and the 30th anniversary of Roger Maris's 61 homers, interesting pieces appeared in publications all over the country. But after that, these articles were no longer timely or salable.

In choosing your angle, avoid covering a sporting event strictly from a news angle, as editors have staff writers who do that. What angles are in demand? Personal experience pieces, particularly for specialty magazines (i.e. boating, skiing and soccer), are marketable, and a fresh statistical analysis angle will often draw editor interest.

Additionally, editors need interviews and player profiles. Find out if any current or retired athletes live in or near your hometown off-season. You need not limit yourself to professional athletes. Many publications are just as interested in material on such amateurs as an outstanding Little Leaguer or a successful disabled athlete.

Pre-game warm-up (research)

I cannot stress enough the importance of thorough research. A good place to start is your local library, where you will find reference books, magazines, newspapers, biographies, clipping files, and a wealth of other sources. You can also get needed information from interviews, letters to Halls of Fame (the major sports halls have extensive libraries, and the information in them is readily available to the public), daily newspapers, television announcers, and even the backs of sports cards.

If you plan to write sports articles regularly, buy some good reference books, such as sports encyclopedias. Not only will this save time, but they will also come in handy when you get an idea at midnight, and you just have to know how many touchdown passes Joe Montana threw from 1984–87.

The accuracy of your research can either help establish or weaken your credibility. If you aren't sure about a statistic or fact, look it up. Sports article readers (and editors) are notorious for their close scrutiny of facts and figures. If you guess wrong about the number of races won by Secretariat, the editor will notice it, and the likelihood of publication will be greatly diminished.

The first quarter (title and lead)

Your article's title is its calling card, so make it count. The title can be a good place for a pun or alliteration. For instance, for a player profile on Isiah Thomas, how about, "There's No Doubting This Thomas," or "Isiah Profits From His NBA Success."

The lead is at least as important as the title. I have been successful with different approaches, including quotes, questions, word definitions, little-known facts and anecdotes. Your lead will often tell the editor whether or not it's worth his or her time to read on, so be innovative.

The second quarter (theme)

This is easy to overlook. Your theme statement may be one short transitional paragraph or it may be part of your lead. Just be sure you inform the reader of your slant before you proceed to the body of the article.

The third quarter (the body)

In a closely contested sports event, the third quarter is often the key in determining the outcome. The team that is most effective in carrying out its game plan will nearly always gain the upper hand in the critical third quarter.

The same holds true in sportswriting. If the editor likes your title, lead, and slant enough to keep reading to this point, a well-organized presentation of your key points in the third quarter may determine whether or not your piece is accepted.

Begin with your strongest point first—a "scoop" about an athlete in a player profile or one or two key facts in a statistical analysis piece.

Editors like quotes, anecdotes, examples, and analogies interspersed throughout a manuscript. And the use of some jargon in a sports article is a plus, because it demonstrates "inside" knowledge of your subject. But don't overdo it, or your article will seem trite and will likely doom your chances of acceptance.

The fourth quarter (the conclusion)

Your conclusion is a good place to use a quote, a pun, or an anecdote. For instance, if you have written a player profile on James Worthy, try something like, "James's three championship rings and 18.6 career scoring average should some day make him Worthy of induction into the Basketball Hall of Fame." A clever conclusion will help the reader and the editor remember your article.

Overtime (sidebars)

Sidebars are used extensively in sportswriting. They are particularly effective for statistical information that might otherwise "clutter" your article—charts, rankings, graphs, and lists.

For example, for the article on the greatest years for running backs, I used sidebars to present the extensive statistical comparisons. This allowed me to provide the reader with "user-friendly" visual aids in comparing the campaigns.

Post-game wrap-up (editing)

Contrary to popular belief, all sports publication editors pay very close attention to diction, grammar, spelling, style, length, transitions, and flow. Therefore, before you attempt to submit your article for publication, read it over several times, and don't be afraid to slash, change, add, and rewrite. You may also want to consider letting someone else edit your piece, whether or not he or she is a sports fan. This can help you hone language, grammar, and even spelling.

As in other markets, it is a good idea to obtain writers' guidelines from sports publications for which you hope to write, and to query them with prospective ideas.

The sports market is extensive, ranging from *Sports Illustrated* (with a circulation of 3.6 million) to specialized publications with circulations of only a few hundred. Most use some free-lance material, but many of the national publications require agent representation, references and/or extensive experience.

For this reason, I recommend that you start with relatively small markets. My first sports article, published in a now-defunct local sports weekly, brought me $10.00. But it was a start, and led to bigger and better sales. Other possible markets for entry-level writers include minor league baseball programs (there are 177 nationwide), college annuals and programs (try your alma mater), and specialty publications. Newspapers are not a good market, because they use staff writers and extensive national wire services.

The best source of potential markets is *Sports Market Place,* a refer-

336

ence guide (available in major libraries) which lists 478 sports publications in 53 specialty markets, as well as 142 general sports publications. You may also want to try obtaining information about or even joining a writers' association, such as the Outdoor Writers' Association of America (2017 Cato Avenue, Suite 101, State College, PA 16801-2768).

68

GIVE READERS WHAT *THEY* WANT— AND NEED

BY SAMM SINCLAIR BAKER

BEST-SELLING NOVELIST Stephen King was quoted in *Publishers Weekly* as saying, "Don't give them what they want—give them what you want." In my opinion, that statement should be reversed if you want to write nonfiction that will sell. Your basic guideline—which can make the difference between sale and rejection—is: *Give them [readers] what they want, not what you [the writer] want.* You must concentrate on serving the reader. That doesn't mean you're greatly restricted in your subject matter: Your articles can inform, elevate, entertain, and teach.

As with every type of writing, you want to attract and involve readers in your articles quickly and personally. A sure way to accomplish that is to appeal to readers' *self-interest,* and show them how they will benefit from what you are telling them in your piece. Keep in mind always the old saying: "Feed your pets what *they* want, not what *you* prefer to eat."

To make your articles most effective, keep the readers' problems and needs foremost and write the best you can, clearly and simply. Above all, focus on the stated or implied you-you-you. In articles and nonfiction books, too much I-I-I is likely to trigger no-no-no from editors. When you recheck and revise your manuscript, cut out every extraneous "I"; insert "you" wherever it fits. That's what will grab and hold editors and readers.

How the YOU-factor works

The superior value of "you" over "I/me" in most nonfiction was proved to me beyond doubt by an ad I worked on years ago for a then new gardening product, "Miracle-Gro." In a preliminary test, the ad was headlined, "How to Grow a Miracle Garden"—a general appeal. The resulting orders were satisfactory, but not great.

We then reran the ad in the same publication, making the headline just one word longer: "How *you* can grow a Miracle Garden." The seemingly minor change increased by many times the draw of the first ad. That dramatic experience taught me the enormous power of the YOU-factor, which I then applied to writing my thirty nonfiction books (including three blockbuster best sellers) and many articles on a variety of subjects.

Since then, the actual word "you" or the implied you has been the guiding sell-word for all my nonfiction. I urge you to consider that in what you write from now on. Also, check your rejected manuscripts for sufficient stress on the YOU-factor. You'll see how even minor changes can often enliven and increase the power of the piece, grab your reader, and sell. Emphasis on *you* can be a significantly valuable guideline in your nonfiction writing.

Concentrate on the reader

Here are two devices I use that you can try for yourself: First, I print the word YOU on a small card and set it up on my desk where I see it intermittently as I write.

Second, I find a newspaper or magazine photo of a person who represents the reader I'm aiming to reach. For a diet article or book, I focus on a photo of an overweight couple. If you are writing about health topics, choose a photo of individuals of varying ages, depending on the market you are addressing.

Whatever the subject, you must make sure that it has an appeal that will grab the reader in a personal way. An article in *Smithsonian Magazine* started this way:

You really feel your age when you get a letter from your insurance agent telling you the car you bought slightly used the year you got out of college can now be considered a "classic." "Your premiums will reflect this change in your classification," the letter said. I went out to look at the car and could almost hear my uncle's disapproving voice. "You should never buy a used car . . ."

Check how many times "you" and "your" keep the reader bound closely to the page. Also note that most individuals are involved at some time in buying a car, new or used, so the topic has universal appeal.

An article on golf in *Modern Maturity* states:

Sharpen your game with seven points from senior pros . . . that will give you power and accuracy. . . . Whatever your problem, you can take the solutions we recommend straight to the practice ground or the course.

Again, note the lure of a popular subject—golf—and how the reader is then brought in intimately by the use of "you" and "your." See how this personalizing technique is far more effective than a general approach.

In the first of my three diet book bestsellers, *The Doctor's Quick Weight Loss Diet,* the reader is hooked in the opening paragraph this way:

The prime aim of this book is to help you take that weight off quickly, and then to help you stay slim, healthy, and attractive. Here you'll learn exactly how in clear, simple, proved ways never told before.

Because the subject of diet is of deep concern to tens of millions of people, I was able to sell dozens of diet articles. The field is wide open for you today. Another point: Never bypass the possibility of milking a subject on which you've scored.

In my inspirational book, *Conscious Happiness,* I had to establish a special, close personal connection with the reader quickly. The opening lines were:

Conscious happiness is free. It can enrich your life tremendously—yet it doesn't cost you a cent from now on. But nobody else can pay for it and give it to you as a gift. You must earn it yourself by wanting it enough so that you work at it daily. Once you attain it, you can keep and enjoy its great benefits for the rest of your more rewarding life.

Note again how the variations of "you" linking the reader to the text repeatedly serve to reach and hold the reader's attention. As for the subject, who doesn't want to be happy?

Convinced more than ever by results I gained in my writing from the selling power of "you," I used those writing techniques for *The Complete Scarsdale Medical Diet,* which started selling immediately

340

after publication and zoomed to become the bestselling diet book of all time.

Right near the start, the writing captured readers this way:

Most meaningful for you are reports from overweight people. Their statements, which came unsolicited through the mail, are all-important as proof that the diet that worked wonderfully for them can do the same for you too. . . .

The clear lesson you can derive from this boils down to three words: *Involve the reader.* Heed this advice and you'll have a far better chance of receiving acceptances instead of rejections on your future nonfiction submissions.

Captions on the covers of major magazines are good examples of the emotional connection that the writer must evoke in the reader. For example, from *Ladies' Home Journal:* "When Your Man Doesn't Give You What You Need." The opening of an article in *McCall's* reads:

Quick! Can your toddler swim? Has your five-year-old expressed an interest in a musical instrument? Does your 12-year-old keep up socially? . . . No? Well, what are you doing wrong?

Note carefully for your future guidance that in another issue of *Ladies' Home Journal,* there are several pages with "you" in the overall headings; *YOU—Relationships & More,* with subsections: *High Anxiety, Ways to Make Your Weekends More Fun . . . Five Things Never to Say in the Height of an Argument.* This is followed by *FINANCE: How Safe is Your Money?*

This is succeeded by an article: "Barbra's New Direction" that starts, "When you first walk into Barbra Streisand's large but cozy apartment . . ." See how the sentence leads *you* personally on the guided tour.

Consider how the following *Reader's Digest* article projects the YOU-factor in the opening line: "Your thoughts influence feelings and behavior and therefore the state of your body. Awareness of this can be an important difference in treating problems of overweight. *Study yourself . . .*" Note the repetition: "*your* thoughts . . . *your* body . . . study *yourself.*"

In short, study the market you are trying to sell to, the subjects that are most timely for that readership, and the best ways to attract the interest of those readers intimately.

Seeking to affect the reader deeply, Walt Whitman wrote, "The whole theory of the universe is directed unerringly to a single individual—namely to You." That wise and enduring concept applies just as effectively today.

The all-important pointers offered to you here will help you profit from your writing now, and from now on.

$ 69

WRITE SHORTS THAT SELL

BY SELMA GLASSER

TURNING A SHORT PHRASE, ORDINARY WORD, or current expression into something humorous, original—and salable—is easy and fun. It can be a gold mine for writers who master this technique. Overworked clichés, songs, proverbs, or often straight quotes are ideal source material. Simply with a twist or change of a letter or sound, you can get published. You can utilize old standbys to create short items that sell because they are quickly recognized in their adapted forms. And best of all, you need not be a mental giant or genius with words: The only qualifications required are alertness, perseverance, and adaptability. The words are all in the dictionary. It's how we choose to "doctor them up" that counts.

Writing shorts is the name of my game. There's no need for me to squirrel myself away for endless hours of writing. It's possible to write on the run, when inspiration hits, wherever I am or whatever I'm doing. Ideas are everywhere, just waiting to be converted, adapted, condensed, parodied, or reversed—with or without embellishment. Major magazines such as *Reader's Digest, The New Yorker,* and even *Playboy* will accept short material, as long as you give the original source and date of publication. While some experts advise writers to start at the bottom, I aim for the big league right from the start, because it pays well. Why not start at the top? You can always go down, if necessary. If you're observant and discerning, you can earn money and bylines from misprints, signs, bumper stickers—plus a little ingenuity.

Be alert and ready to jot down inspirations. You can add your own touches, a new title, or interpretations later. As an example, a trip to Florida enabled me to earn $50.00 for this sign, which I titled, HISTORI-CAL LANDMARK:

"On this site, exactly nothing happened."

343

Sometimes a straight sign that we see often can be worked into a filler. What would you do with these two? AVOID HOME ACCIDENTS. WATCH OUT FOR CHILDREN. Here's how I sold them to *Medical World News:*

SIGNS OF THE TIMES: Planned parenthood isn't anything new. For years, we've observed signs and seen warnings like:
"AVOID HOME ACCIDENTS" and "WATCH OUT FOR CHILDREN"

We hear talk about car pools almost daily. Here's how I used it for a *Good Housekeeping* item:

Where should folks take their cars swimming? IN CAR POOLS.

I thought of a few other commonly used phrases like the "cold war," and my question was:

What do antibiotics fight? THE COLD WAR.

How many times have we heard the expression: "something new under the sun"? A new cleaning product added blue to its formula. I started a prize-winning statement this way:

"First with something blue under the sun . . ."

I usually have pad and pencil with me when I'm driving. It was lucky I did on the day I saw this bumper sticker on the car in front of me:

ANSWER MY PRAYERS, STEAL THIS CAR.

Reader's Digest accepted it for its Bumper Snicker Section of their "Picturesque Speech" page.

When a local radio station offered cash for a reason you'd want to jump back into bed, I thought of someone who was good for nothing. I improved on that hackneyed phrase by submitting:

"Because I'm good for NODDING!"

This is what I did with proverbs to make a sale:

"He who hesitates is last."
"A fool and his money are soon partying."
"Every cloud has a silver airliner."

My favorite fun pursuit is giving unusual or unexpected meanings to ordinary words or phrases. I called a column I sold to *The Saturday Evening Post* "DeFUNitions":

I Do—State of the Union message
English Channel—British TV station
Unmanned vehicle—Car driven by a female
Syntax—Money collected from sinners

I'm not a poet, and I know it. However, by dreaming up all sorts of simple "sound" techniques, I have managed to produce eye-appealing, pun-concealing, rhyme-revealing fillers in the form of light verse, terse verse, or prize-winning rhymes for contests. I changed the spelling and the meaning of the word "deserter" and it served as a pun ending for this poem:

War on Food
No matter how I try
I find dieting pure murder.
It seems there's no amnesty
For this desserter!

Another time, I thought of weather forecasters, and how incorrect they can be, at times. This suggested to me "weather flawcasters," while another popular phrase reworked gave me the punch line I needed. I wrote this light verse:

Weather Flawcasters
Predicting weather they're so wrong,
With each and every scoop;
That's why forecasters all belong
To a non-prophet group!

I write a column I call PHRAZE CRAZE or RIME TIME, which is simply terse verse. For example:

What's a pink flower?   Rosy posy
What's a cheap nose job? Frugal bugle
What's a matchmaker?   Knotter plotter

345

In writing a contest entry for a hair product that called for a statement, I used rhyme to win the prize:

With Protein 21 care,
I've sheen-clean, wash-'n'-wear hair.

In a Royal Cola contest, I created a pun on the sponsor's name, in this way:

I get more energy from this soft drink because it offers me more Royal ColaWATTS per glassful.

My short cut for creating epigrams is describing subjects in terms borrowed from an entirely different field. For example: Here are two epigrams of mine that *Playboy* published:

A guy with money to *burn* usually meets his *match.*

(Note the words "burn" and "match," which sparked the idea for this epigram.)

A man with a *chip* on his shoulder is an indication of *wood* higher up.

You can readily see how the italicized words add interest and creativity here.

There are hundreds of other fields from which you may adapt appropriate words to help you create similar epigrams. For example, ELECTION *(candidate, favorite, platform, win)* or FISHING *(reel, catch, hook, net).*

I hope these examples of the various kinds of short items I've written and had published will help set the stage for you to write shorts that sell.

§70

BREAKING INTO PRINT WITH FEATURE ARTICLES

BY RALPH CORRIGAN

IF YOU'RE ANXIOUS TO GET STARTED as a published writer but don't know where to begin, feature articles for newspapers provide an ideal way to break into print.

Think about the pluses: no credentials are needed (you can be a raw beginner), and features follow an established format so they are easy to write. And believe it or not, editors pay for these stories!

Topics At Your Fingertips

Features are those human interest "soft news" stories tucked into the "Living," "Local," and "Lifestyle" sections of the newspaper that explore the nooks and crannies of our everyday lives. A memorial bridge in town, a local ballet class for kids, remarkable pets, inventions, new businesses, a profile of your neighbor—all qualify as potential sources for feature stories.

Friends, business associates, even family members make excellent feature subjects. What about the beekeeper next door who wins blue ribbons for honey? Or the woman on the next block who started a flower arrangement business in her home? Or the daughter of your co-worker who anchors a TV show?

Local events, another prime source for features, get top billing in hometown papers, and the possibilities are endless. The annual church-sponsored bazaar, the free lecture at a nearby college, the Memorial Day Parade down Main Street, poetry readings at the neighborhood coffeehouse or bookstore, performances at the library—all suggest potential stories to the alert feature writer.

Perhaps you enjoy discovering new sites, or learning more about favorite local haunts, both make excellent stories. Or you could write

347

a feature on a recently renovated park, a historic building, a nearby museum, or even the clam bar opening down the street.

Story ideas lurk where you least expect to find them. One enterprising free lancer sold a piece on the sizes and uses of nails in a hardware store! Someone else delved into the history of a park statue, and another published an article about a prize collection of model ships and still another—about a neighbor who raised rare birds in his cellar.

Writing tips

1) *Seek advice.* Let's say you've come up with a strong idea for a feature and you're seeking expert advice to help you fine-tune it. First, do your homework. Know the most knowledgeable people that should be interviewed and why you think your feature belongs in your hometown paper. Then write a short note to the editor, outlining your idea, and be sure to include your address and phone number, and a self-addressed, stamped envelope (SASE). Most newspaper editors are on the lookout for well-crafted features by free-lance writers, and are happy to offer advice on story angles, sources and length when an idea piques their interest.

2) *Entertain, entertain, entertain.* Whether it's a nostalgic look at the early days of a section of your town or city, or a profile of the much-loved local school-crossing guard at the corner with twenty years of service, readers crave up-beat "success" stories that provide a respite from the mayhem and disasters crowding the front pages. So focus on the good news, tickle the funny bone, or tell a rousing story.

3) *Keep the article timely.* If you offer a special slant on a news story (perhaps a profile on someone featured in a front-page story), or report on a recent lecture, club happening, or town event, timeliness has to be built into the article. When writing on topics with seasonal appeal, keep an eye on the calendar. Talk about skiing and wood stoves in winter, and wind surfing and mulching in the summer.

4) *Be accurate.* Feature writers are the eyes and ears of the readers—collecting facts, conducting interviews, and checking the available "background" information (newspaper clippings, local histories, scrapbooks of people they interview). In a sense, when you affix your byline to the article, you are saying that the information provided, in

the words of journalist Theodore H. White, is "as close to the truth" as you can make it.

So keep the quotes word for word. The pros might shudder at the thought of confirming a quote (get it right the first time, they'd say), but if you are starting out as a writer, rechecking the accuracy of quotations before mailing the manuscript for publication is a wise decision. A little rechecking here and there can save you from headaches later.

5) *Prepare for interviews.* Beginning writers frequently suffer from a case of the jitters before a face-to-face interview. Don't panic. Most interviews are ego trips for the subjects, and besides, you get to prepare beforehand. Find out as much as possible about the person, know the "angle" for your article, then prepare a list of questions you want answered. And if on-the-spot queries uncover a better angle, don't be afraid to jettison your prepared script. Always go for the best story.

6) *Take notes.* How to record the interview is a personal preference. Some writers swear by handwritten notes, others prefer the tape recorder. But relying entirely on a tape recorder is inviting disaster, since they are notorious for jamming or conking out on dead batteries at the most inopportune moments. One writer drove five hours to interview a big-name artist residing in another state. The minute she got in her car to return home she pressed the "play" button on her recorder for a sound check and was horrified to discover a garbled tape. Luckily, she had jotted down notes, and with help from the photographer with her, she was able to salvage enough of the interview for an article. The pros rely on a combination of tape recorder and handwritten notes for interviews.

Devising a plan

After the legwork and research, the next step is to arrange the bits and pieces of information into a solid article. Luckily, features follow a simple pattern: lead, transition, body, and conclusion.

Before beginning to compose the piece, keep in mind that newsprint differs from other forms of writing. Paragraphs (called "grafs") tend to run only a few sentences; avoid long columns of gray print that invariably send readers flipping the page to find something less daunting.

Leads. Start with a bang. An anecdote, a startling statement, an

349

important fact, even a strong quote can hook the reader's attention *and* introduce the story. And above all else, be creative. Unlike the sober, matter-of-fact approach that works with news stories, feature writing calls for a more informal, light-hearted tone.

Here's how Molly O'Neill began her recent *New York Times* front-page feature on the increasing tolerance for messiness in the American home:

Dust bunnies under the couch. Cobwebs in the corner. A grimy shellac over the contents of kitchen cupboards. In a culture where cleanliness has long been equated with godliness, these tell-tale signs should be anathema. But rather than repenting with a vigorous spring cleaning, many Americans are changing creeds.

This sprightly lead paragraph fills in all but the last of the 5 W's (the who, what, when, where, and why questions). O'Neill serves up the "why" in a transitional paragraph deftly highlighted by a quote from an authority:

"Bless the mess," said Mary Ellen Pinkham, whose housecleaning advice column is syndicated in 150 newspapers. While she maintains white-glove standards in her own home, she believes this level of cleanliness is rapidly becoming an anomaly.

"The American home is getting dirtier," she said. "People have better things to do with their time than clean."

A bit of advice: Quote a credible authority near the beginning of your piece, and readers will take notice. It's proof that you've done your homework.

The Body. Aim for a spicy mix of facts, direct quotes, paraphrases, reported information. They all play key roles in keeping the reader from nodding off while the story unfolds.

In a recent Mother's Day feature titled "What Mom Done Told Me . . ." for *The Los Angeles Times,* staff writer Bettijane Levine sets the stage as follows:

No, politeness is not extinct. In fact, a favorite piece of Mom's advice, from readers young and old, is: "Always write a thank-you note."

Then she adds a direct quote from a source:

An Encino woman is one of many who wrote to express amazement at "how touched and grateful people are when you take time to acknowledge them in writing."

And, finally, paraphrases a source, then quotes the source directly:

Judith Martin, who writes the syndicated Miss Manners column, says only ingrates and louts would consider the written thank-you note an obsolete form.
"As long as there are presents given, parties attended, or kindnesses extended in this world, the thank-you note will live."

The above ploy—the paraphrase followed by the direct quote—is a given in news writing, a trick of the trade. First, you introduce what the source is going to say, then you quote the source directly, "According to . . ." is the easiest way to slip into the paraphrasing tactic.

The Ending. Features tend to follow a story line, are meant to be read straight through, and should end with a flourish—a summary, a "refer-back" to the lead, or to a memorable quote from the principal source. Carol Kleiman in a feature on secretaries in the workplace for *The Chicago Tribune,* saves until the very end this quote by professional development authority Susan Fenner:

"I saw a classified ad asking for a secretary able to do financial work, forecasting, software packages, travel extensively, take shorthand and also have other good secretarial skills," said Fenner. "The salary was $70,000 a year. It was breathtaking."

The hot quote tying everything together at the end is called a "clincher." Seasoned reporters are always on the lookout for those blockbuster endings.

When revising the rough draft, aim for a playful style by adding color, sharpness and sparkle to the copy. Take extra time to select words with care. Plans are "altered" instead of "changed," you discover a "niche" instead of a "spot." Vibrant language keeps your reader alert. Use the strongest, most precise action verbs you can, and cut all unnecessary adverbs and adjectives.

Even if the editor gave you a "go ahead" on speculation, unless you are hand-delivering the article, you'll need a brief covering letter to accompany your manuscript. Keep it simple. "Enclosed is a feature

351

on _____, which I hope you will find suitable for publication," is all you need.

Then follow proper manuscript etiquette. Place your name, address, and telephone number in the top left corner of page one, the approximate number of words in the top right, and the title and your byline centered, one-third down the page.

Subsequent pages call for a "slug" in the top left corner (your last name, and the article's title directly underneath), and the page number in the top right corner.

If you've interviewed all your subjects, researched the background information, stressed the human interest angle, and managed to serve up the whole concoction with wit and style, chances are you'll end up published.

And even get a check from an editor!

71

Inside Interviewing

By David Ritz

I've been conducting interviews, writing magazine profiles and collaborating with celebrities on their autobiographies for the past fifteen years. Until now, I've never stopped to understand my techniques. I wasn't even aware of having a technique. It's always been more a matter of feeling my way through the process. So when I was asked to explain my methods of interviewing, I was reluctant. I wasn't sure I had anything to say. Figuring out what I do seemed harder than doing it. Then a friend of my daughters' called, an aspiring journalist named Joey, who told me how he had recently botched an interview. Could I give him some advice? We had a long talk and, after hearing myself, I began to think that maybe I did have a few useful tips after all.

I leveled with Joey. "I'm peculiar," I told him. I'm not exactly sure what I'm doing. I've never written, never even read a "how-to" tract. My temperament won't allow it. Instruction manuals make me crazy. As a ten-year-old pal of mine blurted out as he opened his new video game, throwing the directions to the wind, "I jump in cold!" That's me.

I've learned by doing, and I've been burned. I remember one of my first interviews, back in Buffalo, New York, was with the brilliant and eccentric bebop pianist, Thelonius Monk, an artist I had long admired. I came to that encounter with all the apprehension and eagerness of the uninitiated. My questions were carefully planned, neatly written out. I arrived an hour early, breathing in the stale air of the dark, deserted nightclub. When Monk ambled in, his eyes were hidden behind shades. He nodded at me and sat at the piano, where he began blocking out complex and haunting chord patterns. Whenever he paused, I blurted out questions—"What do you think of John Coltrane, Mr. Monk? Who are your greatest influences, Mr. Monk?"—which Mr. Monk ignored. So it went for two hours. Not a word. Not even a grunt. I left empty-handed.

That's an extreme example, but it brings up the first and most important challenge you face as an interviewer, whether working on a thousand-word profile or a hundred-thousand-word biography: how to get the subject to talk. In my view, you start by being sensitive. Knowing what's happening. *Feeling* what's happening. Obviously, Monk didn't feel like talking—he felt like playing the piano—and I'd have been far wiser to suggest we meet some other time. (Of course I was too petrified to suggest anything.)

At another time, with another interviewee—this one was bluesman Jimmy Reed—I found that my man wasn't interested in responding to my neatly arranged questions. My agenda was far too formal to elicit the information I needed. As Reed, his lady friend, and I sat in the back of an old beat-up Cadillac, riding the turnpike from Dallas to Fort Worth, I saw that the singer felt like talking and sipping whiskey, not fielding questions. So I forgot my canned queries and let him ramble. The result was a decent profile in which hints of his raw speaking voice emerged.

Learning to listen has been the great lesson of my life. I think Jimmy Reed really started to talk because he sensed I was really listening. And you can't capture a subject or render someone life-like, you can't recreate a living voice, with all its unique twists and turns, without listening. Now there are those who listen while waiting breathlessly to break in. For years, that was me. But I'm talking about patient listening, deep-down listening, listening with the heart as well as the head, listening in a way that lets the person know you care, that you want to hear what she has to say, that you're enjoying the sound of her voice.

There are times when you're forced to talk. You sense that your subject is shy, the silences are deadly, and it's up to you to trigger the conversational action. If, for instance, your actress/interviewee is reluctant to discuss embarrassing moments of her childhood, mention a few of your own. Often your example will break the ice and serve as a model for her to follow. Again, the emphasis is on conducting a natural free-flowing conversation, not a static interview. Static interviews make for static writing.

What about tape recorders? I put them in the same category as canned questions. Sometimes they're good, often not. I always take my little Sony, filled with fresh batteries, but first I scope out the situation, seeing whether the presence of a red-blinking machine between me and my interviewee is going to restrict the chatter. If it feels as if the recorder will inhibit, I leave it in my briefcase, scribbling key notes instead. The minute I get home, I type out those notes as fully as possible. If I've taped the meeting, I transcribe the conversation word for word. Either way, I'll reshape the quotes. I realize that for political interviews verbatim quotes are critical. Accurate newspaper reporting depends on literal quotes. But for the magazine profile/interview—and certainly for the celebrity memoir—quotes become a literary device, a character-shaping element, whose test for accuracy is whether the words expressed are true—essentially true—to the speaker's personality and views. (But always proceed with caution. If you're not absolutely certain that your "reshaped" quote is accurate in spirit or letter, call or write the subject for authorization.)

To turn a speaking voice into a literary voice requires craft. For me, it's virtually impossible to accomplish that feat by being literal. I spent hundreds of hours interviewing Ray Charles, for example, for his memoirs, *Brother Ray*. Ray curses profusely, his language a heady mix of back country and big-city street dialect. A sentence or two doesn't go by without a juicy expletive. While my objective was to make it seem as though he is talking to the reader, I also understood that a verbatim transcription of his spoken voice wouldn't do him justice. Obviously the way we read is different from the way we listen. One earthy obscenity every six or seven pages goes a long way to give the authentic flavor of Ray's speech. Profanity every two or three sentences, while literally accurate, would make for an oppressive, monotonous read.

During the interviewing itself, I believe relaxation is a blessing. Enthusiasm also helps. I let my subjects know that it's a treat for me to talk to them, that I'm there as a surrogate for hundreds, thousands, maybe millions of readers, and I consider it a privilege. If I'm relaxed, chances are my interviewee will be relaxed. If I find my plan for the interview—let's say the order in which the subjects are addressed—is suddenly upset or turned on its head, I try to accept it; I try to go with the flow. Eye contact is critical. I believe in looking people in the eye, letting them know that I'm there, I'm learning, I'm listening. I listen for key words or phrases, which are often the key to my subject's individual lexicon.

When writing the article itself, I briefly describe a speech before quoting it: "His soft speaking voice," I wrote about Smokey Robinson, "like his singing voice, is high-pitched, honey-dipped, sweetly seductive." I try to paint a picture of what it feels like to be with the subject, to put the reader in my place. "Smokey looks directly at you; his sea-green eyes are riveting. Riding the band bus or talking till dawn in hotel suites, he tells you his stories with sadness, joy and wonder. He's enthusiastic and animated. He'll leap up and testify; he'll fall down laughing."

Setting is also vital. Sometimes if I find myself in a stagnant setting with a subject, I'll propose we go for a drive or a stroll on the beach, anything to facilitate the easy flow of conversation. Recently, I profiled soul singer Barry White. We were talking about his childhood, and when I learned he was raised only ten miles away from where we were sitting, I suggested we walk the old neighborhood. Once there, Barry started reliving his memories. On one street corner, he stopped dead in his tracks, uttering words I may never have heard if we had remained in his suburban home: "This is where my brother was murdered. It happened on this very spot. He was my best friend. We were a two-man gang, respected and feared. We fell into devilment. For years we ran and ruled these streets."

I strive toward honesty, never pretending to know any more or less than I do about the subject at hand. That doesn't mean I don't prepare; I do. If I'm interviewing a singer, I'll study her work beforehand; I'll learn her records. Celebrities often and justifiably complain about uninformed or naïve queries. Nothing will kill an interview quicker than a dumb question. On the other hand, nothing will foster stimulating responses more than specific questions that demonstrate the writer's familiarity with the subject. "If anyone else askes me whether I'm a jazz singer or a pop singer," Sarah Vaughan once said, "I think I'll strangle him. They should have figured that out before they met me. Instead, why don't they ask me what I was thinking when I sang 'Poor Butterfly' or 'Send in the Clowns'?"

"I like questions that challenge me psychologically," singer Etta James told me. "If someone asks me something he could have just as easily looked up in a book, I figure he ain't that interested in me, so why should I be interested in the interview?"

It isn't always easy to be confident, but confidence helps—confidence to engage another human being in an open-hearted dialogue. If you're prepared, you're more likely to be confident. Not that stressful situations can always be avoided. But these days if I do happen upon an antagonistic interviewee—someone with a lousy attitude about writers, for example—I remind myself that I'm doing this someone a service; I'm publicizing him, bringing him to readers, giving him the benefit of whatever artistry I've developed. I'm not arrogant, but I am proud of what I do—and certainly not apologetic about it.

For me, all these aspects of interviewing—sensitivity, relaxation, preparedness, confidence—are ways of achieving intimacy. My goal is always intimacy. Superficial talk is boring. In dealing with other people, I'm most interested in what's underneath, what they're really thinking or feeling. That's the fascinating part. To me, intimacy is the difference, in life or in print, between the routine and the extraordinary conversation. Gaining intimacy means gaining trust. And I seem to do that by being a good listener, a guy genuinely interested in what you've got to say and willing, at the appropriate time, to reveal as much about myself as you're revealing to me. Ironically, I like keeping my "I" out of the published profile; that makes it easier to focus on the subject. But while I'm managing the interview itself, I want my "I" and my ear to be eager, open, and attentive. I want to forget my own narrow views and give myself—my intelligence and my spirit—over to my subject.

72

SUCCESSFUL ARTICLE WRITING

BY JOHN BOHANNON

I KNOW THE SECRET of good writing, a new and improved method that's guaranteed to help you sell every magazine article you write. And it's yours free.

Got your attention, didn't I? It was merely a sneaky device to illustrate a point, using what New York City advertising agencies call key "power" words: *new, improved,* and *free.* (Pay attention some evening to prime-time television commercials and count how often those three little words jump out at you.)

An article must have a compelling lead, a powerful hook that immediately grabs the reader's attention. These days everyone is busy and in a hurry, with little time to spare and *no* time to waste on reading something that, at a quick glance, might be boring. Readers are exacting. And the *most* exacting reader is the editor, the first person to see your article and decide whether others will see it, too.

The editor can be your most powerful ally or adversary, which means you'd better put all you've got in your lead. This is the most difficult of any writing, so make it appealing, interesting, and inviting. This is the point at which you must beguile your reader, weave that magic spell, entice, seduce, lure, promise—but make no *specious* promises that you can't keep. Take your reader to some secret place that only you know. You're the only expert who knows how to find this fascinating spot, and you're willing to guide the reader there, to explain the wonders of what you've found, then return the reader safely to the place you first met. Do this smoothly, without obvious effort, and your readers will seek you out again, knowing that you have visited intriguing places, talked with interesting people, and will gladly share those experiences with them the next time you meet. But remember, that lead is the door you open to offer the first glimpse of the adventures just down the road; this is where you get either a polite but firm *no thanks* or a *tell me more*. I've had a lot of both. The *tell me mores* are better.

James Thurber offered some wry rules about writing humor, but they apply to *any* type of writing:

1) The reader should be able to find out what the story is about.

2) Some inkling of the general idea should be apparent in the first 500 words.

3) A good way to eliminate confusion is to read the piece over before sending it out.

Rules #1 and #2 are easy: Just say it. At the beginning. In simple declarative sentences, tell your reader what the subject is. Raise the curtain and start the show. Follow rule #3 after you've rewritten your first, second, or even third draft. But put the finished piece aside, let it get cold for a few days, and then read it over. Pretend that you've just picked up a magazine. Be objective. Is the article interesting enough to make *you* read it? If it isn't, rewrite it. The competition in free-lance writing is tough and unforgiving.

There are approximately eleven thousand magazines in print in America, and tens of thousands of writers—all looking for those strong compelling hooks—are trying to attract the immediate attention of editors and, subsequently, readers. Make your lead unique and inviting by polishing it until it dazzles. After you state your thesis, you must defend it with lucid examples, vivid descriptions, and quotes from experts as you fill out the middle. Don't meander or dwell too long at any one spot; you need substance, but keep it streamlined. Treat the middle of your piece with respect and care. Don't let it bulge. When you reach your conclusion, where you wrap everything up, simply stop. Just bring down the curtain when the show is over. Endings are almost as hard as beginnings. Middles are also tricky. Aside from all that, writing is easy.

Actually, writing can be made *somewhat* easier with good preparation. When you have all your research, facts, and background information in front of you, the piece can move along smoothly. I use a tape recorder—an infallible memory—when I interview someone. Then I type a transcript with the date, time, and place of the interview, just in case an editor wants to compare the transcript with my text. And always try to make the editor's job easy. Include the subject's address and phone number in case something has to be verified. For a general-interest piece, a list of sources shows that you've done your homework.

When I finally begin writing an assigned article, I write quickly. My first draft is a bare bones piece, a tight *who, what, where, when, why* type of story. It's the same approach a good photographer uses, getting several "grab" shots immediately to avoid losing the moment or risk having the subject drift away. Then it's time to move in closer, examine, compose carefully, and focus on other aspects, taking dozens of shots from different angles. Eventually, the one picture (or word or phrase) that tells the story, conveys the meaning, triggers an emotion, will stand out.

In writing those first quick drafts of an article, I pay no attention to grammar or spelling. Then I rewrite (many times), making sure that my grammar and spelling are correct and that I've chosen precise words for my final draft.

My final draft is final only to me, though. Editors often make changes that result in a tighter, better piece. Don't argue over your precious words, unless those changes are merely arbitrary and alter the flow, change the slant, or cut out the substance of your piece. Most editors know what they're doing, so don't nitpick. If you do, the editor might reject your later work simply because you're too much trouble. On the other hand, if you run into one who insists on doing more writing than editing, then perhaps it would be best to move on to a different magazine or market.

You've heard this before, but it bears repeating: Target your material to the proper market; know the magazine you want to write for. Magazines are much like people. Each is different, with a distinctive personality and special needs. It's folly to dash off a piece and then frenetically search for a suitable market for it.

Read five or six issues of the magazine you want to sell to. If your query is on a recently published subject, the editor might dismiss you as an amateur. Also check out the advertising. Clients spend hundreds of thousands of dollars to target their magazine ads to specific demographics, and those ads are indicative of readers' interests. The Letters to the Editor, an excellent barometer of the people you hope to reach through your writing, will tell you what has made them angry or happy, what made them laugh or weep.

Query first. You might be wasting your time writing "blind," without knowing how long the piece should be, which slant the editor might be looking for, whether the point of view should be first person or third person.

All rules have exceptions, of course, particularly those you'll find in trying to sell magazine articles. Don't get frustrated. Were it not for rules there would be no exceptions, and life might be a little more predictable . . . but not as interesting.

When you've made that coveted first sale to a major magazine, don't assume that the editor will be eagerly waiting for your next query or submission. You may have a foot in the door, and the editor will take a look at your work faster than at some unknown writer's query; but if you fail to keep your standards high, you'll be left with *only* your foot in the door and the rest of you out in the hallway with all the other writers who are trying to break in. Make sure your next submissions are appropriate.

Think of writing as a business. Your job. Write every day, even if it's only for a few hours. For clear writing, eliminate "speed bumps"; for instance, avoid using the common "he or she" phrase that slows readers down. Show me a sentence with "he or she" or "his or hers," and I'll show you a sentence that can be rewritten without that awkward usage.

Brackets and parentheses are visual speed bumps and are often unnecessary. Avoid words that are spelled the same but have different meanings when pronounced differently, such as making an *entrance* and trying to *entrance* someone.

Now, about that secret of good writing. To be honest, I *do* have a secret. It's perseverance. I sold my first piece to a national publication in 1965. My next major sale was in 1985. In between those two milestones, I still worked as a writer—not free-lance, but as a staff journalist. A few years ago, when I shifted to free-lance writing, I just picked up where I left off, determined to sell my work. So, if you have yet to sell your work to a major market, stay with it. Persevere. You might just stumble upon your *own* secret to good writing—and you'll sell your articles!

§73

SELL YOUR HIDDEN GOLD WITH A QUERY

BY TOM JENKINS

A ONE-PAGE QUERY LETTER IS THE FIRST step in selling your article to a magazine or newspaper. No matter how well you write, you need to market your work; otherwise, it may remain hidden gold.

A written query shows you respect the editor's time—it can be answered at his or her convenience—and indicates your trust that the editor can judge your worth as a writer by reading your writing sample: the query letter.

A query letter should do the following: (1) grab interest; (2) summarize your idea; (3) show you can organize and write simply; (4) sketch your qualifications; and (5) make it easy for the editor to respond.

1. *Grab interest*

No one knows the magazine better than its editor, so in reading a query letter, how long does it take him to know if an article idea fits his publication? The first few words of your query, therefore, are crucial: You may not get another chance. It is obvious you need to grab his interest immediately and keep it throughout the letter. If you can do it in the query, the editor will know you can probably do it in the article you are proposing.

The opener should be brief, arouse a bit of curiosity, and at times suggest a point of view.

Bamboozlement. That was the cry of an English teacher recently as advertising copy writing, a favorite target of the ignorant, became the subject of attack.

This was the opener of my query for an article intending to show the effectiveness of written advertising copy. Acknowledging the flaws and gimmickry of "adblat," I went on to give examples of good advertising copy. The result was an article that appeared in a local news-paper.

Sometimes you can get attention with a single and accurate superlative: "The oldest living organism on earth is alive and well in California: the bristlecone pine." This query opener led to an article published in *Garden* magazine. That was ten years ago.

Since that time, horticulturists have learned that a drab and common shrub growing in the Southwest deserts is older: the creosote bush, one of which is believed to be 11,700 years old. I queried *Garden* again with an opener comparing the bristlecone with the creosote bush, and that led to an article that the magazine bought and published.

Sometimes you can arouse interest and give information at the same time, often in presenting a query about an unusual person. I came across a 52-year-old man whose past nervous condition had caused ulcerative colitis resulting in surgery to remove eight inches of his colon. My query to *Signs of the Times* opened with the following:

> He rides a bicycle, bowls, flies an ultralight and skydives, but he also carries his own portable toilet with him everywhere. This is not a gag but the truth about a courageous man. Robert Kidwell is an ostomate.

The article was published under the title, "Faith Can Fly."

2. *Summarize your idea*

Your query letter should reflect your careful study of the readership, editorial needs, and style of the magazine to which you are writing. A query letter is specific; it is not a form letter sent to multiple publishers simultaneously, hoping for a lucky hit. You are not just proposing an article; you are proposing an article for a particular publication.

Your letter should give an overview of your topic and treatment with just enough details to show the editor you not only know your material but also how to present it.

In a query to *Desert* magazine, I wrote:

> Misunderstood, maligned, and condemned throughout the West, the nation's cleverest wild animal is a needed predator: the coyote.
>
> With hair-trigger reflexes and superbly sensitive senses, the coyote's ability to adjust and survive in the wilds is uncanny. It can sprint at 40 mph and cover 200 miles in a single day in search of food.

A social animal, attached to family and clan, the coyote has been undaunted by the growth of communities, suburban sprawl and compound 1080. Once concentrated almost entirely in the West, the coyote has turned up as far east as Maine, replacing the larger but less intelligent wolf as a wildlife predator.

The response was favorable, asking for the manuscript on speculation. The article appeared under the title, "The Controversial Predator."

Occasionally, a brief listing (but not a separate or complicated outline) in the body of the one-page query letter can give a structured overview some editors prefer. In a query to *Computer Decisions,* I suggested an article about how computerizing geographic data can save money for public utilities that depend upon large numbers of cumbersome, manually controlled maps.

The query included the following list:

With your approval, the article could be organized as follows:
1. Identify the basic problems of costly, nonintegrated and outdated maps that are manually controlled by a gas, electric, telephone or water utility company.
2. Explain how integrating and automating the maps can save money.
3. Give the details of a particular public utility, probably a telephone company, that saves money by using this kind of map management.

The associate editor responded with handwritten comments on the query letter itself, and I wrote the manuscript accordingly. "Big Saving in Computer Management of Maps" appeared in the magazine six months later.

Usually, your article idea is presented—in a kind of extended summary—in the opener and throughout the entire letter. When I read a newspaper item about a local college professor involved in an excavation project in downtown Mexico City, I perked up. I arranged an appointment with him and was impressed, both by him and the article possibilities. My query opened as follows:

Beneath the busy streets of downtown Mexico City, another city is buried. It is the sacred center of an entire empire, including the Great Temple of Tenochtitlan of the Aztec people (circa 1521), a 15-story architectural marvel incongruously devoted to human sacrifice.

I went on to summarize the quest of the University of Colorado's Dr. David Carrasco and his students to accumulate a priceless archive of ritual findings for the college. The managing editor of *Westways* liked the idea, but gave me the assignment only if I collected better photos than those I had submitted with the query. I did so, got an O.K., and the resulting article, "Digging Up a Dynasty," appeared in *Westways*.

3. *Show you can organize and write simply*

Organize your query letter in discrete but related parts, all contributing to the unity of your idea. Then say it simply. Don't try to impress an editor with multisyllabic words and elaborate phrases. Occasionally, you can use a quote to get attention and stress your point. In one query letter, I began with a two-word quote:

"Money walks."
This was the caption of a full-page photo in a national magazine. It was an Easter Seals advertisement showing a small boy, a polio victim, resting on his crutches and looking down at his dog at his side as the dog looked up at him.

The boy's desire to walk was depicted by the photo; the reader's opportunity to give money for research to help make his walking possible was conveyed by the two simple words. The photo by itself was incomplete; the copywriter's words made it complete. I added:

A picture isn't always worth a thousand words. No photo can do what the two words, "Money walks," can do. Those words grab more than the eyes. They grip the mind.
Such use of language is copywriting at its best.

This part of the query became part of the published article, entitled, "In Defense of Advertising Copywriting."
You can use plain words and write a query about a common subject:

It's a simple thing, really. It happens every year. In the fall, aspen leaves turn from green to gold. But the spectacle is stunning no matter how many times you've seen it.

This opener to my query to *Travel & Leisure* became part of the first paragraph of the article as published. The piece described a one-day aspen-viewing trip in the high country of Colorado. After one of the editors made some helpful suggestions, I included side roads, places to eat, and practical advice on what to bring and wear.

365

4. *Sketch your qualifications*

An editor wants to know if you can handle the article you are proposing. Although you can demonstrate your control of language in the query letter, your past success in published articles, as well as your education and work experience, are reasonable indicators of your ability to deal with a chosen subject.

Indicate your qualifications in the query. You can list them or combine the information with your proposed topic in the same paragraph. In a query that proposed a piece about an unorthodox inventor, I wrote as follows:

> Frederick Fisher has built a prototype for a solar-powered crematorium. Yes, a device to make after-the-fact use of the same sun that gave life.
> This kind of irony fits in with other articles I have written about paradox and the oddities of human nature. They include an acre of coffins, an automobile with a 1937 license plate parked in a driveway, untouched for 32 years, and a freelance cartoonist who draws 60 cartoons a week for 60 different newspapers with no written contract for payment.

The article, entitled "Burn Me Up," was accepted and appeared in an alternative newsweekly, *Westword*.

If you have not published anything yet and therefore have no "official" publishing credentials, let your choice of an appropriate idea targeted to a particular magazine contribute to your credibility as a writer. Refer to whatever applicable background you have as a worker, researcher, traveler, collector, hobbyist or adventurer. Remember that your credentials also encompass your imagination, creativity, and intuitive powers. Be alert and observe carefully. You will find article ideas everywhere. An example: An item on a televised news broadcast about a missing railroad train engine caught my interest. I drove to the search site and became even more interested. This led me to the library and an eventual query:

> On a proverbial dark and stormy night in 1878, Kiowa Creek flooded, washing out bridges and sending a Kansas-Pacific railroad train into the raging waters. Afterward, train cars were found, some smashed and almost entirely buried in the sandy creekbed.
> But the locomotive was never recovered.
> Today, 100 years later, a search is taking place.

I went on to tell about the excited people behind the search, including novelist Clive Cussler *(Raise the Titanic)*. The query to *True West* brought a go-ahead. I sent in the article and two weeks later a check came in the mail.

5. *Make it easy for the editor to respond*

It's an old but valid story. Always include an SASE or a self-addressed postcard for the editor who may not want to send a letter back to you. What could be simpler than a self-addressed postcard? You can even type on the reverse of it: Yes _____ No _____ Deadline _____ Photos preferred _____. Or variations of this. All the editor needs to do is make a check mark or two and perhaps indicate a word count. Nothing to dictate or write, no letter or envelope to type, and no stamping or metering. The editor will appreciate your thoughtfulness and assume you are organized and considerate.

I am not without my share of rejections; who isn't? It is unlikely that any of us can be 100 percent efficient in free-lance letter queries, but with practice you can come close. If you can query successfully, you will become a published writer.

There is no shortcut. It isn't an easy process, but it is a workable one. You need to know as much as you can about the publication you are querying. You need to know what articles it has published during the past year; you need to study them. Then you can write a query letter that will reveal your hidden gold.

§74

A BIOGRAPHER'S TALE

BY BETTINA DREW

I FIRST FOUND NELSON ALGREN IN 1983, after reading about his post-humous novel, *The Devil's Stocking,* in *The New York Times Book Review.* His lifelong interest in the outcasts and his depression wander-ings fascinated me; and I soon realized, after scouring the library refer-ence section and writing a letter to his archivist at Ohio State University, that no one was working on Algren at all. In the forties Algren's name appeared next to Dreiser, Farrell, Wright, and Bellow, but most people I knew had never heard of him. Hemingway had ranked Algren next to Faulkner, and his work was translated into doz-ens of languages, but the academics had left him alone. There had been a couple of intermittent dissertations and a tiny Twayne series biography, but Algren seemed to have disappeared. The last of Ameri-can naturalists like Twain, Crane, and Dreiser, Algren had lived through the Depression, served in World War II, and covered Vietnam as a journalist; he'd had a long romantic love affair with this century's great feminist writer, Simone de Beauvoir. Terrific material? Absolutely, so I naïvely embarked on a biography, one of the most underpaid, tedious, and nerve-wracking nonfiction projects possible. A Texas librarian mentioned to a friend that I'd written for some Algren letters, and not long afterwards the University of Texas Press offered me a contract on the basis of ten pages. I sensed possibilities. I wrote to one New York agent and within eight weeks he got me a contract with a major publisher.

In the writing, I found that I could, curiously, make use of my own experiences while discovering the imaginative possibilities of history. I found great pleasure, for instance, in recreating the Depression. Looking for work as a journalist after college, Algren wandered across the Southwest much as I had done in my early twenties, in the 1970s, when so many lost young people tramped out to Boulder or Santa Fe or Berkeley looking for some vague idea of meaning. I had lived in vans and sometimes in the forests of furnished rooms in run-down hotels; and writing Algren's Depression life I felt again the mood of being adrift in a vast indifferent country whose centers of civilization were connected only by highways and a history not quite long enough to offer direction. Like Algren, who learned through the crash that everything he'd been taught about America was a lie, I, too, was disillusioned with the American dream expressed in the suburbs. Fortunately, these episodes of emotional transference occurred early in the book; through them I learned how to place myself into scenes as a silent observer, by which I mean simply to imagine them.

I did so much background reading on the Depression that I almost got stuck there, but I soon discovered that each era had its charms. When I finally finished the long sad night of the 1930s and 40s which for Algren had included more than five years of joblessness, a suicide attempt, a failed marriage, a good novel, an excellent one, and what felt like prison in the army, Algren entered the happiest time in his life. "Oh, Night, Youth, Paris, and the Moon!" I wrote to a friend when, after 1947, Algren had his own place in the Chicago slums and enough time to observe the junkies, produce his best work, fall deeply in love with Simone de Beauvoir, travel to Paris, and win the National Book Award. It was that short time when, with the Nazis defeated, so much felt possible—i.e., before the heavy boom of the Cold War came crashing down.

In the rational universe of the library, I found that I loved investigative work. I spent many hours poring over Algren's papers at Ohio State, afternoons at a beat-up desk in the airless stacks of the archive, oblivious to everything except reconstructing a time even Algren had not remembered clearly. I learned, through interviews, how fallible the average person's memory is when recalling events of twenty or thirty years ago. I loved reading Algren's letters for the laconic references to events of tremendous psychological importance. My discoveries about Algren were all the more rewarding since, though he sometimes kept a reporter's notebook, he never wrote diaries—except once, at Beauvoir's instigation. He was, in fact, a thoroughly guarded individual, who presented to the world a tough-guy face that only just managed to conceal the incredibly sensitive and vulnerable person beneath.

As I've suggested, Algren first interested me as a product of the

369

Depression, and I'm amused now at the reasons I was drawn to him. I saw him as a heroic radical championing the causes of the underdog and social justice. He was that, of course, but more tangentially than one might suppose; if he was first a poet, he was also a gambler, prone to terrifying depressions, and destructive of love relationships. In fact, the very thing that began to horrify me about him in the end made him such a good subject, and that was, of course, the darkness of his inner vision and psychology. For though I believe strongly in the influence of social and economic circumstance on human development, I don't see how anyone could come to biography without being fundamentally interested in the inner man—that is, the place inside each of us where we live life most of the time. "Not to idolize, not to deify, but to humanize, is the supreme task of creative psychological study; not to excuse with a wealth of far-fetched arguments, but to explain, is its true mission," wrote Stefan Zweig, in my mind this century's greatest biographer.

I sometimes felt that people around me, usually my fellow adjuncts teaching subjects and verbs at the City College of New York, wondered—how did *she* get to see Simone de Beauvoir? or some other well-known person, but there really wasn't much to it. I merely wrote saying what I was doing and asking for an interview, and it was usually granted. I met people I would otherwise never have seen, and I managed to avoid feeling intimidated by convincing myself that the famous aren't so different from other people. They were, for instance, fallible. In Paris, almost all the people of color I saw were sweeping the streets, yet when petite, turbaned Simone de Beauvoir opened the door of her quiet, sunny apartment to me, she let me know right off how conformist *Americans* were. In her living room, surrounded by mementos from her travels, she regurgitated what she'd already put in print until I probed a subject that still infuriated her after twenty-five years. Sometimes I would go to an interview, knowing the person had had an affair with Algren, and hear it denied against all evidence. Studs Terkel, friend of the working man, seemed offended by my Radio Shack tape recorder. These glimpses into lives we read about were lucky little educations for me, but I was more impressed, for instance, to meet the deeply insightful late New York City homicide detective Roy Finer, aka "The Big Cop," or Roger Groening, a friend of Algren's who is one of the most well-read individuals I've known. There were many others, three especially who remain among my closest friends today.

Naturally, I encountered sexism, mostly from men twice my age who wondered how this "little girl"—as one Pulitzer-Prize winning author and champion of liberal causes described me when I was thirty—could possibly write accurately about a tough guy. Another American writer, male, questioned every opinion I held about Algren, until, exasperated, I responded to a question by saying that since he'd corrected everything I'd said, I hardly knew how to respond. Fortunately, the interview was just about over. I was later surprised when the same writer wrote two very generous reviews of my book, even saying in one that I had a keen eye for the phony and fatuous. Though a number of professional academics who'd been sitting on Algren material for ten years or more didn't want to share it because they were "planning to do something with it" or demanded free books or placed nit-picking restrictions on speaking to me, most of the hundred or more people I contacted for information were extremely generous with their time and letters, pictures, and memorabilia.

Because Algren lived among and wrote about junkies, prostitutes, gamblers, and others who lived less than legitimate lives, I also wanted to find some of the underworld people who had so inspired him. It was largely impossible. I got tantalizingly close to an army buddy who was the inspiration for Frankie Machine in Algren's *The Man with the Golden Arm,* finally reaching his brother in Blue Island, Illinois. But he told me the man was drunk and homeless, and had just gotten out of the hospital in very poor shape. After a lot of work that included a trip across the decimated slum of West Chicago to the suburban enclave of River Forest, Illinois, I reached, by telephone to California, a former narcotics addict and prostitute who has lived clean for decades. She was suspicious and I had been warned to play dumb about her past. Thus I questioned her about Algren as if I did not know her; then I put all the evidence I had together.

Nothing ever made sense until I wrote it. I worked chapter by chapter, never moving on to the next one until the chapter was finished—which usually meant, with constant revision, I don't know how many drafts; I suppose eight or ten or so. Only when I put down exactly what I wanted to say out of the material at hand could I go on, because only then did I understand what had happened to Algren. A case in point was a letter he wrote in the fifties saying he had "played poker" with $32,000. Since Algren was a compulsive gambler, I took the letter at face value when I first found it; later I realized that he had merely seen his business situation through the gambling metaphor. And so on. Although I had originally begun with the twenty-two-chapter outline used to sell the book, I found that chapter breaks had to be changed to accommodate dramatic content. Wherever I could sacrifice to style I did so, until the facts became the starting point around which the narrative was wrapped.

There were many times when I hated Algren, his sexism, his peevishness and paranoia, but through him I came to understand a great deal about human contradiction, even though sometimes continuing work only by summoning up large doses of compassion. In fact, Algren, whose work is so drenched in compassion, demanded it of me, and I am very, very grateful for that. About halfway through the book, the writing lost its magic because I had learned how to do it. Then sometimes it seemed that my work consisted merely of grouping ideas into paragraphs and finding transitions. But I had too much invested not to go on, and it became, actually, another challenge to hide this from the reader, to hide also that I could not make sense of Algren's last twenty-five years even after writing them, until Algren's friend Roger Groening made me see that the themes I had carried through the book earlier actually did continue later on, a feat of insight for which I dubbed him Roger "The Savior" Groening. I only barely restructured the final sections in time, and it was done so quickly I can't really believe I managed it.

The cuts and editorial and legal revisions, all completed against a rather tight deadline, were, to say the least, physically exhausting. Worry over money, the expense of permissions, and the loss of cordial relations with people who'd helped me, only to be infuriated with what I'd written—a letter from an ex-wife's lawyer comes to mind here— drained me emotionally. In fact, the task of preparing the 500-page manuscript for publication was so overwhelming that, though I accomplished it, I was scarcely able to appreciate the American publication.

For a long time after the book came out, I heard floating in my head James Taylor's words, "I'd have to be some kind of natural-born fool to want to pass that way again." However, *Nelson Algren* appeared in Britain in January 1991 to very positive reviews. *The Spectator* called it "magisterial"; *The London Times,* "first-rate." While Americans, with a sort of hangover from a Cold War culture when criticism about capitalism couldn't be tolerated, felt uneasy about embracing or promoting a man who spoke for and lived among the lost, the British saw Algren's as a quintessentially American life.

I've been working on some essays, but have found that I miss the security of the big project, of waking up in the morning with no doubt about what to work on, of getting out of the house to meet people, of traveling here and there. I haven't been opening anyone's mail, but I have to admit that I've been looking into various lives and snooping around libraries. So who knows?

§75

HOW TO WRITE A HOW-TO THAT SELLS

BY GAIL LUTTMAN

ANY ACTIVITY THAT INTERESTS YOU—from canoeing to cooking to collecting Civil War relics to cutting your own hair—is a potential how-to article. And whether you are an expert or a novice, you are qualified to write about it.

Where to start

The most successful introductions to how-to pieces state a problem and then propose one or more possible solutions, perferably those relating to the seven basic human motivators.

Ego—Does your solution to the problem improve the way you look, the way you feel about yourself, your ability to relate to others?

Economy—Does it save money, protect the environment, improve quality without increasing cost?

Health—Does it give you more energy, promote safety practices, increase your psychological well-being?

Romance—Does it enhance sex appeal, create a cozy atmosphere, improve personal relationships?

Family—Does it entertain children, foster loyalty, help research family history?

Leisure—Does it enliven holiday activities, provide an engrossing hobby, help plan exciting vacations?

Individuality—Does the activity appeal to the universal desire for uniqueness by offering something new, different or better?

These motivators often overlap. A hobby may bring in income. Dieting may improve both health and self-image. An inexpensive bungalow of unusual construction may serve as a romantic retreat. The more motivators you appeal to, the greater interest you will generate in your how-to.

Moving on

After piquing the reader's interest, offer a brief explanation of what the activity involves, couched in enthusiastic words that inspire confidence. Can the skill be learned in five easy steps? Fifteen minutes a day? Does it require a special setting, or will a corner of the garage do? What special tools or materials are needed?

Rather than barrage readers at the beginning with a large number of tools or materials required, you may want to list them in a sidebar, a separate boxed-off article that accompanies the main story. Sidebars are a great way to include data or lengthy explanations without interrupting the narrative flow. Some editors favor articles with one, two, or even three sidebars if the article is very long or complex.

Definitions of unfamiliar terms might go into a vocabulary sidebar, especially when they are numerous; on the other hand, if special words are few or are easy to define, it is better to explain their meanings as you go along.

Whenever possible, describe new concepts by drawing a comparison with something familiar. In a piece about building stone walls, for example, a description of the proper consistency of mortar as "buttery" sparks instant recognition.

Complicated procedures don't seem quite as confusing when written up in short, uncomplicated sentences of the sort found in cookbooks. Explicitness also ensures clarity. Vague directions such as "measure out six to eight cups of water" or "cut two to three yards of string" leave the reader wondering which of the two stated amounts to use.

Clarity is also improved by separating general principles from specific procedures. If you are writing about how to build a chicken coop, for example, after the introductory remarks, explain how the layout and dimensions are established, then include some specific plans. In a how-to about cooking a Christmas goose, first describe how to roast the goose, then offer some favorite recipes. In that way you'll satisfy both the creative reader who likes to improvise and the less adventuresome reader who feels more comfortable with step-by-step instructions.

The final and best way to ensure clarity is with illustrations. The less commonplace the subject, the more important photographs and sketches become, and they are essential when dimensions are involved. In addition, the market is more receptive to illustrated how-tos. But don't despair if you are not an accomplished photographer or artist; many how-to magazines have illustrators who will enhance your article with clear, easy-to-follow illustrations.

Organization

The subject of a how-to usually dictates whether to organize the steps chronologically or to start with simple procedures and work toward difficult ones. If two steps are to be taken at the same time, it is important to make that clear. In bread baking, for instance, point out that yeast should be softening in warm water while the other ingredients are being measured.

Repetition can help or hinder reader understanding. Too much repetition causes readers to lose interest. In a short article, a brief reference to the original explanation is usually all that's needed. But if the article is very long or complex and the explanation is relatively short, repetition is better than asking readers to flip pages back to find the required information.

Include a timetable for each step to help readers gauge their progress. How long does concrete take to set? Eggs to hatch? Wine to ferment? Do varying conditions influence timing? Can or should any deliberate measures be taken to speed things up or slow them down? What specific signs might the reader watch for as the project nears completion?

Finally, what can go wrong? Think twice before including a separate how-not-to section or a trouble-shooting sidebar. Faced with a long list of things that can go wrong, a reader might understandably wonder whether the whole thing is worth the bother. But, in general, as long as a how-to is clearly written and well organized, it doesn't hurt to point out danger spots along the way.

Research, including interviews with appropriate experts, supplies background that adds depth and authority to how-tos, thereby increasing reader interest and credibility. It also helps a writer discover whether his experiences are typical or not. If not, avoid making sweeping or questionable generalizations.

When consulting authoritative sources, watch out for regional variations in the terms and methods you plan to describe, especially when you're writing for a national magazine. Mention chicken wire and a southerner is likely to picture what the westerner calls livestock fencing. Talk about reupholstering a divan or davenport, and there are readers who won't realize you are discussing a couch or a sofa. Before you write your article, look up alternative terminology from other areas.

Voice

Of course, the target audience determines how to approach your subject. If you are describing a new weaving technique to experienced weavers, you may use standard terms freely without defining them. But you should define any words that are specific to the new technique and you should definitely explain why the new technique is worth learning.

It is your job as a how-to writer to make certain that all readers achieve the same level of information by the time they reach the heart of your piece, and to do it without talking down. You can manage this by pretending you are writing a detailed letter to an interested friend.

You will find your most effective how-to voice by writing your article as if you were addressing a particular person who engages you in especially lively conversation. If you can't think of anyone suitable, invent someone. By writing expressly for that single reader, real or fictitious, you will delight all your readers with the personal tone of your how-to.

§76

TRUE CRIME THAT PAYS

BY KRIST BOARDMAN

FOR THE ASPIRING WRITER, CRIME DOES PAY. If you're willing to do some research and master the techniques of detective magazine writing, you can develop a market for yourself that will pay frequently and reasonably. Detective magazines specialize for the most part in true homicide cases. Sold on newsstands, these magazines feature criminal cases in the United States and other countries where police and court records are accessible to the public and journalists.

Usually, these stories are about *closed cases*. This means that a suspect has been arrested, tried, convicted, and sent to prison. There are exceptions to the closed case rule, but beginning true crime writers need not be concerned with them until they have mastered the craft and are contributing to the magazines regularly.

Where do you find a crime story to write about? Any old murder will not do. Though the annual murder rate in the United States now approaches 25,000, you must be selective. To find out what murders have been committed in your area, read the local or metropolitan sections of your newspaper. When you find a case that involves a homicide, clip and date it. Continue to gather clippings. With some practice, you will be able to separate good prospects for true crime features from those that will not work. If the case involves a lot of detective work and has some interesting and unusual twists, it is probably a good possibility for a crime magazine article.

You will notice that crime coverage in metropolitan newspapers usually differs from that in county weeklies. Reading the major dailies—which often publish news of major criminal cases in their home states, not just in their metropolitan areas—is an excellent way to gather leads on cases from all over the state, but those news accounts may be very tersely written, without the details you need for a good true crime article. County weeklies, on the other hand (which cover a smaller area), frequently carry in-depth coverage of particular cases being tried in their communities.

Having identified a good magazine possibility, send a query to a detective magazine editor. Detective magazine editors are usually receptive to new writers who have had some previous writing experience or demonstrate a keen interest in learning how to write these articles. In your query, include the type of crime, names of the victim and suspect, approximate date of the crime, locale, weapon used (if any), a short description of what happened, and the outcome of the case if it has already gone on trial. You can do this prior to the trial, but in that event, don't work on your piece until you get the editor's approval to do it and unless there is a conviction.

The best true crime features are well researched. Go to the courthouse where the criminal case was tried and look up the court file or official record. You can skip over the tedious legal deliberations and go right to what happened, as outlined in the original complaint by the police or prosecutor. Also take careful note of important evidentiary material, such as medical examiner reports, testimony of forensic experts and lab results requested by the police.

In addition, check the files of the county's newspaper of record in the county library. Photocopies of news reports will be helpful when you're describing what happened during the trial.

If the murder case was solved easily, you probably won't have enough material for a 5,000-word story. In that event, remember that there are many other good crimes for you to look into; refocus your efforts on them. More than once, I've found that though my original article never panned out, I nevertheless established new contacts that led me to other publishable ones I was previously not aware of.

Before leaving on a research trip, review your news clips and, if necessary, call ahead to the police department or prosecutor in the jurisdiction concerned to ask if they will talk to you about the case. Your chances of having them cooperate are considerably better if you approach them when their case has already been tried and the criminal has been convicted. An advance call also saves you unnecessary time and expense on trips. Another way to economize is to target several cases in a particular geographical area, so that you can do all your research on them at the same time.

In your research, you want to touch all of the bases, if you can. You may find that interviews are hard to come by, or that court officials are not cooperating in making key documents available, or that the case was not covered in the local media. By consulting all your sources, you will usually be able to get enough material for your story without compromising accuracy.

There is no hard-and-fast way to gain the cooperation of police and prosecutors, but it's always worth a try. Frequently, they appreciate having their firsthand perspectives recorded in a detective magazine. (Police and prosecutors are among the most avid readers of these publications.) Sometimes, police and prosecutors will roll out the red carpet and give you excellent, detailed, accurate accounts of crimes that even their local newspapers missed.

If they can't or won't help you, don't be discouraged; they often operate in highly political environments and under bureaucratic constraints that prevent them from talking to you. You have to learn to take this kind of rejection in stride.

When you have completed your research, you are ready to write your article.

To create a compelling narrative that will keep readers and editors asking for more, there are important techniques to follow.

Begin your manuscript with the commission of the crime, or the events leading up to its discovery. For example: It is five o'clock on a February morning in a medium-sized city. The air is chilly, and the sun has not yet risen. The trash man who comes into the alley to empty a dumpster is shivering and moving quickly to stay warm, exhaling clouds of dimly seen vapor. He notices a body on the ground in front of his truck, and thinking a homeless person is sleeping there, he nudges the body with his foot, but there is no response. He then rolls the body over, and in the murky rays of dawn, sees a bloody, battered face at the head of a lifeless torso. In the headlights of the trash truck, he sees a bloody hammer on the pavement several feet away.

As an editor of a group of detective magazines used to say, there is no need for a true crime writer to write dramatically. Murder is inherently dramatic, without literary embellishment. Just write the facts; in my opinion, understatement is a most powerful form of writing and is appropriate for this medium.

Your article may then explain something about the town where these events occurred, either before or after discovery of the body, to establish setting and also to indicate the frequency of crime in that locale. Perhaps the police have very few homicides to deal with, or maybe murder is commonplace in the area. Either situation will affect the behavior and attitude of the responding investigator and his coworkers.

A uniformed officer arrives first, followed by a detective and a crew of evidence technicians. Usually, the detective takes charge and becomes the central character in your narrative. You adopt him as the protagonist in your account and follow him through his paces until the defendant is apprehended and goes to court.

What kind of identification was on the body? If there was none, what clues were used to establish identity? What about that bloody hammer nearby? Whose fingerprints—if any—were on it? Whose blood? What type? What does the medical examiner establish as the probable time of death, and is the investigator able to find witnesses who saw or heard anything unusual in the area at that estimated time of death? What else did the detective find? How did he respond? These are questions that your investigator will be asking and to which you will want to provide your readers answers all along the investigative trail.

You should also tell your readers something about the primary investigator and his close associates. If you were able to interview the detective, you will have a feel for him, as well as for some specific details about his life and career. The detective may have a partner or a supervisor, and all three may have played unique roles that you will want to explain.

An important element of the police inquiry is the identity of the victim—not just name, address, and occupation, but what in the life of the victim led to his or her murder. Through interviews with his or her friends, coworkers, employers, acquaintances, boyfriends, girlfriends, spouses, the detective will try to reconstruct what the victim's life was like just prior to his death. These different angles produce a profile of the victim's life and world and help narrow the field of suspects to those who interacted with him.

Always remember that except for the victim, suspect, police, and court officials—judges and attorneys—you should not use actual names in your story. A witness identified by name in court documents should be described in your story only as the trash man, a neighbor, a girlfriend, or a relative. The same rule applies to the names of businesses. *This restriction is a must for detective magazines,* because it protects them from lawsuits from persons claiming invasion of privacy.

Avoid revealing the identity and motive of the suspect until you have exhausted every other aspect. I call this style "writing backwards," or backing into the denouement of your story; it prolongs the suspense and pulls the reader along. You want to focus on the clues, the blind alleys of the investigation, other possible suspects, and even possible red herrings, until it's virtually impossible to avoid giving up the identity of the suspect. This keeps the reader in suspense about the resolution of the case until the very end.

This technique is totally different from straight newspaper reporting, which tends to explain the outcome first and then goes back and fills in the details.

Frequently, the most interesting character is the perpetrator of the crime. Once he's been identified as a suspect, you will want to tell more about him and the motivations that led him to commit his crime. His personality often has a direct bearing on the outcome of the case: Is the suspect an abused, mentally disturbed person simply acting in self defense, or is he a vicious and calculating repeat offender who enjoys making his victims suffer? Is he someone in between these extremes? The judge usually takes all of these factors into account when determining a sentence, and the defendant's character might become a point of contention that should be mentioned in your article.

The court trial can be as dramatic as the steps that led up to it. Significant quotations from court testimony, interviews, and news articles can be used to illustrate how the case was resolved.

Now that you have written your 5,000-word manuscript and checked it for factual and grammatical accuracy, get whatever photos you can. This is not always easy, and you must be resourceful. You should ask official sources for crime scene photos, photographs of key evidence, pictures of defendants and suspects. Take your camera to interviews and ask the prosecutor and detectives for permission to photograph them. If they can't give you pictures, ask if you can make copies of their pictures. This is less than ideal but much better than nothing. If official photos are totally unavailable, take your own photos of the scene of the crime and the courthouse where the case was tried. Try to find some pictures of the defendant and victim from local newspapers. Sometimes local newspaper photographers or their newspapers will be willing to share pictures in exchange for a credit line in a national magazine or for nominal payment. If possible, do all this when you are gathering material; being able to mention to an editor that you have photographs or artwork available will increase your article's salability.

The true crime magazine story offers the serious and committed writer the opportunity to get published regularly, and to hone his craft in a market that constantly looks for new material. I also feel that the true crime writer has a mission: to let the world know that the unfortunate victims of murder have not been forgotten, and that serious efforts were made to bring the criminals to justice.

§77

WRITING AND SELLING IN THE NEWSPAPER MARKET

BY JOHANNA S. BILLINGS

ALTHOUGH IT'S NOT EASY TO BREAK INTO the newspaper market as a staff writer, nevertheless, local newspapers are literally begging for free-lance writers, or "stringers," to cover events that the staff writers can't get to.

Both daily and weekly newspapers use stringers. Weeklies generally accept beginning writers because often their staffs are less experienced. Smaller suburban dailies are likely to be receptive to new writers, but the larger dailies usually demand journalism experience.

Breaking in

The best way to sell your work to newspapers is to sell yourself first. Once you have chosen a newspaper, find out who the editor is, and then send a cover letter, including a resumé highlighting your writing credits and "clips" if you have any. A follow-up call should get you an interview, which may be rather informal, especially if you already have some writing experience.

Because most editors are not looking to buy just one article, they seldom want query letters. Instead, they want to cultivate a working relationship with stringers to whom they can give assignments regularly.

As a stringer, you will be doing both "hard news," which refers to government- and other issue-oriented articles, and "features," which include interviews/profiles and community events.

There are no standard rules for article length. Some newspapers have no length guidelines at all; others will tell you before you begin to write exactly how long an article should be.

Article length in newspapers is expressed in inches. The number of words to an inch depends on the size of print and column width of the paper. At the newspaper at which I am currently a stringer, a nine- or ten-inch story is about 800 words, but the same number of words might be eleven or twelve inches at another newspaper.

If you've written for other markets such as magazines, be prepared for a much faster pace. Since newspapers publish roughly thirty times as often as magazines and therefore need thirty times the input, if you want to succeed, you have to write good articles—fast.

Often, particularly at daily newspapers, a stringer will get an assignment without much advance notice. You may get a call Monday afternoon asking if you can cover something that begins at 7:30 that night. And if you're writing for a morning paper, you will be expected to have the story written and in final form by 11 p.m. or midnight.

The "musts"

Both hard news and features are written in much the same way. They must incorporate these elements:

The five W's. *What* is the story about? *Who* is affected by it? *Where* is it happening, and *when*? And most important, *why*? Doing this well means paying attention to details. How much something costs, an address, a person's age, the number of people attending an event are all small details that will make your story complete.

Accuracy. This may seem so basic that it doesn't warrant a mention, but it is crucial. No reader will continue to buy a newspaper if the facts are not reported accurately. And editors will not keep stringers who cannot produce accurate copy.

So, when you conduct an interview or cover a meeting or event, make sure you understand exactly what happened and how, what effects it will have and why it is important. If you have any questions, read previous articles on the subject, or ask sources, editors, and other writers. Then, write your story. When writing about a complicated issue, I try to get phone numbers of key people to call if questions come up while I'm writing.

Balance. Newspapers strive to represent both sides of every story, not the opinion of the writer. If, for example, a zoning board votes to allow an oversized parking lot, explain why the board made that decision. If it wasn't a unanimous vote, be sure to quote people who voted *for* and *against* it. And just as important, be sure to talk to the business people and anyone living nearby who will be affected by the decision.

Let the words of the people you quote speak for themselves, even if you disagree. But remember, the opinions expressed should advance your story, or provide new information, not just repeat information.

The hook. Entice readers at the beginning of your piece with the most interesting item. Newspapers generally present articles in the "inverted pyramid" style, that is, using the most important item first, with the least important at the end. But using the inverted pyramid style is not a hard-and-fast rule. Many of the newspapers I've worked for encourage more flexibility, allowing writers to begin a story with an anecdote or something to catch the reader's attention.

Relevance. Most readers will ask, "What does it mean to me?" before deciding to read on. Put yourself in readers' shoes and ask yourself that question—before you begin writing. For example, what will the zoning hearing mean to the average person reading a story about it— or to the person who is not directly affected but lives or works in the community? Will the new parking lot affect traffic flow? Will a traffic light be necessary? Why did the petitioners need or want a bigger parking lot? Have any residents voiced objections to the new lot? If so, who? Talk to them. Include their opinions in your story.

Generally, the more you include people in a story, the better it will be. If you find that "John Doe" is upset about the new lot, you might lead your story with, "John Doe moved to his present home thirty years ago because he wanted to live in a rural setting. But soon, he will be living next door to So-And-So's new parking lot." Then describe the zoning hearing and decision, moving quickly to represent the views of the zoning board and business owner to make sure your story stays balanced. Personalizing even a hard-news article will make it more interesting to read (and more fun to write).

Do the same with features and stories about community events. Interview people and find out why they came to an event and what they liked or disliked. You might hear about inefficient or rude ticket sales people, something the sponsors would never tell you. Having this information will give your story pizzazz.

The fresh approach. This is particularly important when writing

386

about community events. Without new ideas, the preview and after-the-event story can be essentially the same, year after year. It's your job as a stringer to make sure you don't write the same story that appeared in the paper last year. A fresh approach is especially crucial at a weekly because the story might not appear until six days after the area daily already covered it.

While working for a paper in suburban Philadelphia, I did a preview story on the upcoming annual Philadelphia Folk Festival. I had interviewed some volunteers who camped out on the site months before the festival to get the grounds ready, and began my story by focusing on a couple of them. I then gradually worked my way into the nuts and bolts of the festival—how many people were expected to attend, the dates, and the special attractions. The volunteers' experiences served as the thread that tied all the elements of the story together.

Features about individuals who "overcame great obstacles" or "remain positive despite the obstacles" have been done over and over, so taking a fresh perspective is very important. Don't editorialize; just let the person's words speak for themselves, and readers can form their own conclusions.

One last rule: Stringers are often assigned the stories that staff writers can't get to or don't want. But don't look at this as an obstacle. As a stringer, you'll have the luxury of having the time to develop really interesting features.

At first, all your work will be on assignment by the editor. But once you feel comfortable with the business and the writing, you will feel free to suggest ideas for future articles. If it's a viable idea, you'll get the assignment.

§ 78

Rx for Health Writing

By R. M. Adams

A collection of facts is no more science than a heap of stones is a house.

—Lewis Thomas

IN NO AREA HAS THE INFORMATION explosion been greater than in health and medicine. Scientists always have something new to say, ergo, getting ideas is a cinch. Start by scanning newspapers for 10 days (include two Sunday editions). Pick three or four topics that interest you and decide which one would affect reader health most directly.

Consult the *Readers' Guide to Periodical Literature* under two topics: health and medical/medicine. Make a list of the subcategories. For example, under "medical dynamics" the topics include: education, electronics, equipment, ethics, examinations, facilities, fakers, fees, genetics, geography, histories, and hypnosis. Under each category are titles of published articles. This will give you the "big picture" of health issues in the popular press.

It can also be helpful to visit the pressroom at a medical convention to read the press releases.

When a topic has appeared frequently in these sources, it may mean: 1) the issue has been beaten to death, or 2) reader interest is still high. You must decide, based on the market you wish to target, what is still a viable topic.

Markets

Check the market sections in the back of this book. Peruse newsstands. New publications appear frequently and getting in on the ground floor is easier than approaching an established magazine.

As you study the markets, you'll notice that health/medical publications for the general reader tend to fall into one of two categories:

1. Prevention/lifestyle
2. Disease/treatment

You must pick which fork in the road you wish to take.

Some publications are devoted exclusively to health matters. Because health and medicine are such popular topics, almost any magazine will consider a timely, well-written piece on a health issue that affects its readers, particularly those for older readers such as *Modern Maturity* and *Mature Years*.

Magazines move and change their names and editors, so confirm the current editor and address.

Background

At this point let's say you have decided to write about early detection of breast cancer and have two or three markets in mind. Of course, you will have read back issues and sent for writers' guidelines.

Next, you'll need to read extensively on diagnostic approaches: mammography, breast self-examination, etc.—deep background research. If you have no experience and little knowledge about health issues, this reading is even more important. Research is essential to any good article, but in medical writing, it may *be* the article.

Background research cannot be rushed. In addition to obtaining the latest facts, the object is to gain perspective: Where does your specific topic fit into the general subject? Are there issues related to sociology, psychology, ethics and the law? With breast cancer, early diagnosis is the key; related fields would be the psychology of dealing with a potentially fatal disease or mastectomy, as well as possible complications of treatment.

If you get confused or encounter too much jargon, go to the children's section of the public library and read books on the same topic. Begin with a large city library, then move to a medical school library (anyone has access, but you may not be able to check out materials; plan to spend some money on photocopying key articles).

Other sources of information and free literature are non-profit health agencies like the American Heart Association, American Cancer Society, etc. The government printing office also has inexpensive publications on health and medicine, as do the National Institutes of Health (NIH) in Bethesda, Maryland.

Interviews

You need to consult "experts," because information in books is 18 to 24 months old by the day of publication. One way to find experts is through the commmunications department of a local medical school.

Once you have chosen a few specialists to interview, the following process is recommended:

1. Make appointments to interview them in person; avoid using the phone.

2. Use a tape recorder. This is more important for interviews for health articles than for any other type of inverview, because of the complexity of the subject matter, and the potential for misquoting.

3. Do your homework, both on the topic and the interviewee.

4. Prepare relevant questions in advance.

5. Ask for explanations when anything isn't clear.

6. Repeat what has been said to check your understanding of it.

As long as you give proper credit in the piece, most people will be willing to talk to you.

Putting it together

Before you start writing, make an outline and write the closing. If you can't write a satisfying ending, you either don't have a meaningful theme, or your thinking is still fuzzy. If the former applies, you may have to abandon the project. Often you won't recognize a dead-end piece until you attempt to write the ending.

Assuming you just needed to sharpen your thinking and are able to write a definitive closing, proceed to write the lead. Make it lively but not dramatic. Hook the readers; make them want to know more.

With the lead and ending in good shape, the middle is easy. Given length constraints, this is where you distill and contract (never expand; you should always have more material than you can use).

A word about how to resolve differences of opinion among your experts: DON'T! Just report what they said. Honest differences of opinion enhance your article. Pieces on controversial subjects or presenting major disputes are best. Some timely topics for medical articles might include the following: aging, AIDS, attention deficit disorder, birth

390

control, cancer, computers in medicine, drug abuse, endocrinology, medicine and ethics, health insurance, home remedies, immunology, implants (breast, penile), leisure sports injuries, medical technology, mental health, new drugs, organ transplants, phobias, prenatal diagnosis, profiles (physician/astronaut, Nobel laureates), self-help strategies, space medicine, stress reduction, teen pregnancy, universal health care, use of animals in research, and women's health issues.

Last words

Medical writing is a fertile field because the flow of new information is endless, and the potential for helping thousands of people is rewarding. If you specialize, you'll have a competitive edge over other free lancers.

To begin, publish wherever you can, then with a few clips, move up to loftier periodicals. Use "medicalese" sparingly.

If you continue to write medical articles, you'll soon find you know more medicine than most writers and certainly more journalism than most health professionals.

PLAYWRITING

§79

Blueprint for Writing a Play

By Peter Sagal

IF I WEREN'T A PLAYWRIGHT, I'd be an architect, which on certain days I think is the finest kind of artist there is, because architects create art that is indisputably useful, necessary: Architecture is the art that stitches together the seams of the physical environment. But since I can't draw, I can't do math, and I'm too lazy to undergo all that study, I have to settle for being a playwright. I comfort myself, though, by imagining plays as architecture: art defined by its function, articulated by structure, inspired by the truths about the people who are to use it. Plays, like architecture, are, or should be, useful; they should express their beauty through purpose sheathed with ornament.

So one should go about the business of writing a play with all the dedication, discipline, knowledge, etc. that any fine art requires, but something else, too—something shared again with architecture, and that is a sense of *responsibility*. The architect knows that his or her building may or may not be admired by passers-by, but most definitely it will be used; a mistake on the drawing board may result in discomfort and displeasure for unknown thousands whom the architect failed by making a building that may have been fashionable or pretty but did not *work,* though architects ask people to live and perform their professional and personal functions within such a building. We playwrights ask less but still something substantial: We ask for time. Give us two or three hours of your life, two or three hours that can never be replaced, and we will enclose you in a soundproof room, turn off the lights so you can't read, and forbid you to talk, and we promise that it will be worthwhile.

Your first responsibility as a playwright is to waste no one's time. Consider your audience's attention as a precious gift, a gem, and if you fumble, it's lost forever. Time is a sacred thing, because everyone has only a finite supply of it.

Your job as a playwright, then, is to create a series of events, conversations, and images so important that it's worth asking the audience to give up their lives for a while and listen. I think this is the most difficult task in all writing, with the possible exception of book-length epic poetry. You do not have the expansive freedom of the novelist, or the factual safety net of the journalist. There's no tolerance for sloppiness; writing a play is done with a gun to the head. Here's how to do it:

Love your art

The theater won't pay you, won't comfort you, will provide you with little reward, and for that reward will drain your blood. In the best case your writing will be subject to the whims and caprices of actors, technicians, directors, producers; in the worst case, it will be ignored. If very, very successful, it will reach a tiny fraction of the people who watch "Married With Children" on TV, and your financial remuneration will be an even tinier fraction of the amount received by the writers who produce that work and others like it. Don't write for the theater if you want to write for television or the movies, or even for Broadway, which is a fictional place, like the Big Rock Candy Mountain. Write for yourself; write because if you don't you'll go crazy. Write because nothing else in your life compares to the power of creating your own worlds. Write plays because you believe that the experience of people gathering in a theater to see a play is nothing less than sacred. If you don't have the strength of this quasi-religious conviction, then the trials ahead could well overwhelm you.

Study your art

I am continually amazed by how many aspiring playwrights are ignorant of dramatic writing outside of a narrow canon of recognized giants: Shakespeare, Tennessee Williams, Arthur Miller, David Mamet, Sam Shepard, etc. In many cases, the writer sets out to imitate one or more of them. One problem, of course, is that these writers are geniuses, and you can't just imitate their work.

The other problem is that they *aren't* geniuses at all; they were and are working writers who slogged away for years and years, and most of them did their slogging in the theater. There isn't a single great writer for the theater who did not spend a long apprenticeship: Shakespeare, for example, started with the Lord Chamberlain's Men as an actor, writing plays himself only after he had performed uncounted dozens of other, now unknown works.

Such a lengthy servitude isn't necessary, but it is foolish not to recognize such problems as how to make the stage relevant to your life and the lives around you. If you live in a city with an active theater scene, go all the time, particularly to the new plays; the failures will be as educational as the few successes. If you don't have that luxury, then read as much as you can: Read your peers in American playwriting (Tony Kushner, Marlane Meyer, Neal Bell, Jose Rivera, Migdalia Cruz, Wendy Hammond, etc., etc.) and their counterparts in Great Britain; read plays from non-English speaking and non-Western traditions. You will come across hundreds of good ideas and save yourself from making thousands of mistakes. It is idiotic to try to invent the theater from scratch every time you sit down. Depart and rebel, by all means, but know what you are rebelling against.

I am very skeptical of books and articles that offer "rules" for writing, which is why I refuse to offer any specific suggestions to aspiring playwrights, such as, "start in the middle," "make the exposition active," etc. I have arrived at my own set of principles of dramatic writing, but they describe not so much how to write a play, as the kind of play I like. For every one of those rules, there's an exception, and in many cases, the exceptions are brilliant plays. For example, I don't like to have my characters address the audience, offering information about the other characters. That means I'll never write *The Glass Menagerie* or *The Marriage of Bette and Boo,* or even *Henry V,* among the many other plays I admire. The theater, more than any other form of writing, is a living thing: It grows and changes, departing from what just happened and pointing toward what's next. Rules hinder evolution. Further, when you sit down to write, you should be writing from an interior vision of what *your* play *is,* not some acquired idea of what *a* play is *like.* Television writers follow rules, because people who watch television know what they want and watch TV, expecting to get just that. This is the opposite of theater.

Practice your art

Writers in any form have to confront and control the hunger for acclaim. In the theater, this becomes even more difficult because, first, you are collaborating with actors and other artists who are eager to make their mark, and more important, your work is read out loud to large groups of people who might very well make loud noises that indicate approval (or disapproval). It becomes very tempting to get those words out of the word processor, into the hands of actors, and up in front of the audience, and to let the magic of the moment make up for any shortcomings. However, if you remember what I said about responsibility, you will see that this is a pernicious urge to be avoided. The rules of discipline, writing, and constant revision hold as much in playwriting as in poetry—don't buy into the old adage that a playscript is a "blueprint" and can slide by on heart alone. It *is* a blueprint, and it had better be a perfect blueprint or this house won't stand.

So write, write, write; experiment with sound and language and vision and structure. Do not be indulgent. Do not be lazy. Do not put less than perfect words on a stage and hope that the audience will buy them. Don't try to dazzle. Don't coast. Whatever you put on a page, make it your own. Remember, when you sit down to write a play, you are taking the future of an ancient and fragile art form in your hands: A bad play strikes another blow at it, in these wounded and wounding times; a good play breathes new life into the theater, and sends it striding on into a few more hearts, which may, in turn, nourish it after us.

80

ACT ONE, SCENE ONE: BEGINNING A PLAY

BY JEFFREY SWEET

NOT SO VERY LONG AGO, IT WAS COMMON PRACTICE to start a play with a pair of secondary characters in a scene that ran along these lines:

MARY: Young Gregory was out late last night. He finally came back at three in the morning.
JOHN: Did he say anything about where he was or why there's such a big dent in his car?
MARY: No, but he'd had too much to drink, I can tell you that.
JOHN: I wonder if this has anything to do with the letter he received yesterday. The one that made him turn so pale.
MARY: I couldn't say. But this morning at breakfast you could have cut the tension between him and his parents with a knife.

All right, I'm exaggerating, but not by very much. The introductory conversation between two servants, or two gossips in the neighborhood, or a character newly returned from travels asking about events during his absence often kicked off the action. If you can call this action.

The idea behind such scenes was to pump the audience full of the information necessary to understand the subsequent events. Playgoers used to sit patiently for the first ten minutes or so knowing that enduring this sort of exposition was the price they had to pay in order to get to the good stuff. And I'm not talking only about plays by forgotten hacks. The only reason for the lame passage between Camillo and Archidamus in Act One, Scene One of Shakespeare's *The Winter's Tale* is to help the audience get its bearings. (Just because Shakespeare is the best doesn't mean he didn't make his share of mistakes.)

Generally speaking, plays start faster than they used to.

I think this is partially the result of television. Tune into a prime-time drama series, and you'll see something like this in the pre-credits action:

399

Stand-up comic onstage, telling jokes. Audience laughing. A woman in black carrying a purse slips in through the stage entrance. She moves to a door marked "Dressing Room," enters the room and closes the door behind her. Inside, she switches on the light, looks around, sees a framed photo of an attractive lady sitting on the make-up table. Suddenly, she smashes the photo onto the floor so that the glass from the frame breaks. Onstage, the comic says goodnight and takes his bows. In a cheerful mood, he goes to his dressing room. He switches on the light, takes a step and hears a crunch. He looks down on the floor and sees he has stepped on the glass from the smashed frame. Then he hears a voice: "You were really cooking tonight, Charley. You were killing them." He turns and sees the woman standing behind the door, pointing a small pistol at him. Sweat builds up on his lip. "And I always thought 'die laughing' was an expression," she says. Now she smiles. The camera pulls in on her finger on the trigger. Fade out. Bouncy music kicks in and the credits begin.

Do you want to know who the woman is, why she smashed the picture and whether she's going to ventilate Charley? You've got to stay tuned past the credits and the opening batch of commercials. If you do, you'll probably be willing to sit through some less immediately compelling stuff setting up other characters till the story returns to Charley and his mysterious visitor. And then, odds are, having invested this much time, you'll stick around for the rest of the show. By beginning with a provocative but unexplained incident, the story has been launched, caught your attention and given you enough reason to take the ride to the last stop.

The craft of writing for television has necessarily been affected by the nature of the audience's relation to the medium. Aware that the audience, holding channel changers in their hands, can switch to a competing program at any time, the writers know they have to serve up immediate and pressing reasons for viewers to stick around. Obviously, few are likely to stick around if the show starts with the equivalent of two servants relating offstage events. So a TV script tends to start with a scene that builds to a pressing dramatic question.

Of course, audiences don't come to the theater with channel changers in hand. But, after years of watching the box in their living rooms and getting used to the pacing of tales told there, they come to the theater in the habit of being plunged into the heart of the story quickly. To grab the playgoer fast, many contemporary playwrights have borrowed a leaf from television's book by beginning their plays with characters in the middle of high-energy sequences equivalent to the one introducing Charley's dilemma.

John Guare's remarkable play, *Six Degrees of Separation,* starts with two of the leading characters, Ouisa and Flan Kittredge, excitedly telling the audience about their narrow escape moments before from some unnamed threat, checking to see that none of their valuables has been stolen, savoring how close they may have come to death. Having established their hysteria, Guare then has them take us back several hours to a lower-key scene anticipating the arrival of a friend who is to join them for dinner. With the benefit of hindsight, we know that they will shortly be hyperventilating, and so we watch carefully to see what part this dinner will play in the chain of events that leads to their alarums.

Guare could very well have *started* with the Kittredges discussing their dinner plans and then proceeding with the rest of the play as written. Doing this would not have meant omitting any of his story. But, by kicking the play off with the two in such an agitated state and then flashing back, Guare makes the audience sit up and take notice from the first moment. No coy wooing of the playgoer here; he snares our interest instantly. Knowing that the flashback holds the answer to the question, "What's making the Kittredges so upset?," the audience pays closer attention to the lower-key scene that follows than they would have if the play had started with that scene.

I'm not suggesting that all plays should begin in the middle of action, but quite a few would be improved if they did. I asked the members of a playwriting workshop I run to bring in scripts they were working on, and, as an experiment, we read excerpts from them, each time starting on page ten. In all but two cases, the writers decided their plays actually began better on their tenth pages than on their firsts.

What information was contained in the missing pages? My students discovered that most of it was implicit in the scenes from page 10 on. By beginning in the *middle* of dramatic action—instead of setting up the circumstances in the first ten pages—the playwrights gave the audience the fun of figuring out the circumstances for themselves. Gone were the dull stretches of characters entering the stage, pouring drinks, and slipping in nuggets of self-introduction. Gone, too, were the one-way phone calls designed to sneak in exposition. Rather than switching on and warming up the scripts' motors and then coaxing them up to speed, the plays now had a sense of urgency from the word go, and that urgency made them compelling.

The opening of a play not only gets the story started, it also makes a contract with the audience. The first few minutes virtually announce, "This is the kind of play we're doing," and the audience sets its expectations accordingly. We watch different genres with different expectations. It is very important, then, for the opening of your script to set the audience's expectations correctly. If you break a promise to a friend in real life, you're likely to lose the trust and confidence of that friend. Break a promise to the people who have paid to see your play, and they will respond with confusion and irritation. If, for instance, you begin your play with a pair of bewigged fops trading quips in blank verse, you'd better not suddenly switch in the middle of the second act to a modern psychological thriller. Raising the curtain on a solo figure in black tights on a bare stage miming the life cycle would be a misleading introduction to a Neil Simon-style domestic comedy.

This may sound like very obvious advice, but some very savvy theatrical talents nearly lost a great musical because of such a miscalculation. *A Funny Thing Happened on the Way to the Forum* was trying out in a pre-Broadway engagement in Washington in 1962. According to all accounts, the show was substantially the one we've come to know, but the audiences weren't taking to it. The laughs were few and far between, and each night a dismaying chunk of the audience disappeared at intermission. The perplexed creative team—which included such celebrated figures as George Abbott, Larry Gelbart, Bert Shevelove and Stephen Sondheim—asked director-choreographer Jerome Robbins to take a look and tell them where they were going wrong.

After the performance, Robbins informed them that the problem was with the opening number, a light-hearted little tune called "Love is in the Air," which promised a romantic frolic. What followed instead, however, was an evening of broad jokes, slapstick, and farcical intrigue. Robbins said what was needed was an opening that *promised* broad jokes, slapstick, and farcical intrigue. An opening, he insisted, should promise the audience what in fact a show is going to deliver.

Composer-lyricist Stephen Sondheim went to his piano and wrote a song entitled, "Comedy Tonight," which did just that. According to legend, as soon as it was put in, the reaction to the show turned around completely. What had previously played to indifference now brought cheers. *A Funny Thing Happened* went on to New York, where it received glowing reviews and was proclaimed a hit, all because the opening was changed. It is now counted a classic musical comedy.

Not only do you establish the genre of a show in the first few minutes, you also establish stylistic rights. At the beginning of *Six Degrees of Separation,* Guare swiftly signals the audience that he reserves the right to 1) have any of his characters, at the drop of a hat and without self-consciousness, address the audience directly, and 2) with the briefest of transitions, leap to any other time or place in the story. And, indeed, throughout the script, both major and minor characters feel no compunction about making eye contact with a theater full of playgoers and speaking their minds. What's more, scenes move abruptly back and forth in time and jump, without second thought, from the Kittredges' fancy apartment to Central Park to Greenwich Village and wherever else it is necessary to go to witness the essential events of the story. And, oh yes, the number of laughs at the show's beginning clearly indicates the audience is in for a comedy.

It is a truism among musical theater writers that the opening number is usually the one you write last, because it is only after you've finished the rest of the show that you know what the opening should prepare the audience for. Straight plays are structurally less complicated than musicals, but upon completing a draft, a smart dramatist looks closely at the opening few pages to see if they correctly establish the world and style of the two hours to follow. The audience isn't likely to go through your door if you don't offer them the key to unlock it.

81

NEW WRITING FOR THE THEATRE

BY SHELLEY BERC AND ROBERT HEDLEY

HAVE YOU EVER FOUND YOURSELF SITTING DOWN to write a play and discovered that the ideas and feelings you wished to convey were not served by the traditional route of exposition, development, and denouement; that the world you were perceiving was plotless, fragmented, and collage-like? Perhaps you even felt defeated before you started because you didn't know the "rules"?

One of the most fascinating things we've discovered working with new playwrights, as we do at the Iowa Playwrights Workshop, is that many of their plays or plays-in-progress do not conform to the usual notion of dramatic writing. In fact, when these students attempt to "fix" their plays in conventional ways—a little character development here, a bit more plot there—the plays fall apart. Many of today's playwrights are mapping out a new dramatic territory and are writing the rules of its domain, rather than trying to superimpose a traditional style or structure upon it.

Not since the end of the nineteenth century has there been less consensus over what playwriting is or should be. The realistic play with its concentration on true-to-life, psychologically motivated action is losing its hold on dramatic writing. Playwrights, in increasing greater numbers, are finding themselves attracted to a variety of theatrical styles and approaches that confound our sense of the linear, character-focused play. Many playwrights find that the subject matter and dramatic structure associated with realism do not reflect the fragmented, multisensory, technologically swift nature of life today.

This new writing for the stage is likely to replace psychologically motivated characters with mercurial ones; linear plot with a series of non-linear events that resemble jam sessions on a theme; realistic, informational dialogue with language arias that exist to create momentary metaphysical landscapes. Actually, such elements in one form or

404

another have been a staple of avant-garde theatre for nearly a century. Now, however, they are becoming part of mainstream dramatic writing and can even be called the new classic style. As the world becomes a place where many things are done simultaneously, in which total communication across hemispheres is just a fax away, playwrights are losing patience with single-minded theatre pieces that systematically follow through a central idea or problem for two or three acts, with characters who consistently respond out of psychological motivation.

Internationally acclaimed playwrights such as Heiner Mueller, Irene Fornes, and Manfred Karge are all in their own unique ways creating scripts that speak to today's concerns in a dramatic language and structure that may wholly disregard plot, conflict, dialogue, even character. What then are the elements of postmodern playwriting, and what do they say about the future place of the playwright in the world and on the stage?

Let's take, for example, Manfred Karge's *Man to Man*. The play has only one character, a woman who impersonates her husband after his death so she can take his job and survive in Nazi Germany. As performed at the Royal Court Theatre in London, it opened with a woman lying on the floor amidst the domestic debris of her life. There is no pretense about making the set look like a real room; we see only fragments of the character's life—a few bottles, a record player, a chair, a TV—as if we were sifting through an archaeological site.

For the next fifty minutes (the length of plays is changing, too) this woman tells us the story of her life in terms of its personal, political, economic, and mythological aspects. No single notion of how to perceive her existence is given weight over another. To this end, the text is mercurial in its transitions rather than causal, fragmented in its plot rather than linear, evocative in its development rather than factual.

The text of *Man to Man* hardly looks like a play at all in the usual sense. It is divided into a series of numbered passages that combine prose, verse, slogans, captions, quotes, puns, political references, and a fairy tale. It is a language picked up and spit out like a grab bag of political and cultural history. Several genres of language, from the literary quotation to the billboard advertisement, create the pastiche of this woman's life. More important, the language here does not exist primarily for the purposes of conveying information, developing character, or tracing a tragic flaw. In *Man to Man,* language is both main character and prime action; its forms comment on each other; its vying genres combust and collide, turning the world as we comfortably know it upside down and freeing us to perceive anew.

In many of the new plays that attract critical attention, conventional playwriting wisdom is inadequate. The idea that to write plays that speak eloquently and powerfully, one must start with Aristotle and spend time with Ibsen has not been true for some time and is now particularly untrue. Linearity and character modesty—that is, the assumption that somebody else must reveal the character's story—are less important than ever. Consistency of tone and authorial absence, bulwarks of realism, are directly refused as today's new plays celebrate verbal fluency and imagination. The audience is not asked to suspend its disbelief or allowed to hide voyeuristically behind a "fourth wall."

This is not to suggest that plays of consequence, beauty, power, or outrageousness are not being written in traditional forms, but that impatience or restlessness with those forms is now a part of the young playwright's make-up. It seems no longer possible, for example, to pretend that stage events are taking place without being observed, that a few hundred eyes are not peering out from the darkness. Likewise, it appears to be impossible for characters to restrain the urge to speak directly to their audience. Verbal literacy—that is, a knowledge of what language can be asked to do and a recognition of what it has done in all its uses, misuses, and variations—is on the rise, leading, yet again, to an impatience with plays whose characters are unaware that they inhabit a stage and hence speak only to the fictional point. In the new plays, the boundaries between what is funny and what is sad, what is tragic or trivial, beautiful or trite have been stretched and blurred to an unprecedented extent in direct reflection of our social and historical times.

While the terms in which many of the new plays address the audience are often abstract and complex, their relationship with the audience is astonishingly direct. Characters often tell the audience flat out what it needs to know, rather than going through a long, slow list of clues that become the plot structure. By getting the facts over with quickly (as the Greeks did ages ago in their plays), the playwright can concentrate on the political, historical, and metaphysical concerns he or she wants to relate. Scenes no longer develop one to another in a storylike trance in which all things lead inevitably to the climax.

Rather, they often exist like medieval triptychs in which certain selected images springing from a well-known theme play against each other, illuminating and interpreting the story by its very fracture and incompleteness. Audience response is built through a series of impressions, aural and visceral, carefully arranged to create an idea or image through juxtaposition, irony, parallelism, or repetition.

One of the most interesting trends in new plays is the monodrama, or one-person play. Unlike realism, in which the audience watches the story evolve through key physical and emotional actions, the new monodramas in particular rely heavily on action through language. As storyteller, the playwright uses forms of language in rhythmic variation to provide dynamic action without the trappings of verisimilitude. The monodramas are often a mix of autobiography and cultural mythology. Through a series of impressions, the multiplicity of life is examined, honed down to the microcosm of the lone character. Monodramas examine the self as social creature and the self as mythological hero. Dramatic tension is found in the battle between the disparate identities of the self. Dialogue in the monodrama, when not between these warring selves, is between the character and the audience. Hence, each member of the audience actually becomes a character, and a true dialogue between performer and observer occurs.

The trends and developments are not meant to serve as a prescription nor a set of new rules to replace the old. A play by Irene Fornes, for example, is profoundly different from the Karge play cited here but just as relevant. What is important for the aspiring playwright to recognize is a sense of the freedom and imagination in the newer forms, as well as the reemergence of language as a primary player in the drama.

But let's be more specific. How can beginning playwrights help themselves? First of all it is important to read widely in order to understand what is going on in theater writing today. While publications such as *The Fireside Theatre* are excellent for mainstream writing, the newest pieces can be found in the *Wordplay* collections; the various *PAJ* volumes; *TCG, Plays International, American Theatre,* and other magazines; and in anthologies like *7 Different Plays*. For the inexperienced writer, it is liberating to see the methods and structures used by writers tackling contemporary issues.

In working with their ideas, aspiring playwrights must learn to trust their instincts. While it's not easy for a new playwright to know whether he or she is on the road to creating plays in a nonlinear, lyric, evocative style or merely being sloppy in character delineation and plot development, little good will result from listening to the critical inner voice that compares everything to *Death of a Salesman.* The experience of a new play is a total experience, including its form. Not being a "slice of life," such an experience does not demand consistency of language, place, character, or other normal conditions. Indeed, an impulse or instinct to use multiple forms may indicate the only means of expressing your idea.

But let's conclude with a few basics for you to keep in mind as you write or revise your plays:

1) The one thing traditional playwriting and some of the newer forms have in common is specificity of detail and clarity of expressed ideas.

2) When you are writing a play, make sure you are listening to what *it* is telling *you,* rather than what you think you want to say. Follow your impulses. Listen to your characters. Forget rules, forget doors, forget politeness. Never ask yourself whether it's logical or not.

3) If the play is telling you primarily about the sound and rhythm of a certain day, you must consider that the play may be more of a dramatization of the essence of that day than of the characters or stories you've tried to put in it. The characters and the stories have been there and will be there, at least in your notebook. That day, that flavor, may not. Just because it doesn't resemble plays you know doesn't mean that it won't become a new, important play.

4) Remember that playwrights can and do dramatize anything—from a day to a poem to a piece of architecture. Dramatic action, the mainspring of the theatrical experience, does not necessarily mean physical or psychological action. Action can also mean a movement of ideas or images or words or intentions.

5) Try to put the world you see in your mind on the stage. Explore the thoughts, the words, the visions that own you, and reach for

ways to translate them in terms of actors, sets, and audience. Don't settle for what you know or have seen.

6) Be courageous. You are individual when you write like yourself. When you try to put your ideas in someone else's form you often betray those ideas.

Many of the new techniques are as old as the Greeks, but the varied and joyous way in which styles and genres of the theatre are being put together is wholly new and magical; an invitation to the mind to explore the farthest reaches of its imaginative strength.

82

Before You Try Broadway . . .

By Anna Coates

As a Los Angeles-based writer, script analyst, and devotee of community theater, I see a lot of plays that could have been a lot better, and I read a lot of scripts that probably should have been shredded at birth.

Which is not necessarily a bad thing.

One of the functions of little theater is to give the playwright a chance to see what works and what doesn't—not on the page, but on the stage, with living, fumbling, stumbling actors. The playwright's duty—alas, oft-neglected—is to figure out what doesn't work, and why, and if necessary to cut and chop or even to begin again.

And in a world that seems unjustly biased toward screenwriters— from Joe Eszterhas and his three-million-dollar *Basic Instinct* to Joe Schmoe and his twenty-thousand-dollar B-flick advance—the playwright has one wonderful advantage over the screenwriter. In addition to basic moral superiority, of course.

The playwright can learn as he goes.

The playwright may aspire to Broadway, but he has a crack at many lesser triumphs along the way. He can tinker with his work, tightening here and lengthening there. Even after he surrenders a script to a director's interpretation, he may continue to edit and rewrite, with or without the director's blessing.

Markets for a stage script can be divided into four categories: *community theater, experimental theater, "legitimate theater"* (aka, the Big Time), and *publication/TV.*

Of course, the categories aren't mutually exclusive. Community theater can mean a show performed on a makeshift stage in a church basement, or an elaborate and well-funded production staged as part of the regular "season" of a repertory house. (You understand, of course, that the term "well-funded" is relative!) Student productions

410

are another type of community theater, and in some college towns they are eagerly awaited as the only theater available.

Community theaters like to produce well-known plays by established playwrights. That gets a little tired when you're seeing *Our Town* or *Streetcar* for the fifth time in six years, but if you think about it, it makes sense. Working with tiny budgets, directors tend to pick shows that are proven winners with broad appeal. They keep in mind that audiences—not to mention casts—may be unseasoned, and will react most favorably to mainstream fare.

This doesn't mean your original light comedy or social drama can't find a home with a little theater—of course it can. But you may need extra patience to find the right house to handle its premiere.

And yes, local companies will occasionally get crazy and go for *experimental theater.* But you're more likely to come across it in a city like Los Angeles or New York with a heavy concentration of actors and writers, an abundance of venues, and a weird (whoops, I mean *varied*) range of tastes.

If you're slathering to do your play on the Great White Way, or at least on cable TV, back up and slow down.

The road to Broadway (and Off-, and off-Off) wends its way through many a community theater and college campus. Sure, your play might be one of the fifteen selected by the O'Neill Theatre Center's National Playwrights Conference. On the other hand, it might be one of the fifteen hundred they reject. And it's within the realm of possibility— just faintly, there at the border—that you'll zap out your first rough script to a cable television company and get a fat check and a contract by FedEx a week later. Certainly, if you're confident about the quality of your work you should try.

But for most mere mortals the way to earn a few credits and learn the ropes is to have their work produced by a small local theater or an undergraduate director.

And that should be pretty easy. After all, an undergraduate director is really just a college kid. And local theaters pay nothing—or maybe carfare—and ought to be happy to get what they can get. Right?

Well, no.

The great majority of scripts submitted to student directors, to little theaters, and to contests will never be produced or optioned because they are badly written.

411

It's not because the writers are without talent. There is almost always—no, *always*—something positive I can say about a piece of writing, and I'll go out of my way to figure out what it is. Still, it's frustrating and annoying to read script after script in which plots are direct rip-offs from current movies or standard stage productions, down to characters' names and dialogue. Sure, we all know there are only three basic storylines. The trick is to make yours seem fresh.

What directors and readers and editors look for in a script is a storyline that flows and that is logical *within context*. Think about the eternal *Ten Little Indians*. Now, the idea of a disgruntled murderer gathering nine victims and bumping them off slowly and cleverly, one by one, is a bit preposterous, especially in this day of Uzi machine guns and other high tech timesavers. But so cleverly is this story crafted that contemporary audiences are able to lose themselves in the drama and the terror, and suspend disbelief—for ninety minutes, at least.

Realistic dialogue

Beyond plot, what you should be most concerned with is that your script be peopled by believable characters who use realistic, interesting dialogue. Trust me, if you write a terrific story and a potential producer thinks it needs a modified end, or an older main character, or a different setting, she will let you know. Those are very fixable flaws and an excellent piece of work won't remain homeless because of them.

What will get "no thanks" is a hackneyed plot, flat, stereotyped characters, and trite, wooden dialogue.

Stilted dialogue is a common problem. If you want to know how real people speak, listen to them.

Don't be afraid of contractions! You'll seldom hear a person say, "I do not know what I am going to do about it." Most people will say "I don't know what I'm going to do about it." (The exceptions might be a person speaking stiffly, for emphasis, or a non-native speaker. For instance, on the television series *Star Trek: the Next Generation,* Mr. Data's "un-contracted" speech helps define his android character. This device is effective because the other cast members speak naturally.)

When in doubt, read your dialogue aloud.

People sometimes—uh, pause, when they speak. And sometimes

they begin sentences with *and* or *but*. But I find writers, are, well . . . reluctant to use hesitation in dialogue.

If you want your hero to say, "Gloria, I—I'm confused. This feeling is so strong. And I don't know what's happening between us," then don't write "Gloria, I am confused. This feeling is so strong. I do not know what is happening between us."

Remember that theoretically the actor should utter only the lines you write. Yes, he may get fed up and throw in an ad-lib and the director may decide to use it. In that case you, the playwright, have not done your job. Dialogue that *works* doesn't tempt actors to rewrite.

(As I'm chasing you with the hickory switch, remember that an early production of your play is your chance to cut and polish for later audiences. Maybe the church-basement director won't allow you to rewrite dialogue mid-production, but you certainly may do so before you resubmit your play to larger regional companies.)

The professional look

Budding playwrights I have found avoid commas although I'm not sure why. Without commas the actors may forget to breathe if you follow me or at least they'll be confused.

An occasional *tpyo* is no big deal, but when every other line of a script contains misspellings like "ocaissional," "privledge," "thier," and "perference," can you blame me for concluding that the writer was just too lazy to consult his dictionary?

Grammar mistakes are irksome, too. No, you don't need perfect diction to write a good script. On the other hand, a writer who aspires to be a professional should certainly know the difference between "lie" and "lay." Your heroine may choose to lay on the bed, but that's a pretty good trick if she's alone in the room. And anyway, isn't this a G-rated production?

The writer should know whether his characters are doing well or doing good (or both). He should know whether that cool rebel flaunts rules or flouts them, and why that kid's new puppy can't be a gift from Daddy and I.

He should know if it's proper to contract *it is* as *its* or if it's not.

Of course, people don't speak perfectly, and judiciously placed solecisms make dialogue ring true. But when *every* character confuses literal and figurative, and says fortuitous when he means fortunate, or

413

infer when he means imply, I begin to suspect the blunders aren't the characters' but the writer's own.

Get the simple stuff straight: Split infinitives will continue to easily slip by me. Likewise sentence fragments.

Dialect trips up a lot of playwrights. No, you don't have to be African-American to create a character who speaks "Black English," and you don't have to be Chinese to write about a fellow from Beijing. But spare me your "G'wan, man, I be jivin' yo' funky sef ' " and your "Solly, no speaky Engrish" and most of all, your Southern Belles who say "y'all" when they're speaking to only one person.

If you must indicate a dialect, do it like this:

BELLE

Why, I declare!
(Belle's thick Southern accent makes this sound like, "wha, ah declayuh.")

You need indicate this only once. The director will get the idea, and so will the actress. And both of them will thank you.

Try to keep your set directions to a minimum. Just tell us we're on a pretty beach at sunset, and let the set designer worry about the golden sun and the cry of the gulls and the sails like white wings against the horizon. And keep in mind that the more sets and props your play calls for, the more it will cost to produce.

Keep blocking—the stage directions that show the actors when and how to move—to a minimum. Entrances and exits must be indicated, of course, and long slow clinches are fun to write. But if Tom enters angry, the director will guess that he might slam the door. If Suzy is doing an audience aside, the director will definitely place her downstage. If the phone rings, he can figure out that Jan will need to cross to answer it. O.K.? So indicate movement when necessary to advance the story, and don't leave your actors rooted in place like young saplings. But do have mercy and let the poor director have something to do.

It's scary for a writer to pack up her work and send it out for

414

strangers to peruse. Presumably the fledgling playwright reminds herself that stage companies—local to pro—*want* to like her work. They, like you, are in this biz for the love of the written and spoken word. And besides, who wouldn't like to discover the next Sam Shepard?

What amazes me is that with this in mind, so many scripts are sent out flawed not only in the ways we've discussed above, but badly typed and poorly photocopied.

Neatness counts. Your third-grade teacher told you that and you probably relearned it in college when your psych professor showed you a study indicating that of two term papers *identical* in content the one typed neatly earned higher grades than one full of typos and cross-outs.

So what's the trouble?

I know. It takes a long time to type a hundred pages, doesn't it? It hardly seems worthwhile to retype the whole thing every time you add a couple of paragraphs or take one away.

Stop! You're breaking my heart!

The fact is, if you want to be taken seriously, your script must look professional. That means 8½″ × 11″ white paper, black ink, margins at the top, bottom, and sides, numbered pages, and invisible corrections or none at all. Absolutely no strike-outs.

Submit a photocopy, never the original. If your script is returned to you clean, there's no reason not to send it out again, but spare us the dog-eared, coffee-ringed, penciled fourth-timers! No one likes to feel like last choice.

The standard format for a play script, adjusted according to number of acts and intended medium and audience, is available from many sources, including books from your local library. But you won't be penalized for indenting dialogue seventeen spaces instead of fifteen, or for numbering your pages at the top center instead of at the top right.

Cover letters

Whether you are submitting your work to a little theater, a contest committee, a cable television director, or a magazine editor, address your cover letter to a specific person *with whom you have spoken,* and who has agreed to look at your work. And I don't want to hear any whining about the cost of toll calls. First of all, most of these people aren't going to want to sit and chat (until they've read your script and realize you're brilliant and incredibly talented). And secondly, are you interested in getting produced or in sitting around complaining about an unavoidable business expense?

If you're submitting your script to a contest or television company, write ahead to request specific instructions about format, formal copyright registration, and whether a signed release is required. But when you want a local theater director to look at your work, it's still necessary to call ahead. By calling in advance, you can make sure that you have the correct contact name and address and that the director is willing to consider your work. Why waste time if she's not? Many directors will look at new plays only between seasons, and if you mail your script to a college theater department in June, it's likely to gather dust at least until September. And remember that your work should *always* go out with the copyright symbol (©) that indicates "copyright protected" at the right-hand top of the cover page.

Like your call, your cover letter should be brief. "Here's the script we talked about, and thanks for your time" will do. If you want to, add a few lines to mention your credits, if you have any, or your credentials, if they're germane. If your script is a comedy about a dairy farmer, and you happen to live on a dairy farm, say so.

Don't send a script replete with four-letter words to a children's playhouse, no matter how the kids in your neighborhood talk. And keep in mind that an all-nude sex comedy isn't likely to play in Peoria.

If you've done your homework and kept set and prop requirements to a minimum, you can say so in your cover letter. But don't use your cover letter to sell the script; it must sell itself. Don't write, "This is a wonderful, rip-roaring comedy full of hilarious moments in the wacky life of a dairy farmer."

With all the pitfalls I've described, what's the worst mistake aspiring playwrights make?

It's not confused plotting or flat characterization or trite dialogue. It's not sloppy typing or garbled cover letters. It's not even forgetting to put your name and phone number somewhere it can be found.

The worst mistake budding playwrights make is *not trying*. Not writing that script, or not polishing it, or not sending it out. Or sending it out only once, then giving up.

You may place your first script its first time out. Or you may place your tenth, its tenth time out, then watch it move along through little theaters and repertory ensembles. And as you look back on all the rejections, you'll realize that you learned something from every one.

I'm rooting for you, so get busy. And, hey—see you on Broadway!

§83

CONFLICT: THE HEARTBEAT OF A PLAY

BY D. R. ANDERSEN

EVERY PLAYWRIGHT IS A DR. FRANKENSTEIN trying to breathe life into a page for the stage. In a good play, the heartbeat must be thundering. And the heartbeat of a play is conflict.

Simply put, conflict exists when a character wants something and can't get it. Conflict may sometimes be internal—as when a character struggles to choose between or among opposing desires. For example, Alma in Tennessee Williams's *Summer and Smoke* longs to yield to her sexual yearnings but is prevented by the repressed and conventional side of her nature.

Conflict in drama may also be external—as when a character struggles against another *character* (Oscar and Felix in Neil Simon's *The Odd Couple*); against *society* (Nora in Ibsen's *A Doll's House*); against *nature* (the mountain climbers in Patrick Meyers' *K2*); or against *fate* (Sophocles' *Oedipus*).

In most plays, the conflict is a combination of internal and external struggles. In fact, internal conflict is often externalized for dramatic impact. In Philip Barry's *Holiday,* for instance, the hero's inner dilemma is outwardly expressed in his attraction to two sisters—one who represents the safe but boring world of convention, and the other who is a symbol of the uncertain but exciting life of adventure.

Granted that a conflict may be internal or external; that a character may be in conflict with another character, society, nature or fate; and that most plays are a combination of internal and external conflict, many plays that have these basic elements of conflict do not have a thundering heartbeat. Why? These plays lack one, some, or all of the five magic ingredients of rousing, attention-grabbing-and-holding conflict.

The five magic ingredients

I. *Never let your audience forget what your protagonist wants.*

You can achieve this in a number of ways. Often the protagonist or another character states and periodically restates in dialogue what is at stake. Or in some plays, he explains what he wants directly to the audience in the form of a monologue. As you read or watch plays you admire, take note of the obvious and ingenious techniques playwrights use to tell the reader or audience what the characters' goals are.

Sometimes the method used to keep your audience alerted to your protagonist's goal/concern/need is a direct reflection of the protagonist's personality. In the following three short passages from my play *Graduation Day,*[1] a mother and father with very traditional values have a conversation while waiting to meet their rebellious daughter, who has told them she has a big surprise. Notice how the protagonist—Mrs. Whittaker—nervously and comically manipulates the conversation, reminding her husband and the audience of her concern for her daughter Jane:

MRS. WHITTAKER
(Knocking on the door)
Jane. Jane. It's Mom and Dad.
(Pause)
No answer. What should we do, Tom?
MR. WHITTAKER
Let's go in.
MRS. WHITTAKER
Suppose we find Jane in a compromising situation?
MR. WHITTAKER
Nobody at Smith College has ever been found in a compromising situation.

* * *

MRS. WHITTAKER
Tom, you know, this was my freshman room.
MR. WHITTAKER
Of course, I know.
MRS. WHITTAKER
And Jane's. It was Jane's freshman room too, Tom. Remember?

* * *

MR. WHITTAKER
Mary, you get in the craziest moods at these reunions. I may never bring you back again.

---

1. First produced by Playwrights Horizons in New York, starring Polly Holliday.

MRS. WHITTAKER

Do you know why you fell in love with me, Tom?

MR. WHITTAKER

I fell in love with you the minute I saw you eat pancakes.

MRS. WHITTAKER

That's a sound basis for a relationship. Tom, where do you suppose Jane is? And more frightening, what do you suppose she wants to tell us? She said just enough on the phone to suggest that she's going to be bringing a boy here for us to meet.

MR. WHITTAKER

A man, Mary, a man.

MRS. WHITTAKER

Oh, God. I never even considered that possibility. Suppose Jane brings a fiancé—our age—like Pia Zadora did.

MR. WHITTAKER

Don't you want Jane to live her own life?

MRS. WHITTAKER

No. Especially not her own life. Practically anyone else's. But not her own.

MR. WHITTAKER

What *do* you want for Jane?

MRS. WHITTAKER

I don't see why Jane can't fall in love with a plain Harvard Business School student, let's say. Someone who'll be steady and dependable.

And so it goes. The protagonist discusses a number of topics, but she inevitably leads the conversation back to her overriding concern. Mrs. Whittaker's desire to see her daughter do the right thing and marry wisely is always uppermost in the mind and conversation of the character.

In this one act, a comic effect is achieved by having Mrs. Whittaker insistently remind the audience what she wants. Once you have clearly established what a character wants, you can then write powerful and often hilarious scenes in which the audience, already knowing the character's point of view, is able to anticipate his reaction.

II. *Show your protagonist struggling to achieve what he wants.*

This principle is, of course, the basic writing advice to *show*, not tell, and it was a major concern for me when I was writing *The House Where I Was Born.*[2]

The plot: A young man, Leo, has returned from the Vietnam War, a

---

2. First produced by Playwrights Horizons in New York.

420

psychosomatic mute because of the atrocities he witnessed. He comes back to a crumbling old house in a decaying suburb, a home populated by a callous stepfather; a mother who survives on aphorisms and by bending reality to diminish her despair; a half-crazy aunt; and a grandfather who refuses to buckle under to the pressures from his family to sell the home.

I set out to dramatize Leo's painful battle to free himself of memories of the war and to begin a new life. However, each time I worked on the scene in the play when Leo first comes home, his dialogue seemed to trivialize his emotions.

Then it occurred to me that Leo should not speak at all during the first act; that his inability to speak would *show* an audience his suffering and pain far better than his words could.

At the end of the third act, when Leo regains some hope, some strength to go on, every speech I wrote for him also rang false. The problem, I eventually realized, was that as playwright, I was *telling* the audience that a change had taken place, instead of *showing* the change as it took place.

In the final draft, I solved this dramatic problem by having Leo, who had loved music all his life, sit down at the piano and begin playing and singing Christmas carols while his surprised and relieved family joined in.

First silence, then singing, served my play better than mere telling.

III. *Create honest, understandable, and striking obstacles against which your protagonist must struggle.*

Many plays fail because their characters' problems seem too easily solved. I wrestled with this issue when I was writing *Oh Promise Me,*[3] a play that takes place in a private boarding house for the elderly. The play's original title was *Mr. Farner Wants a Double Bed.* The plot involved the attempt of an elderly man and woman—an unmarried couple—to share a double bed in a rooming house run by a repressed and oppressive owner. I wanted to explore contemporary attitudes toward the elderly, particularly as they concerned sexuality.

The more I played with the idea, the more I repeatedly heard an inner voice saying, "Chances are the couple could find some place to

---

3. Winner of the Jane Chambers Memorial Playwriting Award.

live where nobody cared if they were married or not." This voice—like the audience watching a play without an honest, understandable, convincing obstacle for the protagonist—kept saying, "So what?"

The writer's response: "Suppose, instead of a man and a woman, the couple is two men." Here was a real obstacle: Two elderly, gay men, growing feeble, want to sleep together in a double bed under the roof of an unsympathetic and unyielding landlord.

Suddenly, the play was off and running.

IV. *In the final scene or scenes, make sure your protagonist achieves what he wants; comes to understand that there is something else he wants; or accepts (defiantly, humbly, etc.) that he cannot have what he wants.*

If we spend time in the theater watching a character battle for something, we want to know the outcome—whatever it may be.

In my psychological thriller *Trick or Treat*,[4] Kate, a writer in her forties, has been badly burned in a love affair and is unable to decide whether to accept or reject a new relationship. She is involved at present with Toby, a younger man, but—as the following dialogue reveals—she insists on keeping him at a cool distance.

KATE
That does it, Toby. We're getting out of this place.
TOBY
Okay. Tomorrow we'll check into the local Howard Johnson's.
KATE
I want to go home—to New York—to my own apartment.
TOBY
Okay. Okay. If you insist. Besides, Howard Johnson's is not to be entered into lightly.
KATE
Huh?
TOBY
It's an old college rule. You'd never shell out for a room at Howard Johnson's—unless you were *very* serious about the girl.
KATE
I'll remember that. The day I agree to check into a Howard Johnson's—you'll know I've made a serious commitment to our relationship.

In the course of the play, Kate faces a number of trials—including

---

4. First produced by the Main Street Theater, New York.

422

a threat to her life—as she tries to expose the fraudulent leader of a religious cult. Through these trials—with Toby by her side—Kate comes to realize that she's ready to forget the past and give herself over to a new relationship. This critical decision is humorously expressed in the last seconds of the play:

KATE

Do you love me, Toby?

TOBY

Yes, I do. I found that out tonight . . . when I thought I might be losing you forever. Do you love me?

KATE

Yes. And I can prove it.

TOBY

How?

KATE

Take me to Howard Johnson's—please! Take me to Howard Johnson's!

The curtain falls and the audience knows that the heroine has made an unequivocal decision.

V. *Make sure that the audience ultimately sympathizes with the protagonist's yearning to achieve his goal, however outlandish his behavior.*

This may be the most important of the five magic ingredients of conflict. It may also be the most elusive. To oversimplify, in a good play, the protagonist must be very likable and/or have a goal that is universal.

In the plays I've had produced, one character seems to win the sympathy of the audience hands down. In my romantic comedy *Funny Valentines,*[5] Andy Robbins, a writer of children's books, is that character. Andy is sloppy, disorganized, and easily distracted, and—this is his likable trait—he's painfully aware of his shortcomings and admits them openly. Here's Andy speaking for himself:

ANDY

Judging by my appearance, you might take me to be a complete physical and emotional wreck. Well, I can't deny it. And it's gotten worse—much worse—since Ellen left. You know that's true.

---

5. Published by Samuel French; winner of the Cummings/Taylor Playwriting Award; produced in Canada under the title *Drôles de Valentins.*

Andy is willing to admit his failings to old friends and strangers alike. Here he's talking to an attractive young woman he's just met.

ANDY
You don't have to be consoling just because I haven't finished a book lately. I won't burst into tears or create a scene. No. I lied. I might burst into tears—I'm warning you.
ZAN
I didn't mean to imply . . . *(She laughs.)*
ANDY
Why are you laughing?
ZAN
You stapled your shirt.
ANDY
What's so odd about that? Millions of derelicts do it every day.
ZAN
And your glasses are wired together with a pipe cleaner.
ANDY
I didn't think twine would be as attractive.

In addition to liking Andy, audiences seem to sympathize with his goal of wanting to grow up and get back together with his collaborator and ex-wife, Ellen.

Whether you're wondering where to find an idea for a one-act play or beginning to refine the rough draft of a new full-length work or starting rehearsals of one of your plays, take your cue from the five magic ingredients of conflict. Whatever your experience as a playwright and whatever your current project, understanding the nature of dramatic conflict and how to achieve it will prove invaluable at every point in the writing and staging process.

* * *

Five exercises for creating dramatic conflict

Try these exercises to develop your skill in handling conflict.

1. Choose five plays you like. Summarize each in one sentence, stating what the protagonist wants. For example, Hamlet wants to avenge his father's murder.
2. Write one page of dialogue in which character A asks character B to do something that character B doesn't want to do. Have character A make a request in three different ways, each showing a different emotion—guilt, enthusiasm, humility, anger.

424

3. Write a speech in which a character talks to another character and conveys what he wants without explicitly stating his goal.
4. Choose a famous play you enjoy. Rewrite the last page or two so that the outcome of the conflict for the protagonist is entirely different from the original.
5. Flip through today's newspaper until you find a story about a person—famous or unknown—who interests you. Then summarize the story in one sentence, stating what the person wants. For example: X wants to save an endangered species of bird. Next list the obstacles the person is facing in trying to get what he wants:
   • A developer wants to build a shopping mall where the remaining members of the endangered species live.
   • Pollution from a nearby factory is threatening the birds' food supply.

Finally, write several short scenes in which X (the protagonist) confronts the people (the antagonists) who represent the cause of each obstacle. (In this example, the antagonist would be the developer or the owner of the factory.) Decide which of the scenes you've written is the most dramatically satisfying. Identify the reasons you think it is the best scene.

POETRY

§84

Poets, Learn Your Trade

By Robert Mezey

I HAVE BEEN ASKED TO OFFER some useful advice to beginning writers and I shall address myself to young poets, since poetry is the art I know best. I confess that I feel a little uncomfortable in this role of wise old counselor, being neither particularly old nor particularly wise and, in fact, in want of advice myself. (What wouldn't I give for a conversation with Robert Frost or John Crowe Ransom or W. H. Auden. There are many things I should like to ask them about this beautiful and difficult art.) Also, I am all too aware that the precepts that immediately spring to mind are the ones that veteran writers always hand out to the young. Nevertheless I will mention a few of them; they are easily summarized, they are no less true for being clichés, and they bear repetition.

First of all, live. Experience, observe, reflect, remember—try to be one of those on whom nothing is lost (in Henry James' great phrase). It is not necessary that your experience be wide, only that it be deep. Think what Emily Dickinson managed to live without—sex, travel, drugs, a career, a lifestyle—and yet few Americans have ever lived as fully, as intensely as she. Live your life. One cannot write out of books.

Read, for after all, one does write out of books also, and poetry is made of poetry. Reading and writing are inseparable; if you are not a reader, you are not a writer. Read history, novels, science, whatever you like, and above all, poetry. As in life, so in reading: Deep is better than wide. And read the best—not your mostly dismal contemporaries, but what has lasted hundreds and thousands of years: Homer, Virgil, Dante, Shakespeare, the King James Bible. Read continually.

Revise what you have written, and then revise it again. You don't want to work all the life out of it, but precision and liveliness and an air of spontaneity are the fruit of long hours of writing and rewriting, of trial and error. First thought is *not* best thought, and poetry, unlike

429

jazz, is not improvisation. In fact, first thoughts tend to be banal, unfocused, conventional, not quite coherent. Most poems require a number of drafts—maybe twenty; maybe fifty. Don't be too easily satisfied.

Those are perhaps the three essential commandments. (If they are not easily obeyed, it may be that you are not destined to be a poet.) But I want to tell you something that nowadays not many others would tell you or even assent to. You must learn to write verse. Not "free" verse, but verse—numbers, measures—call it what you will. It is what poetry has always been written in until the last century or so, and indeed it is only over the last few decades that nonmetrical verse has become the norm (if something which, by definition, violates the norm can *be* a norm). Before you break the rules, you need to know the rules; before you seek novelty, you ought to demonstrate that you know the ancient craft. That is no more than simple honesty and humility. You cannot properly call yourself a poet otherwise. A poet who cannot compose in verse is like a painter who cannot draw or a scientist who does not grasp the scientific method. Besides, as you acquire facility, you will find that verse-making supports your sentences, generates ideas, leads you where you might not otherwise have gone; and you will find what many poets have long known, that free verse is not easier than metrical verse, but much more difficult, and very few can write it well. As André Gide said, art is born of constraint and dies of too much freedom.

How can you go about learning to write in meter? As poets have always learned, by reading good verse and trying to imitate its sounds. You may need to count on your fingers at first, to be sure that you have the permitted number of syllables and the accents in the right positions, but soon you will be able to play by ear. It is useful to have some theoretical understanding, but in the end, an iambic pentameter is a line that sounds like an iambic pentameter, and you must know it the way you know the tune of an old familiar song. Be careful where you look for instruction: Many teachers don't know much about the meters, and these days most poets don't either, and the books can be misleading or flat out wrong. George Stewart's book *The Technique of English Verse* (Holt, Rinehart & Winston) is good; so is James McAuley's *Versification* (Michigan State University Press), the shortest and maybe the best; so is Derek Attridge's *The Rhythms of English*

Poetry (Longman). (Remember that good prosodists, though they hear the verse much the same way, may use different terminology or different symbols of scansion.) Be sure you read good models; many contemporary poets who write in meter, or what they call meter, do it atrociously: It is obvious that they don't know how the game is played. You can't go wrong with Marlowe, Herbert, Jonson, Milton, Pope, Tennyson, or Frost, or a hundred others. If you want to read the best of your own times, look for Philip Larkin, Edgar Bowers, Donald Justice, Richard Wilbur, Anthony Hecht, the late distinguished American poet, Henri Coulette, and there are a few others.

All the good poets make up a great free university, which you can attend at any hour of the day or night, choosing whatever teacher you like. Whatever you do, read aloud, both the verse of your models and your own, and listen to it carefully. (It might help to listen to it on tape. It might help to listen to records or tapes of good poets who also read well: Frost, Justice, Larkin, Wilbur, Ransom.)

Once you get the tune fixed in your head, you will have it forever, and you will recognize it in all its many varied patterns. You should, at the very least, be able to write pentameters, tetrameters, and trimeters (the longer and shorter lines are more difficult), and in both strict iambic and loose; common measure and ballad meter; rhymed couplets, tercets, and quatrains; blank verse and passable sonnets. The better you can write in meter, the better you can hear the old verse, and, to some extent, vice versa. And it is essential that you hear the great English poems as they were meant to be heard and that you have some idea of what those poets were trying to do. Otherwise you will have a very imperfect understanding of the poetry of your own language, and that is a serious deficiency in a poet. (Not to say in any cultivated man or woman—after all, accentual-syllabic verse, its invention and development, is one of the glories of our civilization.)

Once you have achieved some mastery of your craft, you can have a go at free verse if you like. Having learnt something about making verse lines that are really lines, you are likelier to do better than if you had never written anything but free. And you may well discover that for all its charms, free verse cannot do nearly as much as metrical verse can, in expressing feeling, in clarifying thought, in varying tempo, in delineating nuances of tone or subtleties of meaning, in emphasizing, modulating, elevating, clinching both ideas and emotions, and above all, in bringing about that perhaps magical phenomenon that poetry alone is capable of: making us feel that the sounds of the words *are* what is being said, that the sounds somehow deepen, enlarge, enact, embody—in a sense, create—the reality behind them. As Henri Coulette once wrote, "Meter is thinking; it is the basis of intimacy between reader and writer."

These are some of the powers of meter and rhyme, and only the profoundest, sincerest, and most original poet can put them aside, and then only if he knows what he is putting aside. I am no Yeats, God knows, but I urge you, young poets, to do what he urged *his* young fellow poets to do: Learn your trade. Sing whatever is well made.

85

REACHING TOWARD FORM IN YOUR POETRY

BY GREG GLAZNER

ANY ASPIRING POET LOVES to read poems. It's safe to guess that if you are writing poetry, you have been keeping a mental list of other people's poems—your favorites—for a while now. My list began when I was ten years old. I was fascinated by several of Robert Frost's poems, thanks to a first-rate teacher. (Mrs. Grimes wasn't perfect; she also taught us a terribly sentimental poem, written by a WWII fighter pilot, which began "Oh, I have slipped the surly bonds of earth / And danced the skies on laughter-silvered wings." I still remember the whole poem verbatim.)

Having ignored poetry during my junior high and high school years, I encountered Frost again during my first year in college. "The woods are lovely, dark, and deep," Dr. Brunner half-chanted over the lectern, and my list of favorite poems began growing again—and changing. Over the next fifteen years, poems by Rilke, Stevens, Whitman, Yeats, Dickinson, Kinnell, Milton, Roethke, and many others surpassed Frost's on my list of favorites, but poetry remains as alive for me now (in different ways, of course) as it was when I was a fourth grader, discovering "Stopping by Woods on a Snowy Evening" for the first time.

The love of reading poems is the first drive you need to become a serious poet. Chances are, if you have read this far, you already possess it. The second drive, the desire to develop craft, is especially important in the beginning years. And the third, a fascination with the way form and style turn into content, implying a world, is especially important after some technical problems have been handled.

Even some of the greats have struggled with technique—and the struggle isn't limited to poets. Early on, Charlie Parker, arguably the greatest musician in the history of jazz, was known as the worst saxo-

433

phone player in Kansas City. Apparently, he was bad enough that after the word got out, he couldn't even get an audition. So for a period of two or three years, he practiced relentlessly with his friend Dizzy Gillespie, racing through scales, working up various classical pieces. He claims to have practiced eleven to fifteen hours a day. No wonder his mature solos would later sound so effortless, so full of vigor and surprise. His reservoir of technique freed him to focus almost all of his immense talent into creating an unprecedented kind of music. He didn't have to think about getting the notes right.

Maybe it's true that poets, like jazz musicians, want nothing more than to break into a spontaneous, intelligent music. If so, the most important lesson to learn at the outset, so that later on it can become as natural and as unconscious as breathing, is this: Almost all of a poem's power comes from what is suggested, not from what is stated outright. And of the many ways that poetry can suggest things, three seem to give beginning poets the most difficulty: voice, tone, and image.

When I use the word "voice," I mean the personality implied by the poems' diction and syntax. Maybe such a distinction already sounds arcane, but it isn't; we instinctively delight in voice in our everyday lives. Consider this fictitious personal example: Over the Christmas holidays, when the whole extended family convenes at my parents' house, somebody gives my mother a new puppy, a three-month-old Great Dane which promptly eats part of the couch. My grandfather happens onto the scene of the crime first, smiles, and says, "I reckon we're just about ready to get shed of a dog." My brother David comes in and says, "So, looks like Rover here jumped the gun on lunch." And my mother addresses the dog directly: "Oh, come on. You know better than that!"

The point is that the way people talk tells us much about their personalities. And the speaker of a poem, while not identical to the poet, must sound authentic in his or her speech patterns. So when a beginning poet brings into one of my workshops a poem which opens, "The moss-infested river flowing forth from the verdant mountains. . . . ," the voice problem jumps out immediately. For starters, the diction is generally pitched too high to be believable. But the overly formal speaker who calls the mountains "verdant" wouldn't use the adjective "moss-infested" in the same breath. So there is a problem with consistency as well. By dropping the diction level and getting the focus away from adjectives, the student writes, "Out of the green mountains, the river choked with moss . . ." and gains much credibility. The voice sounds intelligent, but not stilted.

Beginning poets aren't alone when they encounter substantial difficulties in early drafts of a poem. During the year it took me to write "From the Iron Chair," the nine-page title poem of my book, I filled over three hundred notebook pages with drafts, struggling much of the way. As I worked on the fourth section in particular, the problems in the early drafts all seemed to have to do with tone. By "tone," I mean, of course, the overall mood of a piece of writing.

The first few lines went well enough; only relatively minor changes were necessary. Here are those lines as they appear in the book:

> Down the well of old need,
> down the concrete steps,
> splintered rails, and leaf-rot
>
> of the half-demolished hotel,
> my cousin—one of the last illegal tenants—
> opened the door to his basement.
>
> Inside, there was vodka on his breath
> and a blue-gray static on the air.
> He adjusted a TV wired
>
> to the battery of a car
> and offered me a beer. All I did
> was lean back and take it to my bones,
>
> at twenty that first firing and eviction,
> this last inhabited room
> smelling of booze & glimmering
> like the interior of an age. . . .

Up to this point, the tone was nostalgic, tough, and visceral all at once. It seemed honest. But in what was to follow, the poem took a wrong turn. Here are the next few lines as they appeared in the first draft:

> The weight of twisted beams and bricks
> rose in the mind, at once
> imaginary and real, as if the future

435

had a demolished superstructure—
a brute, invisible weight
and the glut it took to forget it.

What happened to the power of the remembered experience? The tone
of "rose in the mind, at once / imaginary and real, as if the future /
had a demolished superstructure" is detached, cerebral, so that in context,
the lines seem forced and powerless. Here is the same passage rewritten for tone—for the *feel* I had unwittingly abandoned:

We stared into the tube
as if it were enough to change us,

even as the invisible brute weight
of bricks and twisted beams
crushed itself closer like the future.

Twice the ceiling groaned, and I leaned
closer to the sentimental violins.
For an hour my cousin stiffened with me. . . .

While tone and voice work to create the sense that a poem has come
from a believable, human origin, images bring the subject matter alive
through the senses. Imagery is absolutely central to the work of most
poets. Certainly, some great writers have been able to use abstract
statement powerfully in poetry; Wallace Stevens comes to mind as a
modernist who did so. But in most poems written by beginners, a
direct statement of feelings or ideas not embodied in imagery will ring
so false and flat that it will ruin the poem. William Carlos Williams'
directive, "No ideas but in things," seems tailor-made for aspiring
poets learning their craft. Keeping Williams in mind, a young poet
whose love poem contains the line "In your absence, I am sleepless
with longing," revises it to read, "You are gone, and the streetlight sets
off / its blue-white fires across the sheets." The revision gains its power
by appealing to the senses of sight and touch. The poem is an aesthetic
experience, not amateur philosophy and not diary entry. For most
poets, imagery is a crucial way of making a poem live. As the poet
Miller Williams once said, "Film it."

Imagery, tone, voice, and many other aspects of craft are addressed
in poetry workshops available in almost every corner of the country.
A writing workshop can be an excellent way for a poet to improve
rapidly, assuming that the teacher is both a good poet and a good

teacher—and that the student is motivated. But when, after years of hard work, a poet reaches the level of technical competency, writing as well as thousands of poets whose work fills hundreds of literary magazines in America, what next? What follows the long apprenticeship?

In short, transcending one's own self-imposed strictures. Doesn't the serious poet, having learned to write a modest kind of poem, try to live his way beyond it, reaching toward an understanding of the forms that experiences themselves assume? Think of Galway Kinnell's early poems, heavily influenced by the formalism of the 1950s (some of these are very fine, by the way), and his *The Book of Nightmares,* which moves through the most fundamental, archetypal experiences in jagged, free-verse lines, full of a dark, celebratory, American music. Think of Dickinson cloistered in her father's house, fusing the common measure of the church hymn with her intelligence and solitude, forging her small, powerful hymns to doubt. Think of Charlie Parker breathing out rush after rush of chromatic flourishes, sailing beyond the melody like someone discovering a new kind of grace for an age when all the moorings have come loose.

Young, anyone can set out "like something thrown from the furnace of a star," as Denis Johnson puts it. Poetry touches us easily then, as long as we have the good fortune—as I did in the fourth grade—of being exposed to it in an intelligent way. But for some of us, the experience has such power that we go on to become writers ourselves, governing our lives by the rich, unpredictable cadences of the human voice. In the end, we never know for sure whether we succeed in writing important poetry. But the process—reading, crafting, reaching toward form—is a way of aspiring toward meaning with one's whole being. Anything less is just fooling around with verse.

§86

THE SHAPE OF POETRY

BY PETER MEINKE

THERE'S BEEN A LOT OF INTEREST LATELY among young writers in the New Formalism, which is basically a good thing—writers should know what form has to offer, which forms their voice might be compatible with—just as painters and musicians benefit from working with a variety of materials and instruments.

But New Formalism is not an interesting subject, because it's irrelevant to the main question: Are the poems good or not? Writing a villanelle or a sonnet is neither a virtue nor a sin. The point is, does it work? Just as "free verse" often disguises laziness of thought and execution, "formal verse" often sugar-coats a bloodless triviality.

My theory is that every poem, formal or free, has an ideal shape, and the job of the poet is to find it. (I suppose this is partly what Gerard Manley Hopkins meant by his term "inscape"—the "pattern" of a poem.) There is no limit on these shapes but I believe some poems truly want to be free and all over the page, and some want to be haiku or sestinas. A poet, as he or she is working on the early drafts of a poem, has to recognize which way the poem is leaning (of course, to do that, you have to acquaint yourself with the possibilities—no one can write poetry who doesn't spend a lot of time reading it).

Here's the title poem of my book, *Liquid Paper:*

Liquid Paper

Smooth as a snail, this little parson
pardons our sins. Touch the brush tip
lightly and—abracadabra!—a clean slate.

We know those who blot their brains
by sniffing it, which shows
it erases more than ink
and with imagination anything
can be misapplied . . . In the Army,

our topsergeant drank aftershave, squeezing
my Old Spice to the last slow drop.

It worked like Liquid Paper in his head

until he'd glide across the streets of Heidelberg
hunting for the house in Boise, Idaho,
where he was born . . . If I were God
I'd authorize Celestial Liquid Paper
every seven years to whiten our mistakes:
we should be sorry and live with what we've done
but seven years is long enough and all of us

deserve a visit now and then
to the house where we were born
before everything got written so far wrong.

In the first few drafts of this poem, it was all in one stanza, a regular
(or irregular) free verse poem, about half again as long as the final
version. I think it's best to write uncritically for as long as you can,
until you come to a stopping point or run out of steam. When I had
done that, I began to think about what was the best structure for the
poem; it was clear that although the lines tended to be about the same
length, it wasn't going to be regularly rhymed or metered: no clusters of
rhymes or near-rhymes looking to get organized, no iambic pentameter
motor throbbing below the surface.

The next thing I noticed was that the line, "It worked like Liquid
Paper in his head," was more or less in the middle, so I isolated it. I
liked the idea of its being by itself (like Liquid Paper clearing a little
space). Dropping lines and phrases here and there, I shaped the poem
so the same number of lines preceded and followed that line.

Now I had a funny-shaped poem, with two stanzas of about a dozen
lines surrounding a skinny one-line stanza. It was a little hard to read,
to follow. I looked for the first natural break, which came after "a clean
slate" in the third line, so I made that a three-line stanza (that seemed
right: it *was* a clean slate). I then tried writing the poems with three
three-line stanzas surrounding the middle line. That wasn't bad, but
never quite worked just right. The poem didn't want to be in three-
line stanzas.

It took me a while to recognize that this was a poem with a religious
thrust. I had begun just by staring at this familiar little black and white
bottle and seeing what I could think about it, where it would lead me
(poems are seldom really about their ostensible subject, which is just

an excuse to enter the poet's mind). When I realized I had used the number "seven" twice, that led me to the symmetrical final shape of three/seven/one/seven/three—those numbers all having religious significance. The point about all this shifting around is to find the shape in which your poem most clearly and vividly expresses itself. Few readers will notice what you've done—just as no one can see the backbone that holds up your body—but it's extremely important that you've done it: It supports your poem.

One advantage of working in this way is that it's easier to know when you're finished. Although it may be true that poems are not so much finished as simply abandoned, there's a greater chance that the poem will feel finished when you put the last touches on a satisfactory shape. As I stared at "Liquid Paper" in its final stages, I could see that in the (now) second stanza there was a leap of imagination between "misapplied" and "In the Army"; and this was more or less balanced by a similar leap in the fourth stanza, between "born" and "If I were God." I wouldn't have noticed this if I hadn't already broken the poem down into these particular stanzas, but now that I did, I worked on creating a mirror image, dropping a few words, and adding the ellipses, making a sort of four/three: three/four split within the seven-line stanzas. So who cares? I care, the way a painter may stare with dissatisfaction at his painting, and then add a little touch of red to the bottom left hand corner and say, "That's it!" Though no one else will notice, the painter knows he has finished his painting.

I hope when you read "Liquid Paper" it seemed perfectly natural, as if this is just the way it popped out of my head. As Yeats wrote:

> A line will take us hours maybe;
> Yet if it does not seem a moment's thought,
> Our stitching and unstitching has been naught.

The sound of the poem is shaped, too, from the beginning alliterations to the combination at the end of "done," "long," "all," "then," "born," "wrong." Of course, some of these were present in the very first draft, but many were added, and—more importantly—much was jettisoned to outline the sound that I saw already imbedded there.

I hope also the poem sounds "true"—I think it's a true feeling. But some "facts"—as opposed to "truth"—had to be sacrificed for the shape of the sound. For example, my poor old sergeant really did drink my Old Spice, and that fit perfectly well because "Old Spice" goes nicely with "misapplied." But I was stationed in Schweinfurt, not Heidelberg—and I think the sergeant was from Orlando. Obviously, for all kinds of "sound" reasons, Heidelberg and Boise, Idaho, work a lot better here. "Until he'd glide across the streets of Schweinfurt" might have been "true," but the sound is so awkward it breaks up the thought.

Another, maybe simpler, example is the following poem:

Soldiers With Green Leggings
Villa Schifanoia, 1987

Father and daughter marched between
the erect cypresses, moss turning

the dark trunks green
on the north side

like soldiers with green leggings
and he wanted to say

Let us lay down our swords
(how pompous like a father!)

and she wanted to say
Let's open our doors

(how sentimental like a daughter!)
but the music in their heads

kept playing so they held
their chins high, stepping

together left right left right
smart as any parade and soon

the trees marched with them
ground rumbling like distant cannon

birds whirling like bewildered
messengers until a white flag

rose from the castle
and they fell to their knees

to sign the treaty:
any treaty—my treaty, your treaty.

This poem went through many "shapes" until I came up with those couplets, marching unpunctuated side by side down the page, mirroring the two people in the poem. An early draft began like this:

Father and daughter walked between the erect cypresses, moss turning the trunks green on the north side, like soldiers with green leggings. He wanted to say, Let us lay down our swords and she wanted to say, Let us open our doors . . .

Changing it into couplets focused the poem and led to the parenthetical additions, as well as other changes which were much clearer to see with the new structure (i.e., the military emphasis).

There will always be disagreement between those who favor "spontaneity" and little rewriting (Allen Ginsberg, for example), and those (like Yeats) who "labor to be beautiful." Nothing wrong with this. Every poem is a mixture of lines that have just been "given" to us— the inspiration—and those that we have worked on to fulfill the great promise of the original lines—the perspiration. Of course, we tend to be "given" more lines when we're well prepared. Ginsberg began by writing Blakean rhymed poems. As Alexander Pope wrote:

> True ease in writing comes from art, not chance,
> As those move easiest who have learned to dance.

If you are one of those writers whose lines (mostly) come out best on the first try—God bless. I'm jealous. And of course, this happens to everyone, even me, once in a while, like being dealt four aces. But as advice to writers, I'd be lying if I didn't say that I think ninety-nine percent of first drafts benefit from rewriting. Severe rewriting, serious shaping. An inspiration is not a poem, but if it's a real inspiration, with hard work and an eye to the shape it's struggling to be, it can become one.

442

87

YESTERDAY'S NOISE: THE POETRY OF CHILDHOOD MEMORY

BY LINDA PASTAN

How sweet the past is, no matter how wrong, or how sad.
How sweet is yesterday's noise.
　　　　　—Charles Wright, "The Southern Cross"

I WROTE AN ESSAY TEN YEARS AGO CALLED "Memory as Muse," and looking back at it today I am struck by the fact that in the poems I write about childhood now the mood has changed from one of a rather happy nostalgia ("Memory as Muse") to a more realistic, or at least a gloomier, assessment of my own childhood and how it affects me as a writer ("Yesterday's Noise"). Let me illustrate with a poem called "An Old Song," from my most recent book.

An Old Song*

How loyal our childhood demons are,
growing old with us in the same house
like servants who season the meat
with bitterness, like jailers
who rattle the keys
that lock us in or lock us out.

Though we go on with our lives,
though the years pile up
like snow against the door,
still our demons stare at us
from the depths of mirrors
or from the new faces across a table.

And no matter what voice they choose,
what language they speak,
the message is always the same.
They ask "Why can't you do
anything right?" They say
"We just don't love you anymore."

443

As A. S. Byatt said about herself in an interview: "I was no good at being a child." My mother told me that even as a baby I would lie screaming in the crib, clearly terrified of the dust motes that could be seen circling in the sun, as if they were a cloud of insects that were about to swarm and bite me. By the time I was five or six, I had a series of facial tics so virulent that I still can't do the mouth exercises my dentist recommends for fear I won't be able to stop doing them. I'm afraid they'll take hold like the compulsive habits of childhood that led my second-grade teacher to send me from the room until I could, as she put it, control my own face. There was the isolating year (sixth grade) of being the one child nobody would play with, the appointed victim, and there was the even more isolating year (fourth grade) of being, alas, one of the victimizers. There was my shadowy room at bedtime, at the end of a dark hallway, and, until some worried psychologist intervened, no night light allowed.

I thought about calling my last book *Only Child* because something about that condition seemed to define not only me, but possibly writers in general who sit at their desks, necessarily alone, for much of the time. In some ways, of course, it defines all of us, born alone, dying alone, alone in our skins no matter how close we seem to be to others. I tried to capture my particular loneliness as a child, my difficulty in making friends, my search for approval, in what I thought would be the title poem of that book:

Only Child*

Sister to no one,
I watched
the children next door
quarrel and make up
in a code
I never learned
to break.

Go Play!
my mother told me.
Play! said the aunts,
their heads all nodding
on their stems,
a family of rampant
flowers

444

and I a single shoot.
At night I dreamed
I was a twin
the way my two hands,
my eyes,
my feet were twinned.
I married young.

In the fractured light
of memory—that place
of blinding sun or shade,
I stand waiting
on the concrete stoop
for my own children
to find me.

At a reading I gave before a group of Maryland PEN women, someone who had clearly not read beyond the tables of contents of my
books introduced me as a writer of light verse. I remember thinking
in a panic that I hardly had a single light poem to read to those expectant faces, waiting to be amused. Did I have such an unhappy life,
then—wife, mother, grandmother, with woods to walk in, books to
read, good friends, even a supportive editor?

I am, in fact, a more or less happy adult, suffering, thank God, from
no more than the usual griefs age brings. But I think my poems are
colored not only by a possibly somber genetic temperament, but also
by my failure at childhood, even when I am not writing about childhood
per se. And more and more, as I grow older, those memories themselves insist upon inserting themselves into my work. Perhaps it is the
very way our childhoods change in what I called "the fractured light
of memory" that make them such an inexhaustible source of poetry.
For me, it is like the inexhaustible subject of the seasons that can be
seen in the changeable light of the sun, or the versatile light of the
imagination, as benign or malevolent or indifferent, depending upon a
particular poet's vision at a particular moment.

I want to reflect a little then on those poems we fish up from the
depths of our childhoods. And for any teachers reading this, I want to
suggest that assigning poems to student writers that grow out of their
childhoods can produce unusually good results, opening up those frozen ponds with what Kafka called the axe of poetry.

Baudelaire says that "genius is childhood recalled at will." I had a
19-year-old student once who was not a genius but who complained

that he couldn't write about anything except his childhood. Unfortunately, his memory was short, and as a result, all of his poems were set in junior high school. He had taken my course, he told me, in order to find new subjects. I admit that at first glance junior high doesn't seem the most fertile territory for poems to grow in. On the other hand, insecurity, awakening sexuality, fear of failure—many of the great subjects do exist there. It occurred to me that when I was 19, what I usually wrote about were old age and death. Only in my middle years did I start looking back into my own past for the subjects of poems. This started me wondering about the poetry of memory in general. Did other poets, unlike my young students, come to this subject relatively late, as I had? As I looked rather casually and unscientifically through the books on my shelves, it did seem to me that when poets in their twenties and thirties wrote about children, it was usually their own children that concerned them, but when they were in their late forties or fifties or sixties, the children they wrote about tended to be themselves.

Donald Justice, in an interview with *The Missouri Review,* gave as good an explanation of this as anyone. He said, "In the poems I have been thinking of and writing the last few years, I have grown aware that childhood is a subject somehow available to me all over again. The perspective of time and distance alter substance somewhat, and so it is possible to think freshly of things that were once familiar and ordinary, as if they had become strange again. I don't know whether this is true of everybody's experience, but at a certain point childhood seems mythical once more. It did to start with, and it does suddenly again."

There are, first of all, what I call "Poems of the Happy Childhood," Donald Justice's own poem "The Poet At Seven" among them. But for poets less skilled than Justice, there is a danger to such poems, for they can stray across the unmarked but mined border into sentimentality and become dishonest, wishful sort of recollections. When they are working well, however, these "Poems of the Happy Childhood" reflect the Wordsworthian idea that we are born "trailing clouds of glory" and that as we grow older we are progressively despiritualized. Even earlier than Wordsworth, in the mid-17th century, Henry Vaughan anticipated these ideas in his poem, "The Retreat."

I mention Wordsworth and Vaughan because in looking back over

446

the centuries at the work of earlier poets, I find more rarely than I expected poems that deal with childhood at all. Their poems are the exceptions, as are Shakespeare's 30th Sonnet and Tennyson's "Tears, Idle Tears." Perhaps it wasn't until Freud that people started to delve routinely into their own pasts. But nostalgia per se was not so rare, and in a book called *The Uses of Nostalgia: Studies in Pastoral Poetry,* the English critic Laurence Lerner comes up with an interesting theory. After examining pastoral poetry from classical antiquity on, he concludes that pastoral poems express the longing of the poets to return to a childhood arcadia, and that in fact what they longed to return to was childhood itself. He then takes his theory a step further and postulates that the reason poets longed for childhood is simply that they had lost it. He writes, "The list is varied of those who learned to sing of what they loved by losing it. . . . Is that what singing is? Is nostalgia the basis not only of pastoral but of other art too?" Or as Bob Hass puts it in his poem "Meditation at Lagunitas," "All the new thinking is about loss./ In this it resembles all the old thinking."

But though there are some left who think of childhood as a lost arcadia, for the most part Freud changed all of that.

We have in more recent times the idea of poetry as a revelation of the self to the self, or as Marge Perloff put it when describing the poems of Seamus Heaney, "Poetry as a dig."

The sort of poems this kind of digging often provides are almost the opposite of "Poems of the Happy Childhood," and they reflect a viewpoint that is closer to the childhood poems I seem to be writing lately. In fact, a poem like "Autobiographia Literaria" by Frank O'Hara actually consoles the adult by making him remember, albeit with irony in O'Hara's case, how much more unpleasant it was to be a child. If the poetry of memory can console, it can also expiate. In his well-known poem, "Those Winter Sundays," Robert Hayden not only recreates the past but reexamines his behavior there and finds it wanting. The poem itself becomes an apology for his behavior as a boy, and the act of writing becomes an act of repentance.

If you can't expiate the past, however, you can always revise it— and in various and occasionally unorthodox, ways. Donald Justice in the poem "Childhood" runs a list of footnotes opposite his poem, explaining and clarifying. Mark Strand in "The Untelling" reenters the childhood scene as an adult and warns the participants of what is to occur in the future.

Probably the most ambitious thing a poem of childhood memory can accomplish is the Proustian task of somehow freeing us from time itself. Proust is perfectly happy to use random, seemingly unimportant memory sensations as long as they have the power to transport him backwards. When he tastes his madeleine, moments of the past come rushing back, and he is transported to a plane of being on which a kind of immortality is granted. We can grasp for a moment what we can never normally get hold of—a bit of time in its pure state. It is not just that this somehow lasts forever, the way we hope the printed word will last, but that it can free us from the fear of death. To quote Proust: "A minute emancipated from the temporal order had recreated in us for its apprehension the man emancipated from the temporal order." Proust accomplished his journey to the past via the sense or taste, but any sense or combination of senses will do. In my poem "PM/AM," I used the sense of hearing in the first stanza and a combination of sight and touch in the second. Here is the second:

AM**

The child gets up
on the wrong side of the bed.
There are splinters
of cold light on the floor,
and when she frowns
the frown freezes on her face
as her mother has warned her it would.
When she puts her elbows roughly
on the table her father says:
you got up on the wrong side of the bed;
and there is suddenly
a cold river
of spilled milk.
These gestures are merely formal,
small stitches in the tapestry
of a childhood she will remember
as nearly happy. Outside
the snow begins again,
ordinary weather
blurring the landscape
between that time and this,
as she swings her cold legs
over the side of the bed.

448

But did I really say: "A childhood she will remember as nearly happy"? Whom are you to believe, the poet who wrote that poem years ago or the poet who wrote "An Old Song"? As you see, the past can be reinterpreted, the past can be revised, and the past can also be invented. Sometimes, in fact, one invents memories without even meaning to. In a poem of mine called "The One-Way Mirror Back," I acknowledge this by admitting: "What I remember hardly happened; what they say happened I hardly remember." Or as Bill Matthews put it in his poem "Our Strange and Lovable Weather"—

> . . . any place lies about its weather,
> just as we lie about our childhoods,
> and for the same reason: we can't
> say surely what we've undergone
> and need to know, and need to know.

This "need to know" runs very deep and is one of the things that fuels the poems we write about our childhoods.

But the simplest, the most basic thing such poems provide are the memories themselves, the memories for their own sakes. Here is the third stanza of Charles Simic's poem "Ballad": "Screendoor screeching in the wind/ Mother hobble-gobble baking apples/ Wooden spoons dancing, ah the idyllic life of wooden spoons/ I need a table to spread these memories on." The poem itself, then, can become such a table, a table to simply spread our memories on.

Looking back at some of my own memories, I sometimes think I was never a child at all, but a lonely woman camouflaged in a child's body. I am probably more childlike now. At least I hope so.

---

*"An Old Song" and "Only Child" appear in *Heroes In Disguise,* Norton, 1991.
**"AM" is from *PM/AM:New and Selected Poems,* Norton,1982.

88

WRITING FUNNY SERIOUS POEMS

BY HUNT HAWKINS

MUCH CONTEMPORARY POETRY IS HUMORLESS STUFF. Perhaps because we live in an "age of anxiety," as Auden put it, our poets are given to expressing alienation, anguish, angst. But it is well to remember that humor had an important place in past poetry, from the bawdiness of Chaucer, to the wit of the Metaphysical Poets, to the barbs of the eighteenth-century satirists. Maybe one way for poetry to increase its readership, recapturing the audience it once had, is again to find room for humor.

There is of course a tradition of "light" verse that continues to the present day. This verse is always formal (that is, it uses meter and rhyme), and its humor mostly derives from playing with form, as, for example, Ogden Nash does in his delightful couplets. I have nothing at all against light verse—may its tribe increase—but the humor I'm interested in derives more from the poem as a whole than any part of it, from the content as much as the form. It coexists and interacts with that angst mentioned earlier, recognizing as Mark Twain once said, "The secret source of humor itself is not joy but sorrow. There is no humor in heaven." Thus the humorous poems I try to write are not light but heavy; they are funny serious ones.

I've found two ways to go about such poems: a) hyperbolic imagining, and b) compressed narration.

Hyperbolic imagining can take the form of farfetched metaphors. For example, in "My Wife's Shoes" I compare her shoe rack to "a huge immigrant ship entering New York harbor,/the sturdy, honest couples lining the decks." I then extend this metaphor, trying to wring everything I can from it. The whole poem reads:

My Wife's Shoes*

Chasing my errant cat one sloppy afternoon,
I unexpectedly find myself crawling
into my wife's closet, all alien and pink.
Cat gone. Nightgowns tickling my neck.
I start to leave, then spot her aluminum shoerack
like a huge immigrant ship entering New York harbor,
the sturdy, honest couples lining the decks.
So many, so many! How will I ever clothe and feed them?
All my favorites are here: her saddle shoes from the eighth grade,
the blue sling-backs she wore on our first date in San Francisco,
the red pumps I removed the night of the big snow,
innocently to inquire which piggy had roast beef.
Ah, these shoes are as fertile as foreigners,
but they are so appallingly ignorant,
simple peasants come to the land of division of labor.
They have no skills. They will end up like Sacco and Vanzetti.
I think of my own closet.
Maybe the cat has gone there.
It is a humble closet, only three pairs of shoes,
but this pink closet is a tenement.
How will I ever satisfy my wife's lust for shoes?
They are not mere footcoverings.
They have a religious significance like Veronica's handkerchief,
promising relief from this tawdry life.
Where do they come from anyway?
Over the seas. I picture a crew of small men,
singing in Norwegian, wearing stocking caps.
They trudge over the tundra,
rounding up tiny herds of shoe-shaped animals.
Then they patiently shuck the skins.
It is very difficult for us to envision,
but that is the fault of the division of labor
which has kept us apart for so long.
As a poet, my job is to imagine things;
I am never supposed to touch leather.
The shoehunters may seem like foreigners,
but under the skin we are all really brothers and sisters.
This is proved by the exchange of commodities.
Hush, I think my wife is coming.
She mustn't find me like this in her closet.
Here is my poem. I think it is finished.
Quick! Give me your shoes!

Bizarre metaphors should serve some ultimate purpose. They should

---

*Published in *the minnesota review*.

not simply be figures of speech in which "the most heterogeneous ideas are yoked by violence together," as Dr. Johnson (rather unjustly) wrote of metaphysical wit. In "My Wife's Shoes," I play with the idea that the peasant immigrants are coming to a land of division of labor where people are pulled apart by their roles; only imagination can reunite cobblers and poets, husbands (who don't love shoes) and wives (who do). Since the original metaphor is farfetched, the tone throughout remains whimsical, but the topic is serious, being finally about human separation.

Rather than extending a single metaphor, one might string together a series of apparently unrelated ones. In the poem "Ears," I examine my infant daughter's ears and puzzle over their strange shape. I then compare them to spare buttons, anemone, the Roman Coliseum, Van Gogh's stationery, and God's signature. The poem reads:

Ears*

Once in Mankato, Minnesota, I saw men
piling their plates with mashed potatoes.
I was doing the same! Then I noticed their ears
matched their food perfectly.
Since then, I haven't taken ears seriously.
Just for hearing purposes, wouldn't
a pair of plain funnels have been better?
But these gnarled flesh-vegetables! Why?
I seize my infant daughter to study an ear.
The waxy ridges form two C's
overlapping at top but not at bottom
with a hyphen tucked inside.
Perhaps ears are really spare parts
for some convoluted internal organ
sewn on outside like extra buttons.
Or maybe they're a species of anemone
meant to remind us of our underwater origins.
They look something like the Roman Coliseum.
Peering in the folds, I search for
a tiny lion and some cowering Christians.
Or perhaps our ears are curled to suggest
we can only understand each other in twisty ways.
I recall Van Gogh used his as stationery.
Maybe ears are God's signature

---

*Published in *The Madison Review*.

452

scrawled on our heads illegibly
and twice for good measure.
Or it could be ears are a sign
of that inevitable crumpling
which awaits our entire unfortunate flesh.
I'm afraid I've gotten dizzy
thinking about this topic.
Wishing I had never visited Minnesota,
I clutch my daughter to my chest,
then kiss her strange little flaps.

A metaphor's success in any poem depends on its freshness and vividness, and in a series of metaphors, also on some underlying unity. Each image should contribute to a common goal or meaning. In this case, I am trying to make readers realize how odd and miraculous their ears are, and by extension, their whole bodies. The metaphors are all rather off-the-wall and waggish, but they have a common sober purpose: to carry tones of decay, madness, and divinity.

Another form of hyperbolic imagining involves fantastic speculation rather than metaphors. Such a device in a poem may still take the shape of a series or list. An example would be "The Prejohn," in which I am wondering about the function of the little room you pass through in most public buildings before you get to the bathroom. This room, which I believe has no name other than the one I made up, is clearly a waste, so I propose a number of possible uses here:

The Prejohn*

Last night at the movie theater,
going to relieve myself,
I kept thinking what a hard day
Adam must have had
when he was obliged to name all those animals:
kangaroo, porcupine, protozoa, drosophilia, and on and on.
That must be why so many things
remain unnamed;
for example, the little room you enter
before you get to the bathroom.
I paused there, puzzled, pondering—
and hoping no one would come in and get the wrong impression.
What's the purpose of this room? You say

---

*Published in *The Georgia Review.*

it's so outsiders of the different gender
don't catch any untoward sights,
but clearly we don't need a whole room for that—
just a crook or partition.
Why have prejohns
when we don't have precars or prekitchens?
I examined the room carefully.
It had bright lights, flowered wallpaper, white moldings.
I've had friends who lived in worse places than this!
And think of the thousands of prejohns across the country,
empty, going to waste.
We should at least put in shelves
and use them to store jams and jellies.
Or they could house refugees
from countries less fortunate and democratic than our own.
Or we could chain a prisoner in each one.
That way, not only would we relieve prison overcrowding,
but we'd provide a warning against crime
to every citizen going to take a whiz.
But something's wrong here.
It's the room itself we should get rid of.
We've all become Greta Garbos
in our quest for privacy.
We've become islands, not part of the main.
Why do we even need a bathroom
to go to the bathroom?
Shouldn't we be more like Adam's animals,
innocent and free, urinating in the wind,
defecating in the fields,
returning what we don't need
to great Nature from which it came?
O, yes, yes, shouldn't we be more like the French?

The speculations here are meant to be as drolly outlandish as the metaphors in the earlier poems, but they serve a similarly serious purpose: to make us question our exaggerated need for privacy, separation, aloneness.

A second way to write funny serious poems is through compressed narration. Although the epic has virtually died out as a poetic form, it is amazing how many contemporary poems are not simply lyrics but tellers of stories, albeit small ones. In my case, in order to achieve humor, I combine narration with hyperbolic imagining. An example would be "My Neighbor's Pants," in which I tell the (partially fabricated) story of how my divorced and fired former neighbor, who reminds me of my similarly failed father, stays several nights with us.

454

When he leaves, I become convinced he switched pants on me, taking my blue ones and leaving his behind.

After trying the pants on, I madly dash into the backyard, strip them off, and burn them (this is the made-up part). I notice that my other neighbor, the

> gray-haired Baptist lady,
> out raking her lawn,
> looks at me without much surprise.
> Maybe I own all the equipment of middle class life,
> but in her heart she always knew
> this is what poets were like.

In the end, I realize there was no switch, the pants I have burned were really mine, I've been the victim of my own obsessions. The hyperbolic mode of this narrative makes it funny, but the not-so-funny side of it is plain to see.

As a final example of compressed narration I'll offer my mostly autobiographical poem "Honeymoon." The difficulty in writing such poems is to figure out which information is essential and which extraneous, then to compress the story as much as possible. You also have to think up a beginning and end. As Ford Madox Ford once said, "Life does not narrate." Only art packages events into stories, giving them a start and finish. The two snipped-off places of the string have to serve a purpose just as much as any metaphors that may go into it.

In the case of "Honeymoon," I couldn't think of a conclusion, so I just kept writing for a couple of pages, then gave up, laying it aside for more than a year. Then one morning just after I woke up, the ending came out of the blue. Here's how the poem reads:

Honeymoon*

> When we pick up our marriage license,
> the Commonwealth of Pennsylvania, full of wisdom,
> gives us a plastic bag of promotional gifts
> deemed useful to wedded life:
> a roll of Tums, a bottle of Windex, two dozen aspirin.
> As we drive to the Delaware coast,
> my wife finds the true treasure

---

*Published in *The Georgia Review*.

nestled at the bottom of the bag,
a paperback picturing a dark-haired girl on a cliff,
her white dress blowing in the wind, *The Zephyrs of Love.*
For the next two days we hardly leave the room.
We don't even bother to dress.
Instead we take turns reading the book aloud.
It seems the poor English girl, Dominique,
was forced to marry a Greek shipping tycoon
with a scar across his face
because her father owed him lots of money.
She hated Petros with his arrogant ways
and ugly disfiguration
until one night he slipped into her room.
Slowly he ran his swarthy hand
under Dominique's satin nightgown.
When she woke to protest,
he shouted, "But you're my wife!"
As Dominique struggled futilely,
an animal passion seized her soul.
My wife and I stare at each other,
then at my scars:
the knee with the cartilage operation
and the finger I cut on a beer can.
We've taken years to decide to marry,
and we're still not completely sure.
How do Dominique and Petros do it?
They quickly resolve all their differences
as Petros forgives her father's debt
and reveals he received his scar
fighting the Nazis in the Resistance.
Our honeymoon is over.
I think my wife and I are ready
for the Windex, Tums, and aspirin,
knowing our lives will never shine
with the wonderful light of inevitability.
That's all right.
As we take a last walk down the beach,
I practice shouting, "But you're my wife!"

Perhaps I had trouble finishing the poem precisely because our lives
have no inevitability. We can never fully rid ourselves of doubts, second thoughts, irresolution. As you can see, the ending I finally thought
of was to have me practicing shouting Petros's line. The mockery here
is complex, aimed at both romance and me, at once humorous and sad.

I'm sure there are other ways than the ones I've given to generate
funny serious poems. I've never tried my hand, for example, at out-

right parody or satire. Probably I don't have the self-certainty for it. Each poet will have to find the mode and tone that suits him or her best. Still, I would recommend trying some form of humor as a way of opening up the possibilities of poetry and attracting new audiences. Both writing and reading poetry can be marvelous experiences.

§89

WRITING THE POETIC SEQUENCE

BY JEFFREY SKINNER

I'D LIKE TO URGE YOU TO A LITTLE GRAND AMBITION. I realize the oxymoronic character of that phrase, but the poetic sequence as practiced today often contains elements of both transcendence and homeliness, like much of our "postmodern" art, and life. So, please, bear with me.

If we grant that the Adam and Eve of American poetry, Walt Whitman and Emily Dickinson, invented the modern poetic sequence—long, lyrical poems in more or less free-standing sections, connected by tone, texture and theme (rather than by the narrative event and heroic characters of epic)—then it seems natural that every American poet since has at least attempted a long poem to contend with and extend the work of their progenitors.

T. S. Eliot's *The Wasteland,* Ezra Pound's *Cantos,* William Carlos Williams' *Paterson,* Hart Crane's *The Bridge* are some examples of modern poets that come most readily to mind. In the next generation, we might think of John Berryman's *Dream Songs,* Robert Lowell's sonnet sequences, Sylvia Plath's "final" poems. And, to name only a few contemporary examples: Louise Gluck's *Ararat,* Charles Wright's *China Trace,* and Sharon Olds' *The Father.*

This is a cursory list, though even within it one can find an astonishing range of concerns, diction, style, and strategy. I know it's intimidating to begin by mentioning such monuments as *The Wasteland,* but I give them as historical precedent only, not as competitive model. Remember—I said a *little* grand ambition. It is ambitious enough to attempt a sequence on one's own, without bringing Eliot, et al, along for the ride.

We are a diverse and fragmented society, and our poetry reflects this fact. Flexibility of mind and spirit are demanded of us. The juggling act our lives can so easily become is sometimes cause for anxiety, but the other side of this coin is great freedom. At no other moment in history have poets had the opportunity to mix so freely high and low culture, formal and free verse, and language that simultaneously encompasses the diction of the street, the home, the office, the academy and—well, any speech at all—even the jargon of meteorologists.

So—we are free to write a book of sestinas based on the characters in the old Perry Mason television show (*The Whole Truth,* by James Cummins), or a sonnet sequence on rock and roll icons (*Mystery Train,* by David Wojahn). Or we can use free verse and lean more on obsessive character or theme for structuring—as in Sharon Olds' searing vignettes of a father's death *(The Father),* or Charles Wright's book-length sequence of meditative lyrics on the meeting of Eastern and Western views of spiritual regeneration *(China Trace).* The possibilities are infinite. We need not begin with a grand, elevated idea.

How *do* we begin a poetic sequence? Often, the beginnings of a sequence have come for me when I have written a poem I felt did not say all I wanted to say on the subject. But at the same time, I knew that the poem as written was finished: It had a completeness that could not be expanded without distortion. The poem suggested an overarching idea or zone of concern that I wanted to explore from different angles. I sensed that if I continued to build on what the initial poem had established, the resulting group or sequence might acquire an added dimensionality, a depth of field, that the first poem alone did not possess. I felt the pull toward sculpture, if you will, as opposed to the flat canvas.

Here is a poem I wrote some years ago:

Prayer to Owl Hiding in Daylight

Zealot in the trees, hot tiny speck
glowing in the dark of God's endless palm,
forgive me my absences! The clinically depressed
tenements of Bridgeport
ejected me into this calm, and now
there is too much rain, the leaves are pleading,
the green runs. All day, invisibly, you take notes,
like a businessman writing a novel
on his time off, a pale blue spark
snapping between your ears.
When will you visit? We desire visitations
but lack discipline to call them

459

on, and only our best shoes are shining.
I want claw, want your gold
headlights, your roomy coat of feathers.
I want to sleep days and work nights,
praising silence in high branches.
I want the microtonics of steel
drained from my blood. Oh the eclipse
has come and gone: show yourself.
You'll find my true love and me dreaming
on each other's shoulders, as the baby
breathes out tiny flowers in her crib
and the war continues, silently, elsewhere.

I don't know where this poem came from. Or, to be more precise, I don't know where the first line came from—"Zealot in the trees, hot tiny speck." The words drifted into my mind like a song on the radio; I tuned in. I did not discover until later in the writing that the "Zealot" was an owl. When I did, the poem began to move much faster, and I completed the last third rapidly. Only after it was finished did I notice that the poem was a kind of address, or supplication to the owl. That realization gave me the title.

Now I had a poem that was recognizably mine in language and allusion (new baby, Bridgeport tenements, businessman writing a novel), but that also harked back to earlier periods and cultures, when poetry was taken seriously as ritualistic invocation, a concrete way of knitting together the human and natural worlds, often through the mediation of animals. The poem also seemed conscious of the distance between these two worlds; there was a kind of implied acknowledgment of poetry's functional loss, a sad irony that struck me as essentially contemporary in tone.

These contradictions seemed resonant, and I wanted to explore them further. I began writing other "prayers to animals," setting for myself certain "rules": Each poem must address an undomesticated animal (or insect); I must take the animals as they are, without wrenching them from their natural environment or giving them supernatural attributes; each poem must include my world *as it is,* without idealization; and I must ask something of each animal, something I truly desire. I allowed myself to vary the form of the poems: "Prayer to Sparrow in Two Seasons" was written in tercets, with an iambic pentameter base; "Prayer to Cottonmouth Blocking the Road to the Pond" seemed to require couplets; "Prayer to Wasp on the Eve of Its Execution," an extended block of varied two- and three-beat lines; and so forth.

I ended up with about fifteen poems in the sequence. It was exciting to follow the implications of an idea, and writing the poems was, as Frost says, "serious play." I did not think about the "great American poetic sequence." I just looked about me for animal subjects, and wrote the next poem.

And this is the attitude I'd suggest you take when writing a sequence: Let yourself be swept up in the idea, yes, but remember that the section or piece you are currently working on deserves your complete attention, and that, day by day, the whole will take care of itself. *Agi quod agis;* Do what you are doing . . .

I have also written a number of sonnet sequences, a formal challenge that comes down to us trailing a long history and its own set of rules. I don't know exactly why the sonnet remains of perennial interest to poets in succeeding generations, but since its invention and right into the present time, the form has drawn poets to test both its resources and its limits. It may be that the sonnet is, in its compactness, and in the buried logic of its movement, a more accurate analogue of human consciousness than anyone has guessed. The poet David St. John calls poems "maps of consciousness"; perhaps the sonnet is, simply, an ideal grid for the linguistic cartographer. . . .

Theory aside, it's clear to me after years of writing and teaching that the formal strictures of a sonnet or sonnet sequence release a paradoxical freedom in the poet. By concentrating on the "boundaries" of fourteen lines, rough iambic pentameter, and end-rhyme, my students find themselves saying surprising, insightful things they just would not have arrived at by writing "free verse." Such discoveries are compounded in the sonnet sequence, where at a certain point the form itself becomes second nature—no longer an impediment of any kind, but rather a powerful tool for unearthing the new.

I have two daughters, now eight and ten years old, but both toddlers when I wrote this poem:

> I wanted a boy, of course, wanted to create
> in my own image, ambitious little god that I am.
> But the long years spent chasing women immoderate-
> ly stacked karma: now I'm surrounded by them.
> Human flowers, your natural smell intoxicates

461

and the fine blond hair I smooth, reading books,
consoling a fall. My own boyhood aches
in me still, burnished wind of summer dusks
comes back: bike-riding through dinner, stickball,
mumbletypeg in the marvelous junkyard; running,
running the long dark length of Grandma's hall
to leap her scented quilt. . . . Oh I've lost nothing,
and need no small version of myself to keep
boy pleasures. A daughter takes a farther reach.

After reading this over, it occurred to me that it might be the beginning of something larger. It engaged many of the themes important to me at that point in my life: the relation of parenting to one's own childhood; the dangerous tendency to view children as extensions of the self; the eternally fascinating and difficult subject of gender difference; and the anxieties raised by simply bringing children into a complex world.

In addition, the poem gave a hint ("your natural smell intoxicates") of the stance succeeding poems might take: they could be written *to* my daughters. The address to a loved one is a time-honored strategy in sonnet sequences and, as is probably obvious by now, I am in favor of the use of traditional poetic form, as long as that form is refreshed and remade by living, contemporary language.

But at that point in their lives neither of my daughters could read; the younger one was not yet talking. How could I suspend my own disbelief in writing poems to people who could not possibly understand?

The solution came in the form of a title for the sequence: "Sonnets to My Daughters Twenty Years in the Future." The poems, or poem, as I now saw it, would be addressed to the women my daughters would become. I would write a "time capsule" poem. This freed me to speak of adult matters in adult terms, though I would still be writing to my flesh and blood. The prospect was, again, exciting, and I plunged in, writing sonnet after sonnet.

I varied the pattern, using both Shakespearean and Petrarchan models. I relied on an iambic pentameter "back beat," though there is much metrical variation in the finished sequence. I also took considerable liberties with end-rhyme exactness, using off, slant, and approximate rhymes whenever I thought it appropriate. My primary goal, while retaining the strong echo of the sonnet form in the reader's mind, was to stay as close to current American speech (as I hear and use it in conversation) as possible. Whatever interest the resulting sequence has, apart from subject matter, is due in large measure to the tension between traditional form and colloquial usage. Purists may object, but to me there is nothing more boring than the tick-tock of a sonnet written to metronomic perfection. *Make it new!* Pound says, and to do that, whether writing in form or free verse, poets must use the language of the time and place they have been given.

One of the advantages of attempting a sequence is that, whatever the eventual success or shortfall of the piece as a whole, one generally ends up with at least a few sections that are salvageable as poems in their own right. When I was writing the sonnets to my daughters, I made it my goal to write fifty of them. But when I reached somewhere around number forty, I felt the impulse fading; the sonnets were becoming mechanical, repetitive. I wrote to my old mentor and friend Philip Levine for advice. "Stop writing," he replied, "when you get tired of reading them." This seemed like excellent counsel; I closed up shop on the sequence and chose and arranged the twenty best sonnets to include in my second collection of poems.

Writing the poetic sequence allows us a kind of relaxed concentration. We escape the pressure of having to say all we know in a single section or poem. Each section opens the way, associatively, to others. The "grid" of a larger structure frees us from the invention of new form every time we set pen to paper. We have the spur of ambition, tempered by the necessity to attend to whatever specific piece of the whole is before us at the moment.

However you begin your sequence—whether with a line, or a poem in which you sense hidden seams of rich material, or the excitement of a formal pattern, or a subject—at some point you will have to decide whether the *idea* of the sequence is important enough to engage you, deeply, on many levels. The writing of a poetic sequence is the construction of a small world, and the heady intensity of that work can be its own reward. Go ahead—try a little grand ambition. You have nothing to lose, and much of delight and discovery to gain.

❧90

WRITING POETRY FOR CHILDREN AND YOUNG ADULTS

BY PAT LOWERY COLLINS

FOR YOUNG CHILDREN, A POEM IS A DEEPLY SATISFYING way of looking at the world. Fascinated at first by rhyme for its own sake, they soon begin to appreciate poetry that deals with simple concepts. They love slapstick, the wildly impossible, the ridiculous, word play, fanciful questions, clever and unexpected conclusions, twists and turns. They dote on repetition, used to great effect in *A Fine Fat Pig,* by Mary Anne Hoberman, in which the word abracadabra, used as an exclamation, precedes each line describing a zebra.

They revel in the action rhymes, finger play, and later, jump rope games, that depend on onomatopoeia, hyperbole and alliteration, as well as in such farcical verse as *Merry Merry FIBruary,* by Doris Orgel. Using these last two devices and the fun of a deliberate fib, the claim is made that "On the first of FIBruary/Setting out from Hackensack/ My Aunt Selma, in a seashell/ Sailed to Samarkand and back."

Poetry books for this age group are heavily illustrated, not only to complement the words, but also sometimes to explain them. And since poets are usually very visual writers, they will often provide the artist with exciting possibilities for illustrations without really trying.

The combined *Hector Protector* and *As I Went Over the Water* by Maurice Sendak is an unusual case in which poems and illustrations are all of one piece. Words emphasizing the text pepper the illustrations, and much of the action is in the pictures instead of the words. But in most cases, poems, even for the very young, rhymed or unrhymed, should be able to stand on their own.

Sometimes a single poem is used as the entire text for a picture book, illustrated so as to enhance or help to develop a concept or story. The text of my nonfiction book, *I Am an Artist,* is actually one long poem conveying the concept, through the finely detailed paintings

464

of Robin Brickman, that art is a process which begins with our experiences in the natural world.

It's been my observation that children in the middle grades (ages 9–12) are no longer as fascinated by rhyme. To some degree they want a poem to be as profound as what they are experiencing in life, something that takes them seriously. Yet, they still look for poetry that is simple and unlabored. *Haiku,* three unrhymed lines (in Japanese they must consist of 17 syllables) offering an unusual perspective on a spark of reality, is a perfect vehicle. Writing in this form is not as easy as it sounds. To provide an example, I struggled to produce: "Evening/is quietly stitching/the seam of night."

Children of this age are intrigued by the subtlety of haiku, and its shortness is irresistible to those just learning to put their own thoughts on paper.

But humorous, silly verse, either in such traditional forms as the limerick or in new and inventive ways, still holds great appeal. Thus the information that "Oysters/are creatures/without/any features," provided by John Ciardi in *Zoo Doings,* may be better remembered than the multiplication tables.

It is also a good time for books such as *Alice Yazzie's Year,* by Ramona Maher, in which unrhymed poems, each one complete in itself, taken together tell a story of a year in the life of a Navajo girl, a year that holds such mysteries as the birth of a lamb. We are told that "The new lamb sucks/The pinyon burns low/The lamb goes to sleep/His nose is a black star."

Poems about parents quarrelling or grandparents dying are often interspersed with poetry in a lighter vein in collections for this age group. One that does this effectively is *Knock at A Star,* collected by X. J. Kennedy and Dorothy M. Kennedy.

Language for its own sake becomes the focus again for readers about eleven to twelve, when communication with peers, intrigue, and secrets are important. Poetry is then a vehicle to express feelings without exposing them. Tools for this are found in nonsense sounds, obscure meanings, double meanings, rhyme, and, of course, humor. The mystery of nonsense—even an entire made-up language—seems to hold the same allure as it had for the four-year-old. Young readers are all too willing to accept the special logic of Lewis Carroll's "Jabberwocky" and will have no trouble figuring out that when the Jabberwock "came

465

whiffling through the tulgey wood/And burgled as it came," the "beam-ish boy" slays him as his "vorpal blade went snicker-snack!"

But these same children are also looking for poets able to look at life in the ways that they do. The poetry of Walter de la Mare has a timeless appeal because he affirms feelings that are universal. His book *Peacock Pie* was first published in 1913 and has been in print ever since. I'm currently illustrating a collection for Atheneum called *Sports, Power and Dreams of Glory, Poems Starring Girls,* edited by Isabel Joshlin Glaser, that affirms the dreams and aspirations of young women in such poems as "Abigail," by Kaye Starbird*, which ends by saying, "And while her mother said, 'Fix your looks,'/ Her father added, 'Or else write books.'/ And Abigail asked, 'Is that a dare?' And wrote a book that would curl your hair."

Teenagers may establish a passionate identification with one particular poet as they look for role models, a sense of history, a way to understand the world as it changes in and around them. By this time, they have probably been made aware of the mechanics and craft of poetry and are intrigued by experimentation. They can appreciate any poet whose vision is not too obscure. Because of the need of adolescents to deal with strong feelings and disturbing issues such as death and suicide, they are often attracted to poets with dysfunctional lives, for example, Sylvia Plath and Anne Sexton.

Most poetry for this age group appears in anthologies related to a single theme, to a city or to some historical period.

My own feeling is that even though the poetry you are compelled to write may turn out to have a special appeal for this age group, you will be competing with Shakespeare, T. S. Eliot, Walt Whitman, Emily Dickinson, and a cast of thousands. Of course, there is a lot of wonderful poetry out there for young children too, but not enough of it. And here I think the masters of today are a good match for those of yesterday and have an edge because they speak to the familiar.

But knowing your audience is only a beginning. There are a number of other things you should bear in mind in writing poetry for young people.

Don't fall victim to the mistaken notion that writing poetry for chil-

---

*Excerpted from "Abigail," in *The Pheasant on Route Seven,* by Kaye Starbird. Copyright ©1968 by Kaye Starbird. Reprinted by permission of Marian Reiner for the author.

dren of any age is easier than writing for adults. Your perspectives and topics may be different, but the skills you must bring to task are the same, skills honed through years of reading good poetry and working to develop your craft. Your most important assets will be a good memory and a strong awareness of the child within you.

It is a common misconception that almost anyone can write poetry for children. It's true we can get away with serving them peanut butter sandwiches for dinner, but it better be creamy peanut butter or the kind with just the right amount of nuts. Just so, the quality of poetry we give our children should be the best available, from the very beginning of their awareness of language.

Another misconception is that almost any idea for a children's book should be written in rhymed verse. Quite the opposite is true. Although there are exceptions, even reasonably good verse will not necessarily make for a more compelling text, and bad verse can, in fact, be deadly. So many "first" manuscripts in verse are submitted to editors that there is almost a universal resistance to them. Here I must admit to being an offender myself with my first book for children, *My Friend Andrew*. Looking back, I realize that any advantage I may have had was somehow knowing enough to keep it simple.

Things I personally object to, not under the control of the poet, are anthologies that include bad poems simply because they're by "good" poets, and minor poems by major poets because they're short; uneven collections by one poet or many; and anthologists who completely overlook contemporary poems and poets. The inability of some editors to recognize good poetry or to appreciate a child's ability to understand abstract concepts is a real problem.

Besides being as meticulous when writing poetry for children as you would be in writing for adults, you should, under penalty of a one-way trip down the rabbit hole, avoid all of the following:

• Poetry that talks down to the reader or is used as a vehicle to deliver a moral or message, unless it is written with good humor, as when Shel Silverstein, in his *Where the Sidewalk Ends,* admonishes readers to "Listen to the Mustn'ts."

• Near rhymes. They stop children in their tracks and detract from the flow of the poem. An example would be "lion's" rhymed with "defiance" and "cat" with "hate" in the poem "My Old Cat," by Hal Summers. *(Knock at A Star)*

• Rhymes that are too cute, convenient, or overused. "Rain" rhymed with "Spain" comes to mind.

• Lazy images. Even well-known poets sometimes do this, settling for the most obvious image, metaphor, or simile as in "wide as the sky."

• Rhyme for rhyme's sake, not because it will assist in saying what you want to say in the most interesting way. If, as with the book, *Madeline,* by Ludwig Bemelmans, it would be hard to imagine your own story being told in any other way, then, by all means, go for it. (I felt this way about *Andrew.*)

• Subject matter inappropriate for the intended age group, sometimes directed more to the parent than the child, or dealing with subjects outside the child's experience.

• Distorted rhyme that's hard to read aloud. Always read your own work aloud to avoid this.

• Poetry that is florid and old-fashioned, written in the accepted style of an earlier period.

• Poetry that is too complex or obscure. Young readers won't want to struggle to understand what may be very personal imagery.

• Writing presented in the form of a poem that isn't poetry by any stretch of the imagination and isn't even good prose.

• Writers who believe they must write like another poet in order to be published.

There was only one Dr. Seuss. If he had insisted on being another Edward Lear, we would have missed his unique vision and voice. If you aren't sure enough of your own voice, keep studying the work of poets you admire—their pace, rhyme schemes and structure—and keep writing until you find how to say what you want to in ways uniquely yours.

Like Valerie Worth, in her *All the Small Poems,* you may have wonderful, quiet perceptions to express about everyday objects and happenings. Borrow her microscope if you must, but wear your prescription lenses and present the world through your observations and special talents, having in mind that building a poem is much like building a block tower: You will be balancing one word or line against another; arranging and rearranging; dropping one word, adding another, until the poem begins to say what you had in mind all along or what may never before have occurred to you. When a poem really comes together, really "happens," it is a moment like no other. You will feel like the child whose tower at long last has reached the sky.

Today, the market for children's poetry is quite different from what it was in the inhospitable 1980s. Then, there were a few poets who had cracked the barrier somewhat earlier and continued to be published, but a limited number of new names came on the scene. Thanks to the firmer financial footing of most book departments for young readers, to some editors who realize that poetry rounds out a list, and to the demand by teachers and librarians, there is currently greater opportunity for new poets. A number of publishing houses are actively seeking poetry for children, but they are highly selective and still apt to overlook a talented newcomer in favor of a poet more likely to turn a profit.

But the field of poetry has never been considered a lucrative one. There are exceptions, as with any art form, and for some poets, who continue to put their words down on paper napkins and laundry lists, there is really no escape.

§91

WRITING HUMOR AND LIGHT VERSE THAT SELLS

BY ROSEMARIE WILLIAMSON

THERE'S A VERITABLE TREASURE-TROVE of raw material for humorous writing in the world around us; it's just waiting to be garnered, for both pleasure and profit. What subjects lend themselves to this light treatment? Any and all—limited only by our imagination and resourcefulness. When attempting to write light verse and short humor (such as anecdotes and one-liners), it is advisable, at least initially, to draw on situations and observations from your own experience. This gives each concept a basic authenticity, which then may be exaggerated or otherwise altered to suit your particular need.

Consider the home and family, the classroom or work place, as well as social gatherings with friends or neighbors. Familiar premises make promising beginnings. A thoughtful examination of these areas of our lives may conjure up not only some truly amusing incidents and remarks, but also a few not-so-amusing-at-the-time events that seem comical when viewed in perspective. For writers of humor, cloudy moments do have silver linings.

There's often a great deal "going on" in a mere handful of lines. For example, an old saying, a homeowner's chores, and seasonal and neighborhood annoyances all combined to provide the punch in the following verse of mine, which appeared in *Good Housekeeping:*

Ill Wind

With rake in hand I contemplate
The worst of Fall's pet peeves:
We shrewdly planted evergreens—
But get our neighbor's leaves!

470

Another variation of mine on the popular "harried householder" theme was also accepted by *Good Housekeeping:*

A Seedy Story

To concede our neighbor's grass is greener
Drives me nearly wacky—
Despite seeding, feeding, weeding, pleading,
Ours resembles khaki!

A sports fan I'm not. Many of my friends and relatives are, however, which means that over the years I've sat through endless radio and television sportscasts. Adopting the "if you can't beat 'em, join 'em" approach, I decided to immortalize these moments in verse. I wanted to demonstrate that it *is* possible to write marketable humor without an in-depth understanding of a subject. Some peripheral knowledge is necessary, of course, and a few well-paced "buzz words" are definitely a plus. Revenge, if not sweet, has at least been profitable.

From *Golf Journal:*

Pa for the Course

You toted golf clubs all day long.
I find this conduct rash;
Before you left you hadn't strength
To carry out the trash.

From *The American Legion Magazine:*

Saturday's Child

Every fall the same old image—
Pretzels, beer and line of scrimmage!

Selecting a topic for humor may seem like a formidable task for the beginner. It's important to remember, therefore, that few things are *inherently* funny; it's *how you deal* with your chosen theme that indicates professionalism—or lack of it.

The subjects of my published humor have ranged from "ants" to "zebras." The ant enjoyed its "15 minutes of fame" several years ago when *The Carpenter* magazine accepted my "Insecurity Blanket":

471

q: What "bugs" builders at picnics?
a: Carpenter ants.

When the lightning bug demanded equal time, I sold the following to *The Saturday Evening Post:*

A Fiery Courtship

The lightning bug
Luminesces
Till his lady love
Acquiesces.

What's funny about getting married? A traditional wedding has its serious moments, of course, but though emotions run high in prenuptial preparations, there are frequently lighter moments. Minor mishaps occur, which act as tension-breakers and are recalled with laughter at a later date.

At the wedding of my oldest daughter an incongruous thought suddenly popped into my carefully coiffed head. The idea soon took shape as a four-line verse, which was later sent off to the editors at *Good Housekeeping,* and ran on their "Light Housekeeping" page:

A Dress Unknown

Apart from other blessings
That a formal wedding means
Is the chance to see your daughter
In something else but jeans.

Using word play and familiar sayings catches the festive aspect of weddings in general. Intertwined with this lightheartedness, however, are threads of reality: a mother's reluctant acceptance of the "sloppy" clothing favored by today's young people, and wistfulness at "losing" a daughter. Readers can easily relate to these themes.

While firsthand experiences are a logical starting point for writing humor, they're not the *only* situations you can describe with credibility. The experiences of friends and relatives, hand-me-down stories and jokes from acquaintances, and overheard snippets of the conversations of strangers contain slips-of-the-tongue or other language lapses that provide rich sources of material for the alert humorist. It's important

472

to train yourself to be observant and aware of your surroundings. With practice, it becomes a reflexive process and triggers items for humorous verse.

Though I'm not a pet owner, some of my friends are, so I've had several hands-on (or perhaps I should say "paws-on") encounters with cats and dogs. An offbeat thought I once had about cats resulted in the following poem, which I sold to *Cats* magazine:

Once Over Lightly

Black cats that cross your path
Can bring bad luck, they say;
But what if those that cross
Are only charcoal gray?

Here's a personal favorite, which appeared on the "Post Scripts" page of *The Saturday Evening Post:*

Dog Days

School is out, the weather's nippy—
They forecast snow; the kids yell "Yippee!"
And greet the flakes with eager glance,
But Fido views the scene askance—
"Although for kids it has its assets,
It's enough to *bury* us poor bassets!"

Seasonal humor is always in demand. For national magazines, it should be submitted four to six months in advance of publication. Seasonal and other "occasional" verse present a dichotomy. It's both easier and harder to write seasonal and occasional verse than the generic, "no-frills" variety, because there are specific guidelines; the subject (and frequently the predicate—e.g., "I love you, Valentine") is spelled out for you. The difficulty lies in coming up with a fresh approach to a familiar theme. It's also well to keep in mind that family magazines don't want to diverge *too* much in parodies of such old-time favorites as the Easter Bunny, jack-o'-lanterns, and Jolly Old Saint Nick. Holiday images are, after all, "comfort" symbols, and best not tampered with to any great extent.

Since magazine editors sift through mounds of material each holiday season, the canny humor writer uses eye-catching titles and clever turns of phrase. In its quest for humor with a slightly different twist, *Good Housekeeping* bought two of my poems for its holiday pages:

Cookie Crisis

My Christmas cookies baked too long,
They're much too burned to keep;
The twinkle's gone from every star,
And the lambs are poor black sheep!

Halloween Costume Contest

Clothes today are so bizarre—
And that's the reason why,
The kid who walked off with first prize
Had on a SUIT and TIE!

New York Magazine has a popular "Competition" section, a showcase of original humor—including puns, parodies, put-downs, limericks, and lyrics. Not long ago, competitors were invited to select and redefine, humorously, any bona fide English word beginning with the letter "J." After some "J"-walking through the dictionary, I zeroed in on the word "jipijapa," which is defined as a palmlike plant.

The word, of Spanish origin, is pronouced (approximately) "heepy hoppa." A natural, I thought, for the name of the South American Easter Bunny—which became my entry; it won first prize—not in pesos, but a two-year subscription to *New York Magazine*.

The realm of education may not readily come to mind as a subject of humor, although some long-time teachers might be willing to debate this point. I have occasionally come across "educational" tidbits in various news magazines that struck me as "mirth-worthy," and it didn't require a great deal of imagination to turn this "found humor" into salable material. *The American Legion Magazine* accepted the following:

Sometimes you have to wonder about
progress. Take education, for example.
We've gone from "little red school-
houses" to "little-read school books."

474

Live and Learn

We called them "toys,"
As girls and boys,
And they usually sold for low prices.
Now, costly games
Have brand-new names:
"Educational enhancement devices."

And *Good Housekeeping* found this to its liking:

Disturbing Thought

According to a recent news item,
chimpanzees are being taught to read
and write. Terrific . . . and our son
is failing math!

Glancing over my rather extensive house plant collection one day, I asked myself, "Other than their names, what's so funny about a fiddleleaf fern and a ponytail palm?" I proceeded mentally down the "primrose path" of horticultural humor until I felt I had a couple of marketable items. *McCall's* bought the first:

Sun-Room Scenario

They'd catch me talking to myself,
And look at me askance,
But at last I have a fine excuse—
I'm speaking to my plants.

Good Housekeeping selected the following:

Quandary

Live plants wilt and silk ones fade,
I know I cannot trust them.
So the question is, do I prefer
To water them . . . or dust them!

Light verse and short humor can come in a variety of guises and be written on virtually any imaginable subject. The humor itself may be tinged with sarcasm, love, envy, admiration, guilt, etc.—the whole emotional gamut. If there's a single key to successful light verse writing, it's "believability." Readers must be able to identify with the situation in order to be amused by it—even if it's outside their immediate sphere of experience.

They must sense the "logic," however convoluted, that spawned the idea, and feel that it *could* have happened to them. Problems of being overweight or overworked, as well as those of having too little time or money, are universal, and will probably continue to be in perpetuity. For the humor writer—of necessity and inclination an observer of the human condition—these plights can provide a perennial sourse of subjects and ideas.

JUVENILE AND YOUNG ADULT

❧92

NEWS THAT'S FIT FOR FICTION

BY EVE BUNTING

RECENTLY, A PROMOTIONAL POSTER for several of my books, designed to look like the front page of a newspaper, carried this headline:

EXTRA, EXTRA, READ ALL ABOUT IT!
ALL THE FICTION THAT'S FIT TO PRINT

The format was no accident. The editors had already commented on how often the stories I write come straight from newspaper head-lines. . . . well, not straight exactly, but by a fairly direct route. My theory, unconsciously known to me but never actually stated, is that if a story is dramatic enough, heartbreaking, poignant, or funny enough to be considered by newspaper editors and published for millions of people to read, it's a good story.

In my case, I read the newspapers that come to our home rather superficially. But when an article or essay catches my attention, it gets my full attention. Never have I said at this point, "I will write a book about this." What I have said is "Wow! What an interesting story." Sometimes I clip the piece, sometimes I don't. When I don't I'm often sorry and find myself, days or weeks later, trying to track it down on microfilm in my library, unsure of the date when I read it, unsure *where* I read it. I'm tracking down the story because I can't forget it. And that is the key. If I can't forget it, that story has touched me in some deep, heartfelt way. At that point I say: "I want to write about it."

Before I begin, though, there are four questions to consider—the first I've already answered:

(1) Does the story deeply affect me?

(2) Will it also affect young readers, or does it simply touch on my personal interests and concerns?

(3) Can I write it so I have a young person as the protagonist, or is it altogether too adult?

(4) Can I see in this an underlying truth that will unfold as the story unfolds? If not it has only surface value and I don't want to do it.

If all of these questions can be answered in the affirmative I am ready to go on to the "thinking through" process, which to my mind is the most valuable time I spend on any book. I will not know it all when I start. That "miserable middle" will still be shadowy. But I will have a strong skeleton, and the theme or unstated message will be fixed in my mind along with a forceful and unflinching ending that I can work toward.

I was sitting one morning at my breakfast table reading my paper. There was a brief paragraph about two young boys who had been walking home from a party the night before. They walked single file along a road where there was no sidewalk. A car came behind them, on the wrong side of the highway, driving at high speed. It hit and killed one boy. The other jumped to safety. "That was the all of it," as we say in Ireland.

But not for me.

The story took hold of my mind and my heart. I imagined the scene . . . the dark road, the shriek of brakes, the car driving on, the boy who had jumped walking unsteadily to where his friend lay motionless on the road, calling his name, knowing he was dead.

I asked myself the four salient questions and was able to answer "yes" to all of them. When I'd thought it through, I had the outline of a plot that told of a quest to find the driver of the killing car, a story of guilt, of revenge, and the maturing of a boy who realizes that things and people are not always what they seem and that revenge can never truly erase sorrow.

Here is the opening paragraph of *A Sudden Silence,* the scene that I visualized so clearly when I first read that sad article in my morning paper.

It was Saturday the 20th of June at 11:30 pm when my brother, Bry, was killed. I'll never forget that date, not if I live to be an old, old man. Coast Highway, shadowed between its tall pole lights, the car suddenly behind Bry and me as we walked single file in the thick grass at the highway's edge. The glare of its white beams; the roar as it passed me where I'd dived sideways, belly down; the thud as it hit him. I'll never forget it.

Naturally, I did not use the boys' real names or the real setting. But

480

the story began with a real happening in the way that so many of my stories do.

One Sunday, I opened the "View" section of my *Los Angeles Times* and saw a group of bizarre pictures. Life-sized wooden dolls, wide-eyed, staring, stood in the front yard of a small, wooden house. There was a photograph of an elderly couple and a close-up of one of the dolls. The accompanying story told of how the couple had always wanted children but had not been able to have them. The husband, a wood carver, made these dolls for his wife, and they became her children. She found or made clothes for them, she gave them names and talked to them. They "talked" back. I stared at the doll. He stared at me. I was mesmerized, hooked. One of the dolls was on view in an art gallery on La Cienega Boulevard in Los Angeles. I visited it. Oh my! The hook was definitely in place.

Could I give these elderly people a real child who would tell my story? Of course. He could be a nephew who is orphaned and comes to live with his mysterious relatives and their even more mysterious children. I called him Matt and gave him a little sister, someone to protect from ghostly or insane happenings. Would young readers be as entranced by the spookiness of this kind of story as I? I'd bet on it. And what would Matt learn? I saw that clearly from the beginning. Aunt Gerda, who is at first to be feared because she is "not like anyone else," is found to be kind, loving and compassionate to the two orphaned children. Is love stronger than fear? In my stories, yes. In life, too.

"Are the ghost children really real?" children ask in their letters.

"If you think they are," I answer.

It's impossible to give a definitive yes or no. Because the author isn't too sure herself, and it's that kind of uncertainty that makes writing fun! And writing *The Ghost Children* was definitely fun.

Sharing Susan was probably taken more directly from a newspaper article than any other book I wrote. Who didn't read about the little girl, accidentally changed with another baby at birth, everyone unsuspecting until one of the girls died. Then the wrenching, heartbreaking complications arose. Should a child be taken from the only parents she has known for thirteen years and sent to strangers who will be her mother and father from now on? The dramatic, misery-making possibilities tore at my imagination.

481

The writing of *Sharing Susan* presented difficulties. When I write, I usually try to "get rid of the parents" early in the story. That way I am not tempted to have a passive character as my protagonist. I can create one who is independent, who makes decisions on her own, and who can solve her problems without adult help. (Other than her early training, of course, which taught her to be courageous, honest, self-reliant and to ask for help only when it involves her own safety or the safety of others.) I try to send the parents off on a vacation or business trip in Chapter 1 or 2. Or I can have my protagonist go stay with a relative, or go to camp, or keep him or her in school most of the time. Often a mother or father may be out of the picture entirely, and I have a one-parent family that reflects today's society.

In *Sharing Susan*, I had two sets of parents, and many of the decisions being made were *about* Susan, not *by* her. I was forced to have a lot of introspection, slow stuff for young readers. One of my challenges was to keep the plot moving. Strong characterization helped enormously. I had two very different sets of parents with different lifestyles: four complex individuals. My inclination here was to portray one set of parents as mean, demanding, unyielding. That way I could have lots of confrontation and add to Susan's anguish in leaving her familiar home. But I wanted to avoid that trap, which is certainly a cliché and is also scary. A child in such a situation must go where she is sent. What if something like this happened to me, a young reader might ask. Horrifying enough without any additional terror. The book and the idea did spike a lot of imaginations, though, and I must say that most of those who wrote letters to me seemed less than horrified!

Dear Eve:
I've always suspected these weren't my real parents. I am *so different*. Please tell me how I can find out if *I* was changed at birth.
                                                    Your friend. . . .
P.S. Up until now I thought I was adopted or left on their doorstep, but they say no. This seems more likely.

Because I know about children's imaginations, I did try to show how extremely rare such an occurrence would be, and I was careful to portray the adults as wise and caring, making the best of a tragic situation and acting in Susan's best interests—at least the way I hope they would be.

In the book, as in real life, I think, Susan is at first prepared to hate her new, upstart mom and dad. She is totally disinterested in the fact that she will have a brother. She enlists her relatives to help her stay where she thinks she belongs, and when that doesn't work she makes her own plans. She'll be so hateful, so ill-mannered, so rotten to that new little brother that these impostor parents will want to send her back. Susan's efforts gave me an opportunity to have Susan "do" instead of being "done to."

In the resolution, Susan understands that she will always be part of both sets of parents, that it is O.K. to love the new ones, too, and that in no way is it disloyal to the mother and father who have cared for her since they brought her home from the hospital, their wonderful, brand-new little girl. She understands that the more love you give, the more you have left to give. And so, happily, Susan is shared.

"But this really happened. Can't you be sued?" I'm asked.

No, it didn't really happen.

I took reality as a jumping-off place, a springboard to my story. My book has different people, acting out in different ways. I am careful never to use the same characteristics, physical, or as far as I know, psychological, of the original players. For instance, in the newspaper article that sparked *Sharing Susan,* the child's biological parents had six or seven other children. In *Sharing Susan,* they had only one. I knew no follow-up to the "real" story until much later, when my book was completed. This was the reality for me. This was what happened. It was Susan's ordeal, and mine. No one else's.

So, read voraciously and clip like a fiend.

Get excited.

Pause.

Question.

Think.

Write.

Take all that fiction that's fit to print—and make it your own.

483

93

To Be A "Storyteller"

By Zilpha Keatley Snyder

In the years since I began writing books for young people, I have occasionally been referred to by critics and even by friends as a "storyteller." Sometimes as a "natural" or even an "accomplished" storyteller. But even when such an appellation is obviously meant to be complimentary I have found that my reaction is slightly ambiguous.

For me, the sobriquet "storyteller" invokes some particularly poignant and powerful memories, memories of childhood habits and idiosyncrasies that in fact are, I believe, closely related to my present approach to writing fiction for young people. Therefore I thought it might be appropriate to begin a discussion of my writing techniques with a few words about how I happened to have earned, at a rather early age, the not always complimentary title of "storyteller."

As a child, growing up in a rather narrow and limited environment, I learned early on to entertain myself by "making stuff up." I made up games, wildly imaginative scenarios based on everything I had ever heard or read, but winging on past learned facts and data into the realms of sheer illusion. And I also told stories—and soon learned that telling stories can get you in trouble.

I got in trouble when, for instance, in the midst of giving oral book reports, I threw in some really exciting events that the original author might very well have included if he/she had happened to think of them. And I got in even more serious trouble when I succumbed, in the course of describing some interesting occurrence to my parents, to my chronic urge to make any story really worth telling. Even among young friends, who could be quite accepting of my urge to embellish at Halloween when I was esteemed as a concocter of really scary ghost stories, I was at times put down as a "storyteller." And so I was forced long ago to confess to a certain lack of truthfulness as one of my major sins, in spite of the fact that I seldom told lies, which to my way of thinking, is something quite different.

And how does this confession relate to the techniques that I have developed over the years in the course of writing twenty-eight books for children and young adults? It relates, I think, in the following ways.

I still begin a story by indulging in what has always been for me a form of self-entertainment. I look for a character or characters and a beginning situation that cries out to be explored and embellished—or "embroidered," as my mother used to say reprovingly. This beginning situation must be something that connects directly to my long-established urge to find excitement, mystery, and high emotion in the midst of even the most prosaic circumstances. And over the years I have found that if such an element is lacking, I should not look for other reasons to continue work on that particular story idea.

For me at least a theme to develop, a problem to explore, or a message to be delivered, doesn't do it. I know because I've tried. I have started books with a particular message in mind, only to find that my plot mires down and my characters refuse to come to life.

This is not to say that my stories contain no references to problems that have been of concern to me, or causes I would like to promote. I just find it better to start with the joy and excitement of letting my imagination run wild—and let the messages take care of themselves— because they can and will. Messages are, I think, unavoidable. Anything a writer cares or feels deeply about will inevitably find its way into what he or she writes. However, I have found that it is better, when I start out on a new literary journey, to let messages climb into the back seat on their own, rather than to invite them to take the wheel.

So what happens then, after the initial excitement of discovering a sufficiently intriguing combination of characters and setting? Then, of course, comes the hard work—careful methodical plotting, planning and developing. Hard and demanding work, but always buoyed up and carried along by that storytellers' excitement over a situation that simply begs to be "embroidered."

For me, this hard work begins by preparing a looseleaf notebook, taking out the scribbled and doodled-over pages collected during my previous writing endeavor, and adding new, invitingly pristine paper after each of the section dividers. The first section must have blank, unlined paper, because it is there that I will draw maps and/or floor plans.

This urge to draw maps or floor plans may be unique. At least I haven't met any other writers who seem to follow such a strange procedure. I draw town plots when a small town or village is the setting for a new story, clarifying for myself the location of the protagonist's home in relation to other pertinent sites—such as the location of his or her school, best friend's home, sites of important happenings, etc. Then there are the floor plans of a house, if a house is important to the story, particularly a "big old" house, as has been the case in several of my books. Or, as in a recent book, a castle. Drawing that floor plan after studying several castles during the course of a European trip was a particularly intriguing effort.

I don't know what this "map complex" means, except that I know I do have a strong visual sense, and it is important to me to have a vivid mental image of the place I'm writing about. Place or person.

And so—on to persons. The next divider in my notebook is labeled CHARACTER SKETCHES. In this section I start a number of pages with the names of my main characters and begin to jot down what I know about them, not only their general appearance but their strengths and weaknesses, joys and sorrows, loves and hates, family relationships. Everything, down to minor personality quirks. I don't try to finish these descriptions before I begin to write the story. I simply begin with initial impressions, and leave lots of room to add or change information as we get better acquainted.

After the pages for central characters there follow a few pages for minor characters—simply the names I have chosen for them and a sentence or two about their relationship to the story. Such a listing comes in handy when, for instance, you are nearing the end of a book and the occasion requires you to mention a minor character—perhaps a teacher, a mailman, or bus driver—and you find that you have forgotten what you'd named him. Without this list, you'll be endlessly flipping pages, or scrolling through chapters, looking for an elusive name.

Usually after a few days or weeks of daydreaming, map drawing, and character sketching, I begin the actual writing—a preliminary stab at the first chapter or two to get a handle on the tone, style, and feel of the story. But then I pause to work on the all-important next section of my notebook: PLOT.

On the PLOT pages I do what I sometimes describe as "writing the book report before the book is written." I know there are some fine authors who, after getting to know their characters and beginning situation, simply start to write and "just see what happens." I also know it doesn't work for me. It's fun, I'll admit, but it just doesn't work. The usual result is that my characters immediately get themselves into predicaments that I can't get them out of in any logical manner. Also, I really can't understand how one can do the necessary foreshadowing of events, if one is unaware what these events will be.

So as I slowly and carefully (because this is one of the most demanding and crucial steps in the whole process) write the one or two pages of my PLOT section, I clarify in my own mind the barebones storyline that I will be following. Of course I don't, at this point, know everything that is going to happen in the story. Totally unexpected events—surprising and sometimes wonderfully exciting—are certain to occur as the story progresses. But what I must know is the major problem or mystery to be solved—and *in particular,* the final climax of the story and its resolution. Then, the story can zig and zag as new characters come on scene, or minor events occur, without causing the story to wander off into uncharted wastelands—as long as the writer always keeps one eye on the resolution that is the final goal.

Having completed the PLOT section I move on to the CHAPTER OUTLINES, which will be done one at a time as I begin each new chapter.

Each CHAPTER OUTLINE consists of one page divided into two columns, one of which is titled *Action* and the other *Exposition.* On the left-hand side, as I begin each new chapter, I jot down a few notes about the on-scene events that need to happen in the next few pages. And on the right-hand side, I remind myself of information that needs to be presented to the reader—all the background material, descriptions, character development, etc., that should be included in the chapter. I find this brief outline helps me remember to weave expository material into dialogue and action continually, rather than dropping it in occasionally in huge clumps.

The next section of my notebook is labeled REWRITE, and it consists of brief notes that I make as the writing progresses to remind myself that I should, perhaps, "look for a good place to foreshadow Grub's reaction to Robinson's death," for instance. Or perhaps, "go over Chapter Nine to see if some cutting would pick up the pace."

Such notes are usually made when 1) someone in my writer's support group (seven writers who have been meeting twice a month for over twelve years) points out a flaw; 2) after hearing from my editor who has just read the manuscript; 3) I suddenly discover, all by myself, that what I've written is less than perfect.

And that's about it except for one final section labeled RESEARCH, which is self-explanatory. I may refer to this section relatively little when I'm writing a book like *Libby on Wednesday,* a contemporary story set in California, but when I wrote *Song of the Gargoyle,* which has a medieval setting, the research section was almost book length.

So there it is, my own personal "Notebook Method," which has evolved slowly over the years since, at the age of eight, I resolved to be a writer after it dawned on me that there were people in this world who, instead of being scolded for being a "storyteller," actually could make a career of it.

94

THIRTY SECONDS, EIGHT DRAFTS, THREE YEARS—AND THEN A BOOK

By NORMA FOX MAZER

SOME YEARS AGO, I WAS IN A SCHOOL SPEAKING to the youngsters about writing, books, and reading. The librarian had worked hard, the pupils had been reading steadily, and there were countless copies of my books in their hands.

At the end of the day, the librarian drove me back to my motel and on the way told me there'd been an "incident" in the school that day. Two boys had grabbed a girl, pulled her into a corner and molested her. Many people were upset: the girl, the teachers, the principal, the boys, and quite soon it was possible that more people were going to be upset. There were parents to be considered. Newspapers and TV might get wind of this. With her hands off the wheel for a moment, the librarian sketched a "what a mess" statement in the air, and I muttered agreement.

I was tired, and listening to this tale, I became gloomy, angry at those boys and at males in general. When were they going to get it? Not meaning, get the brunt of it, but just *get it*—up there, in the brain. When were they going to wake up, smell the coffee, and start acting like human beings instead of dumb posts with legs?

We were both silent for a few minutes. Then the librarian said, "And you know, the whole thing happened in thirty seconds." All at once, I was alert. All sorts of systems started humming and buzzing in me. My brain woke up with an almost audible click. I flushed and looked at this librarian with intense gratitude and almost as intense suspicion. Did she realize what she had just said? I didn't want her to know that her words had needled their way into my skin.

". . . the whole thing happened in thirty seconds."

Astonishing. My heart beat hard. I was like a dog with a bone, afraid it would be taken from me. I scribbled those words on a piece of paper.

When I looked at it five minutes later, it was indecipherable. No matter. I could no sooner have forgotten what she had said than I could have forgotten the names of my children. But still, taking no chances, I wrote it down, only it came out this way: "Thirty seconds that changed the world."

Then I scribbled a few phrases: "Thirty seconds . . . it all happened in thirty seconds, less than a minute . . . the random and chaotic nature of life . . . the confluence of events and personalities . . . like raging streams that pour together at some point and swell into a flood . . . do one small thing, everything changes. . . ."

From the moment the librarian said those words, I knew I wanted to write a story, and that it would be about those thirty seconds, and I knew, too, that it would be told by one of the boys. Months passed. I wanted to write the book, but I couldn't. I had other commitments, other projects to finish. At last, the time opened up. It was nearly a year later. The only thing I had done in that year to prepare to write this book was to carry around inside me that phrase that was so potent for me. "Thirty seconds that changed the world."

And, then too, I had remembered a retarded woman I'd met in a bookstore in Philadelphia five or six years before. She had come rushing up to tell me with the glowing face of an eight-year-old child that it was her birthday, that she was thirty-three today, that her mommy had given her money to buy a new Nancy Drew book. I smiled at her and wished her happy birthday. She flung her arms around my neck, gave me a smacking kiss, and said, "You are my favorite person! You are a lovely, lovely person!"

Ever since, I'd wanted to write her into a story. I didn't know why she should be in this story, but she had haunted me for so many years, I made up my mind that she would be. I began writing about a boy named Rollo, a nice guy, a big guy, a football player who covers up how much he hates playing. And I wrote about Rollo's two friends and Valerie, a girl he can't stand, who's artistic, short-tempered, outspoken, and tackless. All of these kids come from good homes, are outstanding in school. I didn't know any of this when I started writing. I found out as I wrote. And I found out, too, that Rollo had a retarded sister named Kara.

Now that the book is finished, I see clearly how important Kara is to balancing and building the character of her brother, Rollo, through

490

whom much of the story is told. When we know Kara, and when we know how Rollo acts toward her, we also know that, despite what he will do to Valerie, there's good in him. And Kara is important, also, to the working out of the plot. The gaps that might have been in the story without Kara! No wonder it scares me that her appearance was so seemingly accidental. But then, so much in the writing of a novel is accidental, or at least not deliberate.

Anne Roiphe, the novelist, said of a book she wrote, "The facts were all lies, but the book was all true." That's what I hope for when I write. I don't care about the facts. I don't give a damn about facts. I heard something that day in the car, a tiny piece of truth, a fragment, maybe about thirty seconds worth, and three years and eight drafts later, I had a book called *Out of Control.*

How close is my story to that original incident, to the truth of that school and what those kids did and the details of that day? I have no idea, but I have no reason to think it's close at all. I never saw those kids in the "incident." I never found out what really happened to the girl or what happened to any of them afterwards. I never heard or knew a single other detail than what the librarian had told me on that ten-minute ride. The people in my book are my creations; they are born not to parents but out of my head. The "truth" I hope for concerns the emotions, the feelings, and the thoughts of the characters, and the reverberations of the event. And though it might be discouraging to a young writer for me to say this, I still say that most of these things cannot be planned, but must emerge from the tension between character and story, must emerge as you write.

I was working hard to finish the book when instead of spending every hour in front of the computer, I found myself mesmerized in front of the television, watching the Clarence Thomas confirmation hearings. Listening to Anita Hill tell her story. Watching the wrenching issues of what goes on between men and woman played out on national television.

Since then, the issue of sexual harassment in the schools has gained national attention. *The New York Times* ran a front-page article about sexual harassment; *Seventeen* printed a graphic and deeply disturbing article on the same topic, and *Newsweek* had an article about sexual harassment in the *elementary schools.*

Someone said to me, "Your book is really needed. Great timing!"

but the truth of it is, it was pure dumb luck. I know that if someone had told me to write that book, I wouldn't have done it. I couldn't have. I needed the spur of that phrase about "thirty seconds." I needed the needle in my brain. And should someone come to you today and tell you the market is crying for a book on Subject X and why don't you do it, I would say to you . . . *Don't*.

I believe that the path to publication for the new writer and the secret of survival for the published writer are the same: Follow the yellow brick road. Your heart should go before you. Write what comes to you as passion or curiosity or a nagging of the conscience that you can't put aside. Then you will have something splendid, something that no one else could have written but you.

95

WHAT'S AHEAD FOR CHILDREN'S BOOKS?

BY JAMES CROSS GIBLIN

AS WE MOVE THROUGH THE 90S, THE CHILDREN'S BOOK FIELD is sending out mixed signals.

I'd like to offer a broad overview of some trends I see in the field. It will necessarily be a personal perspective, and somewhat limited, as all such overviews are. But I hope it may provide insights that will be helpful to both beginning and established children's book authors.

The boom in children's books in the last few years has affected every aspect of the field. What caused it? A number of things, in my opinion.

• First, a new generation of enlightened parents wanted their children to be good readers.

• Bookstores specializing in children's books were established to meet these parents' and children's needs, and the major bookstore chains such as B. Dalton and Waldenbooks began to show a new interest in books for children.

• Beginning in California in the mid-1980s, educators proposed a much wider use of children's trade books in the teaching of reading. Instead of getting snippets of children's literature in textbook anthologies, students from preschool through high school were introduced to outstanding examples of picture books, novels, and nonfiction titles.

This innovative method—part of what became known as "the whole language approach"—has since been adopted by educators in many other states and has resulted in greatly increased sales of children's books to schools in both hardcover and paperback editions.

• Children's book publishers responded to this growth in bookstore and school markets by expanding their lists, and many new publishers entered the field in order to get a slice of the pie the boom created. As a result, authors with established reputations have been able to command better contract terms than ever before, and talented new writers have found a more receptive market for their efforts.

However, all is not rosy. Public and school libraries, long the mainstay of the hardcover children's book field, have been hit hard by federal, state, and local budget cuts. They're still buying books, but recently I've noted a disturbing, though understandable, sales pattern. The libraries are purchasing as many if not more copies of the "big" books on a publisher's list: those that have received starred reviews in the library media and won prizes and awards. But they're buying fewer copies of what are sometimes called "midlist" books—the solid, well-done picture books, novels, or nonfiction titles that achieve their goals and deserve to find a readership, even though they may not be of award calibre.

Librarians are also more hesitant about taking a chance on books by unknown authors unless they are greeted by enthusiastic reviews and make a major splash.

In light of these trends, what steps can authors take to insure that their manuscripts will attract first the attention of editors, and then the attention of bookstore customers? What values can they instill in their projects so that librarians will feel they're essential purchases despite tight budgets?

Some answers to these questions can be found by looking in turn at each of the key areas in children's book publishing. Let's start with *picture books*.

1. There's a need for fresh material for children of one to three, but the texts can't be just another introduction to colors and shapes and familiar everyday objects. Editors are looking for more authors who can tell simple but strong stories for this age group, as Cathryn Falwell has done in her books about a little boy named Nicky.

2. Folk and fairy tales attract many writers who retell traditional tales or try to write a new story that follows the classic pattern. But this type of picture book has become more and more the province of illustrators, many of whom write the texts as well as illustrating them. A good example is the 1990 Caldecott Medal winner Ed Young, who translated and also illustrated his own version of the Chinese Red Riding Hood story, *Lon Po Po*.

494

Of course, an illustrator who writes his own text receives the entire royalty and doesn't have to share it with a writer.

3. Instead of retelling an old tale, why not think of a fresh variation on a common family or preschool situation? Careful observation of your own children or incidents that occur in your neighborhood can yield appealing new approaches to such themes as sibling rivalry, parent-child relations, and adjusting to the routines of kindergarten and first grade. Editors are always on the lookout for such stories, especially if told with charm and insight.

4. What other sorts of picture book stories would editors like to see more of?

• Stories with real plots and lots of action that suggest exciting illustrations, all presented in a manuscript of no more than four or five double-spaced, typewritten pages. Anything longer won't allow room for illustrations.

• Genuinely funny stories, like Harry Allard's picture books about Miss Nelson and Jon Scieszka's *The True Story of the Three Little Pigs by A. Wolf.*

• Stories with strong endings. Too many picture book manuscripts start off well but end flatly or just stop in a very unsatisfying way for young children. To avoid this, you should have your ending in mind before you begin. Eve Bunting, author of *A Turkey for Thanksgiving* and *Someday a Tree,* uses this approach. She never begins a picture book until she knows what the last line—the final twist—will be.

5. Another type of picture book in demand today is the story that will lend itself to what I call "beautiful" illustrations. With the bookstore market for children's books growing in importance, especially for picture books, buyers gravitate toward large, strikingly illustrated books that will catch the eye of their customers. Stories set in exotic locales, or in the remote past, or that record dramatic events like a blizzard or a forest fire, all lend themselves to this kind of sweeping pictorial treatment. But they must *first* of all be strong stories in their own right. No picture book has ever been an enduring success on the strength of its illustrations alone.

6. Editors generally prefer stories written in lyrical prose rather

495

than verse. Far too many authors—especially beginners—make the mistake of thinking they'll have a better chance of placing their picture book manuscripts if they're written in verse. They're wrong. Too often the authors get so involved in maintaining the rhyme scheme that they lose the thread of the stories they're trying to tell. They'd stand a much better chance with editors if they wrote their stories in prose instead.

7. Now for some picture book themes that editors definitely *don't* want to see more of because they've been done to death:
• The story that ends with the protagonist waking up and discovering it was all just a dream.

• The text that personifies an inanimate object or substance—"How Gerald Germ Traveled Through Billy's Body," or some such. In most instances, personification should be limited to human beings.

• The story in which the protagonist wants to be something else and imagines a long list of alternatives. Just once, at the end of one of these stories, I wish the hero *wouldn't* decide he'd rather be himself after all.

What about *nonfiction?* How has the boom affected it and its authors?
1. There's been a proliferation of nonfiction series. Running the gamut from biographies, to sports books, to explorations of topical issues, they are being offered by such relatively new publishers as Millbrook Press and Crestwood House, as well as by such established firms as Franklin Watts.
Some of these books are well edited and produced; some aren't. They give many authors the opportunity to be published, some for the first time. But it's difficult for any one title in a series to rise above the rest and get individual critical attention. So if you want your nonfiction book to be noticed, you'll be better off doing it with a house that publishes each title as a separate entity.
2. The boom has also affected the individual book in a positive way. Never has children's nonfiction received as many prestigious prizes and awards as in the past few years. Newbery Honors have gone to Rhoda Blumberg's *Commodore Perry in the Land of the Shōgun* and Patricia Lauber's *Volcano: The Eruption and Healing of Mt. St. Hel-*

ens, and the Newbery Medal itself to Russell Freedman's *Lincoln: A Photobiography.*

3. Why have these and similar nonfiction titles received so much acclaim? It seems to me there are several reasons:

• The texts are not only accurate, but are carefully written with moments of humor and drama, and attention to literary style. They tell true stories that are entertaining as well as informative.

• They find a fresh angle on sometimes familiar subject matter, like Freedman's *Lincoln* with its extensive use of archival photographs that hadn't appeared in other biographies of Lincoln for children. Or else they center on offbeat topics that, for one reason or another, haven't been treated before, like my book *Chimney Sweeps.*

• Where appropriate, they include the contributions of non-Western peoples and cultures. For example, in my book *The Truth About Unicorns,* there's a chapter on the Chinese unicorn, the gentle *ki-lin.* Such multicultural information is much sought after by teachers and librarians.

• Unlike many children's nonfiction titles of the past, books in this category today focus closely on a single topic instead of surveying an entire subject area. They may broaden out to make general points, but they don't attempt to be encyclopedic. For example, Lauber's *Volcano* is about a single volcano, Mt. St. Helens, not volcanoes in general. Such a close focus stands a better chance of getting a reader's attention and making a lasting impression.

• Most important of all, today's nonfiction books are visually inviting. The pages and type are laid out with as much care as a picture book, the paper is of high quality, and the books are elaborately illustrated, usually with photographs. When appropriate to the subject, many of the photographs are being reproduced in full color. But sometimes black-and-white photographs are more effective, like the archival pictures that appear in *Lincoln.*

After most nonfiction writers have finished the texts of their books, they have to do illustration research for them. Finding just the right photos is a time-consuming job, but it is also enjoyable—and it's essential these days if you want your book to be eye-catching and satisfying to readers.

Finally, let's take a look at what's happening in the *fiction* field today.

1. Editors continue to call for chapter books for the 7- to 10-year-old audience. These are short novels divided into six or so chapters, each of which runs to about five or six manuscript pages. They can be any type of story—mystery, adventure, home-and-school—but they all should have appealing characters and fresh dramatic situations at the core. And they don't have to conform to any limited vocabulary lists. Examples of successful chapter books include Jane Resh Thomas's dramatic story, *The Comeback Dog,* Stephen Manes's wacky comedy, *Be a Perfect Person in Just Three Days,* and Sue Alexander's tender story of a lonely girl, *Lila on the Landing.*

A word of warning: Don't make the mistake of thinking a slight, uninvolving story will pass muster with an editor looking for chapter books just because it's short. If anything, a chapter book has to be more compelling than other types of fiction if you want it to catch and hold the attention of beginning readers.

2. Editors are also seeking middle-grade fiction for 8- to 12-year-olds. Contemporary stories featuring characters with whom readers can easily identify dominate this area, but there's room for other types of material including fantasies. However, these must be written with today's young readers in mind and move along at a faster pace than many middle-grade novels of the past. If you're interested in writing for this audience, the novels of Katherine Paterson, Lois Lowry, Betsy Byars, Mary Downing Hahn, and Marion Dane Bauer are excellent models to study.

3. For several reasons, fiction for young adults is a more problematical category today than it was a few years ago. In the paperback area, the fad for teenage romances seems to have run its course, and it isn't clear what new type of story will inspire the same sort of enthusiasm in readers.

Whether published in paperback or hardcover, the "problem novel" has lost its power to shock, since virtually every topic, from drugs to incest to AIDS, has been explored in numerous stories aimed at teenagers. Most damaging of all for the young adult field, library studies show that serious young readers are turning to adult books at earlier ages than ever.

Even so, there continues to be a market, although a limited one, for the hardcover novel for older teens. But to convince an editor to buy your manuscript, you'll need to people it with strong characters, treated in depth, and put them into an unusual dramatic situation. Your writing style will have to be rich and distinctive, too, if it is to win the kind of praise from reviewers that will result in sales to libraries—still the key market for hardcover young adult books. Authors whose novels have earned this kind of critical acceptance, and whose titles merit study in terms of craft, include Richard Peck, Pam Conrad, Bruce Brooks, and M. E. Kerr.

4. Now for two suggestions that can apply to stories for any of the age groups we've discussed:
• Give historical fiction a chance, especially historical novels set during the last forty or so years. The drug scene today may be too unclear and confusing for you to treat in a novel, but what about the choices kids made back in the 1960s, when drugs first became a national concern? You might be able to approach that historical material with the necessary perspective, and use it as the basis of a convincing story.

It's interesting to note that two popular Newbery Medal winners in the last few years—Patricia MacLachlan's *Sarah, Plain and Tall* and Lois Lowry's *Number the Stars*—are both historical novels. And *Number the Stars* takes place in a fairly recent period, the Nazi occupation of Denmark during World War II.

• Don't feel you always have to be serious. Fiction can appeal to a wide range of emotions, and children, like their elders, love to laugh at something funny, or feel a chill run down their spines when something scary happens. In light of this, editors wish more children's fiction writers would turn their attention to humorous stories, to clever mysteries, to ghost stories and stories of suspense—in other words to escape literature. But, of course, it must be done well.

Though the children's book boom may be confusing at times, and authors—especially untried ones—may have a more difficult time placing their manuscripts, I'm sure the majority will rise to the challenge. Knowing the stiff competition they face in the marketplace, they will ask themselves the following questions: Is this a really fresh idea? And

will it result in a truly special book manuscript, one that no editor—
or child—will be able to resist?

If authors find the right answers to these questions, and incorporate
them in their work, chances are they'll be on their way to publishing
success.

§96

WRITING MULTICULTURAL BOOKS
FOR CHILDREN

BY KAREN MCWILLIAMS

LONG BEFORE EUROPEANS, LATIN AMERICANS, and Asians immigrated to this country, the United States was "multicultural." Hundreds of Native-American tribes with unique languages, religions, and customs lived throughout the Americas. Today, with the continuing arrival of immigrants from around the world, most schools have many students from a variety of cultures. Teachers, librarians, and parents, therefore, are demanding more multicultural children's books, so that their pupils can better understand each other as well as learn about and have pride in their own culture. Many publishers are now actively seeking multicultural material in order to meet this growing demand.

All of the mainstream editors I queried stated that 10–20% of their titles are multicultural, and that they would publish more if well-written manuscripts were submitted to them. Furthermore, small presses specializing in multicultural and bilingual books have sprung up within the last decade. Some bilingual publishers publish simultaneously in English and another language, most often Spanish, while others publish bilingually within the book. Some presses specifically look for books about a particular culture that are written by an author belonging to that culture, but most will consider *any* well-written, well-researched manuscript.

Most children's books are classified as preschool and picture books, for kindergarten through third grade; first chapter books for beginning readers; middle-grade novels for more advanced readers; and young-adult novels for preteens through teenagers. But whatever age level you write for, you must make your plot exciting and your characters compelling. And your book should show what the particular culture

501

you are writing about has in common with other cultures, as well as what makes it unique.

Perhaps you wonder how a non-Chinese, for example, can write a convincing middle-grade novel about a Chinese-American family. To do this successfully, you must never write off the top of your head. If you have never lived in China, Taiwan, or Hong Kong, or had Chinese friends, you will have to do extensive research in libraries, archives, and museums. In addition to consulting encyclopedias, books, and watching videos, look in *The Readers' Guide to Periodical Literature* to find the most recent magazine articles about China, especially about Chinese who have relocated to the United States.

Visit the children's section of your library for fiction and nonfiction on China, and other multicultural books written at the grade level in which you are interested. Also, try to locate Chinese or Chinese-Americans living in your region, and talk to people who have lived or traveled in China. You can even visit Chinese restaurants in your area to steep yourself in the culture. Remember, it is better to overdo your research, later omitting most of it from the final version of the manuscript.

The picture book, *I Hate English,* by Ellen Levine, is a perfect example of what it is like to be a foreign child adjusting to life in the United States. Mei Mei had been a good student in her school in Hong Kong, but when her family moved to New York she couldn't understand her teacher or classmates. She hated New York, and she hated English, as revealed in the following excerpt from the book:

> Such a lonely language. Each letter stands alone and makes its own noise. Not like Chinese. Sometimes English letters fight each other. "We will go on a class TRIP," the teacher said in English. T-R-I-P, thought Mei Mei. The letters "T" and "R" bang against each other, and each keeps its own sound. Not like Chinese.

Little by little, Mei Mei understands more English but refuses to speak it. Then her cousin takes her to a Chinatown tutoring center where an American teacher coaxes her—with some difficulty—into speaking English. Once Mei Mei starts to speak English, she becomes a chatterbox in both English and Chinese.

When you have finished your research, how do you make your writing convey the real essence of a Chinese family living in the United

States? Study the many ways in which foreign cultures are presented in multicultural books: Picture books are often written in correct English, and the only way the reader knows the book is multicultural is from the illlustrations. In other cases, writers may occasionally use words and phrases from a particular culture as well as word reversals, such as switching the order of the subject and verb, to give the feeling of a foreigner speaking English.

In the fictional biography, *Ahyoka and the Talking Leaves,* by Peter and Connie Roop, Sequoia, a Cherokee father, and his daughter invent a written language for their tribe. They use words from the Cherokee language as well as description reflecting the Cherokee love of nature:

He must be drawing *agaliha,* sunshine, Ahyoka thought. A difficult word-picture, almost as difficult as anger.

and

Books are as rare around here as wings on bears.

The authors did their research at the Cherokee National Museum, Tsa-La-Gi Ancient Village, the University of Oklahoma, and Sequoia's Home, operated by the Oklahoma Historical Society.

Since middle-grade and young-adult novels are much longer than picture books, they usually include more dialogue and detailed description. In Gary Paulsen's young-adult Newbery Honor Book, *Dogsong,* it is obvious from the following description that the author has either lived on the frozen tundra, where his young Eskimo protagonist lives, or has done extensive research:

On the wall were sealskin mukluks. He took them down and felt inside. The grass bottoms were still good and he pulled them on, tied them up around his calves over the bearskin. Then came the squirrelskin inner parka with the hair out soft and fine, like leather silk . . .

In the young-adult Newbery Honor Book, *The Moves Make the Man,* Bruce Brooks uses dialogue that gives a *sense* of how a poor inner-city African-American boy would speak and think:

I took right to the idea of French class, and I took right to the lingo itself too. The teacher was this white woman named Madame Dupont, but she wasn't French though it was a French name. After three days, which we learned how

503

to pronounce a few basic things and the pronouns and the rules for verbs, after that we were allowed only to speak French in class! Anybody talking in English, they got themselves ignored. Right there in a school and you could not talk English! Man, that room was something special to me, a little world by itself. . . . I never realized before then how much my way of talking was what made me who I thought and other people thought I was.

The mannerisms, vocabulary, and fashions of each new generation differ from earlier ones, so it is important to research and become familiar with the age group for which you're writing. If you don't have contact with middle school or high school students, volunteer at a school or chaperone a youth group to observe them in action. Also, watch television programs popular with teenagers. When writing your book, be careful not to use words unfamiliar or not in common use in other parts of the country or fad words that may soon be out of date. And remember, it is important for you to give your dialogue a *sense of dialect* or the vernacular, but never write exactly the way young people speak or your novel will be unreadable.

Finally, publishers usually require complete manuscripts for picture books and novels, but will accept (and in many cases demand) proposals for nonfiction. If you are not Hispanic but have written a Hispanic novel, include a cover letter stating your qualifications—majoring in Latin American studies in college or experience working with migrant farm workers with Hispanic backgrounds. Include a resumé of your background that is relevant to writing multicultural books for children, and a list of your most recent book or magazine publishing credits, if any, noting the names of the publishers, dates of publication, grade level for which they were intended, number of pages, color photos, number of copies sold, and tearsheets of any reviews. Also, list your multicultural volunteer work or relevant teaching experience.

NOTE: Before submitting your manuscript to a publisher, you may want to consider sending it to The Center for Multicultural Children's Literature, sponsored by HarperCollins and Scott Foresman. First, request an application to submit with your story. A committee of experienced authors and illustrators will then review it, and if the committee feels your story has potential, a mentor will be assigned to you according to the culture, age, level, style, and genre of your manuscript. The CMCL has high standards, too, and cannot accept every submission for review. For an application, write to: The Center for Multicultural Children's Literature, HarperCollins Children's Books, 10 East 53rd Street, New York, NY 10022.

§97

WRITING THE JUVENILE SHORT STORY

BY GLORIA D. MIKLOWITZ

"Now stop that, Blackie," Rufus ordered, crouching before the dog. He wished Blackie would stop straining against the leash holding him to the hydrant. He wished he didn't have to leave him like this. Every time he came to visit Steve at the hospital he felt the same way.

"Down, Blackie, down!" Rufus tried to sound mean. Then he rose and turned his back to the dog. If he didn't hurry, he'd miss visiting hours, and he hadn't seen Steve in two days. Each visit was harder than the last. Ever since the motorcycle accident when Steve lost his arm, it had gotten worse. Rufus would come into the ward and see his friend Steve turned to the wall, closed up, wan. He'd tell him about school, about Karen, about his family. But Steve would only say, "Go away. Leave me alone."

"He just doesn't have the will to live," one of the doctors said. A big lump formed in Rufus's throat. What could he say today to make Steve care again? What could he give him or do that would bring the old spark back?

THERE'S THE OPENING FOR A PURPOSE ACHIEVED plotted story. Rufus's purpose is shown quickly. He loves his friend, but Steve has lost interest in life. The story question becomes: How can Rufus help his friend want to live?

By the end of 2,000 carefully chosen words, about eight double-spaced typed pages, Rufus will have achieved his purpose. He will have done so after making several efforts that fail, always through action. Finally, he will succeed through *ingenuity, courage,* or some *special ability.*

Most short stories and all novels have a shape, a skeletal form, a *plot.* One of the most often used is PURPOSE ACHIEVED.

In my book *After the Bomb* (Scholastic), Philip's purpose is to save his mother, who was badly burned after a nuclear bomb destroyed Los Angeles. Throughout the book, Philip tries, fails, tries again, sometimes making progress toward his goal but often losing ground. Through his persistence and courage, he succeeds in getting his mother to a burn center—a classic PURPOSE ACHIEVED plotline.

Another plot type is MISUNDERSTANDING, DISCOVERY, AND REVER-

506

SAL, in which the hero misunderstands something important—that personal integrity is more important than belonging to a group, for example. Through two-thirds of the story, he acts on this misguided premise, then (through an action scene) discovers he's wrong and reverses his behavior. In a final scene, the hero shows his change of belief, again through action.

No story succeeds, no matter how well worked out the plot, without several other elements, the most important of which are the CHARACTERS. The hero or heroine must be someone the reader likes and cares about. To develop flesh-and-blood people, you need to know a lot about them before you start: age, appearance, attitudes, family, hobbies, likes and dislikes; how they think and feel about themselves and others; what they want from life; what they fear, dislike in themselves and others. In short, you want to create characters like people, like you and your readers. Write a page or two about each character and put it aside. Later, it will help you write more convincingly.

Who is your *antagonist?* In a short story there's room for only one. The antagonist is the person (usually) who tries to prevent the hero from getting what he wants or tries to make the hero do what is wrong. This "villain" supplies much of the opportunity to develop conflict. He needn't be all bad. Even in real life villains often have redeeming features, loving their children, perhaps, or being kind to animals.

An antagonist need not be a person. Imagine a boy who is afraid of heights but must overcome that fear to save a friend. Scaling the height becomes the antagonist. Man against himself or against nature has provided the material for many a story.

When considering the characters in your story, remember: Each must have a reason for being there, or out he goes!

SETTING: Life doesn't happen in a vacuum. A story takes place *somewhere*—in a specific place. Visualize a stage as you begin a scene. What's on it? A couch? Pictures on the wall? An exercise bike? Bring your characters into this setting and *show* through their action, dialogue and inner thoughts what their problems are and how they are dealing with them.

VIEWPOINT: In most short stories, there's a single viewpoint character: your protagonist. He or she will tell the story, but how? In first person ("Now stop that, Blackie," *I* ordered.) or third person personal ("Now stop that, Blackie," *Rufus* ordered.")? In either case, everything must be seen or heard and reacted to by the viewpoint character. No action can take place without the viewpoint person being there to observe it or take part in it. For example, in first- or third-person personal viewpoint, you can't write a scene in which several friends are talking about the hero *unless* the hero is able to hear what's happening.

In juvenile short stories and novels, the main character must solve the problem himself. Wise advice from a parent or friend may be heard but not heeded. The hero must decide on his own what's best for him.

With plot, character, setting, and viewpoint worked out, what next?

Start assembling scenes that will *show* the problem and how the hero is trying to solve it. Each scene must do at least one of three things, preferably two, and even better all three: 1) move the story forward through dialogue, inner thought, and/or action; 2) show us how the character *feels;* 3) give information.

Look at the first paragraphs of the Rufus story. Rufus reprimands his dog, but he does it kindly, so we like him.

The narrative (non-dialogue) gives Rufus's inner thoughts, which provide the reader with information and feelings. (We learn that he visits Steve often and is becoming discouraged.) The narrative moves the story forward to the hospital, where the next scene will take place. By the end of the third paragraph, the story question and plot type are clearly defined. The story question becomes: What can Rufus do to make Steve want to live? The plot type is PURPOSE ACHIEVED. The setting is the hospital, and viewpoint is third person.

By the end of the third paragraph, the reader knows Rufus will attempt all the things he considers. And he does. The rest of the story develops his efforts: He reasons with his friend. It does no good, so he accuses him of cowardice in an effort to shock him out of his lethargy. Failing that, he spends his hard-earned money on a gift, but Steve responds with anger. This is the dark moment. Rufus leaves the hospital certain he can't achieve his purpose. On the way out, he meets Steve's doctor, who remarks that Steve needs a reason to go on, "someone to love, something worth getting on his feet for, something that will make him forget the loss of his hand."

Now Rufus knows what to do. Have you guessed what he'll give Steve? Right. Blackie, the dog he loves almost as much as he loves his friend. In the final scene, he drops Blackie on Steve's bed and tells him the dog is now his. Steve protests, and Rufus turns away. When

Blackie licks Steve's cheek, Steve reaches out with his good arm and pets the dog. The reader knows that everything will be O.K. now.

When the rough draft of your story is done, it's time to look at it with the cold eye of an editor. Maybe you wrote it in one sitting in a white heat. Put it aside for a few days, then read it as if you had never seen it before. Does each scene do what it should? Is each character needed and well defined? Have you gone into too much detail on setting or inner thought? Can you use one word where you've used three?

Is the THEME—the moral statement your story makes, the wisdom you wish to impart—clear? Each story should have a theme buried within it. In *After the Bomb,* the theme is, "never give up"; in the Rufus story, "love is the best gift."

Writing a short story—considering everything that must be part of it—may seem contrived and even confining, but it need not be. Every good story incorporates plot, character, setting, viewpoint, and theme. While some writers instinctively know how to use these elements, most of us need to be reminded.

Master these elements, and you'll write a better short story. Master them and writing the *novel* will even be more manageable.

Short Story Checklist

1. Does your story have a plot type? Is it PURPOSE ACHIEVED (through ingenuity, courage or a special ability?) or MISUNDERSTANDING, DISCOVERY, AND REVERSAL?

2. What is the story question, in one sentence?

3. What is your theme, the moral statement you want to make? Is it developed through the story's action?

4. Have you shown the story problem within the first page? Is there action in those first paragraphs?

5. Do you have conflict through an antagonist, nature, or the main character's personal flaw?

6. Does the hero solve his own problem?

7. Is the story told through one person's viewpoint?

8. Have you avoided solving problems through coincidence?

509

9. Does the story build through several scenes to a climax in which the hero seems to have lost the battle? Then, does the solution follow quickly?

10. Have you checked every word, sentence, paragraph to see if it belongs or can be improved?

§98

WRITING "HIGH" FANTASY: ONCE UPON A TIME TOO OFTEN

BY PATRICIA A. MCKILLIP

THE FORMULA IS SIMPLE. TAKE ONE FIFTEENTH-CENTURY PALACE with high towers and pennants flying, add a hero who talks like a butler, a wizard with fireworks under his fingernails, and a Lurking Evil that threatens the kingdom or the heroine, and there you have it: high fantasy in the making. And there we have all had it up to the proverbial "here." How many times can you repeat the same plot? But how can you write high fantasy without the traditional trappings, characters, and plot that are essential for this kind of fantasy? There are other kinds—fantasies set in the contemporary world, mingling folklore and reality, using familiar language like "rock and roll" and "cholesterol," in which you don't have to worry so much about the clichés of the genre. But this, for perverse reasons I don't fully understand, is not the kind I choose to write. So I am forced to ask myself the same question when I begin a new fantasy: How can it follow the rules of high fantasy and break them at the same time?

The hero

In the *Riddle-Master* trilogy, my impulse was to be as deliberately traditional as possible: A ruler leaves the comforts of his castle to learn from wizards how to fight a Lurking Evil that threatens to destroy his land. The hero, the magic, the danger, are after all elements of fantasy as old as storytelling. But how do you give the Generic Hero— who only has to be high-born, look passable, and fight really well to be a hero—personality? I discarded quite a number of auditioning heroes before settling on Morgon, Prince of Hed, ruler of a tiny island, who liked to make beer, read books, didn't own a sword, and kept the only crown he possessed under his bed. He did not talk like an English butler, he knew which end of a shovel was up, and only a penchant for

511

wanting to learn odd things kept him from being a sort of placid gentleman farmer. That small detail—among all the details of a prosaic, hardheaded life that included farming, trading, pig-herders, backyard pumps and a couple of strong-willed siblings—became the conflict in his personality but ultimately drove him from his land and set him on his questing path. Before I let him set forth, I placed him against as detailed a background as I possibly could. I wanted the reader to see the land Morgon lived in and how it shaped him before he left it and changed himself. So I let him talk about grain and bulls, beer and plowhorses, and his sister's bare feet, before I let him say fairy tale words like tower, wizard, harp, and king, and state his own driving motivation: to answer the unanswered riddle.

The heroine

In *The Sorceress and the Cygnet,* my questing hero found himself falling literally into the path of my questing heroine. She is, in one sense, the princess in the tower whom my hero eventually rescues; in other words, she is very much a piece of the familiar storytelling formula. But she has imprisoned herself in a rickety old house in a swamp, trapped there by her own obsession with the darker side of magic. As she defines herself: "I have been called everything from sorceress to bog hag. I know a great many things but never enough. Never enough. I know the great swamp of night, and sometimes I do things for pay if it interests me." She has pursued her quest for knowledge and power into a dangerous backwater of mean, petty magic, from which, it is clear to everyone but her, she must be rescued. The language she uses, like Morgon's, covers a broad territory between palace and pigherder's hut. Her wanderings have freed her tongue, and she can use words like "sorceress" and "bog hag" in the same sentence.

In the same novel, I also used a female point of view, that of a highborn lady, to contrast with the more earthy, gypsyish, view of my hero. She is the female version of the "friend of the hero"; she frets about the sorceress, gives advice, and fights beside her in the end. She is perhaps the toughest kind of character to work with: genuinely good, honest, and dutiful. Making a point-of-view character both good and interesting is a challenge. Traditionally, a "good" character has a limited emotional range, no bad habits to speak of, and a rather bland vocabulary. As the "friend of the heroine," she is also a sounding board for the heroine's more colorful character. I deliberately chose that kind of character because I wanted to see how difficult it would be to make her more than just a device to move the plot along its necessary path. She turned out to be extraordinarily difficult. I wanted her to be elegant, dignified, calm, responsible. That meant whatever humor a situation sparked would not come from her, but from some conjunction of words in her dialogue, and that to keep her from fading completely into the plot, I constantly had to provide her with events that brought out her best qualities. Manipulating the rhythms in the dialogue also helped to keep her from being overwhelmed with blandness, as in this scene when she is in bed with the Gatekeeper—another good but not nearly so difficult character—who is supposed to be watching the gate:

> "Don't," she pleaded, her eyes closed. "Nothing is out there."
> "I must watch." He sounded still asleep.
> "Stay with me. Don't leave me yet. Not even dawn is at the gate."
> "The gate moved."
> "It's only wind at the gate. Only rain."
> "I must watch."
> "I'll watch," she said, and felt him sink back. She pushed against him; he wound his hand into her hair. "I'll watch . . ."

Keeping her dialogue simple and immediate kept her uncomplicated yet responsive as a character; it also moved the plot forward without dragging along the unnecessary baggage of introspection. She is meant to observe and act; the language should not be more complicated than she is.

The Lurking Evil

Traditionally, the evil in fantasy is personified by someone of extraordinary and perverse power, whose goal in life is to bring the greatest possible misery to the largest number of good honest folk. Sauron of the *Lord of the Rings* trilogy, Darth Vader of the *Star Wars* trilogy, Morgan le Fay of *Le Morte D'Arthur,* are all examples of social misfits from whose destructive powers the hero and heroine must rescue humanity and hobbits and the world as they know it. The problem with the Lurking Evil is that as social misfit, it might become far more interesting than the good and dutiful hero, yet without proper background and personality, the Lurking Evil becomes a kind of unmoti-

513

vated monster vacuum cleaner that threatens humanity simply because it's plugged in and turned on.

I have trouble coming up with genuinely evil characters who are horrible, remorseless, and deserving of everything the hero can dish out. I always want to give them a human side, which puts them in the social misfit category. In the *Riddle-Master* trilogy, I used various kinds of misfits: the renegade wizard Ohm, who was motivated by an unprincipled desire for magical power; the sea-people, whose intentions and powers seem at first random and obscure until they finally reveal their origins; and the ambiguous character Deth, who may be good and may be evil and who keeps my hero off-balance and guessing until the end of the tale.

In *The Sorceress and the Cygnet,* I used much the same kind of device: allowing my hero to define characters as evil until they, in the end, reveal that the evil is not in them, but in my misguided heroine. I do this because evil as a random event, or as the sole motivation for a character, is difficult for me to work with; it seems to belong in another genre, to horror, or mystery. Jung says that all aspects of a dream are actually faces of the dreamer. I believe that in fantasy, the vanquished evil must be an aspect of the hero or heroine, since by tradition, evil is never stronger than the power of the hero to overcome it—which is where, of course, we get the happy endings in high fantasy.

Magic

If you put a mage, sorceress, wizard, warlock, witch, or necromancer into fantasy, it's more than likely that they will want, sooner or later, to work some magic. Creating a spell can be as simple or as difficult as you want. You can write: "Mpyxl made a love potion. Hormel drank it and fell in love." Or you can do research into herb lore and medieval recipes for spells and write: "Mpyxl stirred five bay leaves, an owl's eye, a parsnip, six of Hormel's fingernails and some powdered mugwort into some leftover barley soup. Hormel ate it and fell in love." Or you can consider love itself, and how Mpyxl must desire Hormel, how frustrated and rejected she must feel to be obliged to cast a spell over him, what in Hormel generates such overpowering emotions, why he refuses to fall in love with Mpyxl the usual way, and what causes people to fall in love with each other in the first place. Then you will find that Mpyxl herself is under a spell cast by Hormel, and that she must change before his eyes from someone he doesn't want to someone he desires beyond reason. The language of such a spell would be far different from fingernails and barley soup. The Magic exists only in the language; the spell exists only in the reader's mind. The words themselves must create something out of nothing. To invent a convincing love potion you must, for a moment, make even the reader fall in love.

Why?

Why write fantasy? Because it's there. Fantasy is as old as poetry and myth, which are as old as language. The rules of high fantasy are the rules of the unconscious and the imagination, where good quests, evil lurks, the two clash, and the victor—and the reader—are rewarded. Good might be male or female, so might evil. The battle might be fought with swords, with magic, with wits, on a battlefield, in a tower, or in the quester's heart. At its best, fantasy rewards the reader with a sense of wonder about what lies within the heart of the commonplace world. The greatest tales are told over and over, in many ways, through centuries. Fantasy changes with the changing times, and yet it is still the oldest kind of tale in the world, for it began once upon a time, and we haven't heard the end of it yet.

Author's Postscript

Since I write both fantasy and science fiction, I've often been asked how I deal with the difference between the two. The difference between fantasy and science fiction is like the horizon line, at once very big and very small. There are novels weighted with elements of fantasy which are defined as S/F because they have a technological explanation of how the morning coffee is made. There are nicely researched science fiction novels whose compelling themes of the quest or of the transference of power are straight out of the heritage of fantasy. I tend to weigh the elements in a novel of fantasy or science, and whichever dominate, whichever are most necessary or most moving to me, define its genre for me. I'm not sure that it matters a great deal: Even the contemporary novel is becoming vulnerable to elements of fantasy. For my own purposes, I try to keep the two separate. If I'm writing fantasy I use elements of epic, fantasy, myth, legend; and if I put magic in it, it's magic out of the imagination and out of the heart. When I write S/F, I try to turn my back on traditional fantasy elements and extrapolate a plot from history or everyday life, or whatever science seems to stick in my head. I'm probably more successful at keeping S/F out of my fantasy than keeping fantasy out of my S/F. The heritage, the roots and background of S/F are very different from those of fantasy. The language is different; the images I find in my mind when I contemplate an S/F plot are different. The stars in *Riddle-Master* are a symbol. The stars in science fiction are real.

§99

Is It Good Enough for Children?

By Madeleine L'Engle

A WHILE AGO WHEN I WAS TEACHING A COURSE on techniques of fiction, a young woman came up to me and said, "I do hope you're going to teach us something about writing for children, because that's why I'm taking this course."

"What have I been teaching you?" I asked her.

"Well—writing."

"Don't you write when you write for children?"

"Yes, but—isn't it different?"

No, I assured her, it isn't different. The techniques of fiction are the techniques of fiction, and they hold as true for Beatrix Potter as they do for Dostoevsky.

But the idea that writing for children isn't the same as writing for adults is prevalent indeed, and usually goes along with the conviction that it isn't quite as good. If you're a good enough writer for adults, the implication is, of course, you don't write for children. You write for children only when you can't make it in the real world, because writing for children is easier.

Wrong, wrong, wrong!

I had written several regular trade novels before a publisher asked me to write about my Swiss boarding school experiences. Nobody had told me that you write differently when you write for children, so I didn't. I just wrote the best book I possibly could; it was called *And Both Were Young.* After that I wrote *Camilla,* which has been reissued as a young adult novel, and then *Meet the Austins.* It's hard today for me to understand that this simple little book had a very hard time finding a publisher because it's about a death and how an ordinary family reacts to that death. Death at that time was taboo. Children weren't supposed to know about it. I had a couple of offers of publica-

517

tion if I'd take the death out. But the reaction of the family—children as well as the parents—to the death was the core of the book.

Nowadays what we offer children makes *Meet the Austins* seem pale, and on the whole, I think that's just as well, because children know a lot more than most grown-ups give them credit for. *Meet the Austins* came out of my own family's experience with several deaths. To have tried to hide those deaths from our children would have been blind stupidity. All hiding does is confuse children and add to their fears. It is not subject matter that should be taboo, but the way it is handled.

A number of years ago—the first year I was actually making reasonable money from my writing—my sister-in-law was visiting us, and when my husband told her how much I had earned that year, she was impressed and commented, "And to think most people would have had to work so hard for that!"

Well, it is work, it's most certainly work; wonderful work, but work. Revision, revision, revision. Long hours spent not only in the actual writing, but in research. I think the best thing I learned in college was how to do research, so that I could go right on studying after I had graduated.

Of course, it is not *only* work; it is work that makes the incomprehensible comprehensible. Leonard Bernstein says that for him music is cosmos in chaos. That is true for writing a story, too. Aristotle says that what is plausible and impossible is better than what is possible and implausible.

That means that story must be *true,* not necessarily *factual,* but true. This is not easy for a lot of people to understand. When I was a school child, one of my teachers accused me of telling a story. She was not complimenting me on my fertile imagination; she was accusing me of telling a lie.

Facts are fine; we need facts. But story takes us to a world that is beyond facts, out on the other side of facts. And there is considerable fear of this world.

The writer Keith Miller told me of a young woman who was determined that her three preschool children were going to grow up in the real world. She was not, she vowed, going to sully their minds with myth, fantasy, fairy tales. They were going to know the truth—and for truth, read fact—and the truth would make them free.

One Saturday, after a week of rain and sniffles, the sun came out, so she piled the children into her little red VW bug and took them to the Animal Farm. The parking lot was crowded, but a VW bug is small, and she managed to find a place for it. She and the children had a wonderful day, petting the animals, going on rides, enjoying the sunshine. Suddenly, she looked at her watch and found it was far later than she realized. She and the children ran to where the VW bug was parked, and to their horror, found the whole front end was bashed in.

Outraged, she took herself off to the ranger's office. As he saw her approach, he laughed and said, "I'll bet you're the lady with the red VW bug."

"It isn't funny," she snapped.

"Now, calm down, lady, and let me tell you what happened. You know the elephant your children had such fun riding? She's a circus-trained elephant, and she was trained to sit on a red bucket. When she saw your car, she just did what she was trained to do and sat on it. Your engine's in the back, so you can drive it home without any trouble. And don't worry. Our insurance will take care of it. Just go on home, and we'll get back to you on Monday."

Slightly mollified, she and the kids got into the car and took off. But she was later than ever, so when she saw what looked like a very minor accident on the road, she didn't stop, but drove on.

Shortly, the flashing light and the siren came along, and she was pulled over. "Lady, don't you know that in this state it's a crime to leave the scene of an accident?" the trooper asked.

"But I wasn't in an accident," she protested.

"I suppose your car came that way," she said, pointing to the bashed-in front.

"No. An elephant sat on it."

"Lady, would you mind blowing into this little balloon?"

That taught her that facts alone are not enough; that facts, indeed, do not make up the whole truth. After that she read fairy tales to her children and encouraged them in their games of Make Believe and Let's Pretend.

I learned very early that if I wanted to find out the truth, to find out why people did terrible things to each other, or sometimes wonderful things—why there was war, why children are abused—I was more likely to find the truth in story than in the encyclopedia. Again and again I read *Emily of the New Moon,* by Lucy Maud Montgomery, because Emily's father was dying of diseased lungs, and so was mine. Emily had a difficult time at school, and so did I. Emily wanted to be a writer, and so did I. Emily knew that there was more to the world that provable fact, and so did I. I read fairy tales, the myths of all nations, science fiction, the fantasies and family stories of E. Nesbit. I read Jules Verne and H. G. Wells. And I read my parents' books, particularly those with lots of conversation in them. What was not in my frame of reference went right over my head.

We tend to find what we look for. If we look for dirt, we'll find dirt, whether it's there or not. A very nice letter I received from a reader said that she found *A Ring of Endless Light* very helpful to her in coming to terms with the death of a friend, but that another friend had asked her how it was that I used dirty words. I wrote back saying that I was not going to reread my book looking for dirty words, but that as far as I could remember, the only word in the book that could possibly be construed as dirty was *zuggy,* which I'd made up to avoid using dirty words. And wasn't looking for dirty words an ugly way to read a book?

One of my favorite books is Frances Hodgson Burnett's *The Secret Garden.* I read it one rainy weekend to a group of little girls, and a generation later to my granddaughters up in an old brass bed in the attic. Mary Lennox is a self-centered, spoiled-rotten little heroine, and I think we all recognize at least a little of ourselves in her. The secret garden is as much the garden of Mary's heart as it is the physical walled garden. By the end of the book, warmth and love and concern for others have come to Mary's heart, when Colin, the sick boy, is able to walk and run again. And Dickon, the gardener's boy, looks at the beauty of the restored garden and says, "It's magic!" But "magic" is one of the key words that has become taboo to today's self-appointed censors, so, with complete disregard of content, they would add *The Secret Garden* to the pyre. I shudder. This attitude is extreme. It is also dangerous.

It comes down to the old question of separate standards, separate for adults and children. The only standard to be used in judging a children's book is: *Is it a good book?* Is it good enough for me? Because if a children's book is not good enough for all of us, it is not good enough for children.

100

CALLING IT QUITS

BY LOIS LOWRY

"You put what in it?" my son asked, his fork halfway to his mouth.
"Ginger snaps," I repeated. "Crushed ginger snaps."
"I thought that's what you said." I watched while he put his fork back down on his plate and then pushed the plate away from him. It was clear to me that my son, normally a good sport, was not going to eat my innovative beef stew.

It was clear to me, after I tasted it myself, that he had made the right decision.

SOMETIMES IN THE PROCESS OF CREATING, it is very difficult to know when to quit adding things.

Some years back, I received in the mail the first foreign edition of my first young adult book, *A Summer to Die*. Fortunately it was French. Later I would receive, with a gulp of astonishment, the Finnish, the Afrikaans, the Catalan; but this first one was French. French I can read.

And so I leafed through the pages, savoring the odd, startling sense of recognition that I had, seeing my own words translated into another language.

On the last page, I read the line of dialogue with which I had concluded the book. "'Meg,' he laughed, putting one arm over my shoulders, 'you were beautiful all along.'" There it was, in French.

But there was something else, as well. I blinked in surprise, seeing it. In French, the book concluded: "They walked on."

They walked on? Of course they *had* walked on, those two characters, Meg and Will. I knew they had, and I trusted the reader to know that they had. But I hadn't written that line. The translator had.

I don't know why. I can only guess that the translator simply couldn't resist that urge that makes all of us throw a crushed ginger snap into the stew now and then.

Knowing when to stop is one of the toughest tasks a writer faces.

Is there a rule that one can follow? Probably not. But there is, I think, a test against which the writer can measure his ending, his stopping place.

When something more is going to take place, but the characters have been so fully drawn, and the preceding events so carefully shaped that the reader, on reflection, knows what more will happen, and is satisfied by it—then the book ends.

In essence, you, as writer, will have successfully taught the reader to continue writing the book in his mind.

What about the concept of resolution, then? Isn't the writer supposed to tie up the loose ends of the story neatly at the conclusion? And if everything is neatly packaged and tied, then how on earth can something more take place?

Your story—your plot—your theme—is only a portion of the lives of the characters you have created. Their lives, if you have made them real to the reader, are going to continue in the reader's mind.

Your role is only a part of that process. And you need to know when and how to get out when your role is finished. As author, you tie up and resolve the piece of a life you have chosen to examine. Then you leave, gracefully. The life continues, but you are no longer looking at it.

You have engaged and directed the imagination of the reader; and then you have turned the reader loose.

Writing this, I looked at the endings of some of my own books, to see if they followed any kind of pattern.

In one, *Anastasia on Her Own*, a mother and daughter are laughing and tap-dancing together up a flight of stairs.

In *Find a Stranger, Say Goodbye*, a young girl is packing to go away; she is deciding what to take and what to leave behind.

The narrator and her mother in *Rabble Starkey* are together in a car, heading into a somewhat uncertain future. (Not coincidentally, that book is published in Great Britain under the title *The Road Ahead*.)

The forms of these endings are different. Some are descriptive, some consist of dialogue. Some are lighthearted, others more introspective.

But they do seem to have a few elements in common.

522

They all include the main character—sometimes more than one—in the final scene.

Each of them, in various forms, reflects a sense of motion, of flow, of moving forward.

And each in its own way contains a kind of conclusive statement.

Anastasia fell in behind her mother and tried to follow the complicated hops, turns, and shuffles her mother was doing. Together they tap-danced down the hall and up the stairs. It was silly, she thought; but it was fun. And it sure felt good, having her mother back in charge.

—*Anastasia on Her Own*

It was the throwing away that was the hardest. But she did it, until the trunk was packed, the trash can was filled, and the room was bare of everything except the memories; those would always be there, Natalie knew.

—*Find a Stranger, Say Goodbye*

She sped up a little, driving real careful, and when we went around the curve I looked, and it was all a blur. But there was nothing there. There was only Sweet Hosanna and me, and outside the whole world, quiet in the early morning, green and strewn with brand new blossoms, like the ones on my very best dress.

—*Rabble Starkey*

The common elements that you can see and hear in those ending paragraphs are a little like the basics in a good stew; maybe you could equate them to a garlic clove, a bay leaf, and a dollop of wine.

As for the crushed ginger snaps? The ingredient that qualifies as overkill and makes the whole thing just a little nauseating?

Well, I confess that those three passages have one more thing in common. Each one was tough to end. Like the translator who added another sentence to my book, I wanted to go on, too. I wanted to add crushed ginger snaps: more sentences, more images, embellishments, explanations, embroidery.

And if I had? Take a look:

She sped up a little, driving real careful, and when we went around the curve I looked, and it was all a blur. But there was nothing there. There was only Sweet Hosanna and me, and outside the whole world, quiet in the early morning, green and strewn with brand new blossoms, like the ones on my very best dress.

What would the future hold for us? I had no way of knowing. But I remembered how, in the past years, my mother had worked and saved to bring us this far. I looked at her now, her eyes intent on the road, and I could see the determination . . .

Et cetera. You can't read it—I couldn't *write* it—without a feeling of wanting to push your plate away. It's too much. It's unnecessary. It is, in a word, sickening.

The letters I get so often from kids provide me, unintentionally, with a reminder of the impact of a good ending. Boy, if anyone in the world knows how to *end,* it's a kid writing a letter.

"Well," they say, "I have to quit now."

§101

DISCOVERING STORIES FOR PICTURE BOOKS

BY BARBARA ABERCROMBIE

YOU ASK YOURSELF WHAT COULD BE SO HARD about writing a picture book? It ought to be easy: a short simple story for little kids . . . kind of an apprenticeship for writing adult fiction. So you write a short simple story you think children will like, but when you send it out to publishers it only generates rejection slips. You wonder if there's some sort of trick to discovering stories that will sell. A right way to do it, maybe a formula.

There isn't a trick, of course, or a formula, and if there's a right way to write picture books for children, it's simply being honest about your own feelings. *Your* feelings, not what you think children should or should not feel.

What were *your* secret fantasies when you were little? Did you want to fly? Did you wish you could talk to your cat, or vice versa? Did you want a larger family, or to be an only child? Were you ever confused about who you were and what was expected of you? Did you sometimes have the best intentions in the world but find your actions misinterpreted? Did you want to be bigger? Better? Braver? Did your parents ever embarrass you? Did you feel guilty about being embarrassed? Did you feel too tall, too short, too thin, too fat?

You may notice that things don't change all that much when we grow up. What we dreamed of, found joy in, hid from, or hoped to change as children often still concerns us as adults, and out of these concerns can come the best stories for picture books. It took me a long time to realize this. When I first attempted writing for children, I believed I could think and plan my way into a story. But instead, the idea for my first picture book, *Amanda & Heather & Company*, came to me as an image, a flash of memory: I remembered how it felt to be a little kid on an elevator and able to see only adult knees.

I can't tell you how or why this image popped into my head. But I can tell you that by paying attention to the feeling it gave me, of being very small and not understanding adults and their strange rituals, a story evolved about two little girls puzzled by the strange ways grown-ups enjoy themselves at a party. There's nothing about elevators in the story, but there is an illustration (by Mimi Boswell) showing Heather, very small, looking up at a sea of adult knees.

From writing my first picture book, I learned this lesson: Pay attention to your feelings, respect them, and recognize the paradox of thinking that your emotions are unique, yet at the same time *universal*.

One way to get direction into how you felt in the past is through sense memories—concentrating on whatever you absorbed through your five senses during a specific experience. Try it with the following list (you might want to make up your own list later). After each image, shut your eyes for a few moments, relax, and imagine seeing, smelling, tasting, touching, or hearing whatever the image suggests. Choose a specific period in your childhood and pay attention to the feelings that surface with the memory.
Imagine:

* the smell of your classroom the first day of school
* trying on a brand-new pair of shoes
* listening to the sounds of a summer night after you've gone to bed
* eating hot cereal in your kitchen on a cold winter morning
* holding a kitten and running your fingers through its fur
* walking barefoot through grass
* the sound of your parents' voices when they're angry
* opening a present you've longed for (or not getting a present you've longed for)
* your bedroom: what your bed looks like, the things you collect, your favorite toys, the view from the window
* playing a game with your best friend: the sounds, surroundings, feel of the ball or cards or whatever the game is played with

Notice also from this exercise how few words it takes to evoke feelings and memories.

In a picture book as in a poem, each word counts and echoes. In fact, I think a picture book is closer to a poem than to any other form of writing. The story needs to be compressed, yet at the same time each line requires weight and concentration. Dr. Seuss (Theodor Geisel) spoke of "boiling the thing down to the essentials." Simplicity and specific images (including metaphors) are essential. And your story must entertain as well. The sounds and rhythm of the language are vital. Children like to hear a good picture book read over and over again (something rarely true of novels or other forms of written material), but won't want to listen if the story isn't fun.

To understand the power of a picture book, the range and depth and sheer fun it can offer a child, read Maurice Sendak's *Where the Wild Things Are*. Read it over and over, and you'll understand how and why a picture book can endure and resonate, as a poem can. Read *The Story of Ferdinand* by Munro Leaf, too. Written over fifty years ago, this children's classic about a gentle bull who just wants to sit quietly and smell the flowers is an example of what can be done with plot, character, language, humor, and meaning in less than three pages of text. Read and study picture books that were your favorites when you were a child, then read at least fifty examples of picture books that are being published today—not for formulas or rules, but for information and to see what is possible. The best way to learn how to write is to read what you want to write. (This sounds obvious, but I'm always amazed at how many people try to write for children without ever reading what's being published today.)

How do ideas for picture book stories come to you? All I really know for sure is that out of the writing itself comes the story. You take a flash of memory, a true-life incident, a dream, or an observation, and you start writing. You take a cat from your own life and give it to two children in your imagination. You remember what it feels like when a pet is missing. You try what-ifs. What if the father lives in the city with a new wife? What if the girls visit them every weekend? And then suddenly you realize how that situation would connect to the fact that the cat has two homes.

Sometimes inspiration for picture books can come from experiences we have as adults, and then the story itself grows from a blend of reality and imagination. Charlie, the cat in my picture book *Charlie Anderson,* was actually a cat my parents adopted and that, they later discovered, had a second family. I wrote his story through the eyes of two little girls, but only as I wrote did I discover that Sarah and Elizabeth also have two families—a mother in the country and a father and stepmother in the city. I didn't start out to write about children who have two homes because of a divorce; I followed Charlie's life and discovered a more meaningful story as I wrote.

Another source of inspiration for picture books can be an urge to rewrite history, a need to change a sad, factual ending to a happy or more satisfying one. Newspapers can be gold mines for stories you'd like to rewrite. A few years ago I read a letter to Dear Abby about a pet pig named Hamlet who thought he was a dog. His life came to a sad yet predictable end (his name a self-fulfilling prophecy) when his owner had to give him up because of complaints from her suburban neighbors. The grieving owner wrote to Abby to let the world know how good-hearted pigs are and what wonderful pets they make. I was moved by the letter and couldn't get it out of my mind. Finally, I began a story about a pig that would have a happy ending. I worked on it for a long time before I discovered what the story was really about. My pig, renamed Henry, wants to fit into the family that adopted him. He first tries to be a baby, then one of the cats, and then one of the dogs, but he never really belongs or feels appreciated. He can't find happiness because he's always trying to be something he isn't; he feels he's the wrong color, his fur or tail isn't right, or he's too fat. My happy ending has Henry living out the rest of his natural life in a petting zoo, where he's loved and admired for what he is—a magnificent friendly pink pig.

I wrote this story for myself, to make me feel better about the real-life pig who wanted to be a dog. Picture books aren't written for children *out there* in desperate need of being shown the right way to feel and think and live. The child we're really writing for is right inside us. We're writing for the children we were, and the adults we are now. We still want to hear stories that make us laugh at ourselves and the weirdness of the world; stories that tell us we're not the only ones who get into trouble or danger or feel crazy sometimes; stories that will comfort us in the dark.

102

PUTTING YOUR CHARACTERS TO WORK IN MYSTERY FICTION

BY MARY BLOUNT CHRISTIAN

IF WE HAVE DONE OUR JOBS WELL, our characters are real to our young readers. In fact, they are not "characters" at all, but people—living, breathing people who are bumbling through their troubles like the rest of us and who occasionally triumph, making all of us feel better about ourselves.

I gave as much thought to creating that clever Old English Sheepdog, Sebastian (Super Sleuth), as I have to any of my human characters. Detective John Quincy Jones, his human caretaker, is like a single parent. And while Sebastian is a much better detective than John, he, like my young readers, must depend on the kindness of others for his very existence. Sebastian can't open doors or dog food cans. He has no money of his own, and although he thinks in English, he speaks only Canine, which means he has a difficult time putting his ideas across to people.

He is much smarter than others realize. And he is sharply reprimanded when he does something naughty but is rarely, if ever, applauded for accomplishments. My young readers identify with these experiences and readily accept Sebastian as a peer, ignoring the fact that he's hairy and four-footed.

Reader identification is your best tool in making a story believable. It allows the readers to suspend disbelief in some pretty unbelievable adventures.

It's highly improbable that eight- and ten-year-olds, or even teens (and certainly not dogs), will be faced with the sorts of mysteries I confront them with in my stories. I must create people who are so believable, so real that they make the story work, as improbable as it may seem on the surface.

Introducing these people and their peculiarities to readers should never be rushed. Writers are like anthropologists, slowly brushing away the surface clutter to reveal the wondrous secrets, one layer at a time. That is my favorite part of the writing process, because I find surprises at every layer.

Most of my stories begin with a vague situation and only a general idea about whom I need to carry my story: the gender, the age, the surface flaws and strengths.

I carry a small notebook with me all the time, and I jot down brief reminders of people I've observed with potential for characterization. As a "people collector," I may immediately remember someone I've observed—that toothless waitress with the smear of ketchup across the front of her apron, that shifty-eyed guy with hands the size of hams hanging out from his horse blanket coat—from whom I might get the idea for the fictional character I need.

That image remains blurry, however, until I find the right name for him or her, and I am every bit as attentive to my characters' names as I was to naming my offspring.

For contemporary given names I pore through *Name Your Baby* (Bantam). For popular names, there are the school directories and the birth announcements in the newspapers. If I want a name that is rural and rugged or from a past century, I use *Bible Names* (Ark Products) or *Who's Who in the Bible* (Spire). For more unusual names or ethnic names I consult *The New Age Baby Name Book* (Warner). Last names are as important as first names. Just be sure to select names that fit the origins and backgrounds of your characters. This, too, helps in developing your character.

I go through these books until one of the names finally "connects" with that blurry figure, and the features begin to sharpen. I knew I couldn't name my fictional dog hero after our own dog, though he was the inspiration for the character. Who would have believed a hero named Popsicle? The minute I found my name Sebastian, the image of a not-so-perfect Old English sheepdog, an undercover canine, became clear, and the story began to gel for me.

When I wanted to write a near-slapstick mystery with a hero who took himself a little too seriously, I chose Fenton P. Smith for his name, a mix of the usual and unusual and a bit of mystery thrown in, too, just like my character.

Once I'm sure the name and physical image are properly merged, I do the "Baskin-Robbins" test, probably because I'm a perpetual dieter, and this lets me visit vicariously the forbidden ice cream store. I can learn a lot just by observing my character in that setting.

Does he order vanilla, chocolate, or strawberry when confronted with all those luscious choices? He's probably a traditionalist, slow to take risks. As a mystery hero, he'll need to get pushed to the limit before he'll fight back.

Does he go for the raspberry truffles orange blossom flavor-of-the-month—without asking for a sample first? He's easily influenced and ready to follow the suspect down a dark alley. Does he get a dish or a cone, a double or single dip? Draw your own conclusions; there are no calories.

I go home with him and march right into his room, opening drawers and closet doors, peering under the bed. Are things jammed into drawers or divided and neatly stacked? Is that a stack of automotive magazines shoved under the bed? And is that a pair of hockey skates next to the baseball cleats?

The choice of furniture and curtains may be his mom's, but that poster from the movie *Top Gun* is his own.

I've learned a lot about my character, and I haven't even been through his billfold yet. Of course, I will! We carry our identities with us—in our billfolds, in our purses. There are pictures of our loved ones, our special friends, maybe even our pets. We can tell if he has a driver's license, a student I.D., a private pilot's license, membership in specific organizations, whether or not he has one or several credit cards or any cash.

With these tidbits of information, which I'll jot on a sheet of paper, I will list his position in the family (only, middle, oldest child, etc.), his religious background, his attitudes toward children, the elderly, and animals, his ethnic background, his personal ambitions and needs. When I know enough about him, I may write one or more scenes of conflict, just to hear his voice, listen to his inner thoughts, and watch his physical reactions. Does he slouch when he believes himself alone but stand straight in the presence of others? How does he enter a room? Does he repeat a phrase often? How does he sound when he's talking to his best friend, his teacher, his parent, his girlfriend?

And I won't neglect the other members of my little band of characters, either. The anti-hero has a past that has shaped his attitudes and personality, too. And he won't see himself as the villain. He'll have what are to him valid reasons for behaving as he does. Also, he is a villain because of what he does, not because of what he looks like. So I make a sketch for him, too, and for anyone else who will play a major part in the story.

Imagine all the events in our characters' lives, from birth to death, strung together in a chain; our story is about one tiny link of that chain. We see only that section directly in front of us. Yet, everything our characters do that we can see is influenced by their past experiences. Their futures depend on what they do while we observe them, so if we want them to have reasonably happy futures, it's up to us to send our characters on life's journey with the personalities that will make it so.

You wouldn't send a mountain climber up Pike's Peak without a safety rope and pick. Neither should you send a character into a mystery without curiosity, stamina, and a strong feeling of self-preservation. Whether or not he recognizes these qualities in himself in the beginning, they must already be in place when the story starts, or the glue and Band-Aids will show, and your story will lack believability.

The sheet of information will grow as I write the first draft, peeling away the layers of protective covering that my character, like all of us, has built around himself. When a scene isn't working for me, I go back to my information sheet where I had noted, for example, that at the age of five my character was trapped in a burning house until he was rescued by a firefighter. That's how I knew how he would react now to a house fire. And, because my sketch also indicated that his father had died in a hit-and-run accident, I knew he'd feel strongly about catching a hit-and-run driver.

There is more than just knowing how your character would react to a given situation, though. I had sold several stories with only so-so reviews from the critics until I was lucky enough to attend a workshop given by Tony Hillerman. What he said changed my writing technique and my reviews for the better.

He reminded us that it is sensory detail that bonds the reader to the main character and makes the unbelievable seem true. He told us to write our first drafts, then go back and see that every typed page had at least two sensory details observed through the viewpoint character. Now I experience the story with all my senses: taste, smell, touch, sight, sound. I am thus bonded with my character, and so is my reader.

§103

WRITING CREATIVE NONFICTION BOOKS FOR CHILDREN

BY CHARLENE W. BILLINGS

WRITING NONFICTION BOOKS FOR CHILDREN involves far more than telling just the facts. Part of the challenge is to transform facts into knowledge and insights that excite and compel young readers to want to learn more. Many of the techniques are the same as those used to write fiction.

Accuracy

Accuracy is paramount. The editors of biographies and science books for children are very meticulous about getting the facts straight.

Careful research and documentation are the first steps toward accuracy. Whenever possible, I photocopy information so that I have exact copies for my files, thus averting misquoting a statistic or misspelling a name. If the source is an interview, I ask permission to tape the conversation and later transcribe the material. Usually, a person being interviewed will cooperate if he or she understands that the purpose of the recording is to ensure accuracy.

Of course, facts are not always conveniently in print. Conflicting facts must be interpreted objectively so you can come as close as possible to the truth. One inescapable truth is that inaccuracies undermine the credibility of your work. Sometimes, presenting differing points of view to your readers and letting them reach their own conclusions is a good approach that encourages readers to think for themselves.

Organizing facts

Essential to the creative process of writing a nonfiction book is organizing the facts into a cohesive whole that is more than the sum of its parts, rather like putting together the pieces of a jigsaw puzzle to form a picture. Before all else, it is important for you to be able to summarize the primary point of your book in a few concise sentences.

Your next step is to write a complete outline that includes chapters with their subtopics, a conclusion, appendices, if any, a glossary, a list for further reading, an index, and a bibliography. This discipline forces you to decide what the major topics and subtopics are and how best to arrange them before getting into the actual writing of the book. Preparing an outline helps you to see relationships among the many parts, often in an unexpected new light. It also helps you decide how much emphasis (and therefore, space) to allot to various sections to achieve balance in your book. This is especially important in a children's book, where length and the amount of detail to include are limited by the age of your audience, or by editorial requirements. A good outline should be flexible enough to allow you to add newly discovered, fascinating, and timely information to your book as you proceed with the writing.

Openers

Opening paragraphs are vitally important because it is at the outset that you must engage your readers' interest and attention.

Young readers love to learn about unusual or poisonous animals, and with this idea in mind, I wrote *Scorpions.* The opening paragraphs describe a natural drama:

The chirping cricket is unaware of danger nearby.
Without warning, the giant hairy scorpion seizes the prey with its claws. It flashes the poisonous tip of its tail forward to sting the struggling insect. The lightning attack silences the cricket's song and the scorpion eats its freshly caught supper.

In *Loon: Voice of the Wilderness,* the opening paragraph sets the scene, and immediately, on page one, the young reader is involved sounding out the haunting calls of the loon.

Except for the music of the wind through the forest, few sounds can be heard on the North Country lake in New Hampshire. It is early May. Reflections of spruce, balsam, fir, and white birch trees shimmer on the sunlit surface of the water.
One day, just before dusk, a pair of birds flies in wide circles over the lake, then splash down on the water. They are common loons *(Gavia immer).* Spine-tingling cries pierce the stillness.

"A-a-whoo-quee-quee-whe-oooo-que!"
"A-a-whoo-quee-quee-whe-oooo-que!"

Once you have enticed your readers into your book, how do you keep their attention?

Imaginative chapter titles are one way. For example, in *Scorpions,* Chapter 4 describes the mating ritual of scorpions, but because the male often ends up as a meal for the female, it is called "Courtship—the Dance of Death." Chapter 6 is about survival but is titled "Eating and Being Eaten."

Chapter titles also give an overview of a book; a reader can quickly see what is covered. In *Christa McAuliffe: Pioneer Space Teacher,* chapter titles summarize the biography that I had started months before the launch of the *Challenger* and rewrote after the shuttle disaster as a tribute to Christa (and the crew): "Teacher With the Right Stuff," "Life Before Stardom," "Teacher in Training," "Countdown to the Final Frontier," and "Triumph From Tragedy."

In my book *Superconductivity: From Discovery to Breakthrough,* I made several chapter titles in the form of questions: "What is Superconductivity?"; "What Do We Know About Superconductors?"; and "How Are Superconductors Made?" In *Microchip: Small Wonder,* I ask, "What Is a Chip?" and "Where Are Chips Used?" Such titles encourage readers to seek answers in the text of the book.

Quotations, anecdotes, details and humor

Quotations, anecdotes, and realistic details add substance to science and make your book interesting. Humor offers proof that even serious scientists like to laugh.

In *Grace Hopper: Navy Admiral and Computer Pioneer,* I describe a hot summer day in 1945, when Grace Hopper was working with one of the earliest automated computers, the Mark II, at Harvard University. Because it was wartime, it was vitally important to keep the computer operating around the clock. Moving mechanical parts called relays did the computer's calculations, but suddenly, the computer stopped. A search revealed a moth beaten to death by the moving parts of relay #70. The moth was taped into the Navy logbook, and the entry for that day states, "First actual case of bug being found."

Grace said, "We got a pair of tweezers. Very carefully we took the moth out

535

of the relay, put it in the logbook, and put Scotch tape over it. . . . From then on if we weren't making any numbers, . . . we were debugging the computer." As far as Grace knows, that's where the term *debugging* started.

Historical perspective

Historical accounts enrich science books and biography with invaluable perspective, especially for young readers who, of course, were not alive when the events occurred. For example, four years after he invented the telephone, Alexander Graham Bell tested another communications device. The photophone used a beam of sunlight traveling through the air to carry the sound of human voice from one place to another. In *Fiber Optics: Bright New Way to Communicate* and *Lasers: The New Technology of Light,* I briefly describe how the photophone worked and tell of Bell's enthusiasm expressed in a line from a letter he wrote to his father: "I have heard a ray of sun laugh and cough and sing!" Though Bell thought the photophone was one of his best ideas, the technology to make a practical photophone did not exist while he was alive.

In Chapter 1 of *Superconductivity: From Discovery to Breakthrough,* I introduce the reader to the work of Dutch scientist, Heike Kamerlingh Onnes, who, in 1911, discovered that when mercury is cooled to the extremely low temperature of liquid helium, it suddenly allows electricity to flow through it without loss of energy. From this historical beginning, the reader is led to the more recent breakthroughs in superconductivity research made in the 1980s.

Even from such brief historical accounts, the young reader learns that the foundation of science is built by the efforts of many dedicated researchers through years of time. And the single inspired moment of synthesis, the *Eureka!* of a significant scientific discovery, depends upon this foundation. Such an insight provides the reader with much more than just the scientific facts; it leads the reader to an understanding of science as an ongoing process.

Historical accounts also add perspective to current issues in science. In *Pesticides: Necessary Risk,* I note that DDT was hailed at first because it saved millions of lives by preventing a typhus epidemic in Naples, Italy, in 1944, where it was dusted onto 1,300,000 people. It had also halted an epidemic of plague in Dakar, Africa. By the 1950s, however, doubts arose about the effects of DDT on the environment.

536

In *Silent Spring,* published in 1962, Rachel Carson heightened the public's awareness of environmental problems and warned of the dangers inherent in the indiscriminate use of pesticides. In my book, *Pesticides: Necessary Risk,* I directed young readers to Carson's landmark book, described by Justice William O. Douglas as ". . . the most important chronicle of this century for the human race."

Photographs and illustrations

Another way to keep readers turning pages in a nonfiction book is to provide intriguing illustrations with informative captions. Except for my first book, I have done all of the photo research for my books and written or edited most of the captions.

The research I did for *Salamanders* (the first of my books illustrated with photographs) taught me that locating photographs and obtaining permission to use them in a book is as much work and responsibility as writing the manuscript. Many of the people who provide photographs are also expert sources of current information.

The idea for the opening paragraphs in *Scorpions* came from my seeing a picture of a giant hairy scorpion eating a cricket. Dramatizing the action in a photograph became a wonderful hook to rivet the attention of young readers from the moment they open the book. Other photographs show a scorpion fighting a tarantula, a close-up of a scorpion's stinger, and a female scorpion with her young riding piggyback.

In *Lasers: The New Technology of Light,* I used an electron micrograph of an ant carrying a microchip to emphasize the microscopic miniaturization of devices made possible by laser technology. The same photograph appears opposite the opening page in *Microchip: Small Wonder,* and here, once again, I wrote the opening paragraphs of the book inspired by a remarkable photograph.

A nonfiction book for young readers should have a satisfying conclusion. The ending should summarize the factual information in the book and transmit the excitement of learning about science, history, and human achievements.

Including a list of books and articles for further reading is helpful for readers who want to learn more, and it reinforces the fact that no one book or article can cover everything about a topic. An index will help readers find information in your book, and a bibliography is necessary to lead readers to related information in other sources.

Nonfiction books for children often seem to be viewed as "just facts" and, therefore, as somehow less creative or less important than fiction. But, biographies and books about science or history are as fundamental to children's reading as fiction. In clear language, they present accurate information, intriguing insights, historical perspective, and inspiring role models and, far more than just telling the facts, nonfiction books document the human creative process, celebrate human achievement, and affirm the indomitable nature of the human spirit.

EDITING AND MARKETING

104

GETTING OUT OF THE SLUSH PILE

BY HAROLD UNDERDOWN

AS PART OF MY JOB AS A CHILDREN'S book editor, I read many unsolicited manuscripts. I'd like to pass on some of my experiences, since it's people at my level whom many of you are reaching with submissions, and we, not more senior editors, need new authors.

I'll start where the process begins—the dreaded "Slush Pile": I could be polite and talk about "unsolicited manuscripts," but that is not how people in publishing refer to them, though we use the term with a mix of frustration, bemusement and hope—frustration with the volume of material we have to deal with, bemusement at some of the more misguided submissions, and hope that there'll be something interesting in it today (and if not today, then tomorrow). In any case, the slush is a potential goldmine for a publisher, so most publishers really do read the slush, though they are not always well organized at it.

In the slush pile, certain kinds of manuscripts predominate, and you should aim to distinguish your work from this kind of material, which readers are tired of seeing. So here's a list of some kinds of manuscripts of which I see too many.

Hot topics: Anything in the news brings a brief flurry of manuscripts, from picture books to novels, that in some way "cover" the topic. Desert Storm was one popular source. "Green books" are more generally hot, and often overwhelmingly pedantic and focused on topics like recycling, which is overpublished; a recent submission—"Tony Two-Liter Gets Recycled." The Clintons' cat and the rain forests are big, too. But how many books can be published on a particular topic? Not many. . . .

Personified objects: This category ranges from the mundane (Clyde the Cloud who teaches you about the weather) to the bizarre (Harry the Horizon Line). We get a lot of these simple picture book stories, all of them meant to teach something, either practical information or values. This used to be a common kind of picture book, but it's not being published much today.

Hot characters: New spins on Santa, the Easter bunny, characters from cartoons. Leaving aside the problem with using copyrighted characters, which some people don't seem to be aware of, it is simply difficult to come up with a *truly* original approach to a well-known character.

Anthropomorphized alliterated animals: This includes Sally Squirrel, Carter Carp and Billy the Bossy Beetle. We get hundreds of stories that fall into this category, many by authors who seem to think a story is only a story for children if it has a talking animal with a cute name. But, all too often, their characters work neither as animals nor as stand-ins for children.

Isn't———(insert name) cute?: Authors writing about their own pets or children, or about grandparents who have wonderful relationships with their grandkids, feel their stories are very meaningful, but all too often children would find them like looking at 200 snapshots of a neighbor's little genius.

Verse: Many people will attempt to write like Dr. Seuss; *they try and they try—it just isn't much use.* I can't do it myself. Verse really has to work perfectly in stories or poetry collections for kids, or it sounds just horrible.

Series: Some people put a lot of time and effort into developing a whole series of picture books or novels, as in a recent proposal I saw for 32 picture books about two brothers' adventures on a farm. Unfortunately, hardcover publishers almost never would sign up more than one book at a time, and the effort that went into the series is wasted.

Genre novels: This category includes formulaic middle-grade mysteries and adventure stories, YA romances and memoirs of teenage years by adults. Though competently written and possibly as good as published work, they don't hold the attention of the eager slush reader, who needs to find something *different.*

"Accepting yourself" stories: This is a classic story line in children's books, of course. But how many variations on the story of the Ugly Duckling do we need? We get lots!

Avoid these types if you want to catch the eye of a reader like me. It *is* possible to get a new spin on an old subject, but will your reader necessarily notice that you have done so? Strike out into new territory!

542

Be original and you will get the reader's attention (eventually—though there are many stories of famous books that were rejected before being taken on).

I also see a lot of peripheral material submitted with manuscripts, none of which helps to get my attention:

Illustrations—Unless you are certain you are cut out to be an author/illustrator, don't send any. They can just get in the way of the reader's visualizing the story.

Fancy paper, colorful envelope, Express Mail—all suggest you don't know the standard procedure and convey an unfortunate hint of desperation.

Resumé, qualifications—don't bother to include unless your experience is truly relevant. Writing a technical manual for adults, for example, is not something a reader needs to know about.

Agents—we're getting more and more submissions from people who call themselves agents, but as we don't know them manuscripts are treated like other slush. New authors from *known* agents—same thing. You'll find it hard to get a good agent until you're published, and so you would do better to direct your efforts at publishers.

Cassettes, slides, etc.—these are just a distraction. Most readers don't have the necessary equipment in their offices.

Marketing plans and series ideas—most editors feel they know or their marketing department knows how to market a book and whether a book could become a series.

I have developed a cynical rule of thumb. The more work someone does on peripherals, the less work they have put into the manuscript, and this neglect will probably show.

Does it help to address your submission to a particular editor? I think editors' names are useful only if you have actually made a real contact with someone, either through an encouraging letter or meeting her/him at a conference. Otherwise, the manuscript goes into the slush pile. It can also be counterproductive to use names if your information is not absolutely current or if the person you have sent your middle-grade novel to does only nonfiction. And since beginning editors aren't well known, you can miss them—the ones you want to reach—if you target someone more established. Above all, do not phone and ask for names. Assistants resent it—the implication is that you don't trust them or the reader to pick out the promising stuff—and even if you get a name, you'll probably just end up in the slush, after a slight pause on the editor's desk.

How *can* you get someone's attention? There are two ways that can work:

1. Find a niche, and trumpet this fact in your cover letter (which should be no longer than half a page, or it won't be read). Check *Children's Books in Print,* other reference guides and your library. Find ways to differentiate your manuscript from what is already out there. Do you have a new angle on a familiar subject? Say what it is. This works best in nonfiction, of course, but may also apply with picture books and fiction. In any case, you should always know what similar books exist. Reading the major review magazines—*Horn Book, Booklist, School Library Journal, Publishers Weekly*—can also help keep you up-to-date, and *PW* is particularly useful for news of publishers, gossip, trends, etc.

2. Work on the manuscript. Be tough on yourself. Many manuscripts we get seem not to have been revised, critiqued in any way—writers' workshops are thus a very good idea. As a small side note, local writing contests are not a good measure of your story being ready for publishers. We get occasional manuscripts with a proud cover letter saying it won such-and-such a contest—but these invariably read like good short stories for adults with children as characters, and that is why they won. Feedback from professionals, not friends or family, is probably the most valuable.

In the end, the manuscript has to speak for itself. Simply send your polished manuscript with SASE and a letter pointing out its unique angle to the Submissions Editor (or some such title) of a given imprint.

Try not only new companies, but also regional, specialty, or niche publishers. And do not neglect magazines. You gain valuable experience working with an editor and also get yourself a track record. I know I pay more attention to someone if they have been published; it shows the author is committed to his writing.

The best way, in the end, to get out of the slush pile is to write what you are passionate about. Strive to get beyond competence to something only you can write about in a particular way. Find an editor who shares your passion. If you aren't passionate about your writing, after all, there's simply no reason to be in this field. There's no guarantee that you will get out of the slush pile, and even if you do, you aren't likely to get rich from your writing. So it helps if you get something out of the writing itself. Good luck in your efforts! Luck is another thing that helps. . . .

§105

THE AUTHOR/AGENT RELATIONSHIP

BY JONATHAN DOLGER

IT USED TO BE TRUE, WHEN I FIRST STARTED working in publishing, that the hardest thing to accomplish was finding a publisher. In those days, publishers still accepted unsolicited manuscripts from authors, and they were read by the editorial staff on a weekly basis. There were fewer agents, and contact between the writer and the editor was on a one-to-one basis, simpler than is currently the case.

With the increasing growth and consolidation of publishing companies, publishing has become a more bureaucratic process. Editors' choices are subjected to a review process that includes looking at "profit and loss statements," input from the marketing and sales staff, etc. Rarely can an editor make the final decision on whether or not to publish a manuscript. Instead, we have judgment by consensus, with editors functioning as *de facto* lobbyists.

It's not productive or helpful for the author to worry about these matters. The "gentlemen's business" has become a real business, and that's not so bad. It has produced, from a variety of viewpoints, a collective approach to publishing, which when it works, can be very successful.

The result of this is that many agents have taken over what used to be seen as part of the editorial side of publishing: i.e., reading and evaluating new work. Agents are not magicians, so it would be unreasonable to expect that if an agent agrees to represent you, you will automatically find a publisher. No one can force an editor to buy a book: There has to be reaction to and interaction with the material itself.

What an agent can do, if your work is accepted for publication, is not only make sure that you get the best possible contract, but also continue to protect your interests with the publisher throughout the entire publication process. This is extremely important, since with so many editors changing from one house to another, it is not at all uncommon to have several editors work on your manuscript. Indeed, a client of mine recently had five different editors at the same house, beginning with the one who acquired the book and ending with the one to whom the book was assigned at the time of actual publication.

Now that I've stated just how important an agent can be for a writer, let me also say that a beginning writer can, and should, begin to establish a career before finding an agent. Magazines and newspapers are still the best places for a beginning writer to get published. Don't confine yourself to the few "brand-name" publications, as they may have many of the same problems as book publishers when it comes to screening and reading unsolicited material. It is possible to begin to build your reputation on a local and regional level, develop contacts, and have a good body of work published, at which point you will be in a better position to approach a potential publisher or agent. I recently attended a writers' conference where there were 450 writers, and many of them began their professional careers in just this manner. A good source book here is *The International Directory of Little Magazines and Small Presses,* published by Dustbooks (P.O. Box 100, Paradise, CA 95967).

If you have already reached the point in your professional career where you think you should have an agent, your next hurdle will be to find the right agent and agency for you. You may have contacts who can personally recommend you to some literary agents. If this isn't the case, there are a number of reliable source books that list literary agents and their requirements, including *Literary Market Place* and *The Writer's Handbook.* Most agencies can easily tell you what kind of material they represent and what types of manuscripts you should submit for their consideration. For example, my agency represents adult trade fiction and nonfiction, as well as illustrated books. We do not accept unsolicited manuscripts, but will consider query letters with sample material, and an SASE. So if you are an author of science fiction or children's books, my agency would not be the best choice for you. In general, you should also be aware that most agencies will not charge a reading fee, so double-check any offers to "evaluate" your material for a price.

Once you find the right agency for you, it's time to consider the question of author/agent contracts. Should authors have contracts with agents, and what happens if things don't work out and you want to break the contract? Some agencies insist on having a contract with every client. Generally, the contract will specify what happens if either the author or the agent wants to end the relationship, but if no such language exists, you should ask that it be inserted into the agreement. The contract between you and any agent should not make you liable for work, or options on your work that continue after the agreement is terminated. There are exceptions to this rule: For example, if an agent sells something before the official termination date of a client's agreement, the agent is entitled to the agreed-upon percentage of proceeds from that sale.

One of the main benefits of a writer's contract with an agent (and the reason many authors request such a contract) is that it makes the agent/client relationship clearer and more professional. There should be little reason for disputes if both parties know the responsibilities of the other, what rights are being negotiated, and what percentages the agent charges (percentages vary with the number of services offered— i.e., sales to foreign publishers, sales of film/television rights, etc.— but usually range between 10% and 20% of the author's gross receipts). A simple letter of agreement spelling out these terms should be sufficient. You don't need to sign away your soul on a document that is more convoluted than the tax information provided *gratis* by the IRS.

One of the most important functions an agent performs before sending your material out to publishers is to make sure that it is in the most intelligible and marketable shape. There is a difference between fiction and nonfiction, and I will address these areas separately.

For a nonfiction book by an unpublished author, the publisher can reasonably expect an outline or proposal, and two or three sample chapters that will give him some sense of how the writer will deal with the chosen subject. It doesn't matter whether it's a self-help book or a sociological study of environmental hazards; what these pages must demonstrate is the tone the book will take. To this exent, the agent acts as a "pre-editor," making sure that the ideas are clearly articulated and presented and that the author clearly has a point of view and knows how to communicate it. Also included should be some information about the author: background, other published articles, education. Equally important, the agent can help the author focus the proposal for its potential market.

547

The agent will want to know—just as the publisher will—what competition there might be. Are there similar books in the field that have been or are about to be published? If so, does this one have a special handle that will distinguish it from the others? Are there other markets that the publisher should consider with this book—special premium sales, professional groups, etc.—that will give the book added appeal? Has the book been endorsed or recommended by someone prominent in the field? Does the author have personal contacts with other professionals who would help him obtain information that might not be readily available to others? The proposal should be fifty to seventy-five pages of material that is as good as the author and agent can make it. The agent will add his own perspective and information when the material is sent out to the publisher, but this will serve only to highlight the information in the proposal. The author's voice must be heard on its own.

The handling of fiction is often quite different. In the current diminished and very competitive marketplace, it is rare to sell a novel by an unpublished or even published writer on the basis of a few sample chapters and a synopsis. Most publishers want to see a complete manuscript before making a decision to take on a writer. There are exceptions—mostly in "category" books such as romances or male adventure stories—but these novels are written to a specific formula and therefore are not judged by the same standards and criteria. Also, fiction is a *subjective* art: One editor's taste and sensitivity will vary from another's. Only from reading a completed manuscript can an editor judge what a writer is trying to accomplish.

Here again, the agent can help the author by trying to be sure that the pacing is right, the characters well developed, and that the author makes the reader care and sympathize with his story, but there is less involvement by the agent on this level than with a nonfiction proposal. To a certain extent, the agent's view is also subjective; the agent must take into account that his or her reactions may be personal and that an editor might have a different response.

Once an agent has decided to take you on as a client, whether for fiction or nonfiction, there are several ways to submit your manuscript for publication.

The traditional method has been to choose one publishing house and editor at a time and let them consider the book on an exclusive basis.

If there is no sale, you move on to the second, third, or fourth choice. However, because time is so limited and the publishing process so much more complicated by the many editorial committees that often control selection at a publishing house, the agent may want to submit that material to a number of publishers at the same time. Another obvious reason for multiple submissions is that if the book's subject matter is timely (for example, a current political topic), you want to get the widest amount of exposure as quickly as possible. Some publishers used to be offended by the practice of multiple submissions or auctions, but I don't believe that is a valid viewpoint for the current publishing climate. I try to find the best match between editor, author, and publisher and hope that it works. If it doesn't, I will try a few other houses, but if I still haven't been successful, I will make a limited number of multiple submissions, informing each prospective buyer that other publishers are looking at the material at the same time.

Apart from making the best deal and negotiating the most favorable terms for a client, it is the agent's responsibility to know the publishing network—to make the selection and determination of which editor and house are right for your book. As your link to the publishing community, the agent should shepherd you through the publishing process, looking out for your best interests, but also helping you see the publisher's side of any dispute or disagreement. This requires experience, knowledge, intuition, and often just good diplomatic sense. It has been my experience that authors often do not act in their own best interests when they act alone; they require the objective help of an agent.

Negotiating contracts can vary as much as contracts vary from publisher to publisher. The business points, such as advances and royalties, may be similar, but there are many subtleties in such areas of negotiation as subsidiary rights, warranty, and out-of-print clauses that only an experienced agent can handle. A good agent will also be aware of recent changes in publishing agreements, such as those resulting from the coming of the united European market in 1992, which will make it even more imperative to have an agent's solid, professional advice.

Having your work accepted for representation by an agent and obtaining a publishing contract may seem like the end of a road well-traveled, but in truth it's only the beginning. When the sale is concluded, the publishing process begins. Along the way, there are many decisions that will have to be made regarding editorial changes, book design, promotion, and publicity. In the current publishing climate, even the most sophisticated writer can feel like a new arrival in Oz, where the direction of the Yellow Brick Road has changed, and the Wizard has a boss! In these uncertain times, the good counsel of your literary agent means that you won't travel alone and there'll be someone to help you read the map.

❡106

COMMON QUESTIONS ABOUT COPYRIGHTS

BY HOWARD ZAHAROFF

TO BE A GOOD WRITER, YOU MUST UNDERSTAND THE BASICS OF WRITING. To be a published writer, you must understand the basics of manuscript submission and the editorial process.

And to be a successful writer, the owner of a portfolio of published manuscripts, you must also understand the basics of copyright law. As a lawyer who practices in the field, I promise that this isn't too hard. Let me prove it by answering a dozen questions that free lancers often ask.

Before doing so, a few comments. First, the answers I give are based on U.S. law. International issues are mostly ignored. Second, my focus is mainly on works first published or created after March 1, 1989, the last major revision of the Copyright Act (which I refer to below as the "Act"). Third, although the Copyright Office cannot provide legal advice, its Circulars and Public Information Office (call 202/479-0700) provide guidance on many of the following issues. (Start with Circular 1, "Copyright Basics.") There are also many excellent books available, such as Ellen Kozak's *Every Writer's Guide to Copyright & Publishing Law* (Owl, 1990).

1. *What can be copyrighted?* Copyright protects nearly every original piece you write (or draw, compose, choreograph, videotape, sculpt, etc.): not just your novel, article, story or poem, but the software program you create, the advertisements and greeting cards you published, and the love letters you wrote in high school. But copyright does not protect your ideas, only the way you *express* them.

2. *What protection does copyright provide?* A "copyright" is really a bundle of rights. The copyright owner (whom we'll call the "proprietor") controls not only the right to copy the work, but also the rights

551

to prepare "derivative works" (i.e., adaptations, translations, and other modifications), to perform or display the work publicly, and to make the "first sale" of each copy of the work.

3. *What is the duration of copyright protection, and is it renewable?* For works created or first published after 1977, copyright generally lasts 50 years after the death of the author. However, for anonymous or pseudonymous works, or works made "for hire" (see below), the term expires 100 years from creation or 75 years from publication. There are no renewals. (For works published before 1978, the term is 28 years, with right to renew for 47 additional years. See Circular 15, "Renewal of Copyright.")

4. *How do you obtain a copyright?* Copyright protection arises *automatically* as soon as you put your ideas into tangible form. Thus, once on paper, canvas, video, or computer disk, your creation is protected by law.

5. *Is a copyright notice required for protection?* No. Until recently a notice was required on all *published* copies of a work. ("Published" simply means distributed to the public; it does not require printing in a periodical or book.) However, on March 1, 1989, the United States joined the international copyright treaty known as the Berne Convention and removed this requirement for works published after that date.

Still, including a copyright notice alerts everyone to your claim and prevents an infringer from pleading "innocence" (that is, that he had no idea your work was copyrighted). Thus, good reasons remain for including notices on all published copies of your work, and for insisting that your publisher do so.

If you are concerned that your *unpublished* work may be used or copied without permission (e.g., you are circulating copies of your most timely and accomplished piece within your newly formed writers group), you can't lose by including a notice.

6. *What should my copyright notice say?* A proper notice has three elements:

- The international copyright symbol © or the word "Copyright." Most publishers use both. (The abbreviation "Copr" is also acceptable.)
- The year in which the work is first published. (For unpublished works, you may omit a date.)

• Your name, or a recognizable abbreviation (e.g., International Business Machines Corporation may use "IBM").

In general, notices should be displayed prominently at the beginning of your work, although any reasonable location is acceptable. If your piece will appear in a magazine, anthology, or other collective work, a single notice in the publisher's name will preserve most of your rights. However, including a separate copyright notice in your own name will clarify that only you, *not* the publisher, has the right to authorize further uses of your work.

7. *Must I register my work with the Copyright Office?* Although registration is not required for copyright protection, it is a precondition to suing for infringement of the copyrights in any work first published in the U.S. (and in the unpublished works of U.S. citizens and residents), and enables you to recover both attorneys' fees and "statutory damages" (i.e. damages of up to $100,000, determined by the judge, which the proprietor may elect to recover from the infringer in lieu of proving and recovering actual losses).

You can register your copyrights at any time during the term of copyright. However, registration within three months of publication generally preserves your rights to all infringement remedies, including statutory damages, while registration within five years of publication provides special benefits in legal proceedings.

8. *How do you register a work?* Copyright Office Form TX is the basic form for nondramatic literary works. Form PA is used to register works of the performing arts, including plays and movies. These one-page forms cost $20 to file and are fairly easy to complete (but only if you read the accompanying instructions!). Adjunct Form GR/CP allows writers to reduce costs by making a single registration for all works published in periodicals within a 12-month period. (You can order forms and circulars over the Hotline, 202/707-9100).

When you apply you must submit one copy of the work, if unpublished, and two copies of the "best edition" of the work, if published. (Only one copy of the best edition is required for contributions to collective works.) The "best edition" is the published edition of highest quality, determined by paper quality, binding, and other factors listed by the Copyright Office (see Circular R7b). For example, if the work was published in both hard and soft covers, the hard cover is normally the best edition.

9. *Should I register my work?* In most cases, no. If your work was published, your publisher may have registered it. If not, failure to register costs you mainly the option for *immediate* relief and statutory damages. Moreover, infringement is the exception and, where it occurs, often can be settled without lawsuits or registration. Besides, most writers earn too little to justify the cost of registration (certainly for articles, poems, and other short works).

10. *What is "public domain" and how can you find out what's there?* Works that are not protected by copyright are said to be in the "public domain"—i.e., freely usable by the public, without the need to get permission or pay a fee. This includes works in which copyright has expired or been lost, works for which copyright is not available, and works dedicated to the public. Although there are many exceptions, *in general* the following are in the public domain:

• Works published more than 75 years ago.
• Works published more than 28 years ago, if the copyright was not renewed.
• Works published without a proper copyright notice before 1978.
• Works published without a proper notice between January 1, 1978 and February 28, 1989 (although the Act enables the proprietor to correct this failure).
• Works created by employees of the Federal government as part of their duties.

For a fee the Copyright Office will examine the status of a work. (See Circular 22, "How to Investigate the Copyright Status of a Work.")

11. *What is fair use?* The Act allows the limited use of others' works for research, teaching, news reporting, criticism, and similar purposes. These permitted uses are called "fair use," although the Act never defines that term. Rather, it lists factors to consider, including the purpose and character of the use (e.g., for-profit vs. teaching), the nature of the work (e.g., a science text vs. a poem), the amount and substantiality of the use, and its effect on the market for the work.

Here are some basic rules that should help you stay on the right side of the law (and help you recognize when someone's use of your work doesn't).

• **Copying for noncommercial (e.g., educational) purposes is given wider scope than copying for commercial use.** For example, in general you may quote less of the published writings of a politician in a television docudrama than a history professor may quote in journal articles.

• **Copying factual material gets more latitude than copying fiction.** Fiction contains more of the "originality" protected by the Act: characters and events, sometimes even time and place, derive from the writer's imagination. Facts cannot be copyrighted.

• **Parody is a permissible use, as long as it does not appropriate too much of the original.**

• **Copying from unpublished works without permission is usually considered unfair.** This was illustrated in a 1989 case concerning an unauthorized biography of Scientologist/SF writer L. Ron Hubbard. Referring to an earlier case, in which Random House was enjoined from publishing an unauthorized biography of J. D. Salinger because it infringed copyrights in his unpublished letters, the court wrote that "unpublished works normally enjoy complete protection" from unauthorized publication. (However, legislation is being considered that would expand the application of fair use to unpublished works.)

• **The Act permits certain uses of copyrighted works by libraries, archives, educators, charitable organizations, and others.** See sections 108–110 of the Act and Circular 21.

These rules are complex. Therefore, if you intend to copy more than a negligible amount from another person's work without permission, write to the publisher or copyright owner. Don't take a chance.

12. *What is a "work made for hire," and who owns the rights to these works?* The creator of a work generally owns the copyrights. There is an exception, however, for "works made for hire." Here it is the party who commissions and pays for the work, rather than the actual creator, who owns the copyrights. So when is a work "for hire"?

First, unless expressly excluded by contract, all works created by employees within the scope of their employment are "for hire." (This will normally not include works created on your own time that are unrelated to your employment.) So if you are employed by a newspaper, or hired by a software publisher to write documentation, your employer owns the copyrights in the works you've been paid to create. If you use copies of these works at your next job, you are infringing on your former employer's copyrights.

Second, certain specified categories of works (including translations, compilations, and parts of audiovisual works) are considered "for hire" if they have been specially commissioned and a signed document identifies them as "for hire." Therefore, *if you are not an employee and you haven't agreed in writing that your work is "for hire" (or otherwise assigned your rights), you will generally continue to own the copyrights in your work* even if others paid you to create it (although they will have the right to use your work for the express purposes for which they paid you).

You may wonder about the division of rights when your article, story, or poem is published in a magazine (or other collective work) and there is no written agreement. The Act supplies the answer: The publisher acquires only the right to publish your piece as part of that collective work, of any revision of that work, and of any later collective work in the same series. You retain all other rights, so you are free to revise or remarket your piece.

The above is a *general* discussion of the copyright law as it applies to freelancers. Myriad qualifications and exceptions are not included here. Before making any important copyright decisions consult a knowledgeable copyright lawyer, the Copyright Office, or a trusted publisher or agent with an up-to-date understanding of the law.

§107

DEBUNKING THE WRITING-FOR-CHILDREN-IS-EASY MYTH

BY STEPHANIE OWENS LURIE
Senior Editor, *Little, Brown and Company*

PERHAPS YOU'VE SEEN THEM, THOSE ADS FOR WRITING COURSES that proclaim, "You, too, can be an author. There's no better way to get published than by writing books for children and teenagers." Now, I am in favor of any program that inspires writers, but I do take issue with statements like these. They imply that anyone can get published, and that writing for children is just a stepping stone to getting a contract for a "real" (a.k.a. adult) book. Aspiring writers often fall victim to the myth that children's books are easy to write and even easier to sell. This is a pernicious rumor that has to be stopped, because it bogs down the editorial consideration process for the more dedicated writers out there and also demeans all of us who strive to produce worthwhile children's books.

While the process of writing and publishing a book for children may not be as simple and quick as those ads suggest, it is a rewarding one. If you're serious about breaking into this field, here is some advice that will increase your chances of having your manuscript accepted and published.

1) Don't believe the "writing-for-children-is-easy" myth. The fact that children's books are shorter than books for adults does not mean that they require less time and creative thought. On the contrary, shorter texts are often more difficult to compose, because each word has to be chosen carefully to pack the most punch. Even the most seasoned pro will agree that writing is hard work, no matter how old your intended audience may be.

As for getting that first contract, juvenile editors are just as discriminating as their counterparts in the adult field. In fact, because the market has been inundated with so many children's titles in recent years, booksellers with shrinking shelf space are cutting back their orders, and publishers are being forced to reduce their lists and be even more selective. So, it is more important than ever to try to come up with something strong and unique.

2) One of the best ways you can prepare for the task in front of you is to do research. Understand the market before you approach it. Go to the children's room in your local library and talk to the librarian. Ask him or her which classics you should read. Ask to see some of the recent Caldecott and Newbery Award winners. Ask which books seem to be the most popular with kids today, and what they want but can't find. Next, do the same thing at your local children's bookstore. Watch what parents and kids pick up. Look for the publishers' names on the spines and see if you can get a feel for the kinds of books they produce. Then write to the publishers that appeal to you and ask for their most recent catalogue and their guidelines for submissions. While you're at it, get the name of the children's book editor.

Another important part of your field research is familiarizing yourself with your intended audience—if you don't have children of your own, you can always find some to talk to at a relative's or friend's house, or at a school, library, or day care center. The most successful writers for children have a healthy respect for even the youngest readers. They know better than to condescend or preach to their audience. They avoid writing in a sugary-sweet tone, and they don't automatically choose anthropomorphism or rhyming verse, if a straightforward, true-to-life approach would work better. They know that young children want to learn, are willing to believe, love to laugh, and have boundless imaginations.

3) Although it is important to know what is on the minds of young readers and bookbuyers, I am not suggesting that you write in response to current trends. There are already too many people out there writing about contemporary social issues. By the time you jump on the bandwagon, there will probably be hundreds of manuscripts on the same topic already in circulation, and the trend will be long gone before the typical eighteen months it takes to publish a book are over.

4) When you finally sit down at the keyboard, create for the child

in yourself. The information you have gathered in your research will give you a context in which to write, a yardstick against which you can measure yourself. But the bottom line is that you should write about what you as an individual find funny, delightful, important, etc., not what you as an adult think should appeal to kids. Some of the best manuscripts I've seen came out of the authors' direct experience and were not consciously directed toward kids.

5) Once you've finished your piece, play the part of the publisher for a minute. As you read it over, ask yourself, does this picture book text offer plenty of good opportunities for an illustrator? Would this novel speak to a wide audience? Are there any other books like this on the market? Does it offer a fresh perspective? Is the vocabulary appropriate for the intended audience? Is it fast-paced, believable, authentic? Does it have substance? Is the beginning compelling? Is the ending satisfying? Would I pay $15.00 for this?

6) If you feel that your manuscript meets all of the above criteria and you decide to go ahead and submit it, have enough pride in your work to present it as professionally as possible.

Here are some submission do's and don'ts:

Do . . .
• Type your manuscript (double-spaced).
• Send out a clean, readable photocopy.
• If it is a picture book, it helps to denote page breaks, to show that it will fit into a standard format.
• Include a succinct cover letter, addressed to a specific editor, and listing any publishing credits, credentials, or relevant experience. Briefly explain how your book differs from the competition, if any, and why it would suit this particular publishing house. (This demonstrates your familiarity with the market, and the editor's list.) Mention that you are open to criticism and are willing to revise, if necessary.
• Enclose a self-addressed, stamped envelope.

Don't . . .
• Send out a letter or manuscript with typos or misspellings. (I remember thinking my creative writing professor in college was too nit-picky about typos and misspellings, but now that I'm an editor I've seen the

negative effects both can have on a reader. They give us the impression that you don't care, and if you don't care, why should we?)

• Use erasable bond, or send out an old, yellowed copy that looks as though it has been in circulation for years.

• Attempt to explain your intentions or, worse, offer to come in to present your manuscript to the editor. It should speak for itself.

• Compare your manuscript to a classic.

• Cite the positive reactions of children. Editors are not particularly impressed by this, considering that children will respond favorably to the phone book if it is read aloud to them.

• Ask that the manuscript you are submitting in September be published in time for Christmas or offer to promote your book on *The Today Show* (this shows that you have unrealistic expectations).

• Include instructions for the illustrator, unless the action is unclear, as we encourage illustrators to interpret the text as they see fit, ideally adding an extra dimension to the story.

• Attempt to do the illustrations yourself, unless you've had professional training. We will choose the illustrator—often we try to pair a new author with a well-known illustrator and vice versa, to ensure that the book receives attention.

7) Even after the manuscript is out of your hands, there are things you can do to increase—or decrease—your chances of getting published. Remember that yours is only one of hundreds of manuscripts that the editors have to read, discuss, and respond to. So refrain from calling the editor within two weeks of submitting your manuscript to check on its status. After three months, you have a right to know where it stands. If you get another offer in the meantime, let everyone know so that competitive offers can be made. If an editor expresses an interest in your piece, express your enthusiasm, indicate your willingness to revise or consider editorial changes, and indicate a professional attitude in your questions about contracts and the publication process.

8) If creating books for children is your first love, we at Little, Brown welcome your submissions, whether they be solicited or unsolicited, agented or unagented, single or simultaneous (just let us know if it's

the latter). But if you think of writing for children only as a way to break into publishing, you'd be better off elsewhere. Children's books should be left to the authors who are truly devoted to reaching young readers (infants through young adults), because children don't deserve anything less.

108

AN OPEN LETTER TO FANTASY WRITERS

BY JOSEPHA SHERMAN,
Consulting Editor, Baen Books

SO YOU'VE DECIDED YOU WANT to write fantasy, but you don't know where to start. That's easy. Start by reading. Not just fantasy. Read everything: fiction, nonfiction, cereal boxes—*everything*.

Oh, you've already done that? Good. You've taken the first step on the road to becoming an author. You know what's already been written and have an idea of how a story works or doesn't work.

How do you begin writing? First, think things through a little. You must already have several characters wandering around in your brain in search of a plot, or you wouldn't even have considered writing. But do you know anything about them? I don't mean just their names or even their appearances. How do they feel about honor or patriotism or friendship? Why do they act the way they do?

Let's start by thinking about only one character. Perhaps you've decided that your hero is a human man of middle years who's living in exile. Now the fun begins. *Why* is he in exile? Did he commit a crime? What would his people consider a crime? It doesn't have to be something we'd think of as wrong. Maybe he simply forgot to take part in a ritual or refused to pay tribute to a temple. Or perhaps your hero is of royal blood and is in exile because he's been cast out by a usurper. How did this usurper come to power? Taking over an entire country isn't easy! Take a look at history books to see how conquests did or didn't happen in the real world.

You've figured out how your villain came to power. But if your hero is of the rightful royal line, he's always going to be a danger to that usurper. Why did the villain let your hero live? Or maybe your hero escaped. Maybe the enemy is hunting him even now!

See how a character and his situation can begin to come to life? Now repeat the process with all your other characters. Designing cardboard figures labeled The Brave Hero and The Dastardly Villain is easy. But remember that no one is all good or all bad. Even that wicked usurper is convinced he has a perfectly good reason for taking the throne. Maybe he thinks your hero was too weak to rule a country properly. Or maybe he believes conquering as many lands as possible is his holy mission. You must find out what's going on in the characters' minds before you go any further.

You've done that, you say. You can see your characters in your mind as three-dimensional people, real as the ones you meet every day. And because you took the time to figure out why they are what they are, you have a pretty good idea of the world in which they live. The next thing you have to do is give your characters a job. Don't worry yet about whether this is going to be a short story, a novel, or even, heaven help us, one of those nine-volume trilogies. The growing complexity— or lack of complexity—of your tale will determine its length. But first your characters need a goal. What is it that they're trying to do? Return the exiled ruler to his throne? Defeat the Evil Lord and his Dark Minions? Find the Holy Jewel or Grail or Sword? Their goal doesn't have to be of world-saving size, but it must be something that's of obvious importance to them and to the reader.

Remember that a story has to have a beginning, middle and end. It has to have a *point*. Aimless wandering through a magical forest can be fun for a time, but your characters are going to get pretty bored of trees if they don't see anything else—and so are your readers. Random encounters with hostile creatures don't make a plot, particularly not if those creatures want to do in your characters for no other reason than because you say so! Once again, there has to be a *point* to those encounters. Are they being sent by the Evil Lord? Are they beings of the forest who don't *want* humans traveling through their domain? Think about the reason behind an incident before including it. No matter how much you might like a scene, if it doesn't fit into the plot, grit your teeth and cut it out.

While you're working up a storyline, watch out for the "diary" school of writing: "I got up. I got dressed. I ate breakfast. I went shopping." If your characters go straight from Point A to Point Z with only a few unconnected incidents but no real problems at all, you've written them a diary, not an adventure. A story must have *conflict*. And no, this doesn't mean you must subject your poor characters to a battle on every page. A conflict is simply a problem they must overcome, be it an evil force determined to grind them into the mud, foul weather determined to grind them into the mud, or simply their own inner failings determined to grind them into—you get the picture.

All right. You've written your characters a nice, exciting adventure, getting your hero back on the throne with the help of his friends and the forest creatures he managed to talk into an alliance. And you're feeling pretty good about the whole thing. *Now* what do you do with your six-hundred-page-single-spaced-both-sides-of-the-paper manuscript? You retype it to proper manuscript format! You know the style: your name, story title and page number of the upper right of every page, double-spaced, nice margins on all sides, one side of the page only. Remember, there aren't any magic font sizes or mystic word counts per page that will guarantee publication. Your goal is simply to make your manuscript look as professional as possible—and as easy on the editor's eyes as possible. And of course, always make a copy of every manuscript! Most publishers will happily accept a good, dark, clear photocopy or letter-quality computer printout, so there's really no reason to risk losing an original copy in the mail.

Don't forget to enclose an SASE with every submission. An SASE isn't some arcane charm: It's merely that all-important self-addressed stamped envelope. If you don't want your manuscript copy returned, don't feel squeamish about letting the editor know and simply enclosing a letter-sized SASE rather than one big enough to hold a manuscript. This will *not* prejudice an editor against you. And if you're sending a manuscript out of the country, remember to include either the proper postage *of the foreign country* or sufficient International Reply Coupons, available at every post office.

Fine. You've retyped your manuscript to proper format, remembering to proofread it carefully, and it looks beautiful. You've enclosed an SASE. Where are you going to send it?

It's time to do some homework. Go to the bookstores and magazine stands. Learn which houses publish what. Write a nice note to the publishers (including, of course, an SASE), asking for their writers' guidelines, which are free for the asking, and study them. Those limits on subject matter or story length are there for a good reason. Obey them. If a publisher doesn't want a manuscript under 75,000 words, don't waste time and postage by sending that publisher your 25,000-

word novella. And you certainly aren't going to send your fantasy novel for adults to a house that publishes only picture books for children. Make sure you use *current* reference books to check market listing information. Consult *Literary Market Place* in the library's reference room. Subscribe to the "newszines" of the science fiction and fantasy industry: *Locus* (P.O. Box 13305, Oakland, CA 94661) and *Science Fiction Chronicle* (P.O. Box 2730, Brooklyn, NY 11202–0056). Go to science fiction conventions (both newszines publish information about the dates and sites of these conventions) and keep your ears open.

Of course you know better than to corner editors at a convention to tell them All About Your Book, or to try to force your manuscript on them. There are hundreds of wannabe writers out there. You *don't* want to shoot yourself in the foot by acting like a lout and alienating an editor!

And there you have it. You're going to need the hide of a rhinoceros, the determination of a hungry predator, and the heart of a saint to make it in this maddening, thoroughly illogical business. There aren't any secret handshakes or magic rituals to help you get published. But if you have the right combination of guts, persistence, common sense, and talent, you're well on the road to publication.

Welcome, New Fantasy Writer. It's a tough road you've chosen. But others have traveled it successfully. And the thrill of finally seeing your characters come to life on the printed page is really worth it all!

§109

WHY IT'S HARDER TO FIND AN AGENT THAN A PUBLISHER

BY EDWARD NOVAK

IF YOU'VE NEVER TRIED TO SECURE the services of a literary agent, you should be forewarned that at times you'll feel as if you are searching for the Holy Grail. Getting published for the first time is no picnic—unless you are a former President of the United States or have slept with Elvis's ghost and can prove it. However, finding an agent who will consider your idea for a novel or nonfiction book, read your manuscript or proposal, answer all your questions, provide encouragement and expertise, and yes, sell your book, will not only save you time and money, but you will have gained a valuable, much-needed ally in the swirling, shark-infested waters of publishing.

Why do you need an agent? If you are an unpublished author, here's why: One of the duties of my first job in publishing was to read unsolicited manuscripts sent to Macmillan directly from writers. These manuscripts came in all shapes and sizes, but my directive was the same: Unless you saw another *Gone With the Wind,* forget about it. In my two years in that job, I saw a number of admirable manuscripts, but not one unagented manuscript I read caught the fancy of an editor. You see, editors are extremely busy people: They meet with the sales department, the marketing department, the art department, the publicity department, and the editorial department every week. They meet with agents every day. And, in the evenings and on weekends, they squeeze in time to read manuscripts. Every time I meet an editor for the first time, their first complaint is how little time they get to read *published* books, which is something the rest of the world takes for granted.

Which manuscript do you think they are going to spend time considering seriously: the one sent in over the transom and read by an inexperienced, underpaid reader or the one recommended by an experienced agent?

Put another way: The editor's job, redefined over the years, is to publish writers, not discover them. For better or worse, editors simply have come to rely on agents to discover the next Hemingway, Fitzgerald or Welty and bring them to publishers.

If you are already a published author, here's a good reason for you to get an agent: Imagine how much more productive you would be if you didn't have to oversee the details of getting published; it can take weeks or even months to sell an idea to a publisher and negotiate the contract. Wouldn't you rather be writing than worrying?

How do you get an agent, how do they do business, and what can an agent specifically do for you?

The easiest way to get an agent is through the personal recommendation of a close friend, relative or another writer who has or knows an agent. When I first set up shop as an agent, I depended upon referrals from authors I had worked with in my days as an editor; they either became clients or sent authors my way. If you were looking for a lawyer or an accountant, wouldn't you ask your friends first whom they use and if they're happy with them? That's the easy way.

Step #1: Do a little research. Go to your local library or bookstore and find a copy of one of the dozens of books (such as the grandfather of reference tools, *Literary Market Place*—or *LMP* as we call it) that have lists of reputable agents, the kind of books and/or clients these agents are looking for, and their requirements for submission.

Step #2: After you've narrowed down the list of agents to ones who meet your criteria, write a letter describing your book idea and your background and inquire if they would be interested in it (be sure to include a stamped, self-addressed envelope!). I would advise against trying to describe your book over the telephone; a letter doesn't betray nervousness or forget to mention anything or put any sort of pressure on you. This letter will be very important, so spend some time and thought on it—a strong letter stating your case gives you a chance to include all your thoughts cogently and allows the agent to judge your writing. I always tell writers to state why thousands of people would be willing to spend $18.95 to read their book when they can just as easily spend the same amount of money on someone else's book. You

567

don't have to do that exactly, but keep it in the back of your mind as you compose your letter.

Do not get discouraged if you do not receive an answer from every agent. I cannot speak for every agency, but we respond to every query that includes an SASE, and we are not all that different from a lot of other agencies. Do not be surprised if some tell you they are not looking for new clients. To provide a professional level of service to their current clients, agents must devote most of their time to them.

Step #3: Keep it up. While many publishers no longer consider unagented work, almost every good agent will consider yours if he or she finds it well written and intriguing. If one agent turns your manuscript down, keep trying. There are any number of reasons for an agent to turn down perfectly good books, some having nothing to do with the quality of your work. We don't all think alike or like the same kinds of books, so maybe the second, third, or tenth agent *will* like your book and take it on. Persistence works! I always like to tell people about one of my clients who had written a fine novel in the seventies and got precious little encouragement. She put the novel away in her closet for fifteen years before finally getting up the nerve to show it to an agent—she showed it to me and I sold it to the second editor who read it. This is a story with a happy ending, but I always think about what this author would have accomplished had she been more persistent from the beginning.

[A few words on multiple submissions: Many agents will not consider multiple submissions because they do not want to spend the time reading an entire manuscript only to discover the author decided on another agent two days earlier. If you are going to submit your work to a number of agents at one time, make sure you inform the agents that it is a multiple submission, and be prepared for some very quick rejections. On the other side of the coin, if you have a strong idea— more likely for a nonfiction book than a novel—you may very well get quicker answers from agents who know they are in a competitive situation. And no, agents do *not* hate each other—some of my best friends are agents!]

A fourth suggestion, which will work for some writers but not all, would be to attend a writers' conference. First of all, this will give your writing exposure to professionals who can critique it and work with you; secondly, agents (like me) and editors attend conferences throughout the year looking for new talent. Though it is often difficult to develop any kind of relationship with an agent at a conference, many published authors got their starts at such conferences.

What kind of manuscripts are agents looking for? In one word: salable. Few agents I know really specialize in any one type of book, and most will work with both nonfiction and fiction. (I would venture to guess that most agents deal more in nonfiction than fiction.) In nonfiction, we look for subjects of timely nature, written by authors who have solid credentials in their field. If you want to write your autobiography, you had better either be mentioned regularly in *People* magazine or have lived a secret, incredible life. If you want to write a piece of investigative journalism, it helps if you actually are a reporter. Demonstrated expertise cannot be understated. With novels, however, agents simply look for good writing mixed with a good sense of storytelling— and novelists can be *anyone* with talent.

Most agents I know will not consider magazine articles, poetry or children's books. Major magazines solicit or commission most of the pieces they publish. Poetry can be submitted to literary journals directly by the author; book publishers, however, will consider publishing collections of only the most accomplished and published poets. More agents nowadays are considering children's books because publishers are paying larger advances for them, but these agents are still in the minority. You should definitely consult *LMP* about which agents will consider this kind of work.

I have two pieces of advice for writers looking for subjects: 1) Go to a bookstore and see what is being published. If you see twenty books on a subject, it's a good bet that the market is saturated. For instance, 1990 saw an explosion in the publication of books dealing with the environment; after a while, publishers simply stopped considering new books on this subject, no matter how good their prospects were. 2) Write about something you know about and believe in or care enough about to do the necessary research. If you want to write a novel about soldiering experiences during the Vietnam War, you had better have been there; on the other hand, which science fiction novelist has actually been to Mars or Venus?

Finally, what can you expect from an agent who decides to take on your book? Well, perhaps to become the most important person in your writing life. Years ago, editors such as Maxwell Perkins and publishers such as Bennett Cerf dominated the industry and were the bedrocks of an author's career. Not any more. Certainly, there are many wonderful editors and heady publishers in the business today, but with the rapid and deep changes that have taken place in publishing—takeovers and mergers and "consolidations"—many editors of major firms frequently change jobs and houses before they are able to form close relationships with the authors. Time and time again, I've seen an editor sign up a book and, two months later, announce he or she has landed a new job with another publisher. Nowadays, it is not unusual for an author to write, say, four books and have four or more different editors. The one constant in an author's career is his or her agent.

The most important thing an agent can do for you is to find a publisher for your book and negotiate contract terms and an advance on royalties for you. As a writer, what you want to worry about is your writing; your agent will sweat the details of the business of writing. Successful agents know the industry and will know not to send a first novel to a publisher that specializes in how-to books. A good agent will know not only which publisher is appropriate for your book, but which editor at a particular house is more inclined to consider your book seriously, since editors, unlike agents, tend to specialize in subjects. There are such things as business editors, political editors, fiction editors, and cookbook editors.

Agents can also provide ideas and criticism. Many agents reading a client's new novel, for instance, will suggest changes before submitting it to a publisher. Would you rather have your book submitted to a publisher knowing it was not quite right? Sometimes an agent will read an article in a magazine or newspaper that suggests a book idea and will give the idea to a client who will then write the book. And over the years, we see more books being written by celebrities, but do you think Tip O'Neill took nine months out of his busy schedule to write his memoirs? No, an agent convinced him to get the book done, introduced him to a writer who collaborated with the former Speaker of the House, and negotiated the package with Random House. O'Neill and his collaborator worked together intermittently for a couple of months, and the writer then produced a manuscript, which became a huge bestseller. Without the agent's role in this, the book never would have been published.

Agents also administer the life of a publishing contract, which means this: We keep track of and make sure the publisher pays the advance on time; we also track royalty payments and the issuance of statements. We oversee the selling of various foreign and subsidiary rights to a book: Do you want your book translated and sold in Spain or Japan? How about getting it excerpted in a magazine or newspaper? recorded on audio cassette? or made into a movie? Literary agents handle all these matters for their authors.

All this is the good news. Agents, quite simply, make an author's life easier and their work more commercially viable in return for a commission on all the deals they handle. These commissions usually range from 10–15 percent on domestic sales and licenses and 15–20 percent on all foreign transactions, which often involve "subagents" in other countries who share the commission.

Then there's the bad news, which you saw in the title of this piece. It's tough to get an agent. The arithmetic is against authors. I personally receive roughly thirty query letters a week from writers who have not been referred to me by close friends, relatives or other writers asking me to consider their books. Of this number, I will ask to see anywhere from two to four manuscripts, and, typically, I take on only one manuscript every two months. This does not mean that everything I reject is bad; actually some of it is good, but even good may not be good enough for publishers. And I'm sure the math works the same for most successful agents. Look at it another way: If only one book were published in this country every year, no matter the subject or the quality, it would sell millions and millions of copies. Actually, about fifty thousand books are published here every year, and for every one of those published, I'd bet there are one hundred that are not.

What this means in practical terms for you and for me is that the struggle to get published is often reduced merely to getting a publisher to sit down and seriously consider your book. And oftentimes, alas, talent simply isn't enough. You *will* need an advocate to give you a fighting chance.

So, in closing and recognizing the self-service I am about to perform, I'll just echo the first piece of sound advice given every writer in this country for the last fifty years: Do everything you can to get an agent, because it's a lot harder to get a publisher!

571

§110

ALL I NEEDED TO KNOW ABOUT MARKETING I LEARNED FISHING FOR TROUT

BY JEFFREY A. RASCHE

TROUT FISHERMEN REALLY *should* be the ones who teach writers how to market their work. To think like a trout fisherman is to have the right attitude toward marketing. To watch a successful trout fisherman at work is to witness the image of marketing incarnate.

If writers could pull on some hip waders and slosh along as observers, they might notice three key attitudes:

First, trout fishermen are eternal optimists who, when they toss their bait into a swirling eddy, always seem to believe there is a possibility of catching a fish. Thus, every cast is an expression of hope. The same is true when writers lick a stamp and drop their manuscripts in the mail. No matter how overwhelming the odds may seem, they wouldn't do it if they thought there was no chance.

Second, fishermen must have the patience to endure endless hours without a nibble, hopeless line tangles, and the frustration of big ones getting away. Publishing is a slow, painstaking process. Writers who have the urge to phone editors three times daily or quit after being rejected could learn something from a fisherman's patience.

Third, marketing takes determination, and fishermen demonstrate plenty of that. One frosty October morning I saw a fisherman peel off his clothes and dive into twelve feet of icy water to retrieve a string of trout he had dropped. When writers pursue their goal with such commitment, they are less likely to come home empty-handed, too.

Writers would do well to learn from the attitudes of the fisherman, but they can also profit by applying these trout fishing lessons to the task of marketing:

1) *Read the river.* To increase the odds of catching a trout, it helps

to figure out where the hungry ones are located. For writers, this means finding out what the editors are "hungry" for by reading what they have recently published. If there is a regular editor's column, study it for style. Also, editors will frequently describe their readers, something to keep in mind when you write your articles. It may be useful to think about the people you know. Which three of your friends would be most interested in reading what you write? Then target your material for them.

2) *Keep moving.* A trout fisherman may try dozens of different places along the river each day because "There is more than one fish in the (river)." Likewise, there are thousands of editors and publications. To spend your time wisely, don't show the same type of article to the same editors over and over again (unless they are "biting," of course!).

Instead, list several potential markets for your work (for example, if you write for women's magazines, you might include ten magazines such as *Woman's Day, McCall's,* and *Redbook*). If an article is rejected, revise it, if necessary, and then "drop a line" to the next publisher on the list. While your first article drifts downstream, you should be writing and launching other articles. *Keep moving!* Drop your "bait" in as many places as you can.

3) *Change your bait.* Often a new lure results in a strike where no fish were previously biting. Thus, it is wise to try something different if what you've been doing isn't working.

Try researching a different subject, mailing a query about a fresh article, or modifying an existing article. To make any article suitable for other markets, try these simple exercises:

• Rewrite your idea as a letter to the editor. Shorten and adapt it to the general public. Local publication can give you valuable encouragement and feedback.
• Expand your article into a three-part series. What related subjects would you need to cover? This exercise can provide seeds for a new article, or even a book.
• Rewrite your article as a speech for a specialized group. Changing the slant or intended audience may save your idea from repeated rejec-

tion, or make a previously published article marketable in a new setting.

4) *Try again another day.* Fishermen do! Publishing houses merge, move, and have budget constraints that prevent them from purchasing everything they want. There are many factors that can make an editor more receptive to an article on one day than another.

A rejection slip does not necessarily mean you as a writer are unsuitable for the publication. The phrase "at this time," often included in form-letter rejections, should be understood to mean "try again another day." So don't give up on a publisher too quickly; instead, set a reasonable "rejection time limit" before you start, and then stick to it. Once you reach that limit, try a different publication.

There is one more lesson to learn: *Successful fishermen start early and don't quit until they must.* I know a writer who revised and reshaped a single book for more than ten years without ever submitting it. To market effectively, however, you must have the courage to start and the persistence to continue.

When you market your work over a long period of time, you will certainly have your share of big ones that get away and long days without a nibble; but you will also experience the sense of promise a fisherman feels when dawn breaks on a misty shore. Picture him as he carefully ties on a new lure, works a deep blue hole for a while, then wades upstream with new hope. To follow his example in selling what you write, you must pull out a manuscript, cast it into the river of mail, and try once again to hook the reader.

WHERE TO SELL

Where to Sell

With more markets and listings than ever before, this year's edition of *The Writer's Handbook* has a range of material that will appeal to writers at all levels of experience. The opportunities for free lancers abound, as evidenced by the many markets for articles, fiction, play scripts, children's books, poetry, and op-ed pieces, to name a few. Editors, publishers, and producers all rely on free lancers for much of their material, and many of them are receptive to the work of newcomers.

The field of specialized publications, including city and regional magazines, and those covering such areas as science, consumer issues, sports, and hobbies and crafts, remains one of the best markets for beginning free lancers. Editors of these magazines are in constant need of authoritative articles (for which the payment can be quite high), and writers with experience in and enthusiasm for a particular field, whether it's gardening, woodworking, bicycling, stamp collecting, bridge, or car repair, can turn their knowledge into article sales. Such interests and activities can generate more than one article if a different angle is used for each magazine and the writer keeps the audience and editorial content firmly in mind.

The market for technical, computer, health, and personal finance writing is also very strong, with articles on these topics appearing in almost every publication on the newsstands today. For these subjects, editors are looking for writers who can translate technical material into lively, readable prose, often the most important factor in determining a sale.

While some of the more established markets may seem difficult to break into, especially for the beginner, there are thousands of lesser-known publications where editors will consider submissions from first-time free lancers. City and regional publications offer some of the best opportunities, since these editors generally like to work with local writers and often use a wide variety of material, from features to fillers. Many newspapers accept op-ed pieces, and are most receptive to pieces on topics not covered by syndicated columnists (politics, economics, and foreign affairs); pieces with a regional slant are particularly welcome here.

It is important for writers to keep in mind the number of opportunities that exist for nonfiction, because the paying markets for fiction are somewhat limited. Many general-interest and women's magazines do publish short stories; however, beginners will find these markets extremely competitive, with their work being judged against that of experienced professionals. We highly recommend that new writers look into the small, literary, and college publications, which always welcome the work of talented beginners. Payment usually is made only in copies, but publication in literary journals can lead to recognition by editors of larger circulation magazines, who often look to the smaller publications for new talent. A growing number of regional, specialized, and Sunday magazines use short stories and are particularly interested in local writers.

The market for poetry in general-interest magazines continues to be tight, and the advice for poets, as for fiction writers, is to try to get established and build up a list of publishing credits by submitting material to literary journals. Poets should look also to local newspapers, which often use verse, especially if it is related to holidays or other special occasions.

Community, regional, and civic theaters and college dramatic groups offer new playwrights the best opportunities for staged production in this competitive market. Indeed, many of today's well-known playwrights received their first recognition in regional theaters, and aspiring writers who can get their work produced by one of these have taken a significant step toward breaking into this field. In addition to producing plays and giving dramatic readings, many theaters also sponsor competitions or new play festivals.

The market for television and feature film scripts is limited, and most writers break into it only after a careful study of the medium and a long apprenticeship. Writers should be aware of the fact that this market is inaccessible without an agent, and for this reason, we've listed several agents who are willing to read queries for TV scripts and for screenplays.

While the book publishing field remains competitive, beginners should be especially encouraged by the many first novels published over the past few years, with more editors than ever before seeking out new works of fiction. An increasing number of publishers are broadening their nonfiction lines as well, and editors at many hardcover and paperback houses are on the lookout for new authors, especially those with a knowledge of or training in a particular field. Writers of juvenile and young adult books will be pleased to hear that in response to a growing audience of young readers and increased sales, many publishers are greatly expanding their lists of children's books.

Small presses across the country continue to flourish—in fact, they are currently publishing more books by name authors and more books on mainstream subjects than at any other time in recent years—offering writers an attractive alternative for their manuscripts.

Writers seeking the thrill of competition should review the extensive list of literary prize offers. Many prize sponsors are intent on promoting the as yet unpublished author, and have launched writing contests open only to newcomers. Nearly all of the competitions are for unpublished manuscripts, and offer publication in addition to a cash prize. The prestige that comes with winning some of the more established awards can do much to further a writer's career, as editors, publishers, and agents are likely to consider the future work of the prize winner more closely.

All information in these lists concerning the needs and requirements of magazines, book publishing companies, and theaters comes directly from the editors, publishers, and directors, but editors move and addresses change, as do requirements. No published listing can give as clear a picture of editorial needs and tastes as a careful study of several issues of a magazine or a book catalogue, and writers should never submit material without first thoroughly researching the prospective market. If a magazine is not available in the local library, write directly to the editor for a sample copy (often sent free or at a small cost). Contact the publicity department of a book publisher for an up-to-date catalogue, or a theater for a current schedule. Many companies also offer a formal set of writers guidelines, available for an SASE upon request.

ARTICLE MARKETS

The magazines in the following list are in the market for free-lance articles of many types. Unless otherwise stated in these listings, a writer should submit a query first, including a brief description of the proposed article and any relevant qualifications or credits. A few editors want to see samples of published work, if available. Manuscripts must be typed double-space on good white bond paper (8 ½ × 11), with name, address, and telephone number at the top left- or right-hand corner of the paper. Do not use erasable paper or onionskin, since it is difficult to work with, and always keep a copy of the manuscript, in case it is lost in the mail.

Submit photos or slides *only* if the editor has specifically requested them. A self-addressed envelope with postage sufficient to cover the return of the manuscript or the answer to a query should accompany all submissions. Response time may vary from two to eight weeks, depending on the size of the magazine and the volume of mail it receives. If an editor doesn't respond within what seems to be a reasonable amount of time, it's perfectly acceptable to send a polite inquiry.

Many publications have writers guidelines, outlining their editorial requirements and submission procedures; these can be obtained by sending a self-addressed, stamped envelope (SASE) to the editor. Also, be sure to ask for a sample copy: Editors indicate the most consistent mistake free lancers make is failing to study several issues of the magazine to which they are submitting material.

GENERAL-INTEREST PUBLICATIONS

ACCENT/TRAVELOG—P.O. Box 10010, Ogden, UT 84409. Address Ed. Staff. Articles, 1,000 words, about travel, having fun, fitness, sightseeing, the ordinary and the unusual in foreign and domestic destinations. "Avoid budget approaches and emphasize the use of travel professionals." Must include excellent transparencies. Queries with SASE required. Guidelines. Pays 15¢ a word, $35 for photos, $50 for cover photo, on acceptance.

AIR FORCE TIMES—See *Times News Service.*

AMERICAN HERITAGE—60 Fifth Ave., New York, NY 10011. Richard F. Snow, Ed. Articles, 750 to 5,000 words, on U.S. history and background of American life and culture from the beginning to recent times. No fiction. Pays $300 to $1,500, on acceptance. Query. SASE.

AMERICAN JOURNALISM REVIEW—(formerly *Washington Journalism Review*) 4716 Pontiac St., #310, College Park, MD 20740–2493. Rem Rieder, Ed. Articles, 500 to 3,000 words, on print or electronic journalism, ethics and issues. Pays 20¢ a word, on publication. Query.

THE AMERICAN LEGION—Box 1055, Indianapolis, IN 46206. John Greenwald, Ed. Articles, 750 to 2,000 words, on current world affairs, public policy, and subjects of contemporary interest. Pays $400 to $1,500, on acceptance. Query.

AMERICAN VISIONS, THE MAGAZINE OF AFRO-AMERICAN CULTURE—2101 S St. N.W., Washington, DC 20008–4011. Joanne Harris, Ed. Articles, 1,500 to 2,500 words, and columns, 750 to 2,000 words, on African-American history and culture with a focus on the arts. Pays from $100 to $1,000, after publication. Query.

ARMY TIMES—See *Times News Service.*

THE ATLANTIC MONTHLY—745 Boylston St., Boston, MA 02116. William Whitworth, Ed. Non-polemical, meticulously researched articles on public issues, politics, social sciences, education, business, literature, and the arts. Ideal length: 3,000 to 6,000 words, though short pieces, 1,000 to 2,000 words, are also welcome and longer text pieces will be considered. Pays excellent rates.

BON APPETIT—6300 Wilshire Blvd., Los Angeles, CA 90048. Barbara Fairchild, Exec. Ed. Articles on fine cooking (menu format or single focus), cooking classes, and gastronomically focused travel. Query with samples of published work. Pays varying rates, on acceptance.

BOSTONIA: THE MAGAZINE OF CULTURE AND IDEAS—10 Lenox St., Brookline, MA 02146. Keith Botsford, Ed. Articles, to 3,000 words, on politics, literature, music, art, travel, food, and wine. Pays $150 to $1,000, on publication. Queries required.

CAPPER'S—1503 S.W. 42nd St., Topeka, KS 66609–1265. Nancy Peavler, Ed. Articles, 300 to 500 words: human-interest, personal experience for women's section, historical. Payment varies, on publication.

CAR AUDIO AND ELECTRONICS—21700 Oxnard St., Woodland Hills, CA 91367. Bill Neill, Ed. Features, 1,000 to 2,000 words, on electronic products for the car: audio systems, security systems, CBs, radar detectors, cellular telephones, etc. Pays $300 to $1,000, on acceptance.

CHANGE—1319 18th St. N.W., Washington, DC 20036. Address Ed. Dept. Well-researched features, 2,500 to 3,500 words, on programs, people, and institutions of higher education; and columns, 700 to 2,000 words. "We can't usually pay for unsolicited articles."

CHATELAINE—MacLean Hunter Bldg., 777 Bay St., Toronto, Ont., Canada M5W 1A7. Address Ed. Dept. Articles, 1,500 to 2,500 words, for Canadian women, on current issues, personalities, medicine, psychology, etc., covering all aspects of Canadian life. Send queries to Elizabeth Parr, Sr. Ed. "Upfront" columns, 500 words, on relationships, health, nutrition, fitness, parenting; send queries to Diane Merlevede, Man. Ed. Pays from $350 for columns, from $1,250 for features, on acceptance.

THE CHRISTIAN SCIENCE MONITOR—One Norway St., Boston, MA 02115. Lawrence Goodrich, Features Ed. Articles, 800 words, on arts, education, food, sports, science, and lifestyle; interviews, literary essays for "Home Forum" page; guest columns for "Opinion Page." Pay varies, on acceptance. Original material only.

COLUMBIA—1 Columbus Plaza, New Haven, CT 06510–0901. Richard McMunn, Ed. Journal of the Knights of Columbus. Articles, 500 to 1,500 words, on a wide variety of topics of interest to K. of C. members, their families, and the Catholic layman: current events, religion, education, art, etc., illustrated with color photos. Pays $250 to $500, including art, on acceptance.

THE COMPASS—365 Washington Ave., Brooklyn, NY 11238. J.A. Randall,

Ed. True stories, to 2,500 words, on the sea, sea trades, and aviation. Pays to $600, on acceptance. Query with SASE.

CONSUMERS DIGEST—5705 N. Lincoln Ave., Chicago, IL 60659. John Manos, Ed. Articles, 500 to 3,000 words, on subjects of interest to consumers: products and services, automobiles, health, fitness, consumer legal affairs, and personal money management. Photos. Pays from 35¢ to 50¢ a word, extra for photos, on publication. Buys all rights. Query with resumé and published clips.

COSMOPOLITAN—224 W. 57th St., New York, NY 10019. Helen Gurley Brown, Ed. Guy Flatley, Man. Ed. Articles, to 3,000 words, and features, 500 to 2,000 words, on issues affecting young career women. Query.

COUNTRY—5400 S. 60th, Greendale, WI 53129. Dan Matel, Man. Ed. People-centered articles, 500 to 1,000 words, for a rural audience. "First-person articles about contemporary country experiences especially encouraged." (No articles on farm production techniques.) Taboos: tobacco, liquor, and sex. Pays $75 to $100, on acceptance. Query.

COUNTRY JOURNAL—P.O. Box 8200, Harrisburg, PA 17105. Peter V. Fossel, Ed. Articles, 1,000 to 3,000 words, for country and small-town residents. Helpful, authoritative pieces; issues, humor, how-to, preserving the countryside. Pays $300 to $1,000, on acceptance. Send SASE for guidelines. Query with SASE.

DALLAS LIFE MAGAZINE—*The Dallas Morning News*, Communications Center, P.O. Box 655237, Dallas, TX 75265. Mike Maza, Man. Ed. Well-researched articles and profiles, 1,000 to 3,000 words, on contemporary local issues and personalities. "Dallas peg is a must." Pays from 20¢ a word, on acceptance. Query.

DESTINATION DISCOVERY—(formerly *TDC: The Discovery Channel*) 7700 Wisconsin Ave., Bethesda, MD 20814. Rebecca Farwell, Ed. Amplifies and develops (but does not review or retell) the topics and genres covered by the Discovery cable TV channel, including science and technology, nature and ecology, human adventure, history, people and places. "Our objective is to approach nonfiction subjects in a literary style. We are always looking for writing with strong 'you are there' feeling. Articles are commissioned by staff, though queries are sometimes considered." Send letter of introduction, resumé, areas of expertise, and published clips.

EBONY—820 S. Michigan, Chicago, IL 60603. Lerone Bennett, Jr., Exec. Ed. Articles, with photos, on blacks: achievements, civil rights, etc. Pays from $150, on publication. Query.

THE ELKS MAGAZINE—425 W. Diversey Parkway, Chicago, IL 60614. Fred D. Oakes, Ed. Articles, 3,000 words, on business, sports, and topics of current interest, for non-urban audience with above-average income. Informative or humorous pieces, to 2,500 words. Pays $150 to $400 for articles, on acceptance. Query.

ESQUIRE—1790 Broadway, New York, NY 10019. David Hirshey, Deputy Ed. Michael Hirschorn, Articles Ed. Articles, 2,500 to 4,000 words, for intelligent adult audience. Pay varies, on acceptance. Query with published clips; complete manuscripts from unpublished writers. SASE required.

ESSENCE—1500 Broadway, New York, NY 10036. Stephanie Stokes Oliver, Ed. Provocative articles, 800 to 2,500 words, about black women in America today: self-help, how-to pieces, business and finance, health, celebrity profiles, and political issues. Short items, 500 to 750 words, on work, parenting, and health. Query required. Pays varying rates, on acceptance.

FAMILY CIRCLE—110 Fifth Ave., New York, NY 10011. Susan Ungaro,

Deputy Ed. Articles, to 2,000 words, on "women who have made a difference," marriage, family, and child-rearing issues; consumer affairs, health and fitness, humor and psychology. Query required. Pays top rates, on acceptance.

GLAMOUR—350 Madison Ave., New York, NY 10017. Ruth Whitney, Ed.-in-Chief. Lisa Bain, Articles Ed. Editorial approach is "how-to" for women, 18 to 35. Articles on careers, health, psychology, interpersonal relationships, etc. Fashion, health, and beauty material staff-written. Pays from $1,000 for 1,500- to 2,000-word articles, from $1,500 for longer pieces, on acceptance.

GLOBE—5401 N.W. Broken Sound Blvd., Boca Raton, FL 33487. Robert Taylor, Man. Ed. Factual articles, 500 to 1,000 words, with photos: exposés, celebrity interviews, consumer and human-interest pieces. Pays $50 to $1,500.

GOOD HOUSEKEEPING—959 Eighth Ave., New York, NY 10019. Joan Thursh, Articles Ed. Articles, 2,500 words, on a unique or trend-setting event; family relationships; personal medical pieces dealing with an unusual illness, treatment, and result; personal problems and how they were solved. Short essays, 750 to 1,000 words, on family life or relationships. Pays top rates, on acceptance. Queries preferred. Guidelines.

GRIT—1503 S.W. 42nd St., Topeka, KS 66609. Roberta J. Peterson, Ed.-in-Chief. Articles, 500 to 1,200 words, on health, consumer topics, people, home, garden, friends and family, Americana. Short fiction, 2,500 words (must be addressed to Fiction Ed.). SASE required. Pays 15¢ a word, extra for photos. Guidelines.

HARPER'S BAZAAR—1700 Broadway, New York, NY 10019. Elizabeth Tilberis, Ed.-in-Chief. Articles for sophisticated women on current issues, books, art, film, travel, fashion and beauty. Send queries with one- to three-paragraph proposal; include clips and SASE. Rarely accepts fiction. Payment varies.

HARPER'S MAGAZINE—666 Broadway, New York, NY 10012. Address Ed. Articles, 2,000 to 5,000 words. Query. SASE required. Very limited market.

HARROWSMITH COUNTRY LIFE—Ferry Rd., Charlotte, VT 05445. Address Ed. Dept. Feature articles, 3,000 to 4,000 words, on environment, energy, gardening, rural issues, shelter. How-to and do-it-yourself projects. Short opinion pieces and profiles of country careers, news briefs, and natural history. Pays $500 to $1,500 for features, from $50 to $600 for department pieces, on acceptance. Query with SASE required. Guidelines.

HISTORIC PRESERVATION—1785 Massachusetts Ave. N.W., Washington, DC 20036. Anne Elizabeth Powell, Ed. Feature articles from published writers, 1,500 to 4,000 words, on residential restoration, preservation issues, and people involved in preserving America's heritage. Mostly staff-written. Query.

HOUSE BEAUTIFUL—1700 Broadway, New York, NY 10019. Elaine Greene, Features Ed. Articles related to the home. Pieces on architecture, design, travel, and gardening. One personal memoir each month, "Thoughts of Home," with high literary standards. Pays varying rates, on acceptance. Query with detailed outline and SASE. Guidelines.

INQUIRER MAGAZINE—*Philadelphia Inquirer*, P.O. Box 8263, 400 N. Broad St., Philadelphia, PA 19101. Ms. Avery Rome, Ed. Local-interest features, 500 to 7,000 words. Profiles of national figures in politics, entertainment, etc. Pays varying rates, on publication. Query.

INSIDE MAGAZINE—226 S. 16th St., Philadelphia, PA 19102–3392. Jane Biberman, Ed. Articles, 1,500 to 3,000 words, on Jewish issues, health, finance, and the arts. Queries required; send clips if available. Pays $75 to $600, within four weeks of acceptance.

KEY HORIZONS—Gateway Plaza, 950 N. Meridian, Suite 1200, Indianapolis, IN 46204. Joan Todd, Man. Ed. General-interest articles and department pieces, 300 to 1,500 words, for readers ages 50 and older. Topics include personal finance, cooking, family trends, travel, and puzzles. No nostalgia, domestic humor, fillers, or poetry. Pays $25 to $500, $25 to $50 for photos, on publication.

KIWANIS—3636 Woodview Trace, Indianapolis, IN 46268. Chuck Jonak, Exec. Ed. Articles, 2,500 to 3,000 words, on home; family; international issues; the social, health, and emotional needs of youth (especially under age 6); career and community concerns of business and professional people. No travel pieces, interviews, profiles. Pays $400 to $1,000, on acceptance. Query. Send SASE for guidelines.

LADIES' HOME JOURNAL—100 Park Ave., New York, NY 10017. Jane Farrell, Articles Ed. Articles on contemporary subjects of interest to women. "See masthead for specific-topic editors and address appropriate editor." Query with SASE required.

LIFE IN THE TIMES—See *Times News Service.*

LIFE TODAY—(formerly *Prime Times*) 2802 International Ln., Suite 120, Madison, WI 53704. Rebecca Tavernini, Ed. Articles, 500 to 1,800 words, on health, technology, nature, home, sports, feature interviews, etc. Departments, 850 to 1,000 words. Pays $125 to $750, on publication. Query or send partial manuscript. Guidelines with SASE.

LISTEN MAGAZINE—Pacific Press Pub. Assn., P.O. Box 7000, Boise, ID 83707. Lincoln Steed, Ed. Articles, 1,000 to 1,200 words, on problems of alcohol and drug abuse, for teenagers; personality profiles; self-improvement articles, and drug-free activities. Photos. Pays 5¢ to 7¢ a word, extra for photos, on acceptance. Query. Guidelines.

LOS ANGELES TIMES MAGAZINE—Times Mirror Sq., Los Angeles, CA 90053. Bret Israel, Ed. Articles, to 5,000 words: general-interest news features, photo spreads, profiles, and narratives focusing on current events. Pays to $4,000, on acceptance. Query required.

MCCALL'S—110 Fifth Ave., New York, NY 10011. Kate White, Ed.-in-Chief. Grace Bennett, Sr. Ed. Interesting, unusual, and topical narratives, reports on social trends relating to women of all ages, 1,000 to 3,000 words. Human-interest stories. Pays top rates, on acceptance.

MADEMOISELLE—350 Madison Ave., New York, NY 10017. Joan Feeney, Man. Ed. Articles, 1,500 to 2,500 words, on subjects of interest to single, working women in their twenties. Reporting pieces, essays, first-person accounts, and humor. No how-to or fiction. Query with clips. Pays from $1,500 for full-length articles, on acceptance. Query.

MD MAGAZINE—55 Fifth Ave., New York, NY 10003. Helen Smith, Ed. Articles, 750 to 2,500 words, for doctors, on the arts, travel, history, science, and other aspects of culture; fresh angle required. Payment varies, on publication. Query by mail only.

METROPOLITAN HOME—1633 Broadway, New York, NY 10019. Address Articles Dept. Service and informational articles for residents of houses, co-ops, lofts, and condominiums, on real estate, equity, wine and spirits, collecting, trends, travel, etc. Interior design and home furnishing articles with emphasis on lifestyle. Pay varies. Query with clips.

MODERN MATURITY—3200 E. Carson St., Lakewood, CA 90712. J. Henry Fenwick, Ed. Articles, 1,000 to 2,000 words, on careers, workplace, human interest, living, finance, relationships, and consumerism, for persons over 50 years. Photos. Pays $500 to $2,500, on acceptance. Query.

THE MOTHER EARTH NEWS—24 E. 23rd St., 5th Fl., New York, NY 10010. Michelle Silver, Assoc. Ed. Articles for rural and urban readers: home improvements, how-tos, indoor and outdoor gardening, family pastimes, health, food, ecology, energy, and consumerism. Pays varying rates, on acceptance.

MOTHER JONES—1663 Mission St., San Francisco, CA 94103. Jeffrey Klein, Ed. Investigative articles, political essays, cultural analyses. "OutFront" pieces, 250 to 500 words. Pays on acceptance. Query.

MS.: THE WORLD OF WOMEN—230 Park Ave., 7th Fl., New York, NY 10169. Address Manuscript Ed. Articles relating to feminism, women's roles, and social change; reporting, profiles, essays, theory, and analysis. Pays market rates. Query with resumé, clips, and SASE.

NATIONAL ENQUIRER—Lantana, FL 33464. Address Ed. Dept. Articles, of any length, for mass audience: topical news, the occult, how-to, scientific discoveries, human drama, adventure, personalities. Photos. Pays from $325. Query or send complete manuscript.

NAVY TIMES—See *Times News Service.*

NEW WOMAN—215 Lexington Ave., New York, NY 10016. Karen Walden, Ed.-in-Chief. Articles on personal and professional relationships, health, fitness, lifestyle, money and career issues. Editorial focus is on self-discovery, self-development, and self-esteem. "Read the magazine to become familiar with our needs, and request guidelines with SASE. We look for originality, solid research, and a friendly, accessible style." Pays varying rates, on acceptance.

NEW YORK—755 Second Ave., New York, NY 10017. Edward Kosner, Ed. Peter Herbst, Man. Ed. Feature articles of interest to New Yorkers; focus is on current events in the metropolitan New York area. Pays $850 to $3,500, on acceptance. Query required; not responsible for unsolicited material.

THE NEW YORK TIMES MAGAZINE—229 W. 43rd St., New York, NY 10036. Address Articles Ed. Timely articles, approximately 3,000 words, on news items, forthcoming events, trends, culture, entertainment, etc. Pays to $2,500 for major articles, on acceptance. Query with clips.

THE NEW YORKER—20 W. 43rd St., New York, NY 10036. Address the Fact Editors. Factual and biographical articles for "Profiles," "Reporter at Large," etc. Pays good rates, on acceptance. Query.

NEWSWEEK—444 Madison Ave., New York, NY 10022. Address Ed. Dept. Original opinion essays, 1,000 to 1,100 words, for "My Turn" column; must contain verifiable facts. Submit manuscript with SASE. Pays $1,000, on publication.

OMNI—324 W. Wendover Ave., Suite 205, Greensboro, NC 27408. Keith Ferrell, Ed. Articles, 750 to 3,000 words, on scientific aspects of the future: space, machine intelligence, ESP, origin of life, future arts, lifestyles, etc. Pays $750 to $2,500, on acceptance. Query.

PARADE—750 Third Ave., New York, NY 10017. Amy Sivco, Articles Correspondent. National Sunday newspaper magazine. Factual and authoritative articles, 1,000 to 1,500 words, on subjects of national interest: health, consumer and environmental issues, science, the family, sports, etc. Profiles of well-known personalities and service pieces. No fiction, poetry, games, or puzzles. Pays from $1,000. Query.

PENTHOUSE—1965 Broadway, New York, NY 10023–5965. Peter Bloch, Ed. Nanette Varian, Articles Ed. General-interest or controversial articles, to 5,000 words. Pays to $1 a word, on acceptance.

PEOPLE IN ACTION/SPORTS PARADE—Box 10010, Ogden, UT 84409. Address Ed. Dept. Personality profiles, 1,200 words, of celebrities in sports, entertainment, fine arts, science, etc. Celebrities must be nationally or internationally known for their participation in their field, have positive values, and be making a contribution to society. "High-quality color transparencies are a must; query for details." Pays 15¢ a word, $35 for photos, $50 for cover photos, on acceptance.

PEOPLE WEEKLY—Time-Life Bldg., Rockefeller Ctr., New York, NY 10020. John Saar, Asst. Man. Ed. "Vast majority of material is staff-written." Will consider article proposals, three to four paragraphs, on timely, entertaining, and topical personalities. Pays good rates, on acceptance.

PLAYBOY—680 N. Lakeshore Dr., Chicago, IL 60611. John Rezek, Articles Ed. Sophisticated articles, 4,000 to 6,000 words, of interest to urban men. Humor: satire. Pays to $3,000, on acceptance. Query.

PRIME TIMES—See *Life Today.*

PSYCHOLOGY TODAY—24 E. 23rd St., 5th Floor, New York, NY 10010. Hara E. Marano, Exec. Ed. Bimonthly. Articles, 4,000 words, on timely subjects and news. Pays varying rates, on publication.

QUEEN'S QUARTERLY—Queens Univ., Kingston, Ont., Canada K7L 3N6. Boris Castel, Ed. Articles, to 8,000 words, on a wide range of topics, and fiction, to 5,000 words. Poetry; send no more than six poems. B&W art. Pays to $400, on publication.

READER'S DIGEST—Pleasantville, NY 10570. Kenneth O. Gilmore, Ed.-in-Chief. Unsolicited manuscripts will not be read or returned. General-interest articles already in print and well-developed story proposals will be considered. Send reprint or query to any editor on the masthead.

REAL PEOPLE—950 Third Ave., New York, NY 10022–2705. Alex Polner, Ed. True stories, to 500 words, on the bizarre: occult, UFOs, strange occurrences, everyday weirdness, etc. Pays $50, on publication; send submissions to "Real Bizarre" column. Query for interviews, 1,000 to 1,800 words, with movie or TV actors, musicians, and other entertainment celebrities. Pays $100 to $350, on publication. SASE required.

REDBOOK—224 W. 57th St., New York, NY 10019. Diane Salvatore, Sally Lee, Sr. Eds. Toni Gerber Hope, Health Ed. Articles, 1,000 to 2,500 words, on subjects related to relationships, marriage, sex, current social issues, health, psychology, and parenting. Payment varies, on acceptance. Query with clips.

THE RHODE ISLANDER MAGAZINE—(formerly *Sunday Journal Magazine*) *Providence Sunday Journal*, 75 Fountain St., Providence, RI 02902. Elliot Krieger, Ed. Features on some aspect of life in New England, especially Rhode Island and S.E. Massachusetts. No fiction. Pays $75 to $500, on publication.

ROLLING STONE—1290 Ave. of the Americas, 2nd Fl., New York, NY 10104. Magazine of American music, culture, and politics. No fiction. Query. "We rarely accept free-lance material."

THE ROTARIAN—1560 Sherman Ave., Evanston, IL 60201-3698. Willmon L. White, Ed. Articles, 1,200 to 2,000 words, on international social and economic issues, business and management, human relationships, travel, sports, environment, science and technology; humor. Pays good rates, on acceptance. Query.

THE SATURDAY EVENING POST—1100 Waterway Blvd., Indianapolis, IN 46202. Ted Kreiter, Exec. Ed. Family-oriented articles, 1,500 to 3,000 words: humor, preventive medicine, destination-oriented travel pieces (not personal experience), celebrity profiles, the arts, and sciences. Pieces on sports and home repair (with photos). Pays varying rates, on publication. Queries preferred.

SMITHSONIAN MAGAZINE—900 Jefferson Dr., Washington, DC 20560. Marlane A. Liddell, Articles Ed. Articles on history, art, natural history, physical science, profiles, etc. Query with SASE.

SOAP OPERA DIGEST—45 W. 25th St., New York, NY 10010. Jason Bonderoff, Roberta Caploe, Man. Eds. Investigative reports and profiles, to 1,500 words, about New York- or Los Angeles-based soaps. Pays from $250, on acceptance. Query with clips.

SOAP OPERA UPDATE—270 Sylvan Ave., Englewood Cliffs, NJ 07632. Dawn Mazzurco, Richard Spencer, Exec. Ed. Soap-opera oriented articles, 750 to 1,250 words; fillers to 500 words. Pays $200, on publication. Queries preferred.

SPORTS ILLUSTRATED—1271 Ave. of the Americas, New York, NY 10020. Chris Hunt, Articles Ed. Query; uses very little free-lance material.

SPORTS PARADE—See *People in Action.*

SUNDAY JOURNAL MAGAZINE—See *The Rhode Islander Magazine.*

TDC: THE DISCOVERY CHANNEL—See *Destination Discovery.*

TIMES NEWS SERVICE—Army Times Publishing Co., Springfield, VA 22151. Address R&R Ed. Articles that are informative, helpful, entertaining, and stimulating to a military audience for "R&R" newspaper section (formerly "Life in the Times"). Pays $75 to $100, on acceptance. Also, 1,000-word articles on careers after military service, travel, books and home entertainment, finance, and education for *Army Times, Navy Times,* and *Air Force Times.* Address Supplements Ed. Pays $125 to $200, on acceptance. Guidelines.

THE TOASTMASTER—P.O. Box 9052, Mission Viejo, CA 92690. Suzanne Frey, Ed. Articles, 1,500 to 2,500 words, on decision making, leadership, language, interpersonal and professional communication, humor, logical thinking, rhetorical devices, public speaking in general, profiles of guest orators, speaking techniques, etc. Pays $100 to $250, on acceptance.

TOWN & COUNTRY—1700 Broadway, New York, NY 10019. Pamela Fiori, Ed.-in-Chief. Considers one-page proposals for articles. Include clips and resumé. Rarely buys unsolicited manuscripts. No recent report.

TRAVEL & LEISURE—1120 Ave. of the Americas, New York, NY 10036. Nancy Novogrod, Ed.-in-Chief. Articles, 800 to 3,000 words, on destinations and leisure-time activities. Regional pieces for regional editions. Pays varying rates, on acceptance. Query.

TROPIC—*The Miami Herald*, One Herald Plaza, Miami, FL 33132. Tom Shroder, Exec. Ed. Essays and articles, 1,000 to 4,000 words, on current trends and issues, light or heavy, for sophisticated audience. No fiction or poetry. Limited humor. Pays $200 to $1,000, on publication. SASE. Allow four to six weeks for response.

TV GUIDE—Radnor, PA 19088. Barry Golson, Exec. Ed. Short, light, brightly written pieces about humorous or offbeat angles of television and industry trends. (Majority of personality pieces are staff-written.) Pays on acceptance. Query.

UNION PLUS—Marblehead Communications, 376 Boylston St., Boston, MA 02116. Tony Bogar, Man. Ed. Quarterly. Articles, 500 to 1,500 words, for union members and their families. Consumer, lifestyle, money-related topics. Pays $1 a word, 60 days after acceptance.

VANITY FAIR—350 Madison Ave., New York, NY 10017. Pamela McCarthy, Man. Ed. Articles on celebrities, arts, popular culture, lifestyles. Pays on acceptance. Query.

VILLAGE VOICE—36 Cooper Sq., New York, NY 10003. Sarah Jewler, Man. Ed. Articles, 500 to 2,000 words, on current or controversial topics. Pays $75 to $450, on acceptance. Query or send manuscript with SASE.

VOGUE—350 Madison Ave., New York, NY 10017. Address proposals to Features Ed. Articles, to 1,500 words, on women, entertainment and the arts, travel, medicine, and health. Query.

WASHINGTON JOURNALISM REVIEW—See *American Journalism Review.*

WASHINGTON POST MAGAZINE—*The Washington Post*, 1150 15th St. N.W., Washington, DC 20071. Linton Weeks, Man. Ed. Essays, profiles, and Washington-oriented general-interest pieces, to 5,000 words, on business, arts and culture, politics, science, sports, education, children, relationships, behavior, etc. Pays from $1,000, after acceptance.

WISCONSIN—*The Milwaukee Journal Magazine*, P.O. Box 661, Milwaukee, WI 53201. Alan Borsuk, Ed. Trend stories, essays, humor, personal-experience pieces, profiles, 500 to 2,500 words, with strong Wisconsin emphasis. Pays $75 to $650, on publication.

WOMAN'S DAY—1633 Broadway, New York, NY 10019. Rebecca Greer, Articles Ed. Articles, 500 to 2,000 words, on subjects of interest to women: marriage, education, family health, child rearing, money management, interpersonal relationships, changing lifestyles, etc. Dramatic first-person narratives about women who have experienced medical miracles or other triumphs, or have overcome common problems, such as alcoholism. Query; unsolicited manuscripts not accepted. SASE required. Pays top rates, on acceptance.

YANKEE—Yankee Publishing Co., Dublin, NH 03444. Judson D. Hale, Ed. Articles, to 3,000 words, with New England angle. Photos. Pays $150 to $1,000 (average $750), on acceptance.

YOUR HOME/INDOORS & OUT—Box 10010, Ogden, UT 84409. Address Ed. Dept. Articles, 1,000 words with good color transparencies, on fresh ideas in home decor, ranging from floor and wall coverings to home furnishings. Latest in home construction (exteriors, interiors, building materials, design, entertaining, and lifestyle), the outdoors at home (landscaping, pools, patios, gardens, etc.), home management, and home buying and selling. Avoid do-it-yourself approaches. Emphasize the use of home-improvement professionals. Queries required. Guidelines. Pays 15¢ a word and $35 for photos, $50 for cover photo, on acceptance.

CURRENT EVENTS, POLITICS

AFRICA REPORT—833 U.N. Pl., New York, NY 10017. Margaret A. Novicki, Ed. Well-researched articles by specialists, 1,000 to 2,500 words, with photos, on current African affairs. Pays $150 to $250, on publication.

THE AMERICAN LEGION—Box 1055, Indianapolis, IN 46206. John Greenwald, Ed. Articles, 750 to 2,000 words, on current world affairs, public policy, and subjects of contemporary interest. Pays $500 to $2,000, on acceptance. Query.

THE AMERICAN SCHOLAR—1811 Q St. N.W., Washington, DC 20009–9974. Joseph Epstein, Ed. Non-technical articles and essays, 3,500 to 4,000 words, on current affairs, the American cultural scene, politics, arts, religion, and science. Pays to $500, on acceptance.

THE ATLANTIC MONTHLY—745 Boylston St., Boston, MA 02116. William Whitworth, Ed. In-depth articles on public issues, politics, social sciences, education, business, literature, and the arts, with emphasis on information rather than opinion. Ideal length is 3,000 to 6,000 words, though short pieces, 1,000 to 2,000 words, are also welcome. Pays excellent rates, on acceptance.

CHURCH & STATE—8120 Fenton St., Silver Spring, MD 20910. Joseph L. Conn, Man. Ed. Articles, 600 to 2,600 words, on religious liberty and church-state relations issues. Pays varying rates, on acceptance. Query.

COMMENTARY—165 E. 56th St., New York, NY 10022. Norman Podhoretz, Ed. Articles, 5,000 to 7,000 words, on contemporary issues, Jewish affairs, social sciences, community life, religious thought, culture. Serious fiction; book reviews. Pays on publication.

CURRENT HISTORY—4225 Main St., Philadelphia, PA 19127. William W. Finan, Jr., Ed. Sean Patrick Murphy, Asst. Ed. Country-specific political science articles, to 20 pages. Hard analysis written in a lively manner. "We devote each issue to a specific region or country. Writers should be experts with up-to-date knowledge of the region." Queries preferred. Pays $300, on publication.

ENVIRONMENT—1319 18th St. N.W., Washington, DC 20036–1802. Barbara T. Richman, Man. Ed. Articles, 2,500 to 5,000 words, on environmental, scientific, and technological policy and decision-making issues. Pays $100 to $300, on publication. Query.

FOREIGN SERVICE JOURNAL—2101 E St. N.W., Washington, D.C. 20037. Articles on American diplomacy, foreign affairs, and subjects of interest to Americans representing U.S. abroad. Query.

THE FREEMAN—Foundation for Economic Education, Irvington-on-Hudson, NY 10533. John W. Robbins, Ed. Articles, to 3,500 words, on economic, political, and moral implications of private property, voluntary exchange, and individual choice. Pays 10¢ a word, on publication.

IRISH AMERICA—432 Park Ave. S., Suite 1000, New York, NY 10016. Patricia Harty, Ed. Articles, 1,500 to 2,000 words, of interest to Irish-American audience; preferred topics include history, sports, the arts, and politics. Pays 10¢ a word, after publication. Query.

LABOR'S HERITAGE—10000 New Hampshire Ave., Silver Spring, MD 20903. Stuart Kaufman, Ed. Quarterly journal of The George Meany Memorial Archives. Publishes 15- to 30-page documented articles of original research to be read by labor scholars, labor union members, and the general public. Pays in copies.

MIDSTREAM—110 E. 59th St., New York, NY 10022. Joel Carmichael, Ed. Articles of international and Jewish concern. Pays 5¢ a word, after publication. Allow three months for response.

MOMENT—3000 Connecticut Ave. N.W., Suite 300, Washington, DC 20008. Suzanne Singer, Man. Ed. Sophisticated articles, 2,500 to 5,000 words, on

Jewish topics. Columns, to 1,500 words, on current issues in the Mideast, American Jewry, Israel, pluralism. Pays $50 to $400, on publication.

MOTHER JONES—1663 Mission St., San Francisco, CA 94103. Jeffrey Klein, Ed. Investigative articles and political essays. Pays $1,000 to $3,000 for feature articles, after acceptance. Query required.

THE NATION—72 Fifth Ave., New York, NY 10011. Victor Navasky, Ed. Articles, 1,500 to 2,500 words, on politics and culture from a liberal/left perspective. Pays $75 per published page, to $300, on publication. Query.

NATIONAL REVIEW—150 E. 35th St., New York, NY 10016. Mark Cunningham, Articles Ed. Articles, 1,000 to 5,000 words. "Almost everything we publish was written expressly for the *National Review*. The overwhelming majority of our articles are written by professional, established writers." Payment varies, on publication.

THE NEW YORKER—20 W. 43rd St., New York, NY 10036. Address the Fact Eds. Factual and biographical articles, for "Profiles," "Reporter at Large," "Annals of Crime," "Onward and Upward with the Arts," etc. Pays good rates, on acceptance. Query.

ON THE ISSUES—Choices Women's Medical Center, Inc., 97–77 Queens Blvd., Forest Hills, NY 11374–3317. Beverly Lowy, Man. Ed. "The Magazine of Substance for Progressive Women." Articles, up to 2,500 words, on political or social issues. Movie, music, and book reviews, 500 to 750 words. Query. Payment varies, on publication.

THE PROGRESSIVE—409 E. Main St., Madison, WI 53703. Erwin Knoll, Ed. Articles, 1,000 to 3,500 words, on political and social problems. Pays $100 to $300, on publication.

PUBLIC CITIZEN MAGAZINE—2000 P St. N.W., Suite 610, Washington, DC 20036. Peter Nye, Ed. Investigative reports and articles of timely political interest, for members of Public Citizen: consumer rights, health and safety, environmental protection, safe energy, tax reform, and government and corporate accountability. Photos, illustrations. Pays to $500.

ROLL CALL: THE NEWSPAPER OF CAPITOL HILL—900 2nd St. N.E., Washington, DC 20002. Stacy Mason, Ed. Factual, breezy articles with political or Congressional angle: Congressional history, human-interest subjects, political lore, etc. Political satire and humor. Pays on publication.

THE ROTARIAN—1560 Sherman Ave., Evanston, IL 60201–3698. Willmon L. White, Ed. Articles, 1,200 to 2,000 words, on international social and economic issues, business and management, environment, science and technology. "No direct political or religious slants." Pays good rates, on acceptance. Query.

SATURDAY NIGHT—184 Front St. E., Suite 400, Toronto, Ont., Canada M5A 4N3. John Fraser, Ed. Canada's oldest magazine of politics, social issues, culture, and business. Features, 1,000 to 3,000 words, and columns, 800 to 1,000 words; fiction, to 3,000 words. Must have Canadian tie-in. Payment varies, on acceptance.

VFW MAGAZINE—406 W. 34th St., Kansas City, MO 64111. Richard K. Kolb, Ed. Magazine for Veterans of Foreign Wars and their families. Articles, 1,500 words, on current issues and history, with veteran angle. Photos. Pays to $500, extra for photos, on acceptance. Guidelines.

VILLAGE VOICE—36 Cooper Sq., New York, NY 10003. Sarah Jewler, Man. Ed. Articles, 500 to 2,000 words, on current or controversial topics. Pays $75 to $450, on publication. Query or send manuscript with SASE.

THE WASHINGTON MONTHLY—1611 Connecticut Ave. N.W., Washington, DC 20009. Charles Peters, Ed. Investigative articles, 1,500 to 5,000 words, on politics, government, and the political culture. Pays 10¢ a word, on publication. Query.

WASHINGTON POST MAGAZINE—*The Washington Post*, 1150 15th St. N.W., Washington, DC 20071. Linton Weeks, Man. Ed. Essays, profiles, and general-interest pieces, to 5,000 words, on Washington-oriented politics and related issues. Pays from $1,000, after acceptance. SASE required.

REGIONAL AND CITY PUBLICATIONS

ADIRONDACK LIFE—P.O. Box 97, Jay, NY 12941. Tom Hughes, Ed. Features, to 5,000 words, on outdoor and environmental activities and issues, arts, wilderness, profiles, history, and fiction; focus is on the Adirondack region and north country of New York State. Pays to 25¢ a word, 30 days after acceptance. Query.

ALABAMA HERITAGE—The Univ. of Alabama, Box 870342, Tuscaloosa, AL 35487–0342. Suzanne Wolfe, Ed. Quarterly. Articles, to 5,000 words, on local, state, and regional history: art, literature, language, archaeology, music, religion, architecture, and natural history. Query, mentioning availability of photos and illustrations. Pays an honorarium, on publication, plus 10 copies. Guidelines.

ALASKA—808 E St., Suite 200, Anchorage, AK 99501. Tobin Morrison, Ed. Articles, 2,000 words, on life in Alaska and northwestern Canada. Pays varying rates, on acceptance. Guidelines.

ALOHA, THE MAGAZINE OF HAWAII—49 South Hotel St., #309, Honolulu, HI 96813. Cheryl Chee Tsutsumi, Ed. Articles, 1,500 to 2,500 words, on the life, customs, and people of Hawaii and the Pacific. Poetry. Fiction. Pays $150 to $500 for full-length features, on publication. Query.

AMERICAN DESERT MAGAZINE—P.O. Box 1303, Desert Hot Springs, CA 92240. Joan Brooks, Pub./Ed. Bimonthly. Articles, 1,000 to 2,500 words, related to the southwest deserts: desert history, survival, travel, Native American culture, profiles. Pays 3¢ a word, on publication. Query. Guidelines.

APPRISE—P.O. Box 2954, 1982 Locust Ln., Harrisburg, PA 17105. Jim Connor, Ed. Articles, 1,500 to 3,500 words, of regional (central Pennsylvania) interest, including profiles of notable Pennsylvanians, and broadly based articles of social interest that "enlighten and inform." Pays 10¢ a word, on publication.

ARIZONA HIGHWAYS—2039 W. Lewis Ave., Phoenix, AZ 85009. Robert J. Early, Ed. Articles, 1,600 to 2,000 words, on travel in Arizona; pieces on adventure, humor, lifestyles, nostalgia, history, archaeology, nature, etc. Departments using personal experience pieces include "Mileposts," "Focus on Nature," "Along the Way," "Event of the Month," "Outdoor Recreation," "Back Road Adventures," "Hiking," and "Arizona Humor." Pays 30¢ to 55¢ a word, on acceptance. Guidelines. Query.

ATLANTA—1360 Peachtree St., Suite 1800, Atlanta, GA 30309. Lee Walburn, Ed. Articles, 1,500 to 5,000 words, on Atlanta subjects or personalities. Pays $300 to $2,000, on publication. Query.

ATLANTIC CITY MAGAZINE—P.O. Box 2100, Pleasantville, NJ 08232.

Ken Weatherford, Ed. Lively articles, 200 to 4,000 words, on Atlantic City and the southern New Jersey shore, for locals and tourists: entertainment, casinos, business, recreation, personalities, lifestyle, local color. Pays $50 to $700, on publication. Query.

BACK HOME IN KENTUCKY—P.O. Box 681629, Franklin, TN 37068–1629. Nanci P. Gregg, Man. Ed. Articles on Kentucky history, travel, craftsmen and artisans, Kentucky cooks, "colorful" characters, and limited personal nostalgia specifically related to Kentucky. Pays $25 to $100 for articles with B&W or color photos. Queries preferred.

BAJA EXPLORER—11760 Sorrento Valley Rd., Suite K, San Diego, CA 92121. Landon S. Crumpton, Ed.-in-Chief. Bimonthly. Articles, 800 to 1,200 words, on fishing, sailing, surfing, windsurfing, camping, and natural history, and cultural events of interest to tourists visiting Baja California. Pays 25¢ a word, $50 per slide, on publication.

BALTIMORE MAGAZINE—16 S. Calvert St., Suite 1000, Baltimore, MD 21202. Jonathan Witty, Ed. Articles, 500 to 3,000 words, on people, places, and things in the Baltimore metropolitan area. Consumer advice, investigative pieces, profiles, humor, and personal experience pieces. Payment varies, on publication. Query required.

THE BIG APPLE PARENTS' PAPER—36 E. 12th St., New York, NY 10003. Susan Hodara, Ed. Articles, 600 to 750 words, for New York City parents. Pays $50, on publication. Buys first NY-area rights.

BIRMINGHAM—2027 First Ave. N., Birmingham, AL 35203. Joe O'Donnell, Ed. Personality profiles, features, business, and nostalgia pieces, to 2,500 words, with Birmingham tie-in. Pays $50 to $175, on publication.

BLUE RIDGE COUNTRY—P.O. Box 21535, Roanoke, VA 24018. Kurt Rheinheimer, Ed. Bimonthly. Regional articles, 1,200 to 2,000 words, that "explore and extol the beauty, history, and travel opportunities in the mountain regions of Virginia, North Carolina, West Virginia, Tennessee, Kentucky, Maryland, South Carolina, and Georgia." Color slides or B&W prints considered. Pays $200 for photo/features, on publication. Queries preferred.

BOCA RATON—JES Publishing, Amtec Center, Suite 100, 6413 Congress Ave., Boca Raton, FL 33487. Marie Speed, Ed. Articles, 800 to 3,000 words, on Florida topics, personalities, and travel. Pays $50 to $500, on publication. Query with clips required.

THE BOSTON GLOBE MAGAZINE—*The Boston Globe*, Boston, MA 02107. Ande Zellman, Ed. General-interest articles on local, national, and international topics and profiles, 2,500 to 5,000 words. Query and SASE required.

BOSTON MAGAZINE—300 Massachusetts Ave., Boston, MA 02115. Address the Man. Ed. Informative, entertaining features, 1,000 to 3,000 words, on Boston-area personalities, institutions, and phenomena. Query. Pays to $2,000, on publication.

BOUNDARY WATERS JOURNAL—9396 Rocky Ledge Rd., Ely, MN 55731. Stuart Osthoff, Ed. Articles, 2,000 to 3,000 words, on wilderness recreation, nature, and conservation in Minnesota's Boundary Waters region, including canoe routes, fishing, wildlife, history, and lifestyles of residents. Pays $200 to $400, on publication.

BUSINESS IN BROWARD—2455 E. Sunrise Blvd., Suite 507, Ft. Lauderdale, FL 33304. Reva Weinlaub, Ed. Bimonthly. Articles, 1,000 words, on small business in eastern Florida county. Pay varies, on acceptance. Same address and requirements for *Business in Palm Beach County*.

BUSINESS IN PALM BEACH COUNTY—See *Business in Broward.*

CAPE COD LIFE—P.O. Box 767, Cataumet, MA 02534–0767. Brian F. Shortsleeve, Pub. Articles, to 2,000 words, on current events, business, art, history, gardening, and nautical lifestyle on Cape Cod, Martha's Vineyard, and Nantucket. Pays $40 per column, 30 days after publication. Queries preferred.

CARIBBEAN TRAVEL AND LIFE—8403 Colesville Rd., Silver Spring, MD 20910. Veronica Gould Stoddart, Ed. Articles, 500 to 3,000 words, on all aspects of travel, recreation, leisure, and culture in the Caribbean, the Bahamas, and Bermuda. Pays $75 to $550, on publication. Query with published clips.

CAROLOGUE—South Carolina Historical Society, 100 Meeting St., Charleston, SC 29401–2299. Stephen Hoffius, Ed. General-interest articles, to 10 pages, on South Carolina history. Queries preferred. Pays in copies.

CHESAPEAKE BAY MAGAZINE—1819 Bay Ridge Ave., Annapolis, MD 21403. Jean Waller, Ed. Articles, 8 to 10 typed pages, related to the Chesapeake Bay area. Profiles. Photos. Pays on publication. Query.

CHICAGO—414 N. Orleans, Chicago, IL 60610. Joanne Trestrail, Man. Ed. Articles, 1,000 to 5,000 words, related to Chicago. Pays varying rates, on acceptance. Query.

CHICAGO HISTORY—Clark St. at North Ave., Chicago, IL 60614. Claudia Lamm Wood, Ed. Articles, to 4,500 words, on Chicago's urban, political, social, and cultural history. Pays to $250, on publication. Query.

CITY SPORTS MAGAZINE—2201 Third St., San Francisco, CA 94107. Craig Bystrynski, Ed. Articles, 500 to 2,000 words, on participant sports, family recreation, travel, and the active lifestyle. Pays $100 to $650, on publication. Query. Limited market.

COLORADO BUSINESS—7009 S. Potomac, Englewood, CO 80112. Julie Hutchinson, Ed. Articles, varying length, on business, business personalities, and economic trends in Colorado. Pays on publication. Query.

COLORADO HOMES & LIFESTYLES—7009 S. Potomac, Englewood, CO 80112. Anne McGregor Parsons, Ed. Articles, 1,200 to 1,500 words, on topics related to Colorado: travel, home design and decorating, architecture, gardening, art, antiques, collecting, and entertaining. Pays $125 to $200, on acceptance.

COMMON GROUND MAGAZINE—P.O. Box 99, McVeytown, PA 17051–0099. Ruth Dunmire and Pam Brumbaugh, Eds. Quarterly. General-interest articles, 500 to 5,000 words, related to Central Pennsylvania's Juniata River Valley and its rural lifestyle. Related fiction, 1,000 to 2,000 words. Poetry, to 12 lines. Fillers, photos, and cartoons. Pays $25 to $200 for articles, $5 to $15 for fillers, and $5 to $25 for photos, on publication. Guidelines.

CONCORD AND THE NORTH—See *Network Publications.*

CONNECTICUT—789 Reservoir Ave., Bridgeport, CT 06606. Charles Monagan, Ed. Articles, 1,500 to 3,500 words, on Connecticut topics, issues, people, and lifestyles. Pays $500 to $1,200, within 30 days of acceptance.

CONNECTICUT FAMILY—See *New York Family.*

CORPORATE DETROIT—(formerly *Michigan Business*) 26111 Evergreen, Suite 303, Southfield, MI 48076. Jack Lessenberry, Ed. Articles for owners and top executives of small-to-medium size businesses in southeastern Michigan. Query. Payment varies, on publication.

CRAIN'S DETROIT BUSINESS—1400 Woodbridge, Detroit, MI 48207. Mary Kramer, Ed. Business articles, 500 to 1,000 words, about Detroit, for Detroit business readers. Pays $100 to $200, on publication. Query required.

D—3988 N. Central Expressway, Suite 1200, Dallas, TX 75204. Melissa Houtte, Ed. In-depth investigative pieces on current trends and problems, personality profiles, and general-interest articles on the arts, travel, and business, for upper-class residents of Dallas. "All editorial must have a Dallas focus." Pays $350 to $500 for departments, $800 to $1,200 for features. Queries required.

DALLAS LIFE MAGAZINE—*The Dallas Morning News*, P.O. Box 655237, Communications Ctr., Dallas, TX 75265. Mike Maza, Man. Ed. Well-researched articles and profiles, 1,000 to 3,000 words, on contemporary local issues and personalities. Pays from 25¢ a word, on acceptance. Query required.

DELAWARE TODAY—P.O. Box 2087, Wilmington, DE 19899. Lise Monty, Ed. Service articles, profiles, news, etc., on topics of local interest. Pays $75 to $125 for department pieces, $50 to $500 for features, on publication. Queries with clips required.

DETROIT FREE PRESS MAGAZINE—*Detroit Free Press*, 321 W. Lafayette Blvd., Detroit, MI 48231. Articles, to 5,000 words, on issues, lifestyles. Personality profiles; essays; humor. Pays from $150. Query appreciated.

DETROIT MONTHLY—1400 Woodbridge, Detroit, MI 48207. John Barron, Ed. Articles on Detroit-area people, issues, lifestyles, and business. Payment varies. Query required.

DOWN EAST—Camden, ME 04843. Davis Thomas, Ed. Articles, 1,500 to 2,500 words, on all aspects of life in Maine. Photos. Pays to 20¢ a word, extra for photos, on acceptance. Query.

EASTSIDE PARENT—Northwest Parent Publishing, 2107 Elliott Ave., #303, Seattle, WA 98121. Ann Bergman, Ed. Articles, 300 to 2,500 words, for parents of children ages 12 and under. Queries are preferred. Pays $150 to $500, on publication. Also publishes *Portland Parent* and *Pierce County Parent.*

ERIE & CHAUTAUQUA MAGAZINE—Charles H. Strong Bldg., 1250 Tower Ln., Erie, PA 16505. K. L. Kalvelage, Man. Ed. Feature articles, to 2,500 words, on issues of interest to upscale readers in the Erie, Warren, and Crawford counties (PA), and Chautauqua (NY) county. Pieces with regional relevance. Pays after publication. Query preferred, with writing samples. Guidelines available.

FLORIDA KEYS MAGAZINE—P.O. Box 2921, Key Largo, FL 33037. Gibbons Cline, Ed. Articles, 1,000 to 2,000 words, on the Florida Keys: history, environment, natural history, profiles, etc. Fillers, humor. Photos. Pays varying rates, on publication.

FLORIDA TREND—Box 611, St. Petersburg, FL 33731–0611. Matt Walsh, Ed. Articles on Florida business and businesspeople. Query with SASE required.

FLORIDA WILDLIFE—620 S. Meridian St., Tallahassee, FL 32399–1600. Address the Ed. Bimonthly of the Florida Game and Fresh Water Fish Commission. Articles, 800 to 1,500 words, that promote native flora and fauna, hunting, fishing in Florida's fresh waters, outdoor ethics, and conservation of Florida's natural resources. Pays $50 to $300, on publication.

GEORGIA JOURNAL—Grimes Publications, P.O. Box 27, Athens, GA

30603–0027. Millard B. Grimes, Pub. Conoly Hester, Ed. Articles, 1,000 to 2,000 words, on people, history, events, travel, etc., in and around Georgia. Poetry, to 20 lines. "Designed to promote Georgia writers." Pays $50 to $350, on publication.

GOLDENSEAL—The Cultural Center, 1900 Kanawha Blvd. E., Charleston, WV 25305–0300. Ken Sullivan, Ed. Articles, 1,000 and 3,000 words, on West Virginia history, folklife, folk art and crafts, and music of a traditional nature. Pays to $175, on publication. Guidelines.

GRAND RAPIDS—549 Ottawa N.W., Grand Rapids, MI 49503. Carole Valade Smith, Ed. Service articles (dining guide, travel, personal finance, humor) and issue-oriented pieces related to Grand Rapids, Michigan. Pays $35 to $200, on publication. Query.

GULF COAST GOLFER—See *North Texas Golfer.*

GULFSHORE LIFE—2900 S. Horseshoe Dr., Suite 400, Naples, FL 33942. Lynn Ross, Sr. Ed. Articles, 800 to 3,000 words, on southwest Florida personalities, travel, sports, business, interior design, arts, history, and nature. Pays from $200. Query.

HAMPSHIRE EAST—See *Network Publications.*

HAWAII—Box 6050, Mission Viejo, CA 92690–6050. Dennis Shattuck, Ed. Bimonthly. Articles, 1,000 to 5,000 words, related to Hawaii. Pays 10¢ a word, on publication. Query.

HIGH COUNTRY NEWS—Box 1090, Paonia, CO 81428. Betsy Marston, Ed. Articles on environmental issues, public lands management, energy, and natural resource issues; profiles of western innovators; pieces on western politics. "Writers must take regional approach." Poetry. B&W photos. Pays $2 to $4 per column inch, on publication, for 750-word roundups and 2,000-word features. Query.

HONOLULU—36 Merchant St., Honolulu, HI 96813. Ed Cassidy, Ed./Pub. Features highlighting contemporary life in the Hawaiian islands: politics, sports, history, people, arts, events. Columns and department pieces are mostly staff-written. Queries required. Pays $300 to $700, on acceptance.

HOUSTON METROPOLITAN MAGAZINE—P.O. Box 25386, Houston, TX 77265–5386. Maria Moss, Man. Ed. Chris Kelly, Ed. Articles with strong Houston-area angles. Issue-oriented features, profiles, lifestyle pieces. Department columns: "Art Beat," "City Business," "City Stories" (essays), "Travel," "Habitat" (local environmental issues). Pays $50 to $500 for columns; $600 to $1,000 for features.

ILLINOIS ENTERTAINER—2250 E. Devon, Suite 150, Des Plaines, IL 60018. Michael C. Harris, Ed. Articles, 500 to 1,500 words, on local and national entertainment (emphasis on alternative music) in the greater Chicago area. Personality profiles; interviews; reviews. Photos. Pays varying rates, on publication. Query preferred.

INDIANAPOLIS MONTHLY—950 N. Meridian St., Suite 1200, Indianapolis, IN 46204. Deborah Paul, Ed./Pub. Sam Stall, Man. Ed. Articles, 1,000 words, on health, sports, politics, business, interior design, travel, and Indiana personalities. All material must have a regional focus. Pays varying rates, on publication.

THE IOWAN MAGAZINE—108 Third St., Suite 350, Des Moines, IA 50309. Karen Massetti-Miller, Ed. Articles, 1,000 to 3,000 words, on business, arts, people, and history of Iowa. Photos a plus. Pays $200 to $600, on publication. Query required.

ISLAND LIFE—P.O. Box 929, Sanibel Island, FL 33957. Joan Hooper, Ed. Articles, 500 to 1,200 words, with photos, on wildlife, flora and fauna, design and decor, the arts, shelling, local sports, historical sites, etc., directly related to the islands of Sanibel, Captiva, Marco, Estero, or Gasparilla. No first-person articles. Pays on publication.

JACKSONVILLE MAGAZINE—See *Jacksonville Today.*

JACKSONVILLE TODAY—(Incorporating *Jacksonville Magazine*) White Publishing Co., 1325 San Marco Blvd., Suite 600, Jacksonville, FL 32207. Larry Marscheck, Ed. Service pieces and articles, 2,000 to 2,500 words, on issues and personalities of interest to readers in the greater Jacksonville area. Department pieces, 1,200 to 1,500 words, on business, health, travel, real estate, arts, sports, food. Home and garden articles, 1,000 to 2,000 words. Query required. Pays $200 to $500, on publication. Guidelines.

JOURNAL OF THE WEST—1531 Yuma, Manhattan, KS 66502–4228. Robin Higham, Ed. Articles, to 20 pages, on the history and culture of the West, then and now. Pays in copies.

KANSAS!—Kansas Dept. of Commerce, 700 S.W. Harrison, Suite 1300, Topeka, KS 66603–3957. Andrea Glenn, Ed. Quarterly. Articles, five to seven typed pages, on the people, places, history, and events of Kansas. Color slides. Pays to $250, on acceptance. Query.

KENTUCKY LIVING—P.O. Box 32170, Louisville, KY 40232. Gary Luhr, Ed. Articles, 800 to 2,000 words, with strong Kentucky angle: profiles (of people, places, events), history, biography, recreation, travel, leisure or lifestyle, and book excerpts. Pays $125 to $300, on acceptance. Guidelines.

KEY HORIZONS—Gateway Plaza, 950 N. Meridian, Suite 1200, Indianapolis, IN 46204. Joan Todd, Man. Ed. Quarterly. General-interest articles and department pieces, 300 to 2,500 words, for readers 50 and older. Topics include personal finance, cooking, health, and travel. Pays $25 to $500, $25 to $50 for photos, on publication.

LAKE SUPERIOR MAGAZINE—P.O. Box 16417, Duluth, MN 55816–0417. Paul Hayden, Ed. Articles with emphasis on Lake Superior regional subjects: historical and topical pieces that highlight the people, places, and events that affect the Lake Superior region. Pictorial essays; humor and occasional fiction. Quality photos enhance submission. "Writers must have a thorough knowledge of the subject and how it relates to our region." Pays to $400, extra for photos, after publication. Query.

LOS ANGELES READER—5550 Wilshire Blvd., Suite 301, Los Angeles, CA 90036. James Vowell, Ed. Articles, 750 to 5,000 words, on subjects relating to the Los Angeles area; special emphasis on feature journalism, entertainment, and the arts. Pays $25 to $300, on publication. Query preferred.

LOUISVILLE—One Riverfront Plaza, Louisville, KY 40202. James Oppel, Jr., Ed. Articles, 1,000 to 2,000 words, on community issues, personalities, and entertainment in the Louisville area. Photos. Pays from $50, on acceptance. Query; articles on assignment only. Limited free-lance market.

MANCHESTER—See *Network Publications.*

MARYLAND—2503 Davidsonville Rd., Gambrills, MD 21054. D. Patrick Hornberger, Ed. Dir. Articles, 800 to 2,200 words, on Maryland subjects. Pay varies, on acceptance. Query preferred. Guidelines.

MEMPHIS—MM Corp., Box 256, Memphis, TN 38101. Tim Sampson, Ed. Articles, 1,500 to 4,000 words, on a wide variety of topics related to Memphis and the Mid-South region: politics, education, sports, business, history, etc. Profiles; investigative pieces. Pays $75 to $500, on publication. Query. Guidelines.

MICHIGAN BUSINESS—See *Corporate Detroit.*

MICHIGAN LIVING—1 Auto Club Dr., Dearborn, MI 48126–9982. Len Barnes, Ed. Travel articles, 500 to 1,500 words, on tourist attractions and recreational opportunities in the U.S. and Canada, with emphasis on Michigan: places to go, things to do, costs, etc. Color photos. Pays $150 to $380, extra for photos, on acceptance.

MID-WEST OUTDOORS—111 Shore Dr., Hinsdale, IL 60521–5885. Gene Laulunen, Ed. Articles, to 1,500 words, with B&W photos, on where, when, and how to fish and hunt, within 500 miles of Chicago. Pays $25, on publication.

MILWAUKEE MAGAZINE—312 E. Buffalo, Milwaukee, WI 53202. John Fennell, Ed. Profiles, investigative articles, and service pieces, 2,000 to 6,000 words; local tie-in a must. No fiction. Pays $400 to $500, on publication. Query preferred.

MINNESOTA MONTHLY—15 S. Ninth St., Suite 320, Minneapolis, MN 55402. Jodie Ahern, Man. Ed. Articles, to 4,000 words, on the people, places, events, and issues in Minnesota; fiction, to 3,000 words; poetry, to 50 lines. Pays $50 to $800, on acceptance. Query for nonfiction only.

MONTANA MAGAZINE—P.O. Box 5630, Helena, MT 59604. Carolyn Cunningham, Ed. Where-to-go items, regional profiles, photo essays. Montana-oriented only. B&W prints, color slides. Pays $75 to $350, on publication.

MPLS. ST. PAUL—12 S. 6th St., Suite 400, Minneapolis, MN 55402. Claude Peck, Man. Ed. In-depth articles, features, profiles, and service pieces, 400 to 3,000 words, with Minneapolis-St. Paul focus. Pays to $1,000.

NASHUA—See *Network Publications.*

NEBRASKA HISTORY—P.O. Box 82554, Lincoln, NE 68501. James E. Potter, Ed. Articles, 3,000 to 7,000 words, on the history of Nebraska and the Great Plains. B&W line drawings. Pays in copies. Cash prize awarded to one article each year.

NETWORK PUBLICATIONS—100 Main St., Nashua, NH 03060. Kate Binder, Man. Ed. Lifestyle and business articles with a New Hampshire angle, with sources from all regions of the state, for the company's four regional monthlies: *Nashua, Manchester, Concord and the North,* and *Hampshire East.* Query. Payment varies, on acceptance.

NEVADA—1800 East Hwy. 50, Suite 200, Carson City, NV 89710. David Moore, Ed. Articles, 500 to 700 or 1,500 to 1,800 words, on topics related to Nevada: travel, history, profiles, humor, and place. Special section on Nevada events. Photos. Pay varies, on publication.

NEW JERSEY MONTHLY—P.O. Box 920, Morristown, NJ 07963–0920. Jan Bresnick, Ed. Articles, profiles, and service pieces, 1,500 to 3,000 words; department pieces on health, business, education, travel, sports, local politics, and arts with New Jersey tie-in, 750 to 1,500 words. Pays $25 to $100 for shorts, $400 to $600 for departments, $600 to $1,750 for features, on acceptance. Query with SASE and magazine clips. Guidelines.

NEW JERSEY REPORTER—The Center for Analysis of Public Issues, 16 Vandeventer Ave., Princeton, NJ 08542. Neil Upmeyer, Ed. Lee Seglem, Man. Ed.

In-depth articles, 2,000 to 6,000 words, on New Jersey politics and public affairs. Pays $250 to $500, on publication. Query required.

NEW MEXICO MAGAZINE—Lew Wallace Bldg., 495 Old Santa Fe Trail, Santa Fe, NM 87503. Address Ed. Articles, 250 to 2,000 words, on New Mexico subjects. No poetry or fiction. Pays about 25¢ a word, on acceptance.

NEW ORLEANS MAGAZINE—111 Veterans Blvd., Metairie, LA 70005. Errol Laborde, Ed. Articles, three to 15 triple-spaced pages, on New Orleans area people and issues. Photos. Pays $15 to $500, extra for photos, on publication. Query.

NEW YORK—755 Second Ave., New York, NY 10017. Edward Kosner, Ed. Peter Herbst, Man. Ed. Feature articles on subjects of interest to New Yorkers. Pays varying rates, on acceptance. Query required.

NEW YORK FAMILY—141 Halstead Ave., Suite 3D, Mamaroneck, NY 10543. Felice Shapiro, Pub. Susan Ross, Ed. Stephen Morison, Assoc. Ed. Articles related to family life in New York City. Pays $50 to $100, on publication. Same requirements for *Westchester Family* and *Connecticut Family*.

NORTH DAKOTA HORIZONS—P.O. Box 2467, Fargo, ND 58108. Sheldon Green, Ed. Quarterly. Articles, about 3,000 words, on people, places, and events in North Dakota. Photos. Pays $75 to $300, on publication.

NORTH GEORGIA JOURNAL—65 Roswell St., Bldg. 400, Alpharetta, GA 30201. Olin Jackson, Pub./Ed. History, travel, and lifestyle features, 2,000 to 3,000 words, on North Georgia. History features need human-interest approach and must be written in first person; include interviews. Photos a plus. Pays $75 to $250, on acceptance. Query.

NORTH TEXAS GOLFER—9182 Old Katy Rd., Suite 212, Houston, TX 77055. Steve Hunter, Ed. Articles, 800 to 1,500 words, involving local golfers or related directly to north Texas. Pays from $50 to $425, on publication. Query. Same requirements for *Gulf Coast Golfer* (related to south Texas).

NORTHEAST MAGAZINE—*The Hartford Courant*, 285 Broad St., Hartford, CT 06115. Lary Bloom, Ed. Articles and short essays, 750 to 3,000 words, that reflect the concerns of Connecticut residents. Pays $250 to $1,000, on acceptance.

NORTHERN LIGHTS—Box 8084, Missoula, MT 59807–8084. Address Editor. Articles, 500 to 3,000 words, about the contemporary West. "We look for beautifully crafted personal essays that illuminate what it means to live in the Rocky Mountain West. We're looking to bust the Hollywood stereotypes." Pays 10¢ a word, on publication.

NORTHWEST PARKS & WILDLIFE—See *Northwest Regional Magazines.*

NORTHWEST PRIME TIMES—10829 N.E. 68th St., Kirkland, WA 98033. Neil Strother, Pub./Ed. News and features aimed at those 50 and older. Pays $25 to $50, on publication. Limited market.

NORTHWEST REGIONAL MAGAZINES—P.O. Box 18000, Florence, OR 97439–0130. Address Dave Peden or Judy Fleagle. All submissions considered for use in *Oregon Coast, Northwest Travel,* and *Northwest Parks & Wildlife.* Articles, 800 to 2,000 words, pertaining to the Pacific Northwest, on travel, history, town/city profiles, and nature. News releases, 200 to 500 words. Articles with photos (slides) preferred. Pays $50 to $350, on publication. Guidelines.

NORTHWEST TRAVEL—See *Northwest Regional Magazines.*

OHIO MAGAZINE—62 E. Broad St., Columbus, OH 43215. Ellen Stein

598

Burbach, Ed. Profiles of people, cities, and towns of Ohio; pieces on historic sites, tourist attractions, little-known spots. Lengths and payment vary. Query.

OKLAHOMA TODAY—Box 53384, Oklahoma City, OK 73152–9971. Jeanne M. Devlin, Ed. Articles, 1,000 to 2,000 words: travel; profiles; history; nature and outdoor recreation; and arts. All material must have regional tie-in. Queries preferred. Pays $75 to $750, on acceptance. SASE for guidelines.

ORANGE COAST—245-D Fischer Ave., Suite 8, Costa Mesa, CA 92626. Erik Himmelsbach, Ed. Articles of interest to educated Orange County residents. Pieces, 1,000 to 1,500 words, for regular departments: "Escape" (local travel), "Access" (local services and products), "Selects" (local phenomena), "Guide" (local private schools, weight control centers, art galleries, etc.), and "Focus" (local personality profiles). Feature articles, 1,500 to 2,500 words: investigative, social issues, business trends, and other local topics. Query. Pays $250 for features, $100 for columns, on acceptance. Guidelines.

OREGON COAST—See *Northwest Regional Magazines.*

ORLANDO MAGAZINE—P.O. Box 2207, Orlando, FL 32802. Nancy Long, Ed. Articles and profiles, 1,200 to 1,500 words, on business, lifestyle, home and garden. Photos a plus. Pays $350, on publication. Query required.

OTTAWA MAGAZINE—192 Bank St., Ottawa, Ont., Canada K2P 1W8. Marion Soubliere, Sr. Ed. Articles, investigative journalism, and profiles, 2,000 to 2,500 words, relating to the social issues and cultural and consumer interests of Ottawa City. Query with five or six article ideas, resumé, and published clips. Payment varies, on publication.

PALM SPRINGS LIFE—Desert Publications, 303 North Indian Canyon Dr., P.O. Box 2724, Palm Springs, CA 92263. Jamie Lee Pricer, Ed. Articles, 1,000 to 2,000 words, of interest to "wealthy, upscale people who live and/or play in the desert": food, interior design, luxury cars, shopping, sports, homes, personalities, desert issues, arts, and culture. Pays $150 to $400 for features, $30 to $60 for short profiles, on publication. Query required.

PARENTGUIDE NEWS—475 Park Ave. S., New York, NY 10016. Leslie Elgort, Ed. Articles, 750 to 1,500 words, related to New York families and parenting: trends, profiles, issues, special programs, special products. Payment varies, on publication.

PENNSYLVANIA MAGAZINE—Box 576, Camp Hill, PA 17001. Albert E. Holliday, Ed. General-interest features with a Pennsylvania flavor. All articles must be accompanied by illustrations or photos. Send photocopies of possible illustrations. Photos. SASE required. Guidelines.

PERSIMMON HILL—1700 N.E. 63rd St., Oklahoma City, OK 73111. M.J. Van Deventer, Ed. Published by the National Cowboy Hall of Fame. Articles, 1,500 to 3,000 words, on Western history and art, cowboys, ranching, and nature. Top-quality illustrations a must. Pays from $100 to $250, on publication.

PHOENIX MAGAZINE—5555 N. 7th Ave., Suite B200, Phoenix, AZ 85013. Richard Vonier, Ed. Articles, 1,000 to 3,000 words, on topics of interest to Phoenix-area residents. Pays $300 to $1,000, on publication. Queries preferred.

PIERCE COUNTY PARENT—See *Eastside Parent.*

PITTSBURGH—4802 Fifth Ave., Pittsburgh, PA 15213. Dianne Jacob, Ed. Articles, 850 to 3,000 words, with western Pennsylvania slant, two- to four-month lead time. Pays on publication.

PORTLAND MONTHLY MAGAZINE—578 Congress St., Portland, ME 04101. Colin Sargent, Ed. Articles on local people, legends, culture, and trends. Fiction, to 750 words. Pays on publication. Query preferred.

PORTLAND PARENT—See *Eastside Parent.*

RECREATION NEWS—P.O. Box 32335, Washington, DC 20007–0635. Sam E. Polson, Ed. Articles, 1,500 to 2,000 words, on recreation for government workers in the Washington, D.C. area. Light, first-person accounts, 800 words, for "Sporting Life" column. "Articles should have a conversational tone that's lean and brisk." Queries preferred. Pays $50 for reprints, to $300 for cover articles, on publication. Send SASE for guidelines.

RHODE ISLAND MONTHLY—18 Imperial Pl., Providence, RI 02903. Vicki Sanders, Man. Ed. Features, 1,000 to 4,000 words, ranging from investigative reporting and in-depth profiles to service pieces and visual stories, on Rhode Island and southeastern Massachusetts. Seasonal material, 1,000 to 2,000 words. Fillers, 150 to 250 words, on Rhode Island places, customs, people, events, products and services, restaurants and food. Pays $250 to $1,000 for features; $25 to $50 for shorts, on publication. Query.

THE RHODE ISLANDER MAGAZINE—(formerly *Sunday Journal Magazine*) *Providence Sunday Journal*, 75 Fountain St., Providence, RI 02902. Elliot Krieger, Ed. Articles, 500 to 3,000 words, with a New England focus. Pays $75 to $500, on publication.

ROCKFORD MAGAZINE—331 E. State St., Rockford, IL 61104. Eileen Townsend, Ed. General-interest magazine covering Rockford and northern Illinois. Feature articles, 2,500 to 3,500 words, and departments, 1,500 to 2,000 words, on city and area personalities, politics, events, business, family, travel destinations, home improvement and decor, dining, etc. "Nothing predictable or routine." Query with samples and clips required; no unsolicited manuscripts. Payment varies, on acceptance.

RUNNER TRIATHLETE NEWS—P.O. Box 19909, Houston, TX 77224. Lee Sheffer, Ed. Articles on running for road racing and multi-sport enthusiasts in Texas, Louisiana, Oklahoma, New Mexico, and Arkansas. Payment varies, on publication.

RURAL LIVING—4201 Dominion Blvd., Suite 101, Glen Allen, VA 23060. Richard G. Johnstone, Jr., Ed. Features, 1,000 to 1,500 words, on people, places, historic sites in Virginia and Maryland's Eastern Shore. Queries preferred. Pays $150 to $200 for articles, on publication.

RURALITE—P.O. Box 558, Forest Grove, OR 97116. Address Ed. or Feature Ed. Articles, 800 to 2,000 words, of interest to a primarily rural and small-town audience in Oregon, Washington, Idaho, Nevada, northern California, and Alaska. "Think pieces" affecting rural/urban interests, regional history and celebrations, self-help, profiles, etc. No fiction or poetry. No sentimental nostalgia. Pays $30 to $400, on acceptance. Queries required. Guidelines.

SACRAMENTO MAGAZINE—4471 D St., Sacramento, CA 95819. Karen Coe, Ed. Features, 2,500 words, on a broad range of topics related to the region. Department pieces, 1,200 to 1,500 words, and short pieces, 400 words, for "City Lights" column. Pays $150 to $300, on acceptance. Query.

SAN DIEGO MAGAZINE—4206 W. Point Loma Blvd., P.O. Box 85409, San Diego, CA 92138. Virginia Butterfield, Assoc. Ed. Articles, 1,500 to 3,000 words, on local personalities, politics, lifestyles, business, history, etc., relating to San Diego area. Photos. Pays $250 to $600, on publication. Query with clips.

SAN DIEGO READER—P.O. Box 85803, San Diego, CA 92186. Jim Holman, Ed. Literate articles, 2,500 to 10,000 words, on the San Diego region. Pays $500 to $2,000, on publication.

SAN FRANCISCO BUSINESS TIMES—275 Battery St., Suite 940, San Francisco, CA 94111. Mike Consol, Ed. Business-oriented articles, about 20 column inches. Limited free-lance market. Pays $75 to $100, on publication. Query.

SAN FRANCISCO FOCUS—2601 Mariposa St., San Francisco, CA 94110–1400. Amy Rennert, Ed. Service features, profiles of local newsmakers, and investigative pieces of local issues, 2,500 to 3,000 words. Payment is negotiated, on acceptance. Query required.

SEATTLE—701 Dexter Ave. N., Suite 101, Seattle, WA 98109. Giselle Smith, Ed. City, home, and lifestyle articles, 500 to 2,000 words, relating directly to the greater Seattle area. Pays $100 to $800, on publication. Guidelines.

SEATTLE'S CHILD—Northwest Parent Publishing, 2107 Elliott Ave., #303, Seattle, WA 98121. Ann Bergman, Ed. Articles, 400 to 2,500 words, of interest to parents, educators, and childcare providers of children under 12, and investigative reports and consumer tips on issues affecting families in the Puget Sound region. Pays $75 to $400, on publication. Query required.

SENIOR MAGAZINE—3565 S. Higuera St., San Luis Obispo, CA 93401. Personality profiles and health articles, 600 to 900 words, and book reviews (of new or outstanding older books) of interest to senior citizens of California. Short fiction (to one published page). Pays $1.50 per inch; $10 to $25 for B&W photos; $100 savings bond for fiction, on publication.

SILENT SPORTS—717 10th St., P.O. Box 152, Waupaca, WI 54981. Upper Midwest monthly with regional focus on bicycling, cross-country skiing, running, canoeing, hiking, backpacking, and other "silent" sports; articles, 1,000 to 2,000 words. Pays $40 to $100 for features; $20 to $50 for fillers, on publication. Query.

SOUTH CAROLINA HISTORICAL MAGAZINE—South Carolina Historical Society, 100 Meeting St., Charleston, SC 29401–2299. Stephen Hoffius, Ed. Scholarly articles, to 25 pages with footnotes, on all areas of South Carolina history. Pays in copies.

SOUTH CAROLINA WILDLIFE—P.O. Box 167, Columbia, SC 29202–0167. Address Man. Ed. Articles, 1,000 to 3,000 words, with regional outdoors focus: conservation, natural history and wildlife, recreation. Profiles. Pays from 10¢ a word. Query.

SOUTHERN OUTDOORS—5845 Carmichael Rd., Montgomery, AL 36117. Larry Teague, Ed. How-to pieces, 800 words, and 2,000-word how-to articles on hunting and fishing, for fishermen and hunters in the Southern states. Pays 15¢ a word, on acceptance. Query.

SOUTHWEST ART—5444 Westheimer, Suite 1440, Houston, TX 77056. Susan McGarry, Ed. Articles, 1,200 to 1,800 words, on the artists, art collectors, museum exhibitions, gallery events and dealers, art history, and art trends west of the Mississippi River. Particularly interested in representational or figurative arts. Pays from $400, on acceptance. Query with slides of artwork to be featured.

THE STATE: DOWN HOME IN NORTH CAROLINA—128 S. Tryon St., Suite 2200, Charlotte, NC 28202. Scott Smith, Man. Ed. Articles, 750 to 2,000 words, on people, history, and places in North Carolina. Photos. Pays on publication.

SUNDAY JOURNAL MAGAZINE—See *The Rhode Islander Magazine.*

SUNSET MAGAZINE—80 Willow Rd., Menlo Park, CA 94025. William Marken, Ed. Western regional. Limited free-lance market.

SUNSHINE: THE MAGAZINE OF SOUTH FLORIDA—*The Sun-Sentinel*, 200 E. Las Olas Blvd., Ft. Lauderdale, FL 33301–2293. John Parkyn, Ed. Articles, 1,000 to 3,000 words, on topics of interest to south Floridians. Pays $250 to $1,000, on acceptance. Query. Guidelines.

TALLAHASSEE MAGAZINE—P.O. Box 1837, Tallahassee, FL 32302–1837. Dave Fiore, Ed. Articles, 800 to 1,500 words, with a positive outlook on the life, people, and history of the north Florida area. Pays on acceptance. Query.

TEXAS HIGHWAYS MAGAZINE—Texas Dept. of Transportation, P.O. Box 141009, Austin, TX 78714–1009. Tommie Pinkard, Ed. Texas travel, history, and scenic features, 200 to 1,800 words. Pays about 40¢ to 50¢ a word, $80 to $500 per photo. Query. Guidelines for writers and photographers.

TEXAS MONTHLY—P.O. Box 1569, Austin, TX 78767–1569. Gregory Curtis, Ed. Features, 2,500 to 5,000 words, and departments, to 2,500 words, on art, architecture, food, education, business, politics, etc. "We like solidly researched pieces that uncover issues of public concern, reveal offbeat and previously unreported topics, or use a novel approach to familiar topics." Pays varying rates, on acceptance. Queries required.

TIMELINE—1982 Velma Ave., Columbus, OH 43211–2497. Christopher S. Duckworth, Ed. Articles, 1,000 to 6,000 words, on history of Ohio (politics, economics, social, and natural history) for lay readers in the Midwest. Pays $100 to $900, on acceptance. Queries preferred.

TOLEDO MAGAZINE—*The Blade*, Toledo, OH 43660. Sue Stankey, Ed. Articles, to 5,000 words, on Toledo-area personalities, events, etc. Pays $50 to $150, on publication. Query with SASE.

TORONTO LIFE—59 Front St. E., Toronto, Ont., Canada M5E 1B3. John Macfarlane, Ed. Articles, 1,500 to 4,500 words, on Toronto. Pays $1,500 to $3,500, on acceptance. Query.

TROPIC—*The Miami Herald*, One Herald Plaza, Miami, FL 33132. Tom Shroder, Exec. Ed. General-interest articles, 750 to 3,000 words, for south Florida readers. Pays $200 to $1,000, on acceptance. Send SASE.

TUCSON LIFESTYLE—Old Pueblo Press, 7000 E. Tanque Verde, Tucson, AZ 85715. Sue Giles, Ed.-in-Chief. Features on local businesses, lifestyles, the arts, homes, fashion, and travel in the Southwest. Payment varies, on acceptance. Query preferred.

VALLEY MAGAZINE—16800 Devonshire, Suite 275, Granada Hills, CA 91344. Barbara Wernik, Ed. Articles, 1,000 to 1,500 words, on celebrities, issues, education, health, business, dining, and entertaining, etc., in the San Fernando Valley. Pays $100 to $350, within eight weeks of acceptance.

VENTURA COUNTY & COAST REPORTER—1583 Spinnaker Dr., Suite 213, Ventura, CA 93001. Nancy Cloutier, Ed. Articles, three to five pages, on any locally slanted topic. Pays $10, on publication.

VERMONT LIFE—6 Baldwin St., Montpelier, VT 05602. Tom Slayton, Ed.-in-Chief. Articles, 500 to 3,000 words, on Vermont subjects only. Pays 20¢ a word, extra for photos. Query preferred.

VIRGINIA—(formerly *Virginia Southwest*) P.O. Box 4244, Roanoke, VA 24015. Address the Ed. Bimonthly. "Written for and about people, places, events, and activities in, around, and affecting Virginia." Features, 2,000 to 2,500 words; articles, 1,200 to 1,800 words; humor, folklore, and legend, to 2,000 words; fiction, 1,000 to 1,500 words, with regional setting or reference; related poetry, to 32 lines. Department pieces, 500 to 700 words. Photos. Pays to $300, on publication or within six months, whichever comes first.

VIRGINIA BUSINESS—411 E. Franklin St., Suite 105, Richmond, VA 23219. James Bacon, Ed. Articles, 1,000 to 2,500 words, related to the business scene in Virginia. Pays varying rates, on acceptance. Query required.

VIRGINIA WILDLIFE—P.O. Box 11104, Richmond, VA 23230–1104. Publication of the Dept. of Game and Inland Fisheries. Articles, 1,500 to 2,500 words, with Virginia tie-in, on conservation and related topics, including fishing, hunting, wildlife management, outdoor safety and ethics, etc. Articles must be accompanied by color photos. Query with SASE. Pays 10¢ a word, extra for photos, on publication.

WASHINGTON POST MAGAZINE—*The Washington Post*, 1150 15th St. N.W., Washington, DC 20071. Linton Weeks, Man. Ed. Personal-experience essays, profiles, and general-interest pieces, to 6,000 words, on business, arts and culture, politics, science, sports, education, children, relationships, behavior, etc. Articles should be of interest to people living in Washington, D.C., area. Pays from $100, on acceptance. Limited market.

THE WASHINGTONIAN—1828 L St. N.W., Suite 200, Washington, DC 20036. John Limpert, Ed. Helpful, informative articles, 1,000 to 4,000 words, on DC-related topics. Pays 50¢ a word.

WE ALASKANS MAGAZINE—*Anchorage Daily News*, Box 149001, Anchorage, AK 99514–9001. George Bryson, Ed. Articles, 500 to 1,000 words, and features, 3,000 to 4,000 words, on Alaska topics only. Profiles, narratives, fiction, and humor. Pays $50 to $150 for short articles, $300 to $600 for features, on publication.

THE WEEKLY, SEATTLE'S NEWS MAGAZINE—1931 Second Ave., Seattle, WA 98101. David Brewster, Ed. Articles, 700 to 4,000 words, with a Northwest perspective. Pays $75 to $800, on publication. Query. Guidelines.

WESTCHESTER FAMILY—See *New York Family*.

WESTERN SPORTSMAN—P.O. Box 737, Regina, Sask., Canada S4P 3A8. Brian Bowman, Ed. Informative articles, to 2,500 words, on hunting, fishing, and outdoor experiences in Alberta, Saskatchewan, and Manitoba. How-tos, humor, cartoons. Photos. Pays $75 to $400, on publication.

WESTWAYS—2601 S. Figueroa St., Los Angeles, CA 90007. Eric Seyfarth, Ed. Articles, 1,000 to 3,000 words, and photo essays, on California, western U.S., Canada, and Mexico: history, contemporary living, travel, personalities, etc. Photos. Pays from 25¢ a word, extra for photos, on acceptance. Query.

WINDY CITY SPORTS—1450 W. Randolph, Chicago, IL 60607. Mary Thorne, Pub./Ed. Articles, to 1,500 words, on amateur sports in the Chicago area. Queries required. Pays $100, on publication.

WISCONSIN—*The Milwaukee Journal Magazine*, Journal/Sentinel, Inc., Box 661, Milwaukee, WI 53201. Alan Borsuk, Ed. Articles, 500 to 2,500 words, on business, politics, arts, environment, and social issues with strong Wisconsin emphasis. Personal-experience essays, profiles and investigative articles. Pays $75 to $700, on publication. Query.

WISCONSIN TRAILS—P.O. Box 5650, Madison, WI 53705. Patricia H. McKeown, Assoc. Ed. Articles, 1,500 to 3,000 words, on regional topics: outdoors, lifestyle, events, history, arts, adventure, travel; profiles of artists, craftspeople, and regional personalities. Fillers. Pays $150 to $500, on publication. Query with SASE.

WISCONSIN WEST MAGAZINE—2645 Harlem St., Eau Claire, WI 54703. Articles on current issues for residents of western Wisconsin; profiles of restaurants, weekend leisure activities and getaways, and famous people of western Wisconsin; and historical pieces. Short humor. Payment varies, on publication.

YANKEE—Yankee Publishing Co., Dublin, NH 03444. Judson D. Hale, Ed. Articles and fiction, 500 to 2,500 words, on New England and residents. Pays $500 to $1,200 for features, on acceptance.

YANKEE MAGAZINE'S TRAVEL GUIDE TO NEW ENGLAND—Main St., Dublin, NH 03444. Janice Brand, Ed. Articles, 500 to 2,000 words, on activities, attractions, places to visit in New England. Photos. Pays on acceptance. Query with outline and writing samples required.

TRAVEL ARTICLES

AAA WORLD—1000 AAA Dr., Heathrow, FL 32746–5063. Douglas Damerst, Ed. Articles, 600 to 1,500 words, on consumer automotive and travel concerns. Pays $200 to $800, on acceptance. Query with writing samples required. Articles by assignment only.

ACCENT/TRAVELOG—Box 10010, Ogden, UT 84409. Caroll Shreeve, V.P./Pub. Articles, 1,000 words, on travel destinations, ways to travel, and travel tips. Pays 15¢ a word, $35 for color photos, on acceptance. Query with SASE.

ADVENTURE ROAD—M & A Publishing, 122 E. 25th St., New York, NY 10010. Marilyn Holstein, Ed. Official publication of the Amoco Motor Club. Articles, 1,500 words, on destinations in North America, Mexico, and the Caribbean. Photos. Pays $500 to $1,000, on acceptance. Query required.

AIRFARE: THE MAGAZINE FOR AIRLINE EMPLOYEES—6401 Congress, #100, Boca Raton, FL 33487. Anthony Lederman, Ed. Travel articles, 1,500 words, with photos, on shopping, sightseeing, dining, and nightlife for airline employees. Prices, discount information, and addresses must be included. Pays $250, after publication.

AIR FORCE TIMES—See *Times News Service.*

ARIZONA HIGHWAYS—2039 W. Lewis Ave., Phoenix, AZ 85009. Richard G. Stahl, Man. Ed. Informal, well-researched personal-experience and travel articles, 1,600 to 2,000 words, focusing on a specific city or region in Arizona. Also articles dealing with nature, environment, flora and fauna, history, anthropology, archaeology, hiking, boating, industry. Departments for personal-experience pieces include "Focus on Nature," "Along the Way," "Outdoor Recreation," "Back Road Adventures," "Hiking," and "Arizona Humor." Pays 30¢ to 55¢ a word, on acceptance. Query with published clips. Guidelines.

ARMY TIMES—See *Times News Service.*

ASIA PACIFIC TRAVEL—(formerly *Pacific Travel*) 1540 Gilbreth Rd., Burlingame, CA 94010. Kumar Pati, Pub. Articles, four to six pages, about travel, tourism, entertainment, fashion, culture, and business in Asia and the Pacific Rim countries. Departments include: news in brief, business opportunities, vacation information, etc. Profiles of hotels and restaurants, tourist information, and transportation. "Articles should be written in first person, about personal experience. Submit eight photos, of which we'll publish about four." Payment varies, on publication. Guidelines.

BAJA EXPLORER—11760 Sorrento Valley Rd., Suite K, San Diego, CA 92121. Landon S. Crumpton, Ed.-in-Chief. Bimonthly. Articles, 800 to 1,200 words, on fishing, sailing, surfing, windsurfing, camping, natural history, and cultural events, of interest to tourists visiting Baja California. Pays 25¢ a word, $50 per slide, on publication.

BLUE RIDGE COUNTRY—P.O. Box 21535, Roanoke, VA 24018. Kurt Rheinheimer, Ed. Regional travel articles, 750 to 1,200 words, on destinations in the mountain regions of Virginia, North Carolina, West Virginia, Tennessee, Kentucky, Maryland, South Carolina, and Georgia. Color slides and B&W prints considered. Pays to $200 for photo-features, on publication. Queries preferred.

BRITISH HERITAGE—P.O. Box 8200, Harrisburg, PA 17105–8200. Gail Huganir, Ed. Travel articles on places to visit in the British Isles, 800 to 1,500 words. Include detailed historical information with a "For the Visitor" sidebar. Pays $100 to $200, on acceptance.

CALIFORNIA HIGHWAY PATROLMAN—2030 V St., Sacramento, CA 95818–1730. Carol Perri, Ed. Travel articles, to 2,000 words, focusing on places in California and the West Coast. "We prefer out-of-the-way stops with California Highway Patrol tie-in instead of regular tourist destinations." Query or send complete manuscript with photos. SASE required. Pays 2 ½¢ a word, $5 for B&W photos, on publication.

CANADIAN—199 Avenue Rd., Third Fl., Toronto, Ontario, Canada M5R 2J3. Grant N. R. Geall, Pres./Pub. Inflight magazine of Canadian Airlines International. Travel pieces, 1,000 to 1,500 words. Payment varies, on acceptance. Query.

CARIBBEAN TRAVEL AND LIFE—8403 Colesville Rd., Suite 830, Silver Spring, MD 20910. Veronica Gould Stoddart, Ed. Lively, informative articles, 500 to 2,500 words, on all aspects of travel, leisure, recreation, and culture in the Caribbean, Bahamas, and Bermuda, for upscale, sophisticated readers. Photos. Pays $75 to $550, on publication. Query.

CHILE PEPPER—P.O. Box 4278, Albuquerque, NM 87196. Melissa Jackson, Assoc. Ed. First-person food and travel articles, 1,000 to 1,500 words, about spicy world cuisine. Queries required. Payment varies, on publication.

COLORADO HOMES & LIFESTYLES—7009 S. Potomac, Englewood, CO 80112. Anne McGregor Parsons, Ed. Travel articles, 1,200 to 1,500 words, on cities, regions, establishments in Colorado; roundups and travel pieces with unusual angles, sidebar, and photos. Pays $150, on acceptance. Query.

CONDE NAST TRAVELER—360 Madison Ave., New York, NY 10017. Irene Schneider, Sr. Ed. Uses very little free-lance material.

THE COOL TRAVELER—P.O. Box 11975, Philadelphia, PA 19145. Bob Moore, Pub./Ed. Quarterly. Articles, 1,000 to 1,250 words, including excerpts from diaries and letters written while traveling. "We are a literary magazine about place and experience; we emphasize 'what happened' rather than 'what to see.' " Travel-related poetry. Pays to $20, on publication.

CRUISE TRAVEL—990 Grove St., Evanston, IL 60201. Robert Meyers, Ed. Charles Doherty, Man. Ed. Ship-, port-, and cruise-of-the-month features, 800 to 2,000 words; cruise guides; cruise roundups; cruise company profiles; travel suggestions for one-day port stops. Payment varies, on acceptance. Query with sample color photos.

EARLY AMERICAN LIFE—Box 8200, Harrisburg, PA 17105–8200. Frances Carnahan, Ed. Travel features about historic sites and country inns, 1,000 to 3,000 words. Pays $100 to $600, on acceptance. Query.

ENDLESS VACATION—Box 80260, Indianapolis, IN 46280. Helen W. O'Guinn, Ed. Travel features, to 1,500 words; international scope. Pays on acceptance. Query preferred. Send SASE for guidelines. Limited market.

FAMILY CIRCLE—110 Fifth Ave., New York, NY 10011. Sylvia Barsotti, Sr. Ed. Travel articles, to 1,500 words. Concept travel pieces should appeal to a national audience and focus on affordable activities for families; prefer service-filled, theme-oriented travel pieces or first-person family vacation stories. Pay rates vary, on acceptance. Query.

FRIENDLY EXCHANGE—1912 Grand Ave., Des Moines, IA 50309. Adele Malott, Ed. Articles, 700 to 1,500 words, of interest to active midwestern and western families, on travel and leisure. Photos. Pays $300 to $800, extra for photos. Query preferred. Send SASE for guidelines.

GREAT EXPEDITIONS—Box 18036, Raleigh, NC 27619. George Kane, Ed. Articles, 700 to 2,500 words, on independent, adventurous, budget-conscious travel and unusual destinations. Pays $30 to $80, on publication. Guidelines.

INDIA CURRENTS—P.O. Box 21285, San Jose, CA 95151. Arvind Kumar, Submissions Ed. First-person accounts, 800 words, of trips to India or the subcontinent. Helpful tips for first-time travelers. Prefer descriptions of people-to-people interactions. Pays in subscriptions.

ISLANDS—3886 State St., Santa Barbara, CA 93105. Destination features, 1,000 to 3,000 words, on islands around the world as well as department pieces and front-of-the-book items on island-related topics. Pays from 50¢ a word, within 30 days of acceptance. Query with clips required. Guidelines.

LIFE IN THE TIMES—See *Times News Service*.

MICHIGAN LIVING—Automobile Club of Michigan, 1 Auto Club Dr., Dearborn, MI 48126. Len Barnes, Ed. Informative travel articles, 500 to 1,500 words, on U.S. and Canadian tourist attractions and recreational opportunities; special interest in Michigan.

THE MIDWEST MOTORIST—12901 N. Forty Dr., St. Louis, MO 63141. Michael Right, Ed. Articles 1,000 to 1,500 words, with color slides, on domestic and foreign travel. Pays from $150, on acceptance.

NATIONAL GEOGRAPHIC—17th and M Sts. N.W., Washington, DC 20036. William P.E. Graves, Ed. First-person articles on geography, exploration, natural history, archaeology, and science. Half staff-written; half written by recognized authorities and published authors. Does not consider unsolicited manuscripts.

NATIONAL MOTORIST—Bayside Plaza, 188 The Embarcadero, San Francisco, CA 94105. Jane Offers, Ed. Illustrated articles, 500 to 1,100 words, for California motorists, on motoring in the West, car care, roads, personalities, places, etc. Color slides. Pays from 10¢ a word, on acceptance. Pays for photos on publication. SASE required.

NAVY TIMES—See *Times News Service.*

NEW WOMAN—215 Lexington Ave., New York, NY 10016. Karen Walden, Ed.-in-Chief. Armchair travel pieces; women's personal-experience and "what I learned from this experience" pieces, 800 to 2,500 words. Pays $500 to $2,500, on acceptance. Query required.

NEW YORK DAILY NEWS—220 E. 42nd St., New York, NY 10017. Gunna Bitee Dickson, Travel Ed. Articles, 500 to 700 words, on all manner of travel. Price information must be included. B&W or color photos. Pays $100 to $200 (extra for photos), on publication.

THE NEW YORK TIMES—229 W. 43rd St., New York, NY 10036. Nancy Newhouse, Travel Ed. Queries required; include writer's background, description of proposed article. No unsolicited manuscripts or photos. Pays on acceptance.

NORTHWEST PARKS & WILDLIFE—See *Northwest Regional Magazines.*

NORTHWEST REGIONAL MAGAZINES—P.O. Box 18000, Florence, OR 97439. Address Dave Peden or Judy Fleagle. All submissions considered for use in *Oregon Coast, Northwest Travel*, and *Northwest Parks & Wildlife*. Articles, 1,200 to 2,000 words, on travel, history, town/city profiles, and nature. News releases, 200 to 500 words. Articles with photos or slides preferred. Pays $50 to $300, on publication. Send SASE for guidelines.

NORTHWEST TRAVEL—See *Northwest Regional Magazines.*

OREGON COAST—See *Northwest Regional Magazines.*

PACIFIC TRAVEL—See *Asia Pacific Travel.*

RV TIMES MAGAZINE—Royal Productions, Inc., Box 6294, Richmond, VA 23230. Alice P. Supple, Ed. Articles and fiction, 500 to 2,000 words, related to outdoor or leisure activities, travel attractions in the Maryland, Virginia, New Jersey, New York, Delaware, and Pennsylvania areas. Pays 7¢ a word (to $90), on publication.

SACRAMENTO MAGAZINE—4471 D St., Sacramento, CA 95819. Krista Hendricks Minard, Man. Ed. Articles, 1,000 to 1,500 words, on destinations within a six-hour drive of Sacramento. Pay varies, on publication. Query.

SPECIALTY TRAVEL INDEX—305 San Anselmo Ave., #313, San Anselmo, CA 94960. C. Steen Hansen, Co-Pub./Ed. Semiannual directory of adventure vacation tour companies, destinations, and vacation packages. Articles, 1,000 words, with how-to travel information, humor, and opinion. Pays 20¢ per word, on publication. Slides and photos considered. Queries preferred.

TEXAS HIGHWAYS MAGAZINE—Texas Dept. of Transportation, P.O. Box 141009, Austin, TX 78714–1009. Jack Lowry, Ed. Travel, historical, cultural, scenic features on Texas, 200 to 1,800 words. Pays about 40¢ to 50¢ a word; photos $80 to $500. Guidelines with SASE.

TIMES NEWS SERVICE—Army Times Publishing Co., Springfield, VA 22151. Address R&R Ed. Travel articles, 700 words, on places of distinct interest to military people for use in "R&R" newspaper section (formerly called "Life in the Times"). "We like travel articles to focus on a single destination but with short sidebar covering other things to see in the area." Pays $100, on acceptance. Pays $35 for color slides or prints. Also, travel pieces, 1,000 words, for supplements to *Army Times*, *Navy Times*, and *Air Force Times*. Address Supplements Ed. Pays $125 to $200, on acceptance. Guidelines.

TOURS & RESORTS—See *Travel America.*

TRANSITIONS ABROAD—18 Hulst Rd., Box 344, Amherst, MA 01004. Dr. Clayton A. Hubbs, Ed. Articles for overseas travelers who seek an in-depth experience of the culture: work, study, travel, budget tips. Include practical, first-hand information. Emphasis on establishing meaningful contact with people and socially responsible, ecology-minded travel. "Eager to work with inexperienced writers who travel to learn and want to share information." B&W photos a plus. Pays $1.50 per column inch, after publication. Query preferred. Guidelines.

TRAVEL AMERICA—(formerly *Tours & Resorts*) World Publishing Co., 990 Grove St., Evanston, IL 60201–4370. Randy Mink, Man. Ed. Robert Meyers, Ed. Features, 1,000 to 1,500 words, on U.S. vacation destinations and resorts; also essays, nostalgia, humor, tour company profiles, travel tips, and service articles, 800 to 1,500 words. Pays up to $350, on acceptance. Top-quality color slides a must. Query.

TRAVEL & LEISURE—1120 Ave. of the Americas, New York, NY 10036. Nancy Novogrod, Ed.-in-Chief. Articles, 800 to 3,000 words, on destinations and travel-related activities. Regional pieces for regional editions. Short pieces for "The Last Word" and "First Stop." Pays on acceptance: $2,500 to $4,000 for features; $750 to $1,500 for regionals; $50 to $300 for short pieces. Query; articles on assignment.

TRAVEL SMART—Dobbs Ferry, NY 10522. Short pieces, 250 to 1,000 words, about interesting, unusual and/or economical places. Give specific details on hotels, restaurants, transportation, and costs. Pays on publication. Query.

VISTA/USA—301 E. Hanover Ave., Morristown, NJ 07960. Martha J. Mendez, Ed. Travel articles, 1,200 to 2,000 words, on U.S., Canada, Mexico, and the Caribbean. Also, general-interest topics, hobby/collecting, culture, and Americana. "Flavor of the area, not service oriented." Shorts, 500 to 1,000 words, for "Minitrips," "CloseFocus," "American Vignettes." Pays from $500 for features, from $150 for shorts, on acceptance. Query with SASE, writing sample, and outline. Limited market.

WESTWAYS—2601 S. Figueroa St., Los Angeles, CA 90007. Eric Seyfarth, Ed. Travel articles, 1,300 to 3,000 words, on where to go, what to see, and how to get there, with an emphasis on southern California and the West. Domestic and foreign travel articles are also of interest. Quality color transparencies should be available. Pays 75¢ a word, on acceptance.

INFLIGHT MAGAZINES

ABOARD—North-South Net, Inc., 100 Almeria Ave., Suite 220, Coral Gables, FL 33134. Diana G. Bethel, Ed. Inflight magazine of 10 Latin American international airlines in Chile, Dominican Republic, Ecuador, Guatemala, El Salvador, Bolivia, Nicaragua, Honduras, Peru, and Paraguay. Articles, 1,200 to 1,500 words, with photos, on these countries and on science, sports, home, fashion, and gastronomy. No political stories. Pays $150, with photos, on acceptance and on publication. Query required.

ALASKA AIRLINES MAGAZINE—2701 First Ave., Suite 250, Seattle, WA 98121. Paul Frichtl, Ed. Articles, 800 to 2,500 words, on lifestyle topics, business, travel, and profiles of regional personalities for West Coast business travelers. Query. Payment varies, on publication.

AMERICA WEST AIRLINES MAGAZINE—Skyword Marketing, Inc.,

7500 N. Dreamy Draw Dr., Suite 240, Phoenix, AZ 85020. Michael Derr, Ed. Articles celebrating creativity, 500 to 2,000 words; regional angle helpful. Pays from $250, on acceptance. Query with clips and SASE required. Guidelines.

AMERICAN WAY—P.O. Box 619640, DFW Airport, TX 75261–9640. Doug Crichton, Ed. American Airlines' inflight magazine. Features of interest to the business traveler, emphasizing travel, adventure, business, and the arts/culture. Pays from $900, on acceptance. Query.

CANADIAN—199 Avenue Rd., Third Fl., Toronto, Ontario, Canada M5R 2J3. Grant N. R. Geall, Pres./Pub. Articles, 1,000 to 1,500 words, on travel for Canadian Airlines International travelers. Payment varies, on acceptance. Query.

SKY—600 Corporate Dr., Ft. Lauderdale, FL 33334. Lidia de Leon, Ed. Delta Air Lines' inflight magazine. Articles on business, lifestyle, high tech, sports, the arts, etc. Color slides. Pays varying rates, on acceptance. Query with SASE. Guidelines.

USAIR MAGAZINE—1301 Carolina St., Greensboro, NC 27401. Terri Barnes, Ed. Articles, 1,500 to 2,500 words, on travel, business, sports, entertainment, food, health, and other general-interest topics. No downbeat or extremely controversial subjects. Pays $350 to $800, before publication. Query.

WOMEN'S PUBLICATIONS

BBW: BIG BEAUTIFUL WOMAN—9171 Wilshire Blvd., Suite 300, Beverly Hills, CA 90210. Carole Shaw, Ed.-in-Chief. Articles, 1,500 words, of interest to women ages 25 to 50, especially large-size women, including interviews with successful large-size women and personal accounts of how to cope with difficult situations. Tips on restaurants, airlines, stores, etc., that treat large women with respect. Payment varies, on publication. Query.

BLACK ELEGANCE—475 Park Ave. S., New York, NY 10016. Sharyn J. Skeeter, Ed. Articles, 1,000 to 2,000 words, on fashion, beauty, relationships, home design, careers, personal finance, and personalities, for black women ages 25 to 45. Short interviews. Include photos if available. Pays $150 to $225, on publication. Query. Guidelines.

BRIDAL GUIDE—Globe Communications Corp., 441 Lexington Ave., New York, NY 10017. Deborah Harding, Ed. Susan Sulich, Articles Ed. Bimonthly. Articles, 900 to 1,900 words, on wedding planning, fashion, beauty, contemporary relationships, honeymoon travel, and plans for the first home. Regular departments include: finance, sex, remarriage, and advice for the groom. Prefers queries for articles. Pays $350 to $650, on acceptance.

BRIDE'S & YOUR HOME—350 Madison Ave., New York, NY 10017. Andrea Feld, Man. Ed. Articles, 800 to 3,000 words, for engaged couples or newlyweds, on communication, sex, housing, redecorating, finances, careers, remarriage, step-parenting, health, birth control, pregnancy, babies, religion, in-laws, relationships, and wedding planning. Three major editorial subjects: home, wedding, and honeymoon travel. Pays $300 to $1,000, on acceptance.

CHATELAINE—Maclean Hunter Bldg., 777 Bay St., Toronto, Ont., Canada M5W 1A7. Elizabeth Parr, Sr. Ed. Articles, 1,500 to 2,500 words, on current issues and personalities of interest to Canadian women. Pays from $1,200 for articles; from $350 for 500-word "Up-front" columns (relationships, health, parents/kids), on acceptance. Send query and outline or complete manuscript; include international reply coupon.

COMPENDIUM—5151 N. Oracle Rd., Suite 117A, Tucson, AZ 85704. Jay K. Hiller, Pub. Fiction, 2,000 words, and articles, 600 to 800 words, for women. "We are based on informative articles, humor, and variety." Poetry and fillers. Queries preferred. No payment.

COMPLETE WOMAN—1165 N. Clark, Chicago, IL 60610. Susan Handy, Man. Ed. Articles, 1,500 to 2,000 words, with how-to sidebars, giving practical advice to women on careers, health, personal relationships, etc. Also interested in reprints. Pays varying rates, on publication. Send manuscript or query with SASE.

COSMOPOLITAN—224 W. 57th St., New York, NY 10019. Helen Gurley Brown, Ed. Betty Nichols Kelly, Fiction and Books Ed. Articles, to 3,000 words, and features, 500 to 2,000 words, on issues affecting young career women, with emphasis on jobs and personal life. Fiction on male-female relationships: short shorts, 1,500 to 3,000 words; short stories, 3,000 to 4,000 words; condensed published novels, 25,000 words. SASE required.

COUNTRY WOMAN—P.O. Box 989, Greendale, WI 53129. Kathy Pohl, Man. Ed. Profiles of country women (photo/feature packages), inspirational, reflective pieces. Personal-experience, nostalgia, humor, service-oriented articles, original crafts, and how-to features, to 1,000 words, of interest to country women. Pays $40 to $150, on acceptance.

ELLE—1633 Broadway, New York, NY 10019. Ruth La Ferla, Exec. Ed. Articles, varying lengths, for fashion-conscious women, ages 20 to 50. Subjects include beauty, health, fitness, travel, entertainment, and lifestyles. Pays top rates, on publication. Query required.

ESSENCE—1500 Broadway, New York, NY 10036. Stephanie Stokes Oliver, Ed. Susan L. Taylor, Ed.-in-Chief. Provocative articles, 800 to 2,500 words, about black women in America today: self-help, how-to pieces, business and finance, health, celebrity profiles, art, travel, and political issues. Short items, 500 to 750 words, on work, parenting, and health. Features and fiction, 800 to 2,500 words. Pays varying rates, on acceptance. Query for articles.

EXECUTIVE FEMALE—127 W. 24th St., New York, NY 10011. Basia Hellwig, Ed.-in-Chief. Articles, 750 to 2,500 words, on managing people, time, money, and careers, for women in business. Pays varying rates, on acceptance. Query.

FAMILY CIRCLE—110 Fifth Ave., New York, NY 10011. Susan Ungaro, Deputy Ed. Articles, to 2,000 words, on "women who have made a difference," marriage, family, and child-care and elder-care issues; consumer affairs, psychology, humor, health, nutrition, and fitness. Query required. Pays top rates, on acceptance.

FIRST FOR WOMEN—270 Sylvan Ave., Englewood Cliffs, NJ 07632. Jane Traulsen, Ed. Articles and mainstream stories, 2,500 words, reflecting the concerns of contemporary women; no formula or experimental fiction. "A humorous twist is welcome in fiction." Pay varies, on acceptance. Query for articles. Send manuscript for fiction. Allow eight to 12 weeks for response. SASE required.

GLAMOUR—350 Madison Ave., New York, NY 10017. Lisa Bain, Articles Ed. Ruth Whitney, Ed.-in-Chief. Priscilla Flood, Man. Ed. How-to articles, from 1,500 words, on careers, health, psychology, interpersonal relationships, etc., for women ages 18 to 35. Fashion, entertainment, and beauty pieces staff-written. Query Articles Ed. Pays from $500, on acceptance.

GOOD HOUSEKEEPING—959 Eighth Ave., New York, NY 10019. Joan Thursh, Articles Ed. Lee Quarfoot, Fiction Ed. In-depth articles and features on controversial problems, topical social issues; dramatic personal narratives with unusual experiences of average families; new or unusual medical information, personal medical stories. No submissions on food, beauty, needlework, or crafts. Short stories, 2,000 to 5,000 words, with strong identification for women, by published writers and "beginners with demonstrable talent." Unsolicited fiction not returned; if no response in 6 weeks, assume work was unsuitable. Include SASE with nonfiction submissions. Pays top rates, on acceptance.

HARPER'S BAZAAR—1700 Broadway, New York, NY 10019. Elizabeth Tilberis, Ed.-in-Chief. Articles, 1,500 to 2,500 words, for active, sophisticated women: the arts, world affairs, food, wine, travel, families, education, careers, health, and sexuality. No unsolicited manuscripts; query with SASE. Payment varies, on acceptance.

IDEALS—P.O. Box 140300, Nashville, TN 37214–0300. Tim Hamling, Ed. Articles, 600 to 800 words; poetry, 12 to 50 lines. Light, nostalgic pieces. Payment varies. Guidelines.

IOWA WOMAN—P.O. Box 680, Iowa City, IA 52244. Marianne Abel, Ed. Fiction and articles, 6,500 words, on midwestern history; interviews with prominent women; current social, economic, and environmental issues. Poems, any length (submit up to five); photos and drawings. "We rarely publish work by men, and then only personal essays about their relationships with women." Queries preferred for articles. Pays $5 a page; $25 for illustrations; $75 for cover art, on publication. Guidelines.

LADIES' HOME JOURNAL—100 Park Ave., New York, NY 10017. Myrna Blyth, Pub. Dir./Ed.-in-Chief. Articles of interest to women. Send queries to: Jane Farrell, Articles Ed. (news/general interest); Linda Troiano, Health Ed. (health/medical); Melanie Berger, Asst. Ed. (celebrity/entertainment); Pamela Guthrie O'Brien, Features Ed. (sex/psychology); Lois Johnson, Beauty Dir. (beauty/fashion/fitness); Jan Hazard, Food Ed.; Shana Aborn, Assoc. Ed. (personal experience); Mary Mohler, Man. Ed. (children and families). Fiction accepted through literary agents only. Brief, true anecdotes about amusing things children say for "Kidspeak." True, first-person accounts, 1,000 words, "about the most intimate aspects of our lives" for anonymous "Woman to Woman": Submit typed, double-spaced manuscript with SASE to Box WW, c/o address above; pays $750. Guidelines available; send SASE.

LADY'S CIRCLE—152 Madison Ave., Suite 906, New York, NY 10016. Mary F. Bemis, Ed. How-to, food, and crafts articles for homemakers. Short fiction. "Upbeat" pieces for over-50 audience. Pays $125 for articles, $10 for pet peeves, $5 for recipes or helpful hints, on publication.

LEAR'S—655 Madison Ave., New York, NY 10021. "Literate, lively, and compelling" articles, 800 to 1,200 words, for women, on health, finance, contemporary issues, personalities, and leisure. Query with clips and SASE.

MCCALL'S—110 Fifth Ave., New York, NY 10011. Grace Bennett, Sr. Ed. Articles, 1,000 to 3,000 words, on current issues, human interest, family relationships. "Between Friends" column, about 150 words, on a problem or dilemma you have solved. Pays top rates ($25 to $50 for "Between Friends"), on acceptance.

MADEMOISELLE—350 Madison Ave., New York, NY 10017. Joan Feeney, Man. Ed. Articles, 1,500 to 2,500 words, on work, relationships, health, and trends of interest to single, working women in their mid-twenties. Reporting pieces, essays, first-person accounts, and humor. No how-to or fiction. Submit query with clips and SASE. Pays excellent rates, on acceptance. SASE required.

MODERN BRIDE—249 W. 17th St., New York, NY 10011. Mary Ann Cavlin, Man. Ed. Articles, 1,800 to 2,000 words, for bride and groom, on wedding planning, financial planning, juggling career and home, etc. Query Travel Editor Geri Bain for articles on honeymoon travel. Pays $600 to $1,200, on acceptance.

MS.: THE WORLD OF WOMEN—230 Park Ave., 7th Fl., New York, NY 10169. Address Manuscript Ed. Articles relating to feminism, women's roles, and social change; national and international news reporting, profiles, essays, theory, and analysis. Query with resumé, published clips, and SASE required. No fiction or poetry accepted, acknowledged, or returned.

NA'AMAT WOMAN—200 Madison Ave., Suite 2120, New York, NY 10016. Judith A. Sokoloff, Ed. Articles on Jewish culture, women's issues, social and political topics, and Israel, 1,500 to 2,500 words. Short stories with a Jewish theme. Pays 10¢ a word, on publication.

NEW WOMAN—215 Lexington Ave., New York, NY 10016. Karen Walden, Ed.-in-Chief. Articles for women ages 25 to 49, on self-improvement, self-esteem, self-discovery. Features: relationships, careers, health and fitness, money, fashion, beauty, food and nutrition, travel features with self-discovery angle, and essays by and about women pacesetters. Pays about $1 a word, on acceptance. Query with SASE.

ON THE ISSUES—Choices Women's Medical Center, Inc., 97–77 Queens Blvd., Forest Hills, NY 11374–3317. Beverly Lowy, Man. Ed. "The Magazine of Substance for Progressive Women." Articles, to 2,500 words, on political or social issues. Movie, music, and book reviews, 500 to 750 words. Query. Payment varies, on publication.

RADIANCE: THE MAGAZINE FOR LARGE WOMEN—P.O. Box 30246, Oakland, CA 94604. Alice Ansfield, Ed./Pub. Quarterly. Articles, 1,500 to 2,500 words, that provide information, inspiration, and resources for women all sizes of large. Features include information on health, media, fashion, and politics that relate to issues of body size. Fiction and poetry also welcome. Pays to $100, on publication.

REDBOOK—224 W. 57th St., New York, NY 10019. Dawn Raffel, Fiction Ed. Toni Hope, Health Ed. For mothers, ages 25 to 45. How-to articles on ways a woman can solve the problems of her everyday life. Short stories, to 25 typed pages, and personal-experience pieces, 1,000 to 2,000 words, on solving problems in marriage, family life, or community, for "A Mother's Story." Query with writing samples for articles. SASE required. Pays excellent rates.

SELF—350 Madison Ave., New York, NY 10017. Alexandra Penney, Ed.-in-Chief. "We no longer accept unsolicited manuscripts or queries."

TODAY'S CHRISTIAN WOMAN—465 Gundersen Dr., Carol Stream, IL 60188. Julie A. Talerico, Ed. Jan Senn, Asst. Ed. Articles, 1,500 words, that are "warm and personal in tone, full of real-life anecdotes that deal with the following relationships: marriage, parenting, friendship, spiritual life, and self." Humorous anecdotes, 150 words, that have a Christian slant. Queries required. Payment varies, on acceptance. Guidelines.

VOGUE—350 Madison Ave., New York, NY 10017. Address Features Ed. Articles, to 1,500 words, on women, entertainment and the arts, travel, medicine, and health. General features. No unsolicited manuscripts. Query. Pays good rates, on acceptance.

WOMAN OF POWER—P.O. Box 2785, Orleans, MA 02653. Char McKee, Ed. A magazine of feminism, spirituality, and politics. Articles, to 3,500 words.

612

Each issue explores a special theme. Send SASE for themes and guidelines. Pays in copies and subscription.

WOMAN'S DAY—1633 Broadway, New York, NY 10019. Rebecca Greer, Articles Ed. Human-interest or helpful articles, to 2,000 words, on marriage, child-rearing, health, careers, relationships, money management. Dramatic first-person narratives of medical miracles, rescues, women's experiences, etc. "We will respond to queries; unsolicited manuscripts will be returned unread." Pays top rates, on acceptance. Query.

WOMAN'S OWN—1115 Broadway, New York, NY 10010. Catherine Romano, Man. Ed. Articles, 1,500 to 2,000 words, offering inspirational and practical advice on relationships and career and lifestyle choices for women in their mid-thirties. Common subjects: staying together, second marriages, working women, asserting yourself, meeting new men, "love-styles," sex, etc. Columns, 800 words, for "Suddenly Single," "Moving Up," "Round-Up," "Mindpower," "Dieter's Notes," "Fashion Advisor," "Financial Advisor," and "Shaping Up." Profiles, 250 to 500 words, of women who have overcome great odds for "Woman in the News." Fun, in-depth quizzes. Short pieces on trends and breakthroughs for "Let's Put Our Heads Together." Query. Pays $75 to $300, on acceptance.

WOMAN'S TOUCH—1445 Boonville, Springfield, MO 65802–1894. Sandra G. Clopine, Ed. Aleda Swartzendruber, Assoc. Ed. Inspirational articles, 500 to 1,200 words, for Christian women. Uses some poetry, 50 to 150 words. Pays on acceptance. Allow three months for response. Guidelines and editorial calendar.

WOMEN'S CIRCLE—P.O. Box 299, Lynnfield, MA 01940. Marjorie Pearl, Ed. Success stories on home-based female entrepreneurs. How-to articles on contemporary craft and needlework projects. Unique money-saving ideas and recipes. Pays varying rates, on acceptance.

WOMEN'S SPORTS & FITNESS—2025 Pearl St., Boulder, CO 80302. Kathleen Gasperini, Ed. How-tos, profiles, active travel, and controversial issues in women's sports, 500 to 3,000 words. Fitness, nutrition, and health. Pays on publication.

WORKING MOTHER—Lang Communications, 230 Park Ave., New York, NY 10169. Address Ed. Dept. Articles, to 2,000 words, that help women in their task of juggling job, home, and family. "We like pieces that solve or illuminate a problem unique to our readers." Payment varies, on acceptance.

MEN'S PUBLICATIONS

ESQUIRE—1790 Broadway, New York, NY 10019. David Hirshey, Deputy Ed. Articles, 2,500 to 4,000 words, for intelligent audience. Pays varying rates, on acceptance. Query with clips and SASE.

GALLERY—401 Park Ave. S., New York, NY 10016–8802. Barry Janoff, Ed.-in-Chief. Rich Friedman, Man. Ed. Articles, investigative pieces, interviews, profiles, to 2,500 words, for sophisticated men. Short humor, satire, service pieces, and fiction. Photos. Pays varying rates, on publication. Query. Guidelines.

GENTLEMEN'S QUARTERLY—350 Madison Ave., New York, NY 10017. No free-lance queries or manuscripts.

INSIDE EDGE—50 Church St., Cambridge, MA 02138. Geoffrey Mason, Man. Ed. Fiction, nonfiction, and humor, 1,000 words, for young men ages 18 to 24. Queries preferred. Pays $250, on publication.

MEN'S FITNESS—21100 Erwin St., Woodland Hills, CA 91367. Jim Rosenthal, Fitness Ed. Articles, 1,500 to 2,500 words, and department pieces, 1,000 to 1,500 words: "authoritative and practical articles dealing with fitness, health, and men's lifestyles." Pays $350 to $1,000, on acceptance.

MEN'S HEALTH—Rodale Press, 33 E. Minor Dr., Emmaus, PA 18098. Jeff Csatari, Sr. Ed. Articles, 1,000 to 2,500 words, on fitness, diet, health, relationships, sports, and travel for men ages 25 to 55. Pays from 50¢ a word, on acceptance. Query.

PENTHOUSE—1965 Broadway, New York, NY 10023–5965. Peter Bloch, Ed. Nanette Varian, Articles Ed. General-interest profiles, interviews, or investigative articles, to 5,000 words. Interviews, 5,000 words, with introductions. No unsolicited fiction. Pays on acceptance.

PLAYBOY—680 N. Lakeshore Dr., Chicago, IL 60611. John Rezek, Articles Ed. Articles, 3,500 to 6,000 words, and sophisticated fiction, 1,000 to 10,000 words (5,000 preferred), for urban men. Humor; satire. Science fiction. Pays to $5,000 for articles and fiction, $2,000 for short-shorts, on acceptance. SASE required.

PLAYERS—8060 Melrose Ave., Los Angeles, CA 90046. Joe Nazel, Ed. Articles, 1,000 to 3,000 words, for black men: politics, economics, travel, fashion, grooming, entertainment, sports, interviews, fiction, humor, satire, health, and sex. Photos a plus. Pays on publication.

THE ROBB REPORT—1 Acton Pl., Acton, MA 01720. Janice Stillman, Sr. Ed. Robert R. Feeman, Ed. Lynn Tryba, Ed. Asst. "We are a lifestyle magazine for affluent men." Feature articles on investment opportunities, classic and collectible autos, entrepreneurship, technology, lifestyles, home interiors, boats, travel, etc. Pays on publication. Query with SASE and published clips.

SENIORS' MAGAZINES

DOWN MEMORY LANE—3816 Industry Blvd., Lakeland, FL 33811. Adrian Hoff, Man. Ed. Articles relating to the 1940s, '50s, and '60s. Focus on the human element. Lead features, 800 to 1,000 words; features, 500 to 800 words; pieces, 200 to 500 words. Photos a plus. Also personal anecdotes, remembrances, and articles on collectibles for departments. Pays $75 to $200 per published page for articles; to $150 for departments, within 30 days of publication. Guidelines.

KEY HORIZONS—Gateway Plaza, 950 N. Meridian, Suite 1200, Indianapolis, IN 46204. Joan Todd, Man. Ed. General-interest articles and department pieces, 300 to 1,500 words, for readers ages 50 and over in the Midwest, East, and Southwest. Departments include money, health, finance, travel (no first-person pieces), and better living (gardening, cooking, etc.). No nostalgia or first-person retrospectives. Pays $50 to $500, on publication.

LIFE TODAY—(formerly *Prime Times*) 2802 International Ln., Suite 120, Madison, WI 53704. Rebecca Tavernini, Ed. Articles, 500 to 800 words, on health, technology, nature, home, sports, feature interviews, etc. Departments, 850 to 1,000 words. Pays $125 to $750, on publication. Query required.

MATURE LIVING—127 Ninth Ave. N., Nashville, TN 37234. Al Shackleford, Ed. Fiction and human-interest articles, to 900 words, for senior adults. Must be consistent with Christian principles. Pays 5 ½¢ a word, on acceptance.

MATURE YEARS—201 Eighth Ave. S., P.O. Box 801, Nashville, TN 37202. Marvin W. Cropsey, Ed. Articles of interest to older adults: health and fitness, personal finance, hobbies and inspiration. Anecdotes, to 300 words, poems, cartoons, jokes, and puzzles for older adults. Allow two months for response. "A Christian magazine that seeks to build faith. We always show older adults in a favorable light." Include name, address, and Social Security number with all submissions.

MODERN MATURITY—3200 E. Carson St., Lakewood, CA 90712. J. Henry Fenwick, Ed. Articles, to 2,000 words, on careers, workplace, human interest, living, finance, relationships, and consumerism for readers over 50 years old. Query with SASE. Pays $500 to $2,500, on acceptance.

NEW CHOICES FOR RETIREMENT LIVING—28 W. 23rd St., New York, NY 10010. Allen J. Sheinman, Articles Ed. David A. Sendler, Ed.-in-Chief. News and service magazine for people ages 50 to 65. Articles on planning for retirement, health and fitness, financial strategies, housing options, travel, profiles/interviews (celebrities and newsmakers), relationships, leisure pursuits, etc. Query or send complete manuscript. SASE required. Payment varies, on acceptance.

PRIME TIMES—See *Life Today*.

THE RETIRED OFFICER MAGAZINE—201 N. Washington St., Alexandria, VA 22314. Articles, 800 to 2,000 words, of interest to military retirees and their families. Current military/political affairs, recent military history (especially Vietnam and Korea), humor, travel, hobbies, military family lifestyles, wellness, second careers. Photos a plus. Pays from $500, on acceptance. Queries required; address Manuscript Ed. Guidelines.

RX REMEDY—120 Post Rd. W., Westport, CT 06880. Val Weaver, Ed. Quarterly. Articles, 600 to 2,500 words, on health and medication issues for readers 55 and older. Regular columns include "The Fitness Prescription," and "The Nutrition Prescription." Query. Pays $1 to $1.25 a word, on acceptance.

SENIOR MAGAZINE—3565 S. Higuera St., San Luis Obispo, CA 93401. Personality profiles and health articles, 600 to 900 words, and book reviews of interest to seniors. Fiction, 2,000 words. Pays $1.50 per inch; $10 to $25 for B&W photos; $100 savings bond for fiction, on publication.

YESTERDAY'S MAGAZETTE—P.O. Box 15126, Sarasota, FL 34277. Ned Burke, Ed. Articles and stories, 500 to 1,000 words, set in the 1920s to '70s. "Stories with photos have the best chance of acceptance here." Traditional poetry, to 24 lines. Pays $5 to $25, for articles, on publication. Pays in copies for short pieces and poetry.

HOME & GARDEN/FOOD & WINE

AMERICAN HOMESTYLE—(formerly *Decorating Remodeling*) 110 Fifth Ave., New York, NY 10011. Kathryn George, Karen Saks, Eds.-in-Chief. Articles on home decorating, remodeling, architecture, and gardening. Query. Payment varies, on acceptance.

THE AMERICAN ROSE MAGAZINE—P.O. Box 30,000, Shreveport, LA 71130. William Johnson, Man. Ed. Articles on home rose gardens: varieties, products, helpful advice, rose care, etc.

BETTER HOMES AND GARDENS—1716 Locust St., Des Moines, IA 50309–3023. David Jordan, Ed. Articles, to 2,000 words, on money management, health, travel, pets, and cars. Pays top rates, on acceptance. Query.

615

BRIDE'S & YOUR HOME—350 Madison Ave., New York, NY 10017. Andrea Feld, Man. Ed. Articles, 800 to 3,000 words, for engaged couples or newly-weds on housing, redecorating, etc. Three major editorial subjects: home, wedding, and honeymoon travel. Pays $300 to $1,000, on acceptance.

CANADIAN WORKSHOP MAGAZINE—130 Spy Ct., Markham, Ont., Canada L3R 5H6. Erina Kelly, Ed. Articles, 1,500 to 2,800 words, on do-it-yourself home renovations, energy saving projects, etc., with photos. Payment varies, on publication.

CHILE PEPPER—P.O. Box 4278, Albuquerque, NM 87196. Melissa Jackson, Assoc. Ed. Food and travel articles, 1,000 to 1,500 words. "No general and obvious articles, such as 'My Favorite Chile Con Carne.' We want first-person articles about spicy world cuisine." Queries required. Payment varies, on publication.

DECORATING REMODELING—See *American HomeStyle.*

EATING WELL—Ferry Rd., Charlotte, VT 05445. Scott Mowbray, Ed. Allison Cleary, Man. Ed. Bimonthly. Feature articles, 2,000 to 5,000 words. Departments ("Nutrition Letter: The Science of Eating Well" and "Observer: News from the World of Food"), 200 to 500 words. "We look for strong journalistic voice; authoritative, timely coverage of nutrition issues; healthy recipes that emphasize good ingredients, simple preparation, and full flavor; and a sense of humor." Query. Payment varies, 45 days after acceptance.

ELLE DECOR—1633 Broadway, New York, NY 10019. Charles Bricker, Exec. Ed. Articles, 300 to 1,000 words, on designers and craftspeople. Query with photos of the designers and their work. Articles, 300 to 1,000 words, on houses and apartments "notable for their quirkiness or their beauty, preferably an eclectic combination of the two." Query. Pays $1.25 a word, on publication.

FLOWER & GARDEN MAGAZINE—700 W. 47th St., Suite 310, Kansas City, MO 64112. Practical how-to articles, 1,000 words, on lawn and garden advice. Query. Good photos enhance submission. Pays varying rates, on acceptance (on publication for photos).

FOOD & WINE—1120 Ave. of the Americas, New York, NY 10036. Mary Simons, Ed.-in-Chief. Warren Picower, Man. Ed. Current culinary or beverage ideas for dining and entertaining at home and out. Food-related travel pieces. Submit detailed proposal.

GARDEN DESIGN—4401 Connecticut Ave. N.W., Fifth Fl., Washington, DC 20008. James G. Trulove, Ed.-in-Chief. Garden-related features. Articles, 800 to 1,500 words, on "private and public gardens, interviews with landscape designers and other personalities, and stories on art, architecture, furniture and fashion as they relate to the garden." Pays from 50¢ a word, on acceptance. Guidelines.

GOURMET, THE MAGAZINE OF GOOD LIVING—Conde Nast, 360 Madison Ave., New York, NY 10017. No unsolicited material.

HARROWSMITH COUNTRY LIFE—Ferry Rd., Charlotte, VT 05445. Address Ed. Dept. Investigative pieces, 4,000 to 5,000 words, on issues of ecology and the environment, rural life, gardening, energy-efficient housing, and healthful food. Short pieces for "Screed" (opinions) and "Gazette" (news briefs). Pays $500 to $1,500 for features, from $50 to $600 for department pieces, on acceptance. Query required. Send SASE for guidelines.

HCA NEWS AND VIEWS—Homeowners Club of America, Inc., P.O. Box 5177, Minnetonka, MN 55343. Articles, 500 to 700 words, on how-to projects, renovations, financial issues related to home ownership, gardening/landscaping, and other home ownership topics. Query Articles Ed. Pays 35¢ to 50¢ a word, on acceptance.

THE HERB COMPANION—Interweave Press, 201 E. Fourth St., Loveland, CO 80537. David Merrill, Man. Ed. Bimonthly. Articles, 1,500 to 3,000 words; fillers, 75 to 150 words. Practical horticultural information, original recipes illustrating the use of herbs, thoroughly researched historical insights, step-by-step instructions for herbal craft projects, profiles of notable individuals in the field, book reviews. Pays $100 per published page, on publication.

THE HERB QUARTERLY—P. O. Box 689, San Anselmo, CA 94960. Linda Sparrowe, Ed. Articles, 2,000 to 4,000 words, on herbs: practical uses, cultivation, gourmet cooking, landscaping, herb tradition, medicinal herbs, crafts ideas, unique garden designs, profiles of herb garden experts, practical how-tos for the herb businessperson. Include garden design when possible. Pays on publication. Guidelines; send SASE.

HOME MECHANIX—2 Park Ave., New York, NY 10016. Michael Chotiner, Ed. Home improvement articles. Time- or money-saving tips for the home, garage, or yard; seasonal reminders for homeowners. Pays $50, on acceptance.

HORTICULTURE—98 N. Washington St., Boston, MA 02114. Deborah Starr, Exec. Ed. Authoritative, well-written articles, 500 to 2,500 words, on all aspects of gardening. Pays competitive rates. Query first.

HOUSE BEAUTIFUL—1700 Broadway, New York, NY 10019. Elaine Greene, Features Ed. Service articles related to the home. Pieces on design, travel, and gardening. Query with detailed outline. SASE required. Guidelines.

HOUSEPLANT MAGAZINE—P.O. Box 1638, Elkins, WV 26241. Larry Hodgson, Ed.-in-Chief. Articles, 700 to 1,500 words, on indoor gardening, travel, humor, hydroponics, plant portraits. Query. Payment varies, on publication.

LOG HOME GUIDE FOR BUILDERS & BUYERS—164 Middle Creek Rd., Cosby, TN 37722. Articles, 500 to 1,500 words, on building new, or restoring old log homes, especially with solar or alternative heating systems, as well as pieces on decorating or profiles of interesting builders of log homes. Pays 20¢ a word, extra for photos, on publication. Limited market. Query.

LOG HOME LIVING—P.O. Box 220039, Chantilly, VA 22022. Roland Sweet, Ed. Articles, 1,000 to 1,500 words, on modern manufactured and hand-crafted kit log homes: homeowner profiles, design and decor features. Pays $200 to $500, on acceptance.

THE MOTHER EARTH NEWS—24 E. 23rd St., 5th Fl., New York, NY 10010. Michelle Silver, Assoc. Ed. Articles on country living: home improvement and construction, how-tos, indoor and outdoor gardening, crafts and projects, etc. Also health, ecology, energy, and consumerism pieces; profiles. Pay varies.

NATIONAL GARDENING MAGAZINE—180 Flynn Ave., Burlington, VT 05401. Warren Schultz, Ed. Articles, 800 to 2,500 words, for advanced and beginning gardeners: seed-to-table profiles of major crops; firsthand reports from or profiles of experienced gardeners in this country's many growing regions; easy-to-follow gardening techniques; garden food recipes; coverage of fruits, vegetables, and ornamentals. Pays $100 to $500, on acceptance (on publication for photos). Query preferred.

SELECT HOMES & FOODS—(formerly *Select Homes*) 50 Holly St., Toronto, Ontario, Canada M4S 3B3. Lynette Jennings, Ed. How-to articles, profiles of Canadian homes, renovation, decor, and gardening features, 800 to 1,500 words. Canadian content and locations only. Pays from $400 to $900 (Canadian), on acceptance. Query with international reply coupons. Guidelines.

VEGGIE LIFE—1041 Shary Cir., Concord, CA 94518. David M. Camp, Ed. Bimonthly. Features and profiles, 2,500 words, for "people interested in American and ethnic meatless cuisine, organic gardening, environmental issues, and healthy living." Food features (include eight to 10 recipes); department pieces, 250 to 1,000 words. Queries preferred. Payment varies, on acceptance.

THE WINE SPECTATOR—Opera Plaza, Suite 2014, 601 Van Ness Ave., San Francisco, CA 94102. Jim Gordon, Man. Ed. Features, 600 to 2,000 words, preferably with photos, on news and people in the wine world. Pays from $400, extra for photos, on publication. Query required.

WINE TIDINGS—5165 Sherbrooke St. W., Suite 414, Montreal, Quebec, Canada H4A 1T6. Barbara Leslie, Ed. Published 8 times a year. Articles, 1,000 to 1,500 words, and 400- to 1,000-word shorts, with accurate wine information and written for a Canadian audience. Pays $100 to $300 for features, $30 to $150 for shorts, on publication. Photos, $20 to $50 for B&W or color; $200 to $400 for covers.

WORKBENCH—700 West 47th St., Suite 310, Kansas City, MO 64112. Robert N. Hoffman, Exec. Ed. Illustrated how-to articles on home improvement and woodworking, with detailed instructions. Pays from $150 per printed page, on acceptance. Send SASE for guidelines.

YOUR HOME/INDOORS & OUT —P.O. Box 10010, Ogden, UT 84409. Address Ed. Dept. Articles, 1,000 words with good color transparencies and fresh ideas, in all areas of home decor: the latest in home construction (exteriors, interiors, building materials, design); the outdoors at home (landscaping, pools, patios, gardening); home management, buying and selling. "We are especially interested in articles on choosing a realtor or home builder." No do-it-yourself pieces. Query.

LIFESTYLE AND FAMILY PUBLICATIONS

AMERICAN BABY—475 Park Ave. S., New York, NY 10016. Judith Nolte, Ed. Articles, 1,000 to 2,000 words, for new or expectant parents on prenatal and infant care. Pays varying rates, on acceptance.

AMERICAN HEALTH—28 W. 23rd St., New York, NY 10010. Address Ed. Dept. Lively, authoritative articles, 1,000 to 3,000 words, on scientific and lifestyle aspects of health and fitness; 100- to 500-word news reports. Query with clips. Pays $250 ($50 kill fee) for news stories; 75¢ per word for features, on acceptance.

BABY TALK—636 Ave. of the Americas, New York, NY 10011. Susan Strecker, Ed. Articles, 1,000 to 1,500 words, by parents or professionals, on babies, baby care, etc. Pays varying rates, on acceptance. SASE required.

BAY AREA PARENT—401 Alberto Way, Suite A, Los Gatos, CA 95032–5404. Mary Brence Martin, Ed. Articles, 1,200 to 1,400 words, on local parenting issues for readers in California's Santa Clara County and the South Bay area. Query. Mention availability of B&W photos. Pays 6¢ a word, $10 to $15 for photos, on publication.

THE BIG APPLE PARENTS' PAPER—36 E. 12th St., New York, NY 10003. Susan Hodara, Ed. Articles, 600 to 750 words, for NYC parents. Pays $50, on publication. Buys first NY-area rights.

CAPPER'S—1503 S.W. 42nd St., Topeka, KS 66609–1265. Nancy Peavler, Ed. Human-interest, personal-experience, historical articles, 300 to 700 words. Poetry, to 15 lines, on nature, home, family. Novel-length fiction for serialization. Letters on women's interests, recipes, and hints for "Heart of the Home." Jokes. Children's writing and art section. Pays varying rates, on publication.

CATHOLIC PARENT—Our Sunday Visitor, Inc., 200 Noll Plaza, Huntington, IN 46750. Woodeene Koenig-Bricker, Ed. Humorous features, how-tos, and general-interest articles, 800 to 1,000 words, dealing with the issues of raising children "with solid values in today's changing world. Keep it anecdotal and practical with an emphasis on values and family life." Payment varies, on acceptance.

CHRISTIAN HOME & SCHOOL—3350 East Paris Ave. S.E., Grand Rapids, MI 49512. Gordon L. Bordewyk, Ed. Articles for parents in Canada and the U.S. who send their children to Christian schools and are concerned about the challenges facing Christian families today. Pays $75 to $150, on publication. Guidelines.

CHRISTIAN PARENTING—P.O. Box 850, Sisters, OR 97759. David Kopp, Ed. Articles, 900 to 1,500 words, dealing with raising children with Christian principles. Departments: "Parent Exchange," 25 to 100 words, on problem-solving ideas that have worked for parents; "My Story," 800 to 1,500 words, in first person, of how one family or parent faced a parenting challenge; "Life in our House," insightful anecdotes, 25 to 100 words, about humorous things said at home. Queries preferred for articles. Pays 15¢ to 25¢ a word, on acceptance for assigned articles, on publication for unsolicited articles. Pays $40 for "Parent Exchange," $25 for "Life in our House." Guidelines.

THE CHRISTIAN SCIENCE MONITOR—One Norway St., Boston, MA 02115. Lawrence Goodrich, Features Ed. Newspaper. Articles on lifestyle trends, women's rights, family, and parenting. Pays varying rates, on acceptance.

CONNECTICUT FAMILY—See *New York Family.*

COUNTRY—5400 S. 60th St., Greendale, WI 53129. Dan Matel, Man. Ed. Pieces on interesting rural and country people who have unusual hobbies, 500 to 1,500 words; liberal use of direct quotes. Good, candid, color photos required. Pays on acceptance. Queries preferred.

EASTSIDE PARENT—Northwest Parent Publishing, 2107 Elliott Ave., #303, Seattle, WA 98121. Ann Bergman, Ed. Articles, 300 to 2,500 words, for parents of children under 12. Readers tend to be professional, two-career families. Queries are preferred. Pays $150 to $500, on publication. Also publishes *Portland Parent* and *Pierce County Parent.*

EXCEPTIONAL PARENT—1170 Commonwealth Ave., Boston, MA 02134–4646. Stanley D. Klein, Maxwell J. Schleifer, Eds. Articles, 1,000 to 1,500 words, for parents raising children with disabilities. Practical ideas and techniques on parenting, as well as the latest in technology, research, and rehabilitation. Query. Pays $25, on publication.

FAMILY FUN—Walt Disney Publishing Group, Box 929, Northampton, MA 01061. Alexandra Kennedy, Exec. Ed. Read-aloud stories, to 750 words, and articles, to 1,500 words, on family activities and "creative parenting." Queries preferred. Payment varies, on acceptance.

FAMILY LIFE—Straight Arrow Publishers, Inc. 1290 Ave. of the Americas, New York, NY 10104–0298. Address Editorial Dept. Articles, 1,000 to 4,000 words, on education, travel, money, health, community service, and other subjects of interest to active parents of children ages 3 to 12. Service pieces, 700 to 1,500 words, on sports, lessons, field trips, toys, parties, and pets. Short pieces, 250 to 800 words, on news and activities. Query with clips.

FATE—P.O. Box 64383, St. Paul, MN 55164–0383. Phyllis Galde, Ed. Factual fillers and true stories, to 3,000 words, on strange or psychic happenings and mystic personal experiences. Pays 10¢ a word.

FELLOWSHIP—Box 271, Nyack, NY 10960–0271. Richard Deats, Ed. Published six times a year by the Fellowship of Reconciliation, an interfaith, pacifist organization. Features, 1,500 to 2,000 words, and articles, 750 words, "dealing with nonviolence, opposition to war, and a just and peaceful world community." Photo essays (B&W photos, include caption information). Queries preferred. SASE required. Pays in copies and subscription.

GROWING CHILD/GROWING PARENT—22 N. Second St., Lafayette, IN 47902–0620. Nancy Kleckner, Ed. Articles, to 1,500 words, on subjects of interest to parents of children under 6. No personal experience pieces or poetry. Guidelines.

HEART & SOUL—Rodale Press, Inc., 33 E. Minor St., Emmaus, PA 18098. Catherine Cassidy, Man. Ed. Articles, 800 to 2,000 words, on health, beauty, fitness, nutrition, and relationships for African-American readers. "We aim to be the African-American's ultimate guide to a healthy lifestyle." Queries preferred. Payment varies, on acceptance.

HOME LIFE—127 Ninth Ave. N., Nashville, TN 37234. Charlie Warren, Ed. Southern Baptist. Articles, to 1,500 words, on Christian marriage, parenting, and family relationships. Pays to 5 ½¢ a word, on acceptance.

INDEPENDENT LIVING—150 Motor Parkway, Suite 420, Hauppauge, NY 11788–5145. Anne Kelly, Ed. Articles, 1,000 to 2,000 words, addressing lifestyles of persons who have disabilities. Possible topics: home health care, careers, travel, sports, family life, and sexuality. Pays 10¢ a word, $15 per photo, on publication. Query.

JEWISH CURRENTS—22 E. 17th St., #601, New York, NY 10003. Morris U. Schappes, Ed. Articles, 2,400 to 3,000 words, on Jewish culture or history: Holocaust, resistance commemoration, Black-Jewish relations, Jewish labor struggles. "We are a secular Jewish magazine." No payment.

THE JEWISH HOMEMAKER—705 Foster Ave., Brooklyn, NY 11230. Mayer Bendet, Ed. Bimonthly. Articles, 1,000 words, for a traditional/Orthodox Jewish audience. Humor and fillers. Query. Payment varies, on publication.

JOYFUL CHILD JOURNAL—P.O. Box 5506, Scottsdale, AZ 82561. Peggy Jenkins, Exec. Ed. Quarterly. Fiction and nonfiction, 500 to 1,000 words, that "explore how society and education can more effectively nurture children (and adults) to express their fullest potential, thus releasing their inner joy. Articles on educating and parenting the whole child (body, mind, and spirit)." Some short poetry. Queries preferred. Guidelines. Pays in copies.

L.A. BABY—See *Wingate Enterprises, Ltd.*

L.A. PARENT—See *Wingate Enterprises, Ltd.*

LIFEPRINTS—P.O. Box 5181, Salem, OR 97304. Carol McCarl, Ed. Quarterly. Articles, 1,200 to 1,800 words, and poetry, 20 lines, for visually impaired youth and adults. Career opportunities, educational skills, and recreational activities. "We want to give readers an opportunity to learn about interesting and successful people who happen to be blind." Queries are preferred. Pays $15 for articles; $10 for poetry, on publication.

LIVING WITH CHILDREN—MSN 140, 127 Ninth Ave. N., Nashville, TN 37234. Articles, 800 to 1,200 words, on parent-child relationships, told from a Christian perspective. Pays 5 ½¢ a word, on acceptance.

LIVING WITH PRESCHOOLERS—MSN 140, 127 Ninth Ave. N., Nashville, TN 37234. Articles, 800 to 1,200 words, on Christian family issues. Pays 5 ½¢ a word, on acceptance.

LIVING WITH TEENAGERS—127 Ninth Ave. N., Nashville, TN 37234. Articles, 800 to 1,300 words, from a Christian perspective for parents of teenagers; first-person approach preferred. Poetry, four to 16 lines. Pays 5 ½¢ a word for articles, on acceptance.

MILITARY LIFESTYLE MAGAZINE—4800 Montgomery Ln., Suite 710, Bethesda, MD 20814. Hope Daniels, Ed. Articles, 800 to 1,500 words, for military families in the U.S. and overseas; pieces on child raising, marriage, health, fitness, food, and issues concerning young military families; home decor and "portable" or "instant" gardening articles; fiction. Pays $300 to $700, on publication. Query.

NATIVE PEOPLES MAGAZINE—5333 N. 7th St., Suite C-224, Phoenix, AZ 85014–2804. Gary Avey, Ed. Quarterly. Articles, 1,800 to 2,800 words, on the "arts and lifeways" of the native peoples of the Americas; authenticity and positive portrayals of present traditional and cultural practices necessary. Query, including availability of photos. Pays 25¢ a word, on publication.

NATURAL HEALTH: THE GUIDE TO WELL-BEING—17 Station St., Box 1200, Brookline, MA 02147. Features, 1,500 to 3,000 words, on holistic health, natural foods, herbal remedies, etc. Interviews. Photos. Pays 30¢ a word, extra for photos, on acceptance.

NEW AGE JOURNAL—342 Western Ave., Brighton, MA 02135. Peggy Taylor, Ed. Articles for readers who take an active interest in social change, personal growth, health, and contemporary issues. Features, 2,000 to 4,000 words; columns, 750 to 1,500 words; short news items, 50 words; and first-person narratives, 750 to 1,500 words. Pays varying rates.

NEW CHOICES FOR RETIREMENT LIVING—28 W. 23rd St., New York, NY 10010. Allen J. Sheinman, Articles Ed. David A. Sendler, Ed.-in-Chief. News and service magazine for people ages 50 to 65. Articles on planning for retirement, health and fitness, financial strategies, housing options, travel, profiles/ interviews (celebrities and newsmakers), relationships, leisure pursuits, etc. SASE required. Payment varies, on acceptance.

NEW YORK FAMILY—141 Halstead Ave., Suite 3D, Mamaroneck, NY 10543. Felice Shapiro, Pub. Susan Ross, Ed. Articles related to family life in New York City and general parenting topics. Pays $50 to $100. Same requirements for *Westchester Family* and *Connecticut Family*.

OUT—The Soho Bldg., 110 Greene St., Suite 800, New York, NY 10012. Michael Goff, Ed.-in-Chief. Bimonthly. Articles, 50 to 8,000 words, on various subjects (current affairs, culture, fitness, finance, etc.) of interest to gay and lesbian readers. "The best guide to what we publish is to read previous issues." Query. Guidelines. Payment varies, on publication.

OUT YOUR BACKDOOR—4686 Meridian Rd., Williamston, MI 48895. Jeff Potter, Ed. Articles and fiction, 2,500 words, for thrifty-minded, down-to-earth readers. Budget travel (especially by bicycle), second-hand goods, and "homespun but high-quality culture." Study sample issue before submitting. Pays in copies.

PALM SPRINGS LIFE—Desert Publications, 303 North Indian Canyon Dr., P.O. Box 2724, Palm Springs, CA 92263. Jamie Pricer, Ed. Articles, 1,000 to 3,000 words, of interest to "wealthy, upscale people who live and/or play in the desert." Pays $150 to $400 for features, $30 to $75 for short profiles, on publication. Query required.

PARENTGUIDE NEWS—475 Park Ave. S., New York, NY 10016. Leslie Elgort, Ed. Articles, 1,000 to 1,500 words, related to families and parenting: trends, profiles, issues, special programs and products, etc. Humor, jokes, puzzles, and photos also considered. Payment varies, on publication.

PARENTING—See *Wingate Enterprises, Ltd.*

PARENTING—301 Howard St., 17th Fl., San Francisco, CA 94105. Address Articles Ed. Articles, 500 to 3,500 words, on education, health, fitness, nutrition, child development, psychology, and social issues for parents of young children. Query.

PARENTS—685 Third Ave., New York, NY 10017. Ann Pleshette Murphy, Ed. Articles, 1,500 to 2,500 words, on parenting, family, women's and community issues, etc. Informal style with quotes from experts. Pays from $1,000, on acceptance. Query.

PARENT'S DIGEST—100 Park Ave., New York, NY 10017. Mary E. Mohler, Ed.-in-Chief. Published three times a year by *Ladies' Home Journal.* Articles, 250 to 2,500 words, for parents. Query. Payment varies, on acceptance.

PIERCE COUNTY PARENT—See *Eastside Parent.*

PORTLAND PARENT—See *Eastside Parent.*

QUICK 'N EASY COUNTRY COOKIN'—Parkside Publishing, P.O. Box 66, Davis, SD 57021–0066. Judith Friese, Copy/Production Ed. Family-oriented articles, 400 to 500 words, on cooking, and articles with a human-interest/Christian perspective. Short verse, puzzles, and humorous fillers, to 50 words. Pays $10 for articles, on publication.

THE ROBB REPORT—1 Acton Pl., Acton, MA 01720. Janice Stillman, Sr. Ed. Lynn Tryba, Ed. Asst. "For the Affluent Lifestyle." Feature articles on investment opportunities, classic and collectible autos, entrepreneurship, technology, lifestyles, home interiors, boats, travel, etc. "Lifestyle" column addresses men's fashion, home, trends, food, books, personalities, pets, etc." Pays on publication. Query with SASE and published clips.

SAN DIEGO PARENT—See *Wingate Enterprises, Ltd.*

SEATTLE'S CHILD—Northwest Parent Publishing, 2107 Elliott Ave., #303, Seattle, WA 98121. Ann Bergman, Ed. Articles, 400 to 2,500 words, of interest to parents, educators, and childcare providers of children under 12, plus investigative reports and consumer tips on issues affecting families in the Puget Sound region. Pays $75 to $400, on publication. Query required.

SESAME STREET PARENTS' GUIDE—One Lincoln Plaza, New York, NY 10023. Valerie Monroe, Exec. Ed. Articles, 800 to 2,500 words, on medical, psychological, and educational issues for families with young children (up to 8 years old). First-person pieces on parenting for "Family Portrait." "A Conversation With . . . " columns, to 1,500 words, of questions and answers with professionals (educators, psychologists, authors) who affect the lives of children. Pays 50¢ to $1 per word, up to six weeks after acceptance.

SINGLE GENTLEMEN & WOMEN—3880 Vest Mill Rd., Suite 100, Winston-Salem, NC 27103. Dick Farris, Ed. Quarterly. Articles, to 3,000 words, on travel, food, health, etc., of interest to unmarried men and women ages 35 and older. Fiction, to 3,000 words, and poetry, to 500 words. "Material should be in good taste." Payment varies, after acceptance.

THE SINGLE PARENT—Parents Without Partners, Inc., 8807 Colesville Rd., Silver Spring, MD 20910–4346. Rene McDonald, Ed. Bimonthly. Articles, 1,500 to 2,200 words, addressing the concerns of single parents, including physical and emotional wellness, careers (for adults and youths), and intergenerational issues. Fillers, 300 to 500 words. Prefers pieces that "enlighten and entertain busy people"; no "cutesy or sob stories." Pays $75 to $125 for articles, $25 to $50 for fillers, on publication.

TODAY'S FAMILY—27 Empire Dr., St. Paul, MN 55103. Valerie Hockert, Pub./Man. Ed. Bimonthly. Articles, 750 to 2,000 words, on "hot topics and fun for every family." Pays $10 to $50, on publication. Query preferred.

VIRTUE—P. O. Box 850, Sisters, OR 97759. Marlee Alex, Ed. Articles, 1,000 to 1,500 words, on family, marriage, self-esteem, working mothers, opinions, food, crafts. Fiction and poetry. Pays 15¢ to 25¢ a word, on publication. Query required.

WEIGHT WATCHERS MAGAZINE—360 Lexington Ave., New York, NY 10017. Susan Rees, Sr. Ed., Health and Nutrition. Articles on health, nutrition, fitness, and weight-loss motivation and success. Pays from $350, on acceptance. Query with clips required. Guidelines.

WESTCHESTER FAMILY—See *New York Family*.

WILDFIRE—Bear Tribe Publishing, P.O. Box 199, Devon, PA 19333. Wabun Wind, Ed. Articles, 1,000 to 2,500 words, with a strong nature-based focus on spirituality, personal development, alternative lifestyles, natural healings, and ecology. Poetry, 20 lines. Pay varies, on publication.

WINGATE ENTERPRISES, LTD.—P.O. Box 3204, 443 E. Irving Dr., Burbank, CA 91504. Publishes city-based parenting magazines with strong "service-to-parent" slant. Articles, 1,200 words, on child development, health, nutrition, and education. *San Diego Parent* covers San Diego area. *Parenting* covers the Orange County, CA, area. *L.A. Parent* is geared toward parents of children to age 10; *L.A. Baby* to expectant parents and parents of newborns. Query. Pays $250, on acceptance.

WIRED—544 Second St., San Francisco, CA 94107–1427. Kristin Spence, Ed. Assoc. Lifestyle magazine for the "digital generation." Articles, essays, profiles, fiction, and other material that discusses the "meaning and context" of digital technology in today's world. Guidelines. Payment varies, on publication.

WORKING MOTHER—Lang Communications, 230 Park Ave., New York, NY 10169. Address Ed. Dept. Articles, to 2,000 words, that help women juggle job, home, and family. Payment varies, on acceptance.

YOGA JOURNAL—2054 University Ave., Berkeley, CA 94704. Stephan Bodian, Ed. Articles, 1,200 to 4,000 words, on holistic health, spirituality, yoga, and transpersonal psychology; new age profiles; interviews. Pays $75 to $600, on publication.

SPORTS AND RECREATION

THE AMERICAN FIELD—542 S. Dearborn, Chicago, IL 60605. B.J. Matthys, Man. Ed. Yarns about hunting trips, bird-shooting; articles to 1,500 words, on dogs and field trials, emphasizing conservation of game resources. Pays varying rates, on acceptance.

AMERICAN HANDGUNNER—591 Camino de la Reina, Suite 200, San Diego, CA 92108. Cameron Hopkins, Ed. Semi-technical articles on shooting sports, gun repair and alteration, handgun matches and tournaments, for lay readers. Pays $100 to $500, on publication. Query.

AMERICAN HUNTER—470 Spring Park Pl., Suite 1000, Herndon, VA 22070–5227. Tom Fulgham, Ed. Articles, 1,400 to 2,000 words, on hunting. Photos. Pays on acceptance. Guidelines.

AMERICAN MOTORCYCLIST—American Motorcyclist Assn., Box 6114, Westerville, OH 43081–6114. Greg Harrison, Ed. Articles and fiction, to 3,000 words, on motorcycling: news coverage, personalities, tours. Photos. Pays varying rates, on publication. Query with SASE.

THE AMERICAN RIFLEMAN—470 Spring Park Pl., Suite 1000, Herndon, VA 22070. Ron Keyser, Man. Ed. Factual articles on use and enjoyment of sporting firearms. Pays on acceptance.

AMERICAN SQUAREDANCE MAGAZINE—661 Middlefield Rd., Salinas, CA 93906–1004. Jon Sanborn, Ed. Articles and fiction, 1,000 to 1,500 words, related to square dancing. Poetry. Fillers, to 100 words. Pays $1.50 per column inch.

ATLANTIC SALMON JOURNAL—P.O. Box 429, St. Andrews, N.B., Canada E0G 2X0. Harry Bruce, Ed. Material related to Atlantic salmon: fishing, conservation, ecology, travel, politics, biology, how-tos, anecdotes, cuisine. Articles, 1,500 to 3,000 words. Pays $100 to $400, on publication.

BACKPACKER MAGAZINE—Rodale Press, 33 E. Minor St., Emmaus, PA 18098. John Viehman, Exec. Ed. Articles, 250 to 3,000 words, on self-propelled backcountry travel: backpacking, technique, kayaking/canoeing, mountaineering, nordic skiing, health, natural science. Photos. Pays varying rates. Query.

THE BACKSTRETCH—19899 W. 9 Mile Rd., Southfield, MI 48075–3960. Harriet Dalley, Ed. United Thoroughbred Trainers of America. Feature articles, with photos, on subjects related to thoroughbred horse racing. Pays after publication. Sample issue and guidelines on request.

BACKWOODSMAN—P.O. Box 627, Westcliffe, CO 81252. Charlie Richie, Ed. Articles for the twentieth-century frontiersman: muzzleloading, primitive weapons, black powder cartridge guns, woodslore, survival, homesteading, trapping, etc. Historical and how-to articles. No payment.

BAJA EXPLORER—11760 Sorrento Valley Rd., Suite K, San Diego, CA 92121. Landon S. Crumpton, Ed.-in-Chief. Bimonthly. Articles, 800 to 1,200 words, on fishing sailing, surfing, windsurfing, camping, and natural history, of interest to tourists visiting Baja California. Pays 25¢ a word, $50 per slide, on publication.

BASEBALL FORECAST, BASEBALL ILLUSTRATED—See *Hockey Illustrated.*

BASKETBALL FORECAST—See *Hockey Illustrated.*

BASSIN'—15115 S. 76th E. Ave., Bixby, OK 74008. Simon McCaffery, Man. Ed. Articles, 1,500 to 1,800 words, on how and where to bass fish, for the amateur fisherman. Pays $275 to $400, on acceptance.

BASSMASTER MAGAZINE—B.A.S.S. Publications, P.O. Box 17900, Montgomery, AL 36141. Dave Precht, Ed. Articles, 1,500 to 2,000 words, with photos, on freshwater black bass and striped bass. "Short Casts" pieces, 400 to 800 words, on news, views, and items of interest. Pays $200 to $400, on acceptance. Query.

BAY & DELTA YACHTSMAN—2019 Clement Ave., Alameda, CA 94501. Dana Murphy McNabb, Ed. Cruising stories and features. Must have northern California tie-in. Photos and illustrations. Pays varying rates.

BC OUTDOORS—1132 Hamilton St., #202, Vancouver, B.C., Canada V6B 2S2. George Will, Ed. Articles, to 2,000 words, on fishing, hunting, conservation, and all forms of non-competitive outdoor recreation in British Columbia and Yukon. Photos. Pays from 20¢ to 27¢ a word, on acceptance.

BICYCLE GUIDE—1415 3rd St., Santa Monica, CA 90401. Roy M. Wallack, Ed. "Our magazine covers all aspects of cycling from an enthusiast's perspective: racing, touring, sport riding, product reviews, and technical information. We depend on free lancers for touring articles, personality profiles, race coverage, and photos." Queries are preferred. Pays varying rates, on publication.

BICYCLING—33 E. Minor St., Emmaus, PA 18098. James C. McCullagh, Ed. Articles, 500 to 2,500 words, on recreational riding, fitness training, nutrition, bike maintenance, equipment, racing and touring, for serious cyclists. Photos, illustrations. Pays $25 to $1,000, on acceptance. Guidelines.

BIKEREPORT—Bikecentennial, P.O. Box 8308, Missoula, MT 59807. Daniel D'Ambrosio, Ed. Accounts of bicycle tours in the U.S. and overseas, interviews, personal-experience pieces, humor, and news shorts, 1,200 to 2,500 words. Pays $25 to $65 per published page.

BIRD WATCHER'S DIGEST—P.O. Box 110, Marietta, OH 45750. Mary B. Bowers, Ed. Articles, 600 to 2,500 words, for bird watchers: first-person accounts; how-tos; pieces on endangered species; profiles. Cartoons. Pays from $50, on publication.

BLACK BELT—P.O. Box 918, Santa Clarita, CA 91380–9018. Articles related to self-defense: how-tos on fitness and technique; historical, travel, philosophical subjects. Pays $100 to $300, on publication. Guidelines.

BOAT PENNSYLVANIA—Pennsylvania Fish and Boat Commission, P.O. Box 67000, Harrisburg, PA 17106–7000. Art Michaels, Ed. Articles, 200 to 2,500 words, with photos, on boating in Pennsylvania: motorboating, sailing, waterskiing, canoeing, kayaking, and personal watercraft. No pieces on fishing. Pays $50 to $250, on acceptance. Query. Guidelines.

BOUNDARY WATERS JOURNAL—9396 Rocky Ledge Rd., Ely, MN 55731. Stuart Osthoff, Ed. Articles, 2,000 to 3,000 words, on wilderness recreation, nature, and conservation in Minnesota's Boundary Waters Canoe Area Wilderness and Ontario's Quetico Provincial Park. Regular features include canoe-route journals, fishing, camping, hiking, cross-country skiing, wildlife and nature, regional lifestyles, history, and events. Pays $200 to $400, on publication; $50 to $150 for photos.

BOW & ARROW HUNTING—Box 639, 34249 Camino Capistrano, Capistrano Beach, CA 92629. Roger Combs, Ed. Dir. Articles, 1,200 to 2,500 words, with B&W photos, on bowhunting; profiles and technical pieces. Pays $100 to $300, on acceptance. Same address and mechanical requirements for *Gun World*.

BOWHUNTER MAGAZINE—Box 8200, Harrisburg, PA 17105–8200. M.R. James, Ed. Informative, entertaining features, 500 to 2,000 words, on bow-and-arrow hunting. Fillers. Photos. "Study magazine first." Pays $25 to $300, on acceptance.

BOWHUNTING WORLD—Dept. OU, 601 Lakeshore Pkwy., Suite 600, Minnetonka, MN 55305. Tim Dehn, Ed. Articles, 1,800 to 3,000 words, on all aspects of bowhunting and competitive archery equipment, with photos. "We're interested in features that cover the romance or mechanics of all types of archery gear, from traditional to high tech." Also mini-features, 1,000 to 1,600 words. Pays from $325, on acceptance. Query. Guidelines.

BOWLERS JOURNAL—200 S. Michigan Ave., Chicago, IL 60604. Mort Luby, Ed. Trade and consumer articles, 1,200 to 2,200 words, with photos, on bowling. Pays $75 to $200, on acceptance.

BOWLING—5301 S. 76th St., Greendale, WI 53129. Bill Vint, Ed. Articles, to 1,500 words, on all aspects of bowling, especially human interest. Profiles. "Looking for unique, unusual stories about bowling people and places. Occasionally publishes business articles." Pays varying rates, on publication. Query required.

CALIFORNIA ANGLER—1921 E. Carnegie St., Suite N, Santa Ana, CA 92705. How-to and where-to articles, 2,000 words, for freshwater and saltwater anglers in California: travel, new products, fishing techniques, profiles. Photos. Pays $75 to $400, on publication. Query.

CALIFORNIA HORSE REVIEW—P.O. Box 1238, Rancho Cordova, CA 95741–1238. Articles, 750 to 2,500 words, on horse training, for professional horsemen; profiles of prominent West Coast horses and riders. Pays $35 to $125, on publication.

CANOE—P.O. Box 3146, Kirkland, WA 98083. Jim Thompson, Man. Ed. Features, 1,100 to 2,000 words; department pieces, 500 to 1,000 words. Topics include canoeing or kayaking adventures, destinations, boat and equipment reviews, techniques and how-tos, short essays, camping, environment, humor, health, history, etc. Pays $5 per column inch, on publication. Query preferred. Guidelines.

CAR AND DRIVER—2002 Hogback Rd., Ann Arbor, MI 48105. Csaba Csere, Ed.-in-Chief. Articles, to 2,500 words, for enthusiasts, on new cars, classic cars, industry topics. "Ninety percent staff-written. Query with clips. No unsolicited manuscripts." Pays to $2,500, on acceptance.

CAR CRAFT—8490 Sunset Blvd., Los Angeles, CA 90069. John Baechtel, Ed. Articles and photo features on high performance street machines, drag cars, racing events; technical pieces; action photos. Pays from $150 per page, on publication.

CARIBBEAN SPORTS & TRAVEL—1995 N.E. 150th St., N. Miami, FL 33181. Carol Ozem Hoya, Man. Ed. Articles, 1,000 to 2,500 words, on cruising, recreational boating, golf, travel, covering the Bahamas and the Caribbean. Special sections on the Bahamas, Jamaica, Cayman Islands, and Puerto Rico. Pays varying rates, on publication. Query. Study sample copies. Guidelines.

CASCADES EAST—716 N.E. Fourth St., P.O. Box 5784, Bend, OR 97708. Geoff Hill, Ed./Pub. Articles, 1,000 to 2,000 words, on outdoor activities (fishing, hunting, golfing, backpacking, rafting, skiing, snowmobiling, etc.), history, special events, and scenic tours in Central Oregon Cascades. Photos. Pays 5¢ to 10¢ a word, extra for photos, on publication.

CASINO PLAYER—2524 Arctic Ave., Atlantic City, NJ 08401. Roger Gros, Ed. Articles, 500 to 1,000 words, accompanied by photos, for beginning to intermediate gamblers, on slots, video poker, and table games. No first-person or real-life gambling stories. Pays $100, on publication.

CHESAPEAKE BAY MAGAZINE—1819 Bay Ridge Ave., Annapolis, MD

21403. Jean Waller, Ed. Articles, to 1,500 words, on boating and fishing on Chesapeake Bay. Photos. Pays $85 to $150, on publication. Query.

CITY SPORTS MAGAZINE—2201 Third St., San Francisco, CA 94107. Craig Bystrynski, Ed. Articles, 200 to 2,000 words, on the active lifestyle, including service pieces, trend pieces, profiles, and nutrition. Pays $50 to $650, on publication. Query.

CROSS COUNTRY SKIER—1823 Fremont Ave. S., Minneapolis, MN 55403. Jim Chase, Ed. Published October through February. Articles, to 3,000 words, on all aspects of cross-country skiing. Departments, 1,000 to 1,500 words, on ski maintenance, skiing techniques, health and fitness. Pays $300 to $700 for features, $100 to $350 for departments, on publication. Query.

CURRENTS—212 W. Cheyenne Mountain Blvd., Colorado Springs, CO 80906. Address Greg Moore. Quarterly. "Voice of the National Organization for River Sports." Articles, 500 to 2,000 words, for kayakers, rafters, and river canoeists, pertaining to whitewater rivers and/or river running. Fillers. B&W action photos. Pays $40 and up for articles, $30 to $50 for photos, on publication. Queries preferred.

CYCLE WORLD—1499 Monrovia Ave., Newport Beach, CA 92663. David Edwards, Ed. Technical and feature articles, 1,500 to 2,500 words, for motorcycle enthusiasts. Photos. Pays on publication. Query.

CYCLING U.S.A.—U.S. Cycling Federation, One Olympic Plaza, Colorado Springs, CO 80909. Gina Fedash, Ed. Articles, 300 to 500 words, on bicycle racing. Pays 12¢ to 15¢ a word, on publication. Query.

THE DIVER—P.O. Box 313, Portland, CT 06480. Bob Taylor, Ed. Articles on divers, coaches, officials, springboard and platform techniques, training tips, etc. Pays $15 to $35, extra for photos ($5 to $10 for cartoons), on publication.

EQUUS—Fleet Street Corp., 656 Quince Orchard Rd., Gaithersburg, MD 20878. Laurie Prinz, Man. Ed. Articles, 1,000 to 3,000 words, on all breeds of horses, covering their health, care, the latest advances in equine medicine and research. "Attempt to speak as one horseperson to another." Pays $100 to $400, on publication.

FAMILY MOTOR COACHING—8291 Clough Pike, Cincinnati, OH 45244–2796. Pamela Wisby Kay, Ed. Articles, 1,500 to 2,000 words, on technical topics and travel routes and destinations accessible by motorhome. Query preferred. Payment varies, on acceptance.

FIELD & STREAM—2 Park Ave., New York, NY 10016. Duncan Barnes, Ed. Articles, 1,500 to 2,000 words, with photos, on hunting, fishing. Short articles, up to 1,000 words. Fillers, 75 to 500 words. Cartoons. Pays from $800 for feature articles with photos, $75 to $500 for fillers, $100 for cartoons, on acceptance. Query for articles.

FISHING WORLD—51 Atlantic Ave., Floral Park, NY 11001. Gary Joyce, Ed. Features, 1,500 to 1,800 words, with color transparencies, on fishing sites, technique, equipment. Pays to $350 for major features. Query preferred.

THE FLORIDA HORSE—P.O. Box 2106, Ocala, FL 32678. F. J. Audette, Ed. Articles, 1,500 words, on Florida thoroughbred breeding and racing. Also veterinary articles, financial articles, and articles of general interest. Pays $100 to $200, on publication. Query.

FLY FISHERMAN—6405 Flank Dr., Box 8200, Harrisburg, PA 17105. Philip Hanyok, Man. Ed. Query.

FLY ROD & REEL—P.O. Box 370, Camden, ME 04843. James E. Butler, Ed. Flyfishing pieces, 2,000 to 2,500 words, and occasional fiction; articles on the culture and history of the areas being fished. Pays on acceptance. Query.

THE FLYFISHER—P.O. Box 722, Sandpoint, ID 83864. Chris Bessler, Ed. Articles, 500 to 3,000 words, on techniques, lore, history, and flyfishing personalities; how-to pieces. Serious or humorous short stories related to flyfishing. Pays from $50 to $200, after publication. Queries are preferred. Guidelines.

FOOTBALL DIGEST—Century Publishing Co., 990 Grove St., Evanston, IL 60201. Vince Aversano, Ed. Profiles of pro and college stars, nostalgia, trends in the sport, 1,500 to 2,500 words, aimed at the hard-core football fan. Pays on publication.

FOOTBALL FORECAST—See *Hockey Illustrated.*

FUR-FISH-GAME—2878 E. Main St., Columbus, OH 43209. Mitch Cox, Ed. Illustrated articles, 800 to 2,500 words, preferably with how-to angle, on hunting, fishing, trapping, dogs, camping, or other outdoor topics. Some humorous or where-to articles. Pays $40 to $150, on acceptance.

GAME AND FISH PUBLICATIONS—P.O. Box 741, Marietta, GA 30061. Publishes 30 monthly outdoors magazines for 48 states. Articles, 1,500 to 2,500 words, on hunting and fishing. How-tos, where-tos, and adventure pieces. Profiles of successful hunters and fishermen. No hiking, canoeing, camping, or backpacking pieces. Pays $125 to $175 for state-specific articles, $200 to $250 for multi-state articles, before publication. Pays $25 to $75 for photos.

GOLF DIGEST—5520 Park Ave., Trumbull, CT 06611. Jerry Tarde, Ed. Instructional articles, tournament reports, and features on players, to 2,500 words. Fiction, 1,000 to 2,000 words. Poetry, fillers, humor, photos. Pays varying rates, on acceptance. Query preferred.

GOLF FOR WOMEN—2130 Jackson Ave. W., Oxford, MS 38655. Debra Brumitt, Ed. Dir. Golf-related articles of interest to women; fillers and humor. Instructional pieces are staff-written. Pays from 40¢ a word, on publication. Query.

GOLF JOURNAL—Golf House, P.O. Box 708, Far Hills, NJ 07931–0708. David Earl, Ed. Articles on golf personalities, history, travel. Humor. Photos. Pays varying rates, on publication.

GOLF MAGAZINE—2 Park Ave., New York, NY 10016. Jim Frank, Ed. Articles, 1,000 words with photos, on golf history and travel (places to play around the world); profiles of professional tour players. Shorts, to 500 words. Pays 75¢ a word, on acceptance. Queries preferred.

THE GREYHOUND REVIEW—National Greyhound Assn., Box 543, Abilene, KS 67410. Tim Horan, Man. Ed. Articles, 1,000 to 10,000 words, pertaining to the greyhound racing industry: how-to, historical nostalgia, interviews. Pays $85 to $150, on publication.

GULF COAST GOLFER—See *North Texas Golfer.*

GUN DIGEST—4092 Commercial Ave., Northbrook, IL 60062. Ken Warner, Ed. Well-researched articles, to 5,000 words, on guns and shooting, equipment, etc. Photos. Pays from 10¢ a word, on acceptance. Query.

GUN DOG—P.O. Box 35098, Des Moines, IA 50315. Bob Wilbanks, Man. Ed. Features, 1,000 to 2,500 words, with photos, on bird hunting: how-tos, where-tos, dog training, canine medicine, breeding strategy. Fiction. Humor. Pays $40 to $300 for fillers and short articles, $150 to $400 for features, on acceptance.

GUN WORLD—See *Bow & Arrow Hunting.*

GUNS & AMMO—6420 Wilshire Blvd., Los Angeles, CA 90048. E. G. Bell, Jr., Ed. Technical and general articles, 1,500 to 3,000 words, on guns, ammunition, and target shooting. Photos, fillers. Pays from $150, on acceptance.

HANG GLIDING—U.S. Hang Gliding Assn., P.O. Box 8300, Colorado Springs, CO 80933–8300. Gilbert Dodgen, Ed. Articles, two to three pages, on hang gliding. Pays to $50, on publication. Query.

HOCKEY ILLUSTRATED—Lexington Library, Inc., 233 Park Ave. S., New York, NY 10003. Stephen Ciacciarelli, Ed. Articles, 2,500 words, on hockey players, teams. Pays $125, on publication. Query. Same address and requirements for *Baseball Illustrated, Wrestling World, Pro Basketball Illustrated, Pro Football Illustrated, Baseball Forecast, Pro Football Preview, Football Forecast,* and *Basketball Forecast.*

HORSE & RIDER—1060 Calle Cordillera, Suite 103, San Clemente, CA 92673. Juli S. Thorson, Ed. Articles, 500 to 1,700 words, with photos, on Western riding and general horse care geared to the performance horse: training, feeding, grooming, health, etc. Pays varying rates, on publication. Buys one-time rights. Guidelines.

HORSEMEN'S YANKEE PEDLAR—785 Southbridge St., Auburn, MA 01501. Nancy L. Khoury, Pub. News and feature-length articles, about horses and horsemen in the Northeast. Photos. Pays $2 per published inch, on publication. Query.

HORSEPLAY—P.O. Box 130, Gaithersburg, MD 20884. Cordelia Doucet, Ed. Articles, 700 to 3,000 words, on eventing, show jumping, horse shows, dressage, driving, and fox hunting for horse enthusiasts. Profiles, instructional articles, occasional humor, and competition reports. Pays 10¢ a word for all rights, 9¢ a word for first American rights, after publication. Query. SASE required. Guidelines.

HOT BOAT—Sport Publications, 9171 Wilshire Blvd, #300, Beverly Hills, CA 90210. Peter MacGillivray, Ed. Family-oriented articles, 600 to 1,000 words, on motorized water sport events and personalities; how-to and technical features. Pays $85 to $300, on publication. Query.

HOT ROD—6420 Wilshire Blvd., Los Angeles, CA 90048–5515. Steve Campbell, Ed. How-to pieces and articles, 500 to 5,000 words, on auto mechanics, hot rods, track and drag racing. Photo-features on custom or performance-modified cars. Pays to $250 per page, on publication.

HUNTING—6420 Wilshire Blvd., Los Angeles, CA 90048–5515. Craig Boddington, Ed. How-to articles on practical aspects of hunting. At least 15 photos required with articles. Pays $250 to $500 for articles with B&W photos, extra for color photos, on publication.

THE IN-FISHERMAN—Two In-Fish Dr., Brainerd, MN 56401–0999. Doug Stange, Ed. Published seven times yearly. How-to articles, 1,500 to 4,500 words, on all aspects of freshwater fishing. Humorous or nostalgic looks at fishing, 1,000 to 1,500 words, for "Reflections" column. Pays $250 to $1,000, on acceptance.

INSIDE SPORTS—990 Grove St., Evanston, IL 60201. Vince Aversano, Ed. In-depth, insightful sports articles, player profiles, fillers, and humor. Payment varies, on acceptance. Query.

INSIDE TEXAS RUNNING—9514 Bristlebrook Dr., Houston, TX 77083–6193. Joanne Schmidt, Ed. Articles and fillers on running in Texas. Pays $35 to $100, $10 for photos, on acceptance.

KITPLANES—P.O. Box 6050, Mission Viejo, CA 92690. Dave Martin, Ed. Articles, 1,000 to 4,000 words, on all aspects of design, construction, and performance of aircraft built from kits and plans by home craftsmen. Pays $150 to $350, on publication.

LAKELAND BOATING—1560 Sherman Ave., Suite 1220, Evanston, IL 60201–5047. John Wooldridge, Ed. Articles for powerboat owners on the Great Lakes and other area waterways, on long-distance cruising, short trips, maintenance, equipment, history, regional personalities and events, and environment. Photos. Pays on publication. Query. Guidelines.

MEN'S FITNESS—21100 Erwin St., Woodland Hills, CA 91367. Jim Rosenthal, Fitness Ed. Ted Rand, Health Ed. Features, 1,500 to 2,500 words, and department pieces, 1,000 to 1,500 words: authoritative and practical articles dealing with fitness, health, and men's lifestyles. Pays $350 to $1,000, on acceptance.

MEN'S HEALTH—Rodale Press, 33 E. Minor Dr., Emmaus, PA 18098. Jeff Csatari, Sr. Ed. Articles, 1,000 to 2,500 words, on sports, fitness, diet, health, nutrition, relationships, and travel, for men ages 25 to 55. Pays from 50¢ a word, on acceptance. Query.

MICHIGAN OUT-OF-DOORS—P.O. Box 30235, Lansing, MI 48909. Kenneth S. Lowe, Ed. Features, 1,500 to 2,500 words, on hunting, fishing, camping, and conservation in Michigan. Pays $75 to $150, on acceptance.

MID-WEST OUTDOORS—111 Shore Dr., Hinsdale, IL 60521–5885. Gene Laulunen, Ed. Articles, 1,000 to 1,500 words, with photos, on where, when, and how to fish and hunt in the Midwest. No Canadian material. Pays $15 to $35, on publication.

MOTOR TREND—6420 Wilshire Blvd., Los Angeles, CA 90048–5515. Jeff Karr, Ed. Articles, 250 to 2,000 words, on autos, racing, events, and profiles. Photos. Pay varies, on acceptance. Query.

MOTORCYCLIST—6420 Wilshire Blvd., Los Angeles, CA 90048–5515. Mitch Boehm, Ed. Articles, 1,000 to 3,000 words. Action photos. Pays $150 to $300 per published page, on publication.

MOTORHOME MAGAZINE—3601 Calle Tecate, Camarillo, CA 93012. Barbara Leonard, Ed. Dir. Articles, to 1,500 words, with color slides, on motorhomes. Also travel and how-to pieces. Pays to $600, on acceptance.

MOUNTAIN BIKE—Rodale Press, 33 E. Minor St., Emmaus, PA 18098. Nelson Pena, Man. Ed. Articles, 500 to 2,000 words, on mountain-bike touring; major off-road cycling events; political, sport, or land-access issues; riding techniques; fitness and training tips. Pays $100 to $650, on publication. Query.

MUSCULAR DEVELOPMENT—505-H Saddle River Rd., Saddle Brook, NJ 07662. Alan Paul, Ed. Articles, 1,000 to 3,000 words, personality profiles, training features, and diet and nutrition pieces. Photos. Pays $100 to $400 for articles; $50 for color photos, $25 for B&W, and $300 to $500 for cover photos.

MUSHING—P.O. Box 149, Ester, AK 99725–0149. Todd Hoener, Ed. Dog-driving how-tos, profiles, and features, 1,500 to 2,000 words; and department pieces, 500 to 1,000 words, for competitive and recreational dogsled drivers, weight pullers, and skijorers. International audience. Photos. Pays $20 to $250, on publication. Queries preferred. Guidelines and sample issue on request.

NATIONAL PARKS MAGAZINE—1776 Massachusetts Ave., Washington, DC 20036. Sue E. Dodge, Ed. Articles, 1,500 to 2,500 words, on natural history, wildlife, and conservation as they relate to national parks; illustrated features on the natural, historic, and cultural resources of the National Park System. Pieces about legislation and other issues and events related to the parks. Pays $100 to $800, on acceptance. Query. Guidelines.

THE NEW ENGLAND SKIERS GUIDE—Box 1125, Waitsfield, VT 05673. Andrew Bigford, Ed. Annual (June deadline for submissions). Articles on alpine and nordic skiing, equipment, and winter vacations at New England resorts. Rates vary.

NORTH TEXAS GOLFER—9182 Old Katy Rd., Suite 212, Houston, TX 77055. Steve Hunter, Ed./Pub. Articles, 800 to 1,500 words, of interest to golfers in north Texas. Pays $50 to $250, on publication. Queries required. Same requirements for *Gulf Coast Golfer* (for golfers in south Texas).

NORTHEAST OUTDOORS—P.O. Box 2180, Waterbury, CT 06722–2180. John Florian, Ed. Dir. Articles, 500 to 1,000 words, preferably with B&W photos, on camping and recreational vehicle (RV) touring in northeast U.S.: recommended private campgrounds, camp cookery, recreational vehicle hints. Stress how-to, where-to. Cartoons. Pays $20 to $80, on publication. Guidelines.

OFFSHORE—220 Reservoir St., Needham Heights, MA 02194. Herbert Gliick, Ed. Articles, 1,200 to 2,500 words, on boats, people, and places along the New England, New York, and New Jersey coasts. Writers should be knowledgeable boaters. Photos a plus. Pays 15¢ to 20¢ a word.

ON TRACK—17165 Newhope St., "M," Fountain Valley, CA 92708. Andrew Crask and Tim Tuttle, Eds. Features and race reports, 500 to 2,500 words. Pays $4 per column inch, on publication. Query.

OPEN WHEEL—47 S. Main St., Ipswich, MA 01938. Dick Berggren, Ed. Articles, to 6,000 words, on open wheel drivers, races, and vehicles. Photos. Pays to $400 on publication.

OUTDOOR AMERICA—1401 Wilson Blvd., Level B, Arlington, VA 22209. Address Articles Ed. Quarterly publication of the Izaak Walton League of America. Articles, 1,250 to 1,750 words, on natural resource conservation issues and outdoor recreation; especially fishing, hunting, and camping. Also, short items, 500 to 750 words. Pays 20¢ a word. Query with published clips.

OUTDOOR CANADA—703 Evans Ave., Suite 202, Toronto, Ont., Canada M9C 5E9. Ms. Teddi Brown, Ed. Published nine times yearly. Articles, 1,500 to 2,000 words, on fishing, camping, hiking, canoeing, hunting, and wildlife. Pays $200 to $600, on publication.

OUTDOOR LIFE—2 Park Ave., New York, NY 10016. Vin T. Sparano, Ed.-in-Chief. Articles, 1,400 to 1,700 words, and short, instructive items, 900 to 1,100 words, on hunting, fishing, boats, outdoor equipment, and related subjects. Pays $300 to $550, on acceptance. Query.

OUTSIDE—1165 N. Clark, Chicago, IL 60610. No unsolicited material.

PENNSYLVANIA ANGLER—Pennsylvania Fish and Boat Commission, P.O. Box 67000, Harrisburg, PA 17106–7000. Address Art Michaels, Ed. Articles, 500 to 3,000 words, with photos, on freshwater fishing in Pennsylvania. Pays $50 to $250, on acceptance. Must send SASE with all material. Query. Guidelines.

631

PENNSYLVANIA GAME NEWS—Game Commission, 2001 Elmerton Ave., Harrisburg, PA 17110–9797. Bob Mitchell, Ed. Articles, to 2,500 words, on outdoor subjects, except fishing and boating. Photos. Pays from 6¢ a word, extra for photos, on acceptance.

PETERSEN'S BOWHUNTING—8490 Sunset Blvd., Los Angeles, CA 90069. Greg Tinsley, Ed. How-to articles, 2,000 to 2,500 words, on bowhunting. Also pieces on where to bowhunt, unusual techniques and equipment, and profiles of successful bowhunters will also be considered. Photos must accompany all manuscripts. Query. Pays $300 to $400, on acceptance.

PETERSEN'S HUNTING—6420 Wilshire Blvd., 14th Fl., Los Angeles, CA 90048–5515. Craig Boddington, Ed. How-to articles, 2,500 words, on all aspects of sport hunting. B&W photos; color slides. Pays $300 to $500, on acceptance. Query.

PGA MAGAZINE—The Quartron Group, 2155 Butterfield, Suite 200, Troy, MI 48084. Articles, 1,500 to 2,500 words, on golf-related subjects. Pays $300 to $500, on acceptance. Query.

POWERBOAT—15917 Strathern St., Van Nuys, CA 91406. Lisa Nordskog, Ed. Articles, to 1,500 words, with photos, for high performance powerboat owners, on outstanding achievements, water-skiing, competitions; technical articles on hull and engine developments; how-to pieces. Pays $300 to $1,000, on acceptance. Query.

PRACTICAL HORSEMAN—Box 589, Unionville, PA 19375. Mandy Lorraine, Ed. How-to articles conveying experts' advice on English riding, training, and horse care. Pays on acceptance. Query with clips.

PRIVATE PILOT—P.O. Box 6050, Mission Viejo, CA 92690–6050. Mary F. Silitch, Ed. Technically based aviation articles for general aviation pilots and aircraft owners, 1,000 to 4,000 words, for aviation enthusiasts. Photos. Pays $75 to $250, on publication. Query.

PRO BASKETBALL ILLUSTRATED—See *Hockey Illustrated.*

PRO FOOTBALL ILLUSTRATED, PRO FOOTBALL PREVIEW—See *Hockey Illustrated.*

PURE-BRED DOGS/AMERICAN KENNEL GAZETTE—51 Madison Ave., New York, NY 10010. Beth Adelman, Exec. Ed. Dominique Davis, Features Ed. Articles, 1,000 to 2,500 words, relating to pure-bred dogs. Pays from $100 to $300, on acceptance. Queries preferred.

RESTORATION—P.O. Box 50046, Tucson, AZ 85703–1046. W.R. Haessner, Ed. Articles, 1,200 to 1,800 words, on restoration of autos, trucks, planes, trains, etc., and related building (bridges and structures). Photos. Pays from $25 per page, on publication. Queries required.

RIDER—3601 Calle Tecate, Camarillo, CA 93012. Mark Tuttle Jr., Ed. Articles, to 3,000 words, with slides, on travel, touring, commuting, and camping motorcyclists. Pays $100 to $500, on publication. Query.

RUNNER TRIATHLETE NEWS—P.O. Box 19909, Houston, TX 77224. Lee Sheffer, Ed. Articles on running for road racing and multi-sport enthusiasts in Texas, Oklahoma, New Mexico, Louisiana, and Arkansas. Payment varies, on publication.

RUNNER'S WORLD—Rodale Press, 33 E. Minor St., Emmaus, PA 18098. Bob Wischnia, Sr. Ed. Articles for "Human Race" (submit to Eileen Shovlin), "Finish Line" (to Cristina Negron), and "Health Watch" (to Meg Waldron) columns. Send feature articles or queries to Bob Wischnia. Payment varies, on acceptance. Query.

SAFARI—4800 West Gates Pass Rd., Tucson, AZ 85745. William Quimby, Publications Dir. Articles, 2,000 words, on worldwide big game hunting. Pays $200, extra for photos, on publication.

SAIL—275 Washington St., Newton, MA 02158–1630. Patience Wales, Ed. Articles, 1,500 to 3,500 words, features, 1,000 to 2,500 words, with photos, on sailboats, equipment, racing, and cruising. How-tos on navigation, sail trim, etc. Pays $75 to $1,000 on publication. Guidelines.

SAILING—125 E. Main St., Port Washington, WI 53074. M. L. Hutchins, Ed. Features, 700 to 1,500 words, with photos, on cruising and racing; first-person accounts; profiles of boats and regattas. Query for technical or how-to pieces. Pays varying rates, 30 days after publication. Guidelines.

SALT WATER SPORTSMAN—280 Summer St., Boston, MA 02210. Barry Gibson, Ed. Articles, 1,200 to 1,500 words, on how anglers can improve their skills, and on new places to fish off the coast of the U.S. and Canada, Central America, the Caribbean, and Bermuda. Photos a plus. Pays $350 to $700, on acceptance. Query.

SEA, BEST OF BOATING IN THE WEST—17782 Cowan, Suite C, Irvine, CA 92714. John Vigor, Man. Ed. Features, 800 to 1,500 words, and news articles, 200 to 250 words, of interest to west coast powerboaters: profiles of boating personalities, cruise destinations, analyses of marine environmental issues, technical pieces on navigation and seamanship, news from western harbors. No fiction, poetry, or cartoons. Pays varying rates, on acceptance.

SEA KAYAKER—P.O. Box 17170, Seattle, WA 98107–7170. Christopher Cunningham, Ed. Articles, 400 to 4,500 words, on ocean kayaking. Related fiction. Pays about 10¢ a word, on publication. Query with clips and international reply coupons.

SHOTGUN SPORTS—P.O. Box 6810, Auburn, CA 95604. Frank Kodl, Ed. Articles with photos, on trap and skeet shooting, sporting clays, hunting with shotguns, reloading, gun tests, and instructional shooting. Pays $25 to $200, on publication.

SILENT SPORTS—717 10th St., P.O. Box 152, Waupaca, WI 54981–9990. Articles, 1,000 to 2,000 words, on bicycling, cross country skiing, running, canoeing, hiking, backpacking, and other "silent" sports. Must have regional (upper Midwest) focus. Pays $50 to $100 for features; $20 to $50 for fillers, on publication. Query.

SKI MAGAZINE—2 Park Ave., New York, NY 10016. Steve Cohen, Ed. Articles, 1,300 to 2,000 words, for experienced skiers: profiles, humor, and destination articles. Short, 100- to 300-word, news items for "Ski Life" column. Equipment and racing articles are staff-written. Query (with clips) for articles. Pays from $200, on acceptance.

SKI RACING INTERNATIONAL—Box 1125, Rt. 100, Waitsfield, VT 05673. Articles by experts on race techniques and conditioning secrets. Coverage of World Cup, Pro, Collegiate, and Junior competition. Comprehensive race information. Photos. Rates vary.

SKIN DIVER MAGAZINE—6420 Wilshire Blvd., Los Angeles, CA 90048–5515. Bill Gleason, Pub./Ed. Illustrated articles, 500 to 2,000 words, on scuba diving activities, equipment, and dive sites. Pays $50 per published page, on publication.

SKYDIVING MAGAZINE—1725 N. Lexington Ave., DeLand, FL 32724. Michael Truffer, Ed. Timely news articles, 300 to 800 words, relating to sport and military parachuting. Fillers. Photos. Pays $25 to $200, extra for photos, on publication.

SNOWBOARDER—P.O. Box 1028, Dana Point, CA 92629. Doug Palladini, Assoc. Pub. Bimonthly. Articles, 1,000 to 1,500 words, on snowboarding personalities, techniques, and adventure; color transparencies or B&W prints. Limited fiction market, 1,000 to 1,500 words. Pays $150 to $800, on acceptance and on publication.

SNOWEST—520 Park Ave., Idaho Falls, ID 83402. Steve Janes, Ed. Articles, 1,200 words, on snowmobiling in the western states. Pays to $100, on publication.

SOCCER AMERICA MAGAZINE—P. O. Box 23704, Oakland, CA 94623. Paul Kennedy, Ed. Articles, to 500 words, on soccer news; profiles. Pays $50, for features, within 60 days of publication.

SOCCER JR.—27 Unquowa Rd., Fairfield, CT 06430. Joe Provey, Ed. Articles, fiction, and fillers related to soccer for readers in 5th and 6th grade. Query. Pays $450 for features; $250 for department pieces, on acceptance.

SOUTH CAROLINA WILDLIFE—P. O. Box 167, Columbia, SC 29202–0167. John E. Davis, Ed. Articles, 1,000 to 3,000 words, with state and regional outdoor focus: conservation, natural history, wildlife, and recreation. Profiles, how-tos. Pays on acceptance.

SOUTHERN GAMEPLAN—P.O. Box 13095, Birmingham, AL 35202. Ben Cook, Ed. Sports articles, 1,200 to 1,500 words, with a "southern flair." Queries are preferred. Pay varies, on publication. Guidelines.

SOUTHERN OUTDOORS—5845 Carmichael Rd., Montgomery, AL 36117. Larry Teague, Ed. Essays, 1,200 to 1,500 words, related to the outdoors. Pays 15¢ to 20¢ a word, on acceptance.

SPORT MAGAZINE—6420 Wilshire Blvd., Los Angeles, CA 90048. Cam Benty, Ed. Dir. Query with clips. No fiction, poetry, or first person.

THE SPORTING NEWS—1212 N. Lindbergh Blvd., St. Louis, MO 63132. John D. Rawlings, Ed. Articles, 250 to 2,000 words, on baseball, football, basketball, hockey, and other sports. Queries required, must be timely. "We publish highly personal guest columns, but do not submit a guest column without reading back issues." Pays $150 to $1,000, on publication.

SPORTS ILLUSTRATED—1271 Ave. of the Americas, New York, NY 10020. Chris Hunt, Articles Ed. Query. Rarely uses free-lance material.

SPUR MAGAZINE—P. O. Box 85, Middleburg, VA 22117. Address Editorial Dept. Articles, 300 to 5,000 words, on thoroughbred racing, breeding, polo, show jumping, eventing, and steeplechasing. Profiles of people and farms. Historical and nostalgia pieces. Pays $50 to $400, on publication. Query.

STARTING LINE—P.O. Box 19909, Houston, TX 77224. Lance Phegley, Ed. Quarterly. Articles, to 800 words, for coaches, parents, and children, 8 to 18, on training for track and field, cross country, and racewalking, including techniques, health and fitness, nutrition, sports medicine, and related issues. Payment varies, on publication.

STOCK CAR RACING—47 S. Main St., Ipswich, MA 01938. Dick Berggren, Feature Ed. Articles, to 6,000 words, on stock car drivers, races, and vehicles. Photos. Pays to $400, on publication.

SURFER MAGAZINE—P. O. Box 1028, Dana Point, CA 92629. Court Overin, Pub. Steve Hawk, Ed. Articles, 500 to 5,000 words, on surfing, surfers, etc. Photos. Pays 20¢ to 30¢ a word, $10 to $600 for photos, on publication.

SURFING—P. O. Box 3010, San Clemente, CA 92674. Nick Carroll, Ed. Eric Fairbanks, Man. Ed. Short newsy and humorous articles, 200 to 500 words. No first-person travel articles; knowledge of sport essential. Pays varying rates, on publication.

TENNIS—5520 Park Ave., P. O. Box 0395, Trumbull, CT 06611–0395. Donna Doherty, Ed. Instructional articles, features, profiles of tennis stars, grass-roots articles, humor, 800 to 2,000 words. Photos. Pays from $300, on publication. Query.

TENNIS WEEK—124 E. 40th St., Suite 1101, New York, NY 10016. Eugene L. Scott, Pub. Julie Tupper, Nina Talbot, Merrill Chapman, Man. Eds. In-depth, researched articles, from 1,000 words, on current issues and personalities in the game. Pays $125, on publication.

TRAILER BOATS—20700 Belshaw Ave., Carson, CA 90746–3510. Randy Scott, Ed. Technical and how-to articles, 500 to 2,000 words, on boat, trailer, or tow vehicle maintenance and operation; skiing, fishing, and cruising. Fillers, humor. Pays $100 to $700, on acceptance.

TRAILER LIFE—3601 Calle Tecate, Camarillo, CA 93012. Bill Estes, Ed. Articles, to 2,500 words, with photos, on trailering, truck campers, motorhomes, hobbies, and RV lifestyles. How-to pieces. Pays to $600, on acceptance. Guidelines.

TRAILS-A-WAY—Woodall Publishing Co., P.O. Box 5000, Lake Forest, IL 60045–5000. Ann Emerson, Ed. RV-related travel articles, 1,000 to 1,200 words, for Midwest camping families. Pay varies, on publication.

TRIATHLETE—1415 Third St., Suite 303, Santa Monica, CA 90401. Richard Graham, Ed. Published 11 times yearly. Articles, varying lengths, pertaining to the sport of triathlon. Color slides. Pays 20¢ to 30¢ a word, on publication. Query.

VELONEWS—1830 N. 55th St., Boulder, CO 80301. John Wilcockson, Ed. Articles, 500 to 1,500 words, on competitive cycling, training, nutrition; profiles, interviews. No how-to or touring articles. "We focus on the elite of the sport." Pay varies, on publication.

THE WATER SKIER—799 Overlook Dr., Winter Haven, FL 33884. Greg Nixon, Ed. Feature articles on waterskiing. Pays varying rates, on acceptance.

THE WESTERN HORSEMAN—P.O. Box 7980, Colorado Springs, CO 80933–7980. Pat Close, Ed. Articles, about 1,500 words, with photos, on care and training of horses; farm, ranch, and stable management; health care and veterinary medicine. Pays to $400, on acceptance.

WESTERN OUTDOORS—3197-E Airport Loop, Costa Mesa, CA 92626. Timely, factual articles on fishing and hunting, 1,200 to 1,500 words, of interest to western sportsmen. Pays $400 to $500, on acceptance. Query. Guidelines.

WESTERN SPORTSMAN—P.O. Box 737, Regina, Sask., Canada S4P 3A8. Brian Bowman, Ed. Articles, to 2,500 words, on outdoor experiences in Alberta, Saskatchewan, and Manitoba; how-to pieces. Photos. Pays $75 to $325, on publication.

WIND SURFING—P.O. Box 2456, Winter Park, FL 32790. Debbie Snow, Ed. Features, instructional pieces, and tips, by experienced boardsailors. Fast action photos. Pays $50 to $75 for tips, $250 to $300 for features, extra for photos. SASE for guidelines.

WINDY CITY SPORTS—1450 W. Randolph, Chicago, IL 60607. Shelley Berryhill, Ed. Articles, 1,500 words, on amateur sports in Chicago. Query required. Pays $100, on publication.

WOMAN BOWLER—5301 S. 76th St., Greendale, WI 53129–1191. Jeff Nowak, Ed. Profiles, interviews, and news articles, to 1,000 words, for women bowlers. Pays varying rates, on acceptance. Query with outline.

WOMEN'S SPORTS & FITNESS—2025 Pearl St., Boulder, CO 80302. Kathleen Gasperini, Ed. Outdoor sports how-tos, profiles, adventure travel, and controversial issues in women's sports, 500 to 3,000 words. Fitness, nutrition, and health pieces also considered. Pays on publication.

WRESTLING WORLD—See *Hockey Illustrated*.

YACHTING—2 Park Ave., New York, NY 10016. Charles Barthold, Ed. Articles, 1,500 words, on upscale recreational power and sail boating. How-to and personal-experience pieces. Photos. Pays $350 to $1,000, on acceptance. Queries preferred.

AUTOMOTIVE MAGAZINES

AAA WORLD—AAA Headquarters, 1000 AAA Dr., Heathrow, FL 32746–5063. Douglas Damerst, Ed. Automobile and travel concerns, including automotive travel, purchasing, and upkeep, 750 to 1,500 words. Pays $300 to $600, on acceptance. Query with clips; articles are by assignment only.

AMERICAN MOTORCYCLIST—American Motorcyclist Assn., Box 6114, Westerville, OH 43081–6114. Greg Harrison, Ed. Articles and fiction, to 3,000 words, on motorcycling: news coverage, personalities, tours. Photos. Pays varying rates, on publication. Query with SASE.

CAR AND DRIVER—2002 Hogback Rd., Ann Arbor, MI 48105. William Jeanes, Ed. Articles, to 2,500 words, for enthusiasts, on new cars, classic cars, industry topics. "Ninety percent staff-written. Query with clips. No unsolicited manuscripts." Pays to $2,500, on acceptance.

CAR AUDIO AND ELECTRONICS—21700 Oxnard St., Woodland Hills, CA 91367. Bill Neill, Ed. Features, 1,000 to 2,000 words, on electronic products for the car: audio systems, cellular telephones, security systems, CBs, radar detectors, etc.; how to buy them; how they work; how to use them. "To write for us, you must know this subject thoroughly." Pays $200 to $1,000, on acceptance. Send manuscript or query.

CAR CRAFT—8490 Sunset Blvd., Los Angeles, CA 90069. Chuck Schifsky, Ed. Articles and photo features on high performance street machines, drag cars, racing events; technical pieces; action photos. Pays from $150 per page, on publication.

CYCLE WORLD—1499 Monrovia Ave., Newport Beach, CA 92663. David Edwards, Ed. Technical and feature articles, 1,500 to 2,500 words, for motorcycle enthusiasts. Photos. Pays on publication. Query.

HOT ROD—6420 Wilshire Blvd., Los Angeles, CA 90048–5515. Steve Campbell, Ed. How-to pieces and articles, 500 to 5,000 words, on auto mechanics, hot rods, track and drag racing. Photo features on custom or performance-modified cars. Pays $250 per page, on publication.

MOTORCYCLIST—6420 Wilshire Blvd., Los Angeles, CA 90048–5515.

Mitch Boehm, Ed. Articles, 1,000 to 3,000 words. Action photos. Pays $150 to $300 per published page, on publication.

MOTOR TREND—6420 Wilshire Blvd., Los Angeles, CA 90048–5515. Jeff Karr, Ed. Articles, 250 to 2,000 words, on autos, racing, events, and profiles. Photos. Pay varies, on acceptance. Query.

OPEN WHEEL—See *Stock Car Racing.*

RESTORATION—P.O. Box 50046, Tucson, AZ 85703–1046. W.R. Haessner, Ed. Articles, 1,200 to 1,800 words, on restoration of autos, trucks, planes, trains, etc., and related building (bridges, structures, etc.). Photos. Pays from $25 per page, on publication. Queries required.

RIDER—3601 Calle Tecate, Camarillo, CA 93012. Mark Tuttle Jr., Ed. Articles, to 3,000 words, with color slides, with emphasis on travel, touring, commuting, and camping motorcyclists. Pays $100 to $500, on publication. Query.

ROAD & TRACK—1499 Monrovia Ave., Newport Beach, CA 92663. Ellida Maki, Man. Ed. Short automotive articles, to 450 words, of "timeless nature" for knowledgeable car enthusiasts. Pays on publication. Query.

STOCK CAR RACING—47 S. Main St., Ipswich, MA 01938. Dick Berggren, Ed. Features, technical automotive pieces, up to ten typed pages, for oval track racing enthusiasts. Fillers. Pays $75 to $350, on publication. Same requirements for *Open Wheel*.

TRUCKERS/USA—P.O. Box 323, Windber, PA 15963. David Adams, Ed. Articles, 500 to 1,000 words, on the trucking business and marketing. Poetry and trucking-related fiction. Pays $50 for articles, $10 for poems, on publication.

FITNESS MAGAZINES

AMERICAN FITNESS—15250 Ventura Blvd., Suite 200, Sherman Oaks, CA 91403. Peg Jordan, Ed. Rhonda Wilson, Man. Ed. Articles, 500 to 1,500 words, on exercise, health, sports, nutrition, etc. Illustrations, photos, cartoons.

FITNESS—The New York Times Company Women's Magazines, 110 Fifth Ave., New York, NY 10011. Rona Cherry, Ed. Articles, 500 to 2,000 words, on health, exercise, sports, nutrition, diet, psychological well-being, sex, and beauty for readers in their late twenties. Profiles of athletes and fit celebrities. Queries required. Pays $1 per word, on acceptance.

IDEA TODAY—6190 Cornerstone Ct. E., Suite 204, San Diego, CA 92121–3773. Patricia Ryan, Ed. Practical articles, 1,000 to 3,000 words, on new exercise programs, business management, nutrition, sports medicine, dance-exercise, and one-to-one training techniques. Articles must be geared toward the aerobics instructor, exercise studio owner or manager, or personal trainer. Don't query for consumer or general health articles. Payment is negotiable, on acceptance. Query preferred.

INSIDE TEXAS RUNNING—9514 Bristlebrook Dr., Houston, TX 77083–6193. Joanne Schmidt, Ed. Articles and fillers on running in Texas. Pays $35 to $100, $10 to $25 for photos, on acceptance.

MEN'S FITNESS—21100 Erwin St., Woodland Hills, CA 91367. Jim Rosenthal, Fitness Ed. Features, 1,500 to 2,500 words, and department pieces, 1,000 to 1,500 words: "authoritative and practical articles dealing with fitness, health, and men's lifestyles." Pays $350 to $1,000, on acceptance.

MEN'S HEALTH—Rodale Press, 33 E. Minor Dr., Emmaus, PA 18098. Jeff Csatari, Sr. Ed. Articles, 1,000 to 2,500 words, on fitness, diet, health, relationships, sports, and travel, for men ages 25 to 55. Pays from 50¢ a word, on acceptance. Query.

MUSCULAR DEVELOPMENT—505-H Saddle River Rd., Saddle Brook, NJ 07662. Alan Paul, Ed. Articles, 1,000 to 2,500 words, on competitive bodybuilding, power lifting, sports, and nutrition for serious weight training athletes: personality profiles, training features, and diet and nutrition pieces. Photos. Pays $100 to $400, on publication. Query.

NATURAL HEALTH: THE GUIDE TO WELL-BEING—17 Station St., Box 1200, Brookline, MA 02147. Features, 1,500 to 3,000 words, on holistic health, natural foods, herbal remedies, etc. Interviews. Photos. Pays 30¢ a word, extra for photos, on acceptance.

NEW BODY—1700 Broadway, New York, NY 10019. Nicole Dorsey, Ed. Lively, readable service-oriented articles, 800 to 1,500 words, on exercise, nutrition, lifestyle, diet, and health for women ages 18 to 35. Writers should have some background in or knowledge of the health field. Also considers 500- to 600-word essays for "How I Lost It" column by writers who have lost weight and kept it off. Pays $100 to $300, on publication. Query.

THE PHYSICIAN AND SPORTSMEDICINE—4530 W. 77th St., Minneapolis, MN 55435. Terry Monahan, Man. Ed. News and feature articles. Clinical articles must be co-authored by physicians. Sports medicine angle necessary. Pays $150 to $1,000, on acceptance. Query first. Guidelines.

SHAPE—21100 Erwin St., Woodland Hills, CA 91367–3772. Elizabeth Turner, Asst. Ed. Articles, 1,200 to 1,500 words, with new and interesting ideas on the physical and mental side of getting and staying in shape; reports, 300 to 400 words, on journal research. Payment varies, on publication. Guidelines. Limited market; most bylines by experts.

VEGETARIAN TIMES—P.O. Box 570, Oak Park, IL 60303. Toni Apgar, Pub. Articles, 1,200 to 2,500 words, on vegetarian cooking, nutrition, health and fitness, and profiles of prominent vegetarians. "News Items" and "In Print" (book reviews), to 500 words. "Herbalist" pieces, to 1,800 words, on medicinal uses of herbs. Queries required. Pays $75 to $1,000, on acceptance. Guidelines.

VIM & VIGOR—8805 N. 23rd Ave., Suite 11, Phoenix, AZ 85021. Fred Petrovsky, Ed. Positive articles, with accurate medical facts, on health and fitness, 1,200 to 2,000 words, by assignment only. Writers may submit qualifications for assignment. Pays $450, on acceptance. Guidelines.

WEIGHT WATCHERS MAGAZINE—360 Lexington Ave., New York, NY 10017. Susan Rees, Health and Fitness Editor. Articles on health, nutrition, fitness, and weight-loss motivation and success. Pays from $350, on acceptance. Query with clips required. Guidelines.

WOMEN'S SPORTS & FITNESS—2025 Pearl St., Boulder, CO 80302. Kathleen Gasperini, Ed. Outdoor sports how-tos, profiles, adventure travel, and controversial issues in women's sports, 500 to 3,000 words. Fitness, nutrition, and health pieces also considered. Pays on publication.

YOGA JOURNAL—2054 University Ave., Berkeley, CA 94704. Stephan Bodian, Ed. Articles, 1,200 to 4,000 words, on holistic health, meditation, consciousness, spirituality, and yoga. Pays $50 to $600, on publication.

638

CONSUMER/PERSONAL FINANCE

BETTER HOMES AND GARDENS—750 Third Ave., New York, NY 10017. Margaret V. Daly, Exec. Features Ed. Articles, 750 to 1,000 words, on "any and all topics that would be of interest to family-oriented, middle-income people."

BLACK ENTERPRISE—130 Fifth Ave., New York, NY 10011. Earl G. Graves, Ed. Articles on money management, careers, political issues, entrepreneurship, high technology, and lifestyles for black professionals. Profiles. Pays on acceptance. Query.

CONSUMERS DIGEST—5705 N. Lincoln Ave., Chicago, IL 60659. John Manos, Ed. Articles, 500 to 3,000 words, on subjects of interest to consumers: products and services, automobiles, travel, health, fitness, consumer legal affairs, and personal money management. Photos. Pays from 35¢ to 50¢ a word, extra for photos, on acceptance. Query with resumé and clips.

FAMILY CIRCLE—110 Fifth Ave., New York, NY 10011. Susan Ungaro, Exec. Ed. Susan Sherry, Sr. Ed. Enterprising, creative, and practical articles, 1,000 to 1,500 words, on investing, starting a business, secrets of successful entrepreneurs, and consumer news on smart shopping. Query first with clips. Pays $1 a word, on acceptance.

HOME MECHANIX—2 Park Ave., New York, NY 10016. Michael Chotiner, Ed. Articles on home finances, home improvement, remodeling, maintenance. Also short time- or money-saving tips for home, garage, yard. Pays $250 per page for articles; $50 for tips, on acceptance.

KIPLINGER'S PERSONAL FINANCE MAGAZINE—1729 H St. N.W., Washington, DC 20006. Address Ed. Dept. Articles, of varying lengths, on personal finance (i.e., buying insurance, mutual funds). Query required. Payment varies, on acceptance.

KIWANIS—3636 Woodview Trace, Indianapolis, IN 46468. Chuck Jonak, Exec. Ed. Articles, 2,500 to 3,000 words, on financial planning for younger families and retirement planning for older people. Pays $400 to $1,000, on acceptance. Query required.

MODERN MATURITY—3200 E. Carson St., Lakewood, CA 90712. J. Henry Fenwick, Ed. Articles, 1,000 to 2,000 words, on a wide range of financial topics of interest to people over 50. Pays to $2,500, on acceptance. Queries required.

THE MONEYPAPER—1010 Mamaroneck Ave., Mamaroneck, NY 10543. Vita Nelson, Ed. Financial news and money-saving ideas; particularly interested in information about companies with dividend reinvestment plans. Brief, well-researched articles on personal finance, money management: saving, earning, investing, taxes, insurance, and related subjects. Pays $75 for articles, on publication. Query with resumé and writing sample.

SELF—350 Madison Ave., New York, NY 10017. Anne Field, Money/Careers Ed. Articles, 1,200 to 1,500 words, on money matters for career women in their 20s and 30s. Pays from $1,000, on acceptance. Query first.

WOMAN'S DAY—1633 Broadway, New York, NY 10019. Rebecca Greer, Articles Ed. Articles, to 2,500 words, on financial matters of interest to a broad range of women. Pays top rates, on acceptance. Query; no unsolicited manuscripts.

WORTH—575 Lexington Ave., New York, NY 10022. John Koten, Ed. Dir. Clear, timely, well-argued articles on personal finance. Payment varies, on acceptance. Query with clips and SASE.

YOUR MONEY—5705 N. Lincoln Ave., Chicago, IL 60659. Dennis Fertig, Ed. Informative, jargon-free personal finance articles, to 2,500 words, for the general reader, on investment opportunities and personal finance. Pays 25¢ a word, on acceptance. Query with clips for assignment. (Do not send manuscripts on disks.)

BUSINESS AND TRADE PUBLICATIONS

ABA JOURNAL—American Bar Assn., 750 N. Lake Shore Dr., Chicago, IL 60611. Gary A. Hengstler, Ed./Pub. Articles, to 3,000 words, on law-related topics: current events in the law and ideas that will help lawyers practice better and more efficiently. Writing should be in an informal, journalistic style. Pays from $1,000, on acceptance; buys all rights.

ACCESS CONTROL—6255 Barfield Rd., Atlanta, GA 30328. John Brady, Ed. Comprehensive case studies on large-scale access control installations in industrial, commercial, governmental, retail, and transportational environments: door and card entry, gates and operators, turnstiles and portals, perimeter security fencing and its accessories, perimeter and interior sensors, CCTV technology, system design strategies, integration of hardware, and guard services. Photos. Pays from 20¢ a word, extra for photos, on publication. Query.

ACROSS THE BOARD—845 Third Ave., New York, NY 10022. John Ramos, Asst. Ed. Articles, 1,000 to 4,000 words, on a variety of topics of interest to business executives; straight business angle not required. Pays $100 to $1,000, on publication.

ALTERNATIVE ENERGY RETAILER—P.O. Box 2180, Waterbury, CT 06722. John Florian, Ed. Dir. Feature articles, 1,000 words, for retailers of hearth products, including appliances that burn wood, coal, pellets, and gas; also hearth accessories and services. Interviews with successful retailers, stressing the how-to. B&W photos. Payment varies, extra for photos, on publication. Query.

AMERICAN COIN-OP—500 N. Dearborn St., Chicago, IL 60610–9988. Laurance Cohen, Ed. Articles, to 2,500 words, with photos, on successful coin-operated laundries: management, promotion, decor, maintenance, etc. Pays from 8¢ a word, $8 per B&W photo, two weeks prior to publication. Query. Send SASE for guidelines.

AMERICAN DEMOGRAPHICS—P.O. Box 68, Ithaca, NY 14851–9989. Brad Edmondson, Ed.-in-Chief. Articles, 500 to 2,000 words, on the four key elements of a consumer market (its size, its needs and wants, its ability to pay, and how it can be reached), with specific examples of how companies market to consumers. Readers include marketers, advertisers, and strategic planners. Pays $100 to $500, on acceptance. Query.

AMERICAN FARRIERS JOURNAL—P.O. Box 624, Brookfield, WI 53008–0624. Frank Lessiter, Ed. Articles, 800 to 2,000 words, on general farriery issues, hoof care, tool selection, equine lameness, and horse handling. Pays 30¢ per published line, $10 per published illustration or photo, on publication. Query.

AMERICAN MEDICAL NEWS—515 N. State St., Chicago, IL 60610. Ronni Scheier, Asst. Exec. Ed. Features, 1,000 to 3,000 words, on socioeconomic developments of interest to physicians across the country. No pieces on health, clinical treatments, or research. Query required. Pays $500 to $1,500, on acceptance. Guidelines.

THE AMERICAN SALESMAN—424 N. Third St., P.O. Box 1, Burlington, IA 52601–0001. Barbara Boeding, Ed. Articles, 900 to 1,200 words, on techniques for increasing sales. Author photos requested on article acceptance. Buys all rights. Pays 3¢ a word, on publication. Guidelines.

AMERICAN SCHOOL & UNIVERSITY—401 N. Broad St., Philadelphia, PA 19108. Joe Agron, Ed. Articles and case studies, 1,200 to 1,500 words, on design, construction, operation, and management of school and college facilities. Query.

AREA DEVELOPMENT MAGAZINE—400 Post Ave., Westbury, NY 11590. Tom Bergeron, Ed. Articles for top executives of industrial companies on sites and facility planning. Pays $60 per manuscript page. Query.

ART BUSINESS NEWS—777 Summer St., P.O. Box 3837, Stamford, CT 06905. Fergus Reid, Ed. Articles, 1,000 words, for art dealers and framers, on trends and events of national importance to the art industry, and relevant business subjects. Pays from $100, on publication. Query preferred.

ART MATERIAL TRADE NEWS—See *Arts & Crafts Retailer.*

ARTS & CRAFTS RETAILER—(formerly *Art Material Trade News*) 6151 Powers Ferry Rd. N.W., Atlanta, GA 30339–2941. Ben Johnson, Ed. Articles, from 800 words, for dealers, wholesalers, and manufacturers of arts and crafts materials; must be specific to trade. Pays to 15¢ a word, on publication. Query.

AUTOMATED BUILDER—P.O. Box 120, Carpinteria, CA 93014. Don Carlson, Ed. Articles, 500 to 750 words, on various types of home manufacturers and dealers. Query required. Pays $300, on acceptance, for articles with slides.

BARRISTER—American Bar Assn., 750 N. Lake Shore Dr., Chicago, IL 60611–4403. Vicki Quade, Ed. Articles, 250 to 3,000 words, on legal and social issues, for young lawyers. Pays $250 to $1,000, on acceptance. Query.

BARRON'S—200 Liberty St., New York, NY 10281. Alan Abelson, Ed. National-interest articles, 1,200 to 2,500 words, on business and finance. Query.

BEAUTY EDUCATION—3 Columbia Cir., Albany, NY 12212. Catherine Frangie, Pub. Articles, 750 to 1,000 words, that provide beauty educators, trainers, and professionals in the cosmetology industry with information, skills, and techniques on such topics as hairstyling, makeup, aromatherapy, retailing, massage, and beauty careers. Send SASE for editorial calendar and themes. Pays in copies. Query.

BICYCLE RETAILER AND INDUSTRY NEWS—1444-C South St. Francis Dr., Santa Fe, NM 87501. Marc Sani, Ed. Articles, 50 to 1,200 words, on employee management, employment strategies, and general business subjects for bicycle manufacturers, distributors, and retailers. Pays 17¢ a word, plus expenses (higher rates for complex stories), on acceptance. Query.

BOATING INDUSTRY—Argus Business, 5 Penn Plaza, 13th Floor, New York, NY 10001–1810. Richard W. Porter, Ed. Articles, 1,000 to 2,500 words, on recreational marine products, management, merchandising and selling, for boat dealers. Photos. Pays varying rates, on publication. Query.

BOOKPAGE—ProMotion, Inc., 2501 21st Ave. S., Suite 5, Nashville, TN 37212. Ann Meador Shayne, Ed. Book reviews, 500 words, for a tabloid used by booksellers to promote new titles, authors, and bookstores. Query with writing samples and areas of interest; Editor will make assignments for reviews. Guidelines. Pays in copies.

BUILDER—Hanley-Wood, Inc., 655 15th St. N.W., Suite 475, Washington, DC 20005. Mitchell B. Rouda, Ed. Articles, to 1,500 words, on trends and news in home building: design, marketing, new products, etc. Pays negotiable rates, on acceptance. Query.

641

BUSINESS ATLANTA—6151 Powers Ferry Rd., Atlanta, GA 30339–2941. John Sequerth, Ed. Articles, 1,000 to 3,000 words, with Atlanta business angle, strong marketing slant that will be useful to top Atlanta executives and business people. Pays $300 to $1,000, on publication. Query with clippings.

BUSINESS TIMES—P.O. Box 580, 315 Peck St., New Haven, CT 06513. Joel MacClaren, Ed. Articles on Connecticut-based businesses and corporations. Query.

BUSINESS TODAY—P.O. Box 10010, 1720 Washington Blvd., Ogden, UT 84409. Caroll Shreeve, Pub./Ed.-in-Chief. Informative articles, 1,200 words, on business concerns of the businessperson/entrepreneur in U.S. and Canada. Color photos. Pays 15¢ a word, $35 for photos, $50 for cover photos, on acceptance. Query. Send SASE for guidelines.

CALIFORNIA LAWYER—1390 Market St., Suite 1210, San Francisco, CA 94102. Thomas Brom, Man. Ed. Articles, 2,500 to 3,000 words, for attorneys in California, on legal subjects (or the legal aspects of a given political or social issue); how-tos on improving legal skills and law office technology. Pays $300 to $1,500, on acceptance. Query.

CAMPGROUND MANAGEMENT—P.O. Box 5000, Lake Forest, IL 60045–5000. Mike Byrnes, Ed. Detailed articles, 500 to 2,000 words, on managing recreational vehicle campgrounds. Photos. Pays $50 to $200, after publication.

CHEESE MARKET NEWS—See *Dairy Foods Magazine*.

CHIEF EXECUTIVE—733 Third Ave. 21st Fl., New York, NY 10017. J.P. Donlon, Ed. CEO bylines. Articles, 2,500 to 3,000 words, on management, financial, or business strategies. Departments, 1,200 to 1,500 words, on investments, amenities, and travel. Features on CEOs at leisure, Q&A's with CEOs, other topics. Pays varying rates, on acceptance. Query required.

CHINA, GLASS & TABLEWARE—P.O. Box 2147, Clifton, NJ 07015. Amy Stavis, Ed. Case histories and interviews, 1,500 to 2,500 words, with photos, on merchandising of china and glassware. Pays $50 per page, on publication. Query.

CHRISTIAN RETAILING—600 Rinehart Rd., Lake Mary, FL 32746. Brian Peterson, Ed. Articles, 1,000 to 2,000 words, on new products, industry news, or topics related to running a profitable Christian retail store. Pays $50 to $300, on publication.

CLEANING MANAGEMENT MAGAZINE—13 Century Hill Dr., Latham, NY 12110–2197. Tom Williams, Ed. Articles, 500 to 1,200 words, on managing efficient cleaning and custodial/maintenance operations, profiles, photo features, or general-interest articles directly related to the industry; also technical/mechanical how-tos. Photos encouraged. Query. Pays to $200 for features, on publication. Guidelines.

COMMERCIAL CARRIER JOURNAL—Chilton Way, Radnor, PA 19089. Jerry Standley, Ed. Thoroughly researched, focused articles on private fleets and for-hire trucking operations. Pays from $50, on acceptance. Query required.

COMPUTER GRAPHICS WORLD—10 Tara Blvd., Suite 500, Nashua, NH 03062–2801. Stephen Porter, Ed. Articles, 1,000 to 3,000 words, on computer graphics technology and its use in science, engineering, architecture, film and broadcast, and graphic arts areas. Photos. Pays $600 to $1,200 per article, on acceptance. Query.

CONCORD AND THE NORTH—See *Network Publications.*

CONCRETE INTERNATIONAL—Box 19150, 22400 W. Seven Mile Rd., Detroit, MI 48219–1849. William J. Semioli, Assoc. Pub./Ed. Articles, 6 to 12 double-spaced pages, on concrete construction, design, and technology with drawings and/or photos. Pays $100 per printed page, on publication. Query.

THE CONSTRUCTION SPECIFIER—Construction Specifications Institute, 601 Madison St., Alexandria, VA 22314. Kristina A. Kessler, Ed. Technical articles, 1,000 to 3,000 words, on the "nuts and bolts" of commercial construction, for architects, engineers, specifiers, contractors, and manufacturers. Pays 15¢ per word, on publication.

CONVENIENCE STORE NEWS—7 Penn Plaza, New York, NY 10001. Barbara Francella, Ed. Features and news items, 500 to 750 words, for convenience store owners, and operators. Photos, with captions. Pays $3 per column inch or negotiated price for features; extra for photos, on publication. Query.

COOKING FOR PROFIT—P.O. Box 267, Fond du Lac, WI 54936–0267. Colleen Phalen, Pub./Ed.-in-Chief. Practical how-to articles, 1,500 words, on gas energy management, case studies, etc. Pays $75 to $250, on publication.

CORPORATE CASHFLOW—6151 Powers Ferry Rd. N.W., Atlanta, GA 30339. Richard Gamble, Ed. Articles, 1,250 to 2,500 words, for treasury managers in public and private institutions: cash management; investments; domestic and international financing; credit and collection management; developments in law, economics, and tax. Pays $125 per published page, on acceptance. Query.

CREDIT AND COLLECTION MANAGER'S LETTER—(formerly *Credit and Collection Management Bulletin*) Bureau of Business Practice, 24 Rope Ferry Rd., Waterford, CT 06386. Russell Case, Ed. Interviews, 500 to 1,250 words, for commercial and consumer credit managers, on innovations, successes, and problem solving. Query.

D&B REPORTS—299 Park Ave., New York, NY 10171. Patricia W. Hamilton, Ed. Articles, 1,500 to 2,000 words, for top management of smaller businesses: government regulations, export opportunities, employee relations; how-tos on cash management, sales, productivity; profiles, etc. Pays on acceptance.

DAIRY FOODS MAGAZINE —Delta Communications, 455 N. Cityfront Pl., Chicago, IL 60611. Mike Pehanich, Ed. Articles, to 2,500 words, on innovative dairies, dairy processing operations, marketing successes, new products for milk handlers and makers of dairy products. Fillers, 25 to 150 words. Pays $25 to $300, $5 to $25 for fillers, on publication. Same requirements for *Cheese Market News.*

DEALERSCOPE MERCHANDISING—N. American Publishing Co., 401 N. Broad St., Philadelphia, PA 19108. Richard Sherwin, Ed. Articles, 750 to 3,000 words, for dealers and distributors of audio, video, personal computers for the home, office; satellite TV systems for the home; major appliances on sales, marketing, and finance. How-tos for retailers. Spot news on electronics retailing. Pays varying rates, on publication. Query with clips. Same requirements for *Dealerscope Merchandising First of the Month.*

DENTAL ECONOMICS—P.O. Box 3408, Tulsa, OK 74101. Dick Hale, Ed. Articles, 1,200 to 3,500 words, on business side of dental practice, patient and staff communication, personal investments, etc. Pays $100 to $400, on acceptance.

DRAPERIES & WINDOW COVERINGS—450 Skokie Blvd., Suite 507, Northbrook, IL 60062. Katie Sosnowchik, Ed. Articles, 1,000 to 2,000 words, for retailers, wholesalers, designers, and manufacturers of draperies and window, wall, and floor coverings. Profiles, with photos, of successful businesses in the industry or management and marketing related articles. Pays $150 to $250, after acceptance. Query.

DRUG TOPICS—5 Paragon Dr., Montvale, NJ 07645–1742. Valentine A. Cardinale, Ed. News items, 500 words, with photos, on drug retailers and associations. Merchandising features, 1,000 to 1,500 words. Pays $100 to $150 for news, $200 to $400 for features, on acceptance. Query for features.

THE ENGRAVERS JOURNAL—26 Summit St., P.O. Box 318, Brighton, MI 48116. Rosemary Farrell, Man. Ed. Articles, of varying lengths, on topics related to the engraving industry or small business. Pays $60 to $175, on acceptance. Query.

ENTREPRENEUR—P.O. Box 19787, Irvine, CA 92713–9438. Rieva Lesonsky, Ed.-in-Chief. Articles for established and aspiring independent business owners, on all aspects of running a business. Pay varies, on acceptance. Query required.

EQUIPMENT WORLD—P.O. Box 2029, Tuscaloosa, AL 35403. Marcia Gruver, Ed. Features, 500 to 1,500 words, for contractors who buy, sell, and use heavy equipment; articles on equipment selection, application, maintenance, management, and replacement. Pay varies, on acceptance.

EXECUTIVE FEMALE—127 W. 24th St., New York, NY 10011. Basia Hellwig, Ed.-in-Chief. Articles, 750 to 2,500 words, on managing people, time, money, and careers, for women in business. Pays varying rates, on acceptance. Query.

FARM JOURNAL—230 W. Washington Sq., Philadelphia, PA 19106. Earl Ainsworth, Ed. Practical business articles, 500 to 1,500 words, with photos, on growing crops and raising livestock. Pays 20¢ to 50¢ a word, on acceptance. Query required.

FINANCIAL WORLD—1328 Broadway, New York, NY 10001. Douglas A. McIntyre, Pub. Features and profiles of large companies and financial institutions and the people who run them. Pays varying rates, on publication. Query required.

FISHING TACKLE RETAILER MAGAZINE—P.O. Box 17151, Montgomery, AL 36141–0151. Dave Ellison, Ed. Articles, 300 to 1,250 words, for merchants who carry angling equipment. Business focus is required, and writers should provide practical information for improving management and merchandising. Pays varying rates, on acceptance.

FITNESS MANAGEMENT—P.O. Box 1198, Solana Beach, CA 92075. Edward H. Pitts, Ed. Authoritative features, 750 to 2,500 words, and news shorts, 100 to 750 words, for owners, managers, and program directors of fitness centers. Content must be in keeping with current medical practice; no fads. Pays 8¢ a word, on publication. Query.

FLORIST—29200 Northwestern Hwy., P.O. Box 2227, Southfield, MI 48037–2227. Barbara Koch, Man. Ed. Articles, to 2,000 words, with photos, on retail florist shop management.

FLOWERS &—Teleflora Plaza, Suite 118, 12233 W. Olympic Blvd., Los Angeles, CA 90064. Marie Moneysmith, Ed.-in-Chief. Articles, 1,000 to 3,500 words, with how-to information for retail florists. Pays from $500, on acceptance. Query with clips.

FOOD MANAGEMENT—122 E. 42nd St., Suite 900, New York, NY 10168. Donna Boss, Ed. Articles on food service in hospitals, nursing homes, schools, colleges, prisons, businesses, and industrial sites. Trends, legislative issues, and how-to pieces, with management tie-in. Query.

THE FUTURE, NOW: INNOVATIVE VIDEO—Blue Feather Co., N8494 Poplar Grove Rd., P.O. Box 669, New Glarus, WI 53574–0669. Jennifer M. Jarik, Ed. Bimonthly. Articles, to 2 pages, on new ideas in the video industry. Pays from $75 to $100, on publication.

GARDEN DESIGN—4401 Connecticut Ave. N.W., Fifth Fl., Washington, DC 20008. James Trulove, Ed.-in-Chief. Garden-related features, 800 to 1,500 words, on private and public gardens, interviews with landscape designers and other personalities; also articles on art, architecture, furniture and fashion as they relate to the garden. Pays from 50¢ a word, on acceptance. Guidelines.

GENERAL AVIATION NEWS & FLYER—P.O. Box 98786, Tacoma, WA 98498–0786. Dave Sclair, Pub. Articles, 500 to 2,500 words, of interest to "general aviation" pilots. "Best shot for non-pilot writers is 'destination' series: attractions and activities near airports, not necessarily aviation oriented." Pays to $3 per column inch (approximately 40 words); $10 for B&W photos; to $50 for color photos; within the first month of publication.

GLASS DIGEST—310 Madison Ave., New York, NY 10017. Charles Cumpston, Ed. Articles, 1,200 to 1,500 words, on building projects and glass/metal dealers, distributors, storefront and glazing contractors. Pays varying rates, on publication.

GLOBAL PRODUCTION—1301 Spruce St., Boulder, CO 80302. Kathleen Dunnewald, Ed. Articles, 500 to 2,000 words, on international manufacturing. "We are looking for Spanish-speaking writers who have an interest in writing about manufacturing issues in the Caribbean, Mexico, South and Central America." Query for assignment.

GOLF COURSE NEWS—38 Lafayette St., P.O. Box 997, Yarmouth, ME 04096. Hal Phillips, Ed. Features, 500 to 1,500 words, on all aspects of golf course maintenance, design, building, and management. Pays $200, on acceptance.

GOVERNMENT EXECUTIVE—1730 M St. N.W., Suite 1100, Washington, DC 20036. Timothy Clark, Ed. Articles, 1,500 to 3,000 words, for civilian and military government workers at the management level.

GREENHOUSE MANAGER—P.O. Box 1868, Fort Worth, TX 76101–1868. David Kuack, Ed. How-to articles and success stories, 500 to 1,800 words, accompanied by color slides, of interest to professional greenhouse growers. Profiles. Pays $50 to $300, on acceptance. Query required.

HAMPSHIRE EAST—See *Network Publications.*

HARDWARE AGE—Chilton Way, Radnor, PA 19089. Terrence V. Gallagher, Chief Ed. Articles on merchandising methods in hardware outlets. Photos. Pays on acceptance.

HARDWARE TRADE—10510 France Ave. S. #225, Bloomington, MN 55431. Patt Patterson, Ed. Dir. Articles, 800 to 1,000 words, on unusual hardware and home center stores and promotions in the Northwest and Midwest. Photos. Query.

HEALTH FOODS BUSINESS—567 Morris Ave., Elizabeth, NJ 07208. Gina Geslewitz, Ed. Articles, 1,200 words, with photos, profiling health food stores. Shorter pieces on trends, research findings, preventive medicine, alternative therapies. Interviews with doctors and nutritionists. Pays on publication. Query. Guidelines.

HEALTH PROGRESS—4455 Woodson Rd., St. Louis, MO 63134–3797. Judy Cassidy, Ed. Journal of the Catholic Health Association. Features, 2,000 to 4,000 words, on hospital and nursing home management and administration, medical-moral questions, health care, public policy, technological developments in health care and their effects, nursing, financial and human resource management for health-care administrators, and innovative programs in hospitals and long-term care facilities. Payment negotiable. Query.

HEARTH & HOME—P.O. Box 2008, Laconia, NH 03247. Richard Wright, Pub./Ed. Profiles and interviews, 1,000 to 1,800 words, with specialty retailers selling both casual furniture and hearth products (fireplaces, woodstoves, accessories, etc.). Pays $150 to $250, on acceptance.

HEATING/PIPING/AIR CONDITIONING—2 Prudential Plaza, 180 N. Stetson Ave., Suite 2525, Chicago, IL 60601. Robert T. Korte, Ed. Articles, to 5,000 words, on heating, piping, and air conditioning systems in industrial plants and large buildings; engineering information. Pays $60 per printed page, on publication. Query.

HOME OFFICE COMPUTING—Scholastic, Inc., 730 Broadway, New York, NY 10003. Cathy G. Brower, Man. Ed. Articles of interest to people operating businesses out of their homes: product roundups, profiles of successful businesses, marketing, and financial tips and advice. Payment varies, on acceptance.

HOSPITALS & HEALTH NETWORKS—(formerly *Hospitals*) 737 N. Michigan Ave., Chicago, IL 60611. Mary Grayson, Ed. Articles, 800 to 900 words, for hospital administrators. Query.

HUMAN RESOURCE EXECUTIVE—Axon Group, 747 Dresher Rd., Horsham, PA 19044–0980. David Shadovitz, Ed. Profiles and case stories, 1,800 to 2,200 words, of interest to people in the personnel profession. Pays varying rates, on acceptance. Queries required.

INC.—38 Commercial Wharf, Boston, MA 02110. George Gendron, Ed. No free-lance material.

INCOME OPPORTUNITIES—1500 Broadway, New York, NY 10036–4015. Stephen Wagner, Ed. Helpful articles, 1,000 to 2,500 words, on how to make money full- or part-time; how to start a successful small business, improve sales, etc. Pays varying rates, on acceptance.

INCOME PLUS—73 Spring St., Suite 303, New York, NY 10012. Donna Ruffini, Ed. How-to articles on starting a small business, franchise, or mail-order operation. Payment varies, on publication. Query.

INDEPENDENT BUSINESS—125 Auburn Ct., Suite 100, Thousand Oaks, CA 91362. Daniel Kehrer, Ed. Articles, 500 to 2,000 words, of practical interest and value to small business owners. Pays $200 to $1,500, on acceptance. Query.

INSTANT & SMALL COMMERCIAL PRINTER—P.O. Box 1387, Northbrook, IL 60065. Jeanette Clinkunbroomer, Ed. Articles, 3 to 6 typed pages, for operators and employees of printing businesses specializing in retail printing and/or small commercial printing: case histories, how-tos, technical pieces, small-business management. Pays $150 to $250, extra for photos, on publication. Query.

INTERNATIONAL BUSINESS—500 Mamaroneck Ave., Suite 314, Harrison, NY 10528. David E. Moore, Chairman./Ed. Dir. Articles, 1,000 to 1,500 words, on global marketing strategies. Short pieces, 500 words, with tips on operating abroad. Profiles, 750 to 3,000 words, on individuals or companies. Pays 80¢ to $1 a word, on acceptance and on publication. Query with clips.

JEMS, JOURNAL OF EMERGENCY MEDICAL SERVICES—P.O. Box 2789, Carlsbad, CA 92018. Tara Regan, Man. Ed. Articles, 1,500 to 3,000 words, of interest to emergency medical providers (from EMTs to paramedics to nurses and physicians) who work in the EMS industry worldwide.

LAUNDRY NEWS—Mill Hollow Corp., 19 W. 21st St., New York, NY 10010. Richard Merli, Ed. Articles, 500 to 1,500 words, on the institutional laundering trade as practiced in hotels, hospitals, correctional facilities, and nursing homes. Infection control, government regulation, new technology, major projects, industrial accidents, litigation, and mergers and acquisitions. Query. Pays $100 to $300, on publication.

LLAMAS—P.O. Box 100, Herald, CA 95638. Cheryl Dal Porto Ed. "The International Camelid Journal," published 7 times yearly. Articles, 300 to 3,000 words, of interest to llama and alpaca owners. Pays $25 to $300, extra for photos, on acceptance. Query.

MAINTENANCE TECHNOLOGY—1300 S. Grove Ave., Barrington, IL 60010. Robert C. Baldwin, Ed. Technical articles with how-to information on maintenance of electrical and electronic systems, mechanical systems and equipment, and plant facilities. Readers are maintenance managers, supervisors, and engineers in all industries and facilities. Payment varies, on acceptance. Query.

MANAGE—2210 Arbor Blvd., Dayton, OH 45439. Doug Shaw, Ed. Articles, 800 to 1,000 words, on management and supervision for first-line and middle managers. "Please indicate word count on manuscript and enclose SASE." Pays 5¢ a word.

MANAGING OFFICE TECHNOLOGY—1100 Superior Ave., Cleveland, OH 44114. Lura Romei, Ed. Articles, 3 to 4 double-spaced, typed pages, on new concepts, management techniques, technologies, and applications for management executives. Payment varies, on acceptance. Query preferred.

MANCHESTER—See *Network Publications.*

MANUFACTURING SYSTEMS—191 S. Gary, Carol Stream, IL 60188. Tom Inglesby, Ed. Articles, 500 to 2,000 words, on computer and information systems for industry executives seeking to increase productivity in manufacturing firms. Pays 10¢ to 20¢ a word, on acceptance. Query required.

MEDICAL INDUSTRY EXECUTIVE—1130 Hightower Trail, Atlanta, GA 30350–2910. Elizabeth R. Porter, Ed. Bimonthly. Articles, 750 to 4,000 words, on business, marketing, management, and medical manufacturing, for medical equipment manufacturers and suppliers. Payment varies, on acceptance. Query.

MEMPHIS BUSINESS JOURNAL—88 Union, Suite 102, Memphis, TN 38103. Barney DuBois, Ed. Articles, to 2,000 words, on business, industry trade, agri-business and finance in the mid-South trade area. Pays $80 to $200, on acceptance.

MIX MAGAZINE—6400 Hollis St., Suite 12, Emeryville, CA 94608. David Schwartz, Ed. Articles, varying lengths, for professionals, on audio, video, and music entertainment technology. Pay varies, on publication. Query.

MODERN HEALTHCARE—740 N. Rush St., Chicago, IL 60611. Clark Bell, Ed. Features on management, finance, building design and construction, and new technology for hospitals, health maintenance organizations, nursing homes, and other health care institutions. Pays $200 to $400, on publication. Very limited free-lance market.

MODERN TIRE DEALER—P.O. Box 8391, 341 White Pond Dr., Akron, OH 44320. Lloyd Stoyor, Ed. Tire retailing and automotive service articles, 1,000 to 1,500 words, with photos, on independent tire dealers and retreaders. Query; articles by assignment only. Pays $300 to $350, on publication.

NASHUA—See *Network Publications.*

NATIONAL FISHERMAN—120 Tillson Ave., Rockland, ME 04841. James W. Fullilove, Ed. Articles, 200 to 2,000 words, aimed at commercial fishermen and boat builders. Pays $4 to $6 per inch, extra for photos, on publication. Query preferred.

NATION'S BUSINESS—1615 H St. N.W., Washington, DC 20062. Articles on small-business topics, including management advice and success stories. Pays negotiable rates, on acceptance. Guidelines available.

NEEDLEWORK RETAILER—117 Alexander Ave., P.O. Box 2438, Ames, IA 50010. Anne Brafford, Ed. Bimonthly. Articles, 500 to 1,000 words, on how to run a small needlework business. Payment varies, on acceptance.

NEPHROLOGY NEWS & ISSUES—15150 N. Hayden Rd., Suite 101, Scottsdale, AZ 85260. Mark E. Neumann, Ed. "We publish news articles, human-interest features, and opinion essays on dialysis, kidney transplants, and kidney disease." No payment.

NETWORK PUBLICATIONS—100 Main St., Nashua, NH 03060. Kate Binder, Man. Ed. Lifestyle and business articles with a New Hampshire angle, with sources from all regions of the state, for the company's four regional monthlies: *Nashua, Manchester, Concord and the North,* and *Hampshire East.* Payment varies, on acceptance.

NEVADA BUSINESS JOURNAL—3800 Howard Hughes Pkwy., Suite 120, Las Vegas, NV 89109. Lyle Brennan, Ed. Business articles, 1,500 to 2,500 words, of interest to Nevada readers; profiles, how-to articles. Pays $75 to $150 on publication. Query. Guidelines.

NEW CAREER WAYS NEWSLETTER—67 Melrose Ave., Haverhill, MA 01830. William J. Bond, Ed. How-to articles, 1,500 to 2,000 words, on new ways to succeed at work in the 1990s. Pays varying rates, on publication. Query with outline and SASE. Same address and requirements for *Workskills Newsletter.*

THE NORTHERN LOGGER AND TIMBER PROCESSOR—Northeastern Logger's Assn., Inc., P.O. Box 69, Old Forge, NY 13420. Eric A. Johnson, Ed. Features, 1,000 to 2,000 words, of interest to the forest product industry. Photos. Pays varying rates, on publication. Query preferred.

NSGA RETAIL FOCUS—National Sporting Goods Assoc., 1699 Wall St., Suite 700, Mt. Prospect, IL 60056. Cindy Savio, Man. Ed. Members magazine. Articles, 700 to 1,000 words, on sporting goods industry news and trends, the latest in new product information, and management and store operations. Payment varies, on publication. Query.

NURSINGWORLD JOURNAL—470 Boston Post Rd., Weston, MA 02193. R. Patrick Gates, Ed. Articles, 800 to 1,500 words, for nurses, nurse educators, and students of nursing, etc., on all aspects of nursing. B&W photos. Pays $35, on publication.

OPPORTUNITY MAGAZINE—73 Spring St., Suite 303, New York, NY 10012. Donna Ruffini, Ed. Articles, 900 to 1,500 words, on sales psychology, sales techniques, successful small business careers, self-improvement. Pays $25 to $50, on publication.

OPTOMETRIC ECONOMICS—American Optometric Assn., 243 N. Lindbergh Blvd., St. Louis, MO 63141–7881. Dr. Jack Runninger, Ed. Articles, 1,000 to 2,000 words, on private practice management for optometrists; direct, conversational style with how-to advice on how optometrists can build, improve, better manage, and enjoy their practices. Short humor and photos. Query. Payment varies, on acceptance.

PARTY & PAPER RETAILER—70 New Canaan Ave., Norwalk, CT 06850. Trisha McMahon Drain, Ed. Articles, 800 to 1,000 words, that offer employee, store management, and retail marketing advice to party or stationery store owners: display ideas, success stories, financial advice, legal advice. "Articles grounded in facts and anecdotes are appreciated." Pay varies, on publication. Query with published clips.

PET BUSINESS—5400 N.W. 84th Ave., Miami, FL 33166. Elizabeth McKey, Ed. Brief, documented articles on animals and products found in pet stores; research findings; legislative/regulatory actions; business and marketing tips and trends. Pays $4 per column inch, on publication; pays $20 for photos.

PETS/SUPPLIES/MARKETING—One E. First St., Duluth, MN 55802. Hugh Bishop, Ed. Articles, 1,000 to 1,200 words, with photos, on pet shops, and pet and product merchandising. Pays 10¢ a word, extra for photos. No fiction or news clippings. Query.

PHOTO MARKETING—3000 Picture Pl., Jackson, MI 49201. Margaret Hooks, Man. Ed. Business articles, 1,000 to 3,500 words, for owners and managers of camera/video stores or photo processing labs. Pays $150 to $500, extra for photos, on publication.

PHYSICIAN'S MANAGEMENT—7500 Old Oak Blvd., Cleveland, OH 44130. Bob Feigenbaum, Ed. Articles, about 2,500 words, on finance, investments, malpractice, and office management for primary care physicians. No clinical pieces. Pays $125 per printed page, on acceptance. Query with SASE.

PIZZA TODAY—P.O. Box 1347, New Albany, IN 47151. Danny Bolin, Ed. Articles, to 2,500 words, on pizza business management for pizza entrepreneurs. Pizza business profiles. Pays $75 to $150 per published page, on publication.

P.O.B.—5820 Lilley Rd., Suite 5, Canton, MI 48187–3623. Victoria L. Dickinson, Ed. Technical and business articles, 1,000 to 4,000 words, for professionals and technicians in the surveying and mapping fields. Technical tips on field and office procedures and equipment maintenance. Pays $150 to $400, on acceptance.

POLICE MAGAZINE—6300 Yarrow Dr., Carlsbad, CA 92009–1597. Dan Burger, Ed. Articles and profiles, 1,000 to 3,000 words, on specialized groups, equipment, issues and trends of interest to people in the law enforcement profession. Pays $100 to $300, on acceptance.

POOL & SPA NEWS—3923 W. Sixth St., Los Angeles, CA 90020. News articles for the swimming pool, spa, and hot tub industry. Pays from 10¢ to 15¢ a word, extra for photos, on publication. Query first.

PRIVATE PRACTICE—Box 890547, Oklahoma City, OK 73189–0547. Brian Sherman, Ed. Articles, 1,500 to 2,000 words, on anything that affects doctors' ability to treat their patients. Pays $150 to $300, on publication.

649

PRO—1233 Janesville Ave., Fort Atkinson, WI 53538. Karla Raye Cuculi, Ed. Articles, 1,000 to 1,500 words, on business management for owners of lawn maintenance firms. Pays $150 to $250, on publication. Query.

PROGRESSIVE GROCER—4 Stamford Forum, Stamford, CT 06901. Priscilla Donegan, Man. Ed. Articles related to retail food operations; ideas for successful merchandising, promotions, and displays. Short pieces preferred. Payment varies, on acceptance.

QUICK PRINTING—1680 S. W. Bayshore Blvd., Port St. Lucie, FL 34984. Bob Hall, Ed. Articles, 1,500 to 3,000 words, of interest to owners and operators of quick print shops, copy shops, and small commercial printers, on how to make their businesses more profitable; include figures. Pays from $75, on acceptance.

REAL ESTATE TODAY—National Assoc. of Realtors, 430 N. Michigan Ave., Chicago, IL 60611–4087. Educational, how-to articles on all aspects of residential, finance, commercial-investment, and brokerage-management real estate, to 1,500 words. Query required.

REMODELING—Hanley-Wood, Inc., 655 15th St., Suite 475, Washington, DC 20005. Wendy A. Jordan, Ed. Articles, 250 to 1,700 words, on remodeling and industry news for residential and light commercial remodelers. Pays 20¢ a word, on acceptance. Query.

RESEARCH MAGAZINE—2201 Third St., P.O. Box 77905, San Francisco, CA 94107. Anne Evers, Ed. Articles of interest to stockbrokers, 1,000 to 3,000 words, on financial products, selling, how-tos, and financial trends. Pays from $300 to $900, on publication. Query.

RESTAURANTS USA—1200 17th St. N.W., Washington, DC 20036–3097. Paul Moomaw, Ed. Publication of the National Restaurant Assn. Articles, 1,000 to 1,500 words, on the food service and restaurant business. Restaurant experience preferred. Pays $350 to $750, on acceptance. Query.

ROOFER MAGAZINE—6719 Winkler Rd., Suite 214, Ft. Myers, FL 33919. Mr. Shawn Holiday, Ed. Technical and non-technical articles, human-interest pieces, 1,000 to 1,500 words, on roofing-related topics: new roofing concepts, energy savings, pertinent issues, roofing contractor profiles, industry concern. Humorous items welcome. No general business or computer articles. Include photos. Pays negotiable rates, on publication. Guidelines.

THE SAFETY COMPLIANCE LETTER—24 Rope Ferry Rd., Waterford, CT 06386. Shelley Wolf, Ed. Interview-based articles, 800 to 1,250 words, for corporate safety managers, on solving safety and health problems in the workplace. Pays to 15¢ a word, on acceptance. Query.

SAFETY MANAGEMENT—24 Rope Ferry Rd., Waterford, CT 06386. Margot Loomis, Ed. Interview-based articles, 1,100 to 1,500 words, for safety professionals, on improving workplace safety and health. Pays to 15¢ a word, on acceptance. Query.

SIGN BUSINESS—P.O. Box 1416, Broomfield, CO 80038. Glen Richardson, Ed. Articles specifically targeted to the sign business. Pays $50 to $200, on publication.

SMALL MAGAZINE REVIEW—Dustbooks, P.O. Box 100, Paradise, CA 95967. Len Fulton, Ed./Pub. Reviews, to 200 words, of little and literary magazines; tracks the publishing of small-circulation periodicals. Pays 10¢ a word, on acceptance.

650

SMALL PRESS REVIEW—Dustbooks, P.O. Box 100, Paradise, CA 95967. Len Fulton, Ed./Pub. News pieces and reviews, to 200 words, about small presses and little magazines. Pays in copies.

SOFTWARE MAGAZINE—1900 W. Park Dr., Westborough, MA 01581. John Desmond, Ed. Technical features, to 2,500 words, for computer-literate MIS audience, on how various software products are used. Pays about $500 to $750, on publication. Query required. Calendar of scheduled editorial features available.

SOUTHERN LUMBERMAN—P.O. Box 681629, Franklin, TN 37068–1629. Nanci P. Gregg, Man. Ed. Articles on sawmill operations, interviews with industry leaders, how-to technical pieces with an emphasis on increasing sawmill production and efficiency. "Always looking for 'sweetheart' mill stories; we publish one per month." Pays $100 to $250 for articles with B&W photos. Queries preferred.

SOUVENIRS AND NOVELTIES—7000 Terminal Sq., Suite 210, Upper Darby, PA 19082. Articles, 1,500 words, quoting souvenir shop managers on items that sell, display ideas, problems in selling, industry trends. Photos. Pays from $1 per column inch, extra for photos, on publication.

TEA & COFFEE TRADE JOURNAL—130 W. 42nd St., New York, NY 10036. Jane P. McCabe, Ed. Articles, 3 to 5 pages, on trade issues reflecting the tea and coffee industry. Query. Pays $5 per published inch, on publication.

TEXTILE WORLD—4170 Ashford-Dunwoody Rd. N.E., Suite 420, Atlanta, GA 30319. L.A. Christiansen, Ed. Articles, 500 to 2,000 words, with photos, on manufacturing and finishing textiles. Pays varying rates, on acceptance.

TILE WORLD/STONE WORLD—1 Kalisa Way, Suite 205, Paramus, NJ 07652. John Sailer, Ed. Articles, 750 to 1,500 words, on new trends in installing and designing with tile and stone. For architects, interior designers, and design professionals. Pays $115 per printed page, on publication. Query.

TODAY'S OR NURSE—6900 Grove Rd., Thorofare, NJ 08086. Mary Jo Krey, Man. Ed. Clinical or general articles, from 2,000 words, of direct interest to operating room nurses.

TOURIST ATTRACTIONS AND PARKS—7000 Terminal Sq., Suite 210, Upper Darby, PA 19082. Articles, 1,500 words, on successful management of parks and leisure attractions. News items, 250 and 500 words. Pays 7¢ a word, on publication. Query.

TRAILER/BODY BUILDERS—P.O. Box 66010, Houston, TX 77266. Paul Schenck, Ed. Articles on engineering, sales, and management ideas for truck body and truck trailer manufacturers. Pays from $100 per printed page, on acceptance.

TRAINING MAGAZINE—50 S. Ninth St., Minneapolis, MN 55402. Jack Gordon, Ed. Articles, 1,000 to 2,500 words, for managers of training and development activities in corporations, government, etc. Pays to 20¢ a word, on acceptance. Query.

TREASURY AND RISK MANAGEMENT—253 Summer St., Boston, MA 02210. Ms. Ann Gramm, Ed. Robert Lessor, Art Dir. Bimonthly. Articles, 200 to 3,000 words, on treasury management for corporate treasurers, CFOs, and vice presidents of finance. Pays 50¢ to $1 a word, on acceptance. Query.

TRUCKERS/USA—P.O. Box 323, Windber, PA 15963. David Adams, Ed. Articles, 500 to 1,000 words, on the trucking business and marketing. Trucking-related poetry and fiction. Payment varies, on publication.

VENDING TIMES—545 Eighth Ave., New York, NY 10018. Arthur E.

Yohalem, Ed. Features and news articles, with photos, on vending machines. Pays varying rates, on acceptance. Query.

WINES & VINES—1800 Lincoln Ave., San Rafael, CA 94901. Philip E. Hiaring, Ed. Articles, 1,000 words, on grape and wine industry, emphasizing marketing, management, and production. Pays 5¢ a word, on acceptance.

WOODSHOP NEWS—Pratt St., Essex, CT 06426–1185. Ian C. Bowen, Ed. Features, 1 to 3 typed pages, for and about people who work with wood: business stories, profiles, news. Pays from $3 per column inch, on publication. Queries preferred.

WORKBOAT—P.O. Box 1348, Mandeville, LA 70470. Don Nelson, Ed. Features, to 2,000 words, and shorts, 500 to 1,000 words, providing current, lively information for work boat owners, operators, crew, suppliers, and regulators. Topics include construction and conversion; diesel engines and electronics; politics and industry; unusual vessels; new products; and profiles. Payment varies, on acceptance and on publication. Queries preferred.

WORKSKILLS NEWSLETTER—See *New Career Ways Newsletter.*

WORLD OIL—Gulf Publishing Co., P.O. Box 2608, Houston, TX 77252–2608. T.R. Wright, Jr., Ed. Engineering and operations articles, 3,000 to 4,000 words, on petroleum industry exploration, drilling, or production. Photos. Pays from $50 per printed page, on acceptance. Query.

WORLD SCREEN NEWS—49 E. 21st St., 8th Fl., New York, NY 10010. George P. Winslow, Ed. Features and short pieces on trends in the business of international television programming (network, syndication, cable, and pay). Pays to $750, after publication.

WORLD WASTES—6151 Powers Ferry Rd. N.W., Atlanta, GA 30339. Bill Wolpin, Ed./Pub. Katya Andresen, Assoc. Ed. Case studies, market analysis, and how-to articles, 1,000 to 2,000 words, with photos, of refuse haulers, recyclers, landfill operators, resource recovery operations, and transfer stations, with solutions to problems in field. Pays from $125 per printed page, on publication. Query preferred.

IN-HOUSE/ASSOCIATION MAGAZINES

Publications circulated to company employees (sometimes called house magazines or house organs) and to members of associations and organizations are excellent, well-paying markets for writers at all levels of experience. Large corporations publish these magazines to promote good will, familiarize readers with the company's services and products, and interest customers in these products. And, many organizations publish house magazines designed to keep their members abreast of the issues and events concerning a particular cause or industry. Always read an in-house magazine before submitting an article; write to the editor for a sample copy (offering to pay for it) and the editorial guidelines. Stamped, self-addressed envelopes should be enclosed with any query or manuscript. The following list includes a sampling of publications in this large market.

AMERICAN DANE—The Danish Brotherhood of America, National Headquarters, 3717 Harney St., Omaha, NE 68131–3844. Jennifer Denning-Kock, Ed. Articles and fiction, to 1,500 words, with a Danish "flavor." Queries are preferred. Submit from May through August. Payment varies, to $50, on publication.

652

CALIFORNIA HIGHWAY PATROLMAN—2030 V St., Sacramento, CA 95818–1730. Carol Perri, Ed. Articles on transportation safety, California history, travel, consumerism, past and present vehicles, humor, general items, etc. Photos a plus. Pays 2 ½ ¢ a word, $5 for B&W photos, on publication. Guidelines and/or sample copy with 9″ × 11″ SASE.

COLUMBIA—1 Columbus Plaza, New Haven, CT 06510–0901. Richard McMunn, Ed. Journal of the Knights of Columbus. Articles, 1,500 words, for Catholic families. Must be accompanied by color photos or transparencies. No fiction. Pays to $500 for articles and photos, on acceptance.

THE COMPASS—365 Washington Ave., Brooklyn, NY 11238. J.A. Randall, Ed. Articles, to 2,500 words, on the sea and deep sea trade; also articles on aviation. Pays to $600, on acceptance. Query with SASE.

THE ELKS MAGAZINE—425 W. Diversey Pkwy., Chicago, IL 60614. Judith L. Keogh, Man. Ed. Articles, to 2,500 words, on business, sports, and topics of current interest; for non-urban audience with above-average income. Informative or humorous pieces, to 2,500 words. Pays $150 to $400 for articles, on acceptance. Query.

FIREHOUSE—PTN Publishing Company, 445 Broad Hollow Rd., Melville, NY 11747. Barbara Dunleavy, Ed.-in-Chief. Articles, 500 to 2,000 words: on-the-scene accounts of fires, trends in firefighting equipment, controversial fire-service issues, and lifestyles of firefighters. Pays $100 per typeset page; extra for photos. Query.

FORD NEW HOLLAND NEWS—Ford New Holland, Inc., P.O. Box 1895, New Holland, PA 17557. Address the Ed. Articles, to 1,500 words, with strong color photo support, on production, agriculture, research, and rural living. Pays on acceptance. Query.

THE FURROW—Deere & Co., John Deere Rd., Moline, IL 61265. George R. Sollenberger, Exec. Ed. Specialized, illustrated articles on farming. Pays to $1,000, on acceptance.

KIWANIS—3636 Woodview Trace, Indianapolis, IN 46268. Chuck Jonak, Exec. Ed. Articles, 2,500 words (sidebars, 250 to 350 words), on lifestyle, relationships, world view, education, trends, small business, religion, health, etc. No travel pieces, interviews, profiles. Pays $400 to $1,000, on acceptance. Query.

THE LION—300 22nd St., Oak Brook, IL 60521. Robert Kleinfelder, Sr. Ed. Official publication of Lions Clubs International. Articles, 800 to 2,000 words, and photo essays, on club activities. Pays from $100 to $700, including photos, on acceptance. Query.

NATURE CONSERVANCY—1815 N. Lynn St., Arlington, VA 22209. Mark Cheater, Ed. Membership publication. Articles on wildlife, people, trends in conservation or ecology. Pieces must have connection to The Nature Conservancy's activities or mission. No poetry or fiction. Query with clips required; article lengths, deadlines, and payment determined at time of assignment. Pays on acceptance.

OPTIMIST MAGAZINE—4494 Lindell Blvd., St. Louis, MO 63108. Gary S. Bradley, Ed. Articles, to 1,500 words, on activities of local Optimist Club, and techniques for personal and club success. Pays from $100, on acceptance. Query.

RESTAURANTS USA—1200 17th St. N.W., Washington, DC 20036–3097. Paul Moomaw, Ed. Publication of the National Restaurant Assn. Articles, 1,000 to 1,500 words, on the food service and restaurant business. Restaurant experience preferred. Pays $350 to $750, on acceptance. Query.

THE RETIRED OFFICER MAGAZINE—201 N. Washington St., Alexandria, VA 22314. Address the Manuscripts Ed. Articles, 800 to 2,000 words, of interest to military retirees and their families. Current military/national affairs: recent military history, health/medicine, and second-career opportunities. No fillers. Photos a plus. Pays to $500, on acceptance. Query. Guidelines.

THE ROTARIAN—1560 Sherman Ave., Evanston, IL 60201–3698. Willmon L. White, Ed. Publication of Rotary International, world service organization of business and professional men and women. Articles, 1,200 to 2,000 words, on international social and economic issues, business and management, human relationships, travel, sports, environment, science and technology; humor. Pays good rates, on acceptance. Query.

SILVER CIRCLE—4900 Rivergrade Rd., Irwindale, CA 91706. Jay Binkly, Ed. National consumer-interest quarterly. Consumer service articles, 800 to 2,000 words, on money, health, home, gardening, food, travel, hobbies, etc. Query. Pays $250 to $1,500, on acceptance.

UNION PLUS—Marblehead Communications, 376 Boylston St., Boston, MA 02116. Tony Bogar, Man. Ed. Quarterly. Articles, 500 to 1,500 words, on consumer, lifestyle, and money-related topics for union members and their families. Query. Pays $1 a word, 60 days after acceptance.

VFW MAGAZINE—406 W. 34th St., Kansas City, MO 64111. Richard K. Kolb, Ed. Magazine for Veterans of Foreign Wars and their families. Articles, to 1,500 words, on current issues and military history, with veteran angle. Photos. Pays to $500 for unsolicited articles, extra for photos, on acceptance. Guidelines.

WOODMEN MAGAZINE—1700 Farnam St., Omaha, NE 68102. Scott J. Darling, Asst. V.P. Articles on history, insurance, family, health, science, etc. Photos. Pays 10¢ a word, extra for photos, on acceptance.

RELIGIOUS MAGAZINES

ADVANCE—1445 Boonville Ave., Springfield, MO 65802. Harris Jansen, Ed. Articles, 1,200 words, slanted to ministers, on preaching, doctrine, practice; how-to features. Pays to 8¢ a word, on acceptance.

AMERICA—106 W. 56th St., New York, NY 10019–3893. George W. Hunt, S.J., Ed. Articles, 1,000 to 2,500 words, on current affairs, family life, literary trends. Pays $75 to $150, on acceptance.

AMERICAN BIBLE SOCIETY RECORD—1865 Broadway, New York, NY 10023. Clifford P. Macdonald, Man. Ed. Material related to work of American Bible Society: translating, publishing, distributing. Pays on acceptance. Query.

AMERICAN JEWISH HISTORY—American Jewish Historical Society, 2 Thornton Rd., Waltham, MA 02154. Dr. Marc Lee Raphael, Ed. Academic articles, 15 to 30 typed pages, on the settlement, history, and life of Jews in North America. Queries preferred. No payment.

AMIT WOMAN—817 Broadway, New York, NY 10003-4761. Micheline Ratzersdorfer, Ed. Articles, 1,000 to 2,000 words, of interest to Jewish women: Middle East, Israel, history, holidays, travel. Pays to $75, on publication.

ANGLICAN JOURNAL—600 Jarvis St., Toronto, Ont., Canada M4Y 2J6. Carolyn Purden, Ed. National newspaper of the Anglican Church of Canada. Articles, to 1,200 words, on current events and human-interest subjects in a religious context. Pays $200 to $500, on acceptance. Query.

ANNALS OF ST. ANNE DE BEAUPRÉ—P.O. Box 1000, St. Anne de Beaupré, Quebec, Canada G0A 3C0. Roch Achard, C.Ss.R., Ed. Articles, 1,100 to 1,200 words, on Catholic subjects and on St. Anne. Pays 3¢ to 4¢ a word, on acceptance.

BAPTIST LEADER—American Baptist Churches-USA, P.O. Box 851, Valley Forge, PA 19482-0851. L. Isham, Ed. Practical how-to or thought-provoking articles, 1,200 to 2,000 words, for local church lay leaders, pastors, and Christian education staff.

BIBLE ADVOCATE—P.O. Box 33677, Denver, CO 80233. Roy Marrs, Ed. Articles, 1,000 to 2,500 words, and fillers, 100 to 500 words, on Bible passages and Christian living. Poetry, 5 to 25 lines, on religious themes. Opinion pieces, to 700 words. "Be familiar with the doctrinal beliefs of the Church of God (Seventh Day). For example, they don't celebrate a traditional Easter or Christmas." Pays $10 per page (to $25) for articles, on publication. Guidelines.

BRIGADE LEADER—Box 150, Wheaton, IL 60189. Deborah Christensen, Man. Ed. Inspirational articles, 1,000 words, for Christian men who lead boys, with an emphasis on issues pertaining to men. "Most articles are written on assignment by experts." Pays $60 to $150. Query only.

CATECHIST—2451 E. River Rd., Dayton, OH 45439. Patricia Fischer, Ed. Informational and how-to articles, 1,200 to 1,500 words, for Catholic teachers, coordinators, and administrators in religious education programs. Pays $25 to $75, on publication.

CATHOLIC DIGEST—P.O. Box 64090, St. Paul, MN 55164-0090. Address Articles Ed. Articles, 1,000 to 3,500 words, on Catholic and general subjects. Fillers, to 300 words, on instances of kindness rewarded, for "Hearts Are Trumps"; accounts of good deeds, for "People Are Like That." Pays from $200 for original articles, $100 for reprints, on acceptance; $4 to $50 for fillers, on publication. Guidelines.

CATHOLIC NEAR EAST MAGAZINE—1011 First Ave., New York, NY 10022-4195. Michael La Civita, Ed. A bimonthly publication of Catholic Near East Welfare Assoc., a papal agency for humanitarian and pastoral support. Articles, 1,500 to 2,000 words, on people of the Balkans, eastern Europe, Russia, Ethiopia, Middle East, and India; their faith, religious heritage, culture, and present state of affairs. Special interest in Eastern Christian churches. Color photos for all articles. Query. Pays 20¢ a word.

CATHOLIC PARENT—Our Sunday Visitor, Inc., 200 Noll Plaza, Huntington, IN 46750. Woodeene Koenig-Bricker, Ed. Features, how-tos, and general-interest articles, 800 to 1,000 words, for Catholic parents. "Keep it anecdotal and practical with an emphasis on values and family life. Don't preach." Payment varies, on acceptance.

CATHOLIC TWIN CIRCLE—15760 Ventura Blvd., Suite 1201, Encino, CA 91436. Loretta G. Seyer, Ed. Articles and interviews of interest to Catholic families,

1,000 to 2,000 words, with photos. Opinion or inspirational columns, 800 words. Strict attention to Catholic doctrine required. Enclose SASE. Pays from 10¢ a word for articles, $50 for columns, on publication.

CHARISMA & CHRISTIAN LIFE—600 Rinehart Rd., Lake Mary, FL 32746. John Archer, Ed. Dir. Charismatic/evangelical Christian articles, 1,500 to 2,500 words, for developing the spiritual life. News stories, 300 to 1,500 words. Photos. Pays varying rates, on publication.

THE CHRISTIAN CENTURY—407 S. Dearborn St., Chicago, IL 60605. James M. Wall, Ed. Ecumenical. Articles, 1,500 to 2,500 words, with a religious angle, on political and social issues, international affairs, culture, the arts. Poetry, to 20 lines. Photos. Pays about $25 per printed page, extra for photos, on publication.

CHRISTIAN EDUCATION JOURNAL—Scripture Press Ministries, P.O. Box 650, Glen Ellyn, IL 60138. Ronald R. Ramsey, Exec. Ed. Articles, 5 to 15 typed pages, on Christian education topics. Pays $100, on publication. Guidelines.

CHRISTIAN HOME & SCHOOL—3350 East Paris Ave. S.E., Grand Rapids, MI 49512. Gordon L. Bordewyk, Ed. Articles for parents in Canada and the U.S. who send their children to Christian schools and are concerned about the challenges facing Christian families today. Pays $75 to $150, on publication. Guidelines.

CHRISTIAN MEDICAL & DENTAL SOCIETY JOURNAL—P.O. Box 830689, Richardson, TX 75083–0689. David B. Biebel, D. Min., Ed. Articles, 8 to 10 double-spaced pages, for Christian medical and dental professionals. Queries preferred. Pays to $50, on publication. Guidelines.

CHRISTIAN PARENTING TODAY—P.O. Box 850, Sisters, OR 97759. David Kopp, Ed. Articles, 900 to 1,500 words, dealing with raising children with Christian principles. Departments: "Parent Exchange," 25 to 100 words on problem-solving ideas that have worked for parents; "My Story," 800 to 1,500 words, first-person accounts of how one family or parent faced a parenting challenge; "Life in Our House," insightful anecdotes, 25 to 100 words, about humorous things said at home. Pays 15¢ to 25¢ a word, on acceptance for assigned articles, on publication for unsolicited articles. Pays $40 for "Parent Exchange," $25 for "Life in our House." Guidelines.

CHRISTIAN SINGLE—MSN 140, 127 Ninth Ave. N., Nashville, TN 37234. Stephen Felts, Ed. Articles, 600 or 1,200 words, for single adults about leisure activities, issues related to single parents, inspiring personal experiences, humor, life from a Christian perspective. Payment varies, on acceptance. Query. Guidelines.

CHRISTIAN SOCIAL ACTION—100 Maryland Ave. N.E., Washington, DC 20002. Lee Ranck, Ed. Articles, 1,500 to 2,000 words, on social issues for concerned persons of faith. Pays $75 to $125, on publication.

CHRISTIANITY TODAY—465 Gundersen Dr., Carol Stream, IL 60188. David Neff, Exec. Ed. Doctrinal social issues and interpretive essays, 1,500 to 3,000 words, from evangelical Protestant perspective. No fiction or poetry. Pays $200 to $500, on acceptance. Query.

CHURCH & STATE—8120 Fenton St., Silver Spring, MD 20910. Joseph L. Conn, Man. Ed. Articles, 600 to 2,600 words, on religious liberty and church-state relations. Pays varying rates, on acceptance. Query.

CHURCH EDUCATOR—Educational Ministries, Inc., 165 Plaza Dr., Prescott, AZ 86303. Robert G. Davidson, Ed. How-to articles, to 1,750 words, on

Christian education: activity projects, crafts, learning centers, games, bulletin boards, etc., for all church school, junior and high school programs, and adult study group ideas. Allow 3 months for response. Pays 3¢ a word, on publication.

THE CHURCH HERALD—4500 60th St. S.E., Grand Rapids, MI 49512–9642. Jeffrey Japinga, Ed. Reformed Church in America. Articles, 500 to 1,500 words, on Christianity and culture, politics, marriage, and home. Pays $50 to $125, on acceptance. Query.

CHURCH RECREATION MAGAZINE—127 Ninth Ave. N., Nashville, TN 37234. Lisa Wilson, Ed. Articles, 500 to 1,500 words, on creative how-to ideas for family recreation, social recreation, drama, sports, clowning, puppetry, crafts, camping, retreats, travel, wellness/fitness, games, outdoor education, and administration. Also cartoons and puzzles. "We are interested in the effective use of recreation in the church and daily Christian living." Query preferred. Pays 5 ½¢ a word, after acceptance. Guidelines.

CHURCH TEACHERS—1119 Woodburn Rd., Durham, NC 27705. Shirley H. Strobel, Ed. Articles, 1,000 words, that offer classroom-tested teaching strategies and curriculum ideas for church schools. Book reviews. No simultaneous submissions. Pays $30 to $40 per page, on publication. Guidelines.

CIRCUIT RIDER—P.O. Box 801, Nashville, TN 37202–0801. J. Richard Peck, Ed. Articles for United Methodist pastors, 800 to 1,600 words. Pays $50 to $200, on acceptance. Query preferred; SASE required.

COLUMBIA—1 Columbus Plaza, New Haven, CT 06510–0901. Richard McMunn, Ed. Knights of Columbus. Articles, 1,500 words, for Catholic families. Must be accompanied by color photos or transparencies. No fiction. Pays to $500 for articles with photos, on acceptance.

COMMENTARY—165 E. 56th St., New York, NY 10022. Norman Podhoretz, Ed. Articles, 5,000 to 7,000 words, on contemporary issues, Jewish affairs, social sciences, religious thought, culture. Serious fiction; book reviews. Pays on publication.

COMMONWEAL—15 Dutch St., New York, NY 10038. Margaret O'Brien Steinfels, Ed. Catholic. Articles, to 3,000 words, on political, religious, social, and literary subjects. Pays 3¢ a word, on acceptance.

COMPASS: A JESUIT JOURNAL—10 St. Mary St., #300, Toronto, Ont., Canada M4Y 1P9. Robert Chodos, Ed. Essays, 1,500 to 2,500 words, on current religious, political, and cultural topics. "We are ecumenical in spirit and like to provide a forum for lively debate and an ethical perspective on social and religious questions." Query preferred. Pays $200 to $500, on publication.

THE COVENANT COMPANION—5101 N. Francisco Ave., Chicago, IL 60625. James R. Hawkinson, Ed. Articles, 1,000 words, with Christian implications published for members and attenders of Evangelical Covenant Church, "aimed at gathering, enlightening, and stimulating devotion to Jesus Christ and the living of the Christian life." Poetry. Pays $15 to $35, on publication.

CRUSADER—P.O. Box 7259, Grand Rapids, MI 49510. G. Richard Broene, Ed. Fiction, 900 to 1,500 words, and articles, 400 to 1,000 words, for boys ages 9 to 14 that show how God is at work in their lives and in the world around them. Also, short fillers. Pays 4¢ to 5¢ a word, on acceptance.

DAILY MEDITATION—Box 2710, San Antonio, TX 78299. Ruth S. Paterson, Ed. Inspirational nonsectarian articles, 650 to 2,000 words. Fillers, to 350 words; verse, to 20 lines. Pays ½¢ to 2¢ a word for prose; 14¢ a line for verse, on acceptance. SASE required.

DAILY WORD—Unity Village, MO 64065. Colleen Zuck, Ed. Daily lessons, 25 lines (double-spaced), that may be based on an affirmation, a Bible text, or an idea that has been helpful in meeting some situation in your life. Pays $30, on acceptance, plus copies. Guidelines.

DAUGHTERS OF SARAH—3801 N. Keeler Ave., Chicago, IL 60641. Reta Finger, Ed. Fiction, 750 to 2,000 words, and poetry, to 500 words, from a Christian feminist perspective. Articles, 750 to 2,000 words, on theology and social issues of Christian feminism. Guidelines. Query required.

DECISION—Billy Graham Evangelistic Association, 1300 Harmon Pl., Minneapolis, MN 55403–0779. Roger C. Palms, Ed. Christian testimonies and teaching articles on evangelism and Christian nurturing, 1,500 to 1,800 words. Vignettes, 400 to 1,000 words. Pays varying rates, on publication.

DISCOVERIES—WordAction Publishing Co., 6401 The Paseo, Kansas City, MO 64131. Address the Ed. Asst. Weekly take-home paper designed to correlate with Evangelical Sunday school curriculum. Fiction, 500 to 700 words, for 8- to 10-year-old readers. Stories should feature contemporary, true-to-life characters and should illustrate character building and scriptural application. No poetry. Pays 5¢ a word, on publication. Guidelines.

DREAMS & VISIONS—Skysong Press, RR1, Washago, Ontario, Canada L0K 2B0. Wendy Stanton, Manuscript Ed. New frontiers in Christian fiction. Eclectic fiction, 2,000 to 6,000 words, that "has literary value and is unique and relevant to Christian readers today." Pays in copies and $100 honorarium to best of the year.

EVANGEL—Light and Life Press, Box 535002, Indianapolis, IN 46253–5002. Carolyn Smith, Ed. Free Methodist. Personal experience articles, 1,000 words; short devotional items, 300 to 500 words; fiction, 1,200 words, showing personal faith in Christ to be instrumental in solving problems. Pays 4¢ a word for articles, $10 for poetry, on publication.

EVANGELICAL BEACON—901 E. 78th St., Minneapolis, MN 55420. Carol Madison, Ed. Evangelical Free Church. Articles, 500 to 2,000 words, that fit with the editorial theme. Send SASE for guidelines and editorial calendar. Pays 7¢ a word (3¢ a word for reprints), on publication.

EVANGELIZING TODAY'S CHILD—Warrenton, MO 63383. Articles, 1,200 to 1,500 words, for Sunday school teachers, Christian education leaders, and children's workers. Feature articles should include teaching principles, instruction for the reader, and classroom illustrations. "Impact" articles, 700 to 900 words, show the power of the Gospel in or through the life of a child; "Resource Center" short, original teaching tips. Also short stories, 800 to 1,000 words, of contemporary children dealing with problems; must have a scriptural solution. Pays 8¢ to 10¢ a word for articles; $15 to $25 for "Resource Center" pieces; 6¢ a word for short stories, on publication. Guidelines.

FAITH TODAY—Box 8800, Sta. B, Willowdale, Ontario, Canada M2K 2R6. Brian C. Stiller, Ed. Audrey Dorsch, Man. Ed. Articles, 1,500 words, on current issues relating to the church in Canada. Pays negotiable rates, on publication. Queries preferred.

THE FAMILY DIGEST—(formerly *Parish Family Digest*) P.O. Box 40137, Fort Wayne, IN 46804. Corine B. Erlandson, Ed. Articles, 750 to 1,000 words, on family life, Catholic subjects, seasonal, parish life, prayer, inspiration, etc., for the Catholic reader. Also publishes short humorous anecdotes and light-hearted cartoons. Pays 5¢ a word, on acceptance.

FELLOWSHIP—Box 271, Nyack, NY 10960–0271. Richard Deats, Ed. Bimonthly published by the Fellowship of Reconciliation, an interfaith, pacifist organization. Articles, 750 and 1,500 to 2,000 words; B&W photo essays, on active nonviolence, opposition to war. "Articles for a just and peaceful world community." Queries preferred. SASE required. Pays in copies and subscription.

FELLOWSHIP IN PRAYER—291 Witherspoon St., Princeton, NJ 08542. Articles, to 1,500 words, and poems, to 35 lines, relating to prayer, meditation, and the spiritual life as practiced by any of the world's religions. Pays in copies. Guidelines.

FOURSQUARE WORLD ADVANCE—1910 W. Sunset Blvd., Suite 200, Los Angeles, CA 90026. Ronald D. Williams, Ed. Official publication of the International Church of the Foursquare Gospel. Religious fiction and nonfiction, 1,000 to 1,200 words, and religious poetry. Pays $75, on publication. Guidelines.

FRIENDS JOURNAL—1501 Cherry St., Philadelphia, PA 19102–1497. Vinton Deming, Ed. Articles and fiction, to 2,000 words, reflecting Quaker life today: commentary on social issues, experimental articles, Quaker history, world affairs. Poetry, to 25 lines, and Quaker-related humor and crossword puzzles also considered. Pays in copies. Guidelines.

THE GEM—Box 926, Findlay, OH 45839–0926. Marilyn Rayle Kern, Ed. Articles, 300 to 1,600 words, and fiction, 1,000 to 1,600 words: true-to-life experiences of God's help, of healed relationships, and of growing maturity in faith. For adolescents through senior citizens. Pays $15 for articles and fiction, $5 to $10 for fillers, after publication.

GROUP, THE YOUTH MINISTRY MAGAZINE—Box 481, Loveland, CO 80539. Rick Lawrence, Ed. Interdenominational magazine for leaders of junior and senior high school Christian youth groups. Articles, 500 to 1,700 words, about practical youth ministry principles, techniques, or activities. Short how-to pieces, to 300 words. Pays to $150 for articles, $15 to $25 for department pieces, on acceptance. Guidelines.

GUIDE—Review and Herald Publishing Association, 55 W. Oak Ridge Dr., Hagerstown, MD 21740. Stories, to 1,200 words, for Christian youth, ages 10 to 14. Pays 3¢ to 4¢ a word, on acceptance.

GUIDEPOSTS—16 E. 34th St., New York, NY 10016. Colleen Hughes, Features Ed. True first-person stories, 250 to 1,500 words, stressing how faith in God helps people cope with life. Anecdotal fillers, to 250 words. Pays $100 to $400, $50 for fillers, on acceptance.

HERALD OF HOLINESS—6401 The Paseo, Kansas City, MO 64131. Address Man. Ed. Church of the Nazarene. Articles, 800 to 2,000 words, about distinctive Nazarenes, Christian family life and marriage, a Christian approach to social issues, seasonal material, and short devotional articles. Submit complete manuscript. Pays 4¢ to 5¢ a word, within 30 days of acceptance. Guidelines.

HIGHWAYS—Presbyterian Publishing House, 100 Witherspoon St., Louisville, KY 40202. James S. Clinefelter, Ed. Fiction, 100 to 1,200 words; articles, 600 to 1,000 words; and poetry, to 20 lines. Accepts material for 15- to 18-year-old readers. Pays 3¢ a word, from $3 for poetry, on acceptance. Guidelines.

HOME LIFE—127 Ninth Ave. N., Nashville, TN 37234. Charlie Warren, Ed.

Mary Paschall Darby, Asst. Ed. Southern Baptist. Fiction, personal experience, and articles on Christian marriage, parenthood, and family relationships. Human-interest pieces, 200 to 500 words; cartoons and short verse related to family. Query required. Pays on acceptance.

INDIAN LIFE—Box 3765, Sta. B, Winnipeg, MB, Canada R2W 3R6. Ed Hughes, Ed. Christian teaching articles and testimonials of Native Americans, 1,000 to 1,200 words. "Our magazine is designed to help the North American Indian Church speak to the social, cultural, and spiritual needs of Native people." Writing should be at a seventh-grade reading level. "We prefer Native writers who write from within their culture." Queries required.

INSIDE MAGAZINE—226 S. 16th St., Philadelphia, PA 19102–3392. Jane Biberman, Ed. Articles, 1,500 to 3,000 words, and fiction, 2,000 to 3,000 words, of interest to Jewish adults. Pays $100 to $500, on acceptance. Query.

JEWISH CURRENTS—22 E. 17th St., #601, New York, NY 10003. Morris U. Schappes, Ed. Articles, 2,400 to 3,000 words, on Jewish history, Jewish secularism, progressivism, labor struggle, Holocaust resistance, Black-Jewish relations, Israel, Yiddish culture. "We are pro-Israel though non-Zionist and a secular magazine; no religious articles." Overstocked with fiction and poetry. No payment.

THE JEWISH HOMEMAKER—705 Foster Ave., Brooklyn, NY 11230. Mayer Bendet, Ed. Bimonthly. Articles, 1,000 words, for a traditional/Orthodox Jewish audience. Humor and fillers. Query. Payment varies, on publication.

JOURNAL OF CHRISTIAN NURSING—P.O. Box 1650, Downers Grove, IL 60515. Judy Shelly, Sr. Ed. Articles, 8 to 12 double-spaced pages, that help Christian nurses view nursing practice through the eyes of faith: spiritual care, ethics, values, healing and wholeness, psychology and religion, personal and professional ethics, etc. Priority given to nurse authors, though work by non-nurses will be considered. Opinion pieces, to 4 pages, for "Speaking Out" section. Pays $25 to $80. Guidelines and editorial calendar.

KEY TO CHRISTIAN EDUCATION—8121 Hamilton Ave., Cincinnati, OH 45231–2396. Barbara Bolton and Lowellette Lauderdale, Eds. Articles, to 1,200 words, on teaching methods, and success stories for workers in Christian education. Pays varying rates, on acceptance.

LEADERSHIP—465 Gundersen Dr., Carol Stream, IL 60188. Marshall Shelley, Ed. Articles, 500 to 3,000 words, on administration, finance, and/or programming of interest to ministers and church leaders. Personal stories of crisis in ministry. "We deal mainly with the how-to of running a church. We're not a theological journal but a practical one." Pays $50 to $350, on acceptance.

LIGHT AND LIFE—P.O. Box 535002, Indianapolis, IN 46253–5002. Robert Haslam, Ed. Fresh, lively articles about practical Christian living, and sound treatments of vital issues facing the Evangelical in contemporary society. Pays 4¢ a word, on publication.

LIGUORIAN—Liguori, MO 63057–9999. Rev. Allan Weinert, Ed. Sue Schuster, Man. Ed. Catholic. Articles and short stories, 1,500 to 2,000 words, on Christian values in modern life. Pays 10¢ to 12¢ a word, on acceptance.

THE LIVING LIGHT—U.S. Catholic Conference, Dept. of Education, 3211 4th St. N.W., Washington, DC 20017–1194. Berard L. Marthaler, Exec. Ed. Theoretical and practical articles, 1,500 to 4,000 words, on religious education, catechesis, and pastoral ministry.

THE LOOKOUT—8121 Hamilton Ave., Cincinnati, OH 45231. Simon J. Dahlman, Ed. Articles, 500 to 2,000 words, on spiritual growth, family issues, applying Christian faith to current issues, and people overcoming problems with Christian principles. Inspirational or humorous shorts, 500 to 800 words; fiction, to 2,000 words. Pays 4¢ to 7¢ a word, on acceptance.

THE LUTHERAN—8765 W. Higgins Rd., Chicago, IL 60631. Edgar R. Trexler, Ed. Articles, to 2,000 words, on Christian ideology, personal religious experiences, social and ethical issues, family life, church, and community. Pays $100 to $600, on acceptance. Query required.

MARYKNOLL—Maryknoll, NY 10545. Joseph Veneroso, M. M., Ed. Frank Maurovich, Man. Ed. Magazine of the Catholic Foreign Mission Society of America. Articles, 800 to 1,000 words, and photos relating to missions or missioners overseas. Pays $150, on acceptance. Payment for photos made on publication.

MATURE LIVING—127 Ninth Ave. N., Nashville, TN 37234. Leisure magazine for senior adults. "Unique, creative manuscripts, to 900 words, characterized by human interest, Christian warmth, and humor." Pays 5 ½¢ a word (or per line for poetry). Buys all rights.

MATURE YEARS—201 Eighth Ave. S., P.O. Box 801, Nashville, TN 37202. Marvin W. Cropsey, Ed. Nondenominational quarterly. Articles on retirement or related subjects, 1,500 to 2,000 words. Humorous and serious fiction, 1,500 to 1,800 words, for adults. Travel pieces with religious slant. Poetry, to 14 lines. Include social security number with manuscript. Guidelines.

THE MENNONITE—P.O. Box 347, Newton, KS 67114. Gordon Houser, Ed. Larry Penner, Asst. Ed. Articles, 1,000 words, that emphasize Christian themes. Pays 5¢ a word, on publication. Guidelines.

MESSENGER OF THE SACRED HEART—661 Greenwood Ave., Toronto, Ont., Canada M4J 4B3. Articles and short stories, about 1,500 words, for American and Canadian Catholics. Pays from 4¢ a word, on acceptance.

MIDSTREAM—110 E. 59th St., New York, NY 10022. Joel Carmichael, Ed. Jewish-interest articles and book reviews. Fiction, to 3,000 words, and poetry. Pays 5¢ a word, after publication. Allow 3 months for response.

THE MIRACULOUS MEDAL—475 E. Chelten Ave., Philadelphia, PA 19144–5785. John W. Gouldrick, C.M., Ed. Dir. Catholic. Fiction, to 2,400 words. Religious verse, to 20 lines. Pays from 2¢ a word for fiction, from 50¢ a line for poetry, on acceptance.

MODERN LITURGY—160 E. Virginia St., #290, San Jose, CA 95112. Nick Wagner, Ed. "Articles making the connection between imagination and celebration (faith expression) or worship and 'real' life." Material must be related to Roman Catholic liturgy. Query only. Pays in copies and subscription.

MOMENT—3000 Connecticut Ave. N.W., Suite 300, Washington, DC 20008. Suzanne Singer, Man. Ed. Sophisticated, issue-oriented articles, 2,000 to 4,000 words, on Jewish topics. Nonfiction only. Pays $150 to $400, on publication.

MOMENTUM—National Catholic Educational Assn., 1077 30th St. N.W., Suite 100, Washington, DC 20007–3852. Patricia Feistritzer, Ed. Articles, 500 to 1,500 words, on outstanding programs, issues, and research in education. Book reviews. Pays 4¢ a word, on publication. Query.

MOODY MAGAZINE—820 N. La Salle Blvd., Chicago, IL 60610. Andrew Scheer, Man. Ed. Anecdotal articles, 1,200 to 2,000 words, on the evangelical Christian experience in the home, the community, and the workplace. Pays 15¢ to 20¢ a word, on acceptance. Query.

THE NATIONAL CHRISTIAN REPORTER—See *The United Methodist Reporter.*

NEW COVENANT —200 Noll Plaza, Huntington, IN 46750. Jim Manney, Ed. Articles and testimonials, 1,000 to 4,000 words, that foster renewal in the Catholic Church, especially the charismatic, ecumenical, and evangelical dimensions of that renewal. Queries preferred. Pays from 15¢ a word, on acceptance.

NEW ERA—50 E. North Temple, Salt Lake City, UT 84150. Richard M. Romney, Man. Ed. Articles, 150 to 1,500 words, and fiction, to 2,000 words, for young Mormons. Poetry; photos. Pays 5¢ to 10¢ a word, 25¢ a line for poetry, on acceptance. Query.

NEW WORLD OUTLOOK—475 Riverside Dr., Rm. 1351, New York, NY 10115–0122. Alma Graham, Ed. Articles, 500 to 1,500 words, on United Methodist missions and Methodist-related programs and ministries. Focus on national, global, and women's and children's issues, and on men and youth in missions. Photos a plus. Pays on publication.

OBLATES—15 S. 59th St., Belleville, IL 62223–4694. Priscilla Kurz, Manuscripts Ed. Jacqueline Lowery Corn, Man. Ed. Articles, 500 to 600 words, that inspire, uplift, and motivate through positive Christian values in everyday life. Inspirational poetry, to 16 lines. Send complete manuscript only. Pays $80 for articles, $30 for poems, on acceptance. Send 52¢ SASE for guidelines and sample copy.

THE OTHER SIDE—300 W. Apsley, Philadelphia, PA 19144. Doug Davidson, Nonfiction Ed. Jennifer Wilkins, Fiction Ed. Rod Jellema, Poetry Ed. Independent, ecumenical Christian magazine devoted to issues of peace, justice, and faith. Fiction, 500 to 5,000 words, that deepens readers' encounter with the mystery of God and the mystery of ourselves. Nonfiction, 500 to 4,000 words (most under 2,000 words), on contemporary social, political, economic, or racial issues in the U.S. or abroad. Poems, to 50 lines; submit up to 3 poems. Payment is 2 copies plus $20 to $350 for articles; $75 to $250 for fiction; $15 for poems, on acceptance. Guidelines.

OUR FAMILY—Box 249, Battleford, Sask., Canada S0M 0E0. Nestor Gregoire, Ed. Articles, 1,000 to 3,000 words, for Catholic families, on modern society, family, marriage, current affairs, and spiritual topics. Humor; verse. Pays 7¢ to 10¢ a word for articles, 75¢ to $1 a line for poetry, on acceptance. SAE with international reply coupons required with all submissions. Guidelines.

OUR SUNDAY VISITOR—Huntington, IN 46750. David Scott, Ed. In-depth features, 1,000 to 1,200 words, on the Catholic church in America today. Pays $150 to $250, on acceptance

PARISH FAMILY DIGEST—See *The Family Digest.*

PASTORAL LIFE—Box 595, Canfield, OH 44406–0595. Anthony L. Chenevey, Ed. Articles, 2,000 to 2,500 words, addressing the problems of pastoral ministry. Pays 4¢ a word, on publication. Guidelines.

PATHWAYS—Christian Board of Publication, Box 179, St. Louis, MO 63166. Christine Hershberger Miner, Ed. Fiction, 100 to 1,200 words; articles, 600 to 1,000 words; and poetry, to 20 lines. Accepts material for 12- to 16-year-olds. Pays 3¢ a word for prose, from $3 for poetry, on acceptance. Guidelines.

PENTECOSTAL EVANGEL—1445 Boonville Ave., Springfield, MO 65802. Richard Champion, Ed. Assemblies of God. Religious, personal experience, and devotional articles, 400 to 1,000 words. Verse, 12 to 30 lines; limited poetry market. Pays 7¢ a word, on acceptance.

THE PENTECOSTAL MESSENGER—P.O. Box 850, Joplin, MO 64802. Peggy Allen, Man. Ed. Articles, 500 to 2,000 words, that deal with Christian commitment: human interest, inspiration, social and religious issues, Bible topics, and seasonal material. Pays 1 ½¢ per word, on publication. Guidelines.

PERSPECTIVE—Pioneer Clubs, Box 788, Wheaton, IL 60189. Rebecca Powell Parat, Ed. Articles, 750 to 1,500 words, that provide growth for adult club leaders in leadership and relationship skills and offer encouragement and practical support. Readers are lay leaders of Pioneer Clubs for boys and girls (age 2 to 12th grade). "Most articles written on assignment; writers familiar with Pioneer Clubs who would be interested in working on assignment should contact us." Queries preferred. Pays $40 to $75, on acceptance. Guidelines.

PIME WORLD—17330 Quincy St., Detroit, MI 48221. Paul W. Witte, Man. Ed. Articles, 600 to 1,200 words, on Catholic missionary work in the Orient, West Africa, and Latin America. Color photos. No fiction or poetry. Pays 6¢ a word, extra for photos, on publication.

POWER AND LIGHT—6401 The Paseo, Kansas City, MO 64131. Beula J. Postlewait, Preteen Ed. Fiction, 400 to 800 words, for children (grades 5 and 6), defining Christian experiences and demonstrating Christian values and beliefs. Pays 3 ½¢ a word for first rights; 5¢ a word for multi-use rights, on publication.

THE PREACHER'S MAGAZINE—10814 E. Broadway, Spokane, WA 99206. Randal E. Denny, Ed. Scholarly and practical articles, 700 to 2,500 words, on areas of interest to Christian ministers: church administration, pastoral care, professional and personal growth, church music, finance, evangelism. Pays 3 ½¢ a word, on publication. Guidelines.

THE PRESBYTERIAN RECORD—50 Wynford Dr., N. York, Ont., Canada M3C 1J7. John Congram, Ed. Fiction and nonfiction, 1,500 words, and poetry, any length. Short items, to 800 words, of a contemporary and often controversial nature for "Full Count." The purpose of the magazine is "to provide news, not only from our church but the church at large, and to fulfill both a pastoral and prophetic role among our people." Queries preferred. SAE with international reply coupons required. Pays $50 (Canadian), on publication. Guidelines.

PRESBYTERIAN SURVEY—100 Witherspoon, Louisville, KY 40202–1396. Catherine Cottingham, Man. Ed. Articles, 1,200 words, of interest to members of the Presbyterian Church or ecumenical individuals. Pays to $100, before publication.

THE PRIEST—200 Noll Plaza, Huntington, IN 46750–4304. Robert A. Willems, Assoc. Ed. Viewpoints, to 1,500 words, and articles, to 5,000 words, on life and ministry of priests, current theological developments, etc., for priests, permanent deacons, and seminarians. Pays $50 to $300, on acceptance.

PURPOSE—616 Walnut Ave., Scottdale, PA 15683–1999. James E. Horsch, Ed. Fiction and fillers, to 800 words, on Christian discipleship and church-year related themes, with good photos; pieces of history, biography, science, hobbies, from a Christian perspective; Christian problem solving. Poetry, to 12 lines. "Send complete manuscript; no queries." Pays to 5¢ a word, to $1 a line for poetry, on acceptance.

QUAKER LIFE—Friends United Meeting, 101 Quaker Hill Dr., Richmond, IN 47374–1980. James R. Newby, Ed. Carol Beals, Man. Ed. Articles and news for members of the Society of Friends. Brief poetry considered. "Almost all material is solicited to match theme format." Pays in copies.

QUEEN OF ALL HEARTS—26 S. Saxon Ave., Bay Shore, NY 11706–8993. J. Patrick Gaffney, S.M.M., Ed. Publication of Montfort Missionaries. Articles and fiction, 1,000 to 2,000 words, related to the Virgin Mary. Poetry. Pay varies, on acceptance.

THE QUIET HOUR—850 N. Grove Ave., Elgin, IL 60120. Gary Wilde, Ed. Short devotionals. Pays $15, on acceptance. By assignment only; query.

RECONSTRUCTIONISM TODAY—30 Old Whitfield Rd., Accord, NY 12404. Lawrence Bush, Ed. Articles on contemporary Judaism and Jewish culture. Pays in copies and subscription.

RESPONSE: A CONTEMPORARY JEWISH REVIEW—27 W. 20th St., 9th Fl., New York, NY 10011–3707. Yigal Schleifer, Ed. Adam Margolis, Ed. Fiction, to 25 double-spaced pages, in which Jewish experience serves as controlling influence. Articles, to 25 pages, with a focus on Jewish issues. Poetry, to 80 lines, and book reviews. Pays in 5 copies per article or story; 2 copies per poem. Guidelines.

REVIEW FOR RELIGIOUS—3601 Lindell Blvd., St. Louis, MO 63108. David L. Fleming, S.J., Ed. Informative, practical, or inspirational articles, 1,500 to 5,000 words, from a theological or spiritual point of view. Pays $6 per page, on publication. Guidelines.

ST. ANTHONY MESSENGER—1615 Republic St., Cincinnati, OH 45210–1298. Norman Perry, O.F.M., Ed. Articles, 2,000 to 3,000 words, on personalities, major movements, education, family, religious and church issues, spiritual life, and social issues. Human-interest pieces. Humor; fiction, 2,000 to 3,000 words. Articles and stories should have religious implications. Query for nonfiction. Pays 14¢ a word, on acceptance.

ST. JOSEPH'S MESSENGER—P.O. Box 288, Jersey City, NJ 07303–0288. Sister Ursula Maphet, Ed. Inspirational articles, 500 to 1,000 words, and fiction, 1,000 to 1,500 words. Verse, 4 to 40 lines.

SEEK—8121 Hamilton Ave., Cincinnati, OH 45231. Eileen H. Wilmoth, Ed. Articles and fiction, to 1,200 words, on inspirational and controversial topics and timely religious issues. Christian testimonials. Pays 5¢ to 7¢ a word, on acceptance. SASE for guidelines.

SHARING THE VICTORY—Fellowship of Christian Athletes, 8701 Leeds Rd., Kansas City, MO 64129. John Dodderidge, Ed. Articles, interviews, and profiles, to 1,000 words, for co-ed Christian athletes and coaches in high school, college, and pros. Pays from $50, on publication. Query required.

SIGNS OF THE TIMES—P. O. Box 7000, Boise, ID 83707. Greg Brothers, Ed. Seventh-Day Adventists. Feature articles on Christians who have performed community services; current issues from a biblical perspective; health, home, marriage, human-interest pieces; inspirational articles, 500 to 2,000 words. Pays to 25¢ a word, on acceptance. Send 9x12 SASE for sample and guidelines.

SISTERS TODAY—The Liturgical Press, St. John's Abbey, Collegeville, MN 56321–7500. Articles, 500 to 3,500 words, on theology, social justice issues, and religious issues for women and the church. Poetry, to 34 lines. Pays $5 per printed page, $10 per poem, on publication; $50 for color cover photos and $25 for B&W inside photos. Send articles to: Sister Mary Anthony Wagner, O.S.B., Ed., St. Benedict's Convent, St. Joseph, MN 56374–2099. Send poetry to: Sister Virginia Micka, C.S.J.,1884 Randolph Ave., St. Paul, MN 55105.

SOCIAL JUSTICE REVIEW—3835 Westminster Pl., St. Louis, MO 63108–

3409. Rev. John H. Miller, C.S.C., Ed. Articles, 2,000 to 3,000 words, on social problems in light of Catholic teaching and current scientific studies. Pays 2¢ a word, on publication.

SPIRITUAL LIFE—2131 Lincoln Rd. N.E., Washington, DC 20002–1199. Edward O'Donnell, O.C.D., Ed. Professional religious journal. Religious essays, 3,000 to 5,000 words, on spirituality in contemporary life. Pays from $50, on acceptance. Guidelines.

STANDARD—6401 The Paseo, Kansas City, MO 64131. Articles, 300 to 1,700 words; true experiences; poetry, to 20 lines; fiction with Christian emphasis but not overtly preachy; fillers; short articles with devotional emphasis; cartoons in good taste. Pays 3 ½¢ a word, on acceptance.

SUNDAY DIGEST—850 N. Grove Ave., Elgin, IL 60120. Christine Dallman, Ed. Articles, 1,000 to 1,800 words, on Christian faith in contemporary life; inspirational and how-to articles; free-verse poetry. Anecdotes, 500 words. Pays on acceptance.

SUNDAY SCHOOL COUNSELOR—1445 Boonville Ave., Springfield, MO 65802–1894. Sylvia Lee, Ed. Articles, 1,000 to 1,500 words, on teaching and Sunday school people, for local Sunday school teachers. Pays 5¢ to 10¢ a word, on acceptance.

TEACHERS INTERACTION—3558 S. Jefferson Ave., St. Louis, MO 63118. Jane Haas, Ed. Articles, 800 to 1,200 words; how-to pieces, to 100 words, for Lutheran volunteer church school teachers. Pays $10 to $35, on publication. Limited free-lance market.

TEENS TODAY—Church of the Nazarene, 6401 The Paseo, Kansas City, MO 64131. Short stories that deal with teens demonstrating Christian principles, 1,200 to 1,500 words. Pays 4¢ a word for first rights, 3 ½¢ a word for reprints, on acceptance. Guidelines.

THEOLOGY TODAY—Box 29, Princeton, NJ 08542. Thomas G. Long, Ed. Patrick D. Miller, Ed. Articles, 1,500 to 3,500 words, on theology, religion, and related social and philosophical issues. Literary criticism. Pays $75 to $200, on publication.

TODAY'S CHRISTIAN WOMAN—465 Gundersen Dr., Carol Stream, IL 60188. Julie A. Talerico, Ed. Jan Senn, Asst. Ed. Articles, 1,500 words, that are "warm and personal in tone, full of real-life anecdotes that deal with the following relationships: marriage, parenting, friendship, spiritual life, and self." Humorous anecdotes, 150 words, that have a Christian slant. Queries required. Payment varies, on acceptance. Guidelines.

THE UNITED CHURCH OBSERVER—84 Pleasant Blvd., Toronto, Ont., Canada M4T 2Z8. Factual articles, 1,500 to 2,500 words, on religious trends, human problems, social issues. No poetry. Pays after publication. Query.

THE UNITED METHODIST REPORTER—P.O. Box 660275, Dallas, TX 75266–0275. John Lovelace, Ed. United Methodist newspaper. Religious features, to 500 words. Religious verse, 4 to 12 lines. Photos. "Tight-deadline, time-sensitive, nationally circulated weekly newspaper." Pays 4¢ a word, on publication. Send for guidelines. Same address and requirements for *The National Christian Reporter* (interdenominational).

UNITED SYNAGOGUE REVIEW—155 Fifth Ave., New York, NY 10010. Lois Goldrich, Ed. Articles, 1,000 to 1,200 words, on issues of interest to Conservative Jewish community. Query.

UNITY MAGAZINE—Unity School of Christianity, Unity Village, MO 64065. Philip White, Ed. Articles and poems: inspirational, religious, metaphysical, Bible interpretation, 1,000 to 1,800 words. Pays 20¢ a word, on acceptance.

VIRTUE—P. O. Box 850, Sisters, OR 97759–0850. Marlee Alex, Ed. Articles and fiction for Christian women. Query for articles; SASE required. Guidelines. Send 9x12 SASE with 5 stamps for sample copy.

VISTA MAGAZINE—P. O. Box 50434, Indianapolis, IN 46250–0434. Articles and adult fiction, on current Christian concerns and issues. First-person pieces, 500 to 1,200 words. Opinion pieces from an evangelical perspective, 500 to 650 words. Pays 4¢ a word for first rights, 2¢ a word for reprint. Send SASE for guidelines before submitting material.

THE WAR CRY—The Salvation Army, P.O. Box 269, Alexandria, VA 22313. Address the Ed.-in-Chief. Inspirational articles, to 800 words, addressing modern life and issues. Color photos. Pays 15¢ a word for articles, $75 to $150 for photos, on acceptance.

WITH—722 Main St., Box 347, Newton, KS 67114. Eddy Hall and Carol Duerksen, Eds. Fiction, 500 to 2,000 words; nonfiction, 500 to 1,500 words; and poetry, to 50 lines for Anabaptist-Mennonite teenagers. "Wholesome humor always gets a close read." B&W 8x10 photos accepted. Payment is 4¢ a word, on acceptance (2¢ a word for reprints).

WOMAN'S TOUCH—1445 Boonville, Springfield, MO 65802–1894. Sandra G. Clopine, Ed. Aleda Swartzendruber, Assoc. Ed. Articles, 500 to 1,200 words, that provide help and inspiration to Christian women, strengthening family life, and reaching out in witness to others. Uses some poetry and fillers, 50 to 150 words. Submit complete manuscript. Allow 3 months for response. Payment varies, on acceptance. Guidelines and editorial calendar.

WORLD VISION MAGAZINE—919 W. Huntington Dr., Monrovia, CA 91016. Larry Wilson, Man. Ed. Thoroughly researched articles, 1,200 to 2,000 words, on worldwide poverty, evangelism, the environment, and justice. Include reputable sources and strong anecdotes. "Turning Points," first-person articles, 450 to 700 words, about a life-changing, spiritual experience. "We like articles to offer positive ways Christians can make a difference." Query required. Payment negotiable, made on acceptance or publication.

YOUNG SALVATIONIST—The Salvation Army, 615 Slaters Ln., P.O. Box 269, Alexandria, VA 22313. Deborah Sedlar, Ed. Articles, 600 to 1,200 words, teach the Christian view of everyday living, for teenagers. Short shorts, first-person testimonies, 600 to 800 words. Pays 10¢ a word, on acceptance. SASE required. Send 8 ½x11 SASE (3 stamps) for theme list, guidelines, and sample copy.

YOUR CHURCH—465 Gundersen Dr., Carol Stream, IL 60188. James D. Berkley, Ed. Articles, to 1,000 words, about church business administration. Query required. Pays about 10¢ a word, on acceptance. Guidelines.

HEALTH

ACCENT ON LIVING—P. O. Box 700, Bloomington, IL 61702. Raymond C. Cheever, Pub. Betty Garee, Ed. Articles, 250 to 1,000 words, about physically disabled people, including their careers, recreation, sports, self-help devices, and ideas that can make daily routines easier. Good photos a plus. Pays 10¢ a word, on publication. Query.

AMERICAN BABY—475 Park Ave. S., New York, NY 10016. Judith Nolte, Ed. Articles, 1,000 to 2,000 words, for new or expectant parents on prenatal or infant care. Pays varying rates, on acceptance.

AMERICAN FITNESS—15250 Ventura Blvd., Suite 200, Sherman Oaks, CA 91403. Peg Jordan, Ed. Rhonda Wilson, Man. Ed. Articles, 500 to 1,500 words, on exercise, health, sports, nutrition, etc. Illustrations, photos, cartoons.

AMERICAN HEALTH—28 West 23rd St., New York, NY 10010. Address Ed. Dept. Lively, authoritative articles, 1,000 to 3,000 words, on scientific and lifestyle aspects of health and fitness; 100- to 500-word news reports. Query with clips. Pays $250 ($50 kill fee) for news stories; 75¢ per word for features (kill fee is 25% of assigned fee), on acceptance.

AMERICAN JOURNAL OF NURSING—555 W. 57th St., New York, NY 10019. Florence L. Huey, Ed. Articles, 1,500 to 2,000 words, with photos, on nursing. Query.

ARTHRITIS TODAY—The Arthritis Foundation, 1314 Spring St. N.W., Atlanta, GA 30309. Cindy McDaniel, Ed. Self-help, how-to, general interest, and inspirational articles, 1,000 to 2,500 words, and short fillers, 100 to 250 words, to help people with arthritis live more productive, independent, and pain-free lives. Pays from $450, on acceptance.

BABY TALK—636 Ave. of the Americas, New York, NY 10011. Susan Strecker, Ed. Articles, 1,000 to 1,500 words, by parents or professionals, on babies and baby care, etc. Pay varies, on acceptance. SASE required.

BETTER HEALTH—1384 Chapel St., New Haven, CT 06511. James F. Malerba, Pub. Dir. Wellness and prevention magazine affiliated with The Hospital of Saint Raphael of New Haven. Upbeat articles, 2,000 to 2,500 words, that encourage a healthier lifestyle. Articles must contain quotes and narrative from healthcare professionals at Saint Raphael's and other local services. Pays $300 to $500, on acceptance. Query with SASE.

DIABETES SELF-MANAGEMENT—150 W. 22nd St., New York, NY 10011. James Hazlett, Ed. Articles, 2,000 to 4,000 words, for people with diabetes who want to know more about controlling and managing it. Up-to-date and authoritative information on nutrition, pharmacology, exercise physiology, technological advances, self-help, and other how-to subjects. "Articles must be useful, instructive, and must have immediate application to the day-to-day life of our readers. We do not publish personal experience, profiles, exposés, or research breakthroughs." Query with one-page rationale, outline, writing samples, and SASE. Pays from $500, on acceptance. Buys all rights.

EATING WELL—Ferry Rd., Charlotte, VT 05445. Scott Mowbray, Ed. Allison Cleary, Man. Ed. Bimonthly. A food book with a health perspective. Feature articles, 2,000 to 5,000 words, for readers who "know that what they eat directly affects their well-being, and believe that with the right approach, one can enjoy both good food and good health." Departments ("Nutrition Letter: The Science of Eating Well" and "Observer: News from the World of Food"), 200 to 500 words. "We look for strong journalistic voice; authoritative, timely coverage of nutrition issues; healthy recipes that emphasize good ingredients, simple preparation, and full flavor; and a sense of humor." Query. Pays varying rates, 45 days after acceptance.

EXPECTING—685 Third Ave., New York, NY 10017. Evelyn A. Podsiadlo, Ed. Articles, 700 to 1,800 words, for expectant mothers. Query. Pays $300 to $500, on acceptance.

FITNESS—The New York Times Company Women's Magazines, 110 Fifth Ave., New York, NY 10011. Rona Cherry, Ed. Articles, 500 to 2,000 words, on health, exercise, sports, nutrition, diet, psychological well-being, sex, and beauty. Profiles of athletes and fit celebrities. Average reader is 28 years old. Query required. Pays $1 a word, on acceptance.

HEALTH—(formerly *In Health*) 301 Howard St., 18th Fl., San Francisco, CA 94105. Cassandra Wrightson, Ed. Asst. Articles, 1,200 words, for "Food," "Fitness," "Vanities," "Drugs," "Mind," and "Family" departments. Pays $1,800, on acceptance. Query with clips required.

HEART & SOUL—Rodale Press, Inc., 33 E. Minor St., Emmaus, PA 18098. Catherine Cassidy, Man. Ed. Articles, 800 to 2,000 words, on health, beauty, fitness, nutrition, and relationships for African-American readers. Queries preferred. Pays varying rates, on acceptance.

HOSPITALS & HEALTH NETWORKS—(formerly *Hospitals*) 737 N. Michigan Ave., Chicago, IL 60611. Mary Grayson, Ed. Articles, 800 to 1,500 words, for hospital administrators, on financing, staffing, coordinating, and providing facilities for health care services. Pays varying rates, on acceptance. Query.

IDEA TODAY—6190 Cornerstone Ct. E., Suite 204, San Diego, CA 92121–3773. Patricia Ryan, Ed. Practical articles, 1,000 to 3,000 words, on new exercise programs, business management, nutrition, sports medicine, dance-exercise, and one-to-one training techniques. Articles must be geared toward the aerobics instructor, exercise studio owner or manager, or personal trainer. No queries on topics for the consumer; no general health ideas. Payment negotiable, on acceptance. Query preferred.

IN HEALTH—See *Health.*

LET'S LIVE—P.O. Box 74908, Los Angeles, CA 90004. Court van Rooten, Ed.-in-Chief. Articles, 1,000 to 1,500 words, on preventive medicine and nutrition, alternative medicine, diet, exercise, recipes, and natural beauty. Pays $150, on publication. Query.

MEDIPHORS—P.O. Box 327, Bloomsburg, PA 17815. Dr. Eugene D. Radice, Ed. "A Literary Journal of the Health Professionals." Short stories, essays, and commentary, 3,000 words, related to medicine and health. Poetry, to 30 lines. "We are not a technical journal of science. We do not publish research or review articles, except of a historical nature." Pays in copies. Guidelines.

MUSCULAR DEVELOPMENT—505-H Saddle River Rd., Saddle Brook, NJ 07662. Alan Paul, Ed. Articles, 5 to 10 double-spaced typed pages, geared to serious weight training athletes, on any aspect of competitive body building, power-lifting, sports, and nutrition. Photos. Pays $50 to $400, on publication. Query.

NATURAL FOOD & FARMING—Natural Food Assoc., P.O. Box 210, Atlanta, TX 75551. Lisa Arnold, Janice Elliott, Assoc. Eds. Articles, 2,000 words, on health and nutrition with a focus on naturally grown, chemical-free foods and preventive medicine. Pays $25 on acceptance, plus 5¢ a word, immediately after publication.

NATURAL HEALTH: THE GUIDE TO WELL-BEING—17 Station St., Box 1200, Brookline, MA 02147. Features, 1,500 to 3,000 words, on holistic health, natural foods, herbal remedies, etc., and interviews. Photos. Pays 30¢ a word, extra for photos, on acceptance.

NEW BODY—1700 Broadway, New York, NY 10019. Nicole Dorsey, Ed. Well-researched, service-oriented articles, 800 to 1,500 words, on exercise, nutrition, lifestyle, diet, and health for women ages 18 to 35. Also considers submissions, 500 to 600 words, for "How I Lost It" column, in which writers tell how they lost weight and have kept it off. Writers should have some background in or knowledge of the health field. Pays $100 to $300, on publication. Send detailed query.

NURSING 94—1111 Bethlehem Pike, P.O. Box 908, Springhouse, PA 19477. Patricia Nornhold, Clinical Dir. Most articles are clinically oriented, and are written by nurses for nurses. Also covers legal, ethical, management, and career aspects of nursing; narratives about personal nursing experiences. No poetry. Pays $25 to $300, on publication. Query.

NURSINGWORLD JOURNAL—470 Boston Post Rd., Weston, MA 02193. R. Patrick Gates, Man. Ed. Articles, 500 to 1,500 words, for and by nurses and nurse-educators, on aspects of current nursing issues. Pays $35, on publication.

PATIENT CARE—5 Paragon Dr., Montvale, NJ 07645. Jeffrey H. Forster, Ed. Articles on medical care, for primary-care physicians; mostly staff-written. Pays varying rates, on publication. Query; all articles assigned.

THE PHYSICIAN AND SPORTSMEDICINE—4530 W. 77th St., Minneapolis, MN 55435. Terry Monahan, Man. Ed. News and feature articles; clinical articles coauthored with physician. Sports medicine angle necessary. Pays $150 to $1,000, on acceptance. Guidelines. Query required.

A POSITIVE APPROACH—P.O. Box 910, Millville, NJ 08332. Patricia Johnson, Ed. Articles, 500 words, on all aspects of the positive-thinking disabled/handicapped person's private and business life. Well-researched articles of interest to the visually and hearing impaired, veterans, the arthritic, and all categories of the disabled and handicapped, on interior design, barrier-free architecture, gardening, wardrobe, computers, and careers. No fiction or poetry. Pays in copies.

PSYCHOLOGY TODAY—24 E. 23rd St., 5th Fl., New York, NY 10010. Hara E. Marano, Exec. Ed. Bimonthly. Articles, 4,000 words, on timely subjects and news. Pays varying rates, on publication.

RX REMEDY—120 Post Rd. W., Westport, CT 06880. Val Weaver, Ed. Quarterly. Articles, 600 to 2,500 words, on health and medication issues for readers 55 and older. Regular columns include "The Fitness Prescription," and "The Nutrition Prescription." Query. Pays $1 to $1.25 a word, on acceptance.

TODAY'S OR NURSE—6900 Grove Rd., Thorofare, NJ 08086. Mary Jo Krey, Man. Ed. Clinical or general articles, from 2,000 words, of direct interest to operating room nurses.

VEGETARIAN TIMES—P.O. Box 570, Oak Park, IL 60303. Toni Apgar, Pub. Articles, 1,200 to 2,500 words, on vegetarian cooking, nutrition, health and fitness, and profiles of prominent vegetarians. "News Items" and "In Print" (book reviews), to 500 words. "Herbalist" pieces, to 1,800 words, on medicinal uses of herbs. Queries required. Pays $75 to $1,000, on acceptance. Guidelines.

VIBRANT LIFE—55 W. Oak Ridge Dr., Hagerstown, MD 21740. Features, 750 to 1,500 words, on total health: physical, mental, and spiritual. Seeks upbeat articles on the family and how to live happier and healthier lives; Christian slant. Pays $80 to $250, on acceptance.

VIM & VIGOR—8805 N. 23rd Ave., Suite 11, Phoenix, AZ 85021. Fred Petrovsky, Ed. Positive health and fitness articles, 1,200 to 2,000 words, with accurate medical facts. By assignment only; writers with feature- or news-writing ability may submit qualifications for assignment. Pays $450, on acceptance. Guidelines.

YOGA JOURNAL—2054 University Ave., Berkeley, CA 94704. Stephan Bodian, Ed. Articles, 1,200 to 4,000 words, on holistic health, meditation, consciousness, spirituality, and yoga. Pays $75 to $600, on publication.

YOUR HEALTH—5401 N.W. Broken Sound Blvd., Boca Raton, FL 33487. Susan Gregg, Ed.-in-Chief. Health and medical articles, 1,000 to 2,000 words, for a lay audience. Queries preferred. Pays $75 to $100, on publication.

YOUR HEALTH—1720 Washington Blvd., Box 10010, Ogden, UT 84409. Caroll Shreeve, Pub. Articles, 1,200 words, on individual health care needs: prevention, treatment, low-impact aerobics, fitness, nutrition, etc. Color photos required. Pays 15¢ a word, on acceptance. Guidelines.

EDUCATION

BEAUTY EDUCATION—3 Columbia Cir., Albany, NY 12212. Catherine Frangie, Pub. Articles, 750 to 1,000 words, that provide beauty educators, trainers, and professionals in the cosmetology industry with information, skills, and techniques on such topics as hairstyling, makeup, aromatherapy, retailing, massage, and beauty careers. Send SASE for editorial calendar with monthly themes. Pays in copies. Query.

THE BOOK REPORT—Linworth Publishing, 480 E. Wilson Bridge Rd., Suite L, Worthington, OH 43085–2372. Carolyn Hamilton, Ed./Pub. "The Journal for Secondary School Librarians." Articles by school librarians or other educators about practical aspects of running a school library. Write for themes and guidelines. Also publishes *Library Talk*, "The Magazine for Elementary School Librarians."

CAREER WOMAN—See *Minority Engineer*.

CAREERS & THE DISABLED—See *Minority Engineer*.

CHANGE—1319 18th St. N.W., Washington, DC 20036. Columns, 700 to 2,000 words, and in-depth features, 2,500 to 3,500 words, on programs, people, and institutions of higher education. "We can't usually pay for unsolicited articles."

CHRISTIAN EDUCATION JOURNAL—Scripture Press Ministries, P.O. Box 650, Glen Ellyn, IL 60138. Ronald R. Ramsey, Exec. Ed. Articles, 5 to 15 typed pages, on Christian education topics. Pays $100, on publication. Guidelines.

CHURCH TEACHERS—1119 Woodburn Rd., Durham, NC 27705. Shirley H. Strobel, Ed. Articles, 1,000 words, on classroom-tested teaching strategies for church school. Book reviews related to teaching. Pays $30 to $40 per page, on publication. Guidelines.

THE CLEARING HOUSE—Heldref Publications, 1319 18th St. N.W., Washington, DC 20036. Judy Cusick, Man. Ed. Bimonthly for middle level and high school teachers and administrators. Articles, 2,500 words, related to education: useful teaching practices, research findings, and experiments. Some opinion pieces and satirical articles related to education. Payment is two copies.

EQUAL OPPORTUNITY—See *Minority Engineer*.

GIFTED EDUCATION PRESS NEWSLETTER—P.O. Box 1586, 10201 Yuma Ct., Manassas, VA 22110. Maurice Fisher, Pub. Articles, to 4,000 words, written by educators, laypersons, and parents of gifted children, on the problems of identifying and teaching gifted children and adolescents. "Interested in incisive analyses of current programs for the gifted and recommendations for improving the education of gifted students. Particularly interested in advocacy for gifted children, biographical sketches of highly gifted individuals, and the problems of teaching humanities, science, ethics, literature, and history to the gifted. Looking for highly imaginative and knowledgeable writers." Query required. Pays with subscription.

HOME EDUCATION MAGAZINE—P.O. Box 1083, Tonasket, WA 98855–1083. Helen E. Hegener, Man. Ed. Informative articles, 750 to 2,000 words, on all aspects of the growing homeschool movement. Send complete manuscript or detailed query with SASE. Pays about 2¢ a word, on publication.

THE HORN BOOK MAGAZINE—14 Beacon St., Boston, MA 02108. Anita Silvey, Ed. Articles, 600 to 2,800 words, on books for young readers and related subjects for librarians, teachers, parents, etc. Payment varies, on publication. Query.

INDEPENDENT LIVING MAGAZINE—See *Minority Engineer.*

INSTRUCTOR MAGAZINE—Scholastic, Inc., 730 Broadway, New York, NY 10003. Debra Martorelli, Ed. Articles, 300 to 1,500 words, for teachers in grades K through 8. Payment varies, on acceptance.

ITC COMMUNICATOR—International Training in Communication, P.O. Box 1809, Sutter Creek, CA 95685. JoAnn Levy, Ed. Educational articles, 200 to 800 words, on leadership, language, speech presentation, procedures for meetings, personal and professional development, written and spoken communication techniques. SASE required. Pays in copies.

KEY TO CHRISTIAN EDUCATION—8121 Hamilton Ave., Cincinnati, OH 45231–2396. Barbara Bolton and Lowellette Lauderdale, Eds. Articles, to 1,200 words, on Christian education; tips for teachers in the local church. Pays varying rates, on acceptance.

LEADERSHIP PUBLISHERS, INC.—P.O. Box 8358, Des Moines, IA 50301–8358. Lois F. Roets, Ed. Educational materials for talented and gifted students, grades K to 12. Send SASE for catalogue and guidelines before submitting. Pays in royalty for books, and flat fee for short pieces or booklets.

LEARNING 93/94—1111 Bethlehem Pike, Springhouse, PA 19477. Charlene Gaynor, Ed. How-to, why-to, and personal-experience articles, to 3,000 words, for teachers of grades K through 8. Tested classroom ideas for curriculum roundups, to 600 words. Pays to $300 for features, on acceptance.

LIBRARY TALK—See *The Book Report.*

MEDIA & METHODS—1429 Walnut St., Philadelphia, PA 19102. Andrea Epstein, Man. Ed. Articles, 800 to 1,000 words, on media, technologies, and methods used to enhance instruction and learning in K through 12th grade classrooms. Pays $50 to $200, on publication. Query required.

MINORITY ENGINEER—150 Motor Parkway, Suite 420, Hauppauge, NY 11788–5145. James Schneider, Exec. Ed. Articles, 1,000 to 1,500 words, for college students, on career opportunities in engineering, techniques of job hunting, and role-model profiles of professional minority engineers. Interviews. Pays 10¢ a word, on publication. Query. Same address and requirements for *Equal Opportunity, Career Woman* (query Eileen Nester), and *Careers & the DisABLED.* For *Woman Engineer,* and *Independent Living,* query Editor Anne Kelly.

MOMENTUM—National Catholic Educational Assn., 1077 30th St. N.W., Suite 100, Washington, DC 20007–3852. Patricia Feistritzer, Ed. Articles, 500 to 1,500 words, on outstanding programs, issues, and research in education. Book reviews. Query or send complete manuscript. No simultaneous submissions. Pays 4¢ a word, on publication.

PHI DELTA KAPPAN—8th and Union St., Box 789, Bloomington, IN 47402–0789. Pauline Gough, Ed. Articles, 1,000 to 4,000 words, on educational research, service, and leadership; issues, trends, and policy. Pays from $250, on publication.

SCHOOL ARTS MAGAZINE—50 Portland St., Worcester, MA 01608. Kent Anderson, Ed. Articles, 800 to 1,000 words, on art education with special application to the classroom: successful and meaningful approaches to teaching art, innovative art projects, uncommon applications of art techniques or equipment, etc. Photos. Pays varying rates, on publication. Guidelines.

SCHOOL SAFETY—National School Safety Ctr., 4165 Thousand Oaks Blvd., Suite 290, Westlake Village, CA 91362. Ronald D. Stephens, Exec. Ed. Published 8 times during the school year. Articles, 2,000 to 3,000 words, of use to educators, law enforcers, judges, and legislators on the prevention of drugs, gangs, weapons, bullying, discipline problems, and vandalism; also on-site security and character development as they relate to students and schools. No payment made.

TEACHING K-8—40 Richards Ave., Norwalk, CT 06854. Patricia Broderick, Ed. Dir. Articles, 1,200 words, on the profession of teaching children. Queries are not necessary. Pays to $35, on publication.

TECH DIRECTIONS—Box 8623, Ann Arbor, MI 48107. Paul J. Bamford, Man. Ed. Articles, one to 10 double-spaced typed pages, for teachers and administrators in industrial, technological, and vocational educational fields, with particular interest in classroom projects, computer users, and political issues. Pays $10 to $150, on publication. Guidelines.

TECHNOLOGY & LEARNING—Peter Li, Inc., 2169 E. Francisco Blvd. E., Suite A-4, San Rafael, CA 94901. Holly Brady, Ed. Articles, to 3,000 words, for teachers of grades K through 12, about uses of computers and related technology in the classroom: human-interest and philosophical articles, how-to pieces, software reviews, and hands-on ideas. Pay varies, on acceptance.

TODAY'S CATHOLIC TEACHER—330 Progress Rd., Dayton, OH 45449. Stephen Brittan, Ed. Articles, 600 to 800 words, 1,000 to 1,200 words, and 1,200 to 1,500 words, on education, parent-teacher relationships, innovative teaching, teaching techniques, etc., of use to educators. Pays $65 to $250, on publication. SASE required. Query. Guidelines.

WILSON LIBRARY BULLETIN—950 University Ave., Bronx, NY 10452. GraceAnne A. DeCandido, Ed. Articles, 1,800 to 3,600 words, on libraries, communications, and information systems. News, reports, features. Pays $100 to $300, extra for photos, on publication.

WOMAN ENGINEER—See *Minority Engineer.*

FARMING AND AGRICULTURE

ACRES USA—10008 E. 60 Terrace, Kansas City, MO 64133. Charles Walters, Ed. Articles on biological agriculture: technology, economics, public policy, and current events. "Our emphasis is on production of quality food without the use of toxic chemicals." Pays 6¢ a word, on acceptance. Query.

AMERICAN BEE JOURNAL—51 N. Second St., Hamilton, IL 62341. Joe M. Graham, Ed. Articles on beekeeping, for professionals. Photos. Pays 75¢ a column inch, extra for photos, on publication.

BEEF—7900 International Dr., Minneapolis, MN 55425. Paul D. Andre, Ed.

Articles on beef cattle feeding, cowherds, stocker operations, and related phases of the cattle industry. Pays to $300, on acceptance.

BUCKEYE FARM NEWS—Ohio Farm Bureau Federation, Two Nationwide Plaza, Box 479, Columbus, OH 43216–0479. Lynn Echelberger, Copy Ed. Articles, to 600 words, related to agriculture. Pays on publication. Query. Limited market.

DAIRY GOAT JOURNAL—W. 2997 Markert Rd., Helenville, WI 53137. Dave Thompson, Ed. Articles, to 1,500 words, on successful dairy goat owners, youths and interesting people associated with dairy goats. "Especially interested in practical husbandry ideas." Photos. Pays $50 to $150, on publication. Query.

FARM AND RANCH LIVING—5400 S. 60th St., Greendale, WI 53129. Bob Ottum, Ed. Articles, 2,000 words, on rural people and situations; nostalgia pieces; profiles of interesting farms and farmers, ranches and ranchers. Pays $15 to $400, on acceptance and on publication.

FARM INDUSTRY NEWS—7900 International Dr., Minneapolis, MN 55425. Joe Degnan, Ed. Articles for farmers, on new products, machinery, equipment, chemicals, and seeds. Pays $175 to $400, on acceptance. Query required.

FARM JOURNAL—230 W. Washington Sq., Philadelphia, PA 19106. Earl Ainsworth, Ed. Articles, 500 to 1,500 words, with photos, on the business of farming. Pays 20¢ to 50¢ a word, on acceptance. Query.

FLORIDA GROWER & RANCHER—1331 N. Mills Ave., Orlando, FL 32803. Frank Garner, Ed. Articles and case histories on Florida farmers, growers, and ranchers. Pays on publication. Query; buys little freelance material.

THE FURROW—Deere & Company, John Deere Rd., Moline, IL 61265. George Sollenberger, Exec. Ed. Specialized, illustrated articles on farming. Pays to $1,000, on acceptance.

HARROWSMITH—Telemedia Communications, Inc., Camden East, Ont., Canada K0K 1J0. Arlene Stacey, Ed. Articles, 700 to 3,000 words, on country life, organic gardening, and alternative energy with a Canadian slant. Pays $150 to $1,500, on acceptance. Query with SAE/international reply coupon.

HARROWSMITH COUNTRY LIFE—Ferry Rd., Charlotte, VT 05445. Address Ed. Dept. Investigative pieces, 4,000 to 5,000 words, on ecology, energy, health, gardening, energy-efficient housing, do-it-yourself projects, and the food chain. News briefs for "Gazette." Pays $500 to $2,000 for features, $50 to $600 for department pieces, on acceptance. Query required. Send SASE for guidelines.

NATURAL FOOD & FARMING—Natural Foods Associates, P.O. Box 210, Atlanta, TX 75551. Lisa Arnold, Janice Elliott, Assoc. Eds. Articles, 2,000 words, on health and nutrition with a focus on naturally grown, chemical-free foods and preventive medicine. "We want articles that help develop the interrelationship between the living soil and human health." Pays $25 on acceptance, plus 5¢ a word, immediately after publication.

THE OHIO FARMER—1350 W. Fifth Ave., Columbus, OH 43212. Tim White, Ed. Articles on farming, rural living, etc., in Ohio. Pays $20 per column, on publication.

PEANUT FARMER—P.O. Box 95075, Raleigh, NC 27625. Mary Evans, Man. Ed. Articles, 500 to 2,000 words, on production and management practices in peanut farming. Pays $50 to $350, on publication.

PENNSYLVANIA FARMER—704 Lisburn Rd., Camp Hill, PA 17011. John R. Vogel, Ed. Articles on farmers in Pennsylvania, New Jersey, Delaware,

Maryland, and West Virginia; timely business-of-farming concepts and successful farm management operations. Short pieces on humorous experiences in farming. Payment varies, on publication.

RURAL HERITAGE—281 Dean Ridge Lane, Gainesboro, TN 38562–9685. Gail Damerow, Ed. How-to and feature articles, 1,200 to 1,600 words, related to rural living and draft horses, mules, and oxen. Short pieces, to 800 words, and special features, to 2,000 words also considered. Pays 5¢ a word, $10 for photos, on publication.

SHEEP! MAGAZINE—W. 2997 Markert Rd., Helenville, WI 53137. Dave Thompson, Ed. Articles, to 1,500 words, on successful shepherds, woolcrafts, sheep raising, and sheep dogs. "Especially interested in people who raise sheep successfully as a sideline enterprise." Photos. Pays $80 to $300, extra for photos, on publication. Query.

SMALL FARMER'S JOURNAL—P.O. Box 1627, Dept. 106, Sisters, OR 97759. Address the Eds. How-tos, humor, practical work horse information, livestock and produce marketing, gardening information, and articles appropriate to the independent family farm. "Also actively seeking book-length manuscripts with regional (Northwest) interest." Pays negotiable rates, on publication. Query.

SUCCESSFUL FARMING—1716 Locust St., Des Moines, IA 50309–3023. Gene Johnston, Man. Ed. Articles on farm production, business, and families; also farm personalities, health, leisure, and outdoor topics. Pays varying rates, on acceptance.

TOPICS IN VETERINARY MEDICINE—812 Springdale Dr., Exton, PA 19341–2803. Kathleen Etchison, Ed. Technical articles, 1,200 to 1,500 words, and clinical features, 500 words, on veterinary medicine. Photos. Pays $300, $150 for shorter pieces, extra for photos, on publication.

THE WESTERN PRODUCER—Box 2500, Saskatoon, Saskatchewan, Canada S7K 2C4. Address Man. Ed. Articles, to 800 words (prefer under 600 words), on agricultural and rural subjects, preferably with a Canadian slant. Photos. Pays from 15¢ a word; $20 to $40 for B&W photos; to $100 for color photos, on acceptance.

ENVIRONMENT AND CONSERVATION

THE AMERICAN FIELD—542 S. Dearborn, Chicago, IL 60605. B.J. Matthys, Man. Ed. Yarns about hunting trips, bird-shooting; articles, to 1,500 words, on dogs and field trials, emphasizing conservation of game resources. Pays varying rates, on acceptance.

AMERICAN FORESTS—1516 P St. N.W., Washington, DC 20005. Bill Rooney, Ed. Well-documented articles, to 2,000 words, with photos, on the use, enjoyment, and management of forests. Photos. Pays on acceptance.

THE AMICUS JOURNAL—Natural Resources Defense Council, 40 W. 20th St., New York, NY 10011. Francesca Lyman, Ed. Quarterly. Articles and book reviews on national and international environmental topics. (No fiction, essays, speeches, or product reports accepted.) Query with SASE required. Pays varying rates, on acceptance.

ANIMALS—350 S. Huntington Ave., Boston, MA 02130. Joni Praded, Dir./Ed. Informative, well-researched articles, to 2,500 words, on animal protection, national and international wildlife, pet care, conservation, and environmental issues that affect animals. No personal accounts or favorite pet stories. Pays from $350, on acceptance. Query.

ATLANTIC SALMON JOURNAL—P.O. Box 429, St. Andrews, N.B., Canada E0G 2X0. Harry Bruce, Ed. Articles, 1,500 to 3,000 words, related to Atlantic salmon: fishing, conservation, ecology, travel, politics, biology, how-tos, anecdotes, cuisine. Pays $100 to $400, on publication.

AUDUBON—700 Broadway, New York, NY 10003. Michael W. Robbins, Ed. Bimonthly. Articles, 1,000 to 4,000 words, on conservation and environmental issues, natural history, ecology, and related subjects. Payment varies, on acceptance. Query.

BIRD WATCHER'S DIGEST—P.O. Box 110, Marietta, OH 45750. Mary B. Bowers, Ed. Articles, 600 to 2,500 words, for bird watchers: first-person accounts; how-tos; pieces on endangered species; profiles. Cartoons. Pays from $50, on publication.

BUZZWORM—See *Earth Journal.*

EARTH JOURNAL—(formerly *Buzzworm*) 2305 Canyon Blvd., Suite 206, Boulder, CO 80302. Ilana Kotin, Man. Ed. Bimonthly. Articles on environmental and natural resources issues worldwide: endangered species, new ideas in conservation, personalities, etc. Query with clips and resumé. Pays $25 to $1,050, after publication.

EQUINOX—7 Queen Victoria Rd., Camden East, Ont., Canada K0K 1J0. Alan Morantz, Man. Ed. Articles, 3,000 to 6,000 words, on popular geography, wildlife, astronomy, science, the arts, travel, and adventure. Department pieces, 300 to 800 words, for "Nexus" (science and medicine) and "Habitat" (natural environment). Pays $1,500 to $3,500 for features, $100 to $500 for short pieces, on acceptance.

FLORIDA WILDLIFE—620 S. Meridian St., Tallahassee, FL 32399–1600. Address the Ed. Bimonthly of the Florida Game and Fresh Water Fish Commission. Articles, 800 to 1,200 words, that promote native flora and fauna, hunting, fishing in Florida's fresh waters, outdoor ethics, and conservation of Florida's natural resources. Pays $50 to $400, on publication.

GARBAGE: THE PRACTICAL JOURNAL FOR THE ENVIRONMENT—2 Main St., Gloucester, MA 01930. Patricia Poore, Ed. Articles, 1,500 to 3,000 words, that tailor scientific and technical information to the environmental interests of a lay audience. Topics include food/health; gardening; how-to methods for improving efficiency and cutting down on waste; environmental science and technology. Occasionally publish short news items. Query with published clips or relevant resumé. Payment varies, on acceptance.

HARROWSMITH COUNTRY LIFE—Ferry Rd., Charlotte, VT 05445. Address Editorial Dept. Feature articles, 3,000 to 4,000 words, on environment, energy, gardening, rural issues, shelter. How-to and do-it-yourself projects. Short opinion pieces and profiles of country careers, news briefs, and natural history. Pays $500 to $1,500 for features, from $50 to $600 for department pieces, on acceptance. Query with SASE required. Guidelines.

HOUSEPLANT MAGAZINE—P.O. Box 1638, Elkins, WV 26241. Larry Hodgson, Ed.-in-Chief. Personal experiences and plant profiles, 700 to 1,500 words, for amateur houseplant enthusiasts. Organic solutions should be proposed for any pest problems.

INTERNATIONAL WILDLIFE—8925 Leesburg Pike, Vienna, VA 22184.

Donna Johnson, Assoc. Ed. Short features, 700 words, and 1,500- to 2,500-word articles that make nature, and human use and stewardship of it, understandable and interesting. Pays $500 for one-page features, $1,800 for full-length articles, on acceptance. Query with writing samples. Limited free-lance needs. Guidelines.

NATIONAL GEOGRAPHIC—17th and M Sts. N.W., Washington, DC 20036. William P.E. Graves, Ed. First-person, general-interest, heavily illustrated articles on science, natural history, exploration, and geographical regions. Written query required.

NATIONAL PARKS MAGAZINE—1776 Massachusetts Ave., Washington, DC 20036. Sue E. Dodge, Ed. Articles, 1,500 to 2,500 words, on natural history, wildlife, and conservation as they relate to national parks; illustrated features on the natural, historic, and cultural resources of the national park system. Pieces about legislation and other issues and events related to the parks. Pays $100 to $800, on acceptance. Query. Guidelines.

NATIONAL WILDLIFE—8925 Leesburg Pike, Vienna, VA 22184. Mark Wexler, Ed. Articles, 1,000 to 2,500 words, on wildlife, conservation, environment; outdoor how-to pieces. Photos. Pays on acceptance. Query.

NATURE CONSERVANCY—1815 N. Lynn St., Arlington, VA 22209. Mark Cheater, Ed. Membership publication. Articles on wildlife, people, trends in conservation or ecology. Pieces must have connection to The Nature Conservancy's activities or mission. No poetry or fiction. Query with clips required; article lengths, deadlines, and payment determined at time of assignment. Pays on acceptance.

OH!ZONE—Project Oh!Zone, 420 E. Hewitt Ave., Marquette, MI 49855. Christian Hansen, Ed.-in-Chief. Quarterly. Articles, 200 to 3,000 words, on environmental news, art, and opinion, for readers ages 12 to 21. Special attention given to student submissions. Send SASE for guidelines and list of upcoming themes. Pays $30 to $100 for articles, $10 to $25 for photos or drawings, and $100 for covers, on publication. Contributors receive ten copies and a subscription.

OUTDOOR AMERICA—1401 Wilson Blvd., Level B, Arlington, VA 22209. Address Articles Ed. Quarterly publication of the Izaak Walton League of America. Articles, 1,250 to 1,750 words, on natural resource conservation issues and outdoor recreation; especially fishing, hunting, and camping. Short items, 500 to 750 words. Pays 20¢ a word. Query with published clips.

SEA FRONTIERS—400 S.E. Second Ave., 4th Fl., Miami, FL 33131. Bonnie Bilyeu Gordon, Ed. Illustrated articles, 500 to 3,000 words, on scientific advances related to the sea, biological, physical, chemical, or geological phenomena, ecology, conservation, etc., written in a popular style for lay readers. Send SASE for guidelines. Pays 25¢ a word, on acceptance. Query.

SIERRA—730 Polk St., San Francisco, CA 94109. Jonathan F. King, Ed.-in-Chief. Articles, 750 to 2,500 words, on environmental and conservation topics, travel, hiking, backpacking, skiing, rafting, cycling. Photos. Pays from $500 to $2,000, extra for photos, on acceptance. Query with SASE and clips.

SMITHSONIAN MAGAZINE—900 Jefferson Dr., Washington, DC 20560. Marlane A. Liddell, Articles Ed. Articles on history, art, natural history, physical science, profiles, etc. Query with clips and SASE.

SPORTS AFIELD—250 W. 55th St., New York, NY 10019. Tom Paugh, Ed. Articles, 500 to 2,000 words, with quality photos, on hunting, fishing, natural history, survival, conservation, ecology, personal experiences. How-to pieces; humor, fiction. Pays top rates, on acceptance.

VIRGINIA WILDLIFE—P.O. Box 11104, Richmond, VA 23230–1104. Articles, 1,500 to 2,500 words, on conservation and related topics, including fishing, hunting, wildlife management, outdoor safety, ethics, etc. All material must have Virginia tie-in and be accompanied by color photos. Query with SASE. Pays 10¢ a word, extra for photos, on acceptance.

WILDLIFE CONSERVATION—NYZS/The Wildlife Conservation Society, Bronx, NY 10460. Nancy Simmons, Sr. Ed. First-person articles, 1,500 to 2,000 words, on "popular" natural history, "based on author's research and experience as opposed to textbook approach." Payment varies, on acceptance. Guidelines.

MEDIA AND THE ARTS

AHA! HISPANIC ARTS NEWS—Assoc. of Hispanic Arts, 173 E. 116th St., New York, NY 10029–1302. Dolores Prida, Ed. Editorials, reviews, monthly calendars, feature articles, and listings by artistic discipline. Query required.

THE AMERICAN ART JOURNAL—40 W. 57th St., 5th Fl., New York, NY 10019–4044. Jayne A. Kuchna, Ed. Scholarly articles, 2,000 to 10,000 words, on American art of the 17th through the early 20th centuries. Photos. Pays $200 to $500, on acceptance.

AMERICAN INDIAN ART MAGAZINE—7314 E. Osborn Dr., Scottsdale, AZ 85251. Roanne P. Goldfein, Ed. Detailed articles, 10 typed pages, on American Indian arts: painting, carving, beadwork, basketry, textiles, ceramics, jewelry, etc. Pays varying rates, on publication. Query.

AMERICAN JOURNALISM REVIEW—(formerly *Washington Journalism Review*) 4716 Pontiac St., #310, College Park, MD 20740–2493. Rem Rieder, Ed. Articles, 500 to 3,000 words, on print or electronic journalism, ethics, and issues. Pays 20¢ a word, on publication. Query.

AMERICAN THEATRE—355 Lexington Ave., New York, NY 10017. Jim O'Quinn, Ed. Features, 500 to 4,000 words, on the theater and theater-related subjects. Payment negotiable, on publication. Query.

AMERICAN VISIONS, THE MAGAZINE OF AFRO-AMERICAN CULTURE—2101 S St. N.W., Washington, DC 20008–4011. Joanne Harris, Ed. Articles, 1,500 words, and columns, 750 to 2,000 words, on African-American culture with a focus on the arts. Pays from $100 to $1,000, on publication. Query.

THE ARTIST'S MAGAZINE—1507 Dana Ave., Cincinnati, OH 45207. Greg Albert, Ed. Features, 1,200 to 2,500 words, and department pieces for the working artist. Poems, to 20 lines, on art and the creative process. Single-panel cartoons. Pays $150 to $350 for articles; $65 for cartoons, on acceptance. Guidelines. Query.

ARTS ATLANTIC—P.O. Box 848, Charlottetown, P.E.I., Canada C1A 7L9. Joseph Sherman, Ed. Articles and reviews, 600 to 3,000 words, on visual, performing, and literary arts in Atlantic Canada. Also, "idea and concept" articles of universal appeal. Query.

BLUEGRASS UNLIMITED—Box 111, Broad Run, VA 22014–0111. Peter V. Kuykendall, Ed. Articles, to 3,500 words, on bluegrass and traditional country music. Photos. Pays 8¢ to 10¢ a word, extra for photos.

CAMERA & DARKROOM—9171 Wilshire Blvd., Suite 300, Beverly Hills, CA 90210. Ana Jones, Ed. Articles on photographic techniques and photographic portfolios, 1,000 to 2,500 words, with photos, for all levels of photographers. Pays $100 to $750. Query.

677

CLASSICAL MUSIC MAGAZINE—(formerly *Music Magazine*) Suite 207, 121 Lakeshore Rd. E., Mississauga, Ont., Canada L5G 1E5. Anthony Copperthwaite, Pub. Feature articles, 1,500 to 3,500 words, and short pieces, to 500 words. Interviews, personality profiles, book reviews, historical articles, some human interest. "All articles should pertain to the world of classical music. No academic analysis. A solidly researched historical article with source references, or an interview with a famous classical personality are your best bets." Guidelines. Pays $100 to $500 (Canadian) for articles, $35 to $75 for short pieces, on publication.

CLAVIER MAGAZINE—200 Northfield Rd., Northfield, IL 60093. Kingsley Day, Ed. Practical articles, interviews, master classes, and humor pieces, 2,000 words, for keyboard performers and teachers. Pays $40 to $80 per published page, on publication.

DANCE MAGAZINE—33 W. 60th St., New York, NY 10023. Richard Philp, Ed.-in-Chief. Features on dance, personalities, techniques, health issues, and trends. Photos. Query; limited free-lance market.

DANCE TEACHER NOW—3020 Beacon Blvd., West Sacramento, CA 95691–3436. K.C. Patrick, Ed. Articles, 1,000 to 3,000 words, for professional dance educators, senior students, and other dance professionals on practical information for the teacher and/or business owner, economic and historical issues related to the profession. Profiles of schools, methods, and people who are leaving their mark on dance. Must be thoroughly researched. Pays $200 to $350, on acceptance. Query preferred.

DRAMATICS—Educational Theatre Assoc., 3368 Central Pkwy., Cincinnati, OH 45225–2392. Don Corathers, Ed. Articles, interviews, how-tos, 750 to 4,000 words, for high school students on the performing arts with an emphasis on theater practice: acting, directing, playwriting, technical subjects. Prefer articles that "could be used by a better-than-average high school teacher to teach students something about the performing arts." Pays $25 to $300 honorarium. Complete manuscripts preferred; graphics and photos accepted.

THE ENGRAVERS JOURNAL—26 Summit St., P. O. Box 318, Brighton, MI 48116. Rosemary Farrell, Man. Ed. Articles, varying lengths, on topics related to the engraving industry and small business operations. Pays $60 to $175, on acceptance. Query.

FILM QUARTERLY—Univ. of California Press Journals, 2120 Berkeley Way, Berkeley, CA 94720. Ann Martin, Ed. Historical, analytical, and critical articles, to 6,000 words; film reviews, book reviews. Guidelines.

FLUTE TALK—Instrumentalist Publishing Co., 200 Northfield Rd., Northfield, IL 60093. Kathleen Goll-Wilson, Ed. Articles, 6 to 12 typed pages, on flute performance, music, and pedagogy; fillers; photos and line drawings. Thorough knowledge of music or the instrument a must. Pays honorarium, on publication. Queries preferred.

THE FUTURE, NOW: INNOVATIVE VIDEO—Blue Feather Co., N8494 Poplar Grove Rd., P.O. Box 669, New Glarus, WI 53574–0669. Jennifer M. Jarik, Ed. Bimonthly. Articles, to 2 pages, on new ideas in the video business. Pays from $75 to $150, on publication.

GUITAR PLAYER MAGAZINE—20085 Stevens Creek, Cupertino, CA 95014. Articles, 1,500 to 5,000 words, on guitarists, guitars, and related subjects. Pays $100 to $400, on acceptance. Buys one-time and reprint rights.

INDIA CURRENTS—P.O. Box 21285, San Jose, CA 95151. Arvind Kumar, Submissions Ed. Fiction, to 1,500 words, and articles, to 800 words, on Indian culture in the United States and Canada. Articles on Indian arts, entertainment, and dining. Also music reviews, 300 words; book reviews, 300 to 400 words; commentary on national or international events affecting the lives of Indians, 800 words. Pays in subscriptions. Guidelines.

INDUSTRIAL PHOTOGRAPHY—445 Broadhollow Rd., Melville, NY 11747. Steve Shaw, Ed. Articles on techniques and trends in current professional photography; audiovisuals, etc., for industrial photographers and executives. Query.

KEYBOARD MAGAZINE—20085 Stevens Creek, Cupertino, CA 95014. Dominic Milano, Ed. Articles, 1,000 to 5,000 words, on keyboard instruments, MIDI and computer technology, and players. Photos. Pays $175 to $500, on acceptance. Query.

MEDIA HISTORY DIGEST—c/o *Editor & Publisher*, 11 W. 19th St., New York, NY 10011. Hiley H. Ward, Ed. Articles, 1,500 to 2,000 words, on the history of media, for wide consumer audience. Puzzles and humor related to media history. Pays varying rates, on publication. Query.

MODERN DRUMMER—870 Pompton Ave., Cedar Grove, NJ 07009. Ronald L. Spagnardi, Ed. Articles, 500 to 2,000 words, on drumming: how-tos, interviews. Pays $50 to $500, on publication.

MUSIC MAGAZINE—See *Classical Music Magazine.*

NEW ENGLAND ENTERTAINMENT DIGEST—P.O. Box 313, Portland, CT 06480. Bob Taylor, Ed. News, features and reviews on the arts and entertainment industry in New England. Pays $10 to $25, on publication.

OPERA NEWS—The Metropolitan Opera Guild, 70 Lincoln Center Plaza, New York, NY 10023–6593. Patrick J. Smith, Ed. Articles, 600 to 2,500 words, on all aspects of opera. Pays 20¢ a word, on publication. Query.

PERFORMANCE—1203 Lake St., Suite 200, Fort Worth, TX 76102–4504. Don Waitt, Pub./Ed.-in-Chief. Reports on the touring industry: concert promoters, booking agents, concert venues and clubs, as well as support services, such as lighting, sound and staging companies.

PETERSEN'S PHOTOGRAPHIC—6420 Wilshire Blvd., Los Angeles, CA 90048–5515. Jenni Bidner, Ed. Articles and how-to pieces, with photos, on travel, video, and darkroom photography, for beginners, advanced amateurs, and professionals. Pays $60 per printed page, on publication.

PLAYBILL—52 Vanderbilt Ave., New York, NY 10017. Joan Alleman, Ed.-in-Chief. Sophisticated articles, 700 to 1,800 words, with photos, on theater and subjects of interest to theatergoers. Pays $100 to $500, on acceptance.

POPULAR PHOTOGRAPHY—1633 Broadway, New York, NY 10019. Jason Schneider, Ed.-in-Chief. How-to articles, 500 to 2,000 words, for amateur photographers. Query with outline and photos.

PREVUE—P.O. Box 974, Reading, PA 19603. J. Steranko, Ed. Lively articles, interviews, and illustrated features, 4 to 25 pages, on women and the arts (film and TV actresses, singers, comics, dancers, strippers, artists, celebrities, models, etc.). Pays varying rates, on acceptance. Query with clips.

ROLLING STONE—1290 Ave. of the Americas, 2nd Fl., New York, NY 10104. Magazine of American music, culture, and politics. No fiction. Query; no unsolicited manuscripts. Rarely accepts free-lance material.

SHEET MUSIC MAGAZINE—223 Katonah Ave., Katonah, NY 10536. Josephine Sblendorio, Man. Ed. Pieces, 1,000 to 2,000 words, for pianists and organists, on musicians and composers, how-tos, and book reviews, to 500 words; no hard rock or heavy metal subjects. Pays $75 to $200, on publication.

STORYTELLING MAGAZINE—P.O. Box 309, Jonesborough, TN 37659. Articles, 800 to 2,500 words, related to storytelling. Profiles, 800 words, on people who tell stories via various arts and media. "We publish articles about the people, applications, traditions, and impact of storytelling. No personal essays, travel pieces, fiction, how-tos, or poetry." Pays 8¢ to 10¢ a word.

SUN TRACKS—Box 2510, Phoenix, AZ 85002. Robert Baird, Music Ed. Music section of *New Times*. Long and short features, record reviews, and interviews. Pays $25 to $500, on publication. Query.

TDR (THE DRAMA REVIEW): A JOURNAL OF PERFORMANCE STUDIES—721 Broadway, 6th Fl., New York, NY 10003. Edward David Miller, Man. Ed. Eclectic articles on experimental performance and performance theory; cross-cultural, examining the social, political, historical, and theatrical contexts in which performance happens. Submit query or manuscript with SASE. Pays $100 to $250, on publication.

THEATRE CRAFTS MAGAZINE—135 Fifth Ave., New York, NY 10010. Patricia MacKay, Pub. David Barbour, Ed. Articles, 500 to 2,500 words, on design, technical, and management aspects of theater, opera, dance, television, and film for those in performing arts and the entertainment trade. Pays on acceptance. Query.

U.S. ART—220 S. Sixth St., Suite 500, Minneapolis, MN 55402. Frank J. Sisser, Ed./Pub. Features and artist profiles, 2,000 words, for collectors of limited-edition art prints. Query. Pays $400 to $450, within 30 days of acceptance.

VIDEO MAGAZINE—460 W. 34th St., New York, NY 10001. Stan Pinkwas, Man. Ed. How-to and service articles on home video equipment, technology, and programming. Human-interest features related to above subjects, from 300 to 2,000 words. Pays varying rates, on acceptance. Query.

VIDEOMAKER—P.O. Box 4591, Chico, CA 95927. Stephen Muratore, Ed. Authoritative, how-to articles geared to hobbyist and professional video camera/camcorder users: instructionals, editing, desktop video, audio and video production, innovative applications, tools and tips, industry developments, new products, etc. Pays varying rates, on publication. Queries preferred.

WASHINGTON JOURNALISM REVIEW—see *American Journalism Review*.

HOBBIES, CRAFTS, COLLECTING

ALL ABOUT BEER—Bosak Publishing, 4764 Galicia Way, Oceanside, CA 92056. Bunny Bosak, Assoc. Ed. Bimonthly. Articles on breweries and beer. Queries preferred. Pays varying rates, after publication.

AMERICAN WOODWORKER—Rodale Press, 33 E. Minor St., Emmaus, PA 18098. David Sloan, Ed. "A how-to bimonthly for the woodworking enthusiast." Technical or anecdotal articles, to 2,000 words, relating to woodworking or furniture design. Fillers, drawings, slides and photos considered. Pays from $150 per published page, on publication; regular contributors paid on acceptance. Queries preferred. Guidelines.

ANTIQUE MONTHLY—2100 Powers Ferry Rd., Atlanta, GA 30339.

Cynthia Gorley, Ed.-in-Chief. Articles, 750 to 1,200 words, on trends and the exhibition and sales (auctions, antique shops, etc.) of decorative arts and antiques, with B&W photos or color slides. Heavy emphasis on antique news and timely material. Pays varying rates, on publication.

THE ANTIQUE TRADER WEEKLY—Box 1050, Dubuque, IA 52004. Kyle D. Husfloen, Ed. Articles, 1,000 to 2,000 words, on all types of antiques and collectors' items. Photos. Pays from $25 to $200, on publication. Query preferred. Buys all rights.

ANTIQUES & AUCTION NEWS—P.O. Box 500, Mount Joy, PA 17552. Weekly newspaper. Factual articles, 600 to 1,500 words, on antiques, collectors, collections, and places of historic interest. Photos. Query required. Pays $5 to $20, after publication.

ANTIQUEWEEK—P.O. Box 90, Knightstown, IN 46148. Tom Hoepf, Ed., Central Edition; Connie Swaim, Ed., Eastern Edition. Weekly antique, auction, and collectors' newspaper. Articles, 500 to 1,500 words, on antiques, collectibles, restorations, genealogy, auction and antique show reports. Photos. Pays from $40 to $150 for in-depth articles, on publication. Query. Guidelines.

AOPA PILOT—421 Aviation Way, Frederick, MD 21701. Mark R. Twombly, Ed. Magazine of the Aircraft Owners and Pilots Assn. Articles, to 2,500 words, with photos, on general aviation for beginning and experienced pilots. Pays to $750.

AUTOGRAPH COLLECTOR MAGAZINE—510-A S. Corona Mall, Corona, CA 91720. Kevin Sherman, Ed. Articles, 1,000 to 3,500 words, on all areas of autograph collecting: preservation, framing, and storage, specialty collections, documents and letters, collectors and dealers. Queries preferred. Payment varies.

BIRD TALK—Box 6050, Mission Viejo, CA 92690. Julie Rach, Ed. Articles for pet bird owners: care and feeding, training, safety, outstanding personal adventures, exotic birds in their native countries, profiles of celebrities' pet birds, travel to bird parks or shows. Pays 10¢ a word, after publication. Query or send manuscript; good transparencies a plus.

BIRD WATCHER'S DIGEST—P.O. Box 110, Marietta, OH 45750. Mary B. Bowers, Ed. Articles, 600 to 3,000 words, on bird-watching experiences and expeditions: information about rare sightings; updates on endangered species. Pays from $50, on publication. Allow eight weeks for response.

THE BLADE MAGAZINE—P.O. Box 22007, Chattanooga, TN 37422. J. Bruce Voyles, Pub./Ed. Articles, 500 to 1,500 words: historical pieces on knives and old knife factories, etc.; interviews; celebrities who use/collect knives; trends in knives, handmade and factory; values on collectible knives and knife accessories; how to sharpen knives, etc. Study magazine first. Pays from $200, on publication.

CANADIAN STAMP NEWS—103 Lakeshore Rd., Suite 202, St. Catharines, Ont., Canada L2N 2T6. Ellen Rodger, Ed. Biweekly. Articles, 1,000 to 2,000 words, on stamp collecting news, rare and unusual stamps, and auction and club reports. Special issues throughout the year; ask for guidelines. Photos. Pays from $70, on publication.

CANADIAN WORKSHOP MAGAZINE—130 Spy Ct., Markham, Ont., Canada L3R 5H6. Erina Kelly, Ed. Articles, 1,500 to 2,800 words, on do-it-yourself home renovations, energy saving projects, etc., with photos. Pays varying rates, on publication.

CARD COLLECTOR'S PRICE GUIDE—155 E. Ames Ct., Plainview, NY 11803. Address Ed. Office. Articles, from 800 words, related to non-sports, auto racing, boxing, golf, minor league baseball, and soccer cards; collecting and investing; fillers. Queries preferred. Pays 10¢ a word, on publication.

CARD PLAYER—1455 E. Tropicana Ave., Suite 450, Las Vegas, NV 89119. June Field, Ed./Pub. "The Magazine for Those Who Play to Win." Articles on events, personalities, legal issues, new casinos, tournaments, and prizes. Also articles on strategies, theory and game psychology to improve play. Occasionally use humor, cartoons, puzzles, or anecdotal material. Pays $50 to $200 for articles, $25 to $35 for fillers, on publication. Guidelines.

THE CAROUSEL NEWS & TRADER—87 Park Ave. W., Suite 206, Mansfield, OH 44902. Noreene M. Sweeney, Assoc. Ed. Features on carousel history and profiles of amusement park operators and carousel carvers of interest to band organ enthusiasts, carousel art collectors, preservationists, amusement park owners, artists, and restorationists. Pays $50 per published page, after publication. Guidelines.

CHESS LIFE—186 Rte. 9W, New Windsor, NY 12553–7698. Glenn Petersen, Ed. Articles, 500 to 3,000 words, for members of the U.S. Chess Federation, on news, profiles, technical aspects of chess. Features on all aspects of chess: history, humor, puzzles, etc. Photos. Pays varying rates, on acceptance. Query; limited free-lance market.

COLLECTING TOYS—21027 Crossroads Cir., Waukesha, WI 53187. Jim Bunte, Ed. Bimonthly. Articles of varying lengths for a "nostalgia/collecting magazine that recalls the great toys of the 1940s and '70s." Profiles of toy collectors, designers, and manufacturers; articles for toy collectors. Color photos. Pays 7¢ a word, on acceptance.

COLLECTOR EDITIONS—170 Fifth Ave., New York, NY 10010. Joan Muyskens Pursley, Ed. Articles, 750 to 1,500 words, on collectibles, mainly contemporary limited-edition figurines, plates, and prints. Pays $150 to $350, within 30 days of acceptance. Query with photos.

COLLECTORS NEWS—P.O. Box 156, Grundy Center, IA 50638. Linda Kruger, Ed. Articles, to 1,000 words, on private collections, antiques, and collectibles, especially 20th-century nostalgia, Americana, glass and china, music, furniture, transportation, timepieces, jewelry, farm-related collectibles, and lamps; include B&W photos. Pays $1 per column inch; $25 for front-page color photos, on publication.

COMIC BOOK COLLECTOR—155 E. Ames Ct., Plainview, NY 11803. Address Ed. Dept. Articles, from 800 words, related to comic books, comic characters, cartoons, etc.; collecting and investing; fillers. Queries preferred. Pays 10¢ a word, on publication.

COUNTRY FOLK ART MAGAZINE—8393 E. Holly Rd., Holly, MI 48442–8819. Tanya Lane, Man. Ed. Historical, gardening, collectibles, and how-to pieces, 750 to 2,000 words, with a creative slant on American folk art. Pays $150 to $300, on acceptance. Submit pieces on seasonal topics one year in advance.

COUNTRY HANDCRAFTS—5400 S. 60th St., Greendale, WI 53129. Kathy Pohl, Exec. Ed. All types of craft designs (needlepoint, quilting, woodworking, etc.) with complete instructions and full-size patterns. Pays from $50 to $300, on acceptance, for all rights.

CRAFTS 'N THINGS—Dept. W, 701 Lee St., Suite 1000, Des Plaines, IL 60016–4570. Julie Stephani, Ed. How-to articles on all kinds of crafts projects, with instructions. Send manuscript with instructions and photograph of the finished item. Pays $50 to $250, on acceptance.

CROSS-STITCH SAMPLER—P.O. Box 413, Chester Heights, PA 19017. Deborah N. DeSimone, Ed. Articles, 500 to 1,500 words, about counted cross-stitch, drawn thread, or themes revolving around stitching (samplers, needlework tools, etc.). Queries required. Pays varying rates, on acceptance.

DOLL LIFE—243 Newton-Sparta Rd., Newton, NJ 07860. Michele Epstein, Ed. Bimonthly. Articles, 500 to 1,500 words, on antique, folk, and craft dolls. Profiles of doll artists and how-to pieces for doll makers. Pays 15¢ a word, on publication.

DOLL WORLD—(formerly *International Doll World*) 306 E. Parr Rd., Berne, IN 46711. Beth Schwartz, Ed. Informational articles about doll collecting.

DOLLS, THE COLLECTOR'S MAGAZINE—170 Fifth Ave., New York, NY 10010. Joan Muyskens Pursley, Ed. Articles, 500 to 2,500 words, for knowledgeable doll collectors; sharply focused with a strong collecting angle, and concrete information (value, identification, restoration, etc.). Pays $100 to $350, after acceptance. Query.

EDGES—P.O. Box 22007, Chattanooga, TN 37422. J. Bruce Voyles, Pub. Articles, 500 to 1,500 words, on collectible knives: combat, antique, modern, handmade, and commemorative knives, with value charts for each knife mentioned in the article.

FIBERARTS—50 College St., Asheville, NC 28801. Ann Batchelder, Ed. Published five times yearly. Articles, 400 to 1,200 words, on contemporary trends in fiber sculpture, weaving, surface design, quilting, stitchery, papermaking, felting, basketry, and wearable art. Query with photos of subject, outline, and synopsis. Pays varying rates, on publication.

FINESCALE MODELER—P.O. Box 1612, Waukesha, WI 53187. Bob Hayden, Ed. How-to articles for people who make nonoperating scale models of aircraft, automobiles, boats, figures. Photos and drawings should accompany articles. One-page model-building hints and tips. Pays from $30 per published page, on acceptance. Query preferred.

GAMES—19 W. 21st St., New York, NY 10010. Will Shortz, Ed. Articles on games and playful, offbeat subjects. Quizzes, tests, brainteasers, etc. Pays top rates, on publication.

THE HOME SHOP MACHINIST—2779 Aero Park Dr., Box 1810, Traverse City, MI 49685. Joe D. Rice, Ed. How-to articles on precision metalworking and foundry work. Accuracy and attention to detail a must. Pays $40 per published page, extra for photos and illustrations, on publication. Send SASE for guidelines.

INTERNATIONAL DOLL WORLD—See *Doll World.*

KITPLANES—P.O. Box 6050, Mission Viejo, CA 92690. Dave Martin, Ed. Articles geared to the growing market of aircraft built from kits and plans by home craftsmen, on all aspects of design, construction, and performance, 1,000 to 4,000 words. Pays $60 per page, on publication.

LOST TREASURE—P.O. Box 1589, Grove, OK 74344. Grace Michael, Man. Ed. How-to articles, legends, folklore, and stories of lost treasures. Also publishes *Treasure Facts* (bimonthly): how-to information for treasure hunters, club news, who's who in treasure hunting, tips, etc. *Treasure Cache* (annual): articles on documented treasure caches with sidebar telling how to search for cache highlighted in article. Pays 4¢ a word, $5 for photos, $100 for cover photos.

MILITARY HISTORY—602 S. King St., Suite 300, Leesburg, VA 22075. C.

Brian Kelly, Ed. Bimonthly on the strategy, tactics, and personalities of military history. Department pieces, 2,000 words, on espionage, weaponry, personalities, and travel. Features, 4,000 words, with 500-word sidebars. Pays $200 to $400, on publication. Query. Guidelines.

MODEL RAILROADER—21027 Crossroads Cir., Waukesha, WI 53187. Russ Larson, Ed. Articles on model railroads, with photos of layout and equipment. Pays $90 per printed page, on acceptance. Query.

NEEDLEWORK RETAILER—117 Alexander Ave., P.O. Box 724, Ames, IA 50010. Anne Brafford, Ed. Articles, 500 to 1,000 words, on how to run a small needlework business or anything related to the needlework trade. "Writers must have a background in needlework; we don't want general articles about small businesses." Pays varying rates, on acceptance.

NEW ENGLAND ANTIQUES JOURNAL—4 Church St., Ware, MA 01082. Jody Young, Gen. Mgr. Well-researched articles, to 2,500 words, on antiques of interest to collectors and/or dealers, auction and antiques show reviews, to 1,000 words, antiques market news, to 500 words; photos desired. Pays to $150, on publication. Query or send manuscript. Reports in two to four weeks.

NOSTALGIA WORLD—Box 231, North Haven, CT 06473. Richard Mason, Jr., Ed. Features, 3,000 words, and other articles, 1,500 words, on all kinds of collectibles: records, TV memorabilia (Munsters, Star Trek, Dark Shadows, Elvira, etc.), comics, gum cards, toys, sheet music, monsters, magazines, dolls, movie posters, etc. Pays $10 to $25, on publication.

NUTSHELL NEWS—21027 Crossroads Cir., P.O. Box 1612, Waukesha, WI 53187. Sybil Harp, Ed. Articles, 1,200 to 1,500 words, for dollhouse-scale miniatures enthusiasts, collectors, craftspeople, and hobbyists. Interested in artisan profiles, tours of collections, and how-to projects. "Writers must be knowledgeable miniaturists." Color slides or B&W prints required. Pays $50 per published page, on acceptance. Query.

POPULAR MECHANICS—224 W. 57th St., New York, NY 10019. Deborah Frank, Man. Ed. Articles, 300 to 2,000 words, on latest developments in mechanics, industry, science; features on hobbies with a mechanical slant; how-tos on home, shop, and crafts projects; features on outdoor adventures, boating, and electronics. Photos and sketches a plus. Pays to $1,500; to $300 for short pieces, on acceptance. Buys all rights.

POPULAR WOODWORKING—1041 Shary Cir., Concord, CA 94518. Robert C. Cook, Ed. Project articles, to 2,000 words; techniques pieces, to 1,500 words; anecdotes and essays, to 1,000 words, for the "modest production woodworker, small shop owner, wood craftsperson, advanced hobbyist and woodcarver." Pays $500 to $1,000 for large, complicated projects; $100 to $500 for small projects and other features; half on acceptance, half on publication. Query with brief outline and photo of finished project.

QUICK & EASY CRAFTS—306 E. Parr Rd., Berne, IN 46711. Beth Schwartz, Ed. How-to and instructional needlecrafts and other arts and crafts, book reviews, and tips. Photos. Pays varying rates, before publication.

RAILROAD MODEL CRAFTSMAN—P.O. Box 700, Newton, NJ 07860–0700. William C. Schaumburg, Ed. How-to articles on scale model railroading; cars, operation, scenery, etc. Pays on publication.

R/C MODELER MAGAZINE—P.O. Box 487, Sierra Madre, CA 91025. Patricia E. Crews, Ed. Technical and semi-technical how-to articles on radio-controlled model aircraft, boats, helicopters, and cars. Query.

RESTORATION—P.O. Box 50046, Tucson, AZ 85703–1046. W.R. Haessner, Ed. Articles, 1,200 to 1,800 words, on restoring and building chairs, machines, toys, boats, autos, trucks, planes, trains, toys, tools, etc. Photos and art required. Pays $50 per page, on publication. Query.

SCHOOL MATES—U.S. Chess Federation, 186 Rte. 9W, New Windsor, NY 12553–7698. Jennie L. Simon, Ed. Articles, to 1,000 words, and short fillers, related to chess for beginning chess players (not necessarily children). "Instructive, but there is room for fun puzzles, anecdotes, etc. All chess related. Articles on chessplaying celebrities are always of interest to us." Pays about $40 per 1,000 words, on publication. Query; limited free-lance market.

SEW NEWS—P.O. Box 1790, News Plaza, Peoria, IL 61656. Linda Turner Griepentrog, Ed. Articles, to 3,000 words, "that teach a specific technique, inspire a reader to try new sewing projects, or inform a reader about an interesting person, company, or project related to sewing, textiles, or fashion." Emphasis is on fashion (not craft) sewing. Pays $25 to $400, on acceptance. Queries required; no unsolicited manuscripts accepted.

SPORTS CARD TRADER—155 E. Ames Ct., Plainview, NY 11803. Address Ed. Office. Articles, from 1,000 words, related to baseball, football, basketball, and hockey cards; fillers on collecting and investing. Queries preferred. Pays 10¢ a word, on publication.

SPORTS COLLECTORS DIGEST—Krause Publications, 700 E. State St., Iola, WI 54990. Tom Mortenson, Ed. Articles, 750 to 2,000 words, on old baseball card sets and other sports memorabilia and collectibles. Pays $50 to $100, on publication.

TEDDY BEAR REVIEW—Collector Communications Corp., 170 Fifth Ave., New York, NY 10010. Steve Cronk, Man. Ed. Articles on antique and contemporary teddy bears for makers, collectors, and enthusiasts. Pays $50 to $200, within 30 days of acceptance. Query with photos.

THREADS MAGAZINE—Taunton Press, 63 S. Main St., Box 5506, Newtown, CT 06470. Address the Eds. Bimonthly. Articles and department pieces about materials, tools, techniques, people, and design in sewing and textile arts, especially in garment making, knitting, quilting, and stitchery. Pays $150 per published page, on publication.

TREASURE CACHE, TREASURE FACTS—See *Lost Treasure.*

TROPICAL FISH HOBBYIST—1 T.F.H. Plaza, Neptune City, NJ 07753. Ray Hunziker, Ed. Articles, 500 to 3,000 words, for beginning and experienced tropical and marine fish enthusiasts. Photos. Pays $35 to $250, on acceptance. Query.

WEST ART—Box 6868, Auburn, CA 95604–6868. Martha Garcia, Ed. Features, 350 to 700 words, on fine arts and crafts. No hobbies. Photos. Pays 50¢ per column inch, on publication. SASE required.

WESTERN & EASTERN TREASURES—P.O. Box 1095, Arcata, CA 95521. Rosemary Anderson, Man. Ed. Illustrated articles, to 1,500 words, on treasure hunting and how-to metal detecting tips. Pays 2¢ a word, extra for photos, on publication.

WIN MAGAZINE—16760 Stagg St., #213, Van Nuys, CA 91406–1642. Cecil Suzuki, Ed. Gambling-related articles, 1,000 to 3,000 words. Pays on publication.

WOODENBOAT MAGAZINE—P.O. Box 78, Brooklin, ME 04616. Jonathan Wilson, Ed. How-to and technical articles, 4,000 words, on construction, repair, and maintenance of wooden boats; design, history, and use of wooden boats; and profiles of outstanding wooden boat builders and designers. Pays $150 to $200 per 1,000 words. Query preferred.

WORKBASKET MAGAZINE—700 W. 47th St., Suite 310, Kansas City, MO 64112. Kay M. Olson, Ed. Instructions and models for original knit, crochet, and tat items. (Designs must fit theme of issue.) How-tos on crafts and gardening, 400 to 1,200 words, with photos. Pays on acceptance; negotiable rates for instructional items.

WORKBENCH—700 W. 47th St., Suite 310, Kansas City, MO 64112. Robert N. Hoffman, Exec. Ed. Articles on do-it-yourself home improvement and maintenance projects and general woodworking articles for beginning and expert craftsmen. Complete working drawings with accurate dimensions, step-by-step instructions, lists of materials, in-progress photos, and photos of the finished product must accompany submission. Queries welcome. Pays from $150 per published page, on acceptance.

YELLOWBACK LIBRARY—P.O. Box 36172, Des Moines, IA 50315. Gil O'Gara, Ed. Articles, 300 to 2,000 words, on boys'/girls' series literature (*Hardy Boys, Nancy Drew, Tom Swift*, etc.) for collectors, researchers, and dealers. "Especially welcome are interviews with, or articles by past and present writers of juvenile series fiction." Pays in copies.

YESTERYEAR—P.O. Box 2, Princeton, WI 54968. Michael Jacobi, Ed. Articles on antiques and collectibles for readers in Wisconsin, Illinois, Iowa, Minnesota, and surrounding states. Photos. Will consider regular columns on collecting or antiques. Pays from $10, on publication. Limited market.

ZYMURGY—Box 1679, Boulder, CO 80306–1679. Elizabeth V. Gold, Ed. Articles appealing to beer lovers and homebrewers. Pays in merchandise and books. Query.

POPULAR & TECHNICAL SCIENCE, COMPUTERS

A+/INCIDER—See *MacComputing*.

AD ASTRA—National Space Society, 922 Pennsylvania Ave. S.E., Washington, DC 20003–2140. Richard Wagner, Ed.-in-Chief. Lively, non-technical features, to 3,000 words, on all aspects of international space program. Particularly interested in "Living in Space" articles; space settlements; lunar and Mars bases. Pays $150 to $200, on publication. Query. Guidelines.

AIR & SPACE—370 L'Enfant Promenade, 10th Fl., Washington, DC 20024–2518. George Larson, Ed. General-interest articles, 1,000 to 3,500 words, on aerospace experience, past, present, and future; travel, space, history, biographies, essays, commentary. Pays varying rates, on acceptance. Query.

AMERICAN HERITAGE OF INVENTION & TECHNOLOGY—60 Fifth Ave., New York, NY 10011. Frederick Allen, Ed. Articles, 2,000 to 5,000 words, on history of technology in America, for the sophisticated general reader. Query. Pays on acceptance.

AMIGA WORLD—IDG Communications, 80 Elm St., Peterborough, NH 03458. Dennis Brisson, Ed.-in-Chief. Ann Record, News Ed. Barbara Gefvert, Features Ed. Tim Walsh, Reviews Ed. Articles, 1,500 to 3,000 words: product roundups and comparisons of major products, explanations of new technologies, applications and programming tutorials relating to Amiga systems. Single and comparative reviews, 300 to 1,500 words, on just-released Amiga hardware and software products, 500-word news pieces on Amiga-related events; profiles of interesting Amiga applications/users. Pays $75 to $700, on publication. Query preferred; include credentials.

ARCHAEOLOGY—135 William St., New York, NY 10038. Peter A. Young, Ed.-in-Chief. Articles on archaeology by professionals or lay people with a solid knowledge of the field. Pays $250 to $500, on publication. Query required.

ASSIST—Ziff Institute, 25 First St., Cambridge, MA 02141. Barbara Bourassa, Ed. Articles, 200 to 800 words, focusing on technology, workplace or professional development issues, or trends of interest to computer training and support personnel. Query. Send SASE for sample issue. Pays 50¢ to 75¢ a word.

ASTRONOMY—P.O. Box 1612, Waukesha, WI 53187. Robert Burnham, Ed. Articles on astronomy, astrophysics, space programs, research. Hobby pieces on equipment; short news items. Pays varying rates, on acceptance.

BIOSCIENCE—American Institute of Biological Science, 730 11th St. N.W., Washington, DC 20001. Anna Maria Gillis, Features Ed. Articles, 2 to 4 journal pages, on new developments in biology or on science policy, for professional biologists. Style should be journalistic. Pays $300 per journal page, on publication. Query required.

BYTE MAGAZINE—One Phoenix Mill Ln., Peterborough, NH 03458. Dennis Allen, Ed. Features on new technology, and reviews of computers and software, varying lengths, for technically advanced users of personal computers. Payment is competitive. Query. Guidelines.

COMPUTE—324 W. Wendover Ave., Suite 200, Greensboro, NC 27408–8439. Clifton Karnes, Ed. In-depth feature articles on using the personal computer at home, work, and school. Industry news, interviews with leaders in the PC field, product information, hardware and software reviews. For users of IBM, IBM PC, and compatibles.

COMPUTERCRAFT—76 N. Broadway, Hicksville, NY 11801. Art Salsberg, Ed.-in-Chief. How-to features, technical tutorials, servicing and construction projects related to personal computer and microcontroller equipment and software. Emphasizes enhancements, modifications, and applications. Lengths vary. Query with outline required. Pays $90 to $150 per published page, on acceptance.

DATA COMMUNICATIONS AND DATA COMMUNICATIONS INTERNATIONAL—1221 Ave. of the Americas, New York, NY 10020. Joseph Braue, Ed.-in-Chief. Technical articles, 2,000 words, on communications networks. Readers are managers of multinational computer networks. Payment varies; made on acceptance and on publication.

ELECTRONICS NOW—(formerly *Radio-Electronics*) 500-B Bi-County Blvd., Farmingdale, NY 11735. Brian C. Fenton, Ed. Technical articles, 1,500 to 3,000 words, on all areas related to electronics. Pays $50 to $500 or more, on acceptance.

ENVIRONMENT—1319 18th St. N.W., Washington, DC 20036–1802. Barbara T. Richman, Man. Ed. Factual articles, 2,500 to 5,000 words, on scientific, technological, and environmental policy and decision-making issues. Pays $100 to $300. Query.

THE FUTURIST—World Future Society, 7910 Woodmont Ave., Suite 450, Bethesda, MD 20814. Cynthia G. Wagner, Man. Ed. Features, 1,000 to 5,000 words, on subjects pertaining to the future: environment, education, business, science, technology, etc. Submit complete manuscript with brief bio (or CV) and SASE. Pays in copies.

HOBSON'S CHOICE: SCIENCE FICTION AND TECHNOLOGY—The Starwind Press, P.O. Box 98, Ripley, OH 45167. Address Submissions Ed. Articles and literary criticism, 1,000 to 5,000 words, for readers interested in science and technology. Also science fiction and fantasy, 2,000 to 10,000 words. Query for nonfiction. Pays 1¢ to 4¢ a word, on publication.

HOME OFFICE COMPUTING—Scholastic, Inc., 730 Broadway, New York, NY 10003. Cathy G. Brower, Man. Ed. Articles of interest to people operating businesses out of their homes: product roundups, profiles of successful businesses, marketing and financial tips and advice. Payment varies, on acceptance.

INFOMART MAGAZINE—Infomart Corporate Communications, 1950 Stemmons Fwy., Suite 6038, Dallas, TX 75207. Aaron Woods, Ed. Articles, 800 to 1,200 words, on business applications of information systems and data processing managers. Query. Payment is negotiable.

THE JOURNAL OF IRREPRODUCIBLE RESULTS—Wisdom Simulators, P.O. Box 380853, Cambridge, MA 02238. Marc Abrahams, Ed. Science humor, science reports and analysis, one to four pages. Brief science-related poetry. B&W photos. "This journal is the place to find the mischievous, funny, iconoclastic side of science." Guidelines. No payment.

LINK-UP—2222 River Dr., King George, VA 22485. Loraine Page, Ed. Dir. How-to pieces, hardware and software reviews, and current trends, 600 to 2,500 words, for business professionals who use computers and modems at work and at home. Book reviews, 500 to 800 words. Pays $90 to $220; $55 for book reviews, on publication.

MACCOMPUTING—(formerly *A+/Incider*) Macworld Communications, 80 Elm St., Peterborough, NH 03458. Kelly Sewell, Feature Ed. Paul Statt, Reviews Ed. Features, 2,000 to 3,000 words, of interest to home, small-business, and educational Macintosh computer users. Product reviews, 500 to 2,000 words. Pays $750 to $1,000 for features, $200 to $500 for reviews, on acceptance. Query.

NATURAL HISTORY—American Museum of Natural History, Central Park West at 79th St., New York, NY 10024. Alan Ternes, Ed.-in-Chief. Informative articles, to 3,000 words, by experts, on anthropology and natural sciences. "Strongly recommend that writers send SASE for guidelines and read our magazine, before querying." Pays $1,000 for features, on acceptance. Query.

OMNI—324 W. Wendover Ave., Suite 205, Greensboro, NC 27408. Keith Ferrell, Ed. Articles, 750 to 3,500 words, on scientific aspects of the future: space colonies, cloning, machine intelligence, ESP, origin of life, future arts, lifestyles, etc. Pays $800 to $3,500; $175 for short items, on acceptance. Query.

PCM MAGAZINE—Falsoft, Inc., 9509 US Highway 42, P.O. Box 385, Prospect, KY 40059. Julie Hutchinson, Submissions Ed. Articles and computer programs for Tandy and IBM-compatible computers. Pays varying rates, on publication.

POPULAR ELECTRONICS—500-B Bi-County Blvd., Farmingdale, NY 11735. Carl Laron, Ed. Features, 1,500 to 2,500 words, for electronics hobbyists and experimenters. "Our readers are science and electronics oriented, understand computer theory and operation, and like to build electronics projects." Fillers and cartoons. Pays $25 to $500, on acceptance.

PUBLISH—Integrated Media, Inc., 501 Second St., San Francisco, CA 94107. Jake Widman, Ed.-in-Chief. Features, 1,200 to 2,000 words, and reviews, 300 to 800 words, on all aspects of computerized publishing. Pays $400 for short articles and reviews, $900 and up for full-length features and reviews, on acceptance.

RADIO-ELECTRONICS—See *Electronics Now.*

THE SCIENCES—2 E. 63rd St., New York, NY 10021. Peter G. Brown, Ed. Essays and features, 2,000 to 4,000 words, and book reviews, on all scientific disciplines. Pays honorarium, on publication. Query.

SEA FRONTIERS—400 S.E. Second Ave., 4th Fl., Miami, FL 33131. Bonnie Bilyeu Gordon, Ed. Illustrated articles, 500 to 3,000 words, on scientific advances related to the sea, biological, physical, chemical, or geological phenomena, ecology, conservation, etc., written in a popular style for lay readers. Send SASE for guidelines. Pays 25¢ a word, on acceptance. Query.

SHAREWARE MAGAZINE—1030D E. Duane Ave., Sunnyvale, CA 94086. Michael Callahan, Ed.-in-Chief. Keely Swenson, Asst. Ed. Reviews of shareware programs and articles on related topics, 1,000 to 4,000 words. Payment varies, on publication. Query.

TECHNOLOGY & LEARNING—Peter Li, Inc., 2169 E. Francisco Blvd., Suite A-4, San Rafael, CA 94901. Holly Brady, Ed. Articles, to 3,000 words, for teachers of grades K through 12, about uses of computers and related technology in the classroom: human-interest and philosophical articles, how-to pieces, software reviews, and hands-on ideas. Pay varies, on acceptance.

TECHNOLOGY REVIEW—MIT, W59-200, Cambridge, MA 02139. Steven J. Marcus, Ed. General-interest articles on technology and its implications. Pay varies, on publication. Query.

VERTICAL APPLICATION RESELLER—301 Gibraltar Dr., Box 650, Morris Plains, NJ 07950–0650. Tom Farre, Ed. Bimonthly. Articles, 500 to 1,200 words, that emphasize new technologies and products for readers who are computer systems and software "resellers." "If you know what the title of the magazine means, you probably have a good idea of what we're looking for." Query. Pays from $100, on acceptance.

WINDOWS USER—25 W. 39th St., New York, NY 10018. Rich Santalesa, Ed.-in-Chief. Product reviews and features. Submit two- to three-paragraph query that summarizes proposed article; include clips and/or qualifications. Submissions via MCI Mail (RSantalesa) or CompuServe (75300,3513) preferred. Pays 75¢ a word, on publication.

WORDPERFECT MAGAZINES—270 W. Center St., Orem, UT 84057. Camille Soderquist, Ed. Asst. Features, 1,400 to 1,800 words, and columns, 1,200 to 1,400 words, on how-to subjects with easy-to-follow instructions that familiarize readers with WordPerfect software. Humorous essays, 750 words, for "Final Keystrokes." Pays $400 to $700, on acceptance. Query.

ANIMALS

AMERICAN FARRIERS JOURNAL—P.O. Box 624, Brookfield, WI 53008–0624. Frank Lessiter, Ed. Articles, 800 to 2,000 words, on general farrier issues, hoof care, tool selection, equine lameness, and horse handling. Pays 30¢ per published line, $10 per published illustration or photo, on publication. Query.

ANIMALS—350 S. Huntington Ave., Boston, MA 02130. Joni Praded, Dir./ Ed. Informative, well-researched articles, to 2,500 words, on animal protection, national and international wildlife, pet care, conservation, and environmental issues that affect animals. No personal accounts or favorite pet stories. Pays from $350, on acceptance. Query.

BIRD TALK—Box 6050, Mission Viejo, CA 92690. Julie Rach, Ed. Articles for pet bird owners: care and feeding, training, safety, outstanding personal adventures, exotic birds in their native countries, profiles of celebrities' birds, travel to bird parks or bird shows. Pays 7¢ to 10¢ a word, after publication. Query or send manuscript; good transparencies a plus.

CAT FANCY—P.O. Box 6050, Mission Viejo, CA 92690. Debbie Phillips-Donaldson, Ed. Fiction and nonfiction, to 3,000 words, on cat care, health, grooming, etc. Pays 5¢ to 10¢ a word, on publication.

DAIRY GOAT JOURNAL—W. 2997 Markert Rd., Helenville, WI 53137. Dave Thompson, Ed. Articles, to 1,500 words, on successful dairy goat owners, youths and interesting people associated with dairy goats. "Especially interested in practical husbandry ideas." Photos. Pays $50 to $150, on publication. Query.

DOG FANCY—P. O. Box 6050, Mission Viejo, CA 92690. Kim Thornton, Ed. Articles, 1,500 to 3,000 words, on dog care, health, grooming, breeds, activities, events, etc. Photos. Payment varies, on publication.

EQUUS—Fleet Street Corp., 656 Quince Orchard Rd., Gaithersburg, MD 20878. Laurie Prinz, Deputy Man. Ed. Articles, 1,000 to 3,000 words, on all breeds of horses, covering their health and care as well as the latest advances in equine medicine and research. "Attempt to speak as one horseperson to another." Pays $100 to $400, on publication.

HORSE & RIDER—1060 Calle Cordillera, Suite 103, San Clemente, CA 92673. Juli Thorson, Ed. Sue M. Copeland, Man. Ed. Articles, 500 to 3,000 words, with photos, on western training and general horse care: feeding, health, grooming, etc. Pays varying rates, on publication. Buys one-time rights. Guidelines.

HORSEMEN'S YANKEE PEDLAR—785 Southbridge St., Auburn, MA 01501. Nancy L. Khoury, Pub. News and feature-length articles, about horses and horsemen in the Northeast. Photos. Pays $2 per published inch, on publication. Query.

HORSEPLAY—P.O. Box 130, Gaithersburg, MD 20884. Cordelia Doucet, Ed. Articles, 700 to 3,000 words, on eventing, show jumping, horse shows, dressage, driving, and fox hunting for horse enthusiasts. Profiles, instructional articles, occasional humor, and competition reports. Pays 10¢ a word, buys all rights, after publication. Query with SASE. Guidelines.

LLAMAS—P.O. Box 100, Herald, CA 95638. Cheryl Dal Porto, Ed. "The International Camelid Journal," published 7 times yearly. Articles, 300 to 3,000 words, of interest to llama and alpaca owners. Pays $25 to $300, extra for photos, on acceptance. Query.

MUSHING—P.O. Box 149, Ester, AK 99725–0149. Todd Hoener, Pub. How-tos, profiles, interviews, and features, 1,500 to 2,000 words, and department pieces, 500 to 1,000 words, for competitive and recreational dog drivers and skijorers. International audience. Photos. Pays $20 to $250, after acceptance. Queries preferred. Guidelines.

PRACTICAL HORSEMAN—Box 589, Unionville, PA 19375. Mandy Lorraine, Ed. How-to articles on English riding, training, and horse care. Pays on acceptance. Query with clips.

PURE-BRED DOGS/AMERICAN KENNEL GAZETTE—51 Madison Ave., New York, NY 10010. Beth Adelman, Exec. Ed. Dominique Davis, Features Ed. Articles, 1,000 to 2,500 words, relating to pure-bred dogs. Pays from $100 to $300, on acceptance. Query preferred.

SHEEP! MAGAZINE—W. 2997 Markert Rd., Helenville, WI 53137. Dave Thompson, Ed. Articles, to 1,500 words, on successful shepherds, woolcrafts, sheep raising, and sheep dogs. "Especially interested in people who raise sheep successfully as a sideline enterprise." Photos. Pays $15 to $150, extra for photos, on acceptance. Query.

TROPICAL FISH HOBBYIST—1 T.F.H. Plaza, Neptune City, NJ 07753. Ray Hunziker, Ed. Articles, 500 to 3,000 words, for beginning and experienced tropical and marine fish enthusiasts. Photos. Pays $35 to $250, on acceptance. Query.

WILDLIFE CONSERVATION—NYZS/The Wildlife Conservation Society, Bronx, NY 10460. Nancy Simmons, Sr. Ed. Articles, 1,500 to 2,000 words, that "probe conservation controversies to search for answers and help save threatened species." Payment varies, on acceptance. Guidelines.

TRUE CRIME

DETECTIVE CASES—See *Globe Communications Corp.*

DETECTIVE DRAGNET—See *Globe Communications Corp.*

DETECTIVE FILES—See *Globe Communications Corp.*

FRONT PAGE DETECTIVE—Reese Communications, Inc., 460 W. 34th St., New York, NY 10001. Rose Mandelsberg, Ed.-in-Chief. True detective stories, 5,000 to 6,000 words, with detective work, mystery, and some kind of twist. No fiction. Good color photos of victim, perpetrator, crime scene, or detective may accompany story. Pays $250 to $500 for articles, and up to $200 for photos. Query.

FUGITIVE!—848 Dodge Ave., Suite 240, Evanston, IL 60202. Lawrence Shulruff, Ed. Articles, 600 to 800 words, on unsolved crime and criminals at large. "Provide details about case. We encourage readers to contact police with tips about cases in each issue. Articles shouldn't be gory. Photos or composites of suspect are required." Query required. Pays $50 to $150, on acceptance.

GLOBE COMMUNICATIONS CORP.—1350 Sherbrooke St. West, Suite 600, Montreal, Quebec, Canada H3G 2T4. Dominick A. Merle, Ed. Factual accounts, 3,500 to 6,000 words, of "sensational crimes, preferably sex crimes, either pre-trial or after conviction." All stories will be considered for *Startling Detective, True Police Cases, Detective Files, Headquarters Detective, Detective Dragnet*, and *Detective Cases*. Query with pertinent information, including dates, site, names, etc. Pays $250 to $350, on acceptance; buys all rights.

HEADQUARTERS DETECTIVE—See *Globe Communications Corp.*

INSIDE DETECTIVE—Reese Communications, Inc., 460 W. 34th St., New York, NY 10001. Rose Mandelsberg, Ed.-in-Chief. Timely, true detective stories, 5,000 to 6,000 words, or 10,000 words. No fiction. Color photos of victim, killer, crime scene, or officer who headed investigation. Pays $250 to $500 for articles, and up to $200 for photos, on acceptance. Query.

MASTER DETECTIVE—Reese Communications, Inc., 460 W. 34th St., New York, NY 10001. Rose Mandelsberg, Ed.-in-Chief. Detailed articles, 5,000 to 6,000 words, with photos, on current cases, emphasizing human motivation and detective work. Also publish longer articles, 10,000 words. No fiction. Clear, color photos of victim, crime scene, perpetrator, and officer who led case. Pays to $250 to $500 for articles, and up to $200 for photos, on acceptance. Query.

OFFICIAL DETECTIVE—Reese Communications, Inc., 460 W. 34th St., New York, NY 10001. Rose Mandelsberg, Ed.-in-Chief. True detective stories, 5,000 to 6,000 words, on current investigations, strictly from the investigator's point of view. No fiction. Clear color photos of victim, killer, crime scene, or lead officer on case. Pays $250, to $200 for photos, on acceptance. Query.

P.I. MAGAZINE—755 Bronx Ave., Toledo, OH 43609. Bob Mackowiak, Ed. Profiles of professional investigators containing true accounts of their most difficult cases. Pays $25 to $50, plus copies, on publication.

STARTLING DETECTIVE—See *Globe Communications Corp.*

TRUE DETECTIVE—Reese Communications, Inc., 460 W. 34th St., New York, NY 10001. Rose Mandelsberg, Ed.-in-Chief. Articles, from 5,000 to 10,000 words, with photos, on current police cases, emphasizing detective work and human motivation. No fiction. Photos of perpetrator, victim, crime scene, or officer who spearheaded case. Pays $250 to $500, to $200 for photos, on acceptance. Query.

TRUE POLICE CASES—See *Globe Communications Corp.*

MILITARY

AIR FORCE TIMES—See *Times News Service.*

ARMY MAGAZINE—2425 Wilson Blvd., Arlington, VA 22201–3385. L. James Binder, Ed.-in-Chief. Features, to 4,000 words, on military subjects. Essays, humor, history, news reports, first-person anecdotes. Pays 12¢ to 18¢ a word, $25 to $50 for anecdotes, on publication.

ARMY RESERVE MAGAZINE—1815 N. Ft. Myer Dr., #501, Arlington, VA 22209–1805. Lt. Col. Jim Nielsen, Ed. Articles, 1,000 words, on military training and the history of the Army Reserve; profiles, 250 words, of interesting people in Army Reserve: military family life, humor, and anecdotes. Submit manuscripts with high-quality photos. Query. No payment. Guidelines.

ARMY TIMES—See *Times News Service.*

LEATHERNECK—Box 1775, Quantico, VA 22134–0776. William V.H. White, Ed. Articles, to 3,000 words, with photos, on U.S. Marines. Pays $50 per printed page, on acceptance. Query.

LIFE IN THE TIMES—See *Times News Service.*

MARINE CORPS GAZETTE—Box 1775, Quantico, VA 22134. Col. John E. Greenwood, Ed. Military articles, 500 to 2,000 and 2,500 to 5,000 words. "Our magazine serves primarily as a forum for active duty officers to exchange news on professional, Marine Corps related topics. Opportunity for 'outside' writers is limited." Queries preferred. Pays $50 to $100 for short articles; $200 to $400 for features, on publication.

MILITARY—2122 28th St., Sacramento, CA 95818. Lt. Col. Michael Mark,

Ed. Articles, 600 to 2,500 words, on firsthand experience in military service: World War II, Korea, Vietnam, and all current services. "Our magazine is about military history by the people who served. They are the best historians." No payment.

MILITARY HISTORY—602 S. King St., Suite 300, Leesburg, VA 22075. C. Brian Kelly, Ed. Bimonthly on the strategy, tactics, and personalities of military history. Department pieces, 2,000 words, on espionage, weaponry, personality, and travel. Features, 4,000 words, with 500-word sidebars. Pays $200 to $400, on publication. Query. Guidelines.

MILITARY LIFESTYLE MAGAZINE—4800 Montgomery Ln., Suite 710, Bethesda, MD 20814–5341. Hope Daniels, Ed. Articles, 1,000 to 1,800 words, for active-duty military families in the U.S. and overseas, on lifestyles, child-raising, health, food, fashion, travel, sports and leisure; short fiction. Pays $300 to $800, on publication. Query. No poetry, no historical reminiscences.

NAVY TIMES—See *Times News Service.*

THE RETIRED OFFICER MAGAZINE—201 N. Washington St., Alexandria, VA 22314. Articles, 800 to 2,000 words, of interest to military retirees and their families. Current military/political affairs: recent military history (especially Vietnam and Korea), humor, travel, hobbies, military family lifestyles, wellness, and second-career job opportunities. Photos a plus. Pays to $500, on acceptance. Queries required, no unsolicited manuscripts; address Manuscript Ed. Guidelines.

TIMES NEWS SERVICE—Army Times Publishing Co., Springfield, VA 22151. Address the R&R Ed. Free-lance material for "R&R" newspaper section (formerly called "Life in the Times"). Articles about military life, its problems and how to handle them as well as interesting things people are doing. Travel articles, 700 words, on places of interest to military people. Profiles, 600 to 700 words, on interesting members of the military community. Personal-experience essays, 750 words. No fiction or poetry. Pays $75 to $100, on acceptance. Also articles, 1,000 words, for supplements to *Army Times*, *Navy Times*, and *Air Force Times.* Address Supplements Ed. Pays $125 to $200, on acceptance. Guidelines.

VFW MAGAZINE—406 W. 34th St., Kansas City, MO 64111. Richard K. Kolb, Ed. Magazine for Veterans of Foreign Wars and their families. Articles, 1,500 words, on current events, veteran affairs, and military history, with veteran angle. Photos. Pays to $500, extra for photos, on acceptance. Guidelines. Query.

HISTORY

ALABAMA HERITAGE—The Univ. of Alabama, Box 870342, Tuscaloosa, AL 35487–0342. Suzanne Wolfe, Ed. Quarterly. Articles, to 5,000 words, on local, state, and regional history: art, literature, language, archaeology, music, religion, architecture, and natural history. Query and mention availability of photos and illustrations. Payment is an honorarium, on publication, plus 10 copies. Guidelines.

AMERICAN HERITAGE—60 Fifth Ave., New York, NY 10011. Richard F. Snow, Ed. Articles, 750 to 5,000 words, on U.S. history and background of American life and culture from the beginning to recent times. No fiction. Pays from $300 to $1,500, on acceptance. Query. SASE.

AMERICAN HERITAGE OF INVENTION & TECHNOLOGY—60 Fifth Ave., New York, NY 10011. Frederick Allen, Ed. Articles, 2,000 to 5,000 words, on history of technology in America, for the sophisticated general reader. Query. Pays on acceptance.

AMERICAN HISTORY ILLUSTRATED—6405 Flank Dr., P.O. Box 8200, Harrisburg, PA 17105. Articles, 3,000 to 5,000 words, soundly researched. Style should be popular, not scholarly. No travelogues, fiction, or puzzles. Pays $300 to $650, on acceptance. Query with SASE required.

AMERICAN JEWISH HISTORY—American Jewish Historical Society, 2 Thornton Rd., Waltham, MA 02154. Dr. Marc Lee Raphael, Ed. Articles, 15 to 30 typed pages, on American Jewish history. Queries preferred. No payment.

CAROLOGUE—South Carolina Historical Society, 100 Meeting St., Charleston, SC 29401–2299. Stephen Hoffius, Ed. General-interest articles, to 10 pages, on South Carolina history. Queries preferred. Payment is five copies.

CHICAGO HISTORY—Clark St. at North Ave., Chicago, IL 60614. Claudia Lamm Wood, Ed. Articles, to 4,500 words, on political, social, and cultural history. Pays to $250, on publication. Query.

EARLY AMERICAN LIFE—Box 8200, Harrisburg, PA 17105–8200. Frances Carnahan, Ed. Illustrated articles, 1,000 to 3,000 words, on early American life: arts, crafts, furnishings, architecture; travel features about historic sites and country inns. Pays $50 to $500, on acceptance. Query.

GOLDENSEAL—The Cultural Center, 1900 Kanawha Blvd. E., Charleston, WV 25305–0300. Ken Sullivan, Ed. Features, 3,000 words, and shorter articles, 1,000 words, on traditional West Virginia culture and history. Oral histories, old and new B&W photos, research articles. Pays to $175, on publication. Guidelines.

THE HIGHLANDER—P.O. Box 397, Barrington, IL 60011. Angus Ray, Ed. Bimonthly. Articles, 1,300 to 1,900 words, related to Scottish history. "We are not concerned with modern Scotland or current problems in Scotland." Pays $100 to $150, on acceptance.

HISTORIC PRESERVATION—1785 Massachusetts Ave. N.W., Washington, DC 20036. Anne Elizabeth Powell, Ed. Feature articles from published writers, 1,500 to 4,000 words, on residential restoration, preservation issues, and people involved in preserving America's heritage. Mostly staff-written. Query required.

HISTORY NEWS—AASLH, 530 Church St., Suite 600, Nashville, TN 37219–2325. Susan Cantrell, Ed. History-related articles, 2,500 to 3,500 words, about museums, historical societies and sites, libraries, etc. "Field Notes," 500 to 750 words; "In My Opinion" pieces, 1,000 words; "Technical Leaflets," 5,000 words. B&W photos. Submit two copies of manuscript. No payment made. Guidelines.

JOURNAL OF THE WEST—1531 Yuma, Manhattan, KS 66502–4228. Robin Higham, Ed. Articles, to 20 pages, devoted to the history and the culture of the West, then and now. B&W photos. Pays in copies.

LABOR'S HERITAGE—10000 New Hampshire Ave., Silver Spring, MD 20903. Stuart Kaufman, Ed. Quarterly journal of The George Meany Memorial Archives. Articles, 15 to 30 pages, for labor scholars, labor union members, and the general public. Pays in copies.

MILITARY—2122 28th St., Sacramento, CA 95818. Lt. Col. Michael Mark, Ed. Military history by people who served in the military. First-hand experiences, 600 to 2,500 words, of service in World War II, Korea, Vietnam, and more recent times. No payment.

MILITARY HISTORY—602 S. King St., Suite 300, Leesburg, VA 22075. C. Brian Kelly, Ed. Bimonthly on the strategy, tactics, and personalities of military history. Department pieces, 2,000 words, on espionage, weaponry, personality, perspectives, and travel. Features, 4,000 words, with 500-word sidebars. Pays $200 to $400, on publication. Query. Guidelines.

MONTANA, THE MAGAZINE OF WESTERN HISTORY—225 N. Roberts St., Helena, MT 59620. Charles E. Rankin, Ed. Authentic articles, 3,500 to 5,500 words, on the history of the American and Canadian West; new interpretive approaches to major developments in western history. Footnotes or bibliography must accompany article. "Strict historical accuracy is essential." No fiction. Queries preferred. No payment made.

NEBRASKA HISTORY—P.O. Box 82554, Lincoln, NE 68501. James E. Potter, Ed. Articles, 3,000 to 7,000 words, relating to the history of Nebraska and the Great Plains. B&W line drawings. Allow 60 days for response. Pays in six copies. Cash prize awarded to one article each year.

OLD WEST—P.O. Box 2107, Stillwater, OK 74076. John Joerschke, Ed. Thoroughly researched and documented articles, 1,500 to 4,500 words, on the history of the American West. B&W 5x7 photos to illustrate articles. Queries are preferred. Pays 3¢ to 6¢ a word, on acceptance.

PENNSYLVANIA HERITAGE—P.O. Box 1026, Harrisburg, PA 17108–1026. Michael J. O'Malley III, Ed. Quarterly of the Pennsylvania Historical and Museum Commission. Articles, 3,000 to 4,000 words, that "introduce readers to the state's rich culture and historic legacy and involve them in such a way as to ensure that Pennsylvania past has a future." Pays $300 to $500, up to $100 for photos or drawings, on acceptance.

PERSIMMON HILL—1700 N.E. 63rd St., Oklahoma City, OK 73111. M.J. Van Deventer, Ed. Published by the National Cowboy Hall of Fame. Articles, 1,500 to 2,500 words, on Western history and art, cowboys, ranching, and nature. Top-quality illustrations a must. Pays from $100 to $250, on publication.

PROLOGUE—National Archives, NECP, Washington, DC 20408. Dr. Henry J. Gwiazda, Ed. Quarterly. Articles, varying lengths, based on the holdings and programs of the National Archives, its regional archives, and the presidential libraries. Query. Pays in copies.

SOUTH CAROLINA HISTORICAL MAGAZINE—South Carolina Historical Society, 100 Meeting St., Charleston, SC 29401–2299. Stephen Hoffius, Ed. Scholarly articles, to 25 pages including footnotes, on South Carolina history. "Authors are encouraged to look at previous issues to be aware of previous scholarship." Payment is five copies.

TRUE WEST—P.O. Box 2107, Stillwater, OK 74076–2107. John Joerschke, Ed. True stories, 500 to 4,500 words, with photos, about the Old West to 1930. Some contemporary stories with historical slant. Source list required. Pays 3¢ to 6¢ a word, extra for B&W photos, on acceptance.

THE WESTERN HISTORICAL QUARTERLY—Utah State Univ., Logan, UT 84322–0740. Clyde A. Milner II, Ed. Original articles about the American West, the Westward movement from the Atlantic to the Pacific, twentieth-century regional studies, Spanish borderlands, Canada, northern Mexico, Alaska, and Hawaii. No payment made.

YESTERDAY'S MAGAZETTE—P.O. Box 15126, Sarasota, FL 34277. Ned Burke, Ed. Articles and fiction, to 1,000 words, on the 1920s through '70s, nostalgia and memories of people, places, and things. Traditional poetry, to 24 lines. Pays $5 to $25, on publication. Pays in copies for poetry and short pieces. Guidelines.

COLLEGE, CAREERS

THE BLACK COLLEGIAN—1240 S. Broad St., New Orleans, LA 70125. K. Kazi-Ferrouillet, Man. Ed. Articles, to 2,000 words, on experiences of African-American students, careers, and how-to subjects. Pays on publication. Query.

BYLINE—Box 130596, Edmond, OK 73013. Marcia Preston, Ed.-in-Chief. General fiction, 2,000 to 4,000 words. Nonfiction: 1,500- to 1,800-word features and 300- to 800-word special departments. Poetry, 10 to 30 lines preferred. Nonfiction and poetry must be about writing. Humor, 400 to 800 words, about writing. "We seek practical and motivational material that tells writers how they can succeed, not why they can't. Overdone topics: writers' block, the muse, rejection slips." Pays $5 to $10 for poetry; $15 to $35 for departments; $50 for features and short fiction, on acceptance.

CAREER WOMAN—See *Minority Engineer.*

CAREER WORLD—General Learning Corp., 60 Revere Dr., Northbrook, IL 60062–1563. Carole Rubenstein, Man. Ed. Gender-neutral articles about specific occupations and career development for junior and senior high school audience. Published monthly, September through May. Query with clips and resumé. Payment varies, on publication.

CAREERS & THE DISABLED—See *Minority Engineer.*

CIRCLE K—3636 Woodview Trace, Indianapolis, IN 46268–3196. Nicholas K. Drake, Exec. Ed. Serious and light articles, 1,700 to 2,000 words, on careers, college issues, trends, leadership development, self-help, community service and involvement. Pays $225 to $400, on acceptance. Queries preferred.

COLLEGE BROADCASTER—National Assn. of College Broadcasters, 71 George St., Box 1824, Providence, RI 02912–1824. Bimonthly. Articles, 500 to 2,000 words, on college radio and TV station operations and media careers. Query. Pays in copies.

EQUAL OPPORTUNITY—See *Minority Engineer.*

JOURNAL OF CAREER PLANNING & EMPLOYMENT—62 Highland Ave., Bethlehem, PA 18017. Mimi Collins, Ed. Bill Beebe, Assoc. Ed. Quarterly. Articles, 3,000 to 4,000 words, on topics related to career planning, placement, recruitment, and employment of new college graduates. Pays $100 to $200, on acceptance. Query with clips. Guidelines.

MINORITY ENGINEER—150 Motor Parkway, Suite 420, Hauppauge, NY 11788–5145. James Schneider, Exec. Ed. Articles, 1,000 to 1,500 words, for college students, on career opportunities in engineering fields; techniques of job hunting; developments in and applications of new technologies. Interviews. Profiles. Pays 10¢ a word, on publication. Query. Same address and requirements for *Woman Engineer, Equal Opportunity, Career Woman,* and *Careers & the DisABLED.*

STUDENT LEADERSHIP—P.O. Box 7895, Madison, WI 53707–7895. Jeff Yourison, Ed. Articles, to 2,000 words, and poetry for Christian college students. All material should reflect a Christian world view. Queries required.

WOMAN ENGINEER—See *Minority Engineer.*

OP-ED MARKETS

Op-ed pages in newspapers (those that run opposite the editorials) offer writers an excellent opportunity to air their opinions, views, ideas, and insights on a wide spectrum of subjects and in styles, from the highly personal and informal essay to the more serious commentary on politics, foreign affairs, and news events. Humor and nostalgia often find a place here.

Before submitting material, writers should read the op-ed pages of a number of newspapers to get an idea of the diversity of subjects they cover and a feel for the sort of pieces they publish. Often newspapers will buy exclusive rights in a specific geographic area, and the writer is free to resell the piece outside that area.

THE ARGUS LEADER—P.O. Box 5034, Sioux Falls, SD 57117–5034. Rob Swenson, Editorial Page Ed. Articles, to 850 words, on a wide variety of subjects for "Different Voices" column. Prefer local writers with an expertise in their subject. No payment. Guidelines.

THE ATLANTA CONSTITUTION—P.O. Box 4689, Atlanta, GA 30302. Raman Narayanan, Op-Ed Ed. Articles related to the Southeast, Georgia, or the Atlanta metropolitan area, 200 to 800 words, on a variety of topics: law, economics, politics, science, environment, performing and manipulative arts, humor, education; religious and seasonal topics. Pays $50 to $150, on publication. Submit complete manuscript.

THE BALTIMORE SUN—P.O. Box 1377, Baltimore, MD 21278–0001. Hal Piper, Opinion-Commentary Page Ed. Articles, 600 to 1,500 words, on a wide range of topics: politics, education, foreign affairs, lifestyles, etc. Humor. Payment varies, on publication. Exclusive rights: MD and DC.

THE BOSTON GLOBE—P.O. Box 2378, Boston, MA 02107–2378. Marjorie Pritchard, Ed. Articles, to 700 words, on economics, education, environment, foreign affairs, and regional interest. Send complete manuscript. Pays $100, on publication. Exclusive rights: New England.

BOSTON HERALD—One Herald Sq., Boston, MA 02106. Editorial Page Ed. Pieces, 600 to 800 words, on economics, foreign affairs, politics, regional interest, and seasonal topics. Prefer submissions from regional writers. Payment varies, on publication. Exclusive rights: MA, RI, and NH.

THE CHARLOTTE OBSERVER—P.O. Box 32188, Charlotte, NC 28232. Jane McAlister Pope, Ed. Well-written, thought-provoking articles, to 700 words. "We are only interested in articles on local (Carolinas) issues or that use local examples to illustrate other issues." Pays $50, on publication. No simultaneous submissions in NC or SC.

THE CHICAGO TRIBUNE—435 N. Michigan Ave., Chicago, IL 60611. Dianne Donovan, Op-Ed Page Ed. Pieces, 800 to 1,000 words, on domestic and international affairs, environment, regional interest, and personal essays. SASE required.

THE CHRISTIAN SCIENCE MONITOR—One Norway St., Boston, MA 02115. Shelley Coolidge, Opinion Page Coordinator. Pieces, 750 to 900 words, on domestic and foreign affairs, economics, education, environment, law, and politics. Pays $100, on acceptance. Retains all rights for 90 days after publication.

THE CLEVELAND PLAIN DEALER—1801 Superior Ave., Cleveland, OH 44114. Brent Larkin, Ed. Dir. Pieces, 700 to 900 words, on a wide variety of subjects. Pays $50, on publication.

DALLAS MORNING NEWS—Communications Center, P.O. Box 655237,

Dallas, TX 75265. Carolyn Barta, "Viewpoints" Ed. Pieces, 750 words, on politics, education, foreign and domestic affairs, cultural trends, seasonal and regional issues. No humor. Pay averages $75, on publication. SASE required. Exclusive rights: Dallas/Ft. Worth area.

DENVER POST—P.O. Box 1709, Denver, CO 80201. Bob Ewegen, Ed. Articles, 400 to 700 words, with local or regional angle. Pays $35 to $50, on publication. Query.

DES MOINES REGISTER—P.O. Box 957, Des Moines, IA 50304. "Opinion" Page Ed. Articles, 500 to 850 words, on all topics. Pays $35 to $75, on publication. Exclusive rights: IA.

THE DETROIT NEWS—615 W. Lafayette Blvd., Detroit, MI 48226. Address Anne Abate. Pieces, 600 to 900 words, on a wide variety of subjects. Pays $75, on publication.

THE FLINT JOURNAL—200 E. First St., Flint, MI 48502–1925. David J. Fenech, Opinion Dept. Ed. Articles, 650 words, of regional interest by local writers. Non-local writers should query first. No payment. Limited market.

FRESNO BEE—1626 E St., Fresno, CA 93786–0001. Karen Baker, Ed. Articles, 800 words: human interest, nostalgia, regional interest, and seasonal material. "Our main interest is in material that hasn't been done to death in editorials and syndicated columns; material in which the writer has personal knowledge or experience." Send complete manuscript. Pays $75, on acceptance.

THE HOUSTON POST—P.O. Box 4747, Houston, TX 77210–4747. Fred King, Ed. Opinion pieces, 850 to 875 words, on wide variety of topics. Send complete manuscript. Very limited market. Pays $40, on publication. Exclusive rights: Houston area.

INDIANAPOLIS STAR—P.O. Box 145, Indianapolis, IN 46206–0145. John H. Lyst, Ed. Articles, 700 to 800 words. Pays $40, on publication. Exclusive rights: IN.

LONG BEACH PRESS-TELEGRAM—604 Pine Ave., Long Beach, CA 90844. Larry Allison, Ed. Articles, 750 to 900 words, on lifestyles and regional topics. Writers must be local. Pays $75, on publication. Exclusive rights: Los Angeles area.

LOS ANGELES TIMES—Times Mirror Sq., Los Angeles, CA 90053. Bob Berger, Op-Ed Ed. Commentary pieces, to 750 words, on many subjects. "Not interested in nostalgia or first-person reaction to faraway events. Pieces must be exclusive." Payment varies, on publication. Limited market. SASE required.

LOUISVILLE COURIER-JOURNAL—525 W. Broadway, Louisville, KY 40202. Op-Ed Ed. Pieces, 750 words, on regional topics. Author must live in the area. Pays $25 to $50, on publication. Very limited market.

THE NEW YORK TIMES—229 W. 43rd St., New York, NY 10036. Address Op-Ed Ed. Opinion pieces, 650 words, on any topic, including public policy, science, lifestyles, and ideas, etc. Include your address, daytime phone number, and social security number with submission. "If you haven't heard from us within two weeks, you can assume we are not using your piece. Include SASE if you want work returned." Pays on publication. Buys first North American rights.

NEWSDAY—"Viewpoints," 235 Pinelawn Rd., Melville, NY 11747. Noel Rubinton, "Viewpoints" Ed. Pieces, 700 to 800 words, on a variety of topics. Pays $150, on publication.

THE ORANGE COUNTY REGISTER—P.O. Box 11626, Santa Ana, CA

92711. K.E. Grubbs, Jr., Ed. Articles on a wide range of local and national issues and topics. Pays $50 to $100, on publication.

THE OREGONIAN—1320 S.W. Broadway, Portland, OR 97201. Address Forum Ed. Articles, 900 to 1,000 words, of news analysis. Send complete manuscript. Pays $100, on publication.

PITTSBURGH POST GAZETTE—50 Blvd. of the Allies, Pittsburgh, PA 15222. Editorial Page Ed. Articles, to 800 words, on a variety of subjects. No humor. Pays $75 to $150, on publication. SASE required.

PORTLAND PRESS HERALD—P.O. Box 1460, Portland, ME 04104–5009. Op-Ed Page Ed. Articles, 750 words, on any topic with regional tie-in. Pay is possible, on publication. Query. Exclusive rights: ME.

THE REGISTER GUARD—P.O. Box 10188, Eugene, OR 97440. Don Robinson, Editorial Page Ed. All subjects; regional angle preferred. Pays $10 to $25, on publication. Very limited use of non-local writers.

THE SACRAMENTO BEE—2100 Q St., Sacramento, CA 95852. William Kahrl, Opinion Ed. Op-ed pieces, to 750 words, on state and regional topics only. Pays $150, on publication.

ST. LOUIS POST-DISPATCH—900 N. Tucker Blvd., St. Louis, MO 63101. Donna Korando, Commentary Ed. Articles, 700 words, on economics, education, science, politics, foreign and domestic affairs, and the environment. Pays $70, on publication. "Goal is to have half of the articles by local writers."

ST. PAUL PIONEER PRESS—345 Cedar St., St. Paul, MN 55101. Ronald D. Clark, Ed. Articles, to 700 words, on a variety of topics. Strongly prefer authors with a connection to the area. Pays $75, on publication.

THE SAN FRANCISCO CHRONICLE—901 Mission St., San Francisco, CA 94103. Marsha Vande Berg, Open Forum Ed. Articles, 500 and 700 words, "that represent lively writing, are pertinent to public policy debates, and move the debate forward." Also, well-crafted humor pieces. Pays to $150 (usually $75 to $100 for unsolicited pieces), on publication.

SAN FRANCISCO EXAMINER—110 5th St., San Francisco, CA 94103. Op-Ed Ed. Well-written articles, 500 to 650 words, on any subject. Payment varies, on publication.

SEATTLE POST-INTELLIGENCER—P.O. Box 1909, Seattle, WA 98111. Charles J. Dunsire, Editorial Page Ed. Articles, 750 to 800 words, on foreign and domestic affairs, environment, education, politics, regional interest, religion, science, and seasonal material. Prefer writers who live in the Pacific Northwest. Pays $75 to $150, on publication. SASE required. Very limited market.

TULSA WORLD—P.O. Box 1770, Tulsa, OK 74102. Articles, about 600 words, on subjects of local or regional interest. "We prefer local or regional writers." No payment. Exclusive rights: Tulsa area.

USA TODAY—1000 Wilson Blvd., Arlington, VA 22229. Sid Hurlburt, Ed./ Columns. Articles, 380 to 530 words. Very limited market. Query. Pays $125, on publication.

THE WALL STREET JOURNAL—Editorial Page, 200 Liberty St., New York, NY 10281. Amity Shlaes, Op-Ed Ed. Articles, to 1,500 words, on politics, economics, law, education, environment, humor (occasionally), and foreign and domestic affairs. Articles must be timely, heavily reported, and of national interest by writers with expertise in their field. Pays $150 to $300, on publication.

WASHINGTON TIMES—3600 New York Ave. N.E., Washington, DC 20002. Frank Perley, Articles and Opinion Page Ed. Articles 800 to 1,000 words, on a variety of subjects. No pieces written in the first-person. "Syndicated columnists cover the 'big' issues; find an area that is off the beaten path." Pays $150, on publication. Exclusive rights: Washington, DC, and Balimore area.

ADULT MAGAZINES

FORUM, THE INTERNATIONAL JOURNAL OF HUMAN RELATIONS—1965 Broadway, New York, NY 10023–5965. V. K. McCarthy, Assoc. Pub./Ed. Dir. Erotic fiction with "stunningly memorable, highly explicit sex sculpted with the best possible language skills. Also sexually oriented articles." Pays $600 to $850, on acceptance.

GALLERY—401 Park Ave. S., New York, NY 10016–8802. Barry Janoff, Ed.-in-Chief. Rich Friedman, Man. Ed. Articles, investigative pieces, interviews, profiles, to 2,500 words, for sophisticated men. Short humor, satire, service pieces, and fiction. Photos. Pays varying rates, on publication. Query. Guidelines.

GENESIS—1776 Broadway, 20th Fl., New York, NY 10019. Michael Banka, Ed. Articles, 2,000 words. Sexually explicit nonfiction features, 2,000 words. Photo essays. Pays 60 days after acceptance. Query with clips.

PENTHOUSE—1965 Broadway, New York, NY 10023. Peter Bloch, Ed. General-interest profiles, interviews, or investigative articles, to 5,000 words. Interviews, 5,000 words, with introductions. Pays on acceptance.

PLAYBOY—680 N. Lakeshore Dr., Chicago, IL 60611. John Rezek, Articles Ed. Alice K. Turner, Fiction Ed. Articles, 3,500 to 6,000 words, and sophisticated fiction, 1,000 to 10,000 words (5,000 preferred), for urban men. Humor; satire. Science fiction. Pays to $5,000 for articles, to $5,000 for fiction, $2,000 for short-shorts, on acceptance.

PLAYERS—8060 Melrose Ave., Los Angeles, CA 90046. Joe Nazel, Ed. Articles, 1,000 to 3,000 words, for black men: politics, economics, travel, fashion, grooming, entertainment, sports, interviews, fiction, humor, satire, health, and sex. Photos a plus. Pays on publication.

PLAYGIRL—801 Second Ave., New York, NY 10017. Charlene Keel, Man. Ed. Articles, 1,500 words, for women 18 to 34. Celebrity interviews, 1,500 to 2,000 words. Humor. Pays varying rates, on acceptance.

VARIATIONS, FOR LIBERATED LOVERS—1965 Broadway, New York, NY 10023–5965. V. K. McCarthy, Ed. Dir./Assoc. Pub. First-person true narrative descriptions of "a couple's enthusiasm, secrets, and sex scenes squarely focused within one of the magazine's pleasure catagories." Pays $400 to $500, on acceptance.

FICTION MARKETS

This list gives the fiction requirements of general- and special-interest magazines, including those that publish detective and mystery, science fiction and fantasy, romance and confession stories. Other good markets for short fiction are the *College, Literary and Little Magazines* where, though payment is modest (usually in copies only), publication can help a beginning writer achieve recognition by editors at the larger magazines. Juvenile fiction markets are listed under *Juvenile, Teenage, and Young Adult Magazines*. Publishers of book-length fiction manuscripts are listed under *Book Publishers*.

All manuscripts must be typed double-space and submitted with self-addressed envelopes bearing postage sufficient for the return of the material. Use good white paper; onion skin and erasable bond are not acceptable. *Always* keep a copy of the manuscript, since occasionally a manuscript is lost in the mail. Magazines may take several weeks—often longer—to read and report on submissions. If an editor has not reported on a manuscript after a reasonable amount of time, write a brief, courteous letter of inquiry.

ABORIGINAL SF—P.O. Box 2449, Woburn, MA 01888–0849. Charles C. Ryan, Ed. Stories, 2,500 to 7,500 words, with a unique scientific idea, human or alien character, plot, and theme of lasting value; "must be science fiction; no fantasy, horror, or sword and sorcery." Pays $250. Send SASE for guidelines.

AFTER HOURS—P.O. Box 538, Sunset Beach, CA 90742–0538. William G. Raley, Ed. Quarterly. Fantasy, horror, and macabre humor, 2,000 to 6,000 words, set after sundown. "If it's too weird or off-the-wall for other magazines, send it here." Pays 1¢ per word, on acceptance, plus one copy.

AIM MAGAZINE—P.O. Box 20554, Chicago, IL 60620. Ruth Apilado, Ed. Short stories, 800 to 3,000 words, geared to promoting racial harmony and peace. Pays from $15 to $25, on publication. Annual contest.

ALFRED HITCHCOCK MYSTERY MAGAZINE—1540 Broadway, New York, NY 10036. Cathleen Jordan, Ed. Well-plotted, plausible mystery, suspense, detection and crime stories, to 14,000 words; "ghost stories, humor, futuristic or atmospheric tales are all possible, as long as they include a crime or the suggestion of one." Pays 6 ½¢ a word, on acceptance. Guidelines with SASE.

ALOHA, THE MAGAZINE OF HAWAII—49 S. Hotel St., Suite 309, Honolulu, HI 96813. Cheryl Tsutsumi, Ed. Fiction to 4,000 words, with a Hawaii focus. Pays $150 to $300, on publication. Query.

AMAZING STORIES—Box 111, Lake Geneva, WI 53147. Mr. Kim Mohan, Ed. Janis Wells, Asst. Ed. Original, previously unpublished science fiction, fantasy, and horror, 1,000 to 25,000 words. Pays 6¢ to 10¢ a word, on acceptance.

ANALOG SCIENCE FICTION AND FACT—1540 Broadway, New York, NY 10036. Stanley Schmidt, Ed. Science fiction, with strong characters in believable future or alien setting: short stories, 2,000 to 7,500 words; novelettes, 10,000 to 20,000 words; serials, to 70,000 words. Pays 5¢ to 8¢ a word, on acceptance. Query for novels.

ASIMOV'S SCIENCE FICTION MAGAZINE—1540 Broadway, 15th Fl., New York, NY 10036. Gardner Dozois, Ed. Short science fiction and fantasies, to 15,000 words. Pays 6¢ to 8¢ a word, on acceptance.

THE ATLANTIC MONTHLY—745 Boylston St., Boston, MA 02116. William Whitworth, Ed. Short stories, 2,000 to 6,000 words, of highest literary quality, with "fully developed narratives, distinctive characterization, freshness in language, and a resolution of some kind." SASE required. Pays $2,500, on acceptance.

THE BOSTON GLOBE MAGAZINE—*The Boston Globe*, Boston, MA 02107. Ande Zellman, Ed. Short stories, to 3,000 words. Include SASE. Pays on acceptance.

BOYS' LIFE—P.O. Box 152079, 1325 W. Walnut Hill Ln., Irving, TX 75015–2079. Kathleen Vilim DaGroomes, Fiction Ed. Publication of the Boy Scouts of America. Humor, mystery, science fiction, adventure, 500 to 1,200 words, for 8- to 18-year-old boys; study back issues. Pays from $750, on acceptance. Send SASE for guidelines.

BUFFALO SPREE MAGAZINE—Box 38, Buffalo, NY 14226. Johanna V. Shotell, Ed. Fiction and humor, to 2,000 words, for readers in the western New York region. Pays $100 to $125, on publication.

BYLINE—Box 130596, Edmond, OK 73013. Marcia Preston, Ed.-in-Chief. Kathryn Fanning, Man. Ed. General fiction, 2,000 to 4,000 words. Nonfiction: 1,500- to 1,800-word features and 300- to 800-word special departments. Poetry, 10 to 30 lines preferred. Nonfiction and poetry must be about writing. Humor, 400 to 800 words, about writing. "We seek practical and motivational material that tells writers how they can succeed, not why they can't. Overdone topics: writers' block, the muse, rejection slips." Pays $5 to $10 for poetry; $15 to $35 for departments; $50 for features and short fiction, on acceptance. Guidelines.

CAMPUS LIFE—465 Gundersen Dr., Carol Stream, IL 60188. James Long, Ed. Fiction and humor, reflecting Christian values, 1,000 to 3,000 words, for high school and college students. Pays from $150 to $400, on acceptance. Limited freelance market. Published writers only. Queries required; SASE.

CAPPER'S—1503 S.W. 42nd St., Topeka, KS 66609–1265. Nancy Peavler, Ed. Short novel-length family-oriented or romance stories. Also very limited market for short stories, 7,500 to 12,000 words, that can be divided into two installments. Pays $75 to $400. Submit complete manuscript.

CAT FANCY—P.O. Box 6050, Mission Viejo, CA 92690. Debbie Phillips-Donaldson, Ed. Fiction and nonfiction, to 3,000 words, about cats. Pays 5¢ to 10¢ a word, on publication.

CHESS LIFE—186 Rte. 9W, New Windsor, NY 12553–7698. Glenn Petersen, Ed. Fiction, 500 to 2,000 words, for members of the U.S. Chess Federation. Pays varying rates, on acceptance.

CLINTON STREET—P.O. Box 3588, Portland, OR 97208. David Milholland, Ed. Short stories, 2 to 20 pages: "First-person accounts, thought-provoking, non-rhetorical essays, and idea pieces." Pays varying rates, on publication.

COBBLESTONE—7 School St., Peterborough, NH 03458–1454. Samuel Mead, Ed. Fiction must relate to monthly theme, 500 to 1,200 words, for children aged 8 to 14 years. Pays 10¢ to 17¢ a word, on publication. Send SASE for editorial guidelines.

COMMENTARY—165 E. 56th St., New York, NY 10022. Marion Magid, Ed. Fiction, of high literary quality, on contemporary social or Jewish issues. Pays on publication.

702

COMMON GROUND MAGAZINE—P.O. Box 99, McVeytown, PA 17051–0099. Ruth Dunmire and Pam Brumbaugh, Eds. Quarterly. Fiction, 1,000 to 2,000 words, related to Central Pennsylvania's Juniata River Valley. Pays $25 to $200, on publication. Guidelines.

COSMOPOLITAN—224 W. 57th St., New York, NY 10019. Betty Kelly, Fiction and Books Ed. Short shorts, 1,500 to 3,000 words, and short stories, 4,000 to 6,000 words, focusing on contemporary man-woman relationships. Solid, upbeat plots, sharp characterization; female protagonists preferred. "Submission cannot be returned without SASE." Pays $800 for short shorts; from $1,000 for short stories.

COUNTRY WOMAN—P.O. Box 989, Greendale, WI 53129. Kathy Pohl, Man. Ed. Fiction, 750 to 1,000 words, of interest to rural women; protagonist must be a country woman. "Stories should focus on life in the country, its problems and joys, as experienced by country women; must be upbeat and positive." Pays $90 to $125, on acceptance.

CRICKET—Box 300, Peru, IL 61354–0300. Marianne Carus, Ed.-in-Chief. Fiction, 200 to 1,500 words, for 7- to 14-year-olds. Pays to 25¢ a word, on publication. SASE required.

DISCOVERIES—WordAction Publishing Co., 6401 The Paseo, Kansas City, MO 64131. Address the Ed. Asst. Weekly take-home paper designed to correlate with Evangelical Sunday school curriculum. Fiction, 500 to 700 words, for 8- to 10-year-old readers. Stories should feature contemporary, true-to-life characters and should illustrate character building and scriptural application. No poetry. Pays 5¢ a word, on publication. Guidelines.

EASYRIDERS MAGAZINE—P. O. Box 3000, Agoura Hills, CA 91376–3000. Keith R. Ball, Ed. Fiction, 500 to 1,500 words. Pays from 15¢ a word, on acceptance.

ELLERY QUEEN'S MYSTERY MAGAZINE—1540 Broadway, New York, NY 10036. Janet Hutchings, Ed. High-quality detective, crime, and mystery stories, to 7,000 words. Also "Minute Mysteries," 250 words, short verses, limericks, and novellas, to 17,000 words. "We like a mix of classic detection and suspenseful crime." "First Stories" by unpublished writers. Pays 3¢ to 8¢ a word, on acceptance.

ESQUIRE—1790 Broadway, New York, NY 10019. David Hirshey, Deputy Ed. Send finished manuscript of short story; submit one at a time. No full-length novels. No pornography, science fiction, or "true romance" stories.

EVANGEL—Light and Life Press, Box 535002, Indianapolis, IN 46253–5002. Carolyn Smith, Ed. Free Methodist. Fiction, 1,200 words, with personal faith in Christ shown as instrumental in solving problems. Pays $45, on publication.

FAITH 'N STUFF—c/o *Guideposts*, 16 E. 34th St., New York, NY 10016. Mary Lou Carney, Ed. Bible-based bimonthly for 7- to 12-year-olds. Problem fiction, mysteries, historicals, 1,500 words, with "realistic dialogue and sharp imagery. No preachy stories about Bible-toting children." Pays $125 to $300 for all rights, on acceptance. No reprints.

FAMILY CIRCLE—110 Fifth Ave., New York, NY 10011. Kathy Sagan, Book Ed. "We no longer publish fiction on any regular basis. No manuscripts are currently being considered."

FICTION INTERNATIONAL—English Dept., San Diego State Univ., San Diego, CA 92182–0295. Harold Jaffe, Ed. Post-modernist and politically committed fiction and theory. Submit between September 1st and December 15th.

FIRST FOR WOMEN—270 Sylvan Ave., Englewood Cliffs, NJ 07632. Address Fiction Ed. Well-written, mainstream stories, 2,500 words, reflecting the concerns of contemporary women; no formula or experimental fiction. A humorous twist is welcome. Payment varies, on acceptance. SASE required. Do not query for fiction. Allow 8 to 10 weeks for response. Guidelines.

FLY ROD & REEL—P.O. Box 370, Camden, ME 04843. James E. Butler, Ed. Occasional fiction, 2,000 to 2,500 words, related to fly fishing. Special annual fiction issue published in summer. Payment varies, on acceptance.

GALLERY—401 Park Ave. S., New York, NY 10016–8802. Barry Janoff, Ed. Dir. Rich Friedman, Man. Ed. Fiction, to 3,000 words, for sophisticated men. "We are not looking for science fiction, mystery, 40s-style detective, or stories involving aliens from other planets. We do look for interesting stories that enable readers to view life in an off-beat, unusual, or insightful manner: fiction with believable characters and actions." Pays varying rates, on publication.

GLIMMER TRAIN PRESS—812 S.W. Washington St., Suite 1205, Portland, OR 97205. Susan Burmeister, Ed. Fiction, 1,200 to 6,000 words. "Twelve stories in each quarterly magazine." Pays $300, on acceptance. Submit material in January, April, July, and October; allow 3 months for response. "Send SASE for guidelines before submitting."

GOLF DIGEST—5520 Park Ave., Trumbull, CT 06611. Jerry Tarde, Ed. Unusual or humorous stories, to 2,000 words, about golf; golf "fables," to 1,000 words.

GOOD HOUSEKEEPING—959 Eighth Ave., New York, NY 10019. Lee Quarfoot, Fiction Ed. Short stories, 1,000 to 3,000 words, with strong identification figures for women, by published writers and "beginners with demonstrable talent." Novel condensations or excerpts. "Writers whose work interests us will hear from us within 4 to 6 weeks of receipt of manuscript. Please send inexpensive copies of your work; and do not enclose SASEs or postage. We can no longer return or critique manuscripts. We do accept multiple submissions." Pays top rates, on acceptance.

GRIT—1503 S.W. 42nd St., Topeka, KS 66609. Roberta J. Peterson, Ed.-in-Chief. Short stories, 2,200 to 2,500 words. Pays 12¢ to 25¢ a word, extra for photos, on publication. Guidelines.

HARDBOILED—Gryphon Publications, P.O. Box 209, Brooklyn, NY 11228–0209. Gary Lovisi, Ed. Hard, cutting-edge crime fiction, to 3,000 words, "with impact." Query for articles, book and film reviews. Payment varies, on publication.

HARPER'S MAGAZINE—666 Broadway, New York, NY 10012. Address the Eds. Will consider unsolicited fiction manuscripts. No poetry. SASE required.

HICALL—1445 Boonville Ave., Springfield, MO 65802–1894. Tammy Bicket, Ed. Fiction, to 1,200 words, for 13- to 17-year-olds. Strong evangelical emphasis a must: believable characters working out their problems according to biblical principles. Buys first rights; pays on acceptance. Reprints considered.

HIGHLIGHTS FOR CHILDREN—803 Church St., Honesdale, PA 18431–1824. Kent L. Brown Jr., Ed. Fiction on sports, humor, adventure, mystery, etc., 900 words, for 8- to 12-year-olds. Easy rebus form, 100 to 120 words, and easy-to-read stories, to 500 words, for beginning readers. "We are partial to stories in which the protagonist solves a dilemma through his or her own resources." Pays from 14¢ a word, on acceptance. Buys all rights.

HOMETOWN PRESS—2007 Gallatin St., Huntsville, AL 35801. Jeffrey C. Hindman, M.D., Ed.-in-Chief. Fiction, 800 to 2,500 words, well-crafted and tightly written, suitable for family reading. New and unpublished writers welcome. SASE for guidelines.

ISAAC ASIMOV'S SCIENCE FICTION MAGAZINE—See *Asimov's Science Fiction Magazine.*

LADIES' HOME JOURNAL—100 Park Ave., New York, NY 10017. Fiction generally accepted through agents only. "When submitting material or requesting guidelines, include SASE."

THE LOOKOUT—8121 Hamilton Ave., Cincinnati, OH 45231. Simon J. Dahlman, Ed. Inspirational short-shorts, 500 to 2,000 words. Pays to 7¢ a word, on acceptance. No historical fiction, science fiction, or fantasy.

LOUIS L'AMOUR WESTERN MAGAZINE—1540 Broadway, New York, NY 10036–4021. Elana Lore, Ed. Well-written western short stories, to 10,000 words. "Our focus is on traditional western short stories, but we will also consider Native American, modern, and mystery-oriented westerns." Pays 8¢ a word, on acceptance.

MCCALL'S—110 Fifth Ave., New York, NY 10011. Does not accept fiction submissions.

MADEMOISELLE—350 Madison Ave., New York, NY 10017. No longer accepts fiction.

THE MAGAZINE OF FANTASY AND SCIENCE FICTION—Box 11526, Eugene, OR 97440. Kristine Kathryn Rusch, Ed. Fantasy and science fiction stories, to 15,000 words. Pays 5¢ to 7¢ a word, on acceptance.

MATURE LIVING—127 Ninth Ave. N., Nashville, TN 37234. Al Shackleford, Ed. Fiction, 900 to 1,200 words, for senior adults. Must be consistent with Christian principles. Pays 5 ½¢ a word, on acceptance.

MIDSTREAM—110 E. 59th St., New York, NY 10022. M. S. Solow, Assoc. Ed. Fiction on Jewish themes, to 3,000 words. Pays 5¢ a word, after publication. Allow three months for response.

MILITARY LIFESTYLE MAGAZINE—4800 Montgomery Ln., Suite 710, Bethesda, MD 20814–5341. Hope Daniels, Ed. Fiction, to 1,500 words, for military families in the U.S. and overseas. Pays on publication. Annual fiction contest.

NA'AMAT WOMAN—200 Madison Ave., 21st Fl., New York, NY 10016. Judith A. Sokoloff, Ed. Short stories, approximately 2,500 words, with Jewish theme. Pays 8¢ a word, on publication.

NEW MYSTERY MAGAZINE—The Flatiron Bldg., 175 Fifth Ave., Suite 2001, New York, NY 10010–7703. Charles Raisch, Ed. Quarterly. Short mysteries, crime and suspense stories, 2,000 to 6,000 words, with "sympathetic characters and visual scenes." Book reviews, 250 to 2,000 words, of recently published novels. Pays to 3¢ a word, on publication. No guidelines.

THE NEW YORKER—20 W. 43rd St., New York, NY 10036. Fiction Dept. Short stories, humor, and satire. Payment varies, on acceptance. Include SASE.

OMNI—1965 Broadway, New York, NY 10023. Ellen Datlow, Fiction Ed. Strong, realistic science fiction. Some contemporary hard-edged fantasy. Pays to $2,250, on acceptance.

PENTHOUSE—1965 Broadway, New York, NY 10023. Linda Blanton, Assoc. Ed. Women's erotic fiction. SASE required.

PLAYBOY—680 N. Lakeshore Dr., Chicago, IL 60611. Alice K. Turner, Fiction Ed. Quality fiction, 1,000 to 8,000 words (average 6,000): suspense, mystery, adventure, and sports short stories; stories about contemporary relationships; science fiction. Active plots, masterful pacing, and strong characterization. Pays from $2,000 to $5,000, on acceptance.

PLOUGHSHARES—Emerson College, 100 Beacon St., Boston, MA 02116–1596. Address the Eds. Serious fiction, to 6,000 words. Poetry. Pays $10 per printed page, on publication. Reading periods and themes vary; send SASE for guidelines.

POWER AND LIGHT—6401 The Paseo, Kansas City, MO 64131. Beula J. Postlewait, Preteen Ed. Fiction, 500 to 700 words, for children grades 5 to 6, defining Christian experiences and values. Pays 5¢ a word for multiple-use rights, on publication.

PURPOSE—616 Walnut Ave., Scottdale, PA 15683–1999. James E. Horsch, Ed. Fiction, 800 words, on problem solving from a Christian point of view. Poetry, 3 to 12 lines. Pays up to 5¢ a word, to $1 per line for poetry, on acceptance.

QUEEN'S QUARTERLY—Queens Univ., Kingston, Ont., Canada K7L 3N6. Fiction, to 4,000 words, in English and French. Pays to $300, on publication.

RANGER RICK—8925 Leesburg Pike, Vienna, VA 22184–0001. Deborah Churchman, Fiction Ed. Action-packed nature- and conservation-related fiction, for 6- to 12-year-olds. Maximum: 900 words. No anthropomorphism. "Multi-cultural stories welcome." Pays to $550, on acceptance. Usually buys all rights.

REDBOOK—224 W. 57th St., New York, NY 10019. Dawn Raffel, Fiction Ed. Fresh, distinctive short stories, of interest to women. Pays from $1,500 for short stories (to 30 pages). Allow 6 weeks for reply. Manuscripts without SASE will not be returned. No unsolicited novellas or novels accepted.

ROAD KING—P.O. Box 250, Park Forest, IL 60466. George Friend, Ed. Short stories, to 1,200 words, for and/or about truck drivers. Pays to $400, on acceptance.

ST. ANTHONY MESSENGER—1615 Republic St., Cincinnati, OH 45210–1298. Norman Perry, O.F.M., Ed. Barbara Beckwith, Man. Ed. Fiction that makes readers think about issues, lifestyles, and values. Pays 14¢ a word, on acceptance. Queries or manuscripts accepted.

SASSY—230 Park Ave., New York, NY 10169. Christina Kelly, Fiction Ed. Short stories written in the magazine's style, 1,000 to 3,000 words, for girls age 14 to 19. Pays $1,000, on acceptance.

SCHOOL MATES—U.S. Chess Federation, 186 Rte. 9W, New Windsor, NY 12553–7698. Jennie L. Simon, Ed. Fiction, to 1,000 words, related to chess for beginning chess players (not necessarily children). Pays to $40, on publication.

SEA KAYAKER—P.O. Box 17170, Seattle, WA 98107–7170. Christopher Cunningham, Ed. Short stories exclusively related to ocean kayaking, 1,000 to 3,000 words. Pays on publication.

SEVENTEEN—850 Third Ave., New York, NY 10022. Fiction Ed. High-quality, literary short fiction, to 4,000 words. Pays on acceptance.

SPORTS AFIELD—250 W. 55th St., New York, NY 10019. Tom Paugh, Ed.

Occasional fiction, 1,500 words, on hunting, fishing, and related topics. Humor. Pays top rates, on acceptance.

STRAIGHT—8121 Hamilton Ave., Cincinnati, OH 45231. Carla Crane, Ed. Well-constructed fiction, 1,000 to 1,500 words, showing Christian teens using Bible principles in everyday life. Contemporary, realistic teen characters a must. Most interested in school, church, dating, and family life stories. Pays 3¢ to 7¢ a word, on acceptance. Send SASE for guidelines.

SUNDAY DIGEST—850 N. Grove Ave., Elgin, IL 60120. Christine Dallman, Ed. Short stories, 400 to 1,800 words, with evangelical religious slant. Payment varies, on acceptance.

'TEEN—8490 Sunset Blvd., Los Angeles, CA 90069. Address Fiction Dept. Short stories, 2,500 to 4,000 words: mystery, teen situations, adventure, romance, humor for teens. Pays from $200, on acceptance.

TEENS TODAY—Nazarene Publishing House, 6401 The Paseo, Kansas City, MO 64131. Short stories, 1,000 to 1,200 words, that deal with teens demonstrating Christian principles in real-life situations. Pays 4¢ a word (3 ½¢ a word for reprints), on acceptance.

TQ/TEEN QUEST—Box 3512, Irving, TX 75015. Chris Lyon, Ed. Fiction, 1,000 to 2,000 words, for conservative Christian teens. Pays 10¢ to 15¢ a word, on publication.

TRUCKERS/USA—P.O. Box 323, Windber, PA 15963. David Adams, Ed. Trucking related articles, poetry, and fiction, to 1,000 words. Payment varies, on acceptance.

TRUE CONFESSIONS—233 Park Ave. S., New York, NY 10003. Pat Vitucci, Ed. Romantic stories, 5,000 to 8,000 words: true-to-life drama, passion, intrigue, etc. Also short stories, 1,000 to 2,000 words. Pays after publication. Buys all rights.

VIRGINIA—(formerly *Virginia Southwest*) P.O. Box 4244, Roanoke, VA 24015–0244. Address the Ed. Fiction, 1,000 to 1,500 words, with Virginia setting or reference. Pays to $300, on bimonthly publication or within 6 months, whichever comes first. Limited market.

VIRTUE—P.O. Box 850, Sisters, OR 97759–0850. Marlee Alex, Ed. Fiction with a Christian slant. Pays 15¢ to 25¢ a word, on publication. Query required for articles.

WESTERN PEOPLE—Box 2500, Saskatoon, Sask., Canada S7K 2C4. Short stories, 850 to 1,800 words, on subjects or themes of interest to rural readers in western Canada. Pays $100 to $175, on acceptance. Enclose international reply coupons and SAE.

WILDFOWL—1901 Bell Ave., Suite #4, Des Moines, IA 50315. R. Sparks, Man. Ed. Occasional fiction, humor, related to duck hunters and wildfowl. Pays $200 to $350, on acceptance.

WIN MAGAZINE—16760 Stagg St., #213, Van Nuys, CA 91406–1642. Cecil Suzuki, Ed. Gambling-related fiction. Pays on publication.

WOMAN'S WORLD—270 Sylvan Ave., Englewood Cliffs, NJ 07632. Jeanne Muchnick, Fiction Ed. Fast-moving short stories, about 1,900 words, with light romantic theme. (Specify "short story" on outside of envelope.) Mini-mysteries, 950 words, with "whodunit" or "howdunit" theme. No science fiction, fantasy, or historical romance and no horror, ghost stories, or gratuitous violence. Pays $1,000 for short stories, $500 for mini-mysteries, on acceptance. Submit manuscript with SASE.

YANKEE—Yankee Publishing Co., Dublin, NH 03444. Judson Hale, Ed. Edie Clark, Fiction Ed. High-quality, literary short fiction, to 1,500 words, with setting in or compatible with New England; no sap buckets or lobster pot stereotypes. Pays $1,000, on acceptance.

DETECTIVE AND MYSTERY

ALFRED HITCHCOCK MYSTERY MAGAZINE—1540 Broadway, New York, NY 10036. Cathleen Jordan, Ed. Well-plotted mystery, detective, suspense, and crime fiction, to 14,000 words. Submissions by new writers strongly encouraged. Pays 6 ½¢ a word, on acceptance. Guidelines with SASE.

ARMCHAIR DETECTIVE—129 W. 56th St., New York, NY 10019. Kate Stine, Ed.-in-Chief. Jeffrey Lorber, Man. Ed. Articles on mystery and detective fiction; short stories; biographical sketches, reviews, etc. Pays $10 a printed page for nonfiction; fiction payment varies; reviews are unpaid.

ELLERY QUEEN'S MYSTERY MAGAZINE—1540 Broadway, New York, NY 10036. Janet Hutchings, Ed. Detective, crime, and mystery fiction, approximately 1,500 to 12,000 words. No sex, sadism, or sensationalism. Particularly interested in new writers and "first stories." Pays 3¢ to 8¢ a word, on acceptance.

HARDBOILED—Gryphon Publications, P.O. Box 209, Brooklyn, NY 11228–0209. Gary Lovisi, Ed. Hard, cutting-edge crime fiction, to 3,000 words. Query first for articles, book and film reviews. B&W drawings (send photocopies only). Payment varies, on publication.

NEW MYSTERY MAGAZINE—The Flatiron Bldg., 175 Fifth Ave., Suite 2001, New York, NY 10010–7703. Charles Raisch, Ed. Quarterly. Short mysteries, crime and suspense stories, 2,000 to 6,000 words. Book reviews, 250 to 2,000 words, of upcoming or recently published novels. Pays to 3¢ a word, on publication.

OVER MY DEAD BODY!—P.O. Box 1778, Auburn, WA 98071–1778. Cherie Jung, Features Ed. Mystery, suspense, and crime fiction, to 4,000 words. Author profiles, interviews, and mystery-related travel, 750 to 1,500 words. Fillers, to 100 words. Include B&W photos. "We are entertainment for mystery fans, from cozy to hardboiled and everything in between." Pays 1¢ a word for fiction; $10 to $25 for nonfiction; $5 for fillers; $10 to $25 for illustrations, on publication.

SCIENCE FICTION AND FANTASY

ABERATIONS—Box 8040, 544 Ygnacio Valley Rd., #13, Walnut Creek, CA 94596. Jon L. Herron, Ed. Science fiction, horror, and fantasy, to 8,000 words. "May be gritty, off-beat. Some graphic sex or violence O.K." Guidelines. Pays up to $7, on publication.

ABORIGINAL SF—P.O. Box 2449, Woburn, MA 01888–0849. Charles C. Ryan, Ed. Short stories, 2,500 to 7,500 words, and poetry, one to 2 typed pages, with strong science content, lively, unique characters, and well-designed plots. No sword and sorcery or fantasy. Pays $250 for fiction, $20 for poetry, $4 for science fiction jokes, and $20 for cartoons, on publication.

AFTER HOURS—P.O. Box 538, Sunset Beach, CA 90742–0538. William G. Raley, Ed. Quarterly. Fantasy and horror, 2,000 to 6,000 words, that take place after sundown. "If it's too weird or off the wall for other magazines, send it here." Pays 1¢ a word, on acceptance, plus one copy.

AMAZING STORIES—Box 111, Lake Geneva, WI 53147. Mr. Kim Mohan, Ed. Janis Wells, Asst. Ed. Original, previously unpublished science fiction, fantasy, and horror, 1,000 to 25,000 words. Pays 6¢ to 10¢ a word, on acceptance.

ANALOG SCIENCE FICTION AND FACT—1540 Broadway, New York, NY 10036. Stanley Schmidt, Ed. Science fiction with strong characters in believable future or alien setting: short stories, 2,000 to 7,500 words; novelettes, 10,000 to 20,000 words; serials, to 80,000 words. Also uses future-related articles. Pays to 7¢ a word, on acceptance. Query for serials and articles.

ARGONAUT—P.O. Box 4201, Austin, TX 78765. Michael E. Ambrose, Ed. "Hard" science fiction, to 7,500 words, and science fiction dealing with the sciences, intergalactic or interplanetary adventure. Poetry, to 30 lines, with a science fiction focus. No fantasy, horror, interviews, reviews, or seasonal material. Pays in 3 copies.

ASIMOV'S SCIENCE FICTION MAGAZINE—1540 Broadway, 15th Fl., New York, NY 10036. Gardner Dozois, Ed. Short, character-oriented science fiction and fantasy, to 15,000 words. Pays 5¢ to 8¢ a word, on acceptance. Guidelines.

BEYOND: SCIENCE FICTION & FANTASY—P.O. Box 1124, Fair Lawn, NJ 07410. Roberta Rogow, Ed. Science fiction and fantasy: original, exciting, thought-provoking fiction, 3,000 to 5,000 words, and poems, 10 to 20 lines. Pays ¼¢ a word, on publication.

DRAGON MAGAZINE—P.O. Box 111, Lake Geneva, WI 53147. Roger E. Moore, Ed. Barbara G. Young, Fiction Ed. Articles, 1,500 to 7,500 words, on fantasy and science fiction role-playing games. Fantasy, 1,500 to 8,000 words. Pays 6¢ to 8¢ a word for fiction, on acceptance. Pays 4¢ a word for articles, on publication. SASE for guidelines.

FANGORIA—475 Park Ave. S., 8th Fl., New York, NY 10016. Anthony Timpone, Ed. Published 10 times yearly. Movie previews and interviews, 1,800 to 2,500 words, in connection with upcoming horror films. "A strong love of the genre and an appreciation and understanding of the magazine are essential." Pays $175 to $225, on publication.

FANTASY AND SCIENCE FICTION—Mercury Press, Inc., P.O. Box 11526, Eugene, OR 97440. Kristine Kathryn Rusch, Ed. Short stories, to 20,000 words. "We have no formula, but you should be familiar with the magazine before submitting." For sample copies, write to 14 Jewell St., Cornwall, CT 06753. Pays 5¢ to 7¢ a word, on acceptance.

FANTASY & TERROR—See *Fantasy Macabre.*

FANTASY MACABRE—P.O. Box 20610, Seattle, WA 98102. Jessica Salmonson, Ed. Fiction, to 3,000 words, including translations. "We look for a tale that is strong in atmosphere, with menace that is suggested and threatening rather than the result of dripping blood and gore." Pays 1¢ a word, to $30 per story, on publication. Also publishes *Fantasy & Terror* for poetry-in-prose pieces.

FIGMENT: TALES FROM THE IMAGINATION—Figment Press, P.O. Box 3128, Moscow, ID 83843–0477. Barb and J.C. Hendee, Eds. Mark Coen, Assoc. Ed. Science fiction and fantasy, to 10,000 words, hard or soft, light or dark. Nonfiction, to 2,000 words, of interest to science fiction readers, not writers. Science fiction and fantasy poems, all styles. Pays ½¢ to 1¢ a word, from $5 for poems, within 30 days of acceptance. Send SASE for guidelines before submitting.

FOOTSTEPS PRESS—P.O. Box 75, Round Top, NY 12473. Bill Munster, Ed. Horror, mystery, and ghost story chapbooks, 3,000 to 5,000 words. Royalty (usually from $350 to $500).

GRUE MAGAZINE—Box 370, Times Square Sta., New York, NY 10108. Peggy Nadramia, Ed. Fiction, 6,000 words, and macabre/surreal poetry of any length. "We seek very visceral, original horror stories with an emphasis on characterization and motivation." Pays ½¢ a word for fiction, $5 per poem, on publication. Allow 3 to 6 months for response.

HAUNTS—Nightshade Publications, Box 3342, Providence, RI 02906. Joseph K. Cherkes, Ed. Horror, science/fantasy, and supernatural short stories with strong characters, 1,500 to 8,000 words. No explicit sexual scenes or gratuitous violence. Pays ¼¢ to 1¢ a word, on publication. Manuscripts read January through June.

HOBSON'S CHOICE: SCIENCE FICTION AND TECHNOLOGY—The Starwind Press, P.O. Box 98, Ripley, OH 45167. Address Submissions Ed. Science fiction and fantasy, 2,000 to 10,000 words. Articles and literary criticism, 1,000 to 5,000 words, for readers interested in science and technology. Query for nonfiction. Pays 1¢ to 4¢ a word, on publication.

ISAAC ASIMOV'S SCIENCE FICTION MAGAZINE—See *Asimov's Science Fiction Magazine.*

THE LEADING EDGE—3163 JKHB, Provo, UT 84602. Michael Carr, Ed. Published 3 times a year. Short stories, 3,000 to 12,000 words, and some experimental fiction; poems, to 200 lines; and articles, to 8,000 words, on science, scientific speculation, and literary criticism. Fillers and comics. "Do not send originals; manuscripts are marked and critiqued by staff." Pays ½¢ a word (minimum of $5) for fiction; $5 per published page of poetry; $2 to $4 for fillers, on publication. Guidelines.

THE MAGAZINE OF FANTASY AND SCIENCE FICTION—P.O. Box 11526, Eugene, OR 97440. Kristine K. Rusch, Ed. Fantasy and science fiction stories, to 10,000 words. Pays 5¢ to 7¢ a word, on acceptance.

MAGIC REALISM—P.O. Box 620, Orem, UT 84059–0620. C. Darren Butler, Ed. Julie Thomas, Ed. Published 2 to 3 times a year. Stories, to 7,500 words (4,000 words preferred), of magic realism, exaggerated realism, some genre fantasy/dark fantasy. Occasionally publish glib fantasy like that found in folk, fairy tales, and myths. No occult, sleight-of-hand magicians, or wizards/witches. Pays in one copy.

MARION ZIMMER BRADLEY'S FANTASY MAGAZINE—P.O. Box 249, Berkeley, CA 94701. Marion Zimmer Bradley, Ed. Quarterly. Well-plotted stories, 3,500 to 4,000 words. Action and adventure fantasy "with no particular objection to modern settings." Send SASE for guidelines before submitting. Pays 3¢ to 10¢ a word, on acceptance.

MIDNIGHT ZOO—Box 8040, 544 Ygnacio Valley Rd., #13, Walnut Creek, CA 94596. Jon L. Herron, Ed. Science fiction, horror, and fantasy, 8,000 words. Nonfiction, 1,000 to 2,000 words, including interviews, humor, and general interest. Guidelines. Pays up to $12, on publication.

MODERN MYTHOLOGY—P.O. Box 244, Scottsdale, AZ 85252–0244. Ann Marie Nicastle, Ed. Science fiction, fantasy, horror, and other forms of speculative fiction, to 2,500 words. Topics for regular columns include comics, role playing games, books, television, and films. "Stories should focus on a character, not a specific science; story line should not be based on an existing TV show (ie. Star Trek)." Pays in copies.

NEXT PHASE—Phantom Press Publications, 33 Court St., New Haven, CT 06511. Kim Means, Ed. Science fiction, fantasy, and experimental fiction, to 3,000 words. Poetry, any length. "We prefer environmentally conscious fiction." SASE required. Pays in copies.

OMNI—1965 Broadway, New York, NY 10023. Ellen Datlow, Ed. Strong, realistic science fiction, 2,000 to 10,000 words, with good characterizations. Some fantasy. No horror, ghost, or sword and sorcery tales. Pays $1,250 to $2,250, on acceptance.

PULPHOUSE: A FICTION MAGAZINE—P.O. Box 1227, Eugene, OR 97440. Dean Wesley Smith, Ed./Pub. Fantasy, science fiction, horror, and mysteries, 5,000 words. Articles, essays, interviews, and news items, to 5,000 words. Query for nonfiction only. Pays 4¢ to 7¢, on publication.

SCIENCE FICTION CHRONICLE—P.O. Box 2730, Brooklyn, NY 11202. Andrew Porter, Ed. News items, 200 to 500 words, for science fiction and fantasy readers, professionals, and booksellers. Interviews with authors, 2,500 to 4,000 words. No fiction. Pays 3¢ to 5¢ a word, on publication. Query.

2AM MAGAZINE—P.O. Box 6754, Rockford, IL 61125–1754. Gretta M. Anderson, Ed. Fiction, of varying lengths. "We prefer dark fantasy/horror; great science fiction and sword and sorcery stories are welcome." Profiles and intelligent commentaries. Poetry, to 50 lines. Pays from ½¢ a word, on acceptance. Guidelines.

WEIRD TALES—P.O. Box 13418, Philadelphia, PA 19101. George Scithers, Pub. Darrell Schweitzer, Ed. Fantasy and horror (no science fiction), to 20,000 words. Pays 3¢ to 8¢ a word, on acceptance. Guidelines.

CONFESSION AND ROMANCE

BLACK CONFESSIONS—See *Black Romance.*

BLACK ROMANCE—355 Lexington Ave., New York, NY 10017. Tonia L. Shakespeare, Ed. Romance fiction, 5,800 to 6,700 words, and service articles on beauty, health, and relationship tips, 800 to 1,000 words, for black female readers. Queries preferred. Pays $75 to $125, on publication. Also publishes *Black Secrets, Bronze Thrills, Black Confessions,* and *Jive.* Guidelines.

BLACK SECRETS—See *Black Romance.*

BRONZE THRILLS—See *Black Romance.*

JIVE—See *Black Romance.*

MODERN ROMANCES—233 Park Ave. S., New York, NY 10003. Cherie Clark King, Ed. Confession stories with reader-identification and strong emotional tone, 2,000 to 10,000 words. Pays 5¢ a word, after publication. Buys all rights.

MOONLIGHT ROMANCE—Starlog Communications International, Inc., 475 Park Ave., New York, NY 10016. Milburn Smith, Assoc. Pub. Bimonthly; features one contemporary romance, 75,000 words. Heroines should be American and most action set in the US, but international heroes are fine. "We're looking for romances centering on a relationship, not mainstream contemporary novels centering on a woman's emotional or psychological dilemma." Send outline, first two chapters, and a love scene with SASE. Pays $1,500 ($500 on acceptance, $500 on signing, $500 on publication). Guidelines.

RHAPSODY ROMANCE—Starlog Communications International, Inc., 475 Park Ave., New York, NY 10016. Milburn Smith, Assoc. Pub. Bimonthly; features one historical romance, 75,000 words. "Historicals should be set between 1600 and 1900, but a really good story would make us consider an earlier period." Send outline, first two chapters plus an important love scene, and SASE. Pays $1,500, ($500 on acceptance, $500 on signing, $500 on publication). Buys magazine rights only. Guidelines.

TRUE CONFESSIONS—233 Park Ave. S., New York, NY 10003. Pat Vitucci, Ed. Timely, emotional, first-person stories, 2,000 to 10,000 words, on romance, family life, and problems of today's young blue-collar women. Pays 5¢ a word, after publication.

TRUE EXPERIENCE—233 Park Ave. S., New York, NY 10003. Jeannie A. Wallace, Ed. Jennifer Hampton, Assoc. Ed. Realistic first-person stories, 4,000 to 10,000 words (short shorts, to 2,000 words), on family life, single life, love, romance, overcoming hardships, mysteries. Pays 3¢ a word, after publication.

TRUE ROMANCE—233 Park Ave. S., New York, NY 10003. Pat Byrdsong, Ed. True or true-to-life, dramatic and/or romantic first-person stories, 2,000 to 9,000 words. Love poems. "We enjoy working with new writers." Reports in three to five months. Pays 3¢ a word, a month after publication.

POETRY MARKETS

The following list includes markets for both serious and light verse. Although major magazines pay good rates for poetry, the competition to break into print is very stiff, since editors use only a limited number of poems in each issue. On the other hand, college, little, and literary magazines use a great deal of poetry, and though payment is modest—usually in copies—publication in these journals can establish a beginning poet's reputation, and can lead to publication in the major magazines. Poets will also find a number of competitions offering cash awards for unpublished poems in the *Literary Prize Offers* list.

ALOHA, THE MAGAZINE OF HAWAII—49 S. Hotel St., #309, Honolulu, HI 96813. Cheryl Chee Tsutsumi, Ed. Poetry relating to Hawaii. Pays $25 per poem, on publication.

AMERICA—106 W. 56th St., New York, NY 10019. Patrick Samway, S.J., Literary Ed. Serious poetry, preferably in contemporary prose idiom, 10 to 25 lines. Occasional light verse. Submit 2 or 3 poems at a time. Pays $1.40 per line, on publication. Guidelines.

THE AMERICAN SCHOLAR—1811 Q St. N.W., Washington, DC 20009–9974. Joseph Epstein, Ed. Highly original poetry, 10 to 32 lines, for college-educated, intellectual readers. Pays $50, on acceptance.

THE ATLANTIC MONTHLY—745 Boylston St., Boston, MA 02116. Peter

Davison, Poetry Ed. Previously unpublished poetry of highest quality. Limited market; only 2 to 3 poems an issue. Interested in new poets. Occasionally uses light verse. "No simultaneous submissions; we make prompt decisions." Pays excellent rates, on acceptance.

CAPPER'S—1503 S.W. 42nd St., Topeka, KS 66609–1265. Nancy Peavler, Ed. Traditional poetry and free verse, 4 to 16 lines, with simple everyday themes. Submit up to 6 poems at a time, with SASE. Payment varies, on acceptance.

CHILDREN'S PLAYMATE—P.O. Box 567, Indianapolis, IN 46206. Elizabeth A. Rinck, Ed. Poetry for children, 6 to 8 years old, on good health, nutrition, exercise, safety, seasonal and humorous subjects. Pays from $15, on publication. Buys all rights.

THE CHRISTIAN SCIENCE MONITOR—One Norway St., Boston, MA 02115. Alice Hummer, The Home Forum. Fresh, vigorous nonreligious poems of high quality, on various subjects. Short poems preferred. Pays varying rates, on acceptance. Submit no more than 3 poems at a time.

COMMONWEAL—15 Dutch St., New York, NY 10038. Rosemary Deen, Poetry Ed. Catholic. Serious, witty poetry. Pays 50¢ a line, on publication. SASE required.

COSMOPOLITAN—224 W. 57th St., New York, NY 10019. Rachel Zalis, Poetry Ed. Poetry about relationships and other topics of interest to young, active women. Pays $25, on acceptance. SASE required.

COUNTRY WOMAN—P.O. Box 989, Greendale, WI 53129. Kathy Pohl, Man. Ed. Traditional rural poetry and light verse, 4 to 30 lines, on rural experiences and country living; also seasonal poetry. Poems must rhyme. Pays $10 to $25, on acceptance.

EVANGEL—Box 535002, Indianapolis, IN 46253–5002. Carolyn Smith, Ed. Free Methodist. Devotional or nature poetry, 8 to 16 lines. Pays $10, on publication.

FAMILY CIRCLE—110 Fifth Ave., New York, NY 10011. No unsolicited poetry.

GOOD HOUSEKEEPING—"Light Housekeeping" page, 959 8th Ave., New York, NY 10019. Rosemary Leonard, Ed. Light, humorous verses, quips, and poems. Include phone number and social security number. Pays $25 for 4 lines, $50 for 6 to 8 lines, on acceptance. All unused submissions to "Light Housekeeping" page will be returned to author when accompanied by SASE.

JOURNEY—See *Pathways.*

LADIES' HOME JOURNAL—100 Park Ave., New York, NY 10017. No longer accepts poetry. "Last Laughs" page has been discontinued.

MCCALL'S—110 Fifth Ave., New York, NY 10001. No poetry considered.

MATURE YEARS—201 Eighth Ave. S., P.O. Box 801, Nashville, TN 37202. Marvin W. Cropsey, Ed. United Methodist. Poetry, to 14 lines, on preretirement, retirement, seasonal subjects, aging. No "saccharine" poetry. Pays 50¢ to $1 per line.

MIDSTREAM—110 E. 59th St., New York, NY 10022. Joel Carmichael, Ed. M.S. Solow, Poetry Ed. Poetry of Jewish interest. Pays $25, on publication. Allow 3 months for response.

THE MIRACULOUS MEDAL—475 E. Chelten Ave., Philadelphia, PA

713

19144–5785. John W. Gouldrick, C.M., Ed. Catholic. Religious verse, to 20 lines. Pays 50¢ a line, on acceptance.

MODERN BRIDE—249 W. 17th St., New York, NY 10011. Mary Ann Cavlin, Man. Ed. Short verse of interest to bride and groom. Pays $25 to $35, on acceptance.

THE NATION—72 Fifth Ave., New York, NY 10011. Grace Schulman, Poetry Ed. Poetry of high quality. Pays after publication. SASE requried.

NATIONAL ENQUIRER—Lantana, FL 33464. Michele Cooke, Asst. Ed. Short poems, with traditional rhyming verse, of an amusing, philosophical, or inspirational nature. No experimental poetry. Original epigrams, humorous anecdotes, and "daffynitions." Submit seasonal/holiday material at least two months in advance. Pays $25, after publication. SASE required.

THE NEW REPUBLIC—1220 19th St. N.W., Washington, DC 20036. Mary Jo Salter, Poetry Ed. Pays $75, after publication.

THE NEW YORKER—20 W. 43rd St., New York, NY 10036. First-rate poetry. Pays top rates, on acceptance. Include SASE.

PATHWAYS—(formerly *Journey*) Christian Board of Publication, Box 179, St. Louis, MO 63166. Short poems for 12- to 15-year-olds. Pays 30¢ a line, on publication.

PENTECOSTAL EVANGEL—1445 Boonville, Springfield, MO 65802. Richard G. Champion, Ed. Assemblies of God. Religious and inspirational verse, to 30 lines. Pays to 50¢ a line, on acceptance.

PURPOSE—616 Walnut Ave., Scottdale, PA 15683–1999. James E. Horsch, Poetry Ed. Poetry, to 8 lines, with challenging Christian discipleship angle. Pays 50¢ to $1 a line, on acceptance.

ST. JOSEPH'S MESSENGER—P.O. Box 288, Jersey City, NJ 07303–0288. Sister Ursula Maphet, Ed. Light verse and traditional poetry, 4 to 40 lines. Pays $5 to $15, on publication.

THE SATURDAY EVENING POST—P.O. Box 567, Indianapolis, IN 46206. Steven Pettinga, Post Scripts Ed. Light verse and humor. No conventional poetry. Pays $15, on publication.

THE UNITED METHODIST REPORTER—P.O. Box 660275, Dallas, TX 75266–0275. John Lovelace, Ed. Religious verse, 4 to 16 lines. Pays $2, on acceptance.

WESTERN PEOPLE—P.O. Box 2500, Saskatoon, Sask., Canada S7K 2C4. Michael Gillgannon, Man. Ed. Short poetry, with Western Canadian themes. Pays on acceptance. Send international reply coupons.

YANKEE—Yankee Publishing Co., Dublin, NH 03444. Jean Burden, Poetry Ed. Serious poetry of high quality, to 30 lines. Pays $50 per poem for all rights, $35 for first rights, on publication.

POETRY SERIES

The market for books of poetry is quite small, limited mostly to university presses that publish poetry series, and to foundations that sponsor contests for book-length poetry manuscripts. The following organizations publish book-length collections of poetry, many by writers who have never

714

had a book of poems published. Each has specific rules for submission, and reading fees are often required. Before submitting any material, be sure to write well ahead of the deadline dates for further information. Some organizations sponsor competitions for collections of poems; see *Literary Prize Offers*.

BARNARD COLLEGE—Women Poets at Barnard, Columbia University, 3009 Broadway, New York, NY 10027–6598. Celeste Schenck and Christopher Baswell, Co-Directors. Women writers who have never had a book of poetry published may submit their poetry manuscripts, 50 to 100 pages, for consideration in the New Women Poets Prize contest. Publication in the Women Poets at Barnard series and $1,500 is awarded. Manuscripts are accepted up to September 1. Send SASE for guidelines and reading fee.

CLEVELAND STATE UNIVERSITY POETRY CENTER—Dept. of English, Rhodes Tower, Room 1815, Cleveland, OH 44115. The writer of the best volume of poetry submitted between December 1st and March 1st receives publication in the CSU Poetry Series and $1,000. Reading fee: $10. Send for guidelines prior to submission. The CSU Poetry Center also publishes a Cleveland Poets Series, open only to Ohio poets; write for details.

FOUR WAY BOOKS—P.O. Box 607, Marshfield, MA 02050. Writers who have never had a book of poetry published may enter a book-length collection of poems for consideration in the Intro Series contest, which offers $1,000 and publication. Writers who have had at least one book of poems published are eligible to submit a book-length collection of poems for consideration in the Award Series contest, offering $1,500 plus publication. Both winners receive a two-week residency at Cummington Community for the Arts. Send SASE for guidelines and entry form. Reading fee: $12.50.

NATIONAL POETRY SERIES—P.O. Box G, Hopewell, NJ 08525. Unpublished, book-length poetry manuscripts may be submitted for consideration in the Open Competition. Five winning manuscripts, each selected by a distinguished poet, are published annually. Manuscripts accepted from January 1 to February 15. Reading fee: $25.

NEW YORK UNIVERSITY—Bobst Library, 70 Washington Sq. S., 11th Floor, New York, NY 10012. Rhonda Zangwill, Coordinator. The Elmer Holmes Bobst Awards for Emerging Writers offer publication for a poetry manuscript of 30 to 40 poems, by a writer who has never published a book of poetry. (Book-length fiction is also considered.) There is no reading fee. The contest closes in early April.

PEREGRINE SMITH POETRY SERIES—Gibbs Smith, Publisher, P.O. Box 667, Layton, UT 84041. Offers a $500 prize plus publication for a previously unpublished 64-page poetry manuscript. Manuscripts are accepted during the month of April. Reading fee: $10.

UNIVERSITY OF GEORGIA PRESS—Contemporary Poetry Series, Athens, GA 30602–1743. Poets who have never had a book of poems published may submit book-length poetry manuscripts during the month of September for possible publication. Manuscripts from poets who have published at least one volume of poetry (chapbooks excluded) are considered during the month of January. Send SASE for guidelines. Reading fee: $10. Manuscripts will not be returned.

UNIVERSITY OF MISSOURI PRESS—2910 LeMone Blvd., Columbia, MO 65201–8227. Mr. Clair Willcox, Poetry Ed. Publishes several volumes of poetry each season. From the manuscripts accepted for publication in a given year, one outstanding collection is the recipient of the Devins Award. Submit four to six sample poems, table of contents for entire manuscript, and brief cover letter giving manuscript length and other appropriate information. Submissions accepted year-round. There is no reading fee.

UNIVERSITY OF PITTSBURGH PRESS—Pitt Poetry Series, Pittsburgh, PA 15260. Poets who have never had a full-length book of poetry published may enter a 48- to 100-page collection of poems to the Agnes Lynch Starrett Poetry Prize between March and April. An award of $2,500 and publication of the winning manuscript is offered. Send SASE for guidelines. Reading fee: $12.50.

UNIVERSITY OF WISCONSIN PRESS—Poetry Series, 114 N. Murray St., Madison, WI 53715. Ronald Wallace, Administrator. Manuscripts, 50 to 80 pages, may be submitted during the month of September to the Brittingham Prize in Poetry competition, which offers $1,000, plus publication in the poetry series, for a previously unpublished manuscript. Send SASE for guidelines. Reading fee: $15.

WESLEYAN POETRY PROGRAM—Wesleyan University Press, 110 Mt. Vernon St., Middletown, CT 06459. Considers unpublished book-length (64 to 82 pages) poetry manuscripts by poets who have never had a book published. Response time is two to three months. Manuscripts read year-round. Submit manuscript and SASE. There is no reading fee.

YALE UNIVERSITY PRESS—Box 92A, Yale Sta., New Haven, CT 06520. Attn: Editor, Yale Series of Younger Poets. Conducts Yale Series of Younger Poets Competition, in which the prize is publication of a book-length manuscript of poetry, written by a poet under 40 who has not previously published a volume of poems. Reading fee: $8. Manuscripts are accepted only during the month of February.

GREETING CARD MARKETS

Greeting card companies often have their own specific requirements for submitting ideas, verse, and artwork. In general, however, each verse or message should be typed, double-spaced, on a 3x5 or 4x6 card. Use only one side of the card, and be sure to put your name and address in the upper left-hand corner. Keep a copy of every verse or idea you send. (It's also advisable to keep a record of what you've submitted to each publisher.) Always enclose an SASE, and do not send out more than ten verses or ideas in a group to any one publisher. Never send original artwork.

AMBERLEY GREETING CARD COMPANY—11510 Goldcoast Dr., Cincinnati, OH 45249–1695. Ned Stern, Ed. Humorous ideas for birthday, illness, friendship, anniversary, congratulations, "miss you," etc. Send SASE for guidelines before submitting ideas. Pays $150. Buys all rights.

AMERICAN GREETINGS—10500 American Rd., Cleveland, OH 44144. Kathleen McKay, Editorial Recruitment. Study current offerings and query before submitting.

BLUE MOUNTAIN ARTS, INC.—P.O. Box 1007, Boulder, CO 80306. Address Ed. Staff, Dept. TW. Poetry and prose about love, friendship, family, philosophies, etc. Also material for special occasions and holidays: birthdays, get well, Christmas, Valentine's Day, Easter, etc. Submit seasonal material four months in advance. No artwork or rhymed verse. Pays $200 per poem.

DAYSPRING GREETING CARDS—Outreach Publications, Inc., P.O. Box 1010, Siloam Springs, AR 72761. David Taylor, Ed. Inspirational messages that minister love, encouragement, and comfort to the receiver. Holidays, everyday occasions, and special-occasion cards. SASE for guidelines. Allow four to six weeks for response. Pays $30, on acceptance.

FRAVESSI GREETINGS, INC.—11 Edison Pl., Springfield, NJ 07081. Address Art Dir. Short verse, mostly humorous or sentimental; cards with witty prose. Christmas and everyday material. Pays varying rates, on acceptance.

FREEDOM GREETING CARD COMPANY—P.O. Box 715, Bristol, PA 19007. Jay Levitt, Ed. Dept. Traditional and humorous verse and love messages. Inspirational poetry for all occasions. Pays negotiable rates, on acceptance. Query with SASE.

HALLMARK CARDS, INC.—Box 419580, Mail Drop 216, Kansas City, MO 64141–6580. Write Carol King for submission agreement and guidelines; include SASE, no samples. Not currently soliciting new writers or sentiments. Work is on assignment basis only. Free lancers must show exceptional originality and style not available from in-house employees and must have previous writing experience.

KALAN—97 S. Union Ave., Lansdowne, PA 19050. No longer accepting free-lance submissions.

NOBLE WORKS—113 Clinton St., Hoboken, NJ 07030. Christopher Noble, Ed. Humorous greeting card ideas and copy. "No smut, no verse, nothing sweet or sentimental. We like 'Saturday Night Live' style humor." Pays $150 per complete idea against royalties, on publication. (Other deals and licensing agreements available depending on artist and quality of work.) SASE required.

OATMEAL STUDIOS—Box 138 TW, Rochester, VT 05767. Address the Ed. Humorous, clever, and new ideas needed for all occasions. Send SASE for guidelines.

RED FARM STUDIO—1135 Roosevelt Ave., P.O. Box 347, Pawtucket, RI 02862. Traditional cards for graduation, wedding, birthday, get well, anniversary, friendship, new baby, sympathy, and Christmas. No studio humor. Pays $3 a line. SASE required.

SANGAMON COMPANY—Route 48 W., P.O. Box 410, Taylorville, IL 62568. Address Ed. Dept. "We will send writer's guidelines to experienced free lancers before reviewing any submissions. We work on assignment." Pays competitive rates, on acceptance.

SUNRISE PUBLICATIONS, INC.—P.O. Box 4699, Bloomington, IN 47402. Address Ed. Coordinator. Original copy for holiday and everyday cards. "Submit up to 20 verses, one to four lines; simple, to-the-point ideas that could be serious, humorous, or light-hearted, but sincere, without being overly sentimental. Rhymed verse not generally used." SASE required. Allow four to six weeks for response. Send #10-size SASE for guidelines. Pays standard rates.

TLC GREETINGS—615 McCall Rd., Manhattan, KS 66502–8512. Michele Johnson, Creative Dir. Humorous and traditional cards. General humor cards for women for everyday, Christmas, and Valentine's Day. Very few risqué cards purchased. Pays on acceptance. Guidelines.

VAGABOND CREATIONS, INC.—2560 Lance Dr., Dayton, OH 45409. George F. Stanley, Jr., Ed. Greeting cards with graphics only on cover (no copy) and short punch line inside: birthday, everyday, Valentine's Day, Christmas, and graduation. Mildly risqué humor with double entendre acceptable. Ideas for illustrated theme stationery. Pays $15, on acceptance.

WARNER PRESS PUBLISHERS—1200 E. Fifth St., Anderson, IN 46012. Robin Fogle, Product Ed. Religious themes, sensitive prose, and inspirational verse for boxed cards, posters, and calendars. Pays $20 to $35, on acceptance. Also accepts ideas for coloring and activity books. Must send SASE for guidelines before submitting.

WEST GRAPHICS PUBLISHING—238 Capp St., San Francisco, CA 94110. Address the Ed. Dept. Outrageous humor concepts, all occasions (especially birthday) and holidays, for photo and illustrated card lines. Submit on 3x5 cards: concept on one side; name, address, and phone number on other. Pays $100, 30 days after publication.

WILLIAMHOUSE-REGENCY, INC.—28 W. 23rd St., New York, NY 10010. Nancy Boecker, Ed. Dept. Captions for wedding invitations only. Query for writing specifications sheet. Pays $25 per caption, on acceptance. SASE required.

CAROL WILSON FINE ARTS, INC.—P.O. Box 17394, Portland, OR 97217. Gary Spector, Ed. Carol Wilson, Ed. Humorous copy for greeting cards. Queries preferred. Pays $75 or negotiated royalties, on publication. Guidelines.

COLLEGE, LITERARY, AND LITTLE MAGAZINES

FICTION, NONFICTION, POETRY

The thousands of literary journals, little magazines, and college quarterlies published today welcome work from novices and pros alike; editors are always interested in seeing traditional and experimental fiction, poetry, essays, reviews, short articles, criticism, and satire, and as long as the material is well-written, the fact that a writer is a beginner doesn't adversely affect his or her chances for acceptance.

Most of these smaller publications have small budgets and staffs, so they may be slow in their reporting time—several months is not unusual. In addition, they usually pay only in copies of the issue in which published work appears and some—particularly college magazines—do not read manuscripts during the summer.

Publication in the literary journals can, however, lead to recognition by editors of large-circulation magazines, who read the little magazines in their search for new talent. There is also the possibility of having one's work chosen for reprinting in one of the prestigious annual collections of work from the little magazines.

Because the requirements of these journals differ widely, it is always important to study recent issues before submitting work to one of them. Copies of magazines may be in large libraries, or a writer may send a postcard to the editor and ask the price of a sample copy. When submitting a manuscript, always enclose a self-addressed envelope, with sufficient postage for its return.

For a complete list of literary and college publications and little magazines, writers may consult such reference works as *The International Directory of Little Magazines and Small Presses*, published annually by Dustbooks (P.O. Box 100, Paradise, CA 95967).

AEGEAN REVIEW—220 W. 19th St., Suite 2A, New York, NY 10011. Barbara Fields, Ed. Semiannual. Fiction and nonfiction, to 3,000 words, about Greece or by Greeks in translation. Query for drawings. Pays $50 to $100, on publication.

AFRICAN AMERICAN REVIEW—(formerly *Black American Literature Forum*) Dept. of English, Indiana State Univ., Terre Haute, IN 47809. Joe Weixlmann, Ed. Essays on African-American literature, art, and culture; bibliographies; interviews; poems; fiction; and book reviews. Submit up to 6 poems. Query for book review assignments; send 3 copies of all other submissions. Pays an honorarium and copies. Responds in 3 months.

THE AGNI REVIEW—Dept. TW, Boston Univ., Creative Writing Program, 236 Bay State Rd., Boston, MA 02215. Askold Melnyczuk, Ed. Short stories, poetry, essays, and artwork. Reading period October 1 to April 30 only.

ALABAMA LITERARY REVIEW—Troy State Univ., Smith 253, Troy, AL 36082. Theron Montgomery, Chief Ed. Semiannual. Contemporary, literary fiction and nonfiction, 3,500 words, and poetry, to 2 pages. Thought-provoking B&W photos. Pays in copies. Responds within 3 months.

ALASKA QUARTERLY REVIEW—College of Arts & Sciences, Univ. of Alaska, 3211 Providence Dr., Anchorage, AK 99508. Address Eds. Short stories, novel excerpts, poetry (traditional and unconventional forms). Submit manuscripts between August 15 and May 15. Pays in copies.

ALBATROSS—125 Horton Ave., Englewood, FL 34223. Richard Smyth, Richard Brobst, Eds. High-quality poetry; especially interested in ecological and nature poetry written in narrative form. Interviews with well-known poets. Submit 3 to 5 poems at a time with brief bio. Pays in copies.

AMELIA—329 E St., Bakersfield, CA 93304. Frederick A. Raborg, Jr., Ed. Poetry, to 100 lines; critical essays, to 2,000 words; reviews, to 500 words; belles lettres, to 1,000 words; fiction, to 4,500 words; fine pen-and-ink sketches; photos. Pays $35 for fiction and criticism, $10 to $25 for other nonfiction and artwork, $2 to $25 for poetry. Annual contest.

THE AMERICAN BOOK REVIEW—Publications Center, Univ. of Colorado, English Dept., Box 494, Boulder, CO 80309. Don Laing, Man. Ed. Literary book reviews, 700 to 1,200 words. Pays $50 honorarium and copies. Query with clips.

AMERICAN LITERARY REVIEW—Univ. of North Texas, P.O. Box

13615, Denton, TX 76203. James Ward Lee, Ed. Short stories, to 20 double-spaced pages, and poetry (submit up to 5 poems). Pays in copies.

THE AMERICAN POETRY REVIEW—1721 Walnut St., Philadelphia, PA 19103. Address Eds. Highest quality contemporary poetry. SASE required. Responds in 10 weeks.

AMERICAN QUARTERLY—National Museum of American History, Smithsonian Institution, Washington, DC 20560. Gary Kulik, Ed. Scholarly essays, 5,000 to 10,000 words, on any aspect of U.S. culture. Pays in copies.

THE AMERICAN SCHOLAR—1811 Q St. N.W., Washington, DC 20009–9974. Joseph Epstein, Ed. Articles, 3,500 to 4,000 words, on science, politics, literature, the arts, etc. Book reviews. Pays to $500 for articles, $100 for reviews, on publication.

AMERICAN WRITING—4343 Manayunk Ave., Philadelphia, PA 19128. Alexandra Grilikhes, Ed. Semiannual that "encourages experimentation in writing. We're interested in the voice of the loner (not lonely) and imitation as a subject." Fiction and nonfiction, to 3,500 words, and poetry. Pays in copies.

AMHERST REVIEW—Box 1811, Amherst College, P.O. Box 5000, Amherst, MA 01002–5000. Ismée A. Bartels, Ed. Fiction, to 8,000 words, poetry, artwork, and photographs. Submit material September through March only. SASE required.

ANOTHER CHICAGO MAGAZINE—3709 N. Kenmore, Chicago, IL 60613. Semiannual. Fiction, essays on literature, and poetry. "We want writing that's urgent, new, and lives in the world." Pays $5 to $50, on acceptance.

ANTAEUS—100 West Broad St., Hopewell, NJ 08525. Daniel Halpern, Ed. Short stories, essays, documents, excerpts, translations, poems. Pays on publication.

ANTIETAM REVIEW—7 W. Franklin St., Hagerstown, MD 21740. Susanne Kass and Ann Knox, Eds.-in-Chief. Fiction, to 5,000 words; poetry and photography. Submissions from regional artists only (MD, PA, WV, VA, DE, DC). Pays from $20 to $100. Guidelines. Manuscripts read September through January.

THE ANTIGONISH REVIEW—St. Francis Xavier Univ., Antigonish, N.S., Canada B2G 1C0. George Sanderson, Ed. Poetry; short stories, essays, book reviews, 1,800 to 2,500 words. Pays in copies.

ANTIOCH REVIEW—P.O. Box 148, Yellow Springs, OH 45387–0148. Robert S. Fogarty, Ed. Timely articles, 2,000 to 8,000 words, on social sciences, literature, and humanities. Quality fiction. Poetry. No inspirational poetry. Pays $15 per printed page, on publication. Poetry considered from September to May; other material considered year-round.

APALACHEE QUARTERLY—Apalachee Press, P.O. Box 20106, Tallahassee, FL 32316. Barbara Hamby, Pamela Ball, Mary Jane Ryals, Bruce Boehrer, Paul McCall, Ann Turkle, Eds. Fiction, to 30 manuscript pages; poems (submit 3 to 5). Pays in copies. Manuscripts read year-round.

ARACHNE—162 Sturges St., Jamestown, NY 14701–3233. Susan L. Leach, Ed. Quarterly. Fiction, to 1,500 words. Poems (submit up to 7). "We are looking for rural material and would like first publication rights." No simultaneous submissions. Pays in copies. Manuscripts read January, March, July, and October.

ARIZONA QUARTERLY—Univ. of Arizona, Main Library B-541, Tucson, AZ 85721. Edgar A. Dryden, Ed. Criticism of American literature and culture from a theoretical perspective. No poetry or fiction. Pays in copies.

ARTFUL DODGE—College of Wooster, Wooster, OH 44691. Daniel Bourne and Karen Kovacik, Eds. Annual. Fiction, to 20 pages. Literary essays, especially those involving nonfiction personal narrative, to 15 pages. Poetry, including translations of contemporary poets; submit 3 to 6 poems at a time; long poems encouraged. Pays $5 per page, on publication, plus 2 copies. Manuscripts read year-round.

BAD HAIRCUT—1055 Adams S.E. #4, Olympia, WA 98501–1443. Ray and Kim Goforth, Eds. Articles and fiction, to 4,000 words (2,000 words preferred). Focus on politics, human rights, and environmental themes. Unrhymed poetry, to one page, and drawings also accepted. "We hope that by creating art with these themes we can influence society and help create a better world." Pays in copies.

BAMBOO RIDGE, THE HAWAII WRITERS' QUARTERLY—Bamboo Ridge Press, P.O. Box 61781, Honolulu, HI 96839–1781. Eric Chock, Ed. Poetry, to 10 pages, and short stories, 25 pages, by writers in U.S. and abroad. Submit with SASE. Reports in 3 to 6 months. Pays in small honorarium and 2 copies. Manuscripts read year-round.

BELLES LETTRES—11151 Captain's Walk Ct., N. Potomac, MD 20878–0441. Janet Mullaney, Ed. Reviews and essays, 250 to 2,000 words, on literature by women. Literary puzzles, interviews, rediscoveries, retrospectives, and personal essays. Query required. Pays in copies and subscription.

THE BELLINGHAM REVIEW—The Signpost Press Inc., 1007 Queen St., Bellingham, WA 98226. Knute Skinner, Ed. Semiannual. Fiction, to 5,000 words, and poetry, any length. Pays in copies and subscription. Manuscripts read from September 1 to March 1.

BELLOWING ARK—P.O. Box 45637, Seattle, WA 98145. Robert R. Ward, Ed. Bimonthly. Short fiction, poetry, and essays of varying lengths, that portray life as a positive, meaningful process. B&W photos; line drawings. Pays in copies. Manuscripts read year-round.

THE BELOIT FICTION JOURNAL—Box 11, Beloit College, Beloit, WI 53511. Clint McCown, Ed. Short fiction, one to 35 pages, on all themes. No pornography, political propaganda, religious dogma. Pays in copies. Manuscripts read September to May.

BELOIT POETRY JOURNAL—RFD 2, Box 154, Ellsworth, ME 04605. Strong contemporary poetry, of any length or in any mode. Pays in copies. Guidelines.

BLACK AMERICAN LITERATURE FORUM—See *African American Review.*

BLACK BEAR REVIEW—Black Bear Publications, 1916 Lincoln St., Croydon, PA 19021–8026. Ave Jeanne, Ed. Semiannual. Book reviews and contemporary poetry. "We publish poems with social awareness, but any well-written piece is considered." Pays in one copy.

BLACK RIVER REVIEW—855 Mildred Ave., Lorain, OH 44052–1213. Deborah Glaefke Gilbert, Ed. Contemporary poetry, fiction (to 4,000 words), essays, short book reviews, B&W artwork. No greeting card verse or slick magazine prose. Submit between January 1 and May 1. Pays in copies. Guidelines. SASE required.

THE BLACK WARRIOR REVIEW—The Univ. of Alabama, P.O. Box 2936, Tuscaloosa, AL 35486–2936. Leigh Ann Sackrider, Ed. Fiction; poetry; translations; reviews and essays. Pays per printed page. Annual awards. SASE required. Manuscripts read year-round.

721

THE BLOOMSBURY REVIEW—1028 Bannock St., Denver, CO 80204–4037. Tom Auer, Ed. Marilyn Auer, Assoc. Ed. Book reviews, publishing features, interviews, essays, poetry. Pays $5 to $25, on publication.

BLUE UNICORN—22 Avon Rd., Kensington, CA 94707. Address the Eds. Published in October, February, and June. "We are looking for originality of image, thought, and music; we rarely use poems over a page long." Submit up to 5 poems with SASE. Artwork used occasionally. Pays in one copy.

BLUELINE—English Dept., SUNY, Potsdam, NY 13676. Alan Steinberg, Ed. Essays, fiction, to 3,500 words, on Adirondack region or similar areas. Poems, to 75 lines; submit no more than 5. Pays in copies. Manuscripts read September to November 30.

BOSTON REVIEW—33 Harrison Ave., Boston, MA 02111–2008. Josh Cohen, Ed.-in-Chief. Kim Cooper, Man. Ed. Reviews and essays, 800 to 3,000 words, on literature, art, music, film, photography. Original fiction, to 5,000 words. Poetry. Pays $40 to $100. Manuscripts read year-round.

BOTTOMFISH—21250 Stevens Creek Blvd., Cupertino, CA 95014. Robert Scott, Ed. Annual. Stories, vignettes, and experimental fiction, to 5,000 words. Free verse or traditional poetry, any subject, any length. "Our purpose is to give national exposure to new writers and new styles of creative writing. We publish at the end of March each year." Pays in copies. Manuscripts read July 1 to February 1.

BOULEVARD—P.O. Box 30386, Philadelphia, PA 19103. Richard Burgin, Ed. Published 3 times a year. High-quality fiction and articles, to 30 pages; poetry. Pays to $250, on publication.

THE BRIDGE—14050 Vernon St., Oak Park, MI 48237. Jack Zucker, Ed. Helen Zucker, Fiction Ed. Mitzi Alvin, Poetry Ed. Manon Meilgaard, Assoc. Fiction Ed. Semiannual. Fiction, 7,500 words, and poetry, to 200 lines. Pays in copies.

BUCKNELL REVIEW—Bucknell Univ., Lewisburg, PA 17837. Interdisciplinary journal in book form. Scholarly articles on arts, science, and letters. Pays in copies.

CACANADADADA REVIEW—P.O. Box 1283, Port Angeles, WA 98362. Jack Estes, Ed. Short-shorts, to 800 words, and poetry. Drawings and B&W photos. Pays in copies. Manuscripts read December and June.

CALLALOO—Dept. of English, Univ. of Virginia, Charlottesville, VA 22903. Charles H. Rowell, Ed. Fiction and poetry by, and critical studies on Afro-American, Caribbean, and African artists and writers. Payment varies, on publication.

CALLIOPE—Creative Writing Program, Roger Williams Univ., Bristol, RI 02809–2921. Martha Christina, Ed. Short stories, to 2,500 words; poetry. Pays in copies and subscription. No submissions April through July.

CALYX, A JOURNAL OF ART & LITERATURE BY WOMEN—P.O. Box B, Corvallis, OR 97339. M. Donnelly, Man. Ed. Fiction, 5,000 words; book reviews, 1,000 words (please query with SASE about reviews); poetry, to 6 poems. Include short bio and SASE. Guidelines. Pays in copies. Submissions accepted March 1 to April 15 and October 1 to November 15.

CANADIAN FICTION MAGAZINE—Box 946, Sta. F, Toronto, Ontario, Canada M4Y 2N9. High-quality short stories, novel excerpts, and experimental fiction, to 5,000 words, by Canadians. Interviews with Canadian authors; translations. Pays $10 per page, on publication. Annual prize, $500. Manuscripts read year-round.

THE CAPE ROCK—Dept. of English, Southeast Missouri State Univ., Cape Girardeau, MO 63701. Harvey E. Hecht, Ed. Semiannual. Poetry, to 70 lines, and B&W photography. (One photographer per issue; pays $100.) Pays in copies and $200 for best poem in each issue. Manuscripts read August to April.

THE CARIBBEAN WRITER—Univ. of the Virgin Islands, RR 02, Box 10,000, Kingshill, St. Croix, Virgin Islands, U.S. 00850. Erika J. Waters, Ed. Annual. Fiction (to 15 pages, submit up to 2 stories) and poems (no more than 5); the Caribbean should be central to the work. Blind submissions policy: place title only on manuscript; name, address, and title of manuscripts on separate sheet. Pays in copies. Manuscripts read September though December.

CAROLINA QUARTERLY—Greenlaw Hall CB#3520, Univ. of North Carolina, Chapel Hill, NC 27599–3520. Amber Vogel, Ed. Fiction, to 7,000 words, by new or established writers. Poems, to 300 lines. Manuscripts read year-round.

THE CENTENNIAL REVIEW—312 Linton Hall, Michigan State Univ., East Lansing, MI 48824–1044. R.K. Meiners, Ed. Articles, 3,000 to 5,000 words, on sciences, humanities, and interdisciplinary topics. Pays in copies.

THE CHARITON REVIEW—Northeast Missouri State Univ., Kirksville, MO 63501. Jim Barnes, Ed. Highest quality poetry and fiction, to 6,000 words. Modern and contemporary translations. "The only guideline is excellence in all matters."

THE CHICAGO REVIEW—5801 S. Kenwood Ave., Chicago, IL 60637. David Nicholls, Ed. Andy Winston, Fiction Ed. Essays, interviews, reviews, fiction, translations, poetry. Pays in copies plus one year's subscription. Manuscripts read year-round; replies in 2 to 3 months.

CHIRON REVIEW—Route 2, Box 111, St. John, KS 67576–2212. Michael Hathaway, Ed. Contemporary fiction, to 4,000 words; articles, 500 to 1,000 words; and poetry, to 30 lines. Photos. Pays in copies.

CICADA—329 E St., Bakersfield, CA 93304. Frederick A. Raborg, Jr., Ed. Quarterly. Single haiku, sequences or garlands, essays about the forms, haibun and fiction (one story per issue) related to haiku or Japan. Pays in copies.

CIMARRON REVIEW—205 Morrill Hall, Oklahoma State Univ., Stillwater, OK 74078–0135. Gordon Weaver, Ed. Poetry, fiction, essays. Seeks an individual, innovative style that focuses on contemporary themes. Pays $50 for stories and essays; $15 for poems, plus one-year subscription. Manuscripts read year-round.

CLOCKWATCH REVIEW—Dept. of English, Illinois Wesleyan Univ., Bloomington, IL 61702–2900. James Plath, Ed. Semiannual. Fiction, to 4,000 words, and poetry, to 36 lines. "Our preference is for fresh language, a believable voice, a mature style, and a sense of the unusual in the subject matter." Pays $25 for fiction, $5 for poetry, on acceptance, plus copies. Manuscripts read year-round.

COLLAGES & BRICOLAGES—P.O. Box 86, Clarion, PA 16214. Marie-José Fortis, Ed. Annual. Fiction and nonfiction, plays, interviews, book reviews, and poetry. Surrealistic and expressionistic drawings in ink. "I seek writers who are politically and socially aware and whose writing is not egocentric." Pays in copies. Manuscripts read August through October.

COLORADO REVIEW—English Dept., Colorado State Univ., Fort Collins,

CO 80523. David Milofsky, Ed. Fiction, poetry, essays, and reviews. Pays $5 per printed page. Manuscripts read September to May.

COLUMBIA: A MAGAZINE OF POETRY & PROSE—404 Dodge, Columbia Univ., New York, NY 10027. Address the Eds. Semiannual. Fiction and nonfiction; poetry; essays; interviews; visual art. Pays in copies. SASE required. Guidelines. Manuscripts read September to May.

THE COMICS JOURNAL—Fantagraphics, Inc., 7563 Lake City Way, Seattle, WA 98115. Address Man. Ed. Monthly journal, 90 percent written by freelancers with "working knowledge of the diversity and history of the comics medium." Reviews, 2,500 to 5,000 words; domestic and international news, 500 to 7,000 words; "Opening Shots" editorials, 500 to 1,500 words; interviews; and features, 2,500 to 5,000 words. Query for news and interviews. Pays 1 ½¢ a word, on publication. Guidelines.

CONFRONTATION—Dept. of English, C.W. Post of L. I. U., Brookville, NY 11548. Martin Tucker, Ed. Serious fiction, 750 to 6,000 words. Crafted poetry, 10 to 200 lines. Pays $10 to $100, on publication.

THE CONNECTICUT POETRY REVIEW—P.O. Box 3783, New Haven, CT 06525. J. Claire White and James William Chichetto, Eds. Poetry, 5 to 20 lines, and reviews, 700 words. Pays $5 per poem, $10 per review, on acceptance. Manuscripts read September to January and April to June.

CONNECTICUT RIVER REVIEW—P.O. Box 2171, Bridgeport, CT 06608. Robert Isaacs, Ed. Semiannual. Poetry. Submit 3 to 5 poems, to 40 lines each. Pays in one copy. Guidelines.

THE COOL TRAVELER—P.O. Box 11975, Philadelphia, PA 19145. Bob Moore, Pub./Ed. Quarterly. Articles, 1,000 to 1,250 words, including excerpts from diaries and letters written while traveling. "We are a literary magazine about place and experience; we emphasize 'what happened' rather than 'what to see.' " Travel-related poetry. Pays to $20, on publication.

CRAB CREEK REVIEW—4462 Whitman N., Seattle, WA 98103. Linda Clifton, Ed. Carol Orlock, Fiction Ed. Semiannual. Clear, dynamic fiction, to 4,000 words, with strong voice and imagery. Nonfiction, to 4,000 words, that "uses image and occasion as a reason to share ideas with an intelligent reader." Poetry, to 80 lines. Pays in copies.

CRAZY QUILT—P.O. Box 632729, San Diego, CA 92163–2729. Address the Eds. Fiction, to 4,000 words, poetry, one-act plays, and literary criticism. Also B&W art, photographs. Pays in copies. Manuscripts read year-round.

THE CREAM CITY REVIEW—Box 413, Univ. of Wisconsin, Milwaukee, WI 53201. Mark Drechsler and Brian Jung, Eds.-in-Chief. "We serve a national audience interested in a diversity of writing (in terms of style, subject, genre) and writers (gender, race, class, publishing history, etc.). Both well-known and newly published writers of fiction, poetry, and essays are featured, along with B&W artwork." Payment varies, usually $5 a page plus 2 copies. Manuscripts read year-round; responds in 8 weeks (not as quickly during the summer).

THE CRESCENT REVIEW—1445 Old Town Rd., Winston-Salem, NC 27106–3143. Guy Nancekeville, Ed. Semiannual. Short stories only. Pays in copies. No submissions May to June or November to December.

CRITICAL INQUIRY—Univ. of Chicago Press, Wieboldt Hall, 1050 E. 59th St., Chicago, IL 60637. W. J. T. Mitchell, Ed. Critical essays that offer a theoretical perspective on literature, music, visual arts, and popular culture. No fiction, poetry, or autobiography. Pays in copies. Manuscripts read year-round.

CUMBERLAND POETRY REVIEW—P.O. Box 120128, Acklen Sta., Nashville, TN 37212. Address Eds. High-quality poetry and criticism; translations. No restrictions on form, style, or subject matter. Pays in copies.

DENVER QUARTERLY—Univ. of Denver, Denver, CO 80208. Donald Revell, Ed. Literary, cultural essays and articles; poetry; book reviews; fiction. Pays $5 per printed page, after publication.

DESCANT—Texas Christian Univ., T.C.U. Sta., Fort Worth, TX 76129. Betsy Colquitt, Stanley Trachtenberg, Harry Opperman, and Steve Sherwood, Eds. Fiction, to 6,000 words. Poetry, to 40 lines. No restriction on form or subject. Pays in copies. Frank O'Connor Award ($500) is given each year for best short story published in the volume. Submit material September through May only.

THE DEVIL'S MILLHOPPER—The Devil's Millhopper Press, College of Humanities, USC/Aiken, 171 University Pkwy., Aiken, SC 29801–6399. Stephen Gardner, Ed. Poetry. Send SASE for guidelines and contest information. Pays in copies.

DOG RIVER REVIEW—5976 Billings Rd., Parkdale, OR 97041–9610. Laurence F. Hawkins, Ed. Fiction, plays, book reviews, and related articles, to 2,500 words. Poetry, to 30 lines. B&W art. No religious or greeting card verse. Pays in copies.

DREAMS & VISIONS—Skysong Press, RR1, Washago, Ontario, Canada L0K 2B0. Wendy Stanton, Manuscript Ed. Eclectic fiction, 2,000 to 6,000 words, that is "in some way unique and relevant to Christian readers today." Pays in copies, with $100 honorarium to best of the year.

EARTH'S DAUGHTERS—P.O. Box 41, Central Park Sta., Buffalo, NY 14215. Published 3 times a year. Fiction, to 1,000 words, poetry, to 40 lines, and B&W photos or drawings. "Finely crafted work with a feminist theme." Pays in copies. SASE for guidelines.

ELF: ECLECTIC LITERARY FORUM—ELF Associates, Inc., P.O. Box 392, Tonawanda, NY 14150. C. K. Erbes, Ed. Fiction, 3,500 words. Essays on literary themes, 3,500 words. Poetry, to 30 lines. Allow 4 to 6 weeks for response. Pays in 2 copies.

EMBERS—Box 404, Guilford, CT 06437. Katrina Van Tassel, Mark Johnston, Charlotte Garrett, Eds. Semiannual. Poetry. Interested in original new voices as well as published poets. Chapbook contest in Spring. Manuscripts read year-round.

EVENT—Douglas College, Box 2503, New Westminster, BC, Canada V3L 5B2. Dale Zieroth, Ed. Short fiction, reviews, poetry. Pays $22 per printed page, on publication.

FARMER'S MARKET—P.O. Box 1272, Galesburg, IL 61402. Short stories, essays, and novel excerpts, to 40 pages, and poetry. Pays in copies.

FICTION INTERNATIONAL—English Dept., San Diego State Univ., San Diego, CA 92182–0295. Harold Jaffe, Larry McCaffery, Eds. Post-modernist and politically committed fiction and theory. Pays in copies. Manuscripts read from September 1 to December 15.

THE FIDDLEHEAD—Campus House, Univ. of New Brunswick, Fredericton, N.B., Canada E3B 5A3. Serious fiction, 2,500 words, preferably by Canadians.

Pays about $10 per printed page, on publication. SAE with international reply coupons required. Manuscripts read year-round.

FIELD—Rice Hall, Oberlin College, Oberlin, OH 44074. Stuart Friebert, David Young, Eds. Serious poetry, any length, by established and unknown poets; essays on poetics by poets. Translations by qualified translators. Payment varies, on publication. Manuscripts read year-round.

FINE MADNESS—P.O. Box 31138, Seattle, WA 98103–1138. Poetry, any length; short fiction. Pays in copies. No simultaneous submissions. Guidelines.

FIVE FINGERS REVIEW—P.O. Box 15426, San Francisco, CA 94115. Published once or twice a year. "Writing with a sense of experimentation, an awareness of tradition, and a willingness to explore artistic boundaries." Pays in copies.

FOLIO—Dept. of English, American Univ., Washington, DC 20016. Elizabeth Poliner, Ed. Semiannual. Fiction, poetry, translations, and essays. Photos and drawings. Pays in 2 copies. Submissions read September through March. Contest.

FOOTWORK, THE PATERSON LITERARY REVIEW—Cultural Affairs Dept., Passaic County Comm. College, College Blvd., Paterson, NJ 07505–1179. Maria Mazziotti Gillan, Ed. High-quality fiction and poetry, to 200 pages. Pays in copies. Manuscripts read January through May.

THE FORMALIST—320 Hunter Dr., Evansville, IN 47711. William Baer, Ed. Metrical poetry, to 2 pages, including blank verse, couplets, and traditional forms such as sonnets, ballads, villanelles, etc. "Sound and rhythm make poetry what it is."

FREE INQUIRY—P.O. Box 664, Buffalo, NY 14226. Paul Kurtz, Ed. Tim Madigan, Exec. Ed. Articles, 500 to 5,000 words, for "literate and lively readership. Focus is on criticisms of religious belief systems, and how to lead an ethical life without a supernatural basis." Pays in copies.

FUGUE—Univ. of Idaho, English Dept., Brink Hall, Room 200, Moscow, ID 83843. Address Exec. Ed. Literary digest of the Univ. of Idaho. Fiction, to 7,000 words. Nonfiction, to 2,000 words, on writing. Poetry, any style, 100 lines. "We try to give new writers in all classifications of fiction and poetry a chance at publication." Manuscripts not returned; include SASE for editorial reply. Guidelines. Pays in copies.

THE GEORGIA REVIEW—Univ. of Georgia, Athens, GA 30602–9009. Stanley W. Lindberg, Ed. Stephen Corey, Assoc. Ed. Short fiction; personal and interdisciplinary essays; book reviews; poetry. Novel excerpts discouraged. No submissions in June to September.

THE GETTYSBURG REVIEW—Gettysburg College, Gettysburg, PA 17325. Peter Stitt, Ed. Quarterly. Poetry, fiction, essays, and essay-reviews, 1,000 to 20,000 words. "Review sample copy before submitting." Pays $2 a line for poetry; $25 per printed page for fiction and nonfiction. Allow 3 to 6 months for response.

GLIMMER TRAIN PRESS—812 S.W. Washington St., Suite 1205, Portland, OR 97205. Susan Burmeister, Ed. Quarterly. Fiction, 1,200 to 6,000 words. Twelve stories in each issue. Pays $300, on acceptance. Submit material in January, April, July, and October. Allow 3 months for response.

GRAHAM HOUSE REVIEW—Box 5000, Colgate Univ., Hamilton, NY 13346. Peter Balakian, Ed. Bruce Smith, Ed. Poetry, translations, and essays on modern poets. Payment depends on grants. Manuscripts read year-round; reponds in 2 to 4 weeks.

GRAIN—Box 1154, Regina, Sask., Canada S4P 3B4. Geoffrey Ursell, Ed. Short stories, to 30 typed pages; poems, send up to 8; visual art. Pays $30 to $100 for stories, $100 for cover art, $30 for other art. Self-addressed envelope with international reply coupons required. Manuscripts read year-round.

GRAND STREET—131 Varick St., #906, New York, NY 10013. Jean Stein, Ed. Quarterly. Fiction, essays, and criticism, 10 to 30 pages, and poetry, any length. Pays $200 to $1,000 for fiction and nonfiction; $3 a line for poetry, on publication.

GREEN'S MAGAZINE—P.O. Box 3236, Regina, Sask., Canada S4P 3H1. David Green, Ed. Fiction for family reading, 1,500 to 4,000 words. Poetry, to 40 lines. Pays in copies. International reply coupons must accompany U.S. manuscripts. Manuscripts read year-round.

THE GREENSBORO REVIEW—Dept. of English, Univ. of North Carolina, Greensboro, NC 27412–5001. Jim Clark, Ed. Semiannual. Poetry and fiction. Submission deadlines: September 15 and February 15. Pays in copies. Writer's guidelines and guidelines for literary awards issue available on request.

HALF TONES TO JUBILEE—Pensacola Junior College, English Dept., 1000 College Blvd., Pensacola, FL 32504. Walter F. Spara, Ed. Fiction, to 1,500 words, and poetry, to 60 lines. Pays in copies. Manuscripts read August 15 to May 15. Contest.

HAUNTS—Nightshade Publications, Box 3342, Providence, RI 02906–0742. Joseph K. Cherkes, Ed. Short stories, 1,500 to 8,000 words: horror, science-fantasy, and supernatural tales with strong characters. Pays ¼¢ to 1¢ a word, on publication. Manuscripts read January 1 to June 1.

HAWAII REVIEW—Dept. of English, Univ. of Hawaii, 1733 Donagho Rd., Honolulu, HI 96822. Tamara Moan, Ed.-in-Chief. Quality fiction, poetry, interviews, essays, and literary criticism reflecting both regional and global concerns. Manuscripts read year-round.

HAYDEN'S FERRY REVIEW—Matthew's Center, Arizona State Univ., Tempe, AZ 85287–1502. Salima Keegan, Ed. Semiannual. Fiction, essays, and poetry (submit up to 6 poems). Include brief bio and SASE. Deadline for Spring/Summer issue is September 30; Fall/Winter issue, February 28. Pays in copies.

THE HEARTLANDS TODAY—Firelands Writing Center of Firelands College, Huron, OH 44839. Larry Smith and Nancy Dunham, Eds. Fiction, 1,000 to 4,500 words, and nonfiction, 1,000 to 3,000 words, about the contemporary Midwest. Poetry (submit 3 to 5 poems)."Writing must be set in the Midwest, but can include a variety of themes." B&W photos. Query for current themes. Pays in copies.

HERESIES: A FEMINIST PUBLICATION ON ART AND POLITICS—Box 1306, Canal Street Sta., New York, NY 10013. Thematic issues. Fiction, to 15 double-spaced typed pages; nonfiction; poetry; art; photography. SASE required.

THE HIGHLANDER—P.O. Box 397, Barrington, IL 60011. Angus Ray, Ed. Bimonthly. Articles, 1,300 to 1,900 words, related to Scottish history. "We are not concerned with modern Scotland or current problems in Scotland." Pays $100 to $150, on acceptance.

THE HOLLINS CRITIC—P.O. Box 9538, Hollins College, VA 24020. John

Rees Moore, Ed. Published 5 times a year. Brief book reviews. Poetry. Pays $25 for poetry, on publication.

HOME PLANET NEWS—P.O. Box 415, Stuyvesant Sta., New York, NY 10009. Enid Dame and Donald Lev, Eds. Quarterly art tabloid. Fiction, to 8 typed pages; reviews, 3 to 5 pages; and poetry, any length. "We are looking for quality poetry, fiction, and discerning literary and art reviews." Query for nonfiction. Pays in copies and gift subscription. Manuscripts read year-round.

HOWLING DOG—8419 Rhode, Utica, MI 48317. Dorothy Donovan, Ed. Semiannual. "Strange" fiction, to 1,000 words. Free verse, avant-garde, wild poetry, to 5 pages. "We are looking for pieces with a humorous perspective toward society's problems." Pays in copies.

HURRICANE ALICE: A FEMINIST QUARTERLY—207 Lind Hall, 207 Church St. S.E., Minneapolis, MN 55455. Articles, fiction, essays, interviews, and reviews, 500 to 3,000 words, with feminist perspective. Pays in copies.

THE ILLINOIS REVIEW—(formerly *Illinois Writers Review*) English Dept., Illinois State Univ., Normal, IL 61761–6901. Jim Elledge, Ed. Semiannual. Poems, stories, novel excerpts, one-act plays, translations, essays, and book reviews. "Open to mainstream and alternative material by established or unknown writers." B&W cover art and photos. Pays in copies. Manuscripts read year-round; responds in one to 2 months.

IN THE COMPANY OF POETS—P.O. Box 10786, Oakland, CA 94610. Jacalyn Robinson, Ed./Pub. Quarterly. Fiction and creative essays, to 2,500 words, for a wide multicultural range of readers. Poems of any length. Drawings and photos. Pays in 3 copies. Guidelines. Manuscripts read year-round.

INDIANA REVIEW—316 N. Jordan Ave., Indiana Univ., Bloomington, IN 47405. Cara Diaconoff, Ed. Gretchen Knapp, Assoc. Ed. Fiction with an emphasis on storytelling and sophistication of language. Poems that are well-executed and ambitious. Pays $5 per page. SASE required. Manuscripts read year-round.

INTERIM—Dept. of English, Univ. of Nevada, Las Vegas, NV 89154–5034. A. Wilber Stevens, Ed. Semiannual. Fiction, to 5,000 words, and poetry. Pays in copies and 2-year subscription. Responds in 2 months.

THE IOWA REVIEW—EPB 308, Univ. of Iowa, Iowa City, IA 52242. David Hamilton, Ed. Essays, poems, stories, reviews. Pays $10 a page for fiction and nonfiction, $1 a line for poetry, on publication. Manuscripts read August 15 through May 15.

IOWA WOMAN—P.O. Box 680, Iowa City, IA 52244. Marianne Abel, Ed. Fiction and articles, 6,500 words, on midwestern history; interviews with prominent women; current social, economic, and environmental issues. Poems, any length (submit up to 5); photos and drawings. "We rarely publish work by men, and consider only personal essays from them about relationships with women." Queries preferred for articles. Pays $5 a page; $25 for illustrations; $75 for cover art, on publication. Guidelines.

JACARANDA REVIEW—Dept. of English, Univ. of California, Los Angeles, CA 90024. Bruce Kijewski, Ed. Laurence Roth, Poetry Ed. Semiannual. Fiction, to 50 pages, and poetry (submit up to 3 poems). No payment.

JAPANOPHILE—Box 223, Okemos, MI 48864. Earl R. Snodgrass, Ed. Fiction, to 4,000 words, with a Japanese setting. Each story should have at least one Japanese character and at least one non-Japanese. Articles, 2,000 words, that celebrate Japanese culture. "We seek to promote Japanese-American understanding. We are not about Japan-bashing or fatuous praise." Pays to $20, on publication. Annual contest in December.

A JOYFUL NOISE—Spiritual Quest Publishing, 249 Tamiami Trail S., Venice, FL 34285. Marla Bovinett, Ed. Inspirational and religious poetry, to 20 lines. Submit up to four poems at a time. "We like upbeat, nontraditional, free-verse. Poems should be moving, dramatic, humorous, and thought-provoking. We use all forms of poetry." Guidelines. No payment.

KALEIDOSCOPE—United Disability Services, 326 Locust St., Akron, OH 44302-1876. Darshan Perusek, Ph.D., Ed.-in-Chief. Semiannual. Fiction, essays, interviews, articles, and poetry relating to disability and the arts, to 5,000 words. Photos a plus. "We present balanced, realistic images of people with disabilities and publish pieces that challenge stereotypes." Submissions accepted from writers with or without disabilities. Pays $10 to $125. Guidelines recommended. Manuscripts read year-round; response may take up to 6 months.

KANSAS QUARTERLY—English Dept., Kansas State Univ., Manhattan, KS 66506. Literary criticism, art, and history. Fiction and poetry. Pays in copies. Two series of annual awards.

KARAMU—Dept. of English, Eastern Illinois Univ., Charleston, IL 61920. Peggy Brayfield, Ed. Contemporary or experimental fiction. Creative nonfiction prose, personal essays, and memoir pieces. Poetry. Pays in copies. Manuscripts read year-round; best time to submit is January to May.

THE KENYON REVIEW—Kenyon College, Gambier, OH 43022. Marilyn Hacker, Ed. Quarterly. Fiction, poetry, essays, literary criticism, and reviews. "We appreciate manuscripts from writers who read the magazine." Pays $10 a printed page for prose, $15 a printed page for poetry and reviews, on publication. Manuscripts read September to March.

KIOSK—c/o English Dept., 302 Clemens Hall, SUNY Buffalo, Buffalo, NY 14260. N. Gillespie, Ed. "Quirky experimental fiction and poetry." SASE required. Pays in copies. Manuscripts read from September 1 to April 15.

LATINO STUFF REVIEW—P.O. Box 440195, Miami, FL 33144. Nilda Cepero-Llevada, Ed./Pub. Short stories, 3,000 words; poetry, to one page; criticism and essays on literature, the arts, social issues. Bilingual publication focusing on Latino topics. Pays in copies.

LAUGHING MEDUSA RECORDINGS—23705 Vanowen St., #289, West Hills, CA 91307. Address the Ed. Poetry and prose for multi-disciplinary theme albums. Send SASE for guidelines. Pays in royalties.

THE LEADING EDGE—3163 JKHB, Provo, UT 84602. Michael Carr, Ed. Science fiction and fantasy magazine published 3 times a year. Short stories, 3,000 to 12,000 words; poetry, to 200 lines; and articles, to 8,000 words, on science, scientific speculation, and literary criticism. Fillers and comics. "Do not send originals; manuscripts are marked and critiqued by staff." Pays ½¢ per word ($5 minimum) for fiction; $5 per published page of poetry; $2 to $4 for fillers; on publication. SASE for guidelines.

LIGHT—Box 7500, Chicago, IL 60680. John Mella, Ed. Quarterly. Light verse. Also fiction, reviews, and essays, to 2,000 words. Fillers, humor, jokes, quips. "If it has wit, point, edge, or barb, it will find a home here." Cartoons and line drawings. Query for nonfiction. Pays in copies.

LILITH, THE INDEPENDENT JEWISH WOMEN'S MAGAZINE—250 W. 57th St., New York, NY 10107. Susan Weidman Schneider, Ed. Fiction, 1,500 to 2,000 words, on issues of interest to Jewish women.

LITERARY MAGAZINE REVIEW—English Dept., Kansas State Univ., Manhattan, KS 66506. Reviews and articles concerning literary magazines, 1,000 to 1,500 words, for writers and readers of contemporary literature. Pays modest fees and in copies. Query.

THE LITERARY REVIEW—Fairleigh Dickinson Univ., 285 Madison Ave., Madison, NJ 07940. Walter Cummins, Martin Green, Harry Keyishian, William Zander, Eds. Jill Kushner, Man Ed. Serious fiction; poetry; translations; essays and reviews on contemporary literature. Pays in copies.

LONG NEWS: IN THE SHORT CENTURY—P.O. Box 150–455, Brooklyn, NY 11215. Barbara Henning, Ed. Semiannual. Short experimental essays, 1,000 to 1,500 words. Visual art, poetry, and prose with an emphasis on experimental and urban work. Pays in copies.

LONG SHOT—P.O. Box 6238, Hoboken, NJ 07030. Danny Shot, Jack Wiler, Jessica Chosid, Tom Pulhamus, Eds. Fiction, poetry, and nonfiction, to 10 pages. B&W photos and drawings. Pays in copies.

THE LONG STORY—11 Kingston St., N. Andover, MA 01845. Stories, 8,000 to 20,000 words; prefer stories about poor and working class people. Pays in copies. Manuscripts read year-round.

LOST CREEK LETTERS—Lost Creek Publications, RR 2, Box 373A, Rushville, MO 64484. Pamela Montgomery, Ed. Fiction, to 3,000 words, and poetry, any length. "We are looking for shining gems of contemporary literature. We will not read material sent without SASE." Pays $5 for short stories, $2 for poems, or 2 contributor's copies. Study guidelines before submitting.

MAGIC REALISM—P.O. Box 620, Orem, UT 84059–0620. C. Darren Butler and Julie Thomas, Eds. Published 2 to 3 times a year. Stories, to 7,500 words (4,000 words preferred), of magic realism, exaggerated realism, some genre fantasy/dark fantasy. Occasionally publish glib fantasy like that found in folktales, fairy tales, and myths. No occult, sleight-of-hand magicians, or wizards/witches. Pays in one copy.

THE MALAHAT REVIEW—Univ. of Victoria, P.O. Box 1700, Victoria, BC, Canada V8W 2Y2. Derk Wynand, Ed. Fiction and poetry, including translations. Pays from $20 per page, on acceptance.

MASSACHUSETTS REVIEW—Memorial Hall, Univ. of Massachusetts, Amherst, MA 01003. Literary criticism; articles on public affairs, scholarly disciplines. Short fiction, 15 to 25 pages. Poetry. Pays $50, on publication. SASE required. No submissions between June and October.

MEDIPHORS—P.O. Box 327, Bloomsburg, PA 17815. Eugene D. Radice, MD, Ed. "A literary journal of the health professionals." Short stories, essays, and commentary, 3,000 words. "Topics should have some relation to medicine and health, but may be quite broad." Poems, to 30 lines. Humor. Pays in copies. Guidelines.

MICHIGAN HISTORICAL REVIEW—Clarke Historical Library, Central Michigan Univ., Mt. Pleasant, MI 48859. Address Ed. Semiannual. Scholarly articles related to Michigan's political, social, economic, and cultural history; articles on American, Canadian, and Midwestern history that directly or indirectly explore themes related to Michigan's past. SASE required. Manuscripts read year-round.

MID-AMERICAN REVIEW—Dept. of English, Bowling Green State Univ., Bowling Green, OH 43403. George Looney, Ed. Wayne Burham, Assoc. Ed. High-quality fiction, poetry, articles, translations, and reviews of contemporary writing. Fiction to 5,000 words, (query for longer work). Reviews, articles, 500 to 2,500 words. Pays to $50, on publication (pending funding). No manuscripts read June through August.

MIDWEST QUARTERLY—Pittsburg State Univ., Pittsburg, KS 66762. James B. M. Schick, Ed. Scholarly articles, 2,500 to 5,000 words, on contemporary academic and public issues; poetry. Pays in copies. Manuscripts read year-round.

THE MINNESOTA REVIEW—Dept. of English, East Carolina Univ., Greenville, NC 27858. Address the Editors. "Politically committed fiction, 1,000 to 6,000 words, nonfiction, 5,000 to 7,500 words, and poetry, 3 pages maximum, for readers committed to social issues, including feminism, neomarxism, etc." Pays in copies. Responds in 2 to 4 months.

MISSISSIPPI REVIEW—Center for Writers, Univ. of Southern Mississippi, Southern Sta., Box 5144, Hattiesburg, MS 39406–5144. Frederick Barthelme, Ed. Serious fiction, poetry, criticism, interviews. Pays in copies.

THE MISSISSIPPI VALLEY REVIEW—Dept. of English, Western Illinois Univ., Macomb, IL 61455. John Mann and Tama Baldwin, Eds. Short fiction, poetry (send 3 to 5 poems), and essays. Pays in copies. Manuscripts read September to May.

THE MISSOURI REVIEW—1507 Hillcrest Hall, Univ. of Missouri-Columbia, Columbia, MO 65211. Greg Michalson, Man. Ed. Speer Morgan, Ed. Poems, of any length. Fiction and essays. Pays $20 per printed page, on contract. Manuscripts read year-round.

MODERN HAIKU—P.O. Box 1752, Madison, WI 53701–1752. Robert Spiess, Ed. Haiku and articles about haiku. Pays $1 per haiku, $5 a page for articles. Manuscripts read year-round.

MONTHLY REVIEW—122 W. 27th St., New York, NY 10001. Paul M. Sweezy, Harry Magdoff, Eds. Analytical articles, 5,000 words, on politics and economics, from independent socialist viewpoint. Pays $25 for reviews, $50 for articles, on publication.

MOVING OUT—P.O. Box 21249, Detroit, MI 48221. Poetry, fiction, articles, and art by women. Submit 4 to 6 poems at a time. Pays in copies.

NEBO: A LITERARY JOURNAL—Dept. of English and Foreign Languages, Arkansas Tech. Univ., Russellville, AR 72801–2222. Poems (submit up to 5); mainstream fiction, to 3,000 words; critical essays, to 10 pages. Pays in one copy. SASE required. Guidelines. Offices closed May through August. "Best time to submit is November through February."

NEGATIVE CAPABILITY—62 Ridgelawn Dr. E., Mobile, AL 36608. Sue Walker, Ed. Poetry, any length; fiction, essays, art. Pays $20 per story. Contests.

NEW AUTHOR'S JOURNAL—1542 Tibbits Ave., Troy, NY 12180. Mario V. Farina, Ed. Fiction, to 3,000 words, and poetry. Topical nonfiction, to 1,000 words. Pays in copies and subscription. Manuscripts read year-round.

NEW DELTA REVIEW—c/o Dept. of English, Louisiana State Univ., Baton Rouge, LA 70803–5001. Randi Gray, Nicola Mason, Catherine Williamson, Eds. Semiannual. Fiction and nonfiction, to 5,000 words. Submit up to 4 poems, any length. Also essays, interviews, reviews, and B&W photos or drawings. "We want to see your best work, even if it's been rejected elsewhere." Pays in copies. Manuscripts read year-round.

NEW ENGLAND REVIEW—Middlebury College, Middlebury, VT 05753. T.R. Hummer, Ed. Devon Jersild, Assoc. Ed. Fiction, nonfiction, and poetry of varying lengths. "National, international, literary, political, effectively radical writing." Pays $10 per page, on acceptance, and in copies and subscription. Manuscripts read September to May.

NEW LAUREL REVIEW—828 Lesseps St., New Orleans, LA 70117. Lee Meitzen Grue, Ed. Annual. Fiction, 10 to 20 pages; nonfiction, to 10 pages; poetry, any length. Library market. No inspirational verse. International readership. Pays in one copy.

NEW LETTERS—Univ. of Missouri-Kansas City, Univ. House, Kansas City, MO 64110–2499. James McKinley, Ed.-in-Chief. Fiction, 3,500 to 5,000 words. Poetry, submit 3 to 6 at a time. Send SASE for literary awards guidelines. Manuscripts read October 15 to May 15.

NEW MEXICO HUMANITIES REVIEW—Box A, New Mexico Tech., Socorro, NM 87801. Poetry and fiction, to 30 pages, any theme; personal and scholarly essays; articles dealing with southwestern and Native American themes; book reviews. Pays in subscriptions. Manuscripts read year-round. Annual contests.

NEW ORLEANS REVIEW—Loyola Univ., New Orleans, LA 70118. John Biguenet, Ed. Literary or film criticism, to 6,000 words. Serious fiction and poetry.

THE NEW PRESS LITERARY QUARTERLY—53-35 Hollis Court Blvd., Flushing, NY 11365. Bob Abramson, Pub. Quarterly. Fiction and nonfiction, to 2,500 words. Poetry to 200 lines. Pays $25 for prose. Contests. Manuscripts over 10 pages read from January through June; shorter pieces read year-round.

THE NEW RENAISSANCE—9 Heath Rd., Arlington, MA 02174. Louise T. Reynolds, Ed. An international magazine of ideas and opinions, emphasizing literature and the arts. Query with SASE, outline, and writing sample for articles; send complete manuscript for fiction. Limited poetry market. Payment varies, after publication. Manuscripts read from January 2 to June 30.

THE NEW YORK QUARTERLY—P.O. Box 693, Old Chelsea Sta., New York, NY 10011. William Packard, Ed. Published 3 times a year by The National Poetry Foundation. Poems of any style and persuasion, well written and well intentioned. Pays in copies. Manuscripts read year-round.

NEXUS—Wright State Univ., 006 Univ. Center, Dayton, OH 45435. Ted Cains, Ed. Kayt Hoke, Man. Ed. Poetry, hard-hitting fiction, photography. One-act plays. Essays on obscure poets, artists, and musicians. Pays in copies.

NIGHTSUN—School of Arts & Humanities, Frostburg State Univ., Frostburg, MD 21532–1099. Douglas DeMars, Ed. Annual. Short stories, about 3 pages, and poems, to 40 lines. Payment is 2 copies. Manuscripts read September 1 to May 1.

NIMROD—2210 S. Main St., Tulsa, OK 74114–1190. Publishes 2 issues annually, one awards and one thematic. Quality poetry and fiction, experimental and traditional. Pays $5 a page (to $25) and copies. Annual awards for poetry and fiction. Send SASE for guidelines.

THE NORTH AMERICAN REVIEW—Univ. of Northern Iowa, Cedar Falls, IA 50614–0516. Peter Cooley, Poetry Ed. Poetry of high quality. Pays from $20 per poem, on acceptance. Manuscripts read year-round.

NORTH ATLANTIC REVIEW—15 Arbutus Ln., Stony Brook, NY 11790–1408. John Gill, Ed. Annual. Fiction and nonfiction, to 5,000 words; poetry, any length; fillers, humor, photographs and illustrations. A special section on social issues is a part of each issue. Pays in copies. Responds in 5 or 6 months.

THE NORTH DAKOTA QUARTERLY—Univ. of North Dakota, Grand Forks, ND 58202–8237. Essays in the humanities; fiction, reviews, graphics, and poetry. Limited market. Pays in copies and subscription.

NORTHEASTARTS—Boston Arts Organization, Inc., JFK Sta., P.O. Box 6061, Boston, MA 02114. Mr. Leigh Donaldson, Ed. Fiction and nonfiction, to 750 words; poetry, to 30 lines; and brief humor. "Both professional and beginning writers are considered. No obscene or offensive material." Payment is one copy.

NORTHWEST REVIEW—369 PLC, Univ. of Oregon, Eugene, OR 97403. Hannah Wilson, Fiction Ed. Fiction, commentary, essays, and poetry. Reviews. Pays in copies. Send SASE for guidelines.

OASIS—P.O. Box 626, Largo, FL 34649–0626. Neal Storrs, Ed. Short fiction and literary essays, to 5,000 words, poetry, and translations from French, German, Italian, or Spanish. Nonfiction on any subject. No children's stories. Complete manuscripts preferred. Pays $15 to $50 for prose, $5 per poem, on publication. Guidelines.

OBJECT LESSON—(formerly *West*) Bluestone Press, P.O. Box 1186, Hampshire College, Amherst, MA 01002. John C. Horoschak, Man. Ed. Joshua Saul Beckman, Poetry Ed. Andrew Pollock, Fiction Ed. Semiannual. Fiction and poetry, to 100 pages, one-act plays, essays, interviews, B&W artwork. Annual poetry and fiction contests. Pays in copies.

THE OHIO REVIEW—Ellis Hall, Ohio Univ., Athens, OH 45701–2979. Wayne Dodd, Ed. Short stories, poetry, essays, reviews. Pays $5 per page for prose, $1 a line for poetry, plus copies, on publication. SASE required. Submissions not read in June, July, or August.

ONIONHEAD—Arts on the Park, Inc., 115 N. Kentucky Ave., Lakeland, FL 33801–5044. Address the Editorial Council. Short stories, to 4,000 words; essays, to 2,500 words; and poetry, to 60 lines; on provocative social, political, and cultural observations and hypotheses. Pays in copies. Send SASE for Wordart poetry contest information. Manuscripts read year-round; responds in 8 weeks.

ORANGE COAST REVIEW—Dept. of English, Orange Coast College, 2701 Fairview Rd., Costa Mesa, CA 92628–5005. Short stories, poetry, essays, and interviews, any length. Submit material from December 1 to April 1. Allow 6 to 8 weeks for response. Payment is 2 copies.

OREGON EAST—Hoke College Center, EOSC, La Grande, OR 97850. Short fiction, nonfiction, to 3,000 words, poetry, and high-contrast graphics. Pays in copies. Manuscripts read September though April.

ORPHIC LUTE—Dreamcatcher Multiple Arts, Inc., 1713 14th Ave., Seattle, WA 98112. David Sparenberg, Ed. Lyric poetry, to 40 lines. Special interests include ethnic, ecological, mythic, and dream-related themes. Pays in copies. Submissions read year-round.

OTHER VOICES—Univ. of Illinois at Chicago, Dept. of English (M/C 162), Box 4348, Chicago, IL 60680. Lois Hauselman, Sharon Fiffer, Eds. Semiannual. Fresh, accessible short stories, one-act plays, and novel excerpts, to 5,000 words. Pays in copies and modest honorarium. Reading period is October 1 to April 1.

OUTERBRIDGE—College of Staten Island, English Dept. A324, 715 Ocean Terr., Staten Island, NY 10301. Charlotte Alexander, Ed. Annual. Well-crafted stories, about 20 pages, and poetry, to 4 pages, "directed to a wide audience of literate adult readers." Pays in 2 copies. Manuscripts read September to June.

THE OXFORD AMERICAN—115 1/2 S. Lamar, Oxford, MS 38655. Marc Smirnoff, Ed. Quarterly. Short fiction, nonfiction, and light, humorous poetry. Currently overstocked in fiction; "our interest in good nonfiction is strong." Cartoons, photos, and drawings. Pays from $50 for poetry and art; from $100 for nonfiction, on publication.

PAINTBRUSH—Language & Literature, Northeast Missouri State Univ., Kirksville, MO 63501. Ben Bennani, Ed. Semiannual. Book reviews, to 1,500 words, and serious, sophisticated poems (submit 3 to 5). Query preferred for book reviews. Pays in copies.

PAINTED BRIDE QUARTERLY—230 Vine St., Philadelphia, PA 19106. Marion Wren, Kathleen Volk-Miller, Brian Brown, Eds. Fiction and poetry of varying lengths. Pays in subscription.

PAINTED HILLS REVIEW—P.O. Box 494, Davis, CA 95617. Michael Ishii, Ed. Kara Kosmatka, Ed. Well-crafted fiction and creative nonfiction, to 4,000 words. Poetry, to 100 lines. Pays in one or 2 copies. Manuscripts read year-round. Contests.

PANDORA—2844 Grayson, Ferndale, MI 48220. Meg Mac Donald, Ed. Ruth Berman, Poetry Ed. (2809 Drew Ave. S., Minneapolis, MN 55416). Fiction overstocked; query with SASE. Poetry (send to MN address) and art (to MI address; mark envelope "ART"). "Read magazine before submitting."

PANHANDLER—English Dept., Univ. of West Florida, Pensacola, FL 32514–5751. Michael Yots, Stanton Millet, and Laurie O'Brien, Eds. Semiannual. Fiction, 1,500 to 3,000 words, "that tells a story"; poetry, any length, with a strong sense of colloquial language. Pays in copies. Responds in one to 3 months.

THE PARIS REVIEW—541 E. 72nd St., New York, NY 10021. Address Fiction and Poetry Eds. Fiction and poetry of high literary quality. Pays on publication.

PARNASSUS—41 Union Sq. W., Rm. 804, New York, NY 10003. Herbert Leibowitz, Ed. Critical essays and reviews on contemporary poetry. International in scope. Pays in cash and copies. Manuscripts read year-round.

PARTISAN REVIEW—Boston Univ., 236 Bay State Rd., Boston, MA 02215. William Phillips, Ed. Serious fiction, poetry, and essays. Payment varies. No simultaneous submissions. Manuscripts read year-round.

PASSAGES NORTH—Kalamazoo College, 1200 Academy St., Kalamazoo, MI 49006. Michael Barrett, Ed. Semiannual; published in December and June. Poetry, fiction, essays, interviews, visual art. Pays in copies. Manuscripts read September to June.

THE PENNSYLVANIA REVIEW—Univ. of Pittsburgh, Dept. of English, 526 Cathedral of Learning, Pittsburgh, PA 15260. Fiction, to 5,000 words, book reviews, interviews with authors, and poems (send up to 6 at once). Pays in copies. Manuscripts accepted September through March.

PEQUOD—New York Univ. English Dept., 19 University Pl., 2nd Fl., New York, NY 10003. Mark Rudman, Ed. Semiannual. Short stories, essays, and literary criticism, to 10 pages; poetry and translations, to 3 pages. Pays $10 to $25, on publication.

PIEDMONT LITERARY REVIEW—Bluebird Lane, Rt. #1, Box 1014, Forest, VA 24551. Evelyn Miles, Man. Ed. Quarterly. Prose, to 2,500 words. Submit prose to Dr. Olga Kronmeyer, 25 W. Dale Dr., Lynchburg, VA 24501. Poems, any length and style. Submit up to 5 poems to Gail White, 1017 Spanish Moss Ln., Breaux Bridge, LA 70517. Submit Asian verse to Dorothy McLaughlin, 10 Atlantic Rd., Somerset, NJ 08873. No pornography. Pays one copy.

PIG IRON PRESS—P.O. Box 237, Youngstown, OH 44501–0237. Jim Villani, Ed. Fiction and nonfiction, to 8,000 words. Poetry, to 100 lines. Write for upcoming themes. Pays $5 per published page or poem, on publication. Manuscripts read year-round. Responds in 3 months.

THE PINEHURST JOURNAL—Pinehurst Press, P.O. Box 360747, Milpitas, CA 95036–0747. Michael K. McNamara, Ed. Quarterly. Contemporary and experimental fiction, 750 to 4,000 words. Articles, 1,500 to 3,500 words, on art, music, literature, theater, and opinion; profiles and essays. Poetry, to 24 lines. Line art (no photos). Pays $5, on publication, plus one copy, for fiction and nonfiction; pays in one copy for poetry and art. Send #10 SASE for guidelines. Manuscripts read year-round.

PIVOT—250 Riverside Dr., #23, New York, NY 10025. Martin Mitchell, Ed. Annual. Poetry, to 75 lines. Pays 2 copies. Manuscripts read January 1 to June 1.

PLAINS POETRY JOURNAL—Box 2337, Bismarck, ND 58502–2337. Jane Greer, Ed. Poetry using traditional conventions in vigorous, compelling ways; no greeting card-type verse or prosaic verse. No subject is taboo. Pays in copies.

PLOUGHSHARES—Emerson College, 100 Beacon St., Boston, MA 02116–1596. Pays $10 to $50, on publication, plus 2 copies and subscription. Manuscripts read September through April. Guidelines.

POEM—c/o English Dept., U.A.H., Huntsville, AL 35899. Nancy Frey Dillard, Ed. Serious lyric poetry. Pays in copies. Manuscripts read year-round (best times to submit are December to March and June to September).

POET AND CRITIC—203 Ross Hall, Iowa State Univ., Ames, IA 50011–1201. Neal Bowers, Ed. Poetry, reviews, essays on contemporary poetry. Pays in copies. No manuscripts read June through August.

POET LORE—The Writer's Center, 4508 Walsh St., Bethesda, MD 20815. Philip K. Jason, Exec. Ed. Sunil Freeman, Man. Ed. Original poetry, all kinds. Translations, reviews, and critical essays. Pays in copies. Annual narrative poetry contest.

POET MAGAZINE—P.O. Box 54947, Oklahoma City, OK 73154. Quarterly. "Dedicated to publishing poets at all levels. New and experienced poets encouraged to submit." Submit copies of up to 5 poems, any subject, form, or length, and articles of any length on subjects related to poetry. Include SASE for editorial reply; manuscripts will not be returned. Payment is one copy. Guidelines.

POETRY—60 W. Walton St., Chicago, IL 60610. Joseph Parisi, Ed. Poetry of highest quality. Submit 3 to 4 poems. Allow 8 to 10 weeks for response. Pays $2 a line, on publication.

POETRY EAST—DePaul Univ., 802 W. Belden Ave., Chicago, IL 60614–3214. Marilyn Woitel, Man. Ed. Semiannual. Poetry, essays, and translations.

"Please send a sampling of your best work. Do not send book-length manuscripts without querying first." Pays in copies.

PORTLAND REVIEW—c/o Portland State Univ., P.O. Box 751, Portland, OR 97207. Semiannual. Short fiction, essays, poetry, one-act plays (to 5 pages), photography, and artwork. "Please include a bio." Payment is one copy.

PRAIRIE SCHOONER—201 Andrews Hall, Univ. of Nebraska, Lincoln, NE 68588–0334. Hilda Raz, Ed. Short stories, poetry, essays, book reviews, and translations. Pays in copies. SASE required. Manuscripts read year-round; reponds in 3 months. Annual contests.

PRIMAVERA—Box 37–7547, Chicago, IL 60637. Attn: Editorial Board. Annual. Fiction and poetry that focuses on the experiences of women; "author need not be female." B&W photos and drawings. Pays in 2 copies. Reponds within 3 months.

PRISM INTERNATIONAL—E459-1866 Main Mall, Dept. of Creative Writing, Univ. of British Columbia, Vancouver, B.C., Canada V6T 1Z1. High-quality fiction, poetry, drama, creative nonfiction, and literature in translation, varying lengths. Include international reply coupons. Pays $20 per published page. Annual short fiction contest.

PROOF ROCK—P.O. Box 607, Halifax, VA 24558. Don Conner, Fiction Ed. Serena Fusek, Poetry Ed. Fiction, to 2,500 words. Poetry, to 32 lines. Reviews. Pays in copies.

PUCKERBRUSH REVIEW—76 Main St., Orono, ME 04473. Constance Hunting, Ed. Semiannual. Literary fiction, criticism, and poetry of various lengths, "to bring literary Maine news to readers." Pays in 2 copies. Manuscripts read year-round.

PUDDING MAGAZINE—c/o Pudding House Bed & Breakfast for Writers, 60 N. Main St., Johnstown, OH 43031. Jennifer Bosveld, Ed. "The International Journal of Applied Poetry." Poems on popular culture, social concerns, personal struggle; poetry therapy that has been revised for art's sake; articles/essays on poetry in the human services. Manuscripts read year-round.

PUERTO DEL SOL—New Mexico State Univ., Box 3E, Las Cruces, NM 88003–0001. Kevin McIlvoy, Ed. Short stories and personal essays, to 30 pages; novel excerpts, to 65 pages; articles, to 45 pages, and reviews, to 15 pages. Poetry, photos. Pays in copies. Manuscripts read September 1 to April 1.

PULPHOUSE: A FICTION MAGAZINE—P.O. Box 1227, Eugene, OR 97440. Dean Wesley Smith, Ed./Pub. Fiction, 5,000 words: science fiction, fantasy, horror, mystery, romance, western, and mainstream. Nonfiction, to 5,000 words: articles, essays, interviews, and news items that are controversial or innovative with a futuristic slant. Occasionally uses poetry. Query for nonfiction only. Pays 4¢ to 7¢, on publication.

QUARTERLY WEST—317 Olpin Union, Univ. of Utah, Salt Lake City, UT 84112. Jeffrey Vasseur and M.L. Williams, Eds. Short-shorts and poetry. Biennial novella competition in even-numbered years. Pays $25 to $50 for stories, $25 for poems. Manuscripts read year-round.

RAG MAG—P.O. Box 12, Goodhue, MN 55027–0188. Beverly Voldseth, Ed. Semiannual. Eclectic fiction and nonfiction, art, photos. Poetry, any length. No religious writing. Pays in copies. Manuscripts read year-round.

RAMBUNCTIOUS REVIEW—1221 W. Pratt Blvd., Chicago, IL 60626.

Mary Dellutri, Richard Goldman, Nancy Lennon, Beth Hausler, Eds. Fiction, to 12 pages; poems, submit up to 5 at a time. Pays in copies. Manuscripts read September through May. Contests.

RECONSTRUCTION—1563 Massachusetts Ave., Cambridge, MA 02138. Randall Kennedy, Pub. Quarterly. Articles, 2,000 to 40,000 words, on "important political, social, and cultural issues involving race relations. We are particularly concerned with providing a forum for uninhibited commentary on African-American politics, society, and culture." Payment is negotiable. Queries preferred.

RED CEDAR REVIEW—Dept. of English, 17-C Morrill Hall, Michigan State Univ., East Lansing, MI 48824–1036. Nann Barkiewicz, Ed. Fiction, to 20 pages; poetry (submit up to 4); interviews; book reviews; and graphics. "Submit unpublished work only; no simultaneous submissions." Pays in copies. Manuscripts read year-round.

THE REDNECK REVIEW OF LITERATURE—2919 N. Downer Ave., Milwaukee, WI 53211. Penelope Reedy, Ed. Semiannual. Fiction, to 2,500 words, of the contemporary American West; essays and book reviews, 300 to 1,500 words; poetry. Pays in copies. Manuscripts read year-round.

REED MAGAZINE—Dept. of English, San Jose State Univ., One Washington Sq., San Jose, CA 95192–0090. Address Man. Ed. Fiction, personal essays, and reminiscences, to 10,000 words, and poetry on any subject. "We want material of a literary nature, addressing the human condition." B&W photos. Pays is one copy. Manuscripts read August 1 to November 1.

RESONANCE—P.O. Box 215, Beacon, NY 12508. Evan Pritchard, Ed. Published sporadically. Fiction, to 1,200 words; thematic nonfiction, to 1,200 words; poetry, to 46 lines. Pays one copy.

REVIEW: LATIN AMERICAN LITERATURE AND ARTS—Americas Society, 680 Park Ave., New York, NY 10021. Alfred J. MacAdam, Ed. Semiannual. Work in English translation by and about young and established Latin American writers; essays and book reviews considered. Send queries for 1,000- to 1,500-word manuscripts, and short poem translations. Payment varies, on acceptance.

RHINO—8403 W. Normal Ave., Niles, IL 60648. Kay Meier and Don Hoffman, Eds. "Authentic emotion in well-crafted poetry." Pays in copies. Manuscripts read year-round.

RIVER CITY—Dept. of English, Memphis State Univ., Memphis, TN 38152. J.P. Craig, Man. Ed. Joey Flamm, Assoc. Ed. Poems, short stories, essays and interviews. No novel excerpts. Pay varies according to grants. Manuscripts read September though April. Contests.

RIVER STYX—14 S. Euclid, St. Louis, MO 63108. Address the Ed. Published 3 times a year. Fiction, personal essays, literary interviews, poetry, and B&W photos. Payment is $8 per printed page and 2 copies. Manuscripts read September 1 to October 31; reports in 12 weeks.

RIVERSIDE QUARTERLY—Box 958, Big Sandy, TX 75755. Leland Sapiro, Ed. Science fiction and fantasy, to 3,500 words; reviews, criticism, any length; poetry and letters. "Read magazine before submitting." Send poetry to Sheryl Smith, 515 Saratoga #2, Santa Clara, CA 95050; fiction to Redd Boggs, Box 1111, Berkeley, CA 94701. Pays in copies.

ROANOKE REVIEW—Roanoke College, Salem, VA 24153. Robert R. Walter, Ed. Quality short fiction, to 7,500 words, and poetry, to 100 lines. Pays in copies.

SAN FERNANDO POETRY JOURNAL—18301 Halstead St., Northridge, CA 91325. Richard Cloke, Ed. Quality poetry, 20 to 100 lines, with social content; scientific, philosophical, and historical themes. Pays in copies.

SAN JOSE STUDIES—c/o English Dept., San Jose State Univ., San Jose, CA 95192. John Engell and David Mesher, Eds. Poetry, fiction, and essays on interdisciplinary topics, focusing on Bay Area and California cultures. Occasionally publishes photos and art. Pays in copies. Annual awards. Responds in 2 to 3 months.

SANSKRIT LITERARY/ART PUBLICATION—Univ. of North Carolina/Charlotte, Charlotte, NC 28223–0001. Address the Ed. Annual. Poetry, short fiction, photos, and fine art.

SCANDINAVIAN REVIEW—725 Park Ave., New York, NY 10021. Published 3 times year. Essays on contemporary Scandinavia: arts, sciences, business, politics, and culture of Scandinavia. Fiction and poetry, translated from Nordic languages. Pays from $100, on publication.

THE SEATTLE REVIEW—Padelford Hall, GN-30, Univ. of Washington, Seattle, WA 98195. Donna Gerstenberger, Ed. Short stories, to 20 pages, poetry, essays on the craft of writing, and interviews with northwest writers. Payment varies. Manuscripts read September 1 through May 31.

SENECA REVIEW—Hobart & William Smith Colleges, Geneva, NY 14456. Deborah Tall, Ed. Poetry, translations, and essays on contemporary poetry. Pays in copies. Manuscripts read September 1 to May 1.

SHOOTING STAR REVIEW—7123 Race St., Pittsburgh, PA 15208. Sandra Gould Ford, Pub. Fiction and folktales, to 3,000 words, essays, to 2,000 words, and poetry, to 50 lines, on the African-American experience. Query for book reviews only. Pays $5 for poems; $10 for essays; $10 to $20 for fiction. Send SASE for topic deadlines. Responds to queries in 3 weeks; manuscripts in 4 months.

SHORT FICTION BY WOMEN—Box 1276, Stuyvesant Sta., New York, NY 10009. Rachel Whalen, Ed. Published 3 times a year. Short stories, novellas, and novel excerpts, to 20,000 words, by women writers. No horror, romance, or mystery fiction. Payment varies, on publication. Manuscripts read year-round. Guidelines.

SIN MAGAZINE—432 F St., #411, San Diego, CA 92101. Jeffree Benet, Man. Ed. Fiction and nonfiction, 1,500 to 2,800 words, that "tear apart contemporary society and culture. Our articles are revolutionary, nihilistic, and hilarious." Pays in copies and nominal fee, on publication.

SING HEAVENLY MUSE! WOMEN'S POETRY & PROSE—P.O. Box 13320, Minneapolis, MN 55414. Short stories and essays, to 5,000 words. Poetry. Query for themes and reading periods. Pays in copies.

SKYLARK—2200 169th St., Hammond, IN 46323–2094. Pamela Hunter, Ed. "The Fine Arts Annual of Purdue Calumet." Fiction and articles, to 4,000 words. Poetry, to 21 lines. B&W prints and drawings. Pays in one copy. Manuscripts read December 1 through May 31 for fall publication.

SLIPSTREAM—Box 2071, Niagara Falls, NY 14301. Contemporary poetry, any length. Pays in copies. Query for themes. (Also accepting cassette tape submissions for audio poetics tape series: spoken word, collaborations, songs, audio experimentation.) Guidelines. Annual poetry chapbook contest has a December 1 deadline; send SASE for details.

SMALL MAGAZINE REVIEW—Dustbooks, P.O. Box 100, Paradise, CA

95967. Len Fulton, Ed./Pub. Reviews, 200 words, of little and literary magazines. Query. Pays 10¢ a word, on acceptance.

THE SMALL POND MAGAZINE—P.O. Box 664, Stratford, CT 06497–0664. Napoleon St. Cyr, Ed. Published 3 times a year. Fiction, to 2,500 words; poetry, to 100 lines. Query for nonfiction. SASE required. Include short bio. Pays in copies. Manuscripts read year-round.

SMALL PRESS REVIEW—Box 100, Paradise, CA 95967. Len Fulton, Ed. News pieces and reviews, to 200 words, about small presses and little magazines. Pays in copies.

SNAKE NATION REVIEW—Snake Nation Press, 110 #2 W. Force, Valdosta, GA 31601. Roberta George, Ed. Semiannual. Short stories, novel chapters, and informal essays, 5,000 words, and poetry, to 60 lines. Pays in copies.

SNOWY EGRET—P.O. Box 9, Bowling Green, IN 47833. Karl Barnebey and Michael Aycock, Eds. Poetry, fiction, and nonfiction, to 10,000 words. Natural history from artistic, literary, philosophical, and historical perspectives. Pays $2 per page for prose; $2 to $4 for poetry, on publication. Manuscripts read year-round.

SONORA REVIEW—Dept. of English, Univ. of Arizona, Tucson, AZ 85721. Address Fiction, Poetry, or Nonfiction Ed. Fiction, poetry, translations, interviews, literary nonfiction. Personal essays, memoirs, creative nonfiction. Pays in copies. Annual prizes for fiction, poetry, and nonfiction. No manuscripts read in the summer.

THE SOUTH CAROLINA REVIEW—Dept. of English, Clemson Univ., Clemson, SC 29634–1503. Richard J. Calhoun, Exec. Ed. Semiannual. Fiction, essays, reviews, and interviews of up to 4,000 words. Short poems. Send complete manuscript; query Mark Royden Winchell for book reviews. Pays in copies. Response time is 6 to 9 months. No manuscripts read in summer or December.

SOUTH COAST POETRY JOURNAL—English Dept., CSUF, Fullerton, CA 92634. John J. Brugaletta, Ed. Semiannual. Poetry, to 40 lines. Only unpublished and uncommitted poetry, please. "Our editorial tastes are eclectic, ranging from the strictly metered and rhymed to free verse and including virtually every mixture in between." Payment is in one copy. Manuscripts read September through May.

SOUTH DAKOTA REVIEW—Box 111, Univ. Exchange, Vermillion, SD 57069–2390. John R. Milton, Ed. Exceptional fiction, 3,000 to 5,000 words, and poetry, 10 to 25 lines. Critical articles, especially on American literature, Western American literature, theory and esthetics, 3,000 to 5,000 words. Pays in copies. Manuscripts read year-round; slower response time in the summer.

THE SOUTHERN CALIFORNIA ANTHOLOGY—c/o Master of Professional Writing Program, WPH 404, Univ. of Southern California, Los Angeles, CA 90089–4034. James Ragan, Ed.-in-Chief. Fiction, to 20 pages, and poetry, to 5 pages. Pays in copies. Manuscripts read September to May.

SOUTHERN EXPOSURE—P.O. Box 531, Durham, NC 27702. Eric Bates, Ed. Quarterly forum on "Southern movements for social change." Short stories, to 4,500 words, essays, investigative journalism, and oral histories, 500 to 4,500 words. Pays $25 to $200, on publication. Query.

SOUTHERN HUMANITIES REVIEW—9088 Haley Center, Auburn Univ., AL 36849. Dan R. Latimer, R. T. Smith, Eds. Short stories, essays, and criticism, 3,500 to 5,000 words; poetry, to 2 pages. Responds within 3 months. SASE required.

SOUTHERN POETRY REVIEW—Dept. of English, Univ. of North Carolina, Charlotte, NC 28223. Lucinda Grey and Ken McLaurin, Eds. Poems. No restrictions on style, length, or content. Manuscripts read September through May.

THE SOUTHERN REVIEW—43 Allen Hall, Louisiana State Univ., Baton Rouge, LA 70803. James Olney and Dave Smith, Eds. Emphasis on contemporary literature in United States and abroad with special interest in southern culture and history. Fiction and essays, 4,000 to 8,000 words. Serious poetry of highest quality. Pays $12 a page for prose, $20 a page for poetry, on publication. No manuscripts read in the summer.

SOUTHWEST REVIEW—307 Fondren Library W., Box 4374, Southern Methodist Univ., Dallas, TX 75275. Willard Spiegelman, Ed. "A quarterly that serves the interests of the region but is not bound by them." Fiction, essays, poetry, and interviews with well-known writers, 3,000 to 7,500 words. Pays varying rates. Manuscripts read September 1 though May 31.

SOU'WESTER—Southern Illinois Univ. at Edwardsville, Edwardsville, IL 62026–1438. Fred W. Robbins, Ed. Fiction, to 8,000 words. Poetry, any length. Pays in copies. Manuscripts read year-round; slower response time in the summer.

THE SOW'S EAR POETRY REVIEW—245 McDowell St., Bristol, TN 37620. Address the Eds. Quarterly. Eclectic poetry and art. Submit 1 to 5 poems, any length, plus a brief biographical note. Interviews, essays, and articles, any length, about poets and poetry are also considered. B&W photos and drawings. Payment is 1 copy.

SPARROW MAGAZINE—Sparrow Press, 103 Waldron St., W. Lafayette, IN 47906. Felix Stefanile, Ed./Pub. Contemporary (14-line) sonnets, and formal poems in other structures. Submit up to 5 poems. Pays $3 per poem, on publication. A $25 sonnet prize is awarded to a contributor in each issue.

SPECTRUM—University of California/ Santa Barbara, Box 14800, Santa Barbara, CA 93107. Short stories, to 12 pages, essays on literature, memoirs, poetry. Pays in copies. Annual contest. Manuscripts read September 20 to January 31.

SPECTRUM—Anna Maria College, Box 72-A, Paxton, MA 01612–1198. Robert H. Goepfert, Ed. Scholarly articles, 3,000 to 15,000 words; short stories, to 10 pages; and poetry, to 2 pages; book reviews, photos, and artwork. Pays $20 plus 2 copies. SASE required. Manuscripts read September 1 to May 10.

THE SPOON RIVER POETRY REVIEW—(formerly *The Spoon River Quarterly*) Dept. of English, Stevenson Hall, Illinois State Univ., Normal, IL 61761. Lucia Cordell Getsi, Ed. Poetry, any length. Pays in copies.

SPSM&H—329 E St., Bakersfield, CA 93304. Frederick A. Raborg, Jr., Ed. Single sonnets, sequences, essays about the sonnet form, short fiction in which the sonnet plays a part, books, and anthologies. Pays $10, plus copies.

STAND MAGAZINE—Route 2, Box 122-B, Lacey's Spring, AL 35754. Address the Ed. Fiction, 2,000 to 4,000 words, and poetry to 100 lines. No formulaic verse.

STORY QUARTERLY—P.O. Box 1416, Northbrook, IL 60065. Anne Brashler, Diane Williams, Eds. Short stories and interviews. Pays in copies. Manuscripts read year-round.

STUDIES IN AMERICAN FICTION—English Dept., Northeastern Univ., Boston, MA 02115. James Nagel, Ed. Reviews, 750 words; scholarly essays, 2,500 to 6,500 words, on American fiction. Pays in copies.

THE STYLUS—9412 Huron Ave., Richmond, VA 23294. Roger Reus, Ed. Annual. "An open forum for intelligent, well-researched articles on a variety of authors and literary topics." Query preferred. Limited fiction market. Pays in copies.

THE SUN—The Sun Publishing Co., 107 N. Roberson St., Chapel Hill, NC 27516. Sy Safransky, Ed. Articles, essays, interviews, and fiction, to 10,000 words; poetry; photos, illustrations, and cartoons. "We're interested in all writing that makes sense and enriches our common space." Pays $100 for fiction and essays, $25 for poetry, on publication.

SYCAMORE REVIEW—Purdue Univ., Dept. of English, West Lafayette, IN 47907. Linda Collins Haynes, Ed.-in-Chief. Semiannual. Poetry, short fiction (no genre fiction), personal essays, and translations, to 10,000 words. Pays in copies. Manuscripts read September to April.

TAR RIVER POETRY—Dept. of English, East Carolina Univ., Greenville, NC 27834. Peter Makuck, Ed. Poetry and reviews. "Interested in skillful use of language, vivid imagery. Less academic, more powerful poetry preferred." Pays in copies. Submit from September to November or January to April.

THE TEXAS REVIEW—English Dept., Sam Houston State Univ., Huntsville, TX 77341. Paul Ruffin, Ed. Fiction, poetry, articles, to 20 typed pages. Reviews. Pays in copies and subscription.

THEMA—Box 74109, Metairie, LA 70033–4109. Virginia Howard, Ed. Fiction, to 20 pages, and poetry, to two pages, related to theme. Pays $25 per story; $10 per short-short; $10 per poem; $10 for B&W art/photo, on acceptance. Send SASE for themes and guidelines.

THIRTEEN—Box 392, Portlandville, NY 13834–0392. Ken Stone, Ed. Quarterly. Thirteen-line poetry. Pays in one copy. Manuscripts read year-round.

THE THREEPENNY REVIEW—P.O. Box 9131, Berkeley, CA 94709. Wendy Lesser, Ed. Fiction, to 5,000 words. Poetry, to 100 lines. Essays on books, theater, film, dance, music, art, television, and politics, 1,500 to 3,000 words. Pays to $200, on acceptance. Limited market. Send SASE for guidelines.

TIGHTROPE—323 Pelham Rd., Amherst, MA 01002. Ed Rayher, Ed. Limited-edition, letterpress semiannual. Fiction and nonfiction, to 10 pages; poetry, any length. Pays in copies. Manuscripts read year-round.

TOUCHSTONE—P.O. Box 8308, Spring, TX 77387. Bill Laufer, Pub. Annual. Fiction, 750 to 2,000 words: mainstream, experimental. Interviews, essays, reviews. Poetry, to 40 lines. Pays in copies. Manuscripts read year-round.

TRANSLATION—The Translation Center, 412 Dodge Hall, Columbia Univ., New York, NY 10027. Frank MacShane, Dir. Semiannual. New translations of contemporary foreign fiction and poetry. Query. Payment varies.

TRIQUARTERLY—Northwestern Univ., 2020 Ridge Ave., Evanston, IL 60208–4302. Serious, aesthetically informed and inventive poetry and prose, for an international and literate audience. Pays $20 per page for prose, $1.50 per line for poetry. Reading period October 1 to March 31. Allow 10 to 12 weeks for reply.

TRIVIA—P.O. Box 606, N. Amherst, MA 01059. Erin Rice, Kay Parkhurst, Eds. Semiannual journal of radical feminist writing. Literary essays, experimental prose, translations, interviews, and reviews. "After-readings": personal accounts of the writer's reaction to books or other writings by women. Pays in copies. Guidelines. Manuscripts read year-round.

2AM MAGAZINE—P.O. Box 6754, Rockford, IL 61125–1754. Gretta Anderson, Ed. Poetry, articles, reviews, and personality profiles, 500 to 2,000 words, as well as fantasy, horror, and some science fiction/sword-and-sorcery short stories, 500 to 5,000 words. Pays ½¢ a word, on acceptance. Manuscripts read year-round.

THE UNIVERSITY OF PORTLAND REVIEW—Univ. of Portland, Portland, OR 97203. Thompson M. Faller, Ed. Scholarly articles and contemporary fiction, 500 to 2,500 words. Poetry. Book reviews. Pays in copies.

UNIVERSITY OF WINDSOR REVIEW—Dept. of English, Univ. of Windsor, Windsor, Ont., Canada N9B 3P4. Joseph A. Quinn, Ed. Short stories, poetry. Pays $10 to $50, on publication. Responds in one to 3 months.

URBANUS/RAIZIRR—P.O. Box 192561, San Francisco, CA 94119. Peter Drizhal, Ed. Semiannual. Fiction and nonfiction, 1,000 to 5,000 words, and poetry, to 40 lines, that reflect post-modernist influences for a "readership generally impatient with the mainstream approach." B&W photos and drawings. Pays $5 to $20 for fiction and nonfiction, on publication; pays in copies for prose.

VERVE—P.O. Box 3205, Simi Valley, CA 93093. Ron Reichick, Ed. Contemporary fiction and nonfiction, to 1,000 words, that fits the theme of the issue. Poetry, to two pages; submit up to 5 poems. Pays in one copy. Query for themes.

THE VILLAGER—135 Midland Ave., Bronxville, NY 10708. Amy Murphy, Ed. Fiction, 900 to 1,500 words: mystery, adventure, humor, romance. Short, preferably seasonal poetry. Pays in copies.

VINCENT BROTHERS REVIEW—4566 Northern Cir., Mad River Township, Dayton, OH 45424–5789. Kimberly Willardson, Ed. Published three times a year. Fiction, nonfiction, poetry, fillers, and B&W art. "Read back issues before submitting." Pays from $10 for fiction and nonfiction, plus two copies; payment for all other work is two copies. Guidelines.

VIRGINIA QUARTERLY REVIEW—One W. Range, Charlottesville, VA 22903. Quality fiction and poetry. Serious essays and articles, 3,000 to 6,000 words, on literature, science, politics, economics, etc. Pays $10 per page for prose, $1 per line for poetry, on publication.

VISIONS INTERNATIONAL—1110 Seaton Ln., Falls Church, VA 22046. Bradley R. Strahan, Ed. Published 3 times a year. Poetry, to 40 lines, and B&W drawings. (Query first for art.) "Nothing amateur or previously published." Pays in copies. Manuscripts read year-round.

WASCANA REVIEW—c/o Dept. of English, Univ. of Regina, Regina, Sask., Canada S4S 0A2. Karen Smythe, Ed. Short stories, 2,000 to 6,000 words; critical articles. Pays $3 per page for prose, $10 for poetry, after publication.

WASHINGTON REVIEW—P.O. Box 50132, Washington, DC 20091–0132. Clarissa Wittenberg, Ed. Poetry; articles on literary, performing and fine arts in the Washington, D.C., area. Fiction, 1,000 to 2,500 words. Area writers preferred. Pays in copies. Responds in 3 months.

WEBSTER REVIEW—Webster Univ., 470 E. Lockwood, Webster Groves, MO 63119. Nancy Schapiro, Ed. Fiction; poetry; interviews; essays; translations. Pays in copies. Manuscripts read year-round.

WEST—See *Object Lesson.*

WEST BRANCH—Bucknell Hall, Bucknell Univ., Lewisburg, PA 17837. Karl Patten, Robert Taylor, Eds. Poetry and fiction. Pays in copies and subscriptions.

WESTERN HUMANITIES REVIEW—Univ. of Utah, Salt Lake City, UT 84112. Kristoffer Jacobson, Man. Ed. Quarterly. Fiction and essays, to 30 pages, and poetry. Pays $50 for poetry, $150 for short stories and essays, on acceptance. Manuscripts read year-round; responds in 3 to 6 months.

THE WILLIAM AND MARY REVIEW—P.O. Box 8795, College of William and Mary, Williamsburg, VA 23187–8795. Stacy Payne, Ed. Annual. Fiction, critical essays, and interviews, 2,500 to 7,500 words; poetry, all genres (submit 5 to 8 poems). Pays in copies. Manuscripts read September through April. Responds in 3 months.

WILLOW SPRINGS—MS-1, Eastern Washington Univ., Cheney, WA 99004–2496. Address the Ed. Fiction, poetry, translation, and art. Length and subject matter are open. Pays $10 for poetry; $35 for prose, on publication. Manuscripts read September 15 to May 15.

WIND—RFD #1-Box 809K, Pikeville, KY 41501. Quentin Howard, Ed. Semiannual. Short stories and poems. Reviews of books from small presses, to 250 words. Pays in copies. Manuscripts read year-round.

THE WINDLESS ORCHARD—Dept. of English, Indiana-Purdue Univ., Ft. Wayne, IN 46805. Robert Novak, Ed. Contemporary poetry. Pays in copies. SASE required. Manuscripts read year-round.

WITHOUT HALOS—Ocean County Poets Collective, P.O. Box 1342, Point Pleasant Beach, NJ 08742. Frank Finale, Ed. Submit 3 to 5 poems (to 2 pages) between January 1 and June 30. Pays in copies.

WITNESS—Oakland Community College, 27055 Orchard Lake Rd., Farmington Hills, MI 48334. Peter Stine, Ed. Thematic journal. Fiction and essays, 5 to 20 pages, and poems (submit up to 3). Pays $6 per page for prose, $10 per page for poetry, on publication.

WOMAN OF POWER—P.O. Box 2785, Orleans, MA 02653. Char McKee, Ed. A magazine of feminism, spirituality, and politics. Nonfiction, to 5,000 words. Send SASE for issue themes and guidelines. Pays in copies and subscription. Manuscripts read year-round.

THE WORCESTER REVIEW—6 Chatham St., Worcester, MA 01609. Rodger Martin, Ed. Poetry (submit up to 5 poems at a time), fiction, critical articles about poetry, and articles and reviews with a New England connection. Pays in copies. Reponds within 6 months.

THE WORMWOOD REVIEW—P.O. Box 4698, Stockton, CA 95204–0698. Marvin Malone, Ed. Quarterly. Poetry and prose-poetry, 4 to 400 lines. "We encourage wit and conciseness." Pays 3 to 20 copies or cash equivalent.

WRITERS FORUM—Univ. of Colorado, 1420 Austin Bluffs Pkwy., Colorado Springs, CO 80933–7150. Alex Blackburn, Ed. Annual. Mainstream and experimental fiction, 1,000 to 8,000 words. Poetry (one to 5 poems per submission). Emphasis on western themes and writers. Pays in copies. Send material September through February.

WRITERS ON THE RIVER—P.O. Box 40828, Memphis, TN 38174. Miss Demaris C. Smith, Ed. Catherine Hudgens, Prose Ed. Onida Simmons, Poetry Ed. Fiction (adventure, fantasy, historical, humor, mainstream, mystery/suspense), and nonfiction (profiles, scholarly essays, regional history), to 2,500 words. All types of poetry considered; submit up to 6. "We try to promote good writing and act as a sounding board for Southern writers." Submit 2 copies of manuscripts. Submissions accepted from: AR, AL, MS, LA, TN, KY, and MO. Pays in copies. Manuscripts read year-round.

XANADU: A LITERARY JOURNAL—Box 773, Huntington, NY 11743–0773. Mildred Jeffrey, Barbara Lucas, Weslea Sidon, Mitzie Grossman, Eds. Barry Fruchter, Articles Ed. Poetry on a variety of topics; no length restrictions. Scholarly articles on fiction and poetry. Pays in copies. Manuscripts read September through June.

YALE REVIEW—1902A Yale Sta., New Haven, CT 06520. J.D. McClatchy, Ed. Serious poetry, to 200 lines, and fiction, 3,000 to 5,000 words. Pays average of $300.

YARROW—English Dept., Lytle Hall, Kutztown State Univ., Kutztown, PA 19530. Harry Humes, Ed. Semiannual. Poetry. "Just good, solid, clear writing. We don't have room for long poems." Pays in copies. Manuscripts read year-round.

ZYZZYVA—41 Sutter, Suite 1400, San Francisco, CA 94104. Howard Junker, Ed. Publishes work of West Coast writers only: fiction, essays, and poetry. Pays $50 to $250, on acceptance. Manuscripts read year-round.

HUMOR, FILLERS, AND SHORT ITEMS

Magazines noted for their excellent filler departments, plus a cross-section of publications using humor, short items, jokes, quizzes, and cartoons, follow. However, almost all magazines use some type of filler material, and writers can find dozens of markets by studying copies of magazines at a library or newsstand.

THE AMERICAN FIELD—542 S. Dearborn, Chicago, IL 60605. B.J. Matthys, Ed. Short fact items and anecdotes on hunting dogs and field trials for bird dogs. Pays varying rates, on acceptance.

THE AMERICAN NEWSPAPER CARRIER—P.O. Box 2225, Kernersville, NC 27285. W.H. Lowry, Ed. Short, humorous pieces, to 1,200 words, for preteen, teenage, and adult newspaper carriers. Pays $25, on publication.

ARMY MAGAZINE—2425 Wilson Blvd., Arlington, VA 22201–3385. L. James Binder, Ed.-in-Chief. True anecdotes on military subjects. Pays $25 to $50, on publication.

THE ATLANTIC MONTHLY—745 Boylston St., Boston, MA 02116. Sophisticated humorous or satirical pieces, 1,000 to 3,000 words. Some light poetry. Pays from $500 for prose, on acceptance.

ATLANTIC SALMON JOURNAL—P.O. Box 429, St. Andrews, N.B., Canada E0G 2X0. Harry Bruce, Ed. Fillers, 50 to 100 words, on salmon politics, conservation, and nature. Pays $25 for fillers, on publication.

BICYCLING—33 E. Minor St., Emmaus, PA 18098. Anecdotes, helpful cycling tips, and other items for "Paceline" section, 150 to 250 words. Pays $50, on acceptance.

BIKEREPORT—Bikecentennial, P.O. Box 8308, Missoula, MT 59807. Daniel D'Ambrosio, Ed. News shorts from the bicycling world for "In Bicycle Circles." Pays $5 to $10, on publication.

BYLINE—Box 130596, Edmond, OK 73013. Marcia Preston, Ed.-in-Chief. Humor, 400 to 800 words, about writing. Pays $15 to $35 for humor, on acceptance.

CAPPER'S—1503 S.W. 42nd St., Topeka, KS 66609–1265. Nancy Peavler, Ed. Household hints, recipes, jokes. Pays varying rates, on publication.

CASCADES EAST—716 N. E. 4th St., P. O. Box 5784, Bend, OR 97708. Geoff Hill, Ed. Fillers related to travel, history, and recreation in central Oregon. Pays 5¢ to 10¢ a word, extra for photos, on publication.

CATHOLIC DIGEST—P.O. Box 64090, St. Paul, MN 55164–0090. No fiction. Articles, 200 to 500 words, on instances of unseeking kindness, for "Hearts Are Trumps." Stories about conversions, for "Open Door." Reports of tactful remarks or actions, for "The Perfect Assist." Accounts of good deeds, for "People Are Like That." Humorous pieces, 50 to 300 words, on parish life, for "In Our Parish." Amusing signs, for "Signs of the Times." Jokes; fillers. Pays $4 to $50, on publication. Manuscripts cannot be acknowledged or returned.

CHICKADEE—56 The Esplanade, Suite 306, Toronto, Ont., Canada M5E 1A7. Lizann Flatt, Ed. Humorous juvenile poetry, 10 to 15 lines. (Also humorous fiction, 800 words.) Pays on acceptance. Enclose international reply coupons.

CHILDREN'S PLAYMATE—1100 Waterway Blvd., P. O. Box 567, Indianapolis, IN 46206. Elizabeth Rinck, Ed. Puzzles, games, mazes for 6- to 8-year-olds, emphasizing health, safety, and nutrition. Pays about 10¢ a word (varies on puzzles), on acceptance.

COLUMBIA JOURNALISM REVIEW—Columbia Univ., 700 Journalism Bldg., New York, NY 10027. Gloria Cooper, Man. Ed. Amusing mistakes in news stories, headlines, photos, etc. (original clippings required), for "Lower Case." Pays $25, on publication.

CORPORATE CASHFLOW—6151 Powers Ferry Rd. N.W., Atlanta, GA 30339. Dick Gamble, Ed. Fillers, to 1,000 words, on varied aspects of treasury management and corporate finance, for treasury managers in public and private companies. Pays on acceptance. Query.

COUNTRY WOMAN—P. O. Box 989, Greendale, WI 53129. Kathy Pohl, Man. Ed. Short rhymed verse, 4 to 20 lines, seasonal in nature and country-related. All material must be positive and upbeat. Pays $10 to $25, on acceptance.

CRACKED—Globe Communications, Inc., 441 Lexington Ave., 2nd Fl., New York, NY 10017. Lou Silverstone, Andy Simmons, Eds. Humor, one to five pages, for 12- to 15-year-old readers. "Queries are not necessary, but read the magazine before submitting material!" Pays from $100 per page, on acceptance.

CYCLE WORLD—1499 Monrovia Ave., Newport Beach, CA 92663. David Edwards, Ed. News items on motorcycle industry, legislation, trends. Pays on publication.

THE ELKS MAGAZINE—425 W. Diversey Pkwy., Chicago, IL 60614. Fred D. Oakes, Ed. Informative or humorous pieces, to 2,500 words. No fillers. Pays from $150, on acceptance. Query required.

FACES—Cobblestone Publishing, 7 School St., Peterborough, NH 03458. Carolyn P. Yoder, Ed. Puzzles, mazes, crosswords, and picture puzzles, related to monthly themes, for children. Send SASE for themes before submitting.

FAMILY CIRCLE—110 Fifth Ave., New York, NY 10011. Uses some short humor, to 2,000 words. No fiction. Query required. Payment varies, on acceptance.

THE FAMILY DIGEST—(formerly *Parish Family Digest*) P.O. Box 40137, Fort Wayne, IN 46804. Corine B. Erlandson, Ed. Family- or Catholic parish-oriented humor. Anecdotes, to 250 words, of funny or unusual real-life parish and family experiences. Pays $5 to $10, on acceptance.

FATE—P.O. Box 64383, St. Paul, MN 55164–0383. Phyllis Galde, Ed. Factual fillers, to 300 words, on strange or psychic happenings. True stories, to 300 words, on proof of survival or mystic personal experiences. Pays 10¢ a word. Guidelines.

FIELD & STREAM—2 Park Ave., New York, NY 10016. Duncan Barnes, Ed. Fillers on hunting, fishing, camping, etc., to 500 words. Cartoons. Pays $75 to $250 for fillers, $100 for cartoons, on acceptance.

GALLERY—401 Park Ave. S., New York, NY 10016–8802. Barry Janoff, Ed. Dir. Rich Friedman, Man. Ed. Short humor, satire, and short service features for men. Pays varying rates, on publication. Query. Guidelines.

GAMES—19 W. 21st St., New York, NY 10010. Will Shortz, Ed. Pencil puzzles, visual brainteasers, and pop culture tests. Humor and playfulness a plus; quality a must. Pays top rates, on publication.

GOOD HOUSEKEEPING—959 Eighth Ave., New York, NY 10019. Rosemary Leonard, Ed. Two to 8 lines of witty poetry, light verse, and quips with broad appeal, easy to illustrate for "Light Housekeeping" page. Seasonal material welcome. SASE required for return of material. Pays $25 to $50, on acceptance.

GUIDEPOSTS—16 E. 34th St., New York, NY 10016. Colleen Hughes, Features Ed. Inspirational anecdotes, to 250 words. Pays $10 to $50, on acceptance.

HUMOR MAGAZINE—See *The New Humor Magazine.*

INDEPENDENT LIVING—150 Motor Pkwy., Suite 420, Hauppauge, NY 11788–5145. Anne Kelly, Ed. Short humor, to 500 words, and cartoons for magazine addressing lifestyles and home health care of persons who have disabilities. Pays 10¢ a word, on publication. Query.

THE JOURNAL OF IRREPRODUCIBLE RESULTS—Wisdom Simulators, P.O. Box 380853, Cambridge, MA 02238. Marc Abrahams, Ed. Science humor, science reports and analysis, one to four pages. B&W photos. "This journal is the place to find the mischievous, funny, iconoclastic side of science. An insider's journal that lets anyone sneak into the company of wonderfully mad scientists." Guidelines. No payment.

LADIES' HOME JOURNAL—"Kidspeak," 100 Park Ave., 3rd Fl., New York, NY 10017. Brief, true anecdotes about the amusing things children say for "Out of the Mouths of Babes" column. All material must be original. Pays $50 for children's anecdotes. Due to the volume of mail received, submissions cannot be acknowledged or returned.

MAD MAGAZINE—485 Madison Ave., New York, NY 10022. Address Eds. Humorous pieces on a wide variety of topics. Two- to eight-panel cartoons (not necessary to include sketches with submission). SASE for guidelines strongly recommended. Pays top rates, on acceptance.

MATURE LIVING—127 Ninth Ave. N., MSN 140, Nashville, TN 37234. Brief, humorous, original items; 25-line profiles with action photos; "Grandparents

Brag Board" items; Christian inspirational pieces for senior adults, 125 words. Pays $5 to $15.

MATURE YEARS—201 Eighth Ave. S., P.O. Box 801, Nashville, TN 37202. Marvin W. Cropsey, Ed. Poems, cartoons, puzzles, jokes, anecdotes, to 300 words, for older adults. Allow two months for manuscript evaluation. "A Christian magazine that seeks to build faith. We always show older adults in a favorable light." Include name, address, social security number with all submissions.

MID-WEST OUTDOORS—111 Shore Dr., Hinsdale, IL 60521–5885. Gene Laulunen, Man. Ed. Where to and how to fish and hunt in the Midwest, 400 to 1,500 words, with two photos (no slides). Pays $15 to $35, on publication.

MODERN BRIDE—249 W. 17th St., New York, NY 10011. Mary Ann Cavlin, Man. Ed. Humorous pieces, 500 to 1,000 words, for brides. Pays on acceptance.

MOUNTAIN BIKE—Rodale Press, 33 E. Minor St., Emmaus, PA 18098. Nelson Pena, Man. Ed. Descriptions, 500 words, detailing the routes of off-road rides. Pays $75, on acceptance.

NATIONAL ENQUIRER—Lantana, FL 33464. Michele Cooke, Asst. Ed. Short, humorous or philosophical fillers, witticisms, anecdotes, jokes, tart comments. Original items only. Short poetry with traditional rhyming verse, amusing, philosophical, or inspirational in nature. No obscure or artsy poetry. Submit seasonal/holiday material at least three months in advance. SASE required with all submissions. Pays $25, after publication.

NEW CHOICES FOR RETIREMENT LIVING—28 W. 23rd St., New York, NY 10010. David A. Sendler, Ed.-in-Chief. Short humor pieces for news/service magazine for people ages 50 to 65. Pays $1 a word.

THE NEW HUMOR MAGAZINE—(formerly *Humor Magazine*) Box 216, Lafayette Hill, PA 19444. Edward Savaria, Jr., Ed. Quarterly. Fiction, interviews, and profiles, up to 1,000 words; short poetry, jokes, and fillers. "We would edit out all truly gross humor and anything that elicits loud groans. Please, no X-rated jokes or stories." Pays $50 to $300 for stories and articles, $5 to $25 for jokes and fillers, on acceptance.

NEW JERSEY MONTHLY—P.O. Box 920, Morristown, NJ 07963–0920. Jenny DeMonte, Ed. Short pieces, 750 words, related to life in New Jersey. Pays $400.

NEW YORK—755 Second Ave., New York, NY 10017. Stephen J. Dubner, Assoc. Ed. Short, lively pieces, to 400 words, highlighting events and trends in New York City for "Fast Track." Profiles, to 300 words, for "Brief Lives." Pays $25 to $300, on publication. Include SASE.

THE NEW YORKER—20 W. 43rd St., New York, NY 10036. Address Newsbreaks Dept. Amusing mistakes in newspapers, books, magazines, etc. Pays from $10, extra for headings and tags, on acceptance. Material returned only with SASE.

THE NOSE—Acme Publishing Co., Inc., 1095 Market St., Suite 812, San Francisco, CA 94103. Jack Boulware, Ed. Humorous/investigative pieces with "a shoot-from-the-hip attitude." Features, 1,500 to 4,000 words, on some facet of the bizarre world of the West. Interviews, 1,000 to 3,000 words, that bring out the humorous and outrageous side of the subject. "The Beat," first-person experiences, 350 words. "Wild West," 300 words, random satirical pieces, rewrites of actual news items. Also short, witty reviews of recent videos and books, 150 words. No payment made. Guidelines.

OPTOMETRIC ECONOMICS—American Optometric Assn., 243 N. Lindbergh Blvd., St. Louis, MO 63141. Dr. Jack Runninger, Ed. Short humor on private practice management for optometrists. Payment varies, on acceptance.

OUTDOOR LIFE—2 Park Ave., New York, NY 10016. Vin T. Sparano, Ed. Short instructive items, 900 to 1,100 words, on hunting, fishing, boating, and outdoor equipment; regional pieces focus on lakes, rivers, specific geographic areas that are of special interest to hunters and fishermen. Photos. No fiction or poetry. Pays $300 to $350, on acceptance.

PARISH FAMILY DIGEST—See *The Family Digest.*

PLAYBOY—680 N. Lakeshore Dr., Chicago, IL 60611. Address Party Jokes Ed. or After Hours Ed. Jokes; short original material on new trends, lifestyles, personalities; humorous news items. Pays $100 for jokes, on publication; $50 to $350 for "After Hours" items, on publication.

PLAYGIRL—801 Second Ave., New York, NY 10017. Address Man. Ed. Humorous looks at daily life and relationships from male or female perspective, to 800 words, for "The Men's Room" and "The Women's Room." Query. Pays varying rates.

POPULAR MECHANICS—224 W. 57th St., New York, NY 10019. Deborah Frank, Man. Ed. How-to pieces, from 300 words, with photos and sketches, on home improvement and shop and craft projects. Pays $25 to $300, on acceptance. Buys all rights.

PUNCH DIGEST FOR CANADIAN DOCTORS—14845 Yonge St., Suite 300, Aurora, Ontario, Canada L4G 6H8. Simon Hally, Ed. Humorous pieces, 250 to 2,000 words, for physicians. "Most articles have something to do with medicine." Short humorous verse and original jokes. Pays 30¢ to 40¢ a word; $50 (Canadian) for cartoons, on publication.

READER'S DIGEST—Pleasantville, NY 10570. True, original anecdotes for "Life in These United States," "Humor in Uniform," "Campus Comedy," and "All in a Day's Work." Pays $400, on publication. Original short items for "Toward More Picturesque Speech." Pays $50. Anecdotes, original items, for "Laughter, the Best Medicine," "Personal Glimpses," "Points to Ponder," "Quotable Quotes," etc. Pays $30 per two-column line. No submissions acknowledged or returned. Consult "Contributor's Corner" page for guidelines.

REAL PEOPLE—950 Third Ave., 16th Fl., New York, NY 10022. Alex Polner, Ed. True stories, to 500 words, for "Real Bizarre" column, on the occult, UFOs, strange occurrences, everyday weirdness, etc.; may be funny, sad, or hair-raising. Also short (to 75 words) humorous items taken from small-circulation magazines, newspapers, etc., for "Real Shorts." Write Brad Hamilton, Ed. Pays $50 for "Real Bizarre" items, $25 for "Real Shorts," on publication. Buys all rights.

RHODE ISLAND MONTHLY—18 Imperial Pl., Providence, RI 02903. Vicki Sanders, Man. Ed. Short pieces, to 250 words, on Rhode Island and southeastern Massachusetts: places, customs, people and events; pieces to 150 words on products and services; to 200 words on food, chefs, and restaurants. Pays $25 to $50, on publication.

ROAD & TRACK—1499 Monrovia Ave., Newport Beach, CA 92663. Ellida Maki, Man. Ed. Short automotive articles, to 450 words, of "timeless nature" for knowledgeable car enthusiasts. Pays on publication. Query.

ROAD KING—P. O. Box 250, Park Forest, IL 60466. Address Features Ed. Trucking-related cartoons and anecdotes, to 200 words, for "Trucker's Life." Pays $25 for cartoons, $25 for anecdotes, on publication. SASE required.

THE ROTARIAN—1560 Sherman Ave., Evanston, IL 60201–3698. Willmon L. White, Ed. Occasional humor articles. Payment varies, on acceptance. No payment made for fillers, anecdotes, or jokes.

RURAL HERITAGE—281 Dean Ridge Ln., Gainesboro, TN 38562–9685. Gail Damerow, Ed. Articles, 250 to 300 words, on rural youngsters who have done or are doing remarkable things, for "Country Kids" column. Pays 5¢ a word, on publication.

SACRAMENTO MAGAZINE—4471 D St., Sacramento, CA 95819. Karen Coe, Ed. "City Lights," interesting and unusual people, places, and behind-the-scenes news items, to 400 words. All material must have Sacramento tie-in. Payment varies, on publication.

THE SATURDAY EVENING POST—P.O. Box 567, Indianapolis, IN 46206. Steven Pettinga, Post Scripts Ed. Humor and satire, to 100 words, that is upbeat and positive. No lurid references. Light verse, cartoons, jokes, for "Post Scripts." Original material only. Pays $15, on publication.

THE SINGLE PARENT—Parents Without Partners, Inc., 8807 Colesville Rd., Silver Spring, MD 20910–4346. Rene McDonald, Ed. Fillers, 300 to 500 words, addressing the concerns of the single parent. Pays $25 to $50, on publication.

SKI MAGAZINE—2 Park Ave., New York, NY 10016. Steve Cohen, Ed. Short, 100- to 300-word items on events and people in skiing for "Ski Life" department. Humor, 300 to 2,000 words, related to skiing. Pays on acceptance.

SOAP OPERA UPDATE—270 Sylvan Ave., Englewood Cliffs, NJ 07632. Allison J. Walsman, Man. Ed. Soap-opera oriented fillers, to 500 words. Payment varies, on publication.

SPORTS AFIELD—250 W. 55th St., New York, NY 10019. Unusual, useful tips, anecdotes, 100 to 300 words, for "Almanac" section: hunting, fishing, camping, boating, etc. Photos. Pays on publication.

SPORTS CARD TRADER—155 E. Ames Ct., Plainview, NY 11803. Douglas Kale, Ed. Fillers related to collecting and investing in baseball, football, basketball, and hockey cards. (Also articles on investing in sports cards or memorabilia.) Pays 10¢ a word, on publication.

TECH DIRECTIONS—Box 8623, Ann Arbor, MI 48107. Paul J. Bamford, Man. Ed. Cartoons, puzzles, brainteasers, and humorous anecdotes of interest to technology and industrial education teachers and administrators. Pays $20 for cartoons; $25 for puzzles and other material, on publication.

THOUGHTS FOR ALL SEASONS: THE MAGAZINE OF EPIGRAMS —11530 S.W. 99th St., Miami, FL 33176. Michel P. Richard, Ed. Epigrams and puns, 1 to 4 lines, and poetry, to 1 page. "Writers are advised not to submit material until they have examined a copy of the magazine." Payment is one copy.

TOUCH—Box 7259, Grand Rapids, MI 49510. Carol Smith, Man. Ed. Puzzles based on the NIV Bible, for Christian girls ages 8 to 14. Pays $10 to $15 per puzzle, on acceptance. Send SASE for themes.

TRAILER BOATS MAGAZINE—20700 Belshaw Ave., Carson, CA 90746. Randy Scott, Ed. Fillers and humor, preferably with illustrations, on boating and related activities. Pays $5 per column inch, extra for photos, on publication.

TRAVEL SMART—Dobbs Ferry, NY 10522. Interesting, unusual travel-related tips. Practical information for vacation or business travel. Query for over 250 words. Pays $5 to $150.

TRUE CONFESSIONS—233 Park Ave. S., New York, NY 10003. Pat Vitucci, Ed. Warm, inspirational first-person fillers, 300 to 700 words, about love, marriage, family life, for "The Feminine Side of Things," "My Man," and "Incredible But True." Also short stories, 1,000 to 2,000 words. Pays after publication. Buys all rights.

WISCONSIN TRAILS—P.O. Box 5650, Madison, WI 53705. Short fillers, 300 words, about Wisconsin: places to go, things to see, etc. Pays $75, on publication.

WOMAN'S DAY—1633 Broadway, New York, NY 10019. Address Ed. "Neighbors": heartwarming anecdotes about relationship issues, creative solutions to common community or family problems, true humorous anecdotes, unique party ideas. "Tips to Share": short personal tips, experiences, and practical suggestions for homemakers. Pays $100 for "Neighbors" pieces; $75 for "Tips to Share," on publication.

WOMEN'S GLIB—P.O. Box 259, Bala Cynwyd, PA 19004. Rosalind Warren, Ed. Annual. Feminist humor, two to 10 pages, and brief, rhymed poems. Submissions accepted from women only. No pieces on diet, weight loss, body image, or romance. Cartoons. Pays from $5 per page, on publication, plus copies.

JUVENILE, TEENAGE, AND YOUNG ADULT MAGAZINES

JUVENILE MAGAZINES

AMERICAN GIRL—8400 Fairway Pl., P.O. Box 998, Middleton, WI 53562–0998. Address Publications Dept. Asst. Bimonthly. Articles, to 800 words, and contemporary or historical fiction, to 3,000 words, for girls ages 7 to 12. "We do not want 'teenage' material, i.e. articles on romance, make-up, dating, etc." Query for articles. Payment varies, on acceptance.

BEAR ESSENTIAL NEWS FOR KIDS—P.O. Box 26908, Tempe, AZ 85285–6908. Educational and entertaining articles, 300 to 600 words, for children in grades K through 8, including: world news in kids' terms; unique school projects; profiles of interesting achievers; family entertainment; science; youth sports and health; bilingual and multicultural topics; hobbies/young careers; pets and pet care; cartoon humor; activities, trivia, or puzzles that are educational. Also uses 50- to 150-word companion pieces for a teachers' guide, providing classroom-use ideas related to articles. Pays 10¢ a word, on publication; $10 to $35 for photos. Buys all rights. SASE required.

CALLIOPE: WORLD HISTORY FOR YOUNG PEOPLE—Cobblestone Publishing, Inc., 7 School St., Peterborough, NH 03458. Carolyn P. Yoder, Ed.-in-

Chief. Theme-based magazine, published five times yearly. Articles, 750 words, with lively, original approach to world history (East/West) through the Renaissance. Shorts, 200 to 750 words, on little-known information related to issue's theme. Fiction, to 1,200 words: historical, biographical, adventure, or retold legends. Activities for children, to 800 words. Poetry, to 100 lines. Puzzles and games. Send SASE for guidelines and themes. Pays 10¢ to 17¢ per word, on publication.

CHICKADEE—The Young Naturalist Foundation, 56 The Esplanade, Suite 306, Toronto, Ont., Canada M5E 1A7. Lizann Flatt, Ed. Animal and adventure stories, 300 to 800 words, for 3- to 9-year-olds. Also, puzzles, activities, and observation games. Pays varying rates, on acceptance. Submit complete manuscript with $1.50 check or money order for return postage.

CHILD LIFE—1100 Waterway Blvd., P.O. Box 567, Indianapolis, IN 46206. Stan Zukowski, Ed. Articles, 500 to 1,200 words, for 9- to 11-year-olds. Fiction and humor, to 1,200 words, with emphasis on health, fitness, and sports. General interest. Poetry. Puzzles. Photos. Pays 10¢ a word, extra for photos, on publication. Buys all rights.

CHILDREN'S DIGEST—1100 Waterway Blvd., P.O. Box 567, Indianapolis, IN 46206. Elizabeth Rinck, Ed. Health and general-interest publication for preteens. Informative articles, 500 to 1,200 words, and fiction (especially realistic, adventure, mystery, and humorous), 500 to 1,500 words. Historical and biographical articles. Poetry and activities. Pays from 10¢ a word, from $15 for poems, on publication.

CHILDREN'S PLAYMATE—Editorial Office, 1100 Waterway Blvd., P.O. Box 567, Indianapolis, IN 46206. Elizabeth Rinck, Ed. General-interest and health-related short stories, 500 to 700 words, for 6- to 8-year-olds. Simple science articles and how-to crafts pieces with brief instructions. "All About" features, about 500 words, on health, fitness, nutrition, safety, and exercise. Poems, puzzles, dot-to-dots, mazes, hidden pictures. Pays about 15¢ a word, $15 minimum for poetry, on publication.

CHILDREN'S SURPRISES—275 Market St., Suite 521, Chanhassen, MN 553405. Peggy Simenson, Jeanne Palmer, Eds. "Activities for Today's Kids and Parents." Educational activities, puzzles, games in reading, language, math, science, cooking, music, and art. Articles about history, animals, and geography. Pays $15 to $35, on publication.

CLUBHOUSE—Box 15, Berrien Springs, MI 49103. Elaine Trumbo, Ed. Action-oriented Christian stories: features, 800 to 1,200 words. Children in stories should be wise, brave, funny, kind, etc. Pays $30 to $35 for stories.

COBBLESTONE—7 School St., Peterborough, NH 03458–1454. Samuel Mead, Ed. Theme-related articles, biographies, fiction, and short accounts of historical events, to 1,000 words, for 8- to 15-year-olds. Pays 10¢ to 17¢ a word, on publication. Send SASE for editorial guidelines with monthly themes.

CRICKET—Box 300, Peru, IL 61354–0300. Marianne Carus, Pub./Ed.-in-Chief. Articles and fiction, 200 to 1,500 words, for 6- to 14-year-olds. Poetry, to 30 lines. Pays to 25¢ a word, to $3 a line for poetry, on publication. SASE required. Guidelines.

DISCOVERIES—WordAction Publishing Co., 6401 The Paseo, Kansas City, MO 64131. Address the Ed. Asst. Weekly designed to correlate with Evangelical Sunday school curriculum. Fiction, 500 to 700 words, for 8- to 10-year-olds should feature contemporary, true-to-life character and illustrate character building and scriptural application. No poetry. Pays 5¢ a word, on publication. Guidelines.

751

THE DOLPHIN LOG—The Cousteau Society, 870 Greenbrier Cir., Suite 402, Chesapeake, VA 23320. Elizabeth Foley, Ed. Articles, 400 to 600 words, on a variety of topics related to our global water system: marine biology, ecology, natural history, and water-related subjects, for 7- to 15-year-olds. No fiction. Pays $25 to $150, on publication. Query.

FACES—Cobblestone Publishing, 7 School St., Peterborough, NH 03458–1454. Carolyn P. Yoder, Ed.-in-Chief. In-depth feature articles, 800 to 1,200 words, with an anthropology theme. Shorts, 200 to 800 words, related to monthly themes. Fiction, to 1,500 words, on legends, folktales, stories from around the world, etc., related to theme. Activities, to 1,000 words, including recipes, crafts, games, etc., for children. Pays 13¢ to 17¢ a word for features; 10¢ to 12¢ a word for shorts; 10¢ to 15¢ a word for fiction. Send for guidelines and themes.

FAITH 'N STUFF—c/o *Guideposts*, 16 E. 34th St., New York, NY 10016. Mary Lou Carney, Ed. Bible-based bimonthly. Problem fiction, mysteries, historicals, 1,500 words; articles, 1,500 words, on issues of interest to 7- to 12-year-olds; profiles, 200 to 500 words, of kids doing interesting and unusual activities. "No preachy stories and no Bible games." Pays $125 to $300 for features; $75 to $250 for fiction and fillers; buys all rights, on acceptance. No reprints. Query.

FIELD & STREAM—2 Park Ave., New York, NY 10016. Duncan Barnes, Ed. Articles, to 600 words, on hunting and fishing, real-life adventure, how-to projects, natural phenomena and history, conservation, and sporting ethics for *Field and Stream Jr.*, a special section aimed at 8- to 12-year-olds. Puzzles and fillers, 25 to 100 words. Queries preferred. Pays from $75 to $650, on acceptance.

THE FRIEND—50 E. North Temple, 23rd Floor, Salt Lake City, UT 84150. Vivian Paulsen, Man. Ed. Stories and articles, 1,000 to 1,200 words. Stories, to 250 words, for younger readers and preschool children. Pays from 9¢ a word, from $25 per poem, on acceptance. Prefers completed manuscripts.

HIGHLIGHTS FOR CHILDREN—803 Church St., Honesdale, PA 18431–1824. Beth Troop, Manuscript Coord. Fiction and articles, to 800 words, for 2- to 12-year-olds. Fiction should have strong plot, believable characters, story that holds reader's interest from beginning to end. No crime or violence. For articles, cite references used and qualifications. Easy rebus-form stories. Easy-to-read stories, 300 to 500 words, with strong plots. Pays from 14¢ a word, on acceptance.

HIGHWAYS—Presbyterian Publishing House, 100 Witherspoon St., Louisville, KY 40202. James S. Clinefelter, Ed. Fiction, 100 to 1,200 words; articles, 600 to 1,000 words; and poetry, to 20 lines, for readers ages 15 to 18. Pays 3¢ a word; to $3 for poetry, on acceptance. Guidelines.

HOPSCOTCH, THE MAGAZINE FOR GIRLS—P.O. Box 164, Bluffton, OH 45817–0164. Marilyn Edwards, Ed. Bimonthly. Articles and fiction, 600 to 1,200 words, and short poetry for girls ages 6 to 12. "We believe young girls deserve the right to enjoy a season of childhood before they become young adults; we are not interested in such topics as sex, romance, cosmetics, hairstyles, etc." Pays 5¢ to 7¢ per word; $150 for cover photos, six months before publication.

HUMPTY DUMPTY'S MAGAZINE—1100 Waterway Blvd., P.O. Box 567, Indianapolis, IN 46206. Christine French Clark, Ed. General-interest publication with an emphasis on health and fitness for 4- to 6-years-old. Easy-to-read fiction, to 600 words, some with health and nutrition, safety, exercise, or hygiene as theme; humor and light approach preferred. Creative nonfiction, including photo stories. Crafts with clear, brief instructions. No-cook recipes using healthful ingredients.

Short verse, narrative poems. Pays to 20¢ a word, from $15 for poems, on publication. Buys all rights.

JACK AND JILL—1100 Waterway Blvd., P.O. Box 567, Indianapolis, IN 46206. Steve Charles, Ed. Articles, 500 to 800 words, for 7- to 10-year-olds, on sports, fitness, health, safety, exercise. Features, 500 to 800 words, on history, biography, life in other countries, etc. Fiction, to 1,000 words. Short poems, games, puzzles, projects, recipes. Photos. Pays 10¢ to 20¢ a word, extra for photos, on publication.

JUNIOR TRAILS—1445 Boonville Ave., Springfield, MO 65802–1894. Sinda Zinn, Ed. Fiction, 1,000 to 1,500 words, with a Christian focus, believable characters, and moral emphasis. Articles, 500 to 800 words, on science, nature, biography. Pays 2¢ or 3¢ a word, on acceptance.

KID CITY—Children's Television Workshop, 1 Lincoln Plaza, New York, NY 10023. Address the Eds. Short stories (to 500 words); factual articles; interviews/features on kids in sports, TV, or movies; animal stories; crafts, activities, games and comics that teach. Send complete manuscript for fiction; query for nonfiction. Pays $250 to $350, on acceptance. Guidelines.

LADYBUG—P.O. Box 300, Peru, IL 61354–0300. Marianne Carus, Pub./ Ed.-in-Chief. Paula Morrow, Assoc. Ed. Picture stories, read-aloud stories, fantasy, folk and fairy tales, 300 to 750 words; poetry, to 20 lines; songs and rhymes; crafts, activities, and games, to four pages. Pays to 25¢ a word for stories and articles; to $3 a line for poetry, on publication. SASE required. Guidelines.

MY FRIEND—Daughters of St. Paul, 50 St. Paul's Ave., Boston, MA 02130. Sister Anne Joan, Ed. "The Catholic Magazine for Kids." Readers are 6 to 12 years old. Fiction, to 400 words, for primary readers; 400 to 600 words for intermediate readers. Nonfiction: general-information articles, lives of saints, etc., 150 to 600 words. Some humorous poetry, 6 to 8 lines. Buys first rights. Pays $20 to $150 for stories and articles, $5 to $20 for fillers. Query for artwork. Guidelines available.

NATIONAL GEOGRAPHIC WORLD—1145 17th St. N.W., Washington, DC 20036. Pat Robbins, Ed. Picture magazine for young readers, ages 8 and older. Proposals for picture stories only. No unsolicited manuscripts.

ODYSSEY: SCIENCE THAT'S OUT OF THIS WORLD—Cobblestone Publishing, 7 School St., Peterborough, NH 03458–1454. Carolyn P. Yoder, Ed.-in-Chief. Beth Lindstrom, Assoc. Ed. Features, 250 to 750 words, on astronomy and space science for 8- to 14-year-olds. Short experiments, projects, and games. Pays 10¢ to 17¢ a word, on publication.

OH!ZONE—Project Oh!Zone, 420 E. Hewitt Ave., Marquette, MI 49855. Christian Hansen, Ed.-in-Chief. Quarterly. Articles, 200 to 2,000 words, on environmental news, art, and opinion for grades 7 to 12. Special attention given to student submissions. Send SASE for guidelines and list of upcoming themes. Pays $30 to $100 for articles, $10 to $25 for photos or illustrations, and $100 for covers, on publication. Pays in copies and a subscription.

ON THE LINE—616 Walnut, Scottdale, PA 15683–1999. Mary Clemens Meyer, Ed. Weekly paper for 10- to 14-year-olds. Nature, general nonfiction, and how-to articles, 350 to 500 words; fiction, 900 to 1,200 words; poetry, puzzles, cartoons. Pays to 4¢ a word, on acceptance.

OWL—The Young Naturalist Foundation, 56 The Esplanade, Suite 306, Toronto, Ont., Canada M5E 1A7. Debora Pearson, Ed. Articles, 500 to 1,000 words, for 8- to 12-year-olds about animals, science, people, technology, new discoveries, activities. Pays varying rates, on acceptance. Send for guidelines.

PLAYS, THE DRAMA MAGAZINE FOR YOUNG PEOPLE—120 Boylston St., Boston, MA 02116–4615. Elizabeth Preston, Man. Ed. Wholesome one-act comedies, dramas, skits, satires, farces, and creative dramatic material suitable for school productions at junior high, middle, and lower grade levels. Plays with modern settings and situations preferred. Also uses dramatized classics, folktales and fairy tales, puppet plays. Pays good rates, on acceptance. Buys all rights. Guidelines.

POCKETS—1908 Grand Ave., Box 189, Nashville, TN 37202–0189. Janet McNish, Ed. Ecumenical magazine for 6- to 12-year-olds. Fiction and scripture stories, 600 to 1,500 words; short poems; and articles about the Bible, 400 to 600 words. Pays from 12¢ a word, $25 to $50 for poetry, on acceptance. Guidelines and themes. Annual fiction contest; send SASE for details.

POWER AND LIGHT—6401 The Paseo, Kansas City, MO 64131. Beula J. Postlewait, Preteen Ed. Fiction, 500 to 800 words, for grades 5 and 6, with Christian emphasis. Cartoons and puzzles. Pays 5¢ a word for multi-use rights, 1 3/4¢ a word for reprints. Pays $15 for cartoons and puzzles. Send SASE with manuscript.

RADAR—Standard Publishing, 8121 Hamilton Ave., Cincinnati, OH 45231. Margaret Williams, Ed. Weekly Sunday school take-home paper. Articles, 400 to 650 words, on nature, hobbies, crafts. Short stories, 900 to 1,000 words: mystery, sports, school, family, with 12-year-old as main character; serials, 2,000 words. Christian emphasis. Poems to 12 lines. Pays to 7¢ a word, to 50¢ a line for poetry, on acceptance.

RANGER RICK—National Wildlife Federation, 8925 Leesburg Pike, Vienna, VA 22184–0001. Gerald Bishop, Ed. Articles, to 900 words, on wildlife, conservation, natural sciences, and kids in the outdoors, for 6- to 9-year-olds. Nature-related fiction, mysteries, fantasies, and science fiction welcome. Games (no crosswords or word-finds), crafts, humorous poems, outdoor activities, and puzzles. For nonfiction, query with sample lead, list of references, and names of experts you plan to contact. Pays to $550, on acceptance.

SESAME STREET MAGAZINE—See *3-2-1 Contact.*

SHOFAR—43 Northcote Dr., Melville, NY 11747. Gerald H. Grayson, Ed. Short stories, 500 to 750 words; articles, 250 to 750 words; poetry, to 50 lines; short fillers, games, puzzles, and cartoons for Jewish children, 8 to 13. All material must have a Jewish theme. Pays 10¢ a word, on publication. Submit holiday pieces at least six months in advance.

SKIPPING STONES—P.O. Box 3939, Eugene, OR 97403. Arun N. Toké, Exec. Ed. "A Multi-Cultural Children's Quarterly." Articles, approximately 500 words, relating to nature, cultural celebrations, life in other countries, and traditions for 7- to 13-year-olds. "Especially invited to submit are children from cultural backgrounds other than European-American and/or those with physical challenges. We print art, poetry, songs, games, stories, and photographs from around the world and include many different languages (with English translation)." Payment is one copy, on publication. Send SASE for guidelines.

SOCCER JR.—27 Unquowa Rd., Fairfield, CT 06430. Joe Provey, Ed. Fiction and fillers about soccer for readers ages 8 and up. Pays $450 for a feature or story; $250 for department pieces, on acceptance. Query.

SPARK!—F&W Publications, 1507 Dana Ave., Cincinnati, OH 45207. Beth Struck, Man. Ed. Creative projects for 6- to 12-years-olds. How-to pieces on painting, story writing, sculpture, poetry, drawing, collage, print-making, cartooning, and language games. Art-related features, 350 to 500 words. Columns: "Meet the Masters" and "Draw It!" Queries preferred. Pays $50 to $200 for features; $75 to $150 for columns, on acceptance.

SPORTS ILLUSTRATED FOR KIDS—Time & Life Bldg., Rockefeller Ctr., New York, NY 10020. Stephen Malley, Sr. Ed. Articles, 1,000 to 1,500 words, and short features, 500 to 600 words, for 8- to 13-year-olds. "Most articles are staff-written. Department pieces are the best bet for free lancers." Departments: "My Worst Day," 600 words, an athlete's account as told to a writer; "Curveballs," 150 words, wacky sports trivia; "Tips from the Pros" and "Legends," 400 words, about sports figures of the past. Pays $500 for departments, $1,000 to $1,250 for articles, on acceptance. Query required.

STONE SOUP, THE MAGAZINE BY CHILDREN—Box 83, Santa Cruz, CA 95063–0083. Gerry Mandel, Ed. Stories, free verse poems, plays, book reviews by children under 14. "Preference given to writing based on real-life experiences." Pays $10.

STORY FRIENDS—Mennonite Publishing House, Scottdale, PA 15683. Marjorie Waybill, Ed. Stories, 350 to 800 words, for 4- to 9-year-olds, on Christian faith and values in everyday experiences. Poetry. Pays to 5¢ a word, to $10 per poem, on acceptance.

SUPERSCIENCE BLUE—Scholastic, Inc., 730 Broadway, New York, NY 10003. Science news and hands-on experiments for grades 4 through 6. Article topics are staff-generated and assigned to writers. For consideration, send children's and science writing clips to Editor. Include SASE for editorial calendar. Pays $100 to $500, on acceptance.

3-2-1 CONTACT—Children's Television Workshop, 1 Lincoln Plaza, New York, NY 10023. Curtis Slepian, Ed. Entertaining and informative articles, 600 to 1,000 words, for 8- to 14-year-olds, on all aspects of science, computers, scientists, and children who are learning about or practicing science. Pays $75 to $500, on acceptance. No fiction. Also publishes *Sesame Street Magazine*. Query.

TOUCH—Box 7259, Grand Rapids, MI 49510. Carol Smith, Man. Ed. Up-beat fiction and features, 500 to 1,000 words, for Christian girls ages 8 to 14; personal life, nature, crafts. Poetry, puzzles. Pays 2 ½¢ a word, extra for photos, on acceptance. Query with SASE for theme update.

TURTLE MAGAZINE FOR PRESCHOOL KIDS—1100 Waterway Blvd., Box 567, Indianapolis, IN 46206. Christine French Clark, Ed. Heavily illustrated articles with an emphasis on health and nutrition for 2- to 5-year-olds. Humorous, entertaining fiction. Also crafts and activities pieces and simple science experiments. Simple poems. Stories-in-rhyme and read-aloud stories, to 500 words. Pays to 20¢ a word for stories; from $15 for poems; payment varies for activities, on publication. Buys all rights. Send SASE for guidelines.

U.S. KIDS—1100 Waterway Blvd., P.O. Box 567, Indianapolis, IN 46206. Marta Partington, Ed. Steve Charles, Health/Fitness Ed. Articles, to 1,000 words, on issues related to kids ages 5 to 10, fiction, true-life adventures, science and nature topics. Special emphasis on health and fitness. Fiction with real-world focus; no fantasy.

VENTURE—Christian Service Brigade, P.O. Box 150, Wheaton, IL 60189. Deborah Christensen, Ed. Fiction and nonfiction, 1,000 to 1,500 words, for 10- to 15-year-old boys involved in Stockade and Battalion. "Think like a boy this age. They want action, adventure, and humor. They also need to see how faith in God affects every area of life and is more than just a prayer to get out of trouble." Humor and fillers and B&W 8×10 photos also accepted. Pays 5¢ to 10¢ a word, on publication.

WONDER TIME—6401 The Paseo, Kansas City, MO 64131. Lois Perrigo, Ed. Stories, 200 to 550 words, for 6-to 8-year-olds, with Christian emphasis to correlate with Sunday school curriculum. Pays $25 stories, on production.

YOUNG JUDEAN—50 W. 58th St., New York, NY 10019. Linda Schaffzin, Ed. Quarterly. Articles, 500 to 1,000 words, with photos, for 9- to 12-year-olds, on Israel, Jewish holidays, Jewish-American life, Jewish history. Fiction, 800 to 1,000 words, on Jewish themes. Fillers, humor, reviews. Pays 5¢ a word.

TEENAGE AND YOUNG ADULT

ALIVE NOW!—P.O. Box 189, Nashville, TN 37202. Short essays, 250 to 400 words, with Christian emphasis for adults and young adults. Poetry, one page. B&W photos. Query with SASE for themes. Pays $20 to $30, on publication.

BOYS' LIFE—P.O. Box 152079, 1325 W. Walnut Hill Ln., Irving, TX 75015–2079. Address the Ed. Publication of Boy Scouts of America. Articles and fiction, 500 to 1,500 words, for 8- to 18-year-old boys. Pays from $350 for major articles, $750 for fiction, on acceptance. Query for articles; send complete manuscript for fiction.

CAMPUS LIFE—465 Gundersen Dr., Carol Stream, IL 60188. Jim Long, Ed. Articles reflecting Christian values and world view, for high school and college students. Humor, general fiction, and true, first-person experiences. "If we have a choice of fiction, how-to, and a strong first-person story, we'll go with the true story every time." Photo essays, cartoons. Pays 10¢ to 20¢ a word, on acceptance. Query.

CHALLENGE MAGAZINE—See *Pioneer.*

CRACKED—Globe Communications, Inc., 441 Lexington Ave., 2nd Fl., New York, NY 10017. Lou Silverstone, Andy Simmons, Eds. Humor, one to five pages, for 12- to 15-year-old readers. "Read magazine before submitting." Pays $100 per page, on acceptance.

EXPLORING—1325 W. Walnut Hill Ln., P.O. Box 152079, Irving, TX 75015–2079. Scott Daniels, Exec. Ed. Publication of Boy Scouts of America. Articles, 500 to 1,500 words, for 14- to 21-year-old boys and girls, on teenage trends, college, computer games, music, education, careers, "Explorer" activities (hiking, canoeing, camping) and program ideas for meetings. No controversial subjects. Pays $150 to $500, on acceptance. Query. Send SASE for guidelines.

FREEWAY—Box 632, Glen Ellyn, IL 60138. Amy J. Cox, Ed. First-person true stories, personal experience, how-tos, fillers, humor, fiction, to 1,200 words, for 15- to 22-year-olds. Send photos, if available. Occasionally publishes poetry. Must have Christian emphasis. Pays 7¢ to 10¢ a word.

HICALL—1445 Boonville Ave., Springfield, MO 65802–1894. Tammy Bicket, Ed. Articles, 500 to 1,000 words, fiction, to 1,200 words, and short poetry, for 13- to 17-year-olds; strong evangelical emphasis. Pays on acceptance.

KEYNOTER—3636 Woodview Trace, Indianapolis, IN 46268. Julie A. Carson, Exec. Ed. Articles, 1,500 to 1,800 words, for high school leaders: general-interest features; self-help; contemporary teenage problems. No fillers, poetry, first-person accounts, or fiction. Pays $150 to $300, on acceptance. Query preferred.

LISTEN MAGAZINE—Pacific Press Publishing, P.O. Box 7000, Boise, ID

83707. Lincoln Steed, Ed. Articles, 1,200 to 1,500 words, providing teens with "a vigorous, positive, educational approach to the problems arising from the use of tobacco, alcohol, and other drugs." Pays 5¢ to 7¢ a word, on acceptance.

MERLYN'S PEN: THE NATIONAL MAGAZINES OF STUDENT WRITING—P.O. Box 1058, Dept. WR, East Greenwich, RI 02818. R. James Stahl, Ed. *Intermediate Edition*: writing by students in grades 7 through 10. Short stories, to 3,500 words; reviews; travel pieces; and poetry, to 100 lines. *Senior Edition*: for writers in grades 9 through 12. Fiction, 5,000 words. Poetry, to 200 lines. Responds with a brief critique in 11 weeks. Pays in copies. Guidelines available.

NEW ERA—50 E. North Temple, Salt Lake City, UT 84150. Richard M. Romney, Ed. Articles, 150 to 1,500 words, and fiction, to 2,000 words, for young Mormons. Poetry. Photos. Pays 5¢ to 20¢ a word, 25¢ a line for poetry, on acceptance. Query.

PIONEER—1548 Poplar Ave., Memphis, TN 38104–2493. Jeno Smith, Ed. Southern Baptist. Articles, to 800 words, for 12- and 14-year-old boys, on teen issues, current events. Photo essays on Christian sports personalities. Pays 4 ½¢ a word, extra for photos, on acceptance. Same address and requirements for *Challenge Magazine*.

SASSY—230 Park Ave., New York, NY 10169. Short stories, written in the magazine's style, 1,000 to 3,000 words, for girls ages 14 to 19. Pays $1,000, on acceptance.

SEVENTEEN—850 Third Ave., New York, NY 10022. Sarah Duncan, Articles Ed. Articles, to 2,500 words, on subjects of interest to teenagers. Sophisticated, well-written fiction, 1,500 to 4,000 words, for young adults. Articles, to 1,200 words, by writers 21 and younger for "Voice." Pays varying rates, on acceptance.

STRAIGHT—8121 Hamilton Ave., Cincinnati, OH 45231. Carla J. Crane, Ed. Articles on current situations and issues, and humor, for Christian teens. Well-constructed fiction, 1,000 to 1,200 words, showing teens using Christian principles. Poetry by teenagers. Photos. Pays about 3¢ to 7¢ a word, on acceptance. Send SASE for guidelines.

'TEEN—8490 Sunset Blvd., Los Angeles, CA 90069. Short stories, 2,500 to 4,000 words: mystery, teen situations, adventure, romance, humor for teens. Pays $200, on acceptance. Buys all rights.

TEEN POWER—Box 632, Glen Ellyn, IL 60138. Amy J. Cox, Ed. Take-home Sunday school paper. True-to-life fiction or first-person (as told to), true teen experience stories with Christian insights and conclusion, 700 to 1,000 words. Include photos. Pays 7¢ to 10¢ a word, extra for photos, on acceptance.

TEENS TODAY—Nazarene Headquarters, 6401 The Paseo, Kansas City, MO 64131. Short stories, 1,000 to 1,200 words, dealing with teens demonstrating Christian principles in real-life situations. Stories about relationships and ethics. Pays 3 ½¢ a word, on acceptance.

TIGER BEAT—Sterling/MacFadden Partnership, 355 Lexington Ave., New York, NY 10017. Louise Barile, Ed. Articles, to four pages, on young people in show business and music industry. Pays varying rates, on acceptance. Query. Unsolicited manuscripts sent without SASE will not be returned.

TQ/TEEN QUEST—Box 3512, Irving, TX 75015. Chris Lyon, Ed. Articles, to 1,500 words, and well-crafted fiction, to 2,000 words, for conservative Christian teens. Cartoons and color slides. Pays 10¢ to 15¢ a word, on publication.

757

WRITING!—60 Revere Dr., Northbrook, IL 60062–1563. Alan Lenhoff, Ed. Interviews, 1,200 words, for "Writers at Work" department, for junior high and high school students. Pays $200, on publication. Query.

YM—685 Third Ave., New York, NY 10017. Cathy Cavender, Man. Ed. Articles, to 2,500 words, on entertainment, lifestyle, fashion, beauty, relationships, health, for women ages 14 to 19. Query with clips, SASE. Payment varies, on acceptance.

YOUNG AND ALIVE—4444 S. 52nd St., Lincoln, NE 68506. Richard J. Kaiser, Man. Ed. M. Marilyn Brown, Ed. Quarterly. Feature articles, 800 to 1,400 words, for blind and visually impaired young adults on adventure, biography, camping, careers, health, history, hobbies, holidays, marriage, nature, practical Christianity, sports, and travel. Photos. Pays 3¢ to 5¢ a word, $5 to $20 for photos, on acceptance. Guidelines.

YOUNG SALVATIONIST—The Salvation Army, 615 Slaters Ln., P.O. Box 269, Alexandria, VA 22313. Deborah Sedlar, Ed. Articles for teens, 800 to 1,200 words, with Christian perspective; fiction, 800 to 1,200 words; short fillers. Pays 10¢ a word, on acceptance.

THE DRAMA MARKET

Community, regional, and civic theaters and college dramatic groups offer the best opportunities today for playwrights to see their plays produced, whether for staged production or for dramatic readings. Indeed, aspiring playwrights who can get their work produced by any of these have taken an important step toward breaking into the competitive dramatic field —many well-known playwrights received their first recognition in the regional theaters. Payment is generally nominal, but regional and university theaters usually buy only the right to produce a play, and all further rights revert to the author. Since most directors like to work closely with the authors on any revisions necessary, theaters will often pay the playwright's expenses while in residence during rehearsals. The thrill of seeing your play come to life on the stage is one of the pleasures of being on hand for rehearsals and performances.

Aspiring playwrights should query college and community theaters in their region to find out which ones are interested in seeing original scripts. Dramatic associations of interest to playwrights include the Dramatists Guild (234 W. 44th St., New York, NY 10036), and Theatre Communications Group, Inc. (355 Lexington Ave., New York, NY 10017), which publishes the annual *Dramatists Sourcebook*. *The Playwright's Companion*, published by Feedback Theatrebooks (305 Madison Ave., Suite 1146, New York, NY 10165) is an annual directory of theaters and prize contests seeking scripts. See the *Organizations for Writers* list for other dramatists' associations.

Some of the theaters on the following list require that playwrights submit all or some of the following with scripts—cast list, synopsis, resumé, recommendations, return postcard—and with scripts and queries, SASEs must always be enclosed. Playwrights may also wish to register their material with the U.S. Copyright Office. For additional information about this, write Register of Copyrights, Library of Congress, Washington, DC 20559.

REGIONAL AND UNIVERSITY THEATERS

ACADEMY THEATRE—501 Means St., Atlanta, GA 30318. Elliott J. Berman, Lit. Mgr. Comedies and dramas that "stretch the boundaries of imagination, with poetic language and imagery." Prefers local and regional playwrights or subjects relating to the Southeast. Considers regional and national playwrights for new play premieres. Royalty is negotiable.

ACTORS THEATRE OF LOUISVILLE—316 W. Main St., Louisville, KY 40202. Michael Bigelow Dixon, Lit. Mgr. Ten-minute comedies and dramas, to 10 pages; include SASE. Annual contest. Guidelines.

A. D. PLAYERS—2710 W. Alabama, Houston, TX 77098. Jeannette Clift George, Artistic Dir. Martha Doolittle, Lit. Mgr. Full-length or one-act comedies, dramas, musicals, children's plays, and adaptations with Christian world view. Submit resumé, cast list, and synopsis with SASE. Readings. Pays negotiable rates.

ALABAMA SHAKESPEARE FESTIVAL—The State Theatre, #1 Festival Dr., Montgomery, AL 36117–4605. Kent Thompson, Artistic Dir. Full-length adaptations and plays dealing with southern or black issues. Send resumé and synopsis in June.

ALLEY THEATRE—615 Texas Ave., Houston, TX 77002. Christopher Baker, Lit. Dir. Full-length plays and musicals, including translations and adaptations. No unsolicited scripts; agent submissions or professional recommendations only.

ALLIANCE THEATRE COMPANY—1280 Peachtree St. N.E., Atlanta, GA 30309. Walter Bilderback, Dramaturg. Full-length comedies and dramas, especially those that "deal with moral/spiritual questions of life in multicultural America." Query with synopsis and cast list. Pay varies.

AMERICAN LIVING HISTORY THEATER—P.O. Box 2677, Hollywood, CA 90078. Dorene Ludwig, Artistic Dir. One-act, historically accurate (primary source materials only) dramas dealing with marketable or known American historical and literary characters and events. Submit script with SASE. Reports in one to six months. Pays varying rates.

AMERICAN PLACE THEATRE—111 W. 46th St., New York, NY 10036. Elise Thoron, Dramaturg. "No unsolicited manuscripts accepted. Writers may send a synopsis and the first 20 pages with SASE. We seek challenging, innovative works and do not favor obviously commercial material."

AMERICAN REPERTORY THEATRE—64 Brattle St., Cambridge, MA 02138. Robert Scanlan, Lit. Dir. No unsolicited manuscripts. Submit one-page description of play with 10-page sample. SASE required. Allow four to six months for response.

AMERICAN STAGE COMPANY—FDU, Box 336, Teaneck, NJ 07666. James Vagias, Exec. Prod. Full-length comedies, dramas, and musicals for cast of five or six and single set. No unsolicited scripts.

759

AMERICAN STANISLAVSKI THEATRE—485 Park Ave., #6A, New York, NY 10022. Sonia Moore, Artistic Dir. Full-length or one-act dramas with important message. No offensive language. For cast ages 16 to 45. Submit script with SAS postcard in April and May; reports in September. No payment.

AMERICAN THEATRE OF ACTORS—314 W. 54th St., New York, NY 10019. James Jennings, Artistic Dir. Full-length dramas for a cast of two to six. Submit complete play and SASE. Reports in one to two months.

MAXWELL ANDERSON PLAYWRIGHTS SERIES, INC.—11 Esquire Rd., Norwalk, CT 06851. Muriel Nussbaum, Artistic Dir. Produces six professional staged readings of new plays each year in Greenwich, CT. Send complete script with SASE.

ARENA STAGE—Sixth and Maine Ave. S.W., Washington, DC 20024. Michelle Ward, Lit. Mgr. No unsolicited manuscripts; send synopsis and first 10 pages of dialogue. Allow three to six months for reply.

ARKANSAS REPERTORY THEATRE COMPANY—601 S. Main, P.O. Box 110, Little Rock, AR 72203–0110. Brad Mooy, Lit. Mgr. Full-length comedies, dramas, and musicals; prefer up to eight characters. Send synopsis, cast list, resumé, and return postage; do not send complete manuscript. Reports in three months.

ARTREACH TOURING THEATRE—3074 Madison Rd., Cincinnati, OH 45209. Kathryn Schultz Miller, Artistic Dir. One-act dramas and adaptations for touring children's theater; up to three cast members, simple sets. Submit script with synopsis, cast list, resumé, recommendations, and SASE. Payment varies.

BARTER THEATER—P.O. Box 867, Abingdon, VA 24210. Richard Rose, Producing Dir. Full-length dramas, comedies, adaptations, musicals, and children's plays. Submit synopsis, dialogue sample, and SASE. Allow six to eight months for report. Payment rates negotiable.

BERKELEY REPERTORY THEATRE—2025 Addison St., Berkeley, CA 94704. Sharon Ott, Artistic Dir. No unsolicited manuscripts; agent submissions or professional recommendations only. Reporting time: three to four months.

BOARSHEAD THEATER—425 S. Grand Ave., Lansing, MI 48933. John Peakes, Artistic Dir. Full-length comedies and dramas with simple sets and cast of up to 10. Send precis, five to 10 pages of dialogue, cast list with descriptions, and resumé. SAS postcard for reply.

BRISTOL RIVERSIDE THEATRE—Box 1250, Bristol, PA 19007. Susan D. Atkinson, Producing/Artistic Dir. Full-length plays with up to 10 actors and a simple set. Submit synopsis with return postcard in summer.

CENTER STAGE—700 N. Calvert St., Baltimore, MD 21202. James Magruder, Resident Dramaturg. Full-length comedies, dramas, translations, adaptations. No unsolicited manuscripts. Send synopsis, a few sample pages, resumé, cast list, and production history. Pays varying rates. Allow four to eight weeks for reply.

CHILDSPLAY, INC.—Box 517, Tempe, AZ 85280. David Saar, Artistic Dir. Plays running 45 to 120 minutes: dramas, musicals, and adaptations for young audiences. Productions may need to travel. Four- to eight-person cast. Submissions accepted July through December. Reports in two to six months. Payment varies.

CIRCLE IN THE SQUARE/UPTOWN—1633 Broadway, New York, NY 10019–6795. Theodore Mann, Artistic Dir. Full-length comedies, dramas, and adaptations. Send synopsis with resumé, cast list, and 10-page dialogue sample to Nancy Bosco, Lit. Advisor. No unsolicited scripts. SASE required.

CIRCLE REPERTORY COMPANY—632 Broadway, 6th Fl., New York, NY 10012. Lynn Thomson, Dramaturg/Lit. Mgr. "We accept scripts submitted by agents or accompanied by professional recommendation only." Offers criticism "as often as possible." Reports in six months. Readings.

CLASSIC STAGE COMPANY—136 E. 13th St., New York, NY 10003. Patricia Taylor, Man. Dir. David Esbjornson, Artistic Dir. Full-length adaptations and translations of existing classic literature. Submit synopsis with cast list and SASE, September to May. Offers readings. Pays on royalty basis.

CREATIVE THEATRE—102 Witherspoon St., Princeton, NJ 08540. Eloise Bruce, Artistic Dir. Participatory plays for children, grades K through six; cast of four to six; arena or thrust stage. Submit manuscript with synopsis and cast list. Pay varies.

THE CRICKET THEATRE—1407 Nicollet Ave., Minneapolis, MN 55403. William Partlan, Artistic Dir. Send synopsis, resumé, and 10-page sample of work. Prefers contemporary plays with no more than eight cast members. Reports in six months.

CROSSROADS THEATRE CO.—7 Livingston Ave., New Brunswick, NJ 08901. Ricardo Khan, Artistic Dir. Sydné Mahone, Dir. of Play Development. Full-length and one-act dramas, comedies, musicals, and adaptations; issue-oriented experimental plays that offer honest, imaginative, and insightful examinations of the African-American experience. Also interested in African and Caribbean plays. Queries only, with synopsis, cast list, resumé, and SASE.

DELAWARE THEATRE COMPANY—200 Water St., Wilmington, DE 19801–5030. Cleveland Morris, Artistic Dir. Full-length comedies, dramas, and musicals dealing with interracial dynamics in America. Contemporary or historical settings. Prefer cast of no more than 10. Send synopsis or complete script; SASE required. Reports in six months. Write for details of Connections competition.

DENVER CENTER THEATRE COMPANY—1050 13th St., Denver, CO 80204. Send full-length, previously unproduced scripts June through November. No more than 10 cast members. Stipend and housing. Annual New Play Festival, "US West TheatreFest."

DETROIT REPERTORY THEATRE—13103 Woodrow Wilson Ave., Detroit, MI 48238. Barbara Busby, Lit. Mgr. Full-length comedies and dramas. Enclose SASE. Pays royalty.

STEVE DOBBINS PRODUCTIONS—650 Geary Blvd., San Francisco, CA 94102. Chuck Hilbert, Lit. Dir. Full-length comedies, dramas, and musicals. Cast of up to 12. Query with synopsis and resumé. No unsolicited manuscripts. Reports in six months. Offers workshops and readings. Pays 6% of gross.

DORSET THEATRE FESTIVAL—Box 519, Dorset, VT 05251. Jill Charles, Artistic Dir. Full-length comedies, musicals, dramas, and adaptations for up to eight cast members; simple set preferred. Agent submissions and professional recommendations only. Pays varying rates. Residencies at Dorset Colony House for Writers available October to June. Inquire.

DRIFTWOOD SHOWBOAT—Box 1032, Kingston, NY 12401. Fred Hall, Resident Company Artistic Dir. Full-length family comedies for two- to six-person cast, single setting. No profanity. Submit cast list, synopsis, and return postcard September to June.

EAST WEST PLAYERS—4424 Santa Monica Blvd., Los Angeles, CA 90029. Nobu McCarthy, Artistic Dir. Brian Nelson, Dramaturg. Produces two to three new plays annually. Original plays, translations, adaptations, musicals, and youth theater, "all of which must illuminate the Asian or Asian-American experience, or resonate in a significant fashion if cast with Asian-American actors." Readings. Prefer to see query letter with synopsis and 10 pages of dialogue; complete scripts also considered. Reports in five to six weeks for query; six months for complete script.

ECCENTRIC CIRCLES THEATRE—400 W. 43rd St., #4N, New York, NY 10036. Rosemary Hopkins, Artistic Dir. Full-length and one-act comedies and dramas with simple sets and a cast of no more than 10. Submit manuscript with resumé and SASE. Reports in six weeks.

THE EMPTY SPACE THEATRE—P.O. Box 1748, Seattle, WA 98111–1748. Eddie Levi Lee, Artistic Dir. Unsolicited scripts accepted only from WA, OR, WY, MT, and ID. Outside five-state N.W. region: scripts accepted through agents or established theater groups only.

ENSEMBLE STUDIO THEATRE—549 W. 52nd St., New York, NY 10019. Address Lit. Mgr. Send full-length or one-act comedies and dramas with resumé and SASE, September to April. Rarely pays for scripts. Fifteen readings of new plays per year.

ENSEMBLE THEATRE COMPANY OF MARIN—c/o Tamalpais High School, 700 Miller Ave., Mill Valley, CA 94941. Daniel Caldwell, Artistic Dir. Comedies, dramas, children's plays, adaptations, and scripts addressing high school issues for largely female cast (approx. three women per man). "One-act plays of approximately 30 minutes are especially needed, as we produce 40 short plays each season using teenage actors." Send synopsis and resumé.

FLORIDA STUDIO THEATRE—1241 N. Palm Ave., Sarasota, FL 33577. Steve Ramay, New Play Development. Innovative, small-cast plays that are pertinent and contemporary. Query with synopsis and SASE. Also accepting musicals.

GE VA THEATRE—75 Woodbury Blvd., Rochester, NY 14607. Ann Patrice Carrigan, Festival Coordinator. "Reflections '94, A New Plays Festival." Three American world premieres in rotating repertory. Send script. Allow six months for reply. Readings held during Festival.

WILL GEER THEATRICUM BOTANICUM—Box 1222, Topanga, CA 90290. All types of scripts for outdoor theater, with large playing area. Submit synopsis with SASE. Pays varing rates.

EMMY GIFFORD CHILDREN'S THEATER—3504 Center St., Omaha, NE 68105. James Larson, Artistic Dir. Referrals only.

THE GOODMAN THEATRE—200 S. Columbus Dr., Chicago, IL 60603. Susan V. Booth, Lit. Mgr. Queries from recognized literary agents or producing organizations required for full-length comedies or dramas. No unsolicited scripts or synopses accepted.

THE GROUP THEATRE—(formerly *Seattle Group Theatre*) 305 Harrison St., Seattle, WA 98109. Full-length satires, dramas, musicals, and translations, with no more than 10-person cast and simple set. Special interest in plays suitable for multi-ethnic cast; serious plays on social/cultural issues; satires and comedies with bite. Query with synopsis, sample dialogue, resumé, and SASE. Reporting time: six weeks.

THE GUTHRIE THEATER—725 Vineland Pl., Minneapolis, MN 55403. Full-length comedies, dramas, and adaptations. Manuscripts accepted only from recognized theatrical agents. Query with detailed synopsis and cast size. Reports in one to two months.

HIPPODROME STATE THEATRE—25 S.E. Second Pl., Gainesville, FL 32601. David Boyce, Dramaturg. Full-length plays with unit sets and casts of up to 10. Submit synopsis and resumé in summer and fall. Enclose return postcard.

HOLLYWOOD THEATER COMPANY—12838 Kling St., Studio City, CA 91604–1127. Rai Tasco, Artistic Dir. Full-length comedies and dramas for integrated cast. Include cast list and stamped return postcard with submission.

HONOLULU THEATRE FOR YOUTH—2846 Ualena St., Honolulu, HI 96819. Pam Sterling, Artistic Dir. Plays, 60 to 90 minutes playing time, for young people and family audiences. Adult casts. Contemporary issues, Pacific themes, etc. Unit sets, small cast. Query or send cover letter with synopsis, cast list, and SASE. Royalties negotiable.

HORIZON THEATRE COMPANY—P. O. Box 5376, Station E, Atlanta, GA 30307. Jeffrey and Lisa Adler, Artistic Directors. Full-length comedies, dramas, and satires. Encourages submissions by women writers. Cast of no more than 10. Submit synopsis with cast list, resumé, and recommendations. Pays percentage. Readings. Reports in six months.

HUNTINGTON THEATRE COMPANY—252 Huntington Ave., Boston, MA 02115. Full-length comedies and dramas. Query with synopsis, cast list, resumé, recommendations, and return postcard.

ILLINOIS THEATRE CENTER—400 Lakewood Blvd., Park Forest, IL 60466. Steve S. Billig, Artistic Dir. Full-length comedies, dramas, musicals, and adaptations, for unit/fragmentary sets, and up to eight cast members. Send summary and return postcard. No unsolicited manuscripts. Pays negotiable rates. Workshops and readings offered.

ILLUSTRATED STAGE COMPANY—Box 640063, San Francisco, CA 94164–0063. Steve Dobbins, Artistic Dir. Full-length comedies, dramas, and musicals for a cast of up to 18. Query with synopsis and SASE. No unsolicited manuscripts. Offers workshops and readings.

INVISIBLE THEATRE—1400 N. First Ave, Tucson, AZ 85719. Deborah Dickey, Lit. Mgr. Reads queries for full-length comedies, dramas, musicals, and adaptations, January to May. Cast of up to 10; simple set. Also one-act plays. Pays royalty.

JEWISH REPERTORY THEATRE—1395 Lexington Ave., New York, NY 10128. Ran Avni, Artistic Dir. Full-length comedies, dramas, musicals, and adaptations, with up to 10 cast members, relating to the Jewish experience. Pays varying rates. Enclose SASE.

KUMU KAHUA—Kennedy Theatre, Univ. of Hawaii at Manoa, 1770 East-West Rd., Honolulu, HI 96822. Dennis Carroll, Man. Dir. Full-length plays of special relevance to life in Hawaii. Prefer simple sets for arena and in-the-round productions. Submit resumé and synopsis January through April. Pays $35 per performance. Readings. Contests.

LIVE OAK THEATRE—311 Nueces, Austin, TX 78701. Ms. Amparo Garcia, Lit. Mgr. Full-length plays, translations, and adaptations. "Special interest in producing works of Texan and southern topics and new American plays." No unsolicited scripts; send synopsis, letter of inquiry, and 10 pages of dialogue. Contest. Guidelines.

LOS ANGELES DESIGNERS' THEATRE—P. O. Box 1883, Studio City, CA 91614–0883. Richard Niederberg, Artistic Dir. Full-length comedies, dramas, musicals, fantasies, or adaptations. Religious, political, social, and controversial themes encouraged. Nudity, "adult" language, etc., O.K. "Please detail in the cover letter what the writer's proposed involvement with the production would be if beyond the usual. Do not submit material that needs to be returned." Payment varies.

MANHATTAN THEATRE CLUB—453 W. 16th, New York, NY 10011. Address Kate Loewald. Full-length and one-act comedies, dramas, and musicals. No unsolicited manuscripts. Send synopsis with 10 to 15 pages of dialogue, cast list, resumé, and SASE. Allow six months for reply.

MILL MOUNTAIN THEATRE—One Market Sq., Second Fl., Roanoke, VA 24011–1437. Jo Weinstein, Lit. Mgr. One-act comedies and dramas, 25 to 40 minutes long. For full-length plays, send letter, resumé, and synopsis. Payment varies.

MISSOURI REPERTORY THEATRE—4949 Cherry St., Kansas City, MO 64110. Felicia Londré, Dramaturg. Full-length comedies and dramas. Query with synopsis, cast list, resumé, and return postcard. Royalty.

MUSIC-THEATRE GROUP—29 Bethune St., New York, NY 10014. Innovative works of music-theatre, to one and a half hours long. Query only, with synopsis and return postcard. Best submission time: September to December.

MUSICAL THEATRE WORKS—440 Lafayette St., New York, NY 10003. Andrew Barrett, Lit. Coordinator. Full-length musicals, for a cast of up to 15. Submit manuscript and cassette score with SASE. Responds in two months.

NATIONAL BLACK THEATRE—2033 Fifth Ave., Harlem, NY 10035. Submit to Tunde Samuel. Drama, musicals, and children's plays. "Scripts should reflect African and African-American lifestyle. Historical, inspirational, and ritualistic forms appreciated." Workshops and readings.

NATIONAL PLAYWRIGHTS CONFERENCE, EUGENE O'NEILL THEATRE CENTER—234 W. 44th St., Suite 901, New York, NY 10036. Annual competition to select new stage plays and teleplays/screenplays for development during the summer at organization's Waterford, CT, location. Submission deadline: December 1. Send #10-size SASE in the fall for guidelines to National Playwrights Conference, c/o above address. Pays stipend, plus travel/living expenses during conference.

NEW THEATRE, INC.—755 Boylston St., Suite 309, Boston, MA 02116. New full-length scripts by playwrights for readings, workshop, and main stage productions. Include SASE. Address to NEWorks Submissions Program.

NEW TUNERS/PERFORMANCE COMMUNITY—1225 W. Belmont Ave., Chicago, IL 60657. Allan Chambers, Dramaturg. Full-length musicals only, for cast to 15; no wing/fly space. Send query with brief synopsis, cassette tape of score, cast list, resumé, SASE, and return postcard. Pays on royalty basis.

NEW YORK ACTOR'S NETWORK—c/o FAPC, 6753 Fourth Ave., Brooklyn, NY 11220. Michelle Marotta, Ed. One-act plays with two to five characters and very simple sets for possible production. No payment.

NEW YORK SHAKESPEARE FESTIVAL/JOSEPH PAPP PUBLIC THEATER—425 Lafayette St., New York, NY 10003. Jason Fogelson, Lit. Mgr. Plays and musical works for the theater, translations, and adaptations. Submit manuscript, cassette (with musicals), and SASE. Allow four to six months for response.

NEW YORK STATE THEATRE INSTITUTE—P.O. Box 28, Troy, NY 12181–0028. Query for new musicals and plays for family audiences, with synopsis, cast list. Submit between June and August. Payment varies.

ODYSSEY THEATRE ENSEMBLE—2055 South Sepulveda Blvd., Los Angeles, CA 90025. Ron Sossi, Artistic Dir. Full-length comedies, dramas, musicals, and adaptations: provocative subject matter, or plays that stretch and explore the possibilities of theater. Query Jan Lewis, Lit. Mgr., with synopsis, eight to 10 pages of sample dialogue, and resumé. Pays variable rates. Allow two to six months for reply to script; two to four weeks reply for queries. Workshops and readings.

OLD GLOBE THEATRE—Simon Edison Center for the Performing Arts, Box 2171, San Diego, CA 92112–2171. Address Katie Smalheer. Full-length comedies, dramas, and musicals. No unsolicited manuscripts. Submit through agent, or query with synopsis.

OLDCASTLE THEATRE COMPANY—Southern Vermont College, Box 1555, Bennington, VT 05201. Eric Peterson, Dir. Full-length comedies, dramas, and musicals for a small cast (up to 10) and a single stage set. Submit synopsis and cast list in the winter. Reports in six months. Offers workshops and readings. Pays expenses for playwright to attend rehearsals. Royalty.

PENGUIN REPERTORY COMPANY—Box 91, Stony Point, Rockland County, NY 10980. Joe Brancato, Artistic Dir. Full-length comedies and dramas with cast size to five. Submit script, resumé, and SASE. Payment varies.

PENNSYLVANIA STAGE—837 Linden St., Allentown, PA 18101. Full-length plays with cast of four to ten; no more than two sets. Send synopsis, cast list, and SASE to Outreach/Literary Dept. Pays negotiable rates. Allow six months for reply. Staged readings possible.

PEOPLE'S LIGHT AND THEATRE COMPANY—39 Conestoga Rd., Malvern, PA 19355. Alda Cortese, Lit. Mgr. One-act or full-length comedies, dramas, adaptations. No unsolicited manuscripts; query with synopsis, 10 pages of script required. Reports in six months. Payment negotiable.

PIER ONE THEATRE—Box 894, Homer, AK 99603. Lance Petersen, Lit. Dir. Full-length and one-act comedies, dramas, musicals, children's plays, and adaptations. Submit complete script; include piano score with musicals. New works given staged readings. "We think new works in the theater are extremely important!" Pays 8% of ticket sales for mainstage musicals; other payment varies.

PLAYHOUSE ON THE SQUARE—51 S. Cooper in Overton Sq., Memphis, TN 38104. Jackie Nichols, Artistic Dir. Full-length comedies, dramas; cast of up to 15. Southern playwrights given preference. Contest deadline is April for fall production. Pays $500.

PLAYWRIGHTS HORIZONS—416 W. 42nd St., New York, NY 10036. Address Literary Dept. Full-length, original comedies, dramas, and musicals by American authors. Send resumé and SASE. Off-Broadway contract.

PLAYWRIGHTS' PLATFORM—164 Brayton Rd., Boston, MA 02135. Script development workshops and public readings for New England playwrights only. Full-length and one-act plays of all kinds. No sexist or racist material accepted. Residents of New England, send scripts with short synopsis, resumé, return postcard, and SASE. Readings conducted at Massachusetts College of Art.

POPLAR PIKE PLAYHOUSE—7653 Old Poplar Pike, Germantown, TN 38138. Frank Bluestein, Artistic Dir. Full-length and one-act comedies, dramas, musicals, and children's plays. Submit synopsis with return postcard and resumé. Pays $300.

PORTLAND STAGE COMPANY—Box 1458, Portland, ME 04104. Not accepting unsolicited material at this time.

PRINCETON REPERTORY COMPANY—17 Hulfish St., Suite 260, Palmer Sq. N., Princeton, NJ 08542. Victoria Liberatori, Artistic Dir. Full-length comedies and dramas for a cast of up to five. One set. Submit synopsis with resumé, cast list, and three-page dialogue sample. Do not submit complete script. "Scripts with socially relevant themes that move beyond domestic drama preferred. The treatment of these themes might be lyrical, surreal, realistic, or high concept." Readings offered. Response within one year.

THE PUERTO RICAN TRAVELING THEATRE—141 W. 94th St., New York, NY 10025. Miriam Colon Valle, Artistic Dir. Full-length and one-act comedies, dramas, and musicals; cast of up to 8; simple sets. "We prefer plays based on the contemporary Hispanic experience, material with social, cultural, or psychological content." Payment negotiable.

THE REPERTORY THEATRE OF ST. LOUIS—Box 191730, St. Louis, MO 63119. Query with brief synopsis, technical requirements, and cast size. Unsolicited manuscripts will be returned unread.

THE ROAD COMPANY—Box 5278 EKS, Johnson City, TN 37603. Robert H. Leonard, Artistic Dir. Christine Murdock, Lit. Mgr. Full-length and one-act comedies, dramas with social/political relevance to small-town audiences. Send synopsis, cast list, and production history, if any. Pays negotiable rates. Reports in six to 12 months.

ROUND HOUSE THEATRE—12210 Bushey Dr., Silver Spring, MD 20902. Address Production Office Mgr. Full-length comedies, dramas, adaptations, and musicals; cast of up to 10; prefer simple set. Send one-page synopsis. No unsolicited manuscripts.

SALT AND PEPPER MIME COMPANY/NEW ENSEMBLE ACTORS THEATRE—320 E. 90th St., #1B, New York, NY 10128. Ms. Scottie Davis, Man. Prod. One-acts, all types, especially those conducive to "nontraditional" casting. "Very interested in pieces suitable to surrealistic or mimetic concept in philosophy or visual style." One- or two-person cast. Send resumé, return postcard, cast list, and synopsis. Scripts reviewed from May to September. Payment of royalties based on rates established at beginning of run. Works also considered for readings, storyplayers, experimental development, and readers theater.

SEATTLE GROUP THEATRE—See *The Group Theatre*.

SEATTLE REPERTORY THEATRE—155 Mercer St., Seattle, WA 98109. Daniel Sullivan, Artistic Dir. Full-length comedies, dramas, and adaptations. Submit synopsis, 10-page sample, return postcard, and resumé to Kurt Beattie, Artistic Assoc. New plays series with workshops each spring.

SOCIETY HILL PLAYHOUSE—507 S. 8th St., Philadelphia, PA 19147. Walter Vail, Dramaturg. Full-length dramas, comedies, and musicals with up to six cast members and simple set. Submit synopsis and SASE. Reports in six months. Nominal payment.

SOUTH COAST REPERTORY—P. O. Box 2197, Costa Mesa, CA 92628. John Glore, Lit. Mgr. Full-length comedies, dramas, musicals, juveniles. Query with synopsis and resumé. Payment varies.

SOUTHERN APPALACHIAN REPERTORY THEATRE—P.O. Box 620, Mars Hill, NC 28754. James W. Thomas, Artistic Dir. Full-length comedies, dramas, musicals, and plays with Appalachian theme. Submit resumé, recommendations, full script, and SASE. Send SASE for information on Southern Appalachian Playwright's Conference (held in January each year). Pays $500 royalty if play is selected for production during the summer season. Deadline for submissions is October 1st each year.

THE SPUYTEN DUYVIL THEATRE CO.—P.O. Box 1024, New York, NY 10024. Full-length comedies and dramas with single set and cast size to 10. "Good women's roles needed." SASE required.

STAGE LEFT THEATRE—3244 N. Clark, Chicago, IL 60657. Mike Troccoli and Sandra Verthein, Artistic Dirs. Full-length comedies, dramas, and adaptations for cast of one to 12. "We are committed to producing material that is politically and socially conscious." Offers workshops and readings. No unsolicited scripts. Payment varies.

STAGE ONE: THE LOUISVILLE CHILDREN'S THEATRE—425 W. Market St., Louisville, KY 40202. Adaptations of classics and original plays for children ages four to 18. Submit script with resumé and SASE. Reports in four months.

STAGES REPERTORY THEATRE—3201 Allen Pkwy., #101, Houston, TX 77019. Beth Sanford, Assoc. Dir. Unproduced new works: full-length dramas, comedies, translations, and adaptations, with small casts and simple sets. Texas playwrights' festival held in the spring. Send for guidelines on submitting scripts to the festival.

STUDIO ARENA THEATRE—710 Main St., Buffalo, NY 14202–1990. Comedies and dramas with a cast of up to eight. "Particularly interested in plays of a theatrical/nonrealistic nature." Include synopsis, resumé, cast list, sample dialogue.

TAKOMA PLAYERS, INC.—Box 56512, Washington, DC 20012. Realistic, full-length dramas, comedies, and musicals. Special interest in plays suitable to multi-ethnic casts. Submit manuscript with SASE to Gaynelle Reed Lewis. Payment negotiable.

MARK TAPER FORUM—135 N. Grand Ave., Los Angeles, CA 90012. Oliver Mayer, Lit. Assoc. Full-length comedies, dramas, musicals, juveniles, adaptations. Query.

THE TEN MINUTE MUSICALS PROJECT—Box 461194, W. Hollywood, CA 90046. Michael Koppy, Prod. One-act musicals. Include audio cassette, libretto, and lead sheets with submission. "We are looking for complete short musicals." Pays $250.

THEATER ARTISTS OF MARIN—Box 150473, San Rafael, CA 94915. Charles Brousse, Artistic Dir. Full-length comedies, dramas, and musicals for a cast of two to eight. Submit complete script with SASE. Reports in four to six months. Three showcase productions each year.

THEATRE/TEATRO—Bilingual Foundation of the Arts, 421 N. Ave., #19, Los Angeles, CA 90031. Margarita Galban, Artistic Dir. Full-length plays about Hispanic experience; small casts. Submit manuscript with SASE. Payment varies.

THEATREWORKS/USA—890 Broadway, 7th Fl., New York, NY 10003. Barbara Pasternack, Lit. Mgr. One-hour children's musicals for five-person cast.

Playwrights must be within commutable distance to New York City. Submit outline or treatment, sample scenes, and music in spring, summer. Pays royalty.

WALNUT STREET THEATRE COMPANY—9th and Walnut Sts., Philadelphia, PA 19107. Alexa Kelly, Lit. Mgr. Full-length comedies, dramas, musicals, and adaptations; also, one- to four-character plays for studio stage. Submit 20 sample pages with return postcard, cast list, and synopsis. Musical submissions must include an audio tape. Reports in five months. Payment varies.

THE WESTERN STAGE—156 Homestead Ave., Salinas, CA 93901. Tom Humphrey, Artistic Dir. Joyce Lower, Dramaturg. The Salinas River Playwriting Festival, September through October. Presentations in theater, dance, music, the visual arts, film, poetry. Also workshops, classes, displays, etc. Submissions accepted March through July 15 annually. Write for guidelines and required application.

WOOLLY MAMMOTH THEATRE COMPANY—1401 Church St. N.W., Washington, DC 20005. James C. Byrmes, Lit. Mgr. Looking for offbeat material, unusual writing. Unsolicited scripts accepted. Pay negotiable.

GARY YOUNG MIME THEATRE—23724 Park Madrid, Calabasas, CA 91302. Gary Young, Artistic Dir. Comedy monologues and two-person vignettes, for children and adults, one minute to 90 minutes in length; casts of one or two, and portable set. Pays varying rates. Enclose return postcard, resumé, recommendations, cast list, and synopsis.

PLAY PUBLISHERS

ART CRAFT PLAY COMPANY—Box 1058, Cedar Rapids, IA 52406. Three-act comedies, mysteries, musicals, and farces, and one-act comedies or dramas, with one set, for production by junior or senior high school. Pays on royalty basis or by outright purchase.

BAKER'S PLAYS—100 Chauncy St., Boston, MA 02111. Scripts for amateur production: one-act plays, children's plays, musicals, religious drama, full-length plays for high school production. Three- to four-month reading period. Include SASE.

CHILDREN'S PLAYMATE—1100 Waterway Blvd., P. O. Box 567, Indianapolis, IN 46206. Elizabeth A. Rinck, Ed. Plays, 200 to 600 words, for children ages six to eight. Special emphasis on health, nutrition, exercise, and safety. Pays about 15¢ a word, on publication.

CONTEMPORARY DRAMA SERVICE—Meriwether Publishing Co., Box 7710, 885 Elkton Dr., Colorado Springs, CO 80903. Arthur Zapel, Ed. Easy-to-stage comedies, skits, one-acts, musicals, puppet plays, and full-length plays for schools and churches. (Junior high through college level; no elementary level material.) Adaptations of classics and improvised material for classroom use. Comedy monologues and duets. Chancel drama for Christmas and Easter church use. Enclose synopsis. Books on theater arts subjects and anthologies. Textbooks for speech and drama. Pays flat fee or royalty.

THE DRAMATIC PUBLISHING CO.—311 Washington St., Woodstock, IL 60098. Sarah Clark, Ed. Full-length and one-act plays and musicals for the stock, amateur, and children's theater market. Pays on royalty basis. Reports within three to four months.

DRAMATICS—Educational Theatre Assoc., 3368 Central Pkwy., Cincinnati,

OH 45225–2392. Don Corathers, Ed. One-act and full-length plays for high school production. Pays $100 to $400, on acceptance.

ELDRIDGE PUBLISHING COMPANY—P. O. Drawer 216, Franklin, OH 45005. Nancy Vorhis, Ed. Dept. One-, two-, and three-act plays and operettas for schools, churches, community groups, etc. Special interest in comedies and Christmas plays. Include cassette for operettas. Pays varying rates. Responds in two to three months.

SAMUEL FRENCH, INC.—45 W. 25th St., New York, NY 10010. Lawrence R. Harbison, Ed. Full-length plays for dinner, community, stock, college, and high school theaters. One-act plays (30 to 45 minutes). Children's plays, 45 to 60 minutes. Pays on royalty basis.

HEUER PUBLISHING COMPANY—Drawer 248, Cedar Rapids, IA 52406. C. Emmett McMullen, Ed. One-act comedies and dramas for contest work; three-act comedies, mysteries, or farces, and musicals, with one interior setting, for high school production. Pays royalty or flat fee.

PIONEER DRAMA SERVICE—P. O. Box 22555, Denver, CO 80222. Full-length and one-act plays; plays for young audiences; musicals, melodramas, and Christmas plays. No unproduced plays or plays with largely male casts or multiple sets. Query. Outright purchase or royalty.

PLAYS, THE DRAMA MAGAZINE FOR YOUNG PEOPLE—120 Boylston St., Boston, MA 02116–4615. Elizabeth Preston, Man. Ed. One-act plays, with simple sets, for production by young people, 7 to 17: comedies, dramas, farces, skits, holiday plays, adaptations of classics, biography plays, puppet plays, and creative dramatics. No musicals or plays with religious themes. Maximum lengths: lower grades, 10 double-spaced pages; middle grades, 15 pages; junior and senior high, 20 pages. Send SASE for guidelines. Query first for adaptations. Pays good rates, on acceptance. Buys all rights.

THE RADIO PLAY—Suite 230, 100 Boylston St., Boston, MA 02116. Stanley Richardson, Lit. Mgr. Original radio plays and radio adaptations of American classics in the public domain, 30 to 32 pages, to fit a 30-minute program format. Query for adaptations only. Responds in up to four months for complete manuscripts. Payment varies, on acceptance. Send SASE for style sheet.

THE TELEVISION AND FILM SCRIPT MARKET

The almost round-the-clock television offerings on commercial, educational, and cable TV stations, in addition to the hundreds of films released yearly, may lead free-lance writers to believe that opportunities to sell scripts or program ideas are infinite. Unfortunately, this is not true. With few exceptions, producers and programmers do not consider scripts submitted directly to them, no matter how good they are. In general, free lancers can achieve success in this nearly closed field by concentrating on getting their fiction (short stories and novels) and nonfiction published in magazines or books, combed diligently by television producers for possible adaptations. A large percentage of the material offered over all types of networks (in addition to the motion pictures made in Hollywood) is in the form of adaptations of published material.

Writers who want to try their hand at writing directly for this very limited market should be prepared to learn the special techniques and

769

acceptable format of scriptwriting. Also, experience in playwriting and a knowledge of dramatic structure gained through working in amateur, community, or professional theaters can be helpful.

A knowledge of the TV and film industry is necessary to the script writer, and trade magazines will keep the writer abreast of current events. *The Hollywood Reporter* (5055 Wilshire Blvd., Los Angeles, CA 90036–4396) publishes daily industry news, including information on rewrites underway, book adaptations, deal-making, etc. Writers may also want to check the *Daily Variety* (5700 Wilshire Blvd., Suite 120, Los Angeles, CA 90036) for trade news.

Since virtually all TV and film producers will read scripts and queries submitted only through recognized agents, we've included a list of agents who have indicated to us that they are willing to read queries for TV scripts or screenplays. The agents on this list have indicated that they do not charge a reading fee, and most charge the standard 10% commission for dramatic material; however, writers are advised to write directly for details on each agent's policy. The Association of Authors' Representatives (10 Astor Pl., 3rd Floor, New York, NY 10003) will send a list of member agents upon receipt of a self-addressed, legal-sized envelope with two first-class stamps, and a $5 check or money order. *Literary Market Place* (Bowker), available in most libraries, has a list of agents; and *Literary Agents of North America, Fifth Edition* (Author Aid/Research Associates International, 340 E. 52nd St., New York, NY 10022) provides the most detailed information on agents and their needs. Most of the agents listed below prefer queries and/or synopses; in this case, do not send complete manuscript unless it is requested. A list of network (ABC, NBC, CBS, FOX) shows, agents, and production companies may be found in *Ross Reports Television*, published monthly by Television Index, Inc., (40–29 27th St., Long Island City, NY 11101; (718) 937–3990).

Writers may wish to register their story, treatment, series format, or script with the Writers Guild of America. This registration does not confer statutory rights, but it does supply evidence of authorship and date of authorship. Registration is effective for five years (and is renewable after that). The WGA's registration service is available to guild members and non-members for a reasonable fee. For more information, write to the Writers Guild of America Registration Service East, Inc., 555 W. 57th St., New York, NY 10019. Dramatic material can also be registered with the U.S. Copyright Office (Register of Copyrights, Library of Congress, Washington, DC 20559).

TELEVISION AND FILM SCRIPT AGENTS

BRET ADAMS LTD.—448 W. 44th St., New York, NY 10036. Attn: Mary Harden. Screenplays, teleplays, and stage plays. Query with synopsis, bio, and resumé.

MICHAEL AMATO AGENCY—1650 Broadway, Rm. 307, New York, NY 10019. Attn: Susan Tomkins. Screenplays, teleplays, and stage plays. Query with bio, one-page outline, 5 pages of dialogue, and SASE.

MARCIA AMSTERDAM AGENCY—41 W. 82nd St., #9A, New York, NY 10024. Screenplays and teleplays: comedy, romance, psychological suspense. Query with resumé and SASE.

LOIS BERMAN & JUDY BOALS—Writers House, Inc., 21 W. 26th St., New York, NY 10010. Dramatic material. Query with SASE.

DON BUCHWALD & ASSOCIATES—10 E. 44th St., New York, NY 10017. Attn: Michael Traum. Screenplays, teleplays, and stage plays. Query with resumé and two-paragraph synopsis.

THE CHINA CLARK AGENCY—315 Seventh Ave., Suite 10A, New York, NY 10001. Attn: China Clark. Considers queries for screenplays only.

DOUGLAS, GORMAN, ROTHACKER & WILHELM, INC.—c/o Literary Dept., 1501 Broadway, Suite 703, New York, NY 10036. Screenplays and stage plays. Submit synopsis, bio, and resumé, with SASE. Reporting time is two weeks, *if interested*. "Does not work on a per-project basis. Works only with signed writers. New writers considered." No phone calls.

EARTH TRACKS ARTISTS AGENCY—4809 Avenue N, Suite 286, Brooklyn, NY 11234. Screenplays and teleplays. Query with SASE and syopsis no longer than one page; proposed material should have copyright.

ROBERT A. FREEDMAN DRAMATIC AGENCY, INC.—1501 Broadway, #2310, New York, NY 10036. Screenplays, teleplays, and stage plays. Query with SASE.

PETER HAGAN—P.O. Box 30266, Port Authority Station, New York, NY 10011. Screenplays, teleplays, and stage plays. Send query only, with bio and resumé.

BRIAN KEITH MOODY MANAGEMENT—G.P.O. Box 7996, New York, NY 10116. Attn: Script Dept. Screenplays and teleplays. Query with outline. "Responds to queries only if interested in material."

ARCHER KING, LTD.—10 Columbus Cir., Rm. 1492, New York, NY 10019. Screenplays, teleplays, and stage plays. Query with SASE, outline, and resumé.

OTTO R. KOZAK LITERARY AGENCY—P.O. Box 152, Long Beach, NY 11561. Screenplays and teleplays. Query with outline or treatment and SASE.

LUCY KROLL AGENCY—390 West End Ave., New York, NY 10024. Attn: Lucy Kroll. Screenplays and stage plays. Query with bio, resumé, and SASE.

THE LITERARIUM—332 Bleecker St., Suite E-16, New York, NY 10014. Fiction and screenplays. Query with synopsis, sample pages, bio and resumé, and SASE.

THE SHUKAT COMPANY, LTD.—340 W. 55th St., #1A, New York, NY 10019. Attn: Scott Shukat or Patricia McLaughlin. Screenplays and stage plays. Query with outline, sample pages, and bio. "Since this is a small office, we will reply *only* if we are interested in the material. SASE not necessary."

THE TANTLEFF OFFICE—375 Greenwich St., Suite 700, New York, NY 10013. Attn: Jill Bock; screenplays and teleplays. Attn: John Santoianni; stage plays. Query with outline and SASE.

ANN WRIGHT REPRESENTATIVES—136 E. 56th St., 9J, New York, NY 10022–3619. Dan Wright, Literary Dept. Screenplays and novels with strong motion picture potential; teleplays (no episodic material). Query with SASE.

WRITERS AND ARTISTS AGENCY —19 W. 44th St., Suite 1000, New York, NY 10036. Attn: William Craver. Screenplays, teleplays, and stage plays. Query only, with SASE.

BOOK PUBLISHERS

The following list includes the major book publishers (adult and juvenile fiction and nonfiction) and a representative number of small publishers from across the country.

Before sending a complete manuscript to an editor, it is advisable to send a brief query letter describing the proposed book. The letter should also include information about the author's special qualifications for dealing with a particular topic and any previous publication credits. An outline of the book (or a synopsis for fiction) and a sample chapter may also be included.

It is common practice to submit a book manuscript to only one publisher at a time, although it is becoming more and more acceptable for writers, even those without agents, to submit the same query or proposal to more than one editor at the same time.

Book manuscripts may be sent in typing paper boxes (available from a stationery store) and sent by first-class mail, or, more common and less expensive, by "Special Fourth Class Rate—Manuscript." For rates, details of insurance, and so forth, inquire at your local post office. With any submission to a publisher, be sure to enclose sufficient postage for the manuscript's return.

Royalty rates for hardcover books usually start at 10% of the retail price of the book and increase after a certain number of copies have been sold. Paperbacks generally have a somewhat lower rate, about 5% to 8%. It is customary for the publishing company to pay the author a cash advance against royalties when the book contract is signed or when the finished manuscript is received. Some publishers pay on a flat-fee basis.

ABBEY PRESS—St. Meinrad, IN 47577. Karen Katafiasz, Books Ed. Not considering any new material at this time.

ABINGDON PRESS—Imprint of The United Methodist Publishing House, P.O. Box 801, Nashville, TN 37202. Mary Catherine Dean, Sr. Ed. General-interest books: mainline, social issues, marriage/family, self-help, exceptional people. Query with outline and one or two sample chapters. Guidelines.

ACADEMIC PRESS—Div. of Harcourt Brace, 1250 Sixth Ave., San Diego, CA 92101. Scientific and technical books and journals for research-level scientists, students, and professionals; upper-level undergraduate and graduate science texts. Query.

ACCENT PUBLICATIONS—Box 15337, 12100 W. 6th Ave., Denver, CO 80215. Mary Nelson, Exec. Ed. Nonfiction church resources from evangelical Christian perspective; no trade books. "Request guidelines before querying." Query with sample chapters and SASE. Royalty. Paperback only.

ACCESS PUBLISHERS—1078 E. Otero Ave., Littleton, CO 80122. Kathy Fanchi, Ed. Novels on disk. Science fiction and fantasy, from 40,000 words. "We are looking for highly readable manuscripts that entertain." Query with outline and sample chapters. Royalty.

ACE BOOKS —Imprint of Berkley Publishing Group, 200 Madison Ave., New York, NY 10016. Susan Allison, V.P., Ed.-in-Chief. Science fiction and fantasy. Royalty. Query with first three chapters and outline to Laura Anne Gilman, Asst. Ed.

ADAMA BOOKS—See *Modan Publishing.*

ADDISON-WESLEY PUBLISHING CO.—1 Jacob Way, Reading, MA 01867–3999. Adult nonfiction on current topics including science, health, psychology, business, biography, child care, etc. Specializing in literary nonfiction. Royalty.

AERIAL FICTION—Imprint of Farrar, Straus & Giroux, Inc., 19 Union Sq. W., New York, NY 10003. Wes Adams, Ed. Young adult material. Send query with two or three sample chapters. Paperback reprints of teenage hardcovers; send copy of original edition and reviews. Royalty.

ALADDIN BOOKS—See *Macmillan Children's Book Group.*

ALASKA NORTHWEST BOOKS—A Div. of GTE Discovery Publications, 22026 20th Ave. S.E., Bothell, WA 98021. Marlene Blessing, Ed.-in-Chief. Nonfiction, 50,000 to 100,000 words, with an emphasis on natural world and history of Alaska, Western Canada, Pacific Northwest, and Pacific Rim: travel books; cookbooks; field guides; children's books; outdoor recreation; natural history; native culture; lifestyle. Send query or sample chapters with outline. Guidelines.

ALGONQUIN BOOKS OF CHAPEL HILL—Div. of Workman Publishing Co., Inc., Box 2225, Chapel Hill, NC 27515. Shannon Ravenel, Ed. Dir. Trade books, fiction and nonfiction, for adults.

AMERICAN PARADISE PUBLISHING—P.O. Box 37, St. John, USVI 00831. Gary M. Goodlander, Ed. Useful books, 300 pages, on the Virgin Islands, the Caribbean, and boating in the region. Send query, outline, and sample chapters. Royalty.

THE AMERICAN PSYCHIATRIC PRESS—1400 K St. N.W., Washington, DC 20005. Carol C. Nadelson, M.D., Ed.-in-Chief. Books that interpret scientific and medical aspects of psychiatry for a lay audience and that address specific psychiatric problems. Authors must have appropriate credentials to write on medical topics. Query required. Royalty.

ANCHOR BOOKS—Imprint of Doubleday and Co., 666 Fifth Ave., New York, NY 10103. Martha K. Levin, Pub. Adult trade paperbacks. General fiction and nonfiction, sociology, psychology, philosophy, women's interest, etc. No unsolicited manuscripts.

AND BOOKS—702 S. Michigan, South Bend, IN 46618. Janos Szebedinsky, Ed. Adult nonfiction. Topics include computers, fine arts, health, philosophy, regional subjects, and social justice.

ANDREWS AND MCMEEL—4900 Main St., Kansas City, MO 64112. Matt

Lombardi, Asst. Ed. Humor, how-to, reference, and general adult trade books. Send query letter or proposal with up to three sample chapters. Royalty.

ANHINGA PRESS—P.O. Box 10595, Tallahassee, FL 32302–0595. Rick Campbell, Ed. Poetry books, 48 to 64 pages. (Publishes two books a year.) Query or send complete manuscripts. Flat fee. Annual poetry prize; send SASE for details.

APPALACHIAN MOUNTAIN CLUB BOOKS—5 Joy St., Boston, MA 02108. Regional (New England) and national nonfiction titles, 250 to 400 pages, for adult audience; juvenile and young adult nonfiction. Topics include guidebooks on non-motorized backcountry recreation, nature, mountain history/biography, search and rescue, conservation, and environmental management. Query with outline and sample chapters. Multiple queries considered. Royalty.

ARCADE PUBLISHING—141 Fifth Ave., New York, NY 10010. Richard Seaver, Pub./Ed. Fiction, nonfiction, and children's books. Query required.

ARCHWAY PAPERBACKS—Pocket Books, 1230 Ave. of the Americas, New York, NY 10020. Patricia MacDonald, Ed. Dir. Young adult contemporary fiction (suspense thrillers, survival adventure, strong boy/girl stories) and nonfiction (popular current topics), for ages 11 and up. Query and SASE required; include outline and sample chapter.

ARCO PUBLISHING—Prentice Hall General Reference Group, Paramount Communications Bldg., 15 Columbus Cir., New York, NY 10023. Charles Wall, Ed.-in-Chief. Nonfiction, originals and reprints, from 50,000 words. Career guides, test preparation. Royalty. Query; unsolicited manuscripts not accepted.

ARCSOFT PUBLISHERS—P.O. Box 179, Hebron, MD 21830. Anthony Curtis, Pres. Nonfiction hobby books for beginners: personal computing, space science, desktop publishing, journalism. Hobby electronics for laymen and consumers, beginners and novices. Outright purchase and royalty basis. Query. Paperback books only.

ASTARTE SHELL PRESS—P.O. Box 10453, Portland, ME 04104. Sapphire, Ed. Books on theology, politics, and social issues from a feminist/woman's perspective. No poetry. Send sample chapters or complete manuscripts. Royalty.

ATHENEUM PUBLISHERS—Subsidiary of Macmillan Publishing Co., 866 Third Ave., New York, NY 10022. Mr. Lee Goerner, Pub. General nonfiction, biography, history, current affairs, fiction, belles lettres. Query with sample chapters, outline, and SASE.

THE ATLANTIC MONTHLY PRESS—See *Grove/Atlantic Monthly Press.*

AVALON BOOKS—Imprint of Thomas Bouregy & Co., Inc., 401 Lafayette St., New York, NY 10003. Marcia Markland, Ed. Hardcover library books, 40,000 to 50,000 words: wholesome contemporary romances and mystery romances about young single (never married) women; wholesome westerns. Query with first chapter and outline. SASE required. Guidelines for SASE.

AVERY PUBLISHING GROUP—120 Old Broadway, Garden City Park, NY 11040. Nonfiction, from 40,000 words, on health, childbirth, child care, healthful cooking. Query first with SASE. Royalty.

AVON BOOKS—1350 Ave. of the Americas, New York, NY 10019. Robert Mecoy, Ed.-in-Chief. Genre fiction, general nonfiction, historical romance, 60,000 to 200,000 words. *AvoNova*: science fiction, 75,000 to 100,000 words. Query with synopsis and sample chapters. Ellen Edwards, Historical Romance; John Douglas,

Science Fiction; Chris Miller, Fantasy. *Camelot Books*: Ellen Krieger, Ed. Fiction and nonfiction for 7- to 10-year-olds. Query. *Flare Books*: Ellen Krieger, Ed. Fiction and nonfiction for 12-year-olds and up. Query. Royalty. Paperback only.

AVONOVA—See *Avon Books.*

BACKCOUNTRY PUBLICATIONS—Div. of The Countryman Press, Inc., P. O. Box 175, Woodstock, VT 05091. Robin Dutcher-Bayer, Man. Ed. Regional guidebooks, 150 to 250 pages, on hiking, walking, canoeing, bicycling, mountain biking, cross-country skiing, and fishing covering New England, the mid-Atlantic states, and the Midwest. Send outline and sample chapter with SASE. Royalty.

BAEN BOOKS—Baen Enterprises, P.O. Box 1403, Riverdale, NY 10471–1403. Jim Baen, Pres./Ed.-in-Chief. Strongly plotted science fiction; innovative fantasy. Query with synopsis and manuscript. Advance and royalty. Guidelines available for letter-sized SASE.

BAKER BOOK HOUSE—P. O. Box 6287, Grand Rapids, MI 49516–6287. Allan Fisher, Dir. of Publications. Religious nonfiction: books for trade, clergy, seminarians, collegians. Religious fiction. Royalty.

BALLANTINE BOOKS—201 E. 50th St., New York, NY 10022. Clare Ferraro, Ed.-in-Chief. General fiction and nonfiction. Query.

BALSAM PRESS—One Madison Ave., 25th Fl., New York, NY 10010. Barbara Krohn, Exec. Ed. General and illustrated adult nonfiction. Query. Royalty.

BANTAM BOOKS—Div. of Bantam, Doubleday, Dell, 1540 Broadway, New York, NY 10036. Irwyn Applebaum, Pres./Pub. Adult fiction and nonfiction. Mass-market titles, submit queries to the following imprints: *Crime Line*, crime and mystery fiction; *Domain*, frontier fiction, historical sagas, traditional westerns; *Fanfare*, historical and romantic fiction (see listing); *Spectra*, science fiction and fantasy (see listing); *Bantam Nonfiction*, wide variety of commercial nonfiction, including true crime, health and nutrition, sports, reference. Agented queries and manuscripts only.

BANTAM STARFIRE—See *Laurel-Leaf.*

BARRICADE BOOKS—61 4th Ave., New York, NY 10003. Lyle Stuart, Pub. General nonfiction, celebrity biographies, controversial subjects. No fiction. Send synopsis with SASE. Modest advances against royalties.

BARRON'S—250 Wireless Blvd., Hauppauge, NY 11788. Grace Freedson, Acquisitions Ed. Nonfiction for juveniles (science, nature, history, hobbies, and how-to) and picture books for ages 3 to 6. Nonfiction for adults (business, childcare, sports). Queries required. Guidelines.

BARTON & BRETT—See *Brett Books, Inc.*

BAUHAN, PUBLISHER, WILLIAM L.—Dublin, NH 03444. William L. Bauhan, Ed. Biographies, fine arts, gardening, and history books with an emphasis on New England. Submit query with outline and sample chapter.

BEACON PRESS—25 Beacon St., Boston, MA 02108. Wendy Strothman, Dir. Lauren Bryant, Sr. Ed. General nonfiction: world affairs, women's studies, anthropology, history, philosophy, religion, gay and lesbian studies, environment, nature writing, African-American studies, Asian-American studies, Native-American studies. Series: *Concord Library* (nature writing); *Barnard New Women Poets*; *Black Women Writers* (fiction); *Men and Masculinity* (nonfiction). Query with SASE required.

BEAR & COMPANY, INC.—P.O. Drawer 2860, Santa Fe, NM 87504. Barbara Clow, Ed. Nonfiction "that will help transform our culture philosophically, environmentally, and spiritually." Query with outline and sample chapters. SASE required. Royalty.

BEECH TREE BOOKS—See *William Morrow and Co., Inc.*

BEHRMAN HOUSE—235 Watchung Ave., W. Orange, NJ 07052. Adam Siegel, Projects Ed. Adult and juvenile nonfiction, varying lengths, in English and in Hebrew, that promotes Jewish traditions. Query with outline and sample chapters. Flat fee.

BERKLEY PUBLISHING GROUP —Div. of The Putnam Berkley Group, Inc., 200 Madison Ave., New York, NY 10016. Roger Cooper, Pub. General-interest fiction and nonfiction; science fiction, suspense, and mystery novels; romance. Submit through agent only. Publishes both reprints and originals. Paperback books, except for some hardcover mysteries.

BETHANY HOUSE PUBLISHERS—11300 Hampshire Ave. S., Minneapolis, MN 55438. Address the Ed. Dept. Religious fiction and nonfiction. No unsolicited manuscripts. Royalty.

BETTER HOMES AND GARDENS BOOKS—See *Meredith Corp. Book Group.*

BINFORD & MORT PUBLISHING—1202 N.W. 17th Ave., Portland, OR 97209. J. F. Roberts, Ed. Books on subjects related to the Pacific Coast and the Northwest. Lengths vary. Query. Royalty.

BLACK BUTTERFLY CHILDREN'S BOOKS—Writers and Readers Publishing, 625 Broadway, New York, NY 10012. Address Deborah Dyson or Beth Smith. Titles for black children and other children of color. Picture books for children up to 11; board books for toddlers; juvenile fiction for all ages. Query or send complete manuscript. Royalty.

BLAIR, PUBLISHER, JOHN F.—1406 Plaza Dr., Winston-Salem, NC 27103. Carolyn Sakowski, Pres. Books from 50,000 words: biography, history, folklore, and guidebooks, with southeastern tie-in. Query. Royalty.

BLUEMOON BOOKS, INC.—61 Fourth Ave., New York, NY 10003. Barney Rosset, Pub. Fiction and nonfiction on a variety of topics. Send complete manuscript or sample chapters and SASE.

BONUS BOOKS—160 E. Illinois St., Chicago, IL 60611. Anne Barthel, Assoc. Ed. Nonfiction; topics vary widely. Query with sample chapters and SASE. Royalty.

BOOKS FOR PROFESSIONALS—See *Harcourt Brace.*

BOYDS MILL PRESS—*Highlights for Children*, 815 Church St., Honesdale, PA 18431. Beth Troop, Manuscript Coord. Hardcover trade books for children. Fiction: picture books; middle-grade fiction with fresh ideas and involving story; young adult novels of literary merit. Nonfiction should be "fun, entertaining, and informative." Send outline and sample chapters for young adult novels and nonfiction, complete manuscripts for all other categories. Royalty.

BRADBURY PRESS—866 Third Ave., New York, NY 10022. Barbara Lalicki, Ed. Hardcover: fiction (general, humor, mysteries), grades 4 to 12; nonfiction (science, sports, history) up to grade 6; picture books, to age 8. Submit complete manuscript. Royalty.

BRANDEN PUBLISHING COMPANY—17 Station St., Box 843, Brookline Village, MA 02147. Novels, biographies, and autobiographies. Especially books by or about women, 250 to 350 pages. Also considers queries on history, computers, business, performance arts, and translations. Query only with SASE. Royalty.

BRETT BOOKS, INC.—(formerly *Barton & Brett*) P.O. Box 290–637, Brooklyn, NY 11229–0011. Barbara J. Brett, Pres./Pub. Nonfiction for adult trade market. "Submit a query letter of no more than two pages, stating your professional background and summarizing your book proposal in two to four paragraphs." Royalty.

BRIDGEWATER BOOKS—Imprint of Troll Associates, 100 Corporate Dr., Mahwah, NJ 07430. Hardcover picture books, novels, and anthologies.

BRISTOL PUBLISHING ENTERPRISES—P.O. Box 1737, San Leandro, CA 94577. Patricia J. Hall, Ed. Mature reader series: nonfiction for 50+ population, approximately 40,000 words. *Nitty Gritty Cookbooks*: 120-recipe manuscripts. Query with outline, sample chapters, SASE. Royalty.

BROADMAN PRESS—127 Ninth Ave. N., Nashville, TN 37234. Mike Hyatt, Ed. Dir. Religious and inspirational nonfiction. Query with SASE. Royalty.

BROWNDEER PRESS—Imprint of Harcourt Brace & Co. Children's Books, P.O. Box 80160, Portland, OR 97280–1160. Linda Zuckerman, Ed. Dir. Picture books, humorous middle-grade fiction, and young adult material written from an unusual perspective or about an unusual subject. Query for nonfiction with cover letter, resumé, and sample chapter; send complete manuscript for picture books (avoid rhyming text). For longer fiction, send first three chapters, synopsis, and short cover letter with biographical information. SASE required for all correspondence.

BUCKNELL UNIVERSITY PRESS—Bucknell Univ., Lewisburg, PA 17837. Mills F. Edgerton, Jr., Dir. Scholarly nonfiction. Query. Royalty.

BULFINCH PRESS—Div. of Little, Brown & Co., 34 Beacon St., Boston, MA 02108. Books on fine arts and photography. Query with outline or proposal and vita.

C&T PUBLISHING—5021 Blum Rd., #1, Martinez, CA 94553. Diane Pedersen, Ed. Quilting books, 64 to 200 finished pages. "Our focus is how-to, although we will consider picture, inspirational, or history books on quilting." Send query, outline, or sample chapters. Multiple queries considered. Royalty.

CAMELOT BOOKS—See *Avon Books.*

CANDLEWICK PRESS—2067 Massachusetts Ave., Cambridge, MA 02140. Address the Eds. "Unfortunately, we are no longer able to consider unsolicited material; unsolicited manuscripts will be returned unread."

CAPSTONE PRESS, INC.—P.O. Box 669, N. Mankato, MN 56001–0669. Juvenile theme-books for children in preschool to grade 6. Send SASE for catalogue of series themes. Query required. Flat fee.

CAROLRHODA BOOKS—241 First Ave. N., Minneapolis, MN 55401. Rebecca Poole, Ed. Complete manuscripts for ages 4 to 12: biography, science, nature, history, photo essays; historical fiction, 10 to 15 pages, for ages 6 to 10. Guidelines. Hardcover.

CARROLL AND GRAF PUBLISHERS, INC.—260 Fifth Ave., New York, NY 10001. Kent E. Carroll, Exec. Ed. General fiction and nonfiction. Query with SASE. Royalty.

CASSANDRA PRESS—P.O. Box 150868, San Rafael, CA 94915. New Age, holistic health, metaphysical, and psychological books. Query with outline and sample chapters, or complete manuscript. Include SASE. Royalty (no advance).

THE CATHOLIC UNIVERSITY OF AMERICA PRESS—620 Michigan Ave. N.E., Washington, DC 20064. David J. McGonagle, Dir. Scholarly nonfiction: American and European history (both ecclesiastical and secular); Irish studies; American and European literature; philosophy; political theory; theology. Query with prospectus, annotated table of contents, or introduction and resumé. Royalty.

CHARIOT FAMILY PUBLISHING—A Div. of David C. Cook Publishing Co., 850 N. Grove Ave., Elgin, IL 60120. Catherine Davis, Exec. Ed., *Chariot Children's Books*: fiction that "helps children better understand themselves and their relationship with God"; nonfiction that illuminates the Bible; picture books for ages 1 to 7; fiction for ages 8 to 10, 10 to 12, and 12 to 14. *Life Journey General Titles*: fiction with underlying spiritual theme; books on parenting from a Christian perspective. Lengths and payment vary. Query required. Guidelines.

CHATHAM PRESS—P. O. Box A, Old Greenwich, CT 06870. Roger H. Lourie, Man. Dir. Books on the Northeast coast, New England maritime subjects, and the ocean. Large photography volumes. Query with outline, sample chapters, illustrations, and SASE large enough for the return of material. Royalty.

CHELSEA GREEN PUBLISHING CO.—Route 113, P.O. Box 130, Post Mills, VT 05058–0130. Ian Baldwin, Jr., Ed. Primarily nonfiction: natural history, environmental issues, outdoor recreation, and lifestyle books with strong backlist potential. Query with outline and SASE. Royalty. Not considering any unsolicited manuscripts at this time.

CHICAGO REVIEW PRESS—814 N. Franklin St., Chicago, IL 60610. Amy Teschner, Ed. Nonfiction: activity books for young children, project books for 10- to 18-year-olds, architecture, adoption, how-to, travel, popular science, and regional topics. Query with outline and sample chapters.

CHILTON BOOK CO.—One Chilton Way, Radnor, PA 19089. Christopher J. Kuppig, Gen. Mgr. Antiques and collectibles, sewing and crafts, professional/technical, and automotive topics. Query with outline, sample chapter, and return postage. *Wallace-Homestead Books.*

CHINA BOOKS—2929 24th St., San Francisco, CA 94110. Wendy K. Lee, Sr. Ed. Books relating to China or Chinese culture. Adult nonfiction, varying lengths. Juvenile picture books, fiction, nonfiction, and young adult books. Query. Royalty.

CHRONICLE BOOKS—275 Fifth St., San Francisco, CA 94103. Topical nonfiction, history, biography, fiction, art, photography, architecture, nature, food, regional, and children's books. Send proposal with SASE.

CLARION BOOKS—215 Park Ave. S., New York, NY 10003. Dorothy Briley, Ed.-in-Chief/Pub. Fiction, nonfiction, and picture books: short novels and lively stories for ages 6 to 10 and 8 to 12, historical fiction, humor; picture books for infants to age 7; biography, natural history, social studies, American and world history for readers 5 to 8, and 9 and up. Royalty. Hardcover.

CLARK CITY PRESS—P.O. Box 1358, Livingston, MT 59047. Collections of poems, short stories, and essays; novels, biographies, and some children's books. No unsolicited manuscripts. Royalty.

CLEIS PRESS—P.O. Box 14684, San Francisco, CA 94114. Frédérique Delacoste, Ed. Fiction and nonfiction, 200 pages, by women. No poetry. Send SASE with two first-class stamps for catalogue before querying. Royalty.

CLIFFHANGER PRESS—P.O. Box 29527, Oakland, CA 94604–9527. Nancy Chirich, Ed. Not considering any new material at this time.

CLOVERDALE PRESS—109 W. 17th St., New York, NY 10011. Book packager. Adult nonfiction; young adult, middle- and lower-grade fiction and nonfiction. "Since our requirements vary considerably and frequently according to our publishers' needs, please send query letter before submitting material." Address young adult and juvenile to Marion Vaarn; adult to Lisa Howell.

COBBLEHILL BOOKS—375 Hudson St., New York, NY 10014. Joe Ann Daly, Ed. Dir. Rosanne Lauer, Sr. Ed. Fiction and nonfiction for preschoolers through junior high school. Query with outline and sample chapters. For picture books send complete manuscript. Royalty.

COFFEE HOUSE PRESS—27 N. 4th St., Suite 400, Minneapolis, MN 55401. Address M. Wiegers. Fiction (no genres). Query with SASE. Royalty.

COLLIER BOOKS—See *Macmillan Publishing Co. and Macmillan Children's Book Group.*

COMPCARE PUBLISHERS—3850 Annapolis Ln., Suite 100, Minneapolis, MN 55447. Linda Christensen, Ed. Dir. Adult nonfiction; young adult nonfiction: books on positive living; emotional health; growth in personal, couple, and family relationships. Submit proposal and two sample chapters or complete manuscript. Royalty.

COMPUTE BOOKS—324 West Wendover Ave., Greensboro, NC 27408. PC game books, video game books. Also specializes in Amiga and PC application books.

CONCORDIA PUBLISHING HOUSE—3558 S. Jefferson Ave., St. Louis, MO 63118. Practical nonfiction with explicit religious content, conservative Lutheran doctrine. Children's fiction with explicit Christian content. No poetry. Query. Royalty.

CONFLUENCE PRESS—Spalding Hall, Lewis Clark State College, 500 8th Ave., Lewiston, ID 83502–2698. James Hepworth, Dir. Fiction, nonfiction, and poetry, of varying lengths, "to promote and nourish young writers in particular, to achieve literary and artistic excellence." Send query, outline, and sample chapters. Flat fee or royalty.

CONSUMER REPORTS BOOKS—101 Truman Ave., Yonkers, NY 10703. Sarah Uman, Exec. Ed. Medicine/health, finances, automotive, homeowners, food and cooking topics. Submit complete manuscript, or send contents, outline, three chapters, and resumé.

CONTEMPORARY BOOKS, INC.—180 N. Michigan Ave., Chicago, IL 60601. Nancy Crossman, Ed. Dir. Trade nonfiction, 100 to 400 pages, on health, fitness, sports, cooking, humor, business, popular culture, biography, real estate, finance, women's issues. Query with outline and sample chapters. Royalty.

COUNCIL FOR INDIAN EDUCATION—517 Rimrock Rd., Billings, MT 59102. Hap Gilliland, Ed. Books dealing with Native-American life and culture, for children ages 5 to 18. Picture books, 30 to 60 pages; fiction, nonfiction, and young adult books, 30 to 300 pages. Query or send complete manuscript. Flat fee for short stories included in anthologies; royalty for books. Guidelines. Manuscripts read Oct. to June 1.

CRAFTSMAN BOOK COMPANY—6058 Corte del Cedro, P.O. Box 6500,

Carlsbad, CA 92018. Laurence D. Jacobs, Ed. How-to construction and estimating manuals and software for professional builders, 450 pages. Query. Royalty. Paperback.

CREATIVE ARTS BOOK CO.—833 Bancroft Way, Berkeley, CA 94710. Donald S. Ellis, Pub. Adult nonfiction: women's issues, music, and California topics. Query with outline, sample chapters, SASE. Royalty.

THE CREATIVE COMPANY—123 S. Broad St., P.O. Box 227, Mankato, MN 10104–0298. Nancy Loewen, Ed. Dir. Nonfiction and classic fiction for children in preschool through high school. Nonfiction series. "We usually come up with ideas in-house and then hire writers to complete projects on a flat-fee basis." Submit writing samples and resumé; indicate publishing history and areas of interest and expertise.

CRESTWOOD HOUSE—See *Macmillan Children's Book Group.*

CRIME LINE—See *Bantam Books.*

THE CROSSING PRESS—P.O. Box 1048, Freedom, CA 95019. Elaine Goldman Gill, John Gill, Pubs. Health, men's studies, feminist studies, spiritual works, gay topics, cookbooks; fiction. Royalty.

CROWN BOOKS FOR YOUNG READERS—201 E. 50th St., New York, NY 10022. Simon Boughton, Ed.-in-Chief. Children's nonfiction (science, sports, nature, music, and history), and picture books for ages 3 and up. Send manuscript for picture books. Guidelines.

CRYSTAL RIVER PRESS—P.O. Box 1382, Healdsburg, CA 95448. Tom Watson, Ed.-in-Chief. Juvenile books. Picture books for preschoolers to age 6. Fiction and nonfiction for K through 12. Young adult books, 60,000 words, for readers 14 to 18. Royalty.

CURRENCY BOOKS—See *Doubleday and Co.*

DANIEL AND COMPANY, JOHN—P.O. Box 21922, Santa Barbara, CA 93121. John Daniel, Pub. Books, to 200 pages, in the field of belles lettres and literary memoirs; stylish and elegant writing; essays and short fiction dealing with social issues; one poetry title per year. Send synopsis or outline with no more than 50 sample pages and SASE. Allow 6 to 8 weeks for response. Royalty.

DAW BOOKS, INC.—375 Hudson St., 3rd Fl., New York, NY 10014–3658. Elizabeth R. Wollheim, Ed.-in-Chief. Sheila E. Gilbert, Sr. Ed. Peter Stampfel, Submissions Ed. Science fiction and fantasy, 60,000 to 120,000 words. Royalty.

DEARBORN FINANCIAL PUBLISHING, INC.—Div. of Dearborn Publishing Group Inc., 520 N. Dearborn St., Chicago, IL 60610. Anita A. Constant, Sr. V.P. Books on financial services, real estate, banking, etc. Query with outline and sample chapters. Royalty and flat fee.

DEL REY BOOKS—201 E. 50th St., New York, NY 10022. Shelly Shapiro, Exec. Ed. Veronica Chapman, Sr. Ed. Science fiction and fantasy, 60,000 to 120,000 words; first novelists welcome. Material must be well paced with logical resolutions. Fantasy with magic basic to plotline. Send manuscript or outline with three sample chapters. Royalty.

DELACORTE PRESS—1540 Broadway, New York, NY 10036. Leslie Schnur, Jackie Farber, Emily Reichert, Trish Todd, Jackie Cantor, Eds. Adult fiction and nonfiction. Juvenile and young adult fiction (Craig Virden, Ed.). Accepts fiction (mystery, young adult, romance, fantasy, etc.) from agents only.

DELANCEY PRESS—P.O. Box 40285, Philadelphia, PA 19106. Wesley Morrison, Ed. Dir. Adult genre fiction and all types of nonfiction, 60,000 words. Query. Royalty.

DELL BOOKS—1540 Broadway, New York, NY 10036. Address Editorial Dept., Book Proposal. Commercial fiction and nonfiction, family sagas, historical romances, war action, general fiction, occult/horror/psychological suspense, true crime, men's adventure. Send four-page narrative synopsis for fiction, or an outline for nonfiction. Enclose SASE. Allow 2 to 3 months for response.

DELTA BOOKS—1540 Broadway, New York, NY 10036. Address Editorial Dept., Book Proposal. General-interest nonfiction: psychology, feminism, health, nutrition, child care, science, self-help, and how-to. Send an outline with SASE.

DEVIN-ADAIR PUBLISHERS, INC.—6 N. Water St., Greenwich, CT 06830. C. de la Belle Issue, Pub. J. Andrassi, Ed. Books on conservative affairs, Irish topics, photography, Americana, self-help, health, gardening, cooking, and ecology. Send outline, sample chapters, and SASE. Royalty.

DI CAPUA BOOKS, MICHAEL—See *HarperCollins Children's Books.*

DIAL BOOKS FOR YOUNG READERS—375 Hudson St., New York, NY 10014. Phyllis Fogelman, Pub./Ed.in-Chief. Picture books; easy-to-read books; middle-grade readers; young adult fiction and some nonfiction. Submit complete manuscript for picture books and easy-to-reads; outline and sample chapters for nonfiction and novels. Enclose SASE. Royalty.

DIAL PRESS—Imprint of Dell Publishing, 1540 Broadway, New York, NY 10036. Susan Kamil, Ed. Dir. Quality fiction and nonfiction. No unsolicited material.

DIAMOND BOOKS—Imprint of Berkley Publishing Co., 200 Madison Ave., New York, NY 10012. Leslie Gelbman, Ed.-in-Chief. Suspense fiction, historical romances, regencies, women's contemporary fiction. Westerns. Paperback.

DILLON PRESS—Macmillan Publishing Co., 866 Third Ave., New York, NY 10022. Joyce Stanton, Ed. Juvenile nonfiction, 25 to 100 pages: U.S. history and social studies, social studies topics in European and Third World countries, world geography/places of interest, environmental and science topics, unusual or remarkable animals, contemporary and historical biographies for middle-grade levels. Royalty and outright purchase. Query.

DOMAIN—See *Bantam Books.*

DORLING KINDERSLEY, INC.—232 Madison Ave., New York, NY 10016. Attn: B. Alison Weir. Preschool and children's picture books. Submit through agent only.

DOUBLE D WESTERN—See *Doubleday and Co.*

DOUBLEDAY AND CO.—1540 Broadway, New York, NY 10036. Stephen Rubin, Pub./Pres. David Gernert, Ed.-in-Chief. Hardcover: *Perfect Crime, Double D Western*, romance fiction, mystery/suspense fiction, science fiction, 70,000 to 80,000 words. Send query and outline. Paperback: *Currency Books*, business books for a general audience on "the art of getting things done." No unsolicited manuscripts.

DUNNE BOOKS, THOMAS—Imprint of St. Martin's Press, 175 Fifth Ave., New York, NY 10010. Thomas L. Dunne, Ed. Adult fiction (mysteries, trade, science fiction, etc.) and nonfiction (history, biographies, science, politics, etc.). Query with outline, sample chapters, and SASE. Royalty.

DUQUESNE UNIVERSITY PRESS—600 Forbes Ave., Pittsburgh, PA 15282–0101. Scholarly publications in the humanities and social sciences.

DUTTON ADULT—Div. of Penguin USA, 375 Hudson St., New York, NY 10014. Arnold Dolin, Ed. Dir. Fiction and nonfiction books. Manuscripts accepted only from agents or on personal recommendation.

DUTTON CHILDREN'S BOOKS—Div. of Penguin USA, 375 Hudson St., New York, NY 10014. Lucia Monfried, Ed.-in-Chief. Picture books, easy-to-read books; fiction and nonfiction for preschoolers to young adults. Submit outline and first three chapters with query for fiction and nonfiction, complete manuscripts for picture books and easy-to-read books. Manuscripts should be well written with fresh ideas and child appeal. Include SASE.

EERDMANS PUBLISHING COMPANY, INC., WM. B—255 Jefferson Ave. S.E., Grand Rapids, MI 49503. Jon Pott, Ed.-in-Chief. Protestant, Roman Catholic, and Orthodox theological nonfiction; American religious history; some fiction. For children's religious books, query Amy Eerdmans, Children's Book Ed. Royalty.

EMC CORP.—300 York Ave., St. Paul, MN 55101. Eileen Slater, Ed. Vocational, career, and consumer education textbooks. Royalty. No unsolicited manuscripts.

ENSLOW PUBLISHERS, INC.—Bloy St. & Ramsey Ave., Box 777, Hillside, NJ 07205. Brian D. Enslow, Ed./Pub. Nonfiction books for young people. Areas of emphasis are children's and young adult books for ages 10 to 18 in the fields of social studies, science, and biography. Also reference books for all ages and easy reading books for teenagers.

ERIKSSON, PUBLISHER, PAUL S.—208 Battell Bldg., Middlebury, VT 05753. General nonfiction (send outline and cover letter); some fiction (send three chapters with query). Royalty.

ESTRIN PUBLISHING—1900 Ave. of the Stars, Suite 670, Los Angeles, CA 90067. Dana Graves, Ed. Books, 300 to 400 pages, for paralegal professionals. Query with outline and sample chapters; multiple queries considered. Royalty.

EVANS & CO., INC., M.—216 E. 49th St., New York, NY 10017. Books on humor, health, self-help, popular psychology, and cookbooks. Western fiction for adults; fiction and nonfiction for young adults. Query with outline, sample chapter, and SASE. Royalty.

EVENT HORIZON PRESS—P.O. Box 867, Desert Hot Springs, CA 92240. Joseph Cowles, Ed. Adult fiction and nonfiction. Poetry books, from 50 pages. Juvenile fiction and nonfiction for 7- to 10-year-olds. Not accepting any new material at this time.

EVERGREEN PUBLICATIONS—P.O. Box 220, Davison, MI 48423. Robert Busha, Pub. Evangelical Christian books. Adult fiction and nonfiction, 200 pages, and children's and young adult fiction, 200 pages. Query with outline and sample chapters. Royalty.

EXCALIBUR PUBLICATIONS—Box 36, Latham, NY 12110–0036. Alan M. Petrillo, Ed. Books on military history, firearms history, tactics and strategy, history of battles. Query with outline and sample chapters. Royalty or flat fee.

FABER AND FABER—50 Cross St., Winchester, MA 01890. Novels, anthologies, and nonfiction books on topics of popular culture and general interest. Query with SASE. Royalty.

FACTS ON FILE PUBLICATIONS—460 Park Ave. S., New York, NY 10016. Susan Schwartz, Ed. Dir. Reference and trade books on nature, business, science, health, language, history, the performing arts, etc. (No fiction, poetry, computer books, technical books or cookbooks.) Query with outline, sample chapter, and SASE. Royalty. Hardcover.

FALL CREEK PRESS—P.O. Box 1127, Fall Creek, OR 97438. Sharon Rock, Pub. Anthologies and single-author short story collections. "We publish stories (to 9,000 words) that foster what may be called spiritual growth or personal maturation." Query required. Guidelines. Royalties.

FANFARE—Imprint of Bantam Books, 1540 Broadway, New York, NY 10036. Nita Taublib, Assoc. Pub. Historical and contemporary adult women's fiction, approx. 90,000 to 150,000 words. Study field before submitting. Query required. Paperback and some hardcover.

FARRAR, STRAUS & GIROUX—19 Union Sq. West, New York, NY 10003. Adult and juvenile fiction and nonfiction.

FAWCETT/IVY BOOKS—Imprint of Ballantine Books, 201 E. 50th St., New York, NY 10022. Barbara Dicks, Exec. Ed. Adult mysteries, regencies, and historical romances, 75,000 to 120,000 words. Mysteries and problem novels, 60,000 to 70,000 words, for young adults. Query with outline and sample chapters. Average response time is 2 to 4 months. Royalty.

THE FEMINIST PRESS AT THE CITY UNIVERSITY OF NEW YORK —311 E. 94th St., New York, NY 10128. Florence Howe, Pub. Reprints of significant "lost" fiction, original memoirs, autobiographies, biographies; intercultural anthologies; handbooks; bibliographies. "We are especially interested in international literature, women and peace, women and music, and women of color." Royalty.

FINE, INC., DONALD I.—19 W. 21st St., New York, NY 10010. Literary and commercial fiction. General nonfiction. No queries or unsolicited manuscripts. Submit through agent only.

FIREBRAND BOOKS—141 The Commons, Ithaca, NY 14850. Nancy K. Bereano, Ed. Feminist and lesbian fiction and nonfiction. Royalty. Paperback and library edition cloth.

FLARE BOOKS—See *Avon Books.*

FLORES PUBLICATIONS, J.—P.O. Box 830131, Miami, FL 33283–0131. Eli Flores, Ed. Books, 30,000 to 80,000 words, on business, personal finance, and true crime. Query with outline and sample chapters. Royalty.

FODOR'S TRAVEL GUIDES—201 E. 50th St., New York, NY 10022. Michael Spring, Ed. Travel guides for both foreign and US destinations. "We hire writers who live in the area they will write about." Books follow established format; send writing sample and details about your familiarity with a given area.

FOOTSTEPS PRESS—P.O. Box 75, Round Top, NY 12473. Bill Munster, Ed. Horror, mystery, and ghost story chapbooks, 3,000 to 5,000 words. Royalty (usually from $350 to $500).

FORTRESS PRESS—426 S. Fifth St., Box 1209, Minneapolis, MN 55440. Dr. Marshall D. Johnson, Dir. Books in the areas of biblical studies, theology, ethics, and church history for academic and professional markets, including libraries. Query.

FOUR WINDS PRESS—Imprint of Macmillan Publishing Co., 866 Third

Ave., New York, NY 10022. Virginia Duncan, Ed.-in-Chief. Juveniles: picture books, nonfiction. Fiction for middle grades. Query with SASE required for nonfiction. Hardcover only.

THE FREE PRESS—See *Macmillan Publishing Co.*

FULCRUM PUBLISHING—350 Indiana St., Suite 350, Golden, CO 80401. Address Submissions Dept. Adult trade nonfiction: travel, nature, American history, biography, self-help, and gardening. No fiction. Send cover letter, sample chapters, outline, table of contents, and author credentials. Royalty.

GARRETT PARK PRESS—P.O. Box 190, Garrett Park, MD 20896. Robert Calvert, Jr., Pub. Reference books on career education, occupational guidance, and financial aid only. Query required. Multiple queries considered but not encouraged. Royalty.

GEORGIA STATE UNIVERSITY BUSINESS PRESS—University Plaza, Atlanta, GA 30303–3093. Books, software, research monographs, and directories in the business sciences and related disciplines.

GERINGER BOOKS, LAURA—See *HarperCollins Children's Books.*

GIBBS SMITH PUBLISHER/PEREGRINE SMITH BOOKS—P. O. Box 667, Layton, UT 84401. Madge Baird, Ed. Dir. Adult nonfiction. Query. Royalty.

GINIGER CO. INC., THE K.S.—250 W. 57th St., Suite 519, New York, NY 10107. General nonfiction. Query with SASE; no unsolicited manuscripts. Royalty.

GLENBRIDGE PUBLISHING LTD.—6010 W. Jewell Ave., Lakewood, CO 80232. James A. Keene, Ed. Nonfiction books on a variety of topics, including business, history, and psychology. Query with sample chapter. Royalty.

GLOBE PEQUOT PRESS, THE—6 Business Park Rd., Box 833, Old Saybrook, CT 06475. Laura Strom, Acquisitions Ed. Nonfiction with national and regional focus; nature and outdoor guides; travel; personal finance; business; cooking; home how-tos; gardening. Query with sample chapter, contents, and one-page synopsis. SASE required. Royalty.

GOLD EAGLE BOOKS—See *Worldwide Library.*

GOLDEN PRESS—See *Western Publishing Co., Inc.*

GOLDEN WEST PUBLISHERS—4113 N. Longview, Phoenix, AZ 85014. Hal Mitchell, Ed. Cookbooks and Western history and travel books. Query. Royalty or flat fee.

GRAYWOLF PRESS—2402 University Ave., Suite 203, St. Paul, MN 55114. Scott M. Walker, Ed. Literary fiction (short story collections and novels), poetry, and essays. Query with sample chapters.

GREEN TIGER PRESS—See *Simon & Schuster Children's Book Division.*

GREENWILLOW BOOKS—Imprint of William Morrow and Co., Inc., 1350 Ave. of the Americas, New York, NY 10019. Susan Hirschman, Ed.-in-Chief. Children's books for all ages. Picture books.

GROSSET AND DUNLAP, INC.—Div. of Putnam & Grosset Books, 200 Madison Ave., New York, NY 10016. Craig Walker, Ed.-in-Chief. Mass-market children's books. Query required. Royalty.

GROVE/ATLANTIC MONTHLY PRESS—841 Broadway, New York, NY 10003–4793. Morgan Entrekin, Pub. Distinguished fiction and nonfiction. Query required.

GROVE PRESS, INC.—See *Grove/Atlantic Monthly Press*.

GULLIVER BOOKS—See *Harcourt Brace*.

HAMMOND, INC.—Maplewood, NJ 07040. Charles Lees, Ed. Nonfiction: cartographic reference, travel. Payment varies. Query with outline and sample chapters. SASE required.

HARBINGER HOUSE—2802 N. Alvernon Way, Tucson, AZ 85712. Laurel Gregory, Pub. Manuscripts and queries accepted from agents only.

HARCOURT BRACE—1250 Sixth Ave., San Diego, CA 92101. Adult trade nonfiction and fiction. *Books for Professionals*: test preparation guides and other student self-help materials. Juvenile fiction and nonfiction for beginning readers through young adults under the following imprints: *HB Children's Books, Gulliver Books, Jane Yolen Books, Odyssey Paperbacks*, and *Voyager Paperbacks*. Adult books: no unsolicited manuscripts or queries. Children's books: unsolicited manuscripts accepted by *HB Children's Books* only. No simultaneous submissions. Send query or manuscript to Manuscript Submissions, Children's Book Division, 525 B St., Suite 1900, San Diego, CA 92101-4495. SASE required.

HARCOURT BRACE PROFESSIONAL PUBLISHING—Imprint of Harcourt Brace, 1250 Sixth Ave., San Diego, CA 92101. Professional books for practitioners in accounting, auditing, tax. Query required. Royalty.

HARLEQUIN BOOKS/CANADA—225 Duncan Mill Rd., Don Mills, Ont., Canada M3B 3K9. *Harlequin Romance*: Paula Eykelhof, Ed. Contemporary romance novels, 50,000 to 55,000 words, any setting, ranging in plot from the traditional and gentle to the more sophisticated. Query. *Harlequin "Glitz"*: Dianne Moggy, Sr. Ed. Intense, sensuous dramas set against a backdrop of "glitz and glamour," 100,000 words plus. Query. *Harlequin Superromance*: Marsha Zinberg, Sr. Ed. Contemporary romance, 85,000 words, with a mainstream edge. Query. *Harlequin Temptation*: Birgit Davis-Todd, Sr. Ed. Sensuous, humorous contemporary romances, 60,000 words. Query.

HARLEQUIN BOOKS/U.S.—300 E. 42nd St., 6th Fl., New York, NY 10017. Debra Matteucci, Sr. Ed. Contemporary romances, 70,000 to 75,000 words. Send for tip sheets. Paperback. *Harlequin American Romances*: bold, exciting romantic adventures set in America, "where anything is possible and dreams come true." *Harlequin Intrigue*: set against a backdrop of mystery and suspense, set anywhere in the world. Query.

HARPER PAPERBACKS—HarperCollins, 10 E. 53rd St., New York, NY 10022. Geoff Hannell, Pub. Karen Solem, Ed.-in-Chief. Carolyn Marino, Sr. Ed. Jessica Lichtenstein, Ed. Katie Tso, Ed., Abigail Kamen, Ed. Submissions from agents only.

HARPERCOLLINS CHILDREN'S BOOKS—10 E. 53rd St., New York, NY 10022–5299. Katrin Magnusson, Admin. Coord. Picture books, chapter books, and fiction and nonfiction for middle-grade and young adult readers. "Our imprints (*HarperTrophy* paperbacks, *Michael di Capua Books*, *Laura Geringer Books*, and *Willa Perlman Books*) are committed to producing imaginative and responsible children's books. All publish from preschool to young adult titles." Guidelines. Query, send sample chapters, or complete manuscript. Royalty.

HARPERCOLLINS PUBLISHERS—10 E. 53rd St., New York, NY 10022–5299. Adult Trade Department: Address Man. Ed. Fiction, nonfiction (biography, history, etc.), reference. Submissions from agents only. College texts: Address College Dept. Religion, theology, etc.: Address Harper San Francisco, Ice House

One-401, 151 Union St., San Francisco, CA 94111–1299. No unsolicited manuscripts; query only.

HARVARD COMMON PRESS—535 Albany St., Boston, MA 02118. Bruce Shaw, Ed. Adult nonfiction: cookbooks, travel guides, books on family matters, health, small business, etc. Send outline and sample chapters or complete manuscript. Royalty.

HARVEST HOUSE PUBLISHERS—1075 Arrowsmith, Eugene, OR 97402. Eileen L. Mason, V.P. Editorial. Nonfiction with evangelical theme: how-tos, marriage, women, contemporary issues. Fiction. Children's fiction (ages 9 to 13). No biographies, autobiographies, history, music books, or poetry. Query. SASE required.

HAZELDEN EDUCATIONAL MATERIALS—Box 176, Center City, MN 55012. Address Ed. Dept. Self-help books, 100 to 400 pages, relating to addiction, recovery, and wholeness. Query with outline and sample chapters. Multiple queries considered. Royalty.

HEALTH COMMUNICATIONS, INC.—3201 S.W. 15th St., Deerfield Beach, FL 33442. Marie Stilkind, Ed. Books on self-help recovery and personal growth for adults (250 pages). Query with outline and sample chapter, or send manuscript with SASE. Royalty.

HEALTH PLUS PUBLISHERS—P.O. Box 1027, Sherwood, OR 97140. Paula E. Clure, Ed. No longer considering unsolicited material.

HEALTH PRESS—P.O. Box 1388, Santa Fe, NM 87501. Kathleen Schwartz, Ed. Health-related adult books, 100 to 300 finished pages. "We're seeking cutting-edge, original manuscripts that will excite and help readers. Author must have credentials, or preface/intro must be written by M.D., Ph.D., etc. Controversial topics are desired; must be well researched and documented." Prefer completed manuscript, but will consider queries with outline and sample chapters. Multiple queries considered. Royalty.

HEARST BOOKS, HEARST MARINE BOOKS—See *William Morrow and Co., Inc.*

HEARTFIRE ROMANCES—See *Zebra Books.*

HEINEMANN—361 Hanover St., Portsmouth, NH 03801. Thomas Seavey, Pub. Professional books for teachers and "quality books on education and literacy." Query.

HEMINGWAY WESTERN STUDIES SERIES—Boise State Univ., 1910 University Dr., Boise, ID 83725. Tom Trusky, Ed. Nonfiction relating to the Inter-Mountain West (Rockies) in areas of history; political science; anthropology; environment and natural sciences; racial, gender, and cultural issues; film and fine arts; literary history or criticism.

HERALD PRESS—616 Walnut Ave., Scottdale, PA 15683. Christian books for adults and children: inspiration, Bible study, self-help, devotionals, current issues, peace studies, church history, missions, evangelism, family life, fiction, and personal experience. Send one-page summary and two sample chapters. Royalty.

HIGHSMITH PRESS—P.O. Box 800, Fort Atkinson, WI 53538–0800. Donald Sager, Pub. Adult books, 80 to 360 text pages, on professional library science, education, and reference. Books on multicultural themes or subjects for preschoolers (32 pages) through young adults (120 to 240 pages). Query with outline and sample chapters. Royalty.

HIPPOCRENE BOOKS—171 Madison Ave., New York, NY 10016. George Blagowidow, Ed. Dir. Language instruction books and foreign language dictionaries, travel guides, and military history. Send outline and sample chapters with SASE for reply. Multiple queries considered. Royalty.

HOLIDAY HOUSE, INC.—425 Madison Ave., New York, NY 10017. Margery S. Cuyler, V. P. Ashley Johnson, Asst. Ed. General juvenile and young adult fiction and nonfiction. Submit complete manuscript or three sample chapters and summary. (Buys very few unsolicited picture books.) Hardcover only. Royalty.

HOLT AND CO., HENRY—115 W. 18th St., New York, NY 10011. William Strachan, Ed.-in-Chief. Fiction and nonfiction (mysteries, history, biographies, natural history, travel, and how-to) of highest literary quality. Query with SASE required. Royalty.

HOME BUILDER PRESS—Nat'l Assoc. of Home Builders, 1201 15th St. N.W., Washington, DC 20005–2800. Doris M. Tennyson, Sr. Ed. How-to and business management books, 150 to 200 manuscript pages, for builders, remodelers, and developers. Writers should be experts in homebuilding, remodeling, land development and related aspects of the building industry. Query with outline and sample chapters. Royalty. For guidelines send SASE with $2 postage to Carolyn Poindester, Ed. Asst.

HOUGHTON MIFFLIN COMPANY—222 Berkeley St., Boston, MA 02116–3764. Fiction: literary, historical. Nonfiction: history, biography, psychology. No unsolicited submissions. Children's book division, address Children's Trade Books: picture books, fiction, and nonfiction for all ages. Query. Royalty.

HP BOOKS—Div. of Price Stern Sloan, Inc., 11150 Olympic Blvd., 6th Fl., Los Angeles, CA 90064. Illustrated how-tos on cooking, gardening, automotive topics. Query with SASE. Royalty.

HUNTER PUBLISHING, INC.—300 Raritan Center Pkwy., Edison, NJ 08818. Michael Hunter, Ed. Travel guides. Query with outline.

HYPERION—114 Fifth Ave., New York, NY 10011. Material accepted from agents only. No unsolicited manuscripts or queries considered.

IMPACT PUBLISHERS, INC.—P.O. Box 1094, San Luis Obispo, CA 93406. Address Acquisitions Ed. Popular psychology books, from 200 pages, on personal growth, relationships, families, communities, and health for adults. Children's books for "Little Imp" series on issues of self-esteem. "Writers must have advanced degrees and professional experience in human-service fields." Query with outline and sample chapters. Royalty.

INDIANA UNIVERSITY PRESS—601 N. Morton St., Bloomington, IN 47404–3797. Scholarly nonfiction, especially cultural studies, literary criticism, music, history, women's studies, African-American studies, African studies, Middle East studies, Russian studies, anthropology, regional, etc. Query with outline and sample chapters. Royalty.

INTERNATIONAL MARINE—(formerly *Seven Seas Press*) Box 220, Camden, ME 04843. Jonathan Eaton, Ed. Dir. James Babb, Acquisitions Ed. Books on boating (sailing and power).

ISLAND PRESS—1718 Connecticut Ave. N.W., Suite 300, Washington, DC 20009. Charles C. Savitt, Pub. Nonfiction focusing on the west, natural history, the environment, and natural resource management. "We want solution-oriented material to solve environmental problems." Query or send manuscript. SASE required.

JALMAR PRESS—2625 Skypark Dr., Suite 204, Torrance, CA 90505. Barbara Shores, Dir. Acquisitions & Development. Nonfiction books for parents and teachers. "Our emphasis is self-esteem, under which we publish books to enhance a student's self-awareness." Multiple queries considered. Submit outline. Royalty.

JAMES BOOKS, ALICE—33 Richdale Ave., Cambridge, MA 02140. Kinereth Gensler, Pres. "Shared-work cooperative" publishes books of poetry (64 to 72 pages) by writers living in New England. Manuscripts read in September and February. "We emphasize the publication of poetry by women, but also welcome and publish manuscripts by men." Authors paid with 100 copies of their books. Guidelines.

THE JOHNS HOPKINS UNIVERSITY PRESS—2715 N. Charles St., Baltimore, MD 21218. No unsolicited poetry or fiction considered.

JOHNSON BOOKS, INC.—1880 S. 57th Ct., Boulder, CO 80301. Barbara Mussil, Pub. Nonfiction: environmental subjects, archaeology, geology, natural history, astronomy, travel guides, outdoor guidebooks, fly fishing, regional. Query. Royalty.

JONATHAN DAVID PUBLISHERS, INC.—68–22 Eliot Ave., Middle Village, NY 11379. Alfred J. Kolatch, Ed.-in-Chief. General nonfiction (how-to, sports, cooking and food, self-help, etc.) and books specializing in Judaica. Query with outline, sample chapter, and resumé required. SASE. Royalty or outright purchase.

JUST US BOOKS—301 Main St., Suite 22–24, Orange, NJ 07050. Cheryl Hudson, Ed. Children's books celebrating African-American heritage. Picture books, 24 to 32 pages. Chapter books and biographies, from 2,500 words. Queries with SASE required. Royalty or flat fee.

KAR-BEN COPIES—6800 Tildenwood Lane, Rockville, MD 20852. Judye Groner, Ed. Books on Jewish themes for preschool and elementary children (to age 9): picture books, fiction, and nonfiction. Complete manuscript preferred. Flat fee and royalty. SASE.

KEATS PUBLISHING, INC.—27 Pine St., Box 876, New Canaan, CT 06840. Nathan Keats, Pub. Nonfiction: health, how-to. Query. Royalty.

KENT STATE UNIVERSITY PRESS—Kent State Univ., Kent, OH 44242. John T. Hubbell, Dir. Julia Morton, Sr. Ed. Publishes hardcover and paperback originals and some reprints. Especially interested in scholarly works in history and literary studies of high quality, any titles of regional interest for Ohio, scholarly biographies, archaeological research, the arts, and general nonfiction.

KINGFISHER BOOKS—Grisewood & Dempsey, Inc., 95 Madison Ave., New York, NY 10016. Wendy Barish, Ed. Picture books and juvenile nonfiction. Query or send complete manuscript. Royalty or flat fee.

KNOPF, INC., ALFRED A.—201 E. 50th St., New York, NY 10022. Address Sr. Ed. Distinguished adult fiction and general nonfiction. Query. Royalty.

KNOPF BOOKS FOR YOUNG READERS, ALFRED A.—201 E. 50th, New York, NY 10022. Janet Schulman, Pub. Stephanie Spinner, Assoc. Pub. Frances Foster, Ed.-at-Large. Anne Schwartz, Exec. Ed. Reg Kahney, Sr. Ed., Nonfiction. Sherry Gerstein, Paperback Ed. Distinguished juvenile fiction and nonfiction. Query. Royalty. Guidelines.

KODANSHA AMERICA, INC.—114 Fifth Ave., New York, NY 10011. Address Ed. Dept. Books, 50,000 to 200,000 words, on Asian and other international subjects. Query with outline, sample chapters, and SASE. Royalty.

LAREDO PUBLISHING—22930 Lockness Ave., Torrance, CA 90501. Clara Kohen, Ed. Bilingual and ESL (English as a second language) titles in Spanish and English. Children's fiction and young adult titles. Query with outline. Royalty.

LARK BOOKS—50 College St., Asheville, NC 28801. Rob Pulleyn, Pub. Publishes distinctive books for creative people in crafts, how-to, leisure activities, and "coffee table" categories. Query with outline. Royalty.

LAUREL BOOKS—Imprint of Bantam, Doubleday, Dell Publishing, Co., 1540 Broadway, New York, NY 10036. Address Eds. Nonfiction. History, politics, language, reference. Submissions accepted from agents only.

LAUREL-LEAF—Imprint of Bantam, Doubleday, Dell Publishing Co., 1540 Broadway, New York, NY 10036. Address Eds. Books for children grades 7 through 12. Submissions accepted from agents only. Same guidelines and requirements for *Bantam Starfire*.

LEADERSHIP PUBLISHERS, INC.—P.O. Box 8358, Des Moines, IA 50301-8358. Lois F. Roets, Ed. Educational materials for talented and gifted students, grades K to 12, and teacher reference books. No fiction or poetry. Send SASE for catalogue and writer's guidelines before submitting. Query or send complete manuscript. Royalty for books; flat fee for short pieces or booklets.

LEE & LOW BOOKS—228 E. 45th St., 14th Fl., New York, NY 10017. Philip Lee, Pub. Elizabeth Szabla, Ed.-in-Chief. Focus is on fiction and nonfiction picture books for children ages 4 to 10. "Our goal is to meet the growing need for books that address children of color and to provide books on subjects and stories they can identify with. Of special interest are stories set in contemporary America. Folklore and animal stories discouraged." Query with resumé, writing samples, and SASE. For middle-grade and young adult manuscripts, please send query letter first. Royalty or flat fee.

LEISURE BOOKS—Div. of Dorchester Publishing Co., Inc., 276 Fifth Ave., New York, NY 10001. Frank Walgren, Ed. Historical romance novels, from 100,000 words; futuristic and time-travel romances, from 90,000 words. Query with synopsis, sample chapters, and SASE. Royalty.

LIFE JOURNEY GENERAL TITLES—See *Chariot Family Publishing.*

LIFETIME BOOKS, INC.—2131 Hollywood Blvd., Hollywood, FL 33020. Joyce Sweeney, Ed. Nonfiction (100 to 300 pages): general interest, how-tos, business, health, and inspiration. Query with letter or outline and sample chapter, SASE. Royalty.

LINCOLN-HERNDON PRESS, INC.—818 S. Dirksen Pkwy., Springfield, IL 62703. Shirley A. Buscher, Asst. Pub. American humor that reveals American history. Humor collections. Query.

LION PUBLISHING—1705 Hubbard Ave., Batavia, IL 60510. Robert Bittner, Ed. Fiction and nonfiction written from a Christian viewpoint for a general audience. Guidelines. Royalty.

LITTLE, BROWN & CO.—1271 Ave. of the Americas, New York, NY 10020. Laura Barnes, Ed. Dept. Fiction, general nonfiction, sports books; divisions for law and medical texts. Query only.

LITTLE, BROWN & CO. CHILDREN'S BOOK DEPT.—34 Beacon St., Boston, MA 02108. Address Submissions Ed. Juvenile fiction and nonfiction and picture books. Guidelines.

LITTLE SIMON—See *Simon & Schuster Books for Young Readers.*

LLEWELLYN PUBLICATIONS—P.O. Box 64383, St. Paul, MN 55164–0383. Nancy J. Mostad, Acquisitions Mgr. Books, around 300 pages, on subjects of self-help, how-to, alternative health, astrology, metaphysics, new age, and the occult. Metaphysical/occult fiction. Royalty. Query with sample chapters. Multiple queries considered.

LODESTAR—An affiliate of Dutton Children's Books, a Div. of Penguin Books USA, Inc., 375 Hudson St., New York, NY 10014. Virginia Buckley, Ed. Dir. Fiction (picture books to young adult, mystery, fantasy, science fiction, western) and nonfiction (science, contemporary issues, nature, history) considered for ages 9 to 11, 10 to 14, and 12 and up. Also fiction and nonfiction picture books for ages 4 to 8. "We're looking for strong multicultural books by African-Americans, Hispanics, Asian, and Native-American writers." Send query and sample chapters.

LONGMEADOW PRESS—P.O. Box 10218, 201 High Ridge Rd., Stamford, CT 06904. Attn: Juvenile Ed. Board books, picture books, fiction, and nonfiction for children and young adults. Send complete manuscript. Royalty or flat fee.

LOTHROP, LEE & SHEPARD BOOKS—Imprint of William Morrow & Co., Inc., 1350 Ave. of the Americas, New York, NY 10019. Susan Pearson, Ed.-in-Chief. Juvenile fiction and nonfiction; picture books. Does not review unsolicited material. Royalty.

LOVEGRAM ROMANCES—See *Zebra Books.*

LOVESWEPT—Imprint of Bantam Books, 1540 Broadway, New York, NY 10036. Nita Taublib, Assoc. Pub. Adult contemporary romances, approximately 55,000 words. Study field before submitting. Query required. Paperback only.

LOYOLA UNIVERSITY PRESS—3441 N. Ashland Ave., Chicago, IL 60657–1397. Joseph Downey, S.J., Ed. Religious and ethics-related material for college-educated Christian readers. *Campion Book Series*: art, literature, and religion; contemporary Christian concerns; Jesuit studies; Chicago books. *Values and Ethics Series*: scholarly books centered on the theme of values and ethics, but stressing readability and topical relevance. Nonfiction, 200 to 400 pages. Query with outline. Royalty.

LUCENT BOOKS—P.O. Box 289011, San Diego, CA 92198–0011. Bonnie Szumski, Man. Ed. Lori Shein, Ed. Books, 18,000 to 25,000 words, at 7th- to 12th-grade reading level. "Overview" series: political, social, cultural, economic, moral, historical, and environmental topics. "The Importance Of" biography series presents the lives of the world's most influential men and women in all areas of endeavor. "The Importance Of" world history series presents historical events and their importance to society. Query required; work by assignment only. Flat fee. Guidelines and catalogue available.

LYONS & BURFORD, PUBLISHERS—31 W. 21st St., New York, NY 10010. Peter Burford, Ed. Books, 100 to 300 pages, related to the outdoors (camping, gardening, natural history, etc.) or sports. Query with outline. Royalty.

MCELDERRY BOOKS, MARGARET K.—Macmillan Children's Book Group, 866 Third Ave., New York, NY 10022. Margaret K. McElderry, Ed. Picture books; quality fiction, including fantasy, science fiction, beginning chapter books, humor, and realism; nonfiction. For ages 3 to 5, 6 to 9, 8 to 12, 10 to 14, and 12 and up.

MCFARLAND & COMPANY, INC., PUBLISHERS—Box 611, Jefferson, NC 28640. Robert Franklin, Ed. Scholarly and reference books in many fields, except mathematical sciences. Please do not send new age, inspirational, children's, poetry, fiction, or exposés. Submit double-spaced manuscripts, 225 pages and up, or query with outline and sample chapters. Royalty.

MCGUINN & MCGUIRE PUBLISHING—P.O. Box 20603, Bradenton, FL 34203. Christopher Carroll, Man. Ed. Books, 75,000 to 150,000 words: natural science, history, self-help, business, and how-to titles. "We especially like to see authors who have researched the market as completely as they researched their topic." Send complete manuscript or query with outline and sample chapters. Royalty.

MCKAY COMPANY, DAVID—201 E. 50th St., New York, NY 10022. Unsolicited manuscripts neither acknowledged nor returned.

MACMILLAN CHILDREN'S BOOK GROUP—866 Third Ave., New York, NY 10022. Leslie Ward, Ed. *Aladdin Books*: fiction (except problem novels) for middle grades (age 8 to 12) and young adults (age 12 and up). *Collier Books for Young Adults*: young adult novels. *Crestwood House*: high-interest, low-vocabulary books for reluctant readers through junior high level. Query with outline and sample chapters to Frank Sloan, Ed. Dir. *New Discovery Books*: nonfiction curriculum-related books for grades 6 and up. Query with outline; no multiple queries. Royalty.

MACMILLAN PUBLISHING CO., INC.—866 Third Ave., New York, NY 10022. General Books Division: Religious, sports, science, and reference books. No fiction. Paperbacks: *Collier Books*. College texts and professional books in social sciences, humanities: address *The Free Press*. Royalty.

MADISON BOOKS—4720 Boston Way, Lanham, MD 20706. James E. Lyons, Pub. Full-length nonfiction: on history, biography, contemporary affairs, trade reference. Query required. Royalty.

MEADOWBROOK PRESS—18318 Minnetonka Blvd., Deephaven, MN 55391. Upbeat, useful books, 60,000 words, on pregnancy, childbirth and parenting, humor, cooking, children's activities. Query with outline, sample chapters, and qualifications. Royalty or flat fee.

MEGA-BOOKS OF NEW YORK—116 E. 19th St., New York, NY 10003. Matthew DeBord, Projects Ed. Book packager. Young adult books, 150 pages, children's books. Query for guidelines. SASE with resumé. Flat fee.

MENTOR BOOKS—Imprint of Penguin USA, 375 Hudson St., New York, NY 10014. Address Eds. Nonfiction originals for the college and high school market. Query required. Royalty.

MERCURY HOUSE—201 Filbert St., Suite 400, San Francisco, CA 94133. Thomas Christensen, Exec. Ed. Quality fiction and nonfiction (international politics, literary travel, environment, philosophy/personal growth, and performing arts). Query with outline, sample chapters, and SASE. Limited fiction market.

MEREDITH CORP. BOOK GROUP—(*Better Homes and Gardens Books*) 1716 Locust St., Des Moines, IA 50309–3023. Connie Schrader, Exec. Ed. Books on gardening, crafts, health, decorating, etc., mostly staff-written. "Interested in free-lance writers with expertise in these areas." Limited market. Query with SASE.

MESSNER, JULIAN—Paramount Communications, 15 Columbus Cir., New York, NY 10023. George Rubich, Assoc. Pub. Curriculum-oriented nonfiction. General nonfiction, ages 8 to 14: science, nature, biography, history, and hobbies. Lengths vary. Royalty.

THE MICHIGAN STATE UNIVERSITY PRESS—1405 S. Harrison Rd., Suite 25, E. Lansing, MI 48823–5202. Scholarly nonfiction, with concentrations in history, regional history, African sources, business, and Civil War. Submit prospectus, table of contents, and sample chapters to Editor-in-Chief. Authors should refer to *The Chicago Manual of Style*, 14th Edition, for formats and styles.

MICROTREND—See *Slawson Communications, Inc.*

MILKWEED EDITIONS—430 First Ave. N., Suite 400, Minneapolis, MN 55401–1743. Emilie Buchwald, Ed. "We publish excellent award-winning fiction, poetry, essays, and nonfiction, the kind of writing that makes for good reading." Publishes about 12 books a year. Query with sample chapters. *Milkweeds for Young Readers,* novels and biographies for the middle grades. Royalty.

THE MILLBROOK PRESS—2 Old New Milford Rd., Brookfield, CT 06804. Tricia Bauer, Manuscript Coord. Nonfiction for early elementary grades through grades 7 and up, appropriate for the school and public library market, encompassing curriculum-related topics and extracurricular interests. Query with outline and sample chapter. Royalty.

MILLS & SANDERSON, PUBLISHERS—41 North Rd., #201, Bedford, MA 01730–1021. Jan H. Anthony, Pub. Books, 250 pages, on family problem-solving. Query. Royalty.

MINSTREL BOOKS—Imprint of Pocket Books, 1230 Ave. of the Americas, New York, NY 10020. Patricia MacDonald, Ed. Dir. Fiction for girls and boys ages 6 to 11: scary stories, fantasies, funny stories, school stories, adventures, animal stories. No picture books. Query with detailed plot outline, sample chapter, and SASE. Royalty.

THE MIT PRESS—Acquisitions Dept., 55 Hayward St., Cambridge, MA 02142. Books on computer science/artificial intelligence; cognitive sciences; economics; architecture; aesthetic and social theory; linguistics; technology studies; environmental studies; and neuroscience.

MODAN PUBLISHING—P.O. Box 1202, Bellmore, NY 11710. Bennett Shelkowitz, Man. Dir. Adult nonfiction. Young adult fiction and nonfiction. Children's picture books. Books with international focus or related to political or social issues. Judaica and Hebrew books from Israel, *Adama Books.*

MOON HANDBOOKS—Moon Publications, Inc., 330 Wall St., #1, Chico, CA 95928. Taran March, Sr. Ed. Travel guides of varying lengths. Will consider multiple submissions. Query. Royalty.

MOONLIGHT ROMANCE—Starlog Communications International, Inc. 475 Park Ave. S., New York, NY 10016. Milburn Smith, Assoc. Pub. Bimonthly novels feature one contemporary romance, 75,000 words. Heroines should be American and most action set in the US, but international heroes are fine. "We're looking for romances centering on a relationship, not mainstream contemporary novels centering on a woman's emotional or psychological dilemma." Send outline, first two chapters, and a love scene with SASE. Pays $1,500 ($500 on acceptance, $500 on signing, $500 on publication). Guidelines.

MOREHOUSE PUBLISHING—871 Ethan Allen Hwy., Suite 204, Ridgefield, CT 06877. E. Allen Kelley, Pub. Theology, pastoral care, church administration, spirituality, Anglican studies, history of religion, books for children, youth, elders, etc. Query with outline, contents, and sample chapter. SASE required. Royalty.

MORROW AND CO., INC., WILLIAM—1350 Ave. of the Americas, New York, NY 10019. Adrian Zackheim, Ed. Dir. Adult fiction and nonfiction: no unsolicited manuscripts. *Beech Tree Books* and *Mulberry Books* (children's paperbacks), Amy Cohn, Ed. Dir.; *Hearst Books* (general nonfiction) and *Hearst Marine Books*, Ann Bramsom, Ed. Dir.; *Morrow Junior Books* (children's books for all ages), David Reuther, Ed.-in-Chief.

MOUNTAIN PRESS PUBLISHING—1301 S. 3rd W., P.O. Box 2399, Missoula, MT 59806. Address John Rimel. Nonfiction, 300 pages: natural history, field guides, geology, horses, Western history, Americana, outdoor guides, and fur trade lore. Query with outline and sample chapters; multiple queries considered. Royalty.

THE MOUNTAINEERS BOOKS—1011 S.W. Klickitat Way, Suite 107, Seattle, WA 98134. Margaret Foster, Ed./Acquisitions Mgr. Nonfiction books on noncompetitive aspects of outdoor sports such as mountaineering, backpacking, walking, trekking, canoeing, kayaking, bicycling, skiing; independent adventure travel. Field guides, how-to and where-to guidebooks, biographies of outdoor people; accounts of expeditions. Natural history and conservation. Submit sample chapters and outline. Royalty.

MUIR PUBLICATIONS, JOHN—P.O. Box 613, Santa Fe, NM 87504–0613. Ken Luboff, Ed. Travel guidebooks for adults. Nonfiction books for children, 8 to 12, primarily in the areas of science and intercultural issues. Send manuscript or query with sample chapters. No fiction. Royalty or work for hire.

MULBERRY BOOKS—See *William Morrow and Co., Inc.*

MULTNOMAH PRESS—10209 S.E. Division St., Portland, OR 97266. Conservative, evangelical nonfiction. Send SASE for guidelines and manuscript questionnaire. Royalty. Overstocked; not considering material at this time.

MUSTANG PUBLISHING CO., INC.—Box 3004, Memphis, TN 38173. Rollin A. Riggs, Pres. Nonfiction for 18- to 40-year-olds. Send queries for 100- to 300-page books, with outlines and sample chapters. Royalty. SASE required.

THE MYSTERIOUS PRESS—Imprint of Warner Books, Time and Life Bldg., 1271 Ave. of the Americas, New York, NY 10020. William Malloy, Ed.-in-Chief. Mystery/suspense novels. Agented manuscripts only.

NAIAD PRESS, INC.—Box 10543, Tallahassee, FL 32302. Barbara Grier, Ed. Adult fiction, 52,000 to 60,000 words, with lesbian themes and characters: mysteries, romances, gothics, ghost stories, westerns, regencies, spy novels, etc. Query with letter and one-page précis only. Royalty.

NATIONAL PRESS—7200 Wisconsin Ave., Suite 212, Bethesda, MD 20814. G. Edward Smith, Ed. Nonfiction: history, criminology, reference, and health (*Zenith Editions*); cookbooks; sports and parenting; business, management, and automotive titles (*Plain English Press*). Query with outline and sample chapters. Royalty.

NATUREGRAPH PUBLISHERS—P. O. Box 1075, Happy Camp, CA 96039. Barbara Brown, Ed. Nonfiction: Native-American culture, natural history, outdoor living, land, gardening, health, Indian lore, crafts, and how-to. Query. Royalty.

THE NAVAL INSTITUTE PRESS—Annapolis, MD 21402. Nonfiction, 60,000 to 100,000 words: military histories; biographies; ship guides; how-tos on boating and navigation. Occasional fiction, 75,000 to 110,000 words. Query with outline and sample chapters. Royalty.

NELSON, INC., THOMAS—Nelson Pl. at Elm Hill Pike, P. O. Box 141000, Nashville, TN 37214–1000. Religious and secular fiction and nonfiction for adults. Fiction and nonfiction for teens. Query with outline, sample chapter, and SASE.

NEW DISCOVERY BOOKS—See *Macmillan Children's Book Group.*

NEW HORIZON PRESS—P.O. Box 669, Far Hills, NJ 07931. Joan Dunphy, Ed.-in-Chief. True stories, 96,000 words, dealing with contemporary issues that revolve around a hero or heroine. Royalty. Query.

THE NEW PRESS—450 W. 41st St., New York, NY 10036. Andre Schiffrin, Dir. Serious nonfiction: history, economics, education, politics. Query required.

NEW READERS PRESS—1320 Jamesville Ave., Box 131, Syracuse, NY 13210. Jennifer Lashley, Office Mgr. Fiction and nonfiction, 5,000 to 9,000 words, and poetry for adults who read at low levels, for use in adult basic education programs, volunteer literacy organizations, and job training programs. Query with outline, synopsis, and sample chapters. Read guidelines first. Do not submit material for juvenile or teenage readers. Royalty or flat fee.

NEW RIVERS PRESS—420 N. 5th St., Suite 910, Minneapolis, MN 55401. C.W. Truesdale, Ed./Pub. Collections of short stories, essays, and poems from emerging writers in Upper Midwest. Query.

NEW SOCIETY PUBLISHERS—4527 Springfield Ave., Philadelphia, PA 19143. Nonfiction books on fundamental social change through nonviolent social action. Request guidelines before submitting proposal. SASE required.

NEW WORLD LIBRARY—58 Paul Dr., San Rafael, CA 94903. Submissions Ed. Nonfiction, especially leading edge inspirational/self-help books, enlightened business, Native-American, classic wisdom, environmental awareness. "Aim for intelligent, aware audience, interested in personal and planetary transformation." Query with outline and SASE. Multiple queries accepted. Royalty.

NEW YORK UNIVERSITY PRESS—70 Washington Sq. S., New York, NY 10012. Niko Pfund, Ed.-in-Chief. Scholarly nonfiction. Submit manuscript and/or proposal with sample chapters and curriculum vitae.

NEWCASTLE PUBLISHING—13419 Saticoy St., N. Hollywood, CA 91605. Al Saunders, Pub. Nonfiction manuscripts, 200 to 250 pages, for older adults on personal health, health care issues, and relationships. "We are not looking for fads or trends. We want books with a long shelf life." Multiple queries considered. Royalty.

NEWMARKET PRESS—18 E. 48th St., New York, NY 10017. Esther Margolis, Pub. General nonfiction: arts, lifestyles, self-help, finances. Fiction. Query required. Royalty.

NITTY GRITTY COOKBOOKS—See *Bristol Publishing Enterprises.*

NORTH COUNTRY PRESS—P.O. Box 440, Belfast, ME 04915. William M. Johnson, Pub. Nonfiction with a Maine and/or New England tie-in with emphasis on the outdoors; also limited fiction (Maine-based mystery). "Our goal is to publish high-quality books for people who love New England." Query with SASE, outline, and sample chapters. Royalty.

NORTHLAND PUBLISHING—2900 N. Fort Valley Rd., Flagstaff, AZ 86001. Betti Albrecht, Ed.-in-Chief. Nonfiction books on natural history; fine arts; Native American culture, myth, art, and crafts; and cookbooks. Unique children's books, to 1,500 words, preferably with a Southwest/West regional theme. Query with outline, sample chapter, potential market for proposed book, and SASE for adult books. For children's books, send complete manuscript. Royalty.

NORTHWORD PRESS, INC.—Box 1360, 7520 Highway 51, Minocqua, WI 54548. Greg Linder, Ed. Natural history and natural heritage books, from 25,000 words. Send outline with sample chapters, or complete manuscript. Royalty or flat fee.

NORTON AND CO., INC., W.W.—500 Fifth Ave., New York, NY 10110. Liz Malcolm, Ed. High-quality fiction and nonfiction. No occult, paranormal, religious, genre fiction (formula romance, science fiction, westerns), cookbooks, arts and crafts, young adult, or children's books. Query with synopsis, two to three chapters (including first chapter), and resumé. Return postage and packaging required. Royalty.

ODYSSEY PAPERBACKS—See *Harcourt Brace.*

OPEN COURT PUBLISHING CO.—Box 599, Peru, IL 61354. Scholarly books on philosophy, psychology, religion, eastern thought, history, public policy, education, science, and related topics. Send sample chapters with outline and resumé. Royalty.

ORCHARD BOOKS—95 Madison Ave., New York, NY 10016. Neal Porter, Pres./Pub. Hardcover picture books. Fiction for middle grades and young adults. Nonfiction and photo essays for young children. Submit complete manuscript. Royalty.

OREGON STATE UNIVERSITY PRESS—101 Waldo Hall, Corvallis, OR 97331. Scholarly books in a limited range of disciplines and books of particular importance to the Pacific Northwest. Query with summary of manuscript.

OSBORNE/MCGRAW HILL—2600 Tenth St., Berkeley, CA 94710. Jeffrey M. Pepper, Ed.-in-Chief. Microcomputer books for general audience. Query. Royalty.

THE OVERLOOK PRESS—149 Wooster St., New York, NY 10012. Tracy Carns, Ed. Dir. Literary fiction, some fantasy/science fiction, foreign literature in translation, general nonfiction including art, architecture, design, film, history, biography, crafts/lifestyle, martial arts, Hudson Valley regional interest, and children's books. Query with outline and sample chapters. Royalty.

OWEN PUBLISHERS, INC., RICHARD C.—135 Katonah Ave., Katonah, NY 10536. Janice Boland, Ed., Dept. TW. Fiction and nonfiction. Brief storybooks of 8, 12, and 16 pages (including illustration) suitable for 5-, 6-, and 7-year-old beginning readers for the "Ready to Read" program. Royalties for writers. Flat fee for illustrators. Writers must send SASE for guidelines before submitting.

OXFORD UNIVERSITY PRESS—200 Madison Ave., New York, NY 10016. Authoritative books on literature, history, philosophy, etc.; college textbooks, medical, scientific, technical and reference books. Query. Royalty.

PACER BOOKS FOR YOUNG ADULTS—Imprint of Berkley Publishing Group, 200 Madison Ave., New York, NY 10016. Melinda Metz, Ed. Fiction: horror, suspense, romance, and role-playing fantasy gamebooks. No unsolicited manuscripts; queries only. Paperback only.

PANTHEON BOOKS—Div. of Random House, 201 E. 50th St., New York, NY 10022. Quality fiction and nonfiction. Query required. Royalty.

PAPIER-MACHE PRESS—795 Via Manzana, Watsonville, CA 95076. Sandra Martz, Ed. Fiction, short story collections, and a few poetry books; 4 to 6 books annually. "We emphasize, but are not limited to, the publication of books and related items for midlife and older women." Write for guidelines. Query. Royalty for single-author books; pays in copies for anthologies, plus royalty if book goes into second printing.

PARA PUBLISHING—P.O. Box 4232, Santa Barbara, CA 93140–4232. Dan Poynter, Ed. Adult nonfiction books on parachutes and skydiving only. Author must present evidence of having made at least 1,000 jumps. Query. Royalty.

PARENTING PRESS—11065 Fifth Ave., #F, P.O. Box 75267, Seattle, WA 98125. John Shoemaker, Ed. Choice-oriented parenting books, 112 pages. Skill-building and problem-solving children's books, 30 to 60 pages. "Send SASE for guidelines, then query with outline and sample chapters." Royalty.

PASSPORT BOOKS—4255 W. Touhy Ave., Lincolnwood, IL 60646–1975. Constance Rajala, Ed. Dir. Adult nonfiction, 200 to 400 pages, picture books up to 120 pages, and juvenile nonfiction. Send outline and sample chapters for books on foreign language, travel, and culture. Multiple queries considered. Royalty and flat fee.

PEACHTREE PUBLISHERS, LTD.—494 Armour Circle N.E., Atlanta, GA 30324. Wide variety of children's books, humor, fiction and nonfiction. No religious material, science fiction/fantasy, romance, mystery/detective, historical fiction; no business, scientific, or technical books. Send outline and sample chapters. SASE required. Royalty. No unsolicited submissions at this time.

PELICAN PUBLISHING CO., INC.—1101 Monroe St., Gretna, LA 70053. Nina Kooij, Ed. General nonfiction: Americana, regional, architecture, how-to, travel, cookbooks, inspirational, motivational, music, parenting, etc. Juvenile fiction. Royalty.

PELION PRESS—See *Rosen Publishing Group.*

PENGUIN BOOKS—Imprint of Penguin USA, 375 Hudson St., New York, NY 10014. Address Eds. Adult fiction and nonfiction paperbacks. Also, contemporary verse for *The Penguin Poets* series; submit cover letter, seven sample poems, a bio, list of previous publications, and SASE. Limited market. Royalty.

PERFECT CRIME—See *Doubleday and Co.*

PERLMAN BOOKS, WILLA—See *HarperCollins Children's Books.*

THE PERMANENT PRESS—Noyac Rd., Sag Harbor, NY 11963. Judith Shepard, Ed. Seeks original and arresting novels, biographies. Query. Royalty.

PHILOMEL BOOKS—Div. of The Putnam & Grosset Group, 200 Madison Ave., New York, NY 10016. Patricia Lee Gauch, Ed. Dir. Paula Wiseman, Ed.-in.-Chief. Picture books, young adult fiction, and some biographies. Fresh, original work with compelling characters and "a truly childlike spirit." Query required.

PINEAPPLE PRESS—P.O. Drawer 16008, Southside Sta., Sarasota, FL 34239. June Cussen, Ed. Serious fiction and nonfiction, Florida-oriented, 60,000 to 125,000 words. Query with outline, sample chapters, and SASE. Royalty.

PIPPIN PRESS—229 E. 85th St., Gracie Sta., Box 92, New York, NY 10028. Barbara Francis, Pub. High-quality picture books for preschoolers; small chapter books for ages 6 to 10, emphasizing humor and fantasy, humorous mysteries; imaginative nonfiction for children of all ages. Query required. Royalty.

PLAIN ENGLISH PRESS—See *National Press.*

PLENUM PUBLISHING CORP.—233 Spring St., New York, NY 10013. Linda Greenspan Regan, Sr. Ed. Trade nonfiction, approximately 300 pages, on popular science, criminology, psychology, sociology, and health. Query required. Royalty. Hardcover.

PLUME BOOKS—Imprint of Penguin USA, 375 Hudson St., New York, NY

10014. Address Eds. Nonfiction: hobbies, business, health, cooking, child care, psychology, history, popular culture, biography, and politics. Fiction: serious literary and gay. Query.

POCKET BOOKS—A Paramount Communications Co., 1230 Ave. of the Americas, New York, NY 10020. William R. Grose, Exec. VP/ Ed. Dir. Gina Centrello, Exec. VP/Pub. Original fiction and nonfiction. Mystery line: police procedurals, private eye, and amateur sleuth novels, 60,000 to 70,000 words; query Jane Chelius, Sr. Ed. "We are especially interested in stories with well-drawn and engaging series characters." Royalty.

POPULAR PRESS—Bowling Green State Univ., Bowling Green, OH 43403. Ms. Pat Browne, Ed. Nonfiction, 250 to 400 pages, examining some aspect of popular culture. Query with outline. Flat fee or royalty.

POTTER, CLARKSON —201 E. 50th St., New York, NY 10022. Lauren Shakely, Ed.-in-Chief. General trade books. Submissions accepted through agents only.

PRAEGER PUBLISHERS—Imprint of Greenwood Publishing Group, 88 Post Rd. W., Westport, CT 06880–4232. Ron Chambers, Pub. General nonfiction; scholarly and reference books. Query with outline. Royalty.

PREISS VISUAL PUBLICATIONS, BYRON—24 W. 25th St., New York, NY 10010. Book packager. "We are primarily interested in seeing samples from established authors willing to work to specifications on firm deadlines." Genres: science fiction, fantasy, horror, juvenile, young adult, nonfiction. Pays competitive advance against royalties for commissioned work.

PRENTICE HALL—A Paramount Communications Co., 15 Columbus Cir., New York, NY 10023. General reference and travel books. Query required. Royalty.

PRESIDIO PRESS—505B San Marin Dr., Suite 300, Novato, CA 94945–1340. Nonfiction: military history and military affairs, from 90,000 words. Fiction: selected military and action-adventure works and mysteries, from 100,000 words. Query. Royalty.

PRICE STERN SLOAN, INC.—11150 Olympic Blvd., Los Angeles, CA 90064. Children's books; adult trade nonfiction, including humor and calendars. Query with SASE required. Royalty.

PRIMA PUBLISHING—P.O. Box 1260, Rocklin, CA 95677. Ben Dominitz, Pub. Jennifer Basye, Ed. Nonfiction on variety of subjects, including business, health, and cookbooks. "We want books with originality, written by highly qualified individuals." Royalty.

PRUETT PUBLISHING COMPANY—2928 Pearl, Boulder, CO 80301. Jim Pruett, Pres. Nonfiction: outdoors and recreation, western U.S. history, travel, natural history and the environment, fly fishing. Query. Royalty.

PUFFIN BOOKS—Imprint of Penguin USA, 375 Hudson St., New York, NY 10014. Address Eds. Children's fiction and nonfiction paperbacks. Query required. Royalty.

PUTNAM'S SONS, G.P.—Div. of The Putnam & Grosset Group, 200 Madison Ave., New York, NY 10016. General trade nonfiction, fiction. Query required. Royalty.

PUTNAM'S SONS BOOKS FOR YOUNG READERS, G.P.—Div. of The Putnam & Grosset Group, 200 Madison Ave., New York, NY 10016. Margaret

Frith, Ed.-in-Chief. Picture books, fiction and nonfiction. No unsolicited manuscripts. Query with sample required.

QUEST BOOKS—Imprint of The Theosophical Publishing House, 306 W. Geneva Rd., P. O. Box 270, Wheaton, IL 60189–0270. Brenda Rosen, Sr. Ed. Nonfiction books on Eastern and Western religion and philosophy, holism, healing, transpersonal psychology, men's and women's spirituality, Native-American spirituality, meditation, yoga, ancient wisdom. Query. Royalty.

QUILL TRADE PAPERBACKS—Imprint of William Morrow and Co., Inc., 1350 Ave. of the Americas, New York, NY 10019. Andrew Dutter, Ed. Trade paperback adult nonfiction. Submit through agent only.

RAGGED MOUNTAIN PRESS—Box 220, Camden, ME 04843. Jonathan Eaton, Ed. Dir. Doreas Miller, Acquisitions Ed. Books on outdoor recreation.

RAINTREE STECK-VAUGHN PUBLISHERS—Div. of Steck-Vaughn Co., National Education Corp., 11 Prospect St., Madison, NJ 07940. Walter Kossmann, Ed. Nonfiction books, 5,000 to 30,000 words, for school and library market: biographies for grades 3 and up; and science, social studies, and history books for primary grades through high school. Query with outline and sample chapters; SASE required. Flat fee and royalty.

RANDOM HOUSE, INC.—201 E. 50th St., New York, NY 10022. General fiction and nonfiction. Query with three chapters and outline for nonfiction; complete manuscript for fiction. SASE required. Royalty.

RANDOM HOUSE JUVENILE DIV.—201 E. 50th St., New York, NY 10022. Kate Klimo, Ed.-in-Chief. Fiction and nonfiction for beginning readers; paperback fiction line for 7- to 9-year-olds; 35 pages maximum. Query with three chapters and outline for nonfiction; complete manuscript for fiction. SASE for all correspondence. Royalty.

THE RED SEA PRESS—15 Industry Ct., Trenton, NJ 08638. Kassahun Checole, Pub. Adult nonfiction, 360 double-spaced manuscript pages. "We focus on nonfiction material with a specialty on the Horn of Africa." Query. Royalty.

REGNERY GATEWAY—1130 17th St. N.W., Suite 600, Washington, DC 20036. Nonfiction books on public policy. Query. Royalty.

RENAISSANCE HOUSE—541 Oak St., P. O. Box 177, Frederick, CO 80530. Eleanor H. Ayer, Ed. Regional guidebooks. Currently publishing guidebooks on Colorado, Arizona, California, and the Southwest. "We use only manuscripts written to our specifications for new or ongoing series." Submit outline and short bio. Royalty.

RHAPSODY ROMANCE—Starlog Communications International, Inc. 475 Park Ave., S., New York, NY 10016. Milburn Smith, Assoc. Pub. Bimonthly novels feature one historical romance, 75,000 words. "Historicals should be set between 1600 and 1900, but a really good story would make us consider an earlier period." Send outline, first two chapters plus an important love scene, and SASE. Pays $1,500, ($500 on acceptance, $500 on signing, $500 on publication). Buys magazine rights only. Guidelines.

RISING TIDE PRESS—5 Kivy St., Huntington Sta., New York, NY 11746. Lee Boojamra, Ed. Books for, by, and about lesbians. Fiction, 60,000 to 70,000 words: romance, mystery, and science fiction/fantasy. Nonfiction, 40,000 to 60,000 words. Royalty. Reports in 3 months.

RIZZOLI INTERNATIONAL PUBLICATIONS, INC.—300 Park Ave. S.,

New York, NY 10010. Kimberly Harbour, Children's Book Ed. Seeks manuscripts that introduce children to fine art, folk art, and architecture of all cultures for a small, specialized list. Publishes nonfiction and fiction for all ages. "Particularly interested in stories that can be illustrated with museum art. Fiction should use storytelling as a way of putting art and culture into a vivid, exciting context for kids." Query with SASE or response card. Royalty.

ROC—Imprint of Penguin USA, 375 Hudson St., New York, NY 10014. Address Eds. Horror, science fiction, and fantasy. Query.

RODALE PRESS—33 E. Minor St., Emmaus, PA 18098. Pat Corpora, Pub. Books on health, gardening, homeowner projects, cookbooks, inspirational topics, pop psychology, woodworking, natural history. Query with outline and sample chapter. Royalty and outright purchase. In addition: "We're always looking for truly competent free lancers to write chapters for books conceived and developed in-house"; payment on a work-for-hire basis; address Bill Gottlieb, V.P.

ROSEN PUBLISHING GROUP—29 E. 21st St., New York, NY 10010. Roger Rosen, Pres. Ruth C. Rosen, Ed. Young adult books, 8,000 to 40,000 words, on career and personal guidance, journalism, self-help, etc. *Pelion Press*: music, art, history. Pays varying rates.

RUNNING PRESS—125 S. 22nd St., Philadelphia, PA 19103. Trade nonfiction: art, house and home, science, lifestyles. Children's books. Query required. Royalty.

RUTGERS UNIVERSITY PRESS—109 Church St., New Brunswick, NJ 08901. Literary fiction.

RUTLEDGE HILL PRESS—211 Seventh Ave. N., Nashville, TN 37217. Ronald E. Pitkin, V.P. Southern-interest fiction and market-specific nonfiction. Query with outline and sample chapters. Royalty.

ST. ANTHONY MESSENGER PRESS—1615 Republic St., Cincinnati, OH 45210–1298. Lisa Biedenbach, Man. Ed. Inspirational nonfiction for Catholics, supporting a Christian lifestyle in our culture; prayer aids, education, practical spirituality, parish ministry, liturgy resources. Query with 500-word summary. Royalty.

ST. MARTIN'S PRESS—175 Fifth Ave., New York, NY 10010. General adult fiction and nonfiction. Query. Royalty.

SANDLAPPER PUBLISHING, INC.—P.O. Drawer 730, Orangeburg, SC 29116–0730. Amanda Gallman, Book Ed. Nonfiction books on South Carolina history, culture, cuisine; fiction set in South Carolina. Query with outline, sample chapters, and SASE.

SASQUATCH BOOKS—1931 Second Ave., Seattle, WA 98101. Books, 60,000 to 80,000 words, by Pacific Northwest authors on a wide range of nonfiction topics: travel, natural history, gardening, cooking, history, children's and public affairs. Books must have a Pacific Northwest angle. Query with SASE. Royalty.

SCARECROW PRESS—P.O. Box 4167, Metuchen, NJ 08840. Norman Horrocks, V.P./Editorial. Reference works and bibliographies, from 150 pages, especially in the areas of cinema, TV, radio, and theater, mainly for use by libraries. Query or send complete manuscript; multiple queries considered. Royalty.

SCHOCKEN BOOKS—Div. of Pantheon Books, 201 E. 50th St., New York, NY 10022. General nonfiction: Judaica, women's studies, education, art history. Query with outline and sample chapter. Royalty.

SCHOLASTIC, INC.—730 Broadway, New York, NY 10003. Not currently accepting unsolicited manuscripts.

SCHOLASTIC PROFESSIONAL BOOKS—730 Broadway, New York, NY 10003. Attn: Laureen Harris. Books by and for teachers of kindergarten through eighth grade. *Instructor Books*: practical, activity/resource books on teaching reading, science, math, etc. *Teaching Strategies Books*: 64 to 96 pages on new ideas, practices, and approaches to teaching. Query with outline, sample chapters or activities, contents page, and resumé. Flat fee or royalty. Multiple queries considered. SASE for guidelines.

SCOTT, FORESMAN AND CO.—1900 E. Lake Ave., Glenview, IL 60025. Kate Nyquist, Pres. Elementary and secondary textbooks. Royalty or flat fee.

SCRIBNER'S SONS, CHARLES—866 Third Ave., New York, NY 10022. Barbara Grossman, Pub. Fiction, general nonfiction, science, history, and biography; query first. Clare Costello, Ed., *Books for Young Readers*: fantasy, mystery, science fiction, and problem novels; picture books, ages 5 and up; and nonfiction (science and how-tos). Query with outline and sample chapter.

SEVEN SEAS PRESS—See *International Marine*.

SHAW PUBLISHERS, HAROLD—388 Gunderson Dr., Box 567, Wheaton, IL 60189. Ramona Cramer Tucker, Dir. of Ed. Services. Nonfiction, 120 to 220 pages, with an evangelical Christian perspective. Some teen and adult fiction and literary books. Query. Flat fee or royalty.

SIERRA CLUB BOOKS—100 Bush St., San Francisco, CA 94104. Nonfiction: environment, natural history, the sciences, outdoors and regional guidebooks, nature photography; juvenile fiction and nonfiction. Query with SASE. Royalty.

SIGNET BOOKS AND SIGNET CLASSIC—Imprint of Penguin USA, 375 Hudson St., New York, NY 10014. Address Eds. Commercial fiction (historicals, sagas, thrillers, action/adventure novels, westerns) and nonfiction (self-help, how-to, true crime, etc.). Royalty.

SILHOUETTE BOOKS—300 E. 42nd St., New York, NY 10017. Isabel Swift, Ed. Dir. *Silhouette Romances*: Anne Canadeo, Sr. Ed. Contemporary romances, 53,000 to 58,000 words. *Special Edition*: Tara Gavin, Sr. Ed. Sophisticated contemporary romances, 75,000 to 80,000 words. *Silhouette Desire*: Lucia Macro, Sr. Ed. Sensuous contemporary romances, 53,000 to 60,000 words. *Intimate Moments*: Leslie Wainger, Sr. Ed./Ed. Coord. Sensuous, exciting contemporary romances, 80,000 to 85,000 words. *Silhouette Shadows*: Contemporary gothic style romances, 70,000 to 75,000 words. *Historical romance*: 95,000 to 105,000 words, set in England, France, and North America between 1700 and 1900; query with synopsis and three sample chapters to Tracy Farrell, Sr. Ed. Query with synopsis and SASE to appropriate editor. Tipsheets available.

SIMON & SCHUSTER—1230 Ave. of the Americas, New York, NY 10020. Adult books: No unsolicited material.

SIMON & SCHUSTER CHILDREN'S BOOK DIVISION—15 Columbus Cir., New York, NY 10023. Willa Perlman, Pres./Pub. *Books for Young Readers*: Books for ages preschool through 14. Picture books, fiction from first chapter books to young adult, and nonfiction at all age levels. *Little Simon*: Books for children under 8. Board books, novelty books, picture books, nursery tales, and concept books with a broad market base. *Green Tiger Press*: Illustrated books for all ages. Special content, special art. Unusual fantasy, lyrical prose, offbeat subject matter.

"Unsolicited material discouraged for all three imprints. Long wait for replies. Identify multiple submissions."

SINGER MEDIA CORPORATION—Seaview Business Park, 1030 Calle Cordillera #106, San Clemente, CA 92673. Kurt Singer, Pres. Foreign reprint rights to books in fields of business, management, self-help, romance and mysteries, and psychology. Also, unpublished modern romance novels for foreign licensing. Royalty or flat fee.

SKYLARK BOOKS—See *Yearling Books.*

SLAWSON COMMUNICATIONS, INC.—2075 Corte del Nogal, Suite E, Carlsbad, CA 92009–1414. Sharon Rovario, Asst. to the Pub. *Microtrend*: high-level computer books for professional programmers, 375 to 700 pages. Query with sample chapters. Royalty.

THE SMITH—69 Joralemon St., Brooklyn, NY 11201. Harry Smith, Ed. Fiction and nonfiction, from 64 pages, and poetry, 48 to 112 pages. "While publishing at a high level of craftsmanship, we have pursued the increasingly difficult, expensive and now relatively rare policy of keeping our titles in print over the decades." Query with outline and sample chapters. Royalty.

SOHO PRESS—853 Broadway, New York, NY 10003. Juris Jurjevics, Ed. Adult fiction, mysteries, thrillers, and nonfiction, from 60,000 words. Send SASE and complete manuscript. Royalty.

SOUTHERN ILLINOIS UNIVERSITY PRESS—Box 3697, Carbondale, IL 62902–3697. Curtis L. Clark, Ed. Nonfiction in the humanities, 200 to 400 pages. Query with outline and sample chapters. Royalty.

SOUTHERN METHODIST UNIVERSITY PRESS—Box 415, Dallas, TX 75275. Kathryn Lang, Sr. Ed. Serious literary fiction. Nonfiction: scholarly studies in religion, medical ethics (death and dying); film, theater; scholarly works on Texas or Southwest. No juvenile material, science fiction, or poetry. Query. Royalty.

SPECTACLE LANE PRESS—Box 34, Georgetown, CT 06829. Address the Eds. Cartoon books, 500 to 50,000 words (captions only). "We usually hire cartoonists to illustrate our books, but will consider submissions of writer-cartoonist teams." Royalty.

SPECTRA BOOKS—Imprint of Bantam Books, 1540 Broadway, New York, NY 10036. Lou Aronica, Pub. Science fiction and fantasy, with emphasis on storytelling and characterization. Query with SASE; no unsolicited manuscripts. Royalty.

STANDARD PUBLISHING—8121 Hamilton Ave., Cincinnati, OH 45231. Address Mark Plunkett. Fiction: juvenile, based on Bible or with moral tone. Nonfiction: biblical, Christian education. Conservative evangelical. Query preferred.

STANFORD UNIVERSITY PRESS—Stanford Univ., Stanford, CA 94305–2235. Norris Pope, Ed. "For the most part, we publish academic scholarship." No original fiction or poetry. Query with outline and sample chapters. Royalty.

STARLOG COMMUNICATIONS INTERNATIONAL, INC.—See *Moonlight Romance* and *Rhapsody Romance.*

STEMMER HOUSE PUBLISHERS, INC.—2627 Caves Rd., Owings Mills, MD 21117. Barbara Holdridge, Ed. Juvenile fiction and adult nonfiction. Specializes in art, design, cookbooks, children's, and horticultural titles. Query with SASE. Royalty.

STERLING PUBLISHING CO., INC.—387 Park Ave. S., New York, NY 10016. Sheila Anne Barry, Acquisitions Mgr. How-to, hobby, woodworking, health, fiber arts, craft, wine, nature, oddities, new age, puzzles, juvenile humor and activities, juvenile science, medieval history, Celtic topics, gardening, affirmative lifestyle, business, pets, recreation, sports and games books, reference, and military topics. Query with outline, sample chapter, and sample illustrations. Royalty.

STONE WALL PRESS, INC.—1241 30th St. N.W., Washington, DC 20007. Nonfiction manuscripts, 200 to 300 pages, on natural history, outdoors, conservation. Query. Royalty.

STONEYDALE PRESS—205 Main St., Drawer B, Stevensville, MT 59870. Dale A. Burk, Ed. Adult nonfiction, primarily how-to on outdoor recreation with emphasis on big game hunting. "We're a very specialized market. Query with outline and sample chapters essential." Royalty.

STOREY COMMUNICATIONS—Schoolhouse Rd., Pownal, VT 05261. Gwen Steege, Sr. Ed. How-to books for country living. Adult books, 100 to 350 pages, on gardening, crafts, building, cooking, nature, and how-to. Juvenile nonfiction, 100 to 250 pages, on gardening, crafts, and cooking. Royalty or flat fee.

STORY LINE PRESS—Three Oaks Farm, Brownsville, OR 97327–9718. Robert McDowell, Ed. Fiction, nonfiction, and poetry of varying lengths. Query. Royalty.

STRAWBERRY HILL PRESS—3848 S.E. Division St., Portland, OR 97202–1641. Carolyn Soto, Ed. Nonfiction: biography, autobiography, history, cooking, health, how-to, philosophy, performance arts, and Third World. Query with sample chapters, outline, and SASE. Royalty.

SUNDANCE PUBLISHERS & DISTRIBUTORS—P.O. Box 1326, Newtown Rd., Littleton, MA 01460. Emily Duncan, Ed./Exec. V.P. "We publish 'literature-based' classroom learning programs." Picture books, 16 to 48 pages; children's fiction, 64 to 120 pages; and juvenile nonfiction, 16 to 48 pages. Series include *Sundance Big Books,* which illustrate multicultural characters and themes, for grades K through 2, and *Info Power,* fact-based nonfiction on various subjects for grades 5 through 8. Query. Royalty or flat fee.

TSR, INC.—P.O. Box 756, Lake Geneva, WI 53147. Address Manuscript Ed. Highly original works, 100,000 words, of fantasy or science fiction. Query required.

TAB BOOKS—A Div. of McGraw-Hill, Inc., Blue Ridge Summit, PA 17294. Ron Powers, Ed. Dir. Nonfiction: electronics, computers, vocational how-to, aviation, science fair projects, business start up, science and technology, technician-level automotive, marine and outdoor life, military history, and engineering. Royalty or flat fee.

TAMBOURINE BOOKS—Imprint of William Morrow & Co., Inc., 1350 Ave. of the Americas, New York, NY 10019. Paulette C. Kaufmann, V.P./Ed.-in-Chief. Picture books, fiction, and nonfiction for all ages in general trade market. "We hope to find new talented writers and illustrators who are working outside the New York area."

TAYLOR PUBLISHING CO.—1550 W. Mockingbird Ln., Dallas, TX 75235. Jim Donovan, Sr. Ed. Adult nonfiction: gardening, sports and recreation, health, popular culture, parenting, home improvement, nature/outdoors. Query with outline, sample chapters, relevant author bio, and SASE. Royalty.

TEMPLE UNIVERSITY PRESS—Broad and Oxford Sts., Philadelphia, PA

19122. Michael Ames, Ed. Adult nonfiction. Query with outline and sample chapters. Royalty.

TEN SPEED PRESS—P.O. Box 7123, Berkeley, CA 94707. Self-help and how-to on careers, recreation, etc.; natural science, history, cookbooks. Query with outline, sample chapters, and SASE. Paperback. Royalty.

THUNDER'S MOUTH PRESS—632 Broadway, 7th Fl., New York, NY 10012. Neil Ortenberg, Ed. Mainly nonfiction: current affairs, popular culture, memoirs, and biography, to 200 pages. Royalty.

TICKNOR & FIELDS—Subsidiary of Houghton Mifflin Co., 215 Park Ave. S., New York, NY 10003. John Herman, Ed. Dir. General nonfiction and fiction. Send query letters to Cindy Spiegel. No unsolicited manuscripts accepted. Royalty.

TICKNOR & FIELDS BOOKS FOR YOUNG READERS—215 Park Ave. S., New York, NY 10003. Norma Jean Sawicki, Pub. Juvenile books in any genre, on any subject, and for any age group, as long as the writer is "passionate about what he is writing. We do not think about trends; we want stories well told." Submit complete manuscript. Royalty.

TIMES BOOKS—Div. of Random House, Inc., 201 E. 50th St., New York, NY 10022. Steve Wasserman, Ed. Dir. General nonfiction specializing in economics, politics, science, and current affairs. No unsolicited manuscripts or queries accepted.

TOPAZ—Imprint of Penguin USA, 375 Hudson St., New York, NY 10014. Address Eds. Historical romance. Query.

TOR BOOKS—175 Fifth Ave., 14th Fl., New York, NY 10010. Robert Gleason, Ed.-in-Chief. Patrick Nielsen Hayden, Sr. Ed., science fiction and fantasy. Melissa Ann Singer, Sr. Ed., general fiction. Books from 60,000 words. Query with outline and sample chapters. Royalty.

TRICYCLE PRESS—Imprint of Ten Speed Press, P.O. Box 7123, Berkeley, CA 94707. Nicole Geiger, Ed. Picture books (submit complete manuscript); activity books (submit complete outline and about 20 pages); chapter fiction (submit complete outline with three sample chapters); "real life" books that help children cope with issues. Royalty.

TROLL ASSOCIATES—100 Corporate Dr., Mahwah, NJ 07430. M. Francis, Ed. Juvenile fiction and nonfiction. Query preferred. Royalty or flat fee.

TROUBADOR PRESS—Imprint of Price Stern Sloan, Inc., 11150 Olympic Blvd., Los Angeles, CA 90064. Juvenile illustrated game, activity, paper doll, coloring, and cut-out books. Query with outline and SASE. Royalty or flat fee.

TUDOR PUBLISHERS, INC.—P.O. Box 38366, Greensboro, NC 27438. Eugene E. Pfaff, Jr., Ed. Helpful nonfiction books for senior citizens, teenagers, and minorities. Young adult biographies. Reference library titles. Occasional high-quality fiction. Send proposal or query with sample chapters. Royalty.

TYNDALE HOUSE—351 Executive Dr., Box 80, Wheaton, IL 60189. Ron Beers, V.P. Juvenile and adult fiction and nonfiction on subjects of concern to Christians. Picture books with religious focus for preschool and early readers. Query only.

UAHC PRESS—838 Fifth Ave., New York, NY 10021. Aron Hirt-Manheimer, Ed. Religious educational titles on or related to Judaism. Adult nonfiction; juvenile picture books, fiction, nonfiction, and young adult titles. Query with outline. Royalty.

UNIVERSITY OF ALABAMA PRESS—P.O. Box 870380, Tuscaloosa, AL 35487–0380. Scholarly and general regional nonfiction. Submit to appropriate editor: Malcolm MacDonald, Ed. (history, public administration, political science); Nicole Mitchell, Ed. (English, rhetoric and communication, Judaic studies, women's studies); Judith Knight, Ed. (archaeology, anthropology). Send complete manuscript. Royalty.

UNIVERSITY OF ARIZONA PRESS—1230 N. Park Ave., Suite 102, Tucson, AZ 85719. Joanne O'Hare, Sr. Ed. Christine R. Szuter, Acquiring Ed. Amy Chapman Smith, Acquiring Ed. Scholarly nonfiction: Arizona, American West, anthropology, archaeology, environmental science, Latin America, Native Americans, natural history, space sciences, women's studies. Query with outline and sample chapters or send complete manuscript. Royalty.

UNIVERSITY OF CALIFORNIA PRESS—2120 Berkeley Way, Berkeley, CA 94720. Address Acquisitions Dept. Scholarly nonfiction. Query with cover letter, outline, sample chapters, curriculum vitae, and SASE.

UNIVERSITY OF GEORGIA PRESS—330 Research Dr., Athens, GA 30602–4901. Karen Orchard, Ed. Short story collections and poetry, scholarly nonfiction and literary criticism, Southern and American history, regional studies, biography and autobiography. For nonfiction, query with outline and sample chapters. Poetry collections considered in Sept. and Jan. only; short fiction in June and July only. A $10 fee is required for all poetry and fiction submissions. Royalty. SASE for competition guidelines.

UNIVERSITY OF ILLINOIS PRESS—54 E. Gregory Dr., Champaign, IL 61820. Richard L. Wentworth, Ed.-in-Chief. Short story collections, 140 to 180 pages; nonfiction; and poetry, 70 to 100 pages. Rarely considers multiple submissions. Query. Royalty. "Not considering new work at this time."

UNIVERSITY OF MINNESOTA PRESS—2037 University Ave. S.E., Minneapolis, MN 55455. Biodun Iginla, Ed. Janaki Bakhle, Ed. Nonfiction: media studies, literary theory, critical aesthetics, philosophy, cultural criticism, regional titles, 50,000 to 225,000 words. Query with detailed prospectus or introduction, table of contents, sample chapter, and recent resumé. Royalty.

UNIVERSITY OF MISSOURI PRESS—2910 LeMone Blvd., Columbia, MO 65201–8227. Scholarly books on American and European history; American, British, and Latin American literary criticism; political philosophy; intellectual history; regional studies; and poetry and short fiction. Query Beverly Jarrett, Dir./Ed.-in-Chief, for scholarly studies and creative nonfiction. Query Mr. Clair Willcox, Poetry and Fiction Editor, with 4 to 6 sample poems or one short story, proposed table of contents, and cover letter describing the work and the author's professional background.

UNIVERSITY OF NEBRASKA PRESS—901 N. 17th St., Lincoln, NE 68588–0520. Address Eds. Specializes in the history of the American West, Native-American studies, and literary criticism. Send proposals with summary, two sample chapters, and resumé. Write for guidelines for annual North American Indian Prose Award.

UNIVERSITY OF NEW MEXICO PRESS—Univ. of New Mexico, Albuquerque, NM 87131. Elizabeth C. Hadas, Ed. Dir. David V. Holtby, Larry Ball, Dana Asbury, and Barbara Guth, Eds. Scholarly nonfiction on social and cultural anthropology, archaeology, Western history, art, and photography. Query. Royalty.

UNIVERSITY OF NORTH CAROLINA PRESS—P.O. Box 2288, Chapel Hill, NC 27515–2288. David Perry, Ed. General-interest books (75,000 to 125,000 words) on the lore, crafts, cooking, gardening, travel, and natural history of the Southeast. No fiction or poetry. Query preferred. Royalty.

UNIVERSITY OF NORTH TEXAS PRESS—P.O. Box 13856, Denton, TX 76203–6586. Charlotte M. Wright, Ed. Books on Western Americana, Texan culture, women's studies, multicultural studies, and folklore. Series include: *War and the Southwest* (perspectives, histories, and memories of war from authors living in the Southwest); *Texas Poets* (poetry by Native Texans only); and *Texas Writers* (critical biographies of Texas writers). Send manuscript or query with sample chapters; no multiple queries. Royalty.

UNIVERSITY OF OKLAHOMA PRESS—1005 Asp Ave., Norman, OK 73019–0445. John Drayton, Asst. Dir. Books, to 300 pages, on the history of the American West, Indians of the Americas, congressional studies, classical studies, literary criticism, and natural history. Query. Royalty.

UNIVERSITY OF PITTSBURGH PRESS—127 N. Bellefield Ave., Pittsburgh, PA 15260. Scholarly nonfiction; poetry. Query.

UNIVERSITY OF TENNESSEE PRESS—293 Communications Bldg., Knoxville, TN 37996–0325. Nonfiction, regional trade, 200 to 300 manuscript pages. Query with outline and sample chapters. Royalty.

UNIVERSITY OF WISCONSIN PRESS—114 N. Murray St., Madison, WI 53715–1199. Address Ed. Scholarly nonfiction.

UNIVERSITY PRESS OF COLORADO—P.O. Box 849, Niwot, CO 80544. Scholarly books in the humanities, social sciences, and applied sciences. No fiction or poetry.

UNIVERSITY PRESS OF FLORIDA—15 N.W. 15th St., Gainesville, FL 32611–2079. Walda Metcalf, Ed.-in-Chief/Assoc. Dir. Nonfiction, 150 to 450 manuscript pages, on regional studies, Native Americans, folklore, women's studies, Latin-American studies, contemporary literary criticism, sociology, anthropology, archaeology, international affairs, labor studies, and history. Poetry. Royalty.

UNIVERSITY PRESS OF MISSISSIPPI—3825 Ridgewood Rd., Jackson, MS 39211–6492. Seetha Srinivasan, Ed.-in-Chief. Scholarly and trade titles in American literature, history, and culture; southern studies; African-American, women's and American studies; social sciences; popular culture; folklife; art and architecture; natural sciences; and other liberal arts.

UNIVERSITY PRESS OF NEW ENGLAND—23 S. Main St., Hanover, NH 03755–2048. General and scholarly nonfiction. American, British, and European history, literature, literary criticism, creative fiction and nonfiction, and cultural studies. Jewish studies, women's studies, and studies of the New England region.

VAN NOSTRAND REINHOLD—115 Fifth Ave., New York, NY 10003. Judith R. Joseph, Pres./C.E.O. Business, professional, scientific, and technical publishers of applied reference works. Hospitality, architecture, graphic and interior design, gemology, chemistry, industrial and environmental health and safety, food science and technology, computer science and engineering. Royalty.

VANDAMERE PRESS—P.O. Box 5243, Arlington, VA 22205. Jerry Frank, Assoc. Acquisitions Ed. General trade books, fiction and nonfiction. History, military, parenting, career guides, and travel. Also books about the nation's capital for a national audience. Prefer to see outline with sample chapter for nonfiction; for fiction send 4 or 5 sample chapters. Multiple queries considered. Royalty. SASE required.

VIKING—Imprint of Penguin USA, 375 Hudson St., New York, NY 10014. No unagented manuscripts.

VIKING CHILDREN'S BOOKS—Imprint of Penguin USA, 375 Hudson St., New York, NY 10014. Address Eds. Fiction and nonfiction, including biography, history, and sports, for ages 7 to 14. Humor and picture books for ages 2 to 6. Query Children's Book Dept. with outline and sample chapter. SASE required. Royalty.

VILLARD BOOKS—Div. of Random House, 201 E. 50th St. , New York, NY 10022. Diane Reverand, V.P./Pub./Ed.-in-Chief. Fiction, sports, inspiration, how-to, biography, humor, etc. "We do look for authors who are promotable and books we feel we can market well." Royalty.

VINTAGE BOOKS—Div. of Random House, 201 E. 50th St., New York, NY 10022. Trade fiction and nonfiction. Query with sample chapters.

VOYAGER PAPERBACKS—See *Harcourt Brace.*

WALKER AND COMPANY—720 Fifth Ave., New York, NY 10019. Adult fiction: mysteries, westerns. Adult nonfiction: Americana, biography, history, science, natural history, medicine, psychology, parenting, sports, outdoors, reference, popular science, self-help, business, and music. Juvenile nonfiction, including biography, science, history, music, and nature. Juvenile fiction: Middle grade and young adult novels. Query with synopsis and SASE. Royalty.

WALLACE-HOMESTEAD BOOKS—See *Chilton Book Co.*

WARNER BOOKS—1271 Ave. of the Americas, New York, NY 10020. Mel Parker, Pub., Warner Paperbacks. No unsolicited manuscripts or proposals.

WASHINGTON STATE UNIVERSITY PRESS—Cooper Publications Bldg., Pullman, WA 99164–5910. Glen Lindeman and Keith Petersen, Eds. Books on northwest history, prehistory, and culture, 100 to 250 pages. Send complete manuscript. Royalty.

WASHINGTON WRITERS PUBLISHING HOUSE—P.O. Box 15271, Washington, DC 20003. Address Ed. Poetry books, 50 to 60 pages, by writers in the greater Washington, DC, area. Send SASE for guidelines.

WATERSTON PRODUCTIONS, INC.—1019 N.W. Brooks St., Bend, OR 97701. Carey Vendrame, Ed. Picture books, 200 words, for preschoolers to 8-year-olds; books for young readers, 5 to 8 years old, up to 1,500 words. "We welcome all manuscripts but have particular interest in those with a northwest focus. Manuscripts must be well written, entertaining, and have a unique and endearing quality about them. Cute, condescending or preachy stories are not acceptable." Payment is negotiable. Submit complete manuscript with SASE.

WATTS, INC., FRANKLIN—95 Madison Ave., New York, NY 10016. Emily Dolbear, Submissions. Curriculum-oriented nonfiction for grades K to 12, including science, history, social studies, and biography. Query with SASE required.

WESLEYAN UNIVERSITY PRESS—110 Mt. Vernon St., Middletown, CT 06459–0433. Terry Cochran, Dir. *Wesleyan Poetry*: 64 to 80 pages. Query. Royalty.

WESTERN PUBLISHING CO., INC.—850 Third Ave., New York, NY 10022. Robin Warner, V.P./Pub., Children's Books; Alice Bregman, Marilyn Salomon, Ed. Dirs., Children's Books. Children's books, fiction and nonfiction: picture books, storybooks, concept books, novelty books. Adult nonfiction: field guides. No unsolicited manuscripts. Same address and requirements for *Golden Press*. Royalty or flat fee.

WESTMINSTER/JOHN KNOX PRESS—100 Witherspoon St., Louisville, KY 40202. Davis Perkins, Dir. Stephanie Egnotovich, Man. Ed. Books that inform, interpret, challenge, and encourage Christian faith and living. Royalty. Send SASE for guidelines.

WHISPERING COYOTE PRESS—480 Newbury St., Suite 104, Danvers, MA 01923. Ms. Lou Alpert, Ed. Picture books, 32 pages, for readers ages 4 to 12. Submit complete manuscript with SASE. Royalty.

WHITMAN, ALBERT—6340 Oakton, Morton Grove, IL 60053. Kathleen Tucker, Ed. Picture books for preschool children; novels, biographies, mysteries, and general nonfiction for middle-grade readers. Submit complete manuscript for picture books, three chapters and outline for longer fiction; query for nonfiction. Royalty.

WILDERNESS PRESS—2440 Bancroft Way, Berkeley, CA 94704. Thomas Winnett, Ed. Nonfiction: outdoor sports, recreation, and travel in the western U.S. Royalty.

WILEY & SONS, JOHN—605 Third Ave., New York, NY 10158–0012. Nonfiction, 250 to 350 pages: science/nature; business/management; real estate; travel; cooking; biography; psychology; microcomputers; language; history; current affairs; health; finance. Send proposals with outline, author vita, market information, and sample chapter. Royalty.

WILLOWISP PRESS, INC.—801 94th Ave. N., St. Petersburg, FL 33702. Address Acquisitions Ed. Juvenile books for children in grades K through 8. Picture books, 300 to 800 words. Fiction, 14,000 to 18,000 words for grades 3 through 5; 20,000 to 24,000 words for grades 5 through 8. Requirements for nonfiction vary. Query with outline, sample chapter, and SASE. Guidelines. Royalty or flat fee.

WILSHIRE BOOK COMPANY—12015 Sherman Rd., N. Hollywood, CA 91605. Melvin Powers, Pub. Nonfiction: self-help, motivation, inspiration, psychology, how-to, entrepreneurship, mail order, and horsemanship. Fiction: adult fables, 35,000 to 45,000 words, that teach principles of psychological growth or offer guidance in living. Send synopsis/detailed chapter outline, three chapters, and SASE. Royalty.

WINDSWEPT HOUSE PUBLISHERS—Mt. Desert, ME 04660. Jane Weinberger, Pub. Carl Little, Ed. Children's picture books; young adult novels; adult fiction and nonfiction. Overstocked; not considering new manuscripts until 1995. Query.

WINGBOW PRESS—7900 Edgewater Dr., Oakland, CA 94621. Randy Fingland, Ed. Nonfiction: women's interests, health, psychology. No fiction or poetry. Query preferred. Royalty.

WOODBINE HOUSE—5615 Fishers Ln., Rockville, MD 20852. Susan Stokes, Ed. "Emphasis is increasingly on books for or about people with disabilities, but we will consider nonfiction of all types. No personal accounts or books that can be marketed only through bookstores." Query or submit complete manuscript with SASE. Guidelines for SASE. Royalty.

WORDWARE PUBLISHING—1506 Capital Ave., Plano, TX 75074. Russell A. Stultz, Ed. Computer reference books and Texas regional books. Query with outline and sample chapters. Royalty.

WORKMAN PUBLISHING CO., INC.—708 Broadway, New York, NY 10003. Address Eds. General nonfiction. Normal contractual terms based on agreement.

WORLDWIDE LIBRARY—Div. of Harlequin Books, 225 Duncan Mill Rd., Don Mills, Ont., Canada M3B 3K9. Randall Toye, Ed. Dir. Action adventure series and futuristic fiction for *Gold Eagle Books* imprint; mystery fiction reprints only, no originals. Query. Paperback only.

YANKEE BOOKS—33 E. Minor St., Emmaus, PA 18098. Sarah Dunn, Assoc. Ed. Books relating specifically to New England: travel in the Northeast; New England cooking and recipes, nature and lore. "We are looking for accurate, informative, and practical books that can be used by visitors and would-be visitors to New England, as well as residents of the Northeast." Send proposals only. Royalty.

YEARLING BOOKS—Imprint of Dell Publishing Co., 1540 Broadway, New York, NY 10036. Address Eds. Books for K through 6. Manuscripts accepted from agents only. Same address and requirements for *Skylark Books.*

YOLEN BOOKS, JANE—See *Harcourt Brace.*

ZEBRA BOOKS—475 Park Ave. S., New York, NY 10016. Ann LaFarge, Exec. Ed. Popular fiction: horror; historical romance (*Heartfire Romances*, 117,000 words, and *Lovegram Romances*, 130,000 words); traditional gothics (first person, 100,000 words); regencies (80,000 to 120,000 words); sagas (150,000 words); glitz (100,000 words); men's adventure; westerns; thrillers, etc. Also *To Love Again*, aimed at women over 45. Query with synopsis and sample chapters preferred.

ZENITH EDITIONS—See *National Press.*

ZONDERVAN PUBLISHING HOUSE—5300 Patterson S.E., Grand Rapids, MI 49530. Address Manuscript Review. Christian titles. General fiction and nonfiction; academic and professional books. Query with outline, sample chapter, and SASE. Royalty. Guidelines.

UNIVERSITY PRESSES

University presses generally publish books of a scholarly nature or of specialized interest by authorities in a given field. A few publish fiction and poetry. Many publish only a handful of titles a year. Always query first. Do not send a manuscript until you have been invited to do so by the editor. Several of the following presses and their detailed editorial submission requirements are included in the *Book Publishers* list.

BRIGHAM YOUNG UNIVERSITY PRESS—205 Univ. Press Bldg., Provo, UT 84602.

BUCKNELL UNIVERSITY PRESS—Bucknell University, Lewisburg, PA 17837.

CAMBRIDGE UNIVERSITY PRESS—40 W. 20th St., New York, NY 10011–4211.

THE CATHOLIC UNIVERSITY OF AMERICA PRESS—620 Michigan Ave. N.E., Washington, DC 20064.

COLUMBIA UNIVERSITY PRESS—562 W. 113th St., New York, NY 10025.

DUKE UNIVERSITY PRESS—Box 90660, Durham, NC 27708–0660.

DUQUESNE UNIVERSITY PRESS—600 Forbes Ave., Pittsburgh, PA 15282–0101.

FORDHAM UNIVERSITY PRESS—University Box L, Bronx, NY 10458–5172.

GEORGIA STATE UNIVERSITY BUSINESS PRESS—University Plaza, Atlanta, GA 30303–3093.

HARVARD UNIVERSITY PRESS—79 Garden St., Cambridge , MA 02138–1499.

INDIANA UNIVERSITY PRESS—601 N. Morton St., Bloomington, IN 47404–3797.

THE JOHNS HOPKINS UNIVERSITY PRESS—2715 N. Charles St., Baltimore, MD 21218.

KENT STATE UNIVERSITY PRESS—Kent State Univ., Kent, OH 44242.

LOUISIANA STATE UNIVERSITY PRESS—P.O. Box 25053, Baton Rouge, LA 70894–5053.

LOYOLA UNIVERSITY PRESS—3441 N. Ashland Ave., Chicago, IL 60657–1397.

THE MICHIGAN STATE UNIVERSITY PRESS—1405 S. Harrison Rd., Suite 25, Manly Miles Bldg., E. Lansing, MI 48823–5202.

THE MIT PRESS—Acquisitions Dept., 55 Hayward St., Cambridge, MA 02142.

NEW YORK UNIVERSITY PRESS—70 Washington Sq. S., New York, NY 10012.

OHIO STATE UNIVERSITY PRESS—180 Pressey Hall, 1070 Carmack Rd., Columbus, OH 43210.

OREGON STATE UNIVERSITY PRESS—101 Waldo Hall, Corvallis, OR 97331.

THE PENNSYLVANIA STATE UNIVERSITY PRESS—Barbara Bldg., Suite C, University Park, PA 16802.

PRINCETON UNIVERSITY PRESS—41 William St., Princeton, NJ 08540.

RUTGERS UNIVERSITY PRESS—109 Church St., New Brunswick, NJ 08901.

SOUTHERN ILLINOIS UNIVERSITY PRESS—Box 3697, Carbondale, IL 62902–3697.

SOUTHERN METHODIST UNIVERSITY PRESS—Box 415, Dallas, TX 75275.

STANFORD UNIVERSITY PRESS—Stanford University, Stanford, CA 94305–2235.

STATE UNIVERSITY OF NEW YORK PRESS—State Univ. Plaza, Albany, NY 12246–0001.

SYRACUSE UNIVERSITY PRESS—1600 Jamesville Ave., Syracuse, NY 13244–5160.

TEMPLE UNIVERSITY PRESS—Broad and Oxford Sts., Philadelphia, PA 19122.

UNIVERSITY OF ALABAMA PRESS—P.O. Box 870380, Tuscaloosa, AL 35487–0380.

UNIVERSITY OF ARIZONA PRESS—1230 N. Park Ave., Suite 102, Tucson, AZ 85719.

UNIVERSITY OF CALIFORNIA PRESS—2120 Berkeley Way, Berkeley, CA 94720.

UNIVERSITY OF CHICAGO PRESS—5801 Ellis Ave., Chicago, IL 60637–1496.

UNIVERSITY OF GEORGIA PRESS—330 Research Dr., Athens, GA 30602–4901.

UNIVERSITY OF ILLINOIS PRESS—54 E. Gregory Dr., Champaign, IL 61820.

UNIVERSITY OF MASSACHUSETTS PRESS—Box 429, Amherst, MA 01004.

UNIVERSITY OF MICHIGAN PRESS—P.O. Box 1104, 839 Greene St., Ann Arbor, MI 48106–1104.

UNIVERSITY OF MINNESOTA PRESS—2037 University Ave. S.E., Minneapolis, MN 55455.

UNIVERSITY OF MISSOURI PRESS—2910 LeMone Blvd., Columbia, MO 65201–8227.

UNIVERSITY OF NEBRASKA PRESS—901 North 17th St., Lincoln, NE 68588–0520.

UNIVERSITY OF NEW MEXICO PRESS—University of New Mexico, Albuquerque, NM 87131.

UNIVERSITY OF NORTH CAROLINA PRESS—P.O. Box 2288, Chapel Hill, NC 27515–2288.

UNIVERSITY OF NORTH TEXAS PRESS—P.O. Box 13856, Denton, TX 76203–6586.

UNIVERSITY OF NOTRE DAME PRESS—University of Notre Dame, Notre Dame, IN 46556.

UNIVERSITY OF OKLAHOMA PRESS—1005 Asp Ave., Norman, OK 73019–0445.

UNIVERSITY OF PITTSBURGH PRESS—127 N. Bellefield Ave., Pittsburgh, PA 15260.

UNIVERSITY OF SOUTH CAROLINA PRESS—University of South Carolina, 1716 College St., Columbia, SC 29208.

UNIVERSITY OF TENNESSEE PRESS—293 Communications Bldg., Knoxville, TN 37996–0325.

UNIVERSITY OF UTAH PRESS—101 U.S.B., Salt Lake City, UT 84112.

UNIVERSITY OF WASHINGTON PRESS—P.O. Box 50096, Seattle, WA 98145–5096.

UNIVERSITY OF WISCONSIN PRESS—114 N. Murray St., Madison, WI 53715–1199.

UNIVERSITY PRESS OF COLORADO—P.O. Box 849, Niwot, CO 80544.

UNIVERSITY PRESS OF FLORIDA—15 N.W. 15th St., Gainesville, FL 32611–2079.

THE UNIVERSITY PRESS OF KENTUCKY—663 S. Limestone St., Lexington, KY 40508–4008.

UNIVERSITY PRESS OF MISSISSIPPI—3825 Ridgewood Rd., Jackson, MS 39211–6492.

UNIVERSITY PRESS OF NEW ENGLAND—23 S. Main St., Hanover, NH 03755–2048.

THE UNIVERSITY PRESS OF VIRGINIA—Box 3608, Univ. Sta., Charlottesville, VA 22903.

WAYNE STATE UNIVERSITY PRESS—5959 Woodward Ave., Detroit, MI 48202.

WESLEYAN UNIVERSITY PRESS—110 Mt.Vernon St., Middletown, CT 06459–0433.

YALE UNIVERSITY PRESS—92A Yale Sta., New Haven, CT 06520.

SYNDICATES

Syndicates are business organizations that buy material from writers and artists to sell to newspapers all over the country and the world. Authors are paid either a percentage of the gross proceeds or an outright fee.

Of course, features by people well known in their fields have the best chance of being syndicated. In general, syndicates want columns that have been popular in a local newspaper, perhaps, or magazine. Since most syndicated fiction has been published previously in magazines or books, beginning fiction writers should try to sell their stories to magazines before submitting them to syndicates.

Always query syndicates before sending manuscripts, since their needs change frequently, and be sure to enclose SASEs with queries and manuscripts.

ARKIN MAGAZINE SYNDICATE—300 Bayview Dr., A-8, N. Miami Beach, FL 33160. Joseph Arkin, Ed. Dir. Articles, 750 to 2,200 words, for trade and professional magazines. Must have small-business slant, be written in layman's language, and offer solutions to business problems. Articles should apply to many businesses, not just a specific industry. No columns. Pays 3¢ to 10¢ a word, on acceptance. SASE required; query not necessary.

HARRIS & ASSOCIATES FEATURES—12084 Caminito Campana, San Diego, CA 92128. Dick Harris, Ed. Sports- and family-oriented features, to 1,200 words; fillers and short humor, 500 to 800 words. Queries preferred. Pays varying rates.

HISPANIC LINK NEWS SERVICE—1420 N St. N.W., Washington, DC 20005. Charles A. Ericksen, Ed. Trend articles, opinion and personal experience pieces, and general features with Hispanic focus, 650 to 700 words; editorial cartoons. Pays $25 for op-ed columns and cartoons, on acceptance. Guidelines.

THE HOLLYWOOD INSIDE SYNDICATE—Box 49957, Los Angeles, CA 90049. John Austin, Dir. Feature articles, 750 to 2,500 words, on TV and film personalities with B&W photo(s). Story suggestions for three-part series. Pieces on unusual medical and scientific breakthroughs. Pays on percentage basis for features, negotiated rates for ideas, on publication.

LOS ANGELES TIMES SYNDICATE—Times Mirror Sq., Los Angeles, CA 90053. Commentary, features, columns, editorial cartoons, comics, puzzles and games; news services. Send SASE for submission guidelines.

NATIONAL NEWS BUREAU—P.O. Box 43039, Philadelphia, PA 19129. Harry Jay Katz, Ed. Articles, 500 to 1,500 words, interviews, consumer news, how-tos, travel pieces, reviews, entertainment pieces, features, etc. Pays on publication.

NEW YORK TIMES SYNDICATION SALES—130 Fifth Ave., New York, NY 10011. Gloria Anderson, Exec. Ed. Previously published health, lifestyle, and entertainment articles only, to 1,500 words. Query with published article or tear sheet and SASE. Pays varying rates, on publication.

OCEANIC PRESS SERVICE—Seaview Business Park, 1030 Calle Cordillera, Unit #106, San Clemente, CA 92673. Peter Carbone, General Mgr. Buys reprint rights for foreign markets, on previously published novels, self-help, and how-to books; interviews with celebrities; illustrated features on celebrities, family, health, beauty, personal relationships, etc.; cartoons, comic strips. Pays on acceptance or half on acceptance, half on syndication. Query.

SINGER MEDIA CORP.—#106, 1030 Calle Cordillera, San Clemente, CA 92672. Helen J. Lee, Ed. U.S. and/or foreign reprint rights to published romantic short stories, historical and romantic novels, gothics, westerns, and mysteries (published during last 25 years); business management titles, self-help, and computer. Biography, women's-interest material, all lengths. Home repair, real estate, psychological quizzes. Interviews with celebrities. Illustrated columns, humor, cartoons, comic strips. Pays on percentage basis or by outright purchase.

TRIBUNE MEDIA SERVICES—64 E. Concord St., Orlando, FL 32801. Michael Argirion, Ed. Continuing columns, comic strips, features, electronic databases.

UNITED FEATURE SYNDICATE—200 Park Ave., New York, NY 10166. Diana Loevy, V.P./ Exec. Ed. Syndicated columns; no one-shots or series. Payment by contractual arrangement. Send samples with SASE.

UNITED PRESS INTERNATIONAL—1400 Eye St. N.W., Washington, DC 20005. Robert A. Martin, Man. Ed. No free-lance material.

UNIVERSAL PRESS SYNDICATE—4900 Main St., Kansas City, MO

64112. Attn: Paula Reichler Parker. Articles for "High Impact" feature service, covering lifestyles, trends, health, fashion, parenting, business, humor, the home, entertainment, and personalities. Query. Pays advances or flat fee.

LITERARY PRIZE OFFERS

Each year many important literary contests are open to free-lance writers. The short summaries given below are intended merely as guides; closing dates, requirements, and rules are tentative. Every effort has been made to ensure the accuracy of information provided here. Since submission requirements are more detailed than space allows, writers should send SASE for complete guidelines before entering any contest. Writers are also advised to check the monthly "Prize Offers" column of *The Writer* Magazine (120 Boylston St., Boston, MA 02116–4615) for additional contest listings and up-to-date contest requirements.

ACADEMY OF AMERICAN POETS—Walt Whitman Award, 584 Broadway, Suite 1208, New York, NY 10012. Offers publication and $1,000 cash prize for a book-length poetry manuscript by a poet who has not yet published a volume of poetry. Closes in November.

ACADEMY OF MOTION PICTURE ARTS AND SCIENCES—The Nicholl Fellowships, Dept. WR, 8949 Wilshire Blvd., Beverly Hills, CA 90211–1972. Up to five fellowships of $25,000 each will be awarded for original screenplays that display exceptional craft and engaging storytelling. Closes in May.

ACTORS THEATRE OF LOUISVILLE—Ten-Minute Play Contest, 316 W. Main St., Louisville, KY 40202. Offers $1,000 for previously unproduced ten-page script. Closes in December.

AMELIA MAGAZINE—329 E St., Bakersfield, CA 93304. Attn: Frederick A. Raborg, Jr., Ed. Offers writing awards year-round in poetry, short fiction, and nonfiction, with prizes of up to $250. Contest closings vary.

AMERICAN ACADEMY OF ARTS AND LETTERS—Richard Rogers Production Award, 633 W. 155th St., New York, NY 10032. Offers subsidized production in New York City by a non-profit theater for a musical, play with music, thematic review, or any comparable work other than opera. Closes in November.

AMERICAN RADIO THEATRE—Radio Script Writers' Competition, 3035 23rd St., San Francisco, CA 94110–3315. Prizes of $250, $100, and three $50 awards are offered for the top five radio plays submitted. Closes in June.

THE AMERICAN-SCANDINAVIAN FOUNDATION—Translation Prize, 725 Park Ave., New York, NY 10021. A prize of $2,000 is awarded for an outstanding English translation of poetry, fiction, drama, or literary prose originally written in Danish, Finnish, Icelandic, Norwegian, or Swedish. Closes in June.

ANHINGA PRESS—Anhinga Prize for Poetry, P.O. Box 10595, Tallahassee, FL 32302–0595. A $1,000 prize will be awarded for an unpublished full-length collection of poetry, 48 to 64 pages, by a poet who has published no more than one full-length collection. Closes in March.

THE ASSOCIATED WRITING PROGRAMS—Awards Series, c/o Old Dominion Univ., Norfolk, VA 23529–0079. Conducts Annual Awards Series in Poetry, Short Fiction, the Novel, and Nonfiction. In each category the prize is book publication and a $1,500 honorarium. Closes in February.

ASSOCIATION OF JEWISH LIBRARIES—Sydney Taylor Manuscript Competition, 15 Goldsmith St., Providence, RI 02906. Attn: Lillian Schwartz, Coordinator. Offers $1,000 for the best fiction manuscript, 64 to 200 pages, by an unpublished book author, for readers 8 to 11. Stories must have a positive Jewish focus. Closes in January.

ASTRAEA NATIONAL LESBIAN ACTION FOUNDATION—Lesbian Writers Fund, 666 Broadway, Suite 520, New York, NY 10012. Five Emerging Writers Awards of $11,000 each are given to lesbian writers of fiction or poetry whose work includes some lesbian content. Writers must have published at least one piece in a newspaper, periodical, or anthology, and must not have published more than one book. Closes in March.

BAKER'S PLAYS—High School Playwriting Contest, 100 Chauncy St., Boston, MA 02111. Plays about the high school experience, written by high school students, are eligible for awards of $500, $250, and $100. Closes in January.

BARNARD COLLEGE—New Women Poets Prize, Women Poets at Barnard, Columbia Univ., 3009 Broadway, New York, NY 10027–6598. Attn: Celeste Schenck and Christopher Baswell, Co-Dirs. A prize of $1,500 and publication by Beacon Press is offered for an unpublished poetry manuscript, 50 to 100 pages, by a female poet who has never published a book of poetry. Closes in September.

THE BELLINGHAM REVIEW—The 49th Parallel Poetry Contest, 1007 Queen St., Bellingham, WA 98226. Publication and prizes of $150, $100, and $50 will be awarded for poems up to 40 lines, any style or subject. Closes in December.

BEVERLY HILLS THEATRE GUILD/JULIE HARRIS PLAYWRIGHT AWARD—2815 N. Beachwood Dr., Los Angeles, CA 90068. Attn: Marcella Meharg. Offers prize of $5,000, plus possible $2,000 for productions in Los Angeles area, for previously unproduced and unpublished full-length play. A $2,000 second prize and $1,000 third prize are also offered. Closes in November.

BIRMINGHAM-SOUTHERN COLLEGE WRITER'S CONFERENCE—Hackney Literary Awards, BSC A-3, Birmingham, AL 35254. The Hackney Literary Awards offers $2,000 for an unpublished novel, any length. Closes in September. Also, a $2,000 prize is shared for the winning short story, to 5,000 words, and poem of up to 50 lines. Closes in December.

BOSTON MAGAZINE—Fiction Contest, 300 Massachusetts Ave., Boston, MA 02115. Publication and $500 will is awarded for the best mystery story, up to 3,000 words, set in or around Boston. Closes in September.

BUCKNELL UNIVERSITY—The Philip Roth Residence in Creative Writing, Stadler Ctr. for Poetry, Bucknell Hall, Bucknell Univ., Lewisburg, PA 17837. Attn: John Wheatcroft, Dir. The fall residency may be used by a writer, over 21, not currently enrolled in a university, to work on a first or second book. The residency is awarded in odd-numbered years to a fiction writer, and in even-numbered years to a poet. Closes in March.

CENTER PRESS—Masters Literary Awards, Box 16452, Encino, CA 91416–6452. Awards four quarterly awards of $250 for fiction, poetry and song lyrics, and nonfiction, as well as an annual $1,500 award. Submissions accepted year-round.

CHELSEA AWARDS COMPETITION—P.O. Box 1040, York Beach, ME 03910. Attn: Richard Forester, Assoc. Ed. Prizes of $500 plus publication are awarded for the best unpublished short fiction and poetry. Fiction contest closes in June. Poetry contest closes in December.

THE CHICAGO TRIBUNE—Nelson Algren Awards for Short Fiction, 435 N. Michigan Ave., Chicago, IL 606ll. Offers a first prize of $5,000 and three runner-up prizes of $1,000 for outstanding unpublished short stories, 2,500 to 10,000 words, by American writers. Closes in February.

THE CLAUDER COMPETITION—Theaterworks, Inc., P.O. Box 635, Boston, MA 02117. Awards $3,000 plus professional production for a full-length play by a New England writer. Runner-up prizes of $500 and a staged reading are also awarded. Closes in June of even-numbered years.

CLEVELAND STATE UNIVERSITY POETRY CENTER—Dept. of English, Rhodes Tower, Room 1815, Cleveland, OH 44115. The writer of the best volume of poetry submitted receives publication in the CSU Poetry Series and $1,000. Closes in March.

CMH LITERARY NETWORK—Up and Coming Writer's Short Story Contest, 360 Connecticut Ave., Suite 115, Norwalk, CT 06854. Offers $500 and $250 for original, unpublished fiction, to 2,500 words. Closes in March.

COLONIAL PLAYERS, INC.—99 Great Lake Dr., Annapolis, MD 21403. Attn: Frank Moorman. A prize of $750 plus possible production will be awarded for the best full-length play. Closes in December of even-numbered years.

COMMUNITY CHILDREN'S THEATRE OF KANSAS CITY—8021 E. 129th Terrace, Grandview, MO 64030. Attn: Mrs. Blanche Sellens, Dir. A prize of $500, plus production, is awarded for the best play, up to one hour long, written for elementary school children. Closes in January.

CONNECTICUT POETRY SOCIETY—Joseph E. Brodine Contest, P.O. Box 4827, Waterbury, CT 06704–1992. Awards of $250, $75, and $50, plus publication in the *Connecticut River Review* are offered for unpublished poems, to 40 lines. Closes in July.

THE CRITIC—Short Story Contest, Thomas More Assoc., 205 W. Monroe St., 6th Floor, Chicago, IL 60606–5097. Original, upublished short stories are eligible for the prize of $1,000 plus publication. Closes in September of even-numbered years.

CUMBERLAND POETRY REVIEW—Robert Penn Warren Poetry Prize Competition, P.O. Box 120128, Nashville, TN 37212. Three poems of up to 100 lines each may be submitted for prizes of $500, $300, and $200. Closes in March.

EUGENE V. DEBS FOUNDATION—Bryant Spann Memorial Prize, Dept. of History, Indiana State Univ., Terre Haute, IN 47809. Offers a prize of $1,000 for a published or unpublished article or essay on themes relating to social protest or human equality. Closes in April.

DEEP SOUTH WRITERS CONFERENCE—Contest Clerk, Drawer 44691, Univ. of Southwestern Louisianna, Lafayette, LA 70504–4691. Prizes ranging from $50 to $300 are offered for unpublished manuscripts in the following categories: short fiction, novel, nonfiction, poetry, drama, and French literature. Closes in July. Also offers the $500 Miller Award for a play dealing with some aspect of the life of Edward de Vere (1550–1604), the 17th Earl of Oxford. Closes in July of odd-numbered years.

DELACORTE PRESS—Dept. BFYR, 1540 Broadway, New York, NY 10036. Sponsors Delacorte Press Prize for outstanding first young-adult novel. The prize consists of one Delacorte hardcover and one Dell paperback contract, an advance of $6,000 on royalties, and a $1,500 cash prize. Closes in December.

BARBARA DEMING MEMORIAL FUND, INC.—P.O. Box 40–1043, Brooklyn, NY 11240–1043. Attn: Pam McAllister, Administrator. Grants of up to $1,000 are awarded semiannually to feminists in the arts whose work addresses women's concerns and/or speaks for peace and justice from a feminist perspective. Closes in June and in December.

DOUBLEDAY BOOKS FOR YOUNG READERS—Marguerite de Angeli Prize, Doubleday BFYR, 1540 Broadway, New York, NY 10036. Offers a $1,500 cash prize and a $3,500 advance against royalties for middle-grade fiction that concerns the diversity of the American experience. Closes in June.

DRURY COLLEGE—Playwriting Contest, c/o Sandy Asher, Writer-in-Residence, 900 N. Benton Ave., Springfield, MO 65802. Original, unproduced, unpublished one-act plays are eligible for possible production, a $300 first prize, and two $150 honorable mentions. Closes in December of even-numbered years.

DUBUQUE FINE ARTS PLAYERS—One-Act Playwriting Contest, 569 S. Grandview Ave., Dubuque, IA 52003. Attn: Sally T. Ryan. Prizes of $300, $200, and $100, plus possible production are awarded for unproduced, original one-act plays of up to 40 minutes. Closes in January.

DUKE UNIVERSITY—Dorothea Lange-Paul Taylor Prize Committee, Ctr. for Documentary Studies, Box 90802, Duke Univ., Durham, NC 27708–0802. A grant of up to $10,000 is awarded to a writer and photographer working together in the formative stages of a documentary project that will ultimately result in a publishable work. Closes in January.

EIGHTH MOUNTAIN PRESS—Poetry Prize, 624 Southeast 29th Ave., Portland, OR 97214. A $1,000 advance plus publication is awarded for a poetry manuscript, 50 to 120 pages, by a woman writer. Closes in February of even-numbered years.

ELF: ECLECTIC LITERARY FORUM—Poetry Competition, P.O. Box 392, Tonawanda, NY 14150. Awards of $350, $150, and three $50 prizes are given for poems up to 60 lines. Closes in March.

ELMIRA COLLEGE—Elmira College Playwriting Award, Dept. of Theatre, Elmira College, Elmira, NY 14901. Attn: Prof. Amnon Kabatchnik, Artistic Dir. A prize of $1,000 plus production is awarded for the best original full-length play. Closes in June of even-numbered years.

EMPORIA STATE UNIVERSITY—The Bluestem Award, English Dept., Emporia State Univ., Emporia KS 66801–5087. Offers $1,000 plus publication for a previously unpublished book of poems by a U.S. author. Closes in March.

ENSEMBLE THEATRE—George Hawkins Play Contest, 3535 Main St., Houston, TX 77022. Offers $500 plus production for an original one-act play or musical for African-American audiences, ages 6 to 18. Closes in January.

FLORIDA STATE UNIVERSITY—World's Best Short Short Story Contest, English Dept., Florida State Univ., Tallahassee, FL 32306. Attn: Jerome Stern. A prize of $100, a box of Florida oranges, and publication is offered for the best short short story, 250 words. Closes in February.

FLORIDA STATE UNIVERSITY CREATIVE WRITING PROGRAM—
Richard Eberhart Prize in Poetry, English Dept., F.S.U., Tallahassee, FL 32306.
A $300 prize and publication in *Sun Dog: The Southeast Review*, is awarded for the
best unpublished poem of 30 to 100 lines. Closes in September.

FOUR WAY BOOKS—P.O. Box 607, Marshfield, MA 02050. The Intro
Series in Poetry offers a prize of $1,000 plus publication for a book-length collection
of poems by a poet who has not previously published a book of poetry. The Award
Series in Poetry offers a prize of $1,500 plus publication for a book-length collection
of poems by a poet who has published at least one collection of poetry. Each winner
also receives a two-week residency at the Cummington Community for the Arts.
Closes in April.

GALLERY PLAYERS—Playwriting Prize, The Leo Yassenoff Jewish Community of Greater Columbus, 1125 College Ave., Columbus, OH 43209. A $1,000
award, plus possible production, is offered for the best original, previously unproduced and unpublished full-length play; musicals are not eligible. Closes in September of odd-numbered years.

GLIMMER TRAIN PRESS—Northwest Short-Story Award for New Writers, 812 S.W. Washington St., #1205, Portland, OR 97205. A prize of $1,200 plus
publication is awarded for the best story, 1,200 to 6,000 words, by a writer whose
fiction has not appeared in a nationally distributed publication. Prizes of $500 and
$300 are also awarded. Closes in March.

GROLIER POETRY PRIZE—6 Plympton St., Cambridge, MA 02138. Two
$150 honorariums are awarded for poetry manuscripts of up to 10 pages by poets
who have not yet published a book of poems. Closes in April.

HEEKIN GROUP FOUNDATION—Fiction Fellowships Competition,
68860 Goodrich Rd., Sisters, OR 97759. Offers the $5,000 Tara Fellowship in Short
Fiction and the $10,000 James Fellowship for the Novel in Progress to writers who
have never published a novel, and have not published more than three short stories.
Closes in December.

HELICON NINE EDITIONS—9000 W. 64th Terrace, Merriam, KS 66202.
Attn: Gloria Vando Hickok. Offers the Marianne Moore Poetry Prize of $1,000 for
an original unpublished poetry manuscript of at least 50 pages, as well as the Willa
Cather Fiction Prize of $1,000 for an original fiction manuscript (novella or short
stories) from 150 to 300 pages. Both close in December.

HEMINGWAY SHORT STORY COMPETITION—Hemingway Days
Festival, P.O. Box 4045, Key West, FL 33041. A $1,000 first prize, and two $500
runner-up prizes are offered for short stories, 2,500 words or fewer, in any form or
style. Closes in July.

HIGHLIGHTS FOR CHILDREN—803 Church St., Honesdale, PA 18431.
Conducts children's short fiction contest, with three $1,000 prizes and publication
offered for stories, up to 900 words, on a chosen subject or category. Closes in
February.

HUMBOLDT STATE UNIVERSITY—Raymond Carver Short Story Con-
test, English Dept., Arcata, CA 95521–4957. Offers a $500 first prize, plus publica-
tion in the literary journal *Toyon*, and a $250 second prize for an unpublished short
story, to 25 pages, by a writer living in the U.S. Closes in November.

IOWA WOMAN MAGAZINE—Writing Contest for Women, P.O. Box
2938, Waterloo, IA 50704. Women writers may enter short fiction, essays, or poems
for a $300 first prize, $150 second prize, and publication. Closes in December.

IUPUI CHILDREN'S THEATRE—Playwriting Competition, Indiana Univ.-Purdue Univ. at Indianapolis, 525 N. Blackford St., Indianapolis, IN 46202–3120. Offers four $1,000 prizes plus staged readings for plays for young people. Closes in September of even-numbered years.

JEWISH COMMUNITY CENTER THEATRE IN CLEVELAND—Dorothy Silver Playwriting Competition, 3505 Mayfield Rd., Cleveland Heights, OH 44118. Attn: Elaine Rembrandt, Dir. Offers $1,000 and a staged reading for an original, previously unproduced full-length play, on some aspect of the Jewish experience. Closes in December.

THE CHESTER H. JONES FOUNDATION—National Poetry Competition, P. O. Box 498, Chardon, OH 44024. Offers more than $1,900 in cash prizes (including a $1,000 first prize) for original, unpublished poems, to 32 lines, by unpublished poets. Closes in March.

THE JOURNAL: THE LITERARY MAGAZINE OF O.S.U.—The Ohio State Univ. Press, 180 Pressey Hall, 1070 Carmack Rd., Columbus, OH 43210–1002. Attn: David Citino, Poetry Ed.. Awards $1,000 plus publication for at least 48 pages of original, unpublished poetry. Closes in September.

KALLIOPE—Sue Saniel Elkind Poetry Contest, Florida Community College at Jacksonville, 3939 Roosevelt Blvd., Jacksonville, FL 32205. Publication and $1,000 are awarded for the best poem, under 40 lines, written by a woman. Closes in November.

KEATS/KERLAN MEMORIAL FELLOWSHIP—The Ezra Jack Keats/Kerlan Collection Memorial Fellowship Committee, 109 Walter Library, 117 Pleasant St. S.E., Univ. of Minnesota, Minneapolis, MN 55455. A $1,500 fellowship is awarded to a talented writer and/or illustrator of children's books who wishes to use the Kerlan Collection to further his or her artistic development. Closes in May.

JACK KEROUAC LITERARY PRIZE—Lowell Historical Preservation Commission, 222 Merrimack St., Suite 310, Lowell, MA 01852. A $500 honorarium and festival reading is awarded for an unpublished work of fiction, nonfiction, or poetry relating to themes expressed in Kerouac's work. Closes in July.

MARC. A. KLEIN PLAYWRITING AWARD—Case Western Reserve Univ., Dept. of Theater Arts, 10900 Euclid Ave., Cleveland, OH 44106–7077. A $1,000 prize plus production is offered for an original, previously unproduced full-length play by a student currently enrolled at an American college or university. Closes in May.

LA JOLLA FESTIVAL—International Imitation Raymond Chandler Writing Competition, c/o Friends of the La Jolla Library, 3129 Bremerton Pl., La Jolla, CA 92037. Prizes of $700, $500, and $300 will be awarded for manuscripts, 500 words, that imitate or parody Raymond Chandler's writing style and subject matter. Closes in August.

LEGACIES—Writing Contest, 163 Amsterdam Ave., #107, New York, NY 10023. Awards prizes of $100 to $2,500 for stories by writers over 60. Closes in August.

LIGHT AND LIFE MAGAZINE—Writing Contest, P.O. Box 535002, Indianapolis, IN 46253–5002. Awards of up to $100 and possible publication for essays on Christian themes. Closes in April.

LINCOLN COLLEGE—Billee Murray Denny Poetry Award, Lincoln College, Lincoln, IL 62656. Attn: Janet Overton. Prizes of $1,000, $500, and $250 are offered for original, unpublished poems by poets who have never published a book of poetry. Closes in May.

LITTLE, BROWN, AND CO.—New Voices, New World Contest, 34 Beacon St., Boston, MA 02108. Writers from ethnic minority backgrounds, who have never published a children's book, are eligible to enter previously unpublished children's fiction in the categories of picture book, middle grade, and young adult, for a prize of $5,000 plus publication. Closes in September.

LIVE OAK THEATRE—New Play Awards, 311 Nueces St., Austin, TX 78701. Offers $1,000 each plus possible production for Best American Play and Best Play by a Texas Playwright for unproduced, unpublished, full-length scripts. Closes in November.

LODI ARTS COMMISSION—Drama Festival, 125 S. Hutchins St., Suite D, Lodi, CA 95240. Production plus $1,000 is awarded for a full-length play for adult audiences. Production plus $500 is awarded for a children's play. Closes in April of odd-numbered years.

LOVE CREEK PRODUCTIONS—Short Play Festival, 47 El Dorado Pl., Weehawken, NJ 07087–7004. At least 30 scripts, up to 40 minutes long, are chosen for festival performance; the winner receives a $300 prize. Closes in September.

AMY LOWELL POETRY TRAVELLING SCHOLARSHIP—Choate, Hall & Stewart, Exchange Pl., 53 State St., Boston, MA 02109–2891. Attn: F. Davis Dassori, Jr., Esq. Offers $29,000 to the winning poet to spend the year abroad to advance the art of poetry. Closes in October.

THE MADISON REVIEW—Dept. of English, Univ. of Wisconsin-Madison, Madison, WI 53706. Awards the $500 Felix Pollack Prize in Poetry for a group of three unpublished poems, and the $250 Chris O'Malley Prize in Fiction for an unpublished short story. Winners are published in *The Madison Review*. Closes in September.

MIDWEST RADIO THEATRE WORKSHOP—MRTW Script Contest, 915 E. Broadway, Columbia, MO 65201. Offers $800 in prizes, to be divided among two to four winners, for contemporary radio scripts, 15 to 56 minutes long. Winners also receive $200 scholarship to the annual MRTW conference. Closes in November.

MILKWEED EDITIONS—430 First Ave. N., Suite 400, Minneapolis, MN 55401–1743. The Milkweed National Fiction Prize awards $3,000 plus publication for a novel, novella, or collection of short fiction; open to writers who have previously published a book-length collection of fiction or at least three short stories or novellas in commercial or literary journals with national distribution. Closes in July. The Milkweed Prize for Children's Literature awards $3,000 plus publication for a children's novel or biography that embodies humane values and insights that contribute to cultural understanding; open to writers who have previously published a book-length collection of fiction or nonfiction for children or adults, or at least 3 short stories. Closes in March.

MILL MOUNTAIN THEATRE—New Play Competition, 2nd Floor, One Market Square, Roanoke, VA 24011–1437. Attn: Jo Weinstein, Lit. Mgr. Offers a $1,000 prize and staged reading, with possible full production, for unpublished, unproduced, full-length or one-act play. Cast size to ten. Closes in January.

THE MISSOURI REVIEW—Editors' Prize, 1507 Hillcrest Hall, UMC, Columbia, MO 65211. Publication plus $1,000 is awarded for short fiction and essay manuscripts, 25 pages, and $500 for the winning poetry manuscript, 10 pages. Closes in October.

THE MOUNTAINEERS BOOKS—The Barbara Savage/'Miles from Nowhere" Memorial Award, 1011 S. W. Klickitat Way, Suite 107, Seattle, WA 98134. Attn: Donna DeShazo, Dir. Offers a $3,000 cash award, plus publication and a $12,000 guaranteed advance against royalties for an outstanding unpublished, book-length manuscript of a nonfiction, personal-adventure narrative. Closes in February of even-numbered years.

MULBERRY PRESS—Poetry Prize, 105 Betty Rd., East Meadow, NY 11554–1601. Attn: Contest Chairperson. Offers $500 plus broadside publication for the best previously unpublished poem. Closes in March.

MULTICULTURAL PUBLISHERS EXCHANGE—Children's Book Award, 2215 Atwood Ave., Madison, WI 53204. A $2,000 advance and publication by Highsmith Press is awarded for a previously unpublished children's book, fiction or nonfiction, by an author or illustrator of African American, Hispanic American, Asian American, or Native American heritage. Closes in March.

NATIONAL ENDOWMENT FOR THE ARTS—Nancy Hanks Ctr., 1100 Pennsylvania Ave. N.W., Room 722, Washington, DC 20506. Attn: Dir., Literature Program. Offers fellowships to writers and translators of poetry, fiction, plays, and creative nonfiction. Deadlines vary; write for guidelines.

NATIONAL PLAY AWARD—630 N. Grand Ave., Suite 405, Los Angeles, CA 90012. The National Repertory Theatre Foundation offers a $7,500 first prize, plus five runner-up awards of $500 each, for an original, previously unproduced play. Closes in June of even-numbered years.

NATIONAL POETRY SERIES—Annual Open Competition, P.O. Box G, Hopewell, NJ 08525. Attn: The Coordinator. Five unpublished book-length poetry manuscripts are selected for publication. Closes in February.

NEGATIVE CAPABILITY MAGAZINE—62 Ridgelawn Dr. E., Mobile, AL 36608. Attn: Sue Walker. Sponsors the $1,000 Short Fiction Award for previously unpublished stories, 1,500 to 4,500 words. Closes in December. Also sponsors the Eve of St. Agnes Poetry Competition of $1,000 plus publication for an original, unpublished poem. Closes in January.

NEW DRAMATISTS—L. Arnold Weissberger Playwriting Competition, 424 W. 44th St., New York, NY 10036. Sponsors competition for full-length, unpublished, unproduced scripts; $5,000 is awarded to the winning playwright. Closes in May.

NEW ENGLAND POETRY CLUB—P.O. Box 81275, Wellesley Hills, MA 02181–0002. Attn: Pat Piscitelli. The NEPC sponsors contests for members and nonmembers, with prizes ranging from $100 to $500. Closes in June.

NEW ENGLAND THEATRE CONFERENCE—John Gassner Memorial Playwriting Award Competition, 50 Exchange St., Waltham, MA 02154. A $500 first prize and a $250 second prize are offered for unpublished and unproduced one-act plays. Closes in April.

NEW LETTERS—Univ. of Missouri-Kansas City, Kansas City, MO 64110. Offers $750 for the best short story, to 5,000 words; $750 for the best group of three to six poems; $500 for the best essay, to 5,000 words. The work of each winner and first runner-up will be published. Closes in May.

NEW YORK UNIVERSITY—Elmer Holmes Bobst Awards, Bobst Library,

New York Univ., 70 Washington Sq. S., New York, NY 10012. Attn: Rhonda Zangwill, Coord. Publication is awarded for book-length fiction (novel or short stories) and poetry manuscripts by writers who have not yet had a book published. Closes in April.

NIMROD/HARDMAN AWARDS—Arts and Humanities Council of Tulsa, 2210 S. Main St., Tulsa, OK 74114. Awards a $1,000 first prize and $500 second prize to winners of the Katherine Anne Porter Prize for Fiction (to 7,500 words) and the Pablo Neruda Prize for Poetry (one long poem, or a selection of poems). Closes in April.

NORTH CAROLINA WRITERS' NETWORK—Randall Jarrell Poetry Prize, 3501 Hwy. 54 W., Studio C, Chapel Hill, NC 27516. A $500 prize is awarded for a previously unpublished poem. Closes in November.

NORTHEASTERN UNIVERSITY PRESS—Samuel French Morse Poetry Prize, English Dept., 406 Holmes, Northeastern Univ., Boston, MA 02115. Guy Rotella, Chairman. Offers $500 plus publication for a full-length poetry manuscript by a U.S. poet who has published no more than one book of poems. August is the deadline for inquiries; contest closes in September.

NORTHERN KENTUCKY UNIVERSITY—Year End Series New Play Festival, Dept. of Theatre, Highland Hts., KY 41076. Attn: Joe Conger, Project Dir. Awards three $400 prizes plus production for previously unproduced full-length plays, one-acts, and musicals. Closes in November of even-numbered years.

NORTHERN MICHIGAN UNIVERSITY—Mildred & Albert Panowski Playwriting Competition, Forest Roberts Theatre, Northern Michigan Univ., Marquette, MI 49855–5364. Awards $2,000, plus production for an original, full-length, previously unproduced and unpublished play. Closes in November.

O. HENRY FESTIVAL, INC.—P.O. Box 29484, Greensboro, NC 27429. Publication plus a $1,000 first prize and a $500 second prize is awarded for short stories of under 5,000 words. Closes in August of even-numbered years.

OH!ZONE MAGAZINE—Project Oh!ZONE, 420 E. Hewitt Ave., Marquette, MI 49855. Prizes of $250 and $100 will be awarded for fiction and nonfiction, under 2,500 words, on a given theme, by writers not more than 24 years old. Closes in April.

O'NEILL THEATER CENTER—National Playwrights Conference, 234 W. 44th St., Suite 901, New York, NY 10036. Offers stipend, staged readings, and room and board at the conference, for new stage and television plays. Closes in December.

THE PARIS REVIEW—541 E. 72nd St., New York, NY 10021. Sponsors three annual prizes: The Aga Khan Prize for Fiction awards $1,000, plus publication, for a previously unpublished short story; closes in June. The Bernard F. Connors Prize awards $1,000, plus publication, for a previously unpublished poem; closes in May. The John Train Humor Prize awards $1,500, plus publication, for an unpublished work of humorous fiction, nonfiction, or poetry; closes in March.

PEN FUND FOR WRITERS AND EDITORS WITH AIDS—PEN American Ctr., 568 Broadway, New York, NY 10012. Attn: Joan Danlin. Grants of up to $1,000 are offered to published writers and editors with AIDS. Applications are reviewed every eight weeks. There is no deadline.

PEN/JERARD FUND AWARD—PEN American Ctr., 568 Broadway, New York, NY 10012. Attn: John Morrone, Programs & Publications. Offers $4,000 to beginning female writers for a work-in-progress of general nonfiction. Applicants must have published at least one article in a national magazine or major literary magazine, but not more than one book of any kind. Closes in January of odd-numbered years.

PEN WRITING AWARDS FOR PRISONERS—PEN American Ctr., 568 Broadway, New York, NY 10012. County, state, and federal prisoners are eligible to enter one published manuscript in each of four categories: poetry, fiction, drama, and nonfiction. Prizes of $100, $50, and $25 are awarded in each category. Closes in September.

PEOPLE'S VOICE PRESS—P.O. Box 318, Allentown, NJ 08501. Attn: Sonya Anne Monsen, Pub. Prizes of $1,000, $500, and five $50 prizes are awarded for poems on any subject, to 50 lines. Winning and other selected poems are anthologized. Closes in April and August.

PEREGRINE SMITH POETRY SERIES—Gibbs Smith, Publisher, P.O. Box 667, Layton, UT 84041. Offers a $500 prize plus publication for a previously unpublished 64-page poetry manuscript. Closes in April.

PETERLOO POETS OPEN COMPETITION—Peterloo Poets, c/o Administrator, 2 Kelly Gardens, Calstock, Cornwall PL18 9SA, U.K. A prize of 1,000 British pounds, plus publication is awarded for the best poem up to 40 lines. Prizes of 500, 300, 200, and 100 pounds are also given. Closes in February.

PIG IRON PRESS—Kenneth Patchen Competition, P.O. Box 237, Youngstown, OH 44501. Awards paperback publication, $100, and 50 copies of the winning manuscript of fiction (in even-numbered years) and poetry (in odd-numbered years). Closes in October.

PIRATE'S ALLEY FAULKNER PRIZES FOR FICTION—624 Pirate's Alley, New Orleans, LA 70116–3254. Prizes are $5,000 plus a possible $2,500 advance for unpublished novels of over 50,000 words; $1,500 plus a possible $1,000 advance for novellas of under 50,000 words; and $1,250 plus a possible $250 advance for short stories of under 20,000 words. Closes in April.

PLAYBOY MAGAZINE—College Fiction Contest, 680 N. Lakeshore Dr., Chicago, IL 60611. Sponsors college fiction contest, with first prize of $3,000 and publication, for a short story by a college student; second prize is $500. Closes in January.

PLAYHOUSE-ON-THE-SQUARE—Mid-South Playwriting Contest, 51 S. Cooper, Memphis, TN 38104. Mr. Jackie Nichols, Exec. Dir. A stipend plus production is awarded for a full-length, previously unproduced play or musical; Southern playwrights given preference. Closes in April.

THE PLAYWRIGHTS' CENTER—Jerome Fellowships, 2301 Franklin Ave. E., Minneapolis, MN 55406. Annually awards six emerging playwrights a $5,000 stipend and 12-month residency; housing and travel are not provided. Closes in November.

POCKETS MAGAZINE—Fiction Contest, P.O. Box 189, Nashville, TN 37202–0189. Attn: Lynn W. Gilliam, Assoc. Ed. A $1,000 prize goes to the author of the winning 1,000- to 1,600-word story for children in grades 1 to 6. Closes in September.

POET LORE—John Williams Andrews Narrative Poetry Competition, The Writer's Ctr., 4508 Walsh St., Bethesda, MD 20815. The writers of the best unpublished, original narrative poem to 100 lines, receives $350 plus publication. Closes in November.

POETRY SOCIETY OF AMERICA—15 Gramercy Park, New York, NY

10003. Conducts annual contests (the Celia B. Wagner Memorial Award, the John Masefield Memorial Award, the Elias Lieberman Student Poetry Award, the George Bogin Memorial award, the Robert H. Winner Memorial Award, and the Ruth Lake Memorial Award) for non-members in which cash prizes are offered for unpublished poems. Contests close in December.

EMILY POWELL LITERARY AWARDS—8F Hudson Harbour Dr., Poughkeepsie, NY 12601. Attn: Victor L. Gregurick. Prizes of $200, $150, $100, and $50 will be awarded for unpublished poems, up to 100 lines. Closes in July.

PRISM INTERNATIONAL—Short Fiction Contest, Creative Writing Dept., Univ. of B.C., E466–1866 Main Mall, Vancouver, B.C., V6T 1Z1. A $2,000 first prize and five $200 prizes are awarded for stories of up to 25 pages long. Winning stories are published in *Prism International*. Closes in December.

PURDUE UNIVERSITY PRESS—Verna Emery Poetry Award, 1532 South Campus Courts-B, W. Lafayette, IN 47907–1532. Unpublished collections of original poetry (60 to 90 pages) are considered for an award of $500 plus publication. Closes in January.

QUICK BROWN FOX PUBLISHERS—Short Story and Poetry Contest, Dept. TW, P.O. Box 7894, Athens, GA 30604–7894. Attn: Dr. Charles Connor. Prizes of $500 and $100 are awarded for stories of up to 3,000 words. A $100 prize is awarded for the best poem of up to 16 lines. Closes in February.

RANDOM HOUSE JUVENILE BOOKS—Dr. Seuss Picturebook Award, 225 Park Ave. S., New York, NY 10003. Offers $25,000 plus publication for a picturebook manuscript by an author/illustrator who has not published more than one book. Closes in December of even-numbered years.

RIVER CITY MAGAZINE—Writing Awards in Fiction, Dept. of English, Memphis State Univ., Memphis, TN 38152. Attn: Sharon Bryan, Ed. Awards a $2,000 first prize, plus publication, a $500 second prize, and a $300 third prize, for previously unpublished short stories, to 7,500 words. Closes in December.

THE H.G. ROBERTS FOUNDATION—Roberts Writing Awards, P.O. Box 1868, Pittsburg, KS 66762. Publication plus a $500 first prize, $200 second prize, $100 third prize, and $25 honorable mention are awarded in each category of poetry, short fiction, and informal essay. Closes in September.

ROGER WILLIAMS UNIVERSITY—Women Poets Series Competition, Ampersand Press, Creative Writing Program, School of Fine and Performing Arts, One Old Ferry Rd., Bristol, RI 02809–2921. Publication and $500 is awarded for a 48- to 64-page poetry manuscript by a women who has never published a book of poems. Poems previously published in magazines or journals are eligible. Closes in December.

IAN ST. JAMES AWARDS—c/o The New Writers' Club Ltd., P.O. Box 101, Tunbridge Wells, Kent TN4 8YD, England. Attn: Merric Davidson. Offers ten prizes of 350 to 5,000 British pounds for stories of 5,001 to 10,000 words, plus anthology publication. Also offers six prizes of 200 to 2,000 British pounds for stories of 2,000 to 5,000 words, plus publication. Closes in January.

ST. MARTIN'S PRESS/MALICE DOMESTIC CONTEST—Thomas Dunne Books, 175 Fifth Ave., New York, NY 10010. Offers publication plus a $10,000 advance against royalties, for Best First Traditional Mystery Novel. Closes in November.

ST. MARTIN'S PRESS/PRIVATE EYE NOVEL CONTEST—175 Fifth Ave., New York, NY 10010. Sponsored by Private Eye Writers of America and St.

Martin's Press. Winner receives publication plus $10,000 against royalties; open to previously unpublished writers of private eye novels. Closes in August.

SAN DIEGO POETS PRESS—American Book Series, P.O. Box 8638, La Jolla, CA 92038. For a first book of poetry, the winner receives $500 plus publication. Closes in July.

SIENA COLLEGE—International Playwrights' Competition, Fine Arts Dept., Siena College, Loudonville, NY 12211–1462. Offers $2,000 plus campus residency expenses for the winning full-length script; contemporary settings preferred; no musicals. Closes in June of even-numbered years.

SIERRA REPERTORY THEATRE—Taylor Playwriting Award, P. O. Box 3030, Sonora, CA 95370. Attn: Dennis Jones, Producing Dir. Offers $500, plus possible production, for full-length plays or musicals that have received no more than two productions or staged readings. Closes in August.

SMOKEBRUSH CENTER FOR ARTS AND THEATER—Festival of New Plays for Children, 235 S. Nevada, Colorado Springs, CO 80903. The winning previously unpublished, original children's play is professionally produced, and travel expenses are awarded for the winning playwright to view the production. Closes in February.

SOCIETY OF AMERICAN TRAVEL WRITERS—Lowell Thomas Travel Journalism Award, 1155 Connecticut Ave. N.W., Suite 500, Washington, DC 20036. Prizes total $11,000 for published travel articles and books as well as broadcasted travel pieces by U.S. and Canadian travel journalists. Closes in February.

SONS OF THE REPUBLIC OF TEXAS—Summerfield G. Roberts Award, 5942 Abrams Rd., Suite 222, Dallas, TX 75231. Offers $2,500 for published or unpublished creative writing (fiction, nonfiction, poetry) on the Republic of Texas (1836–1846). Closes in January.

SOUTH COAST POETRY JOURNAL—Annual Poetry Contest, English Dept., California State Univ. at Fullerton, Fullerton, CA 92634. Previously unpublished, original poems, to 40 lines, will be considered for prizes of $200, $100, and $50, plus publication. Closes in March.

SOUTHERN APPALACHIAN REPERTORY THEATRE—P.O. Box 620, Mars Hill, NC 28754–0620. Attn: Mrs. Jan W. Blalock. Invites writers of selected scripts to the Southern Appalachian Playwrights' Conference. All selected scripts are given readings and considered for full production. Closes in October.

THE SOW'S EAR PRESS—19535 Pleasant View Dr., Abingdon, VA 24210–6827. Sponsors annual Chapbook Competition: The prize is $500, plus 50 chapbook copies of the winning 24-page poetry manuscript; closes in April. Also sponsors a $500 poetry prize for the best poem; closes in October.

STAND MAGAZINE—Short Story Competition, 179 Wingrove Rd., Newcastle upon Tyne, NE4 9DA, U.K. Prizes totalling 2,250 British pounds are awarded for previously unpublished stories under 8,000 words. Winning stories are published in *Stand Magazine*. Closes in March of odd-numbered years.

STORY LINE PRESS—Nicholas Roerich Prize, 27006 Gap Rd., Three Oaks Farm, Brownsville, OR 97327–9718. Offers $1,000 plus publication for an original, unpublished book of poetry by a poet who has never published a book. Closes in October.

SUNY FARMINGDALE—The Paumanok Poetry Award, Visiting Writers

Series, Knapp Hall, SUNY Farmingdale, Farmingdale, NY 11735. Offers $750 for seven to ten poems. There is an entry fee. Closes in September.

SYNDICATED FICTION PROJECT—P.O. Box 15650, Washington, DC 20003. Offers $500 for rights to previously unpublished short stories, to 2,500 words, and $100 each time they appear in print. All selected stories are used on the Project's radio show, "The Sound of Writing." Closes in January.

SYRACUSE UNIVERSITY PRESS—John Ben Snow Prize, 1600 Jamesville Ave., Syracuse, NY 13244–5160. Attn: Dir. Awards a $1,500 advance, plus publication, for an unpublished book-length nonfiction manuscript about New York State, especially upstate or central New York. Closes in December.

TAKESHI KAIKO AWARD—Takeshi Kaiko Award Secretariat, c/o TBS Britannica Co., Ltd., Shuwa Sanbancho Bldg., 28–1 Sanbancho, Chiyoda-ku, Tokyo 102, Japan. Three million yen is awarded for a previously unpublished manuscript relating to the observation of human nature; fiction, nonfiction, reviews, or reports up to 80,000 are eligible. Closes in August.

TEN-MINUTE MUSICALS PROJECT—Box 461194, W. Hollywood, CA 90046. Michael Koppy, Producer. Musicals of 8 to 14 minutes are eligible for a $250 advance against royalties and musical anthology productions at theaters in the U.S. and Canada. Closes in August.

THEATRE MEMPHIS—New Play Competition, P.O. Box 240117, Memphis, TN 38124–0117. Conducts New Play Competition for a full-length play or related one-acts. The prize is $1,500 and production. Contest is held every three years. The next deadline is in July 1996.

THEATREWORKS—Playwrights' Forum Awards, Univ. of Colorado, P.O. Box 7150, Colorado Springs, CO 80933–7150. Attn: Whit Andrews, Producing Dir. Two unpublished, unproduced short plays are selected for production; playwrights are awarded $250 plus travel expenses. Closes in December.

THURBER HOUSE RESIDENCIES—The Thurber House, 77 Jefferson Ave., Columbus, OH 43215. Michael J. Rosen, Lit. Dir. Three-month residencies and stipends of $5,000 each will be awarded in the categories of writing, playwriting, and journalism. Winners have limited teaching responsibilities with The Ohio State Univ. Closes in December.

TOWNGATE THEATRE—Playwriting Contest, Oglebay Institute, Oglebay, Wheeling, WV 26003. Offers $300 plus production for an unproduced, full-length, non-musical play. Closes in January.

TRIQUARTERLY—Northwestern Univ., 2020 Ridge Ave., Evanston, IL 60208–4302. The William Goyen Prize for Fiction offers $3,000 plus publication for an unpublished novel, novella, or short story collection, 150 to 400 pages. Closes in June of odd-numbered years. The Terrence Des Pres Prize for Poetry offers $3,000 plus publication for unpublished poetry manuscripts, 48 to 64 pages. Closes in June of even-numbered years.

TRITON COLLEGE—Salute to the Arts Poetry Contest, 2000 Fifth Ave., River Grove, IL 60171–1995. Winning original, unpublished poems, to 60 lines, on designated themes, are published by Triton College. Closes in March.

U.S. NAVAL INSTITUTE—Arleigh Burke Essay Contest, *Proceedings Magazine*, 118 Maryland Ave., Annapolis, MD 21402–5035. Attn: Ed.-in-Chief. Awards $3,000, $2,000, and $1,000 plus publication, for essays on the advancement of professional, literary, or scientific knowledge in the naval or maritime services, and the advancement of the knowledge of sea power. Closes in December.

UNIVERSITY OF ALABAMA AT BIRMINGHAM—Ruby Lloyd Apsey Playwriting Competition, Dept. of Theatre and Dance, Univ. Sta., Birmingham, AL 35294–3340. Attn: Karma Ibsen, Dir. Awards a $500 prize, plus production and travel expenses, for a previously unproduced full-length play. Closes in December.

UNIVERSITY OF ARKANSAS PRESS—Arkansas Poetry Award, 201 Ozark Ave., Fayetteville, AR 72701. Awards a $500 advance and publication of a 50- to 80-page poetry manuscript to a writer who has never had a book of poetry published. Closes in May.

UNIVERSITY OF CALIFORNIA IRVINE—Chicano/Latino Literary Contest, Dept. of Spanish and Portuguese, UCI, Irvine, CA 92717. Attn: Juan Bruce-Novoa, Dir. A first prize of $2,000 plus publication, and prizes of $1,000 and $500 are awarded in alternating years for poetry, drama, novels, and short stories. Closes in April.

UNIVERSITY OF CENTRAL FLORIDA—Florida Poetry Contest, Sigma Tau Delta, Dept. of English, Univ. of Central Florida, Orlando, FL 32816. Attn: Jonathan Harrington. The National English Honor Society awards $500 for the best poem submitted. Closes in February.

UNIVERSITY OF COLORADO—Nilon Award for Excellence in Minority Fiction, Fiction Collective Two, English Dept. Publications Ctr., Campus Box 494, Boulder, CO 80309–0494. Awards $1,000 plus joint publication by Fiction Collective Two and CU-Boulder for original, unpublished, English Language, book-length fiction (novels, novellas, short story collections) by U.S. citizens of the following ethnic minorities: African-American, Hispanic, Asian, Native American, Alaskan Native, and Pacific Islander. Closes in November.

UNIVERSITY OF GEORGIA PRESS—Flannery O'Connor Award for Short Fiction, Athens, GA 30602. Offers two prizes of $1,000, plus publication, for a book-length collection of short fiction. Closes in July.

UNIVERSITY OF HAWAII AT MANOA—Kumu Kahua Playwriting Contest, Dept. of Drama and Theatre, 1770 East-West Rd., Honolulu, HI 96822. Awards $500 for a full-length play, and $200 for a one-act, set in Hawaii and dealing with some aspect of the Hawaiian experience. Also conducts contest for plays written by Hawaiian residents. Closes in January.

UNIVERSITY OF IOWA—Iowa Short Fiction Awards, Dept. of English, 308 English Philosophy Bldg., Iowa City, IA 52242–1492. Offers The John Simmons Short Fiction Award and the Iowa Short Fiction Award, each offering $1,000, plus publication, for an unpublished full-length collection of short stories (150 pages or more). Closes in September.

UNIVERSITY OF IOWA PRESS—The Iowa Poetry Prize, 119 W. Park Rd., 100 Kuhl House, Iowa City, IA 52242–1000. Two $1,000 prizes, plus publication, will be awarded for poetry manuscripts, 50 to 150 pages, by writers who have published at least one book of poetry. Closes in March.

UNIVERSITY OF MASSACHUSETTS PRESS—Juniper Prize, Amherst, MA 01003. Offers $1,000, plus publication, for a book-length manuscript of poetry; awarded in odd-numbered years to writers who have never published a book of poetry, and in even-numbered years to writers who have published a book or chapbook of poetry. Closes in September.

UNIVERSITY OF MISSOURI PRESS—Devins Award, 2910 LeMone Blvd., Columbia, MO 65201–8227. Mr. Clair Willcox, Poetry Ed. From the manuscripts accepted for publication in a given year, one outstanding collection is the recipient of the Devins Award. Submit four to six sample poems, table of contents for entire manuscript, and brief cover letter giving manuscript length and other appropriate information. Submissions accepted year-round.

UNIVERSITY OF NEBRASKA PRESS—North American Indian Prose Award, 327 Nebraska Hall, 901 N. 17th St., Lincoln, NE 68588–0520. Previously unpublished book-length manuscripts of biography, autobiography, history, literary criticism, and essays will be judged for originality, literary merit, and familiarity with North American Indian life. A $1,000 advance and publication are offered. Closes in July.

UNIVERSITY OF PITTSBURGH PRESS—127 N. Bellefield Ave., Pittsburgh, PA 15260. Sponsors Drue Heinz Literature Prize of $10,000, plus publication and royalty contract, for unpublished collection of short stories or novellas. Closes in August. Also sponsors the Agnes Lynch Starrett Poetry Prize of $2,500, plus publication in the Pitt Poetry Series, for a 48- to 100-page collection of poems by a poet who has not yet published a volume of poetry. Closes in April.

UNIVERSITY OF SOUTHERN CALIFORNIA—Ann Stanford Poetry Prize, Master of Professional Writing Program, WPH 404, Univ. of Southern California, Los Angeles, CA 90089–4034. Publication in *The Southern California Anthology* plus prizes of $750, $250, and $100 will be awarded; submit up to five poems. Closes in April.

UNIVERSITY OF WISCONSIN PRESS—Brittingham Prize in Poetry, Poetry Series, 114 N. Murray St., Madison, WI 53715. Attn: Ronald Wallace, Administrator. Offers $1,000, plus publication, for a previously unpublished manuscript, 50 to 80 pages. Closes in September.

THE UNTERBERG POETRY CENTER OF THE 92ND STREET Y—"Discovery"/*The Nation*, 1395 Lexington Ave., New York, NY 10128. Four prizes of $200, publication in *The Nation* Magazine, and a reading at the Poetry Center are offered for original 10-page manuscripts by poets who have not yet published a book of poetry. Closes in February.

VETERANS OF FOREIGN WARS—Voice of Democracy Audio Essay Competition, VFW National Headquarters, 406 W. 34th St., Kansas City, MO 64111. Several national scholarships totalling $88,500 are awarded to high school students for short tape-recorded essays. Themes change annually. Closes in November.

VILLA MONTALVO—Biennial Poetry Competition, P.O. Box 158, Saratoga, CA 95071. Residents of California, Nevada, Oregon, and Washington are eligible to enter poems in any style. Prizes are $1,000 plus an artist residency at Villa Montalvo, $500, and $300, as well as eight prizes of $25. Closes in October of odd-numbered years.

WAGNER COLLEGE—Stanley Drama Award, Dept. of Humanities, 631 Howard Ave., Staten Island, NY 10301. Awards $2,000 plus possible production for an original, previously unpublished and unproduced full-length play. Closes in September.

WASHINGTON PRIZE FOR FICTION—1301 S. Scott St., Arlington, VA 22204. Attn: Larry Kaltman, Dir. Offers $2,000, $1,000, and $500 for unpublished novels or short story collections, at least 65,000 words. Closes in November.

WHITE-WILLIS THEATRE—New Playwrights Contest, 5266 Gate Lake Rd., Ft. Lauderdale, FL 33319. Offers $500 plus production for an unpublished, unproduced full-length play. Closes in November.

TENNESSEE WILLIAMS FESTIVAL—Univ. of New Orleans Conference Services, Metro College-ED 122, New Orleans, LA 70148. A $1,000 prize plus a reading at the festival is offered for an original, unpublished one-act play on an American subject. Closes in January.

WORD WORKS—Washington Prize, P. O. Box 42164, Washington, DC 20015. Offers $1,000 plus publication for an unpublished volume of poetry by a living American poet. Closes in March.

WRITERS AT WORK—Fellowship Competition, P.O. Box 1146, Centerville, UT 84014–5146. Prizes of $1,500 plus publication, and $500, in fiction and poetry categories, are awarded for excerpts of unpublished short stories, novels, or poetry. Open to any writer who has not yet published a book-length volume of original work. Closes in March.

YALE UNIVERSITY PRESS—Yale Series of Younger Poets Competition, Box 92A, Yale Sta., New Haven, CT 06520. Attn: Ed.. The prize is publication for a book-length manuscript of poetry, written by a poet under 40 who has not yet published a volume of poems. Closes in February.

YOUNG PLAYWRIGHTS INC.—Young Playwrights Festival, 321 W. 44th St., Suite 906, New York, NY 10036. Playwrights under the age of 19 are eligible to submit scripts. Winning plays will be given festival production or staged readings. Closes in October.

WRITERS COLONIES

Writers colonies offer isolation and freedom from everyday distractions and a quiet place for writers to concentrate on their work. Though some colonies are quite small, with space for just three or four writers at a time, others can provide accommodations for as many as thirty or forty. The length of a residency may vary, too, from a couple of weeks to five or six months. Most of the following programs have strict admissions policies, and writers must submit a formal application or letter of intent, a resumé, writing samples, and letters of recommendation. As an alternative to the traditional writers colony, a few of the organizations listed offer writing rooms for writers who live nearby. Others operate as guest houses, offering a quiet atmosphere and renting rooms on a first-come basis to writers seeking working vacations. Write for application information first, enclosing a stamped, self-addressed envelope. Residency fees listed are subject to change.

THE EDWARD F. ALBEE FOUNDATION, INC.
14 Harrison St.
New York, NY 10013
(212) 266–2020
David Briggs, *Foundation Secretary*
    "The Barn," or the William Flanagan Memorial Creative Persons Center, on Long Island, is maintained by the Albee Foundation. "The standards for

admission are, simply, talent and need." Sixteen writers are accepted each season for one-month residencies, available from June 1 to October 1; applications, including writing samples, project description, and resumé, are accepted from January 1 to April 1. There is no fee, though residents are responsible for their own food and travel expenses.

ATLANTIC CENTER FOR THE ARTS
1414 Art Center Ave.
New Smyrna Beach, FL 32168
(904) 427–6975
Suzanne Fetscher, *Program Director*
The center is located on the east coast of central Florida, with 67 acres of pristine hammockland on a tidal estuary. All buildings, connected by raised wooden walkways, are handicapped accessible and air conditioned. The center provides a unique environment for sharing ideas, learning, and collaborating on interdisciplinary projects. Master artists meet with mid-career artists for readings and critiques, with time out for individual work. Residencies are three weeks. Fees are $600 for private room/bath; $200 for off-site (tuition only); financial aid is limited. Application deadlines vary.

BELLAGIO STUDY AND CONFERENCE CENTER
Program for Scholars and Artists in Residence
Bellagio Center Office
The Rockefeller Foundation
1133 Avenue of the Americas
New York, NY 10036
(212) 852–8431
Susan E. Garfield, *Coordinator*
Located on Lake Como in the Italian Alps, the Center offers 145 residencies annually to writers, artists, scholars, and scientists who expect their stay to result in publication, exhibition, or performance. Spouses may stay at no cost. Four- and five-week residencies, with free room and board, are available from February 1 to December 20. Residents must provide their own travel and other expenses. Some financial assistance is available. Apply 12 to 14 months prior to residency period. Applicants chosen on the basis of project description, resumé, one sample of published work, and up to three published reviews. Deadlines are March 1, June 1, September 1, and December 1.

BERLINER KUNSTLERPROGRAMM
Artists-in-Berlin Program
950 Third Ave.
New York, NY 10022
(212) 758–3223
Dr. Wedico de Vivanco, *Director*
One-year residencies are offered to well-known and emerging writers, painters, sculptors, and composers to promote cultural exchange. Up to 20 residencies are offered for periods beginning between January 1 and June 30. Room, board, travel, and living expenses are awarded. Residents may bring spouse and children. Application, project description, and copies of publications are due January 1 of the year preceding the residency.

BLUE MOUNTAIN CENTER
Blue Mountain Lake, NY 12812
(518) 352–7391
Harriet Barlow, *Director*
Hosts month-long residencies for artists and writers from mid-June to mid-October. Fiction and nonfiction writers of "fine work which evinces social

and ecological concern" are among the 14 residents accepted per session. Apply by sending a brief biographical sketch, a statement of your plan for work at Blue Mountain, five slides or approximately 10 pages of work, an indication of your preference for an early summer, late summer, or fall residence, and a $20 application fee; applications due February 1. There is no charge to residents for their time at Blue Mountain, although all visitors are invited to contribute to the studio construction fund. Brochure available upon request.

BYRDCLIFFE ARTS COLONY
Artists' Residency Program
Woodstock Guild
34 Tinker St.
Woodstock, NY 12498
(914) 679–2079

The Villetta Inn, located on the 600-acre arts colony, offers private rooms, a communal kitchen, and a peaceful environment for fiction writers, poets, playwrights, visual artists, and craftspeople. Residencies from one to four months are offered from June to September. Fees are $400 to $500 per month; limited financial assistance available. Submit application, resumé, writing sample, reviews, and references; the deadline is mid-April.

CAMARGO FOUNDATION/CASSIS, FRANCE
c/o 64 Main St.
Box 32
East Haddam, CT 06423
Attn: Jane M. Viggiani

The Camargo Foundation offers academics, writers, artists, and composers the opportunity to complete a work-in-progress. Residents are provided a furnished apartment with equipped kitchen on property belonging to the Foundation in the town of Cassis, France. Minimum residency is three months; terms are September to December, or January to May. There are no fees. Applicants chosen on the basis of writing sample, project description, resumé, and three letters of recommendation. Applications due March 1.

CENTRUM
P.O. Box 1158
Port Townsend, WA 98368
(206) 385–3102
Sarah Muirhead, *Program Coordinator*

Centrum sponsors month-long residencies at Fort Worden State Park, a Victorian fort on the Strait of Juan De Fuca in Washington. The program "provides a working retreat for selected artists to create, without distractions, in a beautiful setting." Nonfiction, fiction, and poetry writers may apply for residency awards, which include housing and a $75 a week stipend. Families are welcome, but no separate working space is provided. Application deadlines: October 1 and April 1.

CHATEAU DE LESVAULT
Writers Retreat Program
Onlay
58370 Villapourcon
France
(33) 86–84–32–91
Bibbi Lee, *Director*

This French country residence is located in western Burgundy, in the national park of Le Morvan. Five large rooms, fully equipped for living and

830

working, are available October through April, for one month or longer. Residents in this small artists' community have access to the entire chateau, including the salon, library, and grounds. The fee is 4,500 francs per month, for room, board, and utilities. Applications handled on a first-come basis.

COTTAGES AT HEDGEBROOK
2197 E. Millman Rd.
Langley, WA 98260
(206) 321–4786
Attn: *Director*

Cottages at Hedgebrook provides for women writers, published or not, of all ages and from all cultural backgrounds, a natural place to work. Established in 1988, the retreat is part of Hedgebrook Farm, thirty acres of farmland and woods located on Whidbey Island in Washington State. Each writer has her own cottage, equipped with electricity and woodstove; one cottage is wheelchair accessible. A bathhouse serves all six cottages. Writers gather for dinner in the farmhouse every evening and frequently read in the living room/library afterwards. Limited travel scholarships are available. Residencies range from one week to three months. April 1 is the application deadline for residencies from July 1 to December 10; October 1 for January 11 to June 14. Applicants are chosen by a selection committee composed of writers.

CUMMINGTON COMMUNITY OF THE ARTS
RR#1, Box 145
Cummington, MA 01026
(413) 634–2172
Kirk Stephens, *Executive Director*

Artists of all disciplines use private living spaces and studios in residencies ranging from two weeks to three months, on 110 acres in the Berkshires. Open April through October. Artists with children are encouraged to apply for stays during July and August, when there is a children's program with supervised activities. Fees are $650 to $700 per month (children extra); financial aid and work exchange available. Application deadlines: April 1 for June, July, and August residencies; otherwise, two months prior to month of residency.

CURRY HILL/GEORGIA
c/o 404 Crestmont Ave.
Hattiesburg, MS 39401
(601) 264–7034
Mrs. Elizabeth Bowne, *Director*

This retreat for eight fiction and nonfiction writers is offered for one week each spring (March 20–26, 1994) by writer/teacher Elizabeth Bowne. "I care about writers and am delighted and enthusiastic when I can help develop talent." A $400 fee covers meals and lodging at Curry Hill, a family plantation home near Bainbridge, Georgia. Applications should be sent in early January; qualified applicants accepted on a first-come basis.

DJERASSI RESIDENT ARTISTS PROGRAM
2325 Bear Gulch Rd.
Woodside, CA 94062–4405
(415) 851–8395
Attn: *Executive Director*

The Djerassi Program offers room, board, and work spaces in a rural, isolated setting to writers, visual artists, choreographers, and composers seeking undisturbed time for creative work. Residencies are usually one month; 45 artists are accepted each year. There are no fees, other than the $20 application

831

fee. Applications, with resumé and documentation of recent creative work, are due February 15.

DORLAND MOUNTAIN ARTS COLONY
Box 6
Temecula, CA 92593
(909) 676–5039
Attn: *Admissions Committee*

Dorland is a nature preserve and "primitive retreat for creative people" located in the Palomar Mountains of Southern California. "Without electricity, residents find a new, natural rhythm for their work." Novelists, playwrights, poets, nonfiction writers, composers, and visual artists are encouraged to apply for residencies of two weeks to two months. Fee of $150 a month includes cottage, fuel, and firewood. Application deadlines are March 1 and September 1.

DORSET COLONY HOUSE
Box 519
Dorset, VT 05251
(802) 867–2223
John Nassivera, *Director*

Writers and playwrights are offered low-cost room with kitchen facilities at the historic Colony House in Dorset, Vermont. Residencies are one week to two months, and are available between September 15 and June 1. Applications are accepted year round, and up to eight writers stay at a time. The fee is $75 per week; financial aid is limited. For more information, send SASE.

FINE ARTS WORK CENTER IN PROVINCETOWN
P.O. Box 565
24 Pearl St.
Provincetown, MA 02657
John Skoyles, *Executive Director*

Fellowships, including living and studio space and monthly stipends, are available at the Fine Arts Work Center on Cape Cod, for writers to work independently. Residencies are for seven months (October to May); apply before February 1 deadline. Eight first-year fellows and two second-year fellows are accepted. Send SASE for details.

THE GELL WRITERS CENTER
Writers & Books
740 University Ave.
Rochester, NY 14607
(716) 473–2590
Joe Flaherty, *Director*

The Center, on Canandaigua Lake, is found in the Finger Lakes region of New York, and includes 24 acres of woodlands. Two separate living quarters, with private bath and work area, are available for $35 per night. All serious writers are welcome; reservations made on a first-come basis.

GLENESSENCE WRITERS COLONY
1447 W. Ward Ave.
Ridgecrest, CA 93555
(619) 446–5894
Allison Swift, *Director*

Glenessence is a luxury villa located in the Upper Mojave Desert, offering private rooms with bath, pool, spa, courtyard, shared kitchen, fitness center, and library. Children, pets, and smoking are prohibited. Residencies are offered at $565 per month; meals are not provided. Reservations made on a first-come basis.

THE GUTHRIE CENTRE
Annaghmakerrig, Newbliss
County Monaghan
Ireland
Bernard Loughlin, *Director*
 Set on a 400-acre country estate, the Tyrone Guthrie Centre offers peace and seclusion to writers and other artists to enable them to get on with their work. All art forms are represented. One- to three-month residencies are offered throughout the year, at the rate of 1,000 to 1,350 Irish pounds per month, depending on the season; financial assistance available to Irish citizens only. A number of longer term self-catering houses in the old farmyard are also available at 150 pounds per week. Writers may apply for acceptance year round.

THE HAMBIDGE CENTER
P.O. Box 339
Rabun Gap, GA 30568
(706) 746–5718
Judy Barber, *Director*
 The Hambidge Center for Creative Arts and Sciences is located on 600 acres of quiet woods in the north Georgia mountains. Seven private cottages are available for fellows, who are asked to contribute about $125 per week. Two-week to two-month residencies, from May to October, and limited winter residencies are offered to serious artists from all disciplines. Send SASE for application form. Application reviews begin in March.

HAWTHORNDEN CASTLE INTERNATIONAL RETREAT FOR WRITERS
Hawthornden Castle
Lasswade, Midlothian EH18 1EG
Scotland
031–440–2180
Attn: *Administrator*
 Hawthornden Castle stands on a secluded crag overlooking the valley of the River North Esk. The retreat provides a peaceful setting where creative writers can work without disturbance. The castle houses five writers at a time, and is open ten months out of the year. Writers from any part of the world may apply for full fellowships. Application forms due September 15 for residencies in the following year.

HOMESTEAD GUEST HOUSE
P.O. Box 343
Town Hall Rd.
Beloit, WI 53511
(608) 362–8055
Rolf Lund, *Proprietor*
 The Homestead is located on farmland in southern Wisconsin and is run by three working artists. A two-bedroom cottage and private guest rooms are available for rent at $35 a night; meals are not provided. Reserve at least one week in advance.

KALANI HONUA
Artist-in-Residence Program
RR#2, Box 4500
Pahoa-Kalapana, HI 96778
Michael Fleck, *Program Coordinator*
　　Located in a coastal country setting of 20 botanical acres, Kalani Honua "provides participants with quality educational programs and the aloha experience that is its namesake: harmony of heaven and earth." Residencies range from two weeks to two months and are available throughout the year. Fees range from $26 to $85 per day, depending on accommodations; fee subsidies are available. Applications accepted year round.

LEIGHTON STUDIOS
The Banff Centre
Box 1020-Station 22
Banff, Alberta T0L 0C0
Canada
(403) 762–6180
Susan Adams, *Registrar*
　　Located at the Banff Centre's inspirational Rocky Mountain setting, Banff National Park, the colony provides time and space for artists to produce new work. Residencies last from one week to three months. Applicants are accepted on the basis of project description, resumé, reviews, and writing samples. Three writing studios, and three writing/composing studios are available. Fee is $62 to $83 per day; discounts available for those who demonstrate need. Apply at least six months in advance of desired dates or residencies.

THE MACDOWELL COLONY
100 High St.
Peterborough, NH 03458
(603) 924–3886
Pat Dodge, *Admissions Coordinator*
　　Studios, room, and board at the MacDowell Colony of Peterborough, New Hampshire, are available for writers to work without interruption in a woodland setting. Selection is competitive. Apply by January 15 for stays May through August; April 15 for September through December; and September 15 for January through April. Residencies last up to eight weeks, and 80 to 90 writers are accepted each year. Send SASE for application form.

THE MILLAY COLONY FOR THE ARTS
Steepletop
P.O. Box 3
Austerlitz, NY 12017–0003
(518) 392–3103
Gail Giles, *Assistant Director*
　　At Steepletop in Austerlitz, New York (former home of Edna St. Vincent Millay), studios, living quarters, and meals are provided to writers at no cost. Residencies are for one month. Application deadlines are February 1, May 1, and September 1. Send SASE for more information and an application form.

MISHKENOT SHA'ANANIM
P.O. Box 8215
Jerusalem 91081
Israel
972-2-254–321
　　A 19th century retreat outside the Old City Walls of Jerusalem serves as a place for writers, artists, and scientists to exchange ideas with their Israeli

counterparts. Private room, studio, and apartment are available; write for details. Resumé, references, and project description required. Applications are accepted year round.

MOLASSES POND WRITERS' RETREAT AND WORKSHOP
RR#1, Box 85C
Milbridge, ME 04658
(207) 546–2506
Martha Barron Barrett and Sue Wheeler, *Coordinators*
   Led by writing teachers from the University of New Hampshire, the workshop is one week in June and includes time set aside for writing, as well as manuscript critique and writing classes. Up to nine writers stay in five lakeside cottages with private work space and kitchen. Classes and communal dinner held in the main lodge. The $300 fee covers lodging, dinners, and workshops; scholarships available to Maine residents. Submit statement of purpose, resumé, and writing samples; no children's literature or poetry. The application deadline is May 1.

THE N.A.L.L. ASSOCIATION
232, Boulevard de Lattre
06140 Vence
France
(33) 93–58-13–26
   The international center for writers and artists is located on eight acres of the Mediterranean village of Vence. Residents stay in cottages equipped with kitchen, bath, and private garden. One afternoon a week is set aside for residents to discuss their work with local artists over tea. Cottages are rented by the month to members of the N.A.L.L. (Nature, Art, and Life League); membership is 500 francs per year. Meals are not included. Submit resumé, writing sample, and project description. Applications accepted year round.

THE NORTHWOOD UNIVERSITY
Alden B. Dow Creativity Center
3225 Cook Rd.
Midland, MI 48640–2398
(517) 837–4478
Carol B. Coppage, *Director*
   The Fellowship Program allows individuals time away from their ongoing daily routines to pursue their project ideas without interruption. A project idea should be innovative, creative, and have potential for impact in its field. Four ten-week residencies, lasting from mid-June to mid-August, are awarded yearly. There are no fees and a modest stipend is provided. No spouses or families. Applications are due December 31.

PALENVILLE INTERARTS COLONY
2 Bond St.
New York, NY 10012
(518) 678–3332
Joanna Sherman, *Artistic Director*
   Support is provided for artists of the highest calibre in all disciplines, either working alone or in groups. The admissions panel is interested in interartistic collaboration and intercultural projects. Residencies last from one to eight weeks, and fees range from $125 to $260 per week; scholarships are available. About 50 applicants are accepted for May through October season. Applications due in April; send SASE for details.

RAGDALE FOUNDATION
1260 N. Green Bay Rd.
Lake Forest, IL 60045
(708) 234–1063
Michael Wilkerson, *Director*

Uninterrupted time and peaceful space allow writers a chance to finish works in progress, to begin new works, to solve thorny creative problems, and to experiment in new genres. Located in Lake Forest, Illinois, 30 miles north of Chicago, on 40 acres of prairie. Residencies from two weeks to two months are available for writers, artists, and composers. Fee is $10 per day; some full and partial fee waivers available, based solely on financial need. Send SASE for deadline information. Late applications considered when space is available. Application fee: $20.

SASKATCHEWAN WRITERS' GUILD
Artists Colonies and Retreats
P.O. Box 3986
Regina, Saskatchewan S4P 3R9
Canada
(306) 757–6310

Colonies are at two locations: St. Peter's Abbey, near Muenster, provides month-long retreats year round, as well as a summer colony, with two- to eight-week residencies available; and Emma Lake, near Prince Albert, is the site of a two-week residency in August. The $100 per week fee includes room and board. Submit application form, resumé, project description, references, and writing samples. Saskatchewan residents are given preference. The deadline is April 1 for the St. Peter's summer colony; otherwise, apply three weeks in advance of starting date.

THE JOHN STEINBECK ROOM
Long Island University
Southampton Campus Library
Southampton, NY 11968
(516) 287–8379
Robert Gerbereux, *Library Director*

The John Steinbeck Room at Long Island University provides a basic research facility to writers who have either a current contract with a book publisher or a confirmed assignment from a magazine editor. Use of the room is for a period of six months with one six-month renewal permissible. Send SASE for application.

SYVENNA FOUNDATION
Rte. 1, Box 193
Linden, TX 75563
(903) 835–8252
Barbara Carroll, *Associate Director*

Our purpose is to offer beginning and intermediate women writers the time and space to devote themselves totally to their work. Private cottages with work space, located in the piney woods of Northeast Texas, are provided at no cost; writers receive stipend of $300 per month, and writers are responsible for their personal needs. Residencies last two to three months; eight writers accepted per year. Application deadlines: April 1 for fall residency; August 1, winter; October 1, spring; December 1, summer.

836

THE THURBER HOUSE RESIDENCIES
c/o Thurber House
77 Jefferson Ave.
Columbus, OH 43215
(614) 464–1032
Michael J. Rosen, *Literary Director*
Residencies in the restored home of James Thurber are awarded to journalists, writers, and playwrights. Residents work on their own writing projects, and in addition to other duties, teach one class at The Ohio State University. A stipend of $5,000 per quarter is provided. A letter of interest and resumé must be received by December 15.

UCROSS FOUNDATION
Residency Program
2836 U.S. Hwy. 14–16 East
Clearmont, WY 82835
(307) 737–2291
Elizabeth Guheen, *Executive Director*
Residencies, two to eight weeks, in the foothills of the Big Horn Mountains in Wyoming, allow writers, artists, and scholars to concentrate on their work without interruption. Two residency sessions are scheduled annually: February to May and August to December. There is no charge for room, board, or studio space. Application deadlines are March 1 for fall session and October 1 for spring session. Send SASE for more information.

VALLECITOS RETREAT
P.O. Box 226
Vallecitos, NM 87581
(505) 582–4226
Elizabeth Esquer and Gina Covina, *Proprietors*
The retreat, open October through May, is in an adobe house surrounded by gardens and pastureland, 70 miles north of Santa Fe. Private rooms include writing space; bath, kitchen, living room, and library are communal. Minimum stay is two nights, and weekly rentals are available. Fees are $30 per night; $160 per week; and $400 per month; meals extra. Reserve at least one week in advance.

VERMONT STUDIO CENTER
P.O. Box 613NW
Johnson, VT 05656
(802) 635–2727
Attn: *Registrar*
The Vermont Studio Center offers two-week writing studio sessions led by prominent writers/teachers focusing on the craft of writing. Independent writers' retreats are also available year round for those wishing more solitude. Room, working studio, and meals are included in all programs. Work-exchange fellowships are available. Applications are accepted year-round. Send SASE for more information.

VILLA MONTALVO ARTIST RESIDENCY PROGRAM
P.O. Box 158
Saratoga, CA 95071
(408) 741–3421
Lori A. Wood, *Program Manager*
Villa Montalvo, in the foothills of the Santa Cruz Mountains south of San

Francisco, offers one- to three-month, free residencies to writers and artists. Several merit-based fellowships available. September 1 and March 1 are the application deadlines. Send SASE for application forms.

VIRGINIA CENTER FOR THE CREATIVE ARTS
Sweet Briar, VA 24595
(804) 946–7236
William Smart, *Director*

A working retreat for writers, composers, and visual artists in Virginia's Blue Ridge Mountains. Residencies from one week to three months are available year round. Application deadlines are the 25th of January, May, and September; about 300 residents are accepted each year. A limited amount of financial assistance is available. Send SASE for more information.

THE WRITERS ROOM
153 Waverly Pl., 5th Floor
New York, NY 10014
(212) 807–9519
Renata Miller, *Executive Director*

Located in Greenwich Village, The Writers Room provides "highly subsidized work space to all types of writers at all stages of their careers. We offer urban writers a quiet, benevolent oasis, a place to escape from noisy neighbors, children, roommates, and other distractions of city life." The Room holds 24 desks separated by partitions, a smokers room with four desks, a kitchen, library, and lounge. Open 24 hours a day, 365 days a year. Fee is $165 quarter; several scholarships are available.

THE WRITERS STUDIO
The Mercantile Library Association
17 E. 47th St.
New York, NY 10017
(212) 755–6710
Harold Augenbraum, *Director*

The Studio is a business-like place in which writers can rent quiet space conducive to the production of good work. A carrel, locker, small reference collection, electrical outlets, and membership in The Mercantile Library of New York are available at the cost of $200 per three-month residency. Submit application, resumé, and writing samples; applications considered year round.

HELENE WURLITZER FOUNDATION OF NEW MEXICO
Box 545
Taos, NM 87571
(505) 758–2413
Henry A. Sauerwein, Jr., *Executive Director*

Rent-free and utility-free studios at the Helene Wurlitzer Foundation in Taos, New Mexico, are offered to creative writers and artists in all media. "All artists are given the opportunity to be free of the shackles of a 9-to-5 routine." Length of residency varies from three to six months. The Foundation is open from April 1 to September 30.

YADDO
Box 395
Saratoga Springs, NY 12866–0395
(518) 584–0746
Attn: *Admissions Committee*

Visual artists, writers, choreographers, dancers, composers, and collaborators are invited for stays from two weeks to two months. Room, board, and studio space are provided. Voluntary payment of $20 a day is suggested. No artist deemed worthy of admission by the judging panels will be denied admission on the basis of an inability to contribute. Deadlines are January 15 and August 1. Send SASE for application. An application fee of $20 is required.

WRITERS CONFERENCES

Each year, hundreds of writers conferences are held across the country. The following list, arranged geographically, represents a sampling of conferences; each listing includes the location of the conference, the month during which it is usually held, and the name of the person from whom specific information may be received. Additional conferences are listed annually in the May issue of *The Writer* Magazine (120 Boylston St., Boston, MA 02116–4615).

ALABAMA

WRITING TODAY—Birmingham, AL. April. Write Martha Andrews, BSC A-3, Birmingham Southern College, Birmingham, AL 35254.

ALASKA

SITKA SYMPOSIUM ON HUMAN VALUES AND THE WRITTEN WORD—Sitka, AK. June. Write Carolyn Servid, Island Inst., Box 2420, Sitka, AK 99835.

ALASKA ADVENTURE IN TRAVEL WRITING—Juneau, AK. June. Write Mike Miller, P.O. Box 21494, Juneau, AK 99802.

ARIZONA

PIMA WRITERS' WORKSHOP—Tucson, AZ. June. Write Meg Files, Dir., Pima College, 2202 W. Anklam Rd., Tucson, AZ 85709.

13TH ANNUAL ARIZONA CHRISTIAN WRITERS CONFERENCE—Phoenix, AZ. November. Write Reg Forder, Dir., P.O. Box 5168, Phoenix, AZ 85010.

AMERICAN MEDICAL WRITERS ASSOCIATION ANNUAL CONFERENCE—Phoenix, AZ. November. Write Lillian Sablack, Dir., AMWA, 9650 Rockville Pike, Bethesda, MD 20814.

ARKANSAS

OZARK CREATIVE WRITERS, INC.—Eureka Springs, AR. October. Write Peggy Vining, Dir., 6817 Gingerbread Ln., Little Rock, AR 72204.

ANNUAL WRITERS CONFERENCE—Los Angeles, CA. January. Write Alexandra Cantor, Dir., American Society of Journalists & Authors, Inc., 1501 Broadway, #302, New York, NY 10036.

REMEMBER THE MAGIC—San Diego, CA. January. Write Hannelore Hahn, Dir., IWWG, P.O. Box 810, Gracie Station, New York, NY 10028.

CHAPMAN UNIVERSITY'S ADVANCED SCREENWRITING WORK-SHOP—Orange, CA. January. Send SASE to Mark Axelrod, Dir., Chapman University, Wilkinson Hall 227, Orange, CA 92666.

SANTA BARBARA BOOK PUBLISHING WORKSHOP—Santa Barbara, CA. January, May, August, November. Write Dan Poynter, P.O. Box 4232–196, Santa Barbara, CA 93140.

25TH ANNUAL MOUNT HERMON CHRISTIAN WRITERS CONFER-ENCE—Mount Hermon, CA. March. Write David R. Talbott, Dir., Mount Hermon Assn., Inc., P.O. Box 413, Mount Hermon, CA 95041.

WRITERS' FORUM—Pasadena, CA. March. Write Meredith Brucker, Dir., 1570 E. Colorado Blvd., Pasadena, CA 91106–2003.

12TH ANNUAL IWWG SPRING IN CALIFORNIA CONFERENCE—Sonoma, CA. March. Write Hannelore Hahn, Dir., IWWG, P.O. Box 810, Gracie Station, New York, NY 10028.

"HOW TO GET AND STAY PUBLISHED"—Fresno, CA. April. Write Nannette Potter, Writer's International Network, P.O. Box 26568, Fresno, CA 93729–6568.

"WRITE TO BE READ" WORKSHOP—Hume Lake, CA. July. Write Norman B. Rohrer, 260 Fern Ln., Hume Lake, CA 93628.

GENE PERRET'S ROUND TABLE COMEDY WRITERS CONVEN-TION—Palm Springs, CA. July. Write Linda Perret, Dir., 2135 Huntington Dr., #205, San Marino, CA 91108.

CALIFORNIA WRITERS' CONFERENCE—Pacific Grove, CA. July. Write California Writers' Club, 2214 Derby St., Berkeley, CA 94705.

WRITERS AND ILLUSTRATORS CONFERENCE IN CHILDREN'S LITERATURE—Marina Del Rey, CA. August. Write Lin Oliver, Dir., SCBWI, 22736 Vanowen St., Suite 106, West Hills, CA 91307.

NAPA VALLEY WRITERS' CONFERENCE—Napa, CA. August. Write John Leggett, Dir., Napa Valley Writers' Conference, Napa Valley College, 2277 Napa-Vallejo Hwy., Napa, CA 94558.

COLORADO

COLORADO CHRISTIAN WRITERS CONFERENCE—Boulder, CO. March. Write Debbie Barker, Dir., Box 3303, Lyons, CO 80540.

1994 SUMMER CONFERENCE—Denver, CO. June. Write Sandy Whelchel, Dir., National Writers Club, 1450 S. Havana, Suite 424, Aurora, CO 80012.

STEAMBOAT SPRINGS WRITERS CONFERENCE—Steamboat Springs, CO. August. Write Harriet Freiberger, Dir., P.O. Box 774284, Steamboat Springs, CO 80477.

COLORADO GOLD CONFERENCE—Denver, CO. September. Write Pat MacMillan, Rocky Mountain Fiction Writers, P.O. Box 260244, Denver, CO 80226–0244.

CONNECTICUT

WESLEYAN WRITERS CONFERENCE—Middletown, CT. June. Write Anne Greene, Dir., Wesleyan Writers Conference, Wesleyan University, Middletown, CT 06459.

FLORIDA

12TH ANNUAL KEY WEST LITERARY SEMINAR—Key West, FL. January. Write Monica Haskell, Dir., Key West Literary Seminar, 419 Petronia St., Key West, FL 33040.

CHRISTIAN WRITERS' CONFERENCE—Orlando, FL. February. Write Dottie McBroom, Dir., Christian Writers Inst., 177 E. Crystal Lake Ave., Lake Mary, FL 32746.

SOUTHWEST FLORIDA WRITERS' CONFERENCE—Fort Myers, FL. February. Write Joanne Hartke, Dir., Edison Community College, P.O. Box 06210, Fort Myers, FL 33906–6210.

ANNUAL FLORIDA STATE WRITERS CONFERENCE—Orlando, FL. May. Write Dana K. Cassell, Dir., Florida Freelance Writers Assn., Maple Ridge Rd., N. Sandwich, NH 03259.

14TH ANNUAL SPACE COAST WRITERS CONFERENCE—Cocoa Beach, FL. November. Write Dr. Edwin J. Kirschner, Pres., Space Coast Writers Guild, Box 804, Melbourne, FL 32902.

GEORGIA

CURRY HILL PLANTATION WRITER'S RETREAT—Bainbridge, GA. March. Write Elizabeth Bowne, Dir., 404 Crestmont Ave., Hattiesburg, MS 39401.

SANDHILLS WRITERS' CONFERENCE—Augusta, GA. May. Write Maxine Allen, Augusta College, Cont. Ed. Dept., Augusta, GA 30910.

SOUTHEASTERN WRITERS CONFERENCE—St. Simons Island, GA. June. Write Pat Laye, Rt. 1, Box 102, Cuthbert, GA 31740.

HARRIETTE AUSTIN WRITERS CONFERENCE—Athens, GA. July. Write Jack Huff, University of Georgia, Ctr. for Cont. Ed., Athens, GA 30602.

MOONLIGHT AND MAGNOLIAS WRITER'S CONFERENCE—Atlanta, GA. October. Write Ellen Taber, Dir., 530 Saddle Creek Cir., Roswell, GA 30076.

ILLINOIS

46TH ANNUAL CHRISTIAN WRITERS' CONFERENCE—Wheaton, IL. June. Write Dottie McBroom, Christian Writers' Inst., 177 E. Crystal Lake Ave., Lake Mary, FL 32746.

MISSISSIPPI VALLEY WRITERS CONFERENCE—Rock Island, IL. June. Write David R. Collins, Dir., 3403 45th St., Moline, IL 61265.

AUTUMN AUTHORS' AFFAIR XII—Lisle, IL. October. Write Nancy McCann, Dir., Love Designers/Rendezvous, 1507 Burnham Ave., Calumet City, IL 60409.

INDIANA

MIDWEST WRITERS WORKSHOP—Muncie, IN. July. Write Dr. Earl L. Conn, Dir., Dept. of Journalism, Ball State University, Muncie, IN 47306.

IOWA

IOWA SUMMER WRITING FESTIVAL—Iowa City, IA. June, July. Write Peggy Houston, Dir., University of Iowa, 116 International Ctr., Iowa City, IA 52242.

KANSAS

WRITERS WORKSHOP IN SCIENCE FICTION—Lawrence, KS. July. Write James Gunn, Dir., English Dept., University of Kansas, Lawrence, KS 66045.

KENTUCKY

GREEN RIVER NOVELS-IN-PROGRESS WORKSHOP—Louisville, KY. January. Write Mary E. O'Dell, Dir., 11906 Locust Rd., Middletown, KY 40243.

17TH ANNUAL APPALACHIAN WRITERS WORKSHOP—Hindman, KY. August. Write Mike Mullins, Dir., Box 844, Hindman Settlement School, Hindman, KY 41822.

LOUISIANA

WRITE AWAY: INSTRUCTION AND INSPIRATION FOR WRITERS—Lafayette, LA. March. Write Rosalind Foley, Dir., Writers' Guild of Acadiana, P.O. Box 51532, Lafayette, LA 70505–1532.

MAINE

WELLS WRITERS' WORKSHOP—Wells, ME. May, September. Write Victor Levine, Dir., 69 Broadway, Concord, NH 03301.

ANNUAL STONECOAST WRITERS' CONFERENCE—Portland, ME. July-August. Write Barbara Hope, University of Southern Maine, Summer Session, 98 Falmouth St., Portland, ME 04103.

54TH STATE OF MAINE WRITERS' CONFERENCE—Ocean Park, ME. August. Write Richard F. Burns, Dir., P.O. Box 296, Ocean Park, ME 04063.

MARYLAND

SANDY COVE CHRISTIAN WRITERS CONFERENCE—North East, MD. October. Write Gayle Roper, Dir., RD 6, Box 112, Coatesville, PA 19320.

MASSACHUSETTS

CAPE LITERARY ARTS WORKSHOPS—Centerville, MA. August. Write Marion Vuilleumier, Dir., Cape Cod Writers' Ctr., c/o Cape Cod Conservatory, Rt. 132, W. Barnstable, MA 02668.

CAPE COD WRITERS' CONFERENCE—Craigville, MA. August. Write Marion Vuilleumier, Dir., Cape Cod Writers' Ctr., c/o Cape Cod Conservatory, Rt.132, W. Barnstable, MA 02668.

MICHIGAN

CHRISTIAN WRITERS WORKSHOP—Berrien Springs, MI. June. Write Dr. Kermit Netteburg, Dir., Comm. Dept., Andrews University, Berrien Springs, MI 49104–0800.

MIDLAND WRITERS CONFERENCE—Midland, MI. June. Write Eileen Finzel and Margaret Allen, Dirs., Grace A. Dow Memorial Library, 1710 W. St. Andrews, Midland, MI 48640.

MINNESOTA

SPLIT ROCK ARTS PROGRAM—Duluth, MN. July-August. Write Andrea Gilats, Dir., 306 Wesbrook Hall, 77 Pleasant St. S.E., Minneapolis, MN 55455.

"WRITING TO SELL"—Minneapolis, MN. August. Write Sarie Dale, Dir., MWW Conference, P.O. Box 24356, Minneapolis, MN 55424.

MISSOURI

ANNUAL MARK TWAIN WRITERS CONFERENCE—Hannibal, MO. June. Write Dr. James C. Hefley, Dir., Hannibal-LaGrange College, 921 Center St., Hannibal, MO 63401.

WRITING FOR CHILDREN WORKSHOP—Springfield, MO. October. Write Sandy Asher, Dir., Drury College, 900 N. Benton Ave., Springfield, MO 65802.

MONTANA

YELLOW BAY WRITERS' WORKSHOP—Flathead Lake, MT. August. Write Annick Smith and Judy Jones, Dirs., Ctr. for Cont. Ed., University of Montana, Missoula, MT 59812.

NEVADA

READING AND WRITING THE WEST—Reno, NV. July. Write Stephen Tchudi, Dept. of English, University of Nevada, Reno, NV 89557–0031.

NEW HAMPSHIRE

ANNUAL SEACOAST WRITERS CONFERENCE—Stratham, NH. Fall. Write J. Lynn Makowicz, Dir., Seacoast Writers Assn., P.O. Box 6553, Portsmouth, NH 03802–6553.

NEW JERSEY

25TH ANNUAL NEW JERSEY WRITERS CONFERENCE—Newark, NJ. March. Write Dr. Herman Estrin, Dir., 315 Henry St., Scotch Plains, NJ 07076.

TRENTON STATE COLLEGE WRITERS' CONFERENCE—Trenton, NJ. April. Write Jean Hollander, English Dept., Trenton State College, Hillwood Lakes, CN 4700, Trenton, NJ 08650–4700.

WRITING BY THE SEA—Cape May, NJ. November. Write Natalie Newton, Dir., 7 Chestnut Oak Dr., Cape May, NJ 08210.

NEW MEXICO

WRITERS' CONFERENCE AT SANTA FE—Santa Fe, NM. February. Write Ruth Crowley, Dir., Santa Fe Community College, P.O. Box 4187, Santa Fe, NM 87502–4187.

SOUTHWEST WRITERS WORKSHOP 12TH ANNUAL CONFERENCE—Albuquerque, NM. September. Write Suzanne Spletzer, Dir., SWW Conference, 1336-C Wyoming Blvd. N.E., Albuquerque, NM 87112.

NEW YORK

OMEGA INSTITUTE WINTER WORKSHOPS—Rhinebeck, NY. January, February. Write Omega Inst. for Holistic Studies, 260 Lake Dr., Rhinebeck, NY 12572.

CHILDREN'S LITERATURE CONFERENCE—Hempstead, NY. April. Write Lewis Shena, Dir., 110 Hofstra University, Hempstead, NY 11550.

ANNUAL WRITERS CONFERENCE—New York, NY. June. Write Alexandra Cantor, Dir., American Society of Journalists & Authors, Inc., 1501 Broadway, #302, New York, NY 10036.

WRITERS ON WRITING AT BARNARD—New York, NY. June. Write Ann Birstein, Dir., Barnard College, 3009 Broadway, New York, NY 10027–6598.

WRITERS' WEEK—Purchase, NY. June-July. Write Ruth Dowd, Adult and Special Programs, Manhattanville College, 2900 Purchase St., Purchase, NY 10573.

ROBERT QUACKENBUSH'S CHILDREN'S BOOK WRITING AND ILLUSTRATING WORKSHOP—New York, NY. July. Write Robert Quackenbush, Dir., 460 E. 79th St., New York, NY 10021.

ROMANCE WRITERS OF AMERICA CONFERENCE—New York, NY. July. Write Janet Kuchler, Dir., 13700 Veterans Memorial, Suite 315, Houston, TX 77014.

HIGHLIGHTS FOUNDATION WRITERS WORKSHOP—Chautauqua, NY. July. Write Jan Keen, Dir., Highlights Foundation, 711 Court St., Honesdale, PA 18431.

NORTH CAROLINA

DUKE UNIVERSITY WRITERS' WORKSHOP—Durham, NC. June. Write Marilyn Hartman, Dir., Box 90703, Durham, NC 27708.

OHIO

TRI C WEST WRITERS CONFERENCE—Parma, OH. June. Write Lea Leever Oldham, Dir., 34200 Ridge Rd., #110, Willoughby, OH 44094.

11TH ANNUAL WESTERN RESERVE WRITERS AND FREELANCE CONFERENCE—Mentor, OH. September. Write Lea Leever Oldham, Dir., 34200 Ridge Rd., #110, Willoughby, OH 44094.

MIDWEST WRITERS CONFERENCE—Canton, OH. October. Write Midwest Writers Conference, Kent State University, 6000 Frank Ave. N.W., Canton, OH 44720.

OKLAHOMA

OPPORTUNITY '94—Norman, OK. March. Write Mary Heckendorn, National League of American Pen Women, 828 Cruce St., Norman, OK 73069.

PROFESSIONALISM IN WRITING SCHOOL—Tulsa, OK. March. Write Norma Jean Lutz, Dir., 4308 S. Peoria, Suite 701, Tulsa, OK 74105.

NORTHWEST OKLAHOMA WRITERS WORKSHOP—Enid, OK. March. Write Dr. Earl Mabry, Dir., Box 1308, Enid, OK 73702.

OKLAHOMA WRITER'S FEDERATION STATE CONVENTION— Oklahoma City, OK. May. Write Deborah Camp, 1246 S. Delaware Pl., Tulsa, OK 74105–4130.

OKLAHOMA FALL ARTS INSTITUTE—Lone Wolf, OK. October. Write Mary Frates, Dir., Oklahoma Arts Inst., 720 N.W. 50th, Oklahoma City, OK 73154.

OREGON

FISHTRAP GATHERING—Wallowa Lake, OR. February, July. Write Rich Wandschneider, Dir., Fishtrap, P.O. Box 38, Enterprise, OR 97828.

HAYSTACK WRITING PROGRAM—Cannon Beach, OR. June-August. Write Maggie Herrington, Portland State University Haystack Program, P.O. Box 1491, Portland, OR 97207.

PENNSYLVANIA

PENNWRITERS 7TH ANNUAL CONFERENCE—Hershey, PA. May. Write C.J. Houghtaling, Dir., R.D. 2, Box 241, Middlebury Center, PA 16935.

CUMBERLAND VALLEY FICTION WRITERS WORKSHOP—Carlisle, PA. June. Write Judy Gill, Dir., Dept. of English, Dickinson College, P.O. Box 1773, Carlisle, PA 17013–2896.

SOUTH CAROLINA

WRITE TO SELL IV: THE SOUTHEAST NUTS AND BOLTS WORK-SHOP—Rock Hill, SC. February. Write Ron Chepesiuk, Dir., 782 Wofford St., Rock Hill, SC 29730.

FRANCIS MARION WRITERS' CONFERENCE—Florence, SC. June.

Write David Starkey, Dir., Francis Marion University, English Dept., Florence, SC 29501.

TENNESSEE

RHODES COLLEGE WRITING CAMP—Memphis, TN. June-July. Write Dr. Beth Kamhi, Dir., Dept. of English, Rhodes College, 2000 North Pkwy., Memphis, TN 38112.

WRITER'S WORKSHOP—Nashville, TN. July. Write Dr. Bob Dean, Dir., Church Program Training Ctr., Baptist Sunday School Board, 127 Ninth Ave. N., Nashville, TN 37234.

TEXAS

TCU/CHISHOLM TRAIL WESTERN SEMINAR—Fort Worth, TX. April. Write Diane Lovin, Dir., Box 32927, Fort Worth, TX 76129.

CRAFT OF WRITING CONFERENCE—Richardson, TX. September. Write Janet Harris, Dir., University of Texas, Ctr. for Cont. Ed., P.O. Box 830688, MS CN1.1, Richardson, TX 75083–0688.

VERMONT

SCBWI NEW ENGLAND ANNUAL CONFERENCE—Brattleboro, VT. April. Write Jessie Haas, Dir., RFD 3, Box 627, Putney, VT 05346.

THE OLDERS' TRAVEL WRITING WORKSHOP—Various locations throughout VT. May, June, September. Write Jules and Effin Older, Dirs., Box 163, Albany, VT 05820.

NEW ENGLAND WRITERS CONFERENCE—Windsor, VT. July. Write Dr. Frank Anthony, Dir., P.O. Box 483, Windsor, VT 05089.

ANNUAL BREAD LOAF WRITERS' CONFERENCE—Ripton, VT. August. Write Robert Pack, Dir., Bread Loaf Writers' Conference, Middlebury College, Middlebury, VT 05753.

VIRGINIA

CHRISTOPHER NEWPORT WRITERS' CONFERENCE—Newport News, VA. April. Write Doris Gwaltney, Dir., Christopher Newport University, 50 Shoe La., Newport News, VA 23606.

SHENANDOAH VALLEY WRITERS' GUILD—Middletown, VA. May. Write Prof. F. Cogan, Lord Fairfax Community College, P.O. Box 47, Middletown, VA 22645.

ANNUAL HIGHLAND SUMMER CONFERENCE—Radford, VA. June. Write Dr. Grace Toney Edwards, Dir., Box 6935, Radford University, Radford, VA 24142.

APPALACHIAN WRITERS' ASSOCIATION—Radford, VA. July. Write Dr. Parks Lanier, Dir., Box 6935 RU, Radford, VA 24142–6935.

SHENANDOAH PLAYWRIGHTS RETREAT—Staunton, VA. July-August. Write Robert Graham Small, Dir., Pennyroyal Farm, Rt. 5, Box 167F, Staunton, VA 24401.

846

WRITERS INFORMATION NETWORK—Seattle, WA. February. Write Elaine Wright Colvin, W.I.N., P.O. Box 11337, Bainbridge Island, WA 98110.

WRITERS WEEKEND AT THE BEACH—Ocean Park, WA. February. Write Birdie Etchison, P.O. Box 877, Ocean Park, WA 98640.

CLARION WEST WRITERS' WORKSHOP—Seattle, WA. June-July. Write Clarion West Writers' Workshop, 340 15th Ave. E., Suite 350, Seattle, WA 98112.

PACIFIC NORTHWEST WRITERS CONFERENCE—Seattle, WA. July. Write Judy Bodmer, Dir., PNWC, 2033 6th Ave., #804, Seattle, WA 98121.

PORT TOWNSEND WRITERS' CONFERENCE—Port Townsend, WA. July. Write Carol Jane Bangs, Dir., Centrum, Box 1158, Port Townsend, WA 98368.

GREEN LAKE CHRISTIAN WRITERS CONFERENCE—Green Lake, WI. July. Write Writers Conference, American Baptist Assembly, Green Lake, WI 54941–9599.

SCBWI WISCONSIN 4TH ANNUAL FALL RETREAT—Madison, WI. September-October. Write Sheri Cooper Sinykin, Dir., 26 Lancaster Ct., Madison, WI 53719–1433.

STATE ARTS COUNCILS

State arts councils sponsor grants, fellowships, and other programs for writers. To be eligible for funding, a writer *must* be a resident of the state in which he is applying. For more information, write to the addresses below. Telephone numbers are listed as follows: 1–800 numbers are toll free for in-state calls only; numbers preceded by TDD indicate Telecommunications Device for the Deaf; TTY indicates Teletypewriter.

ALABAMA STATE COUNCIL ON THE ARTS
Albert B. Head, Executive Director
One Dexter Ave.
Montgomery, AL 36130
(205) 242–4076

ALASKA STATE COUNCIL ON THE ARTS
Jean Palmer, Grants Officer
411 W. 4th Ave., Suite 1E
Anchorage, AK 99501–2343
(907) 279–1558

ARIZONA COMMISSION ON THE ARTS
Tonda Gorton, Literature Director
417 W. Roosevelt
Phoenix, AZ 85003
(602) 255–5882

ARKANSAS ARTS COUNCIL
Arthurine Harrison, Assistant Director
1500 Tower Bldg.
323 Center St.
Little Rock, AR 72201
(501) 324–9766

CALIFORNIA ARTS COUNCIL
Public Information Office
2411 Alhambra Blvd.
Sacramento, CA 95817
(916) 227–2550

COLORADO COUNCIL ON THE ARTS
Barbara Neal, Executive Director
750 Pennsylvania St.
Denver, CO 80203–3699
(303) 894–2617

CONNECTICUT COMMISSION ON THE ARTS
John Ostrout, Executive Director
227 Lawrence St.
Hartford, CT 06106
(203) 566–4770

DELAWARE DIVISION OF THE ARTS
Peggy Amsterdam, Director
Carvel State Building
820 N. French St.
Wilmington, DE 19801
(302) 577–3540

FLORIDA ARTS COUNCIL
Ms. Peyton Fearington
Dept. of State
Div. of Cultural Affairs
The Capitol
Tallahassee, FL 32399–0250
(904) 487–2980

GEORGIA COUNCIL FOR THE ARTS
Caroline Ballard, Executive Director
530 Means St. N.W., Suite 115
Atlanta, GA 30318
(404) 651–7920

HAWAII STATE FOUNDATION ON CULTURE AND THE ARTS
Wendell P.K. Silva, Executive Director
335 Merchant St., Room 202
Honolulu, HI 96813
(808) 586–0300

IDAHO COMMISSION ON THE ARTS
Attn: Diane Josephy Peavey
304 W. State St.
Boise, ID 83720
(208) 334–2119

ILLINOIS ARTS COUNCIL
Richard Gage, Director of Communication Arts
James R. Thompson Center
100 W. Randolph, Suite 10–500
Chicago, IL 60601
(312) 814–4990/(800) 237–6994

INDIANA ARTS COMMISSION
Julie Murphy, Director of Programs
402 W. Washington St., Rm. 072
Indianapolis, IN 46204–2741
(317) 232–1268/TDD: (317) 233–3001

IOWA STATE ARTS COUNCIL
Capitol Complex
Des Moines, IA 50319
(515) 281–6787

KANSAS ARTS COMMISSION
Robert T. Burtch, Editor
Jayhawk Tower
700 S.W. Jackson, Suite 1004
Topeka, KS 66603–3758
(913) 296–3335

KENTUCKY ARTS COUNCIL
31 Fountain Pl.
Frankfort, KY 40601
(502) 564–3757/TDD: (502) 564–3757

LOUISIANA STATE ARTS COUNCIL
Gerri Hobdy, Interim Director
Box 44247
Baton Rouge, LA 70804
(504) 342–8200

MAINE ARTS COMMISSION
Alden C. Wilson, Director
State House, Station 25
Augusta, ME 04333–0025
(207) 287–2724

MARYLAND STATE ARTS COUNCIL
Linda Vlasak, Program Director
Artists-in-Education
601 N. Howard St.
Baltimore, MD 21201
(410) 333–8232

MASSACHUSETTS CULTURAL COUNCIL
James McCullough, Literature Coordinator
80 Boylston St., 10th Fl.
Boston, MA 02116–4802
(617) 727–3668/(800) 232–0960
TTY: (617) 338–9153

849

MICHIGAN COUNCIL FOR ARTS AND CULTURAL AFFAIRS
Betty Boone, Executive Director
1200 Sixth St., Suite 1180
Detroit, MI 48226–2461
(313) 256–3731

MINNESOTA STATE ARTS BOARD
Karen Mueller
Artist Assistance Program Associate
432 Summit Ave.
St. Paul, MN 55102
(612) 297–2603/(800) 866–2787

COMPAS: WRITERS & ARTISTS IN THE SCHOOLS
Daniel Gabriel, Director
305 Landmark Center
75 W. 5th St.
St. Paul, MN 55102
(612) 292–3254

MISSISSIPPI ARTS COMMISSION
Jane Crater Hiatt, Executive Director
239 N. Lamar St., Suite 207
Jackson, MS 39201
(601) 359–6030

MISSOURI ARTS COUNCIL
Michael Hunt, Program Administrator for Literature
Wainwright Office Complex
111 N. 7th St., Suite 105
St. Louis, MO 63101–2188
(314) 340–6845

MONTANA ARTS COUNCIL
Martha Sprague, Director, Artists Services Programs
316 N. Park Ave., Suite 252
Helena, MT 59620
(406) 444–6430

NEBRASKA ARTS COUNCIL
Jennifer Severin, Executive Director
3838 Davenport St.
Omaha, NE 68131–2329
(402) 595–2122

NEVADA STATE COUNCIL ON THE ARTS
Attn: Executive Director
329 Flint St.
Reno, NV 89501
(702) 688–1225

NEW HAMPSHIRE STATE COUNCIL ON THE ARTS
Attn: Audrey Sylvester
Phenix Hall, 40 N. Main St.
Concord, NH 03301–4974
(603) 271–2789

NEW JERSEY STATE COUNCIL ON THE ARTS
Grants Office
CN-306
Trenton, NJ 08625
(609) 292-6130

NEW MEXICO ARTS DIVISION
Randy Forrester, Operations Director
228 E. Palace Ave.
Santa Fe, NM 87501
(505) 827-6490

NEW YORK STATE COUNCIL ON THE ARTS
Michael G. Albano, Director, Literature Program
915 Broadway
New York, NY 10010
(212) 387-7023

NORTH CAROLINA ARTS COUNCIL
Deborah McGill, Literature Director
Dept. of Cultural Resources
Raleigh, NC 27601-2807
(919) 733-2111

NORTH DAKOTA COUNCIL ON THE ARTS
Vern Goodin, Executive Director
Black Building, Suite 606
Fargo, ND 58102
(701) 239-7150

OHIO ARTS COUNCIL
Bob Fox, Literature Program Coordinator
727 E. Main St.
Columbus, OH 43205-1796
(614) 466-2613

STATE ARTS COUNCIL OF OKLAHOMA
Betty Price, Executive Director
Jim Thorpe Bldg., Room 640
Oklahoma City, OK 73105
(405) 521-2931

OREGON ARTS COMMISSION
Attn: Peter Sears
550 Airport Rd. S.E.
Salem, OR 97310
(503) 378-3625

PENNSYLVANIA COUNCIL ON THE ARTS
Marcia Salvatore, Literature and Theatre Programs
Diane Young, Artists-in-Education Program
Room 216, Finance Bldg.
Harrisburg, PA 17120
(717) 787-6883

RHODE ISLAND STATE COUNCIL ON THE ARTS
Iona B. Dobbins, Executive Director
95 Cedar St., Suite 103
Providence, RI 02903
(401) 277-3880

SOUTH CAROLINA ARTS COMMISSION
Steven Lewis, Director, Literary Arts Program
1800 Gervais St.
Columbia, SC 29201
(803) 734–8696

SOUTH DAKOTA ARTS COUNCIL
Attn: Dennis Holul
230 S. Phillips Ave., Suite 204
Sioux Falls, SD 57102–0788
(605) 339–6646

TENNESSEE ARTS COMMISSION
Attn: Alice Swanson
320 Sixth Ave., N., Suite 100
Nashville, TN 37243–0780
(615) 741–1701

TEXAS COMMISSION ON THE ARTS
Rita Starpattern, Program Administrator
Visual and Communication Arts
P.O. Box 13406
Austin, TX 78711–3406
(512) 463–5535

UTAH ARTS COUNCIL
G. Barnes, Literary Coordinator
617 East South Temple
Salt Lake City, UT 84102–1177
(801) 533–5895

VERMONT COUNCIL ON THE ARTS
Cornelia Carey, Grants Officer
136 State St.
Montpelier, VT 05602
(802) 828–3291

VIRGINIA COMMISSION FOR THE ARTS
Peggy J. Baggett, Executive Director
223 Governor St.
Richmond, VA 23219
(804) 225–3132

WASHINGTON STATE ARTS COMMISSION
234 E. 8th Ave.
P.O. Box 42675
Olympia, WA 98504–2675
(206) 753–3860

WEST VIRGINIA DEPT. OF EDUCATION AND THE ARTS
Larkin Ray Cook, Executive Director
Culture and History Division
Arts and Humanities Section
The Cultural Center, Capitol Complex
Charleston, WV 25305
(304) 558–0220

WISCONSIN ARTS BOARD
Dean Amhaus, Executive Director
101 E. Wilson St., 1st Floor
Madison, WI 53703
(608) 266–0190

WYOMING ARTS COUNCIL
John Coe, Director
2320 Capitol Ave.
Cheyenne, WY 82002
(307) 777–7742

ORGANIZATIONS FOR WRITERS

THE ACADEMY OF AMERICAN POETS
584 Broadway, Suite 1208
New York, NY 10012
(212) 274–0343
Mrs. Edward T. Chase, *President*
Founded in 1934 to promote American poetry through fellowships, awards programs, public programs, and publications. The Academy offers an annual fellowship for distinguished poetic achievement, the Peter I. B. Lavan Younger Poet Awards, three major book awards, and sponsors prizes for poetry at 176 universities and colleges nationwide. The Academy's readings, lectures, and regional symposia take place at various New York City locations and other locations in the United States. Membership is open to all: $45 annual fee includes subscription to the quarterly newsletter, *Poetry Pilot*, and complimentary copies of award-winning books.

AMERICAN CRIME WRITERS LEAGUE
219 Tuxedo
San Antonio, TX 78209
Barbara Mertz, *President*
Jay Brandon, *Membership Chair*
A national organization of working professional mystery authors. To be eligible for membership in ACWL you must have published at least one of the following: one full-length work of crime fiction or nonfiction; three short stories; or three nonfiction crime articles. The bimonthly *ACWL BULLETin* features articles by reliable experts and an exchange of information and advice among professional writers. Annual dues: $35.

AMERICAN MEDICAL WRITERS ASSOCIATION
9650 Rockville Pike
Bethesda, MD 20814
(301) 493–0003
Lillian Sablack, *Executive Director*
Members of the association are engaged in biomedical communications.

Any person actively interested in or professionally associated with any medium of medical communication is eligible for membership. Annual dues: $75.

AMERICAN SOCIETY OF JOURNALISTS AND AUTHORS, INC.
1501 Broadway, Suite 302
New York, NY 10036
(212) 997–0947
Alexandra Cantor, *Executive Director*

A nationwide organization of independent writers of nonfiction dedicated to promoting high standards of nonfiction writing through monthly meetings, annual writers' conferences, etc. The ASJA offers extensive benefits and services including referral services, numerous discount services, and the opportunity to explore professional issues and concerns with other writers. Members also receive a monthly newsletter with confidential market information. Membership is open to professional free-lance writers of nonfiction; qualifications are judged by Membership Committee. Call or write for application details.

ASSOCIATION OF HISPANIC ARTS, INC.
173 E. 116th St.
New York, NY 10029
(212) 860–5445
Jane Arce Bello, *Executive Director*

Founded in 1975, the AHA serves both Hispanic arts organizations and individual artists at various stages of development, to ensure that the rich array of Hispanic arts and cultural expressions will be preserved. Publishes *Hispanic Arts News*, providing information on events, job opportunities, and other issues. Individual subscription: $20.

THE AUTHORS GUILD, INC.
330 W. 42nd St.
New York, NY 10036–6902
(212) 563–5904
Attn: *Membership Committee*

A professional organization of published authors. Membership offers writers professional advice on book contracts and other publishing affairs. A writer who has published a book in the last seven years with an established publisher, or one who has published several magazine pieces with periodicals of general circulation within the last eighteen months, may be eligible for active voting membership in the Authors Guild. A new writer may be eligible for associate membership. All members of the Authors Guild automatically become members of its parent organization, The Authors League of America, Inc. Annual dues: $90.

THE AUTHORS LEAGUE OF AMERICA, INC.
330 W. 42nd St.
New York, NY 10036–6902
Robin Davis Miller, *Membership*
(212) 564–8350

The Authors League of America is a national organization of over 14,000 authors and dramatists, representing them on matters of joint concern, such as copyright, taxes, and freedom of expression. Membership in the league is restricted to authors and dramatists who are members of The Authors Guild and The Dramatists Guild. Matters such as contract terms and subsidiary rights are in the province of the two guilds.

BLACK THEATRE NETWORK
Box 11502
Fisher Bldg. Station
Detroit, MI 48211
(313) 577–7906
Addell Austin Anderson, *I.P. President*
   The Black Theatre Network is a national non-profit organization devoted to exposing all people to the beauty and complexity of Black theater, and to preserving the art form for future generations. The BTN sponsors an annual national conference, and the Randolph Edmonds Young Scholars Competition. Publications include the quarterly *BTNews*, *The Black Theatre Directory*, and *Black Voices*, a guide to plays by Black authors. Annual dues: $25, *student & retiree*; $40, *individual*.

BRITISH AMERICAN ARTS ASSOCIATION
116 Commercial St.
London E1 6NF
England
(071) 247–5385
Jennifer Williams, *Executive Director*
   An information service and clearing house for exchange between British and American cultural activities in all arts fields, the BAAA provides advocacy and technical assistance to professional artists. The BAAA does not give funds and is not a membership organization.

COUNCIL OF AUTHORS & JOURNALISTS, INC.
P.O. Box 830184
Stone Mountain, GA 30083–0004
(404) 432–0290
Attn: *CAJ Membership*
   The CAJ is a writers' network established to encourage high standards of creative writing and to promote interest in writers, their books, and other literary works. Periodic readings and conferences are held. Annual dues: $15 to $100.

THE DRAMATISTS GUILD
234 W. 44th St.
New York, NY 10036–3909
(212) 398–9366
Peter Stone, *President*
Andrew Farber, *Executive Director*
   America's only professional association of playwrights, composers, and lyricists, the Dramatists Guild was established to protect dramatists' rights and to improve working conditions. Services include use of the Guild's contracts; a toll-free number for members in need of business counseling; a discount ticket service; access to two health insurance programs and a group term life insurance plan; *The Dramatists Guild Quarterly* and *The Dramatists Guild Newsletter*; a reference library; and a Committee for Women. All playwrights (produced or not) are eligible for membership. All Active or Associate members of the Dramatists Guild automatically become members of its parent organization, the Authors League. Annual dues: $125, *active*; $75, *associate*; $50, *subscribing*; $25, *student*.

INTERNATIONAL ASSOCIATION OF THEATRE FOR CHILDREN AND YOUNG PEOPLE
c/o The Open Eye: New Stagings
270 W. 89th St.
New York, NY 10024
Harold Oaks, *President*
    The development of professional theater for young audiences and international exchange are the organization's primary mandates. Provides a link between professional theaters, artists, directors, training institutions, and arts agencies; sponsors festivals and forums for interchange among theaters and theater artists. Annual dues: $50, *individual*; $25, *student and retiree*.

THE INTERNATIONAL WOMEN'S WRITING GUILD
Box 810
Gracie Sta.
New York, NY 10028
(212) 737–7536
Hannelore Hahn, *Executive Director*
    The IWWG is a network for the personal and professional empowerment of women through writing. Services include six issues of a 28-page newsletter, a list of literary agents and publishing services, access to health insurance plans at group rates, annual summer conference at Skidmore College in Saratoga Springs, NY, regional writing clusters, and year-round supportive networking. Writing accomplishment is not a condition of membership. Annual dues: $35; $45 (foreign).

MIDWEST RADIO THEATRE WORKSHOP
KOPN
915 E. Broadway
Columbia, MO 65201
(314) 874–5676
Steve Donofrio, *Director*
    Founded in 1979, the MRTW is the only national resource for American radio dramatists, providing information (referral, technical assistance, educational materials) and workshops. MRTW coordinates an annual national radio script contest, publishes an annual radio scriptbook, and distributes a script anthology with primer. Send SASE for more information.

MYSTERY WRITERS OF AMERICA, INC.
17 E. 47th St., 6th Floor
New York, NY 10017
(212) 888–8171
Priscilla Ridgway, *Executive Director*
    The MWA exists for the purpose of raising the prestige of mystery and detective writing, and of defending the rights and increasing the income of all writers in the field of mystery, detection, and fact crime writing. Each year, the MWA presents the Edgar Allan Poe Awards for the best mystery writing in a variety of fields. The four classifications of membership are: *active* (open to any writer who has made a sale in the field of mystery, suspense, or crime writing); *associate* (for professionals in allied fields/writers in other fields); *corresponding* (for writers living outside the U.S.); *affiliate* (for unpublished writers and mystery enthusiasts). Annual dues: $65; $32.50 *corresponding members*.

NATIONAL ASSOCIATION OF SCIENCE WRITERS, INC.
P.O. Box 294
Greenlawn, NY 11740
(516) 757–5664
Diane McGurgan, *Administrative Secretary*
The NASW promotes the dissemination of accurate information regarding science through all media, and conducts a varied program to increase the flow of news from scientists, to improve the quality of its presentation, and to communicate its meaning to the reading public. Anyone who has been actively engaged in the dissemination of science information is eligible to apply for membership. Active members must be principally involved in reporting on science through newspapers, magazines, TV, or other media that reach the public directly. Associate members report on science through limited-circulation publications and other media. Annual dues: $60.

NATIONAL LEAGUE OF AMERICAN PEN WOMEN
1300 17th St. N.W.
Washington, DC 20036–1973
(202) 785–1997
Muriel C. Freeman, *National President*
Promotes development of the creative talents of professional women in the arts. Membership is by invitation only.

THE NATIONAL WRITERS ASSOCIATION
1450 S. Havana, Suite 424
Aurora, CO 80012
(303) 751–7844
Sandy Whelchel, *Executive Director*
New and established writers, poets, and playwrights throughout the U.S. and Canada may become members of the NWA, a full-time, customer-service-oriented association founded in 1937. Members receive a bimonthly newsletter, *Authorship*, and may attend the annual June conference. Annual dues: $60, *professional*; $50, *regular*; add $20 outside the U.S., Canada, and Mexico.

NATIONAL WRITERS UNION
873 Broadway, #203
New York, NY 10003
(212) 254–0279
Maria Pallante, *Executive Director*
The NWU is dedicated to bringing about equitable payment and fair treatment of free-lance writers through collective action. Its membership is over 3,000 and includes book authors, poets, free-lance journalists, and technical writers in eleven chapters nationwide. The NWU offers its members contract and agent information, health insurance plans, press credentials, grievance handling, a union newspaper, and sponsors events across the country. Membership is open to writers who have published a book, play, three articles, five poems, one short story or an equivalent amount of newsletter, publicity, technical, commercial, government or institutional copy, or have written an equivalent amount of unpublished material and are actively seeking publication. Annual dues: $60 to $150.

NEW DRAMATISTS
424 W. 44th St.
New York, NY 10036
(212) 757–6960
Elana Greenfield, *Director of Artistic Programs*

New Dramatists is dedicated to finding gifted playwrights and giving them the time, space, and tools to develop their craft. Services include readings and workshops; a director-in-residence program; national script distribution for members; artist work spaces; international playwright exchange programs; script copying facilities; and a free ticket program. Membership is open to residents of New York City and the surrounding tri-state area. National memberships are offered to those outside the area who can spend time in NYC in order to take advantage of programs. Apply between July 15 and September 15. No annual dues.

NORTHWEST PLAYWRIGHTS GUILD
Box 9218
Portland, OR 97207–9218
(503) 245–1970
Attn: *Executive Director*
NWPG supports and promotes playwrights living in the Northwest through play development, staged readings, and information networking for play competitions and production opportunities. Members receive monthly and quarterly newsletters. Annual dues: $20.

OUTDOOR WRITERS ASSOCIATION OF AMERICA, INC.
2017 Cato Ave., Suite 101
State College, PA 16801–2768
(814) 234–1011
Sylvia G. Bashline, *Executive Director*
A non-profit, international organization representing professional communicators who report and reflect upon America's diverse interests in the outdoors. Membership (by nomination only) includes a monthly publication, *Outdoors Unlimited*; annual conference; annual membership directory; contests. OWAA also provides scholarships to qualified students.

PEN AMERICAN CENTER
568 Broadway
New York, NY 10012
(212) 334–1660
Karen Kennerly, *Executive Director*
PEN American Center is one of more than 104 centers in 69 countries that make up International PEN, a worldwide association of literary writers, offering conferences, writing programs, and financial and educational assistance. Membership is open to writers who have published two books of literary merit, as well as editors, agents, playwrights, and translators who meet specific standards. (Apply to nomination committee.) PEN sponsors annual awards and grants and publishes the quarterly *PEN Newsletter* and the biennial directory, *Grants and Awards Available to American Writers*.

THE PLAYWRIGHTS' CENTER
2301 Franklin Ave. East
Minneapolis, MN 55406
(612) 332–7481
David Moore, Jr., *Executive Director*
The Playwrights' Center fuels the contemporary theater by providing services that support the development and public appreciation of playwrights and playwriting. Members receive applications for all programs, a calendar of events, eligibility to participate in special activities, including classes, outreach programs, and PlayLabs. Annual dues: $35.

POETRY SOCIETY OF AMERICA
15 Gramercy Park
New York, NY 10003
(212) 254–9628
Elise Paschen, *Executive Director*
Founded in 1910, the PSA seeks through a variety of programs to gain a wider audience for American poetry. The PSA offers 19 annual prizes for poetry (with many contests open to non-members as well as members), and sponsors workshops, poetry readings, and publications. Maintains the Van Voorhis Library of American Poetry. Annual dues: $40.

POETS AND WRITERS, INC.
72 Spring St.
New York, NY 10012
(212) 226–3586
Elliot Figman, *Executive Director*
Poets & Writers, Inc., was founded in 1970 to foster the development of poets and fiction writers and to promote communication throughout the literary community. A non-membership organization, it offers a nationwide information center for writers; *Poets & Writers Magazine* and other publications; as well as readings and workshops.

PRIVATE EYE WRITERS OF AMERICA
330 Surrey Rd.
Cherry Hill, NJ 08002
(609) 482–1018
David S. Masterton, *Membership Chairman*
Robert J. Randisi, *Executive Director*
Private Eye Writers of America is a national organization that seeks to promote a wider recognition and appreciation of private eye literature. Sponsors the annual Shamus Award for the best in P.I. fiction. Writers who have published a work of fiction (short story, novel, TV script, or movie screenplay) with a private eye as the central character are eligible to join as active members. Serious devotees of the P.I. story may become associate members. Annual dues: $30, *active*; $24, *associate*; $30, *international*.

ROMANCE WRITERS OF AMERICA
13700 Veterans Memorial Dr., Suite 315
Houston, TX 77014
(713) 440–6885
Linda Fisher, *Office Supervisor*
The RWA is an international organization with over 120 local chapters across the U.S. and Canada, open to any writer, published or unpublished, interested in the field of romantic fiction. Annual dues of $45, plus $10 application fee for new members; benefits include annual conference, contest, market information, and bimonthly newsmagazine, *Romance Writers' Report*.

SCIENCE-FICTION AND FANTASY WRITERS OF AMERICA, INC.
5 Winding Brook Dr., #1B
Guilderland, NY 12084
Peter Dennis Pautz, *Executive Secretary*
An organization whose purpose it is to foster and further the professional interests of science fiction and fantasy writers. Presents the annual Nebula Award for excellence in the field and publishes the *Bulletin* for its members. Any writer who has sold a work of science fiction or fantasy is eligible for membership. Annual dues: $50, *active* ; $35, *affiliates*; plus $10 installation fee;

send for application and information. The *Bulletin* is available to nonmembers for $15 (four issues) within the U.S.; $18.50 overseas.

SMALL PRESS WRITERS AND ARTISTS ORGANIZATION
2131 S. 227th Dr.
Buckeye, AZ 85326–3872
Cathy Hicks, *Secretary*
Founded in 1977, the SPWAO is an international service organization of approximately 350 writers, artists, poets, and publishers dedicated to the promotion of excellence in the small-press fields of science fiction, fantasy, and horror. Members receive ten issues of the *SPWAO Newsletter*, critiques by fellow members, grievance arbitration, and research assistance free of charge. Annual dues: $17.50 new members, $15 renewal (U.S.); $20 new members, $17.50 renewal (Canada); $20 (overseas).

SOCIETY FOR TECHNICAL COMMUNICATION
901 N. Stuart St., #904
Arlington, VA 22203–1854
(703) 522–4114
William C. Stolgitis, *Executive Director*
A professional organization dedicated to the advancement of the theory and practice of technical communication in all media. The 18,000 members in the U.S. and other countries include technical writers and editors, publishers, artists and draftsmen, researchers, educators, and audiovisual specialists.

SOCIETY OF AMERICAN TRAVEL WRITERS
1155 Connecticut Ave. N.W., Suite 500
Washington, DC 20036
(202) 429–6639
Ken Fischer, *Administrative Coordinator*
The Society of American Travel Writers represents writers and other professionals who strive to provide travelers with accurate reports on destinations, facilities, and services.
Membership is by invitation. Active membership is limited to salaried travel writers and free lancers who have a steady volume of published or distributed work about travel. Initiation fees: $200, *active*; $400, *associate*. Annual dues: $120, *active*; $240 *associate*.

SOCIETY OF CHILDREN'S BOOK WRITERS & ILLUSTRATORS
22736 Vanowen St., Suite 106
West Hills, CA 91307
(818) 888–8760
Lin Oliver, *Executive Director*
A national organization of authors, editors, publishers, illustrators, filmmakers, librarians, and educators, the SCBWI offers a variety of services to people who write, illustrate, or share an interest in children's literature. Full memberships are open to those who have had at least one children's book or story published. Associate memberships are open to all those with an interest in children's literature. Yearly dues are $40.

SOCIETY OF ENVIRONMENTAL JOURNALISTS
7904 Germantown Ave.
Philadelphia, PA 19118
(215) 247–9710
Beth Parke, *Executive Director*
Dedicated to enhancing the quality and accuracy of environmental report-

ing, the SEJ serves 830 members with a quarterly newsletter, an annual conference, computer bulletin board, mentoring program, annual directory. Annual dues: $30.

SOCIETY OF PROFESSIONAL JOURNALISTS
16 S. Jackson St.
Greencastle, IN 46135–0077
(317) 653–3333
Ernie Ford, *Executive Director*
With over 16,000 members and 300 chapters, SPJ serves the interests of print, broadcast, and wire journalists. Services include legal counsel on journalism issues, jobs-for-journalists career search program, professional development seminars, and awards that encourage journalism. Members receive *The Quill*, a monthly magazine that explores current issues in the field. SPJ promotes ethics and freedom of information programs.
Members must spend at least half of their working hours in journalism. Annual dues: $62, *professional*; $31, *student*.

THE SONGWRITERS GUILD OF AMERICA
276 Fifth Ave., Suite 306
New York, NY 10001
(212) 686–6820
George Wurzbach, *Projects Director*
Open to published and unpublished songwriters, the Guild provides members with contracts, reviews contracts, collects royalties from publishers, offers group health and life insurance plans, conducts workshops and critique sessions, and provides a songwriting collaboration service. Annual dues: $55, *associate*; $70 and up, *full member*.

THEATRE COMMUNICATIONS GROUP
355 Lexington Ave.
New York, NY 10017
(212) 697–5230
Peter Zeisler, *Executive Director*
TCG, a national organization for the American theater, provides services to facilitate the work of playwrights, literary managers, and other theater professionals and journalists. Publications include the quarterly bulletin *Play-Source*, which circulates information on new plays, translations, and adaptations to more than 300 TCG constituent theaters and to potential producers. Also publishes the annual *Dramatists Sourcebook*. Individual members receive *American Theatre* Magazine. Annual dues: $30, *individual*.

WESTERN WRITERS OF AMERICA, INC.
416 Bedford Rd.
El Paso, TX 79922–1204
(915) 584–1001
Nancy Hamilton, *Secretary/Treasurer*
Membership is open to qualified professional writers of fiction and nonfiction related to the history and literature of the American West. Its chief purpose is to promote a more widespread distribution, readership, and appreciation of the West and its literature. Holds annual convention in the last week of June. Annual dues: $60. Sponsors annual Spur Awards, Owen Wister Award, and Medicine Pipe Bearer's Award for published work and produced screenplays.

WRITERS GUILD OF AMERICA, EAST, INC.
555 W. 57th St.
New York, NY 10019
(212) 767–7800
Mona Mangan, *Executive Director*

WRITERS GUILD OF AMERICA, WEST, INC.
8955 Beverly Blvd.
West Hollywood, CA 90048
(310) 550–1000
Brian Walton, *Executive Director*
The Writers Guild of America (East and West) represents writers in the fields of radio, television, and motion pictures in both news and entertainment. In order to qualify for membership, a writer must fulfill current requirements for employment or sale of material in one of these three fields.
The basic dues are $25 per quarter for the Writers Guild West and $12.50 per quarter for Writers Guild East. In addition, there are quarterly dues based on percentage of the member's earnings in any one of the fields over which the Guild has jurisdiction. The initiation fee is $1,000 for Writers Guild East and $1,500 for Writers Guild West. (Writers living east of the Mississippi join Writers Guild East, and those living west of the Mississippi, Writers Guild West.)

WRITERS INFORMATION NETWORK
P.O. Box 11337
Bainbridge Island, WA 98110
(206) 842–9103
Elaine Wright Colvin, *Director*
A professional association for Christian writers, W.I.N. was founded in 1983 to provide a link between writers and the religious publishing industry. Offered are a bimonthly newletter, market news, editorial services, advocacy and grievance procedures, referral services, and conferences. Annual dues: $20; $25, *foreign*.

AMERICAN LITERARY AGENTS

The following is a sampling of agents that handle literary and/or dramatic material. Most literary agents do not accept new writers as clients. Since the agent's income is a percentage (10% to 20%) of the amount he receives from the sales he makes for his clients, he must have as clients writers who are selling fairly regularly to good markets. Always query an agent first. Do not send any manuscripts until the agent has asked you to do so; and be wary of agents who charge fees for reading manuscripts.
The Association of Authors' Representatives, Inc., is a merger of the Society of Authors' Representatives with the Independent Literary Agents Association, Inc.; for the most up-to-date list of AAR members and their code of ethics, send a 52¢ legal-size SASE, and a $5 check or money order

to defray handling costs to: Association of Authors' Representatives, Inc., 10 Astor Pl., 3rd Floor, New York, NY 10003.

Addresses that include zip codes in parentheses are located in New York City (many agents in this list are in New York). Individual agents within an agency are listed in italics. An extensive list of agents and their policies can be found in *Literary Market Place*, a directory found in most libraries, and in *Literary Agents of North America, Fifth Edition* (Author Aid/Research Associates International, 340 E. 52nd St., New York, NY 10022).

CAROLE ABEL LITERARY AGENT 160 W. 87th St. (10024) *Carole Abel*

DOMINICK ABEL LITERARY AGENCY 146 W. 82nd St., 1B (10024) *Dominick Abel, Claire Israel*

ACTON, DYSTEL, LEONE & JAFFE, INC. 79 Fifth Ave., 11th Floor (10003) *Edward Acton, Jane Dystel*

BRET ADAMS LIMITED 448 W. 44th St. (10036) *Bret Adams, Mary Harden*

MICHAEL AMATO AGENCY 1650 Broadway, Rm. 307 (10019) *Michael Amato*

MARCIA AMSTERDAM AGENCY 41 W. 82nd St., #9A (10024) *Marcia Amsterdam*

ARCADIA, INC. 20A Old Neversink Rd., Danbury, CT 06811 *Victoria Gould Pryor*

THE AXELROD AGENCY, INC. 66 Church St., Lenox, MA 01240 *Steve Axelrod*

THE BALKIN AGENCY P.O. Box 222, Amherst, MA 01004 *Richard Balkin*

VIRGINIA BARBER AGENCY, INC. 101 Fifth Ave. (10003) *Virginia Barber, Mary Evans, Jennifer Rudolph Walsh*

LORETTA BARRETT BOOKS, INC. 101 Fifth Ave. (10003) *Loretta Barrett*

VICKY BIJUR 333 West End Ave. (10023) *Vicky Bijur*

DAVID BLACK LITERARY AGENCY 220 Fifth Ave., Suite 1400 (10001) *David Black*

GEORGES BORCHARDT, INC. 136 E. 57th St. (10022) *Anne Borchardt, Georges Borchardt, Wendy Schacher Finn, Alexandra Harding, Cindy Klein, Denise Shannon*

BRANDT & BRANDT LITERARY AGENTS 1501 Broadway (10036) *Carl Brandt, Gail Hochman, Marianne Merola, Charles Schlessinger*

THE HELEN BRANN AGENCY, INC. 94 Curtis Rd., Bridgewater, CT 06752 *Helen Brann*

PATTI BREITMAN PUBLISHING PROJECTS 12 Rally Ct., Fairfax, CA 94930 *Patti Breitman*

BROADWAY PLAY PUBLISHING 357 W. 20th St. (10011) *Christopher Gould*

ANDREA BROWN 1081 Alameda, Suite 71, Belmont, CA 94002 *Andrea Brown*

CURTIS BROWN, LTD. 10 Astor Pl. (10003) *Laura Blake, Emilie Jacobson, Ginger Knowlton, Perry Knowlton, Timothy Knowlton, Marilyn Marlow, Christopher McKerrow, Irene Skolnick, Emma Sweeney, Clyde Taylor, Jess Taylor, Maureen Walters*

CURTIS BROWN, LTD. 606 Larchmont Blvd., Suite 309, Los Angeles, CA 90004 *Jeannine Edmunds*

CURTIS BROWN, LTD. 1750 Montgomery St., San Francisco, CA 94111 *Peter Ginsberg*

DON BUCHWALD & ASSOCIATES 10 E. 44th St. (10017) *Don Buchwald*

KNOX BURGER ASSOCIATES, LTD. 39 ½ Washington Square S. (10012) *Knox Burger, Kitty Sprague*

MARIA CARVAINIS AGENCY, INC. 235 West End Ave. (10023) *Maria Carvainis*

MARTHA CASSELMAN P.O. Box 342, Calistoga, CA 94515–0342 *Martha Casselman*

JULIE CASTIGLIA AGENCY 1155 Camino del Mar, Suite 510, Del Mar, CA 92014 *Julie Castiglia*

DIANE CLEAVER, INC. 55 Fifth Ave. (10003) *Diane Cleaver*

RUTH COHEN, INC., LITERARY AGENCY P.O. Box 7626, Menlo Park, CA 94025 *Ruth Cohen*

JOANNA LEWIS COLE 404 Riverside Dr. (10025) *Joanna Lewis Cole*

FRANCES COLLIN LITERARY AGENCY 110 W. 40th St., Suite 1403 (10018) *Frances Collin*

COLUMBIA LITERARY ASSOCIATES 7902 Nottingham Way, Ellicott City, MD 21043 *Linda Hayes*

DON CONGDON ASSOCIATES, INC. 156 Fifth Ave., Suite 625 (10010) *Don Congdon, Michael Congdon, Susan Ramer*

ROBERT CORNFIELD LITERARY AGENCY 145 W. 79th St. (10024) *Robert Cornfield*

RICHARD CURTIS ASSOCIATES, INC. 171 E. 74th St. (10021) *Richard Curtis, Ms. Rob Cohen*

DARHANSOFF & VERRILL LITERARY AGENCY 1220 Park Ave. (10128) *Liz Darhansoff*

JOAN DAVES 67 Clinton Rd., Bedford Hills, NY 10507 *Joan Daves*

ANITA DIAMANT AGENCY, INC. 310 Madison Ave., #1508 (10017) *Anita Diamant, Robin Rue*

SANDRA DIJKSTRA LITERARY AGENCY 1155 Camino del Mar, Suite 515, Del Mar, CA 92014 *Sanda Dijkstra*

THE JONATHAN DOLGER AGENCY 49 E. 96th St., 9B (10128) *Jonathan Dolger*

DONADIO & ASHWORTH, INC. 231 W. 22nd St. (10011) *Eric Ashworth, Candida Donadio*

ANNE EDELSTEIN LITERARY AGENCY 137 Fifth Ave. (10010) *Anne Edelstein*

JOSEPH ELDER AGENCY 150 W. 87th St., 6D (10024) *Joseph Elder*

ANN ELMO AGENCY, INC. 60 E. 42nd St. (10165) *Ann Elmo, Lettie Lee*

FELICIA ETH 555 Bryant St., Suite 350, Palo Alto, CA 94301 *Felicia Eth*

FALLON LITERARY AGENCY 301 W. 53rd St., 13B (10019) *Eileen Fallon*

THE FOGELMAN LITERARY AGENCY 7515 Greenville Ave., Suite 712, Dallas, TX 75231 *Evan M. Fogelman*

THE FOX CHASE AGENCY, INC. Public Ledger Bldg. #930, Independence Square, Philadelphia, PA 19106 *A.L. Hart, Jo C. Hart*

ROBERT A. FREEDMAN DRAMATIC AGENCY, INC. 1501 Broadway, #2310 (10036) *Robert A. Freedman, Selma Luttinger*

SAMUEL FRENCH, INC. 45 W. 25th St. (10010) *William Talbot, Charles R. Van Nostrand*

JAY GARON-BROOKE ASSOCIATES 101 W. 55th St. (10019) *Jay Garon*

GELFMAN SCHNEIDER 250 W. 57th St. (10017) *Jane Gelfman, Deborah Schneider*

GOODMAN ASSOCIATES 500 West End Ave. (10024) *Arnold Goodman, Elise Simon Goodman*

IRENE GOODMAN LITERARY AGENCY 521 Fifth Ave., 17th Fl. (10017) *Irene Goodman*

SANFORD J. GREENBURGER ASSOCIATES 55 Fifth Ave., 15th Floor (10003) *Francis Greenburger, Faith Hornby Hamlin, Heide Lange*

MAXINE GROFFSKY LITERARY AGENCY 2 Fifth Ave. (10011) *Maxine Groffsky*

PETER HAGAN P.O. Box 30266 (10011) *Peter Hagan*

JEANNE K. HANSON LITERARY AGENCY 511 Wooddale Ave. S., Edina, MN 55424 *Jeanne K. Hanson*

HELEN HARVEY 410 W. 24th St., (10011) *Helen Harvey*

JOHN HAWKINS & ASSOCIATES, INC. 71 W. 23rd St., Suite 1600 (10010) *Sharon Friedman, John Hawkins, William Reiss*

HEACOCK LITERARY AGENCY, INC. 1523 Sixth St., Suite 14, Santa Monica, CA 90401 *James Heacock*

JOHN L. HOCHMANN BOOKS 320 E. 58th St. (10022) *John L. Hochmann*

BERENICE HOFFMAN LITERARY AGENCY 215 W. 75th St. (10023) *Berenice Hoffman*

IMG/JULIAN BACH LITERARY AGENCY 22 E. 71st St. (10021) *Julian Bach*

INTERNATIONAL CREATIVE MANAGEMENT, INC. 40 W. 57th St. (10019) *Sam Cohn, Wiley Hausam, Gordon Kato*

SHARON JARVIS & CO. Toad Hall, Inc., Laceyville, PA 18623 *Sharon Jarvis*

JCA LITERARY AGENCY, INC. 27 W. 20th St., Suite 1103 (10011) *Jane Cushman, Jeff Gerecke, Tony Outhwaite*

THE JOYCE KETAY AGENCY 33 W. 89th St. (10024) *Joyce P. Ketay*

KIDDE, HOYT & PICARD 335 E. 51st St. (10022) *Katharine Kidde, Wendy Wylegala*

HARVEY KLINGER, INC. 301 W. 53rd St. (10019) *Harvey Klinger, Laurie Liss, Carol McCleary*

BARBARA S. KOUTS P.O. Box 558, Bellport, NY 11713 *Barbara S. Kouts*

OTTO R. KOZAK LITERARY AGENCY P.O. Box 152, Long Beach, NY 11561 *Otto R. Kozak*

LUCY KROLL AGENCY 390 West End Ave. (10024) *Barbara Hogenson, Lucy Kroll*

PINDER LANE PRODUCTIONS, LTD. 159 W. 53rd St. (10019) *Dick Duane, Robert Thixton*

THE LANTZ OFFICE 888 Seventh Ave. (10106) *Robert Lantz*

THE ROBERT LANTZ-JOY HARRIS AGENCY 156 Fifth Ave., Suite 617 (10010) *Joy Harris*

MICHAEL LARSEN/ELIZABETH POMADA 1029 Jones St., San Francisco, CA 94109 *Michael Larsen*

SARAH LAZIN BOOKS 126 Fifth Ave., Suite 300 (10011) *Sarah Lazin*

LESCHER & LESCHER, LTD. 67 Irving Pl. (10003) *Michael Choate, Robert Lescher, Susan Lescher*

ELLEN LEVINE LITERARY AGENCY, INC. 15 E. 26th St., Suite 1801 (10010–1505) *Anne Dubuisson, Diana Finch, Ellen Levine*

LICHTMAN, TRISTER, SINGER & ROSS 1666 Connecticut Ave. N.W., Suite 501, Washington, DC 20009 *Gail Ross*

WENDY LIPKIND AGENCY 165 E. 66th St. (10021) *Wendy Lipkind*

NANCY LOVE LITERARY AGENCY 250 E. 65th St. (10021) *Nancy Love*

BARBARA LOWENSTEIN ASSOCIATES, INC. 121 W. 27th St., Suite 601 (10001) *Barbara Lowenstein*

DONALD MAASS LITERARY AGENCY 304 W. 92nd St., 8P (10025) *Donald Maass*

MARGARET MCBRIDE LITERARY AGENCY 4350 Executive Dr., Suite 225, San Diego, CA 92121 *Margaret McBride*

GERARD MCCAULEY AGENCY, INC. P.O. Box AE, Katonah, NY 10536 *Gerard McCauley*

ANITA D. MCCLELLAN ASSOCIATES 50 Stearns St., Cambridge, MA 02138 *Anita D. McClellan*

MCINTOSH & OTIS, INC. 310 Madison Ave. (10017) *Julie Fallowfield, Dorothy Markinko, Evva Pryor, Louisa Quayle, Eugene Winick, Renee Cho*

CAROL MANN LITERARY AGENCY 55 Fifth Ave. (10003) *Carol Mann*

ELAINE MARKSON LITERARY AGENCY, INC. 44 Greenwich St. (10011) *Elaine Markson*

MILDRED MARMUR ASSOCIATES LTD. 310 Madison Ave., Suite 607 (10017) *Jennie Dunham, Mildred Marmur*

ELISABETH MARTON AGENCY One Union Sq. W., Rm. 612 (10003–3303) *Tonda Marton*

HAROLD MATSON COMPANY, INC. 276 Fifth Ave. (10001) *Ben Camardi, Jonathan Matson, Elizabeth McKee*

CLAUDIA MENZA LITERARY AGENCY 1170 Broadway (10001) *Claudia Menza*

HELEN MERRILL, LTD. 435 W. 23rd St., #1A (10011) *Helen Merrill*

MARTHA MILLARD LITERARY AGENCY 204 Park Ave., Madison, NJ 07940 *Martha Millard*

BRIAN KEITH MOODY MANAGEMENT G.P.O. Box 7996 (10116) *Brian Keith Moody*

HOWARD MORHAIM LITERARY AGENCY 175 Fifth Ave., Suite 709 (10010) *Howard Morhaim*

WILLIAM MORRIS AGENCY, INC. 1350 Ave. of the Americas (10019) *Mel Berger, Matthew Bialer, Michael Carlisle, Peter Franklin, Robert Gottlieb, Owen Laster, Samuel Liff, Gilbert Parker, Marcy Posner, Esther Sherman, James Stein, Dan Strone*

MULTIMEDIA PRODUCT DEVELOPMENT, INC. 410 S. Michigan Ave., Rm. 724, Chicago, IL 60605 *Jane Jordan Browne*

JEAN V. NAGGAR LITERARY AGENCY, INC. 216 E. 75th St. (10021) *Teresa Cavanaugh, Jean V. Naggar*

RUTH NATHAN AGENCY c/o Van Horn Co., 80 Fifth Ave., Suite 706 (10011) *Ruth Nathan*

NEW ENGLAND PUBLISHING ASSOCIATES, INC. P.O. Box 5, Chester, CT 06412 *Elizabeth Frost Knappman, Edward Knappman*

THE BETSY NOLAN LITERARY AGENCY Wize Acres, P.O. Box 1, 8078 Hudson Ave., Stuyvesant Falls, NY 12174 *Betsy Nolan*

HAROLD OBER ASSOCIATES, INC. 425 Madison Ave. (10017) *Henry Dunow, Patricia Powell, Wendy Schmalz, Peter Shephard, Claire Smith, Craig Tenney, Phyllis Westberg*

ALICE ORR AGENCY, INC. 305 Madison Ave., Suite 1166 (10165) *Alice Orr*

FIFI OSCARD AGENCY, INC. 24 W. 40th St. (10018) *Carmen LaVia, Kevin McShane, Nancy Murray, Fifi Oscard, Peter Sawyer, Ivy Fisher Stone*

THE RICHARD PARKS AGENCY 138 E. 16th St., 5B (10003) *Richard Parks*

L. PERKINS & ASSOCIATES 5800 Arlington Ave., Suite 18J, Riverdale, NY 10471 *Lori Perkins*

JAMES PETER ASSOCIATES, INC. P.O. Box 772, Tenafly, NJ 07670 *Bert Holtje*

THE AARON M. PRIEST LITERARY AGENCY, INC. 122 E. 42nd St., Suite 3902 (10168) *Molly Friedrich, Aaron Priest*

SUSAN ANN PROTTER 110 W. 40th St., Suite 1408 (10018) *Susan Ann Protter*

ROBERTA PRYOR, INC. 24 W. 55th St. (10019) *Roberta Pryor*

RAINES & RAINES 71 Park Ave., Suite 44A (10016) *Mrs. Joan Raines, Theron Raines*

HELEN REES LITERARY AGENCY 308 Commonwealth Ave., Boston, MA 02116 *Helen Rees*

RHODES LITERARY AGENCY 140 West End Ave. (10023) *Joseph Rhodes*

FLORA ROBERTS, INC. 157 W. 57th St., Penthouse A (10019) *Sarah Douglas, Flora Roberts*

ROSENSTONE/WENDER 3 E. 48th St. (10017) *Suzie Perlman Cohen, Howard Rosenstone, Phyllis Wender*

JANE ROTROSEN AGENCY 318 E. 51st St. (10022) *Jane Rotrosen*

PESHA RUBINSTEIN 37 Overlook Terr., #1D (10033) *Pesha Rubinstein*

RUSSELL & VOLKENING, INC. 50 W. 29th St. (10001) *Miriam Altshuler, Timothy Seldes*

RAPHAEL SAGALYN, INC. 4825 Bethesda Ave., Suite 302, Bethesda, MD 20814 *Raphael Sagalyn*

HAROLD SCHMIDT 668 Greenwich St., Apt. 1005 (10014) *Harold Schmidt*

CHARLOTTE SHEEDY LITERARY AGENCY 41 King St. (10014) *Ellen Geiger, Charlotte Sheedy*

THE SHUKAT COMPANY, LTD. 340 W. 55th St., Suite 1A (10019) *Scott Shukat, Patricia McLaughlin*

ROSALIE SIEGEL 111 Murphy Dr., Pennington, NJ 08543 *Rosalie Siegel*

SMITH/SKOLNIK LITERARY MANAGEMENT 23 E. 10th St., #712 (10003) *Nikki Smith*

ELYSE SOMMER, INC. 110–34 73rd Rd., P.O. Box 1133, Forest Hills, NY 11375 *Elyse Sommer*

PHILIP G. SPITZER LITERARY AGENCY 788 Ninth Ave. (10019) *Philip G. Spitzer*

STEPPING STONE LITERARY AGENCY 59 W. 71st St., Apt. 9B (10023) *Sarah Jane Freymann*

STERLING LORD LITERISTIC, INC. One Madison Ave. (10010) *Philippa Brophy, Elizabeth Grossman, Elizabeth Kaplan, Stuart Krichevsky, Peter Matson*

GLORIA STERN AGENCY 1230 Park Ave. (10128) *Gloria Stern*

ROBIN STRAUS AGENCY, INC. 229 E. 79th St. (10021) *Robin Straus*

THE TANTLEFF OFFICE 375 Greenwich St., Suite 700 (10013) *Jack Tantleff*

ROSLYN TARG LITERARY AGENCY, INC. 105 W. 13th St., #15E (10011) *Roslyn Targ*

PATRICIA TEAL LITERARY AGENCY 2036 Vista del Rosa, Fullerton, CA 92631 *Patricia Teal*

RALPH VICINANZA LTD. 111 Eighth Ave., Suite 1501 (10011) *Ralph Vicinanza*

THE WALLACE AGENCY 177 E. 70th St. (10021) *Thomas C. Wallace*

THE WENDY WEIL AGENCY, INC. 232 Madison Ave., Suite 1300 (10016) *Wendy Weil, Claire Needell*

RHODA WEYR AGENCY 151 Bergen St., Brooklyn, NY 11217 *Rhoda Weyr*

AUDREY A. WOLF LITERARY AGENCY 1001 Connecticut Ave. N.W., Washington, DC 20036 *Audrey A. Wolf*

ANN WRIGHT REPRESENTATIVES 136 E. 56th St., 9J (10022–3619) *Dan Wright*

WRITERS AND ARTISTS AGENCY 19 W. 44th St., Suite 1000 (10036) *William Craver, Scott Hudson, Susan P. Urstadt*

WRITERS HOUSE 21 W. 26th St. (10010) *Amy Berkower, Lois Berman, Judy Boals, Susan Cohen, Merilee Heifetz, Fran Lebowitz, Albert Zuckerman*

MARY YOST ASSOCIATES, INC. 59 E. 54th St., #72 (10022) *Mary Yost*

SUSAN ZECKENDORF ASSOCIATES, INC. 171 W. 57th St. (10019) *Susan Zeckendorf*

INDEX TO MARKETS

871